REPORTING CIVIL RIGHTS
PART TWO

Reporting
Civil Rights

PART TWO

AMERICAN JOURNALISM 1963–1973

THE LIBRARY OF AMERICA

Some of the material in this volume is reprinted
with permission of the holders of copyright and publication
rights. Acknowledgments are on pages 935–40.

The paper used in this publication meets the
minimum requirements of the American National Standard for
Information Sciences—Permanence of Paper for Printed
Library Materials, ANSI Z39.48—1984.

Distributed to the trade in the United States
by Penguin Putnam Inc.
and in Canada by Penguin Books Canada Ltd.

Library of Congress Catalog Number: 2002027459
For cataloging information, see end of Index.
ISBN 1–931082–29–4

First Printing
The Library of America—138

Manufactured in the United States of America

Advisory board for *Reporting Civil Rights*

Contents

CONTENTS

CONTENTS

The View from the Front of the Bus

by Marlene Nadle

"There's no place for Uncle Tom on this bus, man." The voice of the Negro echoed down the neon-bathed Harlem street as he mounted the steps of Bus 10 ready to start for Washington.

It was 2 a.m. on the morning of August 28. Anticipation hovered quietly over the 24 buses that lined both sides of 125th Street. Cars and cabs stopped more and more frequently to pour forth bundle-laden, sleepy Marchers. Black, white, old, young zigzagged back and forth across the street trying to find their assigned buses. Bus captains marked by yellow ribbons and rumpled passenger lists stood guard at the bus doors. Small groups huddled around them.

Voices arose above the general din.

"You've got to switch me to Bus 10. It's a swingin' bus. There's nothin' but old ladies on this crate."

"Hey, is this bus air-conditioned?"

"Where can I get seat reservations?"

"Hey, chick, are you on this bus?"

"Yeah."

"Is your husband on this bus?"

"Yeah."

"That's all right. I'll make love to both of you. I'm compatible."

"Who the hell is on this bus?" cried George Johnson, the exasperated 30-year-old Negro captain of Bus 10 and organizer of New York CORE's 24-bus caravan. "People shouldn't be swapping buses, especially CORE members. It only adds to the confusion. Now everybody get in a seat and stay there. You can't save seats. This isn't a cocktail party."

The reaction to George's gruffness was a tongue-in-cheek parody of the Mr. Charlie routine. "Yassir, anything you say, sir." "Don't you fret now, Mr. George." "Don't you go upsetting yourself, boss." "You knows I always listen to you captain sir."

There was a general shuffling of bundles on the bus. Index cards with emergency Washington phone numbers were filled out and kept by everyone. "Sit-In Song Books" were passed back.

Outside the window of Bus 10 an old Negro was standing with outstretched arms reciting an impromptu ode to the Black Woman. "Black Woman, you are the queen of the universe. I would give my life for you." This was less comic than symptomatic. It was just one of many signs of the racial pride which is now surging through the Negro people.

A young Negro in the seat behind me, when asked why he was going on this March, replied, "Because it's like your sweater. It's Black. It's for the cause. If my people are in it, I am going to be in it fighting, even if I get killed."

Outside the window of Bus 10 was also a more extreme reminder of this racial pride. Young members of the Black Muslims, neatly dressed in suits and ties, were hawking copies of Muhammad Speaks. This paper is the official statement of the Black Muslim philosophy: Black is beautiful; Black is best; Black must be separate from white.

I swing off the bus to ask the young Muslim if he was going to Washington. With a faint trace of a smile on his lips, he answered, "No, ma'am, I have to sell papers. You people go to Washington." The implication was clear: he was too busy working for his own cause—separation—to be bothered working for integration.

An older man, converted to a Muslim later in life, was not so emotionally untouched by the March and what it stood for. When I asked him why the Muslims were not participating in the March, he gave all the proper answers. He said: "The Messenger has not spoken. If he says nothing, we sit still. If he says go, we go." But then, asked if as an individual rather than a Muslim he would have gone, he replied: "I would have gone."

Moving through the crowd, I encountered a Negro I knew to be a fence-sitter between the Muslim and integrationist philosophies. I asked him why he had decided to come on the March. He said, "It's like St. Patrick's Day to the Irish. I came out of respect for what my people are doing, not because I believe it will do any good. I thought it would do some good at the beginning, but when the March started to get all the official approval from Mastah Kennedy, Mastah Wagner, and Mastah Spellman, and they started setting limits on how we had to march peacefully, I knew that the March was going to be a mockery. That they were giving us something again. They were letting the niggers have their day to get all this nonsense out of their system, and then planning to go back to things as usual. Well, if the white man continues to sleep, continues to ignore the intensity of the black man's feelings and desires, all hell is going to break loose."

Moving back toward the bus I almost crashed into George Johnson. With a certain Hollywood director flourish, he was telling the driver to rev up the engine. George was being interviewed for radio, and they wanted the sound of departure. Followed by interviewers trailing microphone wires, George shouted, "I feel good because the Negroes are on the march and nothing is going to stop us." With that, he boarded the bus, signaled the driver, and we began to move. It was 3:40 a.m.

The 49 passengers on Bus 10 settled back. Among them were 10 CORE members, including Omar Ahmed and Wayne Kinsler, both typical of Harlem's Angry Young Men. Present also were 10 unemployed workers sent to Washington on money raised by CORE to protest the lack of jobs. Also among the passengers were Jim Peck, author of the book "The Freedom Riders," who took a severe beating on one of the first freedom rides into the Deep South; six members of the Peace Corps who were scheduled to leave for Nigeria; three interviewers from French television, with cameras and sound equipment; and a slightly jaded reporter and a cameraman from the Herald Tribune, both of whom had seen too many Clark Gable reporter movies.

People began to talk and to question one another. Sue Brookway, a white member of the Peace Corps, was standing in the aisle speaking to George Johnson. She said, "I think the biggest influence of the March will be to create a greater national awareness of the issue and get more people to make a commitment to the cause. Although I agreed with CORE's goals, it never occurred to me to become active before this. But now I would join if I weren't going to Nigeria."

Omar Ahmed, who had overheard the word Nigeria, turned around in his seat and said, "The Negro on this March has to be very glad of the existence of the Soviet Union. This government is so worried about wooing the African and Asian mind that it may even give the Negro what he wants."

"I don't think the Civil Rights Bill will get through," commented George Johnson from his seat across the aisle. "I have no faith in the white man. Even Kennedy & Kennedy Inc. isn't doing this for humanitarian reasons, but for political ones."

After a moment he continued: "CORE has been criticized for its new tactics of civil disobedience. Well, as far as I'm concerned, anything done to get our rights is O.K. It's remarkable that the Negro has taken it this long."

The whites in the group were startled at the vehemence in George's statement. Omar, noting their expressions, attempted to explain. "The white power structure has bred a New Negro," he said, "and he is angry and impatient. It's not just the Black Muslims. It's the man on the street. Come down to Harlem some night and listen to what's being said on the street corners. The cops go through and you can see fear on their faces. This isn't Birmingham. If anyone starts anything, we won't be passive."

The kids in the four adjacent seats were twisted around in their chairs listening. Heads pressed together, they formed a roundtable, minus the table. Into this group came Wayne Kinsler, a 19-year-old Negro. He perched on one of the seat arms. Some crumbled cookies and overripe fruit were passed around.

The discussion turned to the Peace Corps. Frank Harman was asked why, since he was white, he wanted to go to Nigeria. He replied, "I want to go to help these people because they are human beings."

Suddenly Wayne shouted, "If this thing comes to violence, yours will be the first throat we slit. We don't need your kind. Get out of our organization."

Completely baffled by the outburst, Frank kept repeating the questions. "What's he talking about? What did I say?"

Wayne, straining forward tensely, screamed, "We don't need any white liberals to patronize us!"

Other Negroes joined in. "We don't trust you." "We don't believe you're sincere." "You'll have to prove yourself."

Frank shouted back, "I don't have to prove myself to anyone except myself."

"We've been stabbed in the back too many times."

"The reason white girls come down to civil rights meetings is because they've heard of the black man's reputation of sex."

"The reason white guys come down is because they want to rebel against their parents."

"I'll tell you this, proving that he is sincere when he is working in the civil rights groups is the last chance the white man has got to keep this thing from exploding."

The other passengers were urging us to stop the argument. Eventually we did. In the lull that followed, the reactions of the whites were mixed. The most widespread one was complete lack of understanding as to why this had all started. There was little comprehension of the effect words like "help you" or "work for you," with all their connotations of the Great-White-Father attitude, could have on the bristling black pride. Another attitude was one of revulsion at the ugliness which had been exhibited. Still others saw the argument as a sign that the walls between the races were beginning to come down, that people were really beginning to communicate instead of hiding behind masks of politeness. They felt that with a greater knowledge of one another's sensitivities, lack of understanding, and desires, it would be easier for the white liberal and the black man to work together.

People began to relax and joke again. Gradually they drifted off into an exhausted sleep. Bus 10 rolled on in silence.

With the coming of dawn, the French TV men started blinding everyone with their lights and interviewing those people who could speak French. Being Gallic, they made sure to get shots of the romantic duos pillowed against one another. Not to be left out, the Herald Tribune's cameraman picked up his light meter and cord and started doing a mock interview of the interviewers.

Someone cheerfully yelled, "Everybody sing."

He was quickly put down by a voice from the lower depths: "You're nuts! At seven o'clock sane people don't even talk."

On we went. Sleeping, talking, anticipating. We passed other buses full of heads covered with caps printed with their organizations' names. On our right was a beat-up old cab with six people in it and March on Washington posters plastered on all its doors.

At 10.30—Washington. The city seemed strangely quiet and deserted except for a few groups of Negro children on corners. They stared curiously at the unending caravan of buses. Police and MPs were everywhere. Traffic moved swiftly. We parked at 117th and Independence, and the people of Bus 10 merged with the crowd moving up the street. The March was on.

The day was full of TV cameras, spontaneous singing, speeches, clapping, the green and white striped news tent, the P.A. system blasting "We Shall Not Be Moved," the ominous Red Cross symbol on a medical tent, March marshals with bright yellow arm bands and little white Nehru hats, the Freedom Walkers in faded blue overalls, Catholic priests in solemn black, posters proclaiming Freedom Now, feet soaking in the reflecting pool, portable drinking fountains, varicolored pennants and hats, warm Pepsi-Cola, the blanket of humanity sprawled in undignified dignity, a Nigerian student with his head bent in prayer, and the echo of Martin Luther King's phrase: "I have a dream . . ."

It was over. The bus moved out slowly. This time there were Negroes on every doorstep. As we passed, they raised their fingers in the victory sign. They clasped their hands over their heads in the prizefighter's traditional gesture. They clapped. They cheered. They smiled and the smile was reflected back from the buses.

On Bus 10 there was no one sitting at "the back of the bus." All the seats were in the front.

"We'll be back," said George Johnson. "If this doesn't work, we'll bring 500,000. And if that doesn't work, we'll bring all 20 million."

The Village Voice, September 5, 1963

Capital Is Occupied by a Gentle Army

by Russell Baker

WASHINGTON, Aug. 28—No one could remember an invading army quite as gentle as the 200,000 civil rights marchers who occupied Washington today.

For the most part, they came silently during the night and early morning, occupied the great shaded boulevards along the Mall, and spread through the parklands between the Washington Monument and the Potomac.

But instead of the emotional horde of angry militants that many had feared, what Washington saw was a vast army of quiet, middle-class Americans who had come in the spirit of the church outing.

And instead of the tensions that had been expected, they gave this city a day of sad music, strange silences and good feeling in the streets.

It was apparent from early morning that this would be an extraordinary day. At 8 A.M. when rush-hour traffic is normally creeping bumper-to-bumper across the Virginia bridges and down the main boulevards from Maryland, the streets had the abandoned look of Sunday morning.

From a helicopter over the city, it was possible to see caravans of chartered buses streaming down New York Avenue from Baltimore and points North, but the downtown streets were empty. Nothing moved in front of the White House, nor on Pennsylvania Avenue.

For the natives, this was obviously a day of siege and the streets were being left to the marchers.

By 9:30, the number of marchers at the assembly point by the Washington Monument had reached about 40,000, but it was a crowd without fire. Mostly, people who had traveled together sat on the grass or posed for group portraits against the monument, like tourists on a rare visit to the capital.

Here and there, little groups stood in the sunlight and sang. A group of 75 young people from Danville, Va., came dressed in white sweatshirts with crudely cut black mourning bands on their sleeves.

"We're mourning injustice in Danville," explained James Bruce, a 15-year-old who said he has been arrested three times for participating in demonstrations there.

Standing together, the group sang of the freedom fight in a sad melody with words that went, "Move on, move on, move on with the freedom fight; move on, move on, we're fighting for equal rights."

Other hymns came from groups scattered over the grounds, but there was no cohesion in the crowd.

Instead, a fair grounds atmosphere prevailed. Marchers kept straggling off to ride the elevators to the top of the monument. Women sat on the grass and concentrated on feeding babies.

Among the younger members of the crowd, beards were in high vogue. "It's just that we're so busy saving the world that we don't have time to shave," Kyle Valkar, 19-year-old Washingtonian, explained.

Up on the slope near the monument's base, Peter Ottley, president of the Building Services International Union, Local 144, in New York City, was ignoring the loudspeaker and holding a press conference before about 100 of his delegates.

He thought the march would "convince the legislators that something must be done, because it is the will of the people to give equality to all."

In the background, the amplifier was presenting Joan Baez, the folk singer.

In one section of the ground a group from Americus and Albany, Ga., was gathered under its own placards singing its own hymn. The placards conveyed an uncharacteristic note of bitterness.

"What is a state without justice but a robber band enlarged?" asked one. Another bore the following inscription: "Milton Wilkerson—20 stitches. Emanuel McClendon—3 stitches (Age 67). James Williams—broken leg."

Charles Macken, 15, of Albany, explained the placard in a deep Georgia accent.

"That's where the police beat these people up," he said.

Over the loudspeaker, Roosevelt Johnson was urged to come claim his lost son, Lawrence.

From the monument grounds the loudspeaker boomed an announcement that the police had estimated that 90,000 marchers were already on the scene.

At 10:56 the loudspeaker announced desperately that "we are trying to locate Miss Lena Horne," and a group from Cambridge, Md., was kneeling while the Rev. Charles M. Bowen of Bethel A.M.E. Church prayed.

"We know truly that we will—we shall—overcome—some day," he was saying.

The Cambridge group rose and began a gospel hymn and clapped and swayed. The loudspeaker was saying, "Lena—wherever you are—."

Many were simply picnicking. They had brought picnic baskets and thermos jugs and camp stools, and lunched leisurely in the soft August sunshine. Some stretched out to doze on the grass.

At 11:10 Bobby Darin, the teen-age pop singer, was being introduced over the amplifier. He was, he announced, "Here as a singer, and I'm proud and kind of choked up."

The marchers by this time, however, had had enough of the Monument grounds. Spontaneously, without advice from the platform, they began to flow away, moving toward the Lincoln Memorial where the official program was to begin at noon.

Thousands simply began to move out into Constitution Avenue, and in a few minutes it was tens of thousands. They trooped leisurely out into the boulevard and moved happily along in a strange mood of quiet contentment.

By 11:55 much of the crowd had regrouped at the Lincoln Memorial, where the speaker's platform was set on the top step under the Lincoln statue.

This made an impressive stage for the star performers, but it was a bad theater for most of the audience, which was dispersed down the sides of the reflecting pool for a third of a mile.

Still the crowd remained in good temper, and many who could not find comfortable space in the open with a clear view up to the Memorial steps filtered back under the trees and sat down on their placards.

On the platform, Roy Wilkins, executive secretary of the National Association for the Advancement of Colored People, surveyed the sea of people and said, "I'm very satisfied. It looks like a Yankee game."

Inside, under the Lincoln statue, the photographers were deployed five deep around Burt Lancaster, Harry Belafonte and Charlton Heston. On metal chairs in the guest sections, Marlon Brando and Paul Newman were submitting to microphone interviewers.

As the crowd on the steps thickened and gradually became an impassable mass, the extraordinary politeness that characterized the day was dramatized every time an elbow was crooked.

People excused themselves for momentarily obstructing a view, excused themselves for dropping cigarette ashes on shoeshines.

When the marshals called for a clear path, hundreds hastened to fall aside with a goodness rarely seen in the typical urban crowd. The sweetness and patience of the crowd may have set some sort of national high-water mark in mass decency.

The program at the Memorial began with more music. Peter, Paul and Mary, a folk-singing trio, were there "to express in song what this meeting is all about," as Ossie Davis, the master of ceremonies, put it.

Then there was Josh White in a gray short-sleeved sportsshirt, singing, "ain't nobody gonna stop me, nobody gonna keep me, from marching down freedom's road."

And the Freedom Singers from Mississippi, a hand-clapping group of hot gospel shouters whom Mr. Davis introduced as "straight from one of the prisons of the South."

"They've been in so many, I forget which one it is," he added.

At 1:19 P.M. there was the Rev. Fred L. Shuttlesworth, president of the Alabama Christian Movement for Human Rights and a leader of the Birmingham demonstrations.

At 1:28 P.M., Miss Baez was singing "Little baby, don't you cry, you know your mama won't die, all your trials will soon be over."

As she sang, Mayor Wagner of New York made his appearance, walking down the Memorial steps.

Miss Baez was followed by Dr. Ralph Bunche.

"Anyone who cannot understand the significance of your presence here today," he said, "is blind and deaf." The crowd roared approval.

Then came Dick Gregory, the comedian.

"The last time I saw this many of us," he said, "Bull Connor was doing all the talking." The reference was to Eugene (Bull) Connor, who was police commissioner of Birmingham during the spring demonstrations there.

To many of the marchers, the program must have begun to seem like eternity, and the great crowd slowly began dissolving from the edges. Mr. Lancaster read a lengthy statement from 1,500 Americans in Europe. They were in favor of the march. Mr. Belafonte read a statement endorsed by a large group of actors, writers and entertainers. They also favored the march.

Bob Dylan, a young folk singer, rendered a lugubrious mountain song about "The day Medgar Evers was buried from a bullet that he caught." Mr. Lancaster, Mr. Belafonte and Mr. Heston found time dragging, stood up to stretch and chat, and set off pandemonium among the photographers. Mr. Brando submitted to another microphone interviewer.

At 1:59 the official speaking began. For those who listened it was full of noble statement about democracy and religious sincerity, but the crowd was dissolving fast now.

Those who left early missed two of the emotional high points of the day. One was Mahalia Jackson's singing, which seemed to bounce off the Capitol far up the mall. The other was the speech of the Rev. Dr. Martin Luther King Jr., president of the Southern Christian Leadership Conference.

Long before that, however, huge portions of the crowd had drifted out of earshot. Thousands had moved back into Constitution Avenue to walk dreamily in the sun. The grass for blocks around was covered with sleepers. Here and there a man sat under a tree and sang to a guitar.

Mostly though, the "marchers" just strolled in the sunshine. Most looked contented and tired and rather pleased with what they had done.

The New York Times, August 29, 1963

200,000 March for Civil Rights in Orderly Washington Rally; President Sees Gain for Negro

by E. W. Kenworthy

WASHINGTON, Aug. 28—More than 200,000 Americans, most of them black but many of them white, demonstrated here today for a full and speedy program of civil rights and equal job opportunities.

It was the greatest assembly for a redress of grievances that this capital has ever seen.

One hundred years and 240 days after Abraham Lincoln enjoined the emancipated slaves to "abstain from all violence" and "labor faithfully for reasonable wages," this vast throng proclaimed in march and song and through the speeches of their leaders that they were still waiting for the freedom and the jobs.

There was no violence to mar the demonstration. In fact, at times there was an air of hootenanny about it as groups of schoolchildren clapped hands and swung into the familiar freedom songs.

But if the crowd was good-natured, the underlying tone was one of dead seriousness. The emphasis was on "freedom" and "now." At the same time the leaders emphasized, para-doxically but realistically, that the struggle was just beginning.

On Capitol Hill, opinion was divided about the impact of the demonstration in stimulating Congressional action on civil rights legislation. But at the White House, President Kennedy declared that the cause of 20,000,000 Negroes had been advanced by the march.

The march leaders went from the shadows of the Lincoln Memorial to the White House to meet with the President for 75 minutes. Afterward, Mr. Kennedy issued a 400-word statement praising the marchers for the "deep fervor and the quiet dignity" that had characterized the demonstration.

The nation, the President said, "can properly be proud of the demonstration that has occurred here today."

The main target of the demonstration was Congress, where committees are now considering the Administration's civil rights bill.

At the Lincoln Memorial this afternoon, some speakers, knowing little of the ways of Congress, assumed that the passage of a strengthened civil rights bill had been assured by the moving events of the day.

But from statements by Congressional leaders, after they had met with the march committee this morning, this did not seem certain at all. These statements came before the demonstration.

Senator Mike Mansfield, of Montana, the Senate Democratic leader, said he could not say whether the mass protest would speed the legislation, which faces a filibuster by Southerners.

Senator Everett McKinley Dirksen of Illinois, the Republican leader, said he thought the demonstration would be neither an advantage nor a disadvantage to the prospects for the civil rights bill.

The human tide that swept over the Mall between the shrines of Washington and Lincoln fell back faster than it came on. As soon as the ceremony broke up this afternoon, the exodus began. With astounding speed, the last buses and trains cleared the city by midevening.

At 9 P.M. the city was as calm as the waters of the Reflecting Pool between the two memorials.

At the Lincoln Memorial early in the afternoon, in the midst of a songfest before the addresses, Josephine Baker, the singer, who had flown from her home in Paris, said to the thousands stretching down both sides of the Reflecting Pool:

"You are on the eve of a complete victory. You can't go wrong. The world is behind you."

Miss Baker said, as if she saw a dream coming true before her eyes, that "this is the happiest day of my life."

But of all the 10 leaders of the march on Washington who followed her, only the Rev. Dr. Martin Luther King Jr., president of the Southern Christian Leadership Conference, saw that dream so hopefully.

The other leaders, except for the three clergymen among the 10, concentrated on the struggle ahead and spoke in tough, even harsh, language.

But paradoxically it was Dr. King—who had suffered perhaps most of all—who ignited the crowd with words that might have been written by the sad, brooding man enshrined within.

As he arose, a great roar welled up from the crowd. When he started to speak, a hush fell.

"Even though we face the difficulties of today and tomorrow, I still have a dream," he said.

"It is a dream chiefly rooted in the American dream," he went on.

"I have a dream that one day this nation will rise up and live out the true meaning of its creed: 'We hold these truths to be self-evident, that all men are created equal.'

"I have a dream . . ." The vast throng listening intently to him roared.

". . . that one day on the red hills of Georgia, the sons of former slaves and the sons of former slave-owners will be able to sit together at the table of brotherhood.

"I have a dream . . ." The crowd roared.

". . . that one day even the State of Mississippi, a state sweltering with the heat of injustice, sweltering with the heat of oppression, will be transformed into an oasis of freedom and justice.

"I have a dream . . ." The crowd roared.

". . . that my four little children will one day live in a nation where they will not be judged by the color of their skin but by the content of their character.

"I have a dream . . ." The crowd roared.

". . . that one day every valley shall be exalted, every hill and mountain shall be made low, the rough places will be made plain, and the crooked places will be made straight, and the glory of the Lord shall be revealed and all flesh shall see it together."

As Dr. King concluded with a quotation from a Negro hymn—"Free at last, free at last, thank God almighty"—the crowd, recognizing that he was finishing, roared once again and waved their signs and pennants.

But the civil rights leaders, who knew the strength of the forces arrayed against them from past battles, knew also that a hard struggle lay ahead. The tone of their speeches was frequently militant.

Roy Wilkins, executive secretary of the National Association for the Advancement of Colored People, made plain that he and his colleagues thought the President's civil rights bill did not go nearly far enough. He said:

"The President's proposals represent so moderate an approach that if any one is weakened or eliminated, the remainder will be little more than sugar water. Indeed, the package needs strengthening."

Harshest of all the speakers was John Lewis, chairman of the Student Nonviolent Coordinating Committee.

"My friends," he said, "let us not forget that we are involved in a serious social revolution. But by and large American politics is dominated by politicians who build their career on immoral compromising and ally themselves with open forms of political, economic and social exploitation."

He concluded:

"They're talking about slowdown and stop. We will not stop.

"If we do not get meaningful legislation out of this Congress, the time will come when we will not confine our marching to Washington. We will march through the South, through the streets of Jackson, through the streets of Danville, through the streets of Cambridge, through the streets of Birmingham.

"But we will march with the spirit of love and the spirit of dignity that we have shown here today."

In the original text of the speech distributed last night, Mr. Lewis had said:

"We will not wait for the President, the Justice Department, nor the Congress, but we will take matters into our own hands and create a source of power, outside of any national structure, that could and would assure us a victory."

He also said in the original text that "we will march through the South, through the heart of Dixie, the way Sherman did."

It was understood that at least the last of these statements was changed as the result of a protest by the Most Rev. Patrick J. O'Boyle, Roman Catholic Archbishop of Washington, who refused to give the invocation if the offending words were spoken by Mr. Lewis.

The great day really began the night before. As a half moon rose over the lagoon by the Jefferson Memorial and the tall, lighted shaft of the Washington Monument gleamed in the reflecting pool, a file of Negroes from out of town began climbing the steps of the Lincoln Memorial.

There, while the carpenters nailed the last planks on the television platforms for the next day and the TV technicians called through the loudspeakers, "Final audio, one, two, three, four," a middle-aged Negro couple, the man's arm around the shoulders of his plump wife, stood and read with their lips:

"If we shall suppose that American slavery is one of the offenses which in the providence of God must needs come but, which having continued through His appointed time, He now wills to remove . . ."

The day dawned clear and cool. At 7 A.M. the town had a Sunday appearance, except for the shuttle buses drawn up in front of Union Station, waiting.

By 10 A.M. there were 40,000 on the slopes around the Washington Monument. An hour later the police estimated the crowd at 90,000. And still they poured in.

Because some things went wrong at the monument, everything was late. Most of the stage and screen celebrities from New York and Hollywood who were scheduled to begin entertaining the crowd at 10 did not arrive at the airport until 11:15.

As a result the whole affair at the monument grounds began to take on the spontaneity of a church picnic. Even before the entertainment was to begin, groups of high school students were singing with wonderful improvisations and hand-clapping all over the monument slope.

Civil rights demonstrators who had been released from jail in Danville, Va., were singing:

> Move on, move on,
> Till all the world is free.

And members of Local 144 of the Hotel and Allied Service

Employes Union from New York City, an integrated local since 1950, were stomping:

> Oh, freedom, we shall not, we shall not be moved,
> Just like a tree that's planted by the water.

Then the pros took over, starting with the folk singers. The crowd joined in with them.

Joan Baez started things rolling with "the song"—"We Shall Overcome."

> Oh deep in my heart I do believe
> We shall overcome some day.

And Peter, Paul, and Mary sang "How many times must a man look up before he can see the sky."

And Odetta's great, full-throated voice carried almost to Capitol Hill: "If they ask you who you are, tell them you're a child of God."

Jackie Robinson told the crowd that "we cannot be turned back," and Norman Thomas, the venerable Socialist, said: "I'm glad I lived long enough to see this day."

The march to the Lincoln Memorial was supposed to start at 11:30, behind the leaders. But at 11:20 it set off spontaneously down Constitution Avenue behind the Kenilworth Knights, a local drum and bugle corps dazzling in yellow silk blazers, green trousers and green berets.

Apparently forgotten was the intention to make the march to the Lincoln Memorial a solemn tribute to Medgar W. Evers, N.A.A.C.P. official murdered in Jackson, Miss., last June 12, and others who had died for the cause of civil rights.

The leaders were lost, and they never did get to the head of the parade.

The leaders included also Walter P. Reuther, head of the United Automobile Workers; A. Philip Randolph, head of the American Negro Labor Council; the Rev. Dr. Eugene Carson Blake, vice chairman of the Commission on Religion and Race of the National Council of Churches; Mathew Ahmann, executive director of the National Catholic Conference for Interracial Justice; Rabbi Joachim Prinz, president of the American Jewish Congress; Whitney M. Young Jr., executive director of the National Urban League, and James Farmer, president of the Congress of Racial Equality.

All spoke at the memorial except Mr. Farmer, who is in jail in Louisiana following his arrest as a result of a civil rights demonstration. His speech was read by Floyd B. McKissick, CORE national chairman.

At the close of the ceremonies at the Lincoln Memorial, Bayard Rustin, the organizer of the march, asked Mr. Randolph, who conceived it, to lead the vast throng in a pledge.

Repeating after Mr. Randolph, the marchers pledged "complete personal commitment to the struggle for jobs and freedom for Americans" and "to carry the message of the march to my friends and neighbors back home and arouse them to an equal commitment and an equal effort."

The New York Times, August 29, 1963

Birmingham Bomb Kills 4 Negro Girls in Church; Riots Flare; 2 Boys Slain

by Claude Sitton

BIRMINGHAM, Ala., Sept. 15—A bomb severely damaged a Negro church today during Sunday school services, killing four Negro girls and setting off racial rioting and other violence in which two Negro boys were shot to death.

Fourteen Negroes were injured in the explosion. One Negro and five whites were hurt in the disorders that followed.

Some 500 National Guardsmen in battle dress stood by at armories here tonight, on orders of Gov. George C. Wallace. And 300 state troopers joined the Birmingham police, Jefferson County sheriff's deputies and other law-enforcement units in efforts to restore peace.

Governor Wallace sent the guardsmen and the troopers in response to requests from local authorities.

Sporadic gunfire sounded in Negro neighborhoods tonight, and small bands of residents roamed the streets. Aside from the patrols that cruised the city armed with riot guns, carbines and shotguns, few whites were seen.

At one point, three fires burned simultaneously in Negro sections, one at a broom and mop factory, one at a roofing company and a third in another building. An incendiary bomb was tossed into a supermarket, but the flames were extinguished swiftly. Fire marshals investigated blazes at two vacant houses to see if arson was involved.

Mayor Albert Boutwell and other city officials and civic leaders appeared on television station WAPI late tonight and urged residents to cooperate in ending "this senseless reign of terror."

Sheriff Melvin Bailey referred to the day as "the most distressing in the history of Birmingham."

The explosion at the 16th Street Baptist Church this morning brought hundreds of angry Negroes pouring into the streets. Some attacked the police with stones. The police dispersed them by firing shotguns over their heads.

Johnny Robinson, a 16-year-old Negro, was shot in the back and killed by a policeman with a shotgun this afternoon. Officers said the victim was among a group that had hurled stones at white youths driving through the area in cars flying Confederate battle flags.

When the police arrived, the youths fled, and one policeman said he had fired low but that some of the shot had struck the Robinson youth in the back.

Virgil Wade, a 13-year-old Negro, was shot and killed just outside Birmingham while riding a bicycle. The Jefferson County sheriff's office said "there apparently was no reason at all" for the killing, but indicated that it was related to the general racial disorders.

Another Negro youth and a white youth were shot but not seriously wounded in separate incidents. Four whites, including a honeymooning couple from Chicago, were injured by stones while driving through the neighborhood of the bombing.

The bombing, the fourth such incident in less than a month, resulted in heavy damage to the church, to a two-story office building across the street and to a home.

Governor Wallace, at the request of city officials, offered a $5,000 reward for the arrest and conviction of the bombers.

None of the 50 bombings of Negro property here since World War II have been solved.

Mayor Boutwell and Chief of Police Jamie Moore expressed fear that the bombing, coming on top of tension aroused by desegregation of three schools last week, would bring further violence.

George G. Seibels Jr., chairman of the City Council's police committee, broadcast frequent appeals tonight to white parents urging them to restrain their children from staging demonstrations tomorrow. He said a repetition of the segregationist motorcades that raced through the streets last Thursday and Friday "could provoke serious trouble, resulting in possible death or injury."

The Rev. Dr. Martin Luther King Jr. arrived tonight by

plane from Atlanta. He had led Negroes, who make up almost one-third of Birmingham's population, in a five-week campaign last spring that brought some lunch-counter desegregation and improved job opportunities. The bombed church had been used as the staging point by Negro demonstrators.

Col. Albert J. Lingo, State director of Public Safety and commander of the troopers, met with Mayor Boutwell and the City Council in emergency session. They discussed imposition of a curfew but decided against it.

The bombing came five days after the descgregation of three previously all-white schools in Birmingham. The way had been cleared for the desegregation when President Kennedy federalized the Alabama National Guard and the Federal courts issued a sweeping order against Governor Wallace, thus ending his defiance toward the integration step.

The four girls killed in the blast had just heard Mrs. Ella C. Demand, their teacher, complete the Sunday school lesson for the day. The subject was "The Love That Forgives."

During the period between the class and an assembly in the main auditorium, they went to the women's lounge in the basement, at the northeast corner of the church.

The blast occurred at about 10:25 A.M. (12:25 P.M. New York time).

Church members said they found the girls huddled together beneath a pile of masonry debris.

Both parents of each of three of the victims teach in the city's schools. The dead were identified by University Hospital officials as:

Cynthia Wesley, 14, the only child of Claude A. Wesley, principal of the Lewis Elementary School, and Mrs. Wesley, a teacher there.

Denise McNair, 11, also an only child, whose parents are teachers.

Carole Robertson, 14, whose parents are teachers and whose grandmother, Mrs. Sallie Anderson, is one of the Negro members of a biracial committee established by Mayor Boutwell to deal with racial problems.

Addie Mae Collins, 14, about whom no information was immediately available.

The blast blew gaping holes through walls in the church

basement. Floors of offices in the rear of the sanctuary appeared near collapse. Stairways were blocked by splintered window frames, glass and timbers.

Chief Police Inspector W. J. Haley said the impact of the blast indicated that at least 15 sticks of dynamite might have caused it. He said the police had talked to two witnesses who reported having seen a car drive by the church, slow down and then speed away before the blast.

The New York Times, September 16, 1963

First of 4 Birmingham Bomb Victims Is Buried

by James D. Williams

BIRMINGHAM—Three thousand eyes were focused on the baby blue casket in the front of St. John's AME Church Tuesday afternoon.

In the casket was the body of Carole Robertson, 14, one of four young girls killed Sunday in the dynamiting of the 16th Street Baptist Church.

She was the first to be buried and an overflow crowd filled the St. John's Church and spilled out into the street where another 1,500 persons waited and listened to the faint sounds that came through the windows.

The coffin, over which had been placed a spray of red and white roses, was not opened during the services.

At 2 p.m., one and a half hours before the start of the services, some 25 people were already in the church. By 3:30 p.m. the area had to be closed to traffic because of the huge number of people at hand.

This was to be a quiet service and the tone was set when the family arrived at St. John's, and with grim and set faces walked into the church through a crowd of photographers.

Carole was a member of the 16th Street Baptist Church but the blast rendered the building useless, hence the necessity of using St. John's, two blocks away.

All week long the leaders of the Human Rights Movement have been urging calmness and warning against any resort to violence.

However, there were many persons in the crowd and in the church who were visibly angered by the cruel death of the four children and were vocal in their bitterness, which harbored on the thin edge of violence.

Present in the audience were the members of the Parker

High School band, dressed in their blue and white uniforms. Carole had been a member of that band and played second clarinet.

The Rev. John H. Cross, pastor of the 16th Street Baptist Church, officiated at the rites.

"Suffer little children to come unto me and forbid them not," the Rev. Hobart E. Oden Jr., assistant pastor of 16th Street Baptist Church said as he read the scripture.

Born in Birmingham on April 24, 1949, Carole was the third child of Mr. and Mrs. Alvin C. Robertson Sr., who survive.

"We come from all walks of life, but our ambitions and desires are the same. In the midst of this confused city, bring us the capacity to walk in a spirit of calmness," said the Rev. C. E. Thomas, pastor of St. John's.

A companion at the side of the mother gently waved a fan. The church was warm and still.

Carole attended the Hill School, and the Wilkerson Elementary School, graduating in May of last year. She was in the tenth grade.

"We live here in a society in which we have not made safe the streets, the homes or the churches," said the Rev. Fred L. Shuttlesworth, president of the Alabama Christian Movement.

Usually a speaker who hurls words of fire, the Rev. Mr. Shuttlesworth spoke simply as he told the family "you, by your loss, have made a payment on this great thing called freedom."

In the audience, as the words rang out, were a number of white persons and clergymen, who had come to add their grief to that of the family.

"We shall work to see their deaths were not in vain. We pledge again our lives, our futures, our sacred consciousness," said the Rev. Mr. Shuttlesworth.

There were cries of "amen" from the audience and it was evident there was agreement with the minister.

The clock raced swiftly ahead and now it was 3:50 and the Rev. Mr. Cross, the child's pastor, stood to deliver the eulogy.

What does one say about a 14-year-old girl who died before she had a chance to live? How does one sum up her life? How does one give meaning to her death?

This is the way the Rev. Mr. Cross did these things.

"When the atrocious act was committed on Sunday morning, it was not commited against us but against all freedom-loving people.

"I believe with my heart that out of this dastardly act, this inhuman deed, somehow we have been brought together as we have never been brought together."

It is not as colored, not as white, not as Catholic and not as Protestant that these people filled the church, but as the Rev. Mr. Cross said "As Children of God".

"This was not an ordinary type of suffering. But here is suffering identified with a cause. The very way they died shows they were caught in a vice. It has been, so to speak, a righteous death.

"It has added to the cause of those who seek the righteous cause."

And now the tears came, slowly at first, but this was a time to cry not only for Carole, who was beyond crying, but for mankind.

The minister spoke on of the crucifixation of Christ and compared Carole's death to His. Both died for causes and both left behind "one great fellowship of love".

The words of the minister died and The Jilters, a group of four young girls—stood up in their fresh green dresses. Laura Poole recited a poem remembering Carole and then the sometimes unsure voices of the girls turned to song.

At the piano was Mrs. Ruth Cowell, a teacher at the Wilkerson school. Carole was once a member of this group and it was fitting that the members should sing the last song for her.

Shortly after four the business at the church was concluded and the casket was carried out. Behind on the floor lay sprigs of greenery.

The Afro-American (Baltimore), September 28, 1963

Birmingham: "My God, You're Not Even Safe in Church"

by Karl Fleming

SPRING came menacingly to Birmingham as the Negro revolution budded, then blossomed violently amid the police dogs and fire hoses. And summer came, a sweaty season of tension and dwindling hope that the new city administration would fulfill spring's agreement to ease the rigid barriers against the Negro. Now summer gave way to a time of darkening fears. Would autumn and the court-ordered desegregation of Birmingham's public schools bring a new harvest of violence?

Schools opened. The Negroes entered. And the first week passed, disrupted only by noisy protests—little violence. But there was still Saturday, a dangerous day when the rednecks, with nothing much to do, would tank up in their jook joints. Anything could happen on Saturday night.

But nothing did. And Sunday dawned quietly, a day of unvarying routine for most of Birmingham's 340,887 people: best clothes, shiny shoes, Sunday school, church, chicken dinner, family visiting. Birmingham has 680 churches (425 white and 255 Negro), and city fathers are given to boasting that they are well attended. So they were as this Sunday came, a chilly overcast day full of the special quiet hustle that goes with getting the kids to Sunday school.

Because his wife was ailing, Claude A. Wesley, 54, gray-haired principal of a Negro school, oversaw the Sunday morning routine for his daughter, a bubbly bright-eyed 14-year-old named Cynthia. Together they did the dishes after a breakfast of bacon, eggs, and coffee before she got into her Sunday best—a ruffled white dress. Cynthia draped a red sweater over her shoulders, and quickly fed her cocker spaniel, Toots. Then she was ready.

After pausing under the sugarberry trees before their brick-front home to wave good-by to Mrs. Wesley, father and

26

daughter climbed in the family's black Mercury and drove to the 16th Street Baptist Church.

Wesley let Cynthia out at the curb and gently shooed her toward the buff brick church. "You go on in, honey," he said. "I'm going to get some gas and I'll be back in a minute."

At 9:22 a.m. Claude Wesley stood by his car at a service station two blocks from the church, watching the attendant fill the tank. Suddenly Sunday blew up. Rocks and glass rattled through the trees. Wesley heard screams and broke into a run toward the church. Someone had dynamited the Sunday school.

Within hours, the explosion sent a shock wave of horror and outrage throughout the South, across the land, around the world. The blast had killed four little Negro girls. There was every sign it would add new intensity to the seething racial turmoil of Birmingham—where bombings have been a commonplace—new fervor to the Negro revolt, new impetus to lagging Federal civil-rights legislation.

The first effect of the bombing, in Birmingham, was a fast-moving phantasmagoria of grief, terror, and hysteria. Pouring out of the church into the chilly street, women and children shrieked amid the debris. Men shouted. A young girl, Sarah Collins, staggered blindly out of the hole ripped by the explosion, her face spewing blood. She stretched her arms in front of her, unseeing, and screamed incoherently.

Negroes by the hundreds swarmed to the scene. Many flung rocks at police cars as they arrived, sirens whining. Half a dozen ambulances and a fire truck raced up into the pandemonium. A Negro woman, heel-deep in glass in the street, screamed: "In church! My God, you're not even safe in church." A slender Negro man with eyes wild with hate shrieked repeatedly: "Let me at the bastards. I'll kill them! I'll kill them!" "Murderers! Murderers!" a Negro woman echoed.

Inside the gutted church, workmen found—in addition to the four horribly battered bodies—blood-splattered copies of kindergarten leaflets bearing the day's prayer ("Dear God, we are sorry for the times when we were unkind") and pages from a religious coloring book. One youngster had been coloring an outline of a girl praying and, with a rough crayon scrawl, had rendered the face black. The main force of the dynamite had struck a dozen girls in a rest room by the downstairs auditorium.

Outside the church, Claude Wesley had been walking around and around looking for Cynthia. Someone finally suggested that Claude Wesley should go to the hospital. There he met his slender wife and they were taken to a room where the dead girls lay covered. "'They asked me if my daughter was wearing a ring," the father said. "I said yes, she was, and they pulled her little hand out and the little ring was there."

So went the melancholy business of identifying the other three victims—Denise McNair, age 11, Carole Robertson, age 14, and Addie Mae Collins, age 14. The blast decapitated one of them, left an apple-size hole in the back of another's head. Mrs. McNair, herself one of the 400 persons in the church when the bomb went off, had also searched desperately for her daughter. Finally, she reported sadly to her father, M. W. Pippen. "Daddy, I can't find Denise." "She's dead, baby," he sobbed. "I've got one of her shoes in here. I'd like to blow the whole town up."

For hours, as the families tended their dead, the city threatened to blow up. Birmingham Negroes had endured many bombings. The latest had been two different blasts within the last month at the home of Arthur D. Shores, an attorney; the best known—until Sunday—the explosion in the A. G. Gaston Motel while Martin Luther King Jr. was a guest last May 11. In all, there have been 50 bombings since World War II and so many in one Negro residential section that it is known as Dynamite Hill. But this time, the aftermath was almost as bloody as the blast itself.

Police and sheriff's deputies armed themselves with shotguns, carbines, rifles, and pistols. They fired over the heads of surging Negro crowds at the church, driving them into adjacent streets and alleys. Back came an answering hail of rocks and glass fragments.

As word of the bombing spread, rock fights between Negroes and whites broke out at street corners. One ended around 4:30 p.m. only when cops arrived. White youths, waving Confederate flags, remained behind, but the Negroes fled down an alley. An officer yelled for one of them, Johnny

Robinson, 16, to halt. When he didn't, the cop shotgunned him in the back. Robinson pitched forward, face down under a clothesline, blood pouring from his mouth. He was dead when they got him to University Hospital.

In the Northwest corner of the city, James Ware, a 16-year-old Negro, was bicycling homeward with his brother Virgil, 13, on the handle bars. On Docena Road a red motorbike, decorated with Confederate stickers and carrying two white youths, approached them. The boy riding double pulled out a pistol, fired twice. Virgil pitched off the handle bars. "Jim, I'm shot," he cried on the ground. "No, you ain't. You ain't shot. Get up, Virg," James said. Virgil, .22-caliber bullets in his head and chest, then died. The next day, two 16-year-old white boys, Michael Lee Farley and Larry Joe Sims, confessed. Farley drove the motorbike. Sims fired the shots. Earlier Sunday they had attended Sunday school. In the afternoon they attended a segregationist rally at a Go Kart track in nearby Midfield. Both were Eagle Scouts and neighbors considered them "model" Birmingham youths. They didn't know Virgil Ware. Why did they kill him? "They didn't give any reason," said the sheriff's office.

Birmingham's bloody Sunday passed, at length, after an anguished night lit by widespread arson and shattered by the crash of rock, glass, and gunfire. Whites shot and wounded two more Negroes during the night, and many whites—including a honeymoon couple going home to Chicago from Florida—were stoned by Negroes. When Monday finally came, nobody around could provide any clear reason for anything that had happened.

The reasons were not far to seek—in the long-steeping racism of Birmingham's whole seamy past; in the failure of the city's officials to implement the agreement ending last spring's bitter Negro demonstrations, in the ugly climate created by Gov. George C. Wallace through his latest defiance of the law and courts.

The city's Mayor Albert Boutwell, an affable lawyer touted as a "moderate," had been moderate indeed about meeting the demands presumably won by the Negroes in their negotiations. So far, desegregation, Birmingham-style, meant Negroes could eat at two white lunch counters; one municipal job had been upgraded.

Boutwell's response to the bombing now seemed characteristic. Graying and thin-mouthed, he wept real tears, but his words were self-exonerating: "All of us are victims," he said, "and most of us are innocent victims." His action only incensed the Negroes further. He called for assistance from Gov. George C. Wallace who promptly dispatched tough, head-knocking Col. Al Lingo and a company of state troopers to the city. "Sending Lingo in here was like spitting in our face," said one Negro.

For days before the bombing, Birmingham's temperament, already inflamed, had been raised to fever pitch by Governor Wallace himself through his illegal efforts to block school desegregation. President Kennedy, expressing a "deep sense of outrage and grief" over the bombing, pinned the responsibility on Wallace without naming him. "It is regrettable," the President said, "that public disparagement of law and order has encouraged violence which has fallen upon the innocent."

News of the bombing and the ensuing terror in Birmingham had hardly broken before the Kennedy Administration's chief racial trouble shooter, Assistant Attorney General Burke Marshall, flew to the scene. What he found was worse then he had imagined. Fear gripped the whole community—white as well as black. The police force's self-appointed job, he discovered, was to protect the whites against the Negroes. Negroes, Marshall found, were patrolling their own neighborhoods as armed vigilantes. Negro children attending newly desegregated schools couldn't get police protection; they had to call on U.S. marshals.

The city's Negro leadership was planning a massive protest march on the capitol in Montgomery. And soon, it was plain, massive demonstrations could well erupt again on Birmingham's streets. "There is a breakdown of law and order in Birmingham and we need Federal troops," a passionately gesturing Rev. Fred L. Shuttlesworth shouted to a Negro rally the day after Bloody Sunday.

Other Negro leaders, such as the Rev. Martin Luther King Jr., who flew in from Atlanta, took up the plea for the President to send in Federal troops. At least, they said, he could attend the funeral himself—or proclaim a day of national mourning for the four dead children.

But the basic urgent need in Birmingham, as Burke Marshall saw it, was to open communications between the races; they had completely broken down. "The police chief or Mayor Boutwell would have fainted if we had even suggested they confer with the Negro leaders," said a Justice Department official. The city, Marshall found, was unwilling even to go along with the suggestion that Negro police be added to the force to restore the Negro community's confidence in local law enforcement.

After Marshall reported the grim picture to Washington, the President agreed to see a delegation of seven Birmingham Negro leaders. Underscoring the Administration's cautious approach to the touchy crisis, the President also arranged to receive a delegation of white leaders from the city this week, and later a group of its white ministers.

Mr. Kennedy announced he was naming a two-man committee as his personal representatives to work for a conciliation of the races in Birmingham. The appointees: former Army football coach Earl H. (Red) Blaik, who has no special ties with the South, and former Army Secretary Kenneth C. Royall, a North Carolinian with an anti-Dixiecrat record.

To many, the naming of a committee seemed a feeble gesture; and there was some groping to understand the special qualifications of its two members. But Administration aides insisted this was a course both practical and indispensable. Marshall's own usefulness as a mediator had become hampered by rising antipathy to the Justice Department in Birmingham. And mediation was a necessity. It was the President's hope that Blaik and Royall, both respected, both men with military backgrounds, could reopen the dialogue between the deadlocked Negroes and whites. The Rev. Martin Luther King Jr., spokesman for the seven-man delegation that visited the White House, agreed it was a crucial objective. But others criticized the President for doing too little.

"We ask for Federal troops," said a Washington Negro bitterly, "and we get two retired officers." Author James Baldwin told an angry Manhattan rally that the appointment of a committee was an "insult to the Negro race." While protests flared, the search for the bombers went quietly and intensively on.

It wouldn't be an easy investigation. Birmingham police, despite their vast experience with bombings, have never solved one. But this time, a special force of fifteen FBI agents was on the scene, and a Justice Department spokesman said it would be the most rigorous manhunt since John Dillinger was bagged.

The reverberations of the crime pursued President Kennedy to New York City, where his appearance before the United Nations General Assembly drew bitter civil-rights pickets into nearby streets. Unaware they were outside, the President put the bombing in a world context in his address to the U.N., urging the organization to safeguard all human rights. "Those rights are not respected," he said, "when a Buddhist priest is driven from his pagoda, when a synagogue is shut down, when a Protestant church cannot open a mission, when a cardinal is forced into hiding, or when a crowded church is bombed."

But it was left to two Southerners to read the portents of Bloody Sunday most eloquently.

One, Charles Longstreet Weltner, a young congressman from Atlanta, Ga., took the bombing as a signal for Southern moderates to begin speaking out. "There was a time when silence amid the denunciations of others was a positive virtue," he said. "But, in face of the events on Sunday, who can remain silent? . . . I know why it happened. It happened because those chosen to lead have failed to lead. Those whose task it is to speak have stood mute. And in so doing, we have permitted the voice of the South to preach defiance and disorder. We have stood by, leaving the field to reckless and violent men. For all our hand-wringing . . . we will never put down violence until we can raise a higher standard."

The other Southerner, Martin Luther King Jr., spoke a moving epitaph for Cynthia Wesley, Denise McNair, Carole Robertson, and Addie Mae Collins. "They are the martyred heroines of a holy crusade for freedom and human dignity," he said. ". . . They have something to say to each of us in their death . . . to every minister of the gospel who has remained silent behind the safe security of stained-glass windows . . . to every politician who has fed his constituents with the stale bread of hatred and the spoiled meat of racism

. . . They say to us that we must be concerned not merely about who murdered them but about the system, the way of life, the philosophy which produced the murderers. Their death says to us that we must work passionately and unrelentingly for the realization of the American dream. And so, my friends, they did not die in vain . . ."

Newsweek, September 30, 1963

The Military's Limited War Against Segregation

by Ruth and Edward Brecher

FOLLOWING World War II, on orders from President Truman, the Army, Navy, and Air Force abolished their traditional Jim Crow units and with very little fanfare integrated themselves. On a recent 3,200-mile tour of the South, we viewed the impressive results.

We saw Negro and white servicemen eating at the same mess-hall tables, drinking at the same on-base bars, playing ball on the same teams. They sleep in the same barracks, share lavatories and showers, borrow money from one another until pay day.

In on-base homes assigned without regard for race, white and Negro families live next door to one another, baby-sit for one another, watch TV together, share backyard barbecues. They swim together in on-base pools, worship together in military chapels. Their children play and squabble happily together on the lawns, attend on-base schools and Sunday schools together. All this has for years been accepted practice on military bases, including many in the Deep South.

Some white service families, to be sure, remain personally aloof; that is their privilege. But "stirring up trouble" on base has become a social misdemeanor. Many Negro servicemen and their wives assured us that nowhere else had they ever experienced such complete or such successful neighbor-to-neighbor integration.

The speed with which Southerners as well as Northerners adapt to this integrated military way of life must be seen to be believed. Negro and white recruits reporting for induction are herded together into buses without prior indoctrination and driven to their first assignment, hours or even days away, in elbow-to-elbow intimacy. From the onset white Southerners take orders from Negro officers and non-coms as a matter of course—a decisive demonstration that abrupt social change is feasible, even when dictated by outside authority rather than inner conviction.

"This must be your first experience associating with Negroes," we remarked to a sandy-haired GI hitchhiking home from Fort Lee—an Army post in Virginia—for a weekend on his father's small farm on the Virginia-Tennessee border.

"Sure is."

"It must have taken quite a while to get used to."

"Sure did—'bout two weeks."

Often white and Negro GIs form firm friendships. "Our best friends at Fort Knox were a white couple from New Orleans," the wife of a Negro lieutenant colonel told us. "We were all heartbroken when we were shipped out—we to Germany and they to Japan. But now we're all back in the States again, and they're bringing their kids for a visit next month." White service families have described similar friendships.

Military integration changes those who experience it. Negroes expect more after they leave the service, and white ex-servicemen are generally willing to yield more. In several Southern cities we found white and Negro ex-officers, ex-GIs, and their wives active in the small but fervent integrationist groups which meet till long past midnight in one another's living rooms to plan their community's next steps toward desegregation. And when such groups negotiate with local officials and business groups for integration concessions, ex-servicemen are commonly found on both sides of the bargaining table.

White segregationists realize that military integration is helping crumble local racial barriers. "My own nephew argues with me about segregation since he's been in the Air Force," an Alabama bank president told us with wry candor. As a guest of the nearby Army base commander recently, this banker for the first time in his life had dinner with a Negro. Though he doesn't like the prospect of integration, he's getting used to the idea.

So, too, are the tens of thousands of Defense Department civil servants who stream into the huge Army, Navy, and Air Force installations each morning. All day they work side by side with Negroes, take orders from Negro supervisors, use integrated washrooms. Evenings and weekends, too, Southern civilians flock to the bases as guests at integrated officers' and enlisted men's clubs. They shake hands with Negro club members, bowl at integrated alleys, play integrated bingo, attend integrated lectures, concerts, art shows, and religious revival meetings. Seeing such activities in the heart of the South, we found it hard to realize that a few miles away, Negroes were being arrested and beaten for seeking a cup of coffee at a lunch counter.

For the sorry truth is that integration stops abruptly at the gates of the military reservations. Just outside those gates, "White Only" signs can be seen on restaurants, bars, and theatres—even drive-in movie theatres—from Maryland to Texas.

We learned at first hand from scores of Negro and white officers and GIs, and from their wives, about the many forms of off-base discrimination, crude and subtle, brutal or merely demeaning, which assail the Negro serviceman and his family. In retelling their stories, we have omitted or altered names of individuals and left locations indefinite for obvious though painful reasons.

The South today is ablaze. Reprisals are daily occurrences. When it was alleged in a local newspaper, for example, that the sister-in-law of the president of a dry-cleaning company had attended an integrated prayer meeting, a boycott was organized against the dry-cleaning company. The small integrationist groups which meet in many Southern communities often receive bombing threats and must change their meeting places frequently. Some integrated meetings have been bombed. Publicity concerning one integrationist group led to tape-recorded attacks on it broadcast all day, every hour on the hour, over a local radio station. To identify a white civilian as an integrationist is to expose him at the very least to a barrage of 2:00 A.M. "hate calls" on the phone and piles of garbage on his lawn. Negro activists, of course, run much graver risks— loss of jobs, police harassment, and "stray" bullets.

Even on the military side of the fence, a man's career may be subtly but significantly affected if he is identified as either an integrationist or a segregationist. At least one influential Southern Congressman is out for the scalp of an Air Force commander who took a step toward integration; another commander suffered transfer to a distant post after he was ac-

cused of "dragging his feet" in carrying out an integration order from Washington. Anonymity is thus a pearl beyond price
in the turbulent South today. The identities of even the officially appointed members of biracial negotiating committees
are commonly kept a closely guarded secret.

Among those who must remain anonymous is an Army
master sergeant we'll call Lincoln Smith. He is typical of the
many dedicated Negro career men on whom the Armed
Forces rely to train recruits and carry out countless other essential military duties. In 1962, after eighteen years' service at
Northern and overseas posts, Master Sergeant Smith got his
bad news: transfer to a base in the South.

On arriving there with his wife and three daughters, he
learned to his dismay that no on-base quarters were available.
This is a common experience; half of all servicemen these days
are married—and the military services have housing for barely
half of their married personnel.

White families who arrived with the Smiths moved temporarily into motels or tourist camps. But most Southern
motels are closed to Negroes. For their first few weeks, as a
result, the Smiths had to swelter in a run-down Negro room-
ing house, in a single room, with a curtain rigged down the
middle; kitchen and bathroom "privileges" were shared with
three other families. The few modern homes and apartments
open to Negroes were full, and waiting lists long. Eventually
the Smiths had to settle for a shack on a dusty unpaved back
street lacking even street lights. It has three small rooms and
a rickety front stoop, a kitchen sink, and a rusty shower stall
but no tub or running hot water. "The only reason I put up
with it is to keep the family together," Mrs. Smith explained.

Overseas, an American commander would do his best to
get his men out of billets like this—but in the South, such accommodations for Negro service families are accepted as a
matter of course.

On his way to the base each morning, Sergeant Smith
passes an attractive air-conditioned FHA-financed housing
project. It was built for service families. Its rents are little
more than the Smiths pay for their shack. And there are half-
a-dozen vacancies—but none for Negroes.

Bad as their housing is, the Smiths worry even more about

education. "We can wait, but our girls' schooling can't; it's now or never," Mrs. Smith said. She herself attended integrated Northern public schools many years ago; that her daughters at this late date should have to attend a Jim Crow school is gall and wormwood for the Smiths.

Master Sergeant Smith is not timid about standing up for his daughters' rights. If he were not in uniform, he might sue to secure their admission to a white school. But as a serviceman in the South, he hesitates. He has eighteen years' seniority at stake. He has heard rumors—and so have we—of Negro servicemen who have taken part in off-base desegregation activities and who have shortly thereafter been labeled "troublemakers" and threatened with reprisals—transfer to some post in Alaska or Greenland, for example, where they cannot have their families with them at all.

These rumors can seldom be confirmed. Some may be apocryphal. But they are widely believed—and no one in authority has ever assured Negro servicemen that they are free to demand their constitutional and off-base human rights. So the rumors have become deterrents; and the Smiths end up feeling even more frustrated than Negro civilians who can at least protest, demonstrate, and sue.

Sergeant Smith has had no trouble personally with the local police force. "I always go straight home nights," he says. And there have been no beatings, jailings, or police-dog attacks in the immediate vicinity during recent months. But an incident or two a year is quite enough to keep a whole population "in its place."

So Sergeant Smith walks the city streets with eyes averted, does not take his daughters to the zoo or other places where they may not be welcome, and avoids looking or sounding "uppity" in the presence of a white man or woman. "If I'd been raised in the South I'd probably catch myself saying, 'Yas, suh, boss,'" he remarked, with an effort to smile.

On base, Master Sergeant Smith must play a very different role—that of a man of dignity and self-assurance, training his troops in the defense of their country. He does his very best. But like tens of thousands of other Negro Americans held in the South by their military orders, his ability to perform his duties boldly and efficiently on base is inevitably impaired by the "disintegration fatigue" from which he suffers off base.

Jim Crow also undermines white morale. A white infantryman from Kentucky stationed in rural Georgia was as bitter on this score as any Negro. "Eleven of us were transferred back from Germany to this hole," he told us. "Three of us are Negroes—great guys, guys you'd trust your life to. We'd been buddying around together all over Europe. First Saturday night here, we headed for town to celebrate with a few beers."

Bar after bar refused to admit them together. When they finally elbowed their way into a Negro spot, the bartender called the police. "Said he'd lose his license if he didn't. The cops jugged us for the night, in segregated cells. When we got back to the base late for drill next morning, the sergeant took away our privileges for a month." The charge was drunkenness. "But hell, we never did finish one beer. Now we go to town separately, and come back mad. The three of them have a grudge against the world, and I don't blame them—but sometimes I wonder what it would be like to go into action with guys nursing grudges. We're all getting out of here the day our time's up. . . ."

"Re-enlist? Hell, no!"

Maxwell Air Force Base in Alabama, Fort Benning in Georgia, and several other large Southern installations serve, in addition to their other functions, as training centers for foreign officers. Among these military guests have been high-ranking Haitians, Liberians, Ethiopians, and others with dark skin. To shield them from affronts, one base supplies foreign officers with handsomely embossed "passports," signed by the mayor, the Chamber of Commerce president, and the base commander. The officers are warned to carry these documents with them whenever they leave the base. But insults, refusals of restaurant service, and other incidents occur despite this and other precautions. And the passport system is peculiarly offensive to Negro American servicemen.

"I had two strikes on me down there," said an MIT graduate who had recently completed his tour of duty. "In addition to being a Negro I was an *American* Negro and wore an *American* uniform. They wouldn't give me a passport so *I* could eat in a decent restaurant or go to a first-run movie." A Negro captain's wife at another base complained: "You can live almost anywhere around here if you speak with a foreign accent. And your kids can go to the white school, even though they're a lot darker than my kids. The only people they discriminate against around here are *American* Negroes."

The Department of Defense took its first short step toward solving off-base discrimination problems in June 1961, when a Pentagon order directed that commanders "make every effort" to secure integrated off-base facilities for their men.

But the order also specified that commanders should use for this purpose their "community relations committees," composed of high-ranking officers and civilian leaders. These committees had previously been devoted to maintaining cordial relations between the bases and their neighboring communities. At many Southern bases, unfortunately, the committees were peculiarly unsuited to their new mission.

Some dated back to the day when a few ruling families still constituted the unchallenged local "power structure." Some had fifty or even a hundred members; inclusion on the committee had become a social honor comparable to listing in the Social Register. Quite a few commanding generals and admirals were themselves born and bred in the South, and kin to the local elite whom they planned to rejoin on retirement. Such officers would hardly venture to trouble their distinguished committee members with the discrimination problems of Master Sergeant Smith—especially if, as was often the case, leading local segregationists sat on the committee. Though the South was rapidly changing, few committee members died and none retired. When the United States Commission on Civil Rights (established by Congress in 1957) checked up on what had been accomplished during the first year of the off-base integration order, it was able to find few signs of progress. Some committees, and even some commanders, were unaware that the order even existed.

This year, following the Civil Rights Commission checkup, the 1961 order was revived and supplemented. On March 6, for example, the Navy instructed "all ships and stations" to "include local leaders of all ethnic groups" on the committees and to establish liaison with ". . . influential local community organizations such as, but not limited to, the Chamber of Commerce, the Rotary, the National Association for the Advancement of Colored People, the Lions, the Urban League, the Young Men's and Young Women's Christian Associations, and the Kiwanis."

On our own recent swing through the South, we noted some resulting harbingers of change. At one base, for example, a commander skilled in social as well as military tactics had first cut his committee down to working size. In the process, he quietly dropped members who might balk at serving with Negroes. He then added two prominent Negro leaders and took the whole group on a two-day military junket to get acquainted with each other. After a few further shakedown dinners and social sessions, he dumped into their laps his most pressing community problems: integrated schooling and the opening of restaurants, hotels, and theatres to all servicemen and their families. The first fruits of the new approach were promptly harvested; courses at the previously all-white university branch near the base were opened to Negro servicemen with barely a ripple of local protest.

At another base we visited, the commander had appointed one Negro to his committee but was hesitating to take the next step. At a third, the commander was balking. "I'd be willing to appoint a Nigra," he told us, "but there isn't a Nigra around here qualified to serve." He was mistaken, of course. During a very brief stay in his area, we met several Negroes capable of serving with distinction.

Some commanders and their staffs displayed a surprising ignorance of conditions outside their gates. "No complaints around here," we were assured at one Georgia base. But ex-GIs who had served there told a different story: they had not dared to complain while still in uniform for fear of reprisals. Currently under consideration by the Defense Department is a proposal that a specially qualified officer on each base— preferably one with legal training, free of personal prejudice— be charged with the duty both of investigating all civil-rights complaints, reprisal threats, and other common grievances of Negro servicemen and their families, and of alerting the commander to abuses even in the absence of formal complaints.

The Defense Department is also seeking in other ways to ease the pressure on its Negro personnel in the South. It has requested an appropriation, for example, to build 12,000 new housing units on bases next year. Congressmen were shocked when Secretary of Defense McNamara, testifying personally in support of this appropriation, showed them photographs of shacks in which service families now live.

But even if the 12,000 new units are built, the surface of the military housing problem will barely be scratched. According to Secretary McNamara's own figures, 106,000 military families live off-base in homes that do not meet military standards because of their physical condition or their small size or their distance from the base. An additional 32,000 families live in substandard on-base housing. And 24,000 married servicemen are living apart from their families because they can't find family housing at all. The brunt of these housing hardships falls with discriminatory weight on Negro service families.

The 12,000 new units should, of course, be built. In addition, private entrepreneurs must be persuaded to build integrated housing near the bases. President Kennedy's Housing Order of November 1962 opens the door for FHA financing of new integrated housing developments throughout the country; but to date, little has been done to put this order to use near military installations. And local commanders, with the help of their reorganized community-relations committees, must be directed to protect the builders from segregationist interference. This is not as formidable an assignment as it might appear to be from a distance. Even the Deep South has for years calmly accepted integrated housing on one side of the military fence; with tactical skill it can no doubt be led to accept it on the other side, too.

Schooling, like housing, is a disgrace to our Armed Forces. Servicemen's children at 248 bases still attend segregated off-base schools; and nine years after the Supreme Court school decision, the federal government is still subsidizing these schools with federal "impacted-area" payments. Worse yet, federal funds are still being furnished for the construction of new segregated schools.

To date, the U.S. Department of Health, Education, and

Welfare has allotted more than $21 million for the construction of such schools in Alabama, more than $33 million for Georgia, and more than $8 million for Mississippi. In addition, generous annual subsidies help meet the operating expenses of these schools—$5.3 million to Alabama school districts last year, $5.6 million to Georgia, and $1.8 million to Mississippi. Negro schools in these districts are likely to be inferior in many respects. Some are not accredited; some use cast-off books from the white schools; some are on double shift. Yet the formula used to compute the subsidies allows as much per Negro pupil as per white pupil.

Fort Lee in Virginia is an example of the system at its worst. The 1,613 children of white servicemen posted there go to bright new Prince George County public schools. The 210 children of Negro servicemen are instead transported by bus to Negro schools in the next county. The Prince George County school board receives federal payments for educating the Negro as well as the white children—but "subcontracts" the Negro children to the Petersburg, Virginia, school board!

School integration throughout the South has been delayed by such practices; for so long as Washington not only tolerates but subsidizes school segregation and discrimination, Southern communities find it hard to believe the government means business on enforcing the Supreme Court decision.

Recently, it is true, the Justice Department has brought suit to desegregate schools receiving federal subsidies in Prince George County and in Huntsville, Madison County and Mobile County, Alabama; Bossier Parish, Louisiana; and Gulfport and Biloxi, Mississippi. Also, the Department of Health, Education, and Welfare is building new integrated elementary schools on eight large Southern reservations—Maxwell Air Force Base, Fort McClellan, and Fort Rucker in Alabama; Robins Air Force Base and Fort Stewart in Georgia; England Air Force Base in Louisiana; and Myrtle Beach Air Force Base and Fort Jackson in South Carolina. Fifteen school boards, in Florida and Texas, have agreed to desegregate "voluntarily," under threat of withdrawal of subsidies or Justice Department suits. But these measures, like the housing measures, barely scratch the surface of the problem. This fall, as in past years, the great majority of children of Negro servicemen stationed in the South at their country's call will be enrolled in segregated schools.

Clearly, new techniques are needed to deal with these ugly situations. One approach as yet untried is the "status of forces agreement" commonly used in foreign countries. Before a base is opened abroad, American officials secure a signed agreement from local authorities safeguarding the rights of military personnel. Similar agreements might be negotiated with American states, cities, and school boards—especially at the strategic moment when Southern lobbyists are in Washington hungrily seeking a new base or the expansion of an existing base. Along with a pleasant climate, safe water supply, and adequate approach highways, federal officials responsible for selecting base locations might consider whether a site assures satisfactory off-base housing, education, public accommodations, and police protection for Negro as well as white personnel. Private industry weighs such factors when choosing plant sites. Had the Defense Department been equally prudent, a disproportionate number of large military bases would not now be crowded into the South.

Strategic opportunities for securing such agreements have been neglected as recently as this spring, when a $400-million installation was allotted to southern Mississippi for military and civilian missile-engine testing. No civil-rights assurances were secured from the Mississippi communities which will boom as a result of the facility's location. The moral issue aside, there is here also a practical issue: it won't be easy to staff the new installation in a turmoil-blighted region.

Another technique often discussed but rarely invoked is use of the power to declare "off-limits" to all servicemen any establishment which refuses to serve Negro servicemen. It is theoretically possible, too, to close down a base altogether and transfer its payroll and purchases to a more hospitable neighborhood.

As a practical matter, however, such steps would no doubt be effectively blocked by powerful Southern Congressmen who are endowed, through their seniority, with the chairmanships of key military affairs and appropriations committees. One measure of their influence is the present weirdly disproportionate crowding of military establishments below the Mason and Dixon line. "If they put any more bases in Alabama, they'll sink the state," an Air Force commander said recently.

Yet another obvious but rarely used remedy for the off-base grievances of Negro GIs is resort to the law of the land. The federal courts, and a few Southern state courts as well, are building magnificent records in safeguarding human rights. A victim of false arrest, a family which cannot rent in a new FHA-financed housing project, or a couple whose child is refused access to a white school can appeal to the courts with considerable likelihood of securing redress eventually. But the prerequisite for court action is skilled legal counsel, a commodity in lamentably short supply for Negroes in the South.

The Armed Forces supply servicemen and their dependents with doctors when they are sick and dentists when they have a toothache—but not with lawyers when they suffer illegal discrimination off-base.

A modest move in this direction has recently been made, it is true. A recent Naval instruction, for example, states: "Legal assistance officers may be employed to assure that members of the Armed Forces are accorded due process of law." The instruction spells out specific steps to be taken "if it appears that civil rights . . . may be infringed on." But these noble phrases refer to legal *advice*, not representation in court—the service which GIs in the South really need.

Recently, too, the Defense Department has been struggling with the problem of whether or not to permit servicemen to participate in peaceful off-base demonstrations when off duty and out of uniform. In June, the Air Force took a small step in this direction; in July (under pressure from Congressmen) the Defense Department modified the June order but did not yield completely. As a result, few servicemen know just where they stand. Orders giving GIs other rights, too, have never been adequately explained to personnel. A right is of little value to a man who doesn't know he has it. A military statement of off-base civil-rights policy, addressed directly to the rank and file, is long overdue.

Also overdue is firm action to clean out the isolated remnants of on-base discrimination which survive in a few commands. They are not common, even in the Deep South, and usually it is the spirit rather than the letter of the integration orders which is violated—but they rankle all the same. No commander these days, for example, would tell Negro officers or non-coms that they are unwelcome in an on-base club. To do so would be to invite court-martial. But there are subtler ways to achieve the same effect. A commander can set up several clubs, staff one of them with a Negro manager, load its jukebox with Negro records, and hire Negro bands for gala events. Negro personnel get the message quickly.

Similarly, no commander would forbid a serviceman to bring a Negro guest to an on-base club. But he can bar guests from within a radius of fifty miles—and then neglect to enforce the order when the guests are white.

Military establishments, like other federal agencies, are under long-standing Presidential directives to hire, promote, and fire civilian employees without regard to race. Yet at one on-base cafeteria we visited, the only Negroes in sight were busboys clearing away dirty dishes. The civil-service employees eating in the cafeteria were without exception white. One way of achieving a lily-white civilian working force, we learned, is by posting notices of civil-service examinations and vacancies only in segregated places where Negroes won't see them. No doubt there are other dodges, too.

Little additional effort would be needed to clean out such anachronistic pockets of discrimination on military bases and thus complete with flying colors the job begun many years ago.

Detailed recommendations for reform, both off base and on, were formulated in June by President Kennedy's Committee on Equal Opportunity in the Armed Forces. In forwarding these recommendations to the Secretary of Defense, the President urged that the military consider them promptly. He called discriminatory practices "morally wrong," and announced: "I am asking the military community to take a leadership role. . . ."

Defense Secretary McNamara in reply promised prompt action and even agreed that in extreme cases businesses or communities discriminating against Negro servicemen might be "declared off-limits" to all servicemen. He gave the three services until August 15 to prepare improvements in their integration policies.

The next moves are thus up to the Army, Navy, and Air Force. Their response during the next few months may have an important impact on the pace of change throughout the South—and in the North as well.

Harper's, September 1963

The Battle-Scarred Youngsters

by Howard Zinn

HAVING just spent a little time in Greenwood, Miss., I felt a certain air of unreality about the March on Washington. The grandiose speeches, the array of movie stars, the big names dropped and bounced several times, the sheer impress of numbers—all added up, technically, to an occasion that one describes as "thrilling." And it must have been so to participants and to the millions who watched on television. Still, while swept up in the spirit myself, I wondered if, to the Negro citizen of Greenwood, Itta Bena and Ruleville; of Albany, Americus and Dawson; of Selma, Gadsden and Birmingham; of Danville and other places, it may not have seemed the most Gargantuan and best organized of irrelevancies.

There was one relevant moment in the day's events at Washington: that was when the youngest speaker on the platform, John Lewis, chairman of the Student Non-Violent Coordinating Committee, lashed out in anger, not only at the Dixiecrats, but at the Kennedy Administration, which had been successful up to that moment in directing the indignation of 200,000 people at everyone but itself.

The depth of Lewis' feeling and the direction of his attack may have baffled Northern liberals, mollified recently by the Administration's new Civil Rights Bill, by its bold words and by the President's endorsement of the great March. But John Lewis knew, because the young SNCC workers in his organization are on the front lines of the conflict, that while the President and the Attorney General speak loud in Washington, their voices are scarcely whispers in the towns and the hamlets of the Black Belt.

Greenwood, Miss., just before the March, revealed in its

own quiet way how the Deep South remains essentially untouched by resonant speeches in the national capital.

Surrounded by cotton plantations, Greenwood overlooks the Delta from a vantage point in west-central Mississippi. It is the headquarters for the Voter Registration Project, in which all the major civil-rights organizations cooperate, and whose working force is supplied mainly by the youngsters of the Student Nonviolent Coordinating Committee (SNCC— affectionately called SNICK). It is the seat of Leflore County, where Negroes are 65 per cent of the population and half the Negro families have an income less than $27 a week. Almost no Negroes vote, and attempts of the past year to register Negroes have been met with torch, shotgun and a dozen varieties of official brutality, intimidation and subterfuge.

The SNICK "office" in Greenwood is like a front company headquarters during wartime. As I came in one evening last August, having driven from Memphis, I was greeted by Annelle Ponder, whose younger sister I taught at Spelman College in Atlanta, and whose path has crossed mine several times in the last few hectic years. The Ponder girls are all tall, black-skinned and beautiful. Annelle has been in Greenwood this past year handling the Southern Christian Leadership Conference's part of the voter registration project. She is quiet and courageous. She has been beaten by police in Winona, Miss. When friends went to the jail one day, they found her sitting there, her face swollen and marked, barely able to speak. She looked up at them, and just managed to whisper one word: "Freedom."

With Annelle at headquarters were a bunch of the SNICK kids. One of them came forward to shake hands and we recognized each other—it was Stokely Carmichael, a tall, slender philosophy student at Howard University, born in the West Indies and reared in the sit-in movement. We had met in Albany, Ga., during the first outburst of trouble there in December, 1961.

What was on for the evening? A mass meeting at one of the Negro churches. And then a party at the home of one of the girls.

They showed my wife and me around the building: on the first floor, a big jumbled room for meetings, with a long table in the center—this was the dining room, too, for whatever voter registration workers were around when mealtime came —and a small kitchen to the side, where Mrs. Johnson cooked the meals. Upstairs were cubicles serving as offices, and a large area with two iron cots in a corner, for travelers in the movement. Cartons of books were on the floor; they had been donated by a Northern college, and were soon to go on new pine bookshelves.

At the church meeting, middle-aged Negroes who had lived forty and fifty years in the Delta without shaking a white person's hand came up to shake hands and say hello. Greenwood has this past year been going through that tense, hopeful process begun recently in many communities of the Deep South—the first contact on an equal basis with white people; an awakening to the possibility of genuine brotherhood. These first white friends have been college students from New England, or ministers from the Middle West, or just interested people passing through—rather than local whites. But it is a start. And among the SNICK youngsters manning battle posts in the Black Belt have been young white Southerners: Bob Zellner from Alabama, Sandra Hayden from Texas. It is a beginning, and credit belongs mostly to the Student Nonviolent Coordinating Committee for blasting open in various parts of the Deep South the first pockets of equal interracial contact.

For Southern whites, watching at the edge of these pockets, it is a painful but inexorable educational process. The first reactions to the sight of Negroes and whites in friendly contact are outrage, fury, often violence. But repetition of the vision dulls the reflex and there begins, not acceptance yet, but at least hesitancy.

Perhaps Greenwood police this past year have begun to move into the second stage. When a police car stopped my wife and me as we were driving away from the SNICK party, they seemed at least a little accustomed to the idea. They flashed their lights again and again into our faces and into the car, and cast looks at the house where the lights were on and the noise of the party could still be heard. They spent some time examining identification papers and then (unlike a previous similar experience in Atlanta, where my companion was a Negro and we were arrested) muttered for us to move on.

*

The next afternoon, a race against time began among the SNICK workers in the Greenwood office. Thirteen youngsters were in Parchman state prison farm, and had been there for two months. Forty-five other Negroes—men and women of all ages—had been on the county prison farm, also for two months. All of them had been arrested in June on charges of "breach of the peace." After much legal delay, release was at hand. A young lawyer, representing the National Council of Churches, had come to Greenwood with bond money for these fifty-eight people. But it turned out that information supplied him by local officials, and transcribed on the bonds, was full of errors, and the county attorney would not accept the bonds. If the transaction could not be completed by that Friday afternoon, the prisoners would have to spend another weekend in jail.

The proper information was quickly compiled, and all available typewriters and people who could type were assembled in the Voter Registration Project office. The new data were typed in. The papers were taken to the sheriff. Just before dusk on Friday the fifty-eight emerged.

The headquarters that night had the eerie quality of a field hospital after a battle. Youngsters out of jail—sixteen and seventeen years old—were sprawled here and there. Two of them lay on the narrow cots upstairs while a few of the SNICK girls dabbed their eyes with boric acid solutions; some dietary deficiency in jail had affected their eyes. One boy nursed an infected hand. Another boy's foot was swollen; he had started to lose feeling in it while in "the hot box" at Parchman, and had stamped on it desperately again and again to restore circulation. Medical attention was refused them in prison. The cold newspaper reports of the past few years about people arrested in various parts of the Deep South for demonstrating have never conveyed the reality of a Black Belt jail.

Three SNICK youngsters, with a tape recorder on the broken-down table near us, told about their arrest, and about life at Parchman. The first was Willie Rogers:

. . . it was twenty minutes to one when the chief came out of his car and across the street in front of the courthouse. It was June 25th —Tuesday. The chief said, I'm askin' you-all to move on. We said that we were up there to get our folks registered. So he said, I'm askin' you-all to move on, you're crowdin' the sidewalk—the sidewalk was clear. We walked up to the courthouse steps so as not to block the sidewalk. He said, I'm askin' you to leave now. We said we came to get them registered and soon as they registered we would leave. So he started placing us under arrest—one by one. . . .

We stayed in jail about two hours before trial came off, and the judge sentenced us to four months and $200 fine for refusing to move on, and about an hour later they came and took us to the penal farm, which we stayed out on the penal farm about a week and worked. . . . Tuesday, without us knowin', they had sentenced us to Mississippi State Penitentiary, Parchman, Mississippi. . . . Two boys named John Hanley and Arthur Jackson and I—he put us in the hot box. We stayed in the hot box two nights. It's about five foot nine inches square, which is why they call it the hot box. Long as they don't turn the heat on—with three in there—you can make it. There's no openings for light or air—there was a little crack under the door, but you couldn't see your hand before your face less you get down on your knees. When they got ready to feed you they hand the tray through a little door which they close—and then you can't eat unless you get down on your knees by the light comin' in the door—then you can see how to eat. And they had a little round hole in the floor which was a commode—about as big around as a six-pound bucket top. After we stayed in there those two nights, the sergeant started pickin' at me: "You're the lyingest nigger in Greenwood, aren't you?" I told him no, I didn't lie, which I had, because I didn't tell him nothing about the movement in Greenwood. . . . The last night he decided to take our T-shirts and things—so we decided not to wear no underwear. So he decided to open all the windows and turn on the fans, and the beds that we were sleepin' on, they didn't have no tick or nothing, just metal, and had round holes in it. So last night I didn't sleep—I stayed up all night and all day today and he came in right after lunch and MacArthur Cotton and I, we weren't saying anything, and the guards came around and handcuffed us to the bar. . . . I'm seventeen.

. . . My name is Jesse James Glover. I live in Itta Bena, Mississippi. I was arrested at the courthouse in Greenwood—charged for likewise, not movin' on. Some of the older people with us, they moved on. But we didn't think it expedient to move, because the courthouse is a public place. So we stayed. . . . We had a trial next morning. We didn't have a lawyer. . . . We stayed at the county farm four days. We dug ditches in the white part of town. We decided among ourselves we weren't going to work or eat any more because we were afraid of being shot from a car passing the road or by one of the guards, because we were all working with SNICK. We didn't eat for two days, neither worked, then they came to take us to Parchman. There was about 25–30 policemen outside with guns and blackjacks and things standing around the bus when we came out— we all put our hands behind our heads and they searched us all, put us on the bus. So we left. . . . We stayed there a week and then I took sick. He didn't let me see a doctor. That's the man in charge. They call him "sergeant." We ate twice a day. At night they put the fan on and it was cold. We were sleepin' on a steel bunk with forty-four holes in it. . . . A week later I was put in a place called the hot box. I stayed in this hot box two days and a half. I was put in because Freddie Harris and Lawrence Guyot and I was whisperin' to each other. Another week I was put in the hot box again. I stayed there four days. About half a week later he said some lice had gotten in the place, so he cut all our hair and gave us some blue ointment and put fourteen of us in a cell—two beds for fourteen of us. We stayed there all night. About another week, I got put into this hot box again—he said we were talkin'. He put nine of us in this box— it's about six by six. Nine of us—we couldn't lie down. . . . Three or four more days they began to take our T-shirts and cut our food in half—so we gave our shorts back because we said what good are shorts without T-shirts. So they put us back in the cell, without our shorts, and turned on the fan again. We were naked. It was real cold. . . . The next day he put thirteen of us in the hole, this six by six hole. We were making it okay about 30 minutes with the fan off —breathing in this oxygen, lettin' out this carbon dioxide—and the air was evaporating on top of the building, and it got so hot the water was falling off the top of the building all around the sides like it was raining. One boy was taken sick in the box. They took the sick boy out—they didn't take him to a doctor—they put him in a cell for that morning. He let us out of the hot box that morning, back in the cell. We told everyone to keep quiet because we didn't want to get in the hot box again—it might cause a death in the hot box. So we all was quiet for a long time. Then a few fellows were talking to each other. He came down and told Lawrence Guyot, I'm going to put these niggers up to this damn bar if I hear any of this racket —so they hung MacArthur Cotton, Arthur Jackson, and Willie Rogers on the bars—MacArthur was singin' some Freedom songs. . . . Altogether, I was thirteen days in the hot box. . . . How did I get in the movement? I was at a mass meeting in Itta Bena. I'd been walkin' and canvassin' on my own. Bob Moses asked me, did I want to work with SNICK. I told him yes. So from then on I been working. Monday I'm startin' school, but in the evening in Itta Bena I'm going to get young people to work with me canvassing—teach the old people how to fill out the forms—try to get my town moving.

. . . My name is Fred Harris. He came around and said, you gonna move? you gonna move? And he frightened the old people. And when we didn't move he arrested us. . . . I stayed in the hole four days. In all I spent 160 hours in the hole—the hot box that is. He told me next time he found paper on the floor in my cell he would hang me up by my arms and my legs. And about a week after that I asked to see the doctor, and he told me, yes, when I die. I'm seventeen. I'll be starting school Monday. I got involved with the movement back in 1960, when SNICK came up. I was fourteen then. Sam Block was talking to me about the movement. I told him, yes, I'd be glad to help, and I started from there on. . . . At first my mother didn't want me to be in it. Then she realized it would be best for her and for me if I were in the movement, so she told me I could go ahead and work in the movement. . . .

While the returned prisoners took turns lying on the bunks, SNICK workers were being delivered to different parts of the Negro section of Greenwood to announce a mass meeting that night to welcome the prisoners back home. You find, roughly, three kinds of SNICK workers in a place like Greenwood: two or three regular staff members, who make $10 or $20 a week—in those weeks when there is money; ten to fifteen students from various parts of the country who have left school temporarily to work with SNICK, and who subsist on $5 or $10 perhaps every other week; indeterminate numbers of young people from the town and the surrounding countryside, who volunteer their time, risk their lives and their liberty, and get an occasional meal at headquarters.

I sat in on the staff meeting next morning, held in the large main room. In one corner was a boiler, in another a rubbish can. On the walls were a map of the City of Greenwood, newspaper clippings on civil rights, photos of Pete Seeger when he was in Greenwood, photos of Jim Forman (executive secretary of SNICK). Scattered around were two typewriters, some broken chairs, books and newspapers and a big pot for Kool-aid.

But if poverty showed in the material possessions at SNICK headquarters, the human resources were something else. Chairing the meeting was Bob Moses, the quiet fighter in charge of the Voter Registration Project, a veteran by now of Mississippi violence and nonviolence. Here was Sam Block, silent, thin, dark, his home deep in the Delta, who did the early reconnaissance for SNICK in the area and almost lost his life for it. Here was Willie Peacock, also from Mississippi, another SNICK veteran. Annelle Ponder was here, representing SCLC (Martin Luther King's group); Martha Prescod, a slender college student from the North; Stokely Carmichael, the fiery young man from Howard; Jean Wheeler, a smiling coed, also from Howard. Here too was a former star student of mine at Spelman College—her home a little town in South Carolina—now just graduated from Yale Law School: Marian Wright. With her was another graduate from Yale, a young white fellow named Oscar Chase. (Chase recently wrote a valuable legal paper which shows how the federal government, by bold, imaginative use of the injunction, could fulfill its responsibility to protect the constitutional rights of Negroes in the Deep South.) In the room also was another of the increasing number of white college students in this essentially Negro-led movement—a California sociology major named Mike Miller, who has done impressive research on civil-rights matters. And five of the youngsters just out of Parchman jail were present.

That afternoon we drove in two cars to Itta Bena, a feudal cotton village outside Greenwood, where Negroes came off the land to meet in a dilapidated little church, welcome back the Parchman prisoners, and sing freedom songs with an overpowering spirit. One of the returned prisoners was Mother Perkins, fragile and small, seventy-five years old, who had just spent, like the rest, two months on the county prison farm for wanting to register.

Cars filled with white men rumbled by along the road that passed by the church door, but the meeting and the singing went on. Anyone who felt the urge got up and spoke. An old man rose on his cane and said: "All these years, going along behind my plow, I thought some day things would change. But I never dreamed I'd see it now."

Bob Moses told them that Negroes—and whites—were without jobs in all the big cities of the nation, that they could not run away any more from the Delta to Chicago and Detroit, that they must stay and wrench from the State of Mississippi what they deserved as human beings. Marian Wright told them a fable about an eagle that for a long time was told it was a chicken and believed it. Stokely Carmichael reminded them that while the Lord might be on their side, they would have to secure their rights by their own intense efforts. Meanwhile, the automobiles kept passing on the road outside.

The crushing conclusion that comes out of Greenwood, Miss.—and Selma, Ala., and Danville, Va., and Americus, Ga.—is that the federal government is but a shadow in the hard-rock places of the Deep South. Standing at the foot of the Lincoln Memorial, John Lewis turned his wrath, not at the easy target, the Dixiecrats, but against the Administration. "It is the *federal government* that indicted nine of our people in Albany." The Democratic Party, Lewis made clear, cannot be treated as a savior as long as it lives with Eastland, nor can the Republicans, harboring Goldwater. "What political leader can stand up and say his party is the party of freedom?" And then, the most dangerous question one can ask in a country boasting of its two-party system: "Where is *our* party?"

To many, the March had been presented as a gigantic lobby for the Administration's Civil Rights Bill, but Lewis pointed quickly, unerringly, to the weaknesses in the bill. Furthermore, by sponsoring a new civil-rights bill, the Administration had skillfully turned attention to Congress, and deflected the erratic spotlight of the civil-rights movement from possibly focusing on inadequacies of the Executive.

The straight, crass fact at which John Lewis was aiming is this: the national government, *without any new legislation*, has the power to protect Negro voters and demonstrators from policemen's clubs, hoses and jails—and it has not used that power.

Despite the welcome new words of concern by the Kennedy Administration, despite several dozen suits filed by the Justice Department in voting cases, the Negro in the Deep South still stands alone and unprotected as he tries to eat in a bus terminal, register to vote, or hand out a leaflet on a street corner. The right to vote, and freedom of expression, are not in themselves solutions to the fundamental problem, which is a rearranging of economic and political power in the South. But they are prerequisites to that rearrangement.

There is a constitutional rock to which the Executive branch can tie its lines and then smash, with all the power at its command, every Wallace, every Barnett, every Chief Pritchett, every Commander Lingo, every Bull Connor, who ever begins to lift a billy club at an American citizen exercising his constitutional rights. That is the Supreme Court's statement in the Debs case of 1895: "The entire strength of the nation may be used to enforce in any part of the land the full and free exercise of all national powers and the security of all rights entrusted by the Constitution to its care."

But to act on that dictum calls for certain traits which the Administration has thus far not shown: imaginativeness in the use of the courts; boldness in the exercise of Executive power; the courage to set new precedents in federal relations; the willingness to by-pass Congress on an issue about which Congress spoke its mind in 1866—when it passed the Fourteenth Amendment.

Above all, it means changing to the offensive. Up to now the Administration has simply *reacted* to every racial crisis. Southern officials have thrown thousands of people into jail, and then put the burden on the civil-rights movement to get them out. The national government needs to *act*, and then put the burden on Southern segregationists to revoke the action; let *them* wrestle with courts, raise money for trial, plead for toleration.

The "equal protection" clause of the Fourteenth Amendment, the Supreme Court's statement in the Debs case, the declaration of Section 242 of the U.S. penal code that any official who deprives a person of his constitutional rights has committed a federal crime: these are the already-existing legal bases for Executive action. That action requires, first, stationing all over the South hundreds of federal agents (replacing the F.B.I., which is incompetent in the field of civil rights) to protect the constitutional rights of Negroes. These agents would have the specific assignment, and the authority granted by the President, to jail any local official who violates the Constitution.

At the same time, the President must begin filling—as he has failed to do so far—the federal judgeships of the Deep South with persons committed to the principle of equality, regardless of the wishes of the region's Senators. Among the outworn political institutions of this nation is that of "Senatorial courtesy," which requires Kennedy to consult Eastland in the appointment of a federal judge in Mississippi, Talmadge and Russell in Georgia. The shattering of precedent can start here. Then, a combination of quick-acting federal agents and determined judges can begin to rivet into the mind of the Deep South, *and into the mind of the nation*, not that Negroes are equal (that will take time), but that if they are not treated equally the consequences will be swift and harsh.

When ten CORE and SNCC people, white and Negro, walked into Alabama to try to establish what Bill Moore, at the cost of his life, had failed to establish—the right to walk safely on a public highway—a cordon of federal marshals should have surrounded them. And when Alabama Safety Director Al Lingo showed up with his electric prod poles and guns, he should have been taken immediately into federal custody.

The burden of legal proof needs to be borne by the segregationists, and this has not yet been done. Any good lawyer knows that the advantage is in the hands of the man who moves first, that delay and bureaucracy and legal complications all work against those who are trying to *undo* an action. Yet the civil-rights movement, which cannot help it, and the Justice Department, which can, have been on the defensive.

The needed initiative is not likely to come from a government whose dedication to racial equality is as circumspect as that of the Kennedy brothers. It took a series of explosive crises throughout the nation to force from them words of moral concern that became part of the Constitution a hundred years ago. It took something close to a revolution to bring forth a moderate civil-rights bill, which will be further moderated by Congress, and by segregationist federal judges, and by a cautious Justice Department.

Basic changes are needed in the social structure of the nation before meaningful racial equality can be established. But in the Deep South, a prerequisite for such changes is the establishment of the right to vote, to organize, to speak, write and assemble freely and without fear of violence. That requires a radical new use of initiative and power by the national government. And because the Administration—and inherently, any administration—lacks the internal motivation for such a seizure of initiative, it will have to be prodded by the increased use of nonviolent direct action.

Right now, those who see this most clearly, feel it most intensely, and are best prepared to move on it, are the young people in the Student Nonviolent Coordinating Committee.

The Nation, October 5, 1963

Gloria, Gloria

by Murray Kempton

LAST July an urban journalist looked upon Mrs. Gloria Richardson in the dungarees that were her command dress and wrote that the Chairman of the Cambridge Non-Violent Action Committee reminded him of Joan of Arc. That comparison is more painful to reasonable white citizens of Cambridge than anything said or written in the summer of Gloria Richardson's uprising that brought their town under martial law.

More white people were shot here last summer than in any of the hundreds of other towns where the Negro's aspirations have brought him into the streets.

Senator Brewster of Maryland came late in October as the newest of the enlightened outsiders to offer himself as mediator and was reported impressed with how rational everyone seemed. The impression of good sense is the general surprise of a visit to Cambridge; there is nothing that can fairly be called irrational except what happens.

The city is governed according to the best aspirations at the command of the border South: its commissioners are entirely aware of the special challenge of the Sixties, which is how to appease the Negro without telling the poor white. Still they have lived through misfortune that continually hinted at becoming catastrophe; and worse public officials in worse towns live at peace. They can be excused, as reasonable men, for blaming all this on Gloria Richardson and everything she has done since she turned the Negro school children out to demonstrate last spring.

"People ask what we did wrong," City Solicitor Awdry Thompson says, "but when you got a woman like Gloria Richardson in your town, it doesn't make much difference what you did wrong."

Gloria Richardson began picketing to open Cambridge's 22

60

restaurants to Negroes last winter. By spring her troop of students was so large that Cambridge commenced arresting great groups of them. Their demonstrations brought the poor whites in from the county; their jailings aroused the adult Negroes. These restless, closed crowds met on Race Street, the Negro district's boundary; Cambridge's last memory of good fortune was that a riot was somehow avoided; but there were gun battles at night. The Governor of Maryland dispatched his National Guard to Cambridge (it is still there) and called the parties to his State House. There official Cambridge offered Gloria Richardson a package it still thinks of as total surrender: an ordinance desegregating restaurants, a promise to complete integration of the schools, a committee to find jobs for Negroes and a Negro public-housing project. Mrs. Richardson could have all this if she would promise not to demonstrate for a year.

Mrs. Richardson refused this offer. A deceptive meditative peace descended; the Governor recalled the guard and Mrs. Richardson led the school children once more to the shopping district. A muster of rural whites came to meet her; that night five white persons were shot. The National Guard came back; Gloria Richardson was called to Washington and capitulation to Robert Kennedy. In return for its deliverance, Cambridge agreed to set up a 12-member biracial committee, with four Negro members to be chosen by Mrs. Richardson, and to sponsor a Charter Amendment desegregating the restaurants but subject to public referendum.

By now, most of what was reasonable in Cambridge had sunk its hopes on desegregating the restaurants as a ritual, remedial sacrifice to peace. Awdry Thompson, who had been a speaker at the founding ceremonies of the not-thereafter-conspicious Dorchester White Citizens Council, was a prominent spokesman for the amendment. He nicely defines the respectability of the cause: "I could go out and try to sell a public accommodations law, but I'd hardly dare this season to go out and try to sell the Kennedys."

The theory was that if barely 35 percent of Cambridges' white voters could be won to this coalition of the practical and the principled, there would be enough Negro votes to pass the law in referendum. Every Negro of substance but one worked to get out the vote. Gloria Richardson announced that she would not ask Negroes to vote on something that was already their constitutional right. In the end, the whites returned a little more than the favorable 35 percent of their vote the public accommodations proposal was supposed to need; but it was defeated because half the Negro voters had abstained. Gloria Richardson, standing almost alone among Negroes with a voice, had managed to hold half her constituency.

"And so," Awdry Thompson reflects, "we can't deal with her and we can't deal without her."

Nothing that happened last summer has changed a single Cambridge custom. Nothing is new except the National Guard, itself by now almost a custom. The biracial committee talks about a meeting this month; the Reverend Mr. Allen Whatley, its chairman, talks about little beyond tables of organization. There is the comfort of the approach of cold weather when people do not normally picket. Gloria Richardson came to Senator Brewster's peace meeting and at the end surprised her enemies by saying that she thought some progress might have been made. Her reason for hope was that the meeting had lasted three hours and 15 minutes. This woman who Cambridge thinks holds it in bondage could not remember a time when its officials had given her case longer than an hour's hearing.

All practical men go on hoping to appease, if not Gloria Richardson herself, at least the memory of what they used to think would appease her. William L. Wise, the fuel dealer who organized the white voters against the public accommodations bill, tried immediately after his victory to persuade the restaurants to desegregate voluntarily, an effort which, of course, failed as soon as it became public. In Cambridge, even the man who rallied the poor whites against the sitting politicians, moves clumsily for some way to appease the Negro without telling the white.

For, that small part of Cambridge which owns property badly needs a clearance from Gloria Richardson. Cambridge had always lived off the farm and the water; its main industries were food processors. But now Dorchester County has 30,000 residents and only 728 farms; Cambridge's largest cannery closed down in the middle Fifties; in 1958, 28 percent of its work force was unemployed. Cambridge's heroic efforts to attract new industries has brought unemployment down to 13 percent, with the Negro rate estimated closer to 25. The campaign for new industries stopped when Gloria Richardson's passion and the subsequent tumult made Cambridge a reproach. Every man of civic spirit—even Wise—knows how much Cambridge's reputation now needs a show of harmony.

Only Gloria Richardson stands outside that consensus. She is a stranger and cannot be engaged, because she is both a Negro and a woman and thus represents the two largest figures in Southern myth and the two smallest in Southern reality. What deepens her mystery is her entire failure at the conventional commercial civic response. She is one of the few militant integrationists who has deliberately made the poor Negro her resource and this choice peculiar to her nature has given her what power she retains.

She is a tall, thin woman, early in the forties, with eyes more sad than hostile. But there sits within her, making her a harder case still, a sense of mischief which obeys no commands but its own. She will, she tells a follower, go to Senator Brewster's meeting. "But I'm not going as a big wheel. I just want to be the little stone that gets in all the big wheels."

She has, on occasion, affronted official Cambridge by seeming to accept a compromise, making it contingent on the approval of her executive committee and then returning from this communion to report that her executive committee has overruled her. Her executive committee is commonly assumed to be a device of Gloria Richardson's guileful and mischievous fancy. Yet the Cambridge Non-Violent Action Committee does have an executive, in whose existence her middle-class fellow citizens may be excused from believing because its members are not Negroes they are likely to know. One works in a packinghouse; another is on public welfare. We can choose to believe either that she picked them because she could manipulate them or because they were persons who had never before been granted a voice. In any case, however brief the hope she may have given them, they returned her the awful power that can inhere in people who had never known the experience and the consequent exhaustion of revolt. Whatever was harsh and terrible in the Negro community last summer—and something seems unprecedentedly to have been—had some of its source in that industrial poor where Gloria Richardson built her strength. A packinghouse worker is not a domestic.

Mrs. Richardson's closest lieutenant last summer was Reginald Robinson, a 22-year-old Student Non-Violent Coordinating Committee official. He has left Cambridge to go South, and she seems resigned to giving him up.

"All this was very rough on Reggie," she explains. "He's very brave, but he really is non-violent. I'm non-violent too, but I guess I'm a little tougher."

An acquaintance, one suspects a Negro acquaintance, is supposed to have said of Gloria Richardson: "She is the only person I have ever known who never seems to have anything good to say about any white man."

Yet, when she talks, the animus that comes through strongest is one of class rather than race. That surprises because she was born a Negro and only chose the poor. Hers is the Negro first family of Maryland; and her grandfather was Cambridge's Negro City Councilman for a generation. She lives in his old house, which is much the most impressive on its block. The funeral parlor, always the most substantial Negro business, remains a family property.

She came here from Baltimore when she was eight to grow up at some remove from ordinary Cambridge Negroes. What society she knew was drawn mostly from the friends who came from more cosmopolitan places to stay with her grandfather. She went to Howard University where she was instructed by Dr. E. Franklin Frazier that she was black bourgeois. Four other girls from the Negro high school went on to college in her time. She thinks that she was the only one to come back to Cambridge to live.

Eight years ago, she and her husband went to worship at Christ Episcopal Church, where the Cambridge biracial Committee's Mr. Whatley was then, as now, rector. Christ Church's vestry quite quickly found a West Indian curate and established a mission in the Negro section, which happens to be closer to the mother church than many of its white parishioners are. Gloria Richardson transferred unprotestingly to the Negro mission and does not seem yet to wonder why the Lord should provide a Negro mission so short a time after her appearance in Christ Church's pew.

She was divorced and thought of going to work. The Negro High School had no place for another teacher; she turned to the United States Employment Service to ask for a job at the new garment factory. "The interviewer said that, since I had a college degree, it would look funny on her records if she put me down as a garment worker, so she registered me instead as a 'public worker.' But, of course, there wasn't any public work." She went to the garment plant, found herself deficient in manual dexterity and went back home for good.

The only experience which could remotely have conditioned her choice of class was this one test of the value of a college degree to the daughter of Cambridge's most substantial Negro family.

Whatever the origin, Gloria Richardson has acquired an identification with the poor that extends even to those country whites who came to Cambridge to drink beer and howl at her demonstrations.

"When there was trouble," she remembers, "and the cops picked up one of *them* they'd be much rougher on him than us. That's because they're poor."

"When even a Negro gets a little property, it's very hard for him not to feel the whites looking at him and he begins to think about words like 'responsibility' and 'culture.' He doesn't want to be considered irresponsible and above all, he doesn't want to seem uncultured. But *my* people know exactly what their problems are."

Morgan College studied the Cambridge Negro's wants, and found out that 60 percent of those interviewed were worried about jobs, and 40 percent about education and only six percent cared about public accommodations. "Oh, sure, those restaurants were right out there and they were something you could hit at. But they weren't the main part of it. The referendum could have meant something only if the Negroes had stayed away and the white people had voted to open the restaurants."

What Gloria Richardson wants would require from Cambridge a passion for the rescue of its poor which reasonable men cannot be expected even to imagine. Reflecting on that seems to have rendered the restaurants irrelevant to her; one reason why she has not yet led her troops back to Race Street may be that the only thing against which she now can raise her banner is everything.

Her meetings are small; the children who were her chief resource are back in school; her subalterns of last summer have gone to simpler, more desperate places like Mississippi. "I think I'll go to Danville," even Gloria Richardson says, "I could be doing something constructive down there in the 9 or 10 days while we're thinking about what to do up here next."

Remembering last summer, Gloria Richardson says just one truly sad thing: "It's funny but during the whole time we were demonstrating actively, there were almost no fights in this ward and almost no crime, not even traffic. Now they've gone back to fighting each other again. They've been thrown back to carrying a chip on their shoulder."

One of Gloria Richardson's friends wondered the other day whether the Negro poor of Cambridge had entered the stage a man reaches when he stops looking for a job any longer. When men see or imagine they see a Joan of Arc, she carries with her the hope of a great new chance for everyone around her. And, when she fades, what is sad is not just that she is going but that the illusion of the chance goes with her.

The New Republic, November 16, 1963

The August 28th March on Washington

by Michael Thelwell

THE now historical March on Washington for Jobs and Freedom was in many ways a social phenomenon that could have taken place, as the *Readers' Digest* is fond of saying, "only in the United States." The true significance of what happened in Washington on that day defies any simple definition. What *really* happened on the tortuous road that the March took to Washington will probably never be made public. This is unfortunate because somewhere along the twisting road that stretched between the first ideas for the March, and the abortion of those ideas that was finally delivered in Washington on August 28, lies the corpse of what could have been a real step forward in the struggle for Negro rights in this country.

It would be useful, especially to Negroes involved in this struggle, to know just who was responsible for what happened to the March, and to know what forces were at work, what kinds of pressures and bribes were tried and by whom. It would be important to know what deals were made, and who made them. Which of the many compromises were the results of inevitable social pressures, and which were forced by the power machinations of the Kennedy administration? Which decisions were sincere mistakes of timidity and of judgment, and which were deliberate attempts to reduce the whole operation to impotence? It would be useful to know, for example, what the real role of the middle-class Negro organizations was in this event, and whose interests they imagined themselves to be representing, and whose interests they did, in fact, end up representing. It would help to know these things, but for understandable reasons, the people who have the information that would indicate these things are silent. But there were some things that are public, like what happened—this the whole world saw, and some of these leaders *did* make public statements that said more than the words spoken.

On the day itself, as the far-flung tentacles of the sprawling organization that had materialized around the idea for the March came together, it was clear to observers that something significant was happening before their eyes. The nature of what was happening was not then, and is still not, clear. On the one hand, there was an undeniable grandeur and awesomeness about the mighty river of humanity, more people than most of us will ever see again in one place, affirming in concert their faith in an idea, and in a hope that is just. And on the other, there was an air of grotesquery as in some kind of carnival where illusion is the stock-in-trade, an impression given sustenance by the huge green and white striped carnival tent and the hordes of hucksters peddling gaudy March pins, pennants, tassels, and similar items more readily associated with sporting events than with serious social protest. It was a day of contrasts, a day of platitude and rhetoric juxtaposed with genuine passion and real anguish, a day of bitterness and disappointment for some, and of hope and inspiration for others.

One looked into the black face of a southern sharecropper, weathered and marked by privation, yet on this day filled with hope and pride, and the belief that a new day was indeed coming. Then one looked at his son, sixteen years old, fresh from the brutality of a southern jail, who did not need the abstractions about oppression and intimidation because his own body bore their marks, and one could not but share in the bitterness in his eyes. And if one looked from these two, to the small army of propagandists, wheeling cameras and masses of equipment around, intent on recording this day as some kind of triumph for the system that has oppressed these people, one could not escape the feeling that somewhere there had occurred a subtle and terrible betrayal. Because, this day that had promised so much was too sweet, too contrived, and its spirit too amiable to represent anything of the bitterness that had brought the people there. And, while the goodwill and amiability of the marchers surmounted race and class and was a heartening thing, there was an overhanging atmosphere of complete political irrelevance.

*

As originally conceived, the March was to come as the climax of the most tumultuous summer of Negro militance in the history of the country, and was to have been the largest single demonstration of social discontent that this government had known.

When I heard the plan articulated for the first time, and it was still embryonic then, I was told that waves of nonviolent demonstrations of civil disobedience were planned to completely immobilize the Congress. The militant student group —the Student Nonviolent Coordinating Committee (SNCC)— was already thinking out stratagems to get huge numbers of demonstrators into the halls of Congress. This is forbidden by law, and the plan was to replace the demonstrators with another wave as soon as the first was removed, and to keep this up until the jails of Washington were filled. Simultaneous with this action there were to be sit-ins in the offices of the Justice Department protesting that agency's failure to protect the constitutional rights of Negroes in the South. Similar sit-ins were planned for the offices of certain politicians from southern states where the constitutional and legal rights of Negroes were being, and are now being, violated each day by local authorities as a matter of official policy. All these activities, which were to be done by the same people who were then manning the lines in demonstrations all over the country, were to be auxiliary to the huge body of the March which would break no laws, but would come to Congress and present to it a petition for the redress of three hundred years of wrongs. The civil disobedience aspect of the demonstrations were intended to dramatize the situation of the Negro: Negroes were there offering their bodies to the jails because in this country they *are* in a jail, because they are not citizens and are not really represented by Congress, because they have no voice in the decisions that govern their living and their dying, and because they have been traditionally and deliberately excluded from full participation in the social processes of the country in which they were born.

Civil disobedience was central. Laws are for those who make them, and who give their consent to them and are protected by them. On this basis, Americans, white and black, fought one revolution, and the Negroes, by symbolically defying the laws, as they have been doing in small communities throughout the South, were again affirming that "government without representation is tyranny." And the attack was to be directed to the seat of government as that is the symbol and residence of power and represents the entire system that persecutes us.

The goal was social dislocation without violence. This is the underlying technique that informs all direct action projects in the movement toward justice for America's disinherited blacks: it is one of rendering the institution under pressure inoperable by the presence of determined black bodies. When demonstrators descend on any establishment, the purpose is to so disrupt its functioning as a segregated institution that it will become nonfunctional and be forced to close and reopen on an integrated basis. So in one sense the demonstrations are aimed at destroying institutions that function unjustly, and replacing them by a different institution, in the sense that the same restaurant once integrated has become a new entity in terms of its function. This was not the idea for the March, since the goal was not to attempt a permanent dislocation of the Congress, but merely to use this kind of pressure for one day. This was in May, and planning was geared toward having this action during the congressional debate on the civil rights legislation that President Kennedy had decided to introduce, largely because of "Ole Miss" and Birmingham.

Certain questions were still to be resolved at this time. The penalty for disrupting the function of the Congress is a sentence of up to five years in jail. Could, from among the thousands of Negroes who were at that time involved in demonstrations all over the country, a sufficiently large number be found who were willing to risk this long sentence? Was it justifiable to ask them to do this? Where would the money come from to stage the kind of complicated and expensive legal battle that would be required to free these demonstrators afterwards? Would the authorities use force to break the demonstrations up? This is the pattern in the South, but not in Washington. But neither is it the pattern to allow demonstrations aimed at Congress. In 1961, when 120 students from Howard University attempted to picket on the steps of the Capitol, the police broke the demonstration up with the threat of the five-year sentence. On the other hand, there was a question of whether Kennedy would risk the kind of adverse publicity that would result if the demonstrators were forcibly removed from the halls of Congress. It has been this administration's posture abroad that it is committed to equality for all Americans. The reality is that it is committed to political expediency and to containing the Negro militance by conciliation. Would it have risked giving the lie to its official image by a picture on the front pages in Africa and Asia, showing ten resisting Negroes being dragged from the steps of the Capitol—the American symbol to the world of democracy and justice? The other alternative would be either to head off the March by making real concessions to Negro demands, or else to allow civil disobedience without any police action that might have triggered off violence. The demands of the March were to be:

"Full employment for all Americans of both races, and an appeal for a massive federal program to train all unemployed . . . in meaningful and dignified jobs at decent wages.

"Integration of all public schools by the end of this year.

"A federal fair employment practices law, outlawing all job discrimination.

"Passage of the Kennedy administration's legislative package . . . without compromise or filibuster."*

As it turns out, the administration was spared having to make this decision. I remember leaving the conversation where the original plan for the March was told to me. I said

---

*The latter is particularly interesting, since this legislation has had an unusual history. Kennedy called it the "most pressing business" of the Congress during the summer's racial turmoil. He recently made the statement that his tax cut is the most necessary, and now that the demonstrations have slowed down, and the polls say that white opinion is that the Negro "is pushing too fast," he and his brother Bobby have indicated that the civil rights legislatoin needs to be "watered down" to ensure that it is passed. A strong bill at this point would not pass they say; what is already an inadequate bill must be further diluted. It is not difficult to see where the two Kennedys are looking—at the presidential elections of '64.

Yet despite this clear betrayal, Kennedy is still supported by his favorite "responsible" Negro leaders. Roy Wilkins and Whitney Young came out this week with statements that sounded alarmingly like Kennedy's, and as though they were saying that the Negro was pushing too hard. It is not difficult to understand why Malcolm X calls Wilkins "Kennedy's Nigger."

to my friend who was to play a central role in organizing the March, "I've told you that when the 'revolution' comes it will be the Negroes who begin it." This was a joke between us, but only partially so, because we were agreed that at the time when the Negro succeeded in forcing the power structure of this country into revising its practices and this society into amending its traditional attitude of exclusion and exploitation toward him, its effects would be so far-reaching and profound as to completely remake society. It is still my conviction that this is so, because no one can look at the deeply entrenched tradition of racial injustice in America and imagine that any gradual evolution of justice is possible. It will take traumatic action of various kinds to wrench society out of the deep channels of segregation in which it moves, and which causes this evil to re-create itself. Early this year, a group of Negro students was told by a Negro official of the federal government that the latter could do nothing to enforce fair employment on one of its contracts, because the kind of extreme action that this would require in the face of the long history of exclusion would disrupt too many of the established socio-economic patterns and affront too many powerful groups within the society. That bureaucrat really meant that the federal government *could* take this action, but that it *would* not. But this illustrates why any meaningful integration of the Negro will be accompanied by social tension, chaos, and will result in the restructuring of the extant social patterns. In this sense it will be "revolutionary" in the deepest sense of that term.

Every Negro leader, except Roy Wilkins and Whitney Young, who has felt the burden of this systematic cultural policy of exclusion, knows that he cannot integrate into this society but into a new and decent one that will have to be created from energy that must be initiated by the Negro people. For this reason, the language of every Negro leader, even those that are incredibly conservative on all other political issues, is couched in the idiom of revolution whenever he talks about integration.

Minister Malcolm X, the fiery and witty leader of the Black Muslim movement, which bases much of its social ideology on the impossibility and undesirability of integration and appeals for complete separation, sums up the totality of the

Negro's exclusion in these terms: "Martin Luther King says that we are second-class citizens. That is not true, we are not citizens at all. The fact that we were here before 1776, and that we are born here does not make us citizens. A cat can have kittens in an oven, but does that mean that they are biscuits?"

It was this entrenchment of discrimination that led me to speak in terms of the "revolution." And this is why I favored, and still do favor, the tactic of disobedience to the civil law on the March, and the use of aggressive nonviolence. If these original plans had not been abandoned, a crisis might have been forced. The mere threat of using five thousand veteran demonstrators who had known jails and police brutality from demonstrations in cities like New York, Birmingham (Alabama), Cambridge (Maryland), and Danville (Virginia), and Negroes from the Deep South where the state quite literally represents a monopoly of violence against the Negro, may well have been enough to pry some action from a reluctant Congress. The history of the United States Congress over the last one hundred years is a history of racism. It has never acted in the interests of the Negro unless it was forced into doing so by political pressure. Like any other institution, its reactions are geared to practical considerations and self-interest and not moral imperatives; therefore, its actions tend to ride on the coattails of public opinion, which means in this country, white opinion and national prejudice. As a body, it will do nothing for the Negro that is likely to move against the mainstream of social momentum. This unwillingness to act for integration is compounded by the structuring of that body, which places southern politicians, who represent areas in which Negroes are effectively disenfranchised, at the head of influential parliamentary committees. Thus Congress is in great measure controlled by men who derive their power from segregation and to whom integration on a political level means the end of the system that brought them to power. The presence of these "Dixiecrats" in the Democratic party, and the essentially schizophrenic and bastard nature of that party within which an allegedly liberal president must live with the most reactionary forces in this country, is one more indication why the Negroes' posture toward the political establishment must be one of attack. It also indicates why no meaningful legislation can be induced out of a Congress with its present political composition, and why the March was originally conceived not as an appeal to conscience, but as an expression of strength.

Such a demonstration as was outlined would not have attracted anything like the 250,000 people who attended on August 28, but there can be no doubt that it would have received widespread support. This was the Negro mood at that time. Newspapers and TV news programs were filled with the story of the "Negro uprising." Demonstrations were erupting in the streets of cities across the nation, North and South. Within a period of two weeks after the March was first mentioned to me, upheavals were recorded in cities as far apart as Albany and Americus in Georgia, Greenwood, Goldsboro, Jackson, and Oxford in Mississippi, and in cities in Florida, Alabama, Louisiana, the Carolinas, California, and the "border" states of Virginia and Maryland. Before the summer was over, outbreaks of varying degrees of violence were to shatter the northern complacency of cities like Chicago, Philadelphia, New York, and Boston.

In Cambridge, Maryland, some of the most critical confrontations took place, and the possibility of a racial war was sufficiently present to warrant the imposition of martial law. In Danville, Virginia, the tactics used by police to break up nonviolent demonstrations were more savage than in Birmingham. On the 10th of June, of sixty-four demonstrators, forty required medical attention after club-wielding police and deputized garbage collectors followed blasts of water poured from fire hoses into the group, clubbing women and children indiscriminately and strewing the street with bloody, soaked bodies. One result of this was that three days later, the demonstrations included 250 Negroes. These two instances illustrate the all-pervading nature of the oppression of Negroes here. I chose them because they are both located within a few hours drive of Washington, D.C., but similar instances of this nature can be found all over the land.

After the much-publicized Birmingham demonstrations, the Negro mood hardened perceptively and became more abrasive and determined. There was more bitterness and less patience; there were also more demonstrations. On these mornings, a glance through the newspapers, which generally subdue their reports of racial unrest, revealed that Negroes, like the spring, "were breaking out all over." Even from the relatively neutral reports, it was evident that the mood of these demonstrations was changing. Incidents of Negroes facing up to the police and to white mobs were more frequent. In the streets, the bars, the homes, the churches, the mood ebony was clearly one of indignation and open anger. The landlady of a friend of mine, a lady of some sixty-five years, and up until then, a veritable stereotype of the respectable, religious, and passive older generation of lower-middle-class Negro, began to seriously investigate the possibilities of purchasing a revolver.

This new mood did not escape the white press, nor did the politicians miss it either. Great concern was expressed about the possibility of a major race riot, or a series of race riots sweeping the country.

President Kennedy had publicly affirmed the right of peaceful demonstrations earlier in the spring. Now, moved as much by the southern and conservative charges that he was encouraging anarchy, as by the possibility that the Negro people would retaliate in kind to their attackers, he took the position that, although legal, demonstrations were irresponsible and that Negroes should return their battle to the arena of the courts, which was, among other things, less visible. The position of the student demonstrators was that there was nothing to be gained by keeping the illusion of "peace." There is no real peace where there is no justice, and the white man's peace is for us a slave's peace. The demonstrations did not stop.

In this position Kennedy was supported by the National Association for the Advancement of Colored People (NAACP), whose national secretary, Roy Wilkins, publicly questioned the effectiveness of street demonstrations. There are two important considerations which militate against this position. One, the simple fact that the white establishment's wish to stop demonstrations is the best possible brief for their continuance; if it becomes sufficiently threatened, it will remove the causes of the demonstrations. The other factor is that discrimination does not exist because of any absence of law affirming Negro rights. It exists, in spite of such laws and the

Constitution, because the federal administration *has never acted to enforce these laws* which are blatantly broken and ignored, unless some kind of crisis seems imminent. Therefore, it is not more laws that are needed, but more pressure.

The 1954 Supreme Court decision on segregated schools directed the integration of the entire school system "with all deliberate speed." Nearly ten years later, there has been little more than token observance of this ruling in the South. One answer is direct action, and even with the schools this is possible. In Englewood, New Jersey, Negro parents took their children out of the Negro kindergarten and into the white school where the children had not been permitted to enroll. The teachers attempted to ignore these illegal infiltrators, but the white infants did not, and after three days the teachers found it simpler to include the "demonstrators" in the class activities. In Boston, Negro citizens set up "freedom schools," and withdrew thousands of Negro children from the official high schools in protest of the inferior facilities given to Negroes. The "freedom schools" included in their curriculum classes in the theory of civil disobedience, social responsibility, and Negro history. The Boston school system hastily came to terms with the Negro community.

The plans for this March were evolved by Bayard Rustin, a Negro militant and pacifist; Tom Kahn, a white student in a Negro university who was a young man with a long history of civil rights activities, and Norman Hill, an executive of the Congress on Racial Equality (CORE), a militant direct action group.

Rustin is one of the most colorful characters in the civil rights movement. In addition to being an astute tactician, and extremely politically sophisticated, he is one of the few real intellectuals that is active. He is essentially not a "leader" figure, but there is no one person who has had more direct effect in defining the direction that the struggle has taken in recent years. He was executive assistant to A. Philip Randolph in planning the March on Washington for the integration of war industries during World War II. He was Martin Luther King's adviser during the Montgomery bus boycott, the director of the Youth March on Washington for integrated schools in

1954, and has organized nonviolent demonstrations in Tanganyika and in England, and, three years ago, led a party of Africans into the Sahara in protest against French nuclear bomb tests. One of the reasons that he is not a publicly acknowledged leader in this struggle—and this does not speak too well of the courage of existing groups—is his association with the American Communist party during the depression, but he is certainly the person with the most realistically radical approach to the struggle, and one of the few adult voices that the students in the struggle respect and will listen to. Another such person is the novelist James Baldwin.

Main opposition to Rustin as organizer of the March came from Roy Wilkins of the NAACP, that huge, middle-class based and essentially conservative Negro organization. Wilkins is the "Negro leader" most appreciated by the middle-class Negro and white liberal community as being "responsible." He is roundly rejected by the students as a tool of the white power structure. It is difficult to understand how anyone can be naïve or nearsighted enough to demand sweeping changes in the area of Negro rights, in a country where any meaningful demand on behalf of the Negro is radical and yet hold conservative attitudes toward all other areas of society.

When I left Washington in June, the plans for the March were not yet made public, and it was my understanding that the first steps were already under way. A. Philip Randolph was approached, and was willing to call on the other five civil rights groups to participate. Since the appeal was for jobs and freedom, it was felt that organized labor should be involved.

Martin Luther King's Southern Christian Leadership Conference (SCLC), which had spearheaded the Birmingham demonstrations, committed itself to the idea eagerly. CORE, another militant organization, and the one responsible for the 1961 Freedom Rides, and the Student Nonviolent Coordinating Committee, which is a student organization which specializes in working only in the deepest South, were also eager to support the March in its unadulterated form. However, the heads of the NAACP and the Urban League, the two most affluent of the civil rights organizations, withheld their support on the basis that it did not appear to be worth the effort or the money. It should be pointed out that the support of these two organizations was considered essential for reasons of politics and finance.

From this point on, the March plans were subjected to the bewildering succession of changes, disputes, and distortions that resulted in the final fiasco that took place on August 28. One meeting of these leaders was described to me in these terms: "Well, we finally pinned Wilkins (of the NAACP) down and finally wrung a commitment from him." By this time he had held up the campaign for several weeks, but the support of the NAACP and the Urban League was on the condition that civil disobedience be abandoned. The first compromise was made: there were to be no sit-ins, pickets, or aggressive activity of any kind. The next issue was a strong objection to Rustin as the deputy organizer. Randolph and King were adamant on this point, and Rustin's services were retained.

My next information was to the effect that although the March was not officially announced, the Kennedys knew about it, and it was in the wind that the administration was against it. The committee was having difficulty getting support or money. "You would be surprised," my informant concluded, "how liberal doors close in your face when Kennedy is opposed to a project." Shortly thereafter, there was a public announcement, and Kennedy publicly disapproved of the idea. A Negro clergyman in New York declared that there were going to be "massive acts of civil disobedience, prostrate bodies on streets and airport runways and railroad tracks, massive and monumental sit-ins at the Congress." The white community was unanimously horrified. It then became a matter of public discussion that SNCC and CORE were preparing for "nonviolent civil disobedience, all day sit-ins at the Justice Department, in Senator Eastland's (of Mississippi) office and in the Congress." The country's reaction was, as nearly as I could observe, one of apprehension, if not open fear. The events of the spring and early summer, especially those in Birmingham, had convinced them that the Negro community was about ready to retaliate in kind. Bloodbaths were predicted, should the March take place.

The Committee for the March, and the leaders of the Urban League and NAACP singly denied any plans for direct action, and CORE and SNCC were chastised for "irresponsibility."

I was told that "the Kennedy administration was putting up unbelievable opposition," and that administration maneuvering was "fantastic." I was not told, nor did I ask, the nature of this opposition. However, after the official rejection of any kind of civil disobedience, public opinion began to veer. The entire idea of the March was no longer condemned as un-American, and groups not normally active in the Negro cause began to hint at support. Liberal columnists began to remember that the Negro had the force of morality and a history of persecution behind him. But the powerful labor federation, the AFL-CIO, still refused, and never came out in support.

Shortly thereafter, the announcement came of the rerouting of the March. Instead of going to the Capitol legally and petitioning Congress, the March would now proceed from the Washington Monument to the Lincoln Memorial and listen to the speeches of the leaders. The leaders alone would *visit* the politicians. Plans to include two unemployed Negroes in the meeting with the president were quietly forgotten. I do not know that they were ever officially changed, but I do know that no unemployed persons made that visit.

With this new announcement, President Kennedy underwent a sudden and dramatic change of heart, and publicly welcomed the March as an expression of support for the legislation that the events of the summer had convinced him to introduce. From this point on, the March became more of an expression of faith in the Kennedy administration. The changing of the route had guaranteed that the whole proceedings would be as unobtrusive as possible and that it could be isolated to one small and relatively unimportant section of Washington.

It was the second week of August before I was able to get to New York. Despite severe doubts about having anything to do with this March, I found myself being pulled, possibly by curiosity, to its headquarters. There the truth of the assertion that "Americans Love a Parade" was made evident. There was great willingness to support the project. The phones buzzed with supporters of this "social revolution" to complain "that the bus that my bridge club has chartered has no air conditioning" or that "our buses have no reclining seats." One group wanted to know if they could carry signs bearing tal-mudic inscriptions and whether their leader could make a speech or see the president. Others wanted to know if they would lose a day's pay by attending. . . .

In the New York headquarters, I found many students whom I knew. Their attitude was one of expectant excite-ment. They were all veterans of the struggle; most had prison records as a result, and were sufficiently aware as to have few illusions about what their relationship as young Negroes was to their environment. Knowing this, I had difficulty deter-mining how they could lend their support to what the project had become. That question is still largely unanswered, but I suspect that the answer has much to do with a personal loy-alty to Rustin, and the manner in which any activity can gen-erate around itself a force and an energy that completely immerses anyone who is in too close proximity to it. For those students, the problem became one of obtaining six more buses, trying to get a train, or getting letters out, and in the solution of these individual problems, the validity of their total meaning passed unnoticed.

The scene at Washington's March headquarters ranged be-tween irony and absurdity. The entire town buzzed with ac-tivity and speculation; the newspapers were filled with little else. In the office, the volunteers of both races, by some queer coincidence, became divided into what appeared to be racial groupings, whites to the North, Negroes to the South. This proved to be the result of coincidence and a personality con-flict between two organizers, rather than any racial tension.

Quite obviously, the March was the best thing that had happened to private enterprise and small business in Wash-ington. Three days before the event, private entrepreneurs started selling the March pins, pennants, and other assorted souvenirs that they had had the foresight to have made. It was a triumph of American ingenuity, and I calculate that the March Committee lost many thousands of dollars to these op-portunists who undersold the official March prices for these items.

Very clearly, the agents of the government were under or-ders to cooperate with the workers. One student volunteer—Stokely Carmichael—received a traffic ticket while driving a

"March" car; the police captain promptly tore the ticket up. This apparently insignificant incident represents a fraudulent inversion of normalcy which can be understood if you know that the student had seen a companion assaulted two months before by a Washington policeman when they protested against brutality in the arrest of a Negro. He was arrested off a picket line a week before in Washington because of the "intimidating" nature of the sign he carried.

The cooperation of various groups was, to say the least, surprising. Huge, luxurious, and air-conditioned cars were loaned to the committee. Two of these came from a firm that had been picketed by CORE that summer because of alleged discrimination in their hiring policy. So much sweetness was generated, in fact, that one woman's conscience was moved. She wanted to help, although her attitudes toward Negroes had not been of the best in the past. She had this huge house so she decided that she'd take in marchers. She phoned the housing committee: "Yes, that's right. I can give housing to twenty marchers. Yes, that's right, twenty. Anything to help a good cause. But, one thing . . . would you please see that you only send me white marchers please?"

But it was most nauseating at the headquarters tent that was pitched by the Washington Monument. White tourists forsook the tour of the monument to photograph and gape at the volunteers at work making signs. The government photographers shot miles of film; they often interrupted the work to pose the volunteers, so as to "integrate" the work teams. "Now smile," they said, "this is going to Africa." So it happened that Negro students from the South, some of whom had still unhealed bruises from the electric cattle prods which southern police use to break up demonstrations, were recorded for the screens of the world portraying "American Democracy at Work."

The sweetness and light was so all-pervading, and the smiling official faces so numerous, that one student volunteer remarked to me: "It's incredible! Look how cooperative they are. When the 'revolution' comes, the government will be cooperating with the revolutionaries."

He was wrong. Whenever it appears that Negroes are about to change the shape of things, and to effect a more equitable distribution of power and privilege—and this is what any kind of Negro freedom in America will require—the real racism will emerge in the form of guns, clubs, police dogs, and the violent suppression that happened in Danville and Birmingham. The March no longer had pretentions of doing that. However, amid this ocean of goodwill, one or two local whites maintained their perspectives. On the night of the 26, the telephone cables into the headquarters tent were cut. On the morning of the 28, some of the buses en route to the demonstration were stoned. The American Nazi party contributed their usual racial abuse until one of their number was arrested. On that morning, a young Virginian was arrested while driving toward the crowd, carrying a sawed-off shotgun. One was almost grateful to these people for reaffirming reality.

Little needs to be said of the events of the day itself. One white marcher gave this account:

"From the headquarters tent they began passing out the placards. They must have had ten thousand of them all neatly lithographed, each bearing one of five officially approved slogans such as 'We March For Jobs For All.' 'If you want a sign please step up,' said a young woman, and the people who had come so far stepped up and were given their officially approved signs.

"'Do you want a program?' asked a busy lady in white, and she made sure that the people who had come so far each had a mimeographed program, showing them which way to march, and telling them how to behave properly.

"And afterwards, through the long hot afternoon, we stood in front of the stolid Memorial while they sang at us and spoke to us of equality and justice; all, it seemed, in officially approved words. And through diligent organization and scrupulous planning, they managed to stage a mass protest against injustice *without offending anyone*.

"I suppose that this is necessary, but I am sad. I had high hopes and I came away sad. I find it sad to live in a society where a man demanding individual freedom must march into battle carrying a mimeographed map, and under a lithographed banner showing an officially approved slogan. And, I feel deeply, that in some way I don't fully understand, the people who had come so far had been betrayed."

These are sentiments that are quite understandable, but suppose the writer instead of being a white Californian, had been a Negro student out of a Mississippi jail? There are two events from the day that are illustrative. James Lee Pruitt is an eighteen-year-old Mississippi Negro. He worked on voter registration for SNCC; his job was to organize Negroes to make the attempt to register. It is dangerous and frustrating work. One student, Jimmy Lee, was shot in Mississippi for doing this two years ago. At the March, Pruitt was stopped by one of the marshals whom the committee had provided to keep the peace.

"Has that sign been approved?" asked the marshal.

"It's my sign," Pruitt said.

He was led silently to the chief marshal for judgment to be passed on his sign which simply said "STOP CRIMINAL PROSE-CUTIONS OF VOTER REGISTRATION WORKERS IN MISSIS-SIPPI." This was something that young Pruitt understood since he had recently spent four months in a five by eight foot cell along with fourteen other SNCC workers. In jail they had been kept without any clothes for forty-seven days, and had the fans trained on their small cell. Pruitt had been placed into a tiny zinc cubicle set in the Mississippi sun until he passed out after twelve hours, with a reported temperature of 104 degrees. When one of the group fell ill and the services of a doctor were requested, the guard said only, "Sure, Nigger, after you are dead."

During his trip to Washington to carry that sign, the car that he was traveling in developed mechanical trouble. No garage in the town would touch the car and it had to be abandoned. Pruitt was one of those who "had come so far" and at great price. It could not have been much consolation to him that the chief marshal, after hearing his story, decided that he had a right to carry the unofficial sign. And this story, while extreme, is symbolic of a great many who had come a long way and at great sacrifice, whose stories were not told and whose anguish was not expressed on that day. There is a small footnote to the Pruitt story. Yesterday, November 15, I heard from a SNCC field secretary that Pruitt was again in Parchman Farm, the Mississippi penal farm of folk song and legend.

The other story concerns another young Negro whose name is John Henry Lewis. He is the twenty-five-year-old national chairman of SNCC, the outfit to which Pruitt belongs. He has been arrested in the South more than twenty-five times and the day of the March was one of the few times that I have seen him without some kind of bandage on his head. He was listed on the "mimeographed program" as a speaker, and, when he spoke, he would tell some of the truth, and at least the stories of the Pruitts would be heard. Of this we were sure.

However, a copy of his speech was seen by the Catholic archbishop of Washington, Patrick O'Boyle, who decided that the speech was "inflammatory" and refused to give the invocation unless it was revised. Over the strong objections of Lewis, supported by Rustin, pressure of the other leaders carried the day and the speech was changed. The final chapter in irrelevance was written. The people who had come so far were to get dreams and visions and rhetoric. Here is some of what Lewis was to have said:

Listen, Mr. Kennedy! Listen, Mr. Congressman! Listen Fellow Citizens! The black masses are on the march for freedom and for jobs. We will march through the South, through the heart of Dixie, the way Sherman did . . . we shall pursue our own scorched earth policy.

We shall take matters into our own hands to create a new source of power outside of any national structure, to splinter the segregated South into thousands of pieces and put the pieces back in the image of democracy.

So there is much to be sad about as regards the magnificent abortion of August 28. It is sad that at the end of so much activity, the best and worst that could be said is that "it was orderly and no one was offended." It is much sadder and a little obscene that if anyone gained from the day's activity it was the U.S. Department of State which converted the proceedings into a great propaganda victory. When the Telestar broadcast of the March was suddenly and inexplicably canceled by Russian TV, this was hailed by the American press and by the State Department as evidence that the "Russians were afraid to show their people this example of democracy in action." But even if this is true, who does this help? Could they not afford to allow their people to see this mammoth crowd of "free" people in a "free society" petitioning their government for the redress of wrongs? No explanation has been offered as to why a free people should need to march for freedom, or why, if the government is really theirs—i.e., really represents them—it has made no move to redress these wrongs. This exploitation of so many angry and sincere people, whose indignation was misrepresented as some kind of testimonial for the system that had oppressed them, and against which they were protesting, must qualify as one of the greatest and most shameless manipulations of recent years.

But the real political waste was that the March became a symbol and a focal point in the minds of Negroes during this explosive summer of our discontent, and in many communities where the Negro temper was right, and where there had begun meaningful protest activity, the militants were diverted into mobilization for the March. In one community the local student group was told in June that the most important activity they could undertake was to make the March preparations their summer project. This was before the emasculation process had begun, and these students decided to set aside their local program and to work toward this end. This happened in too many areas; local action slowed down, and we all looked to Washington for the climax that never came. In this way, much energy and much anger were wasted on the spectacular. Ironically, what was to have been our day of protest served a similar function to the "bread and circuses" of the Roman emperors—it drained the anger of our people into irrelevant channels.

Présence Africaine (Paris), 1er trimestre 1964
[as "Les Meandres de la 'Marche'";
English version from
Duties, Pleasures, and Conflicts (1987)]

A Southern City with Northern Problems

by Hunter S. Thompson

Louisville

QUINO'S CAFE is on Market Street, two blocks up the hill from the river in the heart of Louisville's legal and financial district, and often in the long, damp Ohio Valley afternoons a lot of people who might ordinarily avoid such a place will find themselves standing at Quino's white formica counter, drinking a Fehrs or a Falls City beer, and eating a "genuine twenty cent beercheese sandwich" while they skim through an early edition of the Louisville *Times.* If you stand at the counter and watch the street you will see off-duty cops and courthouse loafers, visiting farmers with five children and a pregnant wife in the cab of a pickup truck, and a well-fed collection of lawyers and brokers in two-button suits and cordovan shoes. You will also see quite a few Negroes, some of them also wearing business suits and cordovan shoes. Louisville takes pride in its race relations, and the appearance of well-dressed Negroes in the Courthouse–City Hall district does not raise any eyebrows.

This city, known as "Derbytown," and "The Gateway to the South," has done an admirable job in breaking down the huge and traditional barriers between the black man and the white. Here in the mint julep country, where the Negro used to be viewed with all the proprietary concern that men lavish on a good coon hound ("Treat him fine when he works good —but when he acts lazy and no-count, beat him till he hollers"), the integration of the races has made encouraging headway.

Racial segregation has been abolished in nearly all public places. Negroes entered the public schools in 1956 with so little trouble that the superintendent of schools was moved to write a book about it, called *The Louisville Story.* Since then, restaurants, hotels, parks, movie theatres, stores, swimming pools, bowling alleys, and even business schools have been opened to Negroes. As a clincher, the city recently passed an ordinance that outlaws racial discrimination in any public accommodation. This has just about done the deed; out of ninety-nine establishments "tested" by NAACP workers, there were only four complaints—two from the same East End bar. Mayor William Cowger, whose progressive Republican administration has caused even Democrats to mutter with admiration, spoke for most of his fellow citizens recently when he said, "The stories of violence in other cities should make us proud to live in Louisville. We enjoy national prestige for sane and sensible race relations."

All this is true—and so it is all the more surprising to visit Louisville and find so much evidence to the contrary. Why, for instance, does a local Negro leader say, "Integration here is a farce"? Why, also, has a local Negro minister urged his congregation to arm themselves? Why do Louisville Negroes bitterly accuse the Federal urban-renewal project of creating "de facto segregation"? Why can't a Negro take out a mortgage to buy a home in most white neighborhoods? And why is there so much bitterness in the remarks of Louisvillians both black and white? "Integration is for poor people," one hears; "they can't afford to buy their way out of it." Or, "In ten years, downtown Louisville will be as black as Harlem."

What is apparent in Louisville is that the Negro has won a few crucial battles, but instead of making the breakthrough he expected, he has come up against segregation's second front, where the problems are not mobs and unjust laws but customs and traditions. The Louisville Negro, having taken the first basic steps, now faces a far more subtle thing than the simple "yes" or "no" that his brothers are still dealing with in most parts of the South. To this extent, Louisville has integrated itself right out of the South, and now faces problems more like those of a Northern or Midwestern city.

The white power structure has given way in the public sector, only to entrench itself more firmly in the private. And the Negro—especially the educated Negro—feels that his victories are hollow and his "progress" is something he reads about in the newspapers. The outlook for Louisville's Negroes may have improved from "separate but equal" to "equal but separate." But it still leaves a good deal to be desired.

The white power structure, as defined by local Negroes, means the men who run the town, the men who control banking and industry and insurance, who pay big taxes and lend big money and head important civic committees. Their names are not well known to the average citizen, and when they get publicity at all it is likely to be in the society sections of the one-owner local press. During the day, their headquarters is the Pendennis Club on downtown Walnut Street, where they meet for lunch, squash, steam baths, and cocktails. "If you want to get things done in this town," according to a young lawyer very much on the way up, "you'd better belong to the Pendennis." On evenings and weekends the scene shifts to the Louisville Country Club far out in the East End, or clear across the county line to Harmony Landing, where good polo and good whiskey push business out of sight if not out of mind.

Anybody who pays dues to at least two of these clubs can consider himself a member in good standing of the white power structure. This is the group that determines by quiet pressure, direct action, and sometimes even default just how far and fast Louisville will move toward integration. Among themselves, it is clear, they are no more integrated now than they were ten years ago, and they are not likely to be at any time in the near future. They have for the most part taken their sons and daughters out of the public schools or moved to suburban areas where the absence of Negroes makes integration an abstract question. The only time they deal actively with Negroes is when they give the maid a ride to the bus stop, get their shoes shined, or attend some necessary but unpleasant confrontation with a local Negro spokesman. Despite an ancient conditioning to prejudice, however, they are, in the main, a far more progressive and enlightened lot than their counterparts in Birmingham or even in a lot of cases than their own sons and daughters.

There is a feeling in liberal circles, especially in New York and Washington, that the banner of racial segregation has little appeal to the younger generation. And Murray Kempton has written that the special challenge of the 1960's "is how to appease the Negro without telling the poor white." But neither theory appears to apply in Louisville. Some of the bitterest racists in town belong to the best families, and no Mississippi dirt farmer rants more often against the "niggers" than do some of Louisville's young up-and-coming executives just a few years out of college. At Bauer's, a fashionable pine-paneled tavern much frequented by the young bucks of the social set, the sentiment is overwhelmingly anti-Negro. Late in the evening some of the habitués may find themselves carried along in the confusion of drink and good-fellowship toward Magazine Street in the heart of the colored section. There, at Oliver's and Big John's and the Diamond Horseshoe, the action goes on until dawn and a carload of jovial racists are as welcome as anybody else, black or white. The Negroes suspend their resentment, the whites suspend their prejudice, and everybody enjoys the music and the entertainment. But there is little or no mingling, and the activities of the night are quite separate from those of the day.

You get a feeling, after a while, that the young are not really serious either about denouncing the "nigger" for "not knowing his place" or about ignoring the color line for nocturnal visits to Magazine Street. Both are luxuries that will not last, and the young are simply enjoying them while they can. Mayor Cowger likes to say: "People are different here. We get along with each other because we don't like trouble." Others will tell you that Louisville has no overt racial problem because the greatest commitment of the majority of white citizens is simply to maintain the status quo, whatever it happens to be.

In such a society, of course, it might be argued that almost anything can happen as long as it happens slowly and inconspicuously without getting people stirred up. All of which naturally frustrates the Negro, who has said that he wants freedom now. If the Negro were patient—and who can tell him he should be?—he would have no problem. But "freedom now" is not in the white Louisville vocabulary.

A good example of the majority viewpoint shows up in the housing situation, which at the moment is inextricably linked with urban renewal. As it happens, the urban-renewal project centers mainly in the downtown Negro district, and most of the people who have to be relocated are black. It also happens that the only part of town to which Negroes can move is the West End, an old and tree-shaded neighborhood bypassed by progress and now in the throes of a selling panic because of the Negro influx. There is a growing fear, shared by whites and Negroes alike, that the West End is becoming a black ghetto.

Frank Stanley, Jr., the Negro leader who said "Integration here is a farce," blames urban renewal for the problem. "All they're doing is moving the ghetto, intact, from the middle of town to the West End." Urban-renewal officials reply to this by claiming the obvious: that their job is not to desegregate Louisville but to relocate people as quickly and advantageously as possible. "Sure they move to the West End," says one official. "Where else can they go?"

It is a fact that whites are moving out of the West End as fast as they can. A vocal minority is trying to stem the tide, but there is hardly a block without a "For Sale" sign, and some blocks show as many as ten. Yet there is "hardly any" race prejudice in the West End. Talk to a man with his house for sale and you'll be given to understand that he is not moving because of any reluctance to live near Negroes. Far from it; he is proud of Louisville's progress toward integration. But he is worried about the value of his property; and you know, of course, what happens to property values when a Negro family moves into an all-white block. So he's selling now to get his price while the getting is good.

Depending on the neighborhood, he may or may not be willing to sell to Negroes. The choice is all his, and will be until Louisville passes an "open housing" ordinance to eliminate skin color as a factor in the buying and selling of homes. Such an ordinance is already in the planning stage.

Meanwhile, the homeowner who will sell to Negroes is a rare bird—except in the West End. And arguments are presented with great feeling that those who will show their homes only to whites are not prejudiced, merely considerate of their neighbors. "Personally, I have nothing against colored people," a seller will explain. "But I don't want to hurt the neighbors. If I sold my house to a Negro it would knock several thousand dollars off the value of every house on the block."

Most Negro realtors deny this, citing the law of supply and demand. Good housing for Negroes is scarce, they point out, and prices are consequently higher than those on the white market, where demand is not so heavy. There are, however, both white and Negro real-estate speculators who engage in "block busting." They will work to place a Negro in an all-white block, then try to scare the other residents into selling cheap. Quite often they succeed—then resell to Negroes at a big profit.

According to Jesse P. Warders, a real-estate agent and a long-time leader in Louisville's Negro community, "What this town needs is a single market for housing—not two, like we have now." Warders is counting on an "open housing" ordinance, and he maintains that the biggest obstacle to open housing without an ordinance is the lack of Negroes on Louisville's Real Estate Board.

In order to be a "realtor" in Louisville, a real-estate agent has to be a member of "the Board," which does not accept Negroes. Warders is a member of the Washington-based National Institute of Real Estate Brokers, which has about as much influence here as the French Foreign Legion.

Louisville, like other cities faced with urban decay, has turned to the building of midtown apartments as a means of luring suburbanites back to the city center. In the newest and biggest of these, called "The 800," Warders tried to place a Negro client. The reaction was a good indicator of the problems facing Negroes after they break the barrier of outright racism.

"Do me a favor," the builder of The 800 told Warders. "Let me get the place fifty per cent full—that's my break-even point—then I'll rent to your client."

Warders was unhappy with the rebuff, but he believes the builder will eventually rent to Negroes; and that, he thinks, is real progress. "What should I say to the man?" he asked. "I know for a fact that he's refused some white people, too. What that man wants is prestige tenants; he'd like to have the mayor living in his place, he'd like to have the president of the board of aldermen. Hell, I'm in business, too. I might not like what he says, but I see his point."

Warders has been on the firing line long enough to know the score. He is convinced that fear of change and the reluctance of most whites to act in any way that might be frowned on by the neighbors is the Negroes' biggest problem in Louisville. "I know how they feel, and so do most of my clients. But do you think it's right?"

The 800 was built with the considerable help of an FHA-guaranteed loan, which places the building automatically in the open housing category. Furthermore, the owner insists that he is color-blind on the subject of tenants. But he assumes none the less that the prestige tenants he wants would not consider living in the same building with Negroes.

It is the same assumption that motivates a homeowner to sell to whites only—not because of race prejudice but out of concern for property values. In other words, almost nobody has anything against Negroes, but everybody's neighbor does.

This is galling to the Negroes. Simple racism is an easy thing to confront, but a mixture of guilty prejudice, economic worries, and threatened social standing is much harder to fight. "If all the white people I've talked to had the courage of their convictions," one Negro leader has said, "we wouldn't have a problem here."

Louisville's lending institutions frustrate Negroes in the same way. Frank Stanley, Jr., claims that there's a gentlemen's agreement among bankers to prevent Negroes from getting mortgages to buy homes in white neighborhoods. The complaint would seem to have a certain validity, although once again less sinister explanations are offered. The lending agencies cite business reasons, not race prejudice, as the reason for their stand. Concern for the reaction of their depositors seems to be a big factor, and another is the allegation that such loans would be a poor risk—especially if the institution holds mortgages on other homes in the neighborhood. Here again is the fear of falling property values.

There is also the question whether a Negro would have any more difficulty getting a mortgage to buy a home in a white upper-class neighborhood than would a member of another minority group—say, a plumber named Luciano, proud possessor of six children, a dirty spitz that barks at night, and a ten-year-old pickup truck with "Luciano Plumbing" painted on the side.

Mayor Cowger, a mortgage banker himself, insists that a Negro would have no more trouble than the hypothetical Mr. Luciano. Another high-ranking occupant of City Hall disagrees: "That's what the mayor would like to think, but it just isn't true. Nobody in Rolling Fields, for instance, would want an Italian plumber for a neighbor, but at least they could live with him, whereas a Negro would be unthinkable because he's too obvious. It wouldn't matter if he were a doctor or a lawyer or anything else. The whites in the neighborhood would fear for the value of their property and try to sell it before it dropped."

Another common contention is that Negroes "don't want to move into an all-white neighborhood." The East End, for instance, remains solidly white except for alley dwellings and isolated shacks. The mayor, who lives in the East End, has said, "Negroes don't want to live here. It wouldn't be congenial for them. There are some fine Negro neighborhoods in the West End—beautiful homes. They don't try to buy homes where they won't be happy. People just don't do things like that." Some people do, however, and it appears that almost without exception they get turned down flat. One Negro executive with adequate funds called a white realtor and made an appointment to look at a house for sale in the East End. Things went smoothly on the telephone, but when the Negro arrived at the realtor's office the man was incensed. "What are you trying to do?" he demanded. "You know I can't sell you that house. What are you up to, anyway?"

No realtor, however, admits to racial prejudice, at least while talking to strangers. They are, they point out, not selling their own homes but those of their clients. In the same fashion, mortgage bankers are quick to explain that they do not lend their own money. A man making inquiries soon gets the impression that all clients, investors, and depositors are vicious racists and dangerous people to cross. Which is entirely untrue in Louisville—although it is hard to see how a Negro, after making the rounds of "very sympathetic" realtors, could be expected to believe anything else.

Housing ranks right at the top among Louisville's racial problems. According to Frank Stanley, Jr., "Housing is basic; once we have whites and Negroes living together, the rest will be a lot easier." Jesse P. Warders, the real-estate agent, however, rates unemployment as the No. 1 problem area, because "Without money, you can't enjoy the other things."

The Louisville Human Relations Commission, one of the first of its kind in the nation, agrees that although the city has made vast strides in the areas of education and public accommodations, the problems of housing and employment are still largely unsolved because "These areas are much more complex and confront long-established customs based on a heritage of prejudice." Of the two, however, the commission sees housing as a bigger problem. J. Mansir Tydings, executive director of the commission, is optimistic about the willingness of merchants and other employers to hire Negroes: "Already —and much sooner than we expected—our problem is training unemployed Negroes to fill positions that are open."

Yet there is still another big hurdle, less tangible than such factors as housing and employment but perhaps more basic when it comes to finding an ultimate solution. This is the pervasive distrust among the white power structure of the Negro leadership's motives. Out in the dove-shooting country, in the suburbs beyond the East End, Stanley is viewed as an "opportunist politician" and a "black troublemaker." Bishop Ewbank Tucker, the minister who urged his congregation to arm themselves, is called an extremist and a Black Muslim. The possibility that some of the Negro leaders do sometimes agitate for the sake of agitation often cramps the avenues of communication between white and Negro leaders.

Even among Negroes, Stanley is sometimes viewed with uneasiness and Bishop Tucker called a racist. A former president of the Louisville NAACP, on hearing the statement that local Negroes "resent the national publicity concerning Louisville's progress in race relations," laughed and dismissed Stanley as a "very nice, very smart young fella with a lot to learn." (Stanley is twenty-six.)

"He wants things to go *properly*," said the NAACP man. "But difficult things never go properly—life isn't that way." He smiled nervously. "Forty years ago I came back here thinking I could be a Black Moses—I thought I was going to set my people free. But I couldn't do it then and it can't be done now. It's not a thing you can do overnight—it's going to take years and years and years."

Nearly everyone agrees with that, and even with all its problems, Louisville looks to be a lot further along the road to facing and solving the "Negro problem" than many other cities. Even Stanley, who appears to make a cult of militant noncompromise, will eventually admit to a visitor that he threatens far more demonstrations than he ever intends to produce.

"The white power structure here tries to cling to the status quo. They keep telling me not to rock the boat, but I rock it anyway because it's the only way to make them move. We have to keep the pressure on them every minute, or we dissipate our strength.

"Louisville isn't like Birmingham," he adds. "I think there's a conviction here that this thing is morally wrong—without that, we'd have real trouble."

The Reporter, December 19, 1963

The Ominous Malcolm X Exits from the Muslims

by Marc Crawford

LAST WEEK the Negro civil rights movement was shaken by a rift in the strong and mystical ranks of the Nation of Islam, the "Black Muslims." Malcolm X, the shrewd and personable Harlem leader of the sect who has been its most prominent national spokesman, abruptly announced he was quitting his ministry and organizing a black nationalist political movement of his own.

Of far greater impact on Negro civil rights leadership than the Muslim split itself was Malcolm's surprising decision to join the civil rights fight this summer—and even try to lead it. Up to now he has been a sideline critic of civil rights demonstrators. He has sneered at them both for their methods of passive resistance and their ultimate aim—integration. Malcolm X, like the leader of the Black Muslims, Elijah Muhammad, is an adamant archsegregationist who insists American Negroes must separate from whites as an independent state in the South or through mass migration to Africa.

The schism between Malcolm and Elijah Muhammad has been growing for months. Elijah, little known personally outside of the Islam movement, suffers from asthma and several times during the past year was rumored to be close to death. Malcolm X had become the Muslims' spokesman and dynamo. And this has reportedly aroused the jealousy of Elijah Muhammad's own family, who expect to inherit the leadership.

Last December Malcolm was temporarily suspended from duties in Harlem's Temple No. 7, ostensibly for intemperate remarks he made after President Kennedy's assassination. During the suspension he scored a coup when Cassius Clay, the new champion, revealed he was a Muslim and that Malcolm had converted him. Shortly after, Malcolm said he was suspended indefinitely from his duties—and he promptly quit the movement.

He took pains to swear continuing loyalty to Elijah Muhammad and to reaffirm his religious faith as a Muslim. But, said Muhammad, "whenever a brother walks away from us, all is gone. Malcolm's doing more running off at the mouth than he can back up."

Many Negroes agree with Muhammad that Malcolm has unplugged himself from his power source and that his fortunes will suffer. But predominant opinion, particularly in Harlem where he is known best, is that Malcolm's violent opposition to white men will prove compelling to many Negroes who until now have gone along with the Rev. Martin Luther King Jr.'s peaceful approach.

"I don't believe in passive resistance," Malcolm X explains, calmly enough. "Every Negro ought to have a weapon in his house—a rifle or a shotgun. Any Negro who is attacked should fight back; if necessary he should be prepared to die like a man, like Patrick Henry. Any Negro leader must be prepared—and must tell the people who are following him to prepare—to go either to jail, the hospital or the cemetery. But not without a fight, not without a reason."

Malcolm expects for the present to find his financial and political base in Harlem where, he contends, "Ninety percent of the people feel as I do, admit it or not."

Then, having announced his move, Malcolm went into seclusion to map out his organizational structure. But already his dialogue was taking form:

▶ On Negroes in the Armed Forces: "If [Martin Luther] King and the others can tell Negroes to boycott buses or industries or schools, I see no reason why they cannot boycott the Army, Navy and Air Force. I don't think any Negro should fight for anything that does not produce for him what it produces for others. Whenever a Negro fights for 'democracy,' he's fighting for something he has not got, never had and never will have. If I'm wrong, then all the other boycotts and civil disobedience are wrong too."

▶ On paying taxes: "If I'm to ride second class on an airplane, I don't pay first-class fare. If I'm a second-class citizen, I should not have to pay first-class taxes."

▶ On separatism: "The American Negro has been unhappily married to the U.S. for 400 years. We can't get along, so let's be intelligent and get a divorce. But let's have a property settlement. Give us our share of what the over-all joint property is worth."

▶ On Americanism: "A cat can have kittens in an oven but that doesn't make them biscuits. I was born in Omaha; that doesn't make me an American. Africa is home."

▶ On the Washington March: "It was a gimmick to hold things in check. It was like putting Novocain in a sore tooth. If the tooth hasn't been pulled or fixed, it's hell when it wears off. The Negro leaders got the people there, put on a show, promised we'd be back in September if there was no civil rights bill. There's still no bill—and no more marching."

▶ On nonviolence: "If you think I'll bleed nonviolently, you'll be sticking me for the rest of my life. But if I tell you I'll fight back, there will be less blood. I'm for reciprocal bleeding."

▶ On the South: "When I speak of the South, I mean south of Canada. The whole U.S. is the South."

▶ On police brutality: "Any dog sicked on to any Negro should be shot. I think there will be dead police dogs before the year is over."

Malcolm X will find scant welcome when and if he offers his help and his ominous philosophy to other Negro leaders. "I think it is very unfortunate," says Martin Luther King, "that Malcolm X continues to predict violence . . . in the past the constant prediction of violence has been a conscious or unconscious invitation to it.

"But if the civil rights bill is watered down at any point, it can lead to a despair and discontent in the Negro community that may well bring about a dark night of social disruption. And responsible Negro leadership will find it much more difficult to keep the struggle disciplined and nonviolent."

Malcolm X puts it more savagely. "This is going to be the hottest summer in history."

Tired of Being Sick and Tired

by Jerry DeMuth

About 20 feet back from a narrow dirt road just off the state highway that cuts through Ruleville, Miss., is a small, three-room, white frame house with a screened porch. A large pecan tree grows in the front yard and two smaller ones grow out back. Butter bean and okra plants are filling out in the gardens on the lots on either side of the house. Lafayette Street is as quiet as the rest of Ruleville, a town of less than 2,000 located in Sunflower County, 30 miles from the Mississippi River. Sunflower County, home of Senator Eastland and 68 per cent Negro, is one of twenty-four counties in the northwestern quarter of the state—the Delta—that make up the Second Congressional District. Since 1941, this district has been represented in Congress by Jamie Whitten, chairman of the House Appropriations Subcommittee on Agriculture, who is now seeking his thirteenth term.

From the house on the dirt road there now comes a person to challenge Jamie Whitten: Mrs. Fannie Lou Hamer. Mrs. Hamer is a Negro and only 6,616 Negroes (or 4.14 per cent of voting-age Negroes) were registered to vote in the Second Congressional District in 1960. But in 1962, when Whitten was elected for the twelfth time, only 31,345 persons cast votes, although in 1960 there were more than 300,000 persons of voting age in the district, 59 per cent of them Negro. Mrs. Hamer's bid is sponsored by the Council of Federated Organizations, a Mississippi coalition of local and national civil rights organizations.

Until Mississippi stops its discriminatory voting practices, Mrs. Hamer's chance of election is slight, but she is waking up the citizens of her district. "I'm showing people that a Negro can run for office," she explains. Her deep, powerful voice shakes the air as she sits on the porch or inside, talking to friends, relatives and neighbors who drop by on the one day each week when she is not out campaigning. Whatever she is talking about soon becomes an impassioned plea for a change in the system that exploits the Delta Negroes. "All my life I've been sick and tired," she shakes her head. "Now I'm sick and tired of being sick and tired."

Mrs. Hamer was born October 6, 1917, in Montgomery County, the twentieth child in a family of six girls and fourteen boys. When she was 2 her family moved to Sunflower County, 60 miles to the west.

The family would pick fifty-sixty bales of cotton a year, so my father decided to rent some land. He bought some mules and a cultivator. We were doin' pretty well. He even started to fix up the house real nice and had bought a car. Then our stock got poisoned. We knowed this white man had done it. He stirred up a gallon of Paris green with the feed. When we got out there, one mule was already dead. T'other two mules and the cow had their stomachs all swelled up. It was too late to save 'em. That poisonin' knocked us right back down flat. We never did get back up again. That white man did it just because we were gettin' somewhere. White people never like to see Negroes get a little success. All of this stuff is no secret in the state of Mississippi.

Mrs. Hamer pulled her feet under the worn, straight-backed chair she was sitting in. The linoleum under her feet was worn through to another layer of linoleum. Floor boards showed in spots. She folded her large hands on her lap and shifted her weight in the chair. She's a large and heavy woman, but large and heavy with a power to back up her determination.

We went back to sharecroppin', halvin', it's called. You split the cotton half and half with the plantation owner. But the seed, fertilizer, cost of hired hands, everything is paid out of the cropper's half.

Later, I dropped out of school. I cut corn stalks to help the family. My parents were gettin' up in age—they weren't young when I was born, I was the twentieth child—and my mother had a bad eye. She was cleanin' up the owner's yard for a quarter when somethin' flew up and hit her in the eye.

So many times for dinner we would have greens with no seasonin' . . . and flour gravy. My mother would mix

flour with a little grease and try to make gravy out of it.
Sometimes she'd cook a little meal and we'd have bread.

No one can honestly say Negroes are satisfied. We've only
been patient, but how much more patience can we have?

Fannie Lou and Perry Hamer have two daughters, 10 and 19, both of whom they adopted. The Hamers adopted the older girl when she was born to give her a home, her mother being unmarried. "I've always been concerned with any human being," Mrs. Hamer explains. The younger girl was given to her at the age of 5 months. She had been burned badly when a tub of boiling water spilled, and her large, impoverished family was not able to care for her. "We had a little money so we took care of her and raised her. She was sickly too when I got her, suffered from malnutrition. Then she got run over by a car and her leg was broken. So she's only in fourth grade now."

The older girl left school after the tenth grade to begin working. Several months ago when she tried to get a job, the employer commented, "You certainly talk like Fannie Lou." When the girl replied, "She raised me," she was denied the job. She has a job now, but Mrs. Hamer explains, "They don't know she's my child."

The intimidation that Mrs. Hamer's older girl faces is what Mrs. Hamer has faced since August 31, 1962. On that day she and seventeen others went down to the county courthouse in Indianola to try to register to vote. From the moment they arrived, police wandered around their bus, keeping an eye on the eighteen. "I wonder what they'll do," the bus driver said to Mrs. Hamer. Half way back to Ruleville, the police stopped the bus and ordered it back to Indianola. There they were all arrested. The bus was painted the wrong color, the police told them.

After being bonded out, Mrs. Hamer returned to the plantation where the Hamers had lived for eighteen years.

My oldest girl met me and told me that Mr. Marlowe,
the plantation owner, was mad and raisin' Cain. He had
heard that I had tried to register. That night he called on
us and said, "We're not ready for that in Mississippi now.
If you don't withdraw, I'll let you go." I left that night but
"Pap"—that's what I call my husband—had to stay on till
work on the plantation was through.

In the spring of last year, Mr. Hamer got a job at a Ruleville cotton gin. But this year, though others are working there already, they haven't taken him back.

According to Mississippi law the names of all persons who take the registration test must be in the local paper for two weeks. This subjects Negroes, especially Delta Negroes, to all sorts of retaliatory actions. "Most Negroes in the Delta are sharecroppers. It's not like in the hills where Negroes own land. But everything happened before my name had been in the paper," Mrs. Hamer adds.

She didn't pass the test the first time, so she returned on December 4, and took it again. "You'll see me every 30 days till I pass," she told the registrar. On January 10, she returned and found out that she had passed. "But I still wasn't allowed to vote last fall because I didn't have two poll-tax receipts. We still have to pay poll tax for state elections. I have two receipts now."

After being forced to leave the plantation, Mrs. Hamer stayed with various friends and relatives. On September 10, night riders fired sixteen times into the home of one of these persons, Mrs. Turner. Mrs. Hamer was away at the time. In December, 1962, the Hamers moved into their present home which they rent from a Negro woman.

Mrs. Hamer had by then begun active work in the civil rights movement. She gathered names for a petition to obtain federal commodities for needy Negro families and attended various Southern Christian Leadership Conference (SCLC) and Student Nonviolent Coordinating Committee (SNCC) workshops throughout the South. Since then she has been active as a SNCC field secretary in voter registration and welfare programs and has taught classes for SCLC. At present, most of her time is spent campaigning.

In June of last year, Mrs. Hamer was returning from a workshop in Charleston, S.C. She was arrested in Winona, in Montgomery County, 60 miles east of Indianola, the county in which she was born. Along with others, she was taken from the bus to the jail.

They carried me into a room and there was two Negro boys in this room. The state highway patrolman gave them a long, wide blackjack and he told one of the boys, "Take this," and the Negro, he said, "This what you want me to use?" The state patrolman said, "That's right, and if you don't use it on her you know what I'll use on you."

I had to get over on a bed flat on my stomach and that man beat me . . . that man beat me till he give out. And by me screamin', it made a plain-clothes man—he didn't have on nothin' like a uniform—he got so hot and worked up he just run there and started hittin' me on the back of my head. And I was tryin' to guard some of the licks with my hands and they just beat my hands till they turned blue. This Negro just beat me till I know he was give out. Then this state patrolman told the other Negro to take me so he take over from there and he just keep beatin' me.

The police carried Mrs. Hamer to her cell when they were through beating her. They also beat Annelle Ponder, a SCLC worker who was returning on the bus with her, and Lawrence Guyot, a SNCC field secretary who had traveled from the Greenwood SNCC office to investigate the arrests.

They whipped Annelle Ponder and I heard her screamin'. After a while she passed by where I was in the cell and her mouth was bleedin' and her hair was standin' up on her head and you know it was horrifyin'.

Over in the night I even heard screamin'. I said, "Oh, Lord, somebody else gettin' it, too." It was later that we heard that Lawrence Guyot was there. I got to see him. I could walk as far as the cell door and I asked them to please leave that door open so I could get a breath of fresh air every once in a while. That's how I got to see Guyot. He looked as if he was in pretty bad shape. And it was on my nerves, too, because that was the first time I had seen him and not smilin'.

After I got out of jail, half dead, I found out that Medgar Evers had been shot down in his own yard.

Mrs. Hamer paused for a moment, saddened by the recollection. I glanced around the dim room. Faded wallpaper covered the walls and a vase, some framed photos, and a large doll were placed neatly on a chest and on a small table. Three stuffed clowns and a small doll lay on the worn spread on the double bed in the corner. Both the small doll and the larger one had white complexions, a reminder of the world outside.

We're tired of all this beatin', we're tired of takin' this. It's been a hundred years and we're still being beaten and shot at, crosses are still being burned, because we want to vote. But I'm goin' to stay in Mississippi and if they shoot me down, I'll be buried here.

But I don't want equal rights with the white man; if I did, I'd be a thief and a murderer. But the white man is the scardest person on earth. Out in the daylight he don't do nothin'. But at night he'll toss a bomb or pay someone to kill. The white man's afraid he'll be treated like he's been treatin' Negroes, but I couldn't carry that much hate. It wouldn't solve any problem for me to hate whites just because they hate me. Oh, there's so much hate. Only God has kept the Negro sane.

As part of her voter-registration work, Mrs. Hamer has been teaching citizenship classes, working to overcome the bad schooling Delta Negroes have received, when they receive any at all. "We just have nice school buildings," she says. In Sunflower County there are three buildings for 11,000 Negroes of high school age, six buildings for 4,000 white high school students. In 1960–61, the county spent $150 per white pupil, $60 per Negro pupil. When applying to register, persons as part of the test must interpret the state constitution but, Mrs. Hamer says, "Mississippi don't teach it in school."

The Negro schools close in May, so that the children can help with the planting and chopping; they open again in July and August, only to close in September and October so that the children can pick cotton. Some stay out of school completely to work in the fields. Mississippi has no compulsory school-attendance law; it was abolished after the 1954 Supreme Court school-desegregation decision. Many Negro children do not attend school simply because they have no clothes to wear.

Mrs. Hamer has helped distribute clothing sent down from the North. "We owe a lot to people in the North," she admits. "A lot of people are wearing nice clothes for the first time. A lot of kids couldn't go to school otherwise."

One time when a shipment arrived for distribution, the Ruleville mayor took it upon himself to announce that a lot of clothes were being given out. More than 400 Negroes showed up and stood in line to receive clothes. Mrs. Hamer, combining human compassion and politicking, told them that the mayor had had nothing to do with the clothing distribution and that if they went and registered they wouldn't have to stand in line as they were doing. Many went down and took the registration test.

"A couple weeks ago when more clothes arrived," she relates, "the mayor said that people could go and get clothing, and that if they didn't get any they should just go and take them. I went and talked to the mayor. I told him not to boss us around. 'We don't try to boss you around,' I told him."

Obviously, Fannie Lou Hamer will not be easily stopped. "We mean to use every means to try and win. If I lose we have this freedom registration and freedom vote to see how many would have voted if there wasn't all this red tape and discrimination." If Mrs. Hamer is defeated by Jamie Whitten in the primary, she will also file as an independent in the general election.

Last fall, SNCC voter-registration workers attempted to register in freedom-registration books all those not officially registered. These Negroes then voted in an unofficial Freedom Vote campaign, choosing between Democrat Paul Johnson, now Governor, Republican Rubel Phillips, and independent Aaron Henry, state NAACP chairman. Henry received 70,000 votes.

The same thing will be done this summer, and if Mrs. Hamer loses, the Freedom Vote total will be used to challenge Whitten's election.

Backing up the discrimination charges are nine suits the federal government has pending in seven Second Congressional District counties, including a suit in Sunflower County where, in 1960, only 1.2 per cent of voting-age Negroes were registered.

A Mississippi Freedom Democratic Party is also being formed which will hold meetings on every level within the state, from precinct on up, finally choosing a delegation to the National Democratic Convention that will challenge the seating of the regular all-white Mississippi delegation.

In addition to Mrs. Hamer, three other Mississippi Negroes are running for national office in the 1964 elections. James Monroe Houston will challenge Robert Bell Williams in the Third Congressional District, the Rev. John E. Cameron faces William Meyers Colmer in the Fifth, and Mrs. Victoria Jackson Gray is campaigning for the Senate seat now held by John Stennis.

This extensive program provides a basis for Negroes organizing throughout the state, and gives a strong democratic base for the Freedom Democratic Party. The wide range of Negro participation will show that the problem in Mississippi is not Negro apathy, but discrimination and fear of physical and economic reprisals for attempting to register.

The Freedom Democratic candidates will also give Mississippians, white as well as Negro, a chance to vote for candidates who do not stand for political, social and economic exploitation and discrimination, and a chance to vote for the National Democratic ticket rather than the Mississippi slate of unpledged electors.

"We been waitin' all our lives," Mrs. Hamer exclaims, "and still gettin' killed, still gettin' hung, still gettin' beat to death. Now we're tired waitin'!"

The Nation, June 1, 1964

Martin Luther King and 17 Others Jailed Trying to Integrate St. Augustine Restaurant

by John Herbers

Sᴛ. Aᴜɢᴜsᴛɪɴᴇ, Fla., June 11—The Rev. Dr. Martin Luther King Jr. was jailed today after he attempted to eat in one of St. Augustine's finer restaurants overlooking Matanzas Bay.

While Dr. King and 17 companions were held on charges of violating Florida's unwanted guest law, other civil rights demonstrators made another night march through crowds of jeering whites.

The whites threw firecrackers into the line of 200 marchers as they circled the old Slave Market. But there were so many helmeted officers—one for every marcher—that the cursing whites made no attempt to assault the demonstrators as they had done previously.

After the march a crowd of white youths attempted to form a march of their own but were blocked by state troopers and police dogs.

"If the niggers can march why can't we?" they shouted.

At one point, the crowd broke through the line and darted toward the Negro neighborhood where the marchers were reassembling in a church. But about 50 troopers and deputies ran in a body for two blocks and cut them off.

Shortly before the march authorities found a cache of weapons including sulphuric acid, chains and clubs hidden beneath a wall along the parade route.

The city had taken two steps to reduce the danger. Workmen removed the bricks that boarded flower beds in the little park that adjoins the old slave market, and an electrician installed seven mercury vapor lights that will illuminate dark corners of the square.

Last night, white men and youths lurking in the shadows hurled bricks at state troopers who were trying to guard civil rights demonstrators from a cursing mob. The whites broke through the police line and slugged and kicked several demonstrators. Other marchers said they were burned by acid thrown from the crowd.

By day downtown St. Augustine is the picture of tranquility with old men playing checkers in the slave market and tourists viewing old Spanish buildings from horse drawn surreys. At night it is the scene of an outpouring of racial hatred and violence.

Dr. King was arrested on the doorstep of the Monson Motor Lodge Restaurant after a 20-minute confrontation with the president and general manager of the concern, James Brock.

Everyone in town had known for 24 hours that Dr. King would be arrested. He had announced yesterday that he would go to jail to dramatize discrimination against Negroes in the nation's oldest city.

When Dr. King and his chief aide, the Rev. Ralph D. Abernathy, arrived shortly after noon, Mr. Brock was waiting.

The night before Mr. Brock, who also is president of the Florida Hotel and Motel Association, had been seen on a downtown street carrying a shotgun, a billy stick, a pistol and a flashlight. He was one of several businessmen in town who were made special deputies yesterday by Sheriff L. O. Davis. The sheriff said he had appealed to the city's civic clubs to help maintain law and order.

Mr. Brock told Dr. King that he and his party of eight persons were not wanted. The two then began a polite debate of the civil rights issue.

Dr. King asked if Mr. Brock understood the "humiliation our people have to go through." Mr. Brock replied he would integrate his business if the substantial white citizens of the community asked him to or if he were served with a Federal Court order.

"You realize it would be detrimental to my business to serve you here," Mr. Brock said. "I have unfortunately had to arrest 84 persons here since Easter."

Then he turned to the television cameras, smiled and said, "I would like to invite my many friends throughout the country to come to Monson's. We expect to remain segregated."

As the cameras and reporters recorded the colloquy, a burly white man, impatient for his lunch, bulled his way through the crowd, violently shoved Dr. King aside and entered the restaurant.

Finally, Sheriff Davis and a deputy arrived and whisked Dr. King and his companions off to jail. Dr. King was expected to remain in jail for a few days while demonstrations continue.

There were indications that the authorities were beginning to crack down on the gangs of whites who have repeatedly set off violence in the town square without arrest or punishment.

State troopers, sent in yesterday by Gov. Farris Bryant, used tear gas to break up the mob that caused last night's outbreak. And for the first time white assailants were arrested.

Sheriff Davis said four St. Augustine youths were charged with disorderly conduct and resisting arrest and a fifth was charged with carrying a concealed weapon, a large chain.

In Tallahassee, Governor Bryant said he had informed the White House law and order would be maintained without use of Federal troops or marshals. Dr. King earlier had asked President Johnson to send marshals because of an apparent breakdown of law enforcement locally.

"It is anticipated there will be more demonstrations," Governor Bryant said. "We cannot guarantee that someone won't throw a rock. We cannot completely stop every overt act. To do that we'd have to line the sidewalks with police. But law and order can be and will be maintained."

Before he went to jail, Dr. King observed that law enforcement had improved since state troopers reinforced the local authorities.

In Jacksonville, Federal District Judge Bryan Simpson said in a court order that there had been a deliberate attempt by law enforcement officers in St. Augustine to break the civil rights movement here by punishing those arrested. Judge Simpson ordered bonds for the defendants in sit-in cases reduced and ordered Sheriff Davis to stop putting prisoners in an outdoor pen in the open sun and in padded cells.

"More than cruel and unusual punishment has been shown," Judge Simpson said in his order. "Here is exposed in its raw ugliness, studied and cynical brutality deliberated and contrived to break men, physically and mentally."

The New York Times, June 12, 1964

Gambler's Choice in Georgia

by Peter de Lissovoy

Albany, Ga.

POSTERS flapping, horn blaring, the King-for-Congress truck rolled suddenly into Harlem—the principal center of business and pleasure on the black side of Albany, Ga.—at about 4:30 on a Saturday afternoon in mid-April. With a gambler named Suitcase and two sharecroppers, I was standing in front of Ware's Place, a bar with few and ill-matched chairs and tables, a great deal of cement floor for dancing, and very fine acoustics. Ware's Place is on Jackson Street, Harlem's main drag. Suitcase was leaning slightly against the doorjamb, all his weight on his feet. He is a young man whose eyes are red at the corners because of the long nights, and both of whose cheeks bear knife scars, memories of sour losers with sharp eyes. His expression is habitually blank, or guarded; now lookout for a card game inside, he was on the watch for cops. The two sharecroppers wore crisp, faded overalls and bright hats. They had hitchhiked into town about a half-hour earlier and were discussing ways of getting some wine. I had been expecting the truck, and when I pointed at it and commented, one of the sharecroppers said, "Ain' no nigger gonna go to Congress."

"Ain' none ever tried," said Suitcase.

The truck pulled into Gibson's Station, parking at a slant. The driver, a high school boy in paint-spattered jeans, jumped out to adjust the loudspeaker atop its cab. A dozen cars followed, made a line behind. After a moment, the other sharecropper mused, "The can'date kin'a favor *Martin Luther King*, don' he?"

The posters made a paper skirt round the trailer of the truck. They masked the cab: REGISTER NOW TO ELECT *Your* CANDIDATE, C. B. KING TO CONGRESS against a background of the candidate's profile. Attorney C. B. King is the legal department of the Negro movement in southwest Georgia. For years he has defended almost every voter registration worker and demonstrator arrested in this corner of the South. He filed the desegregation suit that will effect the integration of the first and second grades in Albany public schools next fall. He has a deep, rounded voice, capable of sarcastic rises, confusing changes of pace; his lower lip has a trick of curling out when he is smiling at some irony—a way of staying sane in the "cracker" courts. He has a prodigious vocabulary, a weapon forged on a peculiar battlefield. (There is nothing quite so red as the cheeks of a cop on the witness stand who, grinning sheepishly at the black attorney questioning him, must say, "Uh, break that down a little, lawyer?") King bears the hopes of thousands for whom "the law" has never meant more than "the cops," and bears, at his hairline, a scar received two years ago at the hands of the late, cane-wielding Sheriff Cull Campbell of Dougherty County. On April 4, he became the first Negro since Reconstruction to seek the Democratic nomination for Representative to Congress from Georgia's Second District.

"Just on the poster," I said to the sharecropper.

"They're like an' they're different," said Suitcase. "Come on," he said to me. Behind us, the first sharecropper was saying, "It ain' nothin' but foolishness, nothin' but!"

High school kids were getting out of cars; SNCC and campaign workers, the campaign singers, movement regulars were crowding round the truck. The driver took a final look at the speaker and leaped back onto the trailer. Some of the girls, the singers, climbed up and began to chorus freedom movement and King campaign songs.

The loud-speaker carried more than a block—from the Cut-Rate Drugstore to Ware's and beyond. All along Jackson Street, cars slowed, heads spun around. A blind gospel singer, picking and shouting in front of Giles's Grocery, lost his audience of old women. The two sharecroppers in front of Ware's separated, the second ambling over to the truck, waving to us, the first shaking his head. Inside, the poker game noticed that its sentry had deserted. It appointed another, and when he too vanished, it came to the door to see what was happening. A part went back to play without cover, and a part started over to the gathering crowd. This Saturday afternoon, as on every Saturday afternoon, and like every bar in Harlem, Ware's Place was full of country folk looking for a good time, factory workers off for the day, barbers and clerks and cab drivers in for a quick one, pool players resting, crap shooters shooting, hustlers, down-and-outs, kings-for-a-day. When the girls started to sing, everyone not too drunk to move came out for a look. Curious, some waited and watched along the sidewalk. Suddenly frightened, or skeptical or indifferent, some moved back inside. Proud, some crossed the street to stand by the truck.

The girl singers swirled down from the truck, and the candidate, in shirt sleeves, got up and stooped slightly to the microphone. He told the people that they had a question for him. Not just those listening, but everybody, all up and down the street: those brave or strong enough to stand around the truck; all those too fearful; the cynical ones; those in the bars who couldn't care less. There was a question in the air.

"Why does a Negro—a black boy—presume to run for the Congress of the United States? How does he dare?" King waited for the question to draw up memories of fear, and then he dispelled them: "Why not? I have the *right* to run." It was a challenge to those inside the bars and pool halls, an affirmation for those gathered by the truck. He waited again, while his audience whooped and applauded. Their response was as strong as their claim to the right of representation has been weak, and as sincere and long as their desire now to assume it at last. King talked about what politics have been in southwest Georgia: long years of representation for and by the rich. Why was a black candidate *needed* in southwest Georgia? That was a better way of asking the question.

"But black's got nothing to do with it. What you and I have in common is our experience, not our skin. I've picked cotton at a half cent a pound. I've shaken peanuts for 50¢ a day. That was years ago, but things aren't much better now. The experience of poverty. . . ."

King's father was relatively well off, a small businessman, but as a boy King was sent to the fields now and then to help meet family expenses. He would usually want to work only one or two days at a time, and so he sought out planters who paid their help every evening. He remembers being deceived by one. When the day's work was over, he went to the white man for his money and was told that Friday was payday. But hadn't the man said he'd pay off tonight? Yeah, he'd said that, but he'd changed his mind. So King had to work out the week in order to make good what he had sunk in the job that first day. When Friday came, the white man handed King his few dollars, and then, a perverse afterthought, shoved him a drink of stump liquor as well. King rolled up the bills and said, no thank you. The man said, "Drink." No, King said, really, he didn't want any. But the white man towered. It'd be funny, a laugh. And besides—and by God—he was being generous to the nigger. "Drink, lil' nigger, drink!" he bellowed. . . .

But why does a black man *bother* to run for Congress? What really might the faraway and inscrutable federal legislature do about poverty in southwest Georgia? King would work for federal aid to education; better job training for the young, retraining for the unemployed; an increase in the funds set aside for the old, sick, infirm; an increase in the minimum-wage law and its extension to cover all domestic and agricultural workers.

"What I propose the whites on the Hill will call communism. But what do they call their subsidies to the cotton industry? Our women who toil in white kitchens, tend and nurse white children for $10 and $12 a week need a subsidy too. . . ."

I raised my eyebrows at Suitcase. It was fine to hear these things being said in Harlem, on a street corner, to these people. He nodded back. "It's a long shot," he said, "but it's worth it. I'm registered. You ever hear of that? A gambler registerin' to vote? It *must* be *worth it.*"

After the rally, we walked back along Jackson Street to Ware's. Clouds of sound—rhythm and blues, rock 'n' roll— waved and swirled in doorways. Men stood about or walked in twos and groups, bright dressed, talking about women, the possibilities of a drink, the campaign.

The cops on the Harlem beat were swaggering up and down, bouncing on their heels, shooting their eyes. The rally had not been announced. It had happened, bang, like a song, and they had had to stand on the corner and listen. The two sharecroppers were back in front of Ware's. The one who had crossed the street to listen to King said to us as we passed, "He be a help up in Washington, sho', but I sho' hate to lose our good lawyer here in Albany."

Inside, Suitcase bawled out the card players who had not bothered to come across to the rally. "It makes me hot, somebody tryin' to *do* somethin' for y'all an' you jus' sit back like you ain' got a care in the worl', you an' the white man on the bes' relation. . . ."

"*Do* somethin'!" interrupted one of the men. "All that meetin' gonna do, gonna make the law mean tonight."

The gamblers in Harlem say that Suitcase is "with the movement." It surprises them a little. (Nothing surprises them a lot.) Last year, he hadn't a kind word to say for it. That was a little surprising too, because the year before he had gone to jail for demonstrating.

Suitcase did not feel one way or the other about the very first demonstrations in Albany. They had had their genesis in the churches and schools, not in Harlem, and though he watched them and listened to the talk, he was not moved to participate. Then one day a cop roughed him up on the street, saying that he had seen him in that "nigger mess." Suitcase protested loudly and the roughing got worse. That was what did it, he says. He saw then that, being black and poor, he was going to be part of the movement whether he liked it or not, and he decided that if he were going to be beaten, he might as well be beaten for something. So he joined a march. It was at least a way of getting back at the cop, a way of affronting the whites.

Leaders of the demonstrations—Martin Luther King, Albany preachers, professional people, students—did not feel themselves affronting anyone exactly. They were exposing social evils, protesting them nonviolently, lovingly, in the spirit breathed by Gandhi and Christ. Even the voter registration drive reflected an essentially religious notion of how society changes. The emphasis was always on registering—the act, pure and simple; little effort was spent to get out the vote, to educate and organize Negro voters. When you registered, you pointed a telling finger at political discrimination. And the effect of it all, presumably, would be a softening of the oppressor's heart, as promised in the Bible.

But Suitcase never supposed his demonstrating would make the crackers see things any differently; he just wanted to shake them up. He saw that if enough Negroes got together in the streets and looked like making trouble, maybe the grays would scare enough to offer some concessions. But he knew that the whites did not need him to tell them they had been preventing Negroes from voting these many years. It was just a very fine feeling, a hard, deep pleasure, to stand in line at the courthouse and look the registrar in the eye. When, after a year of demonstrations, Mr. Charlie did not scare, but just hired more cops and persuaded nearby town and country governments to lend jail space, when there seemed no point to voting, even for kicks, in elections that only offered impossible choices between racists; when the Negro leadership in Albany responded to it all by clinging the more desperately to their worn-out tactics, Suitcase quit the movement.

After that he was full of venom for a leadership that "was leading the people no place but into Chief Pritchett's arms." And he was full of stories about white insurance men being beaten up, or cops and red-neck turnip sellers being shot. A good many of the stories were true. He certainly enjoyed telling them; it was a way of getting back. I remember the night last fall when we watched a Harlem cop shoot up dirt around a little Negro boy suspected of stealing. The cop had chased the boy across the tops of several buildings; the boy had jumped to the ground and then, too frightened to break across the open street, had given up, and was hunched and shaking at the curb. The cop was firing from the roof of the South Grand Bar, directly over our heads, pumping away needlessly at the stunned kid.

Suitcase cursed the cop; then he cursed the crowd for merely gaping and muttering. Finally, he cursed the movement for not organizing the people to do something, and he continued to curse it all night.

Suitcase was no apostate from nonviolence. He had never seen demonstrations that way, did not believe in it. But contrary to the current glib logic, this did not mean that he *be-*

lieved in violence. Suitcase is a gambler. He acquired his name because he does a great deal of traveling. In Columbus, he plays stud poker; in Albany, he plays tonk or shoots dice. Life has come to him too rich in surprises and contradictions, it has been too varied in its demands and rewards to allow his believing absolutely in anything at all. He plays the odds, whatever they are. When he felt the movement was hung up on a single ineffective tactic, he quit as fast as a card player's backer when he sees the kid is playing too straight. Violence and violent talk seemed to him no more the ultimate solution than had demonstrations, but they are a Southern tradition, a significant racial relationship, a familiar way of working out "the problem." When he saw the demonstrations failing, it was easy to revert to them. If you can't win the long money, at least pick up the short.

Suitcase's support of King is a qualified return. And his return reflects a change in the movement. Belatedly, many Negroes who were caught up only a year ago in the nonviolent dogma, have accepted its failure. A certain quaintness has passed. These days, movement thinking in Albany is richer, more pragmatic—in a word, American. Teen-agers, gang boys talk about self-defense, rifle clubs. SNCC is arranging that a group of Africans, touring the country with Operation Crossroads Africa, visit Albany this summer. A delegation attended a nationalist conference in Nashville on May 2 and 3. But, immediately, hopes center upon politics.

During a talent show at a Negro night club on a Saturday night in early April, someone grasped the microphone and announced King's candidacy, concluding, "We got a *point* in registering now!" The Democratic primary will be held in September, but the registration deadline for the primary passed on May 2, and King began serious campaigning as soon as he had filed in order to make the point clear. During the month of April, at night clubs, American Legion posts, in churches, recreation halls, on street corners, King and his campaign speakers explained the significance of a Negro candidate, the possibilities in Congressional representation, the importance of registering. His campaign manager, Thomas Chatmon, a local beautician, toured the Second District, talking with businessmen. Rev. Samuel Wells, who has been registering Negroes since the forties and been jailed literally dozens of times, spoke to the deacon boards. SNCC donated placards, pamphlets, leaflets, and the southwest Georgia SNCC staff distributed them across the Second District. Afternoons in the week following King's announcement, kids in the Albany Student Movement pounded and nailed and painted up wooden booths, at which Negroes might sign up for transportation to the registrar's office, and placed them at strategic points around the city. The chief effect of the campaign thus far has been to crowd the booths. In Albany, from the date of King's announcement to the closing day for registration, nearly 500 Negroes registered. In Tifton, Ga., the only other major town where figures were immediately available, about 350 were registered.

Almost automatically, King receives the support of the middle and lower-middle classes, and of the youth. But he is appealing to the poor, and it is significant that Harlemites, for instance, are registering. Poorer Negroes in southwest Georgia divide into two groups: those who have relatively steady jobs—or a little land; and those who do not. The first is markedly conservative, aware that in a bad show it at least has bit parts. For the second group, the hustlers, all of life that does not obviously and materially touch them has the aspect of a television quiz show—in any given instance, they can turn the set off or root for their side. The people who came out of Ware's Place that Saturday afternoon to listen to King are not afraid of the white man: they play his game according to his laws and customs and cops but, when they can, they cheat. They are likely as not to cheer a black man who is standing up to the white man. The image of King, running verbal circles around the crackers in court, has had them chuckling for years. And their kind of boisterous pride is educable.

Suitcase is back with the movement, but it doesn't mean he wants to become a SNCC field secretary. He figures King will lose, but thinks that a series of such campaigns will make a political force of Negroes in southwest Georgia. He spends some time every day going over these long odds for Harlem people and has taken at least a dozen of them down to register. It is something to do, one hope, a gamble.

Suitcase is a talker. Whenever I want to see him, I look first in Gay's pool hall and on the benches that edge the sidewalk and face the Harlem cafés and cab stands. Whatever the day's topic, he has his view. When asked how the campaign is progressing, he answers by referring to the April killing of Bobby Miller and the effect that it had upon the community.

Bobby was a slight, light-skinned 15 year old, who lived in the impoverished, tracks-fringing section of Albany called CME—C for crime, M for murder and E for the electric chair. He was one of the wild, rambling group of boys who hang around "the Corner" of Flint and Davis, the heart of CME, and the Harlem pool halls: Not a gang exactly—just a like-minded, like-moving circle of youths who attend school rarely because the tired, segregated schools attend so rarely to their needs; who play so much pool because there is so little else to do; who fight often and drink whenever possible, because the conditions of their existences preclude other kinds of intensity; who gamble for power—or its trappings—to overcome, or forget, their birthright of powerlessness.

Early Sunday morning, April 19, the day after King's street rally in Harlem, Bobby left a Harlem pool hall and with a friend, a 14-year-old known in CME as "Pop-bottle," made his way to the Chicken Shack, a CME night spot. After walking up and down in front of the place a few times, building up nerve —and betraying their presence to neighbors and the owner— they made a larkish attempt to enter through a window. The owner called the cops, and when they appeared, the boys tried to run for it. Patrolman J. M. Anderson fired a single shot. A witness heard him yell, "I got him." The police report of the incident claims that Anderson shouted several warnings before shooting. None of the witnesses heard him. The owner, standing next to his establishment, did not hear him.

News of the killing leaped like bullets round the Negro community. Monday, in Harlem, men stood about in groups —a remembrance of the street rally two days before—talking, remonstrating, threatening:

What gonna help, that's what I wanna know. What gonna help it?

Help? I don't know 'bout no help, but I know 'bout need. What I need to do is get me a cracker.

I got my Winchester to the house right now. She sawed off jus' like this. . . . I got my heat on ice, jus' waitin'.

In the late afternoon, more out of shock than calculation, the cops swooped down and shattered a gathering of embittered cab drivers, pool sharks, shoe-shine boys—sent the bitterness calling through the streets.

A mass meeting that evening was full and overflowing. People jammed behind the pulpit in Shiloh Church, stood in the doorway, at the windows. A year or more ago, the meeting might have culminated in a demonstration. Now, from the young particularly, there were cries for vengeance. Yet in the weeks that have passed there has been no serious violence. In CME, when two cops left their car to chase a thief, several of Bobby's friends lifted the spotlight and battery, and went over the body with chains. The same boys have been preventing the delivery in CME of the racist Albany *Herald*, which printed only the police side of the shooting. But there has been nothing more than this, and in the five weekdays that followed Bobby's death, 138 Negroes registered to vote in Albany.

Suitcase is not surprised. "You winnin' that long money, you don' need no short change," he explains. He thinks that people expressed some of their anger by registering or seeing that others did so, that an awareness of the voter registration drive's success satisfied, or at least dulled, a need for vengeance.

At a rally in Tifton, Ga., in late April, Attorney King said, "You'll vote for me because I'm black, and if anyone asks you why, you can say, 'Well, we've tried the other color for 300 years now. . . .'" King is gambling that representation for Negroes will mean something, that our political process, like our legal process, can accommodate certain needs.

Suitcase is gambling too: playing for that long money and hoping that the day won't come again when he must look for nothing but the short.

The Nation, June 22, 1964

3 in Rights Drive Reported Missing

by Claude Sitton

PHILADELPHIA, Miss., June 22—Three workers in a day-old civil rights campaign in Mississippi were reported missing today after their release from jail here last night.

Leaders of the drive said they feared that the three men—two whites, both from New York, and one Negro—had met with foul play.

The three had been held by Neshoba County authorities for four hours following the arrest of one on a speeding charge and the jailing of the others "for investigation."

Agents of the Federal Bureau of Investigation began arriving here in force early tonight after the Justice Department ordered a full-scale search.

The Mississippi Highway Patrol issued a missing-persons bulletin, but a spokesman in Jackson indicated late today that it had no plans at present for further action.

All three missing men arrived in Mississippi late Saturday afternoon from Oxford, Ohio, where they had taken part in a one-week orientation course for the statewide project. They were among the advance group of some 175 workers who are expected to be followed by another 800 participants in the campaign of political action, education and cultural activities among Negroes.

One of the missing whites is Michael Schwerner of Brooklyn, a 24-year-old former settlement-house worker. He came here six months ago with his wife, Rita, to open one of the first community centers for Negroes in Mississippi. Mrs. Schwerner remained at Oxford to take part in the second orientation course for volunteers.

The second missing man is Andrew Goodman, 20, a student volunteer from Queens.

The third is James E. Cheney, 21, a Meridian plasterer and

driver of the late-model Ford station wagon in which they were last seen.

Both Mr. Schwerner and Mr. Cheney are members of a civil rights task force organized by the Congress of Racial Equality, which is cooperating with the Student Nonviolent Coordinating Committee and other organizations in the Mississippi project.

Concern over the fate of the three was heightened by the fact that the two CORE men had always reported their whereabouts before at frequent intervals, according to campaign spokesmen in Jackson. Workers in the Meridian drive headquarters said Mr. Schwerner had repeatedly emphasized the importance of this to the others during their drive here from Oxford.

Further, the prospect of the civil rights campaign had led to an increasing number of violent incidents even before the workers began arriving last Friday.

The three men left Meridian yesterday at about 9:30 A.M. for Philadelphia, about 35 miles away, where they planned to look into the burning of the Mount Zion Methodist Church last Tuesday night. The Negro church was in the Longdale community, some 12 miles east of this town of 5,500 persons in east-central Mississippi.

Cecil Price, the Neshoba County deputy sheriff, said he had halted and arrested the three about 5:30 P.M. yesterday. He said Mr. Cheney had been driving 65 miles an hour in a 30-mile zone on the outskirts of Philadelphia before he stopped them. The whites were held "for investigation."

The three were released from the county jail here at 10:30 P.M. after Mr. Cheney paid a $20 fine.

"I told them to leave the county," said Mr. Price. The three then drove out along State Highway 19 after having told the deputy they were returning to Meridian, according to him.

Sheriff L. A. Rainey, a burly, tobacco-chewing man, showed little concern over the report that the workers were missing.

"If they're missing, they just hid somewhere trying to get a lot of publicity out of it, I figure," he said.

Robert Weil, spokesman for the campaign headquarters in

Jackson, said campaign leaders "definitely fear that there was foul play, perhaps by the local citizens after they were released."

The New York Times, June 23, 1964

"Seeing St. Aug." Proves Exciting

by Snow James

St. Augustine, Fla.—Seeing St. Augustine these days, when Negro rights demonstrations and white counter-demonstrations are virtually on a 'round-the-clock basis, is a thrilling experience, for townfolks and tourists alike.

Often, it is 'most too thrilling, whichever side you are on. Many tourists, alarmed by TV and press stories of race violence, are steering clear and not seeing St. Augustine this season. The fact that practically all of the rough-stuff has been aimed at Negroes, newsmen, and cops does not seem to make the tourists feel any safer.

Neither do the nocturnal serenades of freedom songs, which hundreds of demonstrators have, of late, been presenting outside the big posh lily-white motels, make the occupants sleep any better. Most of them check out first thing in the morning.

The tourist trade, on which this burgh largely depends, is already off at least 50 per cent, according to The Courier's confidential pipeline to the Chamber of Commerce, and many a motel owner is threatened by bankruptcy and foreclosure.

Unable to tolerate this kind of heat any longer, the powers-that-be are looking for some way out of the impasse, without losing face.

To this end they caused to be convened a special session of the St. Johns County Grand Jury, which, after listening to various principals in the titanic struggle, including Martin Luther King, under special escort from the Jacksonville jail—resolved on June 18, that what the Ancient City needs, is a biracial committee. This is, of course, what civil rights forces have been saying for years.

In the hope of saving face, however, the white town spokesmen declare that neither Dr. R. B. Hayling or Martin Luther King—the two men who have done most to create the crack in the wall—are "representative" of the Negro community, and so should not be allowed to participate in any biracial talks.

This is, of course, an attempt to bow to the pressure without giving the appearance of bowing to the pressure.

Just how far this white "acceptance" of the biracial committee idea will get remains to be seen, as other leaders of the Negro community are standing put on a principled refusal to let Negro representatives be "picked" by whites.

Meanwhile the demonstrations continue unabated, while white counter-demonstrations appear to have petered out, for the moment at least.

"We're pulling out," one ring-leader of the Kluxers who have congregated nightly to defend the Old Slave Market for the past ten days, was heard to say in a downtown store.

"Who gave orders to pull out?" a female militant of the local John Birch Society wanted to know.

"Nobody," the man said. "We're pulling ourselves out. I've got to get some rest."

"This is no time to rest," the lady said. "I'm going to get on the phone and call on all the civic leaders to get the white community to turn out and back up you fellows down there. The TV has been trying to make you out to be a lot of riffraff, but you're down there defending us, and we ought to show that we're backing you 100 per cent. People have got to get over being afraid of being labelled KKK or anything else."

This same lady and her husband are working full time to build a "United Front" of hate groups in the Ancient City for a "concerted effort" against desegregation.

This anti-rights coalition includes the Kluxers, Birchites, patriotic societies, and certain elements in the local Goldwater committee.

Already they have plastered the town with reproductions of Alabama Gov. George Wallace's favorite propaganda piece, a photograph of MLK taken at Highlander Folk School in Tennessee, with an alleged communist sitting in the same audience.

They are also pushing a "Support Your Local Police" campaign, with gummed bumper stickers and leaflets stacked free on cigar counters. This item bears the imprint of the Birch Society, and is designed to encourage the use of police dogs, cattle prods, etc.

"The police chief of Birmingham was doing a superb job of maintaining law and order in the midst of a hot situation," these brochures state. "One or more hotheads or dupes among the Negroes went up to the line and deliberately kicked one or more of the dogs."

"The Federal marshals, for another illustration, not only were not needed in Oxford, Miss., but actually created most of the rioting as they obviously were intended to do," the hate sheet adds.

For this sort of poison, the local hate cabal looks not only to the Birch Society, but also to such ultras as the Rev. McIntyre, the Liberty Lobby in Washington, D.C., and to such other ultra centers as Springfield, Mo.

Right now they are writing to the latter for dope to "prove that MLK is not a Christian, but an atheist."

Last week they ran a double-full page spread in the "St. Augustine Record" of the "Dan Smoot Report," which draws its inspiration from FBI Chief J. Edgar Hoover's warning that civil rights demonstrations may be communist-inspired.

The effect of this sort of thing on the white community can readily be imagined.

Ancient City bars and lunch rooms are loaded with seedy characters vieing with one another in purveying all the latest "atrocity" stories, such as:

"That's nothin'—I seen a big limousine with a New Jersey license plate pull into town awhile ago, with a young white woman sitting in the back seat between two n——r men"!

To top that, the next man said he had seen such a car with babies in it.

Sight-seers making the rounds of "points of interest," either by horse-drawn cart or street trains, can get an eyefull of local artistic talent at the Slave Market. On display at the moment, unsigned, is a poster executed in crayon, with the head of MLK mounted on the body of a raccoon, captioned:

> Martin Luther Coon
> And All His Little Coons
> Are Going to Go Down
> Like Good Gas Went Up.

It has hung there for days and days, over the heads of the checker-players, despite the fact that the Slave Mart is public property, and despite the fact that NAACP members were fined not long ago for handing out leaflets advertising a mass meeting.

"Cluttering public property," the judge called it then.

Strange sights and sounds indeed in America's Oldest City today . . .

Every tenth car a State Trooper's—big men, in form-fitting shirts, summer-time straw Stetsons, shiny gold-plated wrist watches and gold-rimmed sun glasses, yakking importantly over their intercoms, speaking of "n——rs" and proud of their mission in saving white civilization.

Tourists in shorts and sun-tan lotion, trying to take a snapshot of a civil war cannon, constantly interrupted by another half-dozen kids coming around the corner to try again to integrate a drug store.

The manager meeting them at the door, telling them they're the 40th within half an hour. The deputy coming up at a trot from the street-corner, leading them off to his car for transport to county jail—signalling his buddy at the next corner to take his place.

King's men arriving from points North, East, South and West; Kluxers arriving in $50 steaming junk-heaps, mostly bearing green Georgia and red Alabama license plates.

The concrete block Elks Rest, GHQ for the demonstrators, a constant procession in and out—gay local kids, a mild-mannered sprinkling of white kids from Ivy League colleges of New England, startling Negro pedestrians by saying "good morning" to them.

The local bank, atop whose sixth story sits the city's "one-man power structure," H. E. Wolffe, lord of all he surveys, insisting that race relations are none of his business, yet warning King's men, there will be blood in the streets unless rights demonstrations are called off.

County jail, clearly visible alongside U.S. 1, north of town, where tourists at Easter were startled to see the sign "Mrs. Peabody Slept Here." Now, the bullpen out back, built of chain-link fence, six feet high with barbed wire on top, hastily built by Sheriff L. O. Davis when King promised to "fill up the jail." Empty now, because U.S. Judge Bryan Simpson forbade him to use it: No shade, one privy, a bucket of drinking water.

Mass meetings every night, at first one church then another, celebrities like Jackie Robinson and Sarah Patton Boyle (author of "The Desegregated Heart"). Ever present, 70-plus Mrs. Altha Eloise Green, white, teacher of Children's Literature at the local Negro college, degrees from Millikin, Illinois State, University of Wisconsin, struck with a brick while marching, refusing all aid.

Of such is America's Oldest City today, as she struggles to cast off old prejudices and ways.

The Pittsburgh Courier, June 27, 1964

The Lone Wolf of Civil Rights

by Martin Mayer

DURING the middle two weeks of April newspapers across the country featured stories about a threat by civil-rights demonstrators to tie up all traffic en route to opening day at the New York World's Fair. The day arrived, but not the thousands of cars that were supposed to "stall-in" on the network of highways leading to the fair. Indeed, traffic moved better on that April 22 than it had on any day for years. One of the civil-rights leaders who had publicly supported the stall-in was cornered by reporters and asked to explain the failure. He praised the organizer of the abortive demonstration, then added, "But let us face the facts—he is no Bayard Rustin. If Bayard had promised two thousand cars, there would have been at least a thousand there."

The comment was a tribute to experience and to talent. Bayard (pronounced "Buy-erd") Rustin, who came to national attention as deputy director and general manager of last summer's March on Washington, has been professionally engaged for a quarter of a century as an organizer of mass movements and demonstrations. Now 54, his stiff brush of hair turning gray over an astonishingly youthful and athletic figure, Rustin is regarded by most civil rights leaders as the indispensable back-office man for any major effort that involves people on the streets. "Nobody will try massive action today," says Norman Hill, the young national program director of CORE, "without trying to get Bayard into it."

Rustin is a free lance in a romantic tradition associated with cheap novels and bad television rather than with real life: He is a fighter whose talents are always available to A Good Cause. Usually the Cause is civil rights or pacifism, though Rustin has also set up picket lines to support strikes, to protest British imperialism, and to denounce German anti-Semitism. He is affiliated permanently with only one organization—the War Resisters League, which lists him as executive secretary on leave to work for others. He has no job. A Quaker group in New York sends him a little money every month, but basically he lives on the fees he is paid for organizing demonstrations.

"I believe in social dislocation and creative trouble," Rustin says; and within these categories he specializes in imagination and invention. The man is an artist as well as an organizer—he made his living for some years as a nightclub singer, working with Josh White and Leadbelly at the old Café Society in New York, and he could make a living tomorrow as an interior decorator specializing in antiques. To Rustin, a demonstration is a piece of theater which will be a memorable experience for the spectators (which is what most people are); and it is an opportunity to find a soft spot where concerted action can make a dent in society.

In this spirit Rustin in 1947 planned and organized the first Freedom Ride (he called it the Journey of Reconciliation). In 1955–56, as the resident idea man of the Southern Christian Leadership Conference, he developed the bag of tricks that sustained Martin Luther King's bus boycott in Montgomery, Ala. On the pacifist side of his career, he set up the first Aldermaston Ban-the-Bomb protest in Britain in 1958, and led the courageous (if perhaps foolish) marchers who set off across the Sahara in 1960 to try to stop the first French nuclear-test explosion. At this moment he is busy with one of the most spectacular of the projects for "the long, hot summer"—an attempt to seat an integrated delegation from Mississippi at the Democratic Convention.

Perhaps the most remarkable of Rustin's contributions has been the discovery of ways to persuade the authorities to cooperate in demonstrations against them. One of the reasons the March on Washington went so smoothly was that Rustin planned it, step by step, with the Washington police, who were too surprised to do anything but follow his instructions. Setting up the first New York school boycott last February, Rustin achieved such excellent liaison with the police that they loaned him a sound truck to use in managing the crowds before school headquarters. In retrospect, it all seems reasonable enough—the authorities and the nonviolent demonstrator both wish to avoid serious trouble on the big day, and because their interests are momentarily identical, they ought to be able to work together. But before Rustin began waving his wand, nobody had even imagined that American bureaucracies could be made to cooperate in their own destruction.

When Rustin signs up to organize a demonstration, he first tries "to analyze the objective situation," and to prepare a written manual, with at least a heading and a cost estimate to cover every contingency. At work he spends most of his time on the telephone and in small meetings, hunting out the people who can be counted on to do a piece of the job. Doing one job for Rustin almost invariably leads to doing others; he keeps a record of all positive contacts in a file of 3-by-5 cards, and he is shameless about soliciting help for a demonstration. He recently called a reporter who knew him only through interviews to ask rather fretfully if the reporter could find him a free sound truck. Rustin's shabby temporary offices pulse with a dozen or more young volunteers of all sizes, shapes and colors. They make a difference in a movement forever starving for funds.

The young flock to Rustin partly because his disheveled personal life and work habits match so well with theirs—like them, he can spend one week working 18 hours a day, and the next week in total idleness—and partly because he is willing to give them responsibility and let them make mistakes. One of the few on salary is Tina Lawrence, Rustin's remarkably pretty secretary, when he has a secretary (in between jobs, she says, "he sends me CARE packages"). Miss Lawrence remembers fondly a moment in the planning of the first school boycott when Rustin flung an important job at her: "He just came out of his office and said, 'My dear, I want you to coordinate all these freedom schools, and I don't care how you do it. Just give me a master list of who's teaching in each one.' You get this feeling," Miss Lawrence adds, "that he has faith in you."

Rustin enjoys educating the young in the intricacies of American social protest. "You work for him a week," Miss Lawrence says, "and unless you're a total idiot, you learn something—economics, politics, the legal structure of the country. It's like a class Socrates might have conducted, except for the hours. Sometimes you start class at three in the morning."

As a result of her first year's education, Miss Lawrence and Blyden Jackson, another Rustin protégé, organized a group called East River CORE, which made the front pages of the newspapers by dumping garbage on New York's Triborough Bridge and tying up traffic to Long Island for two hours on a spring day. They consulted Rustin before they moved, and Rustin advised against their demonstration, on the grounds that it was too complicated, didn't really relate to what they were protesting against (segregated schooling), left no possibility for negotiation, and might actually harm someone by delaying an ambulance or a fire engine. When he finished, Miss Lawrence said, "Do you want us to drop it?"

Rustin said, "Do I convince you?"

"No."

"Then do it," Rustin said. "The only way you'll ever learn anything is by making mistakes."

When the big day came, Miss Lawrence was on salary on one of Rustin's projects, and he came out at about four in the afternoon to dictate a memorandum. "I can't," said Miss Lawrence, shaking her long black hair at him. "I've got to go sit on a bridge."

"Oh, that's right," Rustin said, grinning. "I forgot. Well, good luck, my dear." And he returned to his office to scribble out the memo himself.

The upshot of the Triborough Bridge demonstration was, as Rustin had predicted, a set of screaming headlines in the papers about the dangerous militants of East River CORE— and nothing else. Commenting on this sort of demonstration, A. Philip Randolph, the 75-year-old president of the Brotherhood of Sleeping Car Porters, once said, "It's easy to get people's attention; what counts is getting their *interest.*"

Rustin insists that every demonstration he runs will be related immediately to a specific objective. Freedom rides and lunch-counter sit-ins are ideal, because they call attention directly to the evil being fought and at the same time establish a strong bargaining position for the negotiations which must be the result of any successful demonstration. Schools, jobs and housing, the Negro objectives in the North, are less easily demonstrated for. Though he opposed the "stall-in" as pointless, Rustin went out to the World's Fair on opening day and got himself arrested for blocking the entrance to the New York City pavilion. "We couldn't let that fair open without a protest," he says. "A fair celebrating American affluence, with a third of the country living in poverty." But he felt awful the morning after, because the demonstration was what he calls "grasshopping—just a demonstration, no purpose to it."

The lesson comes from Gandhi, who was Rustin's particu lar idol, and from A. Philip Randolph, who has been Rustin's mentor and protector since 1941. Though his name doesn't get in the newspapers much, Randolph is still the most effective of the Negro leaders. Almost single-handed, Randolph secured what are still by far the most significant governmental actions affecting the Negro American—Franklin Roosevelt's Executive Order 8802, outlawing discrimination on government contracts, and Harry Truman's desegregation of the armed forces in 1948. Randolph won the first by threatening a march on Washington at a time of international crisis, and the second by urging Negroes not to register to be drafted into a Jim Crow army—an action far more "militant" than anything the new razzle-dazzle leadership has ever dared to do.

Alone among the Negro leaders, Randolph has a permanent chair among the seats of the mighty on the executive council of AFL-CIO. He was the only person ever considered by the civil-rights groups to be director of the march on Washington, and it was at his insistence, over the violent objections of everyone else, that Rustin was made deputy director.

The other leaders objected to Rustin's prominence for one reason: They were scared. Even today, after everything has turned out well, they will begin any conversation about Rustin's appointment with the words, "Knowing how vulnerable he is . . ." Probably nobody else in American public life is so easily attacked as Bayard Rustin. He was an organizer for the Young Communist League; refusing to go to a Conscientious Objector camp, he served 28 months in Lewisburg Penitentiary for draft evasion in World War II; and while most of his 23 arrests are the battlestripes of a cause, he was also convicted in California some years ago on a morals charge. This incident cost Rustin his job as race-relations secretary for the

Fellowship of Reconciliation, and some years later forced his departure from the Southern Christian Leadership Conference when Adam Clayton Powell, for his own political reasons, began a campaign of innuendo claiming that Rustin had some "sinister influence" on Martin Luther King.

A politician wishing to accuse Rustin of "disloyalty" can easily convict him out of his own mouth—20 years ago Rustin said and wrote comments about the United States that make Malcolm X look like a narrow-minded piker. "I tell you, brother," Rustin says today, "I fought against it for years, against being American—in my speech, my manner, everything. My experience was like Jimmy Baldwin's, really—it's a hard thing for a Negro to accept, being American, but you can't escape it."

"There's a limit to how big Bayard can become," says George Houser, director of the American Committee on Africa, who has worked with Rustin since 1941. "If Bayard ever gets on a high perch, it's too easy for some Southern senator to knock him off it."

The man who could be knocked off the perch was born in West Chester, Pa. "I come from a very working-class background," he says in the faintly English accent he deliberately acquired during the time he was trying to escape being an American. "I was illegitimate, as so often happens in the Negro community, and I was brought up by my grandparents. My father was from the West Indies. My grandfather was a caterer and extremely poor, but there was always enough to eat because of leftovers from the banquets. Sometimes there would be no real food in the house, but there was plenty of *pâté de foie gras* and Roquefort cheese."

Like many other intelligent working-class Negroes, Rustin went drifting about the country after graduation from high school (where he was on state-championship football and track teams). He returned sporadically to Pennsylvania and accumulated three years at two Negro colleges. At both, he helped pay his bills by singing with traveling groups.

During his drifting, Rustin wandered into the Communist Party, and when he came to New York in 1938, it was as an organizer for the Young Communist League. He enrolled at City College, where for three years "I did just enough work to stay matriculated"; his real job was recruiting evening-school students for the party. He continued to pay his bills by singing, but now he was in the big time at Café Society. "He was really very good, you know," George Houser says. "He had an audience appeal. If he'd wanted to play it that way, he could have been a Belafonte."

Those first years in New York Rustin gave most of his earnings to the party and lived in Harlem with an aunt, moving about the ghetto from one tenement to another. He was and still is immensely excited by the sight of great masses of colored people in one place. "In Harlem," he says, "I thought I'd find this wonderful community, all these colored people bunched together. And at one level, there *is* a strange sense of community—but on another level, there's an absolute isolation and loneliness. There's such a preying upon one another, a kind of necessary preying, but it's terrible."

Hatred for the social system that creates Harlems kept Rustin in the Communist Party through the Trotsky trials and the Hitler-Stalin pact, which shook out much of the membership. What drove him away was the event that made Communism respectable for other Americans, the German attack on Russia in 1941.

"I was brought up a Quaker, you know, by my grandmother, and the Communists had become the great peace party," Rustin says. "I was working on the campaign against segregation in the armed forces, and the Communists were all for it. Then Hitler attacked, and they became a war party. The line was, 'Everybody in the armed forces. People's war. Second front. No domestic issues; forget about discrimination in the Army.'"

For Rustin, leaving the party meant a break with all his friends, his work, his purpose in life. He remembers not knowing what to do with himself for a week, until an acquaintance suggested that he go talk with the Rev. A. J. Muste at the Fellowship of Reconciliation. The Rev. Mr. Muste showed Rustin that there could be a profoundly radical, violently nonviolent movement apart from the Communist Party, and introduced him to the people with whom he is still working. Indeed, CORE was founded in Chicago as a secular arm of Muste's religious Fellowship; its original leaders

were all on the Fellowship payroll. Rustin served as the organizer of the New York branch.

The shock of leaving the party was followed a year later by
the shock of a long jail sentence on the draft charge. In
prison, Rustin taught himself to play the guitar and the lute,
and his interests became less exclusively political. "When
you're dealing with people all the time and nothing is ever
settled," Rustin says, "it's a great pleasure to strike a C chord
and know it's a C chord." Though he seems from the outside
to be wrapped up in the cause, his activist friends are often
disturbed to find that he has private tastes far removed from
politics and meetings and demonstrations. His exotic apartment, his love for music and his wide-ranging tastes in books
make his friends feel that, as one of them says, "Bayard will
give himself unstintingly to the specific project, but for the
long-term follow-through, I think he gets bored with it."

Rustin lives in four-and-a-half rooms in a new (predominantly white) middle-income housing development south of
Penn Station on New York's West Side. His apartment is not
like the others in this development, or in any other development. It is profusely decorated with religious paintings and
objets, ranging in size from small metal crucifixes and miniature African wood carvings to six-foot-high stone and wood
German sculptures of saints, resting on Gothic pedestals. The
furniture is carved dark wood of a German High-Renaissance
style, with crimson plush cushions for the chairs. Outside,
looking very odd on the dusty austerity of a middle-income
terrace, is the one piece of non-Christian art in the place—a
small erotic bas-relief from the Tantric tradition of India.

Most of Rustin's antiques are German, because they were
acquired through an elderly Berlin refugee named Leon Medina, who had a shop on New York's University Place. Rustin
stumbled upon it one day after the war, looking for furniture
to go with his lute, and Medina became probably his dearest
friend. Rustin called Medina "Papa," accompanied him to
auctions, helped him with refinishing jobs, and acted as Medina's purchasing agent with unlimited authority on trips out
of the country. "The best pieces" Rustin owns were left to
him by Medina's will.

Rustin's friends worry about his future. "He was *much*

younger three or four years ago," says Tom Kahn, a lean, intense young man whom Rustin recruited from the Socialist Party for the first Youth March for Integrated Schools in 1958, and who served as Rustin's aide-de-camp ("the man who picked up the pieces") through the March on Washington last year. "The march took an enormous amount out of him. I worked sixteen hours a day with him. I'm a lot younger than he is, and it drove me crazy. But the leaders regard him as possessor of inexhaustible childish energy which never has to be compensated for."

Except for Randolph, civil-rights leaders speak rather coolly of Rustin: "If you want to work with Bayard, you have to know how to *use* him," says the director of one group. "Bayard Rustin is not a Negro leader," Whitney Young of the National Urban League once explained to Tom Kahn, "because a Negro leader is the head of a Negro organization." ("That tells you," Kahn says rather bitterly, "what is wrong with the Negro movement"—but Rustin himself agrees entirely with Young.) Since the March on Washington, however, Rustin has seemed so useful that he is invited to leadership meetings. He was in Washington in April, for example, when the leaders decided not to do anything loud about the filibuster against the Civil Rights Bill. Rustin thought the decision was wrong and said so; but he had to accept the verdict, if only because he came to the meeting representing nobody but himself.

On the other hand, Rustin's independence enables him to call his own shots, and to work for the cause as a whole rather than for any one jealous piece of it. He claims that his lack of affiliation has actually been a help. "If you have five organizations working together," he says, "each of them has to raise money and maintain an image. They can't let somebody from another organization lead their demonstration. But I can be available to all of them." Tom Kahn thinks the argument is silly, because nobody can be an effective fighter without a corner of his own. "Bayard," Kahn says drily, "has always been a great one for making a virtue of necessity."

Rustin probably will have an organization to lead in the near future—an A. Philip Randolph Institute, which is to be established, probably by trade-union money, to perpetuate

Randolph's name, to act as a service center and clearing house for civil-rights groups, and to push such groups toward the non-Communist left. Randolph has approved the plans. "I'm interested in Bayard having some sort of organizational base," he said the other day in the magnificently deep voice that has caught the attention of AFL conventions for more than 40 years. "But the labor movement is a little too prosaic for Bayard. He moves quite expeditiously, and these people want to sit around in committee and talk about it for a day." Randolph thought about it briefly, then smiled and said, "We have to invent something for Bayard."

The Saturday Evening Post, July 11, 1964

"THE LONG, HOT SUMMER": JULY 1964
Harlem Diary

by Lez Edmond

Saturday, night

THE crowds gathered around the 123rd Street Station House in Harlem even before it got dark, and when dark came their anger was like the hot sticky black of the night. "Murphy the Murderer," they screamed. Murphy is the Police Commissioner and they wanted one of his cops—Lt. Thomas Gilligan of Brooklyn's 14th Division. A couple of days before Gilligan had killed a Harlem kid named Jimmy Powell. Jimmy was only 15 and Gilligan shot at him three times and hit him twice. He said the kid had a knife and was going at him. That didn't mean much to the people of Harlem. You don't shoot a kid twice to get rid of his knife.

Jimmy was on his way to a voluntary remedial reading class when he was shot and that made the Harlem people even madder that he was dead. The kid was trying to get ahead, to get out of the ghetto and if he hadn't been shot he might have made it.

The police inside the 123rd Street Station sent for help. When the first of the steel-helmeted cops from outside drove into Harlem with their sirens going, bottles and bricks began to pour down from roof tops. The cops started shooting and that made people in the streets go kind of crazy. They began smashing windows and setting fires and Harlem was in the middle of a riot.

I heard about the trouble around 11 p.m. when getting ready to go out for a late dinner with some friends. I was in the air-conditioned apartment I rent in Queens for $155 a month. For that money in Harlem tenements you're lucky to get indoor plumbing that works. When I heard about the rioting on the radio, I grabbed my tape recorder and I got into Harlem, deep in, quick. I didn't know then that I wouldn't get out for many days.

Sunday, 4 a.m.

The police were shooting up Lenox Avenue. There were so many policemen firing at one time it sounded like automatic weapons going off on a front line and it reminded me of something like Korea. There were hundreds of cops, running in circles, and they all were shooting. People ran into doorways and fell down on the street and crawled under cars. The bullets hit windows and bricks on the old Harlem brownstones and screeched off at sharp angles and all I could hear was screaming. I don't think anybody really expected the cops to shoot. Harlem was surprised and afraid and angry. Some people wanted to shoot back.

A man wearing a straw hat and home-made Bermuda shorts with ragged edges was running down Lenox Avenue and when he saw some people huddled in a doorway he stopped and yelled at them.

"You got to organize. How in the hell are you going to do anything, throwing bottles and running. Remember if we had a damn organization like Marcus Garvey had, you could get a rifle. Or if you wouldn't get a rifle you'll get a piece, and put it aside, Jim, because he can get his, he can get his. Retaliate. Then kill 'em, kill the cops all out. Let them call in their militia."

Sunday, 5 a.m.

New trouble on Lenox Avenue began before dawn when some kids broke into a grocery store. When the police cars came around the corner of 126th Street people up on top of the buildings started throwing bottles. Then more cops came and when somebody threw two Molotov cocktails into the street the cops began shooting again. Some of the bullets went into the windows of hotels and tenements. I turned the corner of 126th Street just as the shooting died down and I saw a big crowd standing in the middle of the street—the police had put up barricades against automobile traffic. I edged my way through the crowd to the middle where a black nationalist leader was talking to Inspector Thomas Prendergast, who was in charge of the 28th Precinct that night. Everybody was trying to listen. I got up close and nobody noticed my tape recorder.

The black nationalist spoke first.

"The children are afraid of those riot helmets. They're having a psychological effect on the children. I knew this. Pull them out of here. You can't do any worse than you're doing now. Let the people of the community, the businessmen, try to straighten this out. Give us a chance."

"You try that. I wish you luck," Prendergast said.

"The businessmen in Harlem don't want Harlem torn up. You must give us a chance to talk to the kids ourselves and get them under control."

"I have to obey orders."

"But there must be someone that you can go to. Someone higher up?"

"There's nothing I can do."

"There has to be someone who will go along with you—so we can stop this thing now."

"Listen, you and I both know who's doing all this. It's the Commies."

"Inspector Prendergast, for Christ's sake, these children wouldn't know Marx or Lenin if they were to come back from the tombs and walk down the streets of Harlem right this minute."

Then there was more shooting up the street and the Inspector ran off towards 125th Street and St. Nicholas Avenue. The police were shooting over the heads of a crowd being led by James Farmer. When I got to 125th Street a Negro was talking to one of the Negro police captains. Negro policemen are always sent to trouble areas in Harlem.

"As long as you have all these policemen, and the majority is white, you're going to have this problem," the man told the Negro Captain.

"I understand this, but this is a problem someone else is going to have to solve."

Sunday, late afternoon

Dr. Yosef Ben Jochannan is a Black Jew. He is also an ardent African Nationalist, and got the biggest hand at Jessie Gray's stormy rally in the Mount Morris Presbyterian Church on 122nd Street and Mount Morris Avenue West. Gray, the Harlem rent strike leader, called for "guerrilla warfare" against the police. The 400 or 500 people who filled the church and overflowed into the street were in no mood for moderation. They booed CORE's James Farmer, and Bayard Rustin, the organizer of last summer's March on Washington. Farmer got the crowd to quiet down a little when he said "they had a right to be mad." Farmer said he saw a woman shot the night before. He said she had asked a policeman to get her a cab so she could get out of the riot area. Farmer said the policeman shot her right in the groin—and then when she fell to the ground and said she had to go to a hospital or die, the policeman told her to "go ahead and die."

That story was the only reason they listened to Farmer. He represented "dealing" with the white Establishment and that afternoon Harlem was in no mood for dealings. Jochannan, a well-educated black Jew from Ethiopia, who is a civil engineer in Harlem, was applauded wildly by the crowd which included many black nationalists. Jochannan attended Cambridge and still has a British accent. He attacked the churches and the crowd loved that because the churches preach moderation. And he touched on some of the black nationalist themes that people in Harlem hear every day—themes from speeches the white man rarely hears.

"There is no group that ever came to the United States even after the Africans were brought here that haven't at one time voted, based upon their race or national origin or religion. The Irish came together on the basis of being Catholic. They had to stick together and they had to vote as Irish in order to survive. The Italians had to vote as Italian—their respectability was built upon the Mafia which they now themselves fight—but that is how they got their money into the community. The original Mafia men, their children and grandchildren are now respectable people of the community.

"The Jews that came to the lower East Side had to fight and vote as Jews in order to survive. The Chinese had the Tong which kept the Chinese in order. Fortunately these people came as a group and they kept their culture and family all together.

"But the Afro-American has been denied this respectable racial solidarity. He has always been taught that only the white man knew anything—and he has always looked forward for them to tell him what to do.

"There are Irish-Americans and Italian-Americans and German-Americans but anyone who calls himself an Afro-American is considered a racist.

"You should never allow any white man to come into a black neighborhood and win an election. I think I read where in Chicago an Afro-American woman was running for office against a white man who had died before the election, yet he was still elected. This should never have happened. I don't care what the ticket is, but we blacks, not the whites, must control our own neighborhoods. Now you may say this is not legal and not part of the constitution, but let me tell you something. Everything was done to suit all the people here and many things were done apart from the constitution and may have made wrong a right, and we too have just as much right to this country as anyone else, for you came here with Columbus and there is no white man who has done more for America than any one black man."

Then Jochannan took off on religion. He said a lot of things that many people in Harlem think but are afraid to say out loud, especially the young people, who think the churches talk too much about moderation. It got the biggest round of applause.

"I was brought up as a religious person. As a matter of fact my family wanted me to be a Rabbi but after growing up and seeing the situation in all religions, I realized that the churches always support the state wherever they are. The churches can't help the people when the chips are down because their interest is with the power structure. In studying American history the only time the so-called ministry backed the people was the time they had the Africans, Methodist and Episcopal churches which had broken away from the white church and ran underground railroads helping slaves escape. Even during Nat Turner's time, the ministry was against him and turned him in when he was trying to burn down the South and assist his people in getting away from slave conditions and since that time the ministry has generally worked against the people.

"In Harlem all of these old theatres are being sold and

turned into some church and the church always pays an exorbitant price—three times as much as the theatre is worth. Now the theatre goes out of business and the building is empty and yet the church comes in and pays these people prices much higher than the building is worth and instead of building a factory or some place to live, which we need desperately, especially the factory, instead we see another hallering place which is to talk only on Sunday and get the people's money. They haller all the time about getting the kids to camp, but do one of them own a camp, own a bus or do they own a hospital? But they are taking the people's money. The ministry does not tell a person on Welfare not to give them money and ask those who can afford to pay to pay. They ask everyone to pay and if you are in the church for 30 years you pay every day and you die, the minister doesn't come to the funeral and if he does it will be just to the funeral parlor. He may come for a minute or two, but he certainly won't waste his gas to go to the burial ground and say a mass when they are throwing dirt on you.

"I say the black man has called upon Jesus Christ for so many years here in America—and now he starts calling on Mohammed and there are many who are calling on Moses—and at no time within this period has the black man's situation changed, nor has the black man any freedom. It is obvious that someone didn't hear his call or isn't interested in that call—either Jesus, Moses or Mohammed.

"Even Jesus when he got hung upon the cross, he said in his own Book—he says, Father, why has Thou forsaken me? He was calling for help. Now if he couldn't help himself how is he going to help you? If I went to a funeral parlor and I saw a dead man there and I asked this dead man to help me, wouldn't you laugh at me when I ask Jesus, Mohammed or Moses to come and help me and they died over thousands of years ago? Yet you would laugh at me if I asked the one who just died yesterday and the body is almost still warm. But you won't laugh at me when I ask for help from someone where the bones are all deteriorated. Our position is not one to ask dead people to come back and help us; our position is to find ways and means to help ourselves."

Monday, afternoon

The tense, battle-torn streets of Harlem looked pale in the daylight--and the people were talking of just two things: what was going to happen tonight, and how much they hate the white cops.

This hate is always there but it only flares to outward violence in extreme times such as this. Harlem people feel that the cops are there for the benefit of the white man, not to guard the Negro against violence. In other communities, cops protect the inhabitants. In Harlem, they police them.

One of the most frequent gripes against the police is that they aren't interested in investigating crimes against Negroes. If a white person is mugged, the police are right there. But if a Negro is mugged, as often happens, it is difficult to get the police to even make out a report.

Harlem thinks that just about every cop is crooked—taking bribes both from pushers and numbers men. One of the many numbers men in Harlem was standing in front of the Hotel Theresa and expressing this elementary resentment in a strange way. He said that when he was younger business was better because the "pads" weren't so high. ("Pads" are pay-offs to the police to operate a number. It can cost from $2000 to $3200 per month, and this entitles you to work out of a candy store or grocery store—but most often out of a hall-way.) The numbers man was complaining that the "white man who came into Harlem" and needed protection had made pads so costly.

"Whenever the cops have to have someone cop a plea (plead guilty for a "show" arrest and get a light sentence), it is usually a Negro or a Puerto Rican who has to do it. If you go into court to some of the trials you would think that only Negroes and Puerto Ricans ran numbers in New York."

Monday, midnight

A distinguished looking Negro was standing in the street complaining to two policemen. The policemen were listening and they don't usually listen to Negroes who are complaining so I went over. The man said he had been hit in the head with a club by the cops and he was angry.

"I was trying to put out a fire. In front of my own building. The kids set those damn barrels on fire, in front of my building and I was trying to put them out. The cops hit me on the head, for trying to stop the fire. I told them I was trying to put out the fire and I asked them where's the protection for the black man that has a business in Harlem? My name is Joseph Monroe. I'm a pioneer of fifty years in Harlem. I've owned a business here for 27 years. I'm no newcomer. It's not the first time this sort of thing has happened, and the idea is this: what protection has the black man got in Harlem? The cops protect all the white man's business in Harlem. You see the white business with big iron rails all in front of them and white policemen standing outside, but a black man gets no protection at all. The police department protects the white businessman in New York City. Now the enterprises that are owned and controlled and operated by Negroes have no protection. I operate a business at 217 West 125th Street. When I tried to put out a fire in front of my building I was hit with a club by the cops. This is in front of my own building and that is the white man's thinking of Harlem. It's entirely different. We are not trying to start anything here in Harlem. This is not a riot. I've seen riots in Harlem and this isn't one. This is something the white man has created to be a riot. They want to make it look like a riot, but we are not here to break up Harlem to satisfy the Police Commissioner. If the Mayor had any integrity he would remove the Police Commissioner. He would direct things that would benefit the community. We haven't got the money to set up a lot of businesses—to pay high insurance. We haven't got the money to compete. Yet everything is guarded through the day and night by the Police Department for the protection of white business. I am a member of the Chamber of Commerce—I own a public relations firm and I'm a member of one of the biggest fraternal organizations on 126th Street. From Captain Winsbury to Captain Flood's time, Inspector Wheeler and all of them know me personally. I've seen the abuse of the people in Harlem. I am not like these ministers that hide in their shadows when you're looking for them to come out and save Harlem. I will do all I can to talk to these kids and save Harlem, and ask for the removal of the

white policemen out of Harlem and get Harlem back to normal and restore it. Whoever incites anything it is not the Negroes in Harlem. In my years in Harlem this is the first of it
that I have seen where the police intimidated Negroes. It
looks to me like the white people are looking for trouble and
not us."

Tuesday, 1 a.m.

I heard moaning in a doorway on 125th Street. I found a
young boy not more than 12 or 13, lying on the ground. His
head was bleeding and there were two friends with him and
they were holding his head. He said he couldn't move his
legs. I asked him what happened to him.

"I was walking down the street when the cop come over to
me and said 'Get out of here.' As I turned to go he hit me
and then they began to beat me up.

"The reason I was beat up is because I didn't run. People
had told me though, if I ran the police would beat me up so
I didn't run. First, one cop was beating me. I grabbed his
stick, and then two other cops start beating me with their
sticks. And then when I was going down the street after
they beat me up some more cops came along and hit me
too."

Shortly after

A Harlem man in an open white shirt with blood on it was
running down 125th Street towards the cops who were lined
up at the corner. The blood was his wife's, and she was running after him, crying. She was bleeding in the face and was
trying to catch her husband before he got down to the cops.
"Let's go home, I don't want any trouble," she cried. But the
man kept running. "If you want to go home go alone. I want
to find the cop that hit you," he said. He ran up to a police
Captain and said that a cop had smashed his wife in the face
with a club for no reason. The Captain said there were too
many policemen around to find out who did it. But the
Harlem man wouldn't go away. So the white Captain sent for
a Negro Captain to calm him down. But all the man kept saying was "Don't tell me a damn thing—just line up all these
white faces and let me show you the one that hit my wife."

Tuesday, 1:30 a.m.

It had been quiet for a while in the 32nd Precinct, then a dozen squad cars raced past me on the street and stopped two blocks ahead at Eighth Avenue. I ran and saw the cops getting out of their cars. They had their guns out and were shooting in the air, like cowboys on a round-up. Then I heard the breaking of glass and people yelling. By the time I was in front of Sam's West Side Bar and Grill there were already a dozen cops inside. I went in as the cops were coming out. Some bystanders had gone in and were helping out six or seven Negroes who were badly beaten up. Everybody inside had a bloody head. One of the persons was the bartender:

"I shut up early because somebody smashed in the window of the supermarket across the street and I was afraid of trouble. I locked the doors from the inside, everybody in here wanted to stay where it was safe. Then maybe twenty, twenty-five minutes later the cops came. They didn't even look across the street to where the trouble had been. They saw the light here, I guess, and shot right through my window. Right through it. Then they took their clubs and broke out the rest of the window. I opened the door and a Lieutenant came in and I told him I was the bartender and he hit me. He hit me with his stick. I kept telling him I was the bartender, but he kept hitting me."

The people inside said that after the bartender got it, all the cops ran in and started beating them, too. One man named Jerry was wiping blood off his face. "I just come here from work, and look, they cracked my head," he said.

I found one man still inside the bar, sitting against the wall. His face was thick with blood and he had a big open gash on the top of his head. His hat was on the floor and it was filled with blood. There was blood right to the brim and when I picked it up the blood poured out slowly like maple syrup. I don't know why, but I wrapped that hat in paper and kept it. I still have it. The man didn't really speak but he kind of wailed.

"They knocked out the glass, forced us to open the door, and began beating on us, with no provocation at all, no provocation, no provocation whatsoever."

I went outside and tried to interview the policeman in

charge. No arrests were made at the bar, and I asked him why.

He wouldn't talk to me, and he wouldn't give his name. Just then a flower pot crashed to the street right by us. All the cops started shooting in the air again and everybody ran for cover.

The next morning the papers said that the police reported they had chased two people into the bar and that was the reason for the trouble there. Nothing was said about the door being locked for 20 minutes before the cops arrived.

Tuesday, 2 a.m.

About ten minutes later Bayard Rustin arrived in front of the bar. Rustin, the man who put together the March on Washington for the civil rights bill, looked dazed. He had been booed in Harlem on Sunday and he couldn't understand why. But now he saw all of the blood and he was visibly shaken. "My God," he said, "I didn't realize it was really like this. I don't blame the people for booing me. I wasn't aware the police actually treated people this way."

Then he asked what he could do to help. He was put into a car with another man to go over to the 32nd Precinct and see what he could do to stop the shooting.

Wednesday, 2 p.m.

Thunder-showers made the heat even stickier, and the pool at a public school gymnasium in Harlem was crowded. One of Harlem's most respected educational leaders, a high school official, was standing by the pool watching the kids splash around. He analyzed the terror ripping his community apart and he was bitter.

"I feel that the trouble is the direct result of the racist policy of the power structure. Not only in New York City, but in New York State and throughout the nation. The manner in which they choose to disregard the legitimate requests of Negro leadership, responsible people of the community driving the long, hard drive to freedom—they choose to label these people as irresponsible radicals. The establishment was told that they should begin to talk to these people, or the brick-throwers would be in the streets, and the real irresponsible element would be on the street in larger numbers. And now the people have taken their case to the streets. They are not demonstrating peacefully as they were doing last summer and this is the long, hot summer that they have been talking about.

"However, the violence has not come from the black community. I think all of the violence—the brutality—has come from the white community as represented by the Police Department. Their brutality, this unnecessary brutality that they are bringing against the black people who have been denied their just rights as citizens for these many years—it is going to cause people to become more and more demanding and more enthusiastic and they are going to stay out in the streets. I think they should stay in the streets and I think the more that we push and the more that we explain the situation as it is now, the faster we are going to get action.

"Dr. Kenneth Clark (the noted Negro educator who helped write the brief that was given to the Supreme Court in the 1954 school desegregation case) has said that he could not let his conscience interfere with his profession as a psychologist, and he could not see how the average Negro leaders could again preach moderation to the Negro people. Now when an eminently qualified man like this who has been identified with the forces of moderation and negotiation speaks out in this manner, we have to be attentive. We have to be aware that what is happening is simply the explosion of long suppressed feelings on the part of Negroes. These Negroes were not told to take to the streets by their leaders. They went on their own.

"Another thing I would like to mention. The press is once again up to its old tactics of—as Harry Truman said when he was President—dragging a red herring across the trail. They play up the question of Communism, and extremists from their white community, supporting, aiding and abetting the Negro movement. One reason they're doing this is to imply that the black community is neither capable nor has the desire to do anything like this. Since America has been conditioned to reject anything labeled Communist since the McCarthy era, they feel that this will tend to divide Negroes among themselves and any white sympathizers. So they label it a red-dominated movement. I say that there may well be Communists involved. But I am sure that they are not leading this.

This is an expression of a frustration of a people who have been denied any consideration for more than 300 years. I don't see how any person with any intelligence could think or expect anything but this, and I marvel that there's been so little violence coming from the black community. But the black community has not yet expressed itself as it will do. The black community in my opinion is being victimized and is the recipient at this point of brutality and violence from the police. They have not yet turned and begun to fight back, but they are going to do this—to fight back.

"The police are operating under the stupid belief that the violent techniques used in the 30's by big business against the labor movement will work today against the Negro movement. They are using this kind of intimidation and force and fear to drive Negroes back into their shells where they will hide, and be afraid to come out again for another century.

"One of the things that most impressed me on the streets in Harlem during the riots was that the police made a tactical error by resorting to the use of firearms—which according to mob-control procedure is the last step that you should take. There are five steps that the police usually take with a mob, and the use of guns is the last. It is the last and only thing that they can turn to when all other things have failed.

"The New York City Police Department decided to use an extreme measure, something that has never happened before and in my view it has backfired on them. I saw Negro people refusing to run when guns were literally placed at their heads, the cops firing at random, and they stood their ground and they had nothing in their hands. They stood their ground and talked back to the cops and they did not move. This means that gunfire has failed to intimidate and cower Negroes and therefore the only thing now that has to happen is for Negroes to begin to fire back. They have no fear of the policemen's guns and the sound of firearms, and it's only logical that they will come out with their own weapons. Then we will see how brave these cops are, the cops that have been volunteering to go into Harlem and Brooklyn. No man in his right mind volunteers for the front line, when he knows that his enemy has the same weapons that he has. He only volunteers to go on a mission when he knows that there is no danger, that there is nothing likely to happen to him. This is why these cops are as eager to get up here where there's 'Coon-hunting season.'"

Wednesday, 9:15 p.m.

A popular eating place on Lenox Avenue is the Chinese Restaurant near 124th Street. Chinese people own it, but they sell all Southern food—Oxtail, piggies, all the special things that you can buy in most colored restaurants. The restaurant was crowded. People were sitting in their shirt sleeves and talking about the riots. Most everybody was listening to a man in a neat business suit who was talking very loudly.

"Everytime something terrible happens, it always happens in your own home Harlem town. On your own land, and why? Because you haven't went past 110th Street and raised no hell yet—you haven't went downtown. You haven't done nothing yet. It's always on your own hometown.

"Three times they've did it here. The cops do everything now, right out in the open, because they don't care, and you know why? Because he's still coming in on your territory. Now let's go downtown and get together and do it.

"So what if some of us gets busted in the head, and get killed, 'cause they keep coming in your own territory and bust you in the head anyway and kill you anytime they get ready."

Wednesday, later

I was at 127th Street and Lenox Avenue and watching a grocery store being looted across the street. The store was right underneath the militant Progressive Labor Movement headquarters at 336 Lenox Avenue and upstairs they were holding a meeting. There were about 25 or 30 people up there and you could see them inside through a big glass window. A young fellow in his middle 20's was standing next to me watching. He had a patch on his head and I asked what had happened to him.

"Last night I was coming from Madison Avenue down 116th Street around 10:30 and all of a sudden I heard a shot, and then a lot of patrol cars came around the block, so naturally everybody began to run. A bunch of us ran up some stairs and curled up in a huddle. The inside door was locked, so we all jammed in there just like sardines in the entrance hallway and waited. I'm the last one, so I'm the first one they grabbed. A Sergeant who had on a black helmet pulled me out and then he threw me through the air right into a big crowd of policemen on the sidewalk and they started wailing me with their clubs and I went unconscious and when I woke up I was in the hospital. I have twelve stitches in my head and I haven't been charged with no crime."

Thursday, about 1 a.m.

The CORE first aid station is on 125th Street in three small up-stairs offices. Normally the place is just an office but since Saturday night it was a first aid station for the injured in Harlem.

Two registered nurses were on duty and medics with walky-talkies went out on the streets during the riots finding the bleeding and the people who had been shot and were still lying on the sidewalk. The medics wore crash helmets to identify them.

There were a few city ambulances at the riots but usually if you were shot or beat up and lying on the sidewalk the police would pick you up when things quieted down and toss you in the back seat of a squad car and take you to the hospital.

There was a young man lying on a cot in the CORE first aid station. I asked what happened to him.

"I was walking down 125th Street near Seventh by the clock between Lenox and Seventh and then I heard shooting and about six or ten cops ran up behind me. They started calling me a nigger bastard and then one hit me in the head with his club. Then they all started hitting me on my back and my legs with clubs. I wasn't running at all, I was just walking, but when I turned around to see they started hitting me and call-ing me 'a nigger bastard.'"

Daytime Thursday

The riots are good for the addicts. Dope addicts form a large part of the Harlem landscape—on any day, at any hour, you can walk into Harlem and see groups of addicts "cool" or "getting ready to sit down." They are standing on street cor-ners, milling about—not bothered by the cops.

Addicts have to steal for a living. Their habits won't allow them to work—they have what they call a "strung-out condition." The jagged open windows in Harlem during these nights of terror gave them the go-sign for looting.

The "cools'" techniques are refined to the finest scientific points—it is well known in Harlem that they can get you any item you want, in any size or color, from any store—and that means from Fifth Avenue to the West Side—within 24 hours.

New York doesn't do anything about its addicts. There must be 50,000 dope addicts in Harlem alone. They operate openly and the police never see them. The police didn't see them Wednesday night, when they started shooting and chasing after the kids smashing windows on Lenox Avenue, and the addicts methodically cleaned out the stores like piranha tearing flesh from a bone.

There is a saying that no white man is safe in Harlem. But the white dope addict is. He runs freely in mixed packs of Puerto Rican and Negro addicts—and the police never seem to think this relationship suspicious.

I talked to a woman who is working to solve Harlem's worst problem and she, like most everybody here who is trying to do something good, is frustrated. Her name is Mrs. Coleman and she works out of the Upper Park Avenue Baptist Church on 125th Street for a Harlem anti-crime, anti-narcotics committee.

"We have for the past few years been working on a program —trying to work on a program—to eliminate narcotics from the community. This committee is concentrated here in Harlem, because here is where we have the greatest dope problem—the greatest in the country. The Harlem and Bedford-Stuyvesant areas have more addicts—far more—than any other part of the United States. The biggest problem in Harlem is the pushers. They work right out on the streets— stand on corners—and allow our children to see them openly pushing drugs in the community. This has become almost socially accepted in Harlem. It goes on everywhere. It isn't easy to get the pushers arrested. They work in a certain building or on a certain corner, and you might be able to give the police his description but you seldom know his name. If he is in a room you are not likely to know what room it is, if he works out of a hotel you are not likely to know what room he occupies in the hotel—and yet you know that he's in the hotel or in the brownstone.

"In the other areas of the city—white areas—if a person was operating a drug business so openly you wouldn't need details for the police to go looking for him. But nothing is done about it in Harlem and we suffer the greatest loss—the loss of numbers of our children to drugs. Our studies show that, each year, of the children who get out of school in June, from one to two percent of them do not return in September. They've been hooked on drugs during the summer. These youths that are lost each year intermingle with the already large addict and criminal element of Harlem and things get worse and worse.

"We who are trying to stop this feel somehow that this condition is allowed purposely to perpetuate itself. It is a wonderful way in the process of demoralizing people to get at its youth and destroy them. It is not easy to cure a drug addict—even a young one—unless you catch them at an early stage. Thousands of our young people are being destroyed by the use of drugs yet there seems to be very little done to stop the flow of drugs into Harlem.

"The availability of drugs here is absolutely ridiculous. You can obtain drugs in the Harlem area on almost every block. On practically every street corner, there is a pusher at various times of the day. This is by now almost accepted by the community. Almost every decent citizen can point you out a drug pusher.

"One thing I'd like to know. How it is that a policeman who is working in an area daily—not those who come in for some other reason, but a man who is on duty daily here— never gets to know that a man is pushing drugs? When the man is pushing drugs out on the street every day? We'd also like to know why it is that when these people are reported to the police very little is done about it. A drug house can run anywhere from 7, 8, 9 or 10 months and you can see a drove of addicts going in three or four times a day and nothing is done about it. Many times they come out and they can't even get down the stoop. They have just had a shot and they have gone into this nod and they can't even get down the stoop. If they make it to the corner, well, they have done good.

"On practically any rooftop in Harlem you can look on the lower rooftops about 1 or 5 o'clock in the afternoon and see a drove of addicts taking to the roof where they use their needles on themselves. This goes on daily. You find the same thing in many hallways, or behind stairs.

"Women often have their pocket-books snatched here by addicts—yet the crimes go on and we still have a flow of drugs in here.

"It seems that it should be possible for the police to stop so many people from pushing drugs in Harlem. We believe that the dope situation is something that is going to keep our people going down with nothing to help them and no one to get to them. We don't have the authority to do anything about someone who is pushing drugs. We cannot go out and arrest them ourselves and we can't do anything that is violent. This is all wrong.

"We are trying to save our youth from being enticed into and talked into and sometimes even forced into drug addiction. It is a fact that a pusher constantly has to have more customers. The more customers the better off he is if he happens to be an addict himself. Yet most pushers must make money for a big man—a man outside of Harlem. There may be one big pusher in the community or even two really big pushers— but we know that these drugs are not brought in here by the Negro community. This is something that comes from outside —because there aren't that many Negroes that are in the position to buy large quantities of drugs coming into the country or even have the contacts to get hold of large quantities of drugs.

"The drugs—the big quantities—seem to be earmarked for the Negro community whether it be Harlem or Brooklyn or Chicago. They are always earmarked for the Negro community and we haven't got a chance of fighting our own juvenile delinquency when the children can see drug pushers standing out on the corners and nothing being done about it by the police.

"The parents are preaching constantly that this is right and this is wrong and you should abide by the right way, and yet the most vicious and the most murderous of all things in Harlem is drug pushing and drug addiction and the kids see nothing done about it—this main and most important problem.

"We have addicts that come to Harlem from Jersey, from Connecticut and from all over, since New York has very liberal narcotic laws compared to many other states. Cars pull up, these people come in here and they line our streets and our corners all day and sometimes all night. On weekends many young people from other areas come into Harlem for dope and they could not get away with doing this anywhere else in the city. This could all be stopped. And we wonder why in a Negro community this sort of thing can continue without interference from our law enforcement."

Ramparts, October 1964

THE SEARCH FOR THE MISSING:
JUNE–AUGUST 1964

from
Three Lives for Mississippi

by William Bradford Huie

IF I live to be a hundred, I'll never forget the attitudes I encountered, the stories I heard and read, and the sensations I felt in Mississippi during the last week in June and the weeks of July 1964. The *Clarion-Ledger* of Jackson calls itself Mississippi's Leading Newspaper for More Than a Century. On June 30 the *Clarion* adorned its front page with four pictures from Philadelphia. One picture showed old men dozing on the courthouse porch, and another showed Cecil Price and four highway patrol officers sprawled in lounge chairs "in conference" under shade trees. Here is the accompanying story:

LIFE GOES ON MUCH AS BEFORE
AT PHILADELPHIA DESPITE EVENTS

A week ago last Monday, Philadelphia was just another typical Mississippi town. The sun rose as usual and there were chores to be done.

A week ago last Monday people in these parts were preparing for the coming work week. Pulpwood trucks began their treck [*sic*] to the forests, store owners were busy sweeping out, the old men began moving to their usual places on the steps of the brick courthouse in the middle of the business district which forms a square.

A week ago diesel trucks braked to a halt on the main highway which runs in front of the courthouse. A few Choctaw Indians had arrived in town early for shopping. A group of young boys skipped down the street thinking about a swim later in the day.

A week ago the main problem facing Philadelphians was the coming Neshoba County Fair. And for Philadelphians, and others, that wasn't really a problem.

A week ago there was some talk around the courthouse about three so-called civil rights workers being arrested for speeding. After they had posted bail, a deputy sheriff had followed them part of the way back to Meridian. The old men, long experts of the courthouse talk, first heard from local officials of the three having disappeared.

157

A week ago that was not much to get excited about. The trio [were] unknown locally, and who knew which way they might have gone when they left Philadelphia?

Then Monday afternoon a burned station wagon, used by the three, was found about 12 miles northeast of town. Since that time Philadelphia has led most news stories all over the world.

During the past seven days, Neshoba Countians have seen hundreds of federal agents, highway patrol personnel, and even members of the U.S. Navy trampling over the countryside. They have heard the President of the United States talk about their town. They have read about a visit by Allen Dulles to Mississippi to discuss their town. They have seen one of the largest groups of news media personnel ever to gather in Mississippi. They have seen their town Philadelphia, through the eyes of national television; they have heard about their town on radio; they have seen their town through the "eyes" of newsprint and pictures.

They have seen their town tried and found guilty by many outsiders . . . an observer can hear phrases of displeasure, particularly concerning national television personnel who have . . . attempted to outdo each other. . . .

An observer . . . immediately gets the feeling that Philadelphians would rather just be left alone. "If people would 'tend to their own business, everything would be alright," one old courthouse sitter said.

"If it was boiled down to gravy there wouldn't be much to it, nohow," another responded.

An inquirer gets the feeling that these Mississippians don't know what happened to the three. And after the treatment they have received from national news media, they wouldn't care to cooperate with visiting television folk.

Monday afternoon was like most Monday afternoons have been in Philadelphia for years. And Philadelphia will be here for many more Mondays to come.

On July 2 the Birmingham *News*, which has a large circulation in east Mississippi, published this Editorial Report on its editorial page:

The Scene: Philadelphia

Four hundred sailors, scores of FBI agents—employes of Uncle Sam—push through dust, weeds, branches, mud and water not far from this national dateline. Eleven hours a day they hunt for clues of three missing men.

Few Mississippians, officials or otherwise, seem to be doing very much active searching.

A Mississippi highway patrolman accompanies each squad of sailors. Their mission, said Gov. Paul Johnson, is to "be certain that the people's houses and property of this area are protected at all times."

Some state investigators, including some brass, spend a good portion of every day under a giant pecan tree behind the small Philadelphia City Hall.

One top investigator, pistol on, lies stretched out in an aluminum, web lounge chair, arms up behind his head. Four or five other chairs under the sheltering tree are for other state men who come and go. . . .

State people for the most part seem to be standing by. Federal agents carry the burden of effort to find the missing men.

It is a distinctly pleasant sort of Southern scene—state investigators behind City Hall eat lunch calmly—sardines, cheese, crackers, dill pickles, cold sweet milk. Sometimes there is baloney and souse meat.

Last Tuesday morning several highway patrol cars stood parked near a church to the west. Maybe more such are present than are needed. These officers only stood around talking to each other. "We were just told to park here," said one.

The Philadelphia police chief and his assistants haven't been evident much in the searching either. Most of the time they seem busy about their duties in town. . . .

The police chief and Philadelphia's mayor provided a small courtroom for state and federal officers, for private phone calls and conferences. Meetings between federal and state men have been increasingly few recently.

The FBI, quite obviously, is keeping almost strictly to itself. Its information is close-guarded. State men give no evidence that federal agents tell them much when they do sit down together.

There is a careful courtesy between local and state officers and federal investigators. But there is an obvious distance between them too. State people appear to feel that the FBI ought to be confiding more in them. Equally apparent, the FBI—which usually says as little as possible—seems to feel its facts are best kept to itself. "Cooperation" in Neshoba County is more ritual than reality.

Gov. Johnson of Mississippi has said, "this [search] is a joint effort. This is a cooperative effort between local, state and federal agents. . . ."

The federal agents do not mix. They attend to their business and mind their tongues. They are quartered in a small motel due west of Philadelphia. They do not tarry long at City Hall when they must visit it.

Monday a federal agent pulled his car up to park near City Hall. His vehicle blocked a woman clerk's car as she worked inside.

A state man suggested someone ought to tell the agent, so he could move his car.

"Wait until he's walked up here," said another state officer under the pecan tree.

"This is a cooperative effort," the governor had said.

How could such officers cooperate in the search for the bodies? Not every state officer knew where the bodies were, but some undoubtedly did and those who didn't probably assumed that other officers did know. A sheriff is a state as well as a county officer; so is his deputy. The Governor of Mississippi can arrest a sheriff, investigate him, replace him. If there was a state police officer assigned to the search who doubted that Sheriff Rainey knew where the bodies were, I didn't meet him. And if there was a state police officer who doubted that Deputy Price had been party to the murders, I didn't meet him either.

How could the FBI cooperate with Sheriff Rainey, Deputy Price, and other state officers who sympathized with the murderers? The FBI represents the free society of the United States. The state officers represent the white-supremacy society of Mississippi. No free society can approve murder, or lynching, or cop-inflicted punishment. Every white-supremacy society tolerates "extremism in its own defense." Mississippi, in effect, approved lynching for decades, as it has approved a hundred cases where "troublemakers" were shot "while resisting arrest."

Since white supremacy cannot now be maintained legally within the United States, how else is it to be maintained except by resort to illegality whenever it feels threatened?

With passage of the Civil Rights Act of 1964, the free society of the United States moved into another showdown with the white-supremacy society of Mississippi. Just as in 1861, when freedom came to a showdown with slavery. This is why the murders were committed: the white-supremacy society trying to protect itself from Invaders it could not repel legally.

How could the "outside press"—the free press of the United States—have pleased the people of Philadelphia? Murder had been committed. The victims were innocent: they were in Mississippi legally and deserved the protection of Mississippi's laws. So the free press felt the bodies should be found and the murderers should be tracked down and punished.

To most, if not all, of the people of Philadelphia no murder had been committed. If killing had been done, it was because the victims had "provoked" the killers. How can killing be called murder "when the victims have come in from the outside just to stir up trouble"? Most of the people of Philadelphia did not want the bodies to be found, and they stood ready to protect and reward the killers.

"Sheriff Rainey is the bravest sheriff in America," announced Circuit Judge O. H. Barnett. Does a sheriff prove he is brave by conspiring to murder three helpless young men, who have broken no law, and who are armed only with opinions the sheriff happens to detest? That is what the federal grand jury indictment, referred to previously, says Sheriff Rainey did. Judge Barnett is another duly elected Mississippi agent, the judge who would charge any state grand jury investigating the case, and the judge who would preside at any Neshoba County trial of the murderers. At a meeting of the State Sheriffs Association, Sheriff Rainey was the hero, "applauded to the rafters."

The only way the national press could have pleased the people of Neshoba County would have been to insist that Sheriff Rainey or Deputy Price, rather than Martin Luther King, deserved the Nobel Peace Prize, and to publish a series of articles or produce a television special proving that Mickey Schwerner and Andy Goodman had been Soviet spies sent to "mongrelize Mississippi."

The FBI could have pleased the people of Mississippi only by respecting that mudsill of white supremacy, states' rights (racist version), and by reporting to and working with Sheriff Rainey and Deputy Price.

In an effort to pretend that cooperation existed between Mississippi and the national press, the Mississippi State Highway Patrol established a press headquarters at the Benwalt Hotel in Philadelphia. Telephones were installed for the visiting press, and a personable young man presented himself as the press representative for the state police. He invited me to attend briefings and use the facilities. I declined with thanks.

Hypocrisy sometimes makes me physically ill. I respect several officers in the Mississippi patrol. They are fine and capable men. They don't like the Ku Klux Klan, and they wouldn't give Lawrence Rainey or Cecil Price the time of day. If they had really been in a position to work on this case, they might have needed an entire afternoon to find those bodies and arrest the first score of these murderers. I'm sure those good men felt embarrassed by the position they were in. Let's just say that the Mississippi state police have done proud work before, and may do proud work again. But not in this case. Here they could accomplish nothing. Because what we had here was a lynching, with police participation.

After the murder, in their treatment of Rita Schwerner the people of Mississippi had to try to degrade her. To risk showing her any sympathy would be to risk showing respect for her murdered husband. Besides, she had slept in "nigger houses."

Asleep in a dormitory in Oxford, Ohio, Rita was awakened about 1 A.M. on Monday morning and asked to come to the office of the Western College for Women. At the office she took the telephone call from Jackson and learned that the three were missing and presumed to be in jail somewhere in Mississippi. She lay on a cot for the rest of the night, taking telephone calls. Sometime after daylight she learned that Neshoba county jail now reported that the three had been detained there during Sunday evening and released at 10:30 P.M. So the three were now said to be "missing."

Rita spent Monday in Oxford, and on Tuesday morning some students drove her the sixty miles to the Cincinnati Airport. There she learned that the burned car had been found.

"I knew then that they were dead," she told me. "I took a plane to Atlanta where I had to spend the night in a motel in order to make the connection to Meridian."

She reached Meridian on Wednesday, and FBI agents questioned her for three hours. Then on Thursday, the twenty-fifth, with a lawyer, she drove to Philadelphia to see Sheriff Rainey. The sheriff ducked her at first; then, accompanied by a highway patrol investigator, Charles Snodgrass, he agreed to talk with her while sitting in his car at the Delphia Motel.

Rainey sat under the wheel; Snodgrass was at his right; and Rita and her lawyer sat in the back seat for perhaps ten minutes. Snodgrass insisted on doing most of the talking.

"Mrs. Schwerner, you mustn't be hard on Sheriff Rainey," Snodgrass said. "He's a worried husband. His wife is in the hospital. He's preoccupied, and he knows very little about this case."

"Well, at least he still has a wife to be concerned about," Rita said. "I ask him only to do me the courtesy of telling me where my husband is."

"But the sheriff doesn't know that," Snodgrass insisted. "He was at the hospital with his wife. How can the sheriff know where your husband decided to go when he left Philadelphia Sunday night?"

Rita persisted in trying to address the sheriff directly. She said: "Sheriff Rainey, I feel that you know what happened. I'm going to find out if I can. If you don't want me to find out, you'll have to kill me."

Rainey's huge knuckles turned white as he tightened his grip on the steering wheel. "I'm very shocked," he said. "I'm sorry you said that."

From Philadelphia Rita went on to Jackson to try to see Governor Johnson. But she waited at the governor's office in vain because he was preoccupied in greeting George Wallace and in helping Wallace address a "mammoth mass meeting" on Thursday evening. "I'm sure Wallace is much more important to Mississippi than three missing men," Rita told reporters at the governor's office.

On Friday every front page in Mississippi carried a three- or four-column cut of Wallace and Johnson "in triumph." Here, in part, is the UPI story as it appeared in the Meridian *Star*:

> ### Gov. Johnson Sides with 'Bama Chief
> #### SOUTH WILL NAME NEXT PRESIDENT, WALLACE TELLS 10,000 IN JACKSON
>
> Jackson, Miss.—Gov. George Wallace of Alabama was backed up by Mississippi Gov. Paul Johnson here Thursday night in telling a roaring crowd of 10,000 that "the South will determine who is the next president of the United States."
>
> Wallace and his wife spent the afternoon as guests at the executive

mansion before the Alabama governor addressed the boisterous turnout of Mississippians at the State Coliseum.

"Certainly I am a candidate for president," Wallace said. "I am running for president because I was born free. I want your children and mine and our posterity to be unencumbered by the manipulations of a soulless state."

Johnson introduced the Alabama governor, assuring the crowd that "the South, with its 112 electoral votes, is the balance of power that will determine who is the next president of the United States."

"It's time the white people of our various states started bloc voting," said Johnson.

Wallace predicted at a news conference earlier in the day that Mississippi would follow the lead of his native state and pledge its electoral votes to him.

"No president of this nation will be elected unless he pays attention to Mississippi and Alabama," he said. "The people are tired of being taken for granted and kicked around by the leaders of both national parties."

Young couples carrying infants and adults leading elderly parents by the arm turned out to hear Wallace's plea for presidential support. They swarmed the speaker's s[t]and at the conclusion of the speech to touch the Alabamian's outstretched arms.

Police estimated the crowd at more than 10,000—possibly the largest throng since the coliseum was built two years ago. A Dixieland band, dancing girls, and "We Love George" cries caused one native of Alabama to remark: "They don't even do this in Alabama. . . ."

Gov. Johnson sided with Wallace in saying "the South has no use for the liberals of either . . . national parties. We want a choice—not of two liberals—but a clear cut choice between a liberal and a conservative. . . ."

Wallace called the 1954 school desegregation ruling by the U.S. Supreme Court "ridiculous and asinine," and said "any person who made such a ruling should have a psychiatric examination. . . ." The Governor noted that the National Press Club presented speakers' certificates to Nikita Khrushchev and Fidel Castro but refused him such a certificate.

The crowd roared when he said: "As far as I'm concerned, they can take their certificate, and you know what they can do with it."

White supremacists like Wallace, Barnett, and Johnson are always repeating the lie that they represent "the South." They long ago captured the term *states' rights*, and in 1964 they tried to capture the word *conservative*. They began implying that all Southerners and all Americans who think of themselves as conservative, or who value the rights of the states, are also white supremacists.

Since Wallace was the Presidential candidate of the white-supremacy terrorists, among the ten thousand who roared for him at Jackson were at least fifty men who knew of the plot to murder Mickey Schwerner and three men who were members of the murder party. When neither Wallace nor Johnson mentioned the disappearance of Schwerner, Chaney and Goodman, every conspirator and murderer left the Coliseum feeling that he had the approval of both Wallace and Johnson.

Here is another UPI story out of Jackson, as carried by the Meridian *Star* June 26.

COULD HAPPEN ANYWHERE, GOVERNOR SAYS

Gov. Paul Johnson said today he was "satisfied" that everything possible was being done to locate the three civil rights workers missing since earlier this week in East-Central Mississippi.

Johnson told newsmen the disappearance of the three was something that "could happen anytime" in any part of the country. "It happens in New York every night," he said, adding that Mississippi has the second lowest crime rate in the nation.

"I'm satisfied that everything is being done that could be done to find them," he said.

Johnson also acknowledged that a second wave of volunteer workers, mostly college students, was expected to arrive in Mississippi during the weekend to participate in the so-called "summer project."

But he said he understood the number may have decreased from earlier expectations. He said he had heard reports that a number of the students had decided against taking part in the project, some on their own and some because of their parents.

The governor was ignoring the characteristics which set the Philadelphia murders apart. The murders committed "nightly" in New York are not the result of plans in which the police have participated. They are not widely approved by the people, and the state seeks to punish the murderers. The governor was failing to note that few Mississippians were extending themselves in the search for the bodies. And by reporting that the number of students coming to Mississippi "may have decreased from earlier expectations," the governor, in effect, was informing the murderers that their action was proving effective.

Rita Schwerner found Governor Johnson Friday afternoon on the steps of the governor's mansion. He and Wallace were still receiving well-wishers, and Rita walked up to meet him. He didn't catch her name at first, so he smiled and extended his hand as though she were a constituent. A highway patrolman shouted a warning, repeating her name, and the governor jerked back his hand and fled, with Wallace, into the house and slammed the door.

"Johnson and Wallace reminded me of two scared children," Rita said. "They stood peeping at me from behind curtains, as though they were curious about me but feared to be seen in public with me."

Not until July 30, in a courtroom in Hattiesburg, did Rita corner Deputy Price. She walked up to him, extended her hand, and said: "I'd like to say hello to you, Mr. Price." He literally jumped away from her and stood gritting his teeth at her. "I don't want to talk to you!" he said in a strangely nervous, high-pitched voice.

For two brave law-enforcement officers, Rainey and Price seemed unduly reluctant to confront the ninety-pound Mrs. Schwerner.

When Rita left the courtroom in Hattiesburg, she found a crowd waiting on the courthouse steps for her. The crowd began jeering as she approached.

"Smell her!" one woman shouted.

"You can actually smell her!" others shouted.

"She stinks!"

Rita walked on down the steps, followed by the calls that she "smelled" and "stank."

As the search moved into its third and fourth weeks, the entire Mississippi press began emphasizing how the civil rights workers "smelled" and "stank." Here is part of another story from the *Clarion-Ledger*:

ODOR OF SWEAT, DIRT FILLS
HATTIESBURG'S COFO OFFICE

Walk into the grey-concrete office of the Council of Federated Organizations at 507 Mobile St. in Hattiesburg [and] the first thing noticed is the odor of sweat and dirt. . . .

Perhaps a dozen Negroes and half a dozen whites meet you at the door to ask your business. The Negroes, as the whites, are poorly dressed. Two white girls with long, straight hair . . . sandals and sack dresses stand by a desk, idly eyeing the intruder.

The appearance of the COFO workers is an affront to most of Hattiesburg's residents . . . a 1964 graduate of the University of Southern Mississippi summed it up like this: "If you don't know them . . . by sight, you could sniff the air and find out."

A police officer, working the Mobile Street beat tabbed the group, "disgusting, just plain disgusting."

The office, from which is controlled COFO's mission to southeast Mississippi, consists of two small rooms and dingy kitchen. A roach scuttles across the floor. A Negro boy—perhaps 18—steps on it with a crackling sound, smiles . . . and says, "Our friends."

A white youth wearing torn blue-jeans, a work shirt and tennis shoes, sits in a corner plucking away tunelessly at a beat-down guitar.

There is much talk about Mississippi as a police state, the cold "brutality" of the people and the superior intelligence of the COFO workers.

COFO's project director, Sanford Leigh of Illinois, is 28 years old and claims to have been in Mississippi since 1961. He is a darker-than-usual Negro, very thin, with black rimmed glasses and a way of looking at his knees when he speaks.

Leigh, who is a college graduate, does most of the group's talking [and is] belligerent.

"Nigger, nigger, nigger, that's what you think while you're standing there," he said. "Just another of the state's yellow journalists working for the state's most condemnatory paper."

Leigh likes the word "condemnatory." He uses it over and over.

[Another spokesman for the group is a white native of Connecticut, Class of '66 at Duke. Tall and rangy, he looks like a beatnik, complete with torn sandals.]

"I'm not down here to impress you or anybody," he said. "If I was, I'd get an ivy-league haircut and some . . . clothes. I don't need . . . clothes to make people realize I'm a human being."

[He] holds hands with a Negro girl. She wears a pin bearing the legend "Student Non-Violent Coordinating Committee—One Man, One Vote." After a while, [he] becomes angry with the . . . reporter, and he and the girl walk out to a car with New York license plates and drive away. Several police officers watch them and jot down the car's license plate.

The white workers, including the girls, live with Negroes in Hattiesburg's Negro section. They say that Negro groups furnish food but not money. COFO pays its workers $9.66 per week after taxes.

The girls spend some of their money on candy bars; the boys spend some of theirs at Negro taverns, drinking beer.

About 20 people work out of the Hattiesburg office. Half are whites. None of the white workers is from Mississippi, and none is old enough to vote.

"We don't need to vote ourselves in order to show others," one said. He was 17, a college freshman.

Because *Life* magazine, in preparing its story on the training at Oxford, Ohio, had photographed Andrew Goodman; and because film footage had been shot by CBS of Goodman at Oxford, an incredible number of Mississippians concluded that a plot had existed for Goodman to come to Mississippi and "become missing." Here is one of many letters to the editor charging a plot that were published:

After watching Walter Cronkite's super-colossal, hate Mississippi newscast, I cannot remain silent. What an array of personalities were presented to jerk tears, play upon emotions, and engender hatred for Mississippi. . . .

However, the master minds seemed to have slipped up a bit and I challenge you to ask this one question. If the planners didn't know prior to Sunday, June 21st, that Andy Goodman was going to "disappear" in Mississippi, then why did the TV cameraman who made pictures at the school in Oxford, Ohio, keep his camera on Goodman close up when there were many other students in the lecture hall with him? He was the only one they focused on and only took the camera off of him briefly to show the Negro speaker . . . telling them that violence could befall them in Mississippi. . . .

The explanation was apparent to all of us in the writing or picture business. Goodman was a particularly attractive, intelligent-looking, obviously sensitive and sincere young man, as is evident in the photo of him at Oxford reproduced in this volume from the CBS film. He was no beatnik. He was the

Film of Andy Goodman at COFO training program in Oxford, Ohio, June 15, 1964 (CBS News)

sort that a commercial photographer spots in a crowd. Then he happened to be caught in the only plot that existed: the plot to murder Michael Schwerner.

Around the middle of July, when the search for the bodies had proceeded unsuccessfully for three weeks, I assumed that the time had come to negotiate with the murderers. The search had never had much chance of succeeding. Where such a murder has been planned; where the murderers have had many hours in which to dispose of the bodies; where there are large stretches of uninhabited countryside; and where the inhabitants are uncooperative because they are hostile to the searchers and/or afraid of the murderers, a search is largely meaningless. Under such circumstances you can't find bodies with helicopters, or with hundreds of young sailors beating bushes, killing snakes, and scratching chigger bites.

"No, we won't find anything," a federal officer said to me. "But we have to keep dragging rivers and beating the bushes while the *real* search goes on: the search for that citizen who, for protection and money, will eventually take us to the bodies."

In a murder case where every knowledgeable survivor is guilty, and where every living witness is a murderer, you obtain information from informers, and you obtain evidence by inducing one murderer to witness against another. And where every witness is under a real threat of death from his fellows if he talks, a witness can be a problem.

In this Mississippi is, in fact, no different from New York. When, because they fear involvement, thirty-eight "decent" New Yorkers neglect to call the police while an innocent woman is murdered before their eyes, how can "decent" Mississippians be expected to witness against terrorists? Bodies hidden by the Mafia and other gangsters are as hard to find as those hidden by Mississippi gangsters; and a thousand murders committed by gangsters have gone unpunished in the United States because "decent" citizens declined to take the risks of giving testimony.

I thought something might be gained by my talking with two or three secure, honorable, sophisticated men in the power structure of Philadelphia—men who were not politicians or preachers, but business or professional men, capable of some degree of objectivity, and with whom I might have mutual friends. It is well known in Mississippi that in order to publish the truth about the Emmett Till murder, I paid those murderers with the assistance of reputable alumni of the Ole Miss Law School. It is also known that in both the Mack Parker case and in the Beckwith case, I had the assistance of Mississippi lawyers and of Mississippi police investigators. For my talks with citizens of Philadelphia to be effective, the talks had to be held away from Philadelphia. I arranged such talks, which went on at some length. I thought I might persuade one of these men to assist at least in finding the bodies if not in obtaining information or evidence.

"Well," one man said, "I'll say this. I'm sorry about the murders. Of course I'm sorry. They were wrong, stupid, and very bad for business in Mississippi. I'm capable of sympathy for the victims. I'm sorry for the families. I'm sure that Schwerner and Goodman were decent, well-meaning young men. They wanted to ride white horses and, right or wrong, they were riding their horses in Mississippi. But here is a fact. On both sides everybody knew that at least one of these young people coming to Mississippi was going to be murdered. I knew it. I assume the fathers of Schwerner and Goodman knew it. I know the instigators of this 'March on Mississippi' expected at least one murder. Joe Alsop wrote that murder was expected, and that the provoking of violence was a tactic deliberately being adopted by the militant Negro organizations."

"But the fact that murder may have been expected doesn't justify it," I said.

"No, but it helps explain it. Mississippi has been a white-supremacy state since its beginning. These rednecks are capable of violence. That's why they make good soldiers; why we use them to lead night patrols in our wars; why so many of them have won Congressional Medals of Honor. They may not read much, but they now own television sets. And when they hear on TV every day that everybody in Mississippi is a stupid, tobacco-chewing bigot, then a murder case like this one here is as predictable as sunrise."

"How about helping find the bodies? For humanitarian reasons if no other?"

"Well," he said, "I'll have to think about that. I suppose I might induce one of these jokers to tell me where they are if I really set my hand to it. But what good can come of it? Maybe the best course for everybody is just to let the bodies lie and let the excitement gradually die down. Once the bodies are found, then there is a great hue and cry to convict somebody . . . to put somebody in jail. And that's a power I don't have. That power doesn't exist in Mississippi. Not even Paul Johnson has any such power. There is no way in the world, in open court, where a twelve-man jury verdict must be unanimous, and where every juror can be polled in open court and made to say how he voted—there's no possible way to ever put anybody in jail. Instead of reducing hate, all a trial can do is spread it. So why should we have all that hue and cry, and a big circus trial, with everybody goddamning Mississippi? What's the use of it? Since a murder like this was expected, why don't we all just admit that we got what we expected and devote ourselves to trying to prevent another one?"

"How do we prevent another one by letting this one go unpunished?"

"This one is going unpunished in any case. That is, the murderers are going unpunished. Mississippi has already been punished, and will continue to be punished."

"So you refuse to help find the bodies?"

"I haven't said that," he answered. "I'll have to think about it. It's a tough question. It's *right* that the bodies should be found. But nothing good can come of finding them."

"Well, here is another of your realities," I said. "The bodies *will* be found. You know it as well as I do. The pressure is great and will get greater. Too many people know where the bodies are. One of them is sure to sell out. There is too much money available."

"How much money?"

"I'd say twenty-five thousand dollars. More if necessary."

"You mean twenty-five thousand dollars for nothing more than the *information* as to where the bodies are? No confession? No public identification of the informer? No signed statement identifying and accusing the others?"

"I think that can be arranged," I said. "If all we can get is the bodies. Naturally, a signed confession which implicates the others would be best, but if we can't get that let's at least get the evidence of murder. The deal will have to be COD. Nobody will pay an informer that amount of money just for an unproved tip. The informer has to pass the information, then wait two or three days while the FBI finds the bodies and identifies them. The informer has to take the calculated risk that he will get his money, but ways can be devised to reduce the risk to a minimum."

"Christ," he said, "maybe I ought to stop what I'm doing and get in the business of finding and selling the bodies of civil rights workers."

"Well, what I'm telling you is no secret," I said. "The FBI

has always paid informers. So does every effective police agency on earth. How else could these bodies ever be found? Or these murderers identified? I think the bodies will be found, and I think that many, perhaps most, of the murderers will eventually be identified even if they are never convicted."

In addition to such talks with substantial citizens of Philadelphia, I spread my Alabama and Mississippi telephone numbers around and let it be widely known that I would pay for information. The FBI agents were doing the same thing. I told them most of what I was doing. They didn't tell me what they were doing: they quite properly never tell anybody.

By July 20 I believed I knew the identity of three of the young men who were in the actual murder and burial parties. I had been told that the bodies had been buried, not submerged; and I had the information that the graves were southwest of Philadelphia. I told one of my publishers that the bodies would be found "not later than August tenth," and I wrote the first draft of a story titled *How the Bodies Were Found in Mississippi.*

I was convinced that by August eighth I would know where the bodies were; and I assumed the FBI agents were as close or closer to a deal than I was.

On July 22 U.S. Senator James O. Eastland of Mississippi made a statement I still can't understand. The Senator is an able, immensely knowledgeable, and powerful man. Not only did he practice skillful law for years in Mississippi before he went to the Senate, but in the Senate he is chairman of the powerful Judiciary Committee and deals daily with the Justice Department. Here is the press association report on his statement:

Sen. James O. Eastland . . . suggested Wednesday that the . . . disappearance of three civil rights workers in Mississippi might have been a hoax.

[He questioned charges that the three had been killed.]

He said an intensive, month-long investigation and search had failed to produce "a shred of evidence" that the three were victims of racial violence.

"Many people in our state assert that there is just as much evidence, as of today, that they are voluntarily missing as there is that they have been abducted," said Eastland.

"No one wants to charge that a hoax has been perpetrated, because there is too little evidence to show just what did happen. But as time goes on, and the search continues, if some evidence of a crime is not produced, I think the people of America will be justified in considering other alternatives more valid solutions to the mystery, instead of accepting as true the accusation of the agitators that heinous crime has been committed."

He claimed that Mississippians were attempting to preserve the peace in the face of a Communist-backed "conspiracy to thrust violence upon them." . . .

Why would Senator Eastland make such a statement as late as July 22? Did the information on which he based his statement come from Governor Johnson? Or from the head of the Mississippi highway patrol? Had the state investigators actually done so little work on the case that they had found "not a shred of evidence that the three were victims of racial violence"? Had it occurred to Senator Eastland or Governor Johnson to call Sheriff Rainey before them and ask what had happened? Or was everybody in Mississippi standing back, averting his eyes, and hoping the FBI would find nothing?

On Saturday, August 1, I was told that FBI agents were guarding the dam. I was told that Deputy Price knew that the FBI had found the bodies; and I was told that FBI agents were not allowing Price near the dam. Sheriff Rainey, for some reason, had picked that week end to go on his vacation, along the Mississippi Gulf Coast.

On Monday, August 3, a federal judge in Biloxi secretly gave the FBI authority to enter the property around the dam and to excavate in the dam. The warrant was issued on the sworn statement of an FBI agent that "an informer" had provided the information that the bodies were in the dam.

On Monday night a truck and trailer left Jackson, Mississippi, carrying a bulldozer and an excavating machine known as a dragline. On Tuesday the dragline lumbered out to the center of the dam and began cutting a perfect V. Eighteen feet down, at the exact bottom of the V, the dragline and bulldozer, then FBI agents with shovels, uncovered a cruel tomb.

In a photograph published around the world—a photograph that should live—Sheriff's Deputy Cecil Price was shown helping to carry the plastic bags in which were the forty-four-day-old remains of Michael Schwerner, James Chaney, and Andrew Goodman.

from *Three Lives for Mississippi* (1965)

Mississippian Relates Struggle of Negro in Voter Registration

by Nan Robertson

ATLANTIC CITY, Aug. 23—Mrs. Fannie Lou Hamer sat in a stifling motel room near the boardwalk here today, mopping her streaming brow and saying:

"Why should I leave Ruleville and why should I leave Mississippi? I go to the big city and with the kind of education they give us in Mississippi I got problems. I'd wind up in a soup line there. That's why I want to change things in Mississippi. You don't run away from problems—you just face them."

Mrs. Hamer, the 46-year-old wife of a Ruleville sharecropper, was seen by millions of Americans on television yesterday as she told the Credentials Committee of the Democratic National Convention how she had been jailed and beaten for trying to register Negroes to vote.

She is a member of the biracial delegation of the Freedom Democratic Party, which is challenging the regular delegation from Mississippi.

The confrontation of the two forces yesterday before the committee produced the most spell-binding moments so far in the convention preliminaries. Mrs. Hamer's testimony was the most dramatic.

The Credentials Committee has not yet decided which of the delegations should be seated as the official representation from Mississippi.

Today, in her husky, powerful voice, Mrs. Hamer spoke of her life, her family and her hopes for the future. She also gave her reactions to the white spokesmen for the regular Mississippi party.

"Maybe plenty people could hate them," she said. "I feel sorry for anybody that could let hate wrap them up. Hate will not only destroy us. It will destroy them."

Mrs. Hamer was the 20th and last child of a Negro farmer, living since her second year in the Mississippi delta town of Ruleville. She began picking cotton with her other brothers and sisters in her father's fields when she was 6. She went to school on and off for eight years.

"It looked like the more we worked the less we would have," she said. For a long time, she said, she wished she was white "so bad."

But with all his children in the fields, Mrs. Hamer's father was finally able to buy mules and cows and wagons and a place of his own. Then one day someone put poison in the feed "and killed everything in our barn, our mules, our cows," she remembers. "My father never was able to get a foothold again."

Mrs. Hamer, a hefty woman weighing 200 pounds, continued to work in the cotton fields. Eventually she was made a checker and time-keeper who paid the other pickers. She became active in voter registration and a field worker for the Student Nonviolent Co-ordinating Committee in December, 1962. She was dismissed from her job shortly thereafter.

This year, the day after she qualified as a Democratic Congressional candidate in the June primary, Mrs. Hamer's husband lost his job.

"I was shocked yesterday when Collins [State Senator E. K. Collins, chief spokesman for the Mississippi regulars] said I got better than 600 votes in the primary," Mrs. Hamer said. "The official count last June was 388 votes. They said we could watch the ballot box but we had to stand across the street to watch it. There's no way of seeing through a concrete wall I know of."

As Mrs. Hamer spoke, her tone ranged from outrage to resignation to hope.

"Is this America?" she asked as she had yesterday before the committee.

"Do you think I came here to compromise and sit in a back seat at this convention? People from all the states are watching us now.

"I'm not proud of being black more than being white, I'm proud of being black because of my heritage. The Negroes are the only race in America that had babies sold from their breasts and mothers sold from their families."

Mrs. Hamer groaned as she took off her shoes and said her feet hurt.

She relaxed and said:

"One day I know the struggle will change. There's got to be a change—not only for Mississippi, not only for the people in the United States, but people all over the world."

The New York Times, August 24, 1964

Mississippi at Atlantic City

by Charles M. Sherrod

IT was a cool day in August beside the ocean. Atlantic City, New Jersey, was waiting for the Democratic National Convention to begin. In that Republican fortress history was about to be made. High on a bill board smiling out at the breakers was a picture of Barry Goldwater and an inscription "In your heart you know he's right." Later someone had written underneath, "Yes, extreme right." Goldwater had had his "moment," two weeks before on the other ocean. This was to be L.B.J.'s "moment," and we were to find out that this was also his convention.

The Mississippi Freedom Democratic Party had been working rather loosely all summer. Money was as scarce as prominent friends. A small band of dedicated persons forged out of the frustration and aspirations of an oppressed people a wedge; a moral wedge which brought the monstrous political machinery of the greatest power on earth to a screeching halt.

The Freedom Democratic Party was formed through precinct, county, district and state conventions. An attempt to register with the state was frustrated. But the party was opened to both black and white voters and non-voters for the State of Mississippi had denied the right to vote to thousands. Ninety-three percent of the Negroes twenty-one years of age or older in Mississippi are denied the right to vote. To show to the Convention and to the country that people want to vote in Mississippi, we held a Freedom Registration campaign. In other words, a voter registration blank from a northern state was used. Sixty-thousand persons signed up in less than three months. We presented our registration books to the Credentials Committee. Both the facts and the law were ably represented by our attorney, Joseph Rauh, Jr., who was also a member of the Credentials Committee.

No one could say that we were a renegade group. We had tried to work within the structure of the state Party. In fact, we were not only trying to be included in the state Party, but we also sought to insure that the state Party would remain loyal to the candidates of the National Democratic Party in November. We attended precinct meetings in several parts of Mississippi.

In eight precincts in six different counties, we went to polling stations before the time legally designated for the precinct meeting, 10:00 A.M., but were unable to find any evidence of a meeting. Some officials denied knowledge of any meeting; others claimed the meeting had already taken place. In these precincts we proceeded to hold our own meetings and elected our own delegates to the county conventions.

In six different counties where we found the white precinct meetings, we were excluded from the meetings. In Hattiesburg we were told that we could not participate without poll tax receipts, despite the recent constitutional amendment, outlawing such provisions.

In ten precincts in five different counties, we were allowed to attend meetings but were restricted from exercising full rights; some were not allowed to vote; some were not allowed to nominate delegates from the floor; others were not allowed to choose who tallied the votes. No one could say that we had not tried. We had no alternative but to form a State Party that would include everyone.

So sixty-eight delegates came from Mississippi—black, white, maids, ministers, carpenters, farmers, painters, mechanics, schoolteachers, the young, the old—they were ordinary people but each had an extraordinary story to tell. And they could tell the story! The Saturday before the convention began, they presented their case to the Credentials Committee, and through television, to the nation and to the world. No human being confronted with the truth of our testimony could remain indifferent to it. Many tears fell. Our position was valid and our cause was just.

But the word had been given. The Freedom Party was to be seated without voting rights as honored guests of the Convention. The Party caucused and rejected the proposed "compromise." The slow and now frantic machinery of the administration was grinding against itself. President Johnson had given Senator Humphrey the specific task of dealing with us. They were desperately seeking ways to seat the regular Mississippi delegation without any show of disunity. The administration needed time!

Sunday evening, there was a somewhat secret meeting held at the Deauville Hotel, for all Negro delegates. The M.F.D.P. was not invited but was there. In a small, crowded, dark room with a long table and a blackboard, some of the most prominent Negro politicians in the country gave the "word", one by one. Then an old man seated in a soft chair struggled slowly to his feet. It was the black dean of politics, Congressman Charles Dawson of Chicago.

Unsteady in his voice, he said exactly what the other "leaders" had said: (1) We must nominate and elect Lyndon B. Johnson for President in November; (2) we must register thousands of Negroes to vote; and (3) we must follow leadership—adding, "we must respect womanhood"—and sat down.

With that a little woman, dark and strong, Mrs. Annie Devine from Canton, Mississippi, standing near the front, asked to be heard. The Congressman did not deny her. She began to speak.

"We have been treated like beasts in Mississippi. They shot us down like animals." She began to rock back and forth and her voice quivered. "We risk our lives coming up here . . . politics must be corrupt if it don't care none about people down there . . . these politicians sit in positions and forget the people put them there." She went on, crying between each sentence, but right after her witness, the meeting was adjourned.

What a nightmare were they having? Here we were in a life-death grip, wrestling with the best political strategists in the country. We needed only eleven votes for a minority report from the Credentials Committee. They postponed their report three times; a sub-committee was working around the clock. If there had been a vote in the Credentials Committee on Saturday, we would have probably had four times as many votes as we needed; Sunday, two times as many; and as late as Tuesday, we still had ten delegates committed to call for the minority report. We had ten states' delegations on record as supporting us. We had at least six persons on the Credentials Committee itself who attended our caucus to help determine the best strategy. We had over half of the press at our disposal. We were the issue, the only issue at that convention! But the black leadership at the convention went the way of the "black" dean's maxim: "Follow leadership." The word had been given.

The Freedom Party had made its position clear, too. They had come to the Convention to be seated in the place of the all-white Party from Mississippi but they were willing to compromise. A compromise was suggested by Congressman Edith Green (D.-Ore.), a member of the Credentials Committee. It was acceptable to the Freedom Party and could have been the minority report: (1) Everyone would be subjected to a loyalty oath, both the Freedom Party and the Mississippi regular party; (2) Each delegate who took the oath would be seated and the votes would be divided proportionally. It was minimal; the Freedom Party would accept no less.

The administration countered with another compromise. It had five points: (1) The all-white Party would take the oath and be seated; (2) The Freedom Democratic Party would be welcomed as honored guests of the Convention; (3) Dr. Aaron Henry and Rev. Edwin King, Chairman and National Committeeman of the Freedom Democratic Party respectively, would be given delegate status in a special category of "delegates at large;" (4) The Democratic National Committee would obligate states by 1968 to select and certify delegates through a process without regard to race, creed, color or national origin; and (5) The Chairman of the National Democratic Committee would establish a special committee to aid the states in meeting standards set for the 1968 Convention and that a report would be made to the National Democratic Committee and be available for the next Convention and its committees.

The "word" had come down for the last time. We had begun to lose support in the Credentials Committee. This came mainly as a result of a squeeze play by the administration.

It was Tuesday morning when the Freedom Democratic Party delegation was hustled to its meeting place, the Union Temple Baptist Church. You could cut through the tension; it was so apparent. People were touchy and on edge. It had been a long fight; being up day and night, running after delegations, following leads, speaking, answering politely, always aggressive, always moving. Now, one of the most important decisions of the convention had to be made.

At one o'clock, it was reported that a group from the M.F.D.P. had gone to talk with representatives of the administration and a report was given; it was the five-point compromise. This was also the majority report from the Credentials Committee. There were now seven hours left for sixty-eight people to examine the compromise, think about it, accept or reject it, propose the appropriate action, and do what was necessary to implement it. The hot day dragged on; there were speeches and speeches and talk and talk—Dr. Martin Luther King, Bayard Rustin, Senator Wayne Morse, Congressman Edith Green, Jack Pratt, James Farmer, James Forman, Ella Baker, Bob Moses. Some wanted to accept the compromise and others did not. A few remained neutral and all voiced total support whatever the ultimate decision. But time had made the decision. The day was fast spent when discussion was opened to the delegation.

The administration had succeeded in baiting us into extended discussion and this was the end. We had no time to sift through over five thousand delegates and alternates, through ninety-eight Credentials Committee members who could have been anywhere in the ocean for all we knew.

The proposal was rejected by the Freedom Democratic Delegation; we had come through another crisis with our minds depressed and our hearts and hands unstained. Again we had not bowed to the "massa." We were asserting a moral declaration to this country that the political mind must be concerned with much more than the expedient; that there are real issues in this country's politics and "race" is one.

One can logically move from this point to others. First of all, the problem of "race" in this country cannot be solved without political adjustment. We must consider the masters of political power at this point and acknowledge that the blacks are not trusted with this kind of power for this is real power. This is how our meat-making and money-making and dress-making and love-making is regulated. A readjustment must be made. One hundred counties where blacks outnumber whites in the South need an example for the future. The real question is whether America is willing to pay its dues. We are not only demanding meat and bread and a job but we are also demanding power, a share in power! Will we share power in this country together in reconciliation or, out of frustration, take a share of power and show it, or the need for it, in rioting and blood?

The manipulation of power in our homeland is in white hands. The white majority controls the decision-making process here. At President Johnson's "coronation" in Atlantic City there were no blacks with power to challenge the position of the administration. Moreover, there was opposition by blacks to any attempt to wield power against the administrative position. There was no black group supporting us; they had no power; they could show no power. But they had positions of power. One would suspect that it is part of the system to give positions meaningless labels and withhold the real power. This is the story of the bond between our country and its black children.

In the South and North, the black man is losing confidence in the intentions of the Federal Government. The case of Byron de la Beckwith is an example of what frustrates our people in this connection. The Klansmen freed in Georgia are another. Both can be explained but the emotions which they aroused in the Negro in this country cannot be explained away. The seating of the Mississippi Freedom Democratic Party would have gone a long way toward restoring the faith in the intentions of our government for many who believe that the Federal Government is a white man. Many Negroes believe that the government has no intention of sharing power with blacks. We can see through the "token." We have had a name for a white man's Negro ever since any white man named one. We want much more than "token" positions or even representations. We want power for our people. We want it out of the country's respect for the ideals of America and love for its own people. We need to be trusted, each for his own worth; this is why we are not chanting everlasting praises for the civil rights bill. We remember all the bills before. In fact, we remember the reconstruction period. This time, we will be our own watchdogs on progress. We will not trade one slavery for another.

Secondly we refuse to accept total responsibility for the conditions of race relations in this country. At the convention we were repeatedly told to be "responsible;" that Goldwater would benefit from our actions. We were told that riots in Harlem and Rochester and Jersey City and Philadelphia must stop. "Responsible" leaders have gotten up and called moratoriums in response to directives to be "responsible." The country is being hurt by the riots, we are told admonishingly.

Who can make jobs for people in our society? Who runs our society? Who plans the cities? Who regulates the tariff? Who makes the laws? Who interprets the law? Who holds the power? Let them be responsible! They are at fault who have not alleviated the causes which make men express their feelings of utter despair and hopelessness. Our society is famous for its white-washing, buck-passing tactics. That is one reason the Mississippi Freedom Democratic Party could not accept the administration's compromise. It was made to look like something and it was nothing. It was made to pacify the blacks in this country. It did not work. We refused to adopt a "victory." We could have accepted the compromise, called it a victory and gone back to Mississippi, carried on the shoulders of millions of Negroes across the country as their champions. But we love the ideals of our country; they mean more than a moment of victory. We are what we are—hungry, beaten, unvictorious, jobless, homeless, but thankful to have the strength to fight. This is honesty, and we refuse to compromise here. It would have been a lie to accept that particular compromise. It would have said to blacks across the nation and the world that we share the power, and that is a lie! The "liberals" would have felt great relief for a job well done. The Democrats would have laughed again at the segregationist Republicans and smiled that their own "Negroes" were satisfied. That is a lie! We are a country of racists with a racist heritage, a racist economy, a racist language, a racist religion, a racist philosophy of living, and we need a naked confrontation with ourselves. All the lies of television and radio and the press cannot save us from what we really are . . . black or white.

It is only now that a voice is being heard in our land. It is the voice of the poor; it is the tongue of the underprivileged; it is from the lips of the desperate. This is a voice of utter frankness: the white man knows that he has deceived himself for his own purposes, yet he continues to organize his own humiliation and ours.

We have no political panaceas. We will not claim that responsibility either. But we do search for a way of truth.

Grains of Salt (Union Theological Seminary), October 12, 1964

Oktibbeha County, Mississippi

by Jeremiah S. Gutman

MY client was Charley Taylor, an eighteen-year-old Negro freedom worker who had been forced off the road by a pickup truck. The driver of the truck had then proceeded to find a highway patrolman, with whom he lodged a complaint of reckless driving against Taylor, who was promptly arrested. He was out on bail posted for him by COFO. The witnesses, local workers and an out-of-state summer volunteer, passengers in his car, substantiated Taylor's story and one of them even claimed to have recognized the pickup truck driver as a local red-neck who had harassed rights workers in the past. The fact that Taylor's car was integrated at the time and the incident occurred after the pickup truck had followed Taylor for some miles made it likely that it was not an accident. By the time we arrived at court, the witnesses, including the defendant, had a pretty fair idea of what to expect and what would be expected of them.

Crimes in Mississippi are either felonies or misdemeanors, distinguished by the severity of potential sentence. Traffic offenses, from improper parking to reckless driving, are misdemeanors. One accused of a misdemeanor is first brought to trial in the local court presided over by a justice of the peace. These men are not legally required to meet any particular educational or other standards, and I know of not one who is a lawyer. Court is held wherever their business is located—in gasoline stations, grocery markets or any other kind of store. In the crossroad towns and villages which are legally cities in Mississippi, the mayors are automatically created justices by virtue of their offices.

Two minutes before 10:00 a.m. we pulled into the parking area of the gasoline station where court was to be held. A group of some eight or ten young white men plus a uniformed sheriff, a highway patrolman and a few others were hanging around the entrance to the office. Taylor and the others waited near the cars. I made my way through the people who blocked the entrance into the courtroom. They made it as uncomfortable as possible by refusing to move in the slightest degree to make way for me and by following my tortuous progress through their phalanx with cold, hostile eyes. Once inside, I found a group of five or six men and one woman, all of whom stared at me without uttering a word of greeting and with stonily angry faces filled with contempt and hatred. I announced to the assembly in general that I was an attorney who had come to defend Charley Taylor. One of the men identified himself as the prosecutor and asked that I wait until the judge was ready. The small room was littered with windshield cleaners, fan belts, fuel additives and, as is usual in Mississippi service stations, boxes of shotgun shells and other ammunition. There were greasy rags, used spare parts, dirty tools and a few bald tires. The only furniture was two small chairs at a table from which all but a few grimy bolts had been removed to make way for a tattered desk pad, a few papers with oily thumb prints and a tin strongbox. The two glass exterior walls looked out, through petroleum product ads taped to the panes, on the pumps in front and the parking lot to the side. Everyone but the woman remained standing silently while we watched a man outside finish a sale of gasoline and wipe the windshield. Calling, "Hurry back and see us, you hear?" and wiping his oily hands on his uniform, His Honor entered his courtroom.

"You the lawyer I spoke with yesterday on the phone? I'm glad to see you're white. I done called your boy's name at ten o'clock and he weren't here so we forfeited his bail, found him guilty, fined him $200 and we was just fixing to get out a warrant for him. Ain't that Charley out there?"

I still had not even said good morning to the judge. I ostentatiously pulled out my pocket watch at the end of a gold chain hanging from my New York vest and asked the lady seated at the desk to please make a record that it was 30 seconds past 10:00 and that I had been waiting several minutes already and that, therefore, any default had been premature. There was a babel of voices as to accuracy of timepieces. I managed to silence the folks by firmly intoning over it, "Unless this matter is reopened and my client afforded a fair trial,

I shall be compelled to force this court to produce for the inspection of the Federal courts all its records of defaults taken since it was created to determine whether, even if the court's clock is correct and I was one minute late, similar actions have been taken with other defendants so that the degree of equal protection of the law provided by this court can be examined." The prosecutor thereupon allowed as how the judge had acted correctly and had no need to give ground, but they wanted to show that everyone was entitled to equal justice in their court, no matter whether he was white, black or green.

The judge sat down behind his cluttered desk on the vacant chair next to his wife. He announced that trial could proceed, and the prosecutor thereupon asked the sheriff to bring in "the boys." The boys turned out to be six of the young men who had been blocking the doorway. I asked who they were and was told that my client had demanded a jury at the time of his arrest and that these were the jurors. (The trial before a justice of the peace is ordinarily without a jury unless the defendant demands one, as Taylor had done.) I inquired as to how many served on a jury and was informed by the prosecutor that all six would serve.

I replied, "I respectfully urge upon this Court that I am entitled to an opportunity to question the jurors as to their ability to render an impartial verdict. If we are to have a trial by jury, I demand a selection from a larger group properly drawn from the entire community so that I may select, in conjunction with the prosecutor, six who are qualified in accordance with the laws of the State of Mississippi, the United States of America and the Constitutions of both."

The judge said, "Now, don't you trouble yourself none about that, son; we done already took care of it so you can just get on with the trial." I refused to permit the prosecutor to proceed and made some of the more obvious objections to drumhead justice and kangaroo courts. Meanwhile, the defendant had been brought in by the highway patrolman who had made the arrest, and by now the tiny room was jammed by participants, jurors, defendant, complainant, sheriff, patrolman and unidentified people whom I did not know but knew not to be on my side. All but the judge and his wife stood crowded together. I finally succeeded in convincing the judge and prosecutor that the complainant, the state highway patrolman, the sheriff, the jurors and the miscellaneous people be cleared from the room while the prosecutor, judge and I discussed the problem. They all went except the sheriff and the highway patrolman, who said they were officers of the state and had a right to be there. The complainant then came back and the judge deputized him as a clerk of the court so that he could stay, too.

My objections to this procedure were overruled and we got down to the next important business, which was my right to practice in the court. The prosecutor advised me that I could not practice unless I had with me two members of the local bar who requested the court to permit me to practice. This, of course, is a perverse reversal of the true situation, which is that an out-of-state attorney may practice unless his qualifications are challenged in a rather technical way by two members of the local bar. I most respectfully disagreed with my learned colleague and pointed out that my understanding of the law was the reverse of his. He stated that he was merely testing to see if I knew the Mississippi law but that I certainly could not practice in that court except for the fact that he would ask His Honor to waive my disqualification and permit the trial to proceed.

Trial in a justice of the peace court is in many ways an unnecessary formality. If you are convicted in that court, you have the right to appeal to the county court. In this second court, the appeal is in reality a trial *de novo*, or from scratch, as though the first trial, of which no minutes are kept, had not occurred. A defendant in the justice court charged with an offense in connection with his civil rights activity (such as trespass or picketing) or accused of an unrelated offense (such as reckless driving) may plead not guilty. He is certain to be convicted. However, there is no legal distinction upon appeal between a plea of not guilty or a plea of *nolo contendere* (or "no contest"). One advantage of a *nolo* plea is that the proceeding is over quickly and the crowd (including jurors) which may have gathered for the spectacle of a trial may be left before it grows into a mob. The chief advantage of a plea of not guilty is that it forces the prosecutor to put on his witnesses and disclose his case without compelling the defendant to do anything but listen and perhaps learn something that may be useful at the second trial upon the appeal. Attempts to keep a record of what the prosecution witnesses say in the JP court (in order to be able to impeach their veracity if they are better "prepared" for the second trial) have backfired into charges of perjury against defense witnesses for allegedly lying about what they heard at the first trial. Effective, even devastating, cross-examination of prosecution witnesses on the first trial has not been known to result in acquittals but has certainly educated prosecutors as to what their witnesses had better say or avoid on the second trial. From the point of view of an attorney defending such a case, the ideal is a plea of not guilty, so that the prosecution witnesses go on and are heard, followed by permission to change the plea to *nolo contendere* so that the defense need not disclose what it may have up its sleeve or put on any witnesses who might be exposed to possible later perjury charges and extrajudicial pressures and harassment.

In the case of Charley Taylor, I was interested above all in speed. The sooner I got him and his friends, including me, out of that tense scene, the better I would like it. As I looked out at the glowering jurors staring through the glass walls of the courtroom at the discussion inside and looked beyond them at the pickup trucks parked at the side of the station with the rifles and shotguns in the rear window-racks, my decision to get this procedure over as fast as possible was reinforced.

Since the prosecutor had withdrawn his objection to my status as attorney for defendant and the room was relatively empty, I adopted a very frank manner with the judge. Of all those present, besides the accused and myself—the prosecutor, the judge, the judge's wife, the two police officers and the deputized complaining driver—only the prosecutor had any but the remotest idea of what I was saying and, as I went on, ostensibly talking to the judge, all of them looked with more and more concern to the prosecutor for a clue of how to react.

My goal was to be permitted to withdraw defendant's jury demand and not-guilty plea and to interpose a *nolo contendere* plea, if I could be sure Taylor would get a small fine and no jail sentence. My method was to exploit what I suspected to be the legal ignorance on the part of all concerned.

"Your Honor," I said, "if we are to proceed with this trial

before you and this jury today, I shall, and do now, interpose objections to the legality of the procedures by which you and the prosecuting attorney were elected; the manner in which the jury panel and jurors were selected; the exclusion from this room of the friends of the defendant; the fact that you have addressed Mr. Taylor by his first name in an insulting manner; the prejudicial atmosphere created by your action prior to my arrival; the fact that you have effectively disqualified yourself by making the complaining witness your clerk; the fact that at least some of the jurors are armed; the fact. . . ."

At this point, the prosecutor, not the judge, interrupted me by, "Well, that's alright, Mr. Gutman, you can make all those objections, but we can go right ahead anyway."

"In addition, sir, I warn you right now, that I regard this entire procedure and all participating in it, from the moment the complainant ran defendant off the road, as part of a conspiracy to deprive defendant and all the passengers in his automobile of their Federal civil rights and I intend immediately upon leaving here today to commence an action for damages against each and every one of you in the Federal court and to file a criminal complaint with the FBI and Department of Justice Civil Rights Division."

"Now, there's no need to get so worked up over a little old driving ticket. Why, we wouldn't deprive Charley here of no rights except a few dollars fine for not driving too good and that hardly seems worth all the fuss you're talking about."

I immediately asked him how much of a fine he had in mind and, since it was within reason, I agreed to let Taylor plead *nolo* and end the case right there. Within the next few minutes the arithmetic was completed, bail had been refunded, the nominal fine had been paid, an appeal bond was posted, a receipt taken and the change pocketed by defendant to be forwarded to Jackson COFO.

The formalities over, Charley Taylor and I left the courtroom together. Side by side, we threaded through the jurors and their friends who were again massed in the doorway. At the far side of the service station parking lot, near the cars, were the integrated group who had come with us, awaiting the result. The judge plucked at my sleeve to stop me as I emerged from the group of immobile, glaring jurors. I told Taylor to keep walking to the cars while I stopped to see what His Honor wanted.

The judge said, "I see you brought some of your friends to see the show. I hope they ain't disappointed."

I assured the judge that no one was disappointed and that we only wished to be on our way so that we could get back to work. The judge said, "I sure hope that you ain't going to say we don't know how to entertain guests what come to see a show." He pointed toward a gully or cut through which railroad tracks passed, behind and about thirty feet below the level on which we were standing. He continued, "These boys here (indicating the jurors) are from our football team and they sure would admire to play a game with your boy. We call it Dropkick the Nigger."

There was much hilarious laughter as I resumed my walk to the automobiles and signaled everyone to get going. The first car had pulled out and the car in which I was riding next to the driver was just about to complete its U-turn out of the parking space when the judge walked up to the side on which I was seated. The highway patrolman and several of the jurors had come forward and were blocking our path of withdrawal when His Honor put his hands upon the side of the car, which had been forced to stop. He said, "That'll be two dollars for parkin', Mister." I said, "I'll pay it, but I promise you I will get it back with interest." He laughed along with all his buddies who stepped aside as he waved us out.

Sometimes in these brushes with Mississippi justice a lawyer gets the feeling that, just perhaps, he is making the local community think and reappraise their actions and attitudes. The positive results of this case include the fact that a young man who would probably have received a jail sentence managed to get off without one, but more important, he, his friends, his neighbors, and many who will hear the tale without ever meeting the people, will have learned that not every white man is an enemy, that the law can be their friend, that they are not alone, that, having been urged to undertake action sure to arouse retaliation, they are not abandoned to face Mr. Charley alone.

from *Southern Justice* (1965)

Personal Terror in Mississippi

by Christopher S. Wren

I HAVE been thoroughly scared three times in my life. The first time was on a hunt for Communist infiltrators in peacetime Korea. The second was when the parachute twisted on my first Army night jump. And the third was on a night ride this summer in Mississippi.

LOOK photographer Tom Koeniges and I had been down in the Delta cotton country, covering the summer volunteers on the preceding pages. The press, particularly from the North, is not welcome in Mississippi. But this trip had been worse than my two previous ones. Cold suspicion became outright hostility. When we paid for a meal, the change was flung back at us. Our car was followed, and the license number copied down. The phones, we suspected, were tapped. We were called "nigger-lovers," "troublemaking bastards," and told "go back where you came from."

One hot evening, as Tom and I left a Negro rally in Ruleville, a white Valiant with three men inside followed us out of town. I had seen it earlier, cruising past the rally. Then the headlights vanished, and we felt better. But as we entered Doddsville, five miles south on Route 49W, the headlights suddenly reappeared. Tom stopped at the traffic light for four precious seconds. He quickly turned left on the shortcut to Greenwood, Route 442. I looked back at the deserted intersection, and saw the white Valiant turn after us without slowing.

We careened down the empty road, the gas pedal to the floor. In the moonlight, the flat cotton fields gave no place to hide. Draped over the wheel, Tom pushed our Ford to 80, then 90 mph. But he had to brake at each curve, and the Valiant, guiding on our taillights, edged closer. Its driver must have known the roads.

We debated why they were after us. The chase had gone

too far—more than 15 miles—to be just a warning. Perhaps they wanted to run us off the road or, as in other incidents, pull us from the car and beat us up. "We could take on three of them," Tom said. But I had been warned that night riders carried guns to fortify their courage. We didn't want to be two more debits in the sum of Mississippi lawlessness. Our speedometer nudged 95.

We must have driven the lonely 14 miles from Doddsville to Schlater in less than 10 minutes. When we slowed for the first cluster of houses, the Valiant caught up. It began to edge us off the narrow road. Tom swung our Ford back into the middle. The white car could not pass us without going into a ditch. Its lights blinked frantically.

We argued about stopping at a plantation, but decided we could expect no help there. In town, the white car dropped back. They would not want to take us where people might see. We thought of jumping out and running into the woods. But if they had guns, we would be targets in the moonlight. We had to keep driving.

As we left Schlater, Tom accelerated. He ran the stop signs and spun onto Route 49E, the Greenwood road. The Valiant squealed after us.

Tom, topping 80 mph, cut in front of a bus, then a truck. We hoped our speed would attract the police. But they must have all been off patrolling the Negro freedom rallies that night.

We lost the Valiant as we passed car after car. With heavier oncoming traffic, it could not keep up. At Greenwood, we swung off the road and waited. The white car never came. "It's worse than Cyprus," said Tom, who a few months before had been shot at by both sides there.

The next morning, a sheriff who wrote down the license number I gave him told me the car was from another county. He quipped that we could take up judo to defend ourselves. A policeman told Tom the car just wanted to pass.

"At 95 miles an hour?" Tom said.

The FBI agent in the sunglasses wasn't interested. And the rental agency would not exchange our Louisiana Ford for a car with local plates. "Afraid of getting shot?" he asked.

We faced a choice. We could give up our story and go

home, or we could take our chances on the roads. If vigilantes had chased us, they would try again. That afternoon, Tom went out and bought a 12-gauge shotgun with six shells.

We kept the gun disassembled in our car trunk during the day. At night, we put it together on the front seat. I don't know whether word got around, but we were not chased again.

When a reporter goes into Mississippi, the questions he asks can suddenly become personal. Why does a white official parry your inquiries with defensive arrogance? Why does a Negro sharecropper welcome you with a glass of cold water, because he has nothing more to give?

And why must you ride through Mississippi after dark with a 12-gauge shotgun on your lap?

Look, September 8, 1964

A Life for a Vote

by John Hersey

To protect the men and women of this story from reprisals, most names and geographic locations have been changed. The events described are literal fact.

ONE April morning last year 17 Negroes, country people, crossed the courthouse square in Athens, Miss., footing stiffly along, conscious of eyes on them, and approached the north door of the county seat, a brooding building of dark red brick with spiked turrets at its corners and a golden-domed cupola with a four-faced clock, which said it was half-past nine. These were cotton-and-soybean farmers from the vicinity of Noonday, 13 men and four women.

Out in front were Randoman Tort, known to Negroes in the county as "a broad-speaking man"—or, as the local rednecks would vehemently put it, a right uppity nigger—and Reverend O. O. Burring, with a straight, cautious carriage, and taciturn Albert Parrisot, who belonged to the N.A.A.C.P., and bear-bodied James Drake, president of the P.T.A. at the Noonday rural school near where the 17 lived. Empria Meeks had her two-year-old, Erma Jean, in her arms, because all her other 11 children were in school or gone, and there was no one to leave the girl with. Mrs. Tulip Caesar, a settled-aged lady, was with the group, and Meshak Lewis, and Billy Head and Elzoda Lee.

And with them, among the others, was Varsell Pleas, a solidly built 44-year-old farmer, a rather aloof man who walked with his head canted slightly back. His brown cheeks seemed festooned up into pronounced bulges, perhaps partly because of a habit he had of pursing his lips in thought before every utterance of speech; the whites of his eyes were yellowed from years of blown loess and bright sun, and the right eye had a disconcerting outward look, ever so slight, a minor cast. Pleas was not among the first, but as the group moved up the concrete path to the courthouse he found himself bunched with those who had been. He slowed his pace. He knew the gravity of what he and his friends were doing. They were putting their lives on the line. They were colored, and they wanted to qualify to vote in one of the roughest corners in all the South—in Ittabala County, Miss.

Varsell Pleas had learned through many hard years that the vote is the real issue in Mississippi. School integration, job opportunities, cotton allotments, social mixing, mongrelization —all other problems, all slogans, all shibboleths give way to the issue of the vote, which is the means to power. In a few counties like Ittabala, the vote is in truth a life-and-death matter, and the reason is twofold. In Ittabala County, as elsewhere in the South ever since the 17th century, Negro labor has made possible a way of life the whites do not wish to give up. And in Ittabala County Negroes outnumber whites 19,100 to 8,200. In all the time since the Mississippi Constitution of 1890 was promulgated, only 26 Negroes have had their names entered in the book of qualified voters in the red courthouse in Athens; about 4,500 whites are registered today. The whites of Ittabala County mean to keep it that way; the Negroes intend to register.

The 17 had slowed down on the path for good cause: On the steps before them, in uniform, armed with a pistol and a billy, stood Sheriff Haralson R. Lee, who is the soul of the county's law and is not given to budging.

Pleas heard one of the Negroes at the front say, "Move on forward, folks."

"Hold on there," Pleas then heard the sheriff call out. "None of that goddamned forward stuff around here. What do you people want?"

Randoman Tort, whom the sheriff knew, now spoke up. "Mr. Lee, we only come to register."

"Register for what, Tort?"

"Register to vote."

"Who you fixing to vote for?"

"We might could vote for you, Mr. Lee, if you was running." Tort smiled as he said this, perhaps to signal deference, perhaps sensing the irony of the offer.

"No use to vote for me. I already been elected." The sheriff gave back the smile of the man who always has the last word. "All right, Tort," he then said, snapping off the good humor, "you all disperse yourselves and go on around to the south side of the courthouse and stop under that shade tree. Don't go in no big crowd, go in twos."

So the 17 did that, and they stood in hushed pairs and threes under the elm tree at the northwest corner of the courthouse yard for a good while, waiting for something to happen. Silent in the sunlight near them, at the head of a slender shaft of stone, a stone man stood, a beautiful young soldier of the War Between the States, at whose unveiling, on December 4, 1905, Miss Annabell Tull of the C. R. Rankin Chapter of the United Daughters of the Confederacy spoke these words in dedication: ". . . From his hands came down to you a wealth of priceless heirlooms: patriotism passed down from his forefathers who fought for rights in 1776, the same true patriotism that shone in 'Sixty-one to 'Sixty-five, heroism that did not fade in all the many changes from wealth to poverty, nobility that rose above defeat, faith in the right, generosity, courage, every trait of a people that make a nation great."

At length the latter-day vessel of those valued heirlooms, Sheriff Haralson R. Lee, came out to the tree, put his hands on his hips, and in what seemed to Pleas a very loud voice said, "All right, now, who wants to go first?"

The Negroes exchanged looks. At first no one seemed to want to volunteer.

Then Tort stepped forward and said he would be first. The sheriff directed him to the office on the right just inside the south door of the courthouse, and Tort walked away.

For two hours nothing happened, and Pleas wondered what the officials inside could be doing with Tort. Pleas knew that the actual process of registration should only take about 15 minutes, long enough to fill out a form with 21 questions. This form was the Mississippi-white-man's means of keeping the Negro from voting. The black man had been fundamentally disfranchised in Mississippi under the state constitution that was adopted in 1890, at a time when most Mississippi Negroes were illiterate, by a clause requiring that every voter should be able to read any section of the state constitution *or* "be able to understand the same when read to him" *or* "give a reasonable interpretation thereof." In 1955, in the angry aftermath of the Supreme Court decision on school desegregation, the state legislature, taking into account the spreading literacy of southern Negroes, passed a bill requiring a written test for registration, on which the applicant must demonstrate that he could read *and* write a clause of the constitution *and* understand it. Whether the clause had been rightly understood was entirely up to the subjective judgment of the registrar, who in Ittabala County was Circuit Clerk James Z. Williams.

At about noon Tort came out and said he had not yet seen the circuit clerk. The lady in the office had said Mr. Williams was busy in court; Tort could sit and wait. Just now, two hours later, the lady had said, "Well, I'm going to dinner now. You can come back after." And he had said, "Yes, ma'am, I'll be back after dinner." So the 17 scattered. Pleas went down with some others to a place kept by a Chinaman on Chickasaw Street to get something to eat.

By the time the circuit clerk's office reopened, the candidates had reassembled under the tree. During the dinner hour policemen had been brought in from other parts of the county; there were now some 10 or 15 uniformed and armed men standing in the shade of the courthouse near the tree, among them the familiar Noonday officer, Town Marshal L. O. Trent. Again there was a long wait; finally Sheriff Lee beckoned to James Drake to go in, and he did.

Standing under the tree, waiting again, Varsell Pleas could not help seeing that the group was causing a sensation in the town. People had come to watch all around one side of the square. Though court was supposed to be standing, white faces appeared in the courthouse windows; Pleas counted nine heads in one window. He wondered, Could Mr. Williams really be so busy? Pleas hated this building. He had lived just outside Athens for three years, from 1944 through 1946, and he remembered two cases that had come to trial here that last year. In the spring a Negro boy named Henry Larkin, crossing a street on a bicycle in Bula, nearby, had bumped into a white man, who had shot him dead; in court the defendant had said that the boy had ridden the bike at him after he had bawled the boy out, and the accused had been acquitted by a jury in less than half an hour. Later that summer four white men had been charged with whipping a Negro man, Brutus Simpson, to death, because he had allegedly stolen some whiskey, and with putting his body in a lake down in the next county; the men had admitted having flogged Simpson but had denied having hurt him enough to kill him, and a jury had acquitted them in 10 minutes.

In midafternoon the Negroes under the tree saw Drake leave the courthouse, but he was not allowed by the policemen to rejoin the group. About an hour later Tort was admitted to take the test; he was out again rather quickly, and he, too, was kept from the others. At 4:30 Sheriff Lee told those who remained that the office was closed, there wouldn't be any more tests that day.

It took three days to test 17 people. The second and third days the police were out in even stronger force than on the first day—at times there were nearly 20 law-enforcement men on hand. Pleas wondered, Whom were they protecting, and from what? The cops were given chairs against the building. The Negroes were kept waiting under the tree.

Midway through the third morning Varsell Pleas's turn came, and he entered the building. At first the circuit clerk's office, with a long counter thrown athwart the entranceway, seemed dark as a crow's throat after the brightness out-of-doors. The circuit clerk was in, but Pleas was told to take a seat. After a few minutes Williams came out and said to the lady in the office, "I have to step across here a minute, be back directly." He was gone an hour. Pleas sat tranquilly; it had long since become obvious to the Negroes that a stretch-out was on, and Pleas knew there was no use getting upset.

Finally the clerk returned, and he beckoned Pleas to the counter and asked him his name. Calling Pleas by his given name from then on, the circuit clerk asked: Why did Varsell want to register? Had he been advised? Had anybody been teaching him? Had he been going to meetings? Were other Negroes from Noonday going to try to register?

A lifetime of practice went into Pleas's noncommittal answers.

Williams took Pleas into a very small room across the hall,

scarcely more than a closet, with a single dim bulb hanging from the high ceiling, and handed him the registration form and assigned him Section 76 of the constitution to copy and explain: "In all elections by the legislature the members shall vote viva voce, and the vote shall be entered on the journals." Pleas had been studying the constitution for several weeks, and he knew several of the 28 sections of Article 3, the state's bill of rights, by heart, but there were 285 clauses in the whole document, and he had never happened to find out the meaning of the phrase "viva voce." Since then he has often wondered how many of the county's registered whites know its meaning.

When Pleas handed in the test, the lady in the office told him to come back in 30 days and find out whether he had passed or not.

A policeman at the courthouse door told him to move on away, stay clear of them niggers under the tree.

Pleas said he had to take some of them home in his pickup.

The constable said, "That don't make no difference. Stay clear, hear?"

So Pleas waited on the other side of the square rest of the day to take his friends home.

Now the sense of danger came strongly out. The Athens *Courier* proclaimed to all the county the names of the 17 Negroes who had attempted to register. The day after the paper appeared, the white owner of the land east of Pleas's, an electrical-equipment dealer from Joshua City, named Rainsford, who did not live on the land but rented it out, and who had long before told Pleas he could fence a small plot for a table garden, drove to Pleas's house, which is in open country six miles northeast of Noonday center.

"Varsell, take that fence down."

"You fixing to sell that land, Mr. Rainsford?"

"Sold it. Sold it to the Government."

"You sold that little old piece to the Government, Mr. Rainsford?"

"Never mind, you just take that fence down."

"Mr. Rainsford, me and my whole family's right busy chopping cotton"—the Negroes' expression for hoeing—"but if you could give me two, three days, I could get that done."

"That'd be all right, Varsell. Just see you do it."

That was the beginning. Two days later Constable Trent came up from Noonday and said, "Varsell, if you should happen to need me for anything, you just call on me. Anytime."

Pleas recognized this as the time-honored offer of protection that served, by underlining the danger, to intimidate.

At the regular citizenship meeting at the Baptist church called Shore of Peace the next Wednesday night, one of the men, in the spirit of the Mississippi state motto, *Virtute et Armis*, "By Virtue and Arms," urged all those who had tried to register to get up on their praying and to have their guns clean and ready.

When Pleas got home, he checked over his three shotguns and his rifle—weapons with which, for years, he and his three older sons had hunted small game in fall and winter months, to supplement the family larder.

One evening about nine o'clock, in the next week, a car drove in by Pleas's house and a white man with a beer can in his hand walked across the headlights. Varsell jumped out one of the back windows and looped around in the dark through his pasture to try to see the car. At the side door the man asked Mrs. Pleas if Varsell was home.

"He was here a minute ago," said Mrs. Pleas, who didn't like the way the man waved his beer can around. "He ain't in the house. Meshak Lewis, he was here a few minutes ago. Varsell was right out here talking to him. Children"—Mrs. Pleas called out at large to any of her 11 children (Varsell Jr., 19, Orsmond, 18, Robert, 17, Cleontha, 15, Pomp, 14, Ervin, 13, James, 12, Edward, 11, Icie, 9, Sussie, 7, and Larnie, 5) who might be within earshot—"where'd your daddy go?" Silence from the children. Actually Varsell Jr. and Orsmond had also gone out a far window, each with a shotgun; Orsmond said later that "if they'd have jumped Daddy," he himself would have aimed at tires first.

"He must have gone up to Noonday."

"How long's he been gone?"

"Must've just left."

"What time'll he be back?"

"I really couldn't tell. He could be gone to Athens." Mrs. Pleas peered out at the car. "Won't you all come in and wait?

Ask your friends in." This was a formality, and both parties knew it; Mrs. Pleas was trying to find out all she could. But the man drove off. Varsell said he'd seen three others in the car.

A few days later—about two weeks after the registration attempt—word came from the domestic-help grapevine in Noonday that "they" were planning something for eight of the people who had tried to register, and Randoman Tort, whose house was near the main highway, Route 57, was first on the list; it was not known exactly what "they" had in mind.

The very next night after these warnings Tort got his. At about three in the morning a fire bomb was thrown in his house, which caught fire. He ran out with a Remington automatic .22 and, seeing two figures, fired at them, and they fired back. The attackers, apparently not having expected gunfire, ran off after having discharged several shots at Tort and into the house. With buckets of water from the hand pump in the yard, the Torts put out the fire.

The following day Tort called the FBI and the sheriff; both came and inspected the damage. That evening Sheriff Lee returned and arrested Tort for arson—for setting fire to his own house. He was in jail for two days and then was released on a $3000 bond. The charges against him were dropped when the case reached Jackson and the Justice Department took a strong hand in it. The involvement of out-of-state FBI in the Tort case apparently caused "them" to call off, at least for the time being, the other attacks they were rumored to have planned.

After Tort was cleared, Varsell Pleas went up to Athens and asked—knowing what the answer would be—whether he had been passed for registration. The lady in the office got out his application and she said, "No, Varsell, you didn't pass."

"Can you tell me, ma'am, just where I didn't pass?"

The lady gave both sides of the sheet a quick look, and she said, "No, it just says, 'Failed.' It doesn't say why. You just failed, that's all."

"Yes, ma'am," said Varsell Pleas, and went home. Not one of the 17 had passed.

After these events, "getting the box," as he and his friends called qualifying to vote, became, more than ever, the central goal of Varsell Pleas's life. He was now 44 years old, he owned his own farm, his older children were leaving home, and he had irrevocably put everything he was and had in jeopardy for this single cause. He felt himself prepared, by the education and experiences he had had, to vote—fully as competent, in his own estimation, as many whites he knew.

He was born on July 16, 1920, near Indianola, Sunflower County, in the rich Delta, seventh child in a family of nine, son of a sharecropper who had made 10 crops for a planter named Spurlack. On that place, as Pleas tells it, the bell rang at foreday, and the boss sat in a chair at the gear house with a leather strop in his hand for the blacks who turned up late. The croppers got six bits a day, and the owner furnished $15 worth of food and clothing a month at his plantation commissary. A family with numerous children to work in the fields might clear $300 when the crop was in; this had to get them through to the following spring.

When Varsell was eight, his father, having raked his shin on a barbed-wire fence, contracted blood poisoning; a doctor cut off his leg to try to save him, but he died. Varsell's mother took her family to Joshua City to live with her father, an industrious man who rented a few acres "for the fourth dollar" —a quarter of what he cleared—from a white named Ratliff, a Freemason and a kind man. In younger years Granddaddy Archer had saved some money to buy mules by making bricks in dry kilns and "getting out" boards for covering houses. Varsell adored him. He taught his grandsons to fish for catfish and grunters and gars in the Delta lakes, and he told stories that his father had told him about slavery. In those Joshua City years Varsell was an everyday companion with a white boy, Jimmy Ratliff, with whom he milked cows and gathered eggs and went fishing, and Mrs. Ratliff helped Varsell with his lessons. He went to school through the seventh grade. He walked five miles to school and five miles back, and he remembers not the weariness but the roadsides fringed with dusty wildflowers—eyebright and pleurisy-root, maypop and spatterdock.

But then "things went out tough and hard"—the depression of the early '30's brought ferocious times for Granddaddy Archer, crowded on a small tenancy with his daughter's family, and in winter croker sacks did for shoes, and the diet was cornbread and sorghum syrup, over and over. In 1934 Varsell left this hardship and went to Jackson, where he found urban hardship even more squalid. He got a job at a white hotel, for one meal a day and six dollars a week and rare nickel tips, running errands on a bicycle, sweeping out the parlors, carrying out trash. He could live. He was 14, and salt fatmeat only cost a nickel a pound in those days, and you could get a 24-pound sack of flour for 40 cents. He even saved a few dollars. But it was not a life—not the kind of life his grandfather had showed him how to live.

In 1936 his mother wrote him from Leflore County to say that Granddaddy Archer had died, and she had married again, and that he should come up and help out his stepfather's farm. And so at 16 Varsell entered a career of cotton farming. He worked hard, sun to sun, and he learned what a man had to do.

Two years later, at 18, he married in haste and soon became a father; his stepfather loaned him $100 to buy a mule, and he found some land he could rent in the vicinity of Noonday, in Ittabala County. He has lived in Ittabala ever since.

Created in 1827, Ittabala County has always been a violent place. It has 795 square miles of good land on the border between the rich Delta and the loam-and-loess hills, land worth fighting for—and Choctaws, Chickasaws and Yazoos fought for it as it was stolen from them. The county has long had a large proportion of Negroes who own land; today 69 percent of the cultivated land is in Negro hands.

After his first crop Pleas cleared $250, and he bought a second mule. By 1941 he had saved enough to put the first installment down on a six-year-old Ford truck, and he began hauling stave blocks and pulpwood, and he was soon earning as much as $40 a week. Then his marriage went bad, and he moved west of Athens, where he rented, alone, a small farm in the hills. He was classified 1A in the draft, but, for some reason that he never understood, the draft board just didn't get to him.

In Athens, in his 23rd year, he met Holly Bell Chronister, a beautiful light-brown-skinned girl from outside of Joshua City, the daughter of capable people, a carpenter and a practical nurse, and herself better educated than most—"promoted to twelfth." She was spirited, emotional, hardworking and bitter-edged. Varsell married her, and the next year, while the announcers were talking on the radio about the invasion of Normandy, Varsell Jr. was born, and the next year Orsmond was born, and the next year Robert was born. Pleas needed a bigger place, and he found one he could rent near Noonday. Landing there changed his life.

Four years earlier, under authority of the Bankhead-Jones Farm Tenant Act of 1937, the New Deal's Resettlement Administration had bought a number of failing plantations in that area—Cincinnatus, Intention, Harper's, Yazoo, The Bogue, Persimmon Tree—and had set up a series of projects for Negroes, men just like Varsell Pleas, who had spent their lives as frequently moving tenants and sharecroppers in a restless search for a stable living. At first the projects were cooperatives and rentals; then, a year after Pleas began renting up nearer Noonday, the Farm Security Administration took them over and made long-term loans to the Negroes to enable them to buy plots of land of about 60 acres each. Pleas soon heard that the red-necks had nicknamed the federal projects Nigger Paradise, and that made him think they must be all right; he went to the FSA office and applied for a unit. But so many had already filed applications that the plots were all gone.

As time passed, "the projects," as the Negroes continued to call them, looked better and better, and Pleas decided to wait out a turn to join one. He worked hard and lived frugally, putting all he could save into building a small herd of Guernsey-Jersey cows. As the years went by, he saw the farmers on the projects begin to work with tractors; he was still mule-farming.

Eight years and five more children after his first application, Pleas got his chance. He heard of a farmer in The Bogue who had fallen behind in his payments, and Pleas arranged with the man and with the Farmers Home Administration, which had taken over the projects, to assume the farmer's indebtedness, $728, and to buy the farm, on a federal 40-year, 5 percent mortgage (the white man's banks in Athens charged Negroes 8 percent and 10 percent) for $6,104. To pay off the

other man's delinquency, he borrowed $460 from Holly
Bell's family and sold three cows. The FHA made him a five-
percent operating loan, with his chattels as securities, for
equipment, seed, fertilizer and pesticides, and he put up five
more cows as down payment on a small Ford tractor.

After these deals his herd, his show for years of sweat, had
dwindled, but for the first time in his life he was his own man.
He now had 59 acres of good, high loam-and-sand earth, with
no low swags or ditches with standing water, and no clayey
"buckshot" soil, and he had an industrious wife, and a tractor,
and a feeling, new and strange, that some white man or men
in Washington, D.C., were aware of him as a human entity.

Now came a time of building up. Since even the most industrious Mississippi Negro could not live on terms of equality with the Mississippi white, the project farmer turned to a
prestige of things. There was an approved order of purchases.
Pressure cooker first. Then, before the first summer was out,
refrigerator—$40 down, with three years to pay. Then, after
the first cotton-and-soybean crop had been sold and the FHA
interest of a little more than $300 had been paid in, a clothes-
washing machine. (Water for the washer came from a hand
pump in buckets and was heated in caldrons over a wood fire
in the yard.) And the next year—emblem of, and contributor
to, prosperity—a freezer, in which, after slaughter, cuts of
hogs, fowl and beef cattle could repose till needed for the
table. More and more, Varsell Pleas was building a life insulated from the whites, whom he saw only in stores. The
FHA even had a Negro supervisor. By his third year in the
project he had a total income of $10,000, and he paid off all
his debts on appliances, and he bought eight cows—money in
the bank.

Varsell Pleas, a Mississippi Negro, could not believe in the
long duration of good times, and sure enough, a turn for the
worse soon came. After the Supreme Court decision in *Brown
vs. Board of Education*, in May, 1954, the white men in the
state, who had long had a saying, "The way to keep a coon
from climbing is to trim his claws," got out their shears and
went to work.

At first the curbs were legalistic and economic. The new
voter-qualification forms were introduced, closing down the

Negro's chances of registering. Credit in stores and for farm goods became tighter. The dirt roads in Negro areas were "pulled" less often than earlier by the road scrapers. A great blow to Pleas came in 1957, when the Federal Government, from whence in the past had come beneficence, introduced crop allotments. Pleas was told that he could plant no more than 11 of his 59 acres in cotton—hardly enough to make tractor farming worthwhile. From then on he began to feel a pinch; he started taking three percent emergency loans from the FHA each summer to pay for "poisoning" his cotton, as the farmers called spraying for armyworms, boll weevil and spider rust.

Then, with the '60's, came violence and outright cheats. Pleas began to hear of the White Citizens Councils and, later, of a resuscitated Ku Klux Klan and of a group that called itself Americans for the Preservation of the White Race. Ugly threats were passed in the towns, and Pleas heard of beatings. Negroes disappeared; bodies were found in lakes. Pleas saw, close at hand, a struggle for the land, as the whites began to use every possible means to drive off Negro landowners. In five years eight families lost their land in The Bogue, and one of them lived next to Pleas.

In this case the farmer, named Cheer, had borrowed $325 from Mr. Rainsford, the merchant, when Cheer's wife had had to go to a hospital for a goiter. Rainsford seemed openhanded, and said there was no hurry about repayments; he later gave Cheer credit to buy a tractor. Two years later, after Cheer had borrowed money a third time, Rainsford agreeably said he could ease the terms and times of repayment on all these loans if Cheer would like to take out a second mortgage on his house; Cheer signed, and Rainsford had "cotched" him. On Cheer's first tardiness in payment of interest, Rainsford's former easygoing manner vanished as with a clap of hands, and the mortgage was foreclosed. Cheer moved his family onto a nearby "good" plantation, Mr. Pine's, where he and his wife and children worked for three dollars a day apiece; he lasted one year there, then drifted to the notorious Sutter plantation, where the hands got two dollars a day; and the next year he left for Chicago. To Ittabala County Negroes, Chicago has always been the symbol of the outside world, and Pleas had noticed that two kinds of Negroes went there—young ones on the way up, and older ones, like Cheer, on the way down.

Not an excitable man, but one in whom there is an inner firmness like a metal armature, Pleas began in the early '60's to talk around with other intelligent Negroes in the projects, "to seek up in," as he puts it, "and see what we could do to eliminate these problems." They agreed on the need to be well informed. Pleas, like most of his neighbors, had a television set, and he listened intently not only to local news but to public-service programs on the race question, to *Meet the Press*, to United Nations debates.

One day in the summer of 1961 Pleas received a notice from the county office of the Agricultural Stabilization and Conservation Service saying he was overplanted in cotton by 4.4 acres. He drove to the ASCS office and said he was not satisfied with the measurements; his oldest two sons, who had studied agricultural surveying in high school, had measured his land, 10 square chains to the acre, and their figures did not agree with the county surveyor's. An official told him that he could put up $15 to have his land remeasured; if he was right, he'd get his $15 back. Pleas decided to risk the money. The surveyor returned, and Pleas and Varsell Jr. and Orsmond followed him as he made the new measurements. Pleas went to the office a few days later and learned that his sons' measurements had been correct, and he got his money back. That saved acreage made $800 difference in Pleas's income that year, and confirmed Pleas's suspicion that the county office of ASCS dealt carelessly, to say the least of it, with Negroes. Ever since then he has been saying to his neighbors, "It's better for the one who stands up for his rights than for the one who keeps it cool."

By now Pleas and his friends realized that their essential helplessness stemmed from their want of the vote, and when, in the early spring of 1963, they heard that The Movement— as the Mississippi Negroes refer to any and all civil-rights efforts—had begun work on voter registration in Leflore County, they drove the more than 50 miles to Greenwood and were directed by Negroes to the office of the Council of

Federated Organizations, an amalgam of the leading civil-rights groups working in Mississippi, and there they asked for help. C.O.F.O. began sending a young teacher, Joe Merriam, from the Student Nonviolent Coordinating Committee, down to Noonday for citizenship classes, and suddenly everything began to fall into place for Varsell Pleas and his friends: They were "going into The Movement."

Joe Merriam found the Noonday Negroes extraordinarily sophisticated about local politics. Pleas could tell him the specific duties of the county sheriff, treasurer, assessor, surveyor, school trustees, and road supervisor, and he knew all the incumbents' names, and which were fairly decent, and which were vicious; he knew that his taxes helped pay for white schools that were far away from, and far better than, his own children's schools, and that he was taxed for a public library to which he was not admissible, and that no one was doing anything about the fact that airplane "poisoning" of cotton was killing the fish in Ittabala Lake, and that school only ran eight months in Noonday. Merriam concentrated on preparing the Noonday people to register. He unfolded to them the intricacies of Mississippi laws on the franchise, and he explained that even if one has registered, he must have paid a poll tax for two years before he can vote in state and local elections. He told of the investigative and protective powers of the Justice Department. He began teaching the state constitution; the first clause Pleas memorized was Section 14: "No person shall be deprived of life, liberty, or property except by due process of law."

In April the 17 went to Lexington and stood under the tree.

The rest of that season Pleas worked unusually hard at his farming, because he had arranged to rent nine acres of cotton land from a Negro widow who lived nearby in The Bogue.

One day in the fall, when he was out picking cotton with his whole family and a number of hired hands—he could have rented a cotton-picking machine but preferred to hire Noonday Negroes to pick by hand, in order to give them work—a boy drove up in a pickup and ran into the field to tell Varsell that some of the red-necks down in Jade County, the border of which lay about 10 miles south of Pleas's farm, had gathered together to kill The Movement's citizenship teacher

down there—would he please call the FBI in Greenwood?
Pleas went to the nearest phone but could not get through.
He drove to Greenwood to the C.O.F.O. office, which was
able to reach the FBI. Its agents drove down and rescued the
man from his mother's barnloft, where he had been hiding.

In the weeks that followed Pleas harvested 44 bales of cotton, which brought him $5,500, and almost exactly two tons
of soybeans, for which he got $2,325. From this crop cash he
had to pay back an FHA short-term operating loan of $1,800,
plus five-percent interest, and an emergency loan of $200 he
had taken out, because during a wet spell he had had to have
his cotton sprayed by airplane, plus three percent interest. He
had had these expenses during the year:

FHA payments	$400
Fertilizer and seed	550
"Poisoning"	300
Gasoline	500
Rent for widow's land	625
Food	400
Payment on a soybean combine (owned with two others)	350
Clothes (for 2 parents, 11 children)	400
Health	100
Insurance	150
Electricity	125
Cooking gas	75
Labor, cotton picking	300
Maintenance of farm equipment	100
Miscellaneous	200
Total	$4,575

Since Pleas's fiscal year is based on crops rather than on the
calendar, a part of his cash surplus had to keep the family
going until the spring, when he could get his next year's operating loan. He had also sent Varsell Jr. off to Alcorn Agricultural and Mechanical College in the fall, and the boy's year
in the trade school would cost $500. It was a fairly favorable
year, thanks to the widow's fields.

Every bit of Pleas's spare time was now devoted to The

Movement. He attended citizenship meetings regularly, called on others to persuade them to go to the courthouse to register, studied further on the constitution, and went himself a second and a third time to take the test. He did not pass either time, nor had he expected to; he thought he should keep trying. In January he went to Athens to pay his poll tax, against the day when he might pass. He went to the ASCS office in Athens and asked that Negroes be represented on the county committee that sets crop allotments; he was told that the matter would have to go to the committee for consideration, and, of course, nothing came of it.

One day on an errand in Joshua City he ran into James Ratliff, his childhood friend, the son of kindly white parents. He had seen Ratliff occasionally over the years, and recently he had heard that his old companion was now a Citizens Council man.

"How do, Mr. Ratliff." Pleas had called him "Jimmy" before their voices had changed.

"What's wrong with you fellows down there?" Ratliff asked.

"What do you mean?"

"You all trying to get up something?"

"What do you mean, Mr. Ratliff?"

"I seen in the paper that you was up to register. You niggers ain't qualified to vote. You don't know what you're doing. I'd stay out of that mess if I was you."

After that Pleas was not so sure that the race problem could be solved simply by having children grow up together in integrated schools. He had heard a note of threat in the voice of his childhood companion.

In the spring reports came that The Movement was going to mount a big Summer Project, for which many Northern students, both colored and white, would come to Mississippi. As the time for the project approached, tension grew, especially as it became known that whites—even white girls—were going to live in Negro homes. Then one day a C.O.F.O. man asked Varsell Pleas if he himself would take a couple of the students into his house; the C.O.F.O. staff man spelled it out that this would be a dangerous hospitality. Pleas said he'd like to think it over.

*

Varsell Pleas made a reckoning of what was at stake—besides his life, to the risk of which he was almost inured by now.

With all of the years' humiliations and strains, there was a priceless tranquillity in the dusty, white six-room house on the curving dirt road in The Bogue. Voices were never raised there. The children knew their chores, and at dawn they fanned sleepily out without having to be told—Orsmond to milk the cow, Robert to sweep the house, Ervin to make the beds, Pomp to fill up the hot-water caldrons in the yard and light the wood fire under them, Cleontha to help Mamma cook, Edward to churn, Icie and Sussie to clean up Mamma's room. James, the seventh, was off in the hills living with Pleas's mother, and caring for his father's herd of 16 cows and calves, the family bank account; Grandma got $50 a month from Social Security.

In the muddy hog pasture around the barn were four fat full-grown swine and five shoats; a milk cow was in the meadow; chickens, guineas and turkeys quarreled under an ancient cottonwood; 20 fruit trees walked out across the table-vegetable field; wax drippings made a sanitary coating on the concrete floor of the outhouse, which the family spoke of as "the lavatory"; the clanking hand pump by the tool-house gave plenty of cool, iron-tasting water.

Mamma had always had a green thumb—though of late years she had had scant time for the borders by the front path, and they had grown ragged; she kept a stand of tropicals on the porch beside the two rocking chairs, one home-caned with intertwined store string, where she and Daddy sat at sunset and talked, screened from the dusty road by a mimosa, a chinaberry, a castor-bean tree, and three sightly varieties of smoke tree. A foxtail pine gave thick afternoon shade across from the back door, for shelling or peeling or sewing.

One son was at Alcorn, a college of sorts; the second would go next fall to Mississippi Valley College, which was not accredited but was better than no school at all.

Now in the spring evenings the whole family gathered in the living room, on whose pale blue wood walls, among framed and cornucopiaed "arrangements" of imitation roses and grapes and poinsettias and calla lilies, hung three separate pictures of John F. Kennedy, one with Jackie and one with

John Jr., and photographs of Varsell Jr. and his girl in the academic caps and gowns of Noonday Attendance Center; beside the television set was an open, gas space heater, and on it were souvenirs—china animals, a miniature wooden churn, a cute little iron model of a coal cooking range. On the linoleum-covered floor was a linoleum scatter rug, with black, white and red checks. The children disposed themselves on the heavy sofas and couches of the living-room "suite" and watched the programs—as the images flickered, Icie combed out and braided Cleontha's hair—until heads began to nod, one by one, and Mamma quietly said, "Sussie, go wash your feet and get in bed. Ervin, put Larnie to bed; put him in with Pomp tonight." It was considered a treat to have the youngest for the night. By 10 all were down, the children in twos and threes.

At a citizenship meeting the next Wednesday night Varsell Pleas raised his hand and said he would take two students, if he could borrow a bed. The widow from whom he rented his extra acres did soon lend him a double bed which, by knocking down two built-in storage closets, he was able to fit in the back room along with the freezer and the washer, and he shifted from the side room, where there were two beds, the four children who had been sleeping there, and distributed them around. The beds in the house would be crowded through the hot summer—except for the guests, who would each have one to himself.

Before the students arrived in Noonday, there came on television one evening the foreboding announcement of the disappearance of three civil-rights workers in Philadelphia over in Neshoba County. It seemed that the worst fears for the summer were going to be realized. Down the domestic-servant grapevine trickled word, a few days later, that the whites were saying those "mixers" had scooted off to Chicago, where they were drinking beer and enjoying the publicity. But Varsell Pleas thought of Henry Larkin and Brutus Simpson and the citizenship teacher hiding in his mother's loft; he had no doubt the three were dead and in a lake or a swamp.

A week later the Summer Project came to Noonday, and

two young men were assigned to Pleas: Tim Shattuck, who was white, a doctor's son from Roslyn, Long Island, a Yale student, quick-witted and intense; and Bud Samson, a light-skinned Negro, a lawyer's son from Michigan who had been through the civil-rights wars as campus chairman of CORE at a midwestern university—he had a 100-day jail sentence on appeal up home, as a subsequence of some sit-ins he had led. Elsewhere around Noonday were deposited two sophisticated Negro girls from Baltimore, who had demonstrated in Cambridge, Md., two California students, three white girls from various eastern colleges, a white Indiana boy and two more white Yale students. The leader of the project in the area was a C.O.F.O. veteran who had spent several weeks in the state prison farm at Parchman for disturbing the peace of Mississippi the previous summer.

Because the Mississippi police were following the Philadelphia pattern of arresting Project volunteers for trivial or trumped-up traffic charges, and because the maximum danger seemed to be upon release from jail after these arrests, the students wanted to follow state driving regulations meticulously. One of the rules was that they would have to replace their out-of-state license plates, on the three cars they had, with Mississippi plates, if they were going to stay in the state more than a month, and a few days after they arrived, Varsell Pleas drove up to Athens with some of the boys to help them with this transaction. When they left the capital, they were followed for some distance, but nothing happened.

The next day, in a grocery store in Athens, Pleas got notice that the whites, too, had a grapevine. The proprietor sauntered over to Pleas and said, "Varsell, it true what they say, you got some of these agitators staying with you?"

"I got me couple of students, yes, sir."

"You ought not to let them stay with you. If they had no place to stay, they'd have to go back where they belong."

But Pleas was long since hardened to white intimidations. He sent all his children to the freedom school that the students set up in the Baptist church and in an abandoned house not far down the road from it. The children's regular public school had never excited them. It had an enrollment for 1963 of 510 but an average daily attendance of only 405.2—many children, especially on the plantations, stayed out to work in the fields. It was housed in a 20-year-old firetrap, with an oil-burning stove in each classroom, and it ran for only eight months of the year. Per-pupil expenditure was less than $50 a year; many first-graders were eight and 10 years old; the Negro principal, who had six children, was paid $4,800 a year; and the poorly trained Negro teachers, who got as little as $3,000, were afraid to try to register to vote for fear of being fired. At the freedom school the children got the first taste they had ever had of unstinting kindness and solicitude from whites, as Yale and Smith students started in with the younger ones on fundamentals of the three R's. Robert, the third boy, a teenager, told his mother that he'd learned more Negro history in two days than he had in 11 years of public school.

Robert Pleas had been apt and keen as a small boy, but he had chugged nearly to a stop in school in recent years. He was a good farm worker, particularly on the tractor, poisoning cotton while the plants were low, but now he talked halfheartedly of finishing high school and of trying to get into the Air Force. He had driven a school bus the previous year for clothing money; had found chemistry and history tolerable but had failed English—he had despised his English teacher, who could not speak as grammatically as his mother and father. What he liked best was hunting. When the muscadines began to ripen, and corn was solid in the ear, and the persimmons were right, then the raccoons would come out, and Robert sometimes winged three or four in an evening. He was a sweet shot—a squirrel would run up a tree to get away from the family Winchester in his hands, but if that squirrel poked two inches of head around to see if the coast was clear, Robert would decap him at 50 feet. Now, however, the freedom school was getting Robert interested, and at meals the two students, Tim and Bud, would fire him up to work for the race. Pretty soon he was saying he thought he'd bone next year, and get to college if he could, and work in The Movement anyway.

Bud and Tim came in excited to the Pleases one night, reporting that at one of the houses over near the highway a white man had been seen fumbling around in the backyard with a flashlight. The owner of the house, with a shotgun on his arm, accosted the man. It turned out to be Bubba Goodheart, a local farmer who had just been made a deputy sheriff in order, it was said, to keep an eye on the invaders. Brought into the cone of a large battery light, Deputy Goodheart shouted that he had had instructions from "higher up" to "protect" a student named Peter Marston. Where was this boy?

One of the Project workers asked Deputy Goodheart why he hadn't just come straight to the front door, if that was his errand.

The deputy said he'd got lost.

There was in fact a Harvard student named Peter Marston in the Noonday contingent, and it came out later that there had indeed been orders from Jackson to look out for him. Pete was the son of a wealthy Boston corporation lawyer, a Harvard graduate, one of whose former college classmates was now a big shot in the White Citizens Council down in Jackson. Pete's father, who disapproved of his being in Mississippi at all, had asked the Citizens Council friend to "keep an eye" on Pete, and an official friend of the friend had obligingly ordered a tail put on the boy. Bubba Goodheart had come blundering forth to carry out this command. Pleas and all his friends believed that the reason he was in the backyard was to try to spy out the sleeping arrangements of white girls in colored homes.

Now a wild man came one night to the Noonday citizenship meeting: Isaac (Zingo) Ostrowski, a 52-year-old contractor from Oregon, who told the Noonday farmers that he was going to build them the nicest meeting hall they'd ever see. Six feet tall, built like a pro-football tackle, Zingo had got a bee in his bonnet the previous winter, had visited Mississippi in the spring and had talked with C.O.F.O. leaders, then had gone back to Oregon and had raised, singlehanded, $10,000. With a carpenter friend whom he had enlisted, and with a station wagon full of building tools, he'd taken off for the Mississippi Delta and had wound up in Noonday.

Mrs. Pleas was elected secretary of the new community center that he was to build, and one of the neighbors leased an acre not far from the main road. Zingo ordered lumber from a Jackson firm, but there followed mysterious delays in delivery; so Zingo made a phone call to Tennessee, and a few days later a big shiny trailer truck from that state drove in and unloaded a heap of things. The farmers at citizenship meetings arranged to procure volunteer labor to help Zingo. Pleas put in a day; workmen began arriving in parties from all over the county, as word went around that a Negro hall was being built where movies would be shown and meetings would be held, and that there was going to be a free library of 7,000 volumes, and a kitchen, and a room for kids, and running water and two flush toilets. When the floor was laid down, everyone turned out with hammers and worked, colored residents and white students together; Randoman Tort said it was the first Integrated Nailing ever held in Mississippi.

Robert was soon head-over-heels in The Movement; a factor in his sudden dedication may have been the attractiveness of one of the Negro girls from Baltimore, Charlotte Bunson, a student at the University of Maryland, daughter of a high-school vice principal. Robert spent much time around the Freedom House, a second abandoned farmhouse, across from the freedom school, where Charlotte and other staff workers lived. There he became interested in what he overheard about the voter-registration canvassing that Tim Shattuck and Bud Samson and others were doing, and soon he got himself excused from freedom school to go out on the voter drive.

The first day he went with Pete Marston to The Bogue. At each house Pete would talk for about 15 minutes about the vote, and about going to the courthouse. His being white was both an advantage and a disadvantage, for though he had to overcome a reflexive suspicion and dislike, he also commanded, even from Negroes three and four times his unripe age, a certain passive respect and obedience, no matter how grudging, that had been bred and drilled into them from birth and from long before birth. Having Robert with him, a local Negro farm boy whom most of The Bogue people knew as the son of Varsell Pleas, was a help.

They took notes:

Mr. Aurelius. Says he backed down but thinks he will go if he has some support. Mr. and Mrs. Aurelius Jr. Both are scared. Should return.

Mrs. Cunninger. Has tried three times.

Mary and T. C. Hampton. Uncertain and fearful. He is reported to be informer to Mr. Pine, white planter. Wife, however, might come around. Man is 85, wife 62. Don't like it here but afraid to vote. Mrs. Shucker. Has tried once. She is 72. Will go down if she feels the energy. She is coming to citizenship meetings.

Mr. Joe Perry Chesnut. Wife works for school. Intimidated through the school system.

Mr. Whitsett. "May have to go to hospital soon."

Mr. and Mrs. Rankin. He works for white builder in town, both scared. Eddy, the son, is very sharp, says he will go in a full car.

Mr. Sam Harbison. Uncle Tom. Will vote when all Negroes are allowed to vote.

For Varsell Pleas and others of the older generation, citizenship meetings continued in the rickety church next to where the studs of the new meeting hall were already being framed. This church, with a slightly tilted steeple, contained five rows of crude benches, and its walls were decorated with offering banners and a calendar with a picture of Jesus protecting a lamb and a C.O.F.O. poster of a Mississippi highway patrolman out of whose eyebeam jumped the question IS HE PROTECTING YOU? Here the Noonday farmers debated whether to try to found a new cooperative store. The farmers felt at the mercy of the white merchants in Athens, and they wanted the economic independence of a low-price supermarket that would belong to Negroes throughout the county. They sought legal advice on this idea from The Movement in Jackson. A miniature power struggle was developing in citizenship meetings between the firebrands and the more cautious heads; Pleas, always an aloof man, was not in either faction. "I'll just try to splice in and get you folks to quit arguing," he said once.

Toward the end of June a large shipment of used clothes, collected in northern drives, came to Noonday, and Pleas volunteered to distribute it. He picked out a few pieces to fill gaps in the wardrobe of his own family—little Larnie was soon sporting a pair of too-large and somewhat frayed sailing shorts, safety-pinned with an overlap at his waist, so that down the sturdy dark thighs ran strings of yacht-club burgees —and then undertook the dangerous work of hauling bundles to the miserable shacks of plantation sharecroppers. The white planters had made bluntly clear their hostility to the Summer Project, and to The Movement as a whole. The threat: "If you want to get in that mess, you'll have to move off my land." Pleas was a Baptist, and he attended, as had numerous plantation Negroes, Fair Heaven Church, which had recently hired an itinerant preacher from downstate named Burroughs, a registered voter who preached voting. When word reached the planters, Mr. Pine and Mr. Sutter, that Reverend Burroughs would get his flock worked up with the spirit to where he could do almost anything with them and then would switch off to registering, the planters refused to let their Negroes go to that church anymore. The half-naked children of these depressed and hopeless people flocked around Pleas like sparrows when he drove up with cartons of clothes.

On the first of July, Robert had an accident with his father's tractor; he collided with a carload of Negroes who had clearly been drinking. The others were let off, but Robert, the son of a Negro who had tried to register, was booked for reckless driving, failure to yield and drunken driving. Pleas went to court with his son and he told the judge that he wouldn't argue with the first two charges, but that Robert never drank.

"I didn't make these charges," the judge said. "Mr. Goodheart made them."

"I didn't think that was fair," Pleas said. "As far as I know, Robert never has taken a drink."

"All right," the judge said, "we won't charge him with that this time."

This was another confirmation, for Pleas, of the importance of standing up to the white man, in cases where he felt he was right. Even so, the fine was $55.

Now the solid summer heat came, with temperatures in the 90's and the air as still as a shameful secret, day after day after day. Mrs. Pleas sat in the shade of the foxtail pine trying to cool herself with a cardboard fan with an ad on it for STROWDER'S FUNERAL HOME AND BURIAL SOCIETY. Summer nuisances hummed and crawled—sandflies and mud daubers, robber flies and stinkbugs. The men worked hard poisoning the cotton, and nerves wore thin.

As the meeting hall arose, a massive affront of raw lumber visible to all eyes from Route 57, so also did tension rise in the area. Red-necks drove their pickups and cars slowly along the dirt road past the building, looking it over.

At four in the morning, on Sunday, July 26, a Negro named T. O. Lacey, who lived not far down the road from the construction, was wakened by a flickering light, and running out, he saw a student's car, which had been parked in front of the house opposite, in flames. He wakened the people across the road, hosts and students, and they tried vainly to put the fire out with water from a hand pump. At daylight nothing was left of the car but a shell. A shattered gallon jug, which had evidently contained kerosene, was found on the front seat.

After that three Negro families, Pittman, Jones and Tort, who lived along the road, set up an armed night watch, some sleeping during the first part of the night, some staying up till late. In early July, The Movement supplied three short-wave radios for these three families, so when an unknown vehicle drove in the head of the road, the word could be passed along. One night Bunell Jones set out in his pickup to patrol, and a Negro student staying in his house jokingly asked him, "You going out in that dark night all alone?"

"No," Jones said, "I got thirty-two brothers with me, and six cousins"—two 16-gauge shotguns and a revolver.

Pleas, who lived three miles from the new building and was not involved in the watches, was putting himself more and more deeply in danger, however, by repeatedly taking people to the courthouse in Athens, on gas furnished by collections at citizenship meetings, to try to register. Because no applicants ever passed, taking people to register came to be called "making a waterhaul"—or, getting no-place. But the whites noticed. "Here comes old Varsell," Pleas heard a deputy sheriff say once. "He sure is up to his ears in it."

One of Pleas's guns was old, and he decided to replace it. (Section 12 of the constitution affirmed "the right of every citizen to keep and bear arms in defense of his home, person, or property," and no license was needed.) But in the hardware store in Noonday the dealer refused to sell him one. "Guns is put up now," he said. Pleas drove to Jackson and bought a new gun, no questions asked, at Hunt and Whitakers. He took to retiring early, so he would be easy to wake from two o'clock on—when most of the violence against Negroes in the state had been taking place. A shotgun stood at the head of his bed, another by Orsmond's, and one by Robert's. Every night four thin dogs and two thin cats lay down in the dust at Pleas's back door, and the racket they raised when anything moved in the neighborhood quickly wakened the house.

One evening late in July, Tim Shattuck, who had been trying to make friends with white-shy Larnie, the five-year-old, and had once heard Larnie muttering about "the wheet," asked his host to tell him honestly what he thought about the white students having come down from the North for the summer.

Pleas, after the usual pause for thought, said in an unemotional voice, "It's the best thing that's happened since there ever was a Mississippi. I just love the students like I love to eat. Listen: They showed they're willing to *die* for us—two of those three at Philadelphia. If more come down here, I'd get out of my bed for them and sleep on a pallet in the tool shed. They're doing things we couldn't do for ourselves in years on end. They've taken away a lot of fear of the courthouse, and people ain't so scared to come to citizenship meetings anymore. They're giving some of our older kids subjects they should have had in school all along—French and typing. And they're so natural—like brothers and sisters. Another thing: The governor is going to have to be more careful what he says now, because a lot of bad smells are getting out to the outside world that never did before. And we got out-of-state FBI in here, and federal lawsuits. It's all changing, it is sure enough changing, right this summer. I hope you can come back another season. If you can't, send somebody else in your place."

Tim asked, "What about the whites? Are we making it worse for you with them?"

"No," Pleas said. "About the whites, there's bad ones and right decent ones. The bad ones been shooting colored people all along and throwing them in lakes, a bunch of students don't change that. The all-right ones, they're kind of gagged

up. But we're going to set them good ones free—ourselves
and them. These white folks have ridiculous fears. I tell you,
we don't want nothing from them but stop. The Negro people ain't going up after them. We country Negroes don't do
people that way. I think we got more real religion in our
blood than the white people; we been told since weaning,
'Don't throw stone for stone.' But they better not come
messing in our homes, setting fire and getting up a big killing
scrape. That won't *never* scare us. That ain't *never* going to
keep me from taking folks up to the courthouse. Because I
tell you something, Tim, we're going to get the vote in three
to five years, and when we do, the Negro man's vote is going
to count just as hard as the white man's vote. I'm paying my
poll tax to keep ready."

A few days later Tim had a story to tell the Pleases; it was
a story which, against the background of the three killed at
Philadelphia, made a big impression on Robert Pleas:

Tim had just got out of one civil-rights car in Athens, that
morning, and was waiting to be picked up by another to go
canvassing in Meeks, when a man of about 40, in a blue
sport shirt and khaki work pants, stepped out of a knot of
men, pointed at Tim's nose and then touched it repeatedly
with a forefinger, and said, "You ain't dung. You ain't even
dung. You ain't as good as dung." Tim, who had been
trained in passive responses to abuse and violence, stood absolutely still and looked straight in the man's blue-gray eyes.
The man began hitting Tim in the face, forehand and back-
hand, and then, as others began closing in with glistening
eyes, Tim suddenly assumed "the nonviolent crouch"—
dropped to his knees and formed a ball of his body, folding
his hands over the nape of his neck, so that as many vital
places as possible were protected. The man, who seemed
startled by this bizarre defense, kicked him halfheartedly a
couple of times and then walked away; the others also drew
back.

At about this time the emphasis of the voter-registration drive
changed. The student canvassers began registering Negroes
for the Freedom Democratic Party, which planned to challenge the seating of the regular Mississippi Democratic Party

delegation at the Democratic National Convention. Robert Pleas began working hard on freedom registrations, and this work took him closer to danger and clinched his commitment to The Movement.

One day he was canvassing in Meeks, a mean town on the eastern border of the county, with Bud Samson, the Negro CORE student. They were standing on the front porch of a house, signing up a Negro woman, when a white deliveryman arrived. He asked the boys what they were doing. Bud explained. The man asked a question.

Bud answered, "Yeah."

The man said, "You mean, 'Yes, sir.'"

Bud said, "Where I live we don't talk that way."

"You're where I live now, boy."

"OK, if it'll make you happy. Yes, sir."

The man asked for identification. Bud gave him a clipping from a Chicago paper, showing his picture and identifying him as a leader of a sit-in.

"This you?"

"Yes." Omission of sir.

"You got a hard head, ain't you, you colorblind little bastard? I might have to soften it up for you."

The man moved toward Bud, and Robert, to his own astonishment, found himself making a definite move. He reached his draft I.D. card out toward the deliveryman as he moved on Bud, and this served to distract the man. With further abuse and warnings he left.

The next week Varsell Pleas was told his son Robert would not be given back his school-bus driver's job in the fall.

Now came two pieces of news that lifted all the Noonday Negroes' spirits. The Mississippi State Democratic Convention, mindful of the challenge to be offered at the national convention by the Freedom Democratic Party, postponed until after Atlantic City the question of how to handle the ballot in November, whether the party's electors should be designated for Johnson or for Goldwater—so that for the first time since Black Reconstruction days Negroes had been able to influence directly the course of Mississippi politics. And then the bodies of the three dead civil-rights workers were found—that showed the FBI really meant business in Mississippi, and maybe the roughest of the whites would think twice before they hurt anyone.

In the hottest weather, in August, came revival time. For a week Varsell Pleas was somewhat turned aside from work for The Movement as he went to revival meetings at Fair Heaven Church every evening at eight. On Saturday night, after meeting, he and Holly Bell sat up late into the night reading the Bible aloud to each other and talking about what they had read. The next morning Varsell went to clean the leaves and scare the water moccasins out of the edge of Mrs. Hodgkins's pond, and at noontime Preacher Burroughs, with Pleas's help for the immersions, reaped 14 souls. The temperature of the air was over 100, and when Pleas got home, he kept his wet clothes on till dinner time.

A white tablecloth was set on the kitchen table that noon, and before dinner a quiet young man from Lockfire, rather scholarly looking, with steel-rimmed glasses, named Louis Weems, drove in with Pleas's 79-year-old mother. All sat down to eat. Pleas said blessing. Then Pleas's mother said, "Louis here just spent five months in Parchman."

"Whatever for?" asked Holly Bell. "You ain't that kind of boy, Louis."

And then, over a baptism-day dinner of chicken and dressing, sweet-potato pie, rutabaga and greens, black-eyed peas, fried tomato, and hot biscuit, Louis Weems, speaking in genteel tones, told the pillar of Fair Heaven Church and his wife, fresh from the week of hymns and conversions, how, having run into debt on his hill-farm wages of three dollars a day, and needing $50 in a matter of hours, he had gone out with two others and stolen three hogs, which they'd sold in Athens for $85. Then he told about life at Parchman, how he'd worked like a slave under a driver in the cotton fields, how he'd become a "walker," counting sleepers inside the wire at Camp Eight, and how he'd been cut on the arm one night by a real bad boy.

When the story and the meal were done, and everyone sat sweating at the table, it had come round to seem to Varsell

Pleas, and he said so, that the crime was not in the hog-rassling but in the pay the man had gotten and the credit squeeze that had driven him to the theft.

"That's right," Holly Bell said. "You ain't never been that kind of boy, Louis."

"I did the wrong thing," Weems said, "and I paid off with my five months."

The roof was on the meeting hall. None of the insurance agents in Athens would write a policy for the building. The sightseers were coming in droves, white men moseying past at five miles an hour. Tort was talking about holding an Integration Ball after the place was opened. Everyone expected a bomb.

On Saturday night, August 8, a Negro man named Stanley Chunn was walking along near the meeting hall, headed out for a beer, when a car drove by and dropped something out on the ground not far from him. He thought it was just some trash, and he walked on. Three or four minutes later—he had nearly reached the highway—there was a sharp explosion back on the road. Negroes gathered from all around—nothing but a hole in the dirt road. Everyone guessed that the white men, intending to bomb the meeting hall, had lit their long fuse in their car, had been startled to see a Negro walking in the road in an area known to be heavily armed, and had dropped the device in the road and skinned out.

The next morning FBI men came to investigate—and word was passed that they were men with out-of-state accents. Within two days the Negro grapevine had told the Noonday people exactly which white man had bungled the bombing—a certain deliveryman from near Athens. He had done a poor job; they'd no doubt be back.

In a farm-equipment store in Joshua City one day the proprietor, Mr. Scott, said, "What are you all going to do when those white people leave you and go back on home?"

Pleas said, "What do you mean?"

"You're going to be coming up here to your old white friends in Joshua City after they've gone, asking for our help. The help just might not be here anymore."

Pleas understood the implied threat. Everyone had been speculating about new outbreaks of violence when the

Summer Project pulled out, but Pleas knew that there would not be a sudden break. Three white students planned to stay on for good in Noonday; what had started as a summer drive was turning into a permanent program. So successful had the summer effort been that the C.O.F.O. people were talking of expanding their project into at least two adjacent states, Alabama and Arkansas.

So Pleas answered with a certain confidence. "It ain't going to be any different, Mr. Scott. I always figured we helped each other: You give me credit, I buy your cultivator and harrow and poisoner and all like that."

This answer, delivered in gentle tones, left Mr. Scott thinking about an implied threat too. Pleas could buy elsewhere.

The great sky cooled as autumn came on. Pleas began picking cotton, the combines moved through the soybeans.

The two oldest left for college, but the younger ones could pick till school began at the end of September. Integration, just beginning in first grade in Jackson, Biloxi and Leale County, was far off for them, but it was rumored that they might be involved in a school boycott in November to protest the conditions of their schooling.

Robert and a local girl, Dearie Mae Jones, of one of the night-watch families, went off in a bus with student friends of the summer to the National Democratic Convention, and Robert, who had never before been farther from home than Jackson, demonstrated on the Atlantic City boardwalk while the politicians seated two Negroes as delegates from Mississippi. Varsell Pleas arranged a $2,300 FHA housing loan, for 33 years at 4 percent, to install running water in his house, add a bathroom, put on a new roof, and build a new front porch. He kept going to citizenship meetings; he was working on the new co-op store, but voting came first with him, as always.

The Justice Department had brought a suit against the circuit clerk in a nearby county, charging discrimination against Negroes in voter registration, under the 1964 Civil Rights Act; and as soon as that case was won, as Pleas confidently expected it to be, he planned to go up and try again to register in the Ittabala Courthouse. They'd find new gimmicks to prevent him, for awhile, he supposed, and they might try to hurt and even kill some Negroes, and he supposed he might be on their list for all he'd been doing, but he was not afraid; some day it would not be a waterhaul.

This year Election Day would pass him by, but with prayer and hard work, keeping guns clean and not venturing away from the house at night, going to the courthouse again and again, he thought that he would, at last, get what he wanted. He expected things to grow worse in Mississippi before they grew better, but he had made his personal reckoning and had long since decided that a vote was worth a life—without a vote a life was not one's own.

The Saturday Evening Post, September 26, 1964

Last Summer in Mississippi

by Alice Lake

THE dialogue occurred in July behind a small white country church with a single spire and a green roof. One of the participants was a man, over six feet and a heavy 200 pounds. He had sandy hair, and a paunch swelling under a sweaty blue shirt with a sheriff's insignia on its sleeve. The other was a slim girl, not quite 22 years old, startlingly pretty, with short, light brown hair, bright blue eyes, crooked teeth, and a smile that lighted up her whole face.

It was an unusual conversation because it was friendly, and these two were not friends. The man was a deputy sheriff in Madison County, 30 miles north of Jackson, the Mississippi state capital. The girl, Ruth Kay Prickett, of Carbondale, Illinois, was a volunteer in the Mississippi Summer Project, which brought to the state over 500 young college students. She had arrived in the county a few days earlier to open a rural Freedom School for Negro teen-agers.

Although these two did not know each other, both had heard stories. In the newspaper the sheriff read, the volunteers were described as dirty, smelly, unwashed beatniks. Looking at Kay, immaculate in a white piqué, V-necked blouse and a sharp-pleated, coffee-colored skirt, he must have wondered. "I had heard ugly things about his kind too," Kay says. "I'd hate to say whether they were true or not. When there is no communication between the races, hearsay stories grow on both sides."

The sheriff drove out from Canton, the county seat, to the one-room church that housed the Freedom School to get Kay and the other two white teachers—Karol Nelson, 25, a tall blonde from Dinuba, California; and Natalie Tompkins, 21, from Melrose, Massachusetts—to register with the local police. This was a requirement of questionable legality for the 42 summer workers in Madison County, who were running a voter-registration drive, manning a community center and seven schools, and organizing a farmers' cooperative among the Negroes, who number almost three quarters of the county's 33,000 population.

The simple task turned out to be more than he had bargained for. When he arrived, Kay and Karol were taking books from cartons and placing them on newly built pine bookshelves. Natalie was giving a French lesson to two Negro girls. While the others continued their chores, Kay took the surprised visitor in hand, deliberately turning on her most naïve manner and the full force of her dazzling smile. She invited him inside to see the school—"we'd both profit from it," she said sweetly. She showed him the library, 1,000 books, mostly on Negro history, and offered to lend him one. He declined hastily. She suggested he visit the school when it met that evening. Again he declined.

Behind the church, where his car was parked, the two talked for over half an hour. Kay asked what he thought of the voter-registration drive. In Madison County only 500 Negroes out of 10,000 eligible are registered to vote, a percentage even lower than the state-wide figure of seven per cent.

"I kind of hate for them to vote," the sheriff answered slowly. "This county is seventy-two per cent nigger. If they get in power, they're really going to be rough on the white people. I just don't trust the nigger. They're not like us."

Kay drew a deep breath but kept on smiling. They talked about the nearby Negro church that had burned to the ground a few days earlier.

"I bet your people burned that church just for the publicity," he said.

Kay answered innocently, "I wasn't there. Were you? Do you have any facts on which to base your opinion?"

The two found one bond. The sheriff was a Mason and so was Kay's father. He brightened. By the time he drove away he was in high good humor. "Now, don't you worry, little girl," he said. "We're not going to come out here and beat you up."

Yet, through the summer Kay and Karol and Natalie had reason to worry. They lived about 12 miles outside of Canton in two Negro farm homes on a dirt country road, surrounded by stalks of waving corn and the dark green leaves of cotton plants. In a nearby community, bomb threats forced three other volunteers to leave Negro homes. A fire bomb was tossed onto the lawn of the Freedom House, Canton headquarters for the civil rights workers. On Canton's main street (named, by some irony, Peace Street), white drivers openly displayed rifles on the back seats of their cars. The girls had one lifeline to summon aid in case of trouble—a telephone in a small Negro grocery store four miles away. Soon after the deputy's visit they lost the lifeline. A sheriff drove up to the store one morning and told its proprietor that he'd be in a peck of trouble if he continued to let those white girls use his phone.

"The nights were the worst," Kay said. "At first we jumped at every noise. Then we got used to the sound of the cows chewing grass outside the window and the clank of the chain dragging at the pony's ankle. But when the dogs started barking at midnight, we turned out the lights and hardly breathed in the dark. Once a car stopped and honked invitingly. Another time we heard footsteps running near the house, with the dogs in growling pursuit."

Kay and Karol shared a big double bed in the front bedroom of the home of John and Mary Higgins, a middle-aged couple. Natalie lived down the road with the Forbes family, who worked 50 acres of their own land, 21 planted in cotton, the rest in corn, butter beans, sweet potatoes, okra. (The Negro families who offered hospitality to the three girls still live in Madison County. For their own protection their names have been altered.) Mr. Forbes, a heavy, friendly man, said firmly, "If I catch someone round my gate, I'm going to take a shot at him." One Sunday night he almost had that opportunity.

"Some of the married sons and their families were down visiting from Jackson," Natalie recalls. "At about eleven P.M. all four dogs started to bark, and we heard someone running. One of the boys went into a bedroom for his rifle. It's like an armory here, rifles in every room. We turned out the lights and saw a dark car parked on the road near the cotton field. The men took their rifles and prowled around outside. Then we heard the motor start up and the car pull away. Just to make sure, two of the boys spent the night in the carport with their rifles ready." Apologetically she added, "I guess I'm the all-time chicken around here, but I was scared."

What made these girls come to hot, humid Mississippi, where people of their own color treated them as enemies? Should they have stayed home, as some advised, and let Mississippi Negroes struggle alone to win their rights? What were their goals? Did they succeed in accomplishing them?

All three girls come from middle-class homes. Kay was a senior at Southern Illinois University at Carbondale; Natalie had just graduated from the University of Massachusetts; and Karol was a teacher in Pacifica, California, after graduating three years earlier from the University of California. From a glance at Kay's animated face, it would be easier to imagine her twisting at a sorority dance than teaching school in a hot little Negro church. Like most girls her age, Kay likes to have fun, loves parties and has a healthy interest in young men.

"Why did I come? I feel segregation is morally wrong," Kay says. "I believe that if we don't help to right that wrong, our democracy may wither away. And I hoped that the summer would make me a better person. Last May a speaker from C.O.F.O. [the Council of Federated Organizations, set up by the four major civil rights groups to run the Mississippi program] spoke on our campus, and when he had finished I raised my hand and asked, 'Where do we get the applications?' Some people had money to help and others had time. I had the time."

Behind the decision lay 21 years of Kay Prickett's life. "I guess my idealism comes from my father," she says. "He has great ideas. He taught us not to throw paper on the highways, and to believe that everybody was equally human, no matter what the color of his skin."

Kay's mother, Juanita, 46, agrees. Mother and daughter look alike, have the same vivacious manner and quick, breathless voice. "I was born in Oklahoma," Mrs. Prickett says, "but my people come from all over the South and I was raised with Southern attitudes. I changed my point of view when I met a wonderful man named Ralph Prickett, a man who used words like 'us' and 'ours' instead of 'I,' 'my,' 'me.' My philosophy is that the world should be a better place because you came through it. That's the way Kay feels too."

Mrs. Prickett did not have an easy time shedding her own racist childhood. In a gym class at Southern Illinois University in 1936, she and other students were asked to clasp hands and form a circle. "When I saw there was a Negro girl beside me, I broke into a cold sweat," she recalls. "But I did it, and I said to myself, 'My land, it doesn't feel any different from any other girl's hand.' I've come a long way since. A few months ago our son Charles, who's twenty, brought home a Negro boy to visit with us. It was a new experience for me. It made me feel ten feet tall."

Nevertheless, neither Juanita nor Ralph Prickett acquiesced easily in Kay's plan to summer in Mississippi. "It wasn't that we were out of sympathy," Mrs. Prickett says. "We were just plain worried about her safety. We tried up to the last minute to persuade her not to go. I was in tears the whole last week."

Only one family member never reconciled himself. Kay's maternal grandfather, 70 years old, is an unreconstructed Southerner who told Kay flatly, "You can choose between the niggers and me." All summer he wrote her pitiful pleading letters. "I love you so much," one read, "that I've hurt ever since you've left. Yet I feel like you've deserted us for the niggers. If you would call me any time of the night and say, 'Grandpa, I want to come home,' I'd drive right through the night until I reached you."

Except for one childhood incident, Kay never knew persons of a different color until she started college. "When I was seven," she recalls, "and my father was a coal chemist with a mining company, he brought home a visitor from Japan. Charlie and I were enchanted, and the next day we took him to see our school. The war had ended only a few years earlier. We were shocked and ashamed when in front of the schoolhouse the other kids yelled, 'Kill the Jap!'"

Kay grew up in De Soto, a community just outside Carbondale which boasted that no Negro would dare spend the night there. Even Carbondale maintained a segregated movie theater until a few years ago. In college some of her friends became interested in civil rights. "For a while," she says, "I dated a boy who was blond and blue-eyed but had almost all Negro friends. At one party we were the only white couple. At first I was self-conscious, but in an hour I really forgot all about it. Last year a group of kids joined the Student Non-Violent Coordinating Committee. I was shy about going to their meetings. I didn't want to go rushing in. One spring day I was sitting in the cafeteria just before a SNCC meeting, and a friend asked me to come. I guess that started my commitment. There are twenty kids in our SNCC chapter at S.I.U. Six of us spent the summer in Mississippi."

The six students needed financial support, $150 each for transportation and living expenses and a $500 pledge of bail money in case of arrest. The Pricketts are not rich. Juanita is a remedial-reading specialist, and Ralph Prickett only recently started a second career as a schoolteacher. But friends on the campus—faculty wives, the university chaplain, the Student Christian Foundation—gave teas to raise funds. Each student received $10 a week during the summer, enough for pocket money and board and room.

The start of the trip seemed a lark—at first. On Sunday, June 21st, Kay arrived by bus at the peaceful green campus of Western College for Women, in Oxford, Ohio, where the National Council of Churches was conducting a week-long orientation session for the summer volunteers. She was one of the second group of 250 youngsters planning to teach in Freedom Schools and man community centers. The first wave, mostly voter-registration workers, was already filtering into Mississippi.

It looked like a gay college weekend. All day buses spilled out youngsters with sleeping bags and guitars. Cars pulled up with stickers from the University of Oregon, Harvard, Yale, Antioch, Oberlin. New York, Massachusetts, Illinois and California were most heavily represented, but students came also from Wyoming, Kansas, Oklahoma. Girls wore bright cottons, and the boys chinos and open-necked shirts. Immediately they began singing. From the start it was a singing movement.

Many had made sacrifices to come. One girl used her college graduation money to finance the summer. Another took the funds she had saved for a trip to Europe. A third arrived on what was to have been her wedding day. She had jilted her fiancé when she found his ardor for civil rights did not match hers.

Greeting the volunteers were sober staff workers familiar with Mississippi jails, scarred by beatings or bullets. They minced no words about the dangers. There was Bob Moses, leader of the project, 29, shy, serious, a New York Negro who had gone to Mississippi in 1961 and never returned to complete his doctorate at Harvard; his pretty wife Donna, 23, tiny, dressed in brief white shorts, her black hair in a single braid down her back; Annell Ponder, 30, dark and beautiful, a crease of worry etched across her forehead; Jesse Morris, slender, tense, with a phenomenal memory; Jimmy Travis, 22, lanky and nervous, only recently recovered from a sniper's bullet that nearly killed him.

On Monday morning Bob Moses spoke to the entire group. "As you come into Mississippi you bring with you the concern of the country. It does not identify with Negroes. It identifies with whites. With that concern comes a little more protection for you. It is still up for grabs whether that protection can be transferred to the Negroes of Mississippi."

He was interrupted by a staff worker approaching the stage. Moses squatted on his haunches and the two whispered briefly. Then for a silent moment Moses remained bent over, rocking back and forth. He straightened wearily and continued, voice flat, unemotional, eyes bleak behind thick glasses. "Three of our people from Meridian, two staff workers and a summer volunteer, have been missing since yesterday afternoon."

Rita Schwerner, 22, painfully thin, dressed in faded blue shorts, her wavy hair piled loosely on top of her head, followed him to the platform. She too seemed unemotional. Later she broke down. "The missing three are my husband Michael Schwerner, James Chaney, of Meridian, and Andrew Goodman, of New York." She wrote their names on the blackboard, and the place—Philadelphia, Neshoba County. In the heat no one stirred. Only a few days earlier Andy Goodman, 20, had sat in one of these auditorium seats. He was in Mississippi a scant 24 hours before he died.

On the surface the volunteers seemed curiously untouched. They jammed the telephone booths to wire their congressmen to demand a federal search. They stood noisily in line for lunch. "I felt tense, like when President Kennedy died," Kay said at the lunch table. "I sort of connected it with myself but sort of not. I thought this might have been done to scare the rest of us away." Had she been scared? She shook her head. "No, I'd never known violence. No one ever threatened to do anything to me. I had no concept of things like that."

Through the week, speaker after speaker urged any youngster who had doubts to return home. "If you don't feel ready for this kind of thing, it is noble, not shameful, to leave," said Vincent Harding, director of the Mennonite House in Atlanta. "Don't worry if you're not ready. No one is ever ready to go to Mississippi." Each evening the telephones shrilled, calls from anxious parents begging their children to leave. Yet not one youngster did.

Subtly the college-weekend air had changed. Volunteers flocked to the bulletin board where the latest news from Neshoba County was displayed. One boy confessed, "I've got cannon balls in my stomach." A worship service, held at 11 P.M. after a tightly scheduled day, was heavily attended. Until 1 A.M. one night the students danced Israeli folk dances taught by a Negro girl from Texas. Then they prowled their dormitories, looking for company.

The days were jammed with classes. Kay attended the general sessions in the morning and the meetings for Freedom School teachers in the afternoon and evening. She learned that her students would be tenth to twelfth graders, and that the curriculum would be equally divided among academic subjects and citizenship education, Negro history and Negro rights. In Mississippi there is no compulsory education law, and the average Negro attends school for only six years. His education costs the state annually less than half what it spends on a white child. One speaker said, "The Negro child is trained to accept without question. Teach him to ask why and the system will fall."

"Friday was our last night in Oxford," Kay says, "and most of us didn't go to bed. I wandered around all evening and ended up in the laundry room of our dorm, where several of us talked until four A.M." On Saturday afternoon the volunteers piled into chartered buses that would take them as far as Memphis. Kay, Karol and Natalie learned that they would proceed from there to Columbus, a town on the eastern border of Mississippi. The bus drove through the night, arriving in Memphis at 5 A.M.

"I kept worrying about my knife," Kay recalls. "It was just an innocent Scout knife, but I cherished it because my brother Charlie gave it to me. Yet I knew I had to get rid of it." Earlier Bob Moses had said, "We will not allow any staff member or volunteer to carry a weapon. This is absolutely bedrock." In the Memphis bus station Kay solved her problem. She asked a woman if it would be all right to give the knife to her little boy. The gift was accepted with delight.

In Memphis the three girls learned that they had been reassigned from Columbus to Greenville, a town near the Mississippi River in the rich Delta country of the northwest. The reason: Columbus Negroes were too frightened to open their homes to civil rights workers. Each volunteer was to be housed in a Negro home. Such hospitality might be perilous. Some hosts lost their jobs. Tear gas was lobbed into one home, and shots fired through the windows of others. Many feared that after the students left, modest homes, built with pennies laboriously saved, might go up in flames.

"As we approached the Mississippi border," Kay recalls, "we kept looking out the window. We weren't exactly scared, but we were thinking of what might happen. When we saw a big billboard reading 'Welcome to Mississippi,' we all laughed nervously."

They arrived in Greenville at noon after two sleepless nights. Immediately Kay saw a friend from Carbondale. "I was too keyed up to sleep, so we walked through town, expecting somebody to jump out and massacre us. But it was quiet—on the surface, at least."

For Mississippi, Greenville is a quiet town. It is the home of Hodding Carter, whose newspaper, the *Delta Democrat-Times*, is one of the few liberal white voices of the state press. Yet even in Greenville there is some harassment. "In my two weeks in the town," Kay says, "I lived in two houses. It was thought safer not to have a civil rights worker remain too long in one place. Negroes there work desperately hard. My first hostess rose at four A.M., and worked from five until mid-afternoon in a restaurant. Then she came home and took in washing, which she scrubbed on an old-fashioned board.

That's the way we did our washing too. A little girl of about six watched Karol the first day, and politely told her that she was using the wrong side of the scrub board. We bought some food in a Negro grocery store. The proprietor was very friendly until white people came in. Then he acted as if he didn't know us."

In Greenville the girls had their first taste of Southern Negro hospitality. One night 35 workers were invited to a fried chicken dinner. Another day they feasted on spaghetti in a local home. Six hundred people jammed into a steaming hall for a dance on the eve of the Fourth of July. Kay danced with the local boys until she was ready to drop. "They were so anxious to dance with us. Most of them had never even shaken hands with a white person."

At Oxford the problem of sexual contacts between white and Negro had been discussed frankly by the ministers. For Kay it soon became a practical dilemma. A 16-year-old boy developed a crush on her. One night he asked if he could kiss her. "I've never kissed a white girl before," he said shyly. Kay's answer was firm. "I don't want you to treat me as a white object any more than I treat you as a black object. I'm a real person and so are you. If the only basis for physical contact is the difference in our color, then there's no basis at all."

Teaching briefly in a Freedom School, Kay learned something about the gaps in Negro education. Federal District Judge Sidney Mize had just ordered three Mississippi school districts to integrate in the fall. His own personal disapproval of the order was implicit in a gratuitous statement that Negro brains were smaller, and thus inferior. Kay and her students decided to write Judge Mize a letter, giving him the true facts. Together they trooped to the white library, where they were pleasantly received, to marshal their evidence. "These were high-school students," Kay says, "but they didn't know how to use an encyclopedia, and they had never been taught how to consult a card catalogue. They're naturally intelligent but they're shy about talking up. I had to be careful not to make the mistake I made in college, that if someone is not verbally adept, he's not quite bright. Everyone doesn't go around yakking the way I do."

In Greenville the three girls were restless. "There were too

many teachers and we felt we were not getting involved with
the movement as much as we'd hoped," Kay explained. When
a phone call came on July 9th from Jackson headquarters,
asking if they would like to start a new Freedom School in
rural Madison County, Kay hesitated only briefly. She had become friendly with a boy, another worker in the Greenville
project. "I was the only one of the three with any ties," she
said, "but I had come to Mississippi for civil rights, not boy
friends." The next day they set off by bus for Canton.

They learned quickly that Canton was not liberal Greenville. Within minutes after the driver dropped them at a gas
station, the police arrived, summoned by the owner, who
spotted "those beatniks from the North." They were questioned briefly and allowed to proceed. They spent their first
night in Canton with a young Negro couple who both had
just lost their jobs for trying to register to vote. In the middle of the living room was a crated bathtub, ordered a month
earlier. Now there was no money to install it. Yet Kay, always
ebullient, was excited by her surroundings. "There's a fig tree
out back, and I ate my first fresh fig," she told a friend
breathlessly.

The story behind their school was exciting too. At the
beginning of the summer, leaders scouted through towns,
hunting students, homes for teachers, a school site. Now Mississippi Negroes were coming to them, begging for more
schools. A thousand youngsters had been expected to enroll.
By midsummer there were already 2,000 in 22 communities.

Two days before the girls reached Canton, a retired Negro
schoolteacher had telephoned the Freedom House there. A
church was available, he had housing for three teachers, and
at least 40 pupils were eager to start. The next day he walked
into the Freedom House and sat down. "I've come for my
teachers," he said firmly.

He drove the girls on July 11th to the Higgins and the
Forbes farms. By Mississippi Negro standards, the home of
John and Mary Higgins, where Kay and Karol lived for the
next six weeks, is middle class. It is a firmly built, green clapboard structure, with a tin roof blazing in the sun. The small
living room has dark red upholstered furniture. A rug covers
the unvarnished floor, and pink and gray paper, peeling near

the ceiling, decorates the walls. ("At night," Kay said, "we listened to the mice scrambling around behind the wallpaper.") There are four bedrooms, a dining room, where the refrigerator sits, a kitchen with a gas stove. Although there is electricity, a television set and a freezer, there is no plumbing. Water is hoisted in a bucket from a deep cistern out back, carried in pails into the kitchen and warmed on the stove. The outhouse is a primitive structure where chickens are frequently underfoot, and where in the heat of the day wasps buzz in swarms. Frequently they also invade the house.

"We took a bath every night," Kay says. "It was so hot you had to. We soon got the trick of lugging in two bucketfuls of water and kneeling in a large washtub to soap ourselves. When we washed our clothes, we used a scrub board and two tubs, one for soaping, the other for rinsing."

The girls helped out with the family chores. Kay hauled the water. Karol sometimes did the family ironing, and they both shared the dishwashing. Often they fixed their own breakfast. "I made an omelet," Kay said, "and Karol promptly burned the toast in the oven. There was a toaster, but the only electrical outlet was the ceiling fixture and the toaster cord was too short to reach."

Two meals were served daily—breakfast, and at midafternoon, dinner. At other times the girls were free to raid the icebox for cheese, watermelon, and raw milk from the Higgins cows. Beef was rarely served, but there were fried chicken, sausage, brains, hominy grits and golden corn bread; and from the garden, tomatoes, okra, potatoes, beans. The diet was starchy, and Kay, who is five feet six and weighs a slim 125 pounds, kept worrying about getting fat. She and Karol vowed to diet, but their resolve broke down as they visited Negro homes where steamy molasses cakes had just been baked.

Security regulations hemmed in their life. Although the Higgins front porch with its comfortable rocker catches a stray breeze, they were discouraged from sitting on it. Passing cars, a potential source of trouble, could see them from the road. They used the Forbes car to drive to school, but they were not allowed to go farther without first notifying the Canton office. When the grocery telephone was forbidden to them, they had no way of notifying Canton at all. Exploring the country roads on foot, except in a small area of Negro homes, was out. After dark they left the house only to go to school or a church meeting.

The girls learned one regulation with some pain. They could not ride alone in a car with a Negro boy. If they drove with Negroes, they sat by themselves either in the front or back. No one had told them this rule when they arrived. One evening after a meeting in a Negro church, Natalie asked a local boy to drive her a quarter of a mile to a grocery store to buy a pack of cigarettes. The innocent trip took ten minutes, but the next day, at the request of the sheriff, the boy was fired from his job. The police spread the word that the two had been seen hugging and kissing in the front seat. (In Oxford, Vincent Harding had warned, "Mississippi whites feel threatened when they see Negro and white together, and they respond to the threat with violence.")

All summer Natalie felt guilty about the incident. "What I worry about most," she said, "is the danger we are to others. Sure, the sheriff says he's not going to kick us, but he might kick someone else because of us. In a way, I'd feel better if we were kicked."

The girls had recurrent moments of cabin fever, particularly on quiet Saturday nights. It was dangerous to be seen with the Negro boys who lived in the farmhouses around them. They could not attend parties of the civil rights staff in Canton because of the hazards of driving at night. This was the time when white boys their own age, who lounged at the gas stations during the day, climbed into their cars and went scouting for trouble. Even receiving and sending mail was uncertain. Mail exchanges were made whenever a civil rights worker drove out from Canton, but the Canton staff never had enough cars for its needs.

On one August day, ready to explode after a week of isolation, Kay and Karol broke security rules and went into Canton to get their mail and telephone their parents. A Negro neighbor drove them three-quarters of the way, and then they started walking in the 100-degree heat. Kay recalls, "On the edge of town we stopped at a gas station to use the bathroom. The attendant started asking questions, and we told him we were civil rights workers. He stared rudely and then said with deliberation, 'If I'd known that, I'd have made you use the colored rest room round back.'

"'That's all right with me,' I said. 'A toilet's a toilet.'

"'Yeah. Next time you use the nigger toilet.'"

To get to the Freedom House they had to walk through the downtown area. Karol had a headache, so they looked for a drugstore. The first one they saw had a sticker on the door reading "White Citizens Council for Racial Integrity." (The Citizens Council, a dominant force in Mississippi, was the first group in the state to call for defiance of the Civil Rights Act of 1964.) They headed for the next place, but it had a Citizens Council sticker too. In fact, all the stores had identical stickers. "We both were shocked," Kay says. "We had no idea that the opposition was so out in the open."

Brief contacts with whites were unpleasant and carried overtones of danger. The girls had hoped to visit white churches and talk to their parishioners, but the experience of other Canton workers was discouraging. One volunteer, turned away from a white church, discovered that the gas tank of his car had been filled with sugar. On another quiet Sunday two volunteers, rebuffed at church, were set upon by hoodlums and beaten.

It soon became instinctive to distinguish friend from enemy. If a car drove down the road with a white arm protruding from the window, Kay and Karol scurried inside to their room. "I always got shook up when white cars came by," Kay said. If the arm was black, they relaxed and waved. The two were walking home from Freedom School one day when a large, sweaty man with a ruddy complexion stopped and offered them a ride. They refused politely. He struck up a conversation. "You're both purty gals," he said, "some of the purtiest I've ever seen. But I seen you the other day up at that nigger store talking to the worst nigger slum in the country. Why, that nigger slum can't even count to ten."

"Yes, we've been talking to Negroes at the store," Karol said, "and we'd be glad to come to your home and talk to your wife and you too."

"I wouldn't let the likes of you in my house. Why don't you go home where you belong?" Then he pulled up the brake and started to get out of the car. The girls didn't wait to discover his intentions. Hearts pounding, they strode away on the double. He stared but did not follow.

Each girl reacted differently to the summer's tension. Natalie was the most cautious. One day white friends of hers, working in the project in another part of the state, drove up for a visit. "Until I saw who they were," she said, "I almost had heart failure."

Small irritations dogged the Freedom School all summer, and Karol met them with impatience. School was held in the evening because many students chopped weeds in the cotton fields all day. (Three dollars for a ten-hour day was good pay.) The girls were always prompt, but their students strolled in a half-hour to an hour late. "I just don't feel I'm doing half the things I could," Karol grumbled. "In Mississippi every day is like Sunday afternoon at home. It's like quicksand, and you can't get out of it."

Kay is a particularly stable young woman. Small setbacks don't usually bother her, and she doesn't worry or get depressed easily. Yet even her equable disposition was ruffled as the lonely summer wore on. "I seem to run a gamut of emotions," she wrote in August to a friend. "Some days I'm easygoing and relaxed, and others I'm impatient and restless with everyone. One afternoon when Karol said it was too hot to walk to Canton, I felt so angry and frustrated that I almost cried."

Occasional parties lightened the monotony. One Sunday the girls and about 20 Negro neighbors went swimming in a nearby pond, after first chasing out a horse and some cows. A few weeks later they joined 300 persons at a large Negro farm for a picnic and county convention of the Freedom Democratic party. Kay and Natalie attended a deer hunters' picnic held on one of the back sloughs of the Pearl River, lined with huge old cypress trees. Food was served from big black iron kettles, one filled with fried fish, the other, a variety stew with meat, lima beans and even lemon peel.

But the heart of the summer was their work, and they loved it. In addition to teaching five evenings a week and preparing their classes, Kay and Karol used free hours for voter-registration work, trudging in the hot sun down miles of dusty roads, knocking on the doors of Negro farmhouses.

Here they met tenant farmers too poor or too tired to attend Freedom School or go to church. Many of the houses were constructed of unpainted, weathered boards, looking as if a light breeze would bring them tumbling down. Front steps were rotting, and milk crates served as porch furniture. Old chamber pots held lovingly tended vines. The rooms were dark, often lighted only from the fireplace or by kerosene lamps. In one house two bulging paper bags were tacked high on a wall. Here Sunday clothing was safe from the mice. Walls were plastered with old newspapers. "In one place the effect was charming," Kay said. "The ceilings were pasted with brightly colored magazine pages, making a collage that would rival some of the pieces in the Chicago Art Institute."

The shacks were swarming with flies and children. "I counted six children in one," Kay said, "the oldest only seven. Their bellies were swollen and their eyes lackluster. They looked like pictures of starving Africans." The mother wore a ragged housedress. She looked close to 40, but she told the girls she was 22. She kept saying, "Yes, ma'am" until Kay could stand it no longer. "I wish you wouldn't call me 'ma'am,'" Kay told her. "The two of us are exactly the same age." It was dangerous to stay long in the houses of tenant farmers. If their employer knew that civil rights workers had visited, they were likely to lose their homes.

The registration drive that engaged Kay's energies was not aimed at bringing Negroes down to the county courthouse to register. In Madison County this is still an almost hopeless task. Their job was to register Negroes in the Freedom Democratic party, formed in the spring of 1964 as an alternative structure to the white Democratic party, which systematically excludes Negroes. The goal was to file 100,000 forms at the national Democratic convention in August in order to challenge the seating of the white Mississippi party. Even the simple form, ten questions long, frightened some persons. "If I fill it out," one widow asked, "are you sure it won't knock out my job or anything?"

At one shack Kay and Karol waited patiently on the porch while an old man walked slowly in from the field where he was ploughing. He had a sad, stoic face, a reddish-bronze cast to his skin and an immense, quiet dignity. When they shook his hand he looked surprised but said nothing. As Kay launched into her glib patter, explaining the Freedom Democratic party, he stood quietly, murmuring an occasional "Yes'm." There was no flicker of recognition when she mentioned the participation of national Negro leaders, such as Dr. Martin Luther King, but his eyes lighted up when she said she lived with the Higgins family. She asked if he wanted to register, and he spoke for the first time. "I don't know about that," he said. "No one ever talked to me before about such things."

Disappointed, the girls shook hands and left. "You're never sure you're getting across," Kay sighed. "You don't ever get any feedback."

But when they returned the following week, the old man greeted them with a smile. He announced proudly that he was ready to sign, and that he also would like to attend the Freedom School. He was 74 years old.

Although the school curriculum was designed for high-school students, the girls constantly revised it for their pupils, who ranged in age from four to 60. Ten adults came regularly and brought their children. There were four age groups: tiny children, just learning to read; those in the upper elementary grades; teen-agers; and adults. Some of the adults were almost illiterate; others were young men and women halfway through college. With 15-mile distances to travel and a paucity of cars, the students usually arrived in groups. One night a young man drove up in a panel truck that disgorged 13 youngsters of assorted ages.

The church that houses the Freedom School is a pleasant one-room structure, its hard wooden benches holding some 75 persons. During the first week the girls realized that anyone seated before an open window, with light streaming out, made an easy target for a shot from a passing car. A few days later they saw a white man peeping in a window. So they set their younger pupils to work making water-color designs on white butcher paper to tack over the windows. The effect was like muted stained glass. One slogan, decorated with curlicues, read simply: "Everybody want freedom. Willie want freedom." Tacked to the pulpit, neatly printed on blue cardboard, was a section of the Declaration of Independence: "We hold these truths to be self-evident. . . ." Below the pulpit were a blackboard and a desk.

Each lesson was tied in to the students' own lives and to the freedom movement. The two French students conjugated "We love freedom." To a science class Kay described the scientific method, emphasizing the necessity for seeking facts before reaching conclusions. A math class centered on installment buying, with an analysis of how much interest a purchaser ended up paying for his stove or television set. Hate was never taught. The groups discussed stereotypes—the rich white man, the poor white, the sheriff—and tried to understand why individual whites acted as they did. Negro history, of which all were abysmally ignorant, was the most popular topic.

There were other shocking areas of ignorance. Most of the adults equated citizenship with voting. Asked if he was a citizen of the United States, one countered, "Well, am I?" Some of the children did not know what state they lived in or what other states bordered on it. There was unanimous disapproval of Barry Goldwater, but few knew why they were against him. The high-school students were sharp in discussion but often deficient in reading ability.

Kay stormed, "These kids are so bright and their school shortchanges them so badly. Their textbooks are second-hand. Their high school has only two typewriters. Last year they finally got the equipment to start a woodworking class for the boys, and then found there was no money to buy wood."

Karol, with three years of experience in teaching middle-class white children, said, "Socially these youngsters are much more mature than my students at home. They've assumed responsibility since childhood. They're very sophisticated in dealing with people. But in academic areas they're far behind. At home some students start off the year with an insolent 'show me' attitude. Here they have a blind faith that you have something to offer them. Working with them sometimes makes me ashamed for myself, because I'm not always sure I can live up to that faith."

If the girls ever had any stereotyped ideas themselves about the Mississippi Negro, the summer dispelled them. "We've heard about how backward the Southern Negro is, how lacking in self-respect," Kay said. "This just hasn't been true among the families we've met. Not one is defeatist or apathetic. When we stand in front of the store and talk to them, it's they who are in danger from a passing white car, but they're quite willing to chance it. They have a caution bred in their bones, but they never cower. One woman I met at church works in the fields, but she has such dignity, such natural manners. She stands like an American Gothic type, straight and spare. And some of the boys—it would be a crime if they didn't get to college."

What did the summer accomplish? All three girls feel that they got more than they gave. Karol said, "Living with Negro people, we learned the meaning of true hospitality. They were willing to take us into their homes before we proved our mettle. Merely by doing this, they showed their belief that all white people were not alike, even though whites they knew lumped Negroes in a single category. Knowing them has made me more hopeful about the future. With the young people freedom is in the air. They won't rest until they achieve it. Perhaps it won't take as long as we had believed."

At Oxford in June, staff officials set modest goals for the Mississippi Summer Project. How many were achieved?

"The most important thing we can do is just to be present," said Vincent Harding. Over 1,000 were present, more than 500 student volunteers, plus staff workers, ministers, doctors, lawyers. Kay says, "We were the first white persons who ever called those Negro women 'Mrs.,' the first to shake many black hands. If we did nothing more than be friendly, if we didn't teach anything at all, it would still be all right."

"We plan to open community centers, Freedom Schools, to stress voter registration, to teach Negro farmers about untapped federal sources for financial aid," said Bob Moses in Oxford. Thirteen community centers functioned, 47 Freedom Schools. Consumer cooperatives were started, and even a Negro chamber of commerce. These will continue. Many community centers will keep their doors open, some under the sponsorship of the National Council of Churches. Schools are still meeting, some in the evening, others as a substitute for inadequate public education. Massive voter registration was not achieved, but federal suits in several areas are expected to forbid registrars from discriminating. Freedom Registration forms, filled out by 65,000, have shown the country unmistakably that the Mississippi Negro wants to vote and the integrated Freedom Democratic party gained a measure of recognition at the Democratic convention, which voted to seat two of its delegates.

"We are working to train leaders in the community," said Staughton Lynd, Freedom School director. Young and old flocked for guidance to the Freedom Houses and then went ahead to develop programs to break the 100-year political, economic and social stranglehold on Mississippi Negroes. Typical is a young longshoreman who now devotes every night in a Gulf town to voter-registration work. Before the advent of the civil rights workers, he spent his nights relaxing in front of his television set.

"We want to give the young people a desire to learn," Staughton Lynd said. Books were a rarity in rural Negro Madison County until Kay and her co-workers opened their library and encouraged students to borrow a book a week. They introduced provocative new names—James Baldwin, Robert Frost. They encouraged youngsters to go to college and told them about available scholarships. They taught their students to ask why.

"Mississippi will not change until there are white people working with Negroes to change it. You had better look for these," Vincent Harding said. This was an area where the project met little success. White moderates—and there are some—were still too fearful to speak up. But the national publicity given the summer project—publicity which stemmed directly from the white skins of its participants—shocked others in the North and West into a realization that a police state existed in America. A C.O.F.O. official said, "Now, for the first time since Reconstruction, we can expect Northern support for Negroes here."

At the end of the summer Kay and Karol went home. Natalie remained, one of more than 100 volunteers to continue the struggle started in the hot summer of 1964. Kay, now back at S.I.U. for her last year of school, is optimistic about Mississippi and the chances of its Negroes to achieve their rights as American citizens. Soberly she knows that outside aid will still be needed for a long time. As for her role?

"I'll be back," she says.

Ollie McClung's Big Decision

by Michael Durham

OLLIE MCCLUNG is a self-effacing 48-year-old lay preacher of the Cumberland Presbyterian Church in Birmingham, Ala., who runs a barbecue restaurant on State Highway 149 on the seedy south side of the city. At lunchtime the 220 seats in Ollie's Barbecue fill up quickly with a loyal clientele that includes corporation executives in dark suits and laborers in work clothes. At night men come and bring their families. Ollie's menu describes the barbecue as "the world's best," and the many customers who agree with this have made Ollie well and respectfully known in his neighborhood.

Now Ollie has become well-known far from the south side —throughout the U.S. He is the first man to challenge the Public Accommodations section of the civil rights law and win. Hearing the case of Ollie McClung Sr. & Ollie McClung Jr. v. Robert Kennedy, a three-judge panel of the federal district court last month held the Civil Rights Act unconstitutional as applied to businesses not engaged in interstate commerce. They ruled that Ollie, whose customers are virtually all local, is not so engaged. (In another case, involving a motel catering to interstate business, courts have upheld the law.) If the Supreme Court upholds him and the lower court, Ollie McClung will have struck a historic blow for segregation.

But Ollie takes no delight in the fact that he has become the champion of segregationists everywhere. It requires a certain arrogance to despise someone just because of the color of his skin, and people who know Ollie will tell you there is not a trace of arrogance in his soul. "Many Negroes," he says, "occupy a higher station in the eyes of God than whites do." That is not the sort of thing that segregationists generally say. Ollie is a little man, sincere and dignified in his beliefs, who has been caught in the currents of a social movement he does not understand.

One thing Ollie does understand is barbecue. The recipe he uses was passed along by his father, who founded the restaurant in 1926. As Ollie sees it, he operates the place as "a trust for our customers." "It is our hope," he says, "that they will leave in a better frame of mind than when they came in." The annual gross of about $350,000 suggests that Ollie's barbecue improves the frame of mind of half a million diners a year. His prices are modest and it takes a man with a stupendous appetite to spend more than a dollar with Ollie, even counting the drinks needed to cool throats heated by Ollie's barbecue sauce—soft drinks because Ollie serves no beer or liquor.

He hasn't since 1946. Just before Christmas that year his wife asked him to take the children to Sunday school. He stayed on, heard the sermon and religion took fire in him. "I had my spiritual experience," he explains.

His whole life changed, and so did his restaurant. One of the first manifestations of the new Ollie occurred on New Year's Day, 10 days after his conversion. He loaded all the beer he had on hand onto a truck and hauled it to the city dump. Thereafter he shut down his restaurant on Sundays: "I now felt that I was in partnership with the Lord, and if the Lord felt he could do better in six days than in seven, we would do the same thing."

These were decisions of pure conscience. And it was again Ollie's conscience—guided by prayer and wrapped around economic considerations that involved his employes as well as himself—that thrust him into the segregation fight.

The civil rights law had posed a dilemma for Ollie. He believes in obeying all laws. On the other hand, he was sure that compliance with this one would wreck his business. Over the years a Negro neighborhood had grown up around the restaurant. He could foresee that once he desegregated, the place would become overrun with Negro teen-agers. His regular customers would stay away.

Ollie wrestled with his conscience and prayed for guidance. Then one night, just before President Johnson signed the bill into law, he called his 26 Negro and 10 white employes together.

"I told them," he recalls, "that I felt the Lord had blessed our business over the years and that He had blessed each one of us greatly. I told them that I didn't feel the Lord felt we should change our method of doing business."

Most of the help has been with Ollie for years. They are paid no wages but draw a percentage of the profits. Some of the money goes into a retirement fund. Ollie works as hard as anybody, spending long hours at the hickory-smoke pit, basting and turning the meat.

At the meeting nobody openly objected to his decision. Several employes, including some Negroes, said they agreed with it.

On the day after the civil rights law took effect a well-dressed young Negro entered the restaurant and asked for the manager. Ollie was at home and his son and partner, Ollie Jr., was in charge. The Negro asked if he could be served at the counter. Ollie Jr. said no and the man left. Within the hour he returned with three other young Negroes. They sat at the counter, and a white customer got up and stalked out. Ollie Jr. asked them to leave and they did, quietly making a notation on a file card.

When his son told him about the incident Ollie started worrying. "I felt we were doing right," he says, "but I didn't want anybody thinking that I was violating the law. I wanted to erase any such thinking." And the only way to do that, he reasoned, was first to alter the law. Ollie and his son went to a lawyer and initiated their suit.

After the judges had decided in his favor, Ollie was thankful that he was no longer violating the law. Then last week Supreme Court Justice Hugo Black issued an order that had the effect of reaffirming the validity of the law until the full Supreme Court could rule. It was only a technical setback for Ollie: He has been advised that he can refuse, without fear of penalty, to serve Negroes until a final ruling is handed down.

Ollie is praying that the Negro community will have the wisdom to go along with his logic: "I don't think that any Christian Negro would want to eat in this restaurant when he knows that it will hurt someone else."

But worries have not kept Ollie from his practice of going

off on Sundays to preach. He has been doing this for years, and in 1961 and 1962 traveled around the country preaching his Fundamentalist doctrines—before Chinese congregations in San Francisco, Indians in Oklahoma. "Some of the hardest preaching I have ever done," he says, "has been in colored churches." Recently he preached a sermon at the Crestline Presbyterian Church on his conflict with the civil rights law. He based his text on I Kings 21, which tells how Ahab, king of Israel, coveted the vineyard owned by Naboth, the Jezreelite. According to Ollie's interpretation, the vineyard is his barbecue and Ahab, who covets it, represents the Federal Government.

Business has not been affected either way by Ollie's suit, nor has the atmosphere of his place. A customer who uses profanity is politely handed a little card asking him not to: "Ladies and children are usually present." A glass case near the cash register displays six editions of the Bible for sale. On the wall is a plaque quoting the Book of Psalms: "O taste and see that the Lord is good: blessed is the man that trusteth in Him." And there is another sign: "We reserve the right to refuse service to anyone."

Life, October 9, 1964

Georgia Boy Goes Home

by Louis E. Lomax

I CAME home to Georgia by jet. The flight from New York to Atlanta was uneventful, but as the plane taxied toward the terminal I felt slightly uneasy. Georgia had just gone for Goldwater; Georgia was still Georgia. Walking along the corridor to the main lobby, I heard cracker twangs all about me; these, in my childhood, were the sound of the enemy, so that even now I react when I hear them, and I immediately suspect any white man who has a Southern drawl. Yet I could see no signs telling me where I should eat, drink, or go to the rest room. The white passengers seemed totally unconcerned with me. I could see a change in their eyes, on their faces, in the way they let me alone to be me.

I was on my way to the Southern Airlines counter to confirm my reservation to Valdosta. Suddenly I saw a brown arm waving at me from a phone booth. There, in the booth, was Martin Luther King, Jr. Martin's family and mine had been Negro Baptist leaders in Georgia for almost fifty years; I first got to know him when I was in college and he was in junior high school. Now I was on my way home to Valdosta for *Harper's* to write about the changes in my town and to give a sermon in my uncle's church; Martin was on the way to the island of Bimini to write his Nobel Prize acceptance speech.

Martin and I stood in the lobby and tried to talk, but to no avail. We were continuously interrupted by white people who rushed over to shake his hand and pat him on the back. I could hardly believe that I was in Atlanta, that these were white people with twangs, and that they were saying what they were saying. Many of them asked for Martin's autograph; a few of them recognized me from television or from the dust jacket of a book and asked me to sign slips of paper. They were an incredible lot: a group of soldiers, five sailors, three marines, a score of civilians including the brother of the present Governor of Georgia, and three Negro girls. One stately old white man walked up to Martin and said, "By God, I don't like all you're doing, but as a fellow Georgian I'm proud of you."

My flight home was several hours away, and I had made a reservation at a motel near the airport. As Martin and I were parting, the loudspeaker announced that the motel bus was waiting for "Dr. Lomax." A Negro porter gathered my baggage and led me to the bus; he put my bags on the ground and I tipped him. A few seconds later I saw the white bus driver, and I knew I had reached a moment of confrontation. It seemed an eternity as I glanced up and down, from the white driver to my baggage; I remembered all those years I had spent serving white people as a bellboy, a shoeshine boy, a waiter. The driver, however, couldn't have cared less about me or my color. He picked up my bags and put them in the bus. This is what the Republic has done to me and twenty million like me—I never felt so equal in all my life when I saw that white man stoop down and pick up *my* bags. "Get right in, sir," he said.

The motel people were the same. They acted as if there had never been such a thing as segregation. I ate and drank where I pleased. Later I had to break away from three white men and their woman companion who latched onto me in the motel dining room and insisted that I party with them until my plane left.

II

I came back home to the land tilled and served by my fathers for four generations. Valdostans, like most people, are children of fixity; as individuals and as a tribe they find a crag, a limb, a spot of earth—physical or emotional or both—and they cling on for dear life. They change without growing, and the more they change the more they remain the same. What frightens them, as with most people, is the sudden discovery that what they are—how they have lived all their lives—stands somehow in the path of history and of progress.

One can go home again if he remembers and accepts the

land of his birth for what it was, if he understands what that land has become and why. The homecoming is more complete if one admits that he and his land have shaped each other, that from it springs much of both his weakness and his strength. Only as I walked down River Street toward the place I was born did I realize how much of a child of this land I am: its mud squished through my toes as I romped on unpaved streets and alleys; its puritanical somnolence settled over my childhood dreams and all but choked me into conformity. It was on the corner of River and Wells Streets, when I was eight years old, that a white man ordered his bulldog to attack me simply because I was a Negro. Judge J. G. Cranford and his wife lived in the big white house on the corner. They saw the incident from the front porch, and Mrs. Cranford ran into the street to my rescue and drove the man away with shame.

River Street has grown old without changing very much. The weed field that stretched between here and Jackson Street Lane is still a weed field; the old warehouse that sat at the edge of the field is now a surplus food distribution center. The houses are the same houses they were when I was a child.

R. F. Lewes, as I shall call him, lived on this block. The summer before my junior year in college I was a handyman in his shop. Mr. Lewes would entertain his customers with dramatic descriptions of lynchings he had attended. His favorite story was about the night three Negroes were killed in a swamp near the Florida line. Lewes would advise his customers to get to a lynching early and stake out a choice spot on the killing ground. "But if the crowd is already there when you get there," he would add, "get down on your all fours and crawl between their legs so you can get up close to the nigger." One night I was cleaning the store when three of Mr. Lewes' cronies came in. "By God," he said to them, "this has been a rough day. Let's get a pint of moonshine and find some nigger bitches and get our luck changed."

Finally the stories became too much, and one day I threw down my shoeshine rag and went home. (After all, I was almost a junior in college and an official in my campus NAACP.) Lewes' son drove to our house and insisted that I return to work. My grandfather, the minister of the Macedonia First African Baptist Church, flatly said I didn't have to work in a place where my race was abused. R. F. Lewes, Jr., assured Grandfather that he would see to it that his father stopped telling lynch stories while I was in the shop. I had hardly returned to work when Lewes walked up to me and put his arms around my shoulders. "Louis," he said, eyeing me as if I were a wounded animal, "I wouldn't hurt *you!*"

During my visit home I saw Mr. Lewes on the street. He is very old and walks with a stick. A few weeks before, a Negro man had sat on a bench on the courthouse lawn next to him. Recoiling in anger, Lewes began jabbing the Negro in the ribs with his walking stick. The Negro called the police, and they told Lewes that the courthouse bench was for all the people, and either to calm down or move on. Mr. Lewes moved on.

III

Ours was a curious ghetto. Jackson Street Lane was the boundary line between the Negro and white sections along River Street. For one block Negroes lived on the north side of the street; the south side was completely white. To compound the oddness—the kind of thing that keeps the South on the thin edge of insanity—the first two families in our block were white. I remember how their menfolk ran into the street rejoicing the night Max Schmeling defeated Joe Louis.

The two white houses are still there, but I cannot for the life of me account for the white people who had lived in them. They were of another world; I did not know their names, who they were, or what they did. For that matter, I can't recall a single white person in the entire town whom I *really knew* when I was a boy. There were a few white people —R. F. Lewes and the man whose bulldog attacked me— whom I truly feared and, more than likely, hated. There were a few white people, Mrs. Cranford for example, whom I trusted and, perhaps, loved. But whatever understanding I had of all of these people was based on nothing more than surface encounter.

The house where I was born is torn down, the land covered with brush. The corner grocery store, built by a grocery chain on land leased from my grandfather, is now an eyesore and a public hazard. This land still belongs to us. My Uncle James, now the preacher at the Macedonia Baptist Church, and I are the last of the Lomaxes. Soon we must sit down and decide what to do about the land. Where my grandmother's living room once was, there are wild weeds; thistles cover the place where my grandfather used to retire on Saturday nights to prepare his sermon. There are tall bushes in the potato patch and creeping vines in the bait bed.

There are other changes. The new freeway that runs from Atlanta to Jacksonville has ruined the sucker and catfish hole where Grandfather and I used to fish. The new city hall and its grounds sprawl over the homesites of more than twenty families, Negro and white. The mud swamp on the Clydesville Road is now the airport, and the Dasher High School from which I was graduated twenty-five years ago is now the J. L. Lomax Junior High School, which is named after my Uncle James.

When I walked these streets as a boy I prided myself in the fact that I knew exactly how many people there were in the town—14,592. (My grandfather used to say that this figure included "Negroes, white people, chickens, cows, two mules, and a stray hound dog.") By 1960 the population had more than doubled, and it is predicted that there may be 75,000 people living here by 1980. Since I was a child the number of people working in agriculture has decreased threefold; the corresponding increase in trades, technical, professional, and government employees is expected to continue.

Despite the occasional new sight, Valdosta, like most American cities and towns, is old and tired and falling down. A few weeks ago, not far from my old home, a chimney fell from a dilapidated building and killed a small child. In October of last year the city manager pleaded with the mayor and the city council for power to initiate a comprehensive housing code. His research showed that 33 per cent of Valdosta's housing is either dilapidated or deteriorating, that less than half of the town's dwelling units are owner-occupied, and that only slightly more than five hundred new housing units will be erected during the rest of the 1960s. The city manager wanted to force the owners of deteriorating properties to fix them up, the owners of dilapidated buildings to tear them down under the threat that if they don't the city will. He wanted to do something about the lack of recreational facilities for young people. So far he has not succeeded, but he is still trying.

A referendum that would have levied two bond issues for parks and recreation recently was defeated, with about 10 per cent of the registered voters participating. But in October a one-million-dollar school bond issue won the voters' approval, although less than two thousand of the city's eight thousand registered women voters bothered to go to the polls.

Apathy plagues the town. The people, both Negro and white, seem to have run out of gas. They simply don't care about civic improvements. The referendum for parks and recreation would have given the city two swimming pools. It was defeated by seventeen votes. Yet one night I walked up and down Patterson Street, the white mecca, and saw scores of boys and girls slinking into darkened store alcoves and alleys. Then I went down along South Ashley Street, the Negro section, and saw even more young people darting into back streets, petting in open lots, dancing to funky music in questionable "soda and ice cream parlors."

IV

As far as public accommodations go, Valdosta is an open town. I ate where I chose and went where I pleased, talking with whomever I wished of both races. Like most Southern towns, this one had moments of racial tension during the first days of integrated cafés, lunch counters, and theaters. But a well-disciplined law force invoked the law of the land. While police chiefs in other Southern towns were rousing the white rabble, the Valdosta police chief was traveling through the swamp farmlands on the town's outskirts telling white men who were most likely to get likkered up and come to town to keep calm. The Negroes were told to eat, not just demonstrate, and the whites were warned to keep the peace. They both did just that. Whenever and wherever Negroes have pressed their case there has been compliance with the Civil Rights Act.

This did not happen all by itself. A loosely organized inter-racial council arrived at reasonable, step-by-step goals. I think the major preventive act took place when the white power structure yielded to demands for Negro policemen. The sight of Negroes whom they knew and trusted policing their community gave Valdosta's Negroes a pride and a sense of personal security they had never had before. My town has not made ugly national and international headlines because the white power structure, led by three key men, took a long look at the turmoil that confronted so many places in the South and decided it would not happen in Valdosta.

E. M. Turner, the seventy-two-year-old editor of the local paper, took the same position with me. I was both astounded and angry. He had been the editor of the paper since I was a child. I had wanted to be a reporter and a writer, to learn the fundamentals of my craft, but I couldn't even get a job as a delivery boy. The first essay I ever wrote won me an honorable mention in a contest sponsored by the paper; they announced that I was a Negro and they misspelled my name. Yet E. M. Turner sat with me now for almost an hour and a half. He traced the rise of Valdosta from a one-crop town that trembled at the thought of the boll weevil to a town which changed its economy to one based on turpentine, pine trees, and resin. He sketched out the semi-industrial era that lies ahead for the town.

Our talk moved on to the race issue. "I've never had any trouble with nigras," Turner said. "I may not like the Civil Rights Bill, but it's the law of the land and it must be obeyed. But let me tell you this," he said. "I talked to my cook; she is a sweet old nigra woman who has been with us for years and she told me she didn't want her grandchildren going to school with white children."

I heard E. M. Turner well, and I thought to myself that I have yet to meet a white man, in the South or the North, whose cook believed in integration. Yet I wondered how, without integrated schools, such a man as Turner expected us to turn out Negroes equally prepared for the American job market. I decided to ask a significant question:

"Would you hire a Negro reporter if he was qualified?"

Turner did not hesitate. "I've never been faced with the issue," he said. "I'm not sure what I would do."

Later that day, when I had a talk with a local businessman,

I saw something of the anguish that afflicts many white Valdostans of my age. His brother-in-law lives in Colombia and is married to a Colombian woman darker than most Negroes. The brother wanted to bring his wife to Valdosta for a visit; the proposed visit was, of course, vetoed with vigor. "Lord, how ashamed I am," he told me. "I'm afraid to have my own brother and sister come to my home."

He is a devout member of a Protestant church in Valdosta. His church raises money each month to keep an impoverished Negro church of the same denomination going. "We raise that money," he told me, "to keep the Negroes from coming to our church. I was just horrified when I saw how my fellow white Christians reacted when the question of integrating the two churches came up."

But it was another realization that really troubled him. "Now take you," he said. "I'd like to have you in my home, to sit down to prayer and break bread with my family. My wife feels the same way. But we'd be afraid to invite you."

"I'd invite you to my home," I told him. "I'm not afraid."

"But I'd be afraid to *come*," he shot back, pounding the desk with anger at his world and himself.

"In other words," I said, "there is a sense in which I, a Negro, have more freedom than you have."

"That's true," he replied. "Everything is so confused down here. They wouldn't bother you and your Uncle James if you invited my family to your home. But they would get after *us* if we came." He turned in his chair, dropping me out of his sight as he faced the wall and let his eyes drift toward the ceiling.

"But I did vote for Goldwater," he added, speaking more to himself than to me. "Somebody has just got to stop the Communists from taking over the world."

V

The Goldwater victory hung like a frightening cloud over the well-meaning white Valdostans who were trying to find a way out of the racial wilderness. One of the men most responsible for Goldwater's carrying Valdosta was George C. Cook, the seventy-three-year-old owner of the radio station. Cook came to town thirty years ago and became a leader in the business community; he has been president of the Chamber of Commerce and has spearheaded the drive to get more industry—"particularly those that will give these nigger women on relief something to do," he explained to me—into Valdosta. He made his station the voice of Goldwater conservatism and the White Citizens' Council. The week before the election, Cook encountered one of Valdosta's most respected Negroes in the post office. "Doctor," Cook said to the Negro, "I want you to go home and call all your friends and tell them to tune in on my station tonight at seven-thirty. We're going to give the niggers and Jews hell tonight and I sure want you and your people to hear it."

I talked with Cook for more than an hour. "Now I came out for Goldwater, but I ain't no Republican," he said. "I'm a Democrat. That," he went on to say, pounding his chest, "is in here, in my heart. I could no more be a Republican than I could fly. But I just couldn't stomach that Kennedy-Johnson crowd and the way they are taking over the rights of the states and the individual.

"Now as for this integration business, I don't see what all the hell's about. We never had any trouble with niggers. I was against the Civil Rights Bill but when it became the law of the land I felt we'd better try and live with it. One of my friends called me up and told me he'd gotten word that the niggers were coming to his lunch counter to demonstrate. He said he was going to feed them if they came there. I told him, by God, to feed them niggers and he'd find out that once he fed them, and they had made their point, they would never come back. And you know," he added, bursting into laughter, "that's exactly what happened. Them niggers ate, then they left and ain't a one of them black sonsabitches been back there since.

"Let me tell you something, Louis," he said suddenly. "I lived with niggers all my life; I grew up with them and played with them; there wasn't a bit of trouble. Why a sweet, old black nigger woman helped raise me; she was as sweet a woman as God ever let live. And if and when I get to heaven I'm going to look up that nigger woman and kiss her on the cheek.

"There ain't going to be no trouble here," he said. "A few

young niggers and young white trash might try to start something; then the old heads, nigger and white, will keep things under control. What we need in this town instead of agitation is some new industries with nigger jobs, so these nigger men can feed their families, so these nigger women on relief can make a pay check. That's what we need to keep Valdosta going. Why, the niggers are pouring into town by the carloads every day, and if we don't find something for them to do we are going to have one hell of a mess in this town before too long. Yes sir, that's what this town needs: nigger jobs, for nigger men and women."

On the subject of jobs, Comer Cherry, a diametrical opposite to Cook among the business community, feels the same way. Cherry has been president of the Chamber of Commerce and the Rotary Club, and a prime mover behind the biracial commission. He is representative of the new thinking among white Valdostans. "The way I see it," he says, "the economy of the nigra community is the root of the problem. Once the nigra can earn a respectable pay check, most of the agitation will die down."

The median income for a Valdosta white family in 1960 was $4,360; for Valdosta Negro families, $2,364. And there is a chilling prophecy in a recent economic study of the town. The study predicts that by 1980 the median income of Valdosta white families will be $9,500, while the income of Negro families will reach only $4,250—more than twice the present disparity. Comer Cherry and George C. Cook have a point. Somebody, somehow, had better do something about Negro income in Valdosta or there will be real trouble in the future.

VI

I found no tension whatsoever in the Valdosta Negro community. The Negro masses undulate along the streets, oblivious to what is going on in the Congo, in Red China, or in Mississippi. The county hospital has been completely integrated, and the authorities have shut down the old back entrance marked "colored." Yet despite the fact that the leaders have told local Negroes to use the front door, one witnesses the pathetic spectacle of their going to the same place to find a back way in. What mainly struck me is that there are more of them, and that they are growing in geometric proportions. They are the citizens of "Niggertown," the habitués of juke joints, of pig-foot alley and crumbling shanties. Their children pour into school, only to drop out. Talking with these dropouts one comes away knowing that they never really dropped in. They don't know anything; they can't do anything. Here, among the black masses, is the greatest monument to my town's—the South's—wickedness. It is a society which continues to grind out hundreds, thousands, millions who are totally defeated, who are alienated from that society from the day they are born.

The Valdosta black bourgeoisie serve the black masses. They teach them in school, pull their teeth, prescribe medicine for their livers, tell them about Jesus on Sunday morning, sell them life insurance when they are young, and bury them when they die. That is the way it was thirty-five years ago; that is the way it is now. Their only saving grace—and this is true all over the country—is that they are willing to accept, without recourse to background, any person who can traverse the maze that leads from Shantytown to professionalism. I was born to the black bourgeoisie; I stumbled and floundered for twenty years; and there were grave doubts that I would ever validate my heritage. Yet I had schoolmates who were up from the trash pile; some of them made it, and they are now solid members of the Valdosta Negro middle class.

It would be wrong for me to say that they don't care about the black masses. They do care; they care, at times, almost to the point of nervous breakdown. Their problem, essentially, is the same as that of the concerned white men of Valdosta: the monster created by the Southern way of life is so terrifying, and becoming so gargantuan, that nobody knows what to do or where to start doing it.

Meanwhile, the Valdosta black bourgeoisie are becoming more and more comfortable, their world more and more secure. They are the ones who can afford to dress up and go out for dinner once a week to a previously "white only" restaurant, who can travel during their vacations and take advantage of the integrated motels, hotels, and travel facilities.

Yet few of them have actually contributed to the Negro revolution that has made these things possible. The Valdosta black bourgeoisie are largely schoolteachers. Despite their new freedom, they must plod away in schoolrooms that are still separate and unequal; they must keep quiet about integration or be fired.

"I'm doing all I can do and still keep my job," one third-grade Negro teacher told me. "When my principal isn't around, I teach my children that four pickets times nine pickets is thirty-six pickets. I just hope and pray they grow up and get the message."

Part of the tragedy of my town is that there is no real Negro leadership to translate to the masses the message this teacher is trying to deliver. Negro leadership in Valdosta is nothing more than ten or twelve men with incomes rooted in the ghetto, who sporadically gather to try to muster general support for programs each of them has presented to the town's white fathers when his fellow Negro spokesmen were not looking. A dozen of these Negro leaders—most of whom I have known since childhood—met with me to discuss the plight of the Valdosta Negro and to describe what they planned to do about it. The more they talked the more it became apparent, as one of them had the courage to say, that Negro leadership was about the same as it was when I was a little boy. There is no NAACP in Valdosta, no Urban League. Nobody would dare let Martin Luther King, Jr., preach in their church, and CORE is something they read about in the newspaper and hear about on television. The Negro leaders, such as they are, turn on each other and accuse one another of being disloyal, apathetic, and indifferent.

VII

What, then, is the next step forward for Valdosta, not just toward integration, but into the world as it really is?

Although the Negro population is 36 per cent, not a single public school is integrated in the town. However, the all-white board of education is ready to accept Negro pupils into any schools they can establish their legal right to attend. Moreover, the white power structure knows precisely where these schools are, and the white students have been prepared for the probability that their schools will one day be integrated. Even more, the white students have accepted the idea and wish the Negroes would get it over with so everybody concerned can settle down to learning his lessons.

White Valdosta businessmen have jobs waiting for Negroes; these jobs will never be filled until Negro leaders stop fighting each other and draw up a unified job program to place before the biracial commission.

At a state college located in Valdosta, I was told, there were only two Negro students, and these were financed by some of the Negro leaders who met with me. No other Negroes had enrolled in two years. This could be changed if Negro spokesmen would unify and make the right demands. There is an integrated county technical and industrial school on the outskirts of Valdosta that is begging for Negro students. There are all too few Negro applicants. The brunt of the burden, I regret to say, rests with the town's Negro middle class. But they, like so many of their white peers, are consumed by fear.

The Valdosta Negro middle class, then, is on the verge of becoming a tribe; its members are fiercely proud of themselves and their own; they couldn't care less about socializing with white people. At a large party given for me one night, I was able to locate only one Negro friend—a woman—who had a social relationship with a white person. She and a white woman have a "luncheon friendship," largely at the urging of the white woman. Even that almost collapsed when the white woman invited other white women to join.

"The other white women smiled dryly at me," she said, "and I was ready to say, like, forget it. My husband makes more than her husband and I wasn't about to grovel just to have some white lunch dates."

"I know what you mean," a county school principal said. "These phony white liberals are about a bitch. They say they love us, that they want to cement relations, that they want to overcome the fact that there has been no communication between us and them, and then they get in that damn voting booth and . . ."

"Vote for Goldwater," several people shouted.

"You think you got problems," a doctor broke in. "I was walking down Patterson Street a few weeks ago and a white man fell to the sidewalk with a heart attack right in front of me. I forgot he was white and tried to help him. A crowd gathered and became hostile because I was a Negro!"

"Did you go away and let him die?" somebody shouted from the back of the room.

"No," the doctor replied, "I did the best I could for the sonofabitch and sent him off to the hospital." Everyone, of course, laughed.

The party music played, but there was surprisingly little drinking or dancing. I was home; these were my brothers and sisters. They knew me and were glad to see me. We talked of the days when we were children, of our fathers and mothers and grandparents who pushed us so far along the way. We told the "in" jokes. Nobody mentioned white people; nobody wanted or needed them there. We would have stayed all night if it had not been Saturday. But at church the next morning one of the school principals was scheduled to sing a solo. One woman was to play the organ, another the piano. Another school principal was to handle the collection, and I was to deliver the sermon.

VIII

The next day I stood in the Macedonia Baptist Church pulpit that has been occupied by a Lomax for more than half a century; some of the people who sat in the congregation had known me before I knew myself. Tribal middle-class pride was running high. Just the Sunday before, Calvin King, one of my younger childhood schoolmates who went on to get his doctorate in mathematics, had been the guest preacher. Uncle James had listened with pride as Calvin told of his travels in the Holy Land, of his work in helping launch a new university in Nigeria.

I told the congregation about my experiences in Africa, behind the Iron Curtain, and in American cities where racial troubles had erupted. White Christianity, I said, had become synonymous with white oppression all over the world, and the black Christians were about all Jesus had left. We were the only ones who could now go about preaching the words of Jesus without being suspected of questionable motives. My plea was that we black Christians become more militant, that we take a courageous stand for human rights, to clarify Christ's name if for no other reason.

It is significant that when I had finished there was a loud congregational "amen." A few white people had come to the service, and one of them was crying. Uncle James issued the invitation for the unchurched to come up and join. But that was not the hour for sinners. Rather, I think, it was a time for the believers to reassess what they were in for.

Change is coming. Having seen many of the troubled places of Africa, America, and the Caribbean, I know social dynamite when I see it. But Valdosta will make it peacefully into tomorrow, partly because the whites themselves are slowly changing, partly because the Negroes are not really pushing. Time nudges them both along. They—the black and the white of my town—are now looking across at each other in estrangement against the day when they might join in frank friendship.

Harper's, April 1965

"This Little Light . . ."

by Peter de Lissovoy

Two hours after the President put his name to the civil rights bill last July, Nathaniel "Spray-man" Beech pulled open the wood-and-glass front door of the Holiday Inn restaurant in Albany, Ga., and dashed, like musical chairs, to the very first table he saw. In a near corner, a plump, brown-suited woman popped a white hand to her full mouth, but let escape: "Oh my soul and body!" To the right, a child pointed, and its mother slapped the tiny hand and whispered urgently. Spray-man tucked a shirt wrinkle into his black, high-pegged trousers, removed his shades, studied a water glass.

In the split moment that the door stood open, Phyllis Martin, a SNCC field worker from New York, had slipped in before him. Her skin is soft mahogany, her hair natural, a silver-black bowl about her head. She stood, dark-eyed, staring around the dining room, and I came up, after Spray-man, and stood next to her. When the wax-smiling head waitress approached, Phyllis raised her eyes a little and pointed sternly, and the waitress obediently led the way to a central table. After a moment Spray-man summoned up his long limbs, rose, breathing deep and joined us; and by the time we had ordered he was holding down a nervous grin.

But when his steak arrived, Spray-man could hardly eat it. "Jus' ain' hungry," he apologized, more to the meat than anything else. He mopped his forehead with a handkerchief, and leaned over to explain: "What it is, I was expectin' everything but this. I was expectin' this waitress to say, 'Would y'all min' fallin' back out that door you jus' come in at?' The niceness got my appetite, I guess."

At this time, Spray-man was operating a shoeshine stand—among other things, for to "spray" is to hustle—in the entrance way of the Beehive Bar in Albany's Harlem. In his few years, he has seen a great deal of this country and taken his meals from many tables; yet here was one at which he had never expected to sit—nor ever wanted to. The white man could walk as he pleased on *his* side of town, but let him watch his step in Harlem: that was the geography of Spray-man's pride. And yet, improvised from a harsh reality though his was, pride hates all boundaries, and I was hardly surprised when he told me he wanted to come along when we tried out the new law. If he was supposed to have a right, he would en-joy it—once anyway. In the car, he was full of cracks; and then, in front of the restaurant, I felt him grow tense. A sense of Southern realities deeper than his pride told him he would have to fight, go to jail perhaps, and he was ready.

But the waitress was icily gracious all during the meal. Such was the strength of the President's signature. Nobody sat at the tables directly adjacent to ours, but nobody got up and left. Everybody stared or took pains to avoid staring. Nearest to us, a family of five giggled and glanced as if galloping through some marvelous adventure.

"Reminds me of up North," said Phyllis.

"What—the stares?" I suggested.

"Yeah . . . and the music." From some hidden orifice, the tensionless, sexless music that you hear in airplanes before take-off was falling like gray rain. We decided that the next thing would be to integrate the *sounds* of places.

Spray-man gave up on his steak about halfway through. When Phyllis finished, the waitress descended upon her plates like a cheery vulture, hurrying us. Abruptly, we were weary. "You 'bout ready?" Phyllis asked. I scraped up a little more and we rose. Spray-man left the waitress an exorbitant tip.

All heads turned to watch us leave. Several white men fol-lowed us from the foyer into the parking lot. I started the motor and we rolled out into the street. Spray-man looked out the window. "Well . . ." he started; and then again, "Well . . ." Phyllis turned to him. "What's the matter? Doesn't progress make you happy?"

At about 2 in the morning, Sunday, July 12, Bo Riggins, man-ager and part-owner of the Cabin in the Pines, tapped me on the shoulder and nodded toward the door. The "Pines" is a bar and dance hall, a key club, a motel, and a restaurant all strung out beneath some scraggly Georgia pine on a lonely road just south of the Albany city limits. With some white money behind it and Bo Riggins fully at the mercy of the Dougherty County police, who are a good deal more rabid than the very rabid city cops, the night-spot had formerly been "black only." When the civil rights bill became law, I took a certain pleasure in seeing it integrated.

But, following me outside this night, Riggins was a frightened man. Sure, he conceded to me, though I had said nothing, there was the new law; but since when had *law* meant anything around here? Somebody might not know who I was. I might get cut, or shot, and where would he be then? He didn't have anything against me personally—nor my color—but he had to think of his business. Couldn't I understand? He paused; but before I could respond, he blurted, "Ah! Here the police now."

Sure enough, a county patrol car had rolled up, and two uniformed men were sauntering over.

"This boy causin' any disturbance?"

"No suh, but I'm scared they be some trouble. It's late. . . ."

"You want him off yo premises?"

"He ain' did nothin', but ita be bes' I think. I don' want him aroun'. . . ."

My mouth full of the irony of it all, I was packed off quickly to the county jail, charged with trespassing and drunk-and-disorderly—the latter a simple frame and the former a matter of law. The chief deputy told me that he didn't know what the country was coming to, and he grew red in the face. He introduced me at the "tank" door ("Comin' up, anothuh nigguh-lovuh . . ."), and I was pitched, biting my lips, into the company of a check-artist, an escapee, a dog-napper, two mattress thieves, a wife-beater, a safe-cracker and assorted winos—all very white and proud of it.

The next day, in Harlem, a collection was started for my bond money; but that was going to take time. A friend of mine, a Baptist deacon and old schoolmate of Bo Riggins, paid the man a call to bawl him out and ask him to drop charges: "Now the whites startin' to do right, we can't one of us keep the wrong alive." This was simplifying matters some-what, because it was white pressure of course that made Riggins do what he had done; but he was the visible opposition. And he was obstinate. Indignation spread in the black community, and was frustrated.

But the reaction among Negroes might have been anticipated. The sentiments of the white men with whom I had to live for a week in jail were a bit more complicated. Had I been arrested while participating in the standard sort of demonstration or sit-in, their response would have been straightforward: open hostility and perhaps the convening of a kangaroo court, with a beating or jail fine as sentence. But as it was, the two initial reactions were a sneering, almost moral disapproval, as if I had been arrested for public indecency, and a simple, stark astonishment that I could have been so stupid, so lacking in imagination, as to think that I could get away with "mixin'" in south Georgia.

Jail is a place for talking, like a barbershop. In a south Georgia jail, all are friends, if not kin, and the jailbirds pass their time reminiscing, berating mutual acquaintances, and reassuring one another of their deeper innocence. There were three real talkers in the cell with me: the escapee, who had sawed through the bars with a file smuggled to him in a bag of crushed ice, only to trip over a sleeping dog a few feet from the jail; one of the mattress thieves, who claimed to have stolen all manner of valuables in his career, only to suffer the irony of being framed as a $5 mattress-pincher; and the fat, hairy safe-cracker, who spent the time he wasn't talking trying to seduce the dognapper, a rosy-cheeked 18-year-old, who threw shoes and tobacco cans at him. Inevitably, my presence injected "race" into every day's bull session. I remember one fragment. The safe-cracker was off chasing his indignant prey; the unsuccessful escapee, the mattress thief and I were leaning on an improvised sofa at one end of the cell:

UE: The new law . . .

MT: What new law?

UE: The nigguh *law. Jesus! The civil rights law. It's gonna change some things, but mos' alla life down heah gonna go on jes' the same. . . .*

MT: It ain' gonna change me. It ain' nothin' but anothuh

civil wah gonna change me an' then they hafta shoot me 'fo I sit down t' table with one a them.

UE: [turning to me]: *You see how it is down heah?* [He reached over and pinched the thief's cheek.] *This heah a Southern white man. But overlook it. S'posin' it works an' we all mixed up in the hotels an' restaur'ants. So what? After a while, somebody gonna get tired a the bad feelin'—nigguhs or the white folk one—an' they'll stop comin'. This law ain't gonna mean shit along the whole run a life.*

I had to agree; after all, I was in jail because of my little bit of confidence in the new law. I didn't tell him that I wished the act had some teeth in it; I didn't tell him that I wanted federal armies to make it work, that I wanted stronger, wider legislation in the future. As a matter of fact, there were a whole lot of banners I wasn't waving. I was doing what in a black man would be called "Tomming"—and I was glad I knew how. I wasn't going to get my head broken trying to re-form men that nobody—from Jesus to Johnson—could have swayed.

Later in the week, a tall, solid fellow with snakes inked up and down his arms was led in to "sober up." He never got the chance—or perhaps it was a ruse from the start. One of the deputies took a good look at his face and build and promised him a pint of whiskey if he would knock me down a few times. But the others were not much for it; they had gotten used to me and, if they weren't about to lay hands on him in my defense, they weren't going to encourage him either. Most of the fun for him would have been in the applause, so I got off with *buying* him a pint. Liquor can always be had for a price on the Dougherty County Jail black market, though you can't be too sure of your brand. It came in a large, waxed dixie cup. He got properly loaded then, and it was necessary to lose heavily at blackjack to keep him peaceful.

In the end, most of the jailbirds came to pity me. "Boy, that ol' judge gonna hang yo' ass. This south *Georgia*, boy, you can't get away with things like maybe in New York. . . ." And when it came to the pinch, it was the law that was the enemy. They kidded me almost warmly when I was called out for the commitment hearing that Attorney C. B. King had arranged. "'Lessen that nigguh lawyer a yours do some mighty fine talkin', we gonna see you back 'fo long. Save you a place in the game."

The judge dismissed both charges. Bo Riggins couldn't remember anyone who had seen me "drunk and disorderly" and I had several witnesses to swear that I was neither. The judge did not seem to have heard of the civil rights law—or at least considered it irrelevant and inapplicable to the trespassing charge; but he had to dismiss it when Riggins admitted that he never actually asked me to leave, but rather just complied with the apparent wishes of the police in the matter.

It seemed to have gone amazingly smoothly. Outside, Attorney King explained why: An election was imminent. My case was virtually unknown in the white community; the newspapers had made nothing out of it. So the judge could gain nothing by sending me back to jail, and he just might catch a few black votes if he did the "nigguh lawyer" a favor. I wondered if the jailbirds would figure it out. A little later I sent them some ice cream. I was going back to the "Pines" and I didn't know but that I would be seeing them again.

Early on a Saturday afternoon some days later, a dark, gawky boy in jeans and sport shirt was rigging a microphone and amplifier in the barren front yard of an unpainted clapboard house in Harlem. He placed two boxes before the mike, sat upon one, lowered the silver head of the device to the level of his mouth, and then produced a guitar which he picked idly until a great, black woman in pink flowing robes and blue-cloth crown poured suddenly from the house porch and heaved down beside him. She took the guitar and commenced tuning it, hummed and tuned, hummed and tuned, until a crowd had started. And then she sang.

Her voice was weary but warm, thick but expressive, a blues voice. She sang religious songs and old ballads and songs made popular by the Movement. Her favorite, the one she repeated most often during the day and evening, was a talking blues that roved around the chorus: "Oh, there was a death in Dallas that day. . . ." It was not so much ominous or foreboding as just terribly regretful, a sighing, head-shaking exclamation of loss. Like each of her songs, the Kennedy-blues worked into a sermon, the substance of which was invariably "trust in the Lord, who giveth and taketh away, for they ain't nothin' else trustworthy" (with a few minor forays into such areas as the evil inherent in woman). Then she passed the hat.

The crowd of listeners was always large. I was in Harlem that day and stayed until nearly midnight, listening to her. At about 8 in the evening, the size of her audience reached its peak, spilling over a curbstone in one direction, backing into a gas station in another. There were sharecroppers, factory workers, housewives; dancing, scurrying children; the celebrated and gently lunatic old woman who checks the doors and windows of all the business establishments in Harlem shortly after midnight every night and reports to the cop on the beat any unusual discoveries, happy tonight, shouting, grinning; and the occasional hipster, sheepish at being in this crowd, at wanting to be there, an eye cocked for the running mate who would most surely call sarcastically, "Hey baby, got 'ligion? Go on now—get happy!" About 8:30, a late-model Chevrolet rolled to a halt at the edge of the gathering, and three young white men got out, slamming doors, and moved into the singing crowd.

One of them immediately engaged a Negro youth in nervous, eyes-flicking conversation. The second, a tall and rake-thin fellow, with long, narrow sideburns, began, modestly, to enjoy himself, clapping and singing in perfect rhythm, his face glowing slightly. The third was drunk. For minutes, he seemed uncertain about what was happening or where he was; then, when things began to clear, he started singing and clapping too—or rather shouting hoarsely and beating his hands together at arbitrary and irregular intervals. At this display, his tall friend was shocked to the point of fright. He tried to get the drunk to the car, gave it up when he grew red and loud and stiffly resistant, and then simply moved away, attempting to dissociate himself.

For a long time, the drunken white boy was merely a tiny shallows in a great, fast river, really offensive only to the thinning few around him. Then, suddenly, as if responding to some vision or internal force, he strode violently forward and demanded the microphone from the ironically—and tolerantly—smiling lady preacher, to ask: "What y'all starin' at us fo'? We white—sho. But that ain' no reason to stare. The bill a rights done been pass'! We got a right. We gonna stay, an I'm gonna as' this kin' lady to sing *This lil' light a mine* fo' the white people a Albany, G-A, who need it, God knows. . . ."

The drunk's two friends were visibly mortified. Not at what he had said, but at his having said anything at all—at his having drawn unnecessary and additional attention to their presence. The first intensified his dialogue with the Negro youth as if to shut out the awful reality of what had just happened. In a moment, the taller, side-burned white man had seized his swaying buddy around the shoulders and bundled him, yelling and protesting, off to their car. The talker trotted to catch up. The car roared and the tall white waved an apologetic and helpless goodby from the driver's wheel. The drunk was slumped in the seat, whooping: "Hooray fo' the nigguhs! Hoo-hoo-hooray fo' the nigguhs!"

But already the singer had taken up where she had left off. Nobody much bothered to hear the drunk's rantings; it was a matter of discipline, a very old discipline.

I was shooting nine-ball in a Harlem poolroom. It was dinner time, family time, on a Friday night in America, and the room was filled with people who had no better place to go. I powdered my hands and sank the winning ball in a combination with the two—and looked up to see five white hustlers appear in the doorway like apparitions out of the foggy night, combing their hair, wiping the water from their foreheads.

"Who wants to shoot?" drawled the skinniest. His voice cracked at the end, and so he repeated the question with force. It sounded belligerent, so he smiled, stupidly.

Eyes blinked. Bodies stirred. Butterball, who had been napping in the corner, rose up and stretched his bulk. He settled his red baseball cap over his eyes. "You got any money, Whitey?" When the white boy flashed a roll, I stepped back from my table. Butter' picked up a stick and called for the houseman to rack.

"What's your name, Whitey?"

For a moment, the white fellow wondered how to answer this question most forcefully, and then he simply let it out, a short nasal squeak. Butter' looked down the row of tables:

"Hey, Rut! You hear that? Go on look up his daddy in the phone book, fin' out how much coin he got. I'm gonna take all Whitey's money tonight!" He leaned back on the heels of his tennis shoes and laughed with all his weight.

"No you aint!" Rut, just as heavy as Butter' and infinitely meaner in the eyes, was heaving down the aisle. "Whitey got way more money'n you can have by y'self, big as you *is*." He stood before the rest of the white team. "Which one a you boys gonna put a ten down on this first game?"

On a Friday night, the poolroom is always crowded by 8. Tonight, when word got around what was happening, old men and young poured in until the house had to close its doors, so that the players might have space to shoot. It looked like the Olympic games; and, in a sense, it was.

Butter' and Whitey were a good match. They played past midnight, and, as it turned out, Butter' lost a little. On other tables, "Schoolboy" Terry and Peter "Rabbit" Harris skinned a blond-headed boy whose nickname really *was* "Whitey," and a laconic, bespectacled, middle-aged hustler with a beautiful if inaccurate stroke. Side bets went round and round. On the whole, the whites lost money, but not nearly as much as would be claimed the next day. When it was all over, Butter', gentleman that he is, took the crew around the corner for drinks. "How 'bout it Whitey?" he asked. "We gonna shoot a little over your side tomorrow?"

"Sure."

"Won't be no shit?"

"Not if you bring your money."

For weeks, the game ran on—the white hustlers appearing in Harlem, black hustlers visiting the white poolrooms. "It's the new law," said Butter'. "Integration always starts over sport."

But not every small-town hustler can shoot nine-ball for $5 and $10 a game. Most make their little money disillusioning country boys, in from the dim lights and hacked tables of south Georgia's tinier hamlets, or the Albany workingmen, tanked up and sure that they are the greatest. "Integrated pool" was only for the best, who could win, or lose big money at big matches. The best soon knew one another and were wary; the novelty wore off and the poolrooms, white and black, returned to their normal, and tedious, business.

It is November. The man who signed a bill and integrated the poolrooms is retained in power. I wonder if Butter' voted. Or Spray-man, taking time off from shining shoes.

That first night, after the Holiday Inn, he had been confused; the experience had not had any immediate meanings. But a few hours later, outside a Negro bar in south Albany, called the Playhouse, he had nodded at the crowded doorway: "Lookit all them Negroes, don't know nothin' 'bout what's happened yet."

A few minutes and a few beers later, he was checking the hand of a girl who was about to drop a dime in the juke box. He carried a chair to the center of the floor, climbed atop it, shouted the crowd silent and the dancing to a halt, and related, in a loud, laughing voice, the events over on the white side. A few applauded. Most listened politely for a minute or two, but soon conversation started again, and Spray-man was struggling against an indifferent current. He looked over at me, apologetically I felt. I waved with great emotion for him to forget it, but he had his hackles up and went on.

A young man with ironic eyes nudged me. "It's fine," he said. "Fine, if you got plenty money to eat at the Holiday Inn. Me, all I got's this one little quarter, an' I ain't expectin' nothin' soon. Tell y' frien' I'm sorry, but I gotta put it in the piccolo. I'm gonna have me 25¢ worth a soun', an' no history. . . ."

When the music started, Spray-man glanced around angrily. But, when it was clear he was overcome, drowned in sound, he grinned reluctantly, then wide. He shrugged, stepped across the floor to replace the chair and, in a moment was dancing.

The Nation, December 21, 1964

A Strange, Tight Little Town, Loath to Admit Complicity

by David Nevin

Philadelphia, Miss.

THERE is little sign that the conscience of this clean and prosperous little town has been touched by murder. Lawrence Rainey is still sheriff and Cecil Price is still deputy; if anything, their arrest in connection with the killing of three decent young men seems to have increased their popularity.

"It took me an hour to get to work this morning," Price said the day after his arrest, "I had to spend so much time shaking hands."

Having posted his bond on the charges, Rainey was on the job as usual last week and nothing really had changed. He fretted about the condition of the county's fire extinguishers. He listened patiently to a townswoman who came in to talk and counseled her gently. He nosed about for an illegal moonshine still and reflected on the drunks who take up his time. Rainey is a heavy man with a hard face and a quick cat-like way of moving. He roams about in his big gray Oldsmobile hung with the trappings of his office—siren, red light, loudspeaker, armament, gilt-lettered doors. Everywhere he went last week men smiled and nodded and shook his hand and told him they were on his side.

This is a strange, tight little town. Its fear and hatred of things and ideas that come from the outside is nearly pathological. As the stranger walks its streets, hostile eyes track him as a swivel gun tracks a target. Yet it is quiet and there is even a certain uniform sense of self-contentment in its conviction that all its troubles are caused by outsiders—by reporters; by militant, uppity Negroes; by the federal government. Philadelphia is barely willing to admit that an inhuman crime did take place, and it is quite unable to feel any collective guilt. It is, in short, a town which has deluded itself endlessly and which is still doing so.

Hardly a Philadelphian will admit even the possibility of a strong Ku Klux Klan organization. Yet in one night last March a large, well-printed bulletin, offering 20 reasons for joining the Klan, was dropped on the porch of nearly every white, non-Catholic home in Neshoba county. It stated bluntly: "Either you're for us or you're for the NAACP." Just a month later eight crosses were burned simultaneously at scattered locations in Philadelphia. It was the Klan's triumphant expression of success: it meant that local Klaverns were formed and operating.

Crosses burned in more than 60 Mississippi counties that month. Yet Mississippi had never been a notably strong Klan state. The Klan's swift growth came out of the genuine hysteria that followed announcement of the Council of Federated Organizations (COFO) summer project, an "invasion" of 800 northern college students coming to help stimulate Negroes to register to vote. But to the insular, frightened Mississippians, it spelled disaster. They visualized a veritable slave uprising—militant Negroes taking over their towns and lives. The fear, however ill-founded, was genuine, and it explains much of Mississippi today.

The first actual "invader" in this area was Mickey Schwerner. He and his wife Rita came to Meridian seven months before the summer project began, and opened a community center for Negroes. Schwerner also began to work among Negroes 39 miles away in Philadelphia, and soon the Klan was watching him. He was a natural enemy: he was a Jew, with a beard, and he was unafraid. Men do not come easily to the point of killing, but feeling against Schwerner grew so intense that the Klan made the formal decision—in its own phrase—to "exterminate" him.

It is clear now that James Chaney and Andrew Goodman died merely because they happened by offhand chance to be with Schwerner when the Klansmen saw their chance. Goodman, a COFO summer volunteer, had been in Mississippi less than 24 hours. Chaney, an active Negro civil rights worker from Meridian, was known—and hated—but there was no formal plan to kill him.

All of this seems to be common knowledge in Philadelphia. Yet the people here do not generally admit the existence of the Klan. Nor do they admit another troubling side of life in Philadelphia—that Negroes here as elsewhere have come openly to resent being treated as a class without rights and that it takes a hard hand to keep them in line. In Philadelphia that hard hand belonged—and still belongs—to Lawrence Rainey.

In August of 1963, when Rainey ran for sheriff, it had become clear that Congress would pass a civil rights bill. Rainey appeared at meetings all over the county, and he would roll his big hat in his big rough hands and say, "I'm Lawrence Rainey and if you elect me sheriff, I'll take care of things for you." He didn't have to say what "things" he meant. Mississippi's only pressing trouble was the race problem, and Rainey's record as a police patrolman and a deputy sheriff in Philadelphia was impressive. He had killed at least two Negroes—in self-defense, he reported—and the Negro community was openly afraid of him.

One night Rainey walked into the light at a Negro county fair attended by 300 men. He stood there without saying a word and gradually the crowd began to thin until every Negro was gone. Rainey was left alone on the grounds; the fair was over.

He was elected sheriff by a handsome majority. He can be likeable, and if you are white and have position, you see this pleasant side. That is what community leaders saw and wanted to see. "I'll tell you what kind of man he is," said Jack Tannehill, editor of the weekly Neshoba *Democrat*. "When he sees a drunk nigger on the street, 'stead of just grabbing him, Lawrence will say, 'Now, boy, you get on home now 'fore I have to run you in.' That's the kind of man Lawrence Rainey is." Thurman Thompson, the druggist, said, "The only people ever complain of him being rough are just jailbirds, that's all."

The classic description of Rainey's gentility comes from a Philadelphia banker. "This nigger woman was trying to cash a forged check," he told a reporter. "I told the teller to call for the sheriff. The nigger woman snatched the check and started to run. The sheriff caught up with her at the corner. She resisted and was slamming him up against a building when I arrived. I don't believe in police brutality, but I told the sheriff, 'Take that club and knock hell out of her.' He didn't do it."

But perhaps the case of Kirk Culberson is more revealing. Culberson, 46, a Negro, owned property and operated a small garage in Philadelphia in addition to working in a sawmill. His testimony before a federal grand jury in Biloxi resulted in an indictment of Rainey and Price for violation of his civil rights. According to the charges and Culberson's testimony, a friend was involved in a shooting using a pistol which belonged to Culberson. Rainey and Price came to Culberson's garage and arrested him.

On the way to the jail Rainey stopped the car on a dark road to question Culberson, who sat alone in the back seat. One of the men—Culberson is not sure which—turned and smashed his head with something hard and heavy, knocking him to the floor. Culberson lifted himself and was smashed down again. He remembers nothing more—but when he came to in a cell his clothes were muddy and his skull was shattered. He believes he was dragged from the car and beaten on the ground while unconscious.

Culberson now has spent many days in hospitals. He has seen X-rays of his head which indicate, as he puts it, that "my skull was split three ways." He is unable to work. Blinding headaches overcome him at the least exertion. His property is gone and he is in debt. He has left Philadelphia, but he is worried about how he will support his wife and four children.

Culberson is deathly afraid of Rainey. "He would say I was drunk and 'Nigger, get in the car.' And I would have to say, 'Yessir, I'm drunk,' and he could beat me up again and nothing would be done about it. It would be a nigger's word against a white sheriff. What he says goes. He's the man."

The fear in Philadelphia is not limited to Negroes. Everyone who fails to conform, white and black alike, learns to fear. Conformity to group thought has become a way of life in Philadelphia, and the Klan pretty much determines group thought. There may be only a few hundred Klansmen, but they reach the whole community. Some of the intimidation is physical, some strikes at men's businesses and livelihoods. But even more important is the structured uniformity of the indoctrinated Mississippian's attitude. To speak out against the

Klan or even to question Lawrence Rainey's treatment of Negroes has come to be equated somehow with disloyalty to one's own. There is no middle ground. A Philadelphia minister said, "A minority has taken over the guidance of thought patterns of our town. It has controlled what was said and what was not said."

Struggling in this mass of pressures, a thoughtful Philadelphian said recently, "I can understand now how Nazi Germany could grow with the good people of Germany knowing more of the atrocities than they would admit—and looking away, always looking away. . . . We have been coerced and intimidated."

A few individuals in Philadelphia, backed by a handful of ministers, are speaking out now for justice and decency. Methodist pastor Clay Lee preached a sermon in which he called pointedly for truth, love and justice as answers to Philadelphia's problems, and people began to respond. But the majority of white people still seems satisfied with what is essentially a Klan point of view. The majority still seems satisfied with Lawrence Rainey as sheriff.

This may account in part for Rainey's confidence in the face of a most serious charge. But even more basic to his casual ease is the fact that the chances of his being convicted are slight indeed. It has nothing to do with his guilt or innocence, which has not yet been determined. It is a simple truth of Mississippi justice that white men are rarely penalized for treatment dealt Negroes and Negro sympathizers. That is the way it is in Mississippi.

So Lawrence Rainey walks around Philadelphia with a wad of tobacco in his jaw and his big .44 pistol on his hip and he wears an easy smile. Everywhere he goes men nod and smile and shake his hand. Lawrence Rainey is likely to be around Philadelphia for a long time. He is the man.

Life, December 18, 1964

from

A Southern Tale

by James Farmer

UNTIL recently Plaquemine was a little town drowsing on the banks of the Mississippi. That difficult balance of social repression with personal benevolence, common to the South, preserved peace and order and a somewhat illusory sense of well-being. The Negroes, at least with one part of their minds, regarded the white people as "good white folks." The whites in turn, with the same part of their minds, thought of the Negroes as jovial and good-natured, content with their lot. They felt honestly surprised when the Negroes began to agitate for the vote.

In the summer of 1963, while many prepared for the famed March on Washington, CORE launched one of its early voter-registration drives in a number of parishes in Louisiana, including Iberville Parish and its principal city of Plaquemine.* Actually there are few Negroes in Plaquemine proper, because the city boundaries have been deliberately engineered to exclude them. The city is horseshoe-shaped, surrounding a Negro community in its midst but refusing to incorporate it legally. As a result this Negro community is deprived of all municipal benefits: the roads are unpaved, sewage runs along the streets in open gutters. Understandably a number of people in this utterly disfranchised Negro community showed interest in the registration drive. A few local professional people —the only Negro doctor in the parish, the Negro school principal—at last were coming forward to assume leadership, despite the jeopardy in which such activity placed their jobs.

As a further stimulus to the drive our field secretary from

---

*The city of Plaquemine is not to be confused with Plaquemines Parish, the county presided over by the savagely segregationist political boss, Judge Leander Perez.

New Orleans, Ronnie Moore, had asked me, in my capacity as National Director (outside agitator number one), to put in an appearance in the area. So I went down to Plaquemine toward the end of August on the first day of what I innocently assumed would be a routine three-day trip. We staged a protest march into town after my speech. When the march was over, all the leaders, myself included, were arrested and taken off to jail in nearby Donaldsonville (which hospitably offered us its facilities in lieu of the already overcrowded Plaquemine jail).

We stayed in jail for a week and a half. As a result, I missed the March on Washington. The timing was unfortunate, but I felt that I really had no choice. Having cast my lot with the people of Plaquemine, I could not simply pull rank and walk out. Moreover, this was my opportunity to reaffirm publicly the insight that CORE had gained during the Freedom Rides of the previous year—that filling the jails could serve as a useful instrument of persuasion. So I sent a message to Washington, which was read by Attorney Floyd B. McKissick, CORE's national chairman, and remained in jail until all the local demonstrators were out. When we came out, the spirit of militancy was spreading in Plaquemine, and two days later a group of young people organized another demonstration, protesting segregation in public places as well as exclusion from the city. This time, however, the marchers did not even get into town. The chief of police stopped them halfway, arrested the leaders, and held the rest of the marchers where they were until state troopers arrived. The troopers came on horseback, riding like cowboys, and they charged into the crowd of boys and girls as if they were rounding up a herd of stampeding cattle. They were armed with billy clubs and cattle prods, which they used mercilessly. Many of the youngsters who fell under the blows were trampled by the horses. (The children of Selma, whose suffering at the hands of police appalled the nation two years later, were but a part of a spiritual community of brave Southern youngsters like these who for years have been deprived of national attention by inadequate press coverage.)

This gratuitous savagery inflicted upon their children immediately aroused the adults to a pitch of militancy much more intense than anything the organizational effort had been able to achieve. The ministers, who had previously hung back, united for the first time. (Only one minister, the Rev. Jetson Davis, had been active in the movement. It was his Plymouth Rock Baptist Church to which the injured boys and girls had fled for comfort and medical assistance.) Apathy or fear or whatever had caused their reluctance dissolved in outrage. The next morning, Sunday, every minister in the Negro quarter preached a sermon extolling freedom and condemning police brutality. After church, according to agreement, they led their congregations to Reverend Davis' church and organized a massive march in protest against the rout of the previous day. As the time approached for the march to begin, some of the ministers began to waver. One of them hesitated on his way to the front of the line. "Where's my wife?" he said, looking around fearfully. "I don't see my wife. I think I'd better just go on home." His wife was standing right behind him. "Man," she said, "if you don't get up there in the front of that line, you ain't got no wife."

He marched, all right, but his presence could not alter the course of events. This time when the troopers intercepted the marchers there was nothing impromptu about the confrontation. They did not even come on horseback; they came in patrol cars and the horses arrived in vans. The troopers mounted their horses and assembled their weapons as if the crowd of unarmed men and women before them were an opposing army; they charged into the mass as they had done the day before, flailing with billy clubs and stabbing with cattle prods. "Get up, nigger!" one would shout, poking a man with an electric prod and beating him to the ground with a club. "Run, nigger, run!"

I was waiting at the Plymouth Rock Church. I watched the Negroes come running back, those who could run, bleeding, hysterical, faint, some of the stronger ones carrying the injured. The nurse started to bandage the wounds and the rest of us began to sing "We Shall Overcome"; but the troopers rode roaring through the streets right up to the door of the church. The Freedom Rock Church, we call it now. They dismounted and broke into the church, yelling and hurling tear gas bombs in front of them—bomb after bomb, poisoning the air. The gas masks protecting the troopers' faces transformed them into monsters as they stood and watched our people growing more and more frantic, screaming with pain and terror, trampling on one another in their frenzied efforts to escape through the back door to the parsonage behind the church. When the people had finally escaped, the troopers set about destroying the empty church. They knocked out the windows, overturned the benches, laid waste everything they could reach, and flooded the gutted building with high-pressure hoses until Bibles and hymnals floated in the aisles.

Then they attacked the parsonage to which we had fled. They sent tear gas bombs smashing through the windows, until all the windows were shattered and almost everyone inside was blinded and choking. The screaming was unbearable. I caught sight of Ronnie Moore administering mouth-to-mouth resuscitation to a young woman. People writhed on the floor, seeking oxygen. A few managed to push through the rear door into the parsonage yard, but the troopers, anticipating them, had ridden around to the back with more bombs to force them in again. And then bombs thrown into the parsonage forced them back out into the yard. All these men and women, who just that morning had resolutely banded together to reach out for freedom and dignity, were reduced now to running from torment to torment, helpless victims of a bitter game.

We tried to telephone for help, but the operators were not putting through any outgoing calls from the Negro section. Within the community, though, there was telephone service, and several calls got through to us in the parsonage. What had appeared to be random and mindless brutality proved to have had a mad purpose after all. It was a manhunt. Troopers were in the streets, kicking open doors, searching every house in the Negro community, overturning chairs and tables, looking under beds and in closets, yelling, "Come on out, Farmer, we know you're in there. Come on out, Farmer! We're going to get you." We could hear the screaming in the streets as the troopers on horseback resumed their sport with the cattle prods and billy clubs: "Get up, nigger! Run, nigger, run!" Holding their victims down with the cattle prod, they were saying, "We'll let you up, nigger, if you tell us where Farmer is." Two of our girls, hiding beneath the church, overheard one trooper saying to another, "When we catch that goddam nigger Farmer, we're gonna kill him."

Spiver Gordon, CORE field secretary in Plaquemine, who, people say, looks like me, told me later that he wandered out of the church into the street at this time. Sighting him, state troopers ran up shouting, "Here he is boys. We got Farmer. We got their m—— f—— Jesus." A trooper beckoned to a crowd of hoodlums who were watching nearby, many holding chains, ropes, clubs. "What post we gonna hang him from?" said one. After Spiver convinced them he wasn't me, he took a good lacing for looking like me. An officer said, "He ain't Farmer. You've beat him enough. Put him in the car and arrest him."

There seemed no prospect of aid from any quarter. We were all suffering intensely from the tear gas, and the troopers kept us running with the bombs. In desperation I sent two people creeping through the grass from the parsonage to a funeral hall half a block away to ask for refuge. The owners of the hall agreed to shelter us (although I doubt that they knew what they were taking on). So we crawled on our bellies through the grass, in twos, threes, fours, making use of guerrilla tactics that some remembered from the war but none of us had ever learned as a technique of non-violent demonstration, until we reached our new sanctuary. Night had fallen by the time all three hundred of us were safely inside, jammed together like straws in a broom into two rooms and a hallway. The sound of screaming still echoed in the streets as the troopers beat down another Negro ("Run, nigger, run!") or invaded another house. The telephones were still useless.

Very shortly the troopers figured out where we were. One of them—a huge, raging, red-faced man—kicked open the back door of the funeral home and screamed, "Come on out, Farmer. We know you're in there. We're gonna get you." I was in the front room. I could look down the hallway, over all the heads, right into his face: it was flushed and dripping with sweat; his hair hung over his eyes, his mouth was twisted. Another trooper burst through the door to stand beside him. "Farmer! Come out!"

I had to give myself up. I felt like a modern Oedipus who, unaware, brought down a plague upon the city. In this hall, their lives endangered by my presence, were three hundred people, many of whom had never even seen me before that day. I began to make my way into the hall, thinking that I would ask to see the warrant for my arrest and demand to know the charges against me. But before I could take three steps the men around me grabbed me silently and pulled me back into the front room, whispering fiercely, "We're not going to let you go out there tonight. That's a lynch mob. You go out there tonight, you won't be alive tomorrow morning."

The trooper, meanwhile, had discovered a large Negro in the back room. He shouted triumphantly: "Here he is, we got that nigger Farmer! Come on in, boys. We got him here."

"I'm not Farmer," the man said. A third trooper came in.

"That ain't Farmer," he said. "I know that nigger." They went through his identification papers. He wasn't Farmer.

Suddenly, to everyone's astonishment, a woman pushed her way through the crowd to the back room and confronted the troopers. It was the owner of the funeral home, a "Nervous Nellie," as they say, who had previously held herself apart from the movement. I can never know—she herself probably does not know—what inner revolution or what mysterious force generated in that crowded room plucked her from her caul of fear and thrust her forth to assert with such a dramatic and improbable gesture her new birth of freedom. A funeral hall is as good a place as any for a person to come to life, I suppose, and her action sparked a sympathetic impulse in everyone who watched as she planted herself in front of the first trooper and shook a finger in his face: "Do you have a search warrant to come into my place of business?"

The trooper stared down at her, confounded, and backed away. "No," he said.

"You're not coming into my place of business without a search warrant. I'm a taxpayer and a law-abiding citizen. I have a wake going on here."

I prayed inwardly that her valiant subterfuge would not prove to be a prophecy.

"This ain't no wake," the trooper said, looking around at the throng of angry, frightened people crushed together before him. "These people ain't at no wake."

"Well, you're not coming into my place of business without a search warrant." The accusing finger pushed him back to the door, where he muttered for a moment to his men outside, then turned and yelled, "All right. We got all the tear gas and all the guns. You ain't got nothin'. We'll give you just five minutes to get Farmer out here. Just five minutes, that's all." He slammed the door.

The door clanged in my ears like the door of a cell in death row. "I'll go out and face them," I said, but once again I was restrained. They would stick by me, these strangers insisted, even if they all had to die, but they would not let me out to be lynched. Someone standing near me pulled out a gun. "Mr. Farmer," he said, "if a trooper comes through that door, he'll be dead."

"If a trooper comes through that door, he may be dead," I conceded. "But what about the trooper behind him and all the ones behind that one? You'll only provoke them into shooting and we won't have a chance." Very reluctantly he allowed me to take the gun from him. It is hard for people to practice non-violence when they are looking death in the face. I wondered how many others were armed.

Then my own private thoughts engulfed me. Reverend Davis was leading a group in the Lord's Prayer; another group was singing "We Shall Overcome." I was certain I was going to die. What kind of death would it be? Would they mutilate me first? What does it feel like to die? Then I grew panicky about the insurance. Had I paid the last installment? How much was it? I couldn't remember. I couldn't remember anything about it. My wife and little girls—how would it be for them? Abbey was only two then—too young to remember; but Tami was four and a half, and very close to me —she would remember. Well, damn it, if I had to die, at least let the organization wring some use out of my death. I hoped the newspapers were out there. Plenty of them. With plenty of cameras.

I was terrified. The five minutes passed. Six. Seven. Eight. A knock at the front door. My lawyers from New Orleans, Lolis Elie and Robert Collins, identified themselves and squeezed in, breathless. New Orleans radio had broadcast the news that a manhunt was in progress in Plaquemine, and they had driven over immediately. The community, they said, was in a state of siege. Everywhere one looked one saw troopers, like an invading army. The two lawyers had crawled through the high grass to seek refuge in the graveyard, but when they got there the place came alive: there was a Negro behind every tombstone ("All find safety in the tomb," sang Yeats, in another context). Apparently everyone had counted on the dead to be more hospitable than the living. Apparently, also, everyone knew where I was, but no one was telling the white men. The troopers, it seemed, had been bluffing; they could not be wholly sure I was in the funeral home. It occurred to me that my physical safety, in some elusive way that had very little to do with me, had become a kind of transcendent symbol to all these people of the possibilities of freedom and personal dignity that existed for them. By protecting me, they were preserving their dreams. But did they understand, I wondered, that through their acts of courage during this desperate night they had taken the first great steps toward realizing these possibilities? Did they sense that they had gained at least some of that freedom for which they longed here, and now?

Just as the lawyers finished their story there was another knock at the door. For a moment I thought the troopers had come at last, until I remembered that troopers don't knock. The two men who entered were recently acquired friends from Plaquemine, and pretty rough characters in their own right: my neighbor from town, whom I shall call Fred, and Bill, a buddy of his, ex-Marines who, I knew, carried several guns in their car at all times. The troopers, they told me, had grown systematic. They had set up roadblocks on every street leading out of town. The men who had been waiting in the back had just driven off in the direction of the sheriff's office, presumably to get a search warrant. In short, if I did not get out right now, my life would not be worth a dime.

I told my lawyers to get in their car and try to drive out through the roadblocks. I thought the troopers might respect their identification as attorneys. If they got through, they were to call New York at once, call my wife and tell her I was all right, call Marvin Rich at CORE and have him get in touch with the FBI, call New Orleans and try to get some kind of federal protection. It was imperative that we make contact with the outside world.

Then Fred and Bill set forth their plan. The woman who owned the funeral home had two hearses. They would send the old one out as a decoy with just a driver, who would take it down the main streets, making sure it was spotted at every roadblock. If pursued, he would speed up. Meanwhile, we would try to escape in the second hearse which was waiting, its motor already running, in a garage which we could reach without going out of the house.

If there was something unsettling about the prospect of riding to safety in a hearse, it was nonetheless the logical conclusion to the macabre events of the day. And we could see no alternative. Fred and Bill led the way to the garage, forcing a passage through the sweating men and women who murmured phrases of encouragement and good wishes as we passed. I prayed that our departure would release them from danger, marveling once more at the courage and devotion shown by these strangers.

It was cool, briefly, in the garage, but the hearse was hot and stuffy again. Ronnie Moore, Reverend Davis, and I crawled into the back and crouched down—three restless, nervous men huddled together in a space meant for one motionless body. I thought I remembered that Huey Long had once escaped from someone in a hearse, and for a moment I almost felt like smiling. Someone climbed into the driver's seat and we were off, speeding down the back roads toward New Orleans. Fred and Bill, heavily armed (although I did not know that at the time), followed us in their car. We took a winding route with countless detours over very rough country roads which the Negroes knew more intimately than the whites. Although you can drive from Plaquemine to New Orleans in less than two hours by highway, it took us four and a half hours, despite the fact that we were going very fast and did not stop at all. Whenever a car approached we flattened out on the floor of the hearse until the road was clear again. Our grim destination was another funeral home; our only protection was blackness, a color which had never before promised immunity to Negroes in the South. At times during that wild ride I thought I was already dead. I don't know what the others thought. But when at last we climbed out of the hearse into the hot New Orleans night, we were, by the grace of God and the extraordinary courage of many ordinary men, still very much alive. And not yet entirely out of danger.

When we finally got in touch with the New Orleans CORE, we discovered that our story was already out. The two lawyers had passed the roadblocks and called the authorities in New Orleans, and the press had picked up the news immediately. They had also called my wife, before she had heard anything, to tell her not to worry: "Jim's all right."

"Oh," said Lula. "Why shouldn't he be?"

"There was a little trouble down in Plaquemine, but there's nothing to worry about now. He's out of danger." Whereupon Lula turned on the television set and learned that there was a house-to-house search reportedly going on in Plaquemine, Louisiana, for CORE National Director, James Farmer . . . and, a little later, that James Farmer was reported missing in Plaquemine, Louisiana. She told me later that she turned off the news broadcast and took the children outside where the voices they would hear were less ominous. Shortly afterward, when she went to call the press to try to find out more, she found they were already waiting for her at the house.

In New York, though, they never carried the complete story. The next morning I held a press conference at the CORE headquarters in New Orleans. Newspaper and TV reporters carefully took down all the details, but what they wrote never got farther than New Orleans. But then the list of stories that the newspapers have overlooked in the South and elsewhere is endless.

A trial was scheduled for me the next day in Plaquemine. I was not exactly eager to return but I announced at the press conference that I intended to appear at the appointed time to be served with the warrant for my arrest and to hear the charges, whatever they might be. The FBI sent a man to New York to find out the details from our national office. Our people told him I was going back into Plaquemine the next day and asked if the FBI could guarantee my safety; our attorney, Lolis Elie, called the FBI regional office in New Orleans with the same request. To both requests, the response was the same: the FBI was an investigatory agency, not a protection agency; they could not guarantee my life. However, since the situation was an extraordinary one, they would see what they could do.

With this ambiguous support, Ronnie Moore, Reverend Davis, and I returned somewhat nervously to Plaquemine the next morning. The city police were waiting for us; as soon as we drove into town we saw a policeman in a squad car in front of us announce our arrival into his radio. To our relief FBI agents were everywhere, questioning people in the Negro section, the white section, and around the courthouse. Two agents came over to me as soon as I walked into the courtroom. But as it turned out the troopers had no warrant for my arrest, no charges against me. Nor could we take any action against them, for their name plates and badge numbers had been taped over during the manhunt. In fact, we learned that many of the men who had been riding that night were not even regular troopers: they were ordinary citizens deputized for the occasion.

The drama of Plaquemine ended there, but its consequences are still alive. A new Negro community grew out of that terrible night, aroused, unified, determined to act. When the parish sheriff was up for re-election, the Negro leaders arranged a meeting with his white opponent to ask him about his platform. There was no question of his being an integrationist, of course, but they wanted to know how he stood on the issue of police brutality. Quite emphatically he replied that he was against it, that he had no use for tear gas, billy clubs, or cattle prods, that he had felt that way all his life, and that if he was elected sheriff he would "put a stop to all this nonsense." Just a few days before the election, in a carefully timed maneuver, Reverend Davis, who was also running, withdrew and threw all his votes to this man. He won, too, by a margin so slim there could be no doubt that he owed his victory to the Negro vote. Since assuming office, moreover, he has kept his word on the question of police brutality and has appointed several Negro deputy sheriffs. He is still an uncompromising segregationist: I want to stress that point. Militant non-violence has not reached his heart, nor is it likely to. But the election of this segregationist sheriff with his policy of decency suggests an important truth which CORE has slowly learned to accept: In the arena of political and social events, what men feel and believe matters much less than what, under various kinds of external pressures, they can be made to *do*. The Negro vote also defeated Jumonville, Iberville's parish state representative and a protégé of Leander Perez, who was alleged by local Negroes to be one of the men deputized to ride that night. Jumonville reportedly accosted one of the Negro leaders after the election with the friendly recommendation that the next time they had a demonstration they had better let him know, because he intended to join them.

But if the hearts of hostile Southerners are likely to be out of reach, the hearts of the men and women involved in the movement are very much within our province. CORE, from its earliest beginnings, has wanted to involve the people themselves, individually, personally, in the struggle for their own freedom. Not simply because it was clear that no one else was going to confer liberty upon them, but because in the very act of working for the impersonal cause of racial freedom, a man experiences, almost like grace, a large measure of private freedom. Or call it a new comprehension of his own identity, an intuition of the expanding boundaries of his self, which, if not the same thing as freedom, is its radical source. This is what happened in Plaquemine to the owner of the funeral home, to the men who kept silence in the graveyard, to the men and women who stood between me and the lynch mob. Gradually, during the course of those two violent days, they made the decision to act instead of being acted upon. The group of people who assembled on Sunday morning were in large part reacting viscerally to the police brutality of the previous day; but the same people that evening, who, although packed together in the funeral hall, refused to be victimized any longer by the troopers, had been transformed into a community of men, capable, despite the severest limitations, of free and even heroic acts. Their subsequent activity at the polls and in initiating a school boycott suggests that this kind of freedom, though essentially personal, will inevitably lead to social action, and that freedom once won is not readily surrendered.

There are also more somber lessons to be drawn from the events at Plaquemine, darker reflections on the future of the movement. CORE is a mass movement now and no longer commands the dedicated allegiance it once did to the principles of non-violence. What will happen when the Negroes, their self-awareness heightened, experience brutality or repression? What do Negroes and whites really see when they look at each other now that the mists of sleep have been brushed aside? Vision is a terrifying gift. All the energy that has been released is in the service of this vision, and it carries with it a payload of violence.

In the funeral hall in Plaquemine, I overheard two people standing by a window, in a conversation that went something like this:

"Did you see who was ridin' one of those horses? Adams' son!"

"No! You're wrong, they're good white people. Adams has been a friend of our family as long as we've been here. I practically brought his son up."

"Just look at him there, riding one of those horses, with a cattle prod in his hand."

And then a third person said something heard more and more from Negroes in Plaquemine: "The only good white man is a dead one."

The humiliation and fury that a man feels when he has been brutally treated are rendered insupportably bitter if he discovers that he has also been betrayed. You may say that the Negroes will not be susceptible to betrayal much longer, for they are rapidly flinging aside all their illusions about the good will of the white man. But to insure oneself unequivocally against betrayal, one must discard more than illusions; one must also abandon any prospect of trust, or faith, in the white man. And many Negroes are hardening their hearts in this way. They have cast off their outgrown shells, like the mollusks on the beach, and are growing new, more formidable armor which protects them not only from illusion but from conciliation and compromise as well, and in very extreme cases from reason and self-control. On another occasion, I spoke at a rally in West Feliciana Parish which was attended by a number of young Negro men from neighboring Plaquemine. After the meeting I discovered that they all had guns in their cars; they had vowed that nothing was going to happen to Mr. Farmer this time. As we stood outside the church where our meeting had taken place, the sheriff of the parish and a carload of rednecks drove slowly back and forth past the church, then parked on the other side of the street and stared, tauntingly. The young men with me stood with their arms folded, staring back. Tension stretched like a wire across the street. No fight broke out that night, but if it had, the Negroes would have grabbed for their guns. And what will prevent that fight the next time, or the time after that?

from *Freedom—When?* (1965)

Malcolm X: The Complexity
of a Man in the Jungle

by Marlene Nadle

MALCOLM X has three faces. One is turned toward Africa, one toward Harlem, and one toward Washington.

His masks are more numerous. They are juggled by both the actor and his audience. He's a charismatic leader. Then a cartoon figure waving a rifle. He's a racist. Then a Black Nationalist gone white. A symbol of hope and Father Divine. An anti-semite and a preacher of brotherhood. An extremist and a man to move the Movement.

In Harlem the people watch the performance.

The black politicians mark the trickle of converts going through the glass doors of the Organization of Afro-American Unity he formed after the split with the Black Muslims in March, 1964. They wait to see if it signals a flood, now that the gates are open to non-Muslims, and now that a separate black state is no longer the destination.

The politicians will not completely associate themselves with him. Nor will they disassociate themselves. The untested potential of Malcolm X keeps people like Adam Clayton Powell careful friends.

A cross-section of Harlem comes to measure the man and his methods on Sunday nights at Audubon Ballroom. Seated on 500 wooden folding chairs are the disinherited people who never had any hope or answers and those, whether Nationalist or non-violent activist, who have run out of both. There are children looking for pride, and there are many older church-goers who, unlike Mahalia Jackson, can't sing, "I found the answer, I learned to pray."

In the bars and grills—Small's and Jock's and the Shalimar on Seventh Avenue, the Palms and Frank's on 125th Street—the debate goes on.

"Malcolm is a genius," said a man at the bar in the Shalimar. "All he cares about is Malcolm X and money."

"Malcolm is a creation of the white press," said a doctor in Frank's.

"Malcolm is a genius," said a lawyer in the back room at Jock's. "He is the most brilliant speaker I have ever heard "

"Malcolm X is a loser," said another man at Jock's. "He'll have to do a lot better than he's doing if he wants to make it in Harlem."

Down the street from Jock's, in his Hotel Theresa headquarters, sat the subject of the debate. With his long frame hunched over a phone in his closet-like inner office, Malcolm made arrangements to speak at Harlem Hospital. He fumbled through the pockets of his dark three-button suit, through his vest and his attache case looking for his pen. Then, hanging up, he pressed his fingers against his eyes and rested.

Remembering the interviewer he apologized and said, "I usually try and get four hours sleep at night. Last night I didn't make it."

The young executive in charge of revolution complained about the pace. About days that too often ran from 9 a.m. to 5 a.m.

Then the mutual testing began. With a half-smile Malcolm said, "A lot of people have warned me about the Village Voice. It's supposed to be a liberal paper, but they say it is very narrow."

"Some people on the staff think you're a con man," I said, and waited for the reaction.

It exploded out of the chair. Now on his feet, he said, "If I wanted to be just a con man, I wouldn't be fool enough to try it on these streets where people are looking for my life, where I can't walk around after dark. If I wanted power, I could have gone anywhere in the world. They offered me jobs in all the African countries.

"Muhammed is the man, with his house in Phoenix, his $200 suits, and his harem. He didn't believe in the black state or in getting anything for the people. That's why I got out."

Do you feel a distorted image of you was created by the press?

"It was created by them and me. The reporters came with

preconceived answers to their questions. They were looking for sensationalism, for something that would sell papers, and I gave it to them. If they had asked probing intelligent questions, they would have gotten different answers."

Why encourage the distortion?

"It's useful. The only person who can organize the man in the streets is the one who is unacceptable to the white community. They don't trust the other kind. They don't know who controls his actions."

The man in the street is the one Malcolm has described as living on the bottom of the social heap. The one who has given up all hope, all ambition, all plans. The one who says, like the old blues song, "I've been down so long till down don't bother me."

Did he plan to use hate to organize the people?

"I won't permit you to call it hate. Let's say I'm going to create an awareness of what has been done to them. This awareness will produce an abundance of energy, both negative and positive, that can then be channeled constructively."

Like the trade-union organizer, Malcolm wants to aggravate the people's frustration and discontent until anger overcomes apathy and they act on their own behalf. This will be done primarily by attacking the whites' treatment of Negroes.

The Jew would seem to be an inevitable scapegoat for his attack. For the Jew, like the policeman, is a visible white in the life of the ghetto. Harlem sees them both not only in terms of their own deeds or misdeeds, but as walking symbols of all whites. It's easy to stir a black audience on both subjects. And stir them is what Malcolm wants to do.

"The greatest mistake of the Movement," he said, "has been trying to organize a sleeping people around specific goals. You have to wake the people up first then you'll get action."

Wake them up to their exploitation?

"No, to their humanity, to their own worth, and to their heritage. The biggest difference between the parallel oppression of the Jew and the Negro is that the Jew never lost his pride in being a Jew. He never ceased to be a man. He knew he had made a significant contribution to the world, and his sense of his own value gave him the courage to fight back. It enabled him to act and think independently, unlike our people and our leaders."

To compensate for the pride and heritage that was aborted by slavery, on almost all occasions, but especially at his Sunday meetings, Malcolm assumes the role of teacher.

Unwinding himself from a hand microphone, without any formal introduction, he comes before his class at the Audubon Ballroom. He chats and kids with them for a while and then gets on with the lessons.

He shows them films of Africa he took on his trip last summer. He tells them, "We have got to get over the brainwashing we had. No matter how much of an Africanist we are, it is hard for us to think of Africa as anything but a place for Tarzan. Look at these films and get out of your mind what the Man put in it."

Narrating from a chair in the first row, he points out the beaches and skyscraping cities and says, "They told us there was nothing but jungle over there. Why, the only jungle I ever saw was right here in New York City."

He reads them an article about James Farmer in U.S. News and World Report. He attacks the magazine for being anti-black like all the press, but he tells his pupils to read it. "Read everything," he said. "You never know where you're going to get an idea. We have to learn how to think. We have to use our heads as well as our bodies in a revolution."

He urges them to watch the kinds of books being used in the schools. "If when we were coming up," he said, "we had a better idea of Africa and our past, we would think more of ourselves."

He closes the meeting with the announcement that child-care classes are going to be taught at the OAAU office.

Before this black audience, Malcolm has a different sound. The extensive vocabulary, the precise grammar, the level resonant voice go. Even the rhythm changes.

Was it deliberate? I asked him. "Sure," he said. "Different audiences have different rhythms. You have to be able to play them, if you don't want to put the people to sleep.

"Now take someone like Bayard Rustin. He's a brilliant man, a real whiz, just like Baldwin. But, he talks white. You know, Oxford accent and all. He came up here to Harlem to debate me. . . . Poor Bayard. . . . He spent so much time trying to figure out how to say things and still sound white that by the time he got the words out, I whipped him."

During the debate, during the speeches on Sundays past, and during the speeches on Sundays future, Malcolm will continue to try to wake Harlem. He will use a negative attack to produce a positive goal. To a white ear the attacks will sound like the ranting of a racist.

To the man who leans casually against the wall at the Theresa, racism is a mask he dons when it will be effective. But even the mask is different from the way it is perceived. To himself he is a racist because he is concerned with the black race. He is a racist because he will attack all people who abuse that race. He is not a racist who hates all non-blacks.

"I care about all people," he said, "but especially about black people. I'm a Muslim. My religion teaches me brotherhood, but doesn't make me a fool."

The white world is not the only place that is concerned with his racism. In the parts of Harlem where white means devil, they are also testing him.

He was challenged at a Sunday meeting. A man stood, rocked back on his heels, and very slowly said, "We heard you changed, Malcolm. Why don't you tell us where you're at with them white folks?"

Without dropping a syllable he gave a black nationalist speech on brotherhood.

"I haven't changed," he said. "I just see things on a broader scale. We nationalists used to think we were militant. We were just dogmatic. It didn't bring us anything.

"Now I know it's smarter to say you're going to shoot a man for what he is doing to you than because he is a white. If you attack him because he is white, you give him no out. He can't stop being white. We've got to give the Man a chance. He probably won't take it, the snake. But we've got to give him a chance.

"We've got to be more flexible. Why, when some of our friends in Africa didn't know how to do things, they went ahead and called in some German technicians. And they had blue eyes.

"I'm not going to be in anybody's strait jacket. I don't care what a person looks like or where they come from. My mind is wide open to anybody who will help get the ape off our backs."

The people he feels that can best help are the students, both black and white. But he considers all militant whites possible allies.

He qualifies the possibility. And woven into the qualifications are the threads of the emotions running through Harlem.

"If we are going to work together, the blacks must take the lead in their own fight. In phase one, the white led. We're going into phase two now.

"This phase will be full of rebellion and hostility. Blacks will fight whites for the right to make decisions that affect the struggle in order to arrive at their manhood and self-respect.

"The hostility is good," Malcolm said. "It's been bottled up too long. When we stop always saying yes to Mr. Charlie and turning the hate against ourselves, we will begin to be free."

How did he plan to get white militants to work with him or even to walk into the Theresa with the kind of slings and arrows he was sending out?

There was the half-smile again. Then, thoughtfully stroking his new-grown beard, he said, "We'll have to try to rectify that."

He admitted it would be difficult to get militant whites and blacks together. "The whites can't come uptown too easily because the people aren't feeling too friendly. The black who goes downtown loses his identity, loses his soul. He's in no position to be a bridge because he has lost contact with Harlem. Our Negro leaders never had contact, so they can't do it.

"The only person who could is someone who is completely trusted by the black community. If I were to try, I would have to be very diplomatic, because there are parts of Harlem where you don't dare mention the idea."

The diplomatic skill of the master juggler will also be needed to get white militant support. For, while wooing it, he must continue to attack whites for the benefit of his Harlem audience.

Bluntly he says, "We must make them see that we are the

enemy. That the black man is the greater threat to this country than Vietnam or Berlin. So let them turn the money for defense in our direcion and either destroy us or cure the conditions that brought our people to this point. For if we cannot live in this house as human beings, we would rather be dead."

As Malcolm finished his comment, he left little doubt that he was willing to go all the way in the fight. Yet he doesn't seem like a man who is in love with violence. On the contrary, as he relaxed during the course of the interview, the impression conveyed by this soft-spoken, non-smoking, non-drinking Muslim was one of gentleness.

When he was not on the stage, another side of the man is revealed. The private rather than the public man is seen when you watch him relate to individuals. He stops and listens to a worried white student despite the fact that the police and his party are trying to hurry him out after a speech. He remembers to buy coffee for everyone in the office when he orders some for himself. He interrupts his sentence on the need for black hostility to ask, with genuine concern, whether I was abused coming to the Theresa.

Violence has no real part in his history. Even the crimes of burglary and larceny he committed as Big Red were mercenary not sadistic.

Why then is he willing to go to such extremes?

"Only violence, or a real threat of it, will get results," he said. "The only time the government moves is in reaction to crises. When it's too costly to let our people continue to suffer, Washington will give the massive federal aid needed to solve the problem."

Violence doesn't mean a huge race war to Malcolm. His strategy is primarily defensive.

He'll work on voter registration in the north and south. But if his people work in a place like Mississippi, they'll be armed. "If the Federal government won't protect the voters," he said, his people will.

He has already begun to offer his services in the south. He addressed a voter-registration rally in Tuskegee, Alabama, on February 3, was in Selma on February 5, and will speak at a Mississippi Freedom Party rally in Jackson on February 19.

Malcolm is also willing to go along with Bayard Rustin's strategy of causing social dislocation in the white community, but he is not willing to do it non-violently. For he says the people in Harlem who are willing to get involved in such activities aren't willing to have a policeman crack their skulls and not fight back.

He will use demonstrations and picketing, but not the kind that play by the rules of the establishment. "Power doesn't back up in the face of a prayer and a smile," he said. "The only demonstrations that they pay attention to are the ones that contain the seeds of violence."

There is another tactic he wants to use. It is the exception in his defensive strategy. He wants bands of invisible guerrillas who would strike and slip back into society. Bands that could match the Klan.

"I'll be the first to join," he said, "and lots of people you don't think will, are going to line up behind me."

It's over the tactics of violence vs. non-violence—or, as Malcolm puts it, self-defense vs. masochism—that he and other civil-rights leaders disagree. This difference is what has prevented the unity that he feels is one of the keys to the struggle.

"It's not that there is no desire for unity, or that it is impossible, or that they might not agree with me behind closed doors. It's because most of the organizations are dependent on white money and they are afraid to lose it.

"I spent almost a year not attacking them, saying let's get together, let's do something. But they're too scared. I guess I will have to go to the people first and let the leaders fall in behind them."

That does not mean ruling out cooperation. He will try and stress the areas and activities where the groups can work together. For he says, "If we are going into the ring, our right fist does not have to become our left fist, but we must use a common head if we are going to win."

Asked if he would support things like a school boycott, he said he would if he agreed with its goals. He would not support it to get more busing. He also wouldn't fight school construction in black communities. Until a better plan for integration is found, he wants more and larger schools built in black neighborhoods. Even more than in comparable white ones, because of the birth rate.

In discussing other things he felt should be done, he said, "We must begin to move into politics and economics. They are two areas where our people are very immature. That's why the OAAU started the liberation school. We want to teach them how to operate."

The political lessons won't be just theory. Malcolm wants to run militant candidates on the local level. They would be race men like the Southern politicians. These candidates would plant angry soap boxes on all the street corners of Harlem. They would make the vote a channel for the discontent for the apolitical man in the streets. Once a political habit is established, it could be a powerful weapon in the struggle.

Would he be a candidate?

"I don't know at this point," he said. "I think I am more effective attacking the establishment. You can't do that as well once you're inside it."

Did he think an all-black party like the Freedom Now Party in Michigan was needed?

"Yes, in some cases you have to create new machinery. In others it's better to take over existing machinery. Either way, we're going to be involved in all levels of politics from '65 on."

Malcolm also wants to take a new economic approach to integration. He thinks blacks should use the same strategy as Jews did in Florida. Instead of spending huge sums of money on lawyers' fees and bail bonds for sit-ins, they should pool their resources and buy housing. Then anybody who wanted to could come in.

He also thinks efforts should be made to have blacks control the food, shelter, and clothing in the communities where they live.

As we spoke and drank the coffee he ordered, it became clear that there is one feature common to all Malcolm's masks. It's determination. Determination to solve the problems of his people at whatever cost. To smash through the deafness of the white world. To force into actions and words the rage that is churning in the guts of the blacks.

On the train I rode downtown, that black rage broke free

in one drunken Negro. He spit his anguish and obscenities into emotionless white faces.

For endless blocks the drunk shrieked against the sound of the subway, "You're full of shit! You're all full of shit! You're killing me! You mothers! You're killing me!"

That rage is what Malcolm wants to shape into a weapon to be used against the continued moral, spiritual, physical, political, cultural, and economic strangulation of the blacks.

Malcolm X Shot to Death at Rally Here

by Peter Kihss

MALCOLM X, the 39-year-old leader of a militant black nationalist movement, was shot to death yesterday afternoon at a rally of his followers in a ballroom in Washington Heights.

Shortly before midnight, a 22-year-old Negro, Thomas Hagan, was charged with the killing. The police rescued him from the ballroom crowd after he had been shot and beaten.

Malcolm, a bearded extremist, had said only a few words of greeting when a fusillade rang out. The bullets knocked him over backward.

Pandemonium broke out among the 400 Negroes in the Audubon Ballroom at 166th Street and Broadway. As men, women and children ducked under tables and flattened themselves on the floor, more shots were fired. Some witnesses said 30 shots had been fired.

The police said seven bullets had struck Malcolm. Three other Negroes were shot.

About two hours later the police said the shooting had apparently been a result of a feud between followers of Malcolm and members of the extremist group he broke with last year, the Black Muslims. However, the police declined to say whether Hagan is a Muslim.

The Medical Examiner's office said early this morning that a preliminary autopsy showed Malcolm had died of "multiple gunshot wounds." The office said that bullets of two different calibers as well as shotgun pellets had been removed from his body.

One police theory was that as many as five conspirators might have been involved, two creating a diversionary disturbance.

Hagan was shot in the left thigh and his left leg was broken, apparently by kicks. He was under treatment in the Bellevue Hospital prison ward last night; perhaps a dozen policemen were guarding him, according to the hospital's night superintendent. The police said they had found a cartridge case with four unused .45-caliber shells in his pocket.

Two other Negroes, described as "apparent spectators" by Assistant Chief Inspector Harry Taylor, in command of Manhattan North uniformed police, also were shot. They were identified as William Harris, wounded seriously in the abdomen, and William Parker, shot in a foot. Both were taken to Columbia Presbyterian Medical Center, which is close to the ballroom.

Capt. Paul Glaser of the Police Department's Community Relations Bureau said early today that Hagan, using a double-barrelled shotgun with shortened barrels and stock, had killed Malcolm X.

Malcolm, a slim, reddish-haired six-footer with a gift for bitter eloquence against what he considered white exploitation of Negroes, broke in March, 1964, with the Black Muslim movement called the Nation of Islam, headed by Elijah Muhammad.

A weapon described as a 12-gauge shotgun was found behind the ballroom stage wrapped in a man's dark gray jacket.

As Hagan fired at Malcolm, Captain Glaser said, Reuben Francis, a follower of Malcolm, drew a .45-caliber automatic pistol and shot Hagan in the leg.

Francis, 33, of 871 East 179th Street, the Bronx, was charged with felonious assault and violation of the Sullivan Law.

Records of the Federal Bureau of Investigation showed that Hagan's real name is Talmadge Hayer, the police said this morning. He was booked as Thomas Hagan.

The F.B.I. records showed that the suspect's address was 347 Marshall Street, Paterson, N.J. He was arrested Nov. 7, 1963, the records showed, in Passaic for possession of stolen property.

Sanford Garelick, Assistant Chief Inspector in charge of the police Central Office Bureau and Squads, said at 5 P.M.—not quite two hours after the shooting—that "this is the result, it would seem, of a long-standing feud between the followers of Elijah Muhammad and the people who broke away from him, headed by Malcolm X."

At 7:30 P.M., Chief of Detectives Philip J. Walsh, who interrupted a vacation to join the hunt for the assassins, predicted "a long drawn-out investigation."

James X, New York spokesman for the Black Muslims, denied that his organization had had anything to do with the killing.

Just one week before the slaying, Malcolm was bombed out of the small brick home in East Elmhurst, Queens, where he had been living. James X suggested that Malcolm had set off firebombs himself "to get publicity."

Assemblyman Percy Sutton, Malcolm's lawyer, said the murdered leader had planned to disclose at yesterday's rally, "the names of those who were trying to kill him."

Mr. Sutton added that Malcolm had taken to carrying a pistol "because he feared for his life" and had notified the police by telephone that he was doing so even though he did not have a permit. Assistant Chief Inspector Taylor, however, said Malcolm was unarmed when he was shot.

Chief Walsh said he believed "proper action was taken on all considerations of protection" for Malcolm, and "many of our requests in this connection were turned down."

Captain Glaser said that since Jan. 27 Malcolm had been offered police protection on seven different occasions, but had refused the guards each time.

One factor in Malcolm's break with the Black Muslims was his comment on the assassination of President Kennedy. He called it a case of "chickens coming home to roost" and an outgrowth of violence that whites had used against Negroes. He was suspended by Elijah Muhammad and then started his own movement.

While the Nation of Islam searches for weapons anyone attending its meetings, Malcolm's new movement emphasized self-defense even with weapons. And so there was no search of anyone at yesterday's rally, a regular Sunday affair of Malcolm's Organization of Afro-American Unity. White persons were barred.

The Audubon Ballroom is in a two-story building on the south side of West 166th Street between Broadway and St. Nicholas Avenue, opposite a small park.

The meeting had been called for 2:30 P.M. in the second-floor hall, where 400 folding wooden chairs had been set up with two aisles going down the sides but no center aisle. At the back of the stage was a mural of a restful country scene.

Witnesses said one of the speakers who preceded Malcolm had asserted: "Malcolm is a man who would give his life for you."

Gene Simpson, a WMCA newsman, said he was sitting in the front row when Malcolm was introduced. He said Malcolm gave the traditional Arabic greeting, "Salaam Aleikum"—"peace be unto you."

"The crowd responded, 'Aleikum Salaam,'" Mr. Simpson said, "and then there was some disturbance about eight rows back. Everybody turned, and so did I, and then I heard Malcolm saying, 'Be cool now, don't get excited.'

"And then I heard this muffled sound, and I saw Malcolm hit with his hands still raised, and then he fell back over the chairs behind him. And everybody was shouting, and I saw one man firing a gun from under his coat behind me as I hit it [the floor] too.

"And he was firing like he was in some Western, running backward toward the door and firing at the same time."

Sharon Six X Shabazz, 19, of 217 Bainbridge Street, who said she was a member of Malcolm's organization, told this story:

"I think he only said 'Brothers and Sisters' when there was a commotion in the back of the room. I thought it was some rowdy drunks."

Some one ran toward the stage, she said, there were loud noises, and she saw blood on Malcolm's face.

"Then everybody started screaming and running and he fell down," she said. "There was blood on his chest, too."

Stanley Scott, a United Press International reporter, said he had been admitted with this admonition by a Malcolm lieutenant: "As a Negro, you will be allowed to enter as a citizen if you like, but you must remove your press badge."

After Malcolm stepped to the rostrum and said a few words, Mr. Scott reported, "there was a scuffle at the back of the auditorium, possibly to distract attention from the assassins.

"Shots rang out," Mr. Scott went on. "Men, women and children ran for cover. They stretched out on the floor and ducked under tables.

"His wife, Betty, who was in the audience, ran about screaming hysterically, 'They're killing my husband!'"

A woman who was wearing a green scarf and a black felt hat with little floral buds, and who would identify herself only as a registered nurse, said she had seen "two men rushing toward the stage and firing from underneath their coats." One, she said, wore a tweed coat.

"I rushed to the stage even while the firing was going on," she said. "I don't know how I got on the stage, but I threw myself down on who I thought was Malcolm—but it wasn't. I was willing to die for the man. I would have taken the bullets myself. Then I saw Malcolm, and the firing had stopped, and I tried to give him artificial respiration.

"I think he was dead then."

Witnesses differed on the number of shots fired; some said as many as 30. Assistant Chief Inspector Taylor estimated the number at nearer eight. Six shots hit Malcolm in the chest and one hit him on the chin; some of the shots struck Malcolm after piercing the plywood rostrum in front of him.

Sgt. Alvin Aronoff and Patrolman Louis Angelos, who were in a radio car, heard the shooting. Sergeant Aronoff said he and his partner got to the ballroom just in time to see four or five persons run out, followed by a mob of perhaps 150, many of them pummeling Hagan.

"I've been shot—help me!" he quoted Hagan as shouting. The sergeant said he fired a warning shot into the air to halt the crowd, then pushed Hagan into the police car and drove him to the Wadsworth Avenue station house. From there the wounded man was quickly taken to Jewish Memorial Hospital and later to the Bellevue prison ward.

"In the car, I found four unused .45 cartridges in Hagan's pocket," Sergeant Aronoff said.

Malcolm was placed on a stretcher and wheeled one block up Broadway to the Vanderbilt Clinic emergency entrance at 167th Street. It was about 3:15 P.M., a Columbia Presbyterian Medical Center spokesman said later, when he reached a third-floor emergency operating room.

A team of doctors cut through his chest to massage his heart. But Malcolm was "either dead or in a death-appearing state," the spokesman said. The effort was given up at 3:30 P.M.

"The person you know as Malcolm X is dead," the spokesman reported.

Malcolm's birth name was Malcolm Little. He considered it a "slave name" and abandoned it when he joined the Black Muslims. At the hospital he was first listed as "John Doe" because he had not been officially identified.

The other wounded men, in addition to Hagan, were believed to have been hit by random shots. Parker was described as being 36 years old and living at 23-05 Thirtieth Avenue, Astoria, Queens. Harris's age was given as 51, and his address as 614 Oak Tree Place, Brooklyn.

The police declined to discuss any suspects.

Patrolman Thomas Hoy, 22, said he had been stationed outside the 166th Street entrance when "I heard the shooting, and the place exploded." He rushed in, saw Malcolm lying on the stage and "grabbed a suspect" who, he said, some people were chasing.

"As I brought him to the front of the ballroom, the crowd began beating me and the suspect," Patrolman Hoy said. He said he put this man—not otherwise identified later for newsmen—into a police car to be taken to the Wadsworth Avenue station.

At the station house later, one man said he had told investigators he believed the killers were "two short fellows, about 5 foot 6," who had been in the audience and who had walked toward the stage with their hands in their pockets.

This witness said he believed the men fired five or six shots from pistols when they were only about eight feet from Malcolm.

An alarm was issued for a 1963 blue Oldsmobile with a New York license plate 1G 2220. The police said the car was registered in the name of a Muslim Mosque, 23-11 97th Street, East Elmhurst, Queens, which was the address of the home Malcolm had occupied until it was burned. The Nation of Islam had him evicted by a Civil Court last week.

According to the police, Malcolm, his wife Betty and their four children moved last week into the Theresa Hotel, 125th Street and Seventh Avenue, and then into the New York Hilton Hotel, Avenue of the Americas and 53d Street. They checked out at noon yesterday, the police said.

The couple was married in January, 1958, in Lansing, Mich.

The children are Attilah, 6; Qubilah, 4, and Lamumbah, 5 months, all daughters, and Ilyasah, a son, 2.

The widow held a brief press conference last night at George's Supper Club, 103-04 Astoria Boulevard, East Elmhurst. She said her husband had received telephone calls at the Hilton Saturday night and yesterday morning saying he had "better wake up before it's too late."

Malcolm's widow, who stayed at an undisclosed site in Elmhurst under police protection last night, was not questioned by the police on the killing.

Assemblyman Sutton, the family lawyer, said:

"Malcolm X died broke, without even an insurance policy. Every penny that he received from books, magazine articles and so on was assigned to the Black Muslims before he broke with them, and after that to the Muslim Mosque, Inc."—the sect Malcolm set up at the Theresa Hotel.

Extra policemen were on duty in Harlem and upper Manhattan yesterday and last night.

At 7:15 P.M. the police left the ballroom. Three cleaning women scrubbed blood off the stage, and overturned chairs were cleared away.

Musical instruments were placed on the stage and a dance sponsored by the Metro Associates, of 230 Tompkins Avenue, Brooklyn, went on as scheduled at 11 P.M.

The New York Times, February 22, 1965

"I Was a Zombie Then—Like All Muslims, I Was Hypnotized"

by Gordon Parks

DEATH was surely absent from his face two days before they killed him. He appeared calm and somewhat resplendent with his goatee and astrakhan hat. Much of the old hostility and bitterness seemed to have left him, but the fire and confidence were still there. We talked of those months two years ago when I had traveled with him through the closed world of Muslimism, trying to understand it. I thought back to the austere mosques of the Muslims, the rigidly disciplined elite guard called the Fruit of Islam, the instruction it received in karate, judo and killing police dogs. I recalled the constant vilification of the "white devil," the machinelike obedience of all Muslims, the suspicion and distrust they had for the outsider. But most of all, I remembered Malcolm, sweat beading on his hard-muscled face, his fist slashing the air in front of his audience: "Hell is when you don't have justice! And when you don't have equality, that's hell! And the devil is the one who robs you of your right to be a human being! I don't have to tell you who the devil is. You know who the devil is!" (*"Yes, Brother Malcolm! Tell 'em like it is!"*)

Malcolm said to me now, "That was a bad scene, brother. The sickness and madness of those days—I'm glad to be free of them. It's a time for martyrs now. And if I'm to be one, it will be in the cause of brotherhood. That's the only thing that can save this country. I've learned it the hard way—but I've learned it. And that's the significant thing."

I was struck by the change; and I felt he was sincere, but couldn't his disenchantment with Elijah Muhammad have forced him into another type of opportunism? As recently as December 20 he had yelled at a Harlem rally: "We need a Mau Mau to win freedom and equality in the United States! . . ." There was an inconsistency here. Could he, in his dread

316

of being pushed into obscurity, have trumped up another type of zealotry? I doubted it. He was caught, it seemed, in a new idealism. And, as time bore out, he had given me the essence of what was to have been his brotherhood speech—the one his killers silenced. It was this intentness on brotherhood that cost him his life. For Malcolm, over the objections of his bodyguards, was to rule against anyone being searched before entering the hall that fateful day: "We don't want people feeling uneasy," he said. "We must create an image that makes people feel at home."

"Is it really true that the Black Muslims are out to get you?" I asked.

"It's as true as we are standing here. They've tried it twice in the last two weeks."

"What about police protection?"

He laughed. "Brother, nobody can protect you from a Muslim but a Muslim—or someone trained in Muslim tactics. I know. I invented many of those tactics."

"Don't you have any protection at all?"

He laughed again. "Oh, there are hunters and there are those who hunt the hunters. But the odds are certainly with those who are most skilled at the game."

He explained that he was now ready to provide a single, unifying platform for all our people, free of political, religious and economic differences. "One big force under one banner," he called it. He was convinced that whatever mistakes he had made after leaving Elijah Muhammad had been in the name of brotherhood. "Now it looks like this brotherhood I wanted so badly has got me in a jam," he said.

Within the last year he had sent me postcards from Saudi Arabia, Kuwait, Ethiopia, Kenya, Nigeria, Ghana and Tanganyika, and I thanked him for them.

"Everybody's wondering why I've been going back and forth to Africa. Well, first I went to Mecca to get closer to the orthodox religion of Islam. I wanted first-hand views of the African leaders—their problems are inseparable from ours. The cords of bigotry and prejudice here can be cut with the same blade. We have to keep that blade sharp and share it with one another." Now he was sounding like the old Malcolm: "Strangely enough, listening to leaders like Nasser,

Ben Bella and Nkrumah awakened me to the dangers of racism. I realized racism isn't just a black and white problem. It's brought blood baths to about every nation on earth at one time or another."

He stopped and remained silent for a few moments. "Brother," he said finally, "remember the time that white college girl came into the restaurant—the one who wanted to help the Muslims and the whites get together—and I told her there wasn't a ghost of a chance and she went away crying?"

"Yes."

"Well, I've lived to regret that incident. In many parts of the African continent I saw white students helping black people. Something like this kills a lot of argument. I did many things as a Muslim that I'm sorry for now. I was a zombie then—like all Muslims—I was hypnotized, pointed in a certain direction and told to march. Well, I guess a man's entitled to make a fool of himself if he's ready to pay the cost. It cost me 12 years."

As we parted he laid his hand on my shoulder, looked into my eyes and said, "A salaam alaikem, brother."

"And may peace be with you, Malcolm," I answered.

Driving home from that last meeting with Malcolm, I realized once more that, despite his extremism and inconsistencies, I liked and admired him. A certain humility was wed to his arrogance. I assumed that his bitterness must have come from his tragic early life. His home in East Lansing, Mich., was burned to the ground by white racists. He had lived for many years with the belief that whites had bludgeoned his father to death and left his body on the tracks to be run over by a streetcar.

Malcolm's years of ranting against the "white devils" helped create the climate of violence that finally killed him, but the private man was not a violent one. He was brilliant, ambitious and honest. And he was fearless. He said what most of us black folk were afraid to say publicly. When he told off "a head-whipping cop"—as he described him—his tongue was coupled with a million other black tongues. When he condemned the bosses of the "rat-infested ghetto," a Harlem full of fervid "amens" could be heard ricocheting off the squalid tenements.

I remember Malcolm's complete devotion to Elijah Muhammad and his words when he was serving as the Muslims' spokesman: "All that Muhammad is trying to do is clean up the mess the white man has made, and the white man should give him credit. He shouldn't run around here calling [Muhammad] a racist and a hate-teacher. White man, call yourself a hate-teacher because you invented hate. Call yourself a racist because you invented the race problem."

Malcolm was not after power in the Muslim organization, but his unquestioning belief in the movement, his personal charm, his remarkable ability to captivate an audience brought him that power. With Elijah aging and ailing, Malcolm became the obvious choice as his successor. But his power and prominence also made him a marked man in the tightly disciplined society. His downfall had started even before his notorious comment on President Kennedy's assassination ("Chickens coming home to roost never did make me sad; they've always made me glad!"). But with that statement he unwittingly made himself more vulnerable.

On the night of Malcolm's death, at the home of friends where his family had taken refuge, I sat with his wife Betty, his two oldest children and a group of his stunned followers, watching a television review of his stormy life. When his image appeared on the screen, blasting away at the injustices of "the enemy," a powerfully built man sitting near me said softly, "Tell 'em like it is, Brother Malcolm, tell 'em like it is."

The program ended and Betty got up and walked slowly to the kitchen and stood staring at the wall. Six-year-old Attillah followed and took her mother's hand. "Is Daddy coming back after his speech, Momma?"

Betty put her arms around the child and dropped her head on the refrigerator. "He tried to prepare me for this day," she said. "But I couldn't bring myself to listen. I'd just walk out of the room. The other day—after they tried to bomb us out of the house—was the only time I could stay and listen. I just closed my eyes and hung onto everything he said. I was prepared. That's why I'm ashamed I cried over him when he was lying there all shot up."

Only Qubilah, the four-year-old, seemed to understand

that her father wouldn't come again. She tugged at her mother's skirt. "Please don't go out, Momma."

"I won't go, baby. Momma won't go out." She gently pushed the child's head into her lap and told her to go to sleep.

"He was always away," Betty went on, "but I knew he would always come back. We loved each other. He was honest—too honest for his own good, I think sometimes." I started to leave and she said, "I only hope the child I'm carrying is just like his father."

"I hope you get your wish," I said.

I rode back to the city with the heavy-set man who had sat near me during the telecast. He slumped in disgust and guilt. "We could have saved him. We could have saved him," he kept mumbling. "How stupid. How stupid."

"What happens now?" I asked.

"Plenty, brother, plenty. *They* made a mistake. We'll rally now like one big bomb. Those zombies are the biggest obstacle in the progress of our people. They're like quicksand. They swallow up people by the dozens. I got into the organization thinking I was going to help promote progress and all the stuff they hand you. The next thing I knew, I was hawking their lying newspaper."

"So, what happens now?" I repeated.

"Six brothers are already on their way for the main visit."

"Main visit?"

"There's always been a standing order. If anything happens to Brother Malcolm, six brothers catch the first plane to Chicago, or Phoenix—wherever he's at."

"Elijah Muhammad, you mean?"

"He's the top zombie. He's the first to be visited."

I thought back to the time in Phoenix when I last saw Muhammad and Malcolm together—the two men warmly embracing, their cheeks touching in farewell. I felt empty.

"And after him?" I asked.

"The names on Brother Malcolm's list—the ones who were trying to kill him."

The list, as the newspapers reported, was taken from Malcolm's pocket as he lay dying.

"They know who they are. They've been properly notified,"

he said solemnly. The list also includes the principal targets for vengeance: the *Muhammad Speaks* newspaper office, the Shabazz Restaurant, Mosque No. 7. "If they're able to hold their meetings at the mosque after tomorrow night," the man said, "I'll join up with them again. Brother, that place will be no more."

I took his word for it—and my despair deepened.

Alabama Police Use Gas and Clubs To Rout Negroes

by Roy Reed

SELMA, Ala., March 7—Alabama state troopers and volunteer officers of the Dallas County sheriff's office tore through a column of Negro demonstrators with tear gas, nightsticks and whips here today to enforce Gov. George C. Wallace's order against a protest march from Selma to Montgomery.

At least 17 Negroes were hospitalized with injuries and about 40 more were given emergency treatment for minor injuries and tear gas effects.

The Negroes reportedly fought back with bricks and bottles at one point as they were pushed back into the Negro community, far away from most of a squad of reporters and photographers who had been restrained by the officers.

A witness said that Sheriff James G. Clark and a handful of volunteer possemen were pushed back by flying debris when they tried to herd the angry Negroes into the church where the march had begun.

[In Washington the Justice Department announced that agents of the Federal Bureau of Investigation in Selma had been directed to make a full and prompt investigation and to gather evidence whether "unnecessary force was used by law officers and others" in halting the march.]

Some 200 troopers and possemen with riot guns, pistols, tear gas bombs and nightsticks later chased all the Negro residents of the Browns Chapel Methodist Church area into their apartments and houses. They then patrolled the streets and walks for an hour before driving away.

The Rev. Dr. Martin Luther King Jr., who was to have led the march, was in Atlanta. After the attack on the marchers, Dr. King issued a statement announcing plans to begin another march Tuesday covering the 50 miles from Selma to Montgomery. He said he had agreed not to lead today's march after he had learned that the troopers would block it. Dr. King also said he would seek a court order barring further interference with the marchers.

John Lewis, chairman of the Student Nonviolent Coordinating Committee, was among the injured. He was admitted to the Good Samaritan Hospital with a possible skull fracture.

Mr. Lewis and Hosea Williams, an aide to Dr. King, led the marchers back to the church after the encounter with the officers. Mr. Lewis, before going to the hospital, made a speech to the crowd huddled angry and weeping in the sanctuary.

"I don't see how President Johnson can send troops to Vietnam—I don't see how he can send troops to the Congo —I don't see how he can send troops to Africa and can't send troops to Selma, Ala.," he said. The Negroes roared their approval.

"Next time we march," he said, "we may have to keep going when we get to Montgomery. We may have to go on to Washington."

The suppression of the march, which was called to dramatize the Negroes' voter-registration drive, was swift and thorough.

About 525 Negroes had left Browns Chapel and walked six blocks to Broad Street, then across Pettus Bridge and the Alabama River, where a cold wind cut at their faces and whipped their coats. They were young and old and they carried an assortment of packs, bedrolls and lunch sacks.

The troopers, more than 50 of them, were waiting 300 yards beyond the end of the bridge.

Behind and around the troopers were a few dozen possemen, 15 of them on horses, and perhaps 100 white spectators. About 50 Negroes stood watching beside a yellow school bus well away from the troopers. The marchers had passed about three dozen more possemen at the other end of the bridge. They were to see more of that group.

The troopers stood shoulder to shoulder in a line across both sides of the divided four-lane highway.

They put on gas masks and held their night sticks ready as the Negroes approached marching two abreast, slowly and silently.

When the Negroes were 50 feet away, a voice came over an amplifying system commanding them to stop. They stopped.

The leader of the troopers, who identified himself as Maj. John Cloud said, "This is an unlawful assembly. Your march is not conducive to the public safety. You are ordered to disperse and go back to your church or to your homes."

Mr. Williams answered from the head of the column.

"May we have a word with the major?" he asked.

"There is no word to be had," the major replied.

The two men went through the same exchange twice more, then the major said, "You have two minutes to turn around and go back to your church."

Several seconds went by silently. The Negroes stood unmoving.

The next sound was the major's voice. "Troopers, advance," he commanded.

The troopers rushed forward, their blue uniforms and white helmets blurring into a flying wedge as they moved.

The wedge moved with such force that it seemed almost to pass over the waiting column instead of through it.

The first 10 or 20 Negroes were swept to the ground screaming, arms and legs flying, and packs and bags went skittering across the grassy divider strip and on to the pavement on both sides.

Those still on their feet retreated.

The troopers continued pushing, using both the force of their bodies and the prodding of their nightsticks.

A cheer went up from the white spectators lining the south side of the highway.

The mounted possemen spurred their horses and rode at a run into the retreating mass. The Negroes cried out as they crowded together for protection, and the whites on the sideline whooped and cheered.

The Negroes paused in their retreat for perhaps a minute, still screaming and huddling together.

Suddenly there was a report, like a gunshot, and a gray cloud spewed over the troopers and the Negroes.

"Tear gas!" someone yelled.

The cloud began covering the highway. Newsmen, who were confined by four troopers to a corner 100 yards away, began to lose sight of the action.

But before the cloud finally hid it all, there were several

seconds of unobstructed view. Fifteen or twenty nightsticks could be seen through the gas, flailing at the heads of the marchers.

The Negroes broke and ran. Scores of them streamed across the parking lot of the Selma Tractor Company. Troopers and possemen, mounted and unmounted, went after them.

Several more tear gas bombs were set off. One report was heard that sounded different. A white civil rights worker said later that it was a shotgun blast and that the pellets tore a hole in the brick wall of a hamburger stand five feet from him.

After about 10 minutes, most of the Negroes were rounded up. They began to move toward the city through the smell of the tear gas, coughing and crying as they stumbled onto Pettus Bridge.

Four or five women still lay on the grass strip where the troopers had knocked them down. Two troopers passed among them and ordered them to get up and join the others. The women lay still.

The two men then set off another barrage of tear gas and the women struggled to their feet, blinded and gasping, and limped across the road. One was Mrs. Amelia Boynton, one of the Selma leaders of the Negro movement. She was treated later at the hospital.

Lloyd Russell of Atlanta, a white photographer who had stayed at the other end of the bridge, said he saw at least four carloads of possemen overtake the marchers as they reentered Broad Street. He said the possemen jumped from the cars and began beating the Negroes with nightsticks.

Two other witnesses said they saw possemen using whips on the fleeing Negroes as they recrossed the bridge.

The other newsmen were finally allowed to follow the retreat.

Ron Gibson, a reporter for The Birmingham News, reached Browns Chapel ahead of the other newsmen. He said later that he had seen Sheriff Clark lead a charge with about half a dozen possemen to try to force the Negroes from Sylvan Street into the church.

Mr. Gibson said the Negroes fell back momentarily, then

surged forward and began throwing bricks and bottles. He said the officers had to retreat until reinforcements arrived. One posseman was cut under the eye with a brick, he said.

Mr. Gibson said that Wilson Baker, Selma's Commissioner of Public Safety, intervened and persuaded the Negroes to enter the church. He said Captain Baker held back Sheriff Clark and his possemen, who were regrouping for another assault.

Mr. Gibson said that Sheriff Clark was struck on the face by a piece of brick but was not injured.

When the other newsmen arrived, more than 100 possemen were packed into Sylvan Street, a block from the church. They were joined shortly by the 50 troopers who had been called back to regroup after turning back the marchers.

The ground floor of the two-story parsonage next to the church was turned into an emergency hospital for an hour and a half.

Negroes lay on the floors and chairs, many weeping and moaning. A girl in red slacks was carried from the house screaming. Mrs. Boynton lay semi-conscious on a table. Doctors and nurses threaded feverishly through the crowd administering first aid and daubing a solution of water and baking soda on the eyes of those who had been in the worst of the gas.

From the hospital came a report that the victims had suffered fractures of ribs, heads, arms and legs, in addition to cuts and bruises.

Hundreds of Negroes, including many who had not been on the march, milled angrily in front of the church.

An old Negro who had just heard that officers had beaten a Negro on his own porch said to a friend, "I wish the bastard would try to come in my house."

The Negro leaders worked through the crowd urging calm and nonviolence.

At the end of the street the possemen and troopers could be seen grouping into a formation. The officers left after an hour, and tonight the Negroes emerged from their houses and poured into Browns Chapel for a mass meeting.

At the meeting Mr. Williams, who was not injured, told the 700 Negroes present about the plans for the Tuesday march.

"I fought in World War II," Mr. Williams said, "and I once was captured by the German army, and I want to tell you that the Germans never were as inhuman as the state troopers of Alabama."

The New York Times, March 8, 1965

Midnight Plane to Alabama

by George B. Leonard

WHEN the wind was right, a peculiar odor spread over the towns that lay near the great crematoria at Auschwitz, Belsen, Dachau. The good people who lived there learned to ignore the stench. They ate, drank, sang, prayed, gave moral instruction to their children. To deny reality, however, is no simple act. Conversation becomes conspiracy. Reality, though denied, always waits nearby, a silent intruder on every group around the fire, every child's bedtime story, every scene of love. In the end, even the senses themselves must join the conspiracy. The people who lived near the gas ovens taught their noses to lie.

Americans, too, have learned to deceive their senses. Sermons have been preached, crusades launched, books on ethics written, systems of morality devised, with no mention whatsoever of how American Negroes are treated. When the senses lie, the conscience is sure to sleep. The chief function, then, of the current Negro movement has been to awaken a nation's conscience, which is to say its ability to smell, see, hear and feel.

Such an awakening is painful. It may take years to peel away the layers of self-deception that shut out reality. But there are moments during this process when the senses of an entire nation become suddenly sharper, when pain pours in and the resulting outrage turns to action. One of these moments came, not on Sunday, March 7, when a group of Negroes at Selma were gassed, clubbed and trampled by horses, but on the following day when films of the event appeared on national television.

The pictures were not particularly good. With the cameras rather far removed from the action and the skies partly overcast everything that happened took on the quality of an old newsreel. Yet this very quality, vague and half-silhouetted, gave the scene the vehemence and immediacy of a dream. The TV screen showed a column of Negroes striding along a highway. A force of Alabama state troopers blocked their way. As the Negroes drew to a halt, a toneless voice drawled an order from a loudspeaker: In the interests of "public safety," the marchers were being told to turn back. A few moments passed, measured out in silence, as some of the troopers covered their faces with gas masks. There was a lurching movement on the left side of the screen; a heavy phalanx of troopers charged straight into the column, bowling the marchers over.

A shrill cry of terror, unlike any sound that had passed through a TV set, rose up as the troopers lumbered forward, stumbling sometimes on the fallen bodies. The scene cut to charging horses, their hoofs flashing over the fallen. Another quick cut: a cloud of tear gas billowed over the highway. Periodically the top of a helmeted head emerged from the cloud, followed by a club on the upswing. The club and the head would disappear into the cloud of gas and another club would bob up and down.

Unhuman. No other word can describe the motions. The picture shifted quickly to a Negro church. The bleeding, broken and unconscious passed across the screen, some of them limping alone, others supported on either side, still others carried in arms or on stretchers. It was at this point that my wife, sobbing, turned and walked away, saying, "I can't look any more."

We were in our living room in San Francisco watching the 6 P.M. news. I was not aware that at the same moment people all up and down the West Coast were feeling what my wife and I felt; that at various times all over the country that day and up past 11 P.M. Pacific Time, that night hundreds of these people would drop whatever they were doing; that some of them would leave home without changing clothes, borrow money, overdraw their checking accounts; board planes, buses, trains, cars; travel thousands of miles with no luggage; get speeding tickets, hitchhike, hire horse-drawn wagons; that these people, mostly unknown to one another, would move for a single purpose: to place themselves alongside the Negroes they had watched on television.

Within the next several hours I was to meet many of these travelers and we were to pass the time telling one another how and why we had decided to come. My own decision was simple. I am a Southerner living away from the South. Many of my friends and relatives have remained there to carry on the grinding day-after-day struggle to rouse the drugged conscience of a stubborn and deluded people. They are the heroes. A trip to Alabama is a small thing.

I had, of course, any number of excellent reasons for *not* going to Selma, not the least of which was a powerful disinclination to be struck on the head and gassed. But as I raised that point and every other negative argument, a matter-of-fact voice answered: "You better get down there."

At midnight, the San Francisco airport was nearly deserted. Three men stood at the Delta Air Lines counter, a Negro and a white man in business suits, and a tall, fair Episcopalian priest. I sensed something dramatic about the tall man; somehow he brought to mind a priest in a Graham Greene story. His companions seemed especially solicitous as they helped him through some complex negotiations with the ticket agent. I introduced myself and learned that the priest alone was going to Selma, that he had decided to go only that night, that he had no idea how he was going to get from Birmingham, where the flight ended, to Selma, ninety miles south. I told him I had wired to both Avis *and* Hertz for cars at Birmingham; somehow I would get him to Selma.

As we started toward the plane, I realized why the priest's companions had seemed worried. Father Charles Carroll of St. Philip's Episcopal Church in San Jose, Calif., walked with a heavy cane; it was an effort for him to maintain our rather slow pace along the runway. Here, then, was the first of our marchers.

Flight 808 to Dixie rose into the cloudless California night. As in countless other flights across America, I pressed my head to the window and wondered at the wilderness below. This nation, the most automated, urbanized civilization in the world, consists mostly of open space. Yet this is appropriate, for America is still unfinished; it is still a huge, untidy experiment, a series of hopeful statements ending with question marks. Most of all, America is the only place in the world where a nonviolent Negro movement could exist. It is the one society that has dared openly confront its own deepest moral wrong, which is also mankind's most ancient prejudice. The great land that lay sleeping some 7 miles beneath me has not yet defined itself, but one thing is sure: it is the only home of a revolution that would correct not laws or governments but the hearts of men. If we can pull this one off, then what is impossible for us? But Selma stood ahead.

"It was the voice of Sheriff Jim Clark on the radio that brought it back to me—that strange feeling in the pit of my stomach." Father Carroll's burning eyes turned inward to the past, to his student days in Germany in the thirties. "I remembered my apartment in Berlin, the Jewish family with whom I lived, the steel that was to be used to bar the front door when 'they' came, the bottle of cyanide in the medicine cabinet—everybody knew why it was there. I remembered my German cousin who had turned Nazi. He had come home one night in 1938 to be asked by his wife what was burning in town. He had said, 'The synagogues,' and she had replied, 'What synagogues?' *Could this be happening here?*

"I went about my rounds today wondering how I could get to Selma and what I would do if I got there. Then I saw the news just as you did and, at that moment, I *knew*. It *is* happening here. I had no more doubts as to what I had to do."

Dawn came in Dallas as we waited between planes. The night had brought other flights from the West, each had its cargo of pilgrims. All of us trooped aboard a rakish, shining Convair 880 for Birmingham—a score of clergymen both Negro and white, a lawyer from Palo Alto, a psychiatrist from Los Angeles, a Bay Area matron who had had a bit too much to drink, a young couple from Berkeley.

Inside the plane, a plump Negro minister from Los Angeles named Bohler kept leaping to his feet to introduce himself and everyone within earshot to each new passenger, most of whom were bound for Selma. Twice he told us that the previous night he had been wanting to go "more than anything," and that the phone had rung at about 10:30 with news that he had been given a ticket—at which he had murmured,

"Oh, He's answered my prayers so quickly!" One of Bohler's companions admitted that "when I told my wife, all she said was buy as much insurance as possible."

There was a stir at the plane's door as a group of rumpled students entered. The newcomers were Mario Savio and some of his followers from the University of California. The bushy-haired student leader and his girl sat across the aisle from me, the door was closed and we took to the sky.

Savio's group, I learned, had decided to come only after watching the 11 P.M. news. They had raced across the Bay Bridge to the airport to catch the flight after ours. Now these young revolutionaries were all over the plane, bursting with news and curiosity. Someone said Governor Wallace and the state of Alabama had been enjoined from interfering with the march. "Looks like somebody may be walking 50 miles today," I said, glancing down at the high heels worn by two of the girls, a sophomore and a junior. "We didn't have time to change," one of them said. "We'll have to march without shoes," added the other. "*Oh* no," said Savio, no doubt considering past criticism of his group's appearance, "we'll buy you shoes."

"How about your shirt tail?" the sophomore said to Savio. "I'll put it in." "And your face," she went on, indicating what appeared to be a two-day growth of beard. "I'll shave," Savio said.

Dark clouds grew into the morning sky and shook our plane as it passed over Texas and into Louisiana. I talked with Savio, a brilliant, uncompromising young man who—aside from matters of etiquette, propriety or procedure and to the considerable dismay of his elders—is right a great deal of the time. "If we're enjoined from marching," he told me firmly, "we should march anyway."

Mississippi. I looked down at the drab fields and forests of late winter and shuddered slightly. Twice in recent years I had gone into that state on story assignments. I experienced again the sick sensation that always came over me when I crossed the state line. It was something like combat in World War II, like flying past that ominous red track across our briefing maps that indicated the point beyond which we could expect to fall into enemy hands if we went down.

To Mississippians, my Southern credentials meant nothing. I represented what they feared most of all: the outside world. To hold to their particular web of self-deception, segregationists must speak only with one another. The very presence of an outside perception threatens the madness to which they cling. That is why no "outsider" can ever feel entirely safe in a place like Mississippi, especially under the following conditions: when it is dark, when the segregationists are armed, when they outnumber their prey, and when they approach from behind. This—God rest my Confederate ancestors—is the present measure of Southern white "courage."

But how can we measure the wrong? When the young Negro civil rights workers from the Student Nonviolent Coordinating Committee first came to work in rural Mississippi, they found that segregationists could spot them immediately and unerringly, even from a distance. No matter that the SNCC workers took pains to dress in the precise manner of the local Negroes; they invariably stood out—*simply because of the way they walked*. And how did they walk? As a human being is supposed to walk: head high, eyes to the front, chest out, feet lifting cleanly from the ground. In the past, during the years of racial "peace" in the South, Negroes have been beaten and killed for less.

And that is one of the things the Southern society has required of its Negroes—that their way of moving on this earth, the very posture of their bodies, proclaim subservience. It is a wrong that goes far deeper than voting rights. But that is a good place to start. On to Selma.

In Birmingham we learned that a federal judge had enjoined Martin Luther King from marching to Montgomery that day. Whether he would march anyway remained in doubt. But nothing could slow our momentum. We had flown all night from the West and were not going to stop now. The airport was in turmoil. People from all over the nation were streaming in. Many others, we learned, were landing in Atlanta, still more in Montgomery. I picked up my car, loaded my passengers and started out on a tricky, uneasy 90 miles through hostile territory.

Father Carroll sat to the right of me, calm and serene. In the back seat was another Episcopal priest, Thomas Steensland. He had left his home in the rural California town of Paso Robles at the last minute, driving south more than 100 miles to catch a plane from Santa Barbara; had missed that plane by ten minutes and had kept going another 100 miles to make a 1 A.M. flight from Los Angeles. Father Steensland also faced a difficult march: as an infantry lieutenant in World War II, he had stepped on a land mine and had lost part of one foot.

Also in the back seat was an older couple who had sat in front of me on the plane from Dallas. I had heard the name, William Morris, and the home town, Malibu Beach, Calif. (*That's* a strange parish, I had mused, assuming Morris to be a clergyman.) Getting in the car, I noticed that Mrs. Morris wore a particularly expensive-looking suit and that she carried a Malaysian Air Lines travel bag. Now I turned and asked lightly: "To what aspect of human life do you minister?"

"Oh, I'm not a minister," Morris said, "I'm in the theatrical business."

A quick realization: He was *the* William Morris of William Morris Agency, the most venerable of theatrical agencies. I wondered what had moved these people, who must live a very comfortable life indeed, to leave Malibu Beach in the middle of the night for a destination that held the clear possibility of tear gas, beating, jail or worse.

"We watched the news," Ruth Morris said, "and then we went in and sat down and were eating dinner. Our home is right on the ocean. It's a very pleasant place to live, rather gay in color. Our dining room is warm and gay and we were sitting down to a very good dinner. We felt sort of guilty about being there enjoying ourselves after what we had just seen on TV.

"We both said it at the same time—it just seemed to come out of the blue: 'Why are we sitting here?' Then I said, 'I'll pack,' and Bill said, 'I'll call for the reservations.'"

The day was more Indian summer than late winter. We were driving south at a careful 50 miles an hour about a hundred yards behind a bus from the Pilgrim Hill Baptist Church of Birmingham. Church members had outlined the procedure for traveling in Alabama in 1965. We were not to have any integrated cars. ("Might attract gunfire.") We were to gas up at a Negro station in Birmingham; no stops would be made along the way. We were to stick to the speed limit; in fact, if the sign said 15, we were to go 14. Two cars loaded with Negroes would scout ahead, returning if necessary to warn us of danger. The most vulnerable vehicle was the bus, for it carried most of those, black and white, who had been on our plane. We of the all-white car were to follow it at a good distance. If it was stopped, we were to pull up behind it and witness whatever happened. The driver of the bus had sketched the route on my map and had shown me the "bad" communities along the way, where we might expect trouble. He would warn me, if anything went wrong, by turning on his blinking yellow loading lights.

Now these lights were flashing. The bus turned off the superhighway we had planned to follow and started down a narrow rural road. We had no way of knowing what the trouble was. We just stayed behind the bus, moving with a turn of the steering wheel into another world, the hazy, dreamy Southland of my childhood. After a night without sleep, I was particularly susceptible to the aching loveliness of the land. We passed run-down Negro shacks, but it was easy not to see them clearly. It took no effort at all to let them fade into the landscape like an old oak or a stand of pines on a rolling hill. Not to see is what our culture has tried to teach us.

I turned to my passengers: "Look at that shack, the holes in the roof, the broken windows, all the children. It gets cold down here."

We turned again. The road became even more lonely. I switched on the radio for news from Selma, but it was difficult to pick out any clear station from the sizzle of static and hillbilly music. At last a faint voice told us Martin Luther King was marching; the march would start in an hour. We could make it.

We never learned why we had followed such a circuitous route, but we entered Selma without ever passing a roadblock or even a city-limits sign, and we stayed on dirt roads all the way to the Negro church district that was our destination. As we pulled to a stop, three slim young Negro women walked past our car. One of them leaned over to us and said with absolute simplicity: "Thank you for coming." Tom Steensland said quietly: "The trip is already worth it."

*

The scene inside the church burst upon me. Every seat, every aisle was packed. They were shoulder to shoulder—the Princeton professor and the sharecropper's child, the Senator's wife and the elderly Negro mammy. The balcony at the left side of the church was like a fresco by a great Renaissance painter. The classic, dizzying angles formed by those who leaned to view the altar were fixed forever, it seemed, against the rich colors of the stained-glass window.

And they were all there at the altar, those who would lead us. For some reason they brought to mind those lines from *John Brown's Body* that introduced the leaders of another time:

Army of Northern Virginia, army of legend,
Who were your captains, that you could trust them so surely,
Who were your battle-flags? Call the shapes from the mist. . . .

Ours were captains of a far gentler army: Charles Evers of the Mississippi NAACP, a martyr's brother and a constant temptation to every cowardly sniper in his state; James Farmer of CORE, the urbane revolutionary with the round face who had walked crying through the streets of Harlem, trying to stop a riot; James Forman of SNCC, the troubled young activist who bears more battle scars than all the rest, now dressed as a poor country boy in overalls; Rev. Ralph Abernathy, Dr. King's trusted lieutenant, a man to soothe the impetuous, possessing iron courage of his own. And, in the center, Dr. King himself.

But now a doctor from New York was speaking; he was giving us, with scientific enthusiasm, our medical briefing. "Tear gas will *not* keep you from breathing. You may *feel* like you can't breathe for a while. Tear gas will not make you *permanently* blind. It may blind you *temporarily*. Do *not* rub your eyes." I looked around at the amused but somber smiles. The doctor's enthusiasm was carrying him away. "If you become unconscious, be sure somebody stays with you." A delighted, outraged laugh rose throughout the church. The doctor laughed, too. "I mean, if you see someone become unconscious, be sure to stay with him." He got the day's greatest ovation.

Martin Luther King stepped forward to the microphones. His slightly oriental eyes glistened in the glaring light. A faint smile, both humble and triumphant, came and went.

As a journalist, I had spent some hours with Dr. King, but had never penetrated the mission to find the man. He was a boy from my home town who had won the Nobel Peace Prize. Some would make him a saint, but it is too early. While the man still lives, one thinks of flaws. I was aware, too, of the narrow, precipitous pathway he walked—between the white leadership, whose ultimate consent he must have, and the Negro activists, who even now rankled with bitter disapproval of his "timidity."

It is too early to beatify him; we must wait for a larger decision. History may take a turn toward harshness. Force and authority may gain sway over men everywhere; in which case Martin Luther King and the Negro movement will rate not even a footnote in history. But if history turns toward the gentler, more subtle controls that we know as love and brotherhood—and it probably must if mankind is to survive—then King's place will be assured.

"Now, we have a problem here in Alabama." Dr. King spoke with restraint and regret. He did not try to stir his audience; they did not need that. He outlined the situation that faced us matter-of-factly. He talked of the decisions all men must make. Next to me a tweedy man with a pipe and British mustache wiped tears from his cheeks. All the faces around me were radiant. Perhaps "the worst sin in life," Dr. King said with a kind of majestic sadness, "is to know right and not to do it."

Outside, in hazy sunlight, the marchers formed. One was to be fatally beaten that night. From a bank I watched the first ranks of four go past. They moved in voiceless exaltation. I exchanged smiles with Jim Forman who walked arm in arm with Dr. King in the front rank. And behind them were all those with whom I had traveled. Tom Steensland went by with another white minister and two Negroes. Bill and Ruth Morris were together and Charles Carroll was with them, supported on the right by a strong Negro minister.

America's conscience has been sleeping, but it is waking up.

In Germany, people did not travel all night across the land to walk with the oppressed. A trip to Alabama is a small thing, but out of many such acts, let us hope, may come a new America. I smiled at my friends and stepped into the ranks.

The Nation, May 10, 1965

Selma: "Ain't Gonna Let Nobody Turn Me 'Round"

by Andrew Kopkind

LAST Tuesday ended with a tall Negro girl in blue overalls crying softly as she walked back into town over the Alabama River bridge. A few minutes later, Dr. Martin Luther King told her, and 2,000 or so fellow marchers, that they had gained a great triumph. "This is the greatest demonstration for freedom, the greatest confrontation so far in the South," he said in those prophetic tones which orchestrate the civil rights movement. "We've been able to do something in Selma today that we've never been able to do before." But if it was triumph for him, it was close to defeat for the young girl, and for many of those who naïvely believed that they could march to Montgomery against the entreaties of President Johnson and the state troopers of Governor Wallace.

Dr. King came to Selma from Atlanta Monday night. Despite brave and encouraging statements, he was in the middle of a serious leadership crisis. His failure to lead the bloody march the day before did not go uncriticized in the militant camp. And there were militants galore in Selma: Student Non-Violent Coordinating Committee teen-agers in jeans, eager clergymen in dog-collars, and a congregation of rope-end Selma Negroes who have been organizing for at least two years.

A "mass meeting" (are there meetings in Selma that are not "mass"?) started at Browns Chapel Methodist Church early in the evening. Before King finally appeared it was nearly midnight, and speaker after speaker had exhorted the crowd to action. The most rousing was James Bevel, a firebrand's firebrand in King's Southern Christian Leadership Conference. Bevel stood at the pulpit in overalls, his shaved head almost covered by a parti-colored West African *yarmulke*, and went over the familiar ground ("Harlem was created in Alabama") with some timely twists. He denounced President Johnson for

339

overreacting in the Congo and Vietnam, and underreacting in Selma. "There are two million white savages here in Alabama," he cried. "Let's tell Johnson, don't play it cheap, 'cause if things get bad we'll walk to see him, too."

There was never any question that Bevel and the others were planning to march the next day, but King was far less certain. His speech was subdued (for him) and strangely personal. "The only way we can achieve freedom is to conquer the fear of death," he said. "Man dies when he refuses to stand up for what is right, for what is just, for what is true." He quoted Langston Hughes: "Life for me ain't been no crystal stair," and he gave the distinct impression that he was involved in some profound struggle with his conscience.

In fact, he had decided to postpone the march. During the day, his leadership group had sought an injunction in federal court prohibiting Wallace from interfering with the next day's plans. An immediate injunction was denied, but there would be a hearing later in the week. Under pressure from the federal government, King had informally agreed to go through with these legal procedures before setting out across the bridge again.

But what was happening in Selma all day and most of the night made inaction unthinkable. Scores of clergymen were hurrying into the city. The lobby of Atlanta's airport, where most of them changed planes for Montgomery, and the ride to Selma, looked like a session of the Ecumenical Council. Civil rights leaders outside the Student Non-Violent Coordinating Committee and the Southern Christian Leadership Conference, which were in charge of the Selma campaign, were joining the fight. When King saw the crowd at the church, he knew that it would be difficult to keep everyone off the bridge the following day. And yet, the meeting ended with the decision to march still unmade.

The confrontation between militants and moderates within the civil rights movement which went on in Selma for the next 12 hours made the confrontation between troopers and marchers look easy by comparison. James Forman's SNCC workers, the coolest cats in town, roamed through the streets in radio cars, coordinating something or other, and generally looking determined. SNCC was all for marching; SCLC was divided. During the night, King realized he had to lead the march. No one could blame him for staying away Sunday—he would surely have been beaten, and perhaps killed—but he blamed himself. Tuesday's march would be a kind of absolution, and it would have the necessary effect of restoring some of the sagging confidence in his leadership.

But the decision was not without some sticky repercussions. Early the next morning, Federal Judge Frank Johnson turned King's petition for an injunction against the state into a prohibition against the march. Again, King went into that state of consultation and meditation which only ministers who are also revolutionists can enjoy. LeRoy Collins, the head of the Civil Rights Commission, and the Justice Department's John Doar, came to town to try to talk King out of marching (and to soften the county and state authorities, too). Attorney General Nicholas deB. Katzenbach practically set up a hot line between King's headquarters at the Torch Motel and the Justice Department in Washington.

What King may not have realized, however, in high agony, was that the decision in large measure was not his to make. It was being made by a lot of singing adolescents and smiling ministers at the church downtown. All morning they waited for the march to begin. The SNCC "freedom chorus" formed on the steps and sang loudly: "Ain't gonna let nobody turn me 'round, I'm gonna keep on walkin', keep on talkin', marching up to freedom land."

No matter what King did, they were going to march, and most of the ministers would, too. "We didn't come from all over the country just to stand around Selma," a young Episcopalian said. At one in the afternoon, King came up the street, walked into the church, and mounted the platform.

"I have no alternative today," he began. "It was a painful decision. There comes a time when a man must decide. I've made my choice this afternoon. I've got to march. I'd rather have them kill me on the highway than make them butcher me in my conscience." The audience cheered, naturally, but his anguish was somehow irrelevant. They knew all along that they would march; he alone doubted his will.

The lines formed on a playing field behind the parsonage.

The volunteer doctors set up an emergency first-aid room in the Baptist Church across the street. Mario Savio and a dozen University of California activists pulled into town. SNCC marshals herded the marchers into order, mixing up the Negroes and the whites for the best effect. King, CORE's James Farmer, Methodist Bishop John Wesley Lord, SNCC's James Forman, and Catholic and Protestant clergymen linked arms and took the head of the column. Governor Collins pulled up in a white car, handed someone a note with a "suggested" line of march, and they were off, down Sylvan Street past rows of shabby Negro public housing, up Water Street to the Edmund Pettus Bridge over the Alabama River. The state's chief deputy federal marshal met them and read excerpts from the injunction; King answered politely that he would go ahead with what he considered the lawful exercise of his constitutional rights. The marshal insisted he would do nothing to enforce the order, nothing at all. He stepped aside, and the march started over the bridge.

Five hundred yards away a double line of state troopers stood across the road. The marchers approached them and stopped. Major John Cloud told them that they could not proceed. King asked if they might pray and sing; Cloud agreed.

If you have never heard 2,000 Negroes and whites sing "We Shall Overcome," hands joined and swaying in eight-abreast rows on US 80 just east of the Alabama River, there is little that can be said to convey the experience. Civil rights demonstrations are now so old hat that hardly anyone not actually participating feels the essential drama. But for about 10 minutes, the incredibly complex, overplanned, overreported, and certainly unresolved Selma voting rights campaign was invested with a kind of profound passion that the world of pseudo-events rarely sees. Then it was over. Like characters in a play, King and Cloud spoke their lines and went through their motions. If it was not rehearsed, it could have been. Passion fled the scene; they were all mechanical men filling their inevitable roles. The troopers stood aside, and the leaders of the long column motioned for their followers to turn back across the river.

Back at the church, there were self-congratulatory but somewhat defensive speeches, many thanks, and appeals for unity ("Division is the favorite trick of Mr. Charlie," said Farmer). "We decided we had to stand up and confront the state troopers who committed the brutality Sunday," said King. "We did march and we did reach the point of the brutality and we had a prayer service and a freedom rally. And we will go to Montgomery next week in numbers that no man can number."

No one could say after Tuesday's march whether a column would ever get through to Montgomery, 50 miles away. But the purpose of the whole campaign—to convince the federal government of the need for voting rights legislation—had already been accomplished. Sunday's violence, as some of the militants like to say, "brought hostility to the surface," and summoned anti-segregation counter-pressure outside the South. Tuesday's march rallied the disarrayed demonstrators and added the really stunning force of the white clergy; the spontaneous response in a matter of hours to the appeal for help—San Francisco's Bishop James Pike chartered a plane and arrived as the march was ending—was the most impressive part of the demonstration. Together, the two unsuccessful attempts to get down yonder on Route 80 will probably provide the impetus to get a voting bill through Congress.

Selma's Sheriff Jim Clark can take much of the credit for the bill—not as much, perhaps, as "Bull" Connor takes for passage of the Civil Rights Act of 1964, but a fair-sized piece nonetheless. Like Birmingham, Selma will have consequences far beyond its borders. For one, it has shaken the civil rights leaders and they have settled into a far more militant alignment. SNCC is now much more than a *kamikaze* squad; it has a position of power in "the movement." For another, it set Negroes to criticize the Johnson Administration, which is no longer a trusted ally.

Ironically, the Negroes of Selma may gain the least from their sufferings. This is too tough a town to have an easy change of heart. It will take a lot of Negro voters to upset Sheriff Clark, or even to convince him of their political power. In the meantime, the Negroes of Selma will have to wait for their freedom. "What do you want?" SCLC's Rev. Ralph Abernathy called to the dispirited marchers on their way back across the bridge. He got the usual liturgical response, "Freedom."

"And when do you want it?" he called. Most of the marchers, on cue, shouted back, "Now." But a few, who were clearly youngsters from Selma, were crying, and they answered, "Next year."

The New Republic, March 20, 1965

Johnson Urges Congress at Joint Session To Pass Law Insuring Negro Vote

by Tom Wicker

WASHINGTON, March 15—President Johnson took the rallying cry of American Negroes into Congress and millions of American homes tonight by pledging that "we shall overcome" what he called "a crippling legacy of bigotry and injustice."

In his slow Southern accent, Mr. Johnson demanded immediate action on legislation designed to remove every barrier of discrimination against citizens trying to register and vote.

He was interrupted 36 times by applause and two standing ovations.

The President said he would send this legislation to Congress Wednesday. It is expected to receive overwhelming bipartisan support.

Before a joint session of Congress and millions watching on television, Mr. Johnson deplored recent violence against Negroes in Selma, Ala., where a voter registration struggle has been going on for six weeks. And he identified the cause of Negroes there and elsewhere with the spirit of the nation.

"Their cause must be our cause too," he said. "Because it's not just Negroes, but really it's all of us who must overcome the crippling legacy of bigotry and injustice.

"And we . . . shall . . . overcome."

To these last words, the title of the great Negro freedom hymn, Mr. Johnson's accent and emphasis imparted an unmistakable determination.

Later, telling of his own experiences as a young teacher in a Mexican-American school in Texas in 1928, Mr. Johnson said he had "never thought then I might be standing here."

"It never occurred to me," he went on, "that I might have the chance to help the sons of those students and people like them all over this country."

Then, forcefully and slowly, he declared:

"But now that I have this chance, I'll let you in on a secret—I mean to use it!"

No other American President had so completely identified himself with the cause of the Negro. No other President had made the issue of equality for Negroes so frankly a moral cause for himself and all Americans.

For "should we defeat every enemy, double our wealth and conquer the stars and still be unequal to this issue," Mr. Johnson said, "then we will have failed as a people and as a nation."

The President's daughter, Lynda Bird Johnson, summed up the impact of the speech in an interview at its conclusion.

She said, "It was just like that hymn, 'Once to every man and nation comes a moment to decide.'"

Mr. Johnson's specific purpose in his fourth appearance before a joint session was to make a dramatic appeal for the legislation he said he would send to Congress.

In passing that legislation, he said, there could be "no delay or no hesitation or no compromise." And he asked the members of the House and Senate, jammed into the chamber of the House of Representatives to hear him, to join with him in working "long hours, nights and weekends if necessary to pass this bill."

But the speech, as delivered, went far beyond that basic purpose and became a moral demand upon the American people to assist in "the effort of American Negroes to secure for themselves the full blessings of American life."

For that goal, he said, "we must not and ought not and cannot wait another eight months."

"We have already waited a hundred years and more," he added. "The time for waiting is gone."

In a printed message accompanying the President's personal appearance he gave a more detailed description of the voting rights legislation on which Administration and Congressional officials were still working today.

It is expected to provide for Federal registration officials to put Negroes' names on the election books in states and districts where discriminatory practices and devices have prevented them from registering and voting.

In addition, the legislation will provide stiff criminal penalties for state and local officials engaging in such discriminatory practices.

Six Southern states would be immediately affected—Alabama, Mississippi, Georgia, Louisiana, Virginia and South Carolina.

For these and other states who wished no Federal action in their communities and wanted to retain local control of elections, Mr. Johnson said, there is a simple course available.

"Open your polling places to all your people," he said. "Allow men and women to register and vote whatever the color of their skin. Extend the rights of citizenship to every citizen of this land."

Anticipating inevitable objections and arguments, he continued: "There is no constitutional issue here. The command of the Constitution is plain.

"There is no moral issue. It is wrong—deadly wrong—to deny any of your fellow Americans the right to vote.

"There is no issue of states' rights or national rights."

Then Mr. Johnson received a standing ovation that went on for nearly a minute after he declared:

"We cannot—we must not—refuse to protect the right of Americans to vote in any election in which they may desire to participate."

But Mr. Johnson—a President who has declared it his goal to be a President of all the people and to end sectional and class antagonisms—refused to aim his remarks solely at Southern states where voting discrimination had occurred.

"There is no Negro problem," he said. "There is no Southern problem or Northern problem. There is only an American problem.

"Let no one, in any section, look with prideful righteousness on the troubles of his neighbors. There is no part of America where the promise of equality has been fully kept. In Buffalo as well as Birmingham, in Philadelphia as well as Selma, Americans are struggling for the fruits of freedom."

The hero of that struggle, he said, is the Negro himself.

"His actions and protests, his courage to risk safety and even to risk his life," Mr. Johnson said, "have awakened the conscience of the nation. His demonstrations have been designed to call attention to injustice, designed to provoke change and designed to stir reform, and who among us can say that we would have made the same progress were it not for his persistent bravery, and his faith in American democracy."

But the President pulled back from a blanket endorsement of all civil rights demonstrations. He intends to protect the right of free speech and the right of free assembly, he said, but they did not include "the right to block public thoroughfares to traffic."

This evoked heavy applause and apparently was a reference to demonstrators who briefly blocked traffic on Pennsylvania Avenue in front of the White House Friday.

Mr. Johnson eliminated, however, a line in his prepared text that said that "the right of free speech does not carry with it the right to endanger the safety of others on a public highway."

This was apparently intended to be a reference and a rebuke to Negroes in Selma who have twice set out on marches to Montgomery, the State Capitol, along the highway. Once they were turned back with violence; once they halted peacefully in front of a line of policemen.

These words were almost the only ones that did not represent a complete endorsement of the Negro cause.

Mr. Johnson, describing himself as "a man whose roots go deeply into Southern soil," said he knew "how agonizing racial feelings are."

But, he said, "the time of justice has now come."

"I believe with all my heart that no force can hold it back," he went on. "It is right in the eyes of man and God that it should come. And when it does, I think that day will brighten the lives of every American."

For it is not only Negroes who are the victims of racial injustice, he said. "How many white children have gone uneducated, how many white families have lived in poverty, how many whites lives have been scarred by fear because we have wasted our energy and substance to maintain the barriers of hatred and terror."

Television viewers got some remarkable views of the reaction of Congress and official Washington to these and other remarks.

They saw Mike Mansfield of Montana, the Senate majority leader, apparently close to tears at one emotional moment.

They saw half the Justices of the Supreme Court applauding one strong line, and the others sitting in judicial stillness.

They saw Senator Albert Gore, Democrat of Tennessee, applauding the President's pledge that "we shall overcome" not only racial bigotry but also "poverty and ignorance and fear."

They saw Senator George Smathers of Florida clap tentatively at one point, then desist quickly.

They saw Senator Sam Ervin of North Carolina sitting with folded arms in massive disapproval.

They saw Senator Allen Ellender of Louisiana slumped gloomily in his seat.

And they saw President Johnson, departing from the chamber, turn to the gallery and blow two quick kisses to his wife and his daughter.

Their party in a special box included J. Edgar Hoover, the director of the Federal Bureau of Investigation; Msgr. George Higgins, director of Social Welfare for the National Catholic Welfare Conference; Dr. Eugene Carson Blake, Stated Clerk of the United Presbyterian Church, and a number of others.

In the printed message that accompanied his speech, Mr. Johnson described fully the voting rights measure that he will propose and the reasons it was needed. In his address, he contented himself with a brief outline of the measure, which he said would "establish a simple, uniform standard" for registration and voting that could not be evaded. It would also eliminate lawsuits in obtaining the right to vote, he said.

Such steps are necessary, he insisted, because in some states, the only way to pass a variety of discriminatory barriers "is to show a white skin" to voting officials.

The outlines of the bill were made clear by officials before Mr. Johnson appeared. In essence, the bill was designed to accomplish these large objectives:

¶ To provide a swift and workable means of registering Negroes and others who have been prevented by discriminatory devices from registering through the usual state and local channels; and of insuring that these persons then could actually vote and have their ballots counted.

¶ To provide stronger criminal penalties against state and

local officials practicing discrimination, in the hope that the discrimination itself might be stopped or lessened.

Officials explained that their object was to get Negroes registered and to have them vote, whether through normal state and local procedures or through the special Federal machinery to be set up by the new legislation.

The bill would apply to all elections, state and local as well as Federal. In that, as well as in its avoidance of cumbersome and time-consuming court procedures, it is unlike any other Federal legislation now on the books.

The practical effect of the legislation would be to abolish literacy tests and other devices of voter qualification wherever these devices have been used in a discriminatory manner.

State and local officials could not apply such devices—for instance, they could not require Negroes to explain involved passages in the Constitution as a prerequisite to voting—under penalty of five years in jail or a $5,000 fine.

Such sentences would be dependent, however, upon the Government's being able to prove a case of discrimination before a Southern jury.

If the devices are applied, however, upon complaint of a sufficient number of Negroes, the Attorney General would have legal grounds to ask the Civil Service Commission, a bipartisan Federal agency, to appoint Federal officials to register them.

The number of Negroes required to file such complaints has not been disclosed but Capitol Hill sources said it would probably be 20.

Upon receiving such complaints, the Attorney General could ask the Civil Service Commission to appoint registration officials in any area where the following conditions existed:

¶ Completion of a literacy or other qualification test—for example, Virginia's complicated registration form, providing for twelve separate entries—was required before registration.

¶ Less than 50 per cent of the voting age population of a state, or elections subdivision within a state, had been registered to vote on Nov. 4, 1964.

But even if 50 per cent of the voting age population was registered, Federal registration officials could be appointed in any state or district applying a discriminatory qualification test if 50 per cent of the voting age population had failed to vote in the general election of Nov. 4, 1964.

The latter provision would make the new law immediately applicable in seven states. They are Mississippi, where only 33 per cent of the voting age population actually voted on Nov. 4, 1964; Alabama, where 39 per cent voted; South Carolina, 38 per cent; Virginia, 41 per cent; Georgia, 43 per cent; Louisiana, 47 per cent; and Alaska, 49 per cent.

In contrast, the national average for voter participation in the general election of 1964 was just above 60 per cent. The highest participation was in Minnesota, where 77 per cent of the voting age population cast ballots in the Presidential election.

Alaska's low percentage is not generally considered due to racial discrimination. One official suggested today that it probably resulted from cold weather and hard traveling conditions in November. There is little chance that the Federal voting machinery will have to be applied in that state.

It could be applied elsewhere than in the six Southern states, however, if election districts within a state met the same conditions—a voter qualification test, and registration of voter participation under 50 per cent.

Certain elections districts in North Carolina, for instance, meet these requirements.

On the other hand, such states as New York and Vermont may continue to apply their nondiscriminatory literacy tests. That is because more than 50 per cent of their populations register and vote and there is no pattern of discrimination against Negroes or any one else.

In practice, the proposed Federal registration procedure would work as follows:

If a Negro was denied the right to register in a state or an elections district where the stated conditions of discrimination existed, he could complain to the Attorney General or to Federal officials in his area.

If a sufficient number of such complaints were received, the Attorney General would request the Civil Service Commission to appoint Federal registration officials in that state or district. In most cases, these would be commission employes or other Federal officials, perhaps postmasters, who lived in the locality.

The Negro denied normal registration would visit this official and fill out a simple form, stating his age, residence and name. This would prove his literacy as well as his basic voting qualifications.

The Federal official would then cause the responsible state or local official to enter the Negro's name on the voting rolls. The law would provide that the Negro could pay at that time any state poll tax required of him, even though state law might have required such payment earlier.

State requirements as to age and length of residence would still be valid. If a Negro registering through the Federal machinery were challenged on these grounds, a hearing would be held within five days to settle the issue.

Hearing examiners would be appointed in the same manner as the Federal registration officials.

States could still refuse to register felons or those shown to be mentally unstable.

If on Election Day, state and local officials refused to permit voting by Negroes registered through the Federal process, or if in a community there had been pressures exerted to keep them from going to the polls, the Federal registration officials would complain to the United States Attorney for the area. He would take the matter into Federal Court.

The proposed legislation would make it mandatory for the court to impound the ballots for the voting district and to suspend their release until the judge was satisfied that all qualified voters had cast a ballot and had it counted.

A state like Mississippi could not evade this law by abolishing its literacy test. In that requirement, as in the insufficient percentages of registration or voting, the vital question is whether the test or the low percentages existed on Nov. 4, 1964.

The New York Times, March 16, 1965

"... It Was Worth the Boy's Dying"

by Paul Good

SELMA, Ala., March 21—It was like a Fourth of July picnic and a pilgrimage, a protest and an exaltation. It was like nothing Selma had ever seen before or dreamed of.

One 82-year-old black man marching at the head of the line perhaps knew better what it was like than anyone else. For him, it was loss and gain to the roots of his soul.

Cager Lee was the grandfather of Jimmie Lee Jackson, the 26-year-old Negro from nearby Marion who died nearly a month ago after being shot by an Alabama State Trooper following a protest demonstration.

Marion Negroes had urged a march to Montgomery to protest his death and today it became a reality.

"Yes, it was worth the boy's dyin'," said Lee as he walked in the front line with the Rev. Dr. Martin Luther King Jr. "He was my daughter's onliest son but she understands. She's takin' it good.

"And he was a sweet boy. Not pushy, not rowdy. He took me to church every Sunday, worked hard. But he had to die for somethin'. And thank God it was for this."

Behind him stretched the column, black and white, pennants fluttering, winding down Broad Street, the main thoroughfare of Selma. A record shop blared "Bye, Bye, Blackbird" over a public address system. And cars carrying white boys went by bearing slogans like "Open Season on Niggers—Cheap Ammo Here" and "Too Bad, Reeb." But Lee seemed not to notice.

"There was but one white man said he was sorry about Jimmie Lee," he said. "He sent me the biggest box of groceries—rice, coffee, sugar, flour. And he called me and said 'I'm so sorry. I don't know what to do.' But no other white man said a word. And I lived and worked in Perry County every day of my life."

The marchers crossed the Edmund Pettus Bridge over the muddy Alabama River. A federalized National Guardsman walked through weeds along the bank below, looking for trouble that never came. At the end of the bridge, where Negroes were routed by State troopers and possemen two Sundays ago, stretches the commercial clutter familiar to the approaches of many American towns: A hamburger stand, gas station and roadside market.

". . . This is the place where the State Troopers whipped us," Hosea Williams, aide to Dr. King, was crying out. "The savage beasts beat us on this spot."

Lee, his thin black cheeks sucked in by age, but his eyes reflecting a mind in full command, paid as little attention to that as he had to "Bye, Bye, Blackbird."

"I wanted to leave here but I waited to raise my seven children and then it was too late," he said. "But now I just want what is mine. In all those years that passed by, I was used as a boy. Never treated as a man. But I ain't mad at white people. No. You have to believe it. I ain't got no evil or spite whatever."

Down the line from him on the other side of Dr. King was an aged Rabbi from New York, bushy white hair and billowing white beard bright in the sun.

Behind them was a blind man tapping with a cane . . . a one-legged man walking on crutches . . . beatniks and patrician ministers. And James Forman, field secretary of the Student Nonviolent Coordinating Committee, giving an interview in French to the Canadian Broadcasting Company on U.S. Rte. 80 in Alabama.

"How could you ever think a day like this would come," asked Lee to himself as to a reporter. "My father was sold from Bedford, Va., into slavery down here. I used to sit up nights till early in the morning to hear him tell of it. He'd tell how they sold slaves like they sold horses and mules. Have a man roll up his shirt sleeves and pants and told: Put on your Sunday walk. So they could see the muscles, you know.

"He was Leftage . . . that was the name of his master in Virginia. But he was sold to a Lee down here. That's where he got his name and I got mine."

And that's where Jimmie Lee Jackson got the middle name he carried to the grave. And that was the beginning of what today's march was all about.

The Washington Post, March 22, 1965

Selma, Alabama:
The Charms of Goodness

by Elizabeth Hardwick

Selma, Ala., March 22

Wʜᴀᴛ a sad countryside it is, the home of the pain of the Confederacy, the birthplace of the White Citizens Council. The khaki-colored earth, the tense, threatening air, the vanquished feeding on their permanent Civil War—all of it brings to mind flamboyant images from Faulkner. Immemorial, doomed streets, policed by the Snopeses and Peter Grimms, alleys worn thin in the sleepless pursuit of a thousand Joe Christmases, and Miss Coldfield and Quentin behind the dusty lattices, in the "empty hall echoing with sonorous, defeated names." As you pass Big Swamp Creek, you imagine you hear the yelp of movie bloodhounds. The cabins, pitifully beautiful, set back from the road, with a trail of wood smoke fringing the sky, the melancholy frogs unmindful of the highway and the cars slipping by, the tufts of moss, like piles of housedust, that hang trembling from the bare winter trees, the road that leads at last to just the dead Sunday afternoon Main Streets you knew were there. We've read it all, over and over. We've seen it in the movies, in the Farm Administration photographs of almost thirty years ago: the voteless blacks, waiting tentatively on the courthouse steps, the angry jowls of the racists, the washed-out children, the enduring Negroes, the police, the same old sheriff: the whole region is fiction, art, dated, something out of a secondhand bookstore. And this, to be sure, is the "Southern way of life," these dated old photographs of a shack lying under a brilliant sky, the blackest of faces, the impacted dirt of the bus station, the little run-down churches, set in the mud, leaning a bit; and the big ones with yellow brick turrets and fat belfries. If this is not it, what else can they mean? The rest might be anywhere, everywhere—mobile homes, dead cars in the yards, little cottages and ranch houses shading their eyes with plastic awnings.

Life arranges itself for you here in the most "conventional" tableaux. Juxtapositions and paradoxes fit only for the most superficial art present themselves over and over. At their best the people who rule Selma, Alabama suffer from a preternatural foolishness and at their worst from a schizophrenic meanness. Just as they use the Confederate flag, so they use themselves in the old pageantry. The tableau (it might have been thought up decades ago by one of the Hollywood Ten): the early morning fog is lifting and a little band of demonstrators stand at their post at the end of the dusty street. A State Highway truck comes up and lets out three desolate Negro convicts wearing black and white striped convict uniforms. The convicts take up their brooms and, with their heads down, jailhouse and penitentiary hopelessness clinging to them, they begin their morose sweeping, up and up to the very shoelaces of demonstrators, the hem of a nun's black skirts. On the heads of the convicts the soft melodies fall: we will overcome, or else go home to our Lord and be free. Great, great! we all say as the convicts and the demonstrators stand as if performing for us. Then off the convicts shuffle, wearing their black and white trousers, part of Alabama's humble devotion to symbolism.

How do they see themselves, we wonder, these posse-men, Sheriff Clark's volunteers, with their guns and sticks and helmets, nearly always squat, fair-faced, middle-aged delinquents and psychopaths? The State Troopers seem one ghostly step ahead of them on the social ladder. They ride around in their cars, their coats hanging primly in the back; they might be salesmen, covering their territory, on to the evening's motel. Who will open the door of the University of Alabama or Clemson or Tulane to the sons of Klansmen? The posse-men live in a joyless night, with no culture or consolation except whiskey. The ignoble posture one observes so frequently in them puzzles. They are strangers to beauty and grace and are indeed the saddest looking people to be seen anywhere in the world. Even the hungry, bone-thin poor of Recife do not present such a picture of deep, almost hereditary, depression. These Southerners have only the nothingness of racist ideas, the burning incoherence, and that is all. No sacred text or hymn book or Armageddon in which all the black devils of the earth are to be swallowed up in some final quicksand of white eternity. Only violence can fill a hole so deep; this bereft, static existence which seems to go back so many generations has its counterpart in the violent, deranged hopelessness of the deprived youth in the cities.

A poor young man, a native of Alabama, in a hot, cheap black suit, and the most insistent of false teeth clinging to gums not over twenty-one years old, back-country accent, pale, with that furry whiteness of a caterpillar, rimless glasses, stiff shoes, all misery and weakness and character armor, said to me, "When I saw those white folks mixed in with the colored it *made me right sick!*" And what could one say in this deprived land: Go see the social worker, find an agency that can help you, some family counsellor, or an out-patient clinic? I did say, softly, "Pull yourself together." And he, too, like the convicts, shuffled off, shaking his head in some primordial perturbation of spirit.

So many of these white people are lost to history, waiting for the light to shine on them, waiting for some release from darkness. Who cares about their destroyed children? What charity can lift them up? When will the students come into the racist home and sleep on the floor and comfort these miserable people? You have to remind yourself that in the madness of the South these outcasts rule. They carry guns and whips and have power over senators and governors. They tell whoever it is that buys the books in the window in Montgomery (*Herzog, Les Mots*) and subscribes to *The New Republic* what they can do and cannot do. They keep in line those Southern queers who are "mad about Negroes" and who collect jazz records. And yet they are a degraded and despised people. This is another of the unbalancing paradoxes we expected to find, as it was, ready at hand.

The intellectual life in New York and the radical life of the Thirties are the worst possible preparation for Alabama at this stage of the Civil Rights movement. In truth it must be said that the demonstrations are an embarrassment of love and brotherhood and hymns and prayers offered up in Jesus' name and evening services after that. Intellectual pride is out of place, theory is simple and practical, action is exuberant and communal, the battlefield is out-of-doors and demands of one a certain youthful athleticism that would, in a morning's work, rip the veins of the old Stalinists and Trotskyites. The political genius of the Reverend Martin Luther King is, by any theory, quite unexpected. The nature of his protest, the quality and extent of his success sprang from a soil of religion and practicality most thinkers had thought to be barren. Looking back, it is curious to remember how small a part the Negro's existence played in the left-wing movements. The concentration on labor problems, the Soviet Union, and the Nazis left the Negro as only a footnote to be acknowledged sometime by the unions or a welfare state. That it could have come to this was unthinkable: this cloud of witnesses, this confrontation between good and evil. Martyred clergymen, Negro children killed at their prayers, the ideas of Gandhi imposed upon restless Negroes and belligerent whites—these appear as some sort of mutation of a national strain. "God will take care of you," they sing, Billy Eckstine style.

In the demonstrations and marches in Alabama you are watching—good people. The foundation is the Civil Rights Movement built by Southern Negroes and into this plot, like so many extras, these fantastic white people have come. On that "hallowed spot," Sylvan Street, you feel you are witness to a new Appomattox played out with the help of overly-refined somewhat feminine Yankee clerics, upright people, marching in their prudent overshoes, some of them wearing coats with velvet collars. The deputy sheriff spoke of these "so-called ministers," but that is a joke. Even a deputy can see that these are preacher faces. On a Sunday after the white churches had turned away the groups of "mixed worshippers" who had knocked at the doors, a Church of Christ found a verse in the Gospel of Matthew that seemed to explain what they had done in the morning. The verse was put up outside the church, in the announcement box, and it said, "When you pray, be not as hypocrites are, standing in the street." But of course hypocrisy is as foreign to these people as vice and that, perhaps, is their story. There is no doubt that they have been, before this chance to be a witness, suffering from some frustration, aching with the shame of the Christian who is busy most of the time ridding the church of the doctrine of the past as he waits for some meaning in the present. The moral justice of the Civil Rights movement, the responsible program of the leaders, the tragic murderous rage of the white people: this was the occasion at last. For the late-comers perhaps the immediate instrument *had* to be the death of a young white idealistic Protestant minister.

In Alabama the cause is right, the need is great, but there is more to it than that. There is the positive attraction between the people. The racists, with their fear of touch, their savage superstition, their strange reading of portents, see before them something more than voting rights. They sense the elation, the unexpected release. Few of us have shared any life as closely as those "on location" in the Civil Rights movement. Shared beds and sofas, hands caressing the shoulders of little children, smiles and this spreading closeness, absorption: this is, as the pilgrims say over and over, a great experience. The police, protected by their helmets, are frightened by these seizures of happiness. The odd thing is that it should not be beatniks and hipsters and bohemians who are sending out the message, but good, clean, downright folk in glasses and wearing tie clasps.

The New York Review of Books, April 22, 1965

Changing the South

by Jimmy Breslin

Montgomery, Ala.

THE sidewalks were nearly empty, with only small groups of Negroes watching, but the white faces were everywhere. They were at the lobby doors of the Jefferson Davis Hotel. And they were looking out from the street level windows of the Dixie Office Supply Company and McGehee's Drug Store and Weiss Opticians. And they looked down from open windows in the Whitley Hotel and the Exchange Hotel, and the big First National Bank building was 12 stories of white faces pressed against windows and looking at the street below.

At first the faces were set and the lips formed curses. Dr. Martin Luther King, the enemy, was coming by. And behind King were some rows of straggly dressed people in shoes that were caked with mud. The faces at the windows smiled, and one face would come up to another and both faces would break into a laugh.

Then the people kept coming. They came in soggy clothes, with mud on their feet, and they walked in silence and with their heads up in the air, high up in the air, with the chins stuck out and the eyes straight ahead, and they came for an hour and a half and the faces at the windows changed.

The cursing was gone and the smiles were gone and the owner of the Ready Shoe Repair Shop stood with his lips apart and he watched the life he knew disappear on the street in front of him. And a man in a white shirt and dark tie was leaning out of the sixth floor window of the bank building, leaning far out so he could see how long the line of marchers was, and he shook his head and pulled it back in and all the faces at the window around him stared blankly.

And Mrs. R. C. Howard sat in a green easy chair at the second floor window of Jay's Dress Shop, sat with one shapely

361

Southern leg over the other, a cigarette held out between
manicured fingers, and the salesgirls stood around her with
their arms folded, and they all tried to see what this thing was
on the street in front of them.

"They are so sloppy," one of the salesgirls said.

"But there are so many of them," Mrs. Howard said

"Look at that white girl holdin' hands with that big ugly
black thing," a salesgirl said.

"I don't know," Mrs. Howard said. "I tell you, I've never
seen this many people together in all my life." She sat motionless and the cigarette burned down while she stared at the
street.

Up Montgomery St. the marchers came. They trailed out
of the Negro section, with its mud roads, and they came onto
the flat asphalt and went by the hotels and office buildings
and they came around the fountain where Montgomery St.
twists into Dexter Ave. and now they came straight up Dexter Ave., up the six-lane street, with their heads high and their
eyes at the white Capitol building at the top of the hill and
they walked through Montgomery and changed the face of
the South yesterday.

John Doar walked first. He was a half block ahead of the
march and he strolled along, a tousled haired white guy in a
quiet green plaid sports jacket and striped tie. He chewed on
an apple. He is the Assistant Attorney General of the United
States in charge of civil rights. He is 42 and he has put in the
last five years, the big years of a man's life, worrying about
these colored people who were behind him. Four years ago,
he came into Montgomery to handle the Freedom Riders and
when he walked out of the bus station for a minute his assistant, John Seigenthaler, was jumped and had his head split
with a lead pipe. But yesterday, John Doar walked up Dexter
Avenue as if he were out for the air and a guy alongside him
kept talking about what was happening.

"It's all gone," the guy said. "The South is all gone. A
whole way of life is going right into memory."

"That's right," Doar said. "That's just what it is."

A few yards behind him, Jim McShane, the chief United
States marshal, stopped and took off his sunglasses and

looked up at something that was sticking out of a building window.

"That's an ABC camera," a man called out from an unmarked car behind McShane.

"Oh, that's right," McShane said. "For a second there . . ."

Then the marchers came. There were the known people, King, and old Phil Randolph, the stiffness of the years in his legs, and Roy Wilkins, and Whitney Young. But there were few that could be recognized. Civil rights, when it comes out of the lecture halls and goes into the backroads of places like Selma, Ala., does not attract many personalities. It attracts only people whose names are nothing, and who have nothing that shows, and they take chances with their lives, and yesterday they walked through Montgomery, these nameless little people who changed the ways of the nation, and with them were people from everywhere, white people and black people, and they walked together in a parade the South never has seen. And they showed, forever, on this humid day in Montgomery, Ala., that what they stand for cannot be stopped.

"I want to get whupped," Alexander McLaughlin said. "I told my wife yesterday that I feels left out of this thing. I want to go out some place and get myself whupped so's I can feel I been in it."

He was an old man with a white card saying "Washington" sticking from the breast pocket of his gray suit.

"Come down with me and you get yourself a good whupping," an old woman in a plaid kerchief called to him. "Oh, ah guarantees you a good whupping."

"Where you from?" McLaughlin said.

"Madison County, Mississippi," the old woman said.

"They whup you for all times in Madison County," somebody in the back yelled out. The old woman shrieked and clapped her hands and everybody laughed and kept walking towards the white capitol building on the top of the hill.

"I'll be in Madison County," McLaughlin said.

Roland Cooper, State Senator from Wilcox County, stood on the white marble steps of the capitol building and watched the line of marchers coming up the hill. Roland Cooper is a solid man. He had on a gray business suit and his hair was cut and combed and his shoes were shined, and he owns an auto agency and a small cattle farm in Camden, Ala.

He is no street-corner redneck. He is a business man and a politician and he shakes hands and says hello affably. He was out on the steps yesterday, watching this long line of sloppy people come up the hill toward him, and when the first rows reached the speakers stand set up in the plaza, they stopped and Roland Cooper, standing for everything that the South used to mean, made fun of them.

"Never saw so many coons all together in mah life," State Sen. Roland Cooper said.

"Damn," he said. "Don't that look like Nigger Penn over yonder there."

"Who?"

"Nigger Penn. Jes' some nigger from mah hometown. If ah catches him here . . ."

He looked to see if the face in the crowd was the one he knew.

"You know something?" Cooper said. "Ah'm good to niggers. Why ah've got two of 'em working for me now at the auto agency. One's been with me 17 years, the other 18. Ah got one on the farm. They like me. Ah'm good to niggers."

"How much do you pay them?"

"Pay them accordin' to the work they do."

Up on the stage at the foot of the steps, Harry Belafonte stepped to a microphone and began to sing.

You waited for Cooper to say it. "Tell you one thing," Cooper said after a while, "'Taint anybody can equal niggers for keepin' time to music."

"What do you think all this means?" he was asked.

"Don't mean nothin'. Don't mean nothin' at all. Jes' take a look at them. They jes' a pack of coons."

He kept looking at them. And they kept coming. Far down the street, around the fountain, the line coiled and the people kept coming up the hill and the sun was breaking through the clouds now and lines of Army troops stood with their rifles at parade rest, and FBI agents walked through the crowd with hand radios, and helicopters flew overhead and Roland Cooper stood and watched his world change and he didn't even know it, and he will not know it until he sees, some day, the registration figures in Wilcox County, Alabama, where niggers never have voted.

But the Roland Coopers were buried yesterday. They were buried on Dexter Avenue, which was decorated with flags of the State of Alabama, a final touch of small-boy toy-breaking which this state loves. And they were buried by people who came winding from a huge field of deep mud behind a Catholic hospital and school in the Negro section, four miles away.

The marchers gathered in a section of town which has places like Council Street. On Council Street yesterday morning, a little boy sat and banged his feet on the tin porch chair they had put him on while he sucked on a smeared plastic bottle. Next door a man dozed on a bench on the porch with a red hat stuck over his face. The house was a tangle of boards nailed together under a tin roof and sat up on cement blocks.

A little girl in a red dress and bare feet stood in the garbage in the weeds at the curb and bent over a pipe that was sticking up. She turned something on the pipe and water came out of its rusted end. She bent over and started to drink the water.

"Don't you have water inside?" she was asked.

"No," she said, "this the water."

On the porch a fat woman in a cotton dress and white butcher's apron held a baby in her arms. The baby woke up when a helicopter flew low over the house and the fat woman began to jiggle the baby back to sleep.

The march started here, and it was going on for people who live on the Council Streets everywhere in this nation. And it wound through the Negro section, past toothless old women who kept calling out, "Ah never thought ah'd see this," and then it came down into the white section, down onto the wide streets, and at a little after 4 o'clock yesterday afternoon the speeches were over and the people started singing "We Shall Overcome."

And when they sang it, they held hands and swayed. Thirty thousand people stood on the main street of Montgomery, Ala., and held hands and swayed and sang "We Shall Overcome" and the voices went out from the street and echoed off the buildings behind them. And the faces in the windows of the buildings were blank, all of them blank now, and these black people singing in the street, these ignorant niggers who would have been shot to death for causing this kind of trouble six months ago, seemed to glow with each word of the song.

You have not lived, in this time when everything is changing, until you see an old black woman with mud on her shoes stand on the street of a Southern city and sing ". . . we are not afraid . . ." and then turn and look at the face of a cop near her and see the puzzlement, and the terrible fear in his eyes. Because he knows, and everybody who has ever seen it knows, that it is over. The South as it has stood since 1865 is gone. Shattered by these people in muddy shoes standing in the street and swaying and singing "We Shall Overcome."

A business man came running down the steps of the capitol building and reached out and grabbed you in the middle of the song.

"Look," he was saying, "I saw you talking to Roland Cooper before. Now Roland Cooper is a sincere man, don't get me wrong. But he just doesn't know. Life has passed him by. This here thing is a revolution. And some of us know it. We really do.

"Now can you please do me a favor. Go over and talk to Red Blount. He's the biggest contractor in town. You see Red Blount, he thinks different. He knows what's going on. Red Blount knows that this is a revolution and he's going to live with it.

"Do me a favor. You saw Roland Cooper. Now please go and see Red Blount. He knows what's going on. The world's just passed Roland Cooper by. It's passed all of us by, unless we start to live with it."

New York *Herald-Tribune*, March 26, 1965

Letter from Selma

by Renata Adler

THE thirty thousand people who at one point or another took part in this week's march from the Brown Chapel African Methodist Episcopal Church in Selma, Alabama, to the statehouse in Montgomery were giving highly dramatic expression to a principle that could be articulated only in the vaguest terms. They were a varied lot: local Negroes, Northern clergymen, members of labor unions, delegates from state and city governments, entertainers, mothers pushing baby carriages, members of civil-rights groups more or less at odds with one another, isolated, shaggy marchers with an air of simple vagrancy, doctors, lawyers, teachers, children, college students, and a preponderance of what one marcher described as "ordinary, garden-variety civilians from just about everywhere." They were insulated in front by soldiers and television camera crews, overhead and underfoot by helicopters and Army demolition teams, at the sides and rear by more members of the press and military, and over all by agents of the F.B.I. Most of them were aware that protection along a route of more than fifty miles of hostile country could not be absolute (on the night before the march, a student who had come here from Boston University was slashed across the cheek with a razor blade), yet few of the thirty-two hundred marchers who set out on Sunday morning seemed to have a strong consciousness of risk. They did not have a sharply defined sense of purpose, either. President Johnson's speech about voting rights and Judge Johnson's granting of permission for the march to take place had made the march itself ceremonial—almost redundant. The immediate aims of the abortive earlier marches had been realized: the national conscience had been aroused and federal intervention had been secured. In a sense, the government of Alabama was now in rebellion, and the marchers, with the sanction and protection of the federal government, were demonstrating against a rebellious state. It was unclear what such a demonstration could hope to achieve. Few segregationists could be converted by it, the national commitment to civil rights would hardly be increased by it, there was certainly an element of danger in it, and for the local citizenry it might have a long and ugly aftermath. The marchers, who had five days and four nights in which to talk, tended for the most part to avoid discussions of principle, apparently in the hope that their good will, their sense of solidarity, and the sheer pageantry of the occasion would resolve matters at some symbolic level and yield a clear statement of practical purpose before the march came to an end.

From this point of view, the first few hours of Sunday morning in Selma were far from satisfying. Broad Street, the town's main thoroughfare, was deserted and indifferent. At the Negro First Baptist Church, on the corner of Sylvan Street and Jefferson Davis Avenue, denim-clad veterans of earlier marches stood wearily aloof from recruits, who ate watery scrambled eggs, drank watery coffee, and simply milled about. On Sylvan Street itself, an unpaved red sand road dividing identical rows of brick houses known as the George Washington Carver Development, crowds were gathering, some facing the entrance to the Brown Chapel Church, others on the steps of the church facing out. Inside the church, more people were milling, while a few tried to sleep on benches or on the floor. For several hours, nothing happened. The church service that was to begin the march was scheduled to take place at ten o'clock, but veterans advised newcomers—in the first of several bitter, self-mocking jokes that became current on the Selma-Montgomery road—that this was C.P.T., Colored People Time, and the service actually began more than an hour behind schedule. In a field behind the housing development, the Reverend Andrew Young, executive director of Dr. Martin Luther King's Southern Christian Leadership Conference (S.C.L.C., referred to by some of the marchers as Slick), which sponsored the march, was giving marshals and night security guards last-minute instructions in the tactics of non-violence. "Keep women and children in the middle," he said. "If there's a shot, stand up and make the others kneel down. Don't be lagging around, or you're going to get hurt. Don't rely on the troopers, either. If you're beaten on, crouch and put your hands over the back of your head. Don't put up your arm to ward off a blow. If you fall, fall right down and look dead. Get to know the people in your unit, so you can tell if somebody's missing or if there's somebody there who shouldn't be there. And listen! If you can't be non-violent, let me know now." A young man in the standard denim overalls of the Student Nonviolent Coordinating Committee (S.N.C.C., otherwise known as Snick) murmured, "Man, you've got it all so *structured*. There seems to be a certain anxiety here about *structure*." Everyone laughed, a bit nervously, and the marshals went to the front of the church.

The crowd there was growing, still arrayed in two lines, one facing in, the other facing out. There were National Guardsmen and local policemen, on foot and in jeeps and cars, along the sides of Sylvan Street and around its corners, at Jefferson Davis and Alabama Avenues. The marchers themselves appeared to have dressed for all kinds of weather and occasions—in denims, cassocks, tweed coats, ponchos, boots, sneakers, Shetland sweaters, silk dresses, college sweatshirts, sports shirts, khaki slacks, fur-collared coats, pea jackets, and trenchcoats. As they waited, they sang innumerable, increasingly dispirited choruses of "We Shall Overcome," "Ain't Gonna Let Nobody Turn Me 'Round," and other songs of the movement. There was a moment of excitement when Dr. King and other speakers assembled on the steps, but a succession of long, rhetorical, and, to a certain extent (when press helicopters buzzed too low or when the microphone went dead), inaudible speeches put a damper on that. An enthusiastic lady, of a sort that often afflicts banquets and church suppers, sang several hymns of many stanzas, with little melody and much vibrato. Exhaust fumes from a television truck parked to the right of the steps began to choke some of the marchers, and they walked away, coughing. Speakers praised one another extravagantly in monotonous political-convention cadences ("the man who . . ."). An irreverent, irritated voice with a Bronx accent shouted, "Would you mind please talking a little louder!" Several members of the crowd sat down in the street, and the march assumed the first of its many moods—that of tedium.

Then Dr. King began to speak, and suddenly, for no apparent reason, several Army jeeps drove straight through the center of the crowd. ("Didn't realize we were interrupting," said one of the drivers, smiling. He had a D.D., for Dixie Division, emblem on his uniform.) The startled crowd, divided in half for a moment, became aware of its size. Dr. King's speech came to an end, and there was a last, unified, and loud rendition of "We Shall Overcome." Then the marshals quickly arranged the crowd in columns, six abreast—women and children in the middle—and the procession set out down Sylvan Street. It was about one o'clock. On Alabama Avenue, the marchers turned right, passing lines of silent white citizens on the sidewalks. On Broad Street, which is also U.S. Route 80 to Montgomery, they turned left, and as segregationist loudspeakers along the way blared "Bye, Bye, Blackbird" and the white onlookers began to jeer, the marchers approached and crossed the Edmund Pettus Bridge. And the march entered another mood—jubilation.

The day was sunny and cool. The flat road, an amalgam of asphalt and the local sand, looked pink. The people in the line linked arms, and the procession was long enough to permit the marchers to sing five different civil-rights songs simultaneously without confusion; the vanguard could not hear what the rear guard was singing. Occasionally, various leaders of the movement broke out of the line to join interviewers from the television networks, which took turns using a camera truck that preceded the line of march. For the first few miles, the highway was flanked by billboards ("Keep Selma Beautiful, Cover It with Dodge"), smaller signs (Rotary, Kiwanis, Lions, Citizens Council), diners, and gas stations. Little clusters of white onlookers appeared at various points along the road, some shouting threats and insults, others silently waving Confederate flags, and still others taking pictures of the marchers, presumably as a warning that their faces would not be forgotten when the march was over. The procession filled the two left lanes of the four-lane highway, but in the two right lanes traffic was proceeding almost normally. A black Volkswagen passed the marchers several times; on its doors and fenders were signs, lettered in whitewash: "MARTIN LUTHER KINK," "WALK, COON," "COONESVILLE, U.S.A.," and "RENT YOUR PRIEST SUIT HERE." Several small children at the roadside waved toy rifles and popguns and chanted "Nigger lover!," "White nigger!," "Half-breed!," and other epithets. A man in front of a roadside diner thumbed his nose for the entire twenty minutes it took the procession to pass him, and a well-dressed matron briefly stopped her Chrysler, got out, stuck out her tongue, climbed in again, slammed the door, and drove off.

Several times, the march came to an abrupt halt, and in the middle ranks and the rear guard there were murmurs of alarm. Then it became clear that these were only rest stops, and the marchers relaxed and resumed their singing. Rented trucks, driven by ministers of the San Francisco Theological Seminary, carried portable toilets up and down the line. When press photographers attempted to take pictures of civil-rights leaders entering the men's rooms, the Reverend Mr. Young shouted, "Can't a man even go to the john in peace?" The photographers moved away. Three tired marchers rode a short distance on the water truck, and James Forman, the executive secretary of S.N.C.C., who was being interviewed in French for Canadian television, broke off his interview to mutter as the truck passed, "Hey, man, you cats could walk." The marchers got down from the truck at once. Forman resumed his interview. "I think he's having trouble with his French," said one of the marchers. "He just said that no Negro in America is allowed to vote." "His French is all right," said another. "But he may be less concerned with the immediate truth than with stirring up the kind of chaos that makes things change."

By sunset of the first day, the caravan was more than seven miles from Selma, and most of the marchers returned by a special train to town, where some of them left for their home communities and others were put up for the night in the Negro development on Sylvan Street. Two hundred and eighty Negroes, representing Alabama counties (a hundred and forty-eight from Dallas County, eighty-nine from Perry, twenty-three from Marengo, and twenty from Wilcox), and twenty whites, from all over the country, who had been chosen to make the entire journey to Montgomery (the court permitted no more than three hundred marchers on the twenty-mile stretch of Route 80 midway between Selma and Montgomery, where it is only a two-lane highway) turned off Route 80 onto a tarred road leading to the David Hall farm —their campsite for the night. Four large tents had already been pitched in a field. As the marchers lined up for supper (three tons of spaghetti), which was served to them on paper plates, from brand-new garbage pails, night fell. Groups of National Guardsmen who surrounded the farm lighted camp-fires. "It looks like Camelot," said one of the younger whites.

Camelot soon became very cold and damp. By nine o'clock, most of the marchers had retired to the tents, but within an hour they had to be roused and sorted out. One tent was for men, another for women, the third for the marchers' own night security patrol, and the fourth for the press. When everyone had been assigned to his or her proper tent, it developed that there was a shortage of blankets, winter clothes, and sleeping bags. A shivering group huddled around an incinerator, the campsite's only source of heat. A few marchers made their way to the loft of a barn beside the Hall farmhouse, to profit from the heat given off by the animals in the stalls below. Five guinea hens perched in a tree outside the barn. The march's security patrol wandered about with walkie-talkies; they had labelled their outposts Able, Baker, Charlie, and Dog, using the Army's old system, to set them apart from Alpha, Bravo, Charlie, and Delta, the out-posts of the National Guard along the perimeter of the field. The night grew colder, damper, and darker, and the group around the incinerator fire grew uneasy.

There was talk of the march ahead through Lowndes County, where swamps and the woods behind them might easily shelter a sniper in a tree or a canoe. Several marchers claimed to have spotted members of the American Nazi Party along the line of march. Someone mentioned the Ku Klux Klan "counter-demonstration" that had taken place in Montgomery that afternoon.

"And the snakes," a man said.

"What snakes?" said a Northern voice.

"Copperheads and cottonmouth. It takes the heat to bring them out, but a trooper told me somebody's caught five baskets full and is letting them go where we camp tomorrow night."

"How'd the trooper hear about it?"

"Spies."

"Well, I suppose there might be spies right here in camp."

"There might. And bombs and mines. They cleared a few this afternoon. Man, this isn't any Boy Scout jamboree. It's something else."

By the time dawn came, the campers were a thoroughly chilled and bleary-eyed group. The oatmeal served at breakfast gave rise to a certain amount of mirth ("Tastes like fermented library paste," said one of the clergymen), and the news that the National Guardsmen had burned thirteen fence posts, two shovel handles, and an outhouse belonging to a neighboring church in order to keep warm during the night cheered everyone considerably. At a press conference held by Jack Rosenthal, the young Director of Public Information of the Justice Department, the rumors about snakes, bombs, and mines were checked out, and it was learned that none of them were true. A reporter waved several racist leaflets that had been dropped from an airplane and asked whether anything was being done to prevent such planes from dropping bombs. "What do you want us to do?" Rosenthal replied. "Use anti-aircraft guns?"

The procession set out promptly at 8 A.M. The distance to the next campsite—Rosa Steele's farm—was seventeen miles. Again the day was sunny, and as the air grew warmer some of the more sunburned members of the group donned berets or Stetsons or tied scarves or handkerchiefs around their heads. To the white onlookers who clustered beside the road, the three hundred marchers must have seemed a faintly piratical band. At the head of the line were Dr. and Mrs. King, wearing green caps with earmuffs and reading newspapers as they walked. Not far behind them was a pale-green wagon (known to the marchers as the Green Dragon) with Mississippi license plates, in which rode doctors wearing armbands of the M.C.H.R. (the Medical Committee for Human Rights). Farther back were some of the younger civil-rights leaders: Hosea Williams, S.C.L.C. director of the march and veteran of the bitter struggle for public accommodations in Savannah, Georgia; the Reverend James Bevel, formerly of S.N.C.C., now S.C.L.C. project director for Alabama (Mr. Bevel was wearing the many-colored yarmulke that has become almost his trademark—"a link," he says, "to our Old Testament heritage"); John Lewis, chairman of S.N.C.C.; and the Reverend Andrew Young. Behind the leaders, some of the main personae of the march had begun to emerge, among them Joe Young, a blind greenhouse worker from Atlanta, Georgia, and Jim Letherer, a one-legged settlement-house worker from Saginaw, Michigan. ("Left! Left! Left!" the segregationist onlookers chanted as Mr. Letherer moved along on crutches.) Chuck Fager, a young worker for S.C.L.C., wearing denims and a black yarmulke, was waving and shouting, "Come march with us! Why don't you come along and march with us?" ("It sets up a dialogue," he explained. "The last time I was in jail, a sheriff pulled me aside and asked me where the hell I was from. Any sort of talk like that sets up a dialogue.") Sister Mary Leoline, a nun from Christ the King parish in Kansas City, Kansas, was talking to John Bart Gerald, a young novelist from New York. "This is a great time to be alive," she said. A few members of the night security guard had somehow acquired cameras, and they were now photographing bystanders who were photographing marchers; it appeared that a sort of reciprocal Most Wanted list was being compiled. From time to time, the marchers were still singing ("Oh-h-h, Wallace, segregation's bound to fall"), and the chief of the Justice Department's Civil Rights Division, Assistant Attorney General John Doar, tall, tanned, and coatless, was striding back and forth along the line of march to see that all was going well.

Around two o'clock, as the middle ranks of marchers passed an intersection just outside Lowndes County, a female bystander apparently could stand it no longer. "They're carrying the flag upside down!" she screamed to the nearest trooper. "Isn't there a law against that? Can't you arrest them? Look at them so-called white men with church collars that they bought for fifty cents! And them de*vir*ginated nuns! I'm a Catholic myself, but it turns my stomach to see them. They said there was thousands yesterday, but there wasn't near a thousand. Them niggers and them girls! I've watched the whole thing three times, and there isn't a intelligent-looking one in the bunch. I feel sorry for the black folks. If they want to vote, why don't they just go out and register? Oh, honey, look! There goes a big one. Go home, scum! Go home, scum!" The procession began to sing a not very hearty version of "A Great Camp Meeting in the Promised Land."

Not all the bystanders along the road were white. At the boundary of Lowndes County (with a population of fifteen thousand, eighty per cent of them Negroes, not one of whom had been registered to vote by March 1, 1965), John Maxwell, a Negro worker in a Lowndes County cotton-gin mill (at a salary of six dollars for a twelve-hour day), appeared at an intersection.

"Why don't you register to vote?" a reporter from the *Harvard Crimson* asked Mr. Maxwell.

"They'd put us off the place if I tried," Mr. Maxwell said.

In the town of Trickem, at the Nolan Elementary School— a small white shack on brick stilts, which had asbestos shingles, a corrugated-iron roof, six broken windows, and a broken wood floor patched with automobile license plates—a group of old people and barefoot children rushed out to embrace Dr. King. They had been waiting four hours.

"Will you march with us?" Dr. King asked an old man with a cane.

"I'll walk one step, anyway," said the man. "Because I know for every one step I'll take you'll take two."

The marchers broke into a chant. "*What* do you *want*?" they shouted encouragingly to the Negroes at the roadside. The Negroes smiled, but they did not give the expected response— "*Freedom!*" The marchers had to supply that themselves.

Late in the afternoon, as Route 80 passed through the swamps of Lowndes County, the marchers looked anxiously at the woods, covered with Spanish moss, which began a few yards back from the road. They reached Rosa Steele's farm at sunset. Many of them seemed dismayed to find that the campsite lay right beside the highway. Fresh rumors began to circulate: a young man had been seen putting a bomb under a roadside bridge; twenty white men, with pistols and shotguns, had been seen prowling through a neighboring field; testing security, a representative of the Pentagon had managed to penetrate the security lines without being asked to show his pass. Mr. Rosenthal again put these fears to rest. "The field has been combed by Army demolition teams," he said. "If anyone from the Pentagon had made it through unchecked, you can bet there would have been one hell of a fuss. And as for the man under the bridge, it was a little boy who got off his bicycle to relieve himself. The troopers found out these things. It's nice to know that they are this aware."

As darkness fell, Dr. King held a press conference. A Negro woman lifted up her three-year-old son so that he might catch a glimpse of Dr. King. She soon grew tired and had to put him down. "I'll take him," said a white man standing beside her, and he lifted the boy onto his shoulders. The boy did not glance at Dr. King; he was too busy gazing down at the white man's blond hair.

Again the night was cold and damp. At the entrance to the field, there was so much mud that boards and reeds had been scattered to provide traction for cars. Most of the marchers went to sleep in their four tents soon after supper, but at Steele's Service Station, across the highway, a crowd of Negroes from the neighborhood had gathered. Some of them were dancing to music from a jukebox, and a few of the more energetic marchers, white and black, joined them.

"This is getting to be too much like a holiday," said a veteran of one of the earlier marches. "It doesn't tell the truth of what happened."

At about ten o'clock, the last of the marchers crossed the highway back to camp. Shortly afterward, a fleet of cars drove up to the service station and a group of white boys got out. Two of the boys were from Georgia, two were from Texas, one was from Tennessee, one was from Oklahoma, one was from Monroeville, Alabama, and one was from Selma. The Reverend Arthur E. Matott, a white minister from Perth Amboy, New Jersey, who was a member of the night patrol, saw them and walked across the highway to where they were standing. "Can I help you fellows?" Mr. Matott asked.

"We're just curious," the boy from Monroeville said. "Came out to see what it was like."

"How long are you planning to stay?" said Mr. Matott.

"Until we get ready to leave," the boy said.

A Negro member of the night patrol quietly joined Mr. Matott.

"I cut classes," said the boy from Tennessee. "Sort of impulsive. You hear all these stories. I wondered why you were marching."

"Well, you might say we're marching to get to know each other and to ease a little of the hate around here," Mr. Matott said.

"You don't need to march for that," said one the boys from Texas. "You're making it worse. The hate was being lessened and lessened by itself throughout the years."

"Was it?" asked the Negro member of the guard.

"It was," the Texas boy said.

"We never had much trouble in Nashville," said the boy from Tennessee. "Where you have no conflict, it's hard to conceive . . ."

"Why don't you-all go and liberate the Indian reservations, or something?" said the boy from Monroeville. "The Negroes around here are happy."

"I don't think they are," said Mr. Matott.

"I've lived in the South all my life, and I know that they are," the boy from Georgia said.

"I'm not happy," said the Negro guard.

"Well, just wait awhile," said the boy from Monroeville.

An attractive blond girl in a black turtleneck sweater, denim pants, and boots now crossed the highway from the camp. "Do you know where I can get a ride to Jackson?" she asked the Negro guard.

"This is Casey Hayden, from S.N.C.C. She's the granddaughter of a Texas sheriff," said the minister, introducing her to the group.

A battered car drove up, and three more white boys emerged.

"I don't mean to bug you," the Negro whispered to the girl, "but did you realize we're surrounded?"

"You fellows from Selma?" Miss Hayden asked, turning to the three most recent arrivals.

"Yeah," said one, who was wearing a green zippered jacket, a black shirt, and black pants, and had a crew cut.

"What do you want?" Miss Hayden asked.

"I don't know," the boy answered.

"That's an honest answer," Miss Hayden said.

"It is," the boy said.

"What do you do?" Miss Hayden asked.

"Well, Miss, I actually *work* for a living, and I can tell you it's going to be hard on all of them when this is over," the boy said. "A lot of people in town are letting their maids go."

"Well, I don't suppose I'd want to have a maid anyway," Miss Hayden said amiably. "I guess I can do most things myself."

"That's not all, though," said another boy. "It's awfully bad down the road. Nothing's happened so far, but you can't ever tell. Selma's a peace-loving place, but that Lowndes County is something else."

"I guess some of these people feel they haven't got that much to lose," Miss Hayden said.

"I know," said the boy.

"Do you understand what they're marching about?" Miss Hayden asked.

"Yeah—fighting for freedom, something like that. That's the idea, along that line. It don't mean nothing," the boy said.

"And to make money," the third young man said. "The men are getting fifteen dollars a day for marching, and the girls are really making it big."

"Is that so?" said Miss Hayden.

"Yeah. Girl came into the Selma hospital this morning, fifteen hundred dollars in her wallet. She'd slept with forty-one."

"Forty-one what?" Miss Hayden asked.

"Niggers," the young man said.

"And what did she go to the hospital for?" Miss Hayden asked.

"Well, actually, Ma'am, she bled to death," the young man said.

"Where did you hear that?" Miss Hayden asked.

"In town," the young man said. "There's not much you can do, more than keep track of everything. It's a big mess."

"Well," Miss Hayden said, "I think it's going to get better."

"Hard to say," said one of the boys as they drifted back to their cars.

At midnight in the camp, Charles Mauldin, aged seventeen,

the head of the Dallas County Student Union and a student at Selma's Hudson High School, which is Negro, was awakened in the security tent by several guards, who ushered in a rather frightened-looking Negro boy.

"What's going on?" asked Charles.

The boy replied that he was trying to found a Negro student movement in Lowndes County.

"That's fine," said Charles.

"The principal's dead set against it," the boy said.

"Then stay underground until you've got everybody organized," Charles said. "Then if he throws one out he'll have to throw you all out."

"You with Snick or S.C.L.C., or what?" the boy asked.

"I'm not with anything," Charles said. "I'm with them all. I used to just go to dances in Selma on Saturday nights and not belong to anything. Then I met John Love, who was Snick project director down here, and I felt how he just sees himself in every Negro. Then I joined the movement."

"What about your folks?" the boy asked.

"My father's a truck driver, and at first they were against it, but now they don't push me and they don't hold me back," Charles said.

"Who've you had personal run-ins with?" the boy asked.

"I haven't had personal run-ins with anybody," Charles said. "I've been in jail three times, but never more than a few hours. They needed room to put other people in. Last week, I got let out, so I just had to march and get beaten on. In January, we had a march of little kids—we called it the Tots' March—but we were afraid they might get frightened, so we joined them, and some of us got put in jail. Nothing personal about it."

"Some of us think that for the march we might be better off staying in school," the boy said.

"Well, I think if you stay in school you're saying that you're satisfied," Charles said. "We had a hundred of our teachers marching partway with us. At first, I was against the march, but then I realized that although we're probably going to get the voting bill, we still don't have a lot of other things. It's dramatic, and it's an experience, so I came. I thought of a lot of terrible things that could happen, because we're committed to non-violence, and I'm responsible for the kids from the

Selma school. But then I thought, If they killed everyone on this march, it would be nothing compared to the number of people they've killed in the last three hundred years."

"You really believe in non-violence?" the boy asked Charles.

"I do," Charles said. "I used to think of it as just a tactic, but now I believe in it all the way. Now I'd just like to be tested."

"Weren't you tested enough when you were beaten on?" the boy asked.

"No, I mean an individual test, by myself," Charles said. "It's easy to talk about non-violence, but in a lot of cases you've got to be tested, and re-inspire yourself."

By 2 A.M., hardly anyone in the camp was awake except the late-shift night security patrol and a group of radio operators in a trailer truck, which served as a base for the walkie-talkies around the campsite and in the church back in Selma. The operators kept in constant touch with Selma, where prospective marchers were still arriving by the busload. Inside the trailer were Norman Talbot, a middle-aged Negro from Selma who had borrowed the trailer from his uncle and was serving as its driver ("I used to work in a junk yard, until they fired me for joining the movement. I've got a five-year-old daughter, but after that I made it my business to come out in a big way"); Pete Muilenberg, a nineteen-year-old white student on leave of absence from Dartmouth to work for C.O.F.O., the Congress of Federated Organizations, in Mississippi; and Mike Kenny, a twenty-nine-year-old white student who had quit graduate school at Iowa State to work for S.N.C.C.

"Snick isn't officially involved in this march," Mr. Kenny said to a marcher who visited him in the trailer early that morning. "Although individual Snick workers can take part if they like. They say Martin Luther King and Snick struck a bargain: Snick wouldn't boycott this march if S.C.L.C. would take part in a demonstration in Washington to challenge the Mississippi members of Congress. We didn't want to bring in all these outsiders, and we wanted to keep marching on that Tuesday when King turned back. Man, there are cats in Selma now from up North saying, 'Which demonstration are you going to? Which one is the best?' As though it were a college prom, or something. I tell them they ought to have sense enough to be scared. 'What do you think you're down here for? For publicity, to show how many of you there are, and to get a few heads bashed in. Nobody needs you to *lead* them. S.C.L.C. has got plenty of leaders.' People need Snick, though, for the technicians. Some of us took a two-day course in short-wave-radio repair from one of our guys, Marty Schiff, so we could set up their radios for them. Then, a lot of Snick cats have come over here from Mississippi, where the romance has worn off a bit and it's time for our experts to take over—running schools, pairing off communities with communities up North, filing legal depositions against the Mississippi congressmen and against the worst of the police. We're called agitators from out of state. Well, take away the connotations and agitation is what we do, but we're not outsiders. Nobody who crosses a state line is an outsider. It's the same with racial lines. I don't give a damn about the Negro race, but I don't give a damn about the white race, either. I'm interested in breaking the fetters of thought. What this march is going to do is help the Alabama Negro to break his patterns of thought. It's also going to change the marchers when they go back home. The students who went back from the Mississippi project became dynamos. It's easier to join the movement than to get out. You have this commitment. There will be Snick workers staying behind to keep things going in Selma. We were here, working, a year and a half before S.C.L.C. came in. Man, there's a cartoon in our Jackson office showing the Snick power structure, and it's just one big snarl. Some of us are in favor of more central organization, but most of us believe in the mystique of the local people. We're not running the C.O.F.O. project in Mississippi next summer, because of the black-white tensions in Snick. Some of the white cats feel they're being forced out, because of the racism. But I can understand it. The white invasion put the Negro cats in a predicament. Not even their movement was their own anymore. I'm staying with it, though. Every Snick meeting is a traumatic experience for all of us, but even the turmoil is too real, too important, for me to get out now. It's what you might call the dramatic-results mentality. Some of

the leaders may be evolving some pretty far-out political philosophy, but it's the workers who get things done—black-
white tensions, left-right tensions, and all."

Later that morning, Tuesday, it began to rain, and the rain
continued through most of the day. When the first drops fell,
whites at the roadside cheered (a Southern adage says that "a
nigger won't stay out in the rain"), but it soon became apparent that, even over hilly country, the procession was going
at a more spirited pace than ever. Jim Letherer, on his
crutches, appeared to be flagging. John Doar walked beside
him for a while, joking and imperceptibly slowing his pace.
Then Mr. Doar said, "Jim, come to the car a minute. I want
to show you something back down the road." Jim disappeared from the march. In twenty minutes, he was walking
again.

Back in Selma, thousands of out-of-towners had arrived
and had been quietly absorbed into the Negro ghetto. On the
outskirts of town, a sign had appeared showing a photograph
of Martin Luther King at the Highlander Folk School and
captioned "Martin Luther King at Communist School." Lying
soggily upon the sidewalks were leaflets reading "An unemployed agitator ceases to agitate. Operation Ban. Selective
hiring, firing, buying, selling." The Selma Avenue Church of
Christ, whose congregation is white, displayed a sign reading
"When You Pray, Be Not As Hypocrites Are, Standing in the
Street. Matt: 6:5," and the Brown Chapel Church displayed a
sign reading "Forward Ever, Backward Never. Visitors Welcome." Inside the church and its parsonage, things were
bustling. There were notes tacked everywhere: "If you don't
have official business here, please leave," "All those who wish
to take hot baths, contact Mrs. Lilly," "Don't sleep here anymore. This is an office," "Please, the person who is trying to
find me to return my suit coat and trenchcoat, not having left
it in my Rambler . . ."

"Everyone here in town is getting antsy," Melody Heaps, a
white girl who had come in from Chicago, said to a reporter.
"We're not allowed to march until Thursday, and there's
nothing to do. On the other hand, we're giving the Selma
Negroes a chance to take it easy. They know what they're
doing, and we don't, so they can order us around a little."

"You know what just happened?" said a white clergyman from Ontario. "Some of those white segs splashed mud all over us. It was so funny and childish we just howled."

A little later, two clergymen picked up their luggage and left the church for the home of Mrs. Georgia Roberts, where, they had been told, they were to spend the night.

"I guess I can put you up," Mrs. Roberts said when they arrived. "Last night, I put up fourteen. I worked as a cook at the Selma Country Club for thirteen years, before they fired me for joining the movement. I've been friendly to all the other guests, so I guess you'll find me friendly, too. I never thought I'd see the day when we'd dare to march against the white government in the Black Belt of Alabama."

At the Tuesday-night campsite, a farm owned by the A. G. Gastons, a Birmingham Negro family who had become millionaires in various businesses, the ground was so wet that the marchers could walk through the clay-like mud only by moving their feet as though they were skating. A Negro family living in the middle of the property had received several intimidating phone calls during the day, and as a consequence, they barred their house to marchers. They held a party in their little front garden to watch the goings on.

The marchers had by then been joined by Mrs. Ann Cheatham, an English housewife from Ealing, who had flown across the Atlantic just to take part in the last two days of marching. "It seems to me an outrage," she said. "I saw it on the telly—people being battered on the head. I came to show that the English are in sympathy. I can see there are a lot of odd bods on this march, but there were a lot in the marches on Aldermaston and Washington. This appalling business of barring white facilities to Negro children! People say it's not my business, but I would deny that. It's everybody's business."

In the early evening, a clergyman became violently ill, and doctors blamed the marchers' water supply. The marchers had all along complained that the water tasted of kerosene, and, upon investigation, it turned out the water was in fact polluted, having come from a truck that was ordinarily used for draining septic tanks. (Fortunately, no other marchers seemed to suffer from the contamination.) Later, the singer Odetta appeared at the campsite, and found all the marchers, including another singer, Pete Seeger, fast asleep.

Wednesday, the fourth and last full day of marching, was sunny again, and the marchers set out in good spirits. In the morning, a minister who had rashly dropped out at a gas station to make a telephone call was punched by the owner, and a free-lance newspaper photographer was struck on the ear by a passerby. (Although he required three stitches, he was heartened by the fact that a Montgomery policeman had come, with a flying tackle, to his rescue.) There seemed, however, to be fewer segregationists by the side of the road than usual—perhaps because the Montgomery *Advertiser* had been running a two-page advertisement, prepared by the City Commissioner's Committee on Community Affairs, imploring citizens to be moderate and ignore the march. The coverage of the march in the Southern press had consistently amused the marchers. "Civil Righters Led by Communists" had been the headline in the Birmingham weekly *Independent*; the Selma *Times-Journal*, whose coverage of the march was relatively accurate, had editorialized about President Johnson, under the heading "A Modern Mussolini Speaks, 'We Shall Overcome,'" "No man in any generation . . . has ever held so much power in the palm of his hand, and that includes Caesar, Alexander, Genghis Khan, Napoleon, and Franklin D. Roosevelt;" and the Wednesday *Advertiser's* sole front-page item concerning the march was a one-column, twenty-one-line account, lower right, of the Alabama legislature's resolution condemning the demonstrators for being "sexually promiscuous." ("It is well known that the white Southern segregationist is obsessed with fornication," said John Lewis, chairman of S.N.C.C. "And that is why there are so many shades of Negro.") At 9 A.M., Ray Robin announced over radio station WHHY, in Montgomery, that "there is now evidence that women are returning to their homes from the march as expectant unwed mothers." Several marchers commented, ironically, on the advanced state of medical science in Alabama.

By noon, most of the marchers were sunburned or just plain weather-burned. Two Negroes scrawled the word "Vote" in sunburn cream on their foreheads and were photographed planting an American flag, Iwo Jima fashion, by the side of the road. Flags of all sorts, including state flags and church flags, had materialized in the hands of marchers. One of the few segregationists watching the procession stopped his jeering for a moment when he saw the American flag, and raised his hand in a salute. The singing had abated somewhat, and the marchers had become conversational.

"This area's a study in social psychopathology," said Henry Schwarzschild, executive secretary of L.C.D.C. (the Lawyers Constitutional Defense Committee). "In a way, they're asking for a show of force like this, to make them face reality."

"And there's the ignorance," said another civil-rights lawyer. "A relatively friendly sheriff in Sunflower County, Mississippi, warned me, confidentially, that my client was a 'blue-gum nigger.' 'Their mouths are filled with poison,' he said. 'Don't let him bite you.'"

"And what did you say?" asked a college student marching beside him.

"What *could* I say?" the lawyer replied. "I said I'd try to be careful."

"The way I see this march," said a young man from S.N.C.C., "is as a march from the religious to the secular—from the chapel to the statehouse. For too long now, the Southern Negro's only refuge has been the church. That's why he prefers these S.C.L.C. ministers to the Snick cats. But we're going to change all that."

"I'm worried, though, about the Maoists," said the student.

"What do you mean by that, exactly?" asked another marcher.

"A Maoist. You know. From the Mau Mau."

In the early afternoon, Dr. King and his wife, who had dropped out for a day in order for him to go to Cleveland to receive an award, rejoined the procession. The singing began again. Marching behind Dr. King was his friend the Reverend Morris H. Tynes, of Chicago, who teased Dr. King continuously. "Moses, can you let your people rest for a minute?" Mr. Tynes said. "Can you just let the homiletic smoke from your cigarette drift out of your mouth and engulf the multitude and let them rest?" Dr. King smiled. Some of the other marchers, who had tended to speak of Dr. King half in joking and half in reverent tones (most of them referred to him conversationally as "De Lawd") laughed out loud.

A Volkswagen bus full of marchers from Chicago ran out of gas just short of the procession. "Now, we all believe in nonviolence," one of the passengers said to the driver, "but if you don't get this thing moving pretty soon . . ."

"Are you members of some sort of group?" asked a reporter, looking inside the bus.

"No," said the driver. "We're just individuals."

At last, on the outskirts of Montgomery, the marchers reached their fourth campsite—the Catholic City of St. Jude, consisting of a church, a hospital, and a school built in a style that might be called Contemporary Romanesque. The four tents were pitched by the time they arrived, and they marched onto the grounds singing "We *Have* Overcome." They also added two new verses to the song—"All the way from Selma" and "Our feet are soaked." Inside the gates of St. Jude's, they were greeted by a crowd of Montgomery Negroes singing the national anthem.

"*What* do you *want?*" the marchers chanted.

This time, the response from the onlookers was immediate and loud: "*Freedom!*"

"*When* do you *want* it?"

"*Now!*"

"How *much* of it?"

"*All* of it!"

On its fourth night, the march began to look first like a football rally, then like a carnival and a hootenanny, and finally like something dangerously close to a hysterical mob. Perhaps because of a new feeling of confidence, the security check at the main gate had been practically abandoned. Thousands of marchers poured in from Selma and Montgomery, some of them carrying luggage, and no one had time to examine its contents. The campsite was cold and almost completely dark, and a bomb or a rifle shot would have left everyone helpless. Word got out that the doctors on the march had treated several cases of strep throat, two of pneumonia, one of advanced pulmonary tuberculosis, and one of epilepsy, and because of the number and variety of sick and handicapped who had made the march a macabre new joke began to go the rounds: "What has five hundred and ninety-nine legs, five hundred and ninety-eight eyes, an indeterminate number of germs, and walks singing? The march from Selma."

An entertainment had been scheduled for nine o'clock that night, but it was several hours late getting started, and in the meantime the crowd of thousands churned about in the mud and chanted. A number of people climbed into trees near the platform where the entertainment was to take place. On the outskirts of St. Jude's, in a section normally set aside as a playground, a few children spun the hand-powered carrousel, or climbed over the jungle gym in the dark. In the wires of the telephone poles around the field, the skeletons of old kites were just visible in the dim lights from the windows of St. Jude's Hospital.

A minister, who had been seeking for several hours to clear the platform, wept with chagrin. "Betcha old Sheriff Clark and his troopers could clear it!" someone shouted. In the darkness, there were repeated cries for doctors, and a soldier stood on top of the radio trailer and beamed a flashlight into the crowd, trying to find the sources of the cries. Thousands crowded around the platform, and several of them were pressed against it and fell. Several others, mostly members of the special group of three hundred marchers, fainted from exhaustion. A number of entertainers, each of whom had been given a dime to use for a phone call in case of an emergency, and all of whom had been instructed to stand in groups of not fewer than six, appeared on the platform. Among them were Shelley Winters, Sammy Davis, Jr., Tony Perkins, Tony Bennett, and Nina Simone. A number of girls in the crowd collapsed and, because there was no other lighted space, had to be carried onstage, where Miss Winters did her best to minister to them. Before long, twenty people, none of them seriously ill or seriously injured, were carried off to the hospital on stretchers. A large group started an agitated march within the campsite.

"I'm tired," said a white college student. "If only I could walk someplace and get a cab!"

"Man, that's not cool," said a Negro. "There are a lot of hostile people outside that gate."

"Inside it, too, for all I know," said the student. "See any white sheets?"

Finally, the entertainment got under way, and the situation improved. Tony Perkins and a few others spoke with well-considered brevity. The crowd clapped along with the singers as they sang folk songs and songs of the movement, and it laughed at the comedians, including Dick Gregory, Nipsey Russell, Mike Nichols, and Elaine May. ("I can't afford to call up the National Guard," said Mike Nichols, impersonating Governor Wallace. "Why not?" said Elaine May, impersonating a telegraph operator. "It only costs a dime.")

At 2 A.M., the entertainment and speeches were over, and the performers left for a Montgomery hotel, which was surrounded for the remainder of the night by shouting segregationists. Most of the crowd drifted off the field and headed for Montgomery, and the tents were left at last to the marchers. Suddenly security tightened up. At one point, the Reverend Andrew Young himself was asked for his credentials. The hours before dawn passed without incident.

On Thursday morning, the march expanded, pulled itself together, and turned at once serious and gay. It finally seemed that the whole nation was marching to Montgomery. Signs from every conceivable place and representing every conceivable religious denomination, philosophical viewpoint, labor union, and walk of life assembled at St. Jude's and lined up in orderly fashion. A Magic Marker pen passed from hand to hand, and new signs went up: "The Peace Corps Knows Integration Works," "So Does Canada," "American Indians" (carried by Fran Poafpybitty, a Comanche from Indiahoma, Oklahoma), "Freedom" in Greek letters (carried by a Negro girl), "Out of Vietnam into Selma" in Korean (carried by a white girl), "The Awe and Wonder of Human Dignity We Want to Maintain" (on a sandwich board worn by a succession of people), and, on two sticks tied together, with a blue silk scarf above it, a sign reading simply "Boston." A young white man in a gray flannel suit hurried back and forth among the platoons of marchers; on his attaché case was written "D. J. Bittner, Night Security."

Near the tents, Ivanhoe Donaldson and Frank Surocco (the

first a Negro project director for S.N.C.C. in Atlanta, the second a white boy, also from S.N.C.C.) were distributing orange plastic jackets to the original three hundred marchers. The jackets, of the sort worn by construction workers, had been bought for eighty-nine cents apiece in Atlanta, and jackets just like them had been worn throughout the march by the marshals, but for the marchers the orange jacket had become a singular status symbol. There was some dispute about who was entitled to wear one. There was also a dispute about the order of march. Some thought that the entertainers should go first, some that the leaders should. Roy Wilkins, of the N.A.A.C.P., demurred on behalf of the leaders. Odetta said, "Man, don't let the morale crumble. The original three hundred deserve to be first." The Reverend Andrew Young was served with a summons in an action by the City of Selma and the Selma Bus Lines protesting the operation of buses in competition with the Selma company. Finally, after another session of virtually inaudible speeches, the parade was ready to go. "Make way for the originals!" the marshals shouted, forming a cordon to hold back the other marchers and the press. Behind the three hundred came Martin Luther King, Ralph Bunche, A. Philip Randolph, the Reverend Ralph Abernathy, the Reverend Fred L. Shuttlesworth, Charles G. Gomillion, the Reverend F. D. Reese, and other civil-rights leaders; behind them came the grandfather of Jimmie Lee Jackson, the Negro boy who had been shot in nearby Perry County, and the Reverend Orloff Miller, a friend of the Reverend James Reeb's, who had been beaten with Reeb on the night of Reeb's murder; and behind them came a crowd of what turned out to be more than thirty thousand people. "We're not just down here for show," said Mr. Miller. "A lot of our people are staying here to help. But the show itself is important. When civil rights drops out of the headlines, the country forgets."

Stationed, like an advance man, hundreds of yards out in front of the procession as it made its way through the Negro section of Montgomery and, ultimately, past a hundred and four intersections was Charles Mauldin, dressed in his Hudson High sweatshirt and blue jeans and an orange jacket, and waving a little American flag and a megaphone. One pocket of his denims was split, and the fatigue in his gentle, intelligent face made him seem considerably younger than his seventeen years. "Come and march with us!" he shouted to Negro bystanders. "You can't make your witness standing on the corner. Come and march with us. We're going downtown. There's nothing to be afraid of. Come and march with us!"

"Tell 'em, baby," said Frank Surocco, who was a few yards back of Charles.

"Is everything safe up ahead?" asked the voice of Ivanhoe Donaldson through a walkie-talkie.

"We watching 'em, baby," said Surocco.

"Come and march with us!" said Charles Mauldin, to black and white bystanders alike.

In midtown Montgomery, at the Jefferson Davis Hotel, colored maids were looking out of the windows and the white clientele was standing on the hotel marquee. Farther along, at the Whitley Hotel, colored porters were looking out of windows on one side of the building and white customers were looking out of windows on the other. Troopers watched from the roof of the Brown Printing Company. The windows of the Montgomery Citizens Council were empty. Outside the Citizens Council building, a man stood waving a Confederate flag.

"What's your name?" a reporter asked.

"None of your goddam business," said the man.

At the intersection of Montgomery Street and Dexter Avenue (the avenue leading to the capitol), Charles Mauldin turned and looked around. "They're still coming out of St. Jude's," a reporter told him. And when the vanguard of the march reached the capitol steps, they were *still* coming out of St. Jude's. "You're only likely to see three great parades in a lifetime," said John Doar to a student who walked beside him, "and this is one of them." A brown dog had joined the crowd for the march up Dexter Avenue. On the sidewalk in front of the capitol, reporters stood on the press tables to look back. Charles and the rest of the orange-jacketed three hundred stood below. Behind them, the procession was gradually drawing together and to a halt. Ahead, a few green-clad, helmeted officers of the Alabama Game and Fish Service and some state officials blocked the capitol steps, at the top of which, covering the bronze that marks the spot where Jefferson Davis was inaugurated President of the Confederacy, was a plywood shield constructed at the order of Governor Wallace—"to keep that s.o.b. King from desecrating the Cradle of the Confederacy," according to a spokesman for the Governor. Martin Luther King had managed to draw a larger crowd than the leader of the Confederacy a hundred years before.

Onto a raised platform—erected by the marchers for the occasion—in a plaza between the crowd and the steps climbed a group of entertainers that included, at one point or another, Joan Baez; the Chad Mitchell Trio; Peter, Paul, and Mary; and Harry Belafonte. As Alabamians peered from the statehouse windows, Negro and white performers put their arms around each other's shoulders and began to sing. Although the songs were familiar and the front rank of the three hundred mouthed a few of the words, none of the crowd really sang along. Everybody simply cheered and applauded at the end of each number. Then Len Chandler, a young Negro folk singer who had marched most of the way, appeared on the platform. He was dressed peculiarly, as he had been on the road—in a yellow helmet, a flaglike blue cape with white stars on it, and denims—and the crowd at once joined him in singing:

"You've got to move when the spirit say move,
    Move when the spirit say move.
    When the spirit say move, you've got to move, oh, Lord,
    You got to move when the spirit say move."

In the subsequent verses, Mr. Chandler changed "move" to "walk," "march," "vote," "picket," "cool it," and "love," and the crowd kept singing. Joan Baez, wearing a purple velvet dress and a large bronze crucifix, even broke into a rather reverent Frug.

After an invocation by a rabbi and speeches by the Reverend Andrew Young and the Reverend Ralph Abernathy, the crowd turned away from the Confederate and Alabama state flags flying from the capitol, faced its own American flags, and sang the national anthem. At its close, the Reverend Theodore Gill, president of the San Francisco Theological Seminary, looked before and behind him and said a simple prayer: "Forgive us our trespasses." One marcher applauded, and was immediately hushed. Then there was the succession of speeches, most of them eloquent, some of them pacific ("Friends of freedom," said Whitney Young, of the Urban League), others militant ("Fellow Freedom Fighters," said John Lewis, of S.N.C.C.), and nearly all of them filled with taunts of Governor Wallace as the list of grievances, intimidations, and brutalities committed by the state piled up.

"This march has become a rescue operation," Charles Mauldin said quietly to a friend as the speeches continued. "Most of those Negroes along the way have joined us, and although this Wallace-baiting sounds like a little boy whose big brother has come home and who is standing outside a bully's window just to jeer, these Negroes are never going to be quite so afraid of the bully again. When the bill goes through, they're going to vote, and the white men down here are going to think twice before they try to stop them. Big brothers have come down from the North and everywhere, and they've shown that they're ready and willing to come down again. I don't think they're going to have to."

"It's good that even a few of the civil-rights *talkers* have joined us," said another marcher. "When those people feel they have to climb on the bandwagon, you know you're on the way to victory."

As one speaker followed another, as Ralph Bunche, who had marched for two full days, and A. Philip Randolph spoke, the civil-rights leaders saluted one another and gave signs of patching up their differences. (Mr. Abernathy, second-in-command of S.C.L.C., slipped once and said, "Now here's James Peck, for James Farmer, to tell us whether CORE is with us." Peck ignored the implications of the "whether" and spoke as eloquently as the rest.) Throughout, the crowd applauded politely but gave no sign of real enthusiasm. S.C.L.C. and S.N.C.C. leaders seemed to be equally popular, but the N.A.A.C.P. and the Urban League, more active in other states than in Alabama, seemed to require a little help from Mr. Abernathy ("Now let's give a big hand to . . .") to get their applause. Some of the marchers crawled forward under the press tables and went to sleep. A Japanese reporter, who had been taking notes in his own language, seized one of the marchers as he crawled under a table. "What do you think of all this?" the reporter asked. "I think it's good," the marcher said. Some fell asleep in their places on Dexter Avenue. (Perhaps remembering the mob scenes of the night before, the crowd left its members ample breathing space in front of the capitol.) A scuffle broke out between marchers and white bystanders in front of Klein's Jewelry Store, but no one was hurt seriously. It rained a little, and Charles Mauldin said, "Wallace is seeding the clouds."

Albert Turner, of Marion, where Jimmie Lee Jackson was murdered, said from the platform, "I look worse than anybody else on this stage. That's because I marched fifty miles." Then he read the Negro voting statistics from Perry County. When he said, "We are not satisfied," the crowd gave him a rousing cheer. He looked down at his orange jacket and smiled. Mrs. Amelia Boynton spoke; during the previous demonstrations, she had been kicked and beaten, and jailed, for what some members of the press have come to call "resisting assault." She read the petition, mentioning the "psychotic climate" of the State of Alabama, that a delegation of marchers was seeking to present to Governor Wallace, and she was roundly applauded. Near the end of the ceremony, Rosa Parks, the "Mother of the Movement," who had set off Dr. King's first demonstration when she was jailed for refusing to yield her seat to a white man on a bus in Montgomery, received the most enthusiastic cheers of all. "Tell it! Tell! Tell!" some of the marchers shouted. "Speak! Speak!" Finally, after an extravagant introduction by Mr. Abernathy, who referred to Dr. King as "conceived by God" ("This personality cult is getting out of hand," said a college student, and, to judge by the apathetic reception of Mr. Abernathy's words, the crowd agreed), Dr. King himself spoke. There were some enthusiastic yells of "Speak! Speak!" and "Yessir! Yessir!" from the older members of the audience when Dr. King's speech began, but at first the younger members were subdued. Gradually, the whole crowd began to be stirred. By the time he reached his refrains—"Let us march on the ballot boxes. . . . We're on the move now. . . . How long? Not long"—and the final, ringing "Glory, glory, hallelujah!," the crowd was with him all the way.

The director of the march, Hosea Williams, of S.C.L.C., said some concluding words, remarking that there should be no lingering in Montgomery that night and exhorting the crowd to leave quietly and with dignity. There was a last rendition of "We Shall Overcome." Within ten minutes, Dexter Avenue was cleared of all but the press and the troopers.

A few hours later, the delegation and its petition were turned away by Governor Wallace. At the airport, where there had been some difficulty during the preceding days (an uncanny number of suitcases belonging to marchers were mislaid by the airlines), new flights had been scheduled to get the marchers out of Montgomery. Still, many marchers had to wait at the airport all night long. They rested on the floor, and on the lawn outside, and as often as the police cleared them away they reappeared and fell asleep again. Word came that Mrs. Viola Liuzzo had been shot. Some of the marchers went back to Selma at once. Others boarded planes for home. At the Montgomery airport exit was a permanent official sign reading "Glad You Could Come. Hurry Back."

The New Yorker, April 10, 1965

McComb, Mississippi

by John Beecher

I. THE COLONEL'S ISSUE

Sister Celestine McComb Ashley is the great-granddaughter of Colonel H. S. McComb, railroad president and founder of the Mississippi town which bears his name. Now in her sixties, Sister Celestine has never voted in an election, nor had her picture in *The Enterprise-Journal*, nor received any other honor due her lineage. This is because her great-grandmother was one of the illustrious Colonel's black concubines.

At the Ark of Safety Missionary Baptist Church in Algiers, a Negro suburb of McComb, where her husband, the Reverend Thomas Ashley, is pastor, Sister Celestine conducts the Sunday School and leads a gospel-singing group comprised of herself, her daughter, Mrs. Lanell Barnes, and three granddaughters, Almadean, Sue Ann, and Tempie. Though only four years old, huge-eyed and with red bows on her pigtails, Tempie leads such spirituals as *Show Some Sign* and *God Don't Want No Coward Soldiers*. Afterwards Sister Celestine's tremendous solo, *I Got Jesus and That's Enough*, gets everybody to clapping and stomping in the squat little edifice crouched under a red clay hill . . .

> *"Oh, there's so many times I didn't have a dime.*
> *Didn't tell nobody but the Lawd."*

Her daughter, Lanell, plays a driving piano accompaniment. Sister Celestine can preach as powerfully as she can sing.

"Since you people know right so well and have came so far to McComb City and let Mayor Burt and Sheriff Warren and Chief Guy know that God doesn't have no respect of persons, that He said from one blood all nations came forth and if He love the white folks He love us too and He don't care no more 'bout one color than He do the other, and since God is fightin' our battles we ain't got nothin' to do but just go and do what we are asked to do through you all and the COFO, and God will be our leanin' post. We might be buffed about and He was. He said if they done that to the green tree you know they goan' do that to us.

"The lesson is this mawnin' 'On the Behalf of a Slave.' We been a slave, I been a slave ever since I been here, Brother and Sister Beecher, but Jesus has a time fixed when we won't have to slave for the other race of people. Jesus said for both of us to work together in unity and in integration. We are already integrated in the kitchen. We can go in there and cook the best meals . . ."

"Amen!" a voice rings out.

". . . make up that bed . . ."

"Amen!"

". . . and we raise the chil'ren . . ."

"Amen!"

"I raised some of the lovelies' white chil'ren they was in McComb City and they loved me better than they did their mother for when she would come in he wouldn't go to her. He still put his little arms aroun' my neck and clings to me and I just wonder today why we can't go in the school house or sit down on the pews. If we are integrated in the kitchen and with the chil'ren what about in the churches and the schools? When it's to come in there and sit down and take a part they think it's a disgrace. But Jesus don't have in His mind like that. God said there's nothin' too hard for Him and He never fails. All we got to do is know *we* are right and go ahead on and He'll fight our battles."

On the hill above the Ark of Safety Church is the eight-room house, largest in Algiers, where Thomas and Celestine Ashley raised their nine children. It is empty now except for themselves, gaunt, sagging, needing paint. A half block away lives the one child still in McComb, Lanell, with her brood including the little girl singers. The other eight Ashley children are all up North, in Chicago and Milwaukee. The Ashleys can't even count their grandchildren up there, and now great-grandchildren are beginning to arrive. Colonel McComb has been blessed with abundant issue.

2. THE PRICE OF COTTON

When the COFO Freedom House was bombed last July, *The Enterprise-Journal* went to the trouble of ferreting out the owner and reported the house to be the property of a certain Willie Mae Cotton, Negro, who had leased it to the outside agitators. Elwin Burt, brother of McComb's Mayor Gordon Burt, and proprietor of the Burt Plumbing Company, called John T. Cotton, one of his Negro employees, into the office. Cotton had started to work for Burt as a plumber's helper when he was 19. Now 41, Cotton was still classed as a plumber's helper although he actually performed the work of a plumber. (No Negro is eligible to become a licensed plumber in the State of Mississippi, although there is nothing to prevent a white man from working him as one, and paying him a small fraction of a plumber's wages.) Instead of $4 an hour Cotton got 67¢. He was classified as a "salaried" employee, received a week's paid vacation each year, and drew $40 every Saturday evening for a work-week of six ten-hour days.

"This Willie Mae Cotton, who rented her house to those COFO troublemakers, and got it blown up like she deserved, she your wife or your sister?" Burt asked Cotton.

"She ain't neither one, Mr. Elwin," Cotton answered.

"Don't give me that crap, John. She must be some kind of kin to you."

"Nawsuh, Mr. Elwin, she no kin of mine."

"Well, you better start on your vacation tomorrow," Burt said.

When John T. Cotton returned from his week's vacation, Burt gave him his time. "Since they done passed that Civil Rights Act you niggers are gittin' out of hand. We don't have anything left for you to do here, John. Maybe President Johnson and them will take care of you now."

After 22 years of service, Cotton was fired without cause. "He ruint the best years of his life crawling under a devilish house," his wife says bitterly. Cotton's former employer was one of the 650 "good white people" who some months later, after the wave of terror-bombings and church-burnings had spent itself, put their names to a statement calling for "law and order" and racial reconciliation. This statement got a lot of attention around the country. Some commentators went so far as to assert that it heralded the dawn of a new era in Mississippi. But John T. Cotton knew different.

3. UPPITY

"A hundred miles from Jackson to McComb,
Further'n that to my good girl's home,
Goan' move to Kansas City . . ."

So goes an old blues in Babe Stovall's repertory. Before he left for New Orleans and became a noted French Quarter troubadour, this guitar-picking singer of Negro country blues share-cropped near Tylertown just east of McComb. Babe's "Goan' move to Kansas City" reflects an exodus. There were fewer people in this part of Mississippi in 1960 than there were in 1910. And still the Negroes "leave out" for the promised land. If anybody should ask you, "What are Mississippi's largest cities?" the right answer is "Chicago, Los Angeles, New Orleans, and Jackson."

Fred Bates' house was the first in McComb to be bombed in the terrible summer of 1964. He was reputed to be "uppity." "Downtown," the succinct Negro word for the white power structure of McComb, had had it in for Fred Bates ever since 1961. In that year Brenda Travis, aged 16, sat in at the segregated Greyhound bus station. The bus station was still segregated when I visited it three years later. Accommodations were not merely separate but far from equal—the white side airy, spacious and modern in furnishings, the Negro side cramped, dingy, with a few beat-up chairs and lunch counter stools. For her contumacy in sitting on the white side, Brenda was sentenced to a year in the Oakland Training School, Mississippi state reformatory for girls.

Bates is an important figure in Burglundtown, the main Negro section of McComb. He owns a nice home, the Standard Oil station for colored and an adjoining café, all on Summit, the Negro main stem. In 1961 Bates also owned and operated the school bus of the all-black Burglund High School, where Brenda had been a student before her commitment. There was a lot of sympathy for Brenda at Burglund High, even among those who hadn't the courage to join her protests. Brenda's entire junior class asked Bates to drive them in the school bus to visit her at Oakland on a weekend, a 450-mile round-trip.

Soon after his return from Oakland, Bates was denied a renewal of his annual bus license. Officials told him it was because he had driven Brenda's classmates to Oakland in the bus. He parked it in front of his service station and hung a big sign on the side, "SCHOOL BUS FOR SALE. THIS IS A FREE COUNTRY BUT THEY WON'T SELL ME A LICENSE."

This "getting smart" made Bates the Number One target when "Downtown" decided the Negro community needed a liberal dose of dynamite to bring it in line and halt the agitation over civil rights. After the bombing of his house, which happened not to kill any of the family, Bates sent his wife and children to Mississippi's second largest city—Los Angeles.

Smog, Proposition 14, Cardinal McIntyre, freeway traffic jams and other Los Angeles blemishes don't bother the Bates family one bit. "L.A. is a paradise," Fred says firmly. And you can't argue him out of that opinion. In fact, he plans to join them in California. His gas station, his café, and his home on Summit are all up for sale. If you'd like to go into business in McComb, Fred Bates will give you a bargain.

4. NAMES, DATES AND PLACES

Wilbert Lewis was grinding valves on a Rambler when the proprietor's son-in-law, Al Sibley, came in the shop of the Mathews Motor Company on Pearl River Avenue and said a man out front had a friend with car trouble. Lewis grabbed a pair of pliers and a screwdriver and got in the car with a strange white man at the wheel.

Two or three miles out of town, on a side road, they came to a dirty 1950 Plymouth in the middle of a wooded area. A man had his head under the raised hood so Lewis couldn't see his face. When Lewis went over, the man straightened up and put a pistol to his head. He was wearing a black hood. Four others in black hoods came out of the woods.

They made Lewis lie down on the floor in the back of the Plymouth and drove about half an hour, until they were in the middle of Holmesville swamp along the Bogue Chitto. They dragged Lewis out of the car and set him down by a tree in the swamp. All they wanted to do was ask him some questions, they said. First they laid out on the ground three objects for his inspection, a grass rope ending in a hangman's noose, a blackjack, and a cat o' nine tails whip. Then they stood him up and tied him to the tree. To put him in the proper mood for answering questions, they dropped his pants and shorts. As the cat o' nine tails wrapped its thongs around him, Lewis screamed.

"Nigger, you holler one more time and we gon'ta leave your brains scattered beside this tree."

Lewis dug his teeth into his arm and kept silent while the whistling thongs scored his flesh again and again. Each of the five hooded men gave him five licks. When they finished, Lewis felt the blood trickling down his legs.

"What we want is names, dates, and places," said the leader of the hooded men. "You're that big nigger preacher Dickey's son-in-law. You know ever'thing that's goin' on, and we aim to whup your black ass till you give us a complete report on all this freedom business. Start talkin'."

They had caught the wrong man. True enough, Wilbert Lewis was married to the Reverend Sylvester Dickey's daughter, but Dickey was no civil rights proponent. In fact, Negroes said Dickey was an Uncle Tom who ran downtown and spilled his guts to Mr. Charley every time he learned some little thing about the movement. This was his way of soliciting white contributions for the new church he was building. Consequently, people took care to keep Dickey as much in the dark as they could.

"Honest to God, white folks," Lewis told the hooded men, "I don't know nothin' about no civil rights business. I stays away from all that agitation. Rev. Dickey he circ'latin' a petition aroun' gittin' cullud peoples to sign that they wants them COFO workers to clear out of town and leave us be."

A sawed-off shotgun dug into Lewis' side.

"Don't say 'colored folks.' You say 'niggers' when you talkin' to us. And don't hand us that stuff about how you don't know nothin'. Give us names, dates, and places 'lessen you want us to beat your God damn black butt plumb off you and then string you up to this cypress tree for buzzard meat."

The hooded men took turns flogging Lewis until they were

worn out. At last they cut him loose and smashed him about the head with the blackjack.

"Nigger, see can you run."

Lewis scrambled away from them through the brush and fell, half-conscious, with his wrists in a creek that ran through the swamp. The cold water revived him some and he staggered out to the road. He started toward McComb when an old pickup came by with a Negro driving. The Negro stopped and recognized the bloody, bedraggled figure as Lewis.

"Son, you headed in the wrong direction," the driver said gently and motioned him in. Lewis got in and collapsed. Next day the FBI took pictures of Lewis' lacerated back and buttocks. That was eight months ago. He kept going back to the office for a while to see if the FBI had found out anything but they always told him no, they were still investigating.

5. GIVE ME LIBERTY

Liberty, the county seat of Amite County, is just west of McComb. Liberty is where Herbert Lee, a 52-year-old Negro landowner, was murdered in 1961 for seeking to register to vote in the county where he had lived all his life. He had carried a load of cotton to the gin and was sitting at the wheel of the truck when Mr. E. H. Hurst, a big white farmer and member of the Mississippi State Legislature at that time, walked up, put a pistol to his head, and shot him dead. Although a great many people witnessed the deed, including a number of Negroes, nobody could be found to testify against Mr. Hurst. The county jury ruled the killing to be "justifiable homicide."

Later, after the FBI opened up an office for Southwest Mississippi, one of the witnesses to Lee's murder, a Liberty Negro named Lewis Allen, found the courage to tell the FBI what he knew. Although information given the FBI is supposedly secret, this is not the case in Southwest Mississippi. It soon leaked back to Liberty that Allen had filed an affidavit with the FBI accusing Representative Hurst of the murder. One morning shortly thereafter Allen was found lying in his driveway. His head had been blown off by a sawed-off shotgun. According to the sheriff and the FBI, Allen met his death at the hands of "parties unknown."

Alma Jackson owns a six-room house in Liberty. It has a bathroom and sinks in the kitchen. Although formerly married, Mrs. Jackson is now, as she puts it, "a single lady with no husban' to he'p support eight head of chil'ren." Altogether she brought ten "head" into the world, but two grown sons have left to raise families of their own. Mrs. Jackson and the eight remaining children, aged 5 to 18, raised cotton and corn on a little farm she inherited from her grandfather out a few miles from Liberty. They also picked cotton up in the Delta every year. They saved enough this way to finish paying out the house and make it comfortable. Nobody had to sleep on a cornshuck mattress or a pallet on the floor.

To make ends meet, Mrs. Jackson also worked in a little store run by an old white man in the colored section of town. He was a foreigner—a Yankee—and suffered from cataracts on both eyes. He had two little white boys who had been working for him and who had taken advantage of his failing eyesight to rob him. He fired them to make room for Mrs. Jackson, and the boys' father was very angry at all this.

A little later a white woman came around to apply for Mrs. Jackson's job, but the old Yankee refused to get rid of Mrs. Jackson. Word began to travel around Liberty that there was something besides business between the old Yankee and Mrs. Jackson. Though a mother of ten and grandmother of six already, she is only 39. Her first child was born when she was 13. She is still attractive, with deep soft eyes, expressive face, and youthful body. The word was spread in Liberty that Mrs. Jackson called the old white man her "husband."

Mrs. Jackson got threatening and obscene phone calls. One night she was wakened by a garish light; it was a cross burning on her lawn. Frightened, she quit her job in the old Yankee's store, and went to work at the box factory over in Fernwood. She stayed with a grown son in nearby McComb, coming home to Liberty, on weekends to visit her children.

One Saturday night when Mrs. Jackson was home for the weekend two cars pulled into her yard. A bunch of white men piled out of them.

"Alma, come on out here. We want to talk with you."

They stormed up on the porch and snatched the screen door loose from the hook. Carrying shotguns, rifles, pistols, and nightsticks, they dragged her out while her children screamed. They put a black mask over her face and made her lie on the floor of one of the cars. They drove off cursing and reviling her and threatened to get her sister and a neighbor named Geneva. (None of the three women had ever been involved in civil rights activity.)

Way out in the woods the cars stopped. The men took Mrs. Jackson and stripped off the house-coat she had round her shoulders. Underneath she had on a blouse, pedal pushers and bedroom slippers. They threw her down on the ground and a man put his foot on her head. Then they started to flog her with a heavy strap. One of the men said, "I want to git at the nekkid meat." He took a switchblade knife and ripped out the seat of her pedal pushers. The knife cut through into her flesh. (She showed me the pedal pushers that had a big jagged flap cut out of the back. They were crusted with blood.)

After the flogging, the men drove away and Mrs. Jackson staggered to a Negro house down the road. A man drove her home. That very night she packed up a few things, crowded all eight of her children into her car, and left Liberty for her son's place in McComb. "I haven't even been back there to look around and see what was going wrong with my house," she says. Because the house was vacant, the insurance company canceled the coverage. Should it burn—or be burned—the fruit of the years Mrs. Jackson and her children slaved in Delta cotton fields will go up in smoke.

The day after Mrs. Jackson left, Geneva, the neighbor whom the men had threatened, left also. Her home is likewise empty and unprotected. A couple of days after Mrs. Jackson's departure, her sister received a telephone call. "You know what happened to Alma. Same thing going to happen to you if you be there when daylight come." She packed a suitcase and got out, leaving her home and everything she had in the world.

Mrs. Jackson tells us of other Negroes forced to leave Liberty in 1964. "Lucius Woodward, the best mechanic in town, was fired from where he'd worked thirty years to make room for a white man. He had to come to McComb to find him a job. Cullud fellow had the onlies' shoe shop in Liberty, they tole him to git out. He was a preacher too. Went to Louziana. Another cullud fellow worked in the pressin' shop. Made him leave out so a white man could git his job. He'd worked there twelve years. Seems like they's running out ev'y cullud person what's got a job in Liberty 'lessen it's fiel' hand work or cookin' for some big white family."

The FBI learned of Alma Jackson's flogging the night it occurred last May when her oldest son reported it. She herself has also sworn out an affidavit. "We knowed who a couple of the white mens was. I guess the FBI jus' don't take an interest in how they does us Negroes here in Mississippi."

Alma Jackson now lives in a dilapidated house in McComb right behind Society Hill Baptist Church. The night the church was bombed and totally destroyed, her home escaped with a few shattered windows. But she and her family were terrified. They couldn't help thinking the dynamite had been intended for them. "I'm livin' like somebody throwed away here in McComb," she says.

6. MAMA QUIN

When Alyene Quin started serving the COFO freedom workers in her South of the Border café, the white owner of the building came and told her, "You've really got things in a mess."

Mama Quin, as the freedom workers call her affectionately, looked around. The café was about as usual. "I don't see any mess," she told the owner.

"I mean about those people," he said. "You're serving white and colored in here. You can't do such as that. When you're in Rome you got to do like the Romans."

"I'm not in Rome, I'm in McComb," Mama Quin said.

After that Mama Quin's home was bombed. Her two youngest, Jackie and Anthony, were almost killed. The roof collapsed around their bed like a tent. A lot of young Negroes congregated at the scene, and since it was the sixteenth bombing to occur in a summer series which also included ten churches burned to the ground, they were incensed. When the police arrived some rocks flew. Chief Guy claimed he got hit on the ankle. One of the auxiliary policemen there later confessed that he had bombed the house. He had rushed home, changed into his uniform, and returned in the guise of a guardian of law and order. (The auxiliary was the same one who at the scene of a previous bombing had threatened to blow Roy Lee's brains out. Roy, who is about six feet four and weighs 265 pounds, was down on his knees praying for strength to keep from attacking the white people. This was enough to provoke any policeman.)

Shortly thereafter, Mama Quin was evicted from her café, the white owner figuring it was next on the list to be bombed. She took over Fred Bates' café further up the street and went on serving the freedom workers, white and black, as before. She was one of the three mothers who went to Washington and told President Johnson to his face about conditions in McComb.

When she got back, the police raided her café. Someone had planted a half-pint of whiskey in the pocket of an old coat hanging from a nail in the men's rest room, but Mama Quin was selling only beer in her new place although she used to sell whiskey in her old café. Whiskey is so illegal in Mississippi that the state collects a tax on bootleg and the distribution monopoly is in the hands of the county sheriffs. Mama Quin used to get her supply from the appropriate source, who put a special mark on the bottle top so so he could check up on whether she was selling anybody else's whiskey. Every week she paid her "license" fees. Now and then she would be hauled in and made to pay a fine as part of the game. This was the basis for Governor Paul Johnson of Mississippi saying that Mama Quin had "a record as long as the I. C. Railroad," which runs from Chicago to New Orleans.

After the last raid Mama Quin paid a heavy fine for the planted bottle. Sheriff Warren also revoked her beer-selling license. This is equivalent to a death sentence for her café. The Negroes tried a beer boycott to get Mama Quin's license restored. It lasted two hours, which is quite a while to go without a drink if you are a Negro and have to live in McComb.

Ramparts, May 1965

Selma Revisited:
4 Months After Their "Finest Hour"
Rights Forces Are in Disarray

by Haynes Johnson

SELMA, Ala.—A new sign stands near the spot in Selma's Negro section where Martin Luther King led the marchers into the street and down the long road to Montgomery last spring. It reads: "FORWARD EVER—BACKWARD NEVER."

Today that sign is more an expression of hope than a statement of fact. While stoutly maintaining their faith in themselves and the civil rights movement, Negroes here are shocked and divided.

The spirit and singleness of purpose they showed when Selma became a byword around the world have been shattered by bickering and scandal. While the victory they scored last spring remains untarnished, the drive to build on it by improving their lot in life has slowed.

Their leaders are struggling to regain precious momentum, but many of those who followed them so patiently are frankly bewildered and disillusioned. Selma's Negro community is, in fact, in an hour of new and more subtle crisis—a tragic crisis when it is contrasted with the soaring hopes and selfless devotion they and their friends demonstrated here such a short time ago.

The reporter returning to Selma finds none of this on the surface. Selma slumbers in the summer heat as if the exciting days of springtime had never occurred. Women with parasols stroll past the small stores. The streets are quiet; there is little movement. Across the Alabama River the hot wind plays across the cotton fields.

Now there are no demonstrators, no barricades, no jeering of chanting crowds, no troopers or armed posses. Now Selma,

Ala., seems merely another trading center in the heart of the black belt of the rural South.

There is no discernible change in the racial climate of the city. The Negroes have scored no real advances in their areas of their greatest need—employment, housing and education. They are discovering that these goals are easier to express than to achieve.

To be sure, there have been some improvements in the Negro position. Volunteer workers of both races are teaching students and adults in improvised classrooms. Leaders of the white and Negro communities have met in an attempt to begin meaningful communications. The Negroes are continuing their voter registration work. More than 20,000 books have been collected from across the country for a Negro library.

And above all is a historical fact. As a result of what the Selma Negroes and their white friends did last spring, the Deep South will never be the same. The demonstrations and the march lifted the spirits of Negroes everywhere.

In part the present dispirited mood in Selma may reflect an inevitable letdown from an emotional peak—what happens when the cheering stops.

It has been aggravated, however, by some specific incidents —the arrest of one of the most prominent local Negro leaders of the protest movement on charges of embezzling civil rights funds and the morals conviction of another Negro who assumed a position of leadership during the demonstrations.

Also, bills incurred by the civil rights movement have mounted. Some have not been paid. The phone in the Southern Christian Leadership Conference office, for instance, was disconnected for non-payment. The SCLC is the national organization headed by Dr. King.

Finally there are stories of widespread misuse of gifts sent to help the Negroes in Selma. Privately, Negroes tell of incidents in which food, clothing and money which poured into Selma during and after the march to Montgomery were sold or used for private gain.

These stories have not been documented; no one has been charged. But the accounts come from reliable sources, and it is fair to report that they are accepted as true within the Negro group.

The first real blow to Negro morale came on June 23 with the morals arrest of William H. Ezra Greer.

At the height of the street encounters early last spring, Greer appeared in the center of the demonstrations. He said he was a minister from Chicago, and a key lieutenant there in King's SCLC. Soon, Greer was standing in front of the crowds delivering fiery speeches in the Billy Sunday manner, fist clenched, crouching, shouting, raising his knee and stamping hard.

He took an active part during a prayer vigil in the streets for the Rev. James J. Reeb, the white Unitarian minister from Boston, who was clubbed to death in Selma. After the march Greer stayed on in Selma, acting as one of the civil rights leaders.

On June 23 Greer was arrested on three charges by Selma's public safety director, Wilson Baker, on warrants filed by Selma Negroes. He was charged with two counts of assault involving the molestation of a Negro girl, one of using obscene language in front of a child, and another of possessing pornographic material.

He was released on $900 bond. The next day, again on warrants filed by Selma Negroes, Greer was arrested on a similar charge of assault.

He was tried, convicted, and sentenced to six months at hard labor and fined $25. The judge suspended the jail sentence, pending good behavior after Greer's lawyer said his client would not continue living in Selma. Greer has left town.

It was an ugly scandal within the civil rights community. But a heavier blow fell days later when Baker arrested the Rev. Frederick D. Reese, president of the Dallas County Voters' League.

Reese, the key man in the Selma rights movement, was charged with three counts of embezzling funds belonging to the Voters' League. Baker says his investigation began when he received tips from Selma Negroes.

Baker turned over information to a special grand jury that Reese had deposited approximately $8,000 over a 40-day period in a Montgomery bank. According to the documents, the first deposit, of $100, was made March 26 when Reese opened a joint checking account in his own and his wife's name. After that he deposited sums such as $2,900, $1,100, and $3,000. He began drawing on the account toward the end of April, Baker says, in checks ranging from $71.88 to $4,073.92.

Baker states that the canceled checks show that every one was for Reese's personal use.

The arrest touched off a storm from Negro leadership. They accused Baker of conspiring to smear the civil rights movement.

Martin Luther King's No. 2 man, the Rev. Ralph Abernathy, flew to Selma after the arrest. At a mass rally he compounded the situation when he was quoted as saying the money belonged to the civil rights movement and they could give it to Reese if they wished.

After that Baker left on a trip to California and the East Coast questioning contributors to the Dallas County Voters' League. He returned with signed statements in which donors said the money was contributed for use only in civil rights work—not for personal use.

In pursuing the investigation, the grand jury subpoenaed the records of the Dallas County Voters' League. According to Baker, few records other than a check book were available. He has hinted that more arrests are forthcoming.

Shaken and clearly unsure of what will come next, Negro leaders in Selma have reacted with a vehemence that in some ways resembles the attitudes of their white antagonists. Any Negro who speaks out about the scandals is branded as a traitor to the cause. Consequently, the voice of the Negro critic is not heard in Selma today.

In a newsletter distributed to Selma Negroes, the Voters' League said editorially:

"There are those in Selma trying to shatter this national symbol of resistance to brutality and oppression. They are the ones who have arrested us. They are the ones who, though they handcuff and jail a Christian minister, neither handcuff, jail, nor punish those who murder in the night."

Even more revealing of present attitudes was a recent night meeting at Brown's Memorial Chapel, the center of civil rights activity. Reese and other officials of the Voters' League were present and spoke.

While members of the audience fanned themselves vigorously in the stifling heat, speaker after speaker took the lectern to excoriate the white community.

"The devil is on the warpath," one Negro said.

From the audience came the murmur of response: "Yeah." "Uh-huh." "Yeah, he is." "That's right."

Then the speaker talked of "secret enemies," of Negroes working "under the table." He worked himself into an emotional pitch and, waving his hands, said the enemy was the Negro—or Negroes—who went to the police.

Who was that Negro? he demanded. Let him show his face. He warned that the Negro—or Negroes—would be "taken care of," and used the phrase "going for a ride."

"Most of us are here tonight because we are on the way to the promised land, the land of freedom," he said. "But we're never going to get to the promised land till we have unity, and we'll never have unity when we slay our leader."

But all the pleas for unity have failed to hide the feeling of dismay that has swept the Negro community.

In the meantime, two key Negro campaigns have slowed to a standstill.

Despite appeals and threats of ostracizing, a boycott of white merchants is a failure. Negroes can be seen at any time of the day buying in the stores.

More important, the voter registration drive has lost its momentum. On the last night of the current Selma schedule for registering voters, for example, SCLC's project director in the city, the Rev. Harold Middlebrook, issued an appeal for Negroes to turn out in the thousands the next morning.

They needed 5,000 registrants, he said, adding that "we are too far now to turn around."

At 9 o'clock the next morning there were some 70 Negroes standing in line outside the Dallas County Court House. By contrast, during January, February, March and April thousands were asked to come—and they did.

Despite the present slowdown, however, the voter registration campaign has been making progress. One comparison illustrates this. Since last February, 7,326 persons—the vast majority Negroes—have signed the registration appearance book in Dallas County. This is more than the total number who voted in the county in the last national election.

Not all who sign the appearance book apply for registration, of course, and many of those who do apply are rejected. Nevertheless, the registration drive has made such an impact that it has brought a counter-reaction from whites.

A group called "Women for Constitutional Government" has been formed to encourage whites in Selma and Dallas County to register. They have taken an office directly across the street from the courthouse. They claim to have contacted 1,000 unregistered whites in the first week of July.

Economically, the outlook for the Negro is still bleak. There are few jobs. There are still no street lights in the Negro sections. The housing and plumbing is abysmal. The streets are still unpaved. The wages are still far below any reasonable minimum. In Selma, a Negro who earns $50 a week is a wealthy man.

Next month when the cotton crop is picked the Negroes who work in the fields will receive $2 a day. A maid in Selma can expect $10 a week. If she works six days a week in a laundry, she will get $12. At one motel, part of a national chain, a maid earns the top figure of $22.50 a week for an eight-hour day.

And outside Selma, in the farmland through which the marchers made their way, the conditions are worse.

After the march some of the Negroes who came to the side of the road to cheer and wave suffered retaliations. Others appear to have been forgotten.

Mrs. Carrie Beaton, 39, sat on the porch of her shack, surrounded by children, and said: "Ain't nobody come to see us noway." Even if they had, she said, "it wouldn't make no difference."

But she, like all the Negroes one talks to, takes great pride in the Selma movement and the march. "It was real good," she said.

Across the field from one of the campsites used on the march, a Negro woman who operates a grocery told how a bakery in Montgomery refused to sell her bread for her store. "The bread man said the white man came to them and told them they better not sell us the bread," she said. "And they said we aren't going to have any school for the little children."

Now the bread deliveries have resumed; things have returned to normal along the Jefferson Davis Highway to Montgomery.

But for Selma and Dallas County, as well as the other rural centers of the South the old days and ways, it seems clear, will never come again.

The white counterattack on voter registration underscores what is perhaps the most basic change in Selma today: a recognition on both sides that despite their present troubles the Negroes are going to exercise power in the future. While the whites, generally speaking, are determined to keep that power at a minimum they tacitly acknowledge—if not accept —the changes to come.

Already, Selma Negroes are talking of the political role they will play.

Middlebrook, the SCLC project director, has said he wants to become State Senator from Dallas County. He has asked for 15,000 Negro votes in the fall to help him go to the Legislature where he can "assist" Gov. George C. Wallace in writing legislation.

Another Negro civil rights leader, the Rev. L. L. Anderson, pastor of the Tabernacle Baptist Church of Selma, has said he wants to be Mayor. Others are talking about and planning for the day when Selma Negroes have a place on the City Council.

One Negro, a man respected throughout Selma, expressed the situation frankly and philosophically.

"Now, racism I despise," he said. "I'm not kidding you, I don't care who it comes from. He can be black as midnight and I despise it. This Black Nationalism you hear here, this killing off the opposition by talking about (Uncle) Toms. It stinks.

"Now, here's the way I look at it: if everything else is lost —and it hasn't been lost—the march and what happened in Selma gave the Negro a sense of dignity he didn't have.

"Yes, sir, he would tell you what you wanted to hear. He was listless. I don't know if you know this but you can't deal with a man as a man unless he regards himself as a man. And this is what has happened, and I rejoice in it.

"Look, this thing has been badly handled after this march. It hasn't been handled well. The way I see it is SCLC has to send in some strong people in here because these people are babes in the wood. . . .

"I predict a good future, I really believe this is going to be one of the best places to live in the world in a few years. You got everything in your favor—good natural resources, good climate and good labor market.

"When we can get over people like George Wallace, get people like (Alabama Atty. Gen. Richmond) Flowers (who has taken a moderate position on race) this is going to be a tremendous place to live.

"Why, I'd rather live here than anywhere in the whole world."

The Washington Star, July 26, 1965

Eight Men Slain; Guard Moves In

by Art Berman

A WHITE deputy sheriff and at least seven Negroes were killed by gunfire Friday night and early today and National Guardsmen moved into the area where riots raged for the third straight night.

A huge section of Los Angeles was virtually a city on fire as flames from stores, industrial complexes and homes lit the skies.

Shootings were being reported with increasing rapidity during the hot, early morning hours and rioting outbursts were reported in Pasadena, Compton and Venice.

Several other people reportedly were shot on the hot, muggy night as Negro mobs fought bloody battles with police, looted stores and set fire to scores of buildings.

Sniper fire and uncontrolled flames were reported over a widening area. It reached almost to City Hall from the south Los Angeles area 10 miles away where the violence began.

Well over 200 people were injured in the three days of terror, including more than 30 peace officers.

Dep. Sheriff Ronald Ernest Ludlow, 27, was shot in the stomach at Imperial Highway and Wilmington Ave. at 9 p.m. and was pronounced dead on arrival at St. Francis Hospital, Lynwood.

Three suspects were arrested in the murder.

Ludlow was the father of two.

Two Negroes died in Oak Park Community Hospital, 369 W. Manchester Blvd., as Negroes rioted outside.

A hospital official said one of them might have been saved if the rioters hadn't prevented an anesthesiologist from reaching the hospital.

Three other gunshot victims were being treated in the hospital.

One of them, an alleged looter, was shot by police in the 2800 block of S. Central Ave. and another was shot at 97th and Figueroa St.

Police made plans to reopen the old Lincoln Heights Jail as those arrested passed the 300 mark.

Damage from fires exceeded $10 million.

Fires blazed from 41st St. to 108th St.

A minor blaze was set at 9th and Main Sts., only nine blocks from City Hall.

The first of 2,000 guardsmen reached the riot area about 9:45 p.m. to bolster the overwhelmed force of 560 police, deputy sheriffs and highway patrolmen.

Another 3,000 guardsmen were on standby alert.

Helmeted guardsmen in jeeps with mounted machine guns established a headquarters at Walter Riis High School and others gathered at Manchester Playground.

By 1 a.m. about 200 guardsmen with fixed bayonets had relieved 200 police officers in an area bounded by Century Blvd., 104th St., Grape St. and Compton Blvd.

Lt. Col. Thomas Haykin of the 1st Battalion called the devastated square "secure." He stationed his troops along streets and at intersections while fires still burned in ruined stores and buildings.

He said there was no immediate plan to expand the perimeter, but he held 250 guardsmen in reserve at Manchester Playground.

A phalanx of guardsmen with fixed bayonets secured a burned out six-block area of 103rd St. without opposition.

With the arrival of the guardsmen, marauding Negro bands seemed to filter out to other areas. The wave of looting, wrecking and burning spread to Vermont Ave., between 35th and 52nd Sts., on Central Ave. as far north as 18th St., and to Pico and Normandie Ave.

The Fire Department called in reserve forces, but up to 45 major blazes went unchecked at a time.

Firemen trying to reach blazes were shot at, battered with rocks and debris and cursed by angry Negroes. Several firemen were treated at hospitals after they were struck by rocks, glass and buckshot.

Two firemen were trapped under a falling wall in a burning

market at 120th St. and Central Ave. Their comrades fought frantically to reach them and then reported by radio:

"One's talking and the other one's quiet."

It was unknown whether that meant he was dead.

At Avalon Blvd. and Santa Barbara Ave., a Negro driver reportedly drove his car into a line of guardsmen, seriously injuring one. Other guardsmen and county marshals opened fire and halted the driver. He was captured, only cut by broken glass.

The injured guardsman, Sgt. Wayne Stewart, was taken to Orthopaedic Hospital with head injuries and a broken leg. His condition is "serious."

Lt. Gov. Glenn M. Anderson called out the National Guard after five hours of pleas from Police Chief William H. Parker and Mayor Samuel W. Yorty. Parker at one point threatened to appeal to President Johnson if Anderson didn't act.

Looters, including women and small children, ran wild throughout the day, grabbing everything in sight—clothes, liquor, drugs, appliances, weapons, shoes, food. Then they burned the empty stores.

Helmeted, shotgun-carrying police formed skirmish lines and cleared various intersections of mobs.

They frequently exchanged gunfire with snipers.

"I'm standing at Vernon and Central and as far as I can see there are buildings on fire—markets, stores, a jewelry store, a record shop," said Robert Richardson, a Times advertising salesman and a Negro.

"Every store has been looted and set fire to, but not all the fires took. Fire trucks are up and down the street.

"Police are holding the mob back about three blocks. Everyone is milling around. There aren't any white people here and there's really nothing for them to do but loot.

"There's a case of whisky on the street in front of me. There are clothing and shoes."

There was no estimate of the number of rioters, but they far surpassed the previous night when the estimate was 7,000.

Many residents of the Negro ghetto were horrified at what was happening and cheers went up when guardsmen entered the area.

The plan was to ring the riot-torn area until dawn, then sweep through with bayonets and tear gas, if necessary, to break up the thousands of rioters.

The Fire Department said 70 fires were reported before midnight, most of them set by Molotov cocktails.

Some fire trucks reached blazes under police guards.

Other fires raged unchecked as mobs blocked streets and taunted police and firemen.

New groups of rioters seemed to spring up spontaneously as the mob fever spread.

Hostility toward authority and toward whites was evident everywhere.

Mobs torched businesses believed owned by Caucasians.

"Burn it down, it's Whitey's," they chanted as the flames glowed.

Sniper fire was widespread, much of it from weapons looted from pawn shops and sporting goods stores.

Police left some areas unpatrolled because they were too dangerous to enter.

The police radio crackled constantly with emergency calls:

"Manchester and Broadway, a mob of 1,000 . . . 51st and Avalon, a mob of 1,000 . . . Vernon and Central, looting . . . 88th and Broadway, gun battle . . . 84th and Vermont, juvenile dispensing guns . . . 48th and Avalon, fire, units can't reach . . ."

And on into the night.

At one point 130 policemen ringed the 77th Street Police Station as well-armed mobs threatened to close in.

Police and news helicopters over the area were fired at from below, but none was hit.

The Watts Post Office on 103rd Street was invaded by a mob and looted.

Forty Caucasians employed in a building at 111th and Avalon Boulevard were besieged during the day, but were rescued by police.

The outcropping of trouble in Pasadena was described early today by Police Chief Samuel H. Addis as the smashing of windows in stores throughout the Negro area there by roving bands of 20 to 30.

Gov. Brown, vacationing in Athens, Greece, notified his

office by telephone that he would fly here by the first available transportation.

President Johnson reportedly was being kept apprised of the situation.

Chief Parker requested the Guard at 10:50 a.m. in a telephone call to Winslow Christian, the governor's executive secretary in Sacramento.

"We have not been able to adequately cope with the lawlessness," Parker told him.

Parker took his action after conferring with Mayor Yorty and reporting that his police force was nearing exhaustion.

The number of policemen in the Avalon Blvd.–Imperial Highway area was reduced sharply at dawn Friday after 700 helmeted and shotgun carrying officers fought a virtual guerrilla war during the night with mobs of frenzied Negroes.

An emergency call for 32 deputy sheriffs was sent out at 11:30 a.m. as roving mobs sacked stores and stoned passing autos virtually unrestrained.

"The situation is completely out of control," the police reported.

Negro comedian Dick Gregory suffered a minor gunshot wound in the thigh as he went to the riot area in an attempt to calm the mobs.

Gregory, a hero of the civil rights movement, met with other Negro leaders Friday in an effort to seek a solution.

But the voices of reason were being drowned out by the surging sea of hatred directed at police and Caucasians.

A white television technician, pulled from his car and beaten by a mob, was in "very critical" condition in Glendale Community Hospital.

Police said Raymond Fahrenkopf, 56, a sound man for a KABC-TV news crew, was beaten, stripped and robbed at 114th St. and Avalon Blvd. late Thursday and was left for dead.

Fahrenkopf reportedly suffered a skull fracture and may lose his eyesight if he recovers, police said.

Various governmental, religious and civil rights groups held meetings Friday to calm the tension but none was successful.

Chief Parker said he thought the riot was being provoked by a hard core of 500 hoodlums as the crowd swelled to an estimated 7,000 early Friday.

The chief said that Negro community leaders have been powerless to cope with the mob.

"It's a result of the terrible conflicts building up with these people," said Parker. "You can't keep telling them that the Liberty Bell isn't ringing for them and not expect them to believe it."

Commenting on long-standing Negro allegations of police brutality, Parker retorted that the riots might not have occurred if police hadn't been handling Negroes "with kid gloves."

"You'll note that few demonstrators have been injured," Parker said.

The chief told the governor's secretary that 103 police cars were used in riot control and all were damaged.

Parker said police will invoke unlawful assembly and riot laws and make mass arrests. He said he would reopen the city jail in Lincoln Heights if necessary.

Even as public officials and civil rights leaders held their various conferences, a mob of 2,000 was forming a new battleground on 103rd St. near Compton Ave. in Watts, a poverty-ridden Negro area.

Rocks and bricks continued flying and police continued grabbing suspects from the retreating fringes of the mobs.

Liquor stores, a drugstore and other businesses were being looted in broad daylight. But police were powerless to interfere because it was necessary to concentrate on the surging mobs.

A Negro reporter, Warren Wilson of United Press International, circulated through the mobs early Friday and told of youths shouting:

"Get that white man. Get that white man."

Wilson told of seeing a white man dragged from his car and beaten with tire irons, bricks and bottles.

A Negro minister saved the white man, driving him off in a car as other Negroes threw a hail of debris at them.

Some youths filled bottles with gasoline and flaming rags— Molotov cocktails—and hurled them into vehicles.

At times, officers formed a skirmish line and charged in with clubs and guns, scattering the mob into alleys and buildings.

Some arrests were made, but new mobs quickly formed elsewhere.

Even churches were not spared by the Negro hoodlums who smashed their windows.

Street lights were broken and residents kept their homes dark as they cowered in fear. The darkened streets were lighted only by the glow of burning autos and buildings.

Police cars darted around the area, their red and orange lights flashing and their sirens wailing.

Los Angeles Times, August 14, 1965

"Burn, Baby, Burn!"

by Robert Richardson

"Get Whitey," Scream Blood-Hungry Mobs

It was the most terrifying thing I've ever seen in my life.

I went along with the mobs, just watching, listening.

It's a wonder anyone with white skin got out of there alive.

I saw people with guns. The cry went up several times—"Let's go to Lynwood!" (an all-white neighborhood) whenever there weren't enough whites around.

Every time a car with whites in it entered the area the word spread like lightning down the street:

"Here comes Whitey—get him!"

The older people would stand in the background, egging on the teen-agers and the people in their early 20s. Then the young men and women would rush in and pull white people from their cars and beat them and try to set fire to their cars.

One white couple, in their 60s, happened to be driving along Imperial before the blockades were put up. They were beaten and kicked until their faces, hands and clothing were bloody. I thought they were going to be killed. How they survived I don't know. Those not hitting and kicking the couple were standing there shouting "Kill! Kill!"

Finally they turned them loose and an ambulance was called and they were taken away.

Two white men driving down Avalon Blvd. ducked when rocks bombarded their car. When they ducked the car hit a car with Negroes.

They were beaten so badly one man's eye was hanging out of the socket. Some Negro ministers made their way through the crowd and carried both men into an apartment building and called an ambulance.

The crowd called the ministers hypocrites. They cussed them and spit on them. Some Negro officers tried to disperse the crowd, but they were jeered at, sworn at, called traitors and stoned.

The Negro officers were given a worse time than the white officers.

Light-skinned Negroes such as myself were targets of rocks and bottles until someone standing nearby would shout, "He's blood," or "He's a brother—lay off!"

As some areas were blockaded during the night, the mobs would move outside, looking for more cars with whites. When there were no whites they started throwing rocks and bottles at Negro cars. Then near midnight they began looting stores owned by whites.

Everybody got in the looting—children, grownups, old men and women, breaking windows and going into stores.

Then everybody started drinking—even little kids 8 or 9 years old. That's when the cry started, "Let's go where Whitey lives!" That's when I began to see guns.

I believe the mobs would have moved into white neighborhoods, but it was getting late and many of them had to go to work Friday morning.

But some said, "Wait till tonight and Saturday. We'll really roll over the weekend. We'll really get Whitey then!"

They knew they had the upper hand. They seemed to sense that the police nor anyone else could stop them.

I heard them say, "Just wait till one of the blood gets shot —then heads will really roll. Then Whitey will get his!"

"Burn, Baby, Burn" Slogan Used as Firebugs Put Area to Torch

Negro arsonists raced autos through otherwise deserted Los Angeles streets, flinging Molotov cocktails into store after store and shouting a hep slogan borrowed from a radio disc jockey:

"Burn, baby, burn!"

It was an eerie scene Friday night. Streets crowded with hundreds of rioters Thursday night were debris-littered but empty. Lighted windows were few. It was almost like a ghost town.

But new flames continued to shoot up. Speeding cars crisscrossed the area. Occupants exchanged the now familiar one, two and three-finger salute and shouted the grim slogan:

"Burn, baby burn!"

(One finger meant he was a Watts man, two meant a Compton man and three fingers meant a man from a Willowbrook area.)

The rioters were burning their city now, as the insane sometimes mutilate themselves.

A great section of Los Angeles was burning, and anyone who didn't return the crazy password was in danger.

I, too, learned to shout "Burn, baby, burn" after several shots were fired at me. Luckily none of the bullets hit my car, and luckier still, none hit me.

At Holmes Ave. and Imperial Highway I saw a looted Safeway Store all but destroyed by fire.

At 120th St. and Central Ave., a Shoprite Market was burning.

Other stores were burning near Manchester Ave. and Broadway, burning alone, with no one apparently paying the least attention. I saw nobody near them.

Near Vernon and Central Aves. several stores were burning over a six-block area from north to south. All had been looted. People had carried off everything, even such commonplace articles as mops, brooms and soap powders.

Firemen here were struggling to combat the flames.

In some spots helmeted police armed with shotguns seemed to have the upper hand.

At Avalon Blvd. and 120th St., I saw five patrol cars converge on a smashed-open liquor store full of looters.

Police arrested nine suspects in the place, five women and four men, and lined them against a wall outside.

For the first time that evening I saw a crowd begin to gather. Half a dozen cars halted and parked. A knot of people gathered on the opposite corner and a few jeered.

But none attempted to throw a rock or interfere with the officers.

In all that area I saw only two businesses open and operating. Both were service stations, one operated by Negroes, the other by whites.

Neither had been disturbed by rioters, and there seemed no explanation for their charmed existences, except that both were familiar in their neighborhoods.

I asked whoever I met, "Where is everybody?" and some said, "Over on Broadway—all up and down Broadway—moving toward the West Side."

They were right. You could follow them by the burning stores.

At 81st St. and Avalon Blvd. a looted liquor store was burning, but there was no crowd. At 76th St. and Central Ave., the White Front Store was pillaged and burning out of control, but still no crowd.

At Manchester Ave. and Central Ave., I found a crowd burning a hotdog stand and a taco place. Teen-agers stood around yelling, "Burn, baby, burn."

I was being shot at again, and it was time to go. Two fire trucks came by with sirens going and I took off right behind them, west on Manchester and north on Broadway.

We passed a furniture store burning out of control and arrived at 48th St. and Broadway. Two furniture stores and a clothing store were burning. They had been cleaned out of everything movable. There were 16 fire trucks on the scene.

I had a flat tire now. One tire had been shot out, and the spare I put on was wiped out by broken glass.

I had to do all of my telephoning from street-corner booths in gas stations. You have no idea how naked you can feel in an exposed, lighted telephone booth.

But I was hep by that time. Whenever a group of Negroes approached to look me over I knew what to do.

You open the door, stick your head out, and shout, "Burn, baby, burn." Then you are safe.

Childhood Vanishes in Embers During Fearful Curfew Hours

The hot summer afternoon is ending. I am talking to Negro residents of the riot-torn area. "Why?" I ask. "Why the riots?"

Some of the answers hit me like a slap in the face. One is a scream:

"We are going to put the fear of the Negro into these white people because they do not have the fear of God."

Now night has fallen. We are moving south on the Harbor Freeway, hearing that snipers are firing on cars there. I'm with three other newsmen. We are all tense and bone-tired.

And we are all Negroes.

Red lights loom abruptly in our rear window and we pull to the side of the freeway, waiting while motorcycle officers come to the side of our car with hands on their guns. One of them checks my I.D. and they tell us to move on.

We turn off the freeway at El Segundo Blvd. and drive east into the curfew area. The streets lie under a strange quietness, without cars or strollers. It's impossible to believe this is Saturday night.

At Willowbrook Ave. and El Segundo something is happening:

Firemen are hauling up hoses and battling to save a building containing a drug store, a barber shop and a liquor store, but they are losing.

Out on the streets behind us—where there had been the deceptive silence—a hostile crowd begins to form. Suddenly, police officers with raised shotguns come striding toward us. "Out of your car. Hands up . . . High!"

We do not know what to do. But we get out, all trying to say at once that we are working newsmen.

"Get the hell out," is the reply from the officers.

We do it. We get back into the car, make a U-turn and drive through the restive crowd that stares at us. Five police officers, helmeted and holding shotguns, watch us warily as we move away.

At 120th St. and Central Ave., I am stunned by the sight of the demolished supermarket that once boasted of its equal hiring practices.

I get out of the car and look at the rubble, thinking, this was the store where I came with my mother as a little boy. . . . where I met with other neighborhood kids and drank soda pop and talked about football. I want to cry.

I am trying to think about that when someone shouts and footsteps come rushing toward me. The guys in the car yell, "Move, man, move!"

Then there is a shotgun in my face and a policeman says, "Move on, mister. Let's go now. Move!"

In the policeman's face there is no awareness that I am trying to see my childhood in the charred wreckage of a supermarket. His eyes are only the eyes of a man with a job to do.

More officers come hurrying over to our car. I can't think of what to tell them, so I get in the car and we get going.

All of us are quiet . . . not saying a thing to each other. We are Negroes, driving past looted stores and burned-out shops and overturned cars and scatterings of debris.

We cruise through the dark streets, empty except for an occasional caravan of police cars and buses. There are the sounds of sporadic shooting and we don't know whether to turn out our lights or keep them on.

In the Watts area, we can see the flicker of flames and we head for it. But suddenly we see helmeted men running across the street with rifles and ducking behind buildings. Out of the darkness comes the command: "Get out of here!" Guardsmen have their rifles pointed at our car.

There is a sign in the street: "Turn left or get shot."

We turn left.

On Manchester Ave., traveling west from Alameda St., we find a service station open and we pull into it. Three or four Negro men are crouched behind cartons of motor oil watching us. They are scared and so are we.

We get out of our car slowly, seeing no weapons but taking no chances. The men come out from behind their barricades just as slowly . . . and suddenly there is a handshake and we are treating each other like old friends.

No one has ordered them to close, so they have stayed open—the only service station for miles around. We get smokes and Cokes from machines and move out following screaming fire engines.

At Manchester and Broadway, we are stopped by a command post and checked out. I look across the street where only Tuesday I bought a new pair of shoes.

Now there is only smoldering rubble.

Going up Broadway from 35th St., we see the sky lighting up with orange. Fire trucks are coming from everywhere. Police caravans are criss-crossing the area. About 10 officers have two Negro teen-agers on the corner, searching them.

"Halt!" comes the bellow over a bullhorn. "Halt!" A second time. I shove the brake to the floorboard. We are ordered out with our hands up. We shout, "Press."

"OK, get back in your car."

The Negro boys are being turned loose and ordered to run double-time away from the area. They move. We head for the fire.

We get there and find a complete block of stores ablaze. Flames are boiling up and thick smoke is spilling into the sky.

But the firemen are hiding under their trucks as the buildings burn. Police are scattering, seeking cover. There are shots.

A store window crashes in near me and my friends are making it back to the car. A policeman charges toward me with a shotgun in one hand and a revolver in the other.

"Who are you people?" he demands.

I show him my identification.

Another window shatters and the glass falls at my feet. We duck. I run for the car. We make another fast U-turn and we're on our way. It's time to go home.

That is, if we still have them.

Los Angeles Times, August 14–16, 1965

August, 1965

by Jerry Farber

"WHAT the hell do the police want?" someone asked.

About 25 squad cars had entirely blocked off Avalon at the corner of Imperial Highway. Policemen and motorcycles lined the street. A growing crowd jammed the sidewalk.

"A riot."

"They gonna get one."

The police had to wait quite a while for their riot. At 11, when we arrived from the N-VAC office, they had already been there maybe an hour. And when we reached the intersection, there was still nothing happening, except that the crowd was growing larger every minute. People had heard about the situation—it was already on television and radio—and were coming to watch. They stood on bus benches or on trucks in the Shell station to get a better view. It was like a parade but with angry spectators. Six of us from N-VAC circulated in the crowd for nearly an hour asking questions. Earlier in the evening, we learned, there had been some rock throwing along Avalon just south of Imperial. Most of the persons we talked to said that it had all started when the police had kicked and slugged a woman. A few insisted that the woman had been pregnant.

Finally—it must have been close to midnight—someone threw a rock. It hit a squad car. A minute or two later a bottle crashed in the street and the newsmen began to leave. From this point on it becomes difficult to remember the sequence of events. But individual scenes are very vivid in my mind. A policeman started to drive his squad car away and someone threw a cigarette butt in it. He stopped, opened the door, located the cigarette and tossed it out. He looked around at the hostile crowd and said, "Thanks a lot!" How can I explain how he said it? He wanted to *get* our ass so bad

428

—but he was afraid. And since he was afraid, he made like it was just a little joke. For me, that was when the whole thing started.

I remember that the tempo of rock and bottle throwing gradually increased. There was also a lot of shouting. I saw a girl about 15 screaming, almost in tears, "*Fuck you, cop! Fuck you!*" Finally, 15 or 20 policemen rushed the crowd with their clubs swinging. They didn't get the rock throwers, who were in back; they grabbed two or three kids out of the crowd and arrested them. During another of these flying raids by the police, I saw someone go down and saw four or five policemen beating him, swinging their clubs high in the air.

At one point, a dozen or so policemen stood in a line facing 40 or 50 of us in the gas station. A couple of them were spinning and twirling their clubs in what they must have regarded as a menacing manner. Someone in the crowd called out, "Hey, you're looking GOOD, motherfucker!" Someone else just missed them with a rock. The police made another rush into the crowd. We scattered; they were arresting, and frequently beating, anyone they could catch. Caroline (also from N-VAC) and I made it over a fence into a back yard next to the Shell station. A man came out of his back door, pointed a pistol at us and said, "I told all of you to get out of my yard. Now get!" I tried to explain about the police but he wasn't listening; he kept waving his damn pistol at me. So we jumped the fence back into the gas station and hid under a truck while the cops rushed around with their clubs in the air.

A little later we emerged and looked around. Robert Hall showed up, furious. He had been taking notes for N-VAC. A cop had ripped the notes out of his hand and torn them up.

At some point after the rock throwing started, the police left. The motorcycle cops took off in a noisy razzle-dazzle—making loops in tight formation near the intersection. It was like a shooting gallery as people in the crowd tried to score with rocks. When the police left, the rock and bottle throwers began checking out passing cars, looking for whitey. Any brother who drove by slowly, holding out a Watts or Compton or Slauson hand signal, was usually safe. The rest were targets; it was hard to make out the color of a driver speeding by at night.

Across the street one group caught a UPI newsman, Nick Beck, in a phone booth and began beating him. Robert Hall pushed his way through, got Beck out of the booth and into his car.

A KTTV mobile unit had been abandoned on the corner. Some kids rolled it onto its side and then, with great effort, on its top. It immediately burst into flames, which lit the entire intersection. A middle-aged lady next to me was talking to a man who had been near the car.

"Look what they done. Somebody in there?"

"No, it's all right. Ain't nobody inside."

"Ain't that something? That truck is burning *up!*"

She was smiling. A lot of people were smiling. The rebellion was well under way.

When we left, around 2:30 a.m., a pattern of guerrilla warfare had been set. There were bands of neighborhood people —teenagers and young men—throwing bottles and rocks at passing cars and beating up whites who stopped and got out of their cars (for hours I had been expecting the police to block off that section of Imperial Highway but they never did). When police came our way, whatever groups were on the street would disappear into houses and yards or would take up a position further down.

Robert and I got a lift back to N-VAC with a photographer from *Muhammad Speaks*. On our way to the car we stopped by a group of rock throwers. One of them, with conked hair, his T-shirt cut off at the sleeves, said, "We been getting hit a long time. Now we hitting back."

He wanted to know what paper the photographer was from. When he found out, he said, "Well listen, man, tell it like it is."

"That's the only thing we print in *Muhammad Speaks*, brother—how it *is*. What are you going to do now?"

"We going to get every white motherfucker comes down this street." He kept glancing up the dark, empty boulevard, looking for cars, looking for the police.

"Listen, brother, the Honorable Elijah Muhammad's been telling you about the devils for years. You brothers got to come on down to the mosque and get with it."

"Ain't no need to go down there. I got my business right

here. You understand? I'm ready to die! You know what I mean? But don't get me wrong. You got a point, brother, you got a point."

By the next night, Thursday, the people of Watts were in possession of a good part of their own community. A carload from N-VAC drove over in the early evening. This time there weren't any white skins in the car. The night before, five white kids had come down. Four of them barely made it out. Dave, convicted, ironically, earlier that day for a civil rights demonstration, had been caught by a group of teenagers. He curled up in the nonviolent position, was kicked a few times and left alone. The fifth Caucasian, Caroline Sweezy, was there almost as long as Robert and I, and had remained unhurt. Someone had spit on her shortly after we arrived but that was all.

Thursday night, however, the white members of N-VAC were talked into staying in the office—even Caroline, who was mad as hell at being segregated out of the riot. Then, driving into Watts, it began to look like nobody was going to make it; we encountered police barricades all around the "riot perimeter." We had to park the car and sneak in one or two at a time. We dropped off Woodrow, then Robert a block further down, then Danny Gray. The three of us who were left parked the car and, one after another, ran like hell across a street that formed the western perimeter. We kept running for a while and eventually found ourselves on a stretch of Avalon just south of Imperial—the area where rock throwing had started the night before. Police held the intersection where the Shell station was but were apparently not leaving their small, well-lit beachhead. Within a stone's throw of the police (literally) the crowd was able to break into stores, set fires and rip out pay phones—under the very eyes of the LAPD.

I stood outside timidly and watched for a police raid as my two friends joined the crowd in emptying a small grocery store. People were coming out with boxes and bags filled with canned goods. One man hung onto his hard liquor but set aside a case of Gallo sauterne to use as ammunition. Men were throwing bottles at street lights too to make the dark street darker. Until the lights were finally out, bottles kept crashing down on either side of the street, bringing startled and angry shouts. But there were no fights. Once, two kids started to square off but someone said, "Save it for whitey, brother," and they stopped.

Four or five hundred persons were roaming up and down that stretch of Avalon or were sitting on their apartment house steps. Women called to their kids to get inside. Teenagers were strolling around the block, shouting out to their friends, looking for news. There were cries—"Kill whitey," "Get whitey"—as well as a lot of talk: awed rumors of dead policemen, reports of other outbreaks on Central Avenue and on 103rd. People were proud as they began to realize the scope and force of what was happening. A woman said, "For the first time in my life, I'm proud to be black."

The looting itself was done with joy but it was no joke. Everybody wanted that food. I remember when two men were carrying a carton of canned goods down the street, people would come up to them: "Come on brother, give me a can of something. Let me have those peaches there. Just one can."

That evening one man looked at me and called out angrily to the people around, "Is that a paddy?" (I'm sort of in-between looking.) I shuddered and answered quickly, "NO, brother!" He said, "Pardon me, brother," but I was sweating like a champ. I began to wonder if this night's excursion might not be the worst mistake I had ever made. What if someone didn't give me a chance to say "NO, brother"? I walked over to find Larry, who was a lot darker than me, and I never got very far away from him for the rest of the evening.

The crowd swirled further south on Avalon to a liquor store that was still open, its lights on. They called for the clerk to come out: "Don't work for the white man, baby. Join us." He didn't come out. Rocks went through the glass front, then a broken-off stop sign, finally a trash can. The clerk stayed inside while the crowd begged him to come out. Then people pulled back as someone shouted, "He's got a gun!" Finally the clerk made it out the back door and everyone rushed in through and over the broken glass. There was pandemonium inside the store but it was cleaned out in minutes, first the money, then the hard liquor, then the wine. Someone standing outside called out, "Goddamn it, Louis, don't be choicy." My friends were very choicy. They stayed in for several minutes and came out with a hand-picked selection of Chivas Regal and other high-ticket merchandise.

We were walking up Avalon again toward Imperial when the police—30 or 40 of them—finally made a flying raid down the street. The crowd disappeared immediately. I found it hard to run holding the four fifths and a pint of Chivas Regal that I was supposed to carry. I remember a series of back yards, holes in fences, thorny bushes, as well as some fancy dodging to get back across the perimeter. The pint had broken and I could have gotten busted just for the way I smelled. It was late. People were going home to party and to get ready for the next day.

On Friday we didn't have to travel. The rebellion spread to N-VAC's neighborhood on Central Avenue near 41st. Fires were burning all the way down Central. A clothing store on the corner three doors from us was broken into and persons of all ages were coming out of it loaded to the eyes with suits, shirts, hats and shoes. A few drove cars up and loaded them. There was the usual rush and flying glass but people were still choicy by and large. Many looked carefully for the right size, the right style.

Not long after the store had been completely emptied, four unmarked cars, filled with policemen, drove up. They stood with drawn guns around and inside the empty store. At one point, a boy of 14 or 15 came out of what looked like the store next to the looted one. He was unarmed and was carrying nothing. The police made a grab for him; he began running down the sidewalk where I was standing in front of the N-VAC office. The police fired several level shots down the sidewalk after him but fortunately missed him as well as those of us who were standing aghast on the sidewalk between him and the cops. The LAPD had always been free with their guns in the ghetto but this week they seemed to feel they had sanction to shoot people at will. Later I talked to a black cop who had previously been working in Hollywood and who had been a big booster of Chief Parker and his force. After three days' riot duty in Watts, my friend changed his mind. He told me about one man who was killed because he didn't raise his hands fast enough. And he told me that on one occasion he had been sitting in a temporary command post and heard two cops approaching who hadn't yet seen him sitting there. They were taking turns bragging about the niggers they had shot.

That evening we received word at the N-VAC office that a man was badly injured near 46th and Central and was getting no medical aid. Clay Carson, Robert Hall and I took a first aid kit and began walking down Central. We got past policemen by showing our N-VAC cards and explaining what we were doing. When we arrived at 46th the man was gone, so we started back to the office. A policeman stopped us. We explained our errand but he said he didn't give a shit what we were doing; he waved his billy club and told us to turn back. There was no point arguing. People were getting shot for less. So we immediately turned around and began walking away. The cop decided to get us anyway. He clubbed Clay on the back of the neck and hit me on the spine and on the back of my leg. I was knocked down toward the sidewalk, which was covered with broken glass, but managed to lurch forward and keep moving.

We finally got back to the N-VAC office and found that a young friend, Danny Grant, had run into similar trouble on Central. The cops had called him "nigger" and "asshole" and had knocked him down and beat him with their nightsticks. When we saw Danny, his shirt was half-covered with blood and he was still bleeding from his forehead and mouth. We all stood around in front of the office comparing notes and got hosed down—accidentally, I guess—by firemen who were trying to put out a fire in the store on the corner.

That night I got to bed at about four in the morning. It had been a hell of a day. I was exhausted but unable to sleep. Instead I lay there, thinking about cops, and let my mind go. Sometime close to dawn I caught myself in a little fantasy about how you would go about killing every cop in Los Angeles. It was a lurid trip: snipers, phony calls for help, howitzers and so on. I *caught* myself, you understand. I'm nonviolent. I wouldn't even step on a cop's toe. But here I was on a mass murder trip. Then I thought about the previous two years. Cops had dragged me around, called me all sorts of nasty names, strangled me, kicked me in the nuts, lied me into jail—and now today I'd gotten clubbed and nearly shot. And I thought: yet and still, I've had it easy. How do you feel when you've had it worse? And what if you're not nonviolent—what if you take violence for granted? What if you don't have that whole middle-class professional bag going for you? Then how do you feel about those uniformed thugs that occupy your community. Shit . . . most Americans can dig violence. In fact, they can even dig killing people they've never seen and don't know a damn thing about. They can say, "Oh boy, we wiped out 178 VC"—halfway around the world—and then those fools want to know why people are rioting in Watts.

I think it was Friday night that the Guard started to move in. I remember sitting in Celes King's bail bond office in the evening when they ran their Operation Clean Sweep down Central Avenue. There was a big loudspeaker telling everybody to get inside. Then there was a sort of parade that followed: some vehicles but mostly men marching with fixed bayonets. Someone was on the phone trying to keep track of the various N-VAC members. Celes and Robert Hall were in back having a little taste. The blinds were shut tight but several of us were curious and opened one slat a little to see what was happening. After a moment one soldier noticed the light and wheeled around, shouting and jabbing his bayonet toward the window. So we gave that up and I went back to join Robert and Celes.

Later, Woodrow called from Watts where there was still a lot of burning and looting going on. Parked cars had been overturned and set on fire. A good stretch of 103rd was going up in flames. Fastidious Woodrow had made his way through the broken glass into one drugstore but left emptyhanded when he found they were out of Viceroys.

The next afternoon we all got a better look when the National Guard made another sweep down Central. We kept inside the doorway of the N-VAC office—all except Danny Gray who walked out to hassle the Guard captain about something chickenshit the captain had called out to us. Danny kept his hands behind his head so that the Guard would have no excuse to shoot him and so that if they did, we would have a stronger case against them. Later, framed in the doorway, the troops marching down Central were like a newsreel of some army marching into a conquered city, with all its inhabitants off the street, peering out behind curtains and blinds. How weird. American GI's moving in . . . on us. We were Americans. Weren't we supposed to be out there in uniform, riding on tanks, taking snapshots, and passing out chewing gum and chocolate bars?

Sunday I left Central Avenue to represent N-VAC at a meeting that Governor Pat Brown had called with "Negro Leaders." N-VAC—a nonviolent group but still, in 1965, regarded as hotheaded militants—N-VAC hadn't been invited by the more respectable Negro Leaders who had arranged this meeting. But we decided to send somebody anyway.

The State Building was mostly empty. Out in front in the hot August sunlight were 30 or 40 suited and vested ministers, doctors, lawyers and political figures, who stood around chatting in quiet tones until the governor arrived. Then we were shown upstairs and through a series of rooms into a large elegant salon with a fireplace and soft carpeting. It was a hell of a room; everything in it murmured "dignity" and "responsibility." Governor Brown's in-person entrance and his attitude of casual good fellowship mellowed the atmosphere even more. We were a long way from Watts. And the governor, he treated us real good.

He spoke for a while. Let us know that he was on our side. But he also confided in us about some of his political problems—let us right into the picture. All about him and Mayor Yorty and Chief Parker and the Chandlers, who publish the *L.A. Times*. He seemed to be setting us up as "political realists" and almost everyone appeared willing to take on the role. Then, after a while, Brown explained that he hadn't come to make speeches and that he wanted to hear what we had to say.

The first speaker, Reverend Brookins, began with a graceful encomium on Governor Brown as Friend of the Negro. Then he briefly explained that "we" were asking for a blue-ribbon commission to investigate the situation. Brown in turn asked for suggestions for a chairman. A number of white men were named. One, I remember, was Dean Acheson. Brown said that he himself had been thinking of Stanley (Mosk). John A. McCone's name, incidentally, did not occur to anyone.

A little later Louis Lomax took the floor and talked about the need for emergency food distribution, since stores were either shut down or burnt out. Then a series of reverends spoke about the need for Brown to call upon all men of good will to work together to solve this tragic problem that had beset us all. This Brown was more than willing to do. Actually, he was being put on as much as we were. The Negro Leaders arrayed there were very reassuring, smiling urbanely, conveying no sense of urgency, prescribing good will instead of tea and toast, and a blue-ribbon commission instead of fruit juices and lots of rest.

There was, however, one point when Brown showed some uncertainty about the advice he was getting. He asked, almost abruptly, if appointing a blue-ribbon commission would stop the rioting. There was an awkward pause. I jumped up without being called on and blurted out some of what I had seen and heard. I said that if Brown really wanted to reach the rioters, he would have to do it by some meaningful action— like trying to put a leash on the LAPD. I suggested that announcing a state attorney general's investigation of LAPD practices in the past and during the riot might—just might— have some meaning to the people who were rioting.

Naturally, the governor didn't disagree. He just didn't agree. He was amiable; in fact, he seemed to know something about the cop problem in L.A.'s ghettos. But he made no secret of his reluctance to antagonize the vast Los Angeles electorate, so thoroughly brainwashed by Yorty, Chief Parker and the Chandlers. It would have taken courage for Brown to go after the police. And that was clearly too much for "political realists" to ask.

The next day N-VAC started distributing food that we and CORE and other groups had collected all over the city. We turned the office into a small grocery store and gave away food all day to huge crowds of people who waited, sometimes for hours, in a line that often went halfway around the block.

The cops were busting people who had merchandise without a sales slip so we had to give out special slips with every bag of groceries. The police were getting really bad. One teenage girl working in the office borrowed my portable radio to listen to as she ran an errand down the street. She got stopped by a carload of shotgun-wielding cops who wanted to see the sales slip for the radio—which, incidentally, was weathered, cracked and had a broken antenna. They were taking her into custody for looting and she was in hysterics and unable to explain herself coherently when Danny Gray happened by. He recognized the girl and also my radio. So he ran back and got me and we went back to identify the radio. At that point they turned the girl loose and asked me where I got it. I said "At The Akron, six months ago." They demanded to see the sales slip. I agreed that it was certainly wise to carry sales slips for all of your possessions in case there might ever be a riot and you got stopped for looting but that, nonetheless, I didn't have one. Eventually, Danny and I managed to keep me from getting busted.

Back at the office the food was going out faster than it came in and there would be long waits and lengthening lines while people were out hustling donations. Some of it came from individuals; some of it came from supermarkets, bakeries and dairies which had developed a sudden interest in creating good will in the black ghetto.

Even after the local markets were open again, we managed to keep the food thing going for a few days. It was great—a kind of organized, legal looting. White housewives, bread companies and markets got rid of some surplus, and raggedy Central Avenue had a temporary windfall. Even when stores began to open, the lines didn't diminish—although the supply did. For mothers on welfare, for men out of work, it was still worth it to stand in the August heat for two hours on the chance of getting a free carton of milk or a loaf of bread.

Downtown, the governor's blue-ribbon commission was forming to investigate why black people would want to riot in Los Angeles.

from The Student as Nigger (1969)

Deacons for Defense

by Hamilton Bims

In Jonesboro, La., one day, Ernest Thomas stood on a hot street corner and watched the Ku Klux Klan parade through town. He stared in amazement as column after column marched by—escorted by police.

Down at Bogalusa, some months later, a steely-eyed trooper watched another kind of demonstration—Negro pickets before a downtown store. Contemplating his billy, he whispered cryptically to a companion, "A nigger's got the hardest head in the world, man."

These two vignettes from the land of the pine trees and bayous are about as good an example as any of the double standard of Louisiana law enforcement. Negroes have become increasingly aware that their fight against racial injustice includes not one, but two foes: white reactionaries and police. As Thomas later put it, "I figured if the power structure would do that for the Klan, we'd better do something for ourselves."

Thomas called a meeting of Jonesboro's Negro males, including several church deacons. They obtained a state charter, bought weapons, ammunition and citizen band radios, and vowed to shoot back at any terrorists threatening their homes. "When a carload of whites would come in," Thomas recounts, "one of the cars would pick it up and follow it through the quarters. Usually, when they knew they were under surveillance, they'd just go on through and not stop." Within months, he claims, harassment had ceased.

In the year or so since, their organization—the Deacons for Defense and Justice—has become one of the strangest, most controversial elements in the civil rights struggle. It is also one of the fastest growing, with a reported 50 to 60 chapters across Louisiana, Mississippi and Alabama. Early this year the group—which has several times lived up to its vow—moved into the most explosive city in the South today, Klan-infested Bogalusa.

Led by bluff, balding Charles Sims, a 41-year-old former insurance man, the Bogalusa Deacons are reportedly armed with pistols, rifles, shotguns and even hand grenades. The actual size of their arsenal is unknown, but a local woman who knows them recounted this experience about two months ago:

"A fellow I know asked me to deliver a package for him to the other side of town. I agreed. They drove this pick-up around the back of a house and about six men started loading it. I saw pistols, rifles, all kind of stuff. It took about ten minutes to get it all on the truck. It was all kind of scary."

In addition to their weapons, the Deacons have walkie-talkies for instant communication, a fleet of ever-ready cars and a membership rumored to include about a tenth of the Negro adult male population (some 9,000 of Bogalusa's 23,000 residents are Negroes).

Sims doesn't like to talk statistics, but he is openly proud of the Deacons' numerical strength. "We don't even have to recruit," he says. "A man who knows he is black and knows he lives in Bogalusa usually knows what to do about it. He comes to us."

The most interesting facet of the Deacons' story, however, and one which has spurred national controversy, has been their strange relationship with CORE and its local affiliate, the Bogalusa Civic and Voters' League.

Cruising through a lily-white area of town one day, A. Z. Young, the League's president, scoffed at charges that the Deacons are a potential liability to civil rights. "If it wasn't for them, I wouldn't have the nerve to be driving around right now. People who say they are destructive seem to forget that they are protecting lives here."

James Farmer, CORE's national director, said during a recent visit to Bogalusa: "I'm glad the Deacons exist. I know that some are comparing them to the Ku Klux Klan. But how many lynchings have they committed? How many homes have they burned—how many churches? The Deacons are not night riders, and anyone who likens them to the Klan is simply evading the issue."

Actually, townsmen consider the Deacons a *deterrent* to

violence in Bogalusa. For one thing, their very existence forces white troublemakers to think twice. For another, by giving the job to mature and restrained men, they discourage Negro hotheads, who otherwise might trigger a racial bloodbath in the tense city. Deacons themselves who prove unfit are dismissed from the organization. "They don't fool around with the wild ones," insists a local housewife.

Before one demonstration, Sims, a grizzled, forbidding man, usually unshaven, climbed to the podium with an icy warning. "I want you to leave your pistols, your knives, your hammers at home," he growled. "Leave the protecting to us. That's our job."

Many outsiders fail to realize, too, just how professional a group the Deacons really are. "They're highly organized," says John Hamilton, a 19-year-old CORE worker from Los Angeles. "Recently, one of our people was reported missing. Within minutes the Deacons had not only found him but delivered him to us."

For all their effectiveness, however, the Deacons have become perhaps the most criticized, and feared, Negro organization since the Black Muslims. Dr. Martin Luther King has complained of their tendency "toward aggressive violence." In a recent trip to Los Angeles, Sims himself was attacked on local television.

"This may be a necessary part of the Negro revolution," said Don Smith of Los Angeles' CORE chapter, "but philosophically I am opposed to all forms of violence, no matter who preaches it." Added the Rev. Thomas Kilgore, head of the Western Christian Leadership Conference: "I disapprove of keeping civil rights workers alive with guns. The Bogalusa movement, under the Deacons—a misnomer—represents a danger to 20 million Negroes."

Why are Bogalusa's vigilantes—only one of numerous Negro gun clubs in America—being viewed with such special apprehension? For one thing, the city in which they operate is unlike any civil rights arena yet brought before the nation. "It's common knowledge that Bogalusa has more Klansmen per capita than any other city of the South," says one observer, and Negroes believe the terrorists have even infiltrated the police department.

In addition, Bogalusa, home of the world's largest paper mill (a unit of Crown Zellerbach Corp.), has attracted more than its share of rednecks. These are wretched, desperate people who feel menaced by Negro demands for equal hiring. They are easily swayed by agitators, one of whom, the Rev. Connie Lynch of the National States' Rights Party, recently told them: "We're gonna clean the niggers out of these streets . . . That means bashing heads or anything else it takes. There's lots of trees around here and we don't mind hangin' 'em . . ."

Fired by tirades like this and unrestrained by local police, Bogalusa's whites have embarked on a campaign of organized terror unparalleled in Louisiana's history.

Early in January, Negroes began testing the public accommodations section of the new civil rights law. CORE's regional bureau in New Orleans reports the following chain of violence and intimidation:

Returning Feb. 3 from a civil rights meeting, two CORE field workers, Bill Yates and Steve Miller, discovered themselves followed by a carload of six whites. A police car assigned to protect them suddenly disappeared, and the workers were chased at high speeds through the Negro area. At an intersection, Yates jumped out and dashed for a restaurant. He was caught by one and beaten severely, suffering a broken hand. The others followed Miller, firing at his car.

Two weeks later, five Negroes sat down at newly integrated Landry's restaurant. Two whites entered with clubs and ordered them to leave. As they departed, one of the Negroes was struck. Later that day a Negro teen-ager entered Landry's. A customer left his seat and put a gun to his head.

On Feb. 28, Robert Hicks, the Voters' League's vice president, and Royan Burris, chairman of its picket committee, strode into the restaurant of the Redwood Hotel. They were refused service, and three minutes later a mob of 20 to 30 whites came looking for them.

In mid-March, Burris returned home from the barber shop he owns. He told CORE he was stopped by Washington Parish (County) K-9 deputies and three city policemen who handcuffed his hands behind his back and drove him to the police station. When he stepped from the car, he says he was slapped and tripped. Once inside, Burris reports, the lawmen formed a circle around him and pushed him from one to the other. Later, when doctors at the city's Community Medical Center learned the cause of his wounds, he says they refused to treat him.

Early in April, as Yates left Hicks' home, three whites pulled up, blocking his truck. One got out with a blackjack. Yates was able to put the truck in reverse and escape. But that night the Klan burned a 10-foot cross and placed two black coffins outside Local 189-A of the United Papermakers and Paperworkers Union (AFL-CIO), the League's headquarters. The coffin bore the names of Yates and Hicks. The next day three carloads of whites shot into Hicks' home.

The following day, April 9, a march to city hall led by Farmer was halted for lack of police protection after a white youth had seized the CORE leader by the shirt, a mob had tried to attack news photographers and a Negro was hospitalized after being struck with a club.

Charles Williams, a Negro, was arrested after a racial altercation. As he entered headquarters, he glanced through a door marked "Private." He reported seeing six men dressed in white robes. One of the costumes was open in front, and Williams claimed he saw a law-enforcement insignia.

One day this writer accompanied about two dozen pickets to Crown Zellerbach. The group, turned away earlier and expecting trouble, made sure to alert police. Upon our arrival, the plant was changing shifts and bands of tough rednecks massed along the sidelines. After some 20 minutes, Elmer Barner, the picket captain, nervously halted the demonstration. Not one policeman had shown up.

The most publicized incident in Bogalusa was the cowardly slaying of O'Neal Moore, one of two Negro deputy sheriffs hired by Washington Parish after pressure. Moore was gunned down from a passing car the night of June 2 as he walked patrol with the other Negro deputy, Creed Rogers. His companion was hospitalized with wounds.

In the wake of such depravity, the Deacons were perhaps inevitable. Likewise their warm reception by the Negro community. "We feel the same about the Deacons as *you'll* feel once you've been here a while," joked Mrs. Valeira Hicks, wife of the League's vice president.

Legally, the Deacons are above board. Article II of the Bill of Rights allows any citizen to bear arms in defense of life and property. Louisiana law also permits ownership of weapons, so long as they are not concealed. As a chartered organization, moreover, the Deacons enjoy the same prestige as any other incorporated movement.

And a measure of their support has been their rapid expansion across the South. Incorporated in March, the Deacons have sent emissaries to practically every trouble spot in the three-state area. In Bogalusa, where Sims already had formed a gun club, they had easy pickings. "We didn't have a charter of our own," explains Sims. "Since getting one would have cost money, we decided to go in with Jonesboro."

Sims, a combat veteran of Europe in World War II, is not surprised at the organization's growth. "The Negro in the South is a brand new breed," he declares. "He's not the same man he was ten years ago."

Ebony, September 1965

Bussing in Boston

by Robert Coles

ON June 15th and 16th, 1964, the last two days of the school year, over two hundred children attending the William Lloyd Garrison School in Boston's Negro section of Roxbury were sent home with notices informing their parents that in September they would be attending the William L. P. Boardman school, also located in Roxbury, but in an area of urban renewal undergoing full-scale demolition and reconstruction. This news surprised and angered many parents who knew all too well the terrain their children would have to cross, and do so only to reach an antiquated, thoroughly inadequate building. A number of them talked to one another and eventually resolved to tell the Garrison School's principal of the fear they had for their children's safety.

Their meeting with the principal was the beginning of a long hassle they were to have with the Boston school system. They were nodded on up the bureaucratic ladder until on July 7th they reached the School Committee itself, in Boston an unsalaried elective office often used as a political launching pad. They reminded the Committee that their children were going to overcrowded schools in a slum area, while thousands of empty seats were available elsewhere in the city. Their complaints were taken "under advisement."

As the opening of school approached about a score of parents decided to meet in a home to consider their coming alternatives. Some talked of refusing to enroll the children at the Boardman school. Others wanted to send their children out of Roxbury, but did not know how it could be done. After much talk they agreed that really the fairest move would be an attempt to re-enroll their children at the Garrison school. It was their children's school; some of them had been going to it for 5 years; they would try to keep them there. They were unanimous in rejecting the Boardman school as an alternative.

Their effort failed. They were denied registration by the teachers who were enrolling children in the school auditorium. When the parents refused to leave, the teachers did, taking their records with them. The parents became enraged, and soon their anger turned into a stubborn determination to stay put. Each day they brought their children to the auditorium. The children were divided into small groups, supervised by parents and taught by volunteers hastily assembled from all over the city. For 13 days the auditorium housed between 50 and 100 children divided into several day-long classes.

The parents were not only "sitting-in" with their children, and appealing for volunteers—from students to housewives—to educate them; in mid-July they had sought an injunction to close the Boardman school. Though it was not granted, a hearing was set for September 14th, four days after school opened. On October 1st the hearing in Boston's Superior Court was concluded. The Boardman school was judged safe, the area around it not unduly hazardous for the entry of children. By this time, however, the entire metropolitan region had an opportunity to see, on the front pages of the newspapers and on television, pictures of the school building and its surrounding acreage of fallen timbers, bricks, shattered glass, and building machines.

Perhaps more significant, the public could see the faces of quite poor, quite ordinary Negro mothers and fathers aroused by one insult, one gratuitous act of inconsideration too many. "Why do they always push us around?" a mother asked shyly yet with insistence. "They move our children out of their school, and tell us the last minute, and then we're supposed to take them over to the new school where they can't even hear themselves think, the machines are making so much noise. And there's glass all over to fall and cut yourself, and you practically have to make a path through the mess of the old buildings. And to tell the truth, why didn't they tear down that Boardman school, while they were at it? Did you see what it's like inside? It's dark like the night and everything is old, old, old. I am against this treatment, period." Playing the tape over again, I hear her beginning voice, plaintive and tentative, then the confidence that increased steadily to a final combativeness.

When they learned of the court order and were told they might be arrested for "aiding and abetting truancy" the parents decided upon another tactic. For many decades Boston has had an "open enrollment policy," whereby any child in the city may attend any school outside his neighborhood, provided there are empty seats to be had where he wants to go. They resolved to take advantage of that law and send their children out of Roxbury altogether to the Peter Faneuil school, clear across the city at the foot of Beacon Hill. Though at first they met as parents confronted with a shared affront to themselves and their children, they had slowly come to know and rely upon one another. I suppose to get categorical about it they had become "a group," a "community-action oriented" one at that.

Thus drawn together, they chose to keep their children so by sending them on a bus. They were by then calling themselves "The Boardman Parents Group." They elected a chairman, a recording secretary and a treasurer. They agreed upon meetings twice a month at different homes or church centers to discuss such issues as finances, transportation, and the progress of their children's education. Of course in the first place they had to raise money to rent a bus and to obtain a driver for it. With the help of local ministers, civic organizations and civil rights groups they managed to get enough for the first weeks, so that by early October they had ventured across the city, enrolled their children in the Faneuil school, sought out a bus driver, learned where they could rent a bus and done that, arranged the details of parking the bus, and set the time and place of its afternoon departure. For poor people, many of the men jobless, the women on relief, a good number without high school degrees, to accomplish such tasks so quickly and efficiently came frankly as a surprise to me. From the start I had watched them come together, then settle down to work. Once again—it has constantly happened to me—I found myself learning as much about my own prejudices and misconceptions as anything else. These people had guts; they had more initiative and perseverance than I expected. A crisis had brought them together, enabling dormant strengths in them to appear, furnishing a direction for their energies and hopes.

I had studied the psychological adjustment of white and Negro Southern families to desegregation, and with this event in Boston embarked upon a similar study in the North, where the issues of de facto segregation and the attempt to end it by bussing children are becoming as universally difficult and touchy as any racial controversy in the South. All last year I rode the bus with the children, also visiting them and their parents at home. (I have just begun doing so again this year.) As in the South, I am trying to find out not only how Negro children from the ghetto get along in the all white or nearly all white schools to which they are bussed, but how white children and teachers come to terms with children whom one blonde six-year-old girl described as "the colored visitors from way over far where we don't go."

We all meet and take our places in the bus between 8:00 and 8:15. The bus driver keeps the bus parked near his home, and drives it each morning to a corner convenient to many of the children. A few have to walk for 10 or 15 minutes to reach the bus, and some others are picked up by the bus on its way to school. The driver is a bright, well-spoken Negro in his fifties; he can be stern yet when necessary kind, the perfect person for the job. The bus carries about 35 of us, more or less from day to day. The children are from six to eleven. Some are neatly and attractively dressed, while others in a glance could be spotted as poor, sorely ignored or rejected at home.

We start in a once prosperous neighborhood, now fast crumbling. Conventional churches have yielded to pente-costal ones. On the first part of the ride we pass by the Board-man school, surrounded by evidence of urban renewal activity, buildings going up or coming down. Sometimes I manage to forget myself and look at the world as the children do, seeing the present reality of decayed tenements and shabby stores. In other moments I cannot banish the comparative memories of my own childhood, when my parents would drive me into Boston along the same route the bus now travels. Then, a quarter of a century ago, the buildings were sound and attractive, the faces of their inhabitants white, the stores new. I told that to a 10-year-old Negro boy one day as we rode along and he replied: "Cities must be like dogs, they live faster and they die before you know it."

In the middle of the trip we plunge into Boston's South End, often riding under the dark, noisy shelter of still-used elevated railroad tracks. Even though it is early in the morning, the skid row derelicts are out, the sidewalks full of sad, dazed and lonely people. The alleyways visible to us reveal the city's worst slums—buildings done for, streets littered, stray dogs and cats as invariable as the garbage they attend. "Why doesn't the city clean these places the way they do the ones that have the hotels on them?" a boy asked his friend one day as we left the ghetto, crossed over the Massachusetts Turnpike and rode through the elegance—fading or mellow, depending upon your point of view—of Back Bay.

The children came to know the Beacon Hill area well during the year. For one thing, their school was located at the foot of the hill. Yet, before the bus reached its destination we invariably moved along the foot of the hill in heavy traffic, so that the sight of antique shops and fancy food stores, the stylish restaurants, bars and houses could all be taken in. The children did so, too, beyond a doubt. I wondered for a while whether they were too absorbed in themselves, in the fun and games they generated inside the bus, to see what was about us as we drove on. A child would bring me up short by commenting on a change of display in a store, a new billboard sign, a bed of flowers in fresh bloom. Or there would be questions: why the doorman in a hotel, or the prevalence of strange small cars unlike any they had ever seen? Almost all the children, I eventually learned, had never before been out of the ghetto, and their curiosity about the rest of the city to this day has not been sated. Indeed, by the time our bus pulls up near their school its eager passengers have already had a rather extensive lesson in urban sociology.

How have they managed their more proper education, embarked upon for the first time with white children? I am right in the middle of my work with these children and some of their white classmates; thus only more observation over the coming months will reveal how these children consolidate— or fail to—the psychological and educational experience of school desegregation. On the other hand, after a year, it must be said that these children are studying as they never have before. They are showing enormous pride in their studies and generally doing excellent work. Many of them have markedly improved their grades, and their earnest, dutiful willingness to do "homework," even seek out extra instruction from volunteer college students has surprised their parents. "My son has gone through a personality change; he has become a fire-ball professor," the mother of a nine-year-old boy observed.

Moreover, the Negro children have come to know white children for the first time, and the Negro and white parents have met at school meetings. Much of what I am now seeing in the children of both races is quite similar to what I saw in the elementary schools of New Orleans: Once again I hear Negro boys and girls express both their desire to be friendly with white children and their fear of them, and once again I hear white children speak the prejudices of their parents, then go on to reveal their own, contradictory friendliness with one or another Negro classmate.

There can be no question that in a year's time the children of the two races have come closer together. When our bus first came in the morning and pulled away in the afternoon the white children watched silently if with evident curiosity. As time wore down distrust, fear or plain shyness, friendships developed that ignored race and toward the end of the year white children would wait for the bus in the morning and escort Negro children to it in the afternoon. They also spoke their envy to the Negroes: "I wish I could get a ride like you do every day," said a girl who lived a block from the school to a Negro girl. The white girl was promptly invited to ride back to Roxbury one afternoon by a girl somewhat ashamed of her home, but proud of her bus. Whatever the academic achievement of these Negro children proves to be, the social and psychological confidence gained in one year by crossing the city on a bus is obvious.

Moreover, with each month's observation of white children I realize how critically important it is to understand *their* moods and attitudes. We sometimes forget that for our children the civil rights struggle has an immediacy, a fresh relevance, hard for older people to comprehend. Just as Negro children all over the country have defied their parents to participate in demonstrations, many white children are ready to stake out their unique generational claim to the solution of the civil rights problem. A white boy I am now interviewing put it this way: "My mother said when she was in school the Negroes were all in the South End; but now they're coming everywhere in the city, so it's different; and she asks me what's happening at school, and I tell her not to worry, we know how to behave."

The issue of bussing figures all over the North in the Negro's struggle to end his apartness from the rest of the nation's life. It is ironic that bussing, once considered by educators a valuable way to consolidate and strengthen rural school districts, now emerges as a bitterly fought source of "harm" in the cities. Some 400,000 children are bussed annually in Massachusetts simply that they may go to the school they desire, or the nearest one available. In Boston many children were routinely bussed last year at city expense for one or another administrative or educational reason. Yet, when Negro parents in Boston show how terribly overcrowded their children's schools are, and request that they be carried elsewhere, to undercrowded schools, they are told that bussing is educationally harmful, some even say hurtful to the child's health. "In the South they just say they don't want us," one Negro mother recently told me, "but up here they give us that lie about how worried they are for our children to take the bus when they can just walk around the corner and be packed in a sardine can. I'll take Georgia. It's more honest."

She is not, however, going back to Georgia, though what she is doing in many ways reminds me of what many Negroes are doing in Georgia. She is becoming stubbornly and even feverishly involved in making sure that her children have a life markedly different from any their ancestors have known. When the Boston schools opened this year the results of her activity, of activity on the part of many others like her, were rather strikingly apparent. During the summer these parents met repeatedly. They talked of the coming year, and explored ways of again raising money. They also talked to friends, relatives, and neighbors, spreading the word of their own success —they are unabashedly proud of it—and their children's new sense of purpose. Working alongside them have been college students, youths with impressive day in and day out dedication. (Some picture these students as impulsively responsive to such circumscribed "dramatic" situations as a week in Selma or a summer in Mississippi, ignoring long months of patient, thoughtful neighborhood work put out by many of them—the tutoring by undergraduates, the advice by medical students, the legal aid by young lawyers, the help, encouragement and example furnished by divinity students scornful of old pieties and hungry for a faith that is relevant.)

By late August it was clear that a major crisis was facing the city, as the School Committee refused to support its own Superintendent's wish to bus some 500 Negro children to white schools outside the ghetto. (As we in the South saw again and again, it takes blind and stupid opposition sometimes to achieve change. Bull Connor of Birmingham and Sheriff Jim Clark of Selma are two of history's all-time integrationists.) When that happened the outraged Negro community responded quickly. By early September Negro parents in overcrowded schools were encouraged to answer the politicians by following the example of the Boardman Parents. "Organize like we did and get a bus on your own, I must have told it to a million people today," one of them said at a meeting just before school opened. "Operation Exodus" it is now called. On the first day of school hundreds of Negro parents took their children all over the city in buses rented by themselves and their friends, thereby also taking many in the city by surprise and commanding the continuing attention of a wide audience, including state and federal officials.

The Boardman Parents are jubilant at the prospect of their direction being followed. They also have become alarmed. "We had better watch out, or we'll become just like all the other groups of parents. We're a year older than them, and we should keep on our own for a while, because we have different problems from the ones they have. We went through theirs *last year*, and next year we might be able to help them on the things we're facing now." When I heard that I felt like stopping the tape recorder. A chapter in survival was over, and one in leadership about to begin.

The New Republic, October 2, 1965

On the Role of Martin Luther King

by August Meier

THE phenomenon that is Martin Luther King consists of a number of striking paradoxes. The Nobel Prize winner is accepted by the outside world as *the* leader of the nonviolent direct action movement, but he is criticized by many activists within the movement. He is criticized for what appears, at times, as indecisiveness, and more often denounced for a tendency to accept compromise. Yet, in the eyes of most Americans, both black and white, he remains the symbol of militant direct action. So potent is this symbol of King as direct actionist, that a new myth is arising about his historic role. The real credit of developing and projecting the techniques and philosophy of nonviolent direct action in the civil rights arena must be given to the Congress of Racial Equality which was founded in 1942, more than a dozen years before the Montgomery bus boycott projected King into international fame. And the idea of mass action by Negroes themselves to secure redress of their grievances must, in large part, be ascribed to the vision of A. Philip Randolph, architect of the March on Washington Movement during World War II. Yet, as we were told in Montgomery on March 25, 1965, King and his followers now assert, apparently without serious contradiction, that a new type of civil rights strategy was born at Montgomery in 1955 under King's auspices.

In a movement in which respect is accorded in direct proportion to the number of times one has been arrested, King appears to keep the number of times he goes to jail to a minimum. In a movement in which successful leaders are those who share in the hardships of their followers, in the risks they take, in the beatings they receive, in the length of time they spend in jail, King tends to leave prison for other important engagements, rather than remaining there and suffering with his followers. In a movement in which leadership ordinarily

devolves upon persons who mix democratically with their followers, King remains isolated and aloof. In a movement
which prides itself on militancy and "no compromise" with
racial discrimination or with the white "power structure,"
King maintains close relationships with, and appears to be in
fluenced by, Democratic presidents and their emissaries, seems
amenable to compromises considered by some half a loaf or
less, and often appears willing to postpone or avoid a direct
confrontation in the streets.

King's career has been characterized by failures that, in the
larger sense, must be accounted triumphs. The buses in
Montgomery were desegregated only after lengthy judicial
proceedings conducted by the NAACP Legal Defense Fund
secured a favorable decision from the U.S. Supreme Court.
Nevertheless, the events in Montgomery were a triumph for
direct action, and gave this tactic a popularity unknown when
identified solely with CORE. King's subsequent major campaigns—in Albany, Georgia; in Danville, Virginia; in Birmingham, Alabama; and in St. Augustine, Florida—ended as
failures or with only token accomplishments in those cities.
But each of them, chiefly because of his presence, dramatically
focused national and international attention on the plight of
the Southern Negro, thereby facilitating overall progress. In
Birmingham, in particular, demonstrations which fell short of
their local goals were directly responsible for a major Federal
Civil Rights Act. Essentially, this pattern of local failure and
national victory was recently enacted at Selma, Alabama.

King is ideologically committed to disobeying unjust laws
and court orders, in the Gandhian tradition, but generally he
follows a policy of not disobeying Federal Court orders. In
his recent Montgomery speech, he expressed a crude, neo-
Marxist interpretation of history romanticizing the Populist
movement as a genuine union of black and white common
people, ascribing race prejudice to capitalists playing white
workers against black. Yet, in practice, he is amenable to compromise with the white bourgeois political and economic Establishment. More important, King enunciates a superficial
and eclectic philosophy and by virtue of it he has profoundly
awakened the moral conscience of America.

In short, King can be described as a "Conservative Militant."

*

In this combination of militancy with conservatism and caution, of righteousness with respectability, lies the secret of King's enormous success.

Certain important civil rights leaders have dismissed King's position as the product of publicity generated by the mass communications media. But this can be said of the successes of the civil rights nonviolent action movement generally. Without publicity it is hard to conceive that much progress would have been made. In fact, contrary to the official nonviolent direct action philosophy, demonstrations have secured their results, not by changing the hearts of the oppressors through a display of nonviolent love, but through the national and international pressures generated by the publicity arising from mass arrests and incidents of violence. And no one has employed this strategy of securing publicity through mass arrests and precipitating violence from white hoodlums and law enforcement officers more than King himself. King abhors violence; as at Selma, for example, he constantly retreats from situations that might result in the deaths of his followers. But he is precisely most successful when, contrary to his deepest wishes, his demonstrations precipitate violence from Southern whites against Negro and white demonstrators. We need only cite Birmingham and Selma to illustrate this point.

Publicity alone does not explain the durability of King's image, or why he remains for the rank and file of whites and blacks alike, the symbol of the direct action movement, the nearest thing to a charismatic leader that the civil rights movement has ever had. At the heart of King's continuing influence and popularity are two facts. First, better than anyone else, he articulates the aspirations of Negroes who respond to the cadence of his addresses, his religious phraseology and manner of speaking, and the vision of his dream for them and for America. King has intuitively adopted the style of the old fashioned Negro Baptist preacher and transformed it into a new art form; he has, indeed, restored oratory to its place among the arts. Second, he communicates Negro aspirations to white America more effectively than anyone else. His religious terminology and manipulation of the Christian symbols of love and non-resistance are partly responsible for his appeal among whites. To talk in terms of Christianity, love, nonviolence is reassuring to the mentality of white America. At the same time, the very superficialities of his philosophy—that rich and eclectic amalgam of Jesus, Hegel, Gandhi and others as outlined in his *Stride Toward Freedom*—makes him appear intellectually profound to the superficially educated middle class white American. Actually, if he were a more profound religious thinker, like Tillich or Niebuhr, his influence would of necessity be limited to a select audience. But by uttering moral cliches, the Christian pieties, in a magnificent display of oratory, King becomes enormously effective.

If his success with Negroes is largely due to the style of his utterance, his success with whites is a much more complicated matter. For one thing, he unerringly knows how to exploit to maximum effectiveness their growing feeling of guilt. King, of course, is not unique in attaining fame and popularity among whites through playing upon their guilt feelings. James Baldwin is the most conspicuous example of a man who has achieved success with this formula. The incredible fascination which the Black Muslims have for white people, and the posthumous near-sanctification of Malcolm X by many naive whites (in addition to many Negroes whose motivations are, of course, very different), must in large part be attributed to the same source. But King goes beyond this. With intuitive, but extraordinary skill, he not only castigates whites for their sins but, in contrast to angry young writers like Baldwin, he explicitly states his belief in their salvation. Not only will direct action bring fulfillment of the "American Dream" to Negroes but the Negroes' use of direct action will help whites to live up to their Christian and democratic values; it will purify, cleanse and heal the sickness in white society. Whites will benefit as well as Negroes. He has faith that the white man will redeem himself. Negroes must not hate whites, but love them. In this manner, King first arouses the guilt feelings of whites and then relieves them—though always leaving the lingering feeling in his white listeners that they should support his nonviolent crusade. Like a Greek tragedy, King's performance provides an extraordinary catharsis for the white listener.

King thus gives white men the feeling that he is their good friend, that he poses no threat to them. It is interesting to note that this was the same feeling white men received from Booker T. Washington, the noted early 20th Century accommodator. Both men stressed their faith in the white man; both expressed the belief that the white man could be brought to accord Negroes their rights. Both stressed the importance of whites recognizing the rights of Negroes for the moral health and well-being of white society. Like King, Washington had an extraordinary following among whites. Like King, Washington symbolized for most whites the whole program of Negro advancement. While there are important similarities in the functioning of both men vis-a-vis the community, needless to say, in most respects, their philosophies are in disagreement.

It is not surprising, therefore, to find that King is the recipient of contributions from organizations and individuals who fail to eradicate evidence of prejudice in their own backyards. For example, certain liberal trade union leaders who are philosophically committed to full racial equality, who feel the need to identify their organizations with the cause of militant civil rights, although they are unable to defeat racist elements in their unions, contribute hundreds of thousands of dollars to King's Southern Christian Leadership Conference (SCLC). One might attribute this phenomenon to the fact that SCLC works in the South rather than the North, but this is true also for SNCC which does not benefit similarly from union treasuries. And the fact is that ever since the college students started their sit-ins in 1960, it is SNCC which has been the real spearhead of direct action in most of the South, and has performed the lion's share of work in local communities, while SCLC has received most of the publicity and most of the money. However, while King provides a verbal catharsis for whites, leaving them feeling purified and comfortable, SNCC's uncompromising militancy makes whites feel less comfortable and less beneficent.

(The above is not to suggest that SNCC and SCLC are responsible for all, or nearly all, the direct action in the South. The NAACP has actively engaged in direct action, especially in Savannah under the leadership of W. W. Law, in South Carolina under I. DeQuincy Newman, and in Clarksdale, Mississippi, under Aaron Henry. The work of CORE—including most of the direct action in Louisiana, much of the nonviolent work in Florida and Mississippi, the famous Freedom Ride of 1961—has been most important. In addition, one should note the work of SCLC affiliates, such as those in Lynchburg, Virginia, led by Reverend Virgil Wood; in Birmingham led by Reverend Fred Shuttlesworth, and in Savannah, by Hosea Williams.

(There are other reasons for SNCC's lesser popularity with whites than King's. These are connected with the great changes that have occurred in SNCC since it was founded in 1960, changes reflected in the half-jocular epigram circulating in SNCC circles that the Student Nonviolent Coordinating Committee has now become the "Non-Student Violent Non-Coordinating Committee." The point is, however, that even when SNCC thrilled the nation in 1960–1961 with the student sit-ins that swept the South, it did not enjoy the popularity and financial support accorded to King.)

King's very tendencies toward compromise and caution, his willingness to negotiate and bargain with White House emissaries, his hesitancy to risk the precipitation of mass violence upon demonstrators, further endear him to whites. He appears to them a "responsible" and "moderate" man. To militant activists, King's failure to march past the State Police on that famous Tuesday morning outside Selma indicated either a lack of courage, or a desire to advance himself by currying Presidential favor. But King's shrinking from a possible bloodbath, his accession to the entreaties of the political Establishment, his acceptance of face-saving compromise in this, as in other instances, are fundamental to the particular role he is playing, and essential for achieving and sustaining his image as a leader of heroic moral stature in the eyes of white men. His caution and compromise keep open the channels of communication between the activists and the majority of the white community. In brief: King makes the nonviolent direct action movement respectable.

Of course, many, if not most, activists reject the notion that the movement should be made respectable. Yet, American history shows that for any reform movement to succeed, it must attain respectability. It must attract moderates, even conservatives, to its ranks. The March on Washington made direct action respectable; Selma made it fashionable. More than any other force, it is Martin Luther King who impressed the civil rights revolution on the American conscience and is attracting that great middle body of American public opinion to its support. It is this revolution of conscience that will undoubtedly lead fairly soon to the elimination of all violations of Negroes' constitutional rights, thereby creating the conditions for the economic and social changes that are necessary if we are to achieve full racial equality. This is not to deny the dangers to the civil rights movement in becoming respectable. Respectability, for example, encourages the attempts of political machines to capture civil rights organizations. Respectability can also become an end in itself, thereby dulling the cutting edge of its protest activities. Indeed, the history of the labor movement reveals how attaining respectability can produce loss of original purpose and character. These perils, however, do not contradict the importance of achieving respectability—even a degree of modishness—if racial equality is ever to be realized.

There is another side to the picture: King would be neither respected nor respectable if there were not more militant activists on his left, engaged in more radical forms of direct action. Without CORE and, especially, SNCC, King would appear "radical" and "irresponsible" rather than "moderate" and "respectable."

King occupies a position of strategic importance as the "vital center" within the civil rights movement. Though he has lieutenants who are far more militant and "radical" than he is, SCLC acts, in effect, as the most cautious, deliberate and "conservative" of the direct action groups because of King's leadership. This permits King and the SCLC to function—almost certainly unintentionally—not only as an organ of communication with the Establishment and majority white public opinion, but as something of a bridge between the activist and more traditionalist or "conservative" civil rights groups, as well. For example, it appears unlikely that the Urban League and NAACP, which supplied most of the funds, would have participated in the 1963 March on Washington if King had not done so. Because King agreed to go along with

SNCC and CORE, the NAACP found it mandatory to join if it was to maintain its image as a protest organization. King's identification with the March was also essential for securing the support of large numbers of white clergymen and their moderate followers. The March was the brainchild of the civil rights movement's ablest strategist and tactician, Bayard Rustin, and the call was issued by A. Philip Randolph. But it would have been a minor episode in the history of the civil rights movement without King's support.

Yet, curiously enough, despite his charisma and international reputation, King thus far has been more a symbol than a power in the civil rights movement. Indeed his strength in the movement has derived less from an organizational base than from his symbolic role. Seven or eight years ago, one might have expected King to achieve an organizationally dominant position in the civil rights movement, at least in its direct action wing. The fact is that in the period after the Montgomery bus boycott, King developed no program and, it is generally agreed, revealed himself as an ineffective administrator who failed to capitalize upon his popularity among Negroes. In 1957, he founded SCLC to coordinate the work of direct action groups that had sprung up in Southern cities. Composed of autonomous units, usually led by Baptist ministers, SCLC does not appear to have developed an overall sense of direction or a program of real breadth and scope. Although the leaders of SCLC affiliates became the race leaders in their communities—displacing the established local conservative leadership of teachers, old-line ministers, businessmen—it is hard for an observer (who admittedly has not been close to SCLC) to perceive exactly what SCLC did before the 1960's except to advance the image and personality of King. King appeared not to direct but to float with the tide of militant direct action. For example, King did not supply the initiative for the bus boycott in Montgomery, but was pushed into the leadership by others, as he himself records in *Stride Toward Freedom*. Similarly, in the late Fifties and early Sixties, he appeared to let events shape his course. In the last two years, this has changed, but until the Birmingham demonstrations of 1963, King epitomized conservative militancy.

SCLC under King's leadership called the Raleigh Conference of April 1960 which gave birth to SNCC. Incredibly, within a year, the SNCC youth had lost their faith in the man they now satirically call "De Lawd," and had struck out on their own independent path. By that time, the Spring of 1961, King's power in the Southern direct action movement had been further curtailed by CORE's stunning Freedom Ride to Alabama and Mississippi.

The limited extent of King's actual power in the civil rights movement was illustrated by the efforts made to invest King with the qualities of a Messiah during the recent ceremonies at the State Capitol in Montgomery. Reverend Abernathy's constant iteration of the theme that King is "our Leader," the Moses of the race, chosen by God, and King's claim that he originated the nonviolent direct action movement at Montgomery a decade ago, are all assertions that would have been superfluous if King's power in the movement was very substantial.

It is, of course, no easier today that it has been in the past few years to predict the course of the Negro protest movement, and it is always possible that the current state of affairs may change quite abruptly. It is conceivable that the ambitious program that SCLC is now projecting—both in Southern voter registration and in Northern urban direct action programs—may give it a position of commanding importance in civil rights. As a result of the recent demonstrations in Selma and Montgomery, King's prestige is now higher than ever. At the same time, the nature of CORE and NAACP direct action activities at the moment has created a programmatic vacuum which SCLC may be able to exploit. Given this convergence of circumstances, SCLC leaders may be able to establish an organizational base upon which to build power commensurate with the symbolic position of their president.

It is indeed fortunate that King has not obtained a predominance of power in the movement commensurate with his prestige. For today, as in the past, a diversity of approaches is necessary. Needed in the movement are those who view the struggle chiefly as a conflict situation, in which the power of demonstrations, the power of Negroes, will force recognition of the race's humanity and citizenship rights, and the achievement of equality. Equally needed are those who see the movement's strategy to be chiefly one of capitalizing on the basic consensus of values in American society by awakening the conscience of the white man to the contradiction between his professions and the facts of discrimination. And just as necessary to the movement as both of these are those who operate skillfully, recognizing and yet exploiting the deeply held American belief that compromise among competing interest groups is the best *modus operandi* in public life.

King is unique in that he maintains a delicate balance among all three of these basic strategy assumptions. The traditional approaches of the Urban League (conciliation of the white businessmen) and of the NAACP (most preeminently appeals to the courts and appeals to the sense of fair play in the American public) basically attempted to exploit the consensus in American values. It would of course be a gross oversimplification to say that the Urban League and NAACP strategies are based simply on attempting to capitalize on the consensus of values, while SNCC and CORE act simply as if the situation were purely a conflict situation. Implicit in the actions of all civil rights organizations are both sets of assumptions—even where people are not conscious of the theoretical assumptions under which, in effect, they operate. The NAACP especially encompasses a broad spectrum of strategies and types of activities, ranging from time-tested court procedures to militant direct action. Sophisticated CORE activists know very well when a judicious compromise is necessary or valuable. But I hold that King is in the middle, acting in effect as if he were basing his strategy upon all three assumptions described above. He maintains a delicate balance between a purely moral appeal and a militant display of power. He talks of the power of the bodies of Negro demonstrators in the streets, but unlike CORE and SNCC activists, he accepts compromises at times that consist of token improvements, and calls them impressive victories. More than any of the other groups, King and SCLC can, up to this point at least, be described as exploiting all three tactical assumptions to an approximately equal degree. King's continued success, I suspect, will depend to a considerable degree upon the difficult feat of maintaining his position as the "vital center" of the civil rights movement.

Viewed from another angle, King's failure to achieve a position of power on a level with his prestige is fortunate because rivalries between personalities and organizations remain an essential ingredient of the dynamics of the movement and a precondition for its success as each current tries to outdo the others in effectiveness and in maintaining a good public image. Without this competitive stimulus, the civil rights revolution would slow down.

I have already noted that one of King's functions is to serve as a bridge between the militant and conservative wings of the movement. In addition, by gathering support for SCLC, he generates wider support for CORE and SNCC, as well. The most striking example is the recent series of demonstrations in Selma where SNCC had been operating for nearly two years with only moderate amounts of publicity before King chose that city as his own target. As usual, it was King's presence that focused world attention on Selma. In the course of subsequent events, the rift between King and SNCC assumed the proportions of a serious conflict. Yet people who otherwise would have been hesitant to support SNCC's efforts, even people who had become disillusioned with certain aspects of SNCC's policies during the Mississippi Summer Project of 1964, were drawn to demonstrate in Selma and Montgomery. Moreover, although King received the major share of credit for the demonstrations, it seems likely that in the controversy between King and SNCC, the latter emerged with more power and influence in the civil rights movement than ever before. It is now possible that the Administration will, in the future, regard SNCC as more of a force to be reckoned with than it has heretofore.

Major dailies like the *New York Times* and the *Washington Post*, basically sympathetic to civil rights and racial equality, though more gradualist than the activist organizations, have congratulated the nation upon its good fortune in having a "responsible and moderate" leader like King at the head of the nonviolent action movement (though they overestimate his power and underestimate the symbolic nature of his role).

It would be more appropriate to congratulate the civil rights movement for *its* good fortune in having as its symbolic leader a man like King. The fact that he has more prestige than power; the fact that he not only criticizes whites but explicitly believes in their redemption; his ability to arouse creative tension combined with his inclination to shrink from carrying demonstrations to the point where major bloodshed might result; the intellectual simplicity of his philosophy; his tendency to compromise and exert caution, even his seeming indecisiveness on some occasions; the sparing use he makes of going to or staying in jail himself; his friendship with the man in the White House—all are essential to the role he plays, and invaluable for the success of the movement. It is well, of course, that not all civil rights leaders are cut of the same cloth—that King is unique among them. Like Randolph, who functions very differently, King is really an institution. His most important function, I believe, is that of effectively communicating Negro aspirations to white people, of making nonviolent direct action respectable in the eyes of the white majority. In addition, he functions within the movement by occupying a vital center position between its "conservative" and "radical" wings, by symbolizing direct action and attracting people to participate in it without dominating either the civil rights movement or its activist wing. Viewed in this context, traits that many activists criticize in King actually function not as sources of weakness, but as the foundations of his strength.

New Politics, Winter 1965

And You, Too, Sidney Poitier!

by Calvin C. Hernton

I REMEMBER the first time I went to the movies, or as they called it in those days, the "picture show." One Friday my step-father and my mother took my younger brother and me down the main street in the Negro section of Chattanooga, Tennessee, past pawnshops and liquor stores, poolrooms and beer joints, past hordes of swarthy Negroes leaning on corners and thronging the littered pavement, to where a long line of colored folks stood outside a great crumbling structure with neon signs flashing on and off. Inside, on the screen, a young beautiful woman, dressed in the most elegant gown, who looked like she was not of the colored race, sang "tick-a-tock-tick-a-tock." Another young woman, very brown and somehow motherly looking, cried and sang softly as she hugged a man's shirt while it hung drying on the washline. A very handsome light-skinned man with long straight black hair, wearing a very loose-fitting suit, pranced and glided across the screen while his hair flopped about his head and face, singing "hi-di-hi-di-ho!"

I learned later that one woman was Lena Horne, the other, Ethel Waters, and the man, the indomitable and flamboyant Cab Calloway. They were Negro personalities that down-South colored folks could be and indeed were proud of. It was all so thrilling. But, somehow, some way, even as a child who knew nothing about acting, I felt that something was lacking in their performance. Despite their great singing and dancing and cooing, and definitely despite their prettiness, they did not strike me as being as *real* in what they were doing as, say, the Negroes I had passed that evening on the street. Although I had enjoyed what I had seen, I was left a little confused.

From that time on I made a point of seeing films in which there were Negroes. Eventually I learned the names of the more prominent film personalities: Ralph Cooper, Herb Jeffries, Mantan Moreland, Stepin Fetchit, Canada Lee, Juan

Hernandez, Rochester, Bo-jangles, Noble Sissle, and the rest. All of them entertained me greatly. In fact, that's all most of them were, entertainers. By this I mean they were either clowns and buffoons with big rolling eyes and invariably afraid of haunted houses, or they were maids and butlers and musicians and singers and tap dancers and band leaders. The few who did not conform to the above stereotypes were poor mimics of white gangsters (Ralph Cooper) and white cowboys (Herb Jeffries); or they struck me as "foreign" black men with strange accents (Hernandez and Lee) who had never lived in America, at least not in the America I knew.

By this time I was fully aware of what had perplexed me as a small boy that day my mother had taken me to see *Stormy Weather*. There had been too much artificiality. It was the absence of the *reality* of Negroes as men and the absence of the *reality* of Negroes as *dramatic* individuals, as I knew them to be in everyday life. In too many instances, it was the negation of the Negro's very humanity in terms of the authentic portrayal of his personality as an entire integrity rather than a fractionary dysfunction. The integrated complexity of the Negro's personality never came to bear upon any one or a variety of situations. Only singular aspects of the Negro—his dancing, or musical, comic, religious, bellicose, or sly characteristics, to name a few—were portrayed, as if they represented the whole of his emotional wellspring.

The first film I saw in which the Negro did not appear as a complete- or semi-caricature was *Home of the Brave*, starring James Edwards. At that time the name of James Edwards was unknown and until his appearance I had begun to grow fearful that perhaps Negroes really did lack the capacity for dramatic portrayal. It was as if they had a deep psychological block, stemming from their racial experiences, that prevented them from performing as straight human beings rather than as mere entertainers. But my fear was dispelled or at least mitigated when I saw James Edwards play the role of a Negro soldier in foreign combat who not only became a hero because of his bravery against the enemy, but who also showed manly prowess in regard to the prejudice of his white comrades. James Edwards was not the best actor I had dreamed of. He was a little too stiff and somewhat slow on cues. Yet he played a proud role in which not merely one but many aspects of his personality (as a *human being* who was a Negro) came through. To me this was a definite sign that Negroes were not necessarily inferior performers. It gave me hope that one day, if Negroes fought diligently, America would have to let black men appear on the screen like bonafide actors with complete integrity regarding their humanity and the essential realism of the situations they might portray.

As is evident now, my hope was not without some degree of realization. There is at least one Negro who has pounced on the American screen and, like a jet, has soared to fame and stardom. What is important here is that Sidney Poitier is not an entertainer, not a singer or a comedian or a musician. Rather, he is strictly an *actor*.

When I first saw him on the screen I was shocked, dumbfounded and delighted. I believe it was around 1955, and Poitier starred in a television drama called *A Man Is Ten Feet Tall*. The story was about a Negro dock worker, a foreman as a matter of fact, who befriends a timid and very insecure white worker against the brutes and roughnecks of the dock, and especially against the southern-born, racist head foreman. The head foreman, of course, hates Poitier because of his color. Moreover, he hates him for his manly attitude in that Poitier does not play the usual role of "Uncle Tom." Envying the friendship between Poitier and the timid white worker, the head foreman proceeds to take out his venom on the white worker whom Poitier defends, ultimately, by way of a hook duel in which the foreman unfairly kills Poitier. In the end the timid worker gains courage and avenges Poitier's death first by beating the foreman, and then by breaking the "silent code" of the docks and literally dragging the murderer to the authorities. The play was later made into a movie entitled *Edge of the City*.

Since that movie Poitier has played, always with great skill and dignity, a variety of starring roles, so that he has become, by all standards, one of America's best actors. His winning of the Academy Award indubitably marked a historic occasion in the annals of Hollywood. What is important about all this is not so much that a Negro has finally won an Academy Award —not this alone; rather, it is the fact that Hollywood and the general public (both white and black) have accepted the *kind* of Negro that Poitier characteristically portrays on the screen. First of all, he is *all* Negro. He is black, his features are markedly Negroid, his body is long and regal, his hands are large and dexterous, his hair is rather "nappy," and he has thick, agile lips. In combination these features make Poitier an unusually powerful figure on the screen. Secondly, his style of acting has involved the entire range of Negro behavior and personality characteristics vehicled by what is known as the "method" technique. Invariably, his role interpretations are rugged, bold, and without the slightest suggestion of "Uncle Tomism," which is to say that everything about his projections definitely lets one know Poitier is authentically Negro. He is no caricature, no stereotyped colored man acting out one or several fractionalized aspects of the Negro personality which whites usually demand of black actors.

For instance, in *Edge of the City* we see Poitier as a laborer, a philosopher, a family man, a friend of the underdog, a dreamer, a man of sensibility, and as a person of courage and dignity. These qualities are projected as only a man who has experienced what it is to be a Negro in America can project them. In other words, with reference to "method" acting, Poitier has what, among others, Paul Newman and Rod Steiger have, plus the added ingredient of his *Negritude*. As a Negro, this makes him more convincing than, say, Belafonte or James Edwards, or even Ossie Davis. In fact, Belafonte and Edwards have something about them that smacks of the nice middle-class Negro; and Ossie Davis reminds one of the old, stereotyped Harlem Theatre Guild Negro actor with the booming voice of a pork chop preacher but without much finesse or genius. Perhaps the only other Negro actor who can rival Poitier in terms of power, genius, and the ability to project himself as an authentic and total human force, is William Marshall. But Marshall is so powerful an actor, in physical stature as well as in role projection, that Hollywood, with the exception of playing him as some kind of warrior or gladiator, simply does not know what to do with him. So Marshall is doing much better in Europe where the fear of the authentic Negro is not so much a part of the European cultural dread, and Poitier is more or less left alone to bear the entire burden and glory of portraying the Negro in America as a true and integral human force.

Even when Poitier plays a role such as the one he played in "Something of Value," where he must be somewhat subservient, it is somehow done with dignity and the full impact of a total, however obsequious, human being—in glaring contrast to, say, Archie Moore's stereotyped, lopsided, artificial portrayal of an Uncle-Tom-type Negro in *The Carpetbaggers*, or *Huckleberry Finn*. Of course, Archie Moore is no actor. And it is revealing why Hollywood would choose him and others like him to play such roles as he has been playing. There is nothing wrong with the Negro being portrayed as an Uncle Tom or as any other derogatory generalization, *so long as the human quality of the characterization comes through*. There is rarely anything artificial and dehumanized about Poitier, neither in his performances as they relate to the art of acting nor as they relate to the human reality of the Negro. This is what makes Poitier great. In all that he does, he does himself justice as an actor and does the Negro justice as a human being, except in one regard. This exception is perhaps the most crucial and sensitive area of our lives.

I have stated that the thing that troubled me about most Negroes in movies was that they, for all of their entertainment value, never seemed real in what they were doing in comparison to the way they are in actual life. I said, something was missing. Sidney Poitier does seem, at first scrutiny, very much real. Yet, when one probes deeply into all the films in which he has played, for every coefficient of Negro life as that life is lived in the real world, one discovers something frightening and terrible. There is something systematically missing, the absence of which turns Poitier, no matter how brilliantly he performs, into a caricature of the Negro that is as artificial and dehumanizing, if not more so, as all the other Hollywood vulgar negations of the black man as a complex, integral human being.

I am talking about the absence, in *all* the Poitier movies, of the primeval emotion, and of that deep psyche-physical yearning to mate with the opposite sex. Why can't Sidney Poitier, since he is such a superb actor, make love in the movies?

No amount of argument can convince me that Poitier is incapable of effectively portraying an amorous involvement on the screen. Neither is it reasonable to say that Poitier is the wrong "type" to make love in the movies. After all, as I have pointed out, Poitier and Paul Newman are the same type of actors, and Newman makes love on the screen constantly. Newman is white. And now we are getting close to the problem—Poitier's blackness, his "Negroness."

The fact that Poitier cannot or does not make love in the movies is a manifestation of American racism as it relates to the sexuality of the Negro. Elsewhere I have written that by and large white America conceives of the Negro as sexually vulgar and repulsive; to see a Negro kiss or pet on the screen would send large numbers of white people, throughout the United States, cringing and recoiling in prurient disgust or excitement. It would be too much for the sexual insecurity and anxiety that the majority of American whites have, not only about the Negro, but about themselves as well. Therefore, the black man in mass media, the cinema especially, must be desexed. And by desexing the Negro, America is denying him his manhood, which ultimately means the negation of his very humanity. This is precisely what Hollywood has done and is doing to, ironically (or is it quite naturally?), the only Negro who has won an Academy Award.

Sidney Poitier and Paul Newman, along with Diahann Carroll and Joanne Woodward, were the stars in a movie called *Paris Blues*. As the story goes, Poitier and Newman are jazz musicians in Paris. One night, after their performance they meet a couple of girls outside the supper club. The two couples confront each other and Diahann Carroll, the colored girl, seems to be fascinated by Paul Newman. For a quick moment it appears as if the foursome is going to pair off interracially. Suddenly Miss Carroll, as if something snaps in her or, better yet, as if on cue from the director, rejects Newman and comes on to her black brother, Poitier.

While there are numerous scenes showing Newman and Miss Woodward hugging, petting, kissing, and even lying around in bed together, there are "equivalent" scenes of Poitier and Miss Carroll walking around Paris, stopping here and there, taking in the sights, and *discussing the race problem*. At one "high" point Poitier *actually* gets a chance to touch Miss Carroll's hand. That's all, brother, that's all.

What is so false and artificial about the entire story is that Poitier, a jazz musician, gets involved, no, gets *associated* with a middle-class, nice-nice, sexually rigid Negro woman who is hung-up about living up to some kind of "race pride." And she convinces Poitier to come back "home" and be a "shining knight" for his people. What a joke! Everybody knows, and I do mean everybody, including Hollywood and the NAACP, that no jazz musician is *that* "nice." There are plenty of Negro women like the one portrayed by Miss Carroll, but you will seldom, if ever, find a jazz musician giving one of them a second thought. Yet I know, we all know, why the pairing-off did not happen interracially. It probably would have caused a riot on Broadway and a slaughter in Alabama. In essence, by denying Poitier the right to make love with either of the women, Hollywood endeavored to play up to the fears of white America, on the one hand, and make the Negro "presentable" to black people, on the other. On both accounts they succeeded only in telling the public a lie. And, incidentally, the movie was the lousiest Poitier film I have seen.

In *The Long Ships* Poitier plays a dashing Moorish prince with not only a beautiful wife but an entire pavilion of pretty girls. He is respected throughout his kingdom. He fights well, and people bow down in his presence. He is the dashing black prince! But for all of that, he is more interested in some golden bell than he is in his most attractive and love-starved wife. In one scene the wife actually begs him and pulls on his arm (nothing else) to stay with her, to give her some of his affection. The black prince stands there rigid like a eunuch; he pushes her aside and runs off looking for gold.

On the other hand, Richard Widmark comes from another land and runs amuck with the women of Poitier's court. Widmark, a white man, ultimately seduces the very wife of the black prince, while the black prince is sitting in a tent talking "intrigue" with Widmark's wife.

All of this is so telling. The sexual stereotypes of black and white are completely reversed: the Negro is "impotent," the white man is "virile." It is not beyond imagination that there might have been some Moorish kings who were homosexuals or "faggots," or what have you. But why did Hollywood have to make such a *point* of this? Why, for instance, did they not put less stress on this aspect, or omit it altogether? I assert that it was no accident. While it may not have been consciously deliberate, it represents a pattern, a systematic attempt to castrate Sidney Poitier in the movies. This signifies, insofar as Poitier in the movies must be a symbolic representation of America's concept of the Negro in general, the outright denial of manhood with reference to all black Americans.

The most "immaculate" version of the desexing of Poitier as an actor is, of course, the role which won him the Academy Award. To me *Lilies of the Field* is a pitiful joke. Picture this— here is a tall, regal, young black man in tight white pants that reveal his every muscle, jumping and running around with a group of nuns. (Incidentally, they are foreigners.) He even shows his naked bulging chest. He is *sexy*, nobody can deny that. One need not belabor the twisted psychological subtleties of this movie. Yet I am compelled to point out that white America can let its imagination run wild, secure in the knowledge that nothing can really happen between that sexy black boy and those white nuns.

No doubt, it appears as if I am being unduly critical about all of this. I don't think so. To illustrate further, let's take a movie (or several movies) where there is some amount of affection between a Negro and a woman. I have in mind *The World, the Flesh, and the Devil* in which Harry Belafonte and a white woman find themselves the only two people left on earth after a strange, presumably nuclear catastrophe. After a great deal of beating around the bush, so to speak, it comes out that the two are definitely interested in each other. There is one scene in which Belafonte cuts the woman's hair—a fine symbolic rite. Although the movie smacks of reality (that is, within the limits of the situation), and is a fine piece of filming and story plotting, the feigned affection between Belafonte and the woman is never realized because a third man pops up, a white man. You know what happens then. Nevertheless the story held together all the way through to the end (mainly because of the skillful plotting) where the woman stops the two men from fighting and takes both the white man's hand and Belafonte's, and leads them off to what can be taken for, under the circumstances, a "brighter horizon."

Although *The World, the Flesh, and the Devil* is the best Hollywood film of its kind, I must point out several things about it that I consider important. First of all, throughout the entire movie the woman is the aggressor, which strikes me as unlikely, or at best, seems like a "neat trick." Secondly, Harry Belafonte is a light-skinned Negro; and granted that if a nuclear situation such as this were to happen, it seems statistically improbable, to say the least, that the one Negro to survive would be a light-skinned, sexually timid type with a morality which comes close to that reputed to be of the respectable white middle class. Especially, since Belafonte's occupation in the movie was as a coal miner and a crack electrician.

Let us examine an extreme example of, for want of a better term, "whitewashing" or "Caucasianizing" the Negro in films that deal with or purport to deal with interracial love. The film is *One Potato, Two Potato*, which was praised by most of the critics (of course, the critics are white). As the story goes, there is this lonely and single Negro living in a small northern town. One day he meets this white divorcée at a picnic. As time goes on they keep running into each other and consequently start dating which leads, after a while, to their getting married. Of course, the woman abandons her friends and the Negro's parents do not accept their white daughter-in-law until she gives birth to a mulatto baby.

Bernie Hamilton (the Negro) did a magnificent job of "acting." I have known him personally for years and I barely recognized him. Although he is an extremely handsome, masculine, dynamic, and rugged type of Negro, in that film he was so middle-class, so sissyfied, so desexed that his metamorphosis would have shocked Kafka. He kissed the white woman once, and it was so artificial, so plastic (that's the word, *plastic*) that one wondered why did they bother at all.

The second factor is the woman's first child (a girl) and the white deserter father. One day he turns up looking for his daughter, now that he has "gotten religion" and wants to fulfill his fatherly responsibilities. Racial-sex rage explodes within him when he finds that his former wife and daughter are living with Negroes. Now this man is a "liberal," and he knows (no doubt in his "heart") that he is wrong. Nevertheless he succumbs right there on the wide screen to all the pathological emotions that racists feel about Negro men and white women. He institutes a law suit to gain custody of his daughter, whom he deserted years ago, on the basis of an "unfit" home. The judge in the suit, who is also no doubt a "liberal," admits that the father is wrong. Nevertheless, he takes the child from the people she has come to love and gives her to the deserter father. Pitifully he rationalizes his decision on the "basis" of "what's going to happen to this little white girl when she grows up if she continues to live with Negroes." The thing I want to know is why, if they really wanted to make an honest movie, didn't the moviemakers (who I am sure conceived of their efforts as "liberal") employ some *positive* gimmicks instead of all of the negative ones? The child, for instance, did not have to be a girl, it could have been a boy, and the judge would not have had to worry about the eventual "pollution" of the chastity of a "darling lily."

Finally—and this is the worst cop-out—while Bernie Hamilton is extremely handsome, the white woman's physical appearance does not match his by any stretch of the imagination. This observation is not intended as a personal slander against Barbara Barrie, who is a fine actress and I would imagine, from the human pathos that shines through her face, a very wonderful person. The fact remains, however, that Miss Barrie looked extremely drab, unattractive, and plain in that movie. This satisfies the stereotype that *any* kind of white woman will do for a Negro, and of any kind it is the most unattractive types that will marry "one." If the moviemakers had any desire to be true to what they pretended to be undertaking, why, since at least Bernie Hamilton is so attractive, did they not employ an actress who equaled or surpassed him in physical qualities? Contrary to the reviewers, *One Potato, Two Potato* is a supreme example of subterranean confirmation of the prejudices, anxieties, and fears that out-and-out racists entertain toward love across the color line. It is the double-talking that characterizes too many would-be white liberals.

But why talk only about racists and so-called white liberals? Negroes tend to adhere to the same systematic mode of de-sexing themselves in the cinema just as whites do and just as the American public seems bent on demanding. Of course,

Negroes who do not adhere to the practice of sterilizing themselves in the visual arts are apt to find that their works will lie around unproduced, or, if produced, will be killed at the box office. But when a few Negroes who have independent means still conform to the same protocol as do the white writers and producers, it means that Negroes have sufficiently internalized the racist concept of, among other things, their sexuality and therefore are ashamed of their nature, and are participating in the denial of one of the bascs of their very humanity.

Sidney Poitier does not have the opportunity to act out love emotions even in an all-Negro movie, because, as it were, the Negro author (the late Lorraine Hansberry) of *A Raisin in the Sun* did not choose to emphasize love and tenderness between men and women as vital aspects of Negro life. And where these aspects are brought up in other all-Negro movies, such as in *The Cool World* and *Nothing but a Man*, the treatment of them is so skimpy and glossed over that one gets the impression that if the moviemakers were to treat sexual emotions of and between black people in America in an authentic and human fashion, all hell would break loose. No doubt it would.

To recognize the *human validity* of Negro sexuality is one of the necessary ways of affirming the Negro's essential manhood. This would constitute a tumultuous psychological revolution with ramifications no less significant than the changes resulting from current civil rights activities.

from White Papers for White Americans (1966)

Fish Are Jumping an' the Cotton Is High: Notes from the Mississippi Delta

by Mike Thelwell

THERE is an immense mural in the Hinds County Courthouse in Jackson, Mississippi. On the wall behind the judge's bench is this mansion. White, gracefully colonnaded in a vaguely classical style, it overlooks vast fields, white with cotton which rows of darkies are busily (and no doubt, happily) picking. In the foreground to the left stands a family. The man is tall, well-proportioned with a kind of benevolent nobility shining from his handsome Anglo-Saxon face. He is immaculate in white linen and a planter's stetson as he gallantly supports his wife, who is the spirit of demure grace and elegance in her lace-trimmed gown. To the right, somewhat in the background to be sure, stands a buxom, grinning handkerchief-headed Aunt Jemima, everyone's good-humored black Mammy. In this mural, progress is represented by a work-gang of Negroes, building under the direction of a white overseer what appears to be an addition to the great house. Although this painting is not wired for sound—a concession, one imagines, to the dignity of the court—it requires little imagination to hear the soothing, homey sound of a spiritual wafting on the gentle wind from the cotton fields. The general tone is certainly one of orderly industry, stability and a general contentment. "Take a good look at them," a Negro lawyer said to me, "because they are the last happy darkies you are likely to see here."

Actually, this mural is so inept in technique and execution, that at first flush one is inclined to mistake it for parody. But Mississippians, especially the politicians, have never demonstrated the sense of security or humor that would permit them consciously to parody themselves, although they seem incapable of escaping this in their public utterances. That this mural, consciously or not, is a burlesque of a parody of a stereotype which has never had historical or social reality goes without saying, but the mere fact that the mural exists and is intended to be taken seriously, or at least with a straight face, is equally important. Because, despite the fact that the Deep South is an area of as vast geographic, economic, and even sociological differentiation as any region in the nation, it is this plantation image of the South that persists in the sentimental subconscious of the American popular imagination. It is this image, or some derivative of it, that people tend to see when the Deep South is mentioned.

In point of fact the area in which huge cotton plantations of "Gone With The Wind" popular fame existed, and to an extent still do, is limited to a relatively small, specific geographic area. This is a narrow band of very level, fertile black earth which runs erratically south, then west from the bottom of Virginia through parts of the Carolinas, central Alabama, picks up in south-west Georgia, and runs through north-western Mississippi and into Arkansas. This very generally describes the region known as the "Black-belt," where the institutional replacements of the huge ante-bellum plantations exist, and where the descendants of the slaves still greatly outnumber the descendants of their masters, and where the relationship between these two groups shows only a superficial formal change. In Mississippi, this area is called the Delta, a term which, in its precise geographic meaning, refers only to the wedge of land between the Mississippi and Yazoo rivers, but which extends in popular usage to most of the north-western quarter of the state. The area of the Delta coincides almost exactly with the Second Congressional District of Mississippi, the home of Senator Eastland, the Citizen's Council, and of the densest population of Negroes in the state. It is here, were it to exist anywhere, that one would find the image of the mural translated into reality.

What can be said about this place that will express the impact of a land so surrealistic and monotonous in its flatness that it appears unnatural, even menacing? Faulkner comes close to expressing the physical impact of the region: ". . . *Crossing the last hill, at the foot of which the rich unbroken alluvial flatness began as the sea began, at the base of its cliffs, dissolving away in the unhurried rain as the sea itself would dissolve away.*"

This description suggests the dominant quality: a flatness like an ocean of land, but within that vast flatness, a sense of confinement, a negation of distance and space that the sea does not have. And there are the rivers—in the east the headwaters of the river called Big Black, and sluggish tributaries, the Skuna, Yalabusha, and Yacona which flow into the Tallahatchie, which in turn meets the Sunflower to become the Yazoo which was called by the Indians the river of the dead. The Yazoo flows south and west until it meets the Mississippi at the city of Vicksburg. These rivers are, in Faulkner's words, ". . . thick, black, slow, unsunned streams almost without current, which once each year ceased to flow at all, then reversed, spreading, drowning the rich land and subsiding again leaving it even richer."

I once entered the Delta from the west, from Arkansas, over a long, narrow old bridge that seemed to go for miles over the wide and uncertain Mississippi. It was mid-summer and a heat that seemed independent of the sun rose from the land. The slightest indentation in the road's surface became a shimmering sheet of water that disappeared as you approached it. The numbing repetition of cotton-fields blurring in the distance wore on one's nerves and perceptions. This has been called the richest agricultural soil in the world. So it may have been, but it also is tough and demanding—no longer boundlessly fecund, it now yields its fruits only after exacting disproportionate prices in human sweat and effort. An old man told me, "for every man it enriches it kills fifty," and some folks joke that "the Delta will wear out a mule in five years, a white man in ten, and a nigger in fifteen."

For long stretches of highway where the fields are unbroken by any structure or sign of habitation, one might be in another century, except that a few things serve to place you in time. Even if tractors are not visible they are suggested by the certainty that there could not be, no, not in all the Southland, enough Negroes and mules to have planted all this. And there are the planes. On smooth strips next to the cotton these toy-like little craft, fragile and buoyant as children's kites, are tethered to the ground. The gentlest wind causes them to rear and buck against their moorings like colts. At times they are seen at absurdly low heights, skimming the top of the crops they are "dusting" against the boll weevil. They are used increasingly on the large plantations. One pilot, unnecessarily reckless, you think, crosses the highway *underneath* the telegraph wires and directly over your car. You remember, in that moment, the outdoor rally in Indianola that was bombed from one of these planes one night.

The billboards along the highway are also indices, not only of time but of place. They exhort you to support your Citizens' Council, to save America by impeaching Earl Warren, and challenge you to deny that "In Your heart, You Know He is Right." "KILLS 'EM FAST, KEEPS 'EM DYING," is the message of another, and it is only when you are nearly abreast of the sign that the small print reveals that an insecticide is being advertised, and nothing larger than a boll weevil is the proposed victim.

But the combination of plane and grisly advertisement reminds you of a report from Panola County, in the heart of the Delta. The SNCC worker who wrote the report is distressed by the fact that many small Negro children in that area are plagued by running, chancre-like sores on their faces or limbs. These lingering and persistent ulcers are attributed by the community to a side-effect of the "pizen" sprayed on the cotton. Children of all ages pick cotton in the Delta, and apparently this insecticide enters any exposed break in the skin and eats away at the flesh like an acid. "What can we do," the report asks, "isn't there some law. . . ." Perhaps, you think, it may be this particular brand of pesticide that "keeps 'em dying."

This is "The Heart of Dixie"—as numerous signs proclaim —the very center of the myth and the image, but what is its reality? For you right now its only reality is heat, and an almost unbearable cumulative discomfort, sweat burning your eyes, oven blasts of dusty air when you open the window, the metal edge of the window that keeps scorching your arm, and all around a punitive white glare that is painful to look into.

For the SNCC workers who are your companions the reality seems to be a certain tense caution. They work the delta and know the road, but in curious terms. Their knowledge is of the condition of the jail, idiosyncrasies of the lawmen, and the make, model and color of the cars they drive. They chose a route, not necessarily the most direct, but one that avoids certain towns and the jurisdictions of certain local officers. They watch the backroad intently for the car that may be the sheriff, the Highway Patrol, or one of the new radio-equipped prowl cars of the Klan. A car or pick-up truck filled with youngish white men, stripped of license tags, is always ominous, especially if they keep passing and inspecting your car. Often, because it is legal to carry openly displayed weapons here, the cars will be fitted with racks on which rifles and shotguns are conspicuous. This should not suggest that violence is an inevitable consequence of using the highways. But the tension is always present, for when a car follows you a few miles, passes you a number of times then streaks off down the highway, you have no way of knowing their intentions. "Man, watch for a '63 chevvy, light grey, no plate on front an' a long aerial. See anything that look like it shout."

The tension in the car draws to a fine edge. All know the car, and the reputation of the patrolman who polices the next fifty or so miles of highway. Two of the young men in the car have been "busted"—arrested by him—and as one says, "Once is enough. That man would rather whup yore head than eat shrimp . . . an' he's a sea-food lover."

This trooper is regarded with a mixture of fear and contempt by the Negroes in the County. He is reputed to stop every Negro he encounters, driving or on foot, to check their licenses and to find out where they are going and why. He is particularly fond of "interrogating" adolescent girls. As your companions talk about him a sort of grim, parodic humor attaches to him. His first statement, they say, is invariably, "All right Nigger, pull to the side, take off your hat, spit out your gum an' lemme see your license." It makes no difference if you are hatless and have never chewed gum. And because, for SNCC workers anyway, the response is either silent compliance or a denial that their name is Nigger, his next utterance is usually "Dammit Nigger, don't you know to say Sir?" But this day he does not appear.

On another occasion I saw him making an arrest. Like most things in the Delta, he verges on being a caricature, drawn with too heavy a hand. He is not tall, but blocky and heavy. His hair is thinning, his face is round, full-cheeked, cherubic save for small pale-blue eyes behind absolutely innocuous gold-rimmed glasses. In the heat his complexion could not be called merely florid, it was red, deeply and truly red. His khaki-colored military-style uniform was too tight and stained with damp circles at the armpits and the seat of his pants. His ponderous, hard-looking belly sags over the belt which slopes down almost to the junction of his thighs. Most striking are his hands: blunt, stubby, very wide—with the skin of the fingers stretched tight, like so many plump, freckled and hairy link sausages. Two images stay with me: one of a boneless, formless, shapeless face; another of the chunky figure, standing spraddle-legged and tugging at the cloth of his trousers where it bunched in tight wrinkles between his thighs. I often wonder about this man. From all accounts he is a sadist, and one with entirely too much opportunity to indulge his impulses, but there is also present a pathetic, somehow pitiable banality about him. Besides, he represents the most easily solved of the problems in the Delta.

Driving along the highways in the Delta you occasionally pass people walking—a single man, two, or sometimes what appears to be an entire family. Usually the man is in front in overalls, or blue denim pants and jacket and with a wide-brimmed straw hat against the sun. The children follow behind in single file, with the woman usually at the end. They often carry tools, but more often cardboard boxes and newspaper-wrapped bundles tied with string. These little caravans become visible while you are some distance down the highway. If they have shoes then they walk on the hot but smooth asphalt, if they are barefoot they take to the weeds. When they hear your car approaching they step off the highway and face the road, motionless, waiting with a quality of dogged, expressionless patience to resume their plodding journey. Sometimes, but rarely, a child will wave, a vague and tentative motion of the arm somewhere between greeting and dismissal, and that is the only sign. No smiles. Often you find such a group miles from any house, village, side road, or anything that might be called a town. One wonders where they sprang from, where they hope to go, and why. They are almost always—I cannot remember seeing any white families walking—Negroes.

*

Indianola is the capital of Sunflower County, a county distinguished because it contains the 4,800-acre plantation of U.S. Senator James O. Eastland, the state prison farm at Parchman, and is the home of Mrs. Fannie Lou Hamer, the ex-plantation worker who has become the symbol of the resistance.

Although this is your first time there, you recognize when you have come home. When the pavement runs out—the streetlights become fewer or nonexistent and the rows of weather-textured, grey-grained clapboard shacks begin—you experience feelings of relief, almost love. This chaotic, dilapidated shanty-town represents community, safety in numbers, friendship, and some degree of security after the exposed vulnerability of the highway.

Even if you wanted to, you could not escape the children of all sizes and shades who abandon their games in the dusty streets or weed-filled lots for the excitement of a new arrival. Noisy with impatient curiosity and quick vitality they surround you, shooting questions. "Is yo' a freedom fighter? Yo' come for the Meeting? Is yo' start up the school? Have any money?" Or proudly, "We does leafletting, yo' want us to give out any?" Big-eyed and solemn they await the answers, ignoring their elders' warnings, shouted from the porches, "Yo' all don't be botherin' that man now, heah?" They must have some bit of information so that they can go scampering importantly up the porches to inform the old people. The community grapevine.

And on the porches, the people are almost always old, at least no longer young. Frequently they are the grandparents of the children because the true parents, the generation in between, are at work, or have left the state in search of work. This gap between generations lies like a blight on every Negro community, and especially in the Delta. You see it in any kind of meeting, in the churches—any gathering of Negroes in Mississippi consists predominantly of teenagers and older people.

So the old people on the porch rock and fan and listen politely, perhaps too politely, expressing a cautious, noncommittal agreement that is somehow too glib and practised. And their eyes flick over your shoulder to see who may be watching. It may be the Man. The quiescent, easy agreement is another aspect of the mask, and one has no right to judge the only practical response that they have fashioned, the only defense they had. For if they survived yessing the white man to death, why not you? "Thou seest this man's fall, but thou knowest not his wrasslin'."

The motion and energy, the openness and thirst to know of the children in the road forms a tragic counterpoint to the neutral caution of the porches. So short a journey and symbolically so final. The problem comes clear: to create within the community those new forms, new relationships, new alternatives that will preserve this new generation from the paralysis of fear and hopelessness.

In all the shanty-towns that cluster on the edge of every delta city and town the population steadily increases as increasing numbers of Negroes are driven off the plantations and off the land. Everywhere you get the impression of hopelessness and waiting. Large numbers of human beings in a kind of limbo, physically present and *waiting*. And what they wait for is the cotton. At planting time, chopping time, and picking time, busses and trucks come into the shanty-towns before the sun is well up. The people—men, women and children—file on in the numbers needed and are taken to the plantations where they work a twelve-hour day for $2.50, or 30 cents an hour. Each year fewer and fewer people are needed for less and less work. If the fall is unusually wet, then it is a little better. The dust becomes a black and adhesive mud miring down the ponderous cotton-picking machines. Then, for a few hectic weeks almost the entire community can find work getting the crop in before it rots. Still, denied education and the skills that would give them mobility, these waiting people are superfluous, the obsolete victims of a vicious system that depended on large numbers of human beings being kept available in case they were needed. One plantation owner in the county is quoted as saying, "Niggers went out like the mule."

One way to understand this primitive and haunting place and the gratuitous human misery that it breeds, is to figure out who is in charge. Two forces rule the Delta: racism and cotton. Though the whitefolks put up a great show of control and dominance they are at the mercy of both. It is Cotton—not even Anglo-Saxon, but an immigrant from Egypt that determines how the society is organized. And as a ruler, he is as ruthless, capricious and sickly as the final issue of some inbred and decadent European House. Delicate, it must be protected from more vigorous hybrid weeds, and from a small beetle from Mexico. Drought will burn it out, water will rot it. Extravagant and demanding, it has—in alliance with human cupidity—all but exhausted a land of once incredible fertility which must now be pampered and fertilized excessively before it will produce. This process is so expensive that the final, grudging yield must be bought by the U.S. government which alone can afford it. The federal government has a surplus at present of some 14,000,000 bales. This spring the federal cotton allotment has been reduced by one-third in the Delta. Even fewer Negroes will have work of any kind. The millionaire planter Eastland and other landlords, however, will still profit handsomely from their federal subsidy. While awaiting a federal check that runs into hundreds of thousands of dollars, the Senator will, if he maintains his average, make three speeches deploring the immorality of government handouts and creeping socialism, by which he must mean the distribution of food surpluses to starving families in his county.

At suppertime the "freedom house" is full of bustle, the local kids pass in and out, a couple of carloads of SNCC workers from other parts of the state have stopped by on their way through. The shouted laughter and greetings are loud, the exchange of news marked by a wry humor. A young man from the southwest corner around Natchez tells stories about a local judge, nicknamed by the lawyers "Necessity," because in Horace's observation "necessity knows no law." But this judge is a favorite, because his records invariably contain so much error that although he never fails to convict, the higher court hardly ever fails to reverse him. Frequently, they say, his mind wanders, and he interrupts the proceedings of his own court with, "Your Honor, I object."

Another worker just down from Sharkey County, which is very rural and contains no city of any size, complains loudly about conditions. "Even the mosquitoes threatening to leave the county. They organized and sent Johnson a telegram saying that if the Red Cross didn't come down and distribute blood, they weren't staying." He wouldn't be surprised, he adds, to find when he returned that they had gotten relief.

The meeting is called for eight, but will not really get started much before nine, as the women must feed their white folks their suppers before going home to feed their own families. But folks start gathering from seven. They use the time to "testify"; to talk about whatever troubles their mind—mostly the absence of food, money, work, and the oppressiveness of the police. They talk about loss of credit, eviction and voting, three things which form an inseparable unity in the Delta. Some young men are there from Washington County. They say the peoples over there got together and told the owners that they wouldn't work anymore for thirty cents. After the evictions they started a tent city, have a "strike fund" collected in the community, and are planting a "freedom garden" for winter food. Everyone cheers. What they want is cooperation. "If they sen' busses from Washington County don't go. Be workin' gainst us if you do."

"Thass right. Nevah. Freedom."

In the clapping, shouting, stomping excitement there is brief release from tension and fear. But over it all hovers an unease, the desperation of the unanswered question, "Whut *is* we gon' do." Winter is coming. "*Whut is we gon' do?*"

A lady wants to know. She is from "out in the rural" she says and two nights ago was awakened by what sounded like people crying. A man, his wife and seven children were coming down the road carrying bundles. The children were crying and tears were in the man's eyes. They had no shoes. He said that that evening the owner had given him twenty dollars and told him to find someplace else. He had worked that plantation all his life, had less than three years of school and had never been outside the county. "Ah tell yo' that man was *shock*, he wuz *confused*. I want to know, what is we gon' do."

A portly, middle-aged lady answers her. This lady is known for a tough nerviness, insouciant streak of daring best characterized by the Yiddish word *chutzpah*, or by the sheriff in the term "smart nigger." She also has a heart condition of some fame and strategic value. (As she gets up, you recall the time she was in jail and convinced the jailor, after two minor attacks and a constant and indignant harangue, that she was quite likely to die, and that he was certain to be held responsible, if she were not allowed to have her "heart prescription." And she got it, too. You remember her, dramatically clutching her ailing heart, breathing laboriously, and accepting with a quick wink the druggist's bottle of sour mash bourbon.) There were two little boys walking down the road, she says. They were throwing stones at everything they met. They came upon a chicken which the larger boy sent off with a well-placed stone. He does the same for a pig, a cow and a mule. Then, they come to a hornets' nest. When the bigger boy makes no effort to hit that target the other asks, "Ain't yo' gonna pop that nes'?" "Nope, sho' ain't." "Why ain't yo' gonna hit thet nes'," the smaller asks. "Well, Ah ain't gonna hit thet nes',"— she pauses, looks at the audience, winks, shakes her head—"I ain't gonna hit thet nes' *because dey's organized*."

They like that story, even if it is only a partial answer, saying *what*, but not *how*. So they nod agreement and murmur that "we'uns gotta be *together*, an' we gotta keep on, keeping on, no matter how mean times git." There is in these Delta communities a great spirit of closeness and cooperation. When a family is evicted, the children may be absorbed into the community, two here, one there. Or an entire family that finds itself suddenly homeless (landlords aren't required by any law to give notice) may be taken in by another family whose home is already too small. Without these traditions the folks could not have endured.

In the meetings, everything—uncertainty, fear, even desperation—finds expression, and there is comfort and sustenance in "talkin' bout hit." A Preacher picks the theme up with a story of his own. "Wunst times wuz very bad fer the rabbits."

"Fo' the *Whut?*" comes a chorus. The old man smiles, "Fer the *rabbits*. Yes Sir, Ah tells yo' they wuz bein' hard *pressed*. Them ol' houn's wuz runnin' them *ragged*. Got so bad it seem like they couldn't git down to the fiel's to nibble a little grass. It looked like they wasn't gonna be able to make it."

"*Yeah, Yeah, Tellit,*" the people shake their heads in sympathy. "They wuz *hard pressed* fo' a fack. So fin'lly, not knowin' what else to do, they calls a meetin'. Yessir, they call a *mass meetin'*."

"*Ahuh, Freedom.*"

"So they talked an' talked, discussed it back an' fo'th, how the houn's wasn't givin' them space even to live."

"*Thass right, tell it.*"

"But they couldn't meet with no solution. It jes' didn't seem like hit was nothin' they could do." The speaker shakes his head. "No, it didn't seem like they could make it. So fin'ly thisyer ol' rabbit, he wuz ol' anyways an' fixin' to die anyhow, he sugges' that since they wuzn't making it *nohow*, they should all jes' join together an' run down to the *river an' drown theyself.*"

Everyone in the church is listening very closely. There is the beginning of a low murmur of rejection.

"But since nobody said any better, they put hit in the form of a motion, an' someone secon' hit an' they take a vote. It passed [pause] *unanimous.* So on the nex' moonlight night, they all git together jes' as the motion call fer, link they arms and start fer the river, fo' to drown theyself. Hit wuz *a-a-l* the rabbits in the county, an' thet wuz a long line, jes' hoppin' along in the moonlight to go drown theyse'f. It wuz somethin' to see, chillun, it sho' wuz. An, yo' know, they hadn't gon far befo' they come upon the houn's, out looking fo' rabbits to chase. Them ol' houn's be so surprise at seein' all them rabbits commin' towards them steady, *they thought they time had come.* They be so surprised they turn roun' an' run so fas' they was outen the county, befo' sun come up. Rabbits had no mo' trouble."

"*Talk 'bout Freedom.*"

There is little of subtlety or delicacy here, it is a region of extremes and nothing occurs in small measure. All is blatant, even the passing of time. Night in the Delta is sudden and intense, an almost tangible curtain of blue-purple darkness that comes abruptly, softening and muting the starkness of the day. The moon and stars seem close, shining with a bright yellow haziness like ripe fruit squashed against a black-board. The wind is warm, very physical and furry as it moves with suggestive intimacy over your face and body. Like the sea, the

Delta is at its most haunting and mysterious in the dark. The air is heavy with the ripe smell of honeysuckle and night-blooming jasmine, at once cloying and aphrodisiac. A woman's voice deep-timbered, husky, and *negro* is singing an old plaintive song of constant sorrow with new words. The song becomes part of the rich-textured night, like the tracings of the fireflies. In the restless and erotic night you believe. For the first time you can believe the blues, tales of furtive and shameful passions, madness, incest, rape and violence. Half-intoxicated by the night, by its sensuous, textured restlessness, it is possible to believe all the secret, shameful history that everyone seems to know and none will admit except in whispers. It is easy to believe that the land is finally and irrevocably cursed. That faceless voice singing to the darkness an old song with new words, "*They say that freedom . . . is a constant sorrow.*"

Just off the road stands the shack. There is a quality of wildness to the scrubby bush around it, and because it is set on short wood piles it appears to have been suddenly set down on the very top of the carpet of weeds around it. The greyed wood siding has long since warped, so that a fine line shows between each plank, giving the shack the appearance of a cage. Crossing the porch you step carefully, avoiding the rotted holes. The woman inside turns dull eyes towards where you stand in the doorway. She is sharing out a pot of greens onto tin plates. The cabin is windowless and dim but is criss-crossed by rays of light beaming through the cracks in the siding and from gaps in the roof where the shingles have rotted and blown away. This light creates patterns of light and shadow on everything in the room. As the woman watches you, at least inclines her head in your direction, her children sidle around her so that she is between them and the door. You see that there are only five—at first it seemed as though the cabin was full. None of them is dressed fully, and the two smallest are completely nude. As the mother gives you the directions back to the highway, she ladles out the greens and each child seizes a plate but stands looking at you. They are all eyes, and these eyes in thin tight faces blaze at you. The full, distended bellies of the children contrasts with the emaciated limbs, big prominent joints, narrow chests in which each rib stands out, the black skin shiny, almost luminous. You cannot leave, so you stand gently talking with the mother, who answers your questions with an unnatural candor. She seems beyond pride. As you talk, she sits on a box and gives her breast to the smallest child even though he seems to be about five. This doesn't surprise you unduly for you have learned that in the Delta Negro mothers frequently do not wean their children until the next one arrives. What will substitute when there is not enough food?

You find out that she is twenty-four, was married at fifteen, had seven children but two died, the father is in Louisiana chopping pulpwood, the nearest work he could find. He sends money when he works. She lives in this abandoned cabin because it was the only rent-free house she could find after they were put off the plantation. As you leave, you see them framed in the doorway, the mother in unlaced man's shoes, one brown, the other black, holding her smallest child with the unnaturally big head and eyes.

You wonder how they are to survive the winter in a cabin with walls that cannot even keep the dust out. But this is Tallahatchie county, where 33 percent of all Negro babies die in the first year of life, where Negroes live, grow old and die without ever being properly examined by a doctor, and children die of cold and hunger in the winter. One reason given for the high infant mortality rate—you meet women who admit to having birthed 10 children of which three or four survived—is that in this completely agricultural county, families survive the winter, when there is no work for the men, on the ten or twelve dollars the mother makes working as a cook or maid. When her time of labor approaches she dares not stop working.

But, all of this was some time ago. All I know of the Delta now is what I hear. I am told that snow blanketed it in January and I am glad I was not there to see it. I am told that in December 250 families were given notice to be off the plantations by January 1st. This means that some 2,200 human beings are without home or livelihood, and none of the programs of the federal government—social security, unemployment compensation, or job retraining—affects them. By spring, they say, some 12,000 people will be homeless. I am glad I was not there to see the ghostly silent caravans trudging through the snow at the side of the highway. A lady in Sunflower County told me on the phone that families were at the tent city asking to be taken in.

Throughout the Delta the plantations are automating, driven by the dual pressure of cutting costs and the potential effect of the 1965 voting rights bill in a region with a Negro majority. The state of Mississippi wants its Negro population thinned out. They make no secret of it. Gov. Johnson has said in praise of his predecessor that under Ross Barnett's regime "116,000 Negroes fled the state." And the state has still not been able to find any way to use the 1.6 million dollars appropriated by the Office of Economic Opportunity to be used to finance the distribution of surplus food in the Delta. Before this grant, it had been Mississippi's position that they simply could not afford the cost of *distributing* the free food. I am just cowardly enough to be glad I am not there to see.

The Massachusetts Review, Spring 1966

2 Veteran Rights Leaders Ousted by SNCC

by Jack Nelson

ATLANTA—The already-militant Student Non-violent Coordinating Committee has dumped unceremoniously its two top leaders in favor of younger Negroes who apparently will more aggressively promote black nationalist politics.

The shakeup, which saw long-time leaders John Lewis and James Forman replaced by Stokely Carmichael and Mrs. Ruby Doris Robinson, coincided with SNCC's emerging policy of de-emphasizing involvement of whites in the civil rights movement in the South.

Carmichael, 24, of New York City, has been the committee's senior field secretary in Alabama where he has organized and promoted an all-Negro political movement, under a Black Panther emblem. He replaced Lewis, 26, as chairman.

Mrs. Robinson, of Atlanta, a graduate of Spelman College here, has worked with SNCC since 1960, when, as a 17-year-old high school senior, she took part in some of the earlier sit-ins. She succeeded Forman, 37, as executive secretary.

The only top official re-elected was Cleveland Sellers, program secretary, formerly of Denmark, S.C.

The elections, held at an all-night session near Nashville, Tenn., Saturday but not announced until Monday, cast the student group further adrift from the mainstream of the civil rights movement.

Lewis, obviously bitter over his ouster, has been SNCC's main link to the more conventional activities of the movement.

He is a member of the executive board of Dr. Martin Luther King's Southern Christian Leadership Conference and has been SNCC's ceremonial head and spokesman since 1963. He has represented the committee with the national Leadership Conference on Civil Rights and in White House meetings between civil rights leaders and President Johnson.

Some leaders of other civil rights organizations have sharply criticized SNCC for its Black Panther activities in Alabama. Hosea Williams, a top aide to Dr. King, calling it "reverse racism," said, "They've run some of the white people out of the movement."

Carmichael Monday issued a statement declaring SNCC would "intensify its efforts in the area of independent politics."

"Our experience organizing in the hard-core racist areas of this country has been one of intimidation by local-elected officials and of inaction by the federal government," he declared.

"We will struggle in the future as we have in the past for human rights and join with those around the world who know the same oppression we know and the same deception on the part of 'the government of the United States in its claims of concern for democracy.'" (The barb at the federal government is a quotation from SNCC's statement of last year which criticized American policy in Vietnam as aggression.)

Carmichael, considered one of the more radical leaders of SNCC, became an activist in the protest movement while a senior at Bronx High School of Science in New York. He joined other students in picketing the House Committee on Un-American Activities in Washington, D.C.

He also participated in some of the earlier sit-ins in the Washington area. He was graduated from Howard University in Washington.

In Lowndes County, Ala., Carmichael helped form the Freedom Organization, an all-Negro party. He called the move necessary because white Democrats in Lowndes had excluded Negroes from party activities and added:

"To ask the Negroes to get in the Democratic Party is like asking Jews to join the Nazi party."

At SNCC headquarters here, an air of petulance greeted newsmen who inquired about the elections. It was obvious that Lewis, always congenial with newsmen, was out of power. He attempted to answer reporters' questions, but stopped when several SNCC members snapped that a newly formed central committee would release all information.

But Lewis said it was true the consensus of the 150 staff members who control SNCC was that the role of whites should be de-emphasized. He indicated he did not agree with this policy.

Lewis and Forman were elected to the central committee, but this may have been little more than a face-saving gesture to two veteran civil rights leaders who had been beaten and jailed many times in the South. There are eight other members on the committee.

The 10-man committee replaces the old 21-men executive committee. Only one white person, Jack Minnis, formerly of Louisiana, was elected to it. Four white persons were on the old executive committee.

Both Lewis and Forman are militants who have taken pride in being called agitators and trouble makers by the white political leaders of the civil rights battlegrounds. But apparently neither would wholeheartedly endorse the more radical, all-Negro direction of some of the younger SNCC members.

Lewis, who has been arrested 40 times in civil rights demonstrations, suffered a fractured skull in March, 1965, while attempting to lead a voting rights demonstration over the Edmond Pettus Bridge at Selma.

Forman shocked visiting white volunteers at a meeting in a Montgomery church last year when he said that if the white man would not let him eat at the table with him, he would "kick the . . . legs out from under it."

Last January Lewis and Forman released the SNCC policy statement accusing the United States of being "deceptive in its claims of concern for freedom of the Vietnamese people," of murdering North Vietnamese in violation of international law, and of being "no respecter of persons or law when such persons or law run counter to its needs and desires."

The statement, which supported persons who refused to respond to draft calls, was disavowed by many other civil rights leaders.

Julian Bond, whose support of the statement led to Georgia House of Representatives action barring him from a seat, said the new leadership does not mean a de-emphasis of SNCC activities in the peace movement. But he said the primary function of SNCC still will be in the field of civil rights.

Bond, SNCC communications director, said, "Forman was just tired of going around the country fund-raising, which is mostly what he has done." Bond said, "Now he'll work in the

South, mostly in the field. Lewis was tired of traveling around and being a speaker. Now he'll be an administrator."

Bond said Carmichael will have two assistant chairmen and Lewis probably will serve as one of them.

However, Lewis declined to say whether he will even remain with SNCC. "I'm here today," he said, "and I'll be here tomorrow and that's all I can say."

Los Angeles Times, May 17, 1966

The Meredith March

by Paul Good

THE marchers did not always know where they were going. But they knew where they were.

On the highways bounded by cotton fields shimmering in the murderous Delta heat, in somnolent towns and awakening cities, and under the tents at night, the marchers knew they were in the middle of a racist reality—Negroes physically segregated in schools, restaurants, and courtrooms, economically throttled by rural peonage and urban discrimination, spiritually demeaned by the preachments and practice of white supremacy. It was bitter knowledge made more bitter because most white Americans not marching seemed unable to grasp it, to comprehend the lesson in social and political geography presented each day along the Mississippi highways.

The majority of Americans from the White House out to the white suburbias of the mind were tired of marchers, of protest, of being reminded that laws were not necessarily realities. They had approved—as certified by surveys—a Supreme Court school decision in 1954, a Civil Rights Act ten years later, a Voting Rights Act in 1965. They had done all that could be expected of good white people and now they preferred to believe the beautiful, that only a little patience was needed to get through the "transition period."

White House Deputy Press Secretary Robert Fleming spoke for President Johnson, who was limiting his public utterances to the Mekong Delta and points north, the problems in a delta nearer Washington expendable.

"The President," said Mr. Fleming, "knows it is going to take a lot of effort to produce understanding down there."

Yes. And so many Americans could not understand why the marchers were behaving with such ill grace. Before they had chanted, "Two, four, six, eight, We wanna integrate." Now it was things like, "Ho-ho, whatta you know, White folks gotta go." Before, in Washington, St. Augustine and Selma, the throat-catching Christliness of "I love everybody, I love everybody, I love everybody in my heart" was a reassurance that the oppressed would not offer hatred but salvation to his oppressor. But now, as the column entered Grenada, a Negro girl was breaking up people around her by singing:

"I love everybody,
I love everybody,
I love everybody in my heart,
I just told a lie,
I just told a lie,
I just told a lie in my heart."

Other songs were more brutal. Christmas and Christ were far away when the Meredith Marchers sang: "Jingle bells, Shotgun shells, Freedom all the way, Oh what fun it is to blast a trooper man away."

But most disturbing, even frightening, was the cry of "Black Power!" from the members of the Student Nonviolent Coordinating Committee. It knifed into the moderate, the liberal white (and sometimes Negro) mind, interpreted as both threat and insult, seeming to undo past efforts at understanding and raising the spectre of violent nights under bloody southern moons. It shocked Dr. Martin Luther King and his Southern Christian Leadership Conference into what appeared a break with SNCC, and left CORE and NAACP wrangling over its meaning. Alarmed national reaction gave the Johnson administration an excuse to lecture the Movement (President Johnson sternly reminding Negroes of their minority status) at a time when its preoccupation with war already was threatening domestic programs that were insufficient to begin with.

So a march that should have been an epic emerged, in much of the nation's press, as an irritant, an ill-considered excursion by competing civil rights groups bent on organizational aggrandizement. But anyone who spent those weeks on Mississippi roads knows it was much more. The march lacked the clean lines of purpose, national backing and surface unity of the Selma-to-Montgomery March. But the Negroes who led it were one year deeper into frustration and disillusion,

Haynes Johnson (*standing at left*) takes notes during the Selma-to-Montgomery
march, March 1965.

Matt Herron, courtesy Haynes Johnson

Peter de Lissovoy outside the county jail in Albany, Georgia, 1964.
Courtesy Sandy Blue de Lissovoy

Christopher Wren (*l.*) talks with James Forman of SNCC, Mississippi, summer 1964.
Courtesy Christopher Wren

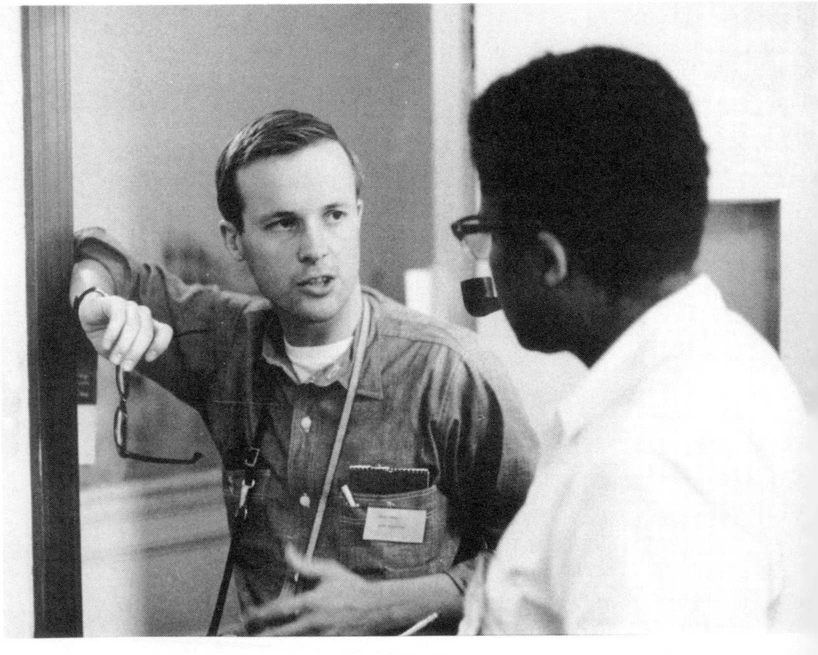

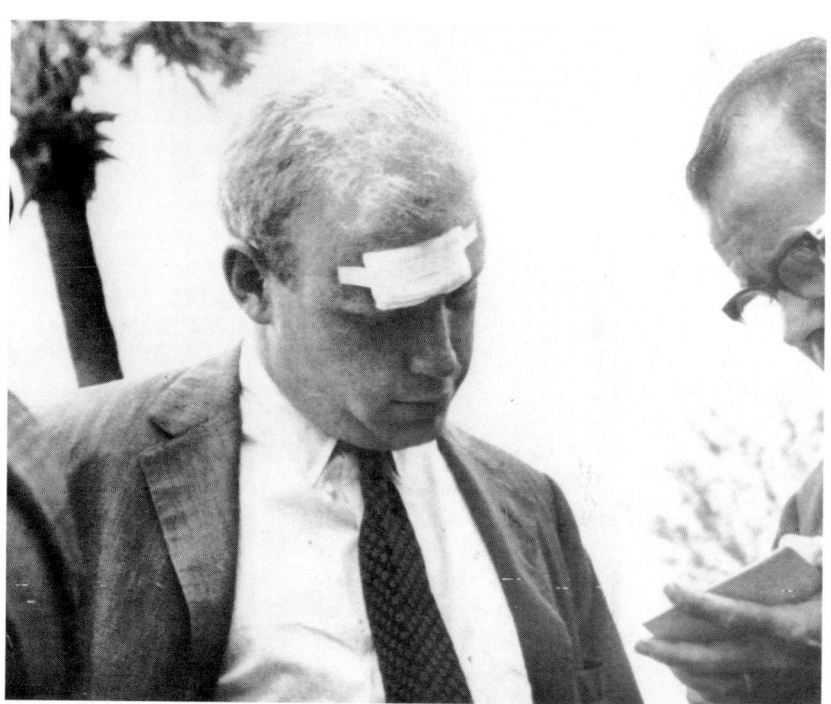

Michael Durham
interviewed after being
beaten during racial
violence in Jacksonville,
Florida, March 24, 1964.
Courtesy Michael Durham

Amsterdam News reporter
George Barner, ca. 1958.
Cecil Layne, courtesy George Barner

Christopher Wren (*with camera*) near Hayneville, Alabama, during the Selma-to-Montgomery march, March 1965.
Courtesy Christopher Wren

David Halberstam,
May 1964.
AP / Wide World Photos

Edward and Ruth Brecher,
1962.
AP / Wide World Photos

C. Gerald Fraser, April 1968.
Courtesy C. Gerald Fraser and Mrs. Herbert Rosenfield

William Bradford Huie, ca. 1960.
Courtesy Martha H. Huie

SNCC workers Charles Sherrod (*standing, right*) and Randy Battle (*seated*) during a voter registration drive in rural southwest Georgia, 1963.

Nora Sayre.
Courtesy Estate of Nora Sayre

Earl Caldwell at
The New York Times, 1970.
AP / Wide World Photos

Murray Kempton, 1961.
Courtesy Library of Congress

Michael Thelwell (*r.*)
with Stokely Carmichael
at the University of
Massachusetts, Amherst,
ca. 1969.
Courtesy Ekwueme Michael Thelwell

Fannie Lou Hamer and Michael Thelwell (*to her left*) outside the U.S. Capitol after Congress rejected the Mississippi Freedom Democratic Party's election challenge, September 17, 1965.
Courtesy Ekwueme Michael Thelwell

Gilbert Moore.
David Parks, courtesy
Gilbert Moore

Nan Robertson
working with
Anthony Lewis,
1960.
Courtesy New York Times

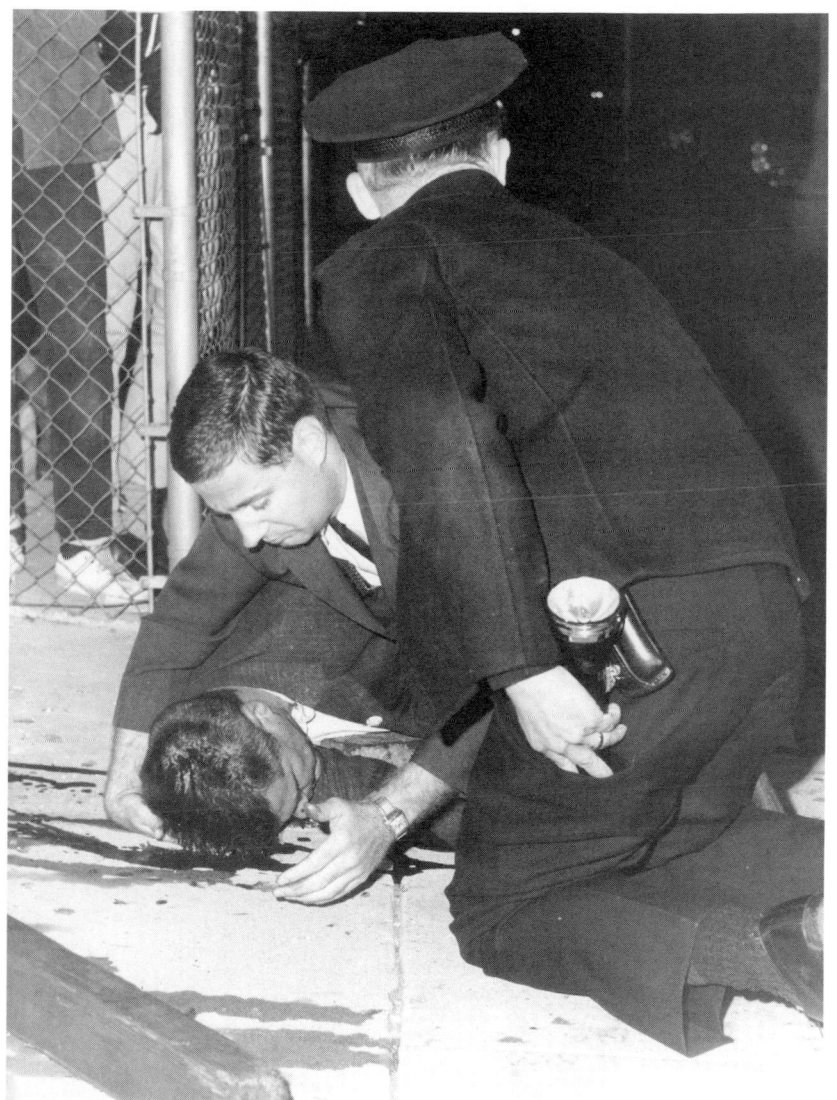

Karl Fleming of *Newsweek* bleeding on the sidewalk after being attacked in Watts, May 17, 1966.

AP / Wide World Photos

Jack Nelson of the
Los Angeles Times in 1965.
Courtesy Los Angeles Times

John Beecher
(*foreground*) at a
demonstration in
support of the
Selma voting rights
campaign, San
Francisco, 1965.
*Clayton Barbeau. Courtesy
Clayton Barbeau*

Marc Crawford (*second from r.*) and others integrating a St. Augustine, Florida, public pool, July 1964.
Stan Wayman / TimePix

Elizabeth Hardwick, December 1967.
AP / Wide World Photos

A federal marshal reads a court order halting a planned Selma-to-Montgomery protest march as Andrew Young (*arms folded*), Martin Luther King Jr. (*behind Young*), James Farmer (*behind King*), and Haynes Johnson (*adjusting camera*) look on. March 9, 1965.
AP / Wide World Photos

Robert Richardson.
Courtesy Los Angeles Times

Joan Didion,
May 1, 1967.
AP / Wide World Photos

Alice Walker, August 1970.
© Corbis/Bettmann

Pat Watters (*far left*) on the way to Washington, D.C., to protest Nixon administration changes in desegregation policy, 1969.
Courtesy Glenda Watters

Louis Lomax (*right*) with Martin Luther King Jr.

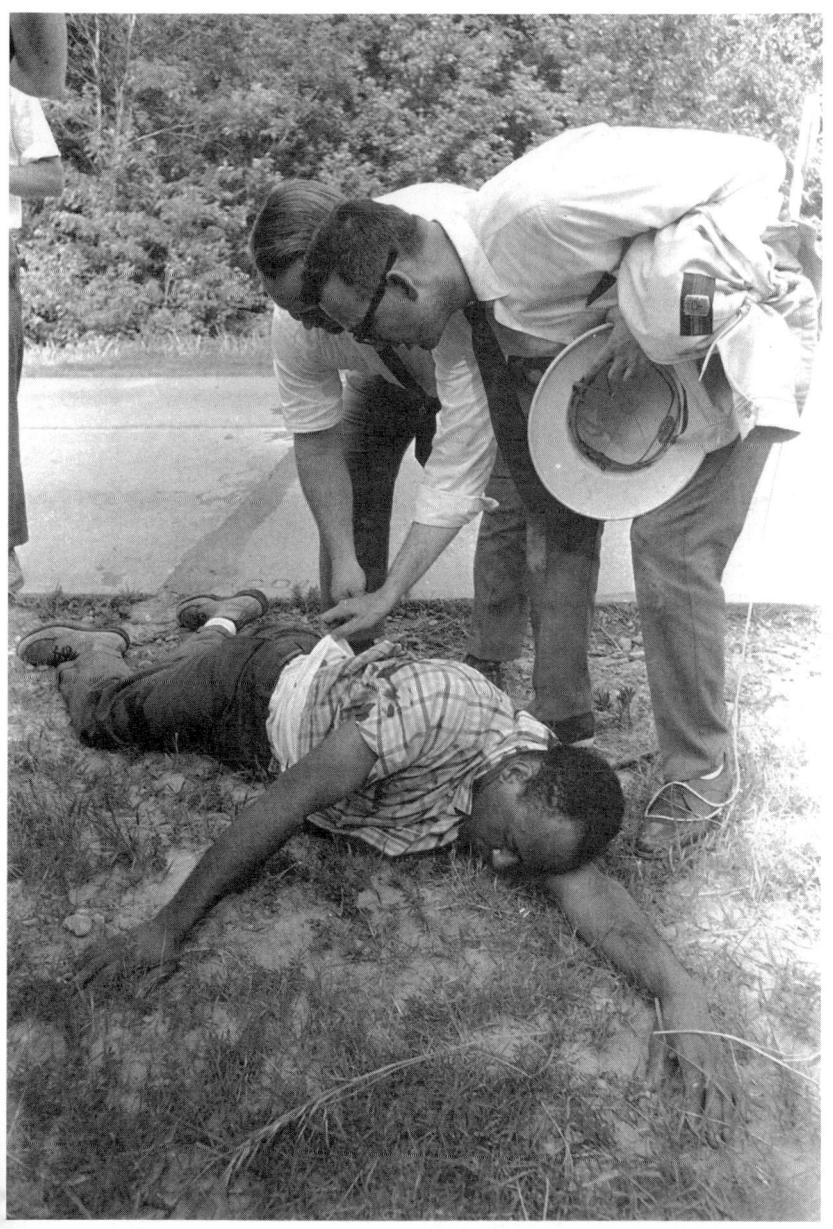

James Meredith lies wounded near Hernando, Mississippi, after being shot, June 6, 1966. *Bottom left:* Meredith's assailant, Aubry James Norvell, crouches at far left.
Jack Thornell, courtesy AP / Wide World Photos

Tom Wicker, September 13, 1963.
George Tames, courtesy New York Times

Jerry Farber, ca. 1968.
Courtesy Jerry Farber

Steve Van Evera,
January 1968.
Courtesy Steve Van Evera

Jerry DeMuth, ca. 1960.
Courtesy Jerry DeMuth

Carol Schmidt.
Courtesy Carol Schmidt

Harper's editor-in-chief Willie
Morris at his desk, 1971.
AP / Wide World Photos

David Nevin with Lyndon Johnson at the LBJ Ranch, ca. 1964.
Courtesy David Nevin

James Farmer demonstrating for CORE at the 1964 World's Fair in New York.

Gordon Parks, 1970.
© Bruce Davidson / Magnum Photos

and this created a desperate atmosphere that encouraged vin-
dictiveness and distrust of the nation's institutions and the
men who controlled them. How does an observer "tell it like
it is" when it was so many different things? In the tangle of
tensions and contradictions, the march reflected truths about
America, north and south, and if they shift in and out of
focus it is because the country is shifting, trying to determine
what it is and wants to be, while the question hangs whether
there is enough time or inclination to truly reform what it
was.

Begin with Grenada on Highway 51 in North Central Mississippi, one week after James Meredith was shot near the
Tennessee border. "Grenada, Population 12,000 and Still
Growing," a city of many churches and the K of C, preserve
of Elk and Moose, its approaches squalid with used car lots
and roadside stands but its residential avenues—its white residential avenues—still imbued with the spell of the Old
South, majestic elms, cool, columned porches, oval windows
in the doors, not quite ante-bellum but charming postwar.
The marchers are approaching a city with half a dozen small,
thriving factories which seemed virtually untouched by the
job section of the 1964 Civil Rights Act. The few black factory
jobs pay $1.25 an hour, Negro domestics get $12 a week, and
what cotton there is gets chopped at $3 a day. The Supreme
Court might not have decided anything in 1954 to judge from
Grenada's unintegrated schools. Its restaurants, theaters, and
courthouse facilities seemed as segregated as they were at the
turn of the century. A great deal of federal law is being broken in this city as the marchers approach, but strangely in an
America that is supposed to be a nation of laws rather than
men, no one is doing anything about it this broiling day.

Behind them at the campsite near the Enid Federal Dam,
their tent is being struck. A bustling white waiter from
Lindy's Restaurant in New York City who is spending his
entire vacation on the march yells across at some young Negro
men rolling canvas:

"Hey boys, come on, we generally get this thing down in
ten minutes."

A young man roars back at him: "*Well*, you better get some
of them *boys* you been working with."

In a nation suffering from racial schizophrenia, it is increasingly hard to be rational. On the highway approaching Grenada, the marchers pass a KKK welcome painted in the pavement. It is Hospitality Month in Mississippi and under their feet they see:

> "Red (sic) nigger and run
> If you can't red run anyway."

A Jewish youth from Coney Island working in the South for a year has a song for it. He had recently been thrown out of a synagogue in Hattiesburg while trying to say a memorial prayer for his father by a shamus who recognized him as a civil rights worker. He has some unique insights into intolerance and to the tune "The Ballad of the Green Beret" he sings:

> "Hooded sheets upon their heads,
> Are these men America's best?
> They kill by night and hate by day,
> The Green Beret and the KKK."

Do all the 150 or so marchers agree with him in condemning the war in Vietnam along with the Klan? Probably, but even with large samples no one can make statements in the name of all the marchers because they are a mixed bag. SCLC, SNCC, CORE, NAACP (excluding, at this point, Charles Evers), Delta Ministry, Mississippi Freedom Democratic Party and freelance demonstrators of every persuasion. There is Mrs. Barbara Kaye, wife of an Englewood, N.J., symphonic composer and one of the original Jackson Freedom Riders. Mrs. Kaye, who brought her beautiful 14-year-old daughter Jennie along, sometimes lets her hair grow out but presently is cutting it African again in her private protest at the "apathetic white and black drift in civil rights." Plodding doggedly along nearby in an old lady's old-fashioned sunbonnet is a 71-year-old white woman from Douglasville, Ga., whose parents were sharecroppers and who has plowed her own moral field at considerable personal cost. Dispensing salt tablets is Miss Helene Richardson, a doe-eyed young Negro girl from Belzoni, Miss. who left a tenant farm to become a registered nurse and is working the Delta with the Medical Committee on Human Rights. A Negro bus driver from Brooklyn, Vincent Young, also is walking his vacation away and carrying a sign, "No Viet Cong Ever Called Me Nigger." There are beards and cleanshaves, sloppy-thinkers and acute ones, bitter black people from Mississippi and Chicago wanting revenge, and others still seeking Dr. King's "beloved community."

All reasons were valid. The existence of Mississippi was excuse enough to be there. Yet many who had come South before stayed home this time. Churchmen and labor groups were sparsely represented. Dr. Homer Jack, director of the Department of Social Responsibility for the Unitarian Universalist Church and a veteran of demonstrations, came and found the march "amorphous."

"The Movement is changing so rapidly," he observed, "that one has to run fast just to keep up."

A CORE worker said the march's ad lib organization was "like trying to fix a car motor with a pair of sprung pliers when you're going down the highway at 60 miles an hour."

If non-segregationist America was not running hard to keep up, the bulk of the press was either plodding or dropping off to snipe. The New York *Times,* The Los Angeles *Times* and one national news magazine had perceptive men in the field. But after that, with exceptions, the quality of reporting dropped off sharply, particularly with the wire services. Since they are the news lifeline for the vast majority of American—and foreign—newspaper readers, the information gap was enormous. It was predictable that the Greenwood *Commonwealth* would write "This is the march that was generated by James Meredith, an ex-Air Force Negro who was responsible for getting two men killed at the University of Mississippi." Or that it would editorialize that "the former winner of the Nobel Peace Prize (Dr. King) can be compared to Joseph Stalin and Mao Tze Tung. This man has created more violence and left more hatred in his path than any other civil rights leader in the country's history."

But what of the UPI story appearing as the column neared Grenada? Readers in Mississippi, California and Washington were told:

"This march has become part movement, part circus. Among the 350-odd marchers . . . are about 50 white youths who wear T-shirts and denims, sandals and weird cowboy hats adorned with Freedom buttons. One is an avowed Marxist. Another is a one-legged redhead who forsook the United States and lives in exile in Mexico.

"There is one marcher who starts each day at the head of the column, then drops out when the news cameras are turned off.

"Another white man approached a reporter to talk about 'the coming sexual revolution' which he said would be centered around homosexuality.

"'This is a great assembly of kooks,' said a Mississippi highway patrolman. Most newsmen agreed."

Perhaps most newsmen in the truck rented by the wire services and TV networks that rolled at the head of the march did agree with UPI's expert appraiser of human behavior. I once saw them shoot from the truck like flushed quail when two marchers almost came to blows. Dissension was a sought-after theme. But mile after uneventful mile they sat there in the truck looking out at the shacks where the essence of the march was made flesh in the lives of Negroes whose median income was $600 a year, whose atrophied political instincts were still held in check despite the Voting Rights Act by threat of dispossession from the land, firing from jobs or other retaliations. And those who marched in their behalf, according to this great newsgathering agency, were kooks. Who? Mrs. Kaye and Jennie? The white sharecropper's daughter? The Negro nurse from Belzoni trying to minister in an area where the U.S. Public Health Service did little or nothing and most Negroes could not get into a hospital without paying a $50 deposit?

The astigmatic press could overlook fieldhand trucks loaded with Negro choppers heading for their $3 day-in-the-sun, serfs in a cotton industry receiving a billion a year in federal subsidies. It would not bother to investigate the Poverty Program. Most of the press could see dissensions and miss needs, point up confusion and stare straight through realities of a Deep South that was changing grudgingly and only when pressure grew too great to bear, pressure sometimes instigated by the federal government but most often by the understaffed and overextended civil rights groups.

So the marchers entered Grenada nationally suspect, if not despised. Yet there was glory in it as they came down Commerce Street, hitting the colored section first from the north, swinging onto Pearl Street past rows of weathered plank shacks, galvanized roofs slick with silver heat, a press helicopter buzzing low over the eternally sleepy street like the Twentieth Century incarnate, ruffling the sunflowers six foot tall and yellow in the narrow yards, the sunflowers waving in the blasted air while on the porches black people looked out at the noise and motion of a parade that had been a century in coming. Civil rights evangelism was an old story to many of us but it was brand new here, new and thrilling and beautiful in its affirmation of things long felt but hidden, whispered, now to be pronounced openly, even shouted. Freedom! Some Auntie Sallies sat and chewed dubiously. But the children and many young grownups yelled it. Freedom! And for a few dusty minutes the word came alive and the march began to have meaning.

"Mr. Charley ain't gonna give you a whippin tonight," a Negro marcher called up to a porch. "Hold your head up, let him know. Come on to the courthouse."

"I got the gout in my foot," an old man in drooping suspenders called back. His shack looked like an oversized, abandoned dollhouse. "Let me go get my lunch, though, an' then I'll come along."

He disappeared. He never came. The glorious parade along Pearl Street passed him by. But many joined. A highway patrolman, ordered to be on good behavior by an image-conscious state, estimated he saw "about a mile of niggers." The crowd swarmed to the courthouse square which was ringed by state and county lawmen, behind them crowds of whites who had been prepared by city fathers for this day of infamy. City Attorney Bradford Dye later described how word was spread to avoid incidents. The county itself was granting concessions to the Negroes all over the place. Roll with the punch. Almost every Grenada white man and woman eligible to vote (6000) was registered but only 700 Negroes out of 4400 eligible. So let them demonstrate for a day and then the parade will be gone and the ineluctable flow of southern time and tradition will again take possession, insuring the perpetuation of those ideals of conduct mythic in the blood, symbolized in the stone of the statue in the square of the young Confederate soldier in forager's dress, musket at parade rest, hand forever grasping his canteen: "To the noble men who marched neath the flag of the stars and bars and were faithful to the end . . . glorious in life, in death sublime."

Behind the statue was a bust of Jefferson Davis. And suddenly Robert Greene, a 32-year-old professor of education at Michigan State University and an SCLC official, Robert Greene, Negro, was laying a dark hand roughly on Jeff Davis' face, you might say slapping it, and then sticking a U.S. flag over his head, crying:

"This joker . . . we want brother Jeff Davison to know that the South he represented will never rise again."

The Negroes of Grenada clustered in the square broke out of their disbelief and cheered. The white citizens watched with disciplined fury the unthinkable desecration. A merchant said: "I saw two of my niggers in there an' they won't have no jobs tomorrow. . . . They get in that march an' that's it. They'll be on relief tomorrow."

The highway patrolmen, all of them white because every highway patrolman in the state of Mississippi is white as every sheriff is white (Are there any Negro sheriffs in the entire Republic?) stood firm between the whites and Negroes. The facade of rectitude, of equal treatment of both races, would be displayed for all the nation, all the northern factory owners looking for locations with cheap labor, to see. Only once would the facade fall to reveal the shell of justice, down the highway in a city called Canton.

"The colored are really trying the patience of this town," a reporter of unknown affiliation said.

The patience of a town tried for a day, the patience of a people tried for a century. Whose patience took precedence in your mind determined how you told the story.

As a direct result of the march, more than 1,300 Grenada Negroes registered as the county graciously provided extra registrars, even colored ones. Of course, barely had the march moved out of town and Negroes were arrested for trying to integrate a theater and rights workers left behind to set up a permanent movement were being attacked. And over the line in Carroll County, by-passed by the march, federal registrars held open office for four straight days without a single Negro applicant appearing. Here were two small, homely examples of what it took to register Mississippi Negroes. Statewide, results were more encouraging with the percentage of eligibles registered since the Voting Act took effect last August jumping from four percent to around thirty. And the increase had come mainly from urban centers like Jackson, Greenville and Greenwood. Rural Negroes, most vulnerable to intimidation, remained at the mercy of white power exerting absolute dominion over their lives. Now on the march an aggressive and often ambiguous cry began to be raised in opposition to these and other facts. The cry was "Black Power" and the source was Stokely Carmichael.

Stokely—as everyone calls him even when mutual antipathy exists, which is often the case—Stokely was 24 and the newly-elected chairman of SNCC. He replaced John Lewis, an ordained preacher and a sober-spoken but courageous militant.

Stokely was a young veteran of 27 arrests who had run the COFO Freedom House in Greenwood during the terrible summer of 1964. He had seen the house firebombed, watched local workers like Silas McGee brutally beaten, had felt deeply the inability of Negroes to function freely or to defend themselves in a place where white people called all the shots—and did all the shooting.

The march gave the new SNCC chairman a great opportunity to get his philosophy across to America because everything he said was delivered within earshot of Dr. King and Dr. King's presence insured fullest press coverage. Not necessarily enlightened but full. As the column made its way into the Delta and neared the city of Greenwood that had tried to break him in 1964, Stokely spread the word to his many followers on the march that Black Power would be the slogan from there on in. The inspiration may have been similar to the one that prompted Robert Greene in Grenada when he slapped the statue of Jeff Davis—a myth-shattering show of black audacity, proof that a Negro could flex his muscle like anyone else and make it stick. Behind the inspiration was a rationale that would be variously interpreted as the march progressed. But now the message boomed out as pure catalyst to self-realization in Negro minds unaccustomed to flaunting a black ego. It seemed to me to say to whites: See me! I'm here now, flesh and blood like you, as good and as tough, and you're never going to get the chance to look through me again.

Stokely was the man to epitomize the message, long-striding, electric with energy, bringing a slashing black style that had been absent since the murder of Malcolm X, perhaps more potent than Malcolm because it was younger. Arrested in Greenwood when police stopped him from putting up the tents, he returned later to a night rally and shouted:

"We're asking Negroes not to go to Vietnam and fight but to stay in Greenwood and fight here. If they put one of us in jail, we're not going to pay a bond to get him out. We're going up there and get him out ourselves . . . We need Black Power. What do we want? (Black Power!) What do we want? (Black Power!)"

When the thunder of the chant died and the press asked just what he meant by getting people out of courthouses or— as he once said—burning them, Stokely would explain that he spoke metaphorically, that he referred to political action.

"It isn't my job to make black people love everybody *or* to pick up guns," he told me. "But to help black people get the things they deserve. Black nationalism? The press has raised that question, not me. I have to address myself to the black people, not to the press or the white bourgeoisie. They aren't responsive because the questions we are raising thrust into areas they don't like to think about. Everybody is in favor of brotherly love because it's humanistic. But whites get nervous when we don't want to keep talking about it. They need re-assurance. But we're not about to divert our energies to give it to them."

Then, Stokely, you're not anti-white?

"I'm not anti-white but I'm pro-Negro. And I know the oppressed has to free himself. The nation has only responded to our demands in all the civil rights legislation. It hasn't initi-ated. Now the demands must become more militant because the opposition stiffens as white people tire of hearing about the struggle. And you can't realistically talk about a coalition, for example, with Mississippi whites. Who are you going to co-alesce with here? Whites don't want to integrate. And integra-tion is an insidious subterfuge when initiated by blacks alone."

This is dogma and it is part of his style to repeat dogma.

"Integration is an insidious subterfuge when initiated by blacks alone. So Negroes must move socially, politically and economically to control neighborhoods, sections, cities, just like any other ethnic group does."

This is basically how he explained the raw slogan, Black Power. But the phrase invited misinterpretation and its application on the march created tensions inside the march leadership. At the Greenwood stage it seemed the Negro ranks still might remain closed, however loosely. SCLC had long taken a Dutch uncle attitude toward SNCC, going to bat for it even when individual SNCC members were vilifying Dr. King at the time of the Selma march. Now an SCLC official told me:

"We understand that SNCC has always represented the politics of protest, just as it's always been divided within by one faction leaning toward moral solutions and another toward political. As long as SNCC was dominated by southern students, the moral or religious element prevailed. But kids coming in from the North changed this and the defeat of John Lewis put the final stamp on it.

"Right now Stokely is trying to fill the militant vacuum left by Malcolm and he has to project an image. He has to stretch Negro protest out to its extreme edge, pulling along white liberals and the Administration as far as they'll go. When they'll go no farther, he can stop and draw back a little. That's almost the history of the entire Movement.

"But on things like Vietnam, Stokely isn't really too far from somebody like Sen. Fulbright. And on Black Power, he's not too far from us. It's just a question how do you best achieve meaningful Negro political power and I think what we have now is basically a hangup on Stokely's style and semantics."

That same day on the steps of the Greenwood courthouse, with hard-faced Negro prison trustees guarding the Civil War memorial, styles began clashing. SCLC's Hosea Williams speaking alongside Dr. King sounded more SNCC than SCLC as he told the demonstrators:

"Get that vote and pin that badge on a black chest. Get that vote . . . Whip that policeman across the head."

Dr. King's voice declared firmly to those around him:

"He means with the vote."

Stokely smiled and said:

"They know what he means."

It was a small exchange. But the roots went deep into the attitudes and the personalities of the two men. Despite Stokely's disavowals of black violence, a feeling of ambiguity persisted in white and Negro minds whether they learned of the Black Power slogan in Greenwood, or Atlanta, or Washington. Or in the tents of the marchers where town meetings under canvas argued the point day and night.

"If you get violent," said a black SCLC adherent, "you'll end up with whites hating Negroes and vice versa."

"Whites do already," snapped a young Negro from Chicago.

"I was trained in a judo school," a Negro from Jackson said. "If one of them crackers pulls one of us out of the line, I'm gonna judo him . . ."

"What if the man in back of him shoots you?" asked a white marcher who had ventured into a discussion where he plainly was not wanted.

"Then I'll just be another dead nigger."

The judo exponent loses the argument rather badly. Embarrassed by being publicly put down, he storms off, saying he will buy a gun. Then Stokely is suddenly in the midst of it with Leon Hall of SCLC.

Stokely: Our country is the most violent in the world. It steals, rapes and murders all over the world. This country has no right to expect Negroes to be moral forces under those circumstances.

Hall: That's all right for you, Stokely Carmichael, to say and understand. But you let some little numbskull like that interpret it and he runs off to buy a gun.

Stokely: So he's a numbskull. Whose fault is it?

Hall: It's the system's fault. Not the white man's fault. Why stoop to the lowest common denominator of violence?

Stokely (waving his arms excitedly): I'm not talking about violence. I'm not talking about violence. I'm talking about getting power.

And like a Greek chorus, some Negro youngsters in a circle outside the tent began chanting under the guidance of SNCC's Cordell Reagan:

"Whatta we want? Black Power. Whatta we want? Black Power . . ."

They reminded the listener of high school cheer leaders, preparing for the big game. Their voices had that same shrill innocence and dedication.

Life in the tents and along the highway was not all polemics and agitation. Neither was it very much fun. It was self-testing and satisfying when you passed, bone-weary and foot-sore satisfaction earned mile after monotonous mile in heat that parched the throat and dizzied the brain. The marchers existed for the water breaks, the truck with the barrels of ice water welcome as a federal registrar. Usually there was too much weariness for singing but sometimes the songs, "Oh-oh Freedom" and "Ain't Gonna Let Nobody Turn me 'Roun'" and "If You Miss Me From . . ." surged up for a quarter mile or so. Sometimes the people roused their spirits with the chants like, "Whatta we want? Freedom! When do we want it? Now!" and in the middle of one broiling stretch of road, the answer to What do we want? burst out—Water! The When? remained unchanged.

Sometimes the fields produced little miracles of rejuvenation, when Negroes would leave their shacks and come up to the road to wave and smile and occasionally walk awhile. And once from the distant rear edge of a field where the cotton met the trees, small figures started running down the long, neat parallel rows of earth between the plants, heading for the highway, and quickly they became larger, became the figures of raggedy children out from some hidden shack to see the parade for colored people, and when they came up big-eyed and dusty and wondering, a marcher felt, by God I'm really touching somebody with my life for a purpose. And it was easier to go on.

By nighttime, anyone who had marched all day wanted only to eat and quickly fall asleep. With few exceptions, local people always provided food, good and plentiful if you hit the line early, sometimes skimpy at the tail end. Observers who came to sniff out sex orgies had to fall back on their imaginations. There was a men's tent and a women's tent, and it stayed that way. I suppose some love was made on the march;

I hope so. The hate all around needed something to bless it. But the women's tent would quiet down early after perhaps an hour of giggliness. Unlike the Montgomery March, there were few guitars and little singing at night around the campfire; when you are living a folk epic you don't have to sing about one.

One wild night in Grenada moonshine got into the men's tent and there was an hour of foul and nearly violent argument, most of it incoherent. The next day the television press reported that the uproar had been over whether violence or nonviolence should be practiced on the march. The subject had never been mentioned during the argument. But there *were* ups and downs among the marchers, and enough white-black strains to pull—but not to tear—the fabric of brotherhood. Some days spirits drooped until you wondered what could one pitifully small column do ranged against the enormity of the problems. Then something, maybe a big, determined reception in a place like Ita Bena, made all things possible again. And always there was, unspoken yet deeply felt, the dream of the march, the fact or fiction—it was never clear—that merely by going on, by covering the miles and never stopping, you were tangibly advancing all the ideals that had brought you into the column. And you wanted the march to keep going on because then the dream was strongest and truest, and it was only when you stopped walking that the realities began again.

On Tuesday, June 22nd, a group of marchers stopped and peeled off to Philadelphia in Neshoba County to hold memorial services for James Chaney, Andrew Goodman and Michael Schwerner, two years to the day after they had been murdered there.

There is no point in dwelling on what happened in Philadelphia that Tuesday. The city represents the lunacy of racism turned homicidal. It was to be expected that police looked on while speeding cars came inches from plowing into the marchers, that law officers, including Deputy Cecil Price, stood by as the crowd threw cherry bombs at Dr. King as he spoke on the main street, that white youths blank-eyed with hate beat Negroes with fists and feet. I was shocked when an elderly Negro man in front of me fell to the street in an epileptic fit; but who could be surprised when a collegiate-looking white in Bermuda shorts said, There's a Mississippi slave for you—can't stand a little Mississippi sun, or when another told a truck driver stopped a few feet from the stricken man, Come on, roll over him, kill him!

President Johnson was not publicly alarmed. Dr. King wired for the protection of federal marshals when the demonstrators would return to Philadelphia later in the week. He was assured, through a White House intermediary, that Gov. Paul Johnson's highway patrol would do the job.

Two days later in Canton, Mississippi highway patrolmen dropped their mask of equal protection for all, put on gas masks, and mounted a brutal attack against the marchers. They had been denied city permission to pitch their tents behind the all-Negro McNeil elementary school. Why there should be a segregated school when the law says there should not be is one of those things you must not question in Mississippi (or elsewhere, north and south) if you would not be considered a crank. Crankily—and still acting in unison—the leaders organized a massive march on the courthouse to defy the ban. Stokely took charge of rounding up demonstrators in the colored section, loping along the streets with contagious energy, clapping the doubtful on the back and urging them to get with it, dominating the scene with his size and verve.

At the courthouse, Stokely and Dr. King and CORE's Floyd McKissick stood arm-in-arm before a great host of local Negroes. I remembered two years before on the first Freedom Day in Canton when an intimidated line of about 300 Negroes were stopped time and again en route to the courthouse by white lawmen giving peremptory orders, motioning them on with waves of deer rifles, halting them, finally letting two or three inside to try to register while the rest stood waiting for ten hours in rigidly controlled lines they were not permitted to leave. Now, blackness spread over the courthouse lawn wherever it wanted to go and in the wave of smiling black faces one white one, tragi-comic like Ned Sparks, a glum investigator for the Mississippi Highway Patrol.

"They said we couldn't pitch our tents on a black school," Stokely cried to the crowd. "Well, we're gonna do it now."

He was wrong. They got the tents off the trucks, Dr. King

and McKissick helping to haul them onto the damp grass, vividly green in a radiant, storm-brooding light that came from behind blooming purple clouds, El Greco colors in Canton, Mississippi. Then the squads of highway patrolmen and county and city officers and conservation men began marching onto the east end of the field. Bolts clicked on their rifles. The men were uniformly big and in their blue and green hardhats holding the guns and with the web belts ringed with tear gas cannisters they looked very formidable. Some of the leaders mounted the top of a rented truck, Dr. King and McKissick silhouetted against the sky's fading radiance, Stokely on the ground starting the chant:

"We're gonna pitch the tents, pitch the tents, pitch the tents."

The marchers and the Canton people joined hands and sang, "We Shall Overcome." Mrs. Kaye asked:

"What do you think they'll do?"

I told her I thought they would throw tear gas.

"Oh no," she said. "They wouldn't do that. Not that I'm frightened. I'm not. This is where I want to be. But I wish I knew just where Jennie was."

Brooklyn bus driver Young was calm; he had been through New York rush hours and he thought: What more can life do to me? The elderly white lady cocked old, expert eyes at the troopers. She had been gassed during a protest in Demopolis, Ala. and knew what to expect. The lawmen put on their masks. It stripped them of any humanity. You thought of Steinbeck's description in "The Grapes of Wrath" of the tractor drivers hired by the eastern banks, masked and goggled, remorselessly ripping up the Okies' farms. Then it started coming, without warning, the psst-boom of exploding tear gas cannisters, some thrown, others fired at point blank range into the scrambling bodies. No one can fight against gas. It leaves no margin for courage or cowardice. One good gulp and you have to run, anywhere but where *it* is. I heard one clarion call of protest ring above the nightmare, a curse at whites.

Then the troopers came, beating, kicking, striking out with rifle butts. They were not arresting anyone. They were punishing people. It was Selma bridge all over again, the casualties fewer but the unleashed hatred just as intense. A heavyset Negro woman in her late 30's, Mrs. Odessa Warrick, was stunned from the gas and as she tried to hold herself up a patrolman kicked her in the back, yelling, "Nigger, you want your freedom, here it is!" She was hospitalized with a possible spinal fracture. A white man, Morris Mitchell, who was 71 that day, had brought to the march some students from an interracial Quaker school on Long Island. He saw a patrolman beating a man on the ground with a rifle butt (Note: apparently Charles Meyer, a white pre-med student who suffered two fractured ribs and a 20 percent collapse of one lung) and said to the patrolman:

"You should be ashamed of yourself."

The patrolman replied to the white-haired Mitchell:

"You get back or I'll put it into you."

As the gas began clearing, a golden crescent moon appeared, hanging calmly beside dark purple and salmon clouds. The discipline of those gassed had been extraordinary. Not one person panicked and no one swerved from nonviolence despite the miles of debate. Stokely, whether from exhaustion or because he took a very heavy dose of gas, was one of the few who seemed to have "lost his cool." He stormed the streets, shouting:

"Start movin', baby. They're gonna shoot again. They're gonna shoot again. The people . . . get the people outa here."

"Keep calm, Stokely," McKissick said.

"Stokely," said Dr. King, himself red-eyed from the gas, "let's go to the nearest house and talk. We can't accomplish anything out here on the street."

It was an emotional moment and dangerous. No one knew what the troopers might do. The Rev. Andy Young, one of SCLC's firmest disciples of nonviolence, confessed later that when he saw the highway patrol cars standing empty along the street, the thought crossed his mind that they should be burned.

"Don't they ever learn?" asked the veteran of St. Augustine and Selma. "Violence can spread just the same as nonviolence did."

Next day, Attorney General Nicholas Katzenbach, speaking

to fill the void of the President's continued silence, said the Canton violence had occurred because Negroes had refused to move from school grounds where they had no right to be. The people who had suffered the brutality were expecting, at the least, indignation; they received from Washington a chiding legalism.

Dr. King said of Katzenbach's reaction:

"Yes, I heard that terrible statement. He's back saying those same things he did when the accused killer of Jonathan Daniels was freed by a Lowndes County jury. That's the price you have to pay for the jury system, he said then . . . Terrible.

"I've heard nothing from President Johnson. It's terribly frustrating and disappointing. The federal government makes my job more difficult every day . . . to keep the Movement nonviolent. Of course, I've lived with this hate and violence for a long time now and I personally can't change. Somebody has *got* to break the chain of hatred. It's not easy and I go through periods when it's very difficult.

"But the fact is that nobody has challenged the concept of nonviolence enough to convince the vast majority of Negroes in this country that it shouldn't remain the way. I think they've come to see that we've made our most tangible gains through nonviolence and can continue to."

And how did "Black Power" affect his thinking?

"I don't think that has touched many of us," Dr. King said. "It has been used on this particular march and I think people generally just use a slogan that anybody projects. I prefer not to use it, not because I don't understand its denotative reasons but because it has connotative implications. I don't use the term 'Black Power' but I do know the Negro must have power if we're gonna gain freedom and human dignity."

SNCC rank-and-file would have howled down his "connotative" and "denotative" as old-fogyism. But more important, Dr. King may have been undermined in his strongest bargaining point in civil rights councils. In the past, he had been able to deliver the power of response in Washington. Not now. If the Johnson Administration had deliberately tried to bolster the burgeoning image of Stokely and SNCC it could not have done better than to turn away from Dr. King's appeal for a federal stand after Canton and Philadelphia. The silent rebuff made the Nobel Prize winner just one more put-down American Negro.

That Friday of disillusion in Canton promised to end with a bang, another confrontation between marchers and troopers over the school campsite. But there was no bang, only whimper. Hundreds of marchers and sympathizers trooped to the school under the impression that they would make another witness in the face of clubs and tear gas, forcing Mississippi to back down or repeat its shoddy performance so that those in the blase national audience who didn't get the point the first time might have a second look. But when the marchers got to the field, they were told that a compromise had been reached with authorities. They would be permitted to hold their rally on the grounds but no camping, the tents had already been sent ahead to Tougaloo in Jackson. The marchers booed; a few cried, "Sellout." Many had brought handkerchiefs soaked in water as makeshift tear gas masks to insure that "we would not be moved." They tossed them away. They heard local leaders like Mrs. Annie Devine explain that because of the doubtful legal basis etc. etc. For the first time, there was suspicion that the marchers were being manipulated. Dr. King did not even appear. John Lewis, lately come to the march, spoke in place of Stokely. No one had much to say that the audience wanted to hear. If the "compromise" had been made for safety's sake, then why hadn't they, the ones who had come to sacrifice, been consulted? And if it had been made for other reasons, to keep the rally on schedule for the big Sunday entry into Jackson before all the network TV cameras, then why not come out and say it? And there was an added insult underfoot. The "compromising" state troopers had attached a water pipe to a drain running from the roof of the school. Water poured out of it, flooding the field, bogging down the demonstrators in mud.

What followed on the march was anti-climax. James Meredith rejoined the march on Saturday, starting out from Canton although technically the march had reached Tougaloo the previous evening. He came in his plastic pith helmet and African walking stick, complaining about "shenanigans" on the part of some leaders but never specifying what he meant. He insisted that his original solitary plan had been a valid one.

I asked him whether he thought he could have made it alone through a town like Philadelphia.

"I have never been any place by myself," he said. "Anywhere there are Negroes I'm not alone."

While he walked his mysterious way, the remnants of civil rights unity were raveled in a motel meeting outside Jackson. The leadership voted on whether the NAACP's Charles Evers would be permitted to speak at the Jackson rally. King wanted him in the interest of unity although Evers had not supported the march in its beginning. But he was outvoted by SNCC, CORE and the Mississippi Freedom Democratic Party, all of whom had been engaged in a blood feud with Evers long before the march. An SCLC official told me after the meeting that all Dr. King wanted to do then was "get the hell away from this atmosphere as fast as he can."

For a few throbbing hours on Sunday, dissensions and disillusions seemed forgotten as the biggest black turnout in the history of the state wound toward toward the capitol from Tougaloo. A band played, "When the Saints Go Marchin' In," battered trombones shining beaten gold in the brilliant sun, and Negroes poured off their porches to march with a show of gleeful release. Big and stirring emotion charged the air along the route but it all seemed to thud to a stop at the capitol. The lawn was saturated with troopers—including many who had taken part in the Canton attack—and National Guardsmen with "U.S. Army" stencilled on their fatigues. Highway patrolmen with their badge numbers covered by black tape had posts directly behind the speakers' stand and they tyrannized all who approached a line of demarcation between white ground and that which was on loan to Negroes for the afternoon.

Speeches were generally lackluster. Dr. King resurrected his "dream" of the March on Washington, found it had turned into a "nightmare," but concluded that he still had a dream that "one day right here in this state of Mississippi justice will become a reality for all." Stokely said that if more black people were shot, "we're gonna move to disrupt this country." Whitney Young announced that the Urban League was finally coming to Mississippi and train people, get them jobs. On and on went the words. The marchers were hot and tired and word of the shattered unity had spread. Many drifted away, their contribution to civil rights history ended, the result in abeyance.

Their walk through Mississippi had achieved many things, tangible and subtle. Four thousand more Negroes were registered and although there still were more than three hundred thousand to go, registration that had been slowed up was put in motion again. Areas untouched by the Movement in the past now had seen civil rights workers in the flesh, though no one could predict how much of this "seeding" would take root. White Mississippi had been pushed a bit further in a direction it did not want to go and sometimes it had responded in a way that would have been impossible even a year before. But it was already pushing back, with troopers clubbing demonstrators in Grenada after the TV cameras left, and the success of its habitual recidivism could not be gauged. Because what happens in Mississippi depends on what happens in Washington and New York and Los Angeles and Atlanta. And what is happening in these places is not at all reassuring. Somehow, Stokely Carmichael and Black Power seem to be becoming the enemy while the enemy of white power unresponsive to just Negro demand skulks off to the side. Already, riot-torn northern cities are blaming "outside agitators" for their ghetto problems. We are coming in on a bad picture we have seen before.

When the march went through Belzoni, I talked to a Negro in his thirties who owned a small cafe on the street where a local civil rights leader named George Lee was murdered a few years ago. The man drove a truck for $1.25 an hour, receiving overtime only after 60 hours, while his wife ran the cafe. He also farmed a little and by pooling everything and working his life away, he made enough for his family to live decently. White power had left its heelmark in his soul and I asked if he hated whites.

"No," he said, "I don't and I never want to. Why? It's hard to say. It's just a meltingness in the heart."

If his kind of heart hardens, the guilt will be on white America and no amount of marches down the highways of this country, North and South, will ever set things right again.

New South, Summer 1966

Which Way in Grenada?

by Robert Analavage

GRENADA, Miss.—There are many small towns still in the South that have not been touched by the Movement. These towns continue to live in traditional, unreconstructed quiet.

They have much in common. Usually there is a black population of 50 per cent or more.

The city officials are of the ignorant, brutal type personified by Jim Clark, the ex-sheriff of Selma, Alabama.

And, most obvious of all, these towns are totally segregated and the black people live in social, political and economic bondage.

Such a town is Grenada, Mississippi, whose population of 8,000 is divided almost equally between black and white.

Only now there is a movement in Grenada. It started when the Meredith March passed through and stirred the black people to move and strike out against the fear and oppression that had ruled their lives.

What kind of movement it will be, what gains it will secure, how it will alter this bastion of white supremacy, may well be an indication of the future course of the Southern freedom movement.

Grenada's reaction to the Meredith March could not have been more disarming.

The city police protected the marchers. Speeches were delivered at the base of the Confederate Memorial in the square. The police even stood by while one marcher placed an American flag on the memorial.

City officials hired six black registrars and allowed 1000 Negroes to register to vote.

When the marchers departed, the six black registrars were fired. The 1000 Negroes whom they registered suddenly discovered they had no proof they were registered, because someone had conveniently forgotten to issue them voting slips.

Organizers from both the Southern Christian Leadership Conference (SCLC) and the Student Non-violent Co-ordinating Committee (SNCC) returned to Grenada at the request of the local people.

Nightly rallies were held and a program for the town was debated and discussed.

Hosea Williams of SCLC argued for a traditional movement, one that would have as its goal total integration and have as its rallying cry the familiar phrase—Freedom Now!

(Throughout the march, Williams consistently opposed using the phrase "Black Power.")

Stokely Carmichael of SNCC argued against the SCLC program with its emphasis on integration and urged the people to work for Black Power and rally around that phrase.

(During the march Carmichael had reiterated that efforts toward integration cannot be achieved unless black people have their own power first.)

The position of Williams and SCLC was accepted by the people largely because of the great personal influence of Martin Luther King which exists in the southern rural areas.

Thus, for the time being, SCLC won the opportunity to demonstrate whether non-violence and the traditional movement approach can be a workable factor in bringing about significant changes in the South.

Carmichael and SNCC, which have worked in Mississippi for the last four years, left Grenada.

In parting, the SNCC chairman said: "When they get tired of marching we'll be back with our program."

Williams and SCLC, which had never organized in Mississippi before, began to put their program into effect. Williams called for an 'open city' with full integration into every aspect of the city's life. The city was presented with 51 demands.

To this, Grenada's power structure replied with a determined—no!

Suggs Ingram, the sheriff of the county and a man who both symbolizes and enforces the old order, said "There will be no concessions of any type or degree made to anyone whatsoever.

"They had it so easy during the march," he said, "they

thought they could come back and take over. We are not going to put up with that even if it takes force."

—The force came with 66 arrests of Negroes during the first week.

—The force came with the burst of a sub-machine gun fired at two civil rights lawyers, which riddled an SCLC staff car with bullets.

—The force came from the gun butts and billy clubs of state troopers who scattered protesting Negroes.

The movement countered with a 'withdrawal of patronage' campaign which would be called a boycott except that it is illegal to boycott in Mississippi.

Groups of pickets appeared daily at all white-owned stores and fully 90 per cent of Grenada's black people 'withdrew their patronage'.

Public accommodations were tested also and Negroes began showing up at downtown cafes and the library, and swimming in the Grenada lake as the whites withdrew from the water.

On Sundays they attempted to integrate the services at several white churches. When they were denied entrance they held prayer sessions on the front lawn hoping to shame the white Christians.

Then Williams began to use the dangerous tactic of staging nightly marches through both the black and white communities to the Confederate Memorial in the center of town.

The marchers' numbers ranged from 400 to 1000 on different nights.

They filed through the black areas first, clapping, chanting, singing such familiar freedom songs as "Never in the World There Is Too Much Love", "Ain't Gonna Let Nobody Turn Me Round", "It May Be the Last Time".

When they got to the white residential areas the clapping and the chanting and the singing gave way to silence and the muffled sounds of feet marching on the concrete.

When they arrived downtown they were greeted by groups of whites clustered on the sidewalk who jeered and hurled curses at the marchers. An occasional missile would be thrown from the crowd.

State troopers and city police stood by with tear gas and sub-machine guns. When the marchers stopped at the courthouse to make their speeches the cops fixed bayonets and held them pointed at the group. The speeches contained much of the same material and were repeated over and over again, night after night.

Williams addressed all of Grenada when he said "It's all over in Grenada, Miss. The Sheriff might as well know, the mayor might as well know, Paul Johnson might as well know, the Ku Klux Klan and the White Citizens' Council might as well know—it is all over in Grenada."

Whites hooted and howled and shouted back that it would never be over in Grenada.

Williams continued: "This country is closer to being destroyed than I ever thought possible. This country is closer to doom than I ever thought possible.

"Negroes are tired. They are tired of being lied to. They are tired of being brutalized in the South. They are tired of being kept in Ghettoes in the North.

"I believe if the black people don't save America she is lost to history. America can tell nobody and no nation anything any more, because nobody believes her any more.

"America owes a bill that she must pay. The bill must be paid even if it must be paid in blood.

"If whites will not yield to nonviolence then they are going to have to deal with the nationalists or Black Power. The choice is yours!"

And night after night, day after day, the struggle goes on with white Grenada determined to resist change and black Grenada determined to create change.

How well SCLC's drive for integration in Grenada will succeed and how much change it will bring into the lives of the black people living there, could well decide which direction the entire Movement takes.

Will it continue to work toward integration as a method for correcting the misuses of 'white power' or will it renounce integration altogether, and instead concentrate on building power in the black community as the only realistic counterbalance against white power?

Part of the answer to this question may be found in this little Mississippi town.

The Southern Patriot, August 1966

Big Changes Are Coming

by James H. Meredith

THE thing I remember most clearly is coming over a rise, with the harsh Mississippi sun baking the pavement of Highway 51, and seeing the town of Hernando lying before me like some Hollywood director's idea of a small town in the American South: a few small stores, some old decaying mansions and many, many unpainted board houses where the Negroes lived. It was the first town I had come to in Mississippi. I saw white faces at windows, and white men standing in front of their shops or staring blankly from the lawns of their homes. I didn't see any Negroes. At least, I didn't see them anywhere around the main street. But they were waiting for me when I walked into the main square of the town. Some of them had been there for two hours, standing together on the far side of the square. There were young men and old, children with pure young faces and old men bent with age. Most were wearing the long blue overalls of cotton-field workers, and they did not seem to know what to do. Some looked away, some stared at the ground. All of them were aware of the group of whites, silent and sullen, who watched us from the far side of the square.

I walked up to the group of Negroes and started shaking hands. Then, after the ice had been broken, I started to explain why I had come back to the Mississippi where I had been born. I told them that a new day was coming, that we were going to get all the rights and privileges we were entitled to, that there were many good whites in the community, but there were also some bad ones, and if society didn't eliminate them, then we would.

I urged them to register to vote, because that was one of the keys to the future, and they said, "We're gonna register, we're gonna register." And then we went around to a café to have something to eat. I was eating a cheeseburger and drinking a glass of milk, when an old Negro farmer came over and pressed a dollar bill in my hand. He had probably never earned more than $300 in a single year, "You just keep that," he said. "You just keep that." I still had that dollar bill in my pocket a few hours later when my back was riddled by shots fired from ambush.

Later I would remember the events in Hernando with greater clarity than even the shooting itself. Hernando represented to me the whole purpose of my return to Mississippi, I had gone there to talk to Negroes, to explain that the old order was passing, that they should stand up as men with nothing to fear. So my sharpest memories remain the faces of those Negro men in Hernando, and the man who gave me the dollar bill, and the way the white people stood in isolation across the street. For both the whites and Negroes of Hernando, nothing like this had ever happened before.

We were an hour out of Hernando, moving south, when Claude Sterrett, a friend from New York, arrived. I was wearing a pith helmet, slacks and working boots, and carrying an ebony-and-ivory cane which had been given to me by a vil lage chief on the banks of the Nile River in the Sudan. The pith helmet had once been the hated symbol of the white man in what he called "darkest Africa." Times, of course, had changed.

"Jay," Sterrett said breathlessly, "I met a man down the road who said someone's waiting for you with a gun. He's gonna shoot you."

I shrugged. In Mississippi, anything was possible. All that day, on the way into Hernando and on the road out again, my walk had been accompanied by a convoy of several cars. These contained some members of the press, some local police and highway patrolmen, and some observers from the FBI. We had passed a number of potential troublemakers, and I had even picked out two men who I expected would give me trouble.

After walking through open farm country, we went down into a long, gradual hollow with thick, almost junglelike foliage on either side. It had rained early that morning and the trees were still damp, and the fresh, earthy smell of the country-side was everywhere. I remember thinking that things were going even better than I had expected. An old farmer and his family came down to the highway and gave me water, in full view of the white people across the road. I remember a Negro maid in one white home who edged down the clothesline to the road and gave me a little wave.

Then something strange happened. The cars that had been following, or leapfrogging alongside me, moved up the road and parked on the shoulder. Some of the men in the cars walked on to a small soft-drinks store. I couldn't see the sheriff's car or the highway patrol. I was left there with Sterrett; Mohammed Rauf of the Washington *Daily News*; Sherwood Ross, a white Washington radio broadcaster who had volunteered to work as my press coordinator; the Rev. Robert O. Weeks, a white Episcopal minister from Monroe, N.Y.; and Joe Crittenden, a Memphis Negro businessman. Suddenly, I heard a voice behind me.

"James," the voice said. "I only want James Meredith. All the rest of you stand aside."

I turned around. A man stood in the roadside foliage, a shotgun cradled in his arms. I've seen a lot of movies, but no director could have made a man look as cold-blooded as this one. This was the face the southern Negro has been staring at through 350 years of history: the hard eyes, the fleshy face, the hard line of mouth. You've seen the same face in dozens of pictures. It is the face of the deputy sheriff, the face of the man freed by an all-white jury after murdering a Negro, the face of those vicious young men carrying Confederate flags who hit civil-rights workers with ax handles.

"Just James Meredith," he said, moving toward the shoulder of the road.

I wished suddenly that I had brought a gun, that I had prepared better. Things were happening so fast that I had no time for fear. I threw myself on the ground, and the gun roared, and I was hit somewhere in the back. I'm still not sure of the sequence of events. I thought four shots were fired; other witnesses said three. I was hit again, and then tried to get across the road and into the safety of a gully. But the last shot hit me in the head and knocked me flat. Then there was absolute silence.

I could hear voices, and people moving past me, and then

I felt someone opening my shirt and shouting for an ambulance. It was, I suppose, as close as I had ever come to being killed. But I knew then what millions of people listening to radios and watching television were not to know for at least an hour. I knew that I was alive.

After the shooting, many people asked: What was Meredith trying to prove? Didn't he know that if he ventured out alone on an open highway in Mississippi, someone would try to kill him? Didn't he know that his reputation as the first Negro ever to be admitted to the University of Mississippi would precede him, and that old simmering hatreds might come to a boil?

Of course I understood those dangers; I am, after all, a Negro American. I was born and reared in Mississippi, and I have learned something about the dark side of human nature. But there are some things a man must do in his life, actions which answer the callings of conscience. There are some feelings that cannot be explained with mere words. Fear is one of them. It was fear, and its consequences for this country, that brought me back to Mississippi.

I just wish there were some way to explain the awful fear that permeates the atmosphere for every Negro in this country, and especially those Negroes who inhabit the American South. I wish there were a way to explain what it is like to be a Negro moving down a deserted highway at night behind the wheel of an automobile, and see car lights blink on in the darkened rear of a service station, and see a car bearing strangers pulling out behind you. I wish I could put into words the sinking feeling in the stomach and the nervous twitching in the face which can come over a Negro when he confronts a southern sheriff. I wish I could explain the long history of murder and castration and death in the night; explain the humiliation and insult of the theory of white supremacy; explain all those things that are the excess baggage of the American Negro's mind, whether he lives in Scarsdale, N.Y., or Philadelphia, Miss. Their root is fear. And in my own way, that morning in June, I hoped that by walking down that road I could remove at least some part of that fear.

I chose Highway 51 because it is the classic route of the Mississippi Negro, a concrete river leading away from home.

Going north, the road spelled hope; going south, it spelled despair. When you read about rioting in Watts and Harlem and Bedford-Stuyvesant, remember that many of those people and their fathers and grandfathers before them made that long trip north along Highway 51 only to find that there are no golden cities. You who live in the North: Do not think that Mississippi has no relevance to you. No Negro, North or South, can hide from its reality. My Mississippi is everywhere.

When I announced my walk, I welcomed any able-bodied man who wanted to join me. I insisted that I did not want women and children, because I felt deeply that women and children should not have to take these risks. It was for this reason that I did not take my wife Mary June or my six-year-old son John. I felt it was time for the American Negro male to assert his manhood, to take his own chances, to risk his own life. I also said that I wanted no one to accompany me who would become a burden to the Negroes of Mississippi, imposing upon them for lodging or food. Any whites who cared to come along were welcome (and at the moment of the shooting three of the men walking that road were white).

The night before setting out I sat in a Memphis hotel room, trying to decide whether I should carry a gun. This question had been on my mind for a long time. I finally decided against it and took instead a Bible. If I had been armed, I could have knocked off the intended killer with one shot. My father, who lived in Mississippi for 74 years and died there, would have prepared himself better than I did.

And so, because I was not properly prepared, I found myself in room 511B of the William F. Bowld Hospital in Memphis. In a matter of hours, three adjacent rooms had been commandeered for use by local police, the FBI, and telephone operators. I tried to call my wife at our apartment in New York City, where I am a student at the Columbia University Law School. She was in a state of shock, believing that I was dead. I assured her I was all right. I tried to call my 62-year-old mother in Kosciusko, Miss., where I had grown up. She had broken down when she heard the reports of my death and was under sedation. It would be two days before she could be told that I was alive.

I must say about the Bowld Hospital that I could not have

wanted better attention and care. The doctors, staff workers and nurses treated me wonderfully. I had 75 to 100 pellets of bird shot in my body, and the doctors decided that cutting out all the pellets would cause more damage than leaving them alone. Some are working their way out. Some I will carry with me all my life.

I slept fitfully through the night. When I woke up, a huge bouquet rested on a shelf across the room. It was from Dick Gregory, an old friend, who had flown in the night before with his wife and children. He was my first visitor, other than those who had been with me on the march.

Dick had left home thinking I was dead. He also had vowed that if nothing else were done, he would pick up the walk from the spot where I had been shot. Now, he said, he was going out to Highway 51, to the place where I was shot, and start a return walk to Memphis.

A short while after Dick left, I was visited by the Rev. Martin Luther King, of the Southern Christian Leadership Conference (S.C.L.C.), Floyd McKissick, national director of the Congress of Racial Equality (C.O.R.E.), and Stokely Carmichael, chairman of the Student Nonviolent Coordinating Committee (S.N.C.C.). I had corresponded with Dr. King briefly when I was a student in Africa, and had met McKissick at the White House Conference on Civil Rights the week before the shooting. I had never met Carmichael.

Dr. King and McKissick came in together, and Carmichael remained outside. My lawyer from Memphis, A. W. Willis, was there, along with one of Dr. King's aides from S.C.L.C., the Rev. James Lawson, of the Centenary Methodist Church in Memphis. We had a two-hour conversation. They apparently did not know that Dick Gregory had already left to start his own walk back from the spot where I had been shot, and when I told them about it, it seemed to upset them a bit. I can understand that; if anything were to be done, it probably should not have been done in a haphazard way.

I explained to them that I had studied the route a long time, and knew that 225 miles was a long way, and that it was not the same as a walk between two large cities like Selma and Montgomery. I explained that as a man who had spent nine years in the Air Force, I was concerned with discipline and order. I was concerned about the logistics of any large march, and the problems of housing and feeding large numbers of people. I also explained why I did not think women and children should be out on that highway.

They listened carefully to what I had to say and then indicated a strong desire to continue. Let me make that clear. They did not want to continue *my* march—they wanted to continue, period. I did not disagree. Whatever they felt they had to do, I was for them. A man has to satisfy his conscience.

All I did was caution them about their responsibilities to the Negroes of Mississippi. Whatever they decided to do— and I certainly could not prevent them from doing anything —I urged them to avoid any acts that would be detrimental to those million human beings who would still be there when the march was over. They agreed. They told me they would attempt to determine the logistics of continuing and would return to see me at four o'clock that afternoon. They assured me that they would not cross the point where I was shot before letting me know their plans.

I did not hear from the leaders again until 8:30 that night, when a telephone call came from Rev. Lawson. It was then that I first became disturbed. Rev. Lawson began to explain to me what "we" had decided, what "we" were going to do. I wanted to know who "we" were—if they were going to make decisions in my name, I wanted to know who "we" were going to be. I made clear my dissatisfaction, and reminded Rev. Lawson of the promise to see me at 4 P.M. He said that Dr. King would come the next morning to see me.

I was still disturbed when Charles Evers came to see me about 30 minutes later. I can never talk to Charles Evers without thinking of his brother Medgar, who had been one of my closest friends and supporters during those crisis-ridden days when I first entered the University of Mississippi. Like so many Negroes in Mississippi in this century, Medgar Evers was murdered, shot in the back from ambush. Charles took over the leadership of the N.A.A.C.P. in Mississippi, and in his own way, is a hard working, effective leader. On this night he was unhappy too. We talked freely about my uneasiness, which seemed to add to his own depression. A few days later he would question the leaders of the march, saying that the Negroes of Mississippi might be left holding the bag when the national leaders and the press had left.

After Charles left, I was visited by Whitney Young, head of the Urban League, and Roy Wilkins, executive secretary of the N.A.A.C.P. They had already made their speeches at the church and did not seem particularly happy about what they had seen and heard. It is no secret that there is a certain amount of tactical disagreement among the major Negro organizations. The N.A.A.C.P. and the Urban League see education, voting and legislation as the keys to Negro freedom. The S.C.L.C. seems to agree, and supports the principles of nonviolence. S.N.C.C. talks increasingly of "black power" and has among its membership young men who are no longer prepared to turn the other cheek. C.O.R.E. lies somewhere in between. Apparently Wilkins and Young felt that the more militant leaders were going to provide the direction to the march. They flew back to New York that night.

The next morning, Dr. King, McKissick and Carmichael came to see me. The night before they had drafted a manifesto for the "Meredith March through Mississippi." Young and Wilkins had not signed it, apparently because they felt that it was anti Administration and too unrealistic in its demand that 600 federal registrars be sent into Mississippi. I told the leaders that the manifesto did not make any difference to me, that it would have been acceptable if it had been written the way Wilkins and Whitney Young wanted it, or the way Carmichael had wanted it. They read it to me, and that was that.

Dr. King and Mr. McKissick stayed behind to tell me why they couldn't come back as they had promised the day before: They had decided that the march had to be resumed immediately, even before the logistical problems were settled. They felt the larger purpose was important enough to risk possible uncertainties and unforeseen difficulties. They did not come to see me because they were marching; in fact, they were scuffling with a pair of Mississippi highway patrolmen at almost exactly the moment of the appointment. I found this perfectly acceptable. And I wished them luck.

At about 8:30 that morning I was told by my attending

doctor that he would keep me until the next day, and possibly until the day after. He said that I seemed to be all right. Then at about 10:30 the security chief told me that I was going to be discharged. Mr. Willis, my lawyer, and the only Negro in the Tennessee Legislature, questioned a hospital procedure in which policemen notified patients of their discharge.

At 10:55 the hospital administrator came in and made it official. He said that my doctor had signed my discharge papers, and they expected me to leave by the 11 A.M. check-out time. That was in five more minutes.

But I didn't leave. Not just then. I followed Willis's advice and stayed there. I was served dinner. Then the administrator returned. He said I could not see the doctor who had been treating me, but that he did have the names of two Negro doctors who might see me. His attitude was so nasty that I said, "All right, give me the papers." I signed them, got dressed and left.

I went upstairs to the seventh-floor doctors' lounge where the press had been waiting for two days to interview me. When I walked into the glare of the TV lights, I began sweating heavily, and I became unsteady on my feet. I had prepared a written statement, five pages long, and was on the fourth page when the accumulation of lights, weakness and tension caught up with me. I fainted. I was taken out of the hospital in a wheelchair, went to a cousin's house for a few hours, and about six that night caught a plane for New York. But I was not through with Mississippi.

I was going back to Mississippi because, like every American Negro, I had to go back. For too many years the American Negro has been like no other citizen in this country. He has been deprived of that most essential of all things: a spiritual homeland. The American of Irish descent can always point with pride to his Irish ancestry; the Italian to his. But the Negro has no home. His history in this country has been dotted with back-to-Africa movements, but they have solved nothing. What Africa? Will he go to Ghana or Nigeria, the Sudan or Kenya? Every American Negro must experience what I experienced during the year I spent in Africa—the feeling that I was, above all, an American. And my homeland, and the homeland of every American Negro, is the South.

The South has formed us and scarred us, but it is where we came from. We carry the South with us wherever we go, to the suburbs of New York, to the ghettos of Detroit, to the charred streets of Watts. Deep inside every one of us is the secret memory of the South. That is why no one can possibly expect conciliation of the races as long as the South remains the way it is.

I can love Mississippi because of the beauty of the countryside and the old traditions of family affection, and for such small things as flowers bursting in spring and the way you can see for miles from a ridge in winter. Why should a Negro be forced to leave such things? Because of fear? No. Not anymore.

The Negro has tried nonviolence, he has turned the other cheek, he has said "love" when the white man said "hate," and it has made no difference. Dr. King is quite an impressive man, but there is much feeling that his philosophy of nonviolence is no longer tenable. There are many Negroes, myself included, who believe that we no longer can guarantee the white man in Mississippi that we will not strike back. The white man cannot hit a Negro, or try to kill him, without expecting to be hit back or killed. Some people are uneasy over the growth of the Deacons for Defense, an organization of Negroes in Louisiana and Mississippi who carry guns and are prepared to meet terror with terror. But when a man lives in a place where violence against him is sanctioned by the law, he will take the law into his own hands.

My own feeling is that nonviolence is incompatible with American ideals. America is a tough country, and a man has to look out for his own, to be his own man. It is not an American ideal to abandon willingly any personal control over your own life; and the philosophy of nonviolence requires this. To ask Negroes to support nonviolence is to ask them to be something different, to be something alien in their own country. I believe that in the next several years you will see fewer and fewer Negroes supporting nonviolence.

The civil-rights movement began as a collaboration between upper- and middle-class Negroes and white liberals within such organizations as the N.A.A.C.P. But in the past few years you have also seen the growth of what I call "the Negro movement." The root of this is a deep pride in one's own race, in one's own traditions, one's own manhood. A pride, if you will, in being Negro. Bravery comes directly from pride, and there will be a lot of Negroes prepared to die before the crisis is over.

It is the conflict between the civil-rights movement (which is rightly the concern of whites and Negroes) and the Negro movement that led to some of the dissension on the march. For one thing, the pretensions of the N.A.A.C.P. to being a mass Negro organization were crumbling with every step the marchers took. The N.A.A.C.P. is not a mass Negro organization: It does not command the emotions or respect of most younger Negroes, and the older Negro is becoming more and more disenchanted. People are tired of the way every American President uses the N.A.A.C.P. national office as the 20th-century house Negro, and the way the N.A.A.C.P. bows to play that role. The N.A.A.C.P. is a civil-rights organization with a white president. I fully support it as a civil-rights organization, but I cannot support its claim to be a Negro organization.

I believe that the march has begun to make lasting changes in Mississippi. Organizations like the Mississippi Freedom Democratic Party are not going to abandon their struggle just because the TV cameras and the reporters have departed. I believe I saw one of these changes when I went back to Mississippi to finish the march.

I arrived in Canton the night after the brave troops of the Mississippi Highway Patrol had tear-gassed and beaten a crowd, including women and children, whose crime was to try to erect a tent in a Negro schoolyard. There was great bitterness and a potential for outright violence. The leaders, under the influence of Dr. King, had decided that to stay in Canton was to risk another outbreak. They had learned that in Mississippi the law was not to protect a citizen as a citizen but to protect the system of white supremacy. In most places in the South the local white supremacists had given in at least a little bit; in Mississippi they had not given an inch. The leaders decided to send an advance party on to Tougaloo, pitch the tents, and make the last lap to Jackson from there.

But I had promised many people that I would walk from Canton to Jackson or at least that I would try. Then, that Friday, I was told there would be no marching on Saturday, and the last lap would be held up until the grand finale on Sunday. I decided to go ahead and do what I had said I would do. On Saturday morning I was in Canton, with three friends, to make the last lap myself.

And it was here that one of the small, hidden, but truly significant occurrences of the march took place. The Mississippi Highway Patrol had refused to offer me any protection whatsoever. So I asked to see the sheriff of Madison County, Jack Cauthen.

The sheriff came over, invited me into his office, and proceeded to astonish me. We sat there, he and I, talking the way human beings talk. He said he had been up for 24 hours, and agreed to give me protection at least to the city limits. When he went outside, he told the people waiting that I was a gentleman, that we had made an agreement, and then he proceeded to carry out the agreement. We marched to the city limits, the four of us growing into more than 500, and we were protected, as citizens should be protected. The police were not surly, there was no cursing, no bad manners, no "nigger-calling." Perhaps for the first time in history the local law-enforcement officials in Mississippi were protecting Negroes with some grace, and without conditions. In its way, that was the most significant part of the march.

That gesture by a Mississippi sheriff was symbolic of what is beginning to happen in the South. He might not have liked me, he might even have hated me; but he treated me as a citizen. He knows that changes are coming. The Negro is finally getting the vote. We now have the legislation, in the wake of the civil-rights acts, and if we still do not have the realities of justice, then I say that we soon will.

I will certainly do everything I can to help bring it about. For the next two years my most important concern is completing my course at Columbia Law School, but at the same time I want to devote all of my spare time to voter registration, particularly in Mississippi and New York. Few people realize this, but the state with the lowest percentage of registered Negroes is not in the Deep South—it is New York. Sometime this summer I hope to lead a voter-registration march through Harlem, to inspire the Negroes there to believe that their votes can be used to improve their lives.

After I leave Columbia, who knows? I want to use my education in the most useful way I can, and I would like to go back to live in my home state of Mississippi. Someday, perhaps, I might want to enter politics there. But for now there is much that must be done, much that we must prepare for.

Negroes are dying bravely alongside whites in Vietnam, and when that generation comes marching back to the small and large towns of America, they will not easily put up with the inequities they have suffered in the past.

That is why, for the good of everyone in this country, the criminal situation in Mississippi must be cleared up immediately. If the Negro's swiftly developing pride in himself is allowed to become hatred for whites, remember that white America taught Negroes how to hate and would not allow them to love. There is still time. But I insist that my Mississippi is everywhere. And the hour is getting late.

The Saturday Evening Post, August 13, 1966

Welfare in Mississippi: *"Tradition" vs. Title VI*

by Robert E. Anderson Jr.

THE main ballroom of the King Edward Hotel in downtown Jackson has the feel, the acoustics, of a college gymnasium, which is to say that it is one cavernous void the length and breadth of a basketball court with no more charm than a detention hall or bus terminal. Yet one could imagine, too, that it was built for gala affairs, the sort of event that the Jackson *Clarion-Ledger* might boost mightily in lead editorials: testimonial banquets, statewide conventions of the various benevolent and fraternal orders which make up so vital a part of the social life of middle class white Mississippi. With little effort one could visualize it, draped in bunting, the state flag and the U.S. flag prominently displayed, tables set for barbecue feasts, while on the floor secret handshakes were exchanged, old acquaintances boisterously renewed.

It was not like that February 17 and 18. White Mississippi was little in evidence those days, no editorial writers were on hand (there was no sign in the press of their presence in any event) and the mood was suggestive more than all else of the waiting room anxiety outside major surgery. No one had come here to enjoy himself but rather to unburden, to testify to present and past grievances—aware of the risk involved in so doing—but hoping after it was all over that things would somehow be better.

A sign outside the door explained the nature of the proceedings: "Mississippi Advisory Committee to the U.S. Civil Rights Commission Hearings on Public Assistance."

Throughout the two days of hearings the faces at the witness table changed many times. Here was a federal spokesman outlining the economic background. Here was a public assistance law expert describing the terrible failure of the federal government to enforce its own regulations. Here was a spokesman for the Mississippi Welfare Department, an ex-state senator who apparently regarded himself as a humanitarian, complaining that when he spoke to civic clubs around the state he had a difficult time answering questions about illegitimacy rates among Negroes, suggesting, too, that it would be a good idea for a committee of this type to probe the promiscuity of welfare mothers. Here were those welfare mothers themselves, the lame, the ailing old people, the civil rights workers who had been dropped from welfare rolls, some speaking out of great despair and hurt; some angry, their words bitter and mocking, others almost indifferent as though certain at the very beginning that their appearance here would come to naught. They felt hostility, they said, whenever they went to the courthouse, no matter if it were to apply for welfare or to buy a license plate; it was as though their mere presence there was an affront, an uppity exhibit of citizenship rights. Courtesy titles for Negroes in welfare offices? They were universally ignored there as they were everywhere else in the state. Many did not know of their right to ask for a fair hearing if their applications for aid were rejected. The welfare "ladies" frowned on such nonsense anyway and did not hesitate to bring pressure upon them to withdraw their requests.

Civil rights professionals agree that the testimony revealed here could have been heard almost verbatim in any of the other four Deep South states, Georgia, Alabama, Louisiana, South Carolina, for increasingly in recent years reports have come from these states, too, of a particularly spiteful attitude in local welfare offices, different in a subtle and insidious way from the indulgent paternalism, the half-amused acceptance of Negro vagaries and dependence on white largesse which went with discrimination only a few years back. Negroes have felt this, it is said, in direct ratio to civil rights gains. Some, indeed, have been denied welfare aid for participating in demonstration marches; others for exercising the basic citizenship right of registering to vote. Sometimes the reasons for rejection have been frankly admitted. More often they have been vaguely disguised with such transparent legerdemain as "the law has been changed." Yet even Negroes who have never identified themselves with civil rights activity have not been immune, so that it is not possible to credit the change in courthouse mood to reaction against civil rights activists alone. Some of it doubtless is the arrogance and hypocrisy of a society which finds self-expression now in shallow slogans about "an honest day's work for an honest day's pay" when the daily wage for chopping cotton is $3.00, when the weekly pay for a household domestic in rural Mississippi, for example, is somewhere in the range of $15.00 a week, depending on individual generosity. Some of it, too, is racism of the old fashioned, undiluted James K. Vardaman kind. Thus a white Mississippi welfare worker recently expressed her disdain for Negroes in a letter to the Memphis *Commercial Appeal*: "Our people underwent hardshps that were unbelievable; took over a new world and worked to achieve what they have only to say to an inferior race, 'Come take it, we've worked for it, but we'll just hand it over to you.'"

Such attitudes at the county courthouse—pernicious as they are and resented as they are—at least disappoint no one but rather are more or less presupposed. The federal role in enforcement of Title VI regulations under the Civil Rights Act of 1964 binding upon all states which accept federal welfare funds is far more puzzling and angering to civil rights advocates. Despite repeated complaints of violations to HEW, they say, few corrective measures have ever been taken. However, it should be noted that the Atlanta regional office is hopelessly understaffed for any effective enforcement procedures and leaves most such activity to the states themselves, a situation which the irreverent have compared to "putting the Mafia on the honor system." The official staff complement at the regional office calls for only one welfare enforcement officer for the whole Southeastern region and until March, 1967, even that one post had never been filled.

Last year in Mississippi, however, it looked as if HEW meant to take bold action. Spurred, no doubt, by increasing Negro complaints, the Department sent a 20-man investigating team from Washington (bypassing the regional office, it is said, to avoid having its future effectiveness with local officials compromised) into the state to make a compliance study of Mississippi welfare agencies. The study was concluded in May,

1966, and civil rights groups in Mississippi awaited the results with some optimism. Today—nearly a year later—they are still waiting, for the findings apparently lie in bureaucratic limbo, never having been made public, or transmitted to the Civil Rights Commission, or presumably to any other department. Attempts to obtain a report on the findings have met with no success. A letter of inquiry from the Southern Regional Council was returned with an unsigned marginal note stating simply: "Not available to send outside the Department." One high HEW official who made a point of not wanting to be named said he doubted if the results would ever be released. A Civil Rights Commission spokesman described the report as "the best kept secret in HEW" and said he knows of only one person in the Civil Rights Commission who has read it. "And he doesn't have a copy."

Thus when the Mississippi Advisory Committee opened its Jackson hearings it was—in a sense—offering another chance to put into the public record what HEW presumably already had discovered in its investigation but for reasons known only to itself wasn't revealing. What went into that record could roughly be divided into two parts—the personal testimony of some forty complainants and the figures, statistics, and legal interpretations of the experts.

—Obviously uncomfortable before a microphone, inhibited even by the largely sympathetic crowd, the Negro mother of seven paused for a moment in her testimony and the audience was quiet—in a way that it had not been all morning—as if it wished almost not to hear the rest, not to have to feel the humiliation and hurt of the woman before them. Like so many others, she had sought aid for her dependent children and the welfare worker had hounded her, asking her "Did she have a man?" "When was the last time she went out with a man?" "Did they have a special place where they went?"; eagerly, obscenely questioning her in a manner reminiscent of Dr. Kinsey about every phrase of her sexual life. And so she had come to the hearings no doubt spurred by a mixture of still-lingering anger and humiliation and now she was having her promised moment of testimony and vindication and yet her tone when she spoke again was not angry at all nor bitter, but weary with a great and terrible weariness that age and hard work alone had not wrought. One felt that more than all else, she wanted simply to be over with it and gone anywhere—out into the drizzle in the streets, back to the little Delta town that she called home—anywhere that she could hide or be alone. "I asked her," she said, "I asked her why I was turned down. She looked at me and said that all we did was go out and get little bastards and then expected them to take care of them. 'Get out,' she says, 'and don't you ever come back.'"

—She had enrolled in the work experience program which was set up under Title V of the Economic Opportunity Act of 1964 to offer work training for those unable to support themselves. In Mississippi, it is completely financed by federal funds. Her work experience was to be as a florist assistant which meant that she was to learn how to arrange bouquets and pot flowers. She looked forward to the training because it had the promise of being paid for creative activity. Her employer—or rather instructor-to-be, since he paid her no wages—was a white man. The training she received, however, had nothing to do with the florist business. Instead, he set her up as a domestic in his house and once when he had a load of gravel that he wanted to be spread over his driveway, he put her to work outside with a shovel. When she complained, he told her he could work her exactly as he pleased. She stayed there three months, the federal government paying her wages, and the white man's wife enjoyed the full time service of a house maid.

—A doctor had examined him following an injury. He was diagnosed as permanently and totally disabled, but the welfare department would not accept the doctor's opinion. Its own medical panel reviewed the written reports on his case and decided that he had improved. Another examination, on his own initiative, confirmed the original medical report. But he was denied disability welfare aid, all the same. "When I got hurt," he said, "it was just like I was a dog."

—In June, 1966, she came to Jackson on a demonstration and was jailed, she said, for twelve days. When she returned home, the "welfare lady" sent word for her to come by the courthouse to see her. "Weren't you on the demonstrations?" she was asked. "Yes," she answered. "Who took care of your children?" But before she could answer what was, she felt, an implied threat to take her children away from her, she was told that if she would work in the fields chopping cotton for $3.00 a day, then she could stay on welfare. She belonged to the Freedom Labor Union, however, and it was on strike and so she refused to work. She was dropped from the welfare rolls because she would not take suitable employment when it was offered to her.

—The welfare worker came to her home and said, "Hmm, you done messed around, got yourself pregnant again. Don't you know you ain't supposed to have no man around?" She lost her head then. All of the prying, the snooping, the patronizing treatment, brought her to make a horrifyingly frank and yet—in its own way—beautiful confession. Sure, she said, she had a man around. She wasn't dead. She had to love.

—Her child was enrolled in a white school and she was cut off welfare rolls the same month. When she asked as to why, she was told that she had been on welfare too long and that a new law had been passed removing her from eligibility.

—She was put off welfare after the birth of her child. This is legal under Mississippi welfare eligibility regulations governing aid to dependent children by a cruel rationalization called the "substitute father clause." Under this rule her child is considered evidence of a continuing relationship with a man who is presumed by the state to be contributing financially to her family. Whether he is or isn't is irrelevant. She could be returned to welfare rolls at the end of six months if she could prove that the relationship had ended. But her other children receive no aid in the interval. What will happen to them, she asked. "That will be your problem," was the answer. However, she was also told that if she would cash her check at a particular store, she could be reinstated. "Who did the store belong to?" a committee member asked. The husband of the county welfare director.

—She had been removed from welfare rolls and decided to exercise her right to ask for a fair hearing. This did not seem to set very well with her case worker who came to her home and suggested that it didn't look as if her children were receiving adequate home care. "You fool around with those doggone civil rights workers and you think they are going to help you. Well, they are not going to help you." She withdrew her request for the hearing, fearing that her children could be taken from her.

—She needed money for glasses, but she had been put off welfare because she had been jailed for her civil rights activities. "Go down to the civil rights workers and let them find you some glasses," she was told. When she appealed to the county health department they turned her down, too, because she had participated in "that march." She had also lost her job as a domestic for the same reason. The welfare lady told her frankly, "If you don't stop that freedom marching, I'm going to take your children from you."

—When you go to get commodities under the surplus food program, she said, you don't get but one issue. The food can be good or bad. The flour can be wet. The meal can have weevils. But you don't get but one issue and you take it and when you are hungry enough, you eat it.

—In 1965, she enrolled three of her nine children in the white school. Immediately thereafter her husband was fired from his job. They were without support and so she went to the county welfare department seeking aid. The first question she was asked was, "How many children do you have in the white school?" The second was, "If you know of anybody else who is planning to send their children there, would you tell us?" "No, ma'm," she replied. To which the welfare "lady" responded, "Well, I can see you are in good shape after all."

The next year she sent all of her children to the white school. Soon afterward, she applied for food under the commodities program and was rejected. Finally one day the welfare worker came to see her again and told her the facts of life. "Look, that's white folks tax money. We can't give you people a living."

The economic and statistical background, torturously read into the record, tells almost a complete story in itself. Less than seven per cent of the Negro labor force works in white collar jobs. Median family income for whites is $4,209; for Negroes, $1,444. One-fourth of all Negro family heads work less than 40 weeks a year. Two-fifths of Negro males are farm laborers. Forty-seven per cent of females are domestics. Four out of five Negro families in 1959 lived on $2,000 a year. More than half lived on $1,000 or less. Mississippi's per capita income in 1965 was $1,608 compared to a national figure of $2,746.

The average monthly payment nationwide to old age recipients in November, 1966, was $67.45. In Mississippi, it was $39.10, lowest in the United States. Mississippi, in fact, puts a $50.00 limit on the amount that can be paid. For the same month, the national average payment in aid to the blind was $86.05, contrasted to $46.15 in Mississippi. Again the state imposes a $50.00 limit. In aid to the permanently and totally disabled, the average monthly payment per recipient in the United States is $73.65. In Mississippi, it is $45.25. As for aid to families with dependent children, the average monthly assistance payment per child in the United States is $36.10; or $148.90 per family. In Mississippi, the average monthly payment per child is $9.25, and the average per family is $38.00. The state pays only 31% of this amount—least in the nation. The federal government provides 83% of all Mississippi welfare funds. What is more, Frank Steninger, director of the Bureau of Family Services of HEW, said that the state does not allow its welfare recipients to take advantage of some aid that federal regulations permit.

Income and resources, as well as any expenses reasonably attributable to the earning of any such income, must be considered in determining the needs of a claimant for assistance. Under the law, however, certain income *may* be disregarded at the option of the individual state. These exceptions are: 1) in all categories, the first $5 of income; 2) for Old Age Assistance and Aid to the Permanently and Totally Disabled, $20 of the first $80 earned, plus one-half of the balance with a maximum disregard of $50; 3) for aid to families with dependent children, $50 earned by each child under 18 with a family maximum of $150; 4) for Aid to the Blind and Aid to the Permanently Disabled, any income or resources by a recipient for 36 months if he is engaged in a plan for self-support approved by the state agency. In Aid to the Blind program, states are required to disregard the first $85 per month of earned income and, in addition, one-half of anything in excess of $85 per month, and for a period of at least one year, any other income or resources of a blind recipient engaged in a plan for self-support approved by the state agency. Mississippi adheres to the mandatory income disregard provision only.

What did it all mean? There were several opinions. Dr. Ed Sparer, widely respected public assistance law authority from Columbia University, pointed out that Mississippi qualifies its eligibility conditions in many and devious ways—from the "employable mother" rule which takes away aid from a woman with children over two years of age should she refuse to accept any employment that the welfare agency wants her to take—to the "substitute father" clause which denies welfare aid to a mother if there is any evidence that an able-bodied male lives in her home or keeps company with her. Given the incredibly low wages that an "employable" mother can earn, given the lack of opportunity for self betterment open to a Negro male in rural Mississippi, the situation roughly amounts to this, Dr. Sparer said: "Before we will give aid, we will make a father desert his home."

Miss Marian Wright of the Mississippi branch of the NAACP Legal Defense and Educational Fund cites ten major ways that the legal rights of Negro welfare applicants and recipients have been violated in Mississippi: 1) by terminating the welfare assistance of eligible Negro citizens because they are active in the civil rights movement; 2) by maintaining all white employment policies in the staffs of the vast majority of public welfare agencies in the state and otherwise maintaining segregationist office policies; 3) by arbitrarily denying welfare assistance to impoverished Negro mothers and children on the ground of vague reports that the mother is friendly with a man; 4) by coercing needy Negro mothers to leave young children in the care of others and accept employment for shockingly low wages; 5) by maintaining welfare application policies and procedures which directly violate federal requirements and elementary due process; 6) by maintaining "fair hearing" policies and procedures which directly violate federal requirements and due process; 7) by imposing arbitrary maximums on the amount of aid for families with young children, which discriminates between families of different sizes and bears no rational relation to the purposes of the public assistance program; 8) by discourteous, rude treatment of Negro applicants and recipients; 9) by violating Mississippi's own regulations where these regulations are beneficial to Negro applicants; 10) by manipulating and suspending the surplus food program with the effect of maintaining the cheapest supply of Negro labor.

A civil rights attorney, citing the fact that aid to dependent children has gone from $9.23 in 1948 to $13.30 in June, 1964, to $11.35 in June, 1965 and back to $9.25 in 1966 questioned whether it was mere coincidence that with increased civil rights activity in the state since 1964 the amount has lessened. Negro migration from the state (48,000 between 1960 and 1965)* indicated to him that the state was saying: "These people are not in our best interests. Let's force them to move away."

One civil rights worker testifying on a remedy panel toward the end of the last session was blunter. It could all be reduced, he said, to "a policy to starve the people to death, or drive them out of the state."

Mr. Steininger, appearing on the same panel, however, didn't see it that way. "I can say with certainty," he said, "that the state of Mississippi—the people of the welfare department—are as sincere and interested in running a good program and treating people with integrity and worth and in following the Mississippi and federal law as you are or I am." He conceded that there were individuals on the county level who did not measure up to his estimation of the state officials. Exactly what his faith in the state officials was based upon, however, was not quite clear, unless he believed as did Mr. Flavius Lambert, information director of the state welfare department, that the complaints "represented sour grapes."

One clue as to HEW's reluctance to force stricter compliance with federal regulations may have been offered in a question and answer session about the work experience training program in Jackson. Had any consideration been given to locating the program at Hinds Junior College, a predominantly white school in downtown Jackson, instead of at Utica Junior College, predominantly Negro, 25 miles out of the city? The federal response to that was that HEW would have little in-

*MISSISSIPPI COUNTY POPULATION ESTIMATES, 1965 by Ellen S. Bryant, published by Mississippi State University Agricultural Experiment Station, August 1966.

fluence with the state since they had had a good deal of trouble launching the program at all. Mississippi, it was then pointed out, had terminated 30 per cent of federal aid to hospitals over federal insistence on the elimination of segregation practices. In other words, the federal government did not want to push Mississippi to the brink of forfeiting all federal welfare funds, a situation that would hurt Negroes in the state far more than whites and would, in fact, probably delight the state's more racist elements who have done their best already to weaken existing welfare programs. Such at least was the implied rationale.

The flaw, of course, is that politicians are still politicians, regardless of their ideological persuasion and power is still what politics is all about. Would the state's politicians so willingly forfeit the tremendous amount of patronage inherent in a program which they completely administer and which is so heavily financed by federal funds? Skillful federal prodding stopped this side of an outright cut-off of funds might reveal a surprising flexibility even at the courthouse level. And if it did not there are those who think that the withdrawal of federal funding might have healthy effects even though the economic pinch on Negro recipients would be far tighter. It could, they reason, unify Negroes at the grass roots level as they have never been before, add impetus to voter registration efforts, strengthen civil rights activity all over the state.

But surely—a committee member asked—there must be legal steps that could be taken short of withdrawing federal funds? None—save mediation—were offered at the hearings. Some civil rights lawyers, however, argue that where a written agreement to comply with the Civil Rights Act exists between state and federal government, the Justice Department could go into federal court charging violation of contract. If a contract breach was proved, officials who refused still to comply could be held in contempt of court.

All of which, of course, goes to the heart of federal resolve in the matter of Civil Rights Act enforcement and finally puts the burden for action on the Justice Department. Every indication, however, is that for the immediate future, compliance with federal welfare regulations will depend solely on HEW's power to mediate with state officials.* This at the very least will mean a federal enforcement official in every state where a pattern of racial discrimination clearly exists. It will also mean a firmer federal commitment to ending welfare program discrimination than has been evident in the past, or was evident in Jackson.

John Mudd, the young director of the Child Development Group of Mississippi (CDGM), put it this way: "It's grotesque. There they sit with their whole lives being bared before everyone, listening to the federal people discussing them as though they were sticks of furniture, as though they weren't present at all."

A good beginning could be made, one thought, if government on all levels could somehow understand that behind their economic graphs and percentages of increase are people such as the Negro mother at the hearings who in telling of her experiences at the county courthouse mentioned that the seats set aside for applicants were turned away from the case workers. "Why," a committee member asked, "do you suppose that was so?"

"I didn't see no reason," she replied, "other than they didn't want to look us in the face."

---

*It is interesting here to note that the federal government officially takes the idiosyncrasies of the states into account in regard to public assistance administration. The 1966–67 edition of the U.S. Government Organization Manual in describing the functions of the Bureau of Family Services states: "Public Assistance includes financial aid, medical care, and other social services to help recipients achieve their potentialities for self-care, self-support, and strong family life. The extent of financial aid and the provision of services vary between States, *reflecting the State's traditions, legislative and administrative structures, community concern, and assistance appropriations.*" (Italics ours: The editors.)

New South, Spring 1967

We're Gonna Rule

by Bob Fletcher

SUNFLOWER CITY, Miss.—For over eight months, a small, militant and determined force of local residents have canvassed the black community of Sunflower City (population 662). They have built a slate, campaigned for it, set up black captains and held meetings. They have explained the action of the Fifth Circuit Federal Court in setting aside the 1966 municipal elections—black people had not been allowed sufficient time to exercise their voting rights, recently clarified by the 1965 Voting Rights Bill, by registering, in time for that election.

The town's 55% registered black voters (out of a potential voting age majority of 75%) were urged to select their own candidates. They nominated a slate of six: 20 year old Otis Brown for Mayor, and for the five aldermanic positions, Elvin Gipson, Mrs. Annie Mae King, Mrs. Willie Mae Smith and the fiery Mrs. Lela Mae Brooks.

A group of northern liberals called the National Committee for Free Elections in Sunflower (headed by William Fitz Ryan and Bayard Rustin) formed and began to apply pressure on the Justice Department to send in federal officials. In an apparent effort to discourage such a likelihood, the local election commission agreed to let Joseph Harris, one of the leading local black organizers, serve as an election official. This meant he would be available to go behind the curtain with any illiterates who requested his help.

On May 1, the day before the election, the JD announced that it would be sending federal observers to Sunflower. That evening, less than twelve hours before the election, the election commission held a special meeting and decided not to let Joe Harris give help after all. This news was brought to the pre-election mass meeting just as the lawyers were confidently explaining that all people had to do was to "ask for Joe." "Oh well," said the lawyers, "you still don't have to worry about a thing; just demand that you and whoever helps you be accompanied by a federal observer." But many poor black people in the Delta are not yet used to demanding anything, and besides, the federal observer was just another white man. There was no longer any guarantee, for illiterates, of a secret ballot, free of reprisals.

Lawyer Morty Stavis explained what had happened. There was a difference of 49 votes between the highest vote for a black candidate (111) and the lowest for a white (160). "Now, there were 38 'spoiled ballots'—THEY said defectively marked. There were 13 challenged ballots. And there were somewhere between 27 and 32 ballots in which people were helped—but only by whites." Stavis argued that there would have been at least 65 more uncontestable votes, more than enough to reverse the difference of 49, if the election officials had not reneged on their agreement to let Joe Harris act as helper. If Joe Harris had been a helper, there could be no challenge of the 27–32 votes where people who asked for help and could only get white help waived all possibility for a secret ballot. If Harris had been a helper, the 38 ballots would not have been improperly marked by people too afraid of whites to ask for help.

"So," said Stavis, "we're going back to federal court. We're going to ask the federal court to set aside this election exactly the same way that we asked the federal court to set aside the last election."

Confusion was further served with the following two letters, both sent out to the black citizens of Sunflower the day before the election. The first one was headed: "Important Notice to Sunflower Citizens:

"In the face of the election of officers to serve the next two years in the department of city government, we want to thank you for the fine support you have given this administration in the past.

"We have had complaints from some of our local citizens that they have been threatened and harassed by people working for the Freedom Democratic Party. As your city officials, we want to take this opportunity to assure our citizens that we will take any and all means to protect the citizens of this community; therefore, your city officials have contacted the proper authorities who have assured us that the highway patrol will assist our local law enforcement in protecting all citizens against their goal. This protection will be guaranteed on election day, after election day and at all other times. We urge all citizens to report any violation or threat to the city officials, county officials, or to the highway patrol so the offenders can be prosecuted to the full extent of the law." (signed, "the mayor and board of Aldermen.")

The second letter was from the chief of police:

"We have had many reports of lies, threats and intimidation directed against the citizens of Sunflower. Threats and intimidation against our citizens will not be tolerated and any such reports are promptly passed on to the proper authorities. As for the lies and falsehoods told our citizens this is the truth and that's the way it is:

•No one, including the United States Government, can MAKE you vote in any election . . .

•If you CHOOSE to vote in any election, NO ONE, including the UNITED STATES GOVERNMENT, can tell you who you HAVE to vote for.

•If you are a duly registered citizen and CHOOSE to vote NO ONE can tell HOW you voted. THE VOTE IS COMPLETELY SECRET. You use your own best judgment and pick the candidate you ALONE think is the best person for the job, best qualified, best experienced, and you vote for that person and not even your own wife or husband will know how you voted unless you tell.

•No person, organization, nor even the United States Government can tell a free citizen how to vote or who to vote for.

"THAT'S JUST THE WAY IT IS. Anyone tries to tell you different or makes threats against you or your property is wrong and should be reported to the authorities at once."

Obviously designed for the nervous fringe of the black community, the letters were apparently intended among other things to 1) implicate the FDP as an unlawful, questionable group in league with ever-insidious "outside agitators", 2) bring to mind the head-beating SS troops of the Delta, the Highway Patrol, 3) further shake what little faith there might have been in the protective presence of the United States Government. "THAT'S JUST THE WAY IT IS."

On May 2, election day, the polls were scheduled to open at 7:00. At least 50 people were up at five for a final prayer meeting, urging the Lord not to forsake the side of righteousness. Students from North Carolina College, a couple of Free Election Committee volunteers, local people and a handful of other outside agitators canvassed their assigned streets for the final time, working with local SNCC people in arranging transportation for all who needed it. Women prepared food for those who had gotten up too early to think about eating. The townspeople came for a final briefing, reviewing the names of the black candidates on their sample ballots. Mrs. Lela Mae Brooks began her final roundup among the community's faint of heart, the not quite confirmed Uncle Toms: "Just want to see if you need a ride down to the headquarters . . . OK, I'll be looking for you now; you know, we can't all live together in Sunflower if we don't get down there and vote, now can we?" "No Ma'm," was the usual nervous reply.

At 6:55, the first wave of people began to move down to the Town Hall polling place to line up for the long-awaited vote. As it turned out, the bailiff was also the chief of police, who, throughout the day, did not hesitate to utilize his position at the polls' entrance to do considerable electioneering, while intimidating Negroes. And so the day began.

Outside and across the street from the Town Hall, Mrs. Fannie Lou Hamer was circulating through the gathering crowd, generating that spirit of determination with which she infects people wherever she travels. This particular day, she and her husband had only to travel 20 minutes from her home in Ruleville, just north of Senator Eastland's 6,000 acre Doddsville Plantation. Mrs. Hamer was the MFDP plaintiff in the court action responsible for this special election.

Kitty-cornered to this group was a service station where about 15–20 crackers had gathered, one with a Brownie camera with which he tried to intimidate blacks on their way to vote. Although reporters and photographers were warned to stay at least 30 feet away from the polling place, nothing was said to the heckling whites, sitting on a pickup truck, less than fifteen feet from the exit door, nor to the mayor's wife, sitting in a parked car just outside the door, very visibly "takin' down names." Inside, things were reported to be very tense, with officials discourteous and uncooperative.

Around 10:00, a group of about 10 whites arrived. A cracker in a pickup truck with a scoped rifle and police dog began circling around the block. Some of the young people began singing rather defiantly. Joe Harris came out and asked them to stop the singing, which he was worried might provoke violence. He told them that they were there to win an election, and nothing more. The 10 whites formed a separate line parallel to blacks who had been patiently waiting their turn. The police chief came out and let the whites in right away. "THAT'S JUST THE WAY IT IS."

By 10:30, only 68 of the eligible black voters had not yet come to the polls. Included among these was the small minority of residents who have some form of employment. They would not be in from work until the afternoon. For the next five hours things went pretty uneventfully in Sunflower City.

Around 4:00 p.m., the whites of Sunflower City began to arrive in large numbers to do their voting. White teenagers, on their way home from school, joined the growing numbers of crackers at the service station. White housewives, on their way home from shopping or picking up their grade-school children, got out of their big cars to take snapshots. During this time, more than 10 whites were spotted by local young people as living outside the legal boundaries. "Next, they'll be hauling them in from the graveyard sure enough," said one girl, when a cripple, whom she identified as living "out in the rurals," was unloaded and wheeled into the polls. Some of the crackers moved from the service station and stationed themselves right outside of the exit door, and of course, nobody ordered them back to the other side of the 30 feet limit.

At 6:00, when the polls closed, Guyot and Mrs. Brooks began to move people off the corner and back to the community center, for fear that the tension of waiting might cause violence to erupt. At that time, everyone involved thought it was touch and go as to who had actually won.

When it was announced that the racist incumbents had taken the election right down the slate, people quieted down into mournful headshaking, groans of sadness or general dull disbelief. In a kind of trance, people "amen'd" Joe Harris as he assured them that "we might not see anybody sitting in the City Hall, but we still won. This is the first time in the history of the city of Sunflower that 97% of the vote turned out in this small town . . . We learned a lot from these elections here in Sunflower . . . and we've got other elections coming up . . . We made a lot of mistakes, but we won't make those mistakes in November."

To this there was polite hand clapping from people who were no longer very optimistic.

The pain and anger in the room began to surface as people who could contain it no longer began to speak. These were the people who drew cheers and shouts. Mrs. Hamer, with tears in her eyes, said "I'm tired of folks comin' and tellin' us to be nice. That we got a symbolic victory. We ain't doin' nothin' symbolic; we doin' this cause our lives are at stake!" She called for a campaign directed at pressuring Negro school teachers (who traditionally in the Deep South have been intimidated by all white school boards) to register and vote in the November elections, by organizing for a boycott of their schools in September.

"I think it's time," said Guyot, "for people who are fighting to survive in the Delta to establish HOW we're going to fight and WHEN we're going to fight, for the first time in our lives. And I'm going to ask that three people from each Delta county come to a meeting . . . so we can talk about lining up a complete black slate, to run as independents throughout this Delta and to STAY THE HELL OUT OF THE GODDAMN DEMOCRATIC PARTY . . .

"I would certainly hope that if we're going to fight for the right of black people to eat and sweat and to live in the Delta, it shouldn't make much difference to us WHICH hunky becomes governor of Mississippi. I just hope that we can understand that what we've got to do now . . . is REGISTER BLACK PEOPLE TO VOTE."

"Now I want y'all to understand something," said Mrs. Lela Mae Brooks. "We did not LOSE the election, the white folks STOLE it; like they stole our land, like they steal our commodities every month, like they stealin' our young men every day to go and fight their war in Viet Nam, like they stole our great, great grandparents from Africa a long, long time ago . . . Now they got nothin' to take from us cept our lives . . .

"They think they can scare us with them guns in their cars; we not scared of them damn guns, and we want them to know it. If we were scared of them guns, we wouldn't even register to vote . . .

"We been running around here talkin that non-violent stuff and this violent stuff. Now, dammit, when THEY get ready to get violent, let's ALL get violent . . . we ain't swore to nobody we wasn't gonna fight . . .

"Now, talk about Viet Nam, it can be Viet Nam right here; in Sunflower; in Mississippi . . . They better believe that, just the same as we can fight over there, we can fight right here . . .

"They think it's over, but it's just startin'. It's time out for sufferin'; we're not afraid of Mississippi anymore . . . We're the majority, and we're gonna rule."

The Movement, June 1967

Whip of Black Power

by Gordon Parks

THE guards had fanned out around the platform at Watts, feet planted apart, arms folded, eyes cutting into the jubilant crowd. I crouched between two of the guards, my back against the platform. More than 4,000 Negroes and a few whites had gathered. Signs with protest slogans jabbed the hot air. The stern image of Malcolm X, stenciled on yellow sweatshirts, wriggled over the bosoms of several girls as they leaped and screamed like cheerleaders. This crowd was tailor-made for Stokely Carmichael. All they wanted was just plain down-home, up-tight, nitty-gritty, git-with-it talk.

"All right! All right! Cool it!" a voice boomed over the loudspeaker. "Before Brother Stokely says a word, all white newsmen, and black newsmen with *one-day contracts* from the white press, and all TV men, move to the back of the crowd! Move quickly! We don't want to have to move you!" The orders were promptly obeyed. A big black man, pushing his luck as a lone dissenter, bawled out at the guards, "You damned incendiaries! You goddamned . . ." Before he could repeat his cry, he was strong-armed off the field.

First Stokely made a modest pitch for money. When the donations came in faster than the small buckets could hold them, Cliff Vaughs, a Snick worker, grabbed an old leather satchel off the platform. When he opened it, his jaw dropped and he quickly snapped the bag shut. "That damn thing is full of equalizers," he whispered to me.

Stokely made his stock speech, which I had heard many times—a fiery cry for Black Power and a vitriolic condemnation of the war in Vietnam. ("McNamara is trying to thin us out. Calls it 'black urban removal.' Well, I've got news for Mister Mac. Ain't no Vietcong ever called me nigger . . . and if I'm going to do any fighting it's gonna be right here at home. We will not fight in Vietnam and run in Georgia!")

On the way out, groups of boys and girls rushed his car. Stokely waved at them. "Those kids will be calling me Uncle Tom in a few years," he said. "People think *I'm* militant. Wait until those kids grow up! There are young cats around here who make me look like a dove of peace."

I nodded. We had seen some of those "young cats" the night before in the back room of an old building just outside Watts. Hard times and distrust marked their faces. Members of various militant organizations, they had come to discuss plans for protecting Stokely during the speech at Watts. He hadn't asked for protection, but a brother explained why he was getting it: "It's kind of voluntarily compulsive-like. We don't want another Malcolm X deal here in Watts." Tommy Jacquette, tall and brooding—a young Watts nationalist leader who was Stokely's self-appointed bodyguard—had stood in the back, eying everyone suspiciously. The planning session, chaired by Ron Karenga, leader of the nationalist group US, had got off to a sullen start with each faction sniping at the others.

"You brothers don't seem too happy with the way security is shaping up," Karenga said. A big fellow sitting to one side of the room cut in: "Trouble is, you jokers are tryin' to run things *your* way." At the touch of Karenga's knee, a young tough beside him stood up. "Bastard!" he snarled. "Call one of us a joker again and I'll knock your goddamned teeth down your throat!" The big fellow chose silence. Then the door opened and the "Sons of Watts," more veterans of the 1965 riots, filed in. About 20 of them lined up against one wall.

"We're discussing security, brothers," Karenga explained. "Got anything to say?" I glanced at Stokely. His eyes played on the ceiling.

"Carmichael's going to be in Watts," the Sons' leader said. "Nobody knows Watts better than us. And we don't intend to be out in left field directing traffic. We're gonna be where the action is or we ain't gonna be there at all. We can't protect the brother unless we're in close."

The argument got hotter. Finally Stokely spoke up, softly, persuasively: "Brothers, let's not argue among ourselves. The leaders of each group should get together, outside this room, and decide how each group will participate." Things cooled.

Later, as we drove into downtown Los Angeles, I said, "Rough session." Stokely nodded: "Now, those are the brothers the crackers had better start worrying about." He began to laugh, beating the dashboard with his fist. "Lord! Tonight, when those tough-looking brothers strolled in, I started praying to May Charles, my dear worrying mother."

Cool, outwardly imperturbable, Stokely gives the impression he would stroll through Dixie in broad daylight using the Confederate flag for a handkerchief. In the four months that I traveled with him I marveled at his ability to adjust to any environment. Dressed in bib-overalls, he tramped the backlands of Lowndes County, Alabama, urging Negroes, in a Southern-honey drawl, to register and vote. The next week, wearing a tight dark suit and Italian boots, he was in Harlem lining up "cats" for the cause, using the language they dig most—hip and very cool. A fortnight later, jumping from campuses to intellectual salons, where he was equally damned and lionized, he spoke with eloquence and ease about his cause, quoting Sartre, Camus and Thoreau.

But wherever he went, Stokely was never very far from his identification with Snick—the Student Nonviolent Coordinating Committee. As its chairman for the past year and a field organizer for five previous years, he has been shaped by Snick's bitter fight for its cause.

Snick, founded in 1960, got its start as an activist organization the next summer when a vanguard of 13 members, most of them Southern college students, spread through the Deep South with the bold idea of breaking the code that since emancipation had sent thousands of Negroes to their deaths simply because they had attempted to vote. The group bedded down in sharecroppers' shacks, scrounged for food and clothing and went to work organizing local Negroes. Snick grew rapidly, and by 1964 there were nearly 1,000 members and volunteers working in the dangerous black belt of the South.

They were not fearless, storybook heroes. The girls screamed when they were beaten. The boys yelled and writhed when the special handcuffs—"wrist breakers"—were clamped on and the protruding screws dug into their veins. They kept singing because singing was sometimes their only link with sanity. The experience left Stokely, who joined Snick at its founding, a complex young rebel. By the time he was 22 he had acquired an ulcer and was close to a nervous breakdown.

Today the official Snick organization numbers only 100—with hundreds of other nonpaid volunteers and sympathizers who send money and help with fund-raising campaigns. The 100 are paid salaries of $20 a week, which they seldom collect. They are still committed to nonviolence—*as a tactical approach*. But, as Stokely points out, "Our organization feels that any man has the right to physically protect his life and his home." At Atlanta headquarters the last few months, while Stokely has been in headlines, the staff has been working on the political organizing they expect to accomplish in the Deep South this summer.

It is this nitty-gritty field work to which Stokely is anxious to return now that he has given up Snick's chairmanship. Long before he announced that decision, he talked about the doubts he had of his leadership role. We were in the home of his friend and adviser Professor Charles V. Hamilton, chairman of the political science department at Lincoln University, located near Oxford, Pa. "I'm an *organizer*," Stokely said. "I want to go back to what I can do best. I'm too young for this job. I don't know enough about the outside world. I need time to read, learn, reflect. I think, perhaps, that more than anything else I'd like to be a college professor."

Stokely's ulcer was acting up and he sipped a glass of milk. "Those black kids," he said gesturing toward students crossing the campus outside the window, "they'll be fighting for a different power, not the kind the Irish and Italian immigrants got. And they'll probably get what they want—although we won't be around to see it. . . . But someone must first teach them to respect themselves, to sit still and listen—otherwise they won't pull off a political revolution."

Stokely was weary after the drive from New York to Oxford, part of which we had made in a snowstorm, and he turned from the window and stretched out on the floor. That afternoon I had seen a flash of the irrepressible humor that helps him keep his balance. Near Oxford the car had skidded and got stuck in a drift. Stokely gunned the motor, but the wheels just spun in their tracks. We tried rocking the car free several times. But we were in good and deep. Finally he cut the motor and we sat there for a few moments. Suddenly the incongruity of the situation struck him. He raised his arms and, shaking both fists violently, shouted, "Black Power! Black Power!"

Now, sprawled on Hamilton's living room rug, Stokely began a rambling recollection of the time in 1961 when he was thrown into a crowded cell at the state farm prison near Parchman, Miss.: "They did everything to us there but lynch us. We're singing one night and in comes this beloved cracker. 'Y'all niggers stop that damn noise or I'm gonna fix you.' We keep right on. Then he says, 'Take the black bastards' blankets!' They grab Hank Thomas first, but he holds on like a leech. They finally shake him off. The cracker points at me. 'You goddamned nigger! I'm gonna see to it that you never get outta here.' Meanwhile, they're clamping wrist-breakers on Freddie Leonard. They're hurting that cat so bad he's twisting around on the floor like a snake. The cracker says to him, 'You tryin' to hit me, nigger?' 'Oh no,' says Freddie, 'I'm just waiting for you to break my arm.' You should have seen that *white man's face!* He was so shook up he just stood there snarling like an animal. All this time we kept singing, *'I'm gonna tell God how you treat me.'* I was leading the singing, so the cracker hollered, 'Git that nigger's mattress!' They bumped me against the floor several times, but I held on. Finally, the old guy gave up. 'Throw him back in the cell!' he shouted. Then he went out the door cussing like hell. We kept singing all night."

Stokely fell silent and his mood changed. He began to describe a march back in 1964, and as he spoke we could feel the billies cracking against the head of John Lewis, Stokely's predecessor as Snick chairman. "As he goes down time and time again, he's moaning, 'I love you. I love you.' And they pick him up again. *Bam! Smack! Bam!* 'You black son-of-a-bitch!' And John, the true believer in nonviolence, sinks half-conscious to the pavement. Now we're retreating. They're coming after us with cattle prods and dogs. 'They've come far enough, baby! Open up.' *Crack! Bam! Pow!* The crackers begin to scatter. 'Shoot out the street lights!' *Bang! Bang!* A big

Army captain is telling them to put on the spotlight. 'Shut that damn light off!' A brother zings a burst past the captain's ankles. The captain hollers, 'Orders changed! Ree-treat! These niggers have gone loco! Ree-treat! Ree-treat!'" We laughed ourselves sick as Stokely rolled back and forth screaming, "Ree-treat!"

Not until he began recounting the fatal church bombings in Birmingham, Ala. in 1963, and the murders the next summer near Philadelphia, Miss., of the three civil rights workers, Chaney, Schwerner and Goodman, did a quiet come to the room. Stokely recalled how in Montgomery he had broken after seeing a pregnant black woman knocked head over heels by water jetting from a fire hose, and other men and women being trampled by police horses. "Suddenly," he said, rubbing his eyelids, "everything blurred. I started screaming and I didn't stop until they got me to the airport. That day I knew I could never be hit again without hitting back."

Stokely was "born smart" in Trinidad on June 29, 1941, and brought to Harlem when he was 11. Later, when his family moved to the Bronx, he became the sole Negro member of the Morris Park Dukes, a neighborhood gang.

Things changed quickly when he was accepted at the Bronx High School of Science, which takes only bright kids: "I broke from the Dukes. They were reading funnies while I was trying to dig Darwin and Marx. But I found myself in another kind of bag at Bronx Science. All those rich kids with their maids and chauffeurs began getting their kicks out of me. 'You're different,' they'd say. I couldn't dance my way out of a potato patch, but let me wiggle one hip—I was their chocolate Fred Astaire! Then I began making the Village scene and parties down on Park Avenue. I felt strange every time a black maid handed me something. My mother, May Charles, was also a maid, making 30 bucks a week.

"I read a lot, but I wasn't hip about many things. In 1960, when I first heard about the Negroes sitting-in at lunch counters down South, I thought they were just a bunch of publicity hounds. But one night when I saw those kids on TV, getting back up on the lunch counter stools after being knocked off them, sugar in their eyes, catsup in their hair— well, something happened to me. Suddenly I was burning.

Then I started picketing all over the place with a bunch of kids from CORE.

"After a few beatings on those picket lines, I realized that it was either them or me. I preferred me. Several white schools offered me scholarships, but I went to Howard University in Washington, D.C. It was a natural. It was black. I could keep in touch with the movement there."

When Stokely was a freshman, he was on his way to his first Freedom Ride to challenge segregated interstate travel. May Charles Carmichael says he just phoned from school one evening and told her he was going to Mississippi to join the Riders.

"'Don't worry, Mom,' he told me. 'I'm going to jail, but you must be proud of me and not ashamed.' I sat by the radio all that night worrying. In a few days I heard that he had been arrested and taken to prison, and then everybody was calling up, asking, 'Is that your boy Stokely they've got down there?' And I would say, 'Yes, that's my boy and I'm so proud of him I don't know what to do!'

"Sometimes now," says May Charles, "I think of him defying anyone for what he believes and I can't figure him out. When he was little, all the kids bullied him. Why, he was even scared of cats! Then, when he found out what he wanted to do, I asked him, 'Son, are you trying to be a big shot or a politician or something like that?' I've never seen him madder. 'I've got one son,' I told him. 'Let other Negroes give of theirs for a while.' He shot right back, 'What's all this religious stuff you taught me about Abraham sacrificing his son? If you really believe that, you shouldn't mind sacrificing your own son.'"

Ever since Stokely first raised the cry of "Black Power," he has had his detractors among the nationally known—and well-respected—Negro leaders. They have viewed his Black Power philosophy and antiwar chanting with consternation, asserting he does more to damage the cause than to help it. An exception among the moderates is Martin Luther King, for whom Stokely has great respect. Dr. King has called Black Power a confusing phrase, but he has never actually denounced it and he has joined with Stokely in linking the Vietnam protest to the civil rights issue.

Roy Wilkins of the NAACP says, "No matter how endlessly they try to explain Black Power, the term means anti-white. . . . It has to mean going it alone. It has to mean separatism. . . . This offers a disadvantaged minority little except the chance to shrivel and die."

I discussed the term—and Stokely—with Whitney Young of the National Urban League at that organization's well-appointed offices in midtown Manhattan. Whitney, a fine-looking, robust man in his early 40s, smiled when I broached the subject. "Well," he said, "Stokely didn't really make the backlash they're all talking about. He just gave them an excuse to come out publicly where they had been hesitant otherwise. But there is no dignity in the withdrawal from society that Stokely preaches. He gives too many Negroes a chance to escape responsibility. We'll have to work hard for what we get. It's better for a black man to reach in his pocket and find a dollar instead of a hole."

The next morning I went to Harlem to talk with Floyd McKissick of CORE in his cluttered little third-floor headquarters. What Floyd says about Stokely isn't much different from what Stokely says about himself, for their philosophy is prac tically the same. Floyd defends the concept of Black Power strenuously. "It's a drive to unite the black man in America in a gigantic effort to erase the causes of alienation, despair and hopelessness," he said. "It's got to be good if the white man is against it."

Stokely has heard so often the charge he is preaching violence that he meets it with a weary shrug: "I'm not advocating violence. I'm just telling the white man he's beat my head enough. I won't take any more. White Power makes the laws and White Power, in the form of white cops with guns and nightsticks, enforces those laws. The white press equates Black Power—the slogan—with racism and separatism, and gives headlines to black leaders, like Wilkins and Young, who attack it. The stories fail to report the productive dialogue taking place in the black community or in the white religions and intellectual areas. As for separatism, what are they talking about? We have no *choice*." He knifed the air with his finger: "They separated us a long time ago. And they sure intend to keep it that way."

He grinned sardonically. "The white man says, 'Work hard, nigger, and you'll overcome.' Well, if that were true, the black man would be the richest man in the world. My old man believed in this work-and-overcome stuff. He was religious, never lied, never cheated or stole. He did carpentry all day and drove taxis all night. They robbed him right and left. May Charles had to bribe an official with 50 bucks and a bottle of perfume to get him into the union. *He didn't know.* 'See,' he said, 'have patience and things will come to you.' The next thing that came to that poor black man was death—from working too hard. And he was only in his 40s."

I reminded Stokely of the remark of Bumpy Johnson, an alumnus of Alcatraz and one of Harlem's legendary figures, now operating a legitimate exterminating business. Bumpy put it this way: "The black man stood on the corner and said, 'Take the world and give me Jesus.' So that's just what the white man did. 'Jesus will help us,' the black people said. Hell, Jesus couldn't even help his own self. He fooled around and got himself nailed to the cross."

I finally asked Stokely, "What do you *really* mean by Black Power?"

"I've given up trying to explain it," he said. "The whites never really listen when I do, anyway."

"But I'm not white and I'm listening," I insisted.

"*For the last time,*" he said, "Black Power means black people coming together to form a political force and either electing representatives or forcing their representatives to speak their needs. It's an economic and physical bloc that can exercise its strength in the black community instead of letting the job go to the Democratic or Republican parties or a white-controlled black man set up as a puppet to represent black people. *We* pick the brother and make sure he fulfills *our* needs. Black Power doesn't mean anti-white, violence, separatism or any other racist things the press says it means. It's saying, 'Look, buddy, we're not laying a vote on you unless you lay so many schools, hospitals, playgrounds and jobs on us.'"

Not long after Stokely had made his controversial appearance at the giant antiwar rally at the United Nations, I dropped in on him one night at his home in the Bronx. He was very tired.

"I don't want personal admiration," he said. "The movement is the important thing. It must live after I'm gone. That was the second tragedy of Malcolm X's death. There was no movement left to carry on."

"You don't expect to go the way he did, do you?"

"The crackers will get me before the summer's over, I'm sure of that. But I'm not worried. There are too many others who believe as I do. I'm expendable."

"You were pretty rough with McNamara, Rusk and Johnson in your speech," I said.

"They deserved every bit of it. My words for them don't start to match the criminal acts they perpetrate against the Vietnamese people. How can McNamara deny racism when proportionately more black boys are dying every day in his stinking war? To black people all over, the U.S. military in Vietnam is international white supremacy. Anyone who thinks otherwise is a victim of U.S. brainwashing."

"Aren't you confusing civil rights issues with the issues for peace?"

"I support Dr. King's theories here," Stokely said. "The people who support the war in Vietnam are the same ones who keep their foot on the black man's neck in this country. Bigotry and death over here is no different from bigotry and death over there."

"What about the Negro soldiers who feel they are fighting for a stake in this country?"

"Our stake will come from the struggle against white supremacy here at home. I'd rather die fighting here tomorrow than live 20 years fighting over there. Why should I go help the white man kill other dark people while he's still killing us here at home?"

I couldn't help thinking about my son who is serving as a tank gunner in Vietnam. A week before, he had received the Purple Heart; his buddy was killed by a sniper. "I now have my fifth kill, dad," he wrote with a kind of frozen passion. "We got the bastard sniper later that afternoon." This from a boy who once said he would never be able to kill. Now, glancing at Stokely, I wondered which boy was giving himself to a better cause. There was no immediate answer. But in the face of death, which was so possible for both of them, I think

Stokely would surely be more certain of why he was about to die.

Stokely said, "Remember, we fought 300 years of American Negro history in a year and a half—organizing, bleeding, starving and educating at the same time. We gave a nation hope. If there is a future for us, we had better face it with hard political lines."

He rubbed his eyes. "Americans cannot face reality. They won't admit to their racism. But it was racism that got me involved in this movement—not love. Maybe we shouldn't be ashamed of hate. Like love, it's a human emotion even if it has a dangerous energy.

"I suppose it's pride, more than color, that binds me to my race. And I'm learning that the concern for blackness is necessary, but the concern has to go further than *that* to reach anyone who needs it.

"Mississippi taught me that one's life isn't too much to give to help rid a nation of fascists. Camus says, 'In a revolutionary period it is always the best who die. The law of sacrifice leaves the last word to the cowards and the timorous, since the others have lost it by giving the best of themselves.' I dig Camus," he said, smiling. Then he stood up, kissed May Charles goodnight and went off to bed.

Life, May 19, 1967

The Second Coming of Martin Luther King

by David Halberstam

HE is perhaps the best speaker in America of this generation, but his speech before the huge crowd in the UN Plaza on that afternoon in mid-April was bad; his words were flat, the drama and that special cadence, rooted in his Georgia past and handed down generation by generation in his family, were missing. It was as if he were reading someone else's speech. There was no extemporizing; and he is at his best extemporaneously, and at his worst when he reads. There were no verbal mistakes, no surprise passions. (An organizer of the peace march said afterwards, "He wrote it with a slide rule.") When he finished his speech, and was embraced by a black brother, it seemed an unwanted embrace, and he looked uncomfortable. He left the UN Plaza as soon as he could.

On that cold day of a cold spring Martin Luther King, Jr. made a sharp departure from his own past. He did it reluctantly; if he was not embittered over the loss of some old allies, he was clearly uneasy about some of his new ones. Yet join the peace movement he did. One part of his life was behind him, and a different and obviously more difficult one lay ahead. He had walked, marched, picketed, protested against legal segregation in America—in jails and out of jails, always in the spotlight. Where he went, the action went too. He had won a striking place of honor in the American society: if he was attacked as a radical, it was by men whose days were past. If his name was on men's room walls throughout the South, he was celebrated also as a Nobel Prize–winner, the youngest one in history; he was our beloved, *Time* Magazine's man of the year; his view of Christianity was accepted by many Americans who could never have accepted the Christianity of Billy Graham. In the decade of 1956 to 1966 he was a radical America felt comfortable to have spawned.

But all that seemed long ago. In the year 1967, the vital issue of the time was not civil rights, but Vietnam. And in civil rights we were slowly learning some of the terrible truths about the ghettos of the North. Standing on the platform at the UN Plaza, he was not taking on George Wallace, or Bull Connor, or Jim Clark; he was taking on the President of the United States, challenging what is deemed national security, linking by his very presence much of the civil-rights movement with the peace movement. Before the war would be ended, before the President and King spoke as one on the American ghettos—if they ever would—his new radicalism might take him very far.

On both these issues there had been considerable controversy and debate within the King organization, especially among those people who care most deeply for King, and see him as the possessor of a certain amount of moral power. On the peace issue none of King's associates really questioned how he felt; rather they questioned the wisdom of taking a stand. Would it hurt the civil-rights movement? Would it deprive the Negroes of King's desperately needed time and resources? And some of these peace people, were they really the kind of people King wanted to play with? On the ghettos there were similar problems.

No one is really going to accomplish anything in the ghettos, goes the argument, until the federal government comes in with massive programs. In the meantime King can only hurt and smear his own reputation; he will get dirt on his hands like the other ward heelers if he starts playing with practical day-by-day politics in the North. In the North, in addition to the white opponents, there are all the small-time Negro operators who will be out to make a reputation by bucking Martin King. Yet the ghettos exist, and to shun them is to lose moral status.

II

After the New York peace rally I traveled with King for ten days on the new paths he had chosen. It was a time when the Negro seemed more than ever rebellious and disenchanted with the white; and when the white middle class—decent, upright—seemed near to saturation with the Negro's new rebellion. The Negro in the cities seemed nearer to riots than ever; the white, seeing the riots on TV, wanted to move further away from the Negro than ever before. A terrible cycle was developing. At press conference after press conference he said no, he didn't think his stand on Vietnam was hurting the civil-rights movement or damaging the Negro cause with the President; no, he didn't think Stokely Carmichael's cry of black power had hurt the Negroes; no, he didn't plan to run for the Presidency. It was a week which began in New York with an announcement that King would go to the Holy Land in the fall on a pilgrimage.

Then came the first question: "And do you relate this to Vietnam?" No, King said, there were no political implications.

A Negro reporter who had been out to St. Albans Hospital in Queens and had talked to the soldiers there said, "The war doesn't bother them. The soldiers are for it."

Later, on the way to the airport (most of King's life is spent going to airports, and it is the only time to talk to him), King's top assistant, Andy Young, commented on the fact that the Vietnam question had come from a Negro reporter. "It always does," he said. "Every time we get the dumb question, the patriot question, it's a Negro reporter." A New York minister said it was the Negro middle class wanting respectability and playing it close on Vietnam. "They're very nervous on Vietnam, afraid they're going to lose everything else." King added, "Yes, they're hoping the war will win them their spurs. That's not the way you win spurs." The ghettos, he said, were better on the war issue than the middle class.

III

The most important stop on King's trip would be Cleveland, where he was thinking of making a major summer effort to break down some of the ghetto barriers. It is a strange thing the way a city can rise to national and international fame over racial problems. Sometimes it is predictable. The word was always out in the South, for instance, that Birmingham was a tough city with a tough police force and Bull Connor;

Negroes in Georgia and Mississippi knew about Bull Connor fifteen years before. Little Rock, which we once heard so much about, was an accident, its crisis deriving from its own succession laws and Orval Faubus' ambition.

Now there are cities imprinted on our memories that we barely know about, cities which we have forgotten, but in the Negro world, and in that part of the white world which is trying to cope with the coming fire, the word is out: Cleveland, where four people died in riots last summer, is likely to be a very tough place with all the worst aspects of the ghetto, and almost none of the safety valves. Unlike New York, where Mayor John Lindsay at least visits the slums, Mayor Ralph Locher seems to have written off the Negro vote, and to depend on the Italians, the Poles, and other white minorities. The Negro ministers there are interested in King's coming in for the summer action program, and though this is early May, a chilly day, and King is asking someone to find him a topcoat, there is a feeling that we will hear a good deal more about Cleveland before the summer is over, probably more than we want to.

King is edgy because the Negro community is divided. He does not want to get caught in a cross fire, and he is sensitive to what happened with his ill-fated organizing effort in Chicago last year.

Yet there are advantages in Cleveland. It is smaller than Chicago, better laid out geographically, and the Mayor is not so smart as Daley. His Chicago machine has enough Negro support to keep the Negro community divided; Locher's indifference to the Negroes in Cleveland may eventually force them to unite. But they must be brought together by someone from the outside. Here, then, is one of the ironies: for years the crisis was in the South, and Northern Negroes sent money and support there. In the process the most skilled leadership rose up in the South, fashioned out of the crises faced there, while in general the Northern leadership, so far lacking such direct and dramatic crises, lacks prestige; it must summon help from the South.

King is met at the airport by one of the older Negro ministers who is representing the Negro Ministers' Association. The preacher is about sixty, very pleased to be meeting King.

As soon as we are in the car he starts talking about an earlier King speech and how much he liked it. Everyone else smiles politely, and there is a murmur of approval from King, which dies as the preacher continues, "I mean the way you got up there, Doctor King, and you told those Negroes they got to improve themselves, they got to help themselves more, isn't anyone else going to help them, and they got to clean up themselves, clean up their houses, clean up the filth in the streets, stop livin' like pigs, they've got to wash up. They can't just wait for someone to come to their doors with a welfare check, they got to help themselves."

There is silence in the car as he continues, his voice gaining in enthusiasm as he carries on, for he is preaching now, and driving a little faster too.

King says nothing, but from the back of the car, quite softly, the Reverend Bernard Lee, a King assistant, says, "You got to have something worth cleaning up, Reverend," almost as an apology.

The tension rises a little in the car; King is silent, and Bernard Lee speaks again. "It's easier said than done, Reverend. You've got six generations just trying to make do, and they've given up fighting."

But the Cleveland Reverend keeps on; the Negroes have got to clean it up; they've lost these homes.

This time it is Andy Young: "You ain't lost it, Reverend. They lost it for you. You never had it."

In all this King has said nothing, letting Lee and Young do the stalking. (Later I am to find that this is his standard technique, holding back, letting others talk themselves out, allowing his men to guide the conversation to the point where it can be finally summed up by him.) "Well, Reverend," King finally says, "these communities have become slums not just because the Negroes don't keep clean and don't care, but because the whole system makes it that way. I call it slummism—a bad house is not just a bad house, it's a bad school and a bad job, and it's been that way for three generations, a bad house for three generations, and a bad school for three generations."

Then Andy Young starts telling of a home-owning community in Atlanta. Recently somewhat lower-class white, it was now turning quickly black, and somewhat middle-class black: "And so, of course, as soon as they've moved they all get together and have a big meeting about how to keep the neighborhood clean . . . and they want that garbage picked up, you know all that, and in the middle of the meeting, a man stands up at the back of the room and he tells them they're kidding themselves. 'Forget it,' he says, 'just forget it, because you're not going to get these services. I work for the sanitation department and I want you to know that they've just transferred twenty men out of this area, so you can just forget it all.'"

"Same old story," Bernard Lee says. "Negroes buy houses and immediately the services stop, and these aren't Negroes on relief, Reverend."

King, to ease the tension, asks about the Negro community of Cleveland, and the preacher becomes so eloquent on the subject of the division within the Negro church community that Andy Young finally says, "Reverend, go back all the way to the New Testament. Even Peter and Paul couldn't get together."

"But *they* got it. They already got theirs, and we're trying to get our share," the preacher says.

King then asks, Is the Mayor a racist? No, says the preacher, it's not racism, "it's just ignorance. He doesn't know the pulse of the new Negro. The wrong kind of people are advising him, telling him handle the Negro this way, give him just a very little bit of this and a very little bit of that; give him a pacifier, not a cure, a sugar tit, that's what we used to call it in the South, a sugar tit, just enough to take away the appetite but doesn't fill you up . . . feed one man, give one man a job, and you've taken care of the Negroes." As he finishes, one can sense the relaxation in the car. The preacher has rehabilitated himself, he's not as much of a Tom as you think.

Then King starts talking about the cities. So very few of the mayors have the imagination to deal with the complexity of the problems, and the handful who do can't really handle it because they lack the resources. The problems are so great that they must go to the federal government, but most of them don't even know the problems in their own cities. It is almost as if they are afraid to try to understand, afraid where that trip would lead them. "Why, this Mayor Locher here in Cleveland," he says, "he's damning me now and calling me an extremist, and three years ago he gave me the key to the city and said I was the greatest man of the century. That was as long as I was safe from him down in the South. It's about the same with Daley and Yorty too; they used to tell me what a great man I was."

IV

That was a simpler time. He had exuded love and Christian understanding during the nation's dramatic assault on legal segregation. In retrospect it was not so much Martin Luther King who made the movement go, it was Bull Connor; each time a bomb went off, a head smashed open, the contributions would mount at King's headquarters. They bombed King's own house, an angry black mob gathered ready to do violence, and King came out and said, "We want to love our enemies. I want you to love our enemies. Be good to them and let them know you love them. What we are doing is right and God is with us." And, of course, it was a time of television, we could tune in for a few minutes and see the cream of Negro youth, the slack-jawed whites answering their love with illiterate threats and violence, shouting what they were going to do to the niggers, and reveling in this, spelling their own doom.

King was well prepared for his part in that war; the weapon would be the white man's Christianity. He knew his people, and he could bring to the old cadences of the Southern Negro preacher the new vision of the social gospel which demanded change in America. He was using these rhythms to articulate the new contemporary subjects they were ready to hear ("America, you've strayed away. You've trampled over nineteen million of your brethren. All men are created equal. Not some men. Not white men. All men. America, rise up and come home"). Before Birmingham, the Montgomery bus strike was a success, and other victories followed. Grouped around King were able young ministers, the new breed, better educated; in a changing South he became the single most important symbol of the fight against segregation, culminating in his great speech before the crowd which had marched to Washington in 1963. Those were heady years, and if not all the battles were won, the final impression was of a great televised morality play, white hats and black hats; lift up the black hat and there would be the white face of Bull Connor; lift up the white hat and there would be the solemn black face of Martin King, shouting love.

v

But in Cleveland in 1967 the Negro ministers are in trouble. They are poorly educated products of another time when a call to preach, a sense of passion, was judged more important than what was being said. Their great strength is organization; they try to hold their own separate congregations together. They get their people out of jail and they get them on welfare, and if that is not very much, there is nothing else.

But now they are divided—by age, by denomination, by style, by petty jealousies. They have not yet found the unifying enemy which bound their contemporaries together in the South, and they are unable to deal with the new young alienated Negroes, for whom their talk about damnation and salvation is at best camp; in the ghettos they cannot help those who need aid most. They are frightened by the Nationalists and Muslims, the anger spawned in the streets, the harshness and bitterness of these new voices, the disrespect to elders, the riots. In the South in the 'fifties all the preachers were on the outside looking in, but here in the North there is sometimes the illusion that they have made it and opened the door to the Establishment. So there is double alienation, not just black from white but black from black middle class.

When King arrives in Cleveland, he is immediately hustled off to a meeting of the ministers. The meeting lasts more than three hours, and there is a general agreement that King should come into Cleveland to organize; there is some doubt expressed because of what happened to his Chicago program, doubts which some of the ministers counter by listing otherwise unknown accomplishments and blaming the white press.*

Afterwards, King has dinner in a Negro restaurant with eight key preachers, some of them old friends. At least one went to Stockholm with him to get the Nobel Prize, and he is letting people know about that. There is something here of a self-consciously jovial atmosphere, curiously reminiscent of white Rotary clubs in the South. King takes the menu and tells one preacher he sees something just right for him. "What's that?" the preacher asks. "*Cat*fish!" King says. There is a considerable ritual of joke telling, most of the jokes dealing with very old wealthy men interested in marriage with young and pretty women. One very wealthy old man is finally permitted to marry, and the Lord says after some deliberation that he can marry a forty-year-old woman. The old man thinks about this some, and then asks, "Lord, would two twenties be all right?"

King laughs enthusiastically, and then tells the story of the young, well-educated minister who visits a church as a guest pastor; he is introduced to the congregation by the pastor as "Dr. So and So." The preacher is embarrassed, and he says, "Sorry, Reverend, I'm not a doctor."

"You're an ordained minister, aren't you?" asks the older man, quite surprised. The younger man nods, and the older preacher says, "Well, then, you're an *automatical* doctor."

Everyone tells King how glad they are to learn what a success the Chicago program was, and that they should have known that the distortions were the fault of the white press. The white press is soundly castigated. "Even here in Cleveland," one of the ministers says, "why, some white reporter

*But many white reporters sympathetic to King, who thought the most important thing that could happen in America last year was for King to succeed in Chicago, consider his Chicago program a failure and a great tragedy. The problems had just been too great, the divisions within the Negro community too sharp, and the Daley machine too clever for him. The Daley machine was like nothing he had ever been up against before, with its roots in the Negro community. To this day there is no love by King for Daley, but there is considerable respect for Daley as a political operator. King sees Daley as a man for whom the machine is an end in itself, a man with little social vision, but with a sense of how social uses can be tailored to the perpetuation of the machine.

asks Martin a question about the Mayor and Martin makes the answer that he thinks the Mayor is apathetic, and the next day the headline says, 'King attacks Mayor.' They got to sell newspapers that way."*

The dinner is pleasant, a discussion of the problems of Cleveland ("the middle-class Negroes are our problem, they've all gone to Shaker Heights and don't give a damn about being Negro anymore"); King says yes, it's the same all over. Finally there is some mild joking and one of the preachers, very dark in skin, points to another and says how much darker the other is. There is almost a reproach in King's remark: "It's a new age," he says, "a new time. Black is beautiful."

Just as they are about to break up one old friend, the one who went to Stockholm, starts talking about what a great man Martin Luther King is, how he is sent to them from Above. Then the preacher tells about the Nobel Prize ceremonies in Stockholm and Martin King, Senior. "There was to be a huge party afterwards," he explains, "and the champagne was all ready to be popped, and Daddy King stopped them. He's a complete teetotaler, and he said, 'Wait a minute before you start all your toasts to each other. We better not forget to toast the man who brought us here, and here's a toast to God.' And then he said, 'I always wanted to make a contribution, and all you got to do if you want to contribute, you got to ask the Lord, and let Him know, and the Lord heard me and in some kind of way I don't even know He came down through Georgia and He laid His hand on me and my wife and He gave us Martin Luther King and our prayers were answered and when my head is cold and my bones are bleached the King family will go down not only in American history but in world history as well because Martin King is a

---

*Yet there is an increasing difficulty in covering racial news. Two years ago if a white reporter even hinted that there was division in the movement, he was accused of trying to create that very division. As the divisions became more obvious, each time you were with an established leader like Roy Wilkins, he would complain how the press *invented* radical leaders, created by the white press because of its guilt feelings. The next day you might be in Harlem talking with one of the more radical Negroes, and he would give a bitter discourse on how the white press played up only Whitney Young and Roy Wilkins; the white press was out to make the Negroes think that this mild leadership was all they had.

Nobel Prize–winner.' When he finished everyone was so moved, why the champagne just stayed there, and they made the toast to God and the champagne just stayed there afterwards. No one drank any, not even Bayard Rustin."

There was a moment of silence, and then one of the other ministers said, "Yes, sir, the Negro preacher is something. He sure is. God has use for him even when the Negro preacher didn't know what he was saying himself."

VI

The Kings of Atlanta are aristocrats of power and influence in the Negro world in the way that the Lodges have been among the Yankees and the Kennedys are among the Irish. The Negro church, particularly in the South, has always been the Negroes' great cultural base. The Baptist church was the church with the largest mass base, untouched by the white man. He did not appoint its preachers, he did not control them. One of the big churches of Atlanta, the greatest city of the South, is the Ebenezer Baptist Church. To have been pastor of it was to have a real base in the Negro community, not just of Atlanta, but in Negro America. Its pastor fifty years ago was a man named A. D. Williams, considered one of the finest preachers of his time; his sweet and gentle daughter married an ambitious young rural Negro from Georgia named Martin Luther King.

Martin King Senior, M. L. Senior, or Daddy King in Atlanta is probably not so outstanding as his son, but he is in many ways more interesting. He is a man of great intensity and willpower, not entirely committed to nonviolence; he goes along with it for his son's sake, but some of those who have physically pushed or hit Martin Junior would regret it if they tried it on his father.

Martin King Junior's reminiscences of his childhood are largely gentle stories; the inevitable hurts are bathed in the love of his parents. But Martin King Senior's stories of his boyhood are stories of violent racial confrontations with the whites of that day. Every angry face is still sketched in full detail, every taunt, every humiliation, every cheating recalled.

As a boy King Senior was the best Bible student around; he

went to Atlanta, worked hard, studied at night, married Reverend Williams' daughter, and became assistant pastor of Ebenezer, where today he is pastor and his son Martin Junior is assistant pastor. By this time his father-in-law was treasurer of the National Baptist Convention, a powerful position which took him all over the country. The Williams family and the Kings came to know the important Negroes in other cities. To this day whenever there is a city in racial trouble King Senior knows the names of all the important people and preachers in town.

Martin King Senior instilled in his family a sense of pride and confidence; every time there was an incident involving the children King Senior repeated to them: Don't be ashamed, you're as good as anyone else. The family grew up well-to-do. "Not wealthy really," says young Martin King, "but Negro-wealthy. We never lived in a rented house and we never rode too long in a car on which payment was due, and I never had to leave school to work."

Six years ago in a loving and prophetic piece about him, James Baldwin quoted a friend's saying of King, quoted and requoted it because Baldwin felt it told so much about King: "He never went around fighting with himself like we all did." (The Baldwin essay was prophetic in that it saw the darkening clouds for any Negro leader; it was also poignant. Baldwin saw King as "a younger much-loved and menaced brother; he seemed slight and vulnerable to be taking on such odds," and one senses, reading it, that King with his happy home as a young man, and with the warmth of his present home, is somebody Baldwin would like to have been.)*

As a young man he grew up in the world of preachers; by the time he went off to college, to Morehouse (father, grandfather, and great-grandfather had gone there; it was where you went) he had decided to become a doctor; he was an agnostic. Part of the reason was a contempt for the Southern Negro preacher, the low level of intellectual training, the intense emotionalism.

He had simply turned on the church: "If God was as all-

---

*See "The Dangerous Road Before Martin Luther King," by James Baldwin, *Harper's*, February 1961.

powerful and as good as everyone said, why was there so much evil on the face of the earth?" Later at Morehouse several teachers, including Dr. Benjamin Mays, the president, and Dr. George Kelsey, a philosophy professor, convinced him that religion could be intellectually respectable; he returned, and then went on to Crozier Theological Seminary in Pennsylvania. There for the first time he entered the white world. He was terribly aware of their whiteness and his blackness, and the stereotypes they had of Negroes. Negroes were always late for things, Martin King was always first in a classroom. Negroes were lazy and indifferent, Martin King worked hard and studied endlessly. Negroes were dirty, Martin King was always clean, always properly, perhaps too properly, dressed. Negroes were always laughing, Martin King was deadly serious. If there was a school picnic, Martin King did not eat watermelon.

He had gone in 1951 from Crozier to Boston University to study for his Ph.D., and entered there the social and intellectual world of the Northern Negro. King felt Morehouse had committed him to work in the South, and besides it was 1955 when he took his degree, the year after the Supreme Court decision outlawing school segregation. King had three offers to stay in the North, including one teaching position, but he chose a small church in Montgomery. He arrived just in time to be there when Rosa Parks' feet hurt, and he was catapulted to national prominence with the bus strike. He was the new boy in a divided city, and he became the leader of the Montgomery Improvement Association precisely because he was both new and yet known and respected through his family.

VII

In Cleveland King was to meet with both the preachers and the Black Nationalists, who have the support of the alienated young people.

The leader of the Nationalists is a tall mystic young man named Ahmed, who has a particular cult of his own combining racism and astrology—the darkness of the white man and the darkness of the skies. Earlier in the year he predicted that May 9 would be the *terrible day* when the black ghetto erupted. He made this prediction partly because there was to be an eclipse of the sun that day. Everyone laughed, old Ahmed, that crazy astrologer, but the police picked up him and a group of his followers that day just in case. Ahmed is mocked not only by the whites, but by the preachers as well. To them he represents nothing, has no job, all he does is talk.

King's people, however, believe Ahmed has a considerable, if somewhat fluid, influence. At first Ahmed and his men put out the word they were not interested in meeting with King; they were down on preachers, and he was a sort of Super-preacher. "He's really a Tom, you know," one of them told a King aide, "and one thing we don't need, that's more lectures from more Toms."

King went out to meet with them, however; he talked with them, but more important he listened to them, and it went surprisingly well. While he spoke nonviolence to them he did tell them to be proud of their black color, that no emancipation proclamation, no act of Lyndon Johnson, could set them free unless they were sure in their own minds they liked being black. And of course he talked with them on Vietnam, and they liked that also. The most important thing, however, was the simple act of paying attention to them. In Cleveland, King's people believe, the Nationalists are extremely important. Cleveland has particularly restless youths, up from Mississippi, either born there, or the first-generation children of parents born there. They are ill prepared for the cities. They come to these compact places like Hough, so that finally the inner ghetto is filled with the completely hopeless, floating, and rootless. It is estimated that one-third of the people in the inner ghetto change residence every year.

"There's a little power in these street gangs," one Negro says, "but power that doesn't go beyond a few blocks. Within those few blocks a man can be pretty big, you know he can shout, 'This is wrong, this is wrong, this is wrong.' But it doesn't go much beyond that. Past Fifty-fifth Street (the ghetto line), they're nothing, so they speak for the poor, but only to the poor."

That night the meeting was stormy. There had been some talk that Ahmed and his people might walk out, but they remained inside and, indeed, dominated the meeting. "The preachers were afraid of them, but they weren't afraid of the preachers," said one of King's aides. Outside one of Ahmed's followers had decided to lecture to other younger Negroes: "Do you think ol' whitey, he's going to come by and say, 'Why there's Chuck Hill. He's a good black man. I'm going to spare that good black Chuck Hill.' No, whitey's not going to do that. He's going to shoot you down like all the others. Whitey doesn't care about any black man."

Inside the meeting, one of the more conservative ones said something about good things coming and the need for only a little more patience, and Ahmed jumped up angrily and said, "How can you trust a man that would kidnap a little child, bring him to a country he raped, put him down on stolen property, and then say, 'Just you wait a few days, I'm going to give you your freedom and lots of other good things'?"

A few minutes later there was a heated debate between Ahmed and a middle-class Negro. Ahmed had been talking, giving his program, when the man rose and shouted:

"Have you got a job? Have you got a job? Have you got a job?"

Ahmed answered, "My job is to free the minds of my people."

"No no no!" the man shouted. "Do you have an eight-hour job? Do you have an eight-hour job?"

"My job is a twenty-four-hour job," Ahmed replied, "and as a matter of fact, it's got just as much risk and danger as your job. Anytime you want to switch I'd be delighted."

The next day King's people were delighted with Ahmed. "He was so warm, so beautiful last night," one of them said, and in the middle of the press conference the next day announcing that King planned to come to Cleveland to organize for better housing and jobs, a King aide suggested to a Negro reporter that he ask Ahmed, sitting next to King, what he thought of King. Ahmed answered that King was a black brother; there was a happy sigh of relief from King's people.

VIII

One wonders whether King's alliance with the Nationalists can last. King is hot and they are cool; he overstates and they understate; he is a preacher and their God is dead. They are of the ghetto the way Malcolm X was, and like

Malcolm they are flawed by it; that was his great strength. King is not of the ghetto, he is not flawed (*he never went around fighting with himself like we all did*), he is of the South. The people he touches most deeply are the people they left behind.

When one raises this question with Andy Young, he talks about the church being a force with young people, but one senses that he shares some of the doubts. He tells of when they went to Rochester, during the riots there. The Negro youths refused to talk with them until they beat them at basketball, beat them at shooting craps, proved they weren't squares. He tells of how the tough kids in Chicago didn't want to meet King. They finally did, and they were impressed with him, with the sheer power of his moral presence, but when he left they slipped right back into the gangs.

"We see the ghettos now as a form of domestic colonialism," Andy Young says. "The preachers are like the civil servants in Ghana, doing the white man's work for them." King has decided to represent the ghettos; he will work in them and speak for them. But their voice is harsh and alienated. If King is to speak for them truly, then his voice must reflect theirs, it too must be alienated, and it is likely to be increasingly at odds with the rest of American society.

His great strength in the old fight was his ability to dramatize the immorality he opposed. The new immorality of the ghettos will not be so easy to dramatize, for it is often an immorality with invisible sources. The slum lords are evil enough, but they will not be there by their homes waiting for King and the TV crews to show up, ready to split black heads open. The schools are terrible, but there is no one man making them bad by his own ill will, likely to wait there in the school yard with a cattle prod. The jobs are bad, but the reasons Negroes aren't ready for decent jobs are complicated; there won't be one sinister hillbilly waiting outside the employment agency grinding cigarettes into the necks of King and his followers.

IX

King admits he is becoming a more radical critic of the society, and that the idea of "domestic colonialism" represents his view of the North. I suggest that he sounded like a nonviolent Malcolm; he says no, he could never go along with black separatism. For better or worse we are all on this particular land together at the same time, and we have to work it out together.

Nevertheless, he and his people are closer to Malcolm than anyone would have predicted five years ago—and much farther from their more traditional allies like Whitney Young and Roy Wilkins. King's people are privately very critical of both men; they realize that both work through the white Establishment to get things for Negroes, that they often have to tolerate things they privately consider intolerable because they feel in the long run this has to be done. The white man is there, he owns 90 per cent of it, and the only course is to work through his Establishment. King's people privately feel that this is fine, but that the trouble is the white Establishment has become corrupt, and in modeling yourself after it and working with it and through it, you pick up the same corruptions.

There are some very basic differences at issue here, much deeper than the war in Vietnam (though King's people see Vietnam as an example of the difference, for they believe that some high-level Negro acceptance of Vietnam is effected not because of agreement with the Johnson Administration's position, but as a price to pay in order to get other things from the Administration). In the split it is King who is changing, not Young or Wilkins. "For years," King says, "I labored with the idea of reforming the existing institutions of the society, a little change here, a little change there. Now I feel quite differently. I think you've got to have a reconstruction of the entire society, a revolution of values."

This means, he says, the possible nationalization of certain industries, a guaranteed annual income, a vast review of foreign investments, an attempt to bring new life into the cities. His view of whites has also changed deeply in the last year; previously he believed that most of America was committed to the cause of racial justice, "that we were touching the conscience of white America," that only parts of the white South and a few Northern bigots were blocking it. But after Chicago he decided that only a small part of white America was truly committed to the Negro cause, mostly kids on the campuses. "Most Americans," he would say, "are unconscious racists."

X

King is a frustrating man. Ten years ago *Time* found him humble, but few would find him that way today, though the average reporter coming into contact with him is not exactly sure why; he suspects King's vanity. One senses that he is a shy and sensitive man thrown into a prominence which he did not seek but which he has come to accept, rather likes, and intends to perpetuate. Colleagues find him occasionally pretentious; and the student leaders have often called him De Lawd, a title both mocking, and at the same time a sign of respect.

Being with him is a little like being with a Presidential candidate after a long campaign; he has been through it all, there has been too much exposure, the questions have all been asked before; the reporters all look alike, as do the endless succession of airport press conferences. King on the inside seems the same as King on the outside—always solemn, always confident, convinced that there is a right way and that he is following it; always those dark, interchangeable suits; the serious shirt and responsible tie.

He has finally come to believe his myth, just as the people in the Pentagon believe theirs and the man in the White House believes his; he sticks to the morality of his life and of his decisions, until there becomes something of a mystic quality to him. His friend, Reverend Wyatt Tee Walker, who is not a mystic, and indeed something of a swinger and finds King almost too serious says, "I am not a mystic but I am absolutely convinced that God is doing something with Martin King that He is not doing with anyone else in this country." And Martin Luther King Senior believes his son is "a prophet. That's what he is, a prophet. A lot of people don't understand what he's doing and don't like it, and I tell them he *has* to do these things, things that aren't popular. Prophets are like that, they have special roles. Martin is just a twentieth-century prophet."

Friends believe King has become decreasingly concerned with worldly things, and has no interest in money. There are many fine Negro homes in Atlanta, but King's is not one of them; he lives in a small house right near one of the ghettos. He takes little money from his church and tends to return a good deal to it; despite this attitude his children are protected because Harry Belafonte, a friend of King's, has set up an educational trust fund for each one.

XI

From Cleveland we flew to Berkeley for a major speech. Berkeley is now the center for the new radicalism in America, and King was likely to get a very warm response there; Berkeley would make him forget about the ghettos. Thousands of cheering young people would be there, applauding him. They would be there not because he led the March on Washington, for those days are easily forgotten (to some of them the March smacks of Tomism now), but because he is saying what they want to hear on Vietnam.

It was Vietnam, of course, which linked him with the new radicalism. His dissent was coming; that had been obvious for some time. Last winter when the peace groups and the New Left planned a major peace demonstration for the spring, the head of it was the Reverend James Bevel, a top King deputy who had organized for King in both Birmingham and Chicago. Bevel is the radical wing of the Southern Christian Leadership Conference, deeply Biblical and mystic, weaving in the new politics with the Old Testament. He is also something of a link between King and SNCC.

Bevel is an intense, fiery man, and these days the words genocide and race war come quickly to his lips, and he is obsessed with Vietnam: *"The war in Vietnam, he has said, will not end until Jesus Christ rises up in the Mekong Delta; the Lord can't hear our prayers here in America, because of all the cries and moans of His Children in the Mekong Delta, and that is all He can hear as long as the war continues, so forget your prayers until the war is over, America."*

King's Southern Christian Leadership Conference is a rather loosely knit organization, and at Atlanta headquarters, there is a certain fear of what are now called Bevelisms. Recently there was a sharp kickback when Bevel spoke at a

Catholic college and apparently made some remarks slurring the Virgin Mary. A young Jesuit questioned him sharply, and Bevel said, yes, he was interested in Mary, "but which Mary, all the thousands of Marys walking the streets of the ghettos, the thousands of peasant Marys being killed in the Mekong Delta, or some chick who lived thousands of years ago?"

The far-left groups who organized the peace march went for Bevel because they wanted King. King had seemed interested himself, but very slightly so. They contacted Bevel and they found he was interested, and ended up coming to their meetings. "Then the question was," one of them said, "could he deliver King? He said he could and he promised, but weeks went by and no King. We began to wonder. Then finally he came through."

They wanted King because they wanted a mass basis; they already had the automatics, the pacifists, their very own, but they wanted a broader constituency. As one peace organizer said, "There were a lot of people we felt wanted to come in on this, you know, good-hearted Americans for whom someone like King would make it easier, be a good umbrella. We could then call some of these unions and church groups and just middle-aged people who were nervous about coming in, who wanted to come in a little bit, but didn't like the whole looks of it, and we could say, Look here, we've got King, and it makes them all breathe easier. They think, Why it's King, it's all right, it's safe."

King repeats over and over again that he does not take stands because of what Stokely Carmichael says. Nonetheless, someone like Carmichael creates pressures to which King must inevitably react in order to retain his position. King would have reacted to the pressures of the ghettos and of Vietnam anyway, but without pressure and the alternative voices of a Stokely or a Floyd McKissick, he might have done it more at his choosing in his own good time. Stokely's outspoken stand on Vietnam made King's silence all the more noticeable. For King is a moralist, a fairly pragmatic one, and he does not intend to lose his position with young, militant, educated Negroes.

What was decisive in Bevel's role was that a trusted lieutenant in the most important of King's projects wanted out so he could join the peace movement. *That* moved King. Here was one more sign that a bright and passionate friend judged Vietnam more important than civil rights. It was symbolic of what King saw the war doing, taking all the time, money, energy, and resources of America away from its ghetto problems and focusing them thousands of miles away on a war the wisdom of which he doubted in the first place.

There are friends who feel that other factors affected him profoundly too, one of these being the right of a *Negro* to speak out. This had come to a point in early March at a fundraising evening in Great Neck. King, Whitney Young, and John Morsell of the NAACP had appeared for an evening of speeches, questions, and answers. The subject of Vietnam came up, and King was asked how he felt. He answered with a relatively mild criticism of the war, the morality of it, and what it was doing to America.

Young was asked the same question and he dissented. There was the other war here in the ghettos, and that was the war the Urban League was fighting; he as an individual couldn't speak for the Urban League, but then he made his personal stand clear: communism had to be stopped just as Hitler should have been stopped in World War II. As the evening was breaking up, Young and King got into a brief but very heated argument. Young told King that his position was unwise since it would alienate the President, and they wouldn't get anything from him. King angrily told him, "Whitney, what you're saying may get you a foundation grant, but it won't get you into the kingdom of truth." Young quite angrily told King that he was interested in the ghettos, and King was not. "You're eating well," Young said.

King told Young that was precisely why he opposed the war, because of what it was doing to the ghettos. The argument, with a number of people still standing around, was so heated that King's lawyer quickly broke it up. Afterwards King felt badly about having spoken so angrily in public, and telephoned Young to apologize. They talked for more than an hour, failing of course to resolve their very basic differences.

This had happened to him once before. In 1965, when he was fresh from the Nobel Prize, King had briefly opposed the war and called for negotiations. There was a violent reaction. President Johnson got in touch with him and persuaded him to talk with that wooer-of-the-strayed, Arthur Goldberg. Goldberg assured him that peace was in the air. Similarly, King admits he was stunned by the extent of the pressure and reaction to him. "They told me I wasn't an expert in foreign affairs, and they were all experts," he said. "I knew only civil rights and I should stick to that." So he backed down, feeling a little guilty and suspecting he had been told that it wasn't a Negro's place to speak on Vietnam. This continued to rankle him, and after the Great Neck meeting he felt that if he had *backed* the war he would have been welcomed aboard, but that if he didn't back the war it was his place to remain silent.

XII

Though King says he could never live under communism, he does not see the chief division in the world as between the communist and capitalist. His is a more U Thantian view, with the division being between the rich and the poor, and thus to a large degree the white and nonwhite (the East European nations would become Have nations, to the surprise of many of their citizens). His view of violence in Vietnam and violence in Angola are quite different. Yet he is also terribly American, more American than he knows; his church is Western, his education is Western, and he thinks as a Westerner, though an increasingly alienated one.

He does not particularly think of the war in Vietnam as a racial one (although the phrase "killing little brown children in Vietnam" slips in); rather he sees the American dilemma there as one of face-saving, of an inability to end a miscalculation and a tendency to enhance it with newer and bigger miscalculations. Because there is a good deal of conservatism in King, there was a lively debate among his advisers as to whether he could go into the Spring Mobilization. The Call to the march had the whole works, genocide and race war; and a number of King allies, traditional liberals, advised him against it. The old ladies in Iowa wouldn't buy it.

But after much negotiating, which King's people clearly enjoyed, it was finally decided he should go in without signing the Call. "I went in because I thought I could serve as a bridge between the old liberals and the New Left," he says. He is still somewhat wary of much of the peace movement, however; he does not know all the people as he does in civil rights, and he lacks a sure touch for the vocabulary of peace. He is also angry about having been ambushed by the New Politics people who leaked to the press in Boston recently that King was considering running for President; he was not yet considering it, and he felt they were trying to push him faster than he wanted to go; he remains wary of some of the peace people, and he realizes they are all out to exploit his name for their own purposes.

His stand on Vietnam is not necessarily the most popular one he has ever taken. It is popular on the campuses, of course, but it has hurt him with the editorial writers (Vietnam and civil rights don't mix), gladdened George Wallace, hurt him in the suburbs, and it has made the ghettos a little uneasy.

Peace is not a sure issue in the ghettos. There have been wars in which the Midwest provided many of the boys, and the small towns rallied around them. There are no picket fences in the ghettos and the American Legion posts are weaker there, but right now *our boys* are coming from the ghettos, and so it is a very delicate issue. One radical Negro leader thought Vietnam would be an easy whipping boy until he began to hang around Harlem bars, where he found you don't knock the war (black faces under green berets) and so he toned down his attacks. But some of King's best friends fear that Roy Wilkins may be wiser than King about how Negroes in the ghetto feel about Vietnam.

XIII

But Berkeley is another country. We went there one sunny day, and they were ready for him. They came to pick him up early in the afternoon, a young Negro dean and some bright young students, and they predicted a great reception for him —a demonstration for a King-Spock ticket.

We rode out together and I relaxed while a young student

editor interviewed King; she had her questions all written down (Declining U.S. moral status in the world? Answer, yes. Doing this because of Stokely? Answer, no). The ride was pleasant, and the students were talking about the dove feeling on the campus, and King said, "I guess it's not too popular to be a hawk at Berkeley," and someone asked if he's for their right of dissent. "I'm too deeply committed to the First Amendment to deny the right of dissent, even to hawks," he said.

On the campus there are a lot of young men wearing pins which say simply, "October 16." That is their day, they explain, when all over the country they plan to go down to recruiting centers and turn in their draft cards. On the campus there are numerous signs saying "King-Spock."

His speech there is an attack on American values; it cites Berkeley as the conscience of the academic community and the center for new values ("we have flown the air like birds, and swum the sea like fishes but we have not learned the simple act of walking the earth like brothers"). It is looser and more natural than the peace-march one, and the biggest ovation of the day comes when King denies that he and Berkeley are against our boys in Vietnam:

"We're for our boys. We're their best friends back home, because we want them to come home. It's time to come home. They've been away too long."

A few minutes later, after answering questions (no, he will not run for President, though he is touched by their support; indeed he says they must be careful who runs against Johnson, perhaps it will be "Mr. Nixon, or your good Governor") he heads for a meeting of the Afro-American students.

Suddenly a white graduate student steps out and blocks his way. "Dr. King," the student says, "I understand your reservations about running for President, but you're a world figure, you're the most important man we've got, you're the only one who can head a third-party ticket. And so when you make your decision, remember that there are many of us who are going to have to go to jail for many years, give up our citizenship, perhaps. This is a very serious thing."

King is stunned; this requires more than a half minute, and the student presses on: "This is the most serious thing in our lives. Politically you're the only meaningful person. Spock isn't enough. So please weigh our jail sentences in the balance when you make your decision."

I have watched King with dozens of people as he nods and half-listens, and this is the first time I have ever seen anyone get to him. He waits for a moment, for the student to say more, and then realizes there is nothing more to say, and he finally says, "Well, you make a very moving and persuasive statement."

That meeting had shaken King a little, and on the way back to San Francisco we talked about the sense of alienation of the students. At the meeting one of the students claimed that the white man was planning to exterminate all American Negroes, every last one, that the war in Vietnam was being used solely for that purpose as a testing ground for weapons. "He really believed that," King said, "really believed that." Another student was deeply committed to separatism—move away from the white community completely, forget all the whites. "What's your program?" King had asked. "What are you offering? But all he had was more radical rhetoric." Another student had advocated more violence, but King had answered "We don't need to talk mean, we need to act mean."

In the car King mused that the trouble with the people who talk mean is that they're always gone when the trouble finally strikes. "They lead you there and then they leave." Then he mentioned a confrontation with Charles Evers, the very able head of the NAACP in Mississippi. He said Charles had really whipped a crowd up one night, putting it to them on violence and the need for it, and King had finally said, "Look here, Charles, I don't appreciate your talking like that. If you're that violent, why you just go up the highway to Greenwood and kill the man who killed your own brother." And they applauded.

The students, King said, were disenchanted with white society, there had been too few victories, and they were losing faith in nonviolence—this and a sense of guilt over their own privileged status. Some of this is good, the fact that they identify with the ghettos much more than they did ten years ago, but there is also the danger of paranoia. One of the white students had mentioned how influential the autobiography of

Malcolm X is with the students, both black and white, and added, "You won't believe this, but my conservative old Republican grandmother has just read it and she thinks it's marvelous, a book of love."

"That is what we call the power to become," King said, "the ability to go on in spite of. It was tragic that Malcolm was killed, he was really coming around, moving away from racism. He had such a sweet spirit. You know, right before he was killed he came down to Selma and said some pretty passionate things against me, and that surprised me because after all it was my own territory down there. But afterwards he took my wife aside, and said he thought he could help me more by attacking me than praising me. He thought it would make it easier for me in the long run."

The car finally reached the hotel. He had covered 3,000 miles in the last few days, and now he was ready to recross the country, five stops on the way. The people, the faces, the audiences, the speeches were already blending into each other; even the cities were becoming interchangeable. Only the terrible constancy of the pressures remained. One sensed him struggling to speak to and for the alienated while still speaking to the mass of America, of trying to remain true to his own, while not becoming a known, identified, predictable, push-button radical, forgotten because he was no longer in the mainstream. The tug on him was already great, and there is no reason to believe that in the days ahead it would become any less excruciating.

Harper's, August 1967

"We Ain't Taking No More"

by George Barner

NEWARK—In these shambles west of the Passaic River something enormous has been awakened even as something else, once equally enormous, has slumbered to the edge of death.

Newly awakened is the hot brash presence of young black anger. It is an anger sharpened between frustration and foreshortened horizons to an edge barely bluntable even by a mass display of police power, and frenzied by the taste of its own formidability to where it drastically destroys its own environs to smash its fist against an authority it has rejected.

"We take. For years we take and take. Now, we're tired of taking. You tell 'em we ain't taking no more. We're dishing, too. I don't care nothing about dying. I'm hardly living. I'd just as soon die here as in Vietnam. If I die I won't know nothing about it."

What is dying is the tired faith of the mature in the usefulness of the ethics of personal responsibility, the precepts of conventional morality, the credibility of promises of progress made in righteous terms for political expediency. It is an abject weariness too spent to be much concerned any longer with where justifiable protest may merge into criminality or at what point every black man's postponed hopes and honest wrath become the mask and excuse for the selfishly cherished sneak thievery of a countable few.

"They're looting and stealing," said a fiftyish woman on Mulberry St. "It doesn't make sense. Who are they hurting but all of us? But maybe it's a way when there's no other way. When they break windows and run wild all night, then they don't say get back there and be patient. Then they come and sit down and talk to you."

The youthful state of mind was embodied in the slight frame of a 16-year-old Weequahic High School junior who would identify himself only as Brother Theodore. He was hunched Friday afternoon over a newspaper in the aisle seat of a Public Service bus bound for Newark from New York intensely reading accounts of the previous two days of riot and actively puffing a big curved pipe oblivious of the No Smoking sign.

Alighting in deathly quiet downtown Newark, Brother Theodore and the reporter who'd made his acquaintance found no buses or taxis immediately heading into the cordoned-off riot area and headed there afoot as Theodore filled the reporter in with a friendliness despite an intense and apparently sincere conviction.

"I'm glad we're waking up at last," said Brother Theodore, whose conventional trousers and workman's footwear were topped by a loose-fitting, collarless, waist-length African blouse which he called a danshiki. It was bright orange with black figures. Around his neck hung a chest-deep necklace of curved white buffalo teeth and oval black beads which he said were from African trees.

"This is a joyous occasion, my brother, this is an awakening," said Brother Theodore as we passed the first battle-clad National Guardsmen and trudged up the long slope of Springfield Ave. which was an appalling shambles from High St. clear back to West 10th and was to spread its blight of havoc over an even wider area in a few short hours.

"Because of this demonstration we will now have more opportunities. There will be jobs now and better places to live, you'll see. This is the sound the white man waited to hear. We have brought it to him."

Brother Theodore, after a moment's hesitation, said he was not a member of "what you could call" a formal organization but was an admirer of Malcolm X and was becoming a student of militant black literature and lore. He was well known to the people—mostly lean-shanked young men no more than five years older than he—who smiled, grinned, joked, greeted and desultorily looted all along the long concrete incline that is the 125th St. of Newark's Central Ward ghetto.

To a cigarette-smoking youth slouching downhill toward us Brother Theodore waved his hand and called: "Made any hits?" The slouching smoker glanced at Brother Theodore's companion and replied that he had not. "Just looking, huh?" asked Brother Theodore, and they both laughed.

Up to Belmont Ave., past Couffel's Custard shop, Hank's Men's Store, the Washington Outfitter and General Vacuum, Brother Theodore and the reporter trudged uphill crunching shards of shattered plate glass underfoot, skirting pulled down metal gratings and peering into the gutted and ravaged interiors of demolished stores and shops. From where we paused at an intersection we saw the cleaned out shelves of Samson's Liquors squatting adjacent to the not noticeably harmed Good Neighbor Rescue Center which proclaimed in fading letters "Jesus Saves" and "established 1958."

Down Springfield Ave. a woman of about 30 stepped gingerly across debris that spilled the width of the sidewalk and, cautiously lifting the hem of her skirt, entered one of the shops to exit in a few moments with a cardboard carton full of contraband.

The militiamen and state troopers at this still daylight hour were within sight of this kind of activity, which was repeated countless times with an almost gleeful abandon by many of its perpetrators, but made no move to come into the blocks where it occurred. They merely sealed it off from exit or entry to most of those who belonged on one side or the other.

Other acquaintances of Brother Theodore's passed and hailed him cheerily, acknowledged that they had indeed participated in the affair of the previous nights and that "everything was cool," or "we scored, man, we scored," or "Where were you?"

Brother Theodore, who said his mother had moved to Newark from New York two years ago, shook hands and departed assuring his local brethren that his inopportune absence had been unplanned and sorely regretted but that he was now back and ready.

At Lincoln Shoes on Springfield Ave. there was the first miracle of what was to be five days of violence, a white-owned store that had escaped virtually unscathed.

The diminutive, sallow-complexioned proprietor, Hy Schwartz, said it was because he was a square shooter.

"I stood here with my property all night, through the whole thing. It was terrible," he said, "but you know what they told me? They told me 'You're on the ball with us.' I've been here for 35 years. I've grown up with all my customers and I got Negro employees." Schwartz said his employees, "young fellows" named Gene Williams, Willie Davidson and Charlie Davidson (brothers), had stood watch with him part of the night.

Standing by the grating, which Schwartz was now locking up tight as the sun started to set and the threatened rain authorities had hoped for began to melt away, was 18-year-old Willie Wiggins, a part-time helper in the store who is classified 1-A in the draft and recently returned from a two-year hitch in the Job Corps.

"That's about the best thing they ever did around here for our people," Wiggins said of the Job Corps. He said he had acquired the beginnings of qualification toward becoming an electrician. He said some of the youths who were loitering about or prancing into and out of the exposed store properties had been in the Job Corps also but had dropped out because they couldn't come home on weekends.

As the unconventional shoppers continued their pickings, Wiggins remarked:

"It's very seldom you see this many Negroes on Springfield Ave. Half of them don't even live in the vicinity." He waved to a passerby and laughed, "Not even on the first of the month when they've all got their check do you see this many."

As we talked, a cream-colored Oldsmobile crowded with several women and a male driver, its chassis almost touching the ground, pulled up a few feet away in front of a haberdashery where three young men were calmly talking. One of the three held an armload of men's and ladies' belts. A passenger in the right rear seat squealed delightedly and extended her right hand imploringly. The youth with the belts sauntered over almost absent mindedly and allowed her to take her pick.

New York Amsterdam News, July 22, 1967

The Killing of Billy Furr, Caught in the Act of Looting Beer

by Dale Wittner

I MET Billy Furr at the corner of Avon and Livingston when he barged into my conversation with a Black Muslim who called himself Haking X. Haking was predicting that the riot would go on "until every white man's building in Newark is burned." But Billy disagreed.

"We ain't riotin' agains' all you whites. We're riotin' agains' police brutality, like that cab driver they beat up the other night," Billy declared. "That stuff goes on all the time. When the police treat us like people 'stead of treatin' us like animals, then the riots will stop."

With that he turned away from me and went with his friends in search of cold beer, which he knew he could not buy legally because of the curfew.

Billy, who was 24, had been stranded in Newark. He came to the city to pick up a $50 unemployment check and look for a job to replace the one he lost at a bakery when it went out of business. When the buses back to Montclair, where he lived with his mother and grandparents, were stopped by the riot, Billy stayed on in Newark with friends.

Photographer Bud Lee and I came on Billy again later—a block farther down Avon at Mack Liquors. He and his friends were looting the store, which already had been broken into the day before. They loaded all the beer they could carry into car trunks and handed it out to passersby. When he noticed me, Billy thrust a can into my hand.

"Have a beer on me," he said. "But if the cops show up get rid of it and run like hell."

I opened the beer and went off to view rat holes and roaches in a cruddy $85-a-month apartment which the tenant, William Jackson, had invited me to inspect. The apartment

593

was only a half a block away, and as we stepped back out the door tires screeched and a city police car skidded to a halt directly in front of Mack Liquors. There had been no warning —it had raced in with its siren silent. This was the first sign of police authority on the block in more than an hour, except for a young Newark police trainee who had sipped beer and watched the looting with me.

In an instant the shotguns that bristled from the cruiser's windows shattered the relative calm. The sudden explosions, rather than clearing the streets, sent mothers screaming out to pull children to safety. Apartment windows that had been empty were now full of dark faces, each of them in danger of being shot.

For the looters caught in the store there was no place to run. They simply fell to the floor or froze in their tracks, hands above their heads. But Billy was standing outside with part of a six-pack in his left hand. He'd been arrested before. This time he ran.

He raced past me down Avon. I was barely 30 feet away from a yellow-helmeted officer with a shotgun pointed toward my head.

"Get down," he screamed. I fell hard to the sidewalk just as a blast from the weapon exploded over me and the officer shouted an order to halt. But apparently Billy kept running behind me. From the ground I looked up into the sweating face of the policeman as he squinted down the long barrel. I prayed he wouldn't shoot. He pulled the trigger.

Tiny pieces of the spent shell fluttered down on me as blue uniform trousers of the Newark Police Department flashed past toward Billy lying on the ground. Already people were screaming obscenities from the windows and bottles arched from the rooftop. More gunfire cleared the windows for a moment, but they quickly filled again.

"Call an ambulance," a policeman yelled back to the car. Up the street the officer who had shot Billy stood over him, the shotgun resting in the crook of his arm. Billy's blood poured onto the dirty sidewalk. Then a girl was beside him sobbing and ignoring the order to "get the hell out of here."

"I'm his girl friend. Help him. Please do something, God, don't let him die," she pleaded.

Back at the corner of Livingston there was more shooting as a line of police reinforcements arrived with an ambulance. I ran toward the crowd being held back at gunpoint on the corner. In the center, blood streaming from his neck, lay little Joe Bass Jr., a 12-year-old who had been shining shoes at home with his brother an hour earlier when playmates asked him to come out.

Two pellets from the same shotgun blast that killed Billy had struck Joey in the neck and thigh. Around his form surged about 50 sobbing men and women, trying to break through the small ring of police. Nearby two other youngsters cried quietly on the curb. The people who wanted to help were clubbed away with rifle and shotgun butts. Their frantic efforts kept the police too busy to help the boy, who we all thought was dying. One Negro appeared to try to snatch the pistol from an officer's holster. He was knocked to the pavement.

I watched as Joey was put in the ambulance and rushed off to the hospital. (His wounds, I learned later, were serious but he is recovering.) I walked back toward Billy's lifeless body. The girl was still kneeling beside it. She would not believe he was dead and ambulance attendants had to pull her away before they could cover Billy Furr.

Life, July 28, 1967

Riot!—A Negro Resident's Story

by Sandra A. West

NEGROES moved into Detroit's near west side because it was "a nice neighborhood."

Yesterday they cried with fear as burning and looting raged all around them.

I have lived in the area since 1954.

Yesterday I saw sights I never dreamed possible. I saw things I had only read about or seen on television.

Raging fires burned out of control for blocks and blocks. Thick black smoke and cinders rained down, at times so heavily they blocked out the vision of homes 20 feet away.

Looters drove pickup trucks loaded with everything from floor mops to new furniture. Price tags still dangled from the merchandise.

Youngsters no more than eight or nine years old rode two on a bicycle with loot under their shirts and clutched in their arms.

There was agony on the faces of those who lived close to the burnings, afraid their homes would be burned, too.

Friends of ours, in and out of the area, set up telephone relay systems with us to pass on any new information. Rumors spread as fast as the flames and it was hard to know what was true.

By 5 p.m. it was necessary to close our home to keep the smoke from saturating the house.

At 6:30 p.m. the electricity went out. We couldn't use our electric fan and were forced to open the house again.

We walked to 12th street where the riots began. There we watched as arsonists touched off fires at two establishments within a one-block area.

Burglar alarms wailed out of control. They went unanswered. Negro-owned stores sported hastily printed signs that read "Soul Brother."

A 12-year-old boy flashed a diamond ring that he said he found on his lawn.

On Linwood, three blocks west of 12th, smoke was so thick it was impossible to see one block away.

Some of the families on the blocks between 12th and Linwood packed their belongings and prepared to leave during the night if it became necessary. We were one of those families.

At the height of the rampage, several homes caught fire from the burning stores.

A man, his wife and two small children stumbled along the street with a suitcase and a bedsheet filled with the few belongings they could grab. Tears streamed down the mother's face.

The acrid odor of smoke burned our lungs and as the sun set we began rummaging around for candles and flashlights. Neighbors told us they planned to sit up on their porches all night.

By the 9 p.m. curfew, the streets were relatively quiet, but fear remained etched on the faces of those of us who had to spend the night there.

Nothing stirred on the streets at 10 p.m. except an occasional police car and jeeps and trucks loaded with national guardsmen. But the residents of "this nice neighborhood" were afraid that the riot wasn't over.

And it wasn't.

The Detroit News, July 24, 1967

The White Community Asks Repeatedly, "Why?"

by Carol Schmidt

WHILE almost all Negroes understood why the riot hit Detroit Sunday, no matter how they felt about it, almost no white people did.

I called my parents Sunday morning to tell them not to worry but they had not yet heard. A communication chain had awakened most Negroes with the news of the flare-up, but whites were insulated from the knowledge by cautious press reports that told only of a raid on a blind pig, adding the phrase, "a place which sells alcoholic beverages after hours" for the benefit of those who did not live in areas where blind pigs were part of a way of life.

Rumors trampled early press reports in the inner-city, but the white community was isolated from knowledge of the scope of the problem until much later, just as the white community had been insulated from the knowledge of the scope of the problem all their lives, knowledge which might have given them answers before now, to their repeated, "Why? What do they want?"

Other newsmen, faces sooty, checking the 10th precinct near which I live, urged me to leave the area when I asked for the latest news. When smoke from Grand River-Joy smothered our yard, and glass tinkled from a liquor store around the corner on Livernois, and a youth tossed a rock from hand to hand, weighing it and the distance to where I stood behind a window, I did leave.

My parents were not surprised when I called around 7; they had been sitting on their hands to keep from calling me, ordering their 24-year-old daughter home from the "no (white) man's land" where she had chosen to live, beyond their comprehension.

There was almost a smug "I told you so" look on my dad's

face, but it faded when I told him the riot had spread to Livernois and was working down Fenkell. A neighbor, though, one of the older white families still making up half the block, positively gloated.

He had sold his house a few days before and was moving to Redford, he smirked. "Let them have the goddam city. I hear they're burning down Woodward now. Those stores won't rebuild, a lot of them will be glad to get their insurance and move to Northland, if they can collect."

Most of them were never able to get insurance, I stated, realizing too late the statement would be used against me, "me" symbolizing for a moment the whole civil rights movement to this neighbor who could not understand, who was afraid.

His harangue branched into an explanation of how it was always "the little guy" who suffered, since he couldn't afford to buy in large quantities or as frequently to compete with the chain stores.

"Then these hoodlums are complaining about the small stores charging too much and not selling fresh goods," he shook his head. "They ought to be glad someone stayed to take care of them. You wouldn't get me working in that area for a million dollars. After today those merchants won't either. Machine gun the looters down, that's the answer."

He stood there, daring me to answer so that he would have fresh ammunition to shoot back, but I saw that it was no use and went back on the porch, sick of the word "they."

Another neighbor on the other side stuck her head out the window at me and cried, "Why? We've been nice enough and let them move into this area. Now they're burning it down. Why?"

I didn't bother to remind her then of the rock-throwing and name-calling and block-busting and pressure by which "we" had "let them move into this area," a process which was being repeated a little further northwest. Maybe we could talk again calmly in a few weeks, but not now while a pillow of smoke heaped the horizon.

The Negro families on the block seemed to stay inside. White neighbors sat on porches, half-expecting a fire-throwing black mob to run down from Fenkell.

Some, like my parents, had gone on earlier in the day as if nothing were wrong, not really knowing from press reports if anything were seriously wrong, and had come back with stories of bricks thrown down on them from expressway overpasses, thwarted picnics to blocked-off Belle Isle, "soul brother" signs going up all over in anticipation of the night.

It took a few minutes to get a phone call through, but the calls came anyway, from suburban friends and relatives asking first if we were okay and then again "why?"

"Those marches were all right, but do they think they're helping their cause by rioting?" came repeatedly. I tried to give the serious questioners a serious answer: some do—you didn't pay any attention to the marches so they have to get your attention somehow. Even those who know the probable repercussion is a retaliatory police state, well—

How do you convey the sense of frustration and alienation a rioter feels, the small sense of exhilaration and retribution that comes with a hurled firebomb against whitey to a person who has never been seriously thwarted in his life?

Everyone left their porches and went inside for the 11 o'clock news. I had driven down 12th earlier in the day, not satisfied with news reports, and the landmarks were still there. Now the TV screen showed charred hulks in their place.

I couldn't help crying when the camera panned over what once was the CORE office, which had apparently caught fire from a neighboring white-owned store. All the memories of 12th came back, the first time I had driven down to the CORE office, car doors locked. If there hadn't been a parking space right in front of the office I'm sure I wouldn't have stopped.

Later I could walk freely on the street, not seeing much difference from similar blocks on Dexter and Livernois, feeling a bit of affection for that kaleidoscopic street. But 12th still had that image in the white community that "anything goes," which drew the men there Friday and Saturday nights.

Sunday night everything went, and the TVs showed the outlying white areas what was happening but not why. At least then, they wanted to know.

I myself turned against a fairly liberal friend who was reacting like an inhibited klansman and who hadn't even tried to answer the barrage of "why?s" he was also getting. I saw this as our role, trying to explain why to whites who ordinarily have no contact with the Negro community what had happened, since for once they seemed genuinely concerned—as long as the smoke drifted northwest.

"Look, I'm not a Negro and neither are you—how can we explain?" he asked. "Beyond the obvious answers—housing, jobs, respect—that these whites have all heard before and ignored, what do you say? Maybe later they'll listen." He didn't sound too convinced himself.

The Michigan Chronicle, July 29, 1967

Breslin on Riot:
Death, Laughter, but No Sanity

by Jimmy Breslin

THERE is no sanity. A national guardsman in an apartment on the first floor fires his M-1 up the dumbwaiter shaft and a guardsman up on the top floor fires down the shaft.

On Linwood, an armored personnel carrier comes out of the blackness and into the glow of a burning building. Only one streetlight still glimmers on the block.

The guardsmen don't like lights around them on the streets. They fire from inside the carrier at the street light. A state policeman on the corner jumps and fires three times in return.

Policemen in helmets tumble out of a car and run along the street shouting for everybody to stop shooting. A guardsman in the carrier fires again.

"Sniper," somebody shouts.

"Where?"

"Up on the roof."

"Sniper on the roof."

The radio in the car says, "At Linwood and Montgomery, hold your fire. Repeat. Hold your fire. Two state policemen in the building."

"Don't shoot," somebody yells.

"Don't shoot, don't shoot, officers in the building."

"Sniper," somebody calls from behind a car.

On a street off Grand River, houses burn. House after house, on both sides of the street, and there are no fire trucks and the fires have been going for an hour and a half. The trees in front of the houses break into flames.

The houses are houses in which normal people live. But a popping sound has been coming from the flames for an hour. All the ammunition the people kept in their houses is exploding.

And at St. Jean and Mack, a fireman named Carl Smith runs to his truck and the sniper shoots him between the eyes. The fireman leaves one child.

All you see is rubble. Once they were buildings and now they are rubble, and fire from the gas main comes up through the tangle. Some places you go along an entire block of houses which have been burned down. Two-family brick houses, with porches and lawns and trees. Now only the chimneys, and parts of the brick walls that didn't fall down, stand in the light from the gas fires.

A tan convertible squeals around the corner, and the policemen jump and scream and aim shotguns and the car stops and a Negro staggers out of it. They grab him and throw him over the fender of a car.

"I'm shot," the man says. "I got shot in the leg."

He opens his belt and his pants fall down. There is a bullet hole in the top of his leg. He pulls the pants back on.

"Stay there," a cop covering him with a shotgun says.

"I'm goin' die here," the man says.

"Stay there."

The man holds his hands in the air and starts walking toward his car in the middle of the street.

"Shoot me," he says.

"Stay there."

"Shoot me!"

It is the fifth largest city in the country and its auto industry is the base of the country's economy, and you reel when you walk on the streets because the city is an asylum. On one avenue, there were so many that looked the same and had the same things happening that the names run together and become forgotten, the people push against each other in the hot daytime sun to get through the broken window of a shoe store.

"Get 'em, get 'em," a man in a white golf cap yells.

"I want my size," somebody inside calls out.

"Who cares what your size is? Get 'em. Just take something. Go on and take it for yourself."

"Yeah, take it.'

"Take everything in the whole mother place."

"Go get 'em, baby, leave me get in there with you."

They laugh and wave shoe boxes and shriek as they come out of the show window.

Four men driving along Grand River are stopped by police, and the car is searched and the police find two packages of bath towels. The men are handcuffed and thrown into a squad car and brought to court and jail.

And all day the looters are shot by the national guardsmen and police, and the death toll climbs, and the people laugh and shriek while they loot.

Very little functions in the insanity.

At 8 o'clock last night, the members of the Trade Union Leadership Council met in a one-story brick building on Joy Road. The people in the council are the Negroes who hold positions in the UAW.

The head of the council is Robert (Buddy) Battle, who is with Local 600. The vice-president is Horace Sheffield, a UAW international representative. Nelson (Jack) Edwards, a UAW board member, also holds a position in the council.

These are Walter Reuther's guys, Negroes who fought for the union and for black status in the union. The idea was that any statement by them would be a hammer in the Negro districts. But Buddy Battle's fights all are in the past and Horace Sheffield can speak more of Harry Bennett's army than he can of the Negro kids out in the street rioting.

And all of them are middle class now and the streets are far away. So the first five hands raised at the meeting were for inquiries about ending the meeting and getting home before the 9 p.m. curfew.

Sheffield had made a statement earlier in the day. The statement deplored the rioting. He now wanted it adopted by the council.

A thin man got up and said, "I don't want this thing classified as a race riot. And I don't want everybody to think this is just Detroit people doing it.

"These looters come in white Cadillacs with license plates from Flint and Saginaw and they stir up everybody and then set fire to it. We've seen quite a few out-of-state license plates too. From Ohio and Illinois."

The man was Negro and he was saying things that even white politicians have learned to drop. "Outside Agitators."

But everybody agreed with him and wanted to go home. Only Sam Dunlap of Local 600 disagreed.

"You've lost contact with the people in the community," he told them. "Some of us have moved out. We're no longer with the community. We better wake up and smell the coffee."

No one paid attention to him. The meeting broke up and nothing was done because the people on whom the white men in the city, state and federal governments always rely on to handle their Negro affairs haven't known street people for years.

The brothers were found a few minutes later, standing on a street corner on Mack Avenue.

"How did it all start?" they were asked.

"It takes too long to tell you," one of the black faces said.

"Yeah, it start 200 years ago," another said.

"Well, why did it start now?"

"It didn't start now. You know a rash? You know how it spread. That's what this is. This is a rash and it spreadin' and spreadin'."

"Were you looting today?"

"What's that mean?"

"It means," one of them cut in, "that you go into a store that has no windows and you emerges with a hi-fi set."

They began laughing. One of them said, "Just put down in the papers that in Detroit there are red flames in the east and black smoke in the west."

Downtown, in a large third-floor office of police headquarters, Gov. Romney sat in a chair in front of a television set and waited for President Johnson to come on television and announce that two brigades of the 101st Airborne were coming into Detroit.

On Sunday, Romney had walked into the same office with an entourage from Lansing. He announced:

"We've got to be firm right from the start here. This reminds me of something Ike once told me. He said that when he ran the Normandy invasion there was a great deal of looting at the start. Ike said he ended it by having them catch a looter, shoot him and then hang him by the heels in the town square. That put an end to it.

"So, let's catch these people right at the start and bring them to court and show them we're tough."

Now, just after midnight this morning, Romney sat in the chair and listened as Mr. Johnson came on the television and said, "I take this action with regret—and only because of the clear, unmistakable and undisputed evidence that Gov. Romney and the local officials have been unable to bring the situation under control."

Mr. Johnson kept saying that Romney was unable to bring matters under control, and Romney sat and watched it and said nothing. When the set was turned off, Romney muttered, "That isn't right. Here I've been working all day and he lays it onto me like that."

At four minutes before 1 a.m., Romney got up from the chair where he had been sitting, bleak-faced and in silence.

"I've been up since 6 this morning," he said. "I'm going to get some sleep."

Jimmy Bannon, an inspector, was in the anteroom waiting to tour the city again.

"When did you get to sleep last?" Bannon was asked later, while he sat with his shotgun out the window and looked at 12th Street, which has been destroyed.

"On Saturday," he said.

The Detroit News, July 25, 1967

Guerilla War Rips 12th

by Jon Lowell

BACKED by tanks and armored personnel carriers, national guardsmen and police last night and early today fought a house-to-house war on 12th Street.

The scene was incredible.

It was as though the Viet Cong had infiltrated the riot-blackened streets.

Snipers in what sounded like at least two dozen locations snapped off rounds as police and riflemen slid past the dingy houses.

They were answered by quick volleys from M-1 carbines, blasts from shotguns and bursts from submachine guns.

Then there was the clanking whine of a tank or a personnel carrier.

A .50-caliber machine gun roared in 30-second bursts, sweeping a roof, building or alley.

Silence for a second, broken only by the soft sounds of moving troops.

Another sniper round and the battle resumed.

Then the darkness vibrated with a sound that made the troops' skin crawl.

"Help . . . help me . . . help me," the voice screamed.

It sounded like the man was about a half-block away.

"It sounds like a white man," a Guard rifleman whispered.

A Negro patrolman clutching a shotgun nodded.

Then the voice stopped.

I crouched under the rear of a Guard jeep at Virginia Park and 12th.

News photographer Craig Wellman crawled back and fourth in the intersection, searching for something he could photograph in the blackness.

He ignored my warnings, the gun battle raging nearby, and

the fact that he was wearing a white shirt. Guardsmen had warned him that the shirt made him an ideal sniper target.

We had gotten into the battle area quite by accident.

Since the riots began on Sunday, police and military units have refused to take newsmen into action with them.

The hundreds of newsmen attempting to report Detroit's agony have improvised a dozen methods of getting to the fighting elsewhere, but the 12th Street area has been tightly sealed off on a wide perimeter.

We got in by simply leaping aboard a Guard truck as it was pulling out on patrol.

The patrol was led by a jeepload of police and guardsmen. We were in the truck behind the jeep with three riflemen and a police officer. A second truck carrying riflemen followed.

With all lights out, the patrol crawled along West Grand Boulevard. Then it turned up Linwood.

"Watch that apartment building on the left," a police officer said. "We took fire from there last night."

The patrol moved slowly past but nothing happened.

Then it wheeled down Virginia Park. The first breath brought the smell of two-day-old fires.

As we rumbled down Virginia Park past darkened homes, a rifleman gave me a short course in sniper warfare in city streets.

It's a technique the young citizen-soldiers have picked up the hard way in the last few days.

"Watch for houses with one screen off a window on the second floor," he said matter-of-factly. "And keep your eye peeled for second floors where one window has the shade down and the other is open a crack."

"Can you spot them by muzzle blasts when they fire?" I asked.

"No, not any more," he said. "They've gotten smart. They open the window a little, move way back in the room and then fire.

"They can snipe away for hours and you can't see them. We were even taking fire from burning buildings last night."

Suddenly the patrol lurched to a halt. Without a word the riflemen leaped out of the trucks and followed police north on 12th, ducking behind parked cars and trees and along buildings as they ran.

After a few moments of lying flat on the floor in the back of the open, slat-sided Army truck and listening to the crack of gunfire, it became obvious to Wellman and me that we were alone with the trucks and jeep.

Wellman slid out and moved up 12th to a spot behind a tree.

I hesitated, then jumped off the back. I slid under the truck, and then thought about what would happen if a slug hit the gasoline tank my head was bumping against.

With buildings possibly containing snipers on all sides of the intersection, it was hard to see anyplace that seemed like a really safe spot.

After deciding one place was as good as another, I sat down on the pavement behind the jeep and started making notes by the light of a still-working neon sign in a looted store.

After about 40 minutes of intermittent gunfire, three riflemen returned to guard the vehicles. Apparently we didn't look formidable enough to take care of Uncle Sam's property.

The rest of the men returned and we scrambled back aboard the trucks. The engines started.

A sniper round cracked over our heads and everyone dived for cover.

"The son of a bitch waited for us to come back," a rifleman said.

An armored personnel carrier wheeled up and blasted out the lights in the looted store that were silhouetting our vehicles.

Riflemen lay prone in the trucks, peering at a half-dozen houses on the north side of Virginia Park, looking for the sniper.

They couldn't find him so we rumbled off down Virginia Park.

The guardsmen seemed remarkably cool considering their youth and the weird battle they were fighting.

"Get the hell out of that window," they shouted when they spotted someone.

The head popped out of sight and no shots were fired.

When we reached the Lodge service drive, the trucks halted and we all piled out.

They were looking for a guardsman who had been standing guard on the corner.

His helmet lay on the ground but there was no sign of him.
Police and riflemen fanned out looking for him.
We caught a ride with a passing squad car back to our auto.
I hope they found the guy that was missing.
I should have stayed but my hands were starting to shake
and one knee was twitching.

The Detroit News, July 26, 1967

Nightmare Journey

by Bob Clark

MY long day's journey into a nightmare began Monday afternoon when I received a phone call from Howard Chapnick of the Black Star Photo Agency. He asked me if I wanted to go to Detroit to cover the riots. I found myself saying yes. Actually, I was in the mood to involve myself in this kind of experience. I really wanted to know what was going on behind the scenes and I wanted to know it first hand. I had covered a race riot in San Francisco and worked on news stories in the deep South. I once interviewed Stokely Carmichael for a German magazine. I thought I had a feel for the current picture of race relations in America. But Newark and Detroit were a new breed of cat. What was happening in our big city ghettos and how far would it go? Chapnick called me back within an hour and we made final arrangements. Soon I was on an early evening flight to Detroit.

Aboard the plane I kept trying to think of someone I could contact in the city. I knew there wouldn't be time to just roam. Things were happening fast and if I expected to get photographs I would have to be on top of things from the beginning. Being a Negro photographer would present special problems. I could expect rejection and hostility from both whites and blacks. I knew from past experience that black people won't hesitate to attack a "black sellout." I also knew that when violence has taken over a community, police don't always bother to ask questions or check carefully. I told myself I had better move around damn carefully or suffer the consequences.

As the plane banked into Metropolitan Airport I could see clouds of dense smoke drifting up from the city. As I think back now, I realize that even seeing that smoke I did not foresee the massive devastation or the enormous danger ahead of me. I remember tensing up and promising myself I would not be gun-shy. I tried to force myself to relax mentally and I vowed to work real loose.

At the Sheraton Cadillac Hotel there were many reporters and photographers in the lobby. The word at the moment was that there were a great many fires around the city but things seemed to have quieted down. I struck up a conversation with a white man who was standing near by. He was short, stockily built and tough-looking and this appearance matched his trade. An ex-boxer turned promoter, Don Elbaum was in town for a boxing show that was canceled after the riots began. Elbaum said he was in the midst of the rioting on Sunday because a lot of his boxers were Negroes from the city's ghetto area. Now he was waiting in the lobby in the hope of meeting some of his boys and he wondered whether I would like to talk with them. I thought this was a good idea so I raced up to my room, changed clothes and returned to the lobby in a few minutes. Elbaum and I waited about half-an-hour but no one came. I began to get edgy about losing time.

I tried calling police headquarters and local television stations to find out where the action was, but either the phones were not answered or no one could offer any precise information.

Don Elbaum is one of those fast-talking, fast-moving sort of people who are in the know about what's going on and always have to be where the action is. When I decided to move on, he came with me. Don knew Detroit very well and guessed that the West side was the hot spot at the moment. We used his car and headed that way. The streets were deserted except for patrols of state troopers and national guardsmen. I was surprised to see that even in the downtown area of the city, buildings were burned and ransacked. I saw cars filled with volunteer sheriffs. These private cars raced about the city, shotguns and rifles protruding from the windows. Just the sight of them made my heart slip into my stomach, because I sensed that these men were my biggest menace.

We arrived somewhere; I don't know exactly where or how we got there. All I know is that all hell broke loose. It was a national guard position and snipers were pouring their fire into it. Guardsmen returned the fire with automatic weapons.

They had a cross-fire going and it was impossible to know who was firing at whom. The guardsmen fired flares into the darkness and there were lengthy fusillades. I couldn't imagine anyone living through all that fire-power. I crawled out of the car and up into a front position. As I dodged from one point of cover to the next, I yelled out, "I'm press, don't shoot!" It was pitch black. I couldn't shoot pictures without using strobe lights and that would mean blinding some of the guardsmen or exposing their positions. I just squatted—listening and watching—for what seemed like an eternal 20 minutes and then went back to the car.

Don and I cruised around again. We spotted fire on the West side and drove toward it. A large warehouse or factory building was burning furiously and before the fire trucks could get into position the sniper-fire began. A small, three-storey house across an alley from the factory began to burn also. Women and children streamed out of this building carrying what belongings they could. Some men who lived in the neighborhood ran up to the house carrying small lawn hoses. The whole scene was like an unreal movie. Now the house was almost completely ablaze but the men refused to stop trying to put out the fire with those ridiculous hoses. I thought they were pathetic and comical. I ran into the building and on the second floor I was stopped by heat and smoke. A guardsman raced past me heading out of the building. "There's an old man in there," he yelled. "He won't come out. He says this is his home." Outside, high voltage wires began to fall and whip about, throwing a spray of deadly sparks. A woman screamed, "My baby, my baby! Where is my baby!" A guardsman tried to comfort her. He looked shaken and frustrated. His commander was shouting for the guardsmen to pull out of the area. The fires raged and the flames seemed to cast shadows of despair over the faces of these homeless black people. I wondered where they would go now. If they tried walking to find help and shelter they could very well be shot in the dark by a frightened guardsman. I could still hear guardsmen shouting about the man who refused to leave his house and I wondered: how could anyone be willing to die for such a dilapidated old building in such a filthy, hot, stinking neighborhood? I felt helpless and wondered why men are not supposed to cry.

Don and I drove around the burning streets for awhile. We were stopped and searched at almost every block by scared guardsmen with trembling rifles. The rows of burning buildings seemed endless in the night. It struck me at this moment that this was war; that finally America was feeling the destruction and despair of war on her own shores.

I don't know how long we drove around but soon we heard gunfire again and headed for the sound. This time state troopers were being fired upon from a burning building. They returned the fire intensely. A cease-fire was ordered and soon a man emerged from around the corner of the building. He was a tall, dark Negro. His shirt was almost completely ripped off and his body was covered with blood. "Don't shoot! Don't shoot!" he yelled. He was seized and searched. While the troopers frisked him he kept yelling, "Them niggers shot me! Them crazy niggers around the corner, they shot me! Please don't hurt me. I ain't no sniper." I moved in for a photograph and a state trooper stepped in front of me. I moved around him and prepared to shoot again. This time I was shoved by the trooper. "You don't want that picture, do you fella?" he growled. I got the message but I played dumb. "I'm press. I have a right to photograph this situation." I pulled out my press card. "I don't give a god-damned who you are! You get off this f—— street or you'll be treated like the rest," he yelled. I could see he was rattled. As he hollered, he kept slamming me with the shotgun barrel. I moved on. I was trembling inside and I wondered if I should have pushed my argument further. I was upset because I missed the picture. As dawn grew near, police and troopers got tougher to deal with. Don and I were driving around in the dark without lights. Police and guardsmen had shot out all the street lamps and we were fair game for all. It was almost dawn when we returned to the hotel.

The next morning I called Howard Chapnick in New York and gave him a brief run down on my experiences. I asked him to send me a telegram stating that I was an accredited photo-journalist. Later, armed with this telegram, I went to police headquarters and spoke with the lieutenant in charge. I asked him if I would need any special kind of permit to work in the riot area and what, if any, restrictions were being laid on the press. He told me that the only restrictions were at night in the vicinity of 12th Street and on Linwood Avenue. These had been among the worst trouble spots and were now completely blocked off to everyone. He checked my telegram from Chapnick, and my press card, and said that I should have no difficulty with these credentials.

I spent the afternoon photographing sporadic fires and sniper action as well as scenes of homeless families. In the late afternoon I was shooting some street scenes when a young guardsman, who looked as though the violent events of the past few days had made him half-crazed, raced up to me and demanded to see my press pass. Singling out me, he had ignored at least half-a-dozen other photographers—all white— who were also working the same area. We argued, and this was one of the few times I pushed the issue. He finally backed off and let me alone. A young Negro who was standing nearby and had been watching this incident sympathetically, came up to me and we began talking. He said he was a Muslim. We spoke about the episode and then he asked me where my sympathies lay. How did I feel about what was happening? I convinced him that I was on the side of Negroes no matter what they did. I expressed the attitude that we are all "soul brothers." I told him I was keenly interested in meeting and talking with young men in the community who were out with the action. The young Muslim said I could walk along with him and he would introduce me to whoever was around.

During our walk I met some youngsters who I later learned were snipers. They laughingly told me that they were spreading rumors that they were planning an attack that night on some suburban communities when in actuality they were going to strike at the downtown district. They told me where they were going to meet later that night and said I could come along if I wished. I photographed these men and then returned to the hotel.

Don Elbaum was still in a mood to stay with the action so we left the hotel together about 9 p.m. We were heading for a meeting with the snipers at a Howard Johnson's somewhere in the downtown district. On our way there, we heard heavy gunfire and followed the sound. As we drew near to the scene our car was fired upon. Shotgun pellets rained on the roof

and pelted the windshield. We stopped and crawled to the
floor of the car. When the firing died down we identified ourselves and pulled up closer. The position was manned by state
troopers and police who were battling snipers. I knew that it's
difficult to take pictures during a gun battle but figured I
might get some dramatic pictures if any snipers were flushed
out and arrested. As Don and I edged closer, the firing started
again. The troopers and police were pinned down by a deadly
crossfire from the rooftops. The snipers were firing automatic
weapons with tracer bullets. We must have stayed pinned for
an hour before we were able to sneak away from this skirmish.

We headed for the meeting with the snipers. We found the
location but they never showed up. I decided to check with
the police department again about my credentials in case the
lieutenant on duty during the afternoon had made a mistake
about night-time regulations. I was again assured my passes
were in order and that I could work during the night.

It was about 10:30 when Don and I left the precinct and
saw a fire truck racing to a call. We followed. Our car was
stopped and searched many times before we finally arrived at
the site of the blaze only to find that the fire truck was returning to its engine house at Warren and Lawton streets.
Again, we followed. The area around the firehouse was under
heavy sniper attack and the firemen were awfully jumpy. We
were checked again and I asked a state trooper at a road block
if I could get out of the car and look around. Another fire engine started to pull out of the station and we decided to follow it. We were still near the engine house when we were
ordered by guardsmen to halt. We were told to spread eagle
against the hood. We showed our press cards and waited. A
trooper passed by and called out that he had just checked us
and that we were press. The guardsmen ignored the trooper
and continued frisking us. Don and I were ordered to lay
down on the ground. A young National Guard lieutenant was
really giving us a going over. I didn't realize what was happening until another car passed by and someone yelled out,
"Halt! Shoot that car! Get them niggers!" There were cries
like this all over the place and suddenly shotgun blasts were
ringing out everywhere. These fellows were really spooked
and acting vicious. They had been under sniper attack all

evening without being able to see a thing. I guess they had to take it out on somebody and the somebody was anybody black that passed by in a car.

Don and I were ordered to stand up, hands behind our backs. When I looked up, I froze with terror. There, ahead of us, stood a gauntlet of two long rows of blood-hungry firemen. They were screaming at the top of their lungs: "Kill the black bastards! Castrate those coons! Shoot 'em in the nuts!" A young guardsman crouched before me, his rifle bayonet thrust forward menacingly. His face was flushed with fear and excitement and I knew that if I so much as stumbled he would blow a hole in me big enough to put a basketball in. "God-dammit, move!" he hollered. I stepped forward and heard someone scream, "What's that nigger smiling at. Wipe the smile off that monkcy's face." A big, red face loomed up in mine. It spit and then suddenly, everyone was spitting, punching, kicking. I don't know how many times I was punched in the groin. I just kept thinking that if I fell I would be shot or stomped to death. I felt the blows on the back of my head. I don't know whether they were rifle butts or what. We must have been far down the gauntlet and near the firehouse door when Don spun around and yelled, "I'll take anyone of you that thinks he's man enough!" I thought they would finish him for sure but a guardsman gave him a crack with a rifle and he was inside the door. We were butted into a small detention room and left with two guardsmen to watch us. The windows were open and the firemen gathered to scream obscenities at us.

My mind was in chaos and couldn't organize what was happening to me. When I had first looked up and seen the gauntlet of firemen standing and screaming before me, I guess a thousand things ran through my mind. I didn't realize I was smiling because certainly I felt a long way from that kind of emotion. I guess I could have been thinking: so this is America! I know that my smug intellectual philosophy about the race problem was destroyed. I kept thinking about the pain, and perhaps even death, on a more real basis than ever before in my life. I knew they wanted me to cringe and beg and cry out: "Please mista boss man, don't hurt me!" And I wanted to. I wanted to run or plead. But I also knew this wouldn't help, that they would still beat me or kill me and that my pleading would only demonstrate to them how tough they were and add to their violent passions. I know that I don't remember most of the pain. What stands out most in my mind is my struggle then to contain my fear.

We were in the room for about ten minutes when the door flew open and two more "niggers" were shoved into the room. They were badly scared; so scared they couldn't follow orders. "Oh, my God, Oh my God! I'm so scared."

There was more gunfire now outside and the guardsmen ordered us to lie down. The firing lasted for about 15 minutes. We sat for over an hour and I tried to find out why we were being held. No one seemed to know. The guardsmen vaguely said something about a gasoline can and a knife. We did have an empty can of gasoline in the car trunk. It was rusty and I doubt it had ever been used. The knife was of Boy Scout manufacture and I carried it as a tool in my camera bag.

A police wagon arrived and a guardsman escorted each of us out individually. One of them grabbed me by the hair, stuck his .45 caliber automatic in the base of my skull and shoved me out. The firemen were lined up outside the door again and we received more beatings before we were pummeled into the police van. Inside the wagon we waited again. No one seemed to know what to do with us. State troopers brought in another Negro. He was a big, middle-aged man and they said he had a rifle in his car. They kicked and punched him into the wagon and called him all sorts of names. A cop walked up and said, "Is this the black son-of-a-bitch with a rifle? He must be a big man on his block. Let's make him run. The bastard doesn't deserve a cell." They hauled him out of the wagon and three of them beat him without mercy. One just whipped away at his head with a black-jack while two others hammered at him with rifle butts. Someone yelled, "Stop! You'll kill the coon." A shrill voice answered, "I don't give a good f—— if I do!" They laughed as the blood seemed to gush from every part of the man's head. He pleaded and cried and then they threw him back into the wagon. I saw that his face and nose looked as though they were split in two. I couldn't look at this.

During the ride to the police station, a national guardsman

sat over me and kept telling me about what they did to niggers in his neck of the woods. He punctuated his remarks with butts on my head with his rifle. We arrived at a police precinct but there was no room. We drove on to another station. This place apparently didn't have an arresting officer to book us on the charges we were to be held for. To simplify matters, the driver was ordered to make out charges and be photographed with us. We were then lined up in a garage and kicked and punched. After being mugged and fingerprinted I was told to sign a card which bore my fingerprints and a charge reading: VIOLATION OF CURFEW. I said I would not sign it without legal counsel and that I didn't understand the charge against me. I showed an officer my press card and Chapnick's telegram. He took them from me and left the room. When he returned he told me to sign the card or else I would spend a long time in jail. Both Don Elbaum and I refused to sign. We were then marched downstairs into the basement where there is a room which is normally used as a pistol firing range. It was damn cold and dirty with no place to sit or lay. About six women were down there and we were only separated by a small railing. By the next morning the room was filled beyond capacity. We were not permitted to make any phone calls or do anything about obtaining legal counsel. Practically everyone in the room was bloody or had been beaten. Most of the men and youths were gangsters and hustlers and practically all of them boasted about looting or sniping they had done.

I spoke to Eddie Dinkins, the man who had been so brutally beaten outside the fire house for having a rifle in his car. Dinkins is 51 years old, has five children and works for a Ford steel mill as a cleaner. He said he was on his way to work on the number one shift, which starts at 12 p.m. Because of the riot and fires next to his home, Dinkins thought it would be best to keep all his valuables with him. In addition to the rifle, he put in his car just about everything that meant something to him. He wanted to keep the rifle, even though he had never used it and the barrel was rusty.

One easily loses track of time in jail. There were no windows so we couldn't have a feeling of day or night. Some of us had had watches so I know that we were brought downstairs about 12:30 Wednesday morning. We received no food until almost 18 hours later. That meal was two slices of bread and one thin slice of lunch meat. Our next meal was 4 p.m. the next day, Thursday, and this was a repeat of the first feast. We had nothing to drink and no decent toilet facilities.

On Thursday afternoon a young white boy, who was arrested for violation of curfew at the same time I was, had an epileptic convulsion. It was a bad one and I knew the danger because my younger sister suffered from the same illness. Both Don and myself administered what first aid we could. We yelled for help and two guards came. I explained the boy's illness and the danger. They looked down at the boy who was foaming at the mouth and one of the guards said, "Tough s—t!" Then they both walked out of the room. I begged for some ice to help pull the youth out of it. Another guard brought me two ice cubes wrapped in a paper towel. I finally managed to force open the boy's mouth and then I massaged him until the convulsions left his body. He just lay there in the filth and fell into a deep sleep. The boy usually takes pills to control convulsions. I told a guard that he needed medical attention badly but like all the rest of our pleas this one also went unheeded.

During the second day our impromptu "cell" stank. We had about 50 men and six women cramped together, some covered with caked blood and everyone dirty from two days of being unable to clean themselves after using the toilet. The guards thought it was a great joke to show off "the Zoo" (as they called it) to national guardsmen. We could hear them eating, drinking and joking about breaking some nigger's ass. They spoke without inhibitions because we were animals and it didn't matter what they did to us or said about us. When some of them were bored, they would come into the cell and shove a shotgun or rifle into someone's face and make them beg. Thursday night a short, slim Negro was brought in. He was there for only about five minutes because he was a known sniper. He was beaten badly. His shirt was torn off and he was covered with blood. There was a deep gash in his head which was so swollen and distorted that the man looked as though he was born with a deformity in which one skull had grown out of the original. He was taken into a corridor and beaten until it was unbearable to listen to his pleas. I saw the same man again on Friday and found it hard to believe that he could have lived through such a beating or even be moving around conscious. His entire body looked like one massive wound.

A white youth was brought in either Wednesday or Thursday. He was suspected of being a sniper and while being booked he received a large gash in his skull from a bayonet-wielding national guardsman. They gave him little peace. Every time a cop came near the basement, the guard at our door would bring him in to see the little white sniper.

On Wednesday, I believe, we received another inmate. Still high from a big night of adventure, he was just popping to brag about his sniping. "Man, I got four of them last night! I sat up there with my bottle of wine and they didn't know what was happening. There was about 35 of us and we waited until a group of five cars came into the block. Nobody fired until they were right in the middle and then our guys in the front opened up. Two cars backed out of it but the rest of them were pinned and so scared they didn't even know what to shoot at. We kept 'em like that until reinforcements got there and then we split. They just didn't know what to do with us. I was having a good time!" He was arrested on his way home, he said, because someone had tipped the police that he was a looter. He just had time to hide his gun.

The "cell" became unbearable. We were starving, dirty and needed desperately to talk with someone about getting out. Everytime a guard showed his face near the door, dozens of inmates would rush to the bars and beg for food. Tempers flared and fights erupted. We were not far from becoming the animals our guards believed us to be. At first I thought all I had to do was be calm until Black Star found me but as the days passed I realized that it might well take the agency weeks to locate me. It hit me that I could well end up in a state prison or perhaps even be shot for trying to escape while being transported from one prison to another. I saw the power these men had and suddenly everything seemed futile. Everything I had believed about this country just didn't seem real anymore.

Thursday afternoon we were moved upstairs into a small

cell that was approximately 20-feet square and hot as an oven. We were given another baloney sandwich and told that we would either be released or sent to court on Friday. That was good news and everyone's spirits rose. I didn't care what they did to me any longer. I just wanted to talk with someone who had some intelligence. I had been holding everything inside of me for three days and I felt as though I had reached my limit and was ready to explode.

Elbaum, four other men and myself had been there longer than anyone else in the group. We were so crowded in our new cell that even floor space was at a premium. If you were lucky enough to find space on the floor so you could stretch your legs out, you just didn't move because someone else would grab it. I bought a paper bag from a guy for a dollar so that I could take notes to occupy my mind.

Most of the prisoners knew each other from their neighborhoods. The majority were hustlers and two-bit gangsters. They boasted about how much loot they got. Listening to them I became convinced there was no outside conspiracy or special organization that had welded them together. Their one common point of focus seemed to be a terrific hate for the Detroit police. Their only "organization" was that they would meet and decide to go out and shoot cops.

Friday morning the guard brought us a new inmate. He looked the role of today's young black revolutionary. Under his arm he held a recording of the late Malcolm X's speeches. It was apparent that he had been drinking the previous night and the liquor was still talking to him loud and clear: "Hey guard, you stupid white bastards, I want out!" His voice echoed down the corridor and he continued with a long tirade of abuses until we all became quite nervous. Everyone began telling him to shut up and sit down before the guards returned for another head-whipping session. He looked at us scornfully and in the grandest manner possible told us how lowly and whipped we were. He began to expound the glory of Mao Tse-Tung and tried to convince us to overpower the guards and take over the whole damn precinct.

In a quiet moment a stocky, powerfully built Negro rose from the floor, calmly looked our young revolutionary in the eye and said: "Boy, if you don't sit down and be nice and quiet, and if they don't feed us because of your big mouth, I'm going to break your neck." I called out: "Motion seconded! All in favor say, 'aye'!" Everyone grunted approval. The young revolutionary sat.

Friday afternoon they gave us another sandwich, making a grand total of four sandwiches in three days. Now the police were taking greater numbers of people out of cells. When the guard started calling names everyone would run to the door and this would be the only time the cell would be quiet. Soon, there were only a few of us remaining. Most of those who had been arrested for violating the curfew had been released. But Don and I were still there and I was beginning to lose hope. About 5:30 Friday night a detective came to the window and called my name and my heart leaped. He told me that someone was there to see me and opened the cell door. My visitor was Jack Kaufman of Benyas-Kaufman, two free-lance photographers who also work with Black Star. Jack was thoughtful enough to take a picture of me in the cell before I was released.

As I was being led out, the Chief of Detectives for the Second Precinct stopped me and asked why I had not identified myself when I was brought in. I told him that I had said over and over again that I was from the press and that I had showed my credentials to the patrolman who was standing right next to him. The patrolman, of course, denied it. The Chief said he was releasing me because my arrest was a mistake but he added: "If I should hear of or read of anything detrimental being said about the Detroit police department, you will have the biggest kick back you've ever seen."

The next afternoon, at my hotel, Mayor Jerome Cavanagh called on me personally to apologize for my arrest. He said, "I'm sorry. It should not have happened."

The way I feel about it, nothing in Detroit should have happened and I'm sorry, too.

Ebony, October 1967

The Call of the Black Panthers

by Sol Stern

San Francisco

IN early May, front pages across America carried the illustrated story of an "armed invasion" of the California Legislature by a group of black men known as the Black Panther Party for Self Defense. What actually happened that day in Sacramento was something less than the beginning of a Negro insurrection, but it was no less important for all that: The appearance of the gun-bearing Panthers at the white Capitol was a dramatic portent of something that is stirring in the Northern black ghettos.

By any yardstick used by the civil-rights movement, the Panther organization is not yet very important or effective. The Panthers' political influence in the Negro community remains marginal. The voice of the Panthers is a discordant one, full of the rhetoric of revolutionary violence, and seemingly out of place in affluent America. But it is a voice that ought to be studied. Like it or not, it is increasingly the voice of young ghetto blacks who in city after city this summer have been confronting cops with bricks, bottles and bullets.

The Panthers came to Sacramento from their homes in the San Francisco Bay Area not to "invade" or to "take over" the Legislature, but simply to exercise their right to attend a session of the Legislature and to state their opposition to a pending bill. The bill was, and is, intended to impose severe restrictions on the carrying of loaded weapons in public—a practice not prohibited by present law so long as the weapons are unconcealed. Since the Panthers have been in the habit of carrying loaded weapons at rallies and public meetings, they regarded the legislation as aimed at them in particular and at black people in general. The only thing that was unusual about their lobbying junket is that they brought their loaded guns with them.

The Panthers arrived in hot, dry, lifeless Sacramento and descended on the Capitol with M-1 rifles and 12-gauge shotguns cradled in their arms, .45-caliber pistols visible on their hips, cartridge belts around their waists. Up the white steps and between the classic marble pillars they marched, in two columns, young, black and tough-looking in their leather jackets, boots and tight-fitting clothes. As they marched grimly down the immaculate halls, secretaries and tourists gaped and then moved quickly out of the way. By the time they were halfway down the corridor, every reporter and cameraman in the building had gathered; they stayed in front of the Panthers, moving backward, snapping pictures as they went.

The Panthers, though all were experts on firearms legislation, did not know their way around the building; they followed the reporters and cameramen who were backing toward the legislative chamber. Instead of veering off toward the spectators' galleries, the group flowed right into the Assembly, past guards who were either too startled or simply too slow to stop them.

Actually, it was the photographers, moving backward, who were the first to move through the large oak doors at the rear of the chamber. The Speaker, seeing the commotion, asked the guards to "clear those cameramen." By the time the legislators realized what was happening behind them, most of the group of cameramen and Panthers had been moved out of the chamber. Outside in the corridor, the guards took some guns away from the Panthers—but since the Panthers were not breaking any law, they had to return them. The Panthers read their statement of protest to the reporters and television cameramen, and left. That would have been all, except for a car that broke down.

A Sacramento police officer spotted the armed Panthers at the gas station at which they stopped for repairs, and sent out a hurried call for reinforcements. This time, the Panthers were arrested on a variety of charges, including some stemming from obscure fish-and-game laws. After they had been in jail overnight, the Sacramento District Attorney changed all the charges; 18 members of the group, now out on bail, await trial for disrupting the State Legislature—a misdemeanor—and for conspiracy to disrupt the Legislature—a felony.

As lobbyists, the Black Panthers are not very effective; but then, the Panthers did not really care much whether the gun bill passed or not. Their purpose was to call attention to their claim that black people in the ghetto must rely on armed self-defense and not the white man's courts to protect themselves.

The adventure at the Capitol assured the passage of the gun legislation, however, and it will soon be signed into law —welcome news to Bay Area police chiefs, who have been frustrated ever since the Panthers first started carrying their loaded weapons in public. In Oakland, across the bay from San Francisco, the police have not waited for the new legislation; they regularly arrest armed Panthers, usually on charges of brandishing a weapon in a threatening manner. The Panthers insist that this is merely harassment, but they have tactically retreated and usually now leave their guns at home.

For the Panthers, their guns have had both real and symbolic meaning—real because they believe they will have to use the guns, eventually, against the white power structure that they charge is suppressing them; symbolic because of the important political effects they think that a few blacks, openly carrying guns, can have in the black community.

"Ninety per cent of the reason we carried guns in the first place," says Panther leader Huey P. Newton, "was educational. We set the example. We made black people aware that they have the right to carry guns."

Only seven years ago, when the head of the Monroe, N.C., chapter of the National Association for the Advancement of Colored People proposed that Negroes should shoot back when armed bands of white rednecks start shooting up the Negro section of town, he set off a furor in the national civil-rights movements and turned himself into a pariah. Robert Williams, eventually charged with kidnapping in what his supporters insist was a frame-up, ultimately left America for Cuba and then China, a revolutionary in exile. It was a short time ago; much has happened in black America since the simple proposal of armed self-defense could provoke so much tumult.

The Black Panther Party for Self Defense was organized principally by 25-year-old Huey Newton and 30-year-old Bobby Seale. Newton looks younger than his years, is tall and lithe, with handsome, almost sculptured features. His title is Minister of Defense, while his darker and more mature-looking friend, Seale, is the chairman. The Minister of Defense is preeminent because, they say, they are in a condition of war. "Black people realize," Newton says, "that they are already at war with the racist white power structure."

Being at war, they are reluctant to give out strategic information about the internal workings of their organization. As they put it, quoting Malcolm X: "Those who know don't say and those who say don't know." Outside estimates of their membership run anywhere from 75 to 200, organized into small units in the various black communities in the Bay area. Each unit has a captain; the captains, along with Newton, Seale and a treasurer, make up an executive committee which sets basic policy for the entire organization. The Panthers get out their message of armed self-defense to the black communities through a biweekly newspaper, and on Saturdays there are outdoor street rallies.

On a sunny Saturday at the end of June, two such rallies were scheduled. The first was on San Francisco's Potrero Hill, at a nearly all black housing project composed of decaying World War II barracks that should have been torn down years ago. Desolate and windy, the project overlooks an industrial section of the city jammed between Potrero Hill and the Bay. It is an ugly and depressing place.

By the time Huey Newton and Bobby Seale arrive from the other side of the Bay, there are about 30 young blacks milling around at the rally site, a dead-end street which serves as a parking lot in the middle of the development. Newton and Seale do not seem disappointed at the turnout. Seale turns over a city garbage can, stands on it and announces that the rally will begin. A half-dozen curious children come running over as the bloods gather. Some women poke their heads out of windows overlooking the street. There is not a white face in sight, nor a policeman, unless someone in the crowd is an undercover agent.

Seale explains the Black Panther Party for Self Defense and the significance of its name. It was inspired, he says, by the example of the Lowndes County Freedom Organization in Alabama, which first adopted the black-panther symbol. That symbol, Seale says, is an appropriate one for black people in America today. "It is not in the panther's nature to attack anyone first, but when he is attacked and backed into a corner, he will respond viciously and wipe out the aggressor."

Seale then introduces the Minister of Defense; Huey Newton provides a 15-minute capsule history of the Negro struggle in America, and then begins to relate it to the world revolution and to the example of the people of Vietnam. "There were only 30 million of them," Newton says of the Vietnamese, "but first they threw out the Japanese, then they drove out the French and now they are kicking hell out of the Americans and you better believe it, brothers." Black people can learn lessons from the fight of the Vietnamese, Newton continues; black people in America also must arm themselves for self-defense against the same racist army. "Every time you go execute a white racist Gestapo cop, you are defending yourself," he concludes.

When Seale returns to the garbage-can platform, the crowd is already with him, shouting "That's right" and "You tell it" as he speaks.

"All right, brothers," he tells them, "let's understand what we want. We have to change our tactics. Black people can't just mass on the streets and riot. They'll just shoot us down." Instead, it is necessary to organize in small groups to "take care of business." The "business" includes among other things "executing racist cops."

Graphically, Seale describes how a couple of bloods can surprise cops on their coffee break. The Negroes march up to the cop and then "they shoot him down—voom, voom—with a 12-gauge shotgun." That, says Seale, would be an example of "righteous power." No more "praying and boot-licking." No more singing of "We Shall Overcome." "The only way you're going to overcome is to apply righteous power."

Seale tells the young crowd not to be impressed by the fact that Negroes are only an 11 per cent minority in America. "We have potential destructive power. Look around at those factories down there. If we don't get what we want, we can make it impossible for the man's system to function. All we got to do is drop some cocktails into those oil tanks and then watch everything go."

No one in the crowd questions the propriety of the Black Panther program. One man says that it sounds O.K. but it's all talk and the trouble is that, when it's time for action, "most of the bloods cut out." Seale says that's true, but "we have to organize."

While a few of the bloods take membership applications and give their names to the local captain, Seale and Newton jump into a car and race across the Bay Bridge to the second rally in Richmond, 20 miles away on the east side of the bay, just north of Berkeley. Only the surroundings are different. It is a ghetto of tiny homes and rundown cottages with green lawns and carports. The rally is held on the lawn of George Dowell, who joined the Panthers after his brother Denzil was shot and killed by the police. Denzil Dowell's body was riddled with six shotgun pellets. The police say he was shot trying to escape after he was caught breaking into a store. The Panthers and many of the people in the neighborhood say simply that he was murdered.

During the rally George Dowell patrols the fringes of the small group, carrying a loaded .30-30 rifle. Another Panther stands on the Dowell roof, demonstrating the loading of a shotgun with a 20-inch barrel—a gun which Bobby Seale tells the group he recommends highly.

Driving away from the rally, a tired Huey Newton jokes with a pretty girl who is his date that evening. She is a member of the Panthers, and has her hair done African style. She says that Richmond reminds her of Watts, where she grew up; the people in Richmond, she adds, are very warm and friendly. Newton agrees.

Asked whether the talk at rallies about killing cops is serious, Newton replies that it is very serious. Then why, he is asked, stake everything, including the lives of the Panthers, on the killing of a couple of cops?

"It won't be just a couple of cops," he says, "when the time comes, it will be part of a whole national coordinated effort." Is he willing to kill a cop? Yes, he answers, and when the time comes he is willing to die. What does he think is going to happen to him?

"I am going to be killed," he says with a smile on his face. He looks very young.

*

To Oakland's chief of police, Robert Preston, the Panthers are hardly worth commenting upon. "It's not the police but society that should be concerned with groups such as this," said Preston, displaying a cool response to the Panthers that perhaps masks a deeper concern. On second thought, Preston said: "They have on occasion harassed police and made some efforts to stir up animosity against us, but they are not deserving of any special treatment. They have made pretty ridiculous assertions which don't deserve to be dignified by anyone commenting on them."

Some of Preston's men on the beat were less reluctant to voice their gut reactions to the Panthers. One of them issued a series of unprintable epithets; another, giggling, suggested, "Maybe those guys ought to pick their best gunman and we pick ours and then have an old-fashioned shoot-it-out."

Despite Huey Newton's fatalism, the Panthers are not simply nihilistic terrorists. When confronted by the police and placed under arrest, as they were in Sacramento, the Panthers have so far surrendered their guns and submitted peacefully. If cops are to be shot—and there is no reason to question the Panthers' willingness to do this—it will be part of a general plan of action which they hope will force revolutionary changes in the society. The Panthers see the white cops in the ghetto as a "foreign occupying army" whose job is to prevent that change by force.

Reflecting on the outbreaks in Northern ghettos recently, Huey Newton said, "They were rebellions and a part of the revolutionary struggle, even though incorrect methods were used. But people learn warfare by indulging in warfare. That's the way they learn better tactics. When people go into the streets in large numbers they are more easily contained. We ought to look to historic revolutions such as Vietnam and learn to wear the enemy down. The way to do that is to break up into groups of threes and fours."

The Panther program calls for the black community to become independent and self-governing. The Negro community in which the Panthers held their second rally that Saturday is an unincorporated part of Contra Costa County; the Panthers are organizing a petition drive that would put the question of incorporation on the ballot. If they should succeed, they will accomplish by legal means one of the goals for which they say they are ultimately willing to engage in violence—removal of the white man's government from the black community.

Like most revolutionaries, the leaders of the Black Panthers do not come from the bottom of the economic ladder. Huey Newton could have escaped from the ghetto, if he had wanted to. He went to the integrated and excellent Berkeley High School, and eventually spent a year in law school. Bright but rebellious, he had numerous run-ins with the authorities (he always remembers them as "white authorities") in high school before he finally was graduated, to go on to Merritt College, a small, rundown two-year institution on the fringes of the Oakland ghetto. That was in the early nineteen-sixties, when Merritt had become a kind of incubator of Negro nationalism.

Both Newton and Seale, who also attended Merritt, remember the time as an exciting period of self-discovery for scores of young Oakland blacks. They would cut classes and sit around the nearby coffee shops, arguing about the black revolution, and reading the classics of black nationalism together.

Both Seale and Newton joined their first organization during that period: a group called the Afro-American Association, which advocated black nationalism and stressed Negro separateness and self-improvement. Seale and Newton both became disillusioned with the group because they felt it did not offer anything but some innocuous cultural nationalism. (The group still functions, led by a lawyer named Donald Warden, whom Seale and Newton scoffingly refer to as a "hard-core capitalist.")

After they had left the Afro-American Association, there was a period of political uncertainty for both Seale and Newton. At one point, Newton was tempted to become a Black Muslim; he had great respect for Malcolm X, but could not "accept the religious aspect." There was also a period of "hustling on the streets" for Newton and frequent arrests for theft and burglary. "But even then I discriminated between black and white property," he says.

Eventually came a year in the county jail on an assault-with-a-deadly-weapon conviction. In jail, again, there was the confrontation with white authority. Newton led riots and food strikes—for which he was placed in solitary confinement. In Alameda County at the time this constituted a unique and degrading form of punishment. The solitary cells were called "soul breakers" by the Negro prisoners. Each was totally bare, without even a washstand. The prisoner was put into it without any clothes and slept on the cement floor. In the middle of the cement floor was a hole which served as a toilet. The prisoners did their time in blocks of 15 days, after which they were allowed out for a shower and some exercise before going back in again.

Newton took it as a challenge. The "white bulls" were out to break him, and he had to resist. He made sure that when they opened the door to his cell he would be doing push-ups. It was also a time for thinking, since there was nothing else to do.

"I relived my life," he says. "I thought of everything I had done. And I realized some new things in that jail. I viewed the jail as no different from the outside. I thought about the relationship between being outside of a jail and being in, and I saw the great similarities. It was the whites who had the guns who controlled everything, with a few Uncle Tom blacks helping them out."

For Newton, as for Malcolm X, the prison experience only confirmed his hostility to the white world and made him more militant. Outside, Newton and Bobby Seale hooked up again and began to talk about the need for a revolutionary party that would represent the black masses and the ghetto youth unrepresented by other civil-rights groups.

"We began to understand the unwritten law of force," says Bobby Seale. "They, the police, have guns, and what the law actually says ain't worth a damn. We started to think of a program that defines and offsets this physical fact of the ghetto. I view black people in America as a colonial people. Therefore we have to arm ourselves and make the colonial power give us our freedom."

San Francisco's Hunters Point riot of last summer galvanized Newton and Seale into action. They viewed the disorganized half-hearted attempts of the Negroes to fight back against the cops as a waste. A new strategy was needed. After the riots they moved around the Bay Area talking to groups of bloods and gangs from the ghettos. The young bloods would ask Seale and Newton: "Tell us how we are going to do something. Tell us what we are going to do about the cops." The answer was the Black Panthers.

"The dream of the black people in the ghetto is how to stop the police brutality on the street," says Bobby Seale. "Can the people in the ghetto stand up to the cops? The ghetto black isn't afraid because he already lives with violence. He expects to die any day."

To someone who is not black, the issue of police brutality and police malpractice in the ghetto cannot be disposed of by checking a sociologist's statistics or the records of police review boards. It remains, an unrecorded fact that lurks in unlit ghetto streets, in moving police cars, in the privacy of police stations. It is recorded in the eyes of the young Negroes at Black Panther rallies who do not even blink when the speaker talks of "executing a cop"; it is as if every one of them has at least one memory of some long unpunished indignity suffered at the hands of a white cop.

To these young men, the execution of a police officer would be as natural and justifiable as the execution of a German soldier by a member of the French Resistance. This is the grim reality upon which the Panthers build a movement.

To the blood on the street, the black man who can face down the white cop is a hero. One of the early tactics of the Panthers was the "defense patrol." Four Panthers, armed with shotguns, would ride around in a car following a police car in the ghetto. If the police stopped to question a Negro on the street, the Panthers with their guns drawn would get out and observe the behavior of the police. If an arrest was made, the Panthers would try to raise the money to bail the Negro out.

On the basis of such acts, new members were recruited, taught the rudiments of the law on search and seizure, the right to bear arms and arrest procedure, and introduced to the standard works of militant black revolution: Frantz Fanon, Malcolm X, W. E. B. Du Bois, Marcus Garvey. Currently, Panthers are reading and digesting Mao Tse-tung's Little Red Book. Seale and Newton admit that the rank and file of the Panthers, many of whom are members of street gangs, are not sophisticated politically, but insist that they are "wise in the ways of power."

To Newton and Seale the identification with world revolution is a serious business. They see the United States as the center of an imperialist system which suppresses the world-wide revolution of colored people. And, says Newton: "We can stop the machinery. We can stop the imperialists from using it against black people all over the world. We are in a strategic position in this country, and we won't be the only group rebelling against the oppressor here."

If the Panthers are no more than a tiny minority even among militant Negroes, it does not seem to affect their revolutionary fervor. Theirs is a vision of an American apocalypse in which all blacks are forced to unite for survival against the white oppressors. Newton puts it this way: "At the height of the resistance they are going to be slaughtering black people indiscriminately. We are sure that at that time Martin Luther King will be a member of the Black Panthers through necessity. He and others like him will have to band together with us just to save themselves."

In the meantime, all is not smooth among the black militants. The Panthers have had running feuds with other black nationalist groups, one of them a Bay Area group which has also used the name "Black Panthers," and which has been attacked by Newton and Seale for its overly intellectual approach and for its unwillingness to carry guns in the open. "Cultural nationalists" is the epithet that Newton and Seale use for black nationalists who they claim never try to develop grass-roots support in the ghetto community, but are content to live in an intellectual milieu of black nationalism.

In turn, the Panthers have been criticized for their provocative and public actions by other black militants. One Negro leader in the area said privately, "These cats have just been playing cowboys and Indians." But opinions among black leaders are sharply divided on the subject. When asked about the Panthers on a recent trip to the Bay Area, H. Rap Brown, the new national chairman of the Student Nonviolent Coordinating Committee, had only favorable things to say about them. "What they're doing is very important," said Brown. "Black people are just beginning to get over their fear of the police and the Panthers are playing an important role in helping them to surmount that fear." (Eleven days ago, Brown was arrested on charges of inciting Negroes to riot in Cambridge, Md.)

How does the ordinary, nonpolitical Negro respond to the Panthers? Consider, not because he is representative, but for the quality of the reaction, 22-year-old Billy John Carr, once a star athlete at Berkeley High School. Carr lives in Berkeley's Negro ghetto, has a wife and child now, and tries to keep his family together with sporadic work as a laborer. He has never been a member of any political organization and knows the Panthers only by reputation. Of the Panthers he says: "As far as I'm concerned it's beautiful that we finally got an organization that don't walk around singing. I'm not for all this talking stuff. When things start happening I'll be ready to die if that's necessary and it's important that we have somebody around to organize us."

The Sacramento incident clearly won the Panthers grudging respect and put them on the map in the ghetto. Recently, when traditional civil-rights organizations and Negro politicians in California organized what they called a "Black Survival Conference," the Panthers were invited to speak and got an enthusiastic response.

Are the Panthers racists? Both Huey Newton and Bobby Seale deny it. "Black people aren't racists. Racism is primarily a white man's problem," says Seale, perhaps begging the question. Whatever the root causes of American racism, there *are* Negroes in the society who simply hate whites as a matter of principle, and would commit indiscriminate violence against them merely for their color. The violent rhetoric of the Panthers—which pits the black man against the white cop —undoubtedly fans such feelings.

Yet the fact is that the Panthers, unlike certain other black nationalist groups, have not allowed themselves to indulge in baiting the "white devil." They are race-conscious, they are exclusively "pro-black," but they also seem conscious of the dangers of simple-minded antiwhite hostility.

Though the Panthers will not allow whites to attend their

membership meetings, they have had friendly relations with groups of white radicals in the area. They participated in a meeting with leaders of the San Francisco "hippie" community, in which common problems were discussed. The hippies had been concerned about trouble with young Negroes in the area who were starting fights and harassing the hipples. "We went around and told these guys that the hippies weren't the enemy, that they shouldn't waste their time on them," says Newton.

The Panthers' relations with the local chapter of S.N.C.C., which has a number of whites in it, have been friendly. Terry Cannon, a white member of the editorial board of The Movement, a newspaper affiliated with S.N.C.C., and long a Bay Area activist, sees the Panthers' initial action as necessary. "The Panthers have demonstrated something that was very much needed in Northern cities," says Cannon. "They have effectively demonstrated that the black community is willing to defend itself."

Though they claim to have started chapters in Los Angeles, Harlem and elsewhere in the North, the Panthers remain pitifully small in numbers and their organizational resources meager. Frequent arrests have brought severe financial strain in the form of bail money and legal fees—and police harassment is certain to continue. If the Panthers increasingly "go underground" to escape such pressures, they will find it that much more difficult to broaden their contact with the rest of the black community.

But to write off the Panthers as a fringe group of little influence is to miss the point. The group's roots are in the desperation and anger that no civil-rights legislation or poverty program has touched in the ghetto. The fate of the Panthers as an organization is not the issue. What matters is that there are a thousand black people in the ghetto thinking privately what any Panther says out loud.

The New York Times Magazine, August 6, 1967

U.S. Letter: Cleveland

by Calvin Trillin

October 6

By the time Ralph S. Locher, the incumbent mayor of Cleveland, had decided to run again for the Democratic mayoralty nomination, those who sit in judgment on public officials here had accused him of almost every municipal offense except being dishonest or colored. Ostensibly, Locher made his appeal to the voters on the basis of his unchallenged honesty—a characteristic that has been widely celebrated as his chief qualification for public office. The only real issue, though, was that his principal opponent, an articulate and aggressive young State Representative named Carl B. Stokes, does not share the second of Locher's saving graces—an incontrovertible whiteness. From the outset of the campaign, it was taken for granted that most white people in Cleveland would not vote for a Negro candidate for mayor under any circumstances, and that Cleveland's Negroes, who now make up more than a third of the city's registered voters, would vote for a Negro candidate even if he were, in the words of one local politician, "a Black Muslim, a black dog, or a black automobile."

Locher seemed sincerely puzzled about why he had to enter the campaign with little more than his whiteness intact. He is, after all, in the line of succession of mayors that Cleveland found perfectly acceptable for a quarter century—men distinguished by their honesty, their frugality, their popularity with the Southern and Eastern European ethnic groups that make up a third of the city's population (known as the cosmopolitan, or cosmo, vote), their fondness for the status quo, and their selection by Louis B. Seltzer, who was the editor of the Cleveland *Press* until his retirement last year. Locher— Rumanian-born, honest, frugal, and the rest—was reëlected once, in 1963, without opposition, but a few years later he happened to be the man in office when the Urban Crisis finally caught up with Cleveland. In the past year or so, Cleveland has endured, among other civic disasters, a riot in its awesomely deteriorated Hough ghetto, a bungling of its urban-renewal program so monumental that the federal government finally cut off funds, and a series of Civil Rights Commission hearings, national magazine articles, and local citizens'-committee reports that supported Carl Stokes's claim that Cleveland had become "a symbol of the failure of American cities to cope with their human and physical problems." Cleveland businessmen began to realize that they might be luxuriously quartered on a sinking ship. A few of them publicly backed the Democratic primary campaign of Frank P. Celeste, a white former suburban mayor, as an alternative to Locher. The Cuyahoga County Democratic Executive Committee, which had reportedly tried to persuade Locher to accept less controversial employment, eventually endorsed him, but the Cleveland *Plain Dealer* endorsed Stokes early in the campaign, and the Cleveland *Press*, a journalistic watchdog that had not opposed an incumbent mayor in twenty-five years, advised its readers to vote for anybody except Ralph Locher.

Locher went right ahead with the traditional cultivation of the party workers and the cosmo voters which is called for in the Cleveland election formula perfected by Bronis J. Klementowicz—the Locher campaign manager, the Law Director of Cleveland, and, in the judgment of both friends and enemies, the shrewdest cultivator of them all. ("This is a very cosmopolitan city," Klementowicz explains to visitors, tapping on the cigarette holder that is his trademark. "I'm Polish myself.") Locher made the rounds of the Polish Falcons and the Croatian Club and the Twenty-third Ward Democratic Club, meeting at the Slovenian National Home. At a meeting of the Ninth Ward Democratic Club, Locher slapped the back of his right hand into his left palm with every word as he shouted, "Ralph S. Locher is not for sale!" ("Very prompt," Klementowicz said when he was asked what Ninth Ward Democrats were like. "There's a lot of elderly girls and whatnot in that club, and when they say eight o'clock they're right there at eight o'clock.") At the Alliance of Poles Hall—in a pale-green basement meeting room whose walls are decorated with a half-dozen flowery murals and with a small framed rectangle of rough material on which is written "Please Strike Matches Here"—the Mayor was cheered as he told the members of Polish America, "I said to you that if we had the financial capabilities, we'd have combined rubbish-and-garbage collection—*and we have it!*" Locher ordinarily came no closer to raising the race issue than to promise that hoodlums would not take over the town or to complain that Ford Foundation money had been used for a voting drive only in "certain wards," but when the county Democratic committee began to accuse Celeste of being a vote-splitter, nobody had any doubt about which vote he was being accused of splitting.

Stokes—an independent legislator who has sponsored not only a fair-housing law but also a law that permits the governor to dispatch the National Guard to potential riot areas whenever a show of force seems needed—attempted to become a biracial candidate. He talked to both black and white audiences about law and order, he spoke in the detached tone of a visiting urbanologist about how to solve the complex problems created by "a high incidence of low-income Appalachian whites and Southern Negroes," and he more or less ignored his color except for one attempt to neutralize the issue at the start with a full-page advertisement headlined, "DON'T VOTE FOR A NEGRO." ("Vote for a Man. Vote for Ability.") Publicly, Stokes campaigned on what he called Locher's "internationally documented record of failure," but he acknowledged that his real campaign was to demonstrate to whites that "Negroes don't have two heads and a tail" and that "this is not a Black Power takeover." Through constant exposure in the white community, he hoped to pick up fifteen or twenty per cent of the white vote and—perhaps more important—to "calm the fears" of those whites who might not bother to vote at all unless they became alarmed. In the 1965 mayoral election—when he ran as an independent against three white candidates and astonished the local political experts by coming within about two thousand votes of beating Locher—Stokes had campaigned almost exclusively in East Side Negro wards and had got only about three per cent of the white vote. It is taken for granted in Cleveland that campaigning by a Negro candidate in the tight East Side Polish and Italian neighborhoods adjoining the bulging Negro ghetto would be at least fruitless and probably dangerous. But the West Side, the neighborhoods west of where the bright-brown waters of the Cuyahoga River flow into Lake Erie, is virtually all white and somewhat less strictly cosmo than the East Side. Stokes's policy this year was to accept every invitation he received from the West Side, and he received more invitations than anyone had expected. Night after night, he sat in church basements or Y.M.C.A. meeting rooms, demonstrating his polish and his impressive knowledge of urban problems and his lack of an extra head and a tail, as white West Siders asked questions about the problem of air pollution or the problem of industry's leaving the city —until it seemed impossible that someone in the audience, suddenly remembering all the hatred that everyone took for granted, would not stand up and ask, "What do you expect to do about the problem of being a Negro?"

The West Side strategy was based on the belief that the Negro wards, organized down to the block-leader level by Stokes volunteers, would maintain enough enthusiasm to turn out a huge vote even if Stokes spent most of his time courting whites—the question being not whom Negroes would vote for but how many of them would vote. Last summer, when Cleveland was regarded as the logical spot for a serious ghetto disturbance, even the Hough militants, who consider Stokes a "bourgie" and consider elections a form of white pacification, decided to "cool it for Carl"—while Martin Luther King ran a cooling, nondemonstrative employment campaign and helped register voters. Stokes, an attorney and a former Assistant City Prosecutor, had been too remote from the ghetto to draw folk-hero adulation, but early in the campaign it became clear that, anti-riot bill or no anti-riot bill, a great many Negroes, of varying outlooks, would work for his election. Many Negroes believed that there would simply have to be some change in their lives if the mayor was a black man who had grown up in the ghetto instead of a white man who refused to talk to them. Militant Negroes supported Stokes partly because of the impression that his election could make on Negroes—on black children, who would be able to see a black man in City Hall, or on the black masses, who would finally realize the hopelessness of the system when they saw that having a Negro mayor made no difference at all—and middle-class Negroes supported him partly because of the impression his election would make on everyone else. ("You have been a gentleman," one Negro woman said to Stokes in the final days of the campaign. "You haven't shown that low element that white people think the colored man carries. You have shown we have culture and intelligence.") A couple of days before the election, CORE placed an advertisement in the Negro paper headed, "If You Don't Vote This Tuesday, Forget It."

The Stokes campaign was run not from the ghetto but from an elaborate downtown office—where white housewives from Shaker Heights mailed out slick campaign brochures, and table-of-organization charts on the walls listed participants like "operations managers," and a visitor half expected to hear one of the earnest young white men in attendance say how nice it would be if a good-looking and well-spoken Negro happened to be elected president of the student-government association. In a sense, the Stokes campaign, like Locher's courting of the cosmos, was a throwback—a kind of electoral March on Washington, a relic of the days when it was thought that well-meaning black people and well-meaning white people could work things out, and that the enemy was Bull Connor. Like any local hero of Bull Connor days, Stokes took it for granted that New York was the logical place to raise money and that his Democratic Party ties were with Hubert Humphrey rather than with the county chairman. (The Cuyahoga County Democratic chairman, as befits a man whose rank-and-file voters are about as far from the national party's official racial attitudes as Bull Connor's supporters used to be, called Stokes a racist and complained that the National Administration wants a Negro mayor in order to influence the Negro urban swing vote—an Ohio echo of complaints about the pressure of "all them niggra votes up North.") Stokes's connection with the white liberals of New York sounded just as evil when Locher described it to the Ninth Ward Democratic Club as it would have sounded a few years ago in Alabama; as Locher recalled Stokes's presence in "that spacious, sunken apartment on Central West Park, with murals on the walls," the members of the Ninth Ward Democratic Club shuddered.

Early in the week before the primary, the Cleveland papers reported that Stokes was making some headway on the West Side, with what passes in Cleveland for the middle-class white vote. (Actually, Cleveland is noted for not having a middle class within the city limits. Of the twenty-one cities in the United States with populations over five hundred thousand, it ranks twenty-first in percentage of white-collar workers. One indication of the almost total middle-class exodus from the city is that the generally accepted figure for the Jewish population of Cleveland is five hundred—with eighty-five thousand in the suburbs.) By the weekend, both Cleveland papers had published polls predicting a narrow victory for Locher. Celeste, whose campaign had never developed, was running a bad third in the polls—losing the support of people interested in voting for whichever white man had the better chance of stopping Stokes. Some whites told the poll-takers that they would vote against Stokes because of his lack of administrative experience, and some whites would obviously vote *for* Locher rather than against Stokes, being less interested in having a mayor who seemed to know the modern methods of getting federal money than in having a familiar regime that could be counted on to leave them alone unless they needed something from the city. But, as the mock discussions melted away in the week before the primary, it was clear that for most voters the campaign would end as it had begun, with a black man against a white man. The only street-corner campaigner among the candidates, Celeste continued to hand out his literature—walking in and out of stores with European names over their doors and black-bordered pictures of John F. Kennedy on their walls, and finding, as he had found throughout the campaign, that virtually everyone who engaged him in conversation said something like "You're just splitting the vote and letting the nigger in" or "Better you than that black boy." The county Democratic committee, completing its imitation of Bull Connor, put out an issue of its newsletter saying "Will Dr. Martin Luther King actually be the mayor of Cleveland if Carl B. Stokes is elected Tuesday?

This would give the noted racist control of his first city in the United States." A Republican politician predicted to some visiting reporters that Stokes would win, basing the prediction partly on the argument that the Democratic Party "doesn't have the muscle to put on the kind of hate campaign it would take to beat him."

At 9 P.M. on the day of the primary, a local television station said that Mayor Locher had won the nomination. At nine-fifteen, Stokes—displaying his customary self-assurance, despite the fact that the Board of Elections count showed him considerably behind—announced that he had won, and thanked the citizenry for its confidence in him. By ten-thirty, when the count from the East Side Negro wards had come in, the Stokes victory had been announced officially, and Mayor Locher came to offer his congratulations. It turned out that Stokes's strategy had worked well enough to give him a clear majority of the vote. A huge vote had come out in the Negro wards, and Stokes had got nearly fifteen per cent of the less imposing white turnout—a reaffirmation of the faith he had often expressed to campaign workers that in America a Negro candidate "like a Carl Stokes or an Edward Brooke" can always count on the presence of a certain number of decent white people (although in Cleveland it might be unwise to count on the number's being as high as fifteen per cent). Hundreds of whites and Negroes celebrated in the street in front of Stokes's headquarters. Some of the white housewives who had been manning the telephones and electronic calculators in the Stokes communications center began to cry, and Hubert Humphrey phoned from Washington to offer his help in the forthcoming general election.

Although the Democratic nominee for mayor has ordinarily beaten the Republican by at least three to one, some Cleveland politicians believe that Stokes is not absolutely guaranteed to win the election against Seth B. Taft, an earnest and civic-minded lawyer whose views on the city's problems are quite close to Stokes's own. In the provincial, blue-collar politics of Cleveland, Taft has the disadvantage of being a Republican, a Taft, an Establishment lawyer, a transplanted suburbanite, and an Urban League liberal on racial matters; he has the advantage, somewhat to his embarrassment, of being as white as Ralph Locher.

Stokes is, as usual, completely confident. His white liberal supporters believe that they are about to "make history" by electing the first Negro mayor of a major American city, and that they will, at the same time, bring in an administration with the intelligence and imagination to make a start on solving Cleveland's problems. There are, of course, people in Cleveland who believe that Cleveland's problems—like the problems of Detroit or New Haven—have gone too far to be greatly affected by any mayor working with the tools now available, and that next summer white people in Cleveland will be demanding to know why the Negroes are burning everything down less than a year after Cleveland was liberal enough to elect a Negro mayor. "If the crisis is as serious as we think it is, how can it be affected by having a Negro mayor?" one of the few whites who are deeply involved in the ghetto here said a few days before the primary. "The cops might get a little better for a while, and there might be a few more jobs, but in the long term the election is irrelevant." Then he went to Stokes's headquarters to help with the campaign.

The New Yorker, October 14, 1967

Martin Luther King Is Slain in Memphis

by Earl Caldwell

MEMPHIS, Friday, April 5—The Rev. Dr. Martin Luther King Jr., who preached nonviolence and racial brotherhood, was fatally shot here last night by a distant gunman who then raced away and escaped.

Four thousand National Guard troops were ordered into Memphis by Gov. Buford Ellington after the 39-year-old Nobel Prize–winning civil rights leader died.

A curfew was imposed on the shocked city of 550,000 inhabitants, 40 per cent of whom are Negro.

But the police said the tragedy had been followed by incidents that included sporadic shooting, fires, bricks and bottles thrown at policemen, and looting that started in Negro districts and then spread over the city.

Police Director Frank Holloman said the assassin might have been a white man who was "50 to 100 yards away in a flophouse."

Chief of Detectives W. P. Huston said a late model white Mustang was believed to have been the killer's getaway car. Its occupant was described as a bareheaded white man in his 30's, wearing a black suit and black tie.

The detective chief said the police had chased two cars near the motel where Dr. King was shot and had halted one that had two out-of-town men as occupants. The men were questioned but seemed to have nothing to do with the killing, he said.

A high-powered 30.06-caliber rifle was found about a block from the scene of the shooting, on South Main Street. "We think it's the gun," Chief Huston said, reporting it would be turned over to the Federal Bureau of Investigation.

Dr. King was shot while he leaned over a second-floor railing outside his room at the Lorraine Motel. He was chatting with two friends just before starting for dinner.

One of the friends was a musician, and Dr. King had just asked him to play a Negro spiritual, "Precious Lord, Take My Hand," at a rally that was to have been held two hours later in support of striking Memphis sanitationmen.

Paul Hess, assistant administrator at St. Joseph's Hospital, where Dr. King died despite emergency surgery, said the minister had "received a gunshot wound on the right side of the neck, at the root of the neck, a gaping wound."

"He was pronounced dead at 7:05 P.M. Central standard time (8:05 P.M. New York time) by staff doctors," Mr. Hess said. "They did everything humanly possible."

Dr. King's mourning associates sought to calm the people they met by recalling his messages of peace, but there was widespread concern by law enforcement officers here and elsewhere over potential reactions.

In a television broadcast after the curfew was ordered here, Mr. Holloman said, "rioting has broken out in parts of the city" and "looting is rampant."

Dr. King had come back to Memphis Wednesday morning to organize support once again for 1,300 sanitation workers who have been striking since Lincoln's Birthday. Just a week ago yesterday he led a march in the strikers' cause that ended in violence. A 16-year-old Negro was killed, 62 persons were injured and 200 were arrested.

Yesterday Dr. King had been in his second-floor room— Number 306—throughout the day. Just about 6 P.M. he emerged, wearing a silkish-looking black suit and white shirt.

Solomon Jones Jr., his driver, had been waiting to take him by car to the home of the Rev. Samuel Kyles of Memphis for dinner. Mr. Jones said later he had observed, "It's cold outside, put your topcoat on," and Dr. King had replied, "O.K., I will."

Dr. King, an open-faced, genial man, leaned over a green iron railing to chat with an associate, Jesse Jackson, standing just below him in a courtyard parking lot.

"Do you know Ben?" Mr. Jackson asked, introducing Ben Branch of Chicago, a musician who was to play at the night's rally.

"Yes, that's my man!" Dr. King glowed.

The two men recalled Dr. King's asking for the playing of

the spiritual. "I really want you to play that tonight," Dr. King said, enthusiastically.

The Rev. Ralph W. Abernathy, perhaps Dr. King's closest friend, was just about to come out of the motel room when the sudden loud noise burst out.

Dr. King toppled to the concrete second-floor walkway. Blood gushed from the right jaw and neck area. His necktie had been ripped off by the blast.

"He had just bent over," Mr. Jackson recalled later. "If he had been standing up, he wouldn't have been hit in the face."

"When I turned around," Mr. Jackson went on, bitterly, "I saw police coming from everywhere. They said, 'where did it come from?' And I said, 'behind you.' The police were coming from where the shot came."

Mr. Branch asserted that the shot had come from "the hill on the other side of the street."

"When I looked up, the police and the sheriff's deputies were running all around," Mr. Branch declared.

"We didn't need to call the police," Mr. Jackson said. "They were here all over the place."

Mr. Kyles said Dr. King had stood in the open "about three minutes."

Mr. Jones, the driver, said that a squad car with four policemen in it drove down the street only moments before the gunshot. The police had been circulating throughout the motel area on precautionary patrols.

After the shot, Mr. Jones said, he saw a man "with something white on his face" creep away from a thicket across the street.

Someone rushed up with a towel to stem the flow of Dr. King's blood. Mr. Kyles said he put a blanket over Dr. King, but "I knew he was gone." He ran down the stairs and tried to telephone from the motel office for an ambulance.

Mr. Abernathy hurried up with a second larger towel.

Policemen were pouring into the motel area, carrying rifles and shotguns and wearing riot helmets.

But the King aides said it seemed to be 10 or 15 minutes before a Fire Department ambulance arrived.

Dr. King was apparently still living when he reached the St. Joseph's Hospital operating room for emergency surgery. He was borne in on a stretcher, the bloody towel over his head.

It was the same emergency room to which James H. Meredith, first Negro enrolled at the University of Mississippi, was taken after he was ambushed and shot in June, 1966 at Hernando, Miss., a few miles south of Memphis. Mr. Meredith was not seriously hurt.

Outside the emergency room some of Dr. King's aides waited in forlorn hope. One was Chauncey Eskridge, his legal adviser. He broke into sobs when Dr. King's death was announced.

"A man full of life, full of love, and he was shot," Mr. Eskridge said. "He had always lived with that expectation—but nobody ever expected it to happen."

But the Rev. Andrew Young, executive director of Dr. King's Southern Christian Leadership Conference, recalled there had been some talk Wednesday night about possible harm to Dr. King in Memphis.

Mr. Young recalled: "He said he had reached the pinnacle of fulfillment with his nonviolent movement, and these reports did not bother him."

Mr. Young believed that the fatal shot might have been fired from a passing car. "It sounded like a firecracker," he said.

In a nearby building, a newsman who had been watching a television program thought, however, that "it was a tremendous blast that sounded like a bomb."

There were perhaps 15 persons in the motel courtyard area when Dr. King was shot, all believed to be Negroes and Dr. King's associates.

Past the courtyard is a small empty swimming pool. Then comes Mulberry Street, a short street only three blocks away from storied Beale Street on the fringe of downtown Memphis.

On the other side of the street is a six-foot brick restraining wall, with bushes and grass atop it and a hillside going on to a patch of trees. Behind the trees is a rusty wire fence enclosing backyards of two-story brick and frame houses.

At the corner at Butler Street is a newish-looking white brick fire station.

Police were reported to have chased a late-model blue or white car through Memphis and north to Millington. A civilian in another car that had a citizens band radio was also reported to have pursued the fleeing car and to have opened fire on it.

The police first cordoned off an area of about five blocks around the Lorraine Motel, chosen by Dr. King for his stay here because it is Negro-owned. The two-story motel is an addition to a small two-story hotel in a largely Negro area.

Mayor Henry Loeb had ordered a curfew here after last week's disorder, and National Guard units had been on duty for five days until they were deactivated Wednesday.

Last night the Mayor reinstated the curfew at 6:35 and declared:

"After the tragedy which has happened in Memphis tonight, for the protection of all our citizens, we are putting the curfew back in effect. All movement is restricted except for health or emergency reasons."

Governor Ellington, calling out the National Guard and pledging all necessary action by the state to prevent disorder, announced:

"For the second time in recent days, I most earnestly ask the people of Memphis and Shelby County to remain calm. I do so again tonight in the face of this most regrettable incident.

"Every possible action is being taken to apprehend the person or persons responsible for committing this act.

"We are also taking precautionary steps to prevent any acts of disorder. I can fully appreciate the feelings and emotions which this crime has aroused, but for the benefit of everyone, all of our citizens must exercise restraint, caution and good judgment."

National Guard planes flew over the state to bring in contingents of riot-trained highway patrolmen. Units of the Arkansas State Patrol were deputized and brought into Memphis.

Assistant Chief Bartholomew early this morning said that unidentified persons had shot from rooftops and windows at policemen eight or 10 times. He said bullets had shattered one police car's windshield, wounding two policemen with flying glass. They were treated at the same hospital where Dr. King died.

Sixty arrests were made for looting, burglary and disorderly conduct, chief Bartholomew said.

Numerous minor injuries were reported in four hours of clashes between civilians and law enforcement officers. But any serious disorders were under control by 11:15 P.M., Chief

Bartholomew said. Early this morning streets were virtually empty except for patrol cars riding without headlights on.

In his career Dr. King had suffered beatings and blows. Once—on Sept. 20, 1958—he was stabbed in a Harlem department store in New York by a Negro woman later adjudged insane.

That time he underwent a four-hour operation to remove a steel letter opener that had been plunged into his upper left chest. For a time he was on the critical list, but he told his wife, while in the hospital, "I don't hold any bitterness toward this woman."

In Memphis, Dr. King's chief associates met in his room after he died. They included Mr. Young, Mr. Abernathy, Mr. Jackson, the Rev. James Bevel and Hosea Williams.

They had to step across a drying pool of Dr. King's blood to enter. Someone had thrown a crumpled pack of cigarettes into the blood.

After 15 minutes they emerged. Mr. Jackson looked at the blood. He embraced Mr. Abernathy.

"Stand tall!" somebody exhorted.

"Murder! Murder!" Mr. Bevel groaned. "Doc said that's not the way."

"Doc" was what they often called Dr. King.

Then the murdered leader's aides said they would go on to the hall where tonight's rally was to have been held. They wanted to urge calm upon the mourners.

Some policemen sought to dissuade them.

But eventually the group did start out, with a police escort.

At the Federal Bureau of Investigation office here, Robert Jensen, special agent in charge, said the F.B.I. had entered the murder investigation at the request of Attorney General Ramsey Clark.

Last night Dr. King's body was taken to the Shelby County morgue, according to the police. They said it would be up to Dr. Derry Francisco, county medical examiner, to order further disposition.

The New York Times, April 5, 1968

Martin Luther King Is Still on the Case!

by Garry Wills

Of course, Mailer had an instinct for missing good speeches—at the Civil Rights March in Washington in 1963 he had gone for a stroll just a little while before Martin Luther King began, "I have a dream," so Mailer—trusting no one else in these matters, certainly not the columnists and the commentators—would never know whether the Reverend King had given a great speech that day, or revealed an inch of his hambone.

—Norman Mailer
The Armies of the Night

"NIGGER territory, eh?" He was a cabdriver, speculative; eyed the pistol incongruous beside him on the seat, this quiet spring night; studied me, my two small bags, my raincoat. The downtown streets were empty, but spectrally alive. Every light in every store was on (the better to silhouette looters). Even the Muzak in an arcade between stores reassured itself, at the top of its voice, with jaunty rhythms played to no audience. Jittery neon arrows, meant to beckon people in, now tried to scare them off. The curfew had swept pedestrians off the street, though some cars with white men in them still cruised unchallenged.

"Well, get in." He snapped down every lock with four quick slaps of his palm; then rolled up his window; we had begun our safari into darkest Memphis. It *was* intimidating. Nothing stirred in the crumbling blocks; until, almost noiseless—one's windows are always up on safari—an armored personnel carrier went nibbling by on its rubber treads, ten long guns bristling from it (longer because not measured against human forms, the men who bore them were crouched behind the armored walls); only mushroom helmets showed, leaning out from each other as from a single stalk, and, under each, bits of elfin face disembodied.

At last we came to lights again: not the hot insistence of

downtown; a lukewarm dinginess of light between two buildings. One was modern and well-lit; a custodian sat behind the locked glass door. This is the headquarters of a new activism in Memphis, the Minimum Salary Building (designed as national headquarters for raising the pay of ministers in the African Methodist Episcopal Church and now encompassing other groups). Its director, Reverend H. Ralph Jackson, was a moderate's moderate until, in a march for the striking sanitation workers, he was Maced by police. Since then his building has been a hive of union officials, Southern Christian Leadership Conference staff, and members of various human-rights organizations.

Next to it is the Clayborn Temple, a church from which marchers have issued almost daily for the past two months. Marchers fell back to this point in their retreat from the scuffle that marred Dr. King's first attempt to help the strikers. Some say tear gas was deliberately fired into the church; others that it drifted in. But the place *was* wreathed with gas, and a feeling of violated sanctuary remains. Churches have been the Negro's one bit of undisputed terrain in the South, so long as they were socially irrelevant; but this church rang, in recent weeks, with thunderous sermons on the godliness of union dues.

I pay the cabdriver, who resolutely ignores a well-dressed young couple signaling him from the corner, and make my way, with bags and coat, into the shadow of the church porch. In the vestibule, soft bass voices warn me. I stop to let my eyes, initiated into darkness, find the speakers and steer me through their scattered chairs. They are not really conversing; their meditative scraps of speech do not meet each other, but drift off, centripetally, over each one's separate horizon of darkness. This uncommunicative, almost musical, slow rain of words goes on while I navigate my way into the lighted dim interior of the church.

About a hundred people are there, disposed in every combination: family groups; clots of men, or of women; the lean of old people toward each other, the jostle outward of teenagers from some center (the church piano, a pretty dress on a hanger); or individuals rigid in their pews as if asleep or dead. The whole gathering is muted—some young people try to pick out a hymn on the piano, but halfheartedly. There are boxes of food, and Sunday clothes draped over the backs of pews. The place has the air of a rather lugubrious picnic—broken up by rain, perhaps, with these few survivors waiting their chance to dash out through the showers to their homes. Yet there is a quiet sense of purpose, dimly focused but, finally, undiscourageable. These are garbage collectors, and they are going to King's funeral in Atlanta. It is ten P.M.; in twelve hours the funeral will begin, 398 miles away.

They have been told different things, yesterday and today, by different leaders (some from the union, some from S.C.L.C.). They have served as marshals in the memorial march that very afternoon, and preparations for that overshadowed any planning for this trip. Some have been told to gather at ten o'clock; some at eleven. They believe there will be two buses, or three; that they will leave at eleven, or at twelve; that only the workers can go, or only they and their wives, or they and their immediate families. Yesterday, when they gathered for marshals' school, a brusque young Negro shouted at them to arrive sharply at ten: "We're not going by C. P. Time—Colored People's Time. And if you don't listen now, you won't find out how to get to Atlanta at all, 'cause *we'll* be on the *plane* tomorrow night." The speaker seemed to agree with much of white Memphis that "you have to know how to talk to these people."

And so they wait. Some came before dark, afraid to risk even a short walk or drive after curfew. Some do not realize the wait will be so long; they simply know the time they were asked to arrive. Most will have waited three hours before we start; some, four or five. I try to imagine the mutters and restlessness of a white group stranded so long. These people are the world's least likely revolutionaries. They are, in fact, the precisely *wrong* people—as the Russian fieldworker was the wrong man to accomplish Marx's revolt of the industrial proletariat.

People such as these were the first "Memphians" I had met in any number. That was four days ago. And my first impression was the same as that which nagged at me all night in the church: these Tennessee Negroes are not unlikely, they are impossible. They are anachronisms. Their leaders had objected for some time to J. P. Alley's "Hambone" cartoon in the local paper; they say, rightly, that it offers an outdated depiction of the Negro. Nonetheless, these men *are* Hambones. History has passed them by.

I saw them by the hundred, that first morning, streaming past the open casket in a hugger-mugger wake conducted between the completion of the embalmer's task and the body's journey out to the Memphis airport. I had arrived in Memphis several hours after King's death; touched base at the hotel, at the police station, at the site of the murder—dawn was just disturbing the sky; flashbulbs around and under the balcony still blinked repeatedly against the room number—306—like summer lightning. As the light strengthened, I sought out the funeral home police had mentioned—R. S. Lewis and Sons.

Clarence Lewis is one of the sons; he has been up all night answering the phone, but he is still polite; professionally sepulchral, calm under stress. "They brought Dr. King here because we have been connected with the Movement for a long time. We drove him in our limousines when he was here last week [for the ill-fated march]. They brought the body to us from the morgue at ten-thirty last night, and my brother has been working on it ever since. There's so much to do: this side [he pulls spread fingers down over his right cheek and neck] was all shot away, and the jawbone was just dangling. They have to reset it and then build all that up with plaster." I went through the fine old home (abandoned to trade when the white people moved from this area) into a new addition— the chapel, all cheap religious sentiment, an orange cross in fake stained glass. There are two people already there, both journalists, listening to the sounds from the next room (Clarence calls it, with a mortician's customary euphemism, "the Operating Room"), where a radio crackles excerpts from Dr. King's oratory, and men mutter their appreciation of the live voice while they work on the dead body. We comment on the ghoulishness of their task—knowing ours is no less ghoulish. We would be in there, if we could, with lights and cameras; but we must wait—wait through an extra hour of desperate cosmetic work. We do it far less patiently than Memphis garbage men wait in their church. "Hell of a place for Dr. King to end up, isn't it?" the photographer says. "And one hell of a cause—a little garbage strike."

When, at eight o'clock, the body is brought out, bright TV lights appear and pick out a glint of plaster under the cheek's powder. Several hundred people file past; they have sought the body out, in their sorrow, and will not let it leave town without some tribute. But not one white person from the town goes through that line.

Those who do come are a microcosm of the old Southern Negro community. Young boys doff their hats and their nylon hair caps—their "do rags"—as they go by. A Negro principal threatened to expel any child from a local high school who came to class with an "Afro" hairdo. Possessive matrons take up seats in the back, adjust their furs, cluck sympathetically to other women of their station, and keep the neighborhood record straight with bouts of teary gossip. They each make several passes at the coffin; sob uncontrollably, whip out their Polaroid cameras, and try an angle different from that shot on their last pass. One woman kisses the right cheek. Clarence Lewis was afraid of that: "It will spoil the makeup job. We normally put a veil over the coffin opening in cases of this sort; but we knew people would just tear that off with Dr. King. They want to see him. Why, we had one case where the people lifted a body up in the coffin to see where the bullet had gone into a man's back."

Outside, people mill around, making conversation, mixing with stunned friendliness, readjusting constantly their air of sad respect. Again, the scene looked like a disconsolate picnic. Some activists had called him "De Lawd." He always had to be given either his title (*"Doctor* King," even the *Reverend Doctor* King") or his full historic name ("Luther Martin King" one prim lady mourner called him in the funeral home, understandably stumbling over the big mouthful). Even that title "Doctor"—never omitted, punctiliously stressed when whites referred to him, included even in King's third-person references to himself—had become almost comical. He was not only "De Lawd," but "De Lawd High God Almighty," and his Movement was stiff with the preacher-dignities of the South; full of Reverends This and Bishops That and Doctors The-Other. No wonder the militants laughed at it all. And now, damned if he hadn't ended up at a Marc Connelly *fish fry* of a wake—right out of *The Green Pastures.*

Connelly learned to read by poring over the pages of the Memphis *Commercial Appeal* and he learned his lesson well: he was able to create a hambone God: "Dey's gonter to be a deluge, Noah, an' dey's goin' to be a flood. De Levees is gonter bust an' everything dat's fastened down is comin' loose." These are unlikely people, I thought at that sad fish fry, to ride out the deluge whose signs had already thundered from several directions on the night King died. But then, so was Noah an unlikely candidate. Or Isaac, who asked: "Does you want de brainiest or the holiest, Lawd?" "I want the holiest. I'll make him brainy." And there was one note, at King's makeshift wake, not heard anywhere in Connelly's play. As one of the mammy types waddled out the front door, she said with matter-of-fact bitterness to everyone standing nearby: "I wish it was Henry Loeb lying there"—handsome lovable Henry Loeb, the city's Mayor, who would later tell me, in his office, how well he liked his Negroes; unaware, even now, that they are not his. Connelly's "darkies" do not hate white people: "the white folk" simply do not exist in his play, which was meant to fortify the Southern conviction that "they have their lives and we have ours," an arrangement convenient to the white and (so whites tell themselves) pleasant for all. The whites get servants, and the blacks get fish fries. That whole elaborate fiction was shattered by the simple words, "I wish it was Henry Loeb." Massah's not in the cold, cold ground. She wishes he were. These people may be Hambones, but not J. P. Alley's kind. They are a paradox, a portent white Memphis still must come to grips with—hambone militants, "good darkies" on the march. When even the stones rise up and cry out, the end has come for Henry Loeb's South.

The signs of it are everywhere—at the Lorraine Motel, where King died; it is an extension of the old Lorraine Hotel, once a white whorehouse. Then, when the neighborhood began to go black, it was thrown to a Negro buyer as, in the South, old clothes are given to "the help." A man named William Bailey bought it, and laboriously restored it to respectability. King stayed there often on his visits to Memphis. It is now a headquarters for the S.C.L.C.'s Project Memphis, a program designed—as its assistant director says—"to make Memphis pay for the death of Dr. King." Yet the Lorraine is run by a man who could pose for "Uncle Ben" rice ads—an ex–Pullman porter who is still the captain of porters at a Holiday Inn. He works for the white man, and does it happily, while he owns and runs a black motel where activists plot their campaigns. "I'm very proud to be part of the Holiday Inn family," he told me. "Why, the owners of the whole chain call me Bill Bailey." That's the Negro Henry Loeb has always known. It is the other side of him—the owner of the Lorraine, the friend of Dr. King—that is the mystery.

King made the mistake of staying, on his penultimate visit to Memphis, at one of the posher new Holiday Inns—in the kind of place where Bill Bailey works, not in the motel he owns. The Memphis paper gleefully pointed out that King *could* stay in the Inn because it had been integrated—"without demonstrations." But the Lorraine is not integrated (except in theory). Neither was the white flophouse in which the sniper lurked. It is good that King came back to the real world, the de-facto segregated world, to die. He was in the right place, after all. Memphis indeed, had taught him to "stay in his place"—a thing it will come to regret. For "his place" is now a command post, a point where marches are planned, and boycotts, and Negro-history classes.

These garbage men are that new thing. Hambones in rebellion—and they have strange new fish to fry. The people who filed past King's body had said no to the whole city of Memphis; said it courteously, almost deferentially (which only made it more resounding); they had marched every day under their employers' eyes; boycotted the downtown; took on, just for good measure, firms like Coca-Cola and Wonder Bread and Sealtest Milk; and were ready, when the time came, to join with King in taking on Washington. Patience radiates from them like a reproach. Perhaps that is why the white community does not like to see them in a mass—only in the single dimension, the structured encounter that brings them singly into the home or the store for eight hours of work. These Negroes seem almost too patient—wrong people for rebels. Yet their like has already made a rebellion. A tired woman in Birmingham was the wrong sort to begin all the modern civil-rights activism; but Rosa Parks did it. King was drawn into that first set of marches and boycotts almost by accident—as he was involved, finally, in the garbage men's strike: "Dat's always de trouble wid miracles. When you pass one you always gotta r'ar back an' pass another."

The buses were late. They were supposed to arrive at eleven-thirty for loading baggage (each man had been told to bring toothbrush, change of underwear, change of outer clothes if he wanted it, and most wanted it). Besides, there had been talk of a bus for teen-agers, who were now giggling and flirting in the dark vestibule (surrendered to them by their elders). Jerry Fanion, an officer of the Southern Regional Conference, scurried around town looking for an extra bus; like all Negroes, he was stopped everywhere he went. Police recognized him, and they had been alerted about the men who would be leaving their homes for the funeral; but they made him get out of the car anyway, and laboriously explain himself. He never did get the bus. Later in the week, the teen-agers made a pilgrimage to King's grave.

Meanwhile, the wives in the Clayborn Temple still did not know whether they could go with their husbands. About eleven-thirty, T. O. Jones showed up, with P. J. Ciampa. Jones is the spheroid president of the sanitation local—a man too large in some ways and too small in others for any standard size of shirt, coat, pants. He is content with floppy big pants and a windbreaker that manages to get around him, but only by being too long in the sleeves and too wide in the shoulders. He is a quiet man in his early forties, determined but vague, who began the strike by going to the office of the Director of Public Works and—when the Director told him there was an injunction against any strike by city employees—changing into his "prison clothes" on the spot.

Ciampa is the fiery Italian organizer who came into town for the union and amused people with televised arguments against Mayor Loeb (who insisted that all negotiations be carried on in public). Jones and Ciampa have lost the list of men signed up for the buses; they don't know how many buses are coming, how many can ride on each. They try to take two counts—of workers alone, and workers with their wives; but it's difficult to keep track of those who wander in and out of shadows, doors, anterooms.

After an hour of disorder, it becomes clear that everyone can fit into the three buses if folding chairs are put down the aisles. T. O. had told me to save a seat for him, but the chairs in the aisle barricade us from each other. I sit, instead, with a sleepy young man who describes the route we *have* to take, and then finds confirmation of his theory, with a kind of surprised triumph, all along the way. The route one travels through Mississippi and Alabama is a thing carefully studied by Southern Negroes. After giving T. O. a check for the bus drivers, Ciampa went back to the hotel. T. O. swung onto the lead bus, and we pulled out.

In the seat behind me, a woman is worried over the teenagers still standing by the church, hoping they will get a bus. "How they gonna get home?" she asks. "Walk, woman," her husband growls. "But what of the curfew?" "What of it?" "I don't trust those police. If I hadn't got on the bus with you, I'd have stayed all night in the church." As the bus rolls through downtown Memphis, on its way South, the woman sees cars moving. "What are they doing out during the curfew? Why aren't *they* stopped?" She knows, of course. Her husband does not bother to answer her.

In our bus, all the animation comes from one voice in the back. A tall laughing man I had watched, in the church, as he moved from one cluster to another, mixing easily, asked to sit beside me while I was still saving a seat for T. O. I was sorry later I had not said yes. As the riders shouldered sleepily into their chair backs, he joked more softly, but showed no signs of fatigue himself—though he had been a marshal all the long afternoon of marching. And as fewer and fewer responded to him, he moved naturally from banter and affectionate insults to serious things: "That Dr. King was for us." The response is a sigh of yesses. "He didn't have to come here." A chorusing of noes. As he mused on, the crowd breathed with him in easy agreement, as if he were thinking for them. This "audience participation" is what makes the Southern preacher's sermon such an art form. I had been given a dazzling sample of it three days before in the garbage men's meeting at the United Rubber Workers Union Hall. That was the day after King's death, and a formidable lineup of preachers was there to lament it. They all shared a common language, soaked in Biblical symbol: Pharaoh was Mayor Loeb, and Moses was Dr. King, and Jesus was the Vindicator who would get them their dues checkoff. But styles were different, and response had to be earned. The whole hall was made up of accompanists for the improvising soloist up front. When he had a theme that moved them, they cheered him on: "Stay there!" "Fix it." "Fix it up." "Call the roll." "*Talk* to me!" "Talk *and a half*." The better the preacher, the surer his sense of the right time to tarry, the exact moment to move on; when to let the crowd determine his pace, when to push against them; the lingering, as at the very edge of orgasm, prolonging, prolonging; then the final emotional breakthrough when the whole audience "comes" together.

Memphis is not really the birthplace of the blues, any more than Handy was the father of them; but these are the same people who created the form—the triple repeated sighing lines, with a deep breathing space between each, space filled in with the accompanists' "break" or "jazz." That is the basic pattern for the climactic repetitions, subtle variations, and refrains of the preacher's art. That kind of sermon is essentially a musical form; and the garbage men are connoisseurs. When a white pastor from Boston got up, he gave them slogans and emotion; but without a response from the audience—he didn't know the melody.

Nor did all the black preachers succeed, or win equal acceptance. The surprise of the afternoon, at least for me, came when an S.C.L.C. delegation reached the hall, and the Reverend James Bevel got up to preach. He and his associates looked almost out of place there amid the "do rags" and scarred ebony skulls; they were immaculately dressed, with educated diction, wearing just the proper kind of "natural" and a beard.

Bevel was the fourteenth, and last, speaker of the afternoon. It seemed that earlier emotional talks would have drained these men of all response left them after the shock of the preceding night. But Jim Bevel slowly built them up, from quiet beginnings, to an understanding of what it means to be "on the case." (This is a phrase he invented a year ago to describe musicians who are perfectly interacting; it is now an S.C.L.C. phrase of wide applicability.) "Dr. King died on the case. Anyone who does not help forward the sanitation workers' strike is not on the case. You getting me?" (They're getting him.) "There's a false rumor around that our leader is dead. *Our* leader is not dead." ("No!" They know King's *spirit* lives on —half the speeches have said that already.) "That's a *false* rumor!" ("Yes!" "False." "Sho' nuff." "*Tell* it!") "Martin Luther King is not—" (yes, they know, not dead; this is a form in which expectations are usually satisfied, the crowd arrives at each point *with* the speaker; he outruns them at peril of losing the intimate ties that slacken and go taut between each person in the room; but the real artist takes chances, creates suspense, breaks the rhythm deliberately; a snag that makes the resumed onward flow more satisfying)—"Martin Luther King is not our *leader*!" ("No!" The form makes them say it, but with hesitancy. They will trust him some distance; but what does he mean? The "Sho' nuff" is not declamatory now; not fully interrogatory, either; circumflexed.) "*Our* leader—("Yes?")—is the *man*—("*What* man?" "Who?" "Who?" Reverend Abernathy? Is he already trying to supplant King? The trust is almost fading)—who led *Moses* out of *Israel*." ("*Thass* the man!" Resolution; all doubt dispelled; the bridge has been negotiated, left them stunned with Bevel's virtuosity.) "*Our* leader is the man who went with Daniel into the lions' den." ("Same man!" "Talk some.") "Our leader is the man who walked out of the grave on Easter morning." ("Thass the leader!" They have not heard, here in hamboneland, that God is dead.) "Our leader never sleeps nor slumbers. He cannot be put in jail. He has never lost a war yet. *Our* leader is *still on the case*." ("*That's* it!" "*On* the case!") "Our leader is not dead. One of his prophets died. We will not stop because of that. Our staff is not a funeral staff. We have friends who are undertakers. We *do business*. We *stay on the case*, where our leader is."

It is the most eloquent speech I have ever heard. I was looking forward, a day later, to hearing Bevel again, before a huge audience in the Mason Temple. He was good—and gave an entirely different speech. But the magic of his talk to the sanitation workers was gone. It was not merely the size of the crowd (though that is important—the difference between an intimate combo and some big jazz band only partially rehearsed). The makeup of the crowd was also different. Those in the Union Hall were predominantly male. Men accompany; women compete—they talk over the preacher's rhythms. Their own form is not the jazz combo, but the small group of gospel singers, where each sister fights for possession of the song by claiming a larger share of the Spirit. In a large place like the Mason Temple, women set up nuclei around the hall and sang their own variations on the sermon coming out of the loudspeakers.

But that night in the bus, there was no fighting the jolly voice that mused on "Dr. King's death." Responses came, mingled but regular, like sleepy respirations, as if the bus's sides were breathing regularly in and out. This is the subsoil of King's great oratory, of the subtly varied refrains: "I have a *dream* . . . *I* have a dream today." He must have been a great preacher in his own church; he could use the style out in the open, before immense crowds. He made the transition more skillfully than Bevel had—and far better than Abernathy does. That very day, the Monday before King's funeral, Abernathy had paused long on the wrong phrases: "I do not *know* . . . I do not *know*." He had let the crowd fool him by their sympathy; he took indulgence for a *demand* to linger. He did not have King's sure sense of when to move.

I suppose I heard thirty or forty preachers on that long weekend of religious eloquence; but not one of them reached King's own level of skill in handling a crowd. That was the mystery of King. He was the Nobel Prize winner and a Southern Baptist preacher; and, at places like the Washington Mall in 1963, the two did not conflict but worked together. As the man in the bus kept saying, "He was for *us*." ("Unh-*hmmn!*") "He was *one* with us." ("That he was." "That he was.")

But King's rapport with his people was not the natural thing it seems now. He had to learn it, or relearn it. The man's voice rose behind us in the bus: "You know what Dr. King said?" ("What?") "He said not to mention his Nobel Prize when he died." ("Thass what he *said*.") "He said, 'That don't mean nothin.'" ("Sho' nuff.") "What matters is that *he* helped *us*." ("Thass the truth." "That *is* the truth." "*That* is.")

In several ways. King was very bright, a quick study. He skipped two grades to finish high school at the age of fifteen. He was ordained at eighteen; graduated from college at nineteen. It was a fast start, for a career that is one long quick record of youthful accomplishment. He got his theology degree at the age of twenty-two. While a pastor (from the age of twenty-five), he got his Ph.D. from Boston University at twenty-six. And he went direct from graduate school to a position of national leadership. His major achievements were already behind him when he became the youngest man (thirty-five) to receive the Nobel Prize. He was dead before he reached the age of forty; and there are constant little surprises in remembering how young he was—as when Harry Belafonte, speaking in Memphis, referred to King as his junior by a year. Was "De Lawd" really younger than that baby-faced singer? And why did we never think of him as young?

He had the strained gravity of the boy who has moved up fast among his elders. That unnatural dignity is in his writing, too, which labors so for gravity that it stretches grammar: "President Kennedy was a strongly contrasted personality . . . trying to sense the direction his leadership could travel." His acceptance speech will not rank with the great Nobel speeches: "transform this *pending* cosmic elegy into a creative psalm . . . unfolding events which surround . . . spiral down a militaristic stairway . . . blood-flowing streets. . . ."

The young King wanted to study medicine. He majored in sociology at Morehouse College. He thought preachers not quite intellectually respectable, though his father and grandfather and great-grandfather had all been preachers. Even when he accepted ordination, he thought he should become a theologian-minister, perhaps a professor, rather than a mere preacher. He took his first parish—in Montgomery—to get "pastoring background" before accepting a teaching post. To the end of his life he talked of turning to an academic career.

But he was never convincing as a scholar. An account of his own intellectual development reads as if it were lifted from a college catalog: "My intellectual journey carried me through new and sometimes complex doctrinal lands, but the pilgrimage was always stimulating, gave me a new appreciation for objective appraisal and critical analysis, and knocked me out of my dogmatic slumber." He was not even a very perceptive commentator on the men who created his doctrine of civil disobedience—Thoreau and Gandhi. When he began the Montgomery boycott, he liked to refer vaguely to Hegel as the prophet of "creative tensions." It was not till someone suggested more likely patrons of nonviolent rebellion that he began referring to Gandhi and Gandhi's American forerunner —*referring* to them— as saints. He never really discusses their philosophy. And his most ambitious defense of civil disobedience—the Letter from a Birmingham Jail, written eight years after the Montgomery boycott—does not even *refer* to Gandhi or Thoreau. Instead, King uses tags from Augustine and Aquinas (hardly anti-authoritarians). Nor does the Letter deserve high marks for logic. It offers as the model of civil disobedience, not Gandhi, but Socrates, the stock Platonic figure suborned for all noble causes, but something of an embarrassment in this context, since Plato makes him preach history's most rigorous sermon against civil disobedience in the *Crito*. The Letter gives three qualifications for a valid act of civil disobedience: 1) that it be open, 2) that it be loving (nonviolent), and 3) that those engaged in it accept their punishment willingly. Then he gives as a historical example of this the Boston Tea Party, whose perpetrators: 1) were clandestine (they disguised themselves as Indians), 2) were armed for violence (they forced wharf guards away and were ready to repel any interruption), and 3) evaded all punishment (Sam Adams and his Committee of Correspondence *dared* England to attempt punishment). Indeed, none of the historical examples of civil disobedience given in King's Letter meets the three requirements he had just set up.

Like Moses, he was not "de brainiest." He only knew one book well—the Bible. It was enough. All the other tags and quotes are meant to give respectability to those citations that count—the phrases sludged up in his head from earliest days like a rich alluvial soil. He could not use these with the kind of dignity he aspired to unless he were more than "just a preacher." Yet the effect of that *more* was to give him authority *as* a preacher. By trying to run away from his destiny, he equipped himself for it. He became a preacher better educated than any white sheriff; more traveled, experienced, poised. He was a Hambone who could say "no" and make it sound like a cannon shot.

It is interesting to contrast him with another preacher's son —James Baldwin. Baldwin became a boy preacher himself as a way of getting out into the secular world. King became a student as a way of getting into a larger world of *religion*, where the term "preacher" would not be a reproach. He needed a weightiness in his work which only that "Doctor" could give him. He needed it for personal reasons—yes, he had all along aspired to be "De Lawd"—and in order to make Southern religion relevant. That is why King was at the center of it all: he was after *dignity*, which is the whole point of the Negro rebellion. His talent, his abilities as a "quick study," his versatility, his years studying philosophy and theology (for which he had no real natural bent) were means of achieving power. His books and degrees were all tools, all weapons. He had to put that "Doctor" before his name in order to win a "Mister" for every Southern Negro. They understood that. They rejoiced in his dignities as theirs. The Nobel Prize *didn't* matter except as it helped them. As T. O. Jones put it, "There can never be another leader we'll have the feeling for that we had for him."

Our three buses had a long ride ahead of them—ten hours, an all-night run, through parts of Mississippi, Alabama, and Georgia. They were not luxury buses, with plenty of room; the Greyhound company had run out of vehicles and leased these from a local firm. One could not even stretch one's legs in the aisle; the folding chairs prevented that. Ten hours there. Ten hours back.

Minutes after our departure, the man behind me said, "We're in Mississippi now." "Oh no!" his wife groaned. It is well to be reminded that our citizens are afraid to enter certain states. The man most frightened was T. O. Jones. He knows what risks an "uppity" Negro takes in the South. He does not give out his address or phone number. The phone is changed automatically every six months to avoid harassment. He has lived in a hotel room ever since the beginning of his union's strike, so his wife and two girls will not be endangered by his presence in the house. "This is risky country," he told me. "And it gets more dangerous as you go down the road. That Mississippi!" We were going down the road.

The lead bus had no toilet, and the chairs in the aisle effectively barricaded it from anyone's use in the other buses. The technique for "rest stops" was for all three buses to pull off into a darkened parking lot; the chairs were folded; then people lined up at the two toilets (one bus for men, one for women). At our first stop, some men began to wander off into the trees, but T. O., sweating in the cool night, churning all around the buses to keep his flock together, warned them back. "Better not leave the bus." I asked him if he expected trouble. "Well, we're in Mississippi, and folk tend to get flustered at—" He let it hang. He meant at the sight of a hundred and forty Negroes pouring out of buses in the middle of the night. "You didn't see that man over there, did you—in the house by the gas station? There was a man at the door." Some had tried to go near the dark station, to get Cokes from an outdoor vending machine. T. O. pulled them back to the buses. He carries his responsibility very self-consciously.

Back in the bus, there was a spasm of talk and wakefulness after our stop. The deep rumbling voice from the rear got chuckles and approval as he mused on the chances of a strike settlement. "We got Henry Loeb on the run now." ("Yeah!" "Sure do!") "He don't know what hit him." Fear is not surprising in the South. This new confidence is the surprising thing. I had talked to a watery little man, back in the church, who seemed to swim in his loose secondhand clothes—a part-time preacher who had been collecting Memphis' garbage for many years. What did he think of the Mayor? "Mr. Loeb doesn't seem to do much thinking. He just doesn't *understand*. Maybe he can't. The poor man is just, y'know—kinda—*sick*." It is King's word for our society, a word one hears everywhere among the garbage men; a word of great power in the Negro community—perhaps the key word of our decade. It is no longer a question of courage or fear, men tell each other; of facing superior white power or brains or resources. It is just a matter of understanding, of pity. One must be patient with the sick.

Henry Loeb does not look sick. He is vigorous, athletic, bushy-browed, handsome in the scowling-cowboy mold of William S. Hart and Randolph Scott. And he has a cowboy way of framing everything as part of his personal code: "*I* don't make deals. . . . *I* don't believe in reprisals. . . . *I* like to conduct business in the open." There is an implicit contrast, in that repeatedly emphasized pronoun, with all the other shifty characters in this here saloon. He even has a cowboy's fondness for his "mount"—the P.T. boat he rode during the war, a loving if unskilled portrait of which hangs behind his desk. (His office biography makes the inevitable reference to John F. Kennedy.)

Loeb is an odd mixture of the local and the cosmopolitan. He comes from a family of Memphis millionaires; he married the Cotton Carnival Queen. Yet as a Jew he could not belong to the Memphis Country Club (he has become an Episcopalian since his election as Mayor); and he went East for his education. A newsman who knows him made a bet with me: "When he hears you are from a national magazine he will not let five minutes go by without a reference to Andover or Brown." When I went into his office, he asked for my credentials before talking to me (he would later boast that he talks to anyone who wants to come see him). Then he asked where I live. Baltimore. "Oh, do you know so-and-so?" No. Why? "He was in my class at Andover, and he came from Baltimore." That newsman could clean up if he made his bets for money.

Loeb did not mention Brown. But he did not need to. As I waited for him in his office, his secretary took the Dictaphone plug out of her ear and began flipping through her dictionary, and confided to me, as she did so, "The Mayor was an English major at Brown University, and he uses words so big I can't even find them." Later, his executive assistant found occasion to let me know that his boss was "an English major at Brown University."

But the Mayor also plays the role of local boy protecting his citizens from carpetbaggers out of the North. He has the disconcerting habit of leaving his telephone amplifier on, so that visitors can hear both ends of a conversation; and when a newspaperman with a pronounced Eastern accent called him for some information, he amused local journalists, who happened to be in his office, by mimicking the foreigner in his responses. When a group of white suburban wives went to his office to protest his treatment of the garbage strikers, he listened to them, then slyly asked the five who had done most of the talking where they were from; and his ear had not betrayed him—not one was a native "Memphian." He has a good ear for classes, accent, background. He wanted to know where I had gone to college. The South is very big on "society."

But Loeb has no ear at all for one accent—the thick, slow drawl of men like T. O. Jones. He knows they haven't been to college. I asked him whether he thought he could restore good relations with the Negro community after the sanitation workers settlement. "There is good understanding now. I have Negroes come to me to firm up communications—I won't say to reestablish them, because they had not lapsed." I told him I attended a mass rally at Mason Temple, where more than five thousand Negroes cheered as preacher after preacher attacked him. "Well, you just heard from a segment of the community whose personal interests were involved. Why, I have open house every Thursday, and just yesterday I had many Negroes come in to see me about different things." Imagine! And Massah even talked to them! And they came right in the front door, too! It is the conviction of all Henry Loebs that the great secret of the South, carefully hidden but bound to surface in the long run, is the Negro's profound devotion to Henry Loeb. After all, look at everything he has done for them. "*I* took the responsibility of spending fifteen thousand dollars of city money—multiplied many times over by federal food stamps—to feed the strikers." *Noblesse oblige.*

The odd thing is that white Memphis really *does* think that —as citizen after citizen tells you—"race relations are good." Its spokesman cannot stop saying, "How much we have done for the Negro" (the Southern bigot is nothing but the Northern liberal caricatured—we have *all* done so much for the Negro). A journalist on the *Press-Scimitar*, the supposedly "liberal" paper in town, says, "We have been giving Negroes the courtesy title" (that is, calling Mr. and Mrs. Jones *Mr.* and *Mrs.* Jones) "ever since the Korean War." (It embarrassed even the South to call the parents of a boy killed in action *John* and *Jane* Jones.) But the executive secretary of the local N.A.A.C.P. was considered a troublemaker when, arrested in a demonstration supporting the strikers, she held up the booking process time after time by refusing to answer the officer's call for "Maxine" instead of Mrs. Smith. ("Why, *isn't* your name Maxine?" one honestly befuddled cop asked her.)

Mrs. Smith is one of the many Negroes who protested the morning paper's use of the "Hambone" cartoon. But she ran up against the typical, infuriating response: "Hambone" was actually the white man's way of saying how much he *loves* the Negro. It was begun in 1916 by J. P. Alley, who—this is meant to settle the question once for all—won a Pulitzer Prize for attacking the Klan. It was kept up by the Alley family (one of whom is married to the morning paper's editor), and Memphis felt it would lose a precious "tradition" if their favorite darkie disappeared from their favorite newspaper—as, at last, a month after King's death, he did; with this final salute from the paper: "Hambone's nobility conferred a nobility upon all who knew him."

Nowhere is the South's sad talk of "tradition" more pitiful than in Memphis. The city was founded as part of a land deal that brought Andrew Jackson a fortune for getting Indians to give up their claims to the site. The city's great Civil War hero —to whom Forrest Park is dedicated—could not belong to the antebellum equivalent of the Memphis Country Club because he was not a "gentleman"—that is, he was not a slave *owner* but a slave *trader*. After the war, however, he took command of the Ku Klux Klan, which made him "society." The Memphis Klan no doubt boasted of all the things it did for the Negro, since it *was* more selective and restrained than the Irish police force, which slaughtered forty-six Negroes in as many hours during 1866. Later in the century, yellow fever drove the cotton traders out of town; and Irish riffraff took over; the municipality went broke, surrendered its charter, and ceased to exist as a city for a dozen years. Then, just as Memphis regained its right of self-government, a small-town boy from Mississippi, Ed Crump, came up the pike and founded the longest-lasting city "machine" of this century. The main social event for the town's "aristocracy"—the Cotton Carnival—goes back only as far as 1931, when it was begun as a gesture of defiance to the Depression: the city is built on a bluff, and run on the same principle.

When Dr. King's planned second march took place, four days after his death, men built the speaker's platform inconveniently high up, so Mrs. King would be standing before the city emblem, above the doors of City Hall, when she spoke. It was meant, of course, as a rebuke to the city. But her standing there, with that background, is henceforth the only tradition Memphis has worth saving.

Yet the city keeps telling itself that "relations are good." If that is so, why was Henry Loeb guarded by special detectives during and after the strike? (One sat in during my session with him; they stash their shotguns under his desk.) Why did some white ministers who supported the strike lose their jobs? Why are black preachers called Communists in anonymous circulars? But the daily papers will continue to blink innocently and boast on the editorial page: "Negro football and basketball players figure prominently in all-star high-school teams selected by our Sports Department." What *more* do they want?

When dawn came, our buses had reached Georgia, the red clay, the sparse vegetation. By the time we entered Atlanta, it was hot; the funeral service had already begun at Ebenezer Church. The bus emptied its cramped, sleepy load of passengers onto a sidewalk opposite the courthouse (Lester Maddox is hiding in there behind *his* bodyguard, conducting the affairs of office on a desk propped up, symbolically, with shotguns). The garbage men who brought their good clothes have no opportunity to change. The women are especially disappointed; the trip has left everyone rumpled. Men begin to wander off. T. O. does not know what to do. He ends up staying where the bus stopped, to keep track of his flock. Some men get the union's wreath over to the church. Others walk to Morehouse College. But for most, the long ride simply puts them in the crowd that watches, at the Capitol, while celebrities march by.

It was a long ride for this; and the ride back will seem longer. The buses leave Atlanta at eight-thirty on the night of King's burial, and do not reach Memphis until six the next morning. But no one regretted the arduous trip. T. O. told me he *had* to go: "We were very concerned about Dr. King's coming to help us. I talked with the men, and we knew he would be in danger in Memphis. It was such a saddening thing. He was in Memphis for only one reason—the Public Works Department's work stoppage. This is something I lay down with, something I wake up with. I know it will never wear away."

A week after the funeral, Mayor Loeb finally caved in to massive pressures from the White House. The strike was settled, victoriously. At the announcement, T. O. blubbered without shame before the cameras. It was the culmination of long years—almost ten of them—he had poured into an apparently hopeless task, beginning back in 1959 when he was fired by the city for trying to organize the Public Works Department. After the victory I went with him to an N.A.A.C.P. meeting where he was introduced, to wild applause, by Jesse Turner, head of the local chapter: "Our city fathers tell us the union has been foisted on us by moneygrubbing outsiders. Well, here's the outsider who did it all, Carpetbagger Jones." The applause almost brought him to tears again: "I was born in Memphis, and went to school here. I haven't been out of the state more than three days in the last ten years. Is that what they mean by an outsider?" A man got up in the audience and said, "When my wife saw you on television, she said 'I feel sorry for that fat little man crying in public.' But I told her, 'Don't feel sorry for him. I've seen him for years trying to get something going here, and getting nowhere. *He* just *won*.'"

When the strike was still on, Henry Loeb, if asked anything about it, liked to whip out his wallet and produce the first telegram he got from the union's national office, listing nine demands. He would tick off what he could and couldn't do under each heading, giving them all equal weight, trying to bury in technicalities the two real issues—union recognition and dues checkoff. When I went to see him after the settlement, he brought out the tired old telegram, now spiderwebbed with his arguments and distinctions. Then he searched the grievance-process agreement for one clause that says the final court of appeal is the Mayor (still built on a bluff). He assured me that, no matter how things look, *he* does not make deals. They really settled on *his* terms. But isn't there a dues checkoff? No. The *city* does not subtract union dues before pay reaches the men; their credit union does (a device the union had suggested from the outset). What about recognition of the union; wasn't that guaranteed? No, it was not. There is no contract, only a memorandum signed by the City Council. Well, is that not a binding agreement—i.e., a contract? "No, it is a *memorandum*" (see how useful it is to be an English major?) "but we have a way of honoring our commitments." The code. Well, then, didn't the union get a larger raise than the Mayor said it would? Not from the *city*. Until July 1, when all city employees were scheduled for a raise, the extra demands of the union will be met by a contribution of local businessmen. *Noblesse oblige*—see what we have done for our Negroes. Will the Mayor handle promised union agitation by the hospital and school employees in a new way, after the experience of the garbage strike? "No. Nothing has changed."

Wrong again, Henry. Everything has changed. The union is here to stay, it will spread: Jesse Epps and P. J. Ciampa and T. O. Jones will see to that. The S.C.L.C. is here to stay: Jim Bevel is in charge of Project Memphis. The city is his case now, and he is on it. A coalition of local preachers that backed the strikers has made itself a permanent organization, Community on the Move for Equality; preachers like James Lawson, better educated than some Brown graduates, are convinced that the God of Justice is not dead, not even in Memphis. Most important, Memphis is now the place where Dr. King delivered one of his great speeches—those speeches that will outlive his labored essays.

The excerpt most often published from that last speech told how King had been to the mountaintop. But those who were there at the Mason Temple to hear him, the night before he died, remember another line most vividly.

He almost did not come to that meeting. He was tired; the weather was bad, he hoped not many would show up (his first march had been delayed by late spring *snows* in Tennessee); he sent Ralph Abernathy in his stead. But the same remarkable people who rode twenty hours in a bus to stand on the curb at his funeral came through storm to hear him speak on April 4. Abernathy called the Lorraine and told King he could not disappoint such a crowd. King agreed. He was on his way.

Abernathy filled in the time till he arrived with a long introduction on King's life and career. He spoke for half an hour—and set the mood for King's own reflection on the dangers he had faced. It was a long speech—almost an hour —and his followers had never heard him dwell so long on the previous assassination attempt, when a woman stabbed him near the heart. The papers quoted a doctor as saying that King would have died if he had sneezed. "If I had sneezed," he said, he would not have been in Birmingham for the marches. "If I had sneezed—" ("Tell it!" He was calling the roll now, talking "and a half," tolling the old cadences.) He could never, had he sneezed, have gone to Selma; to Washington for the great March of 1963; to Oslo. Or to Memphis.

For the trip to Memphis was an important one. He did not so much climb to the mountaintop there as go back down into the valley of his birth. Some instinct made him return to the South, breathing in strength for his assault on Washington, which he called the very last hope for nonviolence. He was learning, relearning, what had made him great—learning what motels to stay at; what style to use; what were his roots. He was learning, from that first disastrous march, that he could not come in and touch a place with one day's fervor; that he had to *work with* a community to make it respond nonviolently as Montgomery had, and Birmingham, and Selma.

It is ironic that the trouble on that first march broke out on Beale Street, where another man learned what his roots were. W. C. Handy did not come from Memphis, like Bessie Smith; he did not grow up singing the blues. He learned to play the trumpet in Alabama from a traveling bandmaster, a real Professor Harold Hill. Then he went North, to tootle transcribed Beethoven on "classical cornet" afternoons in Chicago. It was only when he came back South, and saw that the native songs *worked* better with audiences, that he began to write down some of those songs and get them published.

King, after largely ineffectual days in Chicago, returned to Memphis, the deracinated Negro coming home. Home to die. His very oratory regained majesty as he moved South. He had to find out all over what his own movement was about— as Marc Connelly's "Lawd" learns from his own creation: "Dey cain't lick you, kin dey Hezdrel?" Bevel said the leader was not Martin King. That was true, too, in several ways. In one sense, Rosa Parks was the true leader. And T. O. Jones. All the unlickable Hezdrels. King did not sing the civil-rights blues from his youth. Like Handy, he got them published. He knew what *worked*—and despite all the charges of the militants, no other leader had his record of success. He was a leader who, when he looked around, had armies behind him.

This does not mean he was not authentic as a leader. On the contrary. His genius lay in his ability to articulate what Rosa Parks and T. O. feel. Mailer asks whether he was great or was hamboning; but King's unique note was precisely his *ham* greatness. That is why men ask, now, whether *his* kind of greatness is obsolete. Even in his short life, King seemed to have outlived his era. He went North again—not to school this time, but to carry his movement out of Baptist-preacher territory—and he failed. The civil-rights movement, when it left the South, turned to militancy and urban riots. Men don't sing the old songs in a new land.

Yet it may be too soon to say that the South's contribution has been made. After all, the first two riots in 1968 were in South Carolina and Tennessee. The garbage strike opens a whole new possibility of labor-racial coalition in those jobs consigned exclusively to Negroes throughout the South. And, more important, the Northern Negro, who has always had a love-hate memory for the South, begins to yearn for his old identity. The name for it is "soul."

The militant activists insist on tradition (Africa) and religion (Muslimism, black Messianism, etc.) and community (the brothers). Like the young King, many Negroes feel the old Baptist preachers were not dignified. Better exotic headdress and long gowns from Africa than the frock coat of "De Lawd." But the gowns and headgear *are* exotic—foreign things that men wear stiffly, a public facade. There are more familiar Negro traditions and religion and community. Black graduate students have earned the right to go back to hominy and chitlins and mock anyone who laughs. The growth of "soul" is a spiritual return to the South—but a return with new weapons of dignity and resistance. Religion, the family, the past can be reclaimed now without their demeaning overtones. In this respect, the modern Negro is simply repeating, two decades later, King's brilliant maneuver of escape and reentry. He got the best of both worlds—the dignity that could only be won "outside," and the more familiar things which that dignity can transform. King was there before them all.

He remained, always, the one convincing preacher. Other civil-rights pioneers were mostly lawyers, teachers, authors. They learned the white man's language almost too well. King learned it, too; but it was always stiff. He belonged in the pulpit, not at the lectern. Bayard Rustin, with his high dry professional voice and trilled r's, cannot wear the S.C.L.C.'s marching coveralls with any credibility. The same is true, in varying measure, of most first-generation "respectable" leaders. Some of them would clearly get indigestion from the thinnest possible slice of watermelon. Adam Powell, of course, can ham it with the best; but his is a raffish rogue-charm, distinguished by its whiff of mischief. King, by contrast, was an Uncle Ben with a degree, a Bill Bailey who came home—and turned the home upside down. That is why he infuriated Southerners more than all the Stokelys and Raps put together. In him, they saw *their* niggers turning a calm new face of power on them.

King had the self-contained dignity of the South without its passivity. His day is not past. It is just coming. He was on his way, when he died, to a feast of "soul food"—a current fad in Negro circles. But King was there before them. He had always loved what his biographer calls, rather nervously, "ethnic delicacies." He never lost his "soul." He was never ashamed. His career said many things. That the South cannot be counted out of the struggle yet. That the Negro does not have to go elsewhere to find an identity—he can make his stand on American soil. That even the Baptist preacher's God need not yield, yet, to Allah. God is not dead—though "De Lawd" has died. One of His prophets died.

Esquire, August 1968

Black Panther

by Joan Didion

AROUND five o'clock on the morning of October 28, 1967, in the desolate district between San Francisco Bay and the Oakland estuary that the Oakland police call Beat 101A, a 25-year-old black militant named Huey P. Newton was stopped and questioned by a white police officer named John Frey Jr. An hour later Huey P. Newton was under arrest at Kaiser Hospital in Oakland, where he had gone for emergency treatment of a gunshot wound in his stomach, and a few weeks later he was indicted by the Alameda County grand jury on charges of murdering John Frey, wounding another officer, and kidnapping a bystander. He is now awaiting trial in the Alameda County jail.

I went to see him there not long ago. I suppose I went because I was interested in the alchemy of issues, for an issue is what Huey P. Newton had by then become. To understand how that had happened, you must first consider Huey Newton, who he is. He comes from an Oakland family, and for a while he went to Merritt College. In October of 1966 he and a friend named Bobby Seale organized what they called the Black Panther Party. They borrowed the name from the emblem used by the Freedom Party in Lowndes County, Ala., and, from the beginning, they defined themselves as a revolutionary political group. The Oakland police know the Panthers, and have a list of the 20 or so cars they drive. I am telling you neither that Huey Newton killed John Frey nor that he did not kill John Frey, for in the context of revolutionary politics Huey Newton's guilt or innocence is irrelevant. I am telling you only how Huey Newton happened to be in the Alameda County jail, and why rallies were held in his name, demonstrations organized whenever he appeared in court. LET'S SPRING HUEY, the buttons said (50 cents each), and here and there on the courthouse steps, among the Black Panthers with their berets and sunglasses, the chants would go up:

Get your M-31,
'Cause baby we gonna have some fun,
BOOM, BOOM, BOOM, BOOM.

"Fight on, brother," a woman would add in the spirit of a good-natured amen. "Bang, bang." There were always whites there as well, some of them the cause-proud who had spent all their adult lives shoring up their virtue by passing out leaflets on rainy mornings around Oakland and Berkeley and San Francisco. Others were functionaries of the Peace and Freedom Party (the Peace and Freedom Party got onto the California ballot at about the same time George Wallace's party did), young bureaucrats whose *patois* seemed based exclusively on phrases like "steering committee" and "plenary session" and who, cognizant of the issue Huey P. Newton had become, were talking about running him in the Seventh Congressional District for the House of Representatives.

It was at the night rallies, of course, that the big names came out. James Forman came, and told the Panthers and their black and white admirers that whereas the retaliation they were to extract in the case of his own death should be only 10 war factories, 15 power plants, 30 police stations, one southern governor, two mayors and 50 cops, "for Huey Newton the sky's the limit." Rap Brown came. "The only thing that's gonna free Huey Newton," he told them, "is gun powder." Stokely Carmichael came, and he told them this: "Huey Newton laid down his life for us."

But of course Huey Newton had not yet laid down his life at all, was just sitting there in the Alameda County jail waiting to be tried, and I wondered if the direction these rallies were taking ever made him uneasy, ever made him suspect that in many ways he was more useful to the revolution behind bars than on the street. It was the fact of his being behind bars, after all, that attracted attention, that enabled Huey Newton to give, as he was giving the day I saw him, press conferences. There was a Los Angeles *Times* man there that morning, and a radio newscaster, and we all signed the police register and sat around a scarred pine table and waited for Huey Newton. When he came in, he seemed an extremely likable young man, engaging, direct, and I did not get the sense that he had intended to become a political martyr. He smiled at us all and waited for the tape recorder, and then he smoked and talked, running the words together because he had said them so many times before, about "the American capitalistic materialistic system" and "so-called free enterprise" and "the fight for the liberation of black people throughout the world." His lawyer was there, too, and Eldridge Cleaver, the Black Panthers' Minister of Information. (Huey Newton was still the Minister of Defense.) Eldridge Cleaver wore a black sweater and one gold earring and spoke in an almost inaudible drawl and was allowed to see Huey Newton because he had press credentials from *Ramparts*. Actually his interest was in getting "statements" from Huey Newton, "messages" for the faithful, and every now and then he would signal Huey Newton and say something like, "There are a lot of people interested in the Executive Mandate Number Three you've issued to the Black Panther Party, Huey. Care to comment on that?"

And Huey Newton, like a bright child with a good memory, would comment. "Yes, Mandate Number Three is this demand from the Black Panther Party speaking for the black community. Within the mandate we admonish the racist police force. . . ." I kept wishing that he would talk about himself, hoping to break through the wall of rhetoric, but he seemed to be one of those autodidacts for whom all things specific and personal present themselves as minefields to be avoided even at the cost of coherence, for whom safety lies in generalization. The newspaperman, the radio man, they tried:

Q. *Tell us something about yourself, Huey. I mean your life before the Panthers.*

A. *Before the Black Panther Party my life was very similar to that of most black people in the country.*

Q. *Well, your family, some incidents you remember, the influences that shaped you . . .*

A. *Living in America shaped me.*

Q. *Well, yes, but more specifically—*

A. *It reminds me of a quote from James Baldwin: "To be black and conscious in America is to be in a constant state of rage."*

"To be black and conscious in America is to be in a constant state 'of rage,'" Eldridge Cleaver wrote down then. "Huey P. Newton quoting James Baldwin." I could see it emblazoned above the speakers' platform at a rally, imprinted on the letterhead of an *ad hoc* committee still unborn. As a matter of fact almost everything Huey Newton said had that same odd ring of being a "quotation," a "pronouncement" ready to be employed whenever the need arose, wherever the troops faltered. I seemed to be listening to one of those educational fun-fair machines, where pressing a button elicits great thoughts on selected subjects. I heard Huey P. Newton On Racism ("The Black Panther Party is against racism"), Huey P. Newton On Cultural Nationalism ("The Black Panther Party believes that the only culture worth holding onto is revolutionary culture"), Huey P. Newton On White Radicalism, Police Occupation of the Ghetto, The European *vs.* The African. "The European started to be sick when he denied his sexual nature," Huey Newton said, and his lawyer interrupted then, bringing it back to first principles. "Isn't it true, though, Huey," he said, "that racism got its start for *economic* reasons?"

There was a window between where we sat and the sheriff's deputies at the jail desk, and I had the sense that we were acting out some dumb show for them behind the glass. The small room was hot and the fluorescent light hurt my eyes and I still did not know to what extent Huey Newton understood the nature of the role in which he had been cast. As it happened I had always appreciated the logic of the Panther position, based as it is on the notion that political power begins with the barrel of a gun (exactly what guns had even been specified, in an early memorandum from Huey P. Newton: "Army .45; carbine; 12-gauge Magnum shotgun with 18" barrel, preferably the brand of High Standard; M-16; .357 Magnum pistol; P-38"), and I could appreciate as well the particular beauty in Huey Newton as "issue." In the politics of revolution everyone is expendable, but I doubted that Huey Newton's political sophistication extended to seeing himself that way; the value of a Scottsboro boy is easier to see if you are not yourself the Scottsboro boy. "Is there anything else you want to ask Huey?" the lawyer said. There did not seem to be. The lawyer adjusted his tape recorder. "I've had a request, Huey," he said, "from a high-school student, a reporter on his school paper, and he wanted a statement from you, and he's going to call me tonight. Care to give me a message for him?"

Huey Newton regarded the microphone. There was a moment in which he seemed not to remember what button had been pushed, and then he brightened. "I would like to point out," he said, and I could see how the memory disks had clicked, *high school, student, youth, message to youth*, "that America is becoming a very young nation. . . ."

The Saturday Evening Post, May 4, 1968

"No Man Can Fill Dr. King's Shoes"
—But Abernathy Tries

by Paul Good

MORNING dawned gray in Memphis April 5. Dr. Martin Luther King Jr. had been dead 11 hours, and in the same Lorraine Motel where he was fatally wounded, a squat black man with a broad, dolorous face dictated his speech of accession to the presidency of the Southern Christian Leadership Conference. The Rev. Ralph David Abernathy did not look like a leader at that moment. Numb from lack of sleep, jowls unshaven, he spoke haltingly as some staff members gathered around to help while others drifted off to their private griefs.

"The assassination of Martin Luther King Jr. has placed upon my shoulders the task—" he began. "No, make that 'the awesome task.' The awesome task of directing the organization which he established, which has given—what do we say here—'hope'? So much hope to the black people—to the oppressed people of this nation. Even after 15 years of sharing the struggle with Dr. King, I—I tremble as I move forward to accept this responsibility. No man can fill Dr. King's shoes."

A few weeks later in Selma, Ala., Abernathy was leading S.C.L.C.'s Poor People's Campaign to Washington. He wore two strands of yellow and white African beads. An armband reading "Mississippi God Damn" circled the sleeve of his blue denim jacket. Sweating under the glare of television lights, his expression tragicomic, Abernathy wagged his head and declared to a black church audience:

"Don't ever get it in your mind it was Martin Luther King's dream only. It was Ralph David Abernathy's dream too. So no need of asking me to be Martin Luther King. I never tried to preach like him and he never tried to preach like me. I've been Ralph David Abernathy for 42 years and each time I look in the mirror in the morning I look better and better. I have two little girls and a boy, and they tell me

I'm the sweetest daddy in the world and they wouldn't swap me for Lyndon Baines Johnson. So we better get adjusted to each other. I'm not gonna be anybody but Ralph Abernathy and, Lord knows, with me you're gonna have hell on your hands."

The contrast in attitude from uncertain to bombastic was a measure of the dilemma Abernathy faced as he replaced a revered Negro martyr: how to assert himself while keeping fresh the King legend. For nearly 15 years, he had labored in the shadow of Dr. King. The substance in that shadow eluded the public eye although those close to the movement always understood that Dr. King and Abernathy had achieved a unique human symbiosis. Together the two Baptist ministers had begun the 1955 Montgomery bus boycott. Together they helped found S.C.L.C. For a dozen dangerous and exhilarating years they marched, preached and were jailed together as they cracked the monolith of Southern racism. S.C.L.C. Mobilization Director Hosea Williams, a goateed former truck driver, describes the relationship this way:

"They were just the greatest team, and Ralph was the unsung hero of the civil-rights movement. Martin wouldn't make a decision without him. He trusted Ralph like he trusted Jesus. And Ralph ran interference for Martin, going out to meet a hostile audience so he wouldn't have to, and most times turning it around for Martin. Ralph gave him confidence, security, a strong soul to lean on. On the other hand, he gave Ralph his brilliance, his eloquence and intellectual depth, that charisma the white press is always talking about. Look, he had to be a terribly powerful man to develop this kind of association with the *most* powerful spirit of our times.

"And it showed two days after Martin's death. The S.C.L.C. staff went into a retreat in Hampden, Ga. You read all these press lies about us arguing over nonviolence. It never happened. We were just crushed. And then Ralph talked to us. He was militant and nonviolent and filled with substance. The staff was rising from their chairs as Martin finished and we hoisted him up on our shoulders. There's the dissension you hear about."

He stopped.

"Did I say Martin? I meant Ralph. We all do that sometimes. It touches him."

To the public at large, there seemed no confusion of identity. Comparisons between the two men were inevitable, and on the surface all they revealed were differences. Abernathy is a thoroughly black man where Dr. King was light skinned. Dr. King's speech was polished, his bearing poised and his intellectuality apparent. There is an earthiness about Abernathy from his thick Alabama accent to the informality of his words and gestures. "Bearish" is an adjective commonly applied to him; it fits a voice that sometimes growls and arms that encircle friends in ponderous hugs. Dr. King, for all his radical assault on American racism, was cast in a sophisticated Negro mold that many white Americans found reassuring; it even flattered their own liberal self-image to accept him and his dream. But for many of these same people, it is jarring, threatening when black man Abernathy emerges from the shadows to sloganeer:

"Dr. King wanted to reel and rock and shake the nation until everything fell into place. But under this leadership we're going to turn it upside down and right side up."

"Right side up" often gets lost to white listeners in the rush of applause from blacks. So do the similarities between the two men. Like most social revolutionaries (including Stokely Carmichael), they came from middle-class families. Abernathy's father had the most prosperous Negro farm in Marengo County, Ala., and his 12 children never lacked for food or education. Abernathy eventually earned a master's degree in sociology, an academic notch below Dr. King's Ph.D. in philosophy. Both men became masters of the homily early in their ministries. Dr. King's ran along more erudite lines (Bryant's "Truth, crushed to earth, shall rise again," or Carlyle's "It seems that God sits in His heaven and does nothing"), with Abernathy favoring more homely observations ("If everything is moving smoothly in your life, you aren't doing anything," or "We spend too much time trying to make a living rather than trying to make a life"). But the transcendent similarity between Martin Luther King and Ralph Abernathy lay in their shared belief that militant nonviolence could bring salvation to black and white America.

Their friendship had begun in Montgomery before the epic bus boycott and their nonviolent philosophy grew with it. The vehicle for carrying that philosophy into action was a wondrous machine called the Southern Christian Leadership Conference. No one could be certain precisely how it worked. A ministerial staff grew by accretion around Dr. King and Abernathy, and decisions evolved through group debate with Abernathy's intuitive judgments a strong influence on Dr. King's final authority.

Beyond the inner circle, S.C.L.C. was and is an exercise in organized chaos. The quality of a largely volunteer office and field staff varies wildly, the delivery of telephone messages is a sometime thing and if anyone has ever been dismissed for incompetence, no one can remember who. But through the zeal of its collective leadership, variable support from Southern black churches and financial help from Americans of conscience, it not only survived from its founding in 1957 but achieved some remarkable victories, like the Voting Rights Act of 1965.

However, all past movements—Birmingham, St. Augustine, Selma—were only preludes to a present infinitely more complex and dangerous than confronting a peckerwood sheriff or shifty registrar. The Poor People's Campaign was planned to probe the essence of the American system, to see whether it could make a massive material and spiritual readjustment to change the lives of its poverty-stricken millions and construct a rational future where base poverty would not coexist with stupendous wealth. Shortly before his death, Dr. King confided to intimates his fear that America might not be able to respond to S.C.L.C.'s nonviolent call for change, that it might have to burn. The prevailing national mood, he felt, was to view with alarm the prospect of a few thousand white, black and Indian poor demonstrating in the capital, but to regard with equanimity 35 million poor spread throughout the country.

Still, the staff carefully prepared position papers for Congressional perusal on welfare reforms, a guaranteed income, agriculture practices. Dr. King, aware that nonviolent militancy could be volatile, achieved an accord with Stokely Carmichael and his Black United Front in Washington. Carmichael's forces would not participate in P.P.C., but neither would they disrupt its nonviolent course.

While Carmichael's rejection of nonviolence as an outmoded and discredited weapon precluded any coalition with S.C.L.C., the *entente* demonstrated Dr. King's accelerating search for a *modus vivendi* with militants. His plans for mass civil disobedience in Washington if officials proved unresponsive were decried by organizations like the Urban League and N.A.A.C.P. He was laying his immense prestige on the line, chancing a violent accident or deliberate sabotage that could come from either left or right. Then on the eve of the test he was gone and the leadership he had willed to Ralph Abernathy was inherited in a moment of peril.

Two former staff members, both mature men still dedicated to S.C.L.C., rallied to Abernathy's side. But their evaluations of him differed. One said: "If Ralph tries to cut the mustard by himself, he's going to fail. He lacks Doc's allround abilities, and he's going to have to rely heavily on the staff to see him through. He can't dominate the situation as Doc did, and he must adjust to that fact."

The other said: "The man who held the staff together was Ralph. Dr. King never put out the fires when there was conflict. He'd say, 'Ralph, you do it.' And Ralph would. He has the kind of personality that cuts through disagreements and resolves them. Intellectually, he was far behind Dr. King, but in terms of native intelligence he was way ahead."

As the caravans of the poor started rolling toward their present encampment in Washington and whatever destiny awaits them, the dimensions of Abernathy became a national concern. What was he really like? What had he done? What would he do?

The Rev. Ralph Abernathy's West Hunter Street Baptist Church in Atlanta is bright and handsome with polished pine pews filled for the 10:45 Sunday service by a well-dressed black congregation. The ladies' hats are floral bourgeois masterpieces. The usherettes wear lime green dresses and little white gloves.

Abernathy is leaving for Mississippi in the afternoon to lead a Poor People's march out of Mt. Beaulah next day. He has already baptized new church members at the 7:30 service, beginning a long day. Now his children have come to hear their daddy preach before he goes away. Donzaleigh Avis, 7, is radiantly beautiful with lustrous black hair and her father's soft brown eyes in a tan face. She examines herself in a mirror in the rectory office and, complimented, replies: "I look gross."

The service begins with the processional hymn, "We're Marching to Zion," and before his sermon on "A New Heaven and a New Earth," Abernathy announces that at 3 P.M. he will perform a marriage, the groom a legal counsel for S.C.L.C.

"The news has gotten out," he says, "that when I put you together, you stay put."

The congregation smiles. There is obvious affection between them and their pastor.

His sermon is mostly concerned with the Poor People's Campaign. A listener who has often heard Dr. King preach begins the game of comparisons and then abandons it. Abernathy sets his own rough-hewn style.

"The life of a Christian is a hard life," he preaches. "You must get ready to live dangerously for God. Because if a man has not found something he's willing to die for, then he's not fit to live. . . . Do you know what I'm talkin' about? We're goin' to Washington and we're saying to the President and the Congress, 'We're goin' all the way. We'll bring in all our rats and roaches and we're gonna build a shantytown and call it the City of Hope.' Now some of you middle-class Negroes *don't* seem to know what I'm talkin' about. But let me tell you— you only got out of there about a week and half ago yourself."

Later, when the choir sings "Take My Hand, Precious Lord, Lead Me On," Abernathy raises a hand to his glistening eyes.

The air is turbulent between Atlanta and Jackson, Miss. As the DC-8 falls and rises like a wayward elevator, Abernathy sips a glass of milk and reminisces about the tragedy.

"I had thought they would kill us together," he says. "I never thought the day would come I'd live without Martin. But he always told me they would get him first.

"We had started out of the motel room together, and I went back to get some shave lotion. Before I could put it on, I heard it. I was the first one to him. I patted his left cheek. I said, 'Martin, Martin, this is Ralph; everything's going to be all right.' He knew I was there. He looked at me but he couldn't talk. Still, I'm certain he tried to talk to me with his eyes. He gave me a good, long, solid look as if to say, 'See, Ralph, didn't I tell you it would happen this way?'"

The plane is over Alabama, a state Abernathy says he loves despite its racist antecedents. Childhood was apparently secure and happy.

"I never farmed," he recalls. "I was always reading and writing, and my father gave up on me early as far as the farm went. A stern, wonderful man. I taught Sunday school at 10, but he didn't believe in boy preachers. Still, I knew deep down I would one day end up preaching. I just had to have a platform ready-made. I'm a preacher and I love to preach."

Preaching brought a pulpit at the First Baptist Church in Montgomery, a short while before Dr. King was called to the Dexter Avenue Baptist Church there. Their friendship was already established that day in 1955 when Mrs. Rosa Parks refused to give up her bus seat to a white woman and became the catalyst for America's racial reformation.

Abernathy recalls how the Montgomery bus boycott began with a phone call to him from a Pullman porter named E. D. Dixon protesting Mrs. Park's arrest. Abernathy talked to Dr. King and together they organized the boycott. Each was preoccupied with his religious duties and neither wanted the leadership. Each suggested another man, but at the meeting that organized the Montgomery Improvement Association (the precursor to S.C.L.C.), Dr. King's choice declined and nominated Dr. King. It was amicably agreed on, and Ralph Abernathy took the secondary role as director of programming.

Although he was destined to remain in that secondary role, Abernathy would be the first to be arrested, his home and church destroyed by bombs. But the glory of international renown and a Nobel Peace Prize went to Dr. King. Was there never a twinge of envy during all those years of marching in his shadow?

Abernathy shakes his head.

"You have to understand one thing. We were so honest with each other. No decisions were ever taken without him asking my thinking and vice versa. My wife, Juanita, and Coretta—Mrs. King—couldn't understand it but that's how we worked. I never tried to duplicate him or steal the show.

In press conferences, he'd take all the questions without referring any to me. We just tried to be ourselves and to help each other."

I remember how a former staff member, analyzing the present staff around Abernathy, told me of the camaraderie created by memories of perils and triumphs shared. At the same time, he pointed out that there were often personality clashes between Hosea Williams, militant-minded and only tactically nonviolent, and the Rev. Andrew Young, the S.C.L.C. executive vice president, who had been spiritually and intellectually close to Dr. King. He mentioned the Rev. James Bevel, another member of that inner group, a brilliant tactician with his own highly individual visions of what must happen to America. Could Abernathy control them and prevent a schism now that the unifying presence of Dr. King was gone?

"I'm nothing new to them," he says. "Most of us have been together a long time now. So far, nobody's gone."

Is he convinced that Stokely Carmichael's pledge not to interfere with the P.P.C. in Washington will be honored?

"I love Stokely," Abernathy says. "He's a wonderful guy. A real, likable personality. A brilliant young man. I may disagree with individuals like him on strategy, but not on goals. All I know is we will remain nonviolent."

The plane slips and lurches toward a landing. A down-draft brings it perilously close to trees. Even the stewardess—especially the stewardess—looks frightened. Abernathy smiles at his uneasy seatmate.

"O ye of little faith," he says. "Course, maybe it's easier for me. I know the Man who owns the airspace."

There is a welcoming committee of Negroes at the Jackson Airport who sing: "Who's our leader? Aber-*na*-thy." Before, the refrain had ended, "Martin Luther King!" A fast press conference has been called. The press and television, it seems, have been sniping at the P.P.C.: The Montgomery Advertiser has called Abernathy an "unprincipled and unspeakable bum"; N.B.C.'s Sander Vanocur has been harping on disorganization and hinting at failure. Abernathy is tired now and cranky, and when someone reports that a newspaperman has bet that he will be late for the conference, he growls: "I'm not running a movement for the press."

A TV reporter tells him there has been some "criticism" that the campaign has lost its impetus. Heralded plans for a mule caravan and a Freedom Train appear to be disintegrating.

"The trouble with the press," Abernathy replies, "is, if you try to make things logical, you're always gonna be wrong. A movement moves with the spirit, not with some organizational table."

Abernathy falls into a deep sleep as we drive through the night to Mt. Beaulah, a former Negro junior college outside Edwards that currently is operated as a training center by the militant Delta Ministry. He is still foggy as he enters the meeting hall. The hall is crowded, the ancient wooden balcony seeming to sag under the weight of black youngsters, but for all the crowd the applause for him is mild. Hosea Williams warms up the audience for Abernathy with freedom songs, just as Abernathy used to warm them up for Dr. King with preaching:

> If you miss me from the back of the bus
> And you can't find me nowhere,
> Come on over to the front of the bus,
> And I'll be riding up there.

For a moment, it seems like the old movement of the early nineteen-sixties with its infinite hope. An elderly black man in a cast-off Army jacket and baggy pants claps along, not knowing the words but his eyes shining, and old black women, come in from Mississippi shacks, stomp in time. But it is not the old movement. Now there are black boys in African regalia, some wearing earrings, and girls stunning in their natural hair, and P.P.C. marshals with the armbands reading "Mississippi God Damn." (The official explanation is that God will damn Mississippi unless the state straightens out, but more direct renderings are acceptable.)

The young people, in particular, watch Abernathy closely as he begins to speak, judgment in their eyes. He has come wide awake, loose before this audience, teetering as he slowly builds the intensity of his speech, sometimes plucking at the tails of his suitcoat like a boy reciting.

"They freed us as slaves and promised us 40 acres and a mule. I haven't got my mule. You haven't got your 40 acres. But we're going to Washington to get our mule and 40 acres —plus interest," he tells them.

The audience applauds, then cheers when he says:

"I'm nonviolent, and I don't care much about boxing. But we say to white America: 'We want our black champion back.' We say: 'If you don't want Cassius Clay, then get a white man and let him beat him.'"

That hits the button with the kids and they explode. He follows by talking about the stewardess who served him on the plane, pointing out that she is little more than a waitress. "But the white man gives a white girl like her some dignity," he says. "He dresses her up fine, and gives her a fancy title. But when they put our women in a restaurant, they dress 'em up to look like Aunt Jemima."

This time, the balcony shakes. The press still is rankling him and he good-naturedly chides a TV cameraman about the Sander Vanocur criticism. Inconveniently, the cameraman is from another network.

"You know," he continues, "the press asks me, 'Well, what bills do you want written in Washington?' It's not my job to write bills. My job is to raise questions. Eastland makes $30,000 a year to write 'em and if he hasn't got enough sense to write a good bill, he better learn. But even though it's not my job, lemme tell you somethin'—when they do write the bills they got to write them to *my* satisfaction."

By the time he finishes, Abernathy appears to have won over most of his audience. It is a process he must repeat over and over in the days ahead.

Early next morning, Andy Young stands in a pale sunshine watching the poor people gathering for the short march into Edwards and then the bus ride on to Selma and, eventually, Washington. They have the patience of the poor as they stand with cardboard suitcases and bulging paper bags on a street called Medgar's Way in honor of the slain Mississippi civil-rights leader, Medgar Evers. Young, a bright and courageous man in his mid-30's, left a New York job with the National Council of Churches in 1963 to come South and attach himself to Dr. King. Few persons loved or admired Dr. King more, but now he says:

"At this time, Ralph might be the better man to identify with Negroes. He can get on easily with the militants, his attitude is right. The brothers in the street, or out here, remember things he says, even when they don't know his name or who he is. With Dr. King, it was often the other way around. His language and concepts sometimes sailed over their heads. Ralph can talk the language."

Abernathy appears in blue work denims and heavy brogans, with "Mississippi God Damn" encircling his arm. Another march is about to begin—like so many they had led together. How did he feel?

"It still really hasn't hit me. It hasn't sunk in. I've been so busy, so little sleep. . . . It might sound hard, but there hasn't been time to let myself go. I know what I'd like to do is walk into those pine woods over there and talk to him, commune with him. You share so many agonies, and this morning just to talk to him again would feel good."

He moves to a pair of mules donated by a local black farmer to lead the march. They are promptly named Eastland and Stennis after Mississippi's Senators.

"Come on, Stennis," Abernathy says, grasping the bridle. "Let's go."

The march moves down dirt roads fragrant with sprays of honeysuckle and mimosa, past ramshackle houses where black families cluster, watching, waving. The motion of a march going forward revives memories of simpler days in the movement, when political and economic complexities were not so apparent, and when physically moving forward produced the illusion you were getting some place. Edwards is a stark little town with a few cafes and gas stations. Local Negroes and a few hard-eyed whites have congregated for the big event. Five years earlier—even four years—Abernathy might have been mobbed for what he says from the mule cart:

"That mule there is named Eastland. I didn't know why. Then I found out he's old and forgetful, and he don't even want to carry his part of the load. The other's Stennis. They gave me the task to lead him. Now, Stennis is still full of life. But he's so stubborn. He wanted to get off the road to eat grass. I said, 'All these years, you been leading us around, but today, thanks be to God, we're leading you.'"

Even after the speech has ended and the buses have pulled out, the black people of Edwards are standing around, smiling at one another, shaking their heads over what that preacher Abernathy said.

En route to Selma by car, Andy Young drives part of the way, with Abernathy beside him, while Hosea Williams and Abernathy's white secretary, Terry Randolph, sit in the back. Abernathy goes out of his way to introduce her at all rallies, although S.C.L.C.'s integrated staff is anathema to many black militants. The conversation in the car revolves around church stories; scripture is quoted back and forth—and some tales not found in scripture.

Williams, an enthusiastic if erratic singer, tells how he used to sing his own version of the Lord's Prayer during worship, to the delight of the doting aunt who raised him. Then he entered the Army. Three years later, on his first Sunday home after discharge, the deacon called on him to perform, while his aunt sat beaming. But Williams found his voice register had changed, and he decided to flee after croaking a few notes.

"There was that pot-bellied nigger deacon waiting for me to go on," he says. "And there I was, so ashamed, crawling out of the church on my hands and knees so nobody would see, and my poor old aunt wondering where I went to."

Abernathy laughs along with his two assistants, alleged antagonists in a power struggle. Later, the talk turns to Washington and a questioner reminds Abernathy that for the last two years of Dr. King's life he had never once been invited to the White House by President Johnson. At the same time, conservative Negroes like Whitney Young of the Urban League were regular visitors, were named to commissions and were consulted. Was Abernathy disturbed by this Administration favoritism?

"Oh, no," he replies. "There are lots of paper leaders. But to be a real leader, you have to have people in back of you. If some of these paper leaders want to lead people, let them get out and lead. It never bothered Martin that the White House didn't invite him. He was glad not to go and get compromised for a bunch of tea and cookies. And I feel the same way. It's just another handout.

"Also, you take the way Senator Kennedy and Governor Rockefeller supplied the planes to carry Coretta to Memphis and bring back the body. We're appreciative for what they did. But it takes more than kindness to solve our problems, and attending to the burial of Martin Luther King is not enough to determine who will be the next President of the United States. Kennedy people have already asked me for an endorsement, but I turned it down. I'm not giving my endorsement until I hear somebody's poverty program in detail. And if I hear the right program, this year S.C.L.C. may come out with a political endorsement for the first time in our history."

In Selma, where three S.C.L.C. supporters were murdered in the campaign that produced the Voting Rights Act and where Abernathy and Dr. King shared a jail cell for three days, officials try to limit the march. They back down when Abernathy tells them to get a few hundred jail cells ready because all the marchers are going ahead anyway.

That night, at a church rally, a trumpeter plays a solo, "How Great Thou Art," in tribute to Dr. King. The church where he had preached is silent as the notes pour forth, reverential but laced with a current of blues. Abernathy's face is grim as he begins to speak. He manages a few sentences, but when he tries to refer to Dr. King, the delayed reaction at last hits. His mouth opens, but no words come out. The audience understands and waits. A slow minute goes by—then two, while fat tears run down his cheeks.

An old man in a front pew chants: "Jesus has all power. . . . Lord, keep us together." "Amen," people respond. Finally, it passes and Abernathy says: "It has been so lonely since he went away. But with your help and with God's help we have made up our minds we are going on until victory is won."

It is not so emotional two days later in Boston. Abernathy is making his first Northern excursion. The occasion is a $100-a-plate luncheon at Northeastern University, which raises $15,000 for S.C.L.C. Those gathered include former Gov. and

Mrs. Thomas Peabody, university Brahmins, some latter-day Abolitionists and a sprinkling of middle-class Boston Negroes.

Abernathy is good and late, and he enters preceded by a squad of Boston black militants called the Youth Alliance Patrol. They have come uninvited, but Abernathy blandly accepts their presence. Some carry weighted canes and walkie-talkies, and the leader is swathed in fabric of African design revealing only his eyes, so that he looks a cross between Rudolph Valentino and the Mummy's Revenge. The sensation in the dining room is obvious but it is quickly smothered by proper Bostonian *noblesse oblige.*

Abernathy has brought with him a written speech he had recited the day before at a Y.M.C.A. luncheon in Atlanta. It is a speech without soul—not really a bad speech, but a boring one—and he reads it badly. Its pleas for economic justice and its reiteration of the nonviolent creed all are predictable, and even Abernathy seems bored reading it. He tries an ad lib:

"Unless my mind fails and my tongue cleaves to the roof of my mouth, I will not disappoint you and I will not let America down."

The applause is mild.

A line that always gets a good response in Southern black churches, no matter how often it is used, concerns Bull Connor, the public safety commissioner of Birmingham in 1963, who became a symbol of villainy through his use of police dogs and fire hoses against demonstrating Negroes. "With the knife of nonviolence," Abernathy says, "we took Bull Connor and turned him into a steer."

The diners are not amused.

And when he ends by saying, "Let us walk together, children. And don't get weary. 'Cause there's a great camp meeting in the Promised Land," the lack of response indicates they may choose to miss the meeting.

S.C.L.C. and what is left of the movement obviously are not going to be the same with Abernathy. The bullet that killed Dr. King halved a whole made up of two compatible personalities and left the leadership shorn of an image that had been building for 15 years. What may not be obvious is that Dr. King today would be as much a captive of the times as Abernathy is.

It may not strike certain whites—or Negroes—as seemly when Abernathy puts on African prayer beads instead of a clerical collar, taunts white boxing prowess and does not rebuff the attention of swathed black militants with loaded canes. But Dr. King was being moved in the same direction. Dr. King's prestige would confer a distinction on the deeds, while Abernathy's lack of identity suggests to some that he is pandering to extremists and indulging in demagoguery.

An exquisite and sinister sense of timing removed Dr. King in the moment he had made a peace, of sorts, with Stokely Carmichael, and at the same time had issued a black challenge to the Federal Government and the white nation at large. With the strongest leader removed, a lesser leader like Abernathy elevated, and would-be leaders encouraged to make their bids, nascent black unity could get lost in the shuffle. Small wonder that black suspicions run deep over who really pulled the trigger in Memphis. Many Negroes are convinced, while offering no proof, that the C.I.A. murdered Malcolm X just as he was moving to forge a oneness of blackness. They do not consider it outlandish that Dr. King might have paid the same price for striking a bargain with Stokely Carmichael.

Abernathy plainly lacks—to use the vogue word—charisma. At least, for white people. But this may no longer be relevant, and the disdainful white sniff sensed in the air of the Boston luncheon could work to his advantage. He is a thoroughgoing, straight-talking black man of intuitive intelligence and acquired authority in moving black people. No other black man in America today has his experience or his credentials.

How well he will use his background is impossible to predict, and it is unfair to expect miracles of demonstrated leadership in seven weeks. Past performance may provide some measure and an impartial evaluation comes from John Doar, a former civil-rights trouble-shooter with the Justice Department and a legend in his own right.

"I saw him frequently in the Selma campaign," Doar says, "and while I never sat in on the S.C.L.C. councils, his public judgment always seemed good, tough and sensible. He did not equivocate but said what he thought. He was committed to substantial changes in existing institutions through non-violence. I felt he had compassion and considerable feeling for the little people of the South he was trying to help."

Today, Abernathy's public voice still is uncertain because he is trying to be all things to all people, black and white. But his character suggests that he will settle on something close to that image he sees in the mirror, each day looking better and better to him. How good it looks to old-time allies of S.C.L.C. and those blacks still under the spell of Dr. King is something else. Clearly, he is more at home among Southern black people than he is among blacks or whites in the North.

Muddying any judgment about him is the fact that he has been physically exhausted since April 4, making nonstop public appearances, sometimes contradicting himself, occasionally undermining through blunders the image of dependable leadership he must create. When police attacked marchers in Marks, Miss., for example, he rushed to announce that three marchers had been killed. It proved untrue.

Part of the problem here is that his staff, however loyal, is not protecting him as it did Dr. King from the pitfalls of continual public exposure. He needs an occasional shield, and an occasional respite from making all declarations in the name of S.C.L.C.

Even care for his physical safety has been slack. Two weeks ago, at the Jackson, Miss., airport, he was left alone to park the staff car, and was subjected to verbal harassment from police—and even from a drawling parking-lot attendant. The potential for a dangerous incident was obvious. Dr. King would never have been exposed to such a danger.

This problem probably will be resolved in time as his new role solidifies and staffers make the necessary mental transition, transferring their past solicitudes from Dr. King to Abernathy.

Inside his own organization, he certainly wields unchallenged authority. He is in control of the Poor People's Campaign as well as anybody can control such an amorphous undertaking. Because he is a tougher administrator than Dr. King—who could never bring himself to chastise, much less fire, anybody—Abernathy may reduce S.C.L.C.'s organizational chaos. Inevitably, there will be staff changes. No one will leave until the Poor People's Campaign ends, out of loyalty to Dr. King and dedication to the ideals that brought them to S.C.L.C. in the first place. S.C.L.C. is not General Motors, and no board-of-directors battle is raging. But when a leader like Dr. King goes, balances are upset, not so much along moderate-militant lines as in the more subtle area of personality.

The final question is: Can S.C.L.C. under Abernathy survive as a black force for nonviolence in American life? One crass impediment is money. S.C.L.C. is spending vast sums on the Poor People's Campaign with no guarantee they can be readily replenished. In the past, Dr. King's fund-raising magic always worked miracles of loaves and fishes; Abernathy's skills are untested. Much will depend on his acceptability to the whites who provided the largest share of past financing.

But more critical to S.C.L.C.'s future is what will happen in Washington. Without a significant victory, survival will be difficult. Southern blacks are getting tired of marching miles while change in their lives is measured in millimeters. Most Northern blacks have long regarded nonviolence as an aberration of Southern Christers and are cynical about Washington's ability to respond to the peaceful lobbying of the poor.

So the answer to the question does not rest with Abernathy of S.C.L.C. but with the American essence now being tested in Washington. The Congressional and executive reaction to the Poor People's Campaign—if it reflects the white American majority—indicates that white America has learned little about blacks and less about itself in the past decade of civil-rights activity.

A recent photograph in the New York Times showed antiriot troops being trained at Ft. Gordon, Ga. Some of the units are probably on call for Washington duty today, should the poor people demonstrate. The photograph depicted a group of "enemy" demonstrators being assaulted by antiriot troops. Lest there be any confusion in identity, the mock enemies carried a placard. The slogan it bore was not "Black Power" or "Up the Vietcong." It was the title of a hymn that

Dr. King and Ralph Abernathy had sung a thousand times together and that the President of the United States had quoted twice in an address to Congress:

"We Shall Overcome."

The New York Times Magazine, May 26, 1968

THE BLACK PANTHER PARTY: JUNE 1968

from

A Special Rage

by Gilbert Moore

THERE was a distinct click on the line the first time I tried to telephone Eldridge Cleaver; it was the familiar sound of a wire-tap being engaged. A peculiar feeling comes from knowing that you are speaking to at least two people when you choose to speak to only one.

Eldridge, as I expected, was not home, but Kathleen, his wife, invited me to stop by. The Cleavers lived then on Oak Street in San Francisco. As instructed, we rang the downstairs doorbell three times. Kathleen peeped out of the window from three floors up, and I suppose that photographer Howard Bingham and I looked unforbidding enough so she let us in. Upstairs she apologized for all the cloak-and-dagger, but they had to be careful she said because the pigs were closing in. I nodded casually as though I knew perfectly well how it felt when "the pigs were closing in."

Their living room was dominated by a grand wicker rattan chair and floor-to-ceiling shelves of books—Fanon, the *Autobiography* of Malcolm X, *The Confessions of Nat Turner*, Dostoyevsky, Sartre, Mailer, Baldwin, *Black Rage*, *The Economic Transformation of Cuba*, among many others.

Kathleen sat on the wicker chair and handed me a folder full of newspaper clippings. She seemed so thoroughly in command of her movements, with elegant black boots hugging her legs to the knees and reddish-brown hair coiling to majestic heights above her head. And yet in another moment she looked so very frail, the belt around her waist drawn to its thinnest girth, her face looking so very soft. She was very young; twenty-three really is very young.

We didn't catch up with Eldridge until the next day. He had so many appearances to make that neither he nor anyone around him was ever quite sure where he would be from one

699

moment to the next. Anyway, we got to the Berkeley campus just in time to watch him leaving the podium before a crowd of three hundred cheering students. He looked tall and mighty in the familiar black leather jacket and boots and the beginnings of a beard, but the thundering blackness of his clothing and dark glasses was softened by a beige turtleneck sweater and tiny multicolored beads around his neck.

I told him who we were, what we had come for. (Howard, meanwhile, had assumed his wide-angle crouch position and had begun shooting.) Eldridge smiled and nodded his tentative approval to our presence, but the hopeless feeling came over me that I was addressing an oak tree.

Abruptly he asked me: "Have you ever written about the black liberation struggle, man?"

And with as much authority as I could summon on such short notice I said, "Yes, of course I have." The moment froze, and we simply walked side by side to his car with nothing else to say to each other. He was too busy with his own private thoughts and I with mine.

We returned to the Berkeley campus the next day. The Berkeley City Council was holding public hearings to determine whether the Black Panthers, the Peace and Freedom Party, the hippies, the Yippies and assorted student groups against the war in Vietnam should be allowed to hold an outdoor rally on July 4. Bobby Seale was there. Three watchful Panthers were standing around him as he awaited his turn outside the campus building to appear before the Council. Seale looked as though he hadn't slept in a week. His hair was uncombed; his gaunt face was heavy with fatigue. Good photograph! I nudged Howard, who raised his camera about to shoot.

"You not taking no pictures in here—mother*fucker*," a voice behind us said. We spun around to confront another Panther. He couldn't have been more than eighteen, but his voice had all of the raspy authority of an Army master sergeant. Howard whipped out his press credentials. In his haste to show that he was "clean," his hand obscured half of the press pass. The visible portion read: "Los Angeles Police Department."

The Panther was astonished. "You a pig?" he asked. "Now I *know* you not takin' no pictures 'round here."

Bobby Seale came over, smiling. "It's all right, brother," he said to the young Panther.

"But these cats are pigs, Chairman Bobby. They—"

"No, it's okay," Bobby said.

"If you cats are gonna be taking pictures," Bobby warned us later, "better watch your step. These brothers are not playin'."

The main office of the Black Panther Party was then a cramped store front on Grove Street in West Oakland, sandwiched between a tiny soul-food joint and an alley. A huge poster of Huey Newton stared at you as you walked in. Signs on the walls reminded the membership that alcohol or the drinking of it was not permitted on the premises. Nor would the presence of any form of narcotics be tolerated. Signs also reminded the membership that it was time to intensify the struggle and that power grew out of the barrel of the gun. Another sign demanded strict adherence to party rules:

1. No party member can have narcotics or weed in his possession while doing party work.

2. Any member found shooting narcotics will be expelled from this party.

3. No party member can be drunk while doing daily party work.

4. No party member will violate rules relating to office work and general meetings of the Black Panther Party, and meetings of the Black Panther Party anywhere.

5. No party member will point or fire a weapon unnecessarily at anyone other than the enemy.

6. No party member can join any other army or force other than the Black Liberation Army.

7. No party member can have a weapon in his possession while drunk or loaded on narcotics or weed.

8. No party member will commit any crimes against other Black people at all, and cannot steal or take from the people; not even a needle and a piece of thread.

9. When arrested, Black Panther Party members will give only name and address and will sign nothing. Legal first aid must be understood by all party members.

10. The Ten Point Program and platform of the Black
Panther Party must be known and understood by each
party member.

The telephone rang constantly. There was a sister seated at
the cluttered desk to answer all the calls. Periodically she
would come outside to inquire whether anyone had seen
"Chairman Bobby" or "Captain David." Like her male fellows
she wore black and powder blue and a rifle shell dangled from
a chain around her neck. All telephone conversations ended
with her saying "Power to the people!" or "Panther power!"

There was the loud screech of automobile tires coming
from outside the office. An enormous yellow chariot pulled
up to the curb. A man of about thirty-five sprang out of the
freshly polished Cadillac. He wore the conventional Panther
uniform, complete with beret and dark glasses. He had a limp
in his right leg. He was introduced simply as "Captain
Crutch." It amazed me that Captain Crutch looked so out of
keeping with his fellow Panthers with his show of "middle-
class decadence," brazenly parked curbside, and, what was
more, his head was (as we used to say) "gassed." Where was
his proud Afro haircut? I wondered.

We shook hands, whereupon he frowned impatiently and
said, "We don't shake hands like that, brother. You better get
yourself together." And then he demonstrated: a firm conventional handshake first, then a kind of upturned handshake,
grasping thumbs, then another ordinary handshake, then a
grasping of fingers, of shoulders, ordinary handshake again,
then a snapping of fingers . . . it was an old African tribal
ritual. I decided then that in the future I would use the first
three steps, which struck me as adequate enough a fraternal
greeting, and that I would skip the rest.

"See that fine yellow bitch over there?" Captain Crutch
asked. "I got that when I was pimping. Now I use her in the
struggle. She serves the people now."

The Black Panther political education classes for that area
were held in St. Augustine's church, the Episcopal church in
the black community of Oakland. Thirty brothers and sisters
attended the class on this first day that I went. They were as
young as sixteen. They were as old as forty-seven. They en-

tered the church variously laughing, talking, reading. Each of them carried a tiny red volume—the Red Book, the *Quotations from Chairman Mao Tse-tung*. In an orderly procession they each took a folding chair from the corner rack, placing them in classroom-style rows of five and six. At the table in the front of the room sat the conductors of the class, David Hilliard, then National Headquarters Captain, and George Murray, Minister of Education. They were going to deal today with the *Catechism of the Revolutionist* by Mikhail Bakunin, a contemporary of Karl Marx, Minister Murray said.

And the brothers and sisters listened attentively to learn what their attitudes as revolutionists should be:

The revolutionist is a doomed man. He has no personal interests, no affairs, sentiments, attachments, property, not even a name of his own. Everything in him is absorbed by one exclusive interest, one thought, one passion—the revolution. . . . He despises public opinion. He despises and hates the present-day code of morals with all its motivations and manifestations. To him, whatever aids the triumph of the revolution is ethical; all that which hinders it is unethical and criminal. . . . The nature of a real revolutionist precludes every bit of sentimentality, romanticism, of infatuation and exaltation. It precludes even personal hatred and revenge. Revolutionary passion having become a normal phenomenon, it must be combined with cold calculation. At all times and places the revolutionist must not be that towards which he is impelled by personal impulses, but that which the general interests of the revolution dictate.

They were also going to get into what Chairman Mao had to say about "liberalism," Minister Murray said. Captain Hilliard reminded the brothers and sisters that in coming up to address the class they should not be ashamed or afraid to use their own words and the language they were used to.

And according to Chairman Mao, what is liberalism?

One young brother thought he had the answer. He was only eighteen and new to the party, but he seemed determined not to look eighteen and new. On his way up to the front of the class he tucked his shirt in and glanced at his proud "Free Huey" button to see if it was straight.

"There's lots of different kinds, different types o' liberalism," he began. "Like say I come into the party with another cat and we been friends, we been tight for a long time and we're still tight and I see this cat breaking the rules o' the party. Like say I see him smokin' pot or somethin' while he's workin' for the party. If I don't say somethin' to the brother about it, tryin' to stay tight with the cat and if I don't bring the thing up with somebody else in the party, it would be bad for the cat and bad for the party and bad for the people and jus' bad for everybody. And if I acted like that, Chairman Mao says that I would be 'gaging in a type of liberalism."

The young brother paused to gauge reaction to his performance before returning to his seat. The class approved and voiced their approval: "Right on, brother, right on!"

After that meeting in the church I began to wake up. After reading more, in the Panther paper, I began to wake up:

Black people have already judged you, America . . . and have condemned you to death. And we also know that history has selected us, your slaves and chief victims, to be your executioner, the instrument of your destruction. . . .

Read on, read on.

What a laugh! America the beautiful. Home of the brave. Friend of the underdog. You once had a beautiful dream—but even then, while you dreamed that dream, you were foul and corrupt and rotten in your heart, but you were a minor league brigand and then when you compared yourself to the tyrannies in the world, you looked innocent by contrast to their greater evil. The innocent blood they had shed was a vast and ancient ocean, and yours was a fresh new stream. But now your little stream has become vaster than the sky and your evil dwarfs everything that has gone before. Now you stand naked before the world, before yourself, a predatory, genocidal Dorian Gray, stripped of all egalitarian democratic makeup. . . .

America, you will be cleansed by fire, by blood, by death. . . .

Now how do you make that palatable to the readers of *Life* magazine? How do you make that palatable to potato farmers in Idaho and little old Presbyterian ladies in Massachusetts and construction workers in Pittsburgh? And isn't there an enormous absurdity about your even trying?

I began to look for soft chinks in the granite. Sometimes I found them. "We do not claim the right to indiscriminate violence. We seek no bloodbath," Eldridge once said to me.

"The Panthers is a political organization; it's a third party.

The Republican Party, the Democratic Party, we find, do not answer the desires of black people. We find it necessary to create a third party—or really we think of it as a second party because there's not very much difference between the Republicans and the Democrats." Huey Newton himself said that once in an interview, and wasn't that a pretty mild thing to say?

But for each soft chink I found there were ten cold nuggets of steel to offset them. There was absolutely no way that I could tell everything I was learning about the Black Panthers and somehow make it digestible to America. The realization was slow in coming, but it was coming.

from *A Special Rage* (1971)

"Keep on A-walking, Children"

by Pat Watters

I HAD decided during the week after they killed Dr. King that I would go to Washington for the Poor People's Campaign—whenever it would be they wanted white people there. What prompted me to go was not my respect for Dr. King's life, the special feeling that Southerners in the civil rights movement had for his style and spirit. It was not even the sense of our loss, or the knowledge (never to be shaken) of all the hope—Southern and, in the way of Southern hopes and lost causes, naïve—which had been destroyed. In those nightmare days of the spring of 1968, I felt too despondent or too angry for these motives to have much force. Acting out of numbness, I went to find out what would happen now, what there was left to hold onto, what the future of the civil rights movement could possibly be.

There was a time of strong hope that what Dr. King preached—his grandly universalist faith in mankind, couched in a Southern Negro Baptist idiom—might, if not prevail, at least enter and renew the core of American culture. At the very least, the greatest of the Southern nonviolent demonstrations (and most of these were organized not by his SCLC, but by SNCC and CORE) had dramatized for the nation, like a man teetering on a high wire, the precarious course that American democracy had now taken, the fateful tension between the spirit that Dr. King preached and the spirit of obscene violence attracted to these demonstrations. The bullet through John Kennedy's brain signaled the breaking point of the teetering balance. From then on, violence—obscene violence—became more and more dominant, and the spirit that Dr. King embodied progressively declined until the bullet that destroyed him made us recognize that it was defeated. (I make a distinction about violence, calling "obscene" the kind which has come to prevail in the American psyche: a hysterical objectiveless, morbid, unrealistic, *neurotic* violence, in quality much the same as the Southern racist violence I happen to know well.)

Our poets know about the killing of the spirit of nonviolence, the capture of America by the spirit of obscene violence —especially those whose medium is journalism, whose muse is paranoia. They have told it, like the Old Testament prophets, over and over in the course of filing their suspicions, their distrust, their theories of national and international conspiracy. Whether the intricate webs of facts and surmises by which they weave their poetry are in themselves true or not is irrelevant: it is the metaphor these poets of paranoia make that holds the truth, and the nation, in its avid reading of all this stuff about Oswald, Garrison, etc., in its enthusiasm for the play *MacBird!*, knows the truth of that metaphor. The CIA, it is often said in their poetry, engineered the assassinations, as it has engineered violent events around the world, for its own ugly purpose. This purpose, in sum, is to make prevalent and permanent in this land the spirit of violence whose medium is the Cold War, whose rationale is that there is a strategy, an ideology, more important than all and any human life, and whose ultimate obscenity is nuclear holocaust. True, not true —in the factual sense? Who is to say? True, metaphorically? Look about you. When they killed Robert Kennedy, when that obscene spirit killed him, if it said anything at all, it said: do not even allow yourself to hope, against all evidence, just to hope there might be chance for something else, for the spirit embodied in the words, the efforts, the life of Dr. King.

And when the time came to attend the sad finale to his efforts, the Poor People's Campaign, there was no longer even any of the rage I had intermittently felt; nor the idea of going there not as a journalist but as a participant—white, Southern, middle-aged, middle class, without ideology, really, not radical only radically angry—to show them, by God, they just couldn't get away with it, couldn't kill what Dr. King stood for. That was gone. For the knowledge was there, underscored by the assassination of Robert Kennedy, that they had indeed killed it, that it was gone in this nation, and that violence, obscene violence, nuclear violence controlled.

*

So when I arrived in Washington on June 18, it was with much the same feeling that has hung over the liberal establishment for some time now, and has spread to those varieties of left-of-center people who had thought they were better than the liberals: numbness, let us call it, weariness, the sense of going through the motions because there is not even energy enough, will enough, to call a halt, to say no more of this, it is hopeless. I had not understood this malaise in the liberals before, seeing diabolical motives in their willingness these past several years to keep on trying all those obsolete methods—study groups, pilot studies, conferences, papers—in situations that demanded drastic action, certainly not more words. But now I was in Washington, a notebook in my inside coat pocket, though stuck there indecisively. I had always gone to these events as a reporter—first as a newspaperman, later as a representative of the Southern Regional Council and its small magazine, *New South*. The Southern Regional Council is a civil rights organization whose role has been mainly fact-gathering, setting the record straight rather than direct action. Normally, I had worked with the conviction that trying to tell the truth had importance, could make a difference. But this time I didn't know that I would act even as a reporter, knowing that I wouldn't participate as a marcher—would perhaps just stand around, observe, absorb the full meaning of the thing.

"This will be the whimper," a friend who had observed a good bit of the Poor People's Campaign heretofore in Washington during the spring and the summer had said, "with which the Movement will die." I had once before just stood there and taken in the full impact of an event. That had been John Kennedy's assassination. Until a month before I had been a newspaperman for eleven years, and when the flash came from Dallas, my every instinct was to get up from my new job, rush out, and begin putting together a story. Instead I had to sit there and just feel what had happened. Journalism is a cold and callous calling; out of the necessity to get the news while it is breaking, the best workers have a conditioning and an ability to divert all the energy of their emotion into the skills of gathering information and writing it coherently. Sometimes this can be a blessing.

My notes on the three days in Washington reflect my inner ambivalence; they are fragmentary, disinterested, without passion. (On the first view of Resurrection City: "A-frame huts. Mud. Handball mud-encrusted in the middle of mudhole. Sewage pipes in mud alongside ditch. Mess tent: dried mud on plywood floor. Sign: 'Please Brother, Clean Up.'") I was neither participant, fully feeling observer, nor reporter. On the eve of the Solidarity Day march, I stepped out of the Dupont Plaza (not the best of hotels but luxurious enough to make ludicrous the notion that I was there in solidarity with the starving children of Mississippi). Over in Dupont Circle a demonstration was being formed, a line of maybe two hundred ready to go, an even mixture of white and black, mostly young, excited, even ebullient. They were a contingent of the National Welfare Rights Organization, a group recently formed to organize welfare recipients. A young Negro had given fliers to a good-looking girl, and he was trying to get the older guy beside her on the bench—in a business suit, frowning, shaking his head—to take one of them. "At least read it, get both sides of things," he was saying to the man. Conditioned by what I had read and heard of the Poor People's Campaign, the Black Power attempts at bullying the Indians and Mexicans, conditioned by encounters with Southern varieties of Negroes emancipated into an ability to express racial animosity, bad manners, or strong-arm predilections, I had been walking warily amid this crowd of demonstrators, as among Southern whites at a Citizens' Council meeting or a straight political rally. I was waiting for one of those ugly, defeating episodes of inane nastiness which has become the coin of all social intercourse in our cities and has spread finally into the nonviolent movement that Dr. King founded. But here this young Negro, proffering his flier about welfare rights, was smiling, was sincere, was simply trying to get the guy to read the thing—truth in open encounter. The guy kept refusing it; the Negro looked at the girl, who was dutifully glancing over hers. "He with you?" he asked, as though she could do something about the other's intransigence, but she only nodded, sloe-eyed, smiling up. No intimidation here, nor white guilty fear. Just people. (In the next two days I would keep coming back to Dupont Circle—

a circle of sanity, a place of the future where people might just be people.)

The line had started moving out, cops all over the place directing it, with gaps every twenty people or so. I asked the young Negro where they were going. "We are going to have dinner with Wilbur Mills," he said, his accent Northern. The Welfare Rights people had just gotten to town for the march the next day, and were taking the opportunity to embarrass the member of the House of Representatives they held most to blame for their many, I am certain, just grievances. Mills lived, he said, about a mile away. I was to meet some friends who might be able to fill me in on Resurrection City; since I was going in the same direction, I fell in behind a segment of the march, my notebook hidden.

It was a good-natured crowd moving along the sidewalk, and the residents of the area (a lot of them, I was to learn, Washington's hippies and students) seemed to welcome the diversion of the demonstration and to support the marchers. But after we got about a block, the cops intervened and began to hold things up. I stood around awhile, and got to thinking it would be this way at every intersection, and felt impatient, then felt how futile it was to try to embarrass a man like Mills who would measure any such effort down to the most minute calibers of power, and conclude quickly that here was no threat, no power, that could affect him. ("Congress Wake Up To What's Going On," said a big sign.) So I left the march, not having really joined it, and went over to the next block and watched it from each parallel intersection. An old crazy-hair lady stood alongside it at one intersection, hands on hips, not liking it at all. One of the friends I was to meet was watching it outside the restaurant, and we stood together as it went by, a segment singing weakly, "Ain't goin' let nobody turn me 'round," one young man throwing his whole soul into the song, his thin shoulders squared, head thrown back, his pinched face suggesting the fanatical college student drawn inevitably to the Movement, but his close-clipped, home-style haircut belying this, suggesting that he was a bona-fide welfare recipient. "Ain't goin' let nobody turn me 'round," and it occurred to me that nobody much but the crazy-hair old lady seemed to want to, she now moving on by us, muttering, stopping to pick up a bit of paper littered there by some bad citizen, then dropping it angrily, as she would like to drop the demonstration, in a garbage can. Later, I read in the paper that some of these demonstrators were arrested, in some technical contretemps with the cops over where it was improper for them to be.

There had been a familiar feeling about that walking out of the hotel into a demonstration. It was like arriving in Selma or Albany during Dr. King's direct-action campaigns, the plunging from the gray world of everyday into a world where everyday wrongs had been disinterred, brought forth for confrontation, the demonstrations a focus for seeing what is ordinarily not seen, for making tension and conflict the norm of every day (often every hour), as in a battle. Washington has known some of this, I thought, with the Poor People's Campaign. But then I learned that the march I had stumbled on was a rarity, not the minor skirmish I had supposed.

Much of the malaise afflicting Resurrection City, I was also to learn, stemmed from the lack of action for people who had come for a crusade of direct action. It was not the much-publicized mud, which was no different from niggertown alley mud, fragranced with garbage and excretion whenever rain comes in the South; no worse than ghetto filth. Nor was it the social pathology said to be stalking the encampment at night—sped by wine, drugs, and other torments. Nor was it even the cruel and heartbreaking irony of the discovery in the muddy misery of the place that their own "brothers" named to the role of security police, given clubs and power over them, became suddenly the beasts that all white cops were known to be. No, none of these. We know even from the pale empathy of print that the culture of poverty contains all of this and worse, and has its mechanisms—not only brutalization, the blunting of sensibility—whereby people deal with it, even as the culture of affluence contains its own versions of viciousness and has its martini mechanisms for coping. It was the lack of action that had sent so many away, back to familiar mud, and hunger and crime and *idleness*. The capacity of Resurrection City was three thousand. At the peak of occupancy around May 20, about a month after Dr. King's murder, there were 2650 residents, and many more had been turned away. By the time of the Solidarity Day march, there were no more than eight hundred people left. Some had gone home; others had drifted off to the Washington ghetto; nearly all remaining were Negro, with maybe twenty or twenty-five whites, mostly from West Virginia, some from Chicago, still dwelling among them. Indians and Mexican-Americans, out of bureaucratic ineffectiveness, out of dismay at conditions, and out of hostility from the Negroes, never had lived in any number in Resurrection City, but had encamped in nearby schools and churches. Of 125 Indians who came, no more than fifteen or twenty were still there for Solidarity Day; of four hundred Mexican-Americans, two hundred were left.

Idleness, maybe we will come to know from the Poor People's Campaign, is, along with hunger, the bane of the poor. Robert Coles has written of an organizing instinct in the human mind which tries to impose a routine on the days of idleness, of nothing to do, of purposelessness, among the starving people of the rural South. Murray Kempton, standing about with reporters (in our isolation) at Resurrection City, spoke of that sense of disorder that comes upon the ghetto, upon individual souls in the ghetto as afternoon starts, as the hope of the morning dies and the realization sinks in that here is another day wasted, another day that will come to nothing; this is the time that the wine-drinking starts, the pathology begins to stir. How much of what had moved the poor to far-off, unfriendly Washington, to Resurrection City, I now asked myself, was merely the hope of something to do, a surcease from futility? (They go, said my good friend who had helped recruit them in rural Alabama, because they know that things at the campaign can't be any worse than back home. We both had thought it was only food that they hungered for.)

Occasionally during those long weeks a demonstration would be announced on the rarely idle loudspeaker system of the "City," and people would bestir themselves, begin to build a life of a day on the announcement, getting ready, girding themselves. Then there would be delays and falterings, and usually the thing would be called off. But more often, there would not even be the announcement of a demonstration. The people were getting enough to eat (although the fine plans for three hot meals a day never were realized; not always, even, was supper hot). From an adequate diet there was unaccustomed energy. But the energy was not used, was frustrated.

The few "good" demonstrations that had occurred stood out in the memory of those involved; they hinted at what might have been. There had been the time, about two weeks before Solidarity Day, when everyone was together. The march was on the Justice Department to protest the unconstitutional arrest of Mexican-American youngsters in a Los Angeles school walkout. Mexican-Americans were at the head of the march, behind them, whites, and then blacks. There was a driving rain. The singing, the solidarity defied the rain, and for the moment defied Washington—shook a mighty fist at all its alien grandeur and haughtiness.

So the little march that I saw on the eve of Solidarity Day was a big thing, and I suppose I should have known this merely from having seen the physical setting of Resurrection City, the reification of all the South's niggertowns, the Northern city ghettos. I had earlier in the day walked down one side of it, up the other. They had finally laid a trail of planks and plywood through the mud, leading by the huts of habitation, the larger huts of headquarters and officialdom, and the gathering places, like Martin Luther King Plaza—a wooden platform from which Dr. Ralph Abernathy made his pronouncements. I notice that I headed my notes "Tent City," a nostalgic slip, harking back to the desperate little enterprise of 1966, in Lowndes County, Alabama, where Negroes evicted from the land for attempting to register to vote took refuge in tents and sought in vain to call attention to their plight. There were other unsuccessful Southern antecedents. Strike City in Tribbett, Mississippi, was a tent encampment for the farm laborers who in 1965, in a grandly hopeless gesture against the law of supply and demand, attempted to bargain collectively with the planters. And then there was the Tent City, also in 1966, set up in Washington itself, a little band of the dispossessed and hungry people who had tried to take over an abandoned air force base in Greenville, Mississippi, and had been efficiently carried out of it, old folks and little children, by the United States military.

Our time is expanded, broadened out, filled almost to the bursting point with event; that was all two and three years ago as time has been measured since antiquity—linearly—but how many years of antiquity's slim pacing of event? It seems like a decade, even a century ago. When that Washington Tent City was encamped on Lafayette Square, the newly formed Citizens Crusade Against Poverty was holding a poor people's convention—incongruously, indeed surrealistically—within the luxurious confines of the International Inn. In one of the first public displays of the unruliness and just plain undeservingness of the poor (there was considerable comment in the liberal press), the delegates there, led by some of the toughest of Mississippi's grass-roots Negro leaders—which is to say some of the most misused and lied-to people in the world—set upon such speakers as Walter Reuther with boos and catcalls and an alarming disregard for parliamentary procedure. How long ago, how far back in our innocence; we were sorry the President and the nation and its Congress didn't respond to those various tent cities. But we had other things going; the Poverty Program seemed so hopeful, founded in the notion that the poor, with proper direction and encouragement, could democratically rid themselves of the taints and defects that prevented them from sharing in the affluent society. There was little thought then that it was the society itself that was tainted and defective.

Tents are honest temporary shelters. Somehow, plywood built into the shape and size of tents has no honesty, no integrity. A man is not demeaned by having to bend over to get into a tent; he does so for the sake of being able to strike the thing in the morning and go on his way. But permanent plywood tents press down on the soul, bend heads and shoulders toward indignity. Middle-class mindlessness designed and built those abominations and set them down on lawn grass with the same insensitivity that housed a crusade against poverty in a plastic and glass-bubble modern motel, and with the same deadly unrealism that expected democratic procedures, used against the poor a million times, to sustain them, to hold up under them.

Resurrection City itself felt like an African village seen in the movies—that sense of imperfect planning conveyed by the huts, of an unknown communal culture, perhaps more sociable than ours, with black babies waddling barefoot in the mud. There also was a feel of the South, the porch somebody had incongruously stuck out in front of one of the huts, three men seated on it, chairs tilted back to the plywood wall. And there was a sense of the circus—controlled chaos, the big top soon to rise—the same as there was on the Selma to Montgomery march produced by the essential Americanism of Dr. King and the metaphors of protest he had projected.

Little groups were gathered in discussion, one felt endless discussion: tableaux of black young men, a white in their group; or two whites sitting on their haunches; or an old garrulous Southern Negro woman talking at once to everyone and no one. There was hostility toward the stranger—the white, the besuited, unbearded with press tag affixed, notebook out in the open—but mostly I was struck by the aloofness of these people, the demand that their privacy in this place be respected. There had been the time when, as a reporter, I would have, without second thought, moved among such people, talked with them. In part I would have done so simply because I was interested in them, glad of the chance to meet them, to hear what they had to say, to share a common view. That part had been genuine and good; but there had also been another, not very pretty part: the unspoken, maybe even, for some of them, unrecognized enactment of a mutually demeaning ritual: of my eliciting, their showing, the pathos, the tragedy, the ugliness of their situation, and the humor and braveness and beauty of their response: this to be put down in my notebook, to be filled out, built up, bodied forth in quotes, the alive words of suffering people for the American consumers of words, of authenticity, of real human material. No more. Or at least not here. The people had apparently been exposed too much in Washington to the truth of how little America cares about their humanity. So they do not speak to the straight stranger, nor look at him, even in the intimacy of the one waiting while the other negotiates a single plank through a mud puddle. Or they show contempt by demanding a cigarette or money.

I remember my shock, the first upsetting of my conditioned expectations of the Movement Negroes of the South, and most of all, of SNCC, when in the summer of 1964, Freedom Summer, I went into the SNCC-run office of COFO in Jackson, Mississippi, and had a Negro youth ask me for money. That was not the way the Movement had been run heretofore; there was too much mutual respect for that sort of thing, despite my expense account and good living made out of writing about the Movement, despite their poverty and their beyond-belief braveness. I had not learned then to be aware of the implications of our relative positions, their incongruity in the real meanings of that movement to which we were both devoted; and he had not learned that begging might have utility beyond the momentary need for money, that begging by such as him from such as me could be an exquisite insult. For a time the activists of the Movement accepted those white Southerners (and there were damn few of them) who were able to support direct action. In this context, some of us, reporters and others, developed a sort of proprietary feeling about the Movement; we liked to advise and criticize it, using as a standard those best and most beautiful moments of it that we had seen. Sometimes we could be relevant and constructive; but sometimes our attitude degenerated into that of the connoisseur—carping and superficial. In any case, the Movement's penetration to ever deeper and more painful truth about American society has ended this rule. We have come a ways since, that long-ago kid at COFO and myself.

Wordlessly, I handed out cigarettes to three young black men before one of the huts, and we all four lit up, and I tried to think of some way not to get just a quote. I could not. They read my press tag. (I had decided to wear it out of dread of some mean, stupid scene with the security police.) One of the young men said, "Tell the truth about us when you write." I had heard that so many times from the whites in the South; there was no longer any shock at hearing it, too, from Negroes, and with probably more justification, but again renouncing the old politeness, the old mutual respect that had been so pleasant. "He can write anything he wants to," another of them said, turning, disgusted, cynical, bending his head down to go into his hut. "It's a free country."

An old Negro man, from the South, from the country, unlearned in or maybe too wise for blanket hostility, the gratuitous, meaningless insult, asked politely for a cigarette, and then went on to say that he was praying for rain on Solidarity Day "so all them visitors can get baptized in our mud." He laughed, and I laughed. Maybe he was paying for his cigarette in the old unconscious ways with a quote. Maybe he wasn't. But it was like old times.

There was a faint sense in Resurrection City of a struggle of wills, of the constructive and, let us say, softer side of humanity against the harsh and destructive. A dribble painting executed with skill on a hut's outer wall was carefully signed. The God's Eye Bakery was dispensing hot brown bread and apple butter to all comers, straight strangers even, with a joy in the goodness of it. At the Child Care Center, a large, three-room plywood construction with a blessedly squared-off roof, not cramping down on the children, there was a sense of purpose, of busy people. Crayon and fingerpaint art was all over the walls; children were moving about in the random way of preschoolers; a sign on the wall said to take a free toothbrush. A boy of about five in a corner cried all the woe of his time in life, and one of a number of pretty, mud-stained white girls went quickly to him, knelt to him, comforted him, ended sitting on the floor and engaging him in some game. Two middle-aged, middle-class local Negro women were in charge, both with experience in professional day-care work. They talked of their thirty-five charges, including some infants, in that gentle way—not condescending, nor pitying, but more nearly awed—that their middle-aged, middle-class counterparts in the Child Development Group of Mississippi speak of theirs: these selfsame bright-eyed little kids flowering forth their potential, their beauty, freed for a time from torpor and listless quarrelsomeness by the advent in their lives of one hot meal a day.

Back outside, an old white man with dancing eyes began to

talk of the greatness of America, that it could produce such a thing as Resurrection City. Another of his kind interrupted a conversation of a beautiful young woman with straight black hair, high cheekbones, and tan skin, a Negro professional civil rights worker who had been assigned to work with the Indians. She had been telling how every time an Indian got singled out for any role of leadership he was immediately discredited with the others, and she was saying, as the old man hove up, "I'm just a token Indian." "No, no," he reassured her. "You're an Indian—" as though nothing could be worse than what she really was. He went on his way, had an afterthought, returned to tell it. "If it weren't for the Indians, we wouldn't have this country, would we? We stole it from them."

Shortly before they killed Dr. King, I heard that he had been made hopeful once more by the success in recruiting the other races for the Poor People's Campaign; he regarded it as evidence that his dream of welding all the poor together could be achieved. There had been little enough during the past few years to encourage him. His organization (if the scattering of outposts and individual preachers across the South could be called an organization) and funds had shrunk. His Chicago adventures had been near disasters (the old tactic of exposing at its most vicious the normally hidden brutality of segregation had worked as dramatically in Chicago as it had in the South, but there was little willingness in the nation even to acknowledge the brutality it was shown, let alone act upon the Northern ghetto problems). His influence in the White House was long since gone, the condemnation of the Vietnam war having ended all contact. He had been badly used by Stokely Carmichael *et al.* during the Meredith March of 1966, his presence having drawn the press and thus given the leaders of the Black Power schism a national platform as well as a stalking horse for their new doctrine. Finally, Dr. King and his movement undoubtedly had been hurt by the riots in the Northern ghettos. Almost nowhere in the South had there been anything like them.

We know in the South (from the beginning of our lives) that it is insanity we fight when we oppose racism, when we exercise our civil liberties. You handle insanity as delicately, cautiously as you can, not out of political moderation or humane feeling, but out of self-preservation. This was at the essence of the strategy (as distinct from the philosophy) of Dr. King's nonviolent movement. To have that self-preserving caution, that pitting of the sane against the insane, suddenly blown up by outbursts of an answering insanity from the ghettos must have been to know anguish and despair of an exquisite kind. Back in 1965, Bayard Rustin had stated with Southern clarity the case against black violence when he remarked of the new breed of black militants: "They think [Malcolm X] can frighten white people into doing the right thing. To believe this, of course, you must be convinced, even if unconsciously, that at the core of the white man's heart lies a buried affection for Negroes—a proposition one may be permitted to doubt." Not the least of the reasons Dr. King found himself in Memphis in the fateful spring of 1968 was the pressure on him to show, as in a staging ground for the Washington campaign, that nonviolent demonstrations could still be achieved, could resist the agents and impulses of the riot insanity. And of course the insanity did arise, preparing the ground for that more effective, lethal white variant of it that ended his life.

Naturally enough, in the process of all the vicissitudes of recent years, Dr. King's headquarters staff had shown signs of demoralization. Unlike the old SNCC and CORE, Dr. King's organization had always had a tendency toward soft middle-class living. I remember my innocent shock (the same connoisseur's shock of being panhandled by a SNCC kid) at overhearing a big SCLC leader in 1963 in Albany, Georgia, where the demands on the people for sacrifice and suffering were great, speak of dreading to go into the heat, the noise of the nightly mass meetings which the people loved so much, this being his form of sacrifice and suffering. There were other men of power on the SCLC staff of whom there was universal agreement among us bystanders that SCLC, Dr. King, and the Movement would long have been better off without. There was never any hint that Dr. King would get rid of such men. Ralph Abernathy was to show a similar disinclination: some said it was because Mr. Abernathy felt more comfortable around such men, lesser men than himself, than around the lean, aggressive younger activists who came back to SCLC for the Poor People's Campaign. I don't think this motive was ever part of Dr. King's tolerance for them. I think that in a way so genuine it was innate with him, he believed in the good, the positive in all men to a degree that made of little significance to him those gradations in demonstrated goodness—or more to the point here, ability—by which the rest of us judge individuals. His leadership was to draw the best from each man, not seek better and better men. This is the *ne plus ultra*, of course, of radical leadership, a concept ancient enough, but in our time of *surplus* human beings, an entirely alien one.

After his death, reports came from the spontaneous drawing together in grief of his staff, from their staff meetings, a retreat they held, that there was to be a renaissance of the old movement spirit, a renewed unity and dedication. Everything one now heard in Washington about the staff seemed to deny this, or to indicate a deterioration of the new spirit. The most public criticism was that of the unwillingness of the staff to live in the squalor of Resurrection City. There were gleeful reports of a bill of at least fifteen thousand dollars run up by the staff at the motel where most of them stayed. More devastating to the effect of the campaign was the confusion of command, the absence of leadership and authority which developed in Washington, manifest in the failures to get demonstrations going, to satisfy the hunger for purposefulness in the poor people. The style of the Southern movement had always included a fine little bit of chauvinism, a deliberate baiting of the Northern fetish for efficiency. In all its major campaigns, SCLC had indulged this indifference to routines and planning to dangerous degrees. Apparently in Washington it got out of hand. Previously it had been the defect of a greater virtue—a spontaneity that provided energy, morale. Now it seemed the expression of collapsed morale from whatever wide variety of causes among the individuals on the staff.

Thus, the connoisseur of the Movement might make his pronouncements and judgments, like a literary critic or sportswriter. The press is expert at this; the Poor People's Campaign has been subjected to it everywhere, from *The Village Voice* to

Business Week. What do any of us know of the real forces at work on any group, any organization, any collection of people, even on that most intimate grouping of all, our own families? What happens to the men who make such a movement? I speak of hopelessness. What do we know of the dimensions of hopelessness (or hope) in a man at the head of a demonstration line in the Black Belt South marching into the face of his worst childhood fears? I remember Dr. King's inarticulateness in Albany during one of the first arrests there: the words, the inspiration, the incredible bravery coming that time not from him but from one of those he led, seeking the best in them—an unlettered country preacher falling on his knees in the street, praying in the breath-gasping, ungrammatical idiom of his religious tradition, inchoate, wild-sounding prayer, pulling the demonstrators to his own exalted state.

I do not presume to judge, then, or even to insist that these surface things I have told even begin to explain what happened to the Poor People's Campaign. It is fair and accurate to report, though, that on the eve of the Solidarity Day march, no one was hopeful, no one was predicting, from the performance of SCLC in the simple mechanics of organizing for such an event, much of a crowd. It will be the whimper, my friend had said. It happened, though, that I had had occasion the previous week to be reading a random assortment of out-of-town papers, and I had been struck with how nearly all of them—in the South, New England, Pittsburgh, such places—had their little stories saying a thousand from here, a busload from there, were getting themselves ready to go to the march. Apparently much of this was spontaneous, with no great organizational effort behind it—a minister here, a Negro leader there, getting it up. So I had a hunch that the crowd would be better than anyone had a right to hope; and through the hot morning, watching the people gathering around the Washington Monument, seeing them steadily coming, like so many picnickers, I felt some little sense of satisfaction, and, seeing such a quietly ordered and decent-looking crowd, I found myself, in an old reflex of the Movement's magic, beginning to hope. We had counted crowds so many times, the numbers in a church, the size of the demonstration, as though to find some mystical, magical number, as though to quantify the miracle occurring before our eyes was somehow to solidify it, certainly Americanize it. The essence of Dr. King's movement—perhaps like that of his people, the Negro South—derived more from the East than the West: spiritual, indeed mystical, involving the absorbing of the individual in the will and consciousness of the many, just as his demonstrations made use of methods and mechanisms not much drawn on anymore in the West— singing, chanting, religious exaltation. I can still see Claude Sitton of the New York *Times* running up and down the line of the demonstrations in St. Augustine, Florida, sweating in the balmy, tropical night heat, counting the number that was willing, incredibly, night after night, to march to the town square and get beaten with clubs and steel pipe and bicycle chains, and then be arrested for their pains. It was important to get the exact number. During the morning in Washington people kept saying, "How would you estimate the crowd?" "Would you say fifty thousand?" We had sat up late the night before, talking, dolefully talking, as we had so many nights since the assassinations, and the hangover I had was like so many since then, indeed one big one since then, a hangover of impotent grief and anger that would not sweat away in that godawful morning of Washington humidity. So I tended to be short with my stock answer, that I don't think it's possible to estimate a crowd, that if you can't count them (count their legs and divide by two, we used to say), then you just don't know, and it becomes a guessing game, an issue of contention between those who are for the crowd and those against it. Sure enough, the next day, Ralph Abernathy called a press conference to quarrel with the Washington *Post*'s estimate of fifty thousand.

Less was said about the quality of the crowd. There was, as always at these things, the most recent one having been Dr. King's funeral, the sense of being at a reunion, or convention, the seeing and greeting and talking with members of a community who came from all over, mostly up and down the Eastern seaboard—people with ties to the Movement, with mutual memories. Occasionally, one of them would say of the day's crowd that—yes, it was different, different from that great, joyous throng in 1963 in Washington, for example.

Some would say that it was better—younger, more serious. Others would say it seemed lifeless, hopeless, going through the motions. I couldn't tell. My notes at one point say flatly, "not young predominantly, not poor—the same kind of middle-class, well-intentioned, naïve crowd that has always turned out for these things—maybe even more whites than there used to be."

The crowd flowed slowly around the Washington Monument. At the base, one of those inevitable "entertainment" sessions went on, with maybe half the crowd gathered around it. Pete Seeger sang, the good Southern idiom of "The Crawdad Song" ("You git a line, I'll git a pole . . . We'll go down to that crawdad hole . . .") ringing out over the more than ordinarily inhuman loudspeaker system. There is a verse to "The Crawdad Song" that Seeger understandably refrained from using: "Yonder comes a nigger with a sack on his back; yonder comes a nigger with a sack on his back . . . Got more crawdads than he can pack . . ." There is a spirit in which that verse can be sung which would not be offensive to Negroes, Southern Negroes, a spirit of white and black sharing subtleties of humor, the anomaly of a nigger ever having more of anything than he can pack, the humbleness of that creature, the crawdad, diminutive cousin of the lobster, capable in the tradition of turnip greens, pigs' snouts, of being cooked into exquisite fare, as in crayfish bisque. We have not seen the time, even that joyous time of the March on Washington in 1963, when such an explanation could be broached to such a crowd. We shall not likely see it, ever. To try it even in print is to risk offending good people and court the contumely of various kinds of fools, including Black Power ones. And yet—who wants to live in a land where you can't try to say the unsayable?

In the headquarters tent, around noon, I watched Ralph Abernathy being greeted, hugged, posed for pictures, being treated like a potentate by various old friends of his, and new ones. He looked tired, as Dr. King used to look during these climaxes of his adventures in innovative political action. Ralph Abernathy is a likable man, more so on the level of how-de-do, haven't seen you in a long time, than Dr. King ever was.

I always admired his preaching. He gets a tone of the sardonic and at the same time of Elizabethan, Gargantuan outrage into his voice that is eloquent; it sang for a while in his speech later in the day. His children and Dr. King's have been among the tiny token of desegregation at the grammar school where my children go; he and I sat together one PTA meeting and listened to his daughter and my son and two of Dr. King's youngsters in a choral group on the stage singing "Dixie." We looked at each other, shook our heads, laughed. I watched him and Dr. King once in Albany, going to all the Negro dives and poolrooms to plead that there be no repetition of the previous night's disruption of a demonstration by throwing bricks at police. That was in 1962, and in those innocent, pre-Northern riots, pre-Black Power times, the plea prevailed; in these encounters, we reporters, connoisseurs, agreed, Abernathy, of the two men of God down among the sinners, had the surest common touch, was the most effective. It was said that much of the ineffectiveness and the doldrums in Resurrection City stemmed from a flaw in the command system which demanded that he make every decision, however minor, although he was nearly always unavailable, caught as now in talk by handwringers and hangers-on. Be that as it may, the march was, true to form, to cliché, going to be late.

When, finally, the Reverend Jesse Jackson got the march officially under way, fully half the marchers had already ambled the short distance of its course across the green and alongside the reflecting pool to the Lincoln Memorial. With marvelous ability to ignore this plain reality, Jackson was officiously instructing who should be where in the march—the Resurrection City residents first, the Mule Team people (their mule team in some bureaucratic snag left across the river in a Washington suburb) second, etc.

I noticed, ambling along the march route, that many of the Resurrection City residents were sitting it out in the familiarity of the shade of their huts, some of them standing along the fence, looking at, even talking to the marchers. There was a clear division: the march was in one tradition (that of the old, lately lamented coalition of white liberals, labor and religious figures, and Negro sacrifices, the former unable to deliver such crucial items as votes but ever able to bargain, the latter depended upon to deliver whatever was demanded—votes, lives); Resurrection City was in another tradition, one that was done with coalition. "We marched at Selma, 1965, Washington, 1968," said what may have been the saddest of all the hand-lettered signs on the plywood of the A-frame huts. A button to complement it was worn by a middle-aged, middle-class lady, innocent of innocents: "Think Poor."

The dust, the crowding, the heat were worse than even in the morning's hangover dread I had imagined. Finally I sat down in some shade, apart from all of it; there were maybe a hundred of us along there. They played "The Star-Spangled Banner." I stood up. I always have, though never since the age of twelve, I reckon, with any meaning in it. Maybe six others in our shade did too.

About this time two buses marked "Congressional Delegation" pulled up, and I watched the occupants descend from their air-conditioning right into the worst of the heat and crowdedness. To a man, they stood a moment, staring down at what they (and there were precious few of them) had come here to be part of. I watched their faces—these politicians' faces, whore-trained to simulate any desired emotion—one after the other falter and fall for an instant into honest expressions, mostly of dismay, a few of panic, fear. And then I watched Senator McCarthy arrive. He had given us the first faint, fitful start of real hope since the assassinations with the news that morning of the New York primary returns. The Secret Service men and the soldiers were scurrying before and after him, their heads swinging unnaturally fast in sweeps of observation, scanning like electronic instruments for killers. McCarthy's face as he scurried along was all twisted, maybe squinting in the glare—but maybe showing his distaste for this ritual of his arrival, along with all the rest of ritual which he has so eloquently disdained.

When Humphrey arrived a little later, they booed him. It was one of the few good moments. Another was when a large group, more than a hundred, did their marching through the length of the reflecting pool, waving their signs, clapping, singing the old Movement songs, "Sing A-men . . . Amen . . . Amen. Amen. Amen." They were refreshed, alive—having fun. The filthy water sparkled in their hair.

I ran into John Lewis, who was the old SNCC's brave, gentle leader. Of all the young activists who were inspired by Dr. King (SNCC sprang full-grown from the belly of an SCLC conference), Lewis was probably the closest to him in spirit and in a still unfaltering ability to accept each person as he is, on his own terms. More than one automatically ironic reporter was to note that the famous words that were stricken from John Lewis' speech at the 1963 march would have been pale beside the inflammatory idiom of this day's speeches. One reporter somehow got into print in a paper that should have known better the comment that John Lewis had become in the years since that 1963 speech entirely respectable, a man who now wore an Ivy League suit. He always had. I remember seeing him, still dazed, still in pain, wearing such a suit a few days after the most spectacular of his countless brave acts: he and Hosea Williams leading the march that tried to cross the Edmund Pettus bridge in Selma, and was beaten back and trampled by Alabama troopers and other savages on horseback. John Lewis had been with Robert Kennedy, had talked with him just before they killed him. His grief, as it had been over Dr. King, was terrible to see. I had somewhere in one of those long days of all our grief snarled out, "Why in the hell doesn't somebody put a bullet through the brain of one of theirs, the worst of theirs," and John turned on me, as harsh as I ever heard him speak, and said, "Hush that kind of talk. We're sick—sick with violence." This most hopeful of all the men I have known in the Southern movement spoke of going to this march but not expecting much. I had seen him during the morning. He confided that he had noticed a lot of bureaucrat types in the crowd, the kind who come to anything only as a command performance. "It wouldn't surprise me," John Lewis said wistfully, "to see the President show up."

A sign, "Jobs Or Income For All," had been abandoned, stuck on its flimsy stick in the middle of a mud puddle. I made notes: a big Negro man with a hand that dwarfs his sign stick: "America Why Not Now?" A stooped middle-class white woman, kerchief on her gray head, a bearded kid behind her, a gray-haired priest, a solemn Negro man, hand on hip, head bent, listening to Roy Wilkins, four girls sitting in grass, the day's dust coating their mini-skirts, an elderly nun, a middle-class Negro woman with glasses on a chain around her neck, a white mother and son eating sandwiches, a news cameraman asleep. A banner proclaiming that Ripon Republicans Join Poor People's Struggle is held by three young men, somehow looking fresh in their business suits, like a television commercial. A Negro man from out of the Washington wilderness paces slowly with his sandwich board: "I am the true prophet. This land is going to be bombed with nuclear. This is the end for the nations of Christianity. This is the meaning of doom's day."

It was the alienated young, in all their modes of hairstyle and dress, who got to me most: a tall young Negro in a robe, his happy discovery of a style really expressive of himself, a princeliness, ferociousness formerly denied him; or the young in Resurrection City in all their brooding privacy and silence. They stirred buried sources of anxiety I didn't know I had. I began to feel that this nation was going off the track. I had been reared in the surly listlessness of the Southern Depression, had come of age in the hysteria of World War II, had matured in the Southern civil rights struggle, had witnessed the insurrection of the white South after the 1954 Supreme Court decision and Dr. King's counterrevolution. But here in Washington I felt for the first time that the orderly path, those parallel lines between which our struggles had been confined, seemed certain always to be confined, twisting and turning, moving forward and backward, those lines that seemed so certainly, so permanently drawn—really could be ripped apart, torn away, and new ones drawn. Perhaps they would be more stirring lines, but they would lead through the air there in Resurrection City, all of that nameless hostility. Knowing the Southern darkness, the murderous insanity that had created this hostility in its image and now awaited it, lips pursed; considering the sad inevitabilities of revolution; considering some of the psychological specimens I had known of the nucleus of the New Left in the South; considering that being *under* thirty no more assures a sense of consequences than being Negro or white does, or being poor, I felt a fear of the future like none I had ever known.

The speeches were as dull, as remote from the reality of Resurrection City as the routine program designed them to be. There was the usual gossip among the connoisseurs about the mighty power struggle going on within SCLC, exemplified by Mrs. Coretta King's taking so much time for her part of the program (her speech was acutely intelligent, her courage and beauty that had shown through all the obscene spectacle of the assassination's aftermath on display once more). Such talk of power struggles trailed Dr. King through his career, struggles that seem integral to any organized effort of Southerners, white and black, their zest for exaggerating the ordinary maneuverings of clique and faction in any human endeavor being one of their more debilitating traits. By far the best of the speeches was the fiery tirade of Reies Lopes Tijerina, by all accounts a monomaniac, centering on lands swindled from his ancestors: "I stand before the eyes of the world to accuse the United States of America of organized criminal conspiracy against my people. I accuse the United States of cultural genocide against the Spanish-American people. . . . I accuse the U.S.A. of violating all the human rights of the people of the Southwest." The ellipsis marks one of those lapses into the ludicrous, the noting of which proved irresistible to some of the best of reporters covering the Poor People's Campaign, stimulated as they were by all the incongruities of American society's disparate body of castoffs, misfits, not-neededs: Indians whose ancestors practiced slavery denouncing it, Negroes cheering Mexicans in denunciations of the Supreme Court. In the counts of his indictment Lopes Tijerina accused America of slaughtering sixty million buffaloes to divide the Indians into poverty and genocide.

But the dominant presences, haunting the event, hovering over it, were not the suffering poor but the martyred dead. *Their* theme was played in endless variations by the crowd, the man in a business suit festooned with buttons as big as saucers in memory of John F. Kennedy and Martin Luther King, Jr., a family grouping, grandparents to babies, sitting under a tree with their homemade sign propped up that said "This Family Believes in That Dream," and that displayed magazine photographs of both Kennedys and Dr. King. Ralph Abernathy in his oration at the end of the day evoked the memory of a few of the many lesser-known martyrs: "four little girls in the Sunday School of the Sixteenth Street Baptist Church in Bir-

mingham, Alabama, died at the hands of a mad bomber. . . .
We met with some success in Selma. But it cost us the lives of
Reverend James Reeb, Mrs. Viola Liuzzo, and Jimmy Lee
Jackson. . . . Medgar Evers was murdered, and hundreds of
unknown black men sleep in the bloody soil and waters of the
Southland." Over it all, looking down on it with his mourn-
ful, gravedigger's face, was the first martyr of them all, the
seated Lincoln.

Dr. Abernathy's speech was probably the best he has ever
made. But by the time the program wound its weary way to
him, it was evening and at least half the crowd had wandered
away: many, no doubt, back to their air-conditioned hotels
and motels to sanely watch the program wind down on television; the people from Resurrection City were nearly all back
in the heat and stench and mud of their turf. Those who had
remained were mostly unheeding, sunk in the heat torpor.
The program, I realized, had been built on the old model
that accommodated Dr. King—building up slowly, lengthily,
to his appearance, last on the program, longest to speak. But
Dr. King was a celebrity they would wait to see; Dr. King was
an orator capable of pulling back the long-since-wandered attention, reviving energy, bringing to climax and fruition all
the day's walking, talking, weary waiting, all the day's emotion. Dr. Abernathy could not evoke this excitement; he remains a preacher, one of the best in the Negro Southern
Baptist tradition of virtuosity, but he is no celebrity. Who
even heard what he had to say out there in the weary
afternoon heat, his preacher rhythm ringing all kinds of nu-
ances out of his words, like early jazz: "We have been taught
by two hundred and five years of bitter experience that we
cannot trust the leadership of this nation. We cannot trust the
elected representatives of Congress. We cannot trust the administration—whether Democratic or Republican—to fulfill
the promise to the disinherited. . . ."
And who in the restless crowd there was listening, even
when the moments of thunder came: "I see nothing in my
Bible about the riches of the world or this nation belonging
to Wilbur Mills or Russell Long; nor do they belong to General Motors, the grape growers in California, the cotton kings

in Mississippi, and the oil barons in Texas. But I read in my Bible that the earth is the Lord's and the fullness thereof, and there is no need of God's children going hungry in 1968."

Who listened to Dr. Abernathy say: "I will not sink so low as to imitate the very worst of white Western civilization violence. The United States Government is the leader of the violent movement in the world. They believe in fire power. . . ."

Maybe the poets of paranoia were listening. Maybe the seated Lincoln, who had his own powerful prophetic style. A nation cannot survive half slave, half free. Nor can an individual. Yet that was precisely our predicament, we out there in the innocent, unaware middle-class crowd, just as much as the most beset citizen of Resurrection City. We talk about economic intimidation of Negroes in the Black Belt. But consider as well the poor young devil, white and privileged, graduated by the skin of his teeth a few years before from a second-rate college, with two babies and a third on the way, a mortgage on the house, and a superfluity of installment-credit appliances and vehicles. Then think of his political position vis-à-vis that of the manager of his office (no need to go up the chain of intimidation to the president of the company). Then speak of economic intimidation, half slave, half free. A middle-aged friend had said, look to the kids, not the Negroes. (C. Wright Mills said it, too.) The main question of our time, my friend had said, is whether the kids are going to decide to free us or enslave us. Either way, the nation could stand—but not as now, full of people divided against themselves.

The Solidarity Day march ended in anticlimax, the familiar mournful music of "We Shall Overcome" floating lifeless over the reflecting pool where a Washington Negro slum kid, fully clothed, swam slowly in the muck. "We are not afraid" floated into Resurrection City, arousing what memories there? What derision? Or perhaps no reaction at all, the most chilling characteristic of its somber mood, the blank stare of depression's rage. They swayed, hand in middle-class hand, black and white innocents together, singing the swan song of the Movement as I had known it, loved it, Dr. King's movement that came cutting through the edge of all my conditioned resistance to emotion, to belief, to such a thing as hope, and consumed my life for a long time, shaped it, put me down at one specified reference point on the map of the world of my times, and held me there, South-caught. No one had heard Ralph Abernathy. They never really heard Dr. King either, most of the middle class, half slave and half free, even the most sensitive and human of them who had comprised the Movement's crowds over the years, like the one dwindling away now from the Lincoln Memorial. And those who had heard him, his people, the basis of all he said and the way he said it—they were over there in Resurrection City.

I had watched a group of six or so young blacks standing in the street in front of the Lincoln Memorial during Dr. Abernathy's sermon. They were typical of their generation—slim, full of nervous energy, a sense of freedom of motion that was well beyond the American norm, with all the eccentricity of adornment that is their conformity. They were having a great time of it, cheering the speech, intoning with perfect timing the amen's, the "Yes, tell it, brother" responses which weld the crowd in a Negro church into one personality, one being —greater than the sum of the individuals, perhaps; certainly different from it. These kids were not listening to the honest, harsh, just words of the speech, its tedious linear development of meaning, but were responding to the familiar rhythms of the preacher's style, and their responses were mocking, jeering—as much of themselves and the best of their vaunted black heritage as of poor old preacher Abernathy. A friend came along and pointed one of them out as the young gentleman known as Sweet Willie, who was leader of that gang which in Memphis disrupted the last attempt of Dr. King to work his miracle of nonviolence. My friend called him over and presented me to him (in the way of these things, a recommendation of me for future reference, wherever our paths might cross). I shook his hand, looked into his unfriendly, glancing-away eyes. To a segregationist white Southerner, shaking hands with a nigger has been the most anathematic gesture of all, and I sensed in the listless hand I shook there as Abernathy spoke, as Lincoln looked down, the same loathfulness of contact. The Urban Coalition, the latest of the Establishment's teams to wrestle with race relations, has taken unto its breast such fellow power politicians as Sweet Willie;

so have the centers of American innocence like the liberal church and sincere liberal politics; somehow I found myself not charmed with him.

The sensed violence (which was only the more volatile and less evil aspect of the mood of Resurrection City) broke loose that night, after a storm had rung down the curtain on the Solidarity Day march. I read about it in the Washington *Post*: six "youths" with tent poles confronting six cops, the youths talking about getting whiteys, honkies; the cops pushing them back; a crowd coming from Resurrection City, throwing bottles; fifty more cops rushing in; a tense confrontation, as we say, finally ending without, as we say, serious mishap. The story also noted "seventeen reported assaults" within Resurrection City that night, but contained no details because the Resurrection City residents acting as "security police" would not let reporters in, or tell them anything. The story also noted that some security police were drunk during the previous day's march, and pushed around tourists as well as Resurrection City residents. Subsequently, the *Post* carried a story quoting a security policeman who alleged that violence, theft, and rape had been commonplace throughout the existence of Resurrection City and who was now quitting because of the lack of law enforcement there. The story would be subsequently cited the following week by the authorities bent on getting Resurrection City gone forever. The SCLC people would point out that whatever pathology was on display in Resurrection City was typical of all the hidden environments of poverty they were protesting. The speaker who, early in the campaign, had said that Resurrection City was better than the ghettos if there were no murders nor death from overdose of drugs there was much quoted.

But this would seem a trifle disingenuous; after all, Resurrection City had not been planned by Dr. King as a showcase of the criminality of the poor. There had been talk of a "model city." Haunting the failure of responsibility in regard to the security police situation and general welfare (the showers that never materialized, the less adequate than promised diet, for example) was the memory of the old faith, held most militantly by SNCC, that all the evils of this world could be cured if the poor people could only be put in charge. If you know the wisdom, the resources of strength, courage, and doggedness in the poor people of the rural South with whom the old SNCC worked (it being more clear in the South than elsewhere that poverty is not the fault of the poor, not a signal of failure, but the result of systematic repression, and the inability of the economic system to provide adequate jobs and wages), you can understand that old SNCC romanticism of the poor. I remember defending it to a friend in New York and having him, as we drove the intricate complexity of the expressways there, wave his hands about at all the arranged system of signals and signs, and say in exasperation, "Do you think Mrs. Hamer could run all this?" And of course I could wave my hands and holler, "Who needs all this?" But the point is, the main point perhaps of Resurrection City, is that we do need all of the social organization, social responsibility, humane planning, intelligent administration we can get. The one point on which the Right and the Left agree is that the social system is breaking down, like an old locomotive being driven at faster and faster speeds. We most likely will see it run off the tracks. But we won't likely see the system abolished. From what I have seen of the thinking that would make the revolution, we would end up with the same old malfunctioning society in new hands. Give Sweet Willie his choice of blowing up the Pentagon or becoming the head general in charge of it. His swagger-stick and systems analysis would be the envy of the military world.

I went back to Resurrection City the next day, in the hope that seeing it on the morning after might reveal more of its truth, make it somehow seem less unhealthy. But the violence of the early morning hours, while I slept, was apparently the only thing that was left to happen there. In the morning's muggy sun and mud, that same silent torpor was upon it. Once more, I walked its length and back again: the same few unfriendly encounters, and the same unwillingness, inability, on my part to invade the privacy of the people. At the front gate, a number of the families, looking like Southerners, were gathered with their paper-bag baggage: the stout Negro women, thinly strong Negro men, solemn-eyed Negro children of the rural South, apparently going home. Had they come only for the march? Or had they been there all along, and finally had had enough of Resurrection City last night? Or had they decided, like me, that the march proclaimed the end of what had once been the one bright hope in their lives? I looked into the fatigued, introspective eyes of one of those women, wanting to ask—but not able to.

A young guy demanded a cigarette, and then started in on his need for money. I heard my name shouted and then apparently his, and a laughing Southern voice saying, "What a pair to find here together." It was Lawrence Guyot from Mississippi, the head of the Mississippi Freedom Democratic Party. He had also been part of the Mississippi challenge at Atlantic City in 1964, which had been an earlier ending, the killing of the hope in SNCC, the final convincing evidence to them that you couldn't work within the system, between those lines of orderly progress, reform, and that you couldn't trust white people—from the most powerful man of them all on down. The other man, it seemed, was from Greenwood, Mississippi, where the bravest of all the voter registration campaigns had been double-crossed by the Kennedy Justice Department, where Jimmy Travis had been shot in the neck with an automatic rifle, where for the first time national attention had been paid to the desperate, child-starving poverty of the rural South—followed by a brief, fitful spurt of free food and clothing. That was in 1963. Some of the toughest SNCC workers had wept at seeing the people coming with rags tied on their feet in lieu of shoes, grateful for whatever had been given; the workers were also grieved to see the entirely to be expected results of privation that showed in some of the poor, the trickery, the taking any way they could, some of them, more than their share of the Thanksgiving basket, missionary largesse sent down from rich America. Conditions were no less desperate in 1963 than in 1968 or the years between in the rural South. Now the nation's attention was attracted again. But the old SNCC was gone; they had killed all that good in it, that young, hard-boiled, tough good which, nurtured on the unexpected, stupendous success of the sit-ins, had for a time behind it the belief that anything—no limits, no caution—could be achieved, or at least tried. The good in the poor people could prevail. What organization now, what leader, could be said to elicit and speak for that good? Now, the violence that is built into the victim of injustice and neglect, the greediness that had so grieved SNCC, seems more likely to be the poor people's contribution to the new order. Guyot soon went his way, a good guy, full of talk about plans for the delegate challenge—this time in Chicago.

All morning the loudspeakers had been heralding a demonstration. It was to have started around lunchtime; I had resigned myself to another no-lunch day when it still had not started a good two hours later. People had formed their line; they were waiting for the word to go. In charge was Hosea Williams, a brave SCLC activist from Savannah, Georgia, as well as a self-promoter of prodigious energy, a man with a knack for antagonizing people needlessly, the kind of man you want in a revolution to lead troops but somehow not get back in time to help form the new government. Finally he gave the order for the line of about fifty people to start marching through Resurrection City, from the front gate toward the back one, and off we set, the old familiar formation: we reporters, notebooks in hand, off to the side; they marching, singing the good old songs—"Ain't goin' let nobody turn me 'round," "If you miss me in the back of the bus and you can't find me nowhere, Come on up to the front of the bus, and I'll be driving up there," "Come by here, my Lord, Come by here, oh, Lord, Come by here. . . ." It was to these very songs, in coincidental fact, that I had responded most in that personal religious experience which had been my introduction to Dr. King's movement, a long time ago. It seemed a mockery to hear those songs now, dodging along through the mud, seeing the blank looks that the vast majority of Resurrection City's residents gave the demonstrators and their song, summing up so many betrayals of good words, good people, so many disappointments, disillusionments.

The march through the mud of Resurrection City added no more than fifteen people to the little line. Hosea called them into a huddle in the grass just outside the rear gate. Then he strode over ostentatiously to the press contingent (consisting of me, a lanky young man from the Washington

Post, and a very black young man from some African publication) and yelled, "Y'all go on over away from us so we can discuss things." I stuck my hand out to him, said howdy. "Yeah," he said in a tone suggesting he wished I hadn't stuck my hand out to him. "Y'all go on over yonder."

I thought this would be where they called the march off, but no, it started off again, Hosea heading back into Resurrection City, and a tall young man who looked remarkably like Stokely Carmichael (but no kin—somebody finally asked him) in charge. We went through the field that had been yesterday's staging area for the march, up the hill toward the Washington Monument. They kept singing those good old songs, cops bumping alongside on motorcycles, motors roaring. We passed three Negro teen-agers with Afro haircuts, sitting under a tree; one had a saxophone, and blew riffs at the demonstration. "Get a gun, brother," yelled one of the demonstrators, last of the legions of Dr. King's nonviolent army.

"Michael, row the boat ashore," they sang, approaching the Washington Monument. I got my first inkling, then, of something else that might be considered a prime cause of what ailed Resurrection City. There were rows of tourists sitting on little benches all around the base of the monument, and the brave song of the little marching band wavered as they approached those tourists, sitting in their slick-magazine informal wear—melting-pot American families, American primitives, all kinds—and before the marchers had got past all those cold eyes, the song had died completely. The only sound was the flapping of all those American flags ringing the monument, so gallantly streaming. It was not like marching down to the courthouse, through the familiarity of the town square in the South, every inch of the way known, every nuance of the angry, hostile, sneering response of those ol' crackers just as familiar. In the South, we have shared the physical world, every town and city being two towns, black Atlanta, white Atlanta, the business section common property, and the rivers and the woods used separately but jointly, with all that intricacy of rules of separation over which so much of the energy of the Southern civil rights movement was consumed. Up here, godamighty, in the ghetto cities of the North, they don't even do that, don't share the land: this pile of monument concrete, these big, rich-as-a-bank-looking buildings.

The Department of Agriculture proved to be the target of this demonstration, the lair of that most evildoing of all the middle-class innocents, Orville W. Freeman, standing accused on national television of starving little newborn babies to death in the interest of showing his boss one of those two-million-dollar bookkeeping gains so dear to the boss's not at all innocent heart. The entrance at which the march stopped had marble columns (the big house of the plantation), and behind these, taller than a man, gates of close iron rods; then the building itself, tall, marble, intimidating. The cops were in clusters (I counted twenty-two at one point) across the street in the park (orderly and forbidding-looking, these parks, not like the woods, not like parks back home), and there were about a dozen men in business suits standing and watching the demonstrators in front of the building, no more than four of these newsmen, the others looking like cops, like FBI, like authority. One uniformed cop kept walking up close to the demonstrators, standing in a long line thinly stretched across the front of that wide building; he poked a Polaroid camera at one or another of them, and then stepped back quickly to peel off his print, as you might take a picture of an alligator as close-up as you could. A young Negro man who had made the march on crutches broke out in a sudden tirade, perhaps in defiance of the bigness, the business suits, the strangeness surrounding him. He hollered something about America being the richest nation in the world, veins standing out on his forehead, and then his voice died out, like the song back at the monument, and, self-consciously, he hollered out: "I'm tryin' to tell it like it is, Brother."

There was a little flurry of surprise, and style, when a gleaming truck rolled up, and, within a few minutes, a beautiful buffet lunch was laid out on a long table. The demonstrators quietly formed a line, and with no show of exuberance over this fine little fillip, with that same subdued mood of their singing, they filled their plates and sat down to eat around the entranceway of the place. Workers within looked down from high windows on the scene, blank, white faces. No one would say who had provided the food, paid for it. The truck was from a Negro-owned catering service; its three attendants were Negro, one of them a squat, big-shouldered man wearing a sweat shirt with "Black Liberation" lettered on it, and an inked-on design of stars and a crescent. While they ate, he stared with hating eyes, like white Southerners when they can catch your eye, at all the whites bustling around in their business suits. I long ago had learned how to avoid such eyes. My stomach was gnawing in its own faint, middle-class knowledge of hunger. In the old days, the press would have been offered food, would have had to make one of those delicate little decisions of whether partaking would impair the image, the myth of their objectivity (getting both sides of questions about which there can be no debate, like the right of Negroes to register to vote). Now none was offered.

The demonstrators were about half white, half Negro, all ages, the whites including a mother with her baby, and a stringy, tough-looking lady who looked like she was from the hill country. Their differences were eclipsed by the familiar larger separation of the two realities, the two worlds of such a situation: the demonstrators in theirs, a crisis scene of long-built emotion, one that was soon to culminate in a high, fearful, brave moment of life, maybe the highest of a lifetime; and the rest of us in ours, just a little out of the ordinary routine, doing the job, getting along, making a day, one in ten thousand of them. While we were waiting for the demonstrators to finish their lunch, a photographer spoke to one of the cops about how, thank God, in just two hours he would be out on a boat fishing, then about getting his daughter married the coming weekend. In the South during the Movement's past, these moments before the confrontation would have tremendous dramatic tension, for there was always a real sense of the drum-stir, the chain-rattle, the death-touch of totalitarianism, the shivering awareness that in this world, the limitlessness of human cruelty can be unleashed in licensed, uniformed, drilled numbers on the helpless, the hapless, the normal, decent run of no-better-and-no-worse-than-they-should-be humanity. Violence would victimize them all: the demonstrators but also the bureaucrats, the cops, the tourist come up with his green cap on to take a picture of this whole thing, his wife harping at him to get on up closer, ask that man to move out of the way. And this destruction of decency would be done at the will not of a monster, a De Sade, but at the behest of merely the type of life-hating, twisted, mean little son-of-a-bitch that we have all known, some stingy little storekeeper, some smirking little clerk. You can almost taste that meanness in your mouth, horrible and human, in the South, the George Wallaces squeezing their abominable ways up out of it every generation, the real horror of our heritage down there. But here in official, marble Washington, the potential horror had a further dimension, something purely mechanical and alien, a monstrosity of machines and mathematics that had moved on beyond any humanly evil origins, beyond human control —the efficient, functional *technique* that was starving Southern children, burning Vietnamese ones, and moving inevitably on to its own final and total solution.

After lunch, one of the bustling little business-suit men came forward and took charge. He was a baldheaded gent who had stared with some puzzlement previously at my press badge, which said I represented *New South*, a publication not likely known in his circles. I had put him down at the time as a bureaucrat (a cop would have asked about the badge, or not been so obviously staring). He turned out to be Joseph M. Robertson, assistant secretary for administration. The leaders of the march told him they wanted an audience with Secretary Freeman. He said to give him fifteen minutes, and with ten of them still to go, he bustled back and said to the leaders that he was sorry but he had to report that the secretary would not see the demonstrators. Mr. Freeman would be happy to confer with Mr. Abernathy at any time but not . . . he didn't say "rabble" but the inference was plain.

The leaders, some of the demonstrators, the press, the cops, we were all gathered around him for the announcement. "But these are the people," the young man who resembled Stokely said. "The people . . ." Robertson shook his head, the gesture signifying how entirely futile it was to argue with him; it was out of his hands. So the leader ended with:

"I'll tell the people there's nothing you can do. This is just a small minority of the people in this country who are starving." He threw the words at the bald, bland-faced Robertson, and I harkened to that, to the insult and accusation in his voice. Maybe it would move the man.

The confrontation was reminding me of a time when I had helped two men try to get a boat for Daufuskie Island, South Carolina. It was in a spring of the long ago in Washington, the very same time that the poor were first showing some of the less benign side of what hunger and hurt does to people, that time of the convention of the poor staged by the Citizens Crusade Against Poverty. Could it have been only two years ago, way back there in 1966? Two citizens of Daufuskie Island had come to the convention to try out a scheme they had. Their island lies just above Hilton Head, which is a notable new resort whose development in the 1950's resulted forthwith in that action of state and federal authority in mutual accord and purposefulness necessary to the construction of a causeway to connect it to the mainland and all its tourist money. I cherish the memory of Hilton Head and its splendid, entirely untouched beach, and the assemblage of tourists every day around the luxury motel swimming pool, their finely, fashionably tanned backs to the beach.

Well, Daufuskie had not yet been bought up for development and exploitation. Most of its inhabitants are Negro; some of the few whites there, like most of the Negroes, trace their ancestry on the island back to the days of slavery. The two citizens who came to Washington shared this distinction: the ancestors of the white one of them (a rough-hewn gentleman with a game leg, beyond middle-age, articulate in his coastal brogue) had owned the ancestors of the black one of them (a grave, elderly black farmer, articulate with his eyes and the wrinkling of his brows but seldom-spoken). Their island had no causeway, inhabited as it was just by poor people, and no other means beyond motor boats of getting to and back from the mainland. Daufuskie's two citizens in Washington wanted no part of a causeway; what they wanted was a boat, a big boat, big enough to haul crops and cars and the other heavy cargo necessary to develop farming on Daufuskie. The United States Government, they understood, had a lot of boats, just the kind they needed, sitting around unused in harbors. So, since they were up here in Washington anyhow for the convention, they thought they would just ask their government if they couldn't have one of those boats. They thought they would ask the President.

I got drawn into the boat thing by a friend of mine who had a penchant for this kind of situation, a feeling for the people we call poor, like the two Daufuskie Islanders, who fit none of the imagery of the word. In an ebullient mood, we bundled into a taxi and set off to see the President. All four of us were in the way of Southerners richly delighted with the scheme, capable of laughing at it and at the same time of believing in the possibility of confounding mighty Washington and all its ambiguous marble bigness and complexity by this specific, simple-minded need of a boat. Someday the rest of the nation will realize that it has been by this keen sense of the specific—the refusal ever to get embroiled in generalities, in dangerous abstraction, principle, ideals—that the Southerner has ever out-tricked them; out-traded them: losing the war but winning the peace; spreading the taint of systematized racism through the nation; corrupting, capturing, ruining the Congress; making fools of all adversaries.

The taxi driver was not amused, hearing us. They will put you'uns in jail, he warned. Better not try to go in his office. Find a phone booth and call him up. He deposited us at one, shaking his head. We spent the morning around the phone booth, the white man of the Daufuskie team doing all the calling, telling his story with its insulting threat over and over to startled receptionists on down a line (the President, it seemed, was gone to South America, darn the luck, he reported early on), not getting angry but being plenty forceful, emphasizing his words occasionally by banging on the metal tray of the phone booth with his stubby fist, saying loudly enough for us to hear once, "Well, don't you see, we want to be part of the United States, we're drifting off, we may wind up in Cuba." The other member of the team stood straight as a pole, patient and solemn through it all, glancing occasionally at the sun, measuring all the time this was taking. I stood alongside him, thinking of a couple of former newspaper colleagues of mine who were now fancy Presidential correspondents, wondering what they would think to find me here, standing, waiting with the Daufuskie fellows, after a boat. Finally, the talker emerged, grinning. "The Vice President's gonna see us." He had an appointment; there was just time for a gleeful, hopeful lunch.

Humphrey's outer office told much of what the world was later to learn from his actions about the essential gimcrackery of his soul. I recollect a replica of a wagon train; a lot of pharmaceutical paraphernalia; a number of those certificates and diplomas by which Americans convince themselves that they know more than they know they know, that they have achieved more than they know they have; and an Indian motto, appropriately engraved, something to the effect that you shouldn't criticize a fellow until you've walked in his moccasins. (How many times, one wonders, did Hubert Humphrey in those four years console himself with this wisdom?)

We presented the spectacle that we were, and our little story, to a receptionist who recovered her aplomb quickly, and said she was sorry to inform us that the Vice President actually couldn't see us but that an aide of his would—a very important one, she implied. We went on into his office, some of our impertinency having been chipped away by that same combination of big-building, big-people, big-nation awesomeness whose effect on the demonstrators I was later in my life to note. The Negro farmer of the Daufuskie team showed the effect most openly, the fingers of his big, strong farmer's hands clinched together, the knuckles taut knots, and his forehead wrinkled into an eloquent tight knot of concentration and, yes, awe.

The aide looked at us and listened to us with something of the air of a man suffering from the phobia that haunts a friend of mine, that his daily hangover has come at last to be of such severe proportions that it has snapped his mind, unhinged him at last from reality. At one point he said, "A *boat?*" with exquisite expressiveness, and at another, "Now let me get this straight, you say you need a boat?" The white Daufuskie Islander did most of the talking, telling the story straight through, about how the young people were leaving, a paradise for them lost, how the people who stayed were suffering, all for the lack of a boat, of how it didn't used to matter about not having a boat because most of the livings on the island were made by oyster fishing, but now there was only farming to do, and hence the need of the boat to haul the crops ashore, because the United States Government—and here was our punch line, our threat, our insult, and the old islander pushed it hard at the aide—had forbidden oyster fishing anymore because the water around the island is so polluted that the oysters will kill you if you eat them. It was a time when the administration of which Mr. Humphrey's office was so elevatedly a part was still claiming vehemently that it wished to do things about such domestic problems as pollution, and the story about the oysters had its effect on the aide, his eyes walling even more than when we walked in. He plunged into the kind of crisp summing-up questions and ordering of the facts of the case that is a ritual with his kind. At one point, all engrossed in the thing, he asked, "How many now are there of you on the island?" And being told, he asked, "And how many of these have incomes below the poverty level?" And being told, "Ever' one of 'em, ever' last one of us," he exclaimed, "Good. Good."

He sent us finally to a man in the Office of Economic Opportunity, a man he called with a great display of how important it was, how much it meant for him to call the man, not just send us over there. Seeing us out the door with his eyes still walling, he made a little joke about "have to be careful how you pronounce the name of that island of yours, heh heh," which did not sit well with the two Daufuskie Islanders at all, impressed as they were, jubilant as they were. Letting out some of their steam, they pegged along, the game-legged one setting the pace, through seemingly endless tunnels that whistled with unearthly subterranean winds. "This is where they send everybody who dares to come up here asking for a boat," said my friend who had got me into all this.

We ended up, the four of us and the high-ranking bureaucrat to whom we had been sent, on our knees on the floor of his office, studying an elaborate mariner's map of the island that the white islander had brought. When the bureaucrat tried to unsettle him with highly specific questions about the kind of boat he wanted, he was easily able to unsettle the bureaucrat with a knowledgeable, well-prepared list of specifications for exactly the kind of boat needed. We left with the man's words ringing in our ears: "Now I'm not sure, you understand, I can't say for certain, but I think it can be done, I think we can swing it—but don't get your hopes up, don't be too hopeful."

Hopeful. Actually, he did swing it; Daufuskie did get its boat. I was in Charleston a short while before Solidarity Day, and heard how a fine brand-new boat and other improvements for the island had resulted from our venture. I was to read a short while later another bit of news about Daufuskie Island: in the Democratic primary, a qualified and peace-campaigning Negro candidate for Congress had run against the incumbent from their district; and all the islanders, "ever' last one of 'em," had voted for the warmonger, racist L. Mendel Rivers. Maybe it was out of gratitude at getting the boat. I also read, not a long while after our call on the Humphrey aide, that he had been forced to resign, because of some indiscretion in the politics of his, and Mr. Humphrey's, home state. I like to think he was indiscreet on the side of decency, and that our confronting him with the reality of the need for a boat in the unreality of that office, that world he dwelt in, might have had something to do with it.

But all of that might have occurred in another age, even another country. Nobody at the Department of Agriculture (already implicated in just about every racist practice against Negroes in the rural South through every administration of every liberal President over the years) was about to be pushed around by any Southern specifics of starvation, any mere insults, any reality. The demonstrators huddled and very briefly decided what they would do: "We're going to go on to the next order of business," they warned Robertson, and formed a line of march, singing "Do What the Spirit Say Do." They were in a column of twos, and in the same bookkeeper's voice that would say it outside of a gas chamber, a minor bureaucrat said to the major bureaucrat, Robertson, "Now we've got a chance at last for a reasonably accurate count of them."

I thought they were folding up—another demonstration,

another day come to naught—and I asked a middle-aged Negro man if they were going back to Resurrection City. "Ask the man at the front of the line," he snapped, in that almost shamefaced nastiness of any minor functionary under orders not to talk to outsiders. I trailed along as they turned the corner, not back toward that wretched place I guess they called home. I watched with admiration as they turned another corner and gravely began peeling off to sit in all the many doorways of the Agriculture Department buildings on both sides of the street. Somewhere along the way they had become supplied with the personal belongings that demonstrators take to jail, toothbrushes, combs, the like. It was well-organized, clean, efficient, as were the arrests that began quickly to follow. With the dignity and style of the old movement, the demonstrators passively resisted the police, some going limp, some walking slowly, one Negro man standing as he was frisked. Then, as he was led to a police bus, he began to sing: "Oh Freedom, oh Freedom, oh Freedom over me, Before I'll be a slave, I'll be buried in my grave, and go home to my Lord and be free," singing over and over the old brave words, alive for a hopeful little moment there again.

I watched Robertson's face as he ordered the beginning of the arrests; he had the look of a man trying to clean rats out of his cellar. The white cops' faces had that look of grim, morbid excitement worn by their Southern counterparts in similar circumstances. One Negro cop was holding back people on the sidewalk while demonstrators were being removed from the door. A nondescript Negro man was among these he held back; he growled something about Black Power to the cop. This cop's face was flinty; he had the flat nose, the flesh tones of an Indian. He was angry—surely in part at being where he was, doing what he was doing (not what the spirit say do).

They sang as they waited, in twos and threes blocking each of the doorways, to be arrested. A blonde girl, college-age, was among those going limp. A cop said, "I'd grab that broad by the hank of the hair." Two Negro cops did the removal job at one of the doorways; talking to the kids, preparing to lift them, their faces seemed friendly. One of the kids did the little jerking motions that make such a task more difficult. "Don't act like a child," one of the Negro cops grunted.

Faces were peering down from all the windows. You would expect them to be full of concern, or anger, or sympathy—or something. For the most part, they were not. As four cops lifted a young Negro, a pretty black girl looked down and smiled. While these arrests were taking place, other demonstrators had lain down in the driveways to the parking lots of some of the buildings. A car was unable to get out and the driver, a middle-aged guy with his gray-faced wife beside him, was sitting on his horn. I moved with the cops and the press toward this development, and in the middle of the street, I heard from above a voice of anger—at last—coming from one of the windows. A pretty blonde was yelling down, "No. No. You're not going to arrest them." She was angry not because of the suppression of decency, of reality going on down there, but because the cops were getting the man out of his car. But it wasn't to arrest him. He had to sign something, a complaint, I suppose, so they could begin removing the driveway blockers.

A fat Negro man, spectator of all this, yelled up at the blonde: "Shut yo' mouth. Mind yo' business."

She yelled back at him: "I work."

It seemed to sum it all up, both sides of the shibboleth. I watched the orderly, systematic clearing of one driveway after another. In one, there were three girls and two boys of college age, black and white together, and a country-looking, older white woman. All their faces, so disparate—the white girls' full of that innocent bloom of assured middle-class security—had a shared calmness, coolness. Here is the best hope, I thought. Here is the other side of the prophecy made by my friend: the basis for believing that the young might free us, or help us find courage to fight for our freedom. The quiet calm of their absolute conviction was what struck this muddled and fearful middle-aged observer; this was the way it had been in SNCC, this was the way it must have been through history, for those who were able, really able, to resist tyranny and stupidity. They could laugh at what made me cringe; they could march through tear gas and get their heads beat with the same sort of apparent inner certainty that it doesn't matter that what they believe in will prevail. And what they believe in—here, around the world, South African whites among them even—has been so uniformly right: against war, against racism, against poverty; against the monstrosity of *technique*; and being for, in every conceivable context, the liberation and enhancement of the human spirit. I noticed that the elderly country-looking lady was right there with them. It was not really a matter of chronological age. It was a matter of the best in people coming out, quietly fighting, serenely sure. They won't kill this, I thought.

It was getting toward my plane time. I didn't regret having to leave, as once I would have—indeed would not have left, back when these dramas demanded the reporter's loyalty to see them through, to be there as witness to whatever might be the worst atrocity, to be there as witness so the worst atrocity might not occur. The press by this time was on the scene in great numbers. I chatted a few moments with Charlayne Hunter, who, after making news by integrating the University of Georgia, had covered a lot of these demonstrations in the South. "I'm leaving," I said. "I've seen all this before." As the arrests got started, as the bureaucrat Robertson jerked his stiff face around, as the cops pushed their pistol-strength into the demonstrators, as the inevitable white loudmouth heckled unhindered behind police lines, I had felt a good and healthy rise in me of Southern chauvinism, a desire to yell at the cops, the bureaucrats, "You're no better, no better than the worst of ours." It was the first time I had seen this Northern ability to duplicate, down to the last self-righteous gesture, Southern racism, Southern dehumanization. In a few short minutes there, I had lost something, a part of my provinciality, the Southerner's collective inferiority complex: and I had lost something else, too—a little more of the respect for and confidence in men and institutions that is the glue which holds a society together. Long weak and watery in the South, the glue was becoming the same, evidently, in Washington and in the rest of the nation. Once the Southerner opposed to racism could console himself with the thought: I am virtually alone down here, but I am of the majority in the nation. No more.

I had left my bags at a friend's office near my hotel. I decided to take one last walk through Resurrection City, hoping maybe to get a better feel of it, or to get a better feeling about it, before catching a cab. But when I got to the back gate, a cop was there who refused to let me enter. I started to begin one of those contests of authority with him, using my press card, but realized it wasn't worth it, no more than trying to talk with those silent, bitter people.

I went away and sat in the cool green of Dupont Circle, watching all its diversity of types, like colorful and busy birds: the hippies; a boy on his knees patiently following a pigeon across the grass; the old people of both races; one Negro with an empty golf bag, not new, enigmatically on the bench beside him; the straight people, mostly walking through—a beautiful blonde baby-girl type, so young, so slim, carrying a big bag of groceries; a tall young man in his Haspel cord carrying a courier case under one arm, a shopping sack in the other hand, walking long strides, head back, a farmer, a pioneer. And there were even a few of those I sensed to be a new breed, a blend of what the hippies seek, what old people come to after finally getting their values settled, what the young straights have in the way of confidence and control: a plump young mother in an indifferent dress that sagged and rippled all around the hem, her black hair unfashionably long, watching her two fat babies playing in the sandpile; a young Negro with three Negro girls beside him, sketching the park scene. Someone began a loud, melodious, free whistling. This, I thought, is what a Resurrection City should be like: this tolerance in all these people in all their diversity, each for the others.

I went on to get my bag, and at the next corner, a drab little drama ensued. A slovenly young white woman was yelling at a group of six or seven people waiting at the bus stop. I saw that she was yelling at the one Negro among them, a stout, dignified matriarchal woman. "Communists," the fat girl screamed drunkenly. "Communists. Why don't you go back to Africa?" All the worst of the racist insults poured out of the girl, anachronistic, almost refreshing in their direct ugliness. The Negro woman stood there, swollen with outrage. "We never come from Africa," she said finally in that voice Southern Negroes use with drunks of theirs, with idiots and the insane, with unruly white children. When I came out of my office with my bag, the fat drunk white girl was out in the middle of the street, the light against her. A young white guy at the bus stop yelled at her, "Hey you— you're the one breaking the law." The girl wheeled back around: "Faggot. Faggot. You burned your draft card. You faggot." She passed me at the next corner where I was trying to catch my cab, crossed with the light, and then stood, face blank with all her meaningless rage, as the light changed three times. She was still standing there, hulking, murderous, pitiful, when I got my cab.

The episode had the feel of the worst I had experienced at Resurrection City, standing by the main gate, listening to Murray Kempton, who was extemporizing his bedazzling sort of intricate instant analysis of everything I had been seeing. An old Negro man—thin, city-looking, defeated in his face— came up to us. Drunk, wine-drunk by the look of his eyes, he said to get out. We both had been through these minor moments of nastiness many times before; I from whites, mostly, but blacks in recent times, Kempton I guess, plenty of both, and we knew that the only thing to do was avoid any personal touch with this drunk, like avoiding the hate stare of the racist when you walk into a Southern restaurant in the company of a Negro. We moved away slowly, the old guy behind us, cursing us, his voice low, as though if he properly yelled, it would end the magic of our obeying him. We wouldn't look back at him, kept walking slowly, continuing our conversation. He came closer and put his hand on my shoulder, still saying to get out, cursing us, and walking in a pantomime of pushing me out, no force in his hand, no ability really to heave me the hell out of there.

The feebleness of his anger reminded me of the time I sat listening to a racist harangue from the state superintendent of schools in Georgia, shortly after the 1954 school decision. He was an old man, a good, gentle product of white Southern Methodism, a good educator by Southern standards, which meant that he really cared about the children rather than merely for the prerogatives and power of his job. His tirade was of that same weak and feeble quality as the drunk Negro's heave-ho; somewhere in the midst of it, he got Jesus into it, as was natural for his generation and his religious tradition, and I burst out, surprised at myself: "Leave Jesus out of this." His old eyes were startled for a minute, and then hurt, and for a long time afterward I felt bad about hurting him needlessly, for he was old, and unregenerate on the race thing, and, I thought, harmless. Later I came to know how harmful such innocent old men in positions of power were to be to the South, to humanity, how ruinous the workings of the innocent were in America. And now I finally knew, too, that to burst out at him, on the most elemental of human terms, was better than not to—better than not to fight him, not even to look at him.

The radio in the taxicab described what happened to the demonstration after I left it, how it attracted other columns of marchers, more police, how it spread into the street, how the police had to use "necessary restraint with their billy clubs." Some who were there later told me the cops started it; others said it was one group of Negroes bent on violence. Either way, it is the same: the violence is the thing, neither side anymore has any real control of it.

I read a few days later of Abernathy's final march and arrest, and of the expeditious way that they ran the few remaining people out of Resurrection City, and then destroyed it, and got grass to growing there again almost overnight. Out of that sorry episode, Jack Nelson of the Los Angeles *Times* wrote the best single newspaper story on the civil rights movement I have ever read—about how efficient the government was in enforcing the penny-ante law it used to clear Resurrection City out of the landscape and consciousness of Washington, D.C., but how inefficient that same government had been over many long years in enforcing the vital, basic laws (voter registration, protection of civil rights, not to mention human life; farm programs and job opportunities; the feeding of hungry children) that would make life livable for the poor. How sorry a record of incredible failure.

It was like reading about the old regime leading up to the French or Russian revolution: the Greek-tragedy sense of disaster drawing on, of forces and events out of control. I passed the White House on one of the nights there in Washington, and a Washington friend in the car exclaimed that he never had seen it so lit up before, spotlights like they use in prison yards illuminating every inch of the grounds, this bastion of the greatest of all the nickel-nursing switchers-off of unused forty-watt bulbs in America. We all surmised that he was afraid, that man in there, of the poor people down in Resurrection City, and afraid of all the gatherings of the innocents who had come spontaneously, out of the last saving remnants of decency and goodness within America. One of the main reasons he did not run again, I was told by a Washington friend privy to such secrets, was that he was afraid he would be killed during the campaign and not just embarrassed to death by those demonstrations that followed him everywhere the police and military didn't keep them out.

As my plane climbed above Washington, I pondered the valedictory feeling about the Movement that had been dogging me for the past two days and nights, the sense of an ending. It was not dead in its organizational forms or its plans and campaigns (John Lewis would come back from Washington two weeks after I did, quietly optimistic, telling of the fine new scheme for the poor people's embassy up there). It was just dead within me. It had acquainted me with a kind of hope, a universal kind of hope for humanity, that my generation had been conditioned not to know. My life, my work had fed on that hope through crucial years of my lifetime. Now that hope was gone. I had never, like the innocents, been a niggerlover. It seems to me that the premise underlying all that Dr. King knew and taught was that to love everybody without ever loving anybody is as meaningless as hating everybody. Black Power is deep in that meaninglessness, which the riots so graphically express. So do the assassinations. Black violence has not killed a single real enemy of black people, of humanity; it has killed its own. And the vehemence of the verbal violence of Black Power has been much less a threat than an advantage to these enemies, while only the true friends of the Black Powerists, black and white masochistically together, expect it to overcome.

It would be cathartic to draw lines and say I am the enemy

of all these, Black Powerists and white niggerlovers, just as I have been the enemy of all the white racists in the South. But the Southern sun bores itself into your bones, sweats such dogmatism out of you. Like all liberals down there, Negro and white, Dr. King included, I know that humanity is too complex, too mysterious to draw rigid lines and expect to contain much reality in them. The lines have to be drawn on principles, not on people.

There was a time when just about every black person I saw agreed with me on principles, which involved essentially the Bill of Rights and the failure to exercise and enforce it where Negro citizens of the South were concerned. Thus I felt we were united in a struggle, the Movement, to achieve those principles, that enforcement, which denied to some were meaningless to all. This unity no longer exists. So now it is necessary to judge each Negro I meet on the criteria by which we judge all other people—a natural and, indeed, better way: some are with you, some are enemies of your most important principles and values. And so one looks among them, as one looks among whites, for those who believe in what is summed up in the Bill of Rights, and who are aware of all the ways the Bill of Rights is raped in America, not just as regards Negroes, but whites as well. This, then, has been Black Power's most constructive effect: that it has removed from whites the last shred of romantic, paternalistic, indiscriminate idealization of Negroes, and that it has removed Negroes from the obligations, the expectations unrealistically put upon them by whites, to do, in sum, the impossible.

There was some justification for the expectation. In the South, Negro leaders and Negro people fought for their civil liberties with the kind of courage, the kind of selflessness that white liberals were incapable of when the Cold War insanity, and its first agent, Joe McCarthy, clenched a fist around *their* civil liberties. Whites, the likes of me, looked at the Negro movement, Dr. King's movement, once it had stirred hope within them, to do more than oppose the racial injustices of the South. What we came to expect was that Negroes, with their demonstrations, their new-found ability to force action by the offering of their bodies to the clubs of the cops and the murderousness of the unlicensed terrorists, would change

American society, would right its wrongs, would correct the fatal malfunctions of its systems. Despite all that hopelessness I carried up there to Washington, I must have had some small hope left that the Movement, spread now to the poor of all races, still might just do it, might reactivate the conscience of society. This had been the ultimate delusion: that the least powerful, and then, even, the least able could do a job that may well not be accomplished even should it be tackled by the most powerful, the most able. At last, the delusion was dead.

I got my two drinks fetched as fast as tourist accommodations allow, and ignored my seat-mate, a young soldier, through most of the first one. But the soldier asked me for a cigarette (damn it, I seemed to be counting out my last hopes for the Movement in bummed cigarettes) and seemed as anxious as I was for the stewardess to bring the drinks. We got to talking. His voice was Southern, which sounded good to me. He had drunk, he said, the day before, a full quart of grain alcohol, and still hadn't quite got over it. He said that the first drink just about burned out his whole mouth and throat and head.

"I took it straight," he said.

"Should have cut it with grapefruit juice," I said out of the vastness of my own military experience.

"Yeah, I did after that first one."

He mentioned that he was a cook. Oh-oh, I thought, remembering that all the army cooks of my time had been certifiably insane.

A colored man, he said, had given him the grain alcohol as a going-away present for his leave. "He comes around every night and I give him all the food we have left over. His family needs it, other families. I don't see any harm in that. We waste so damn much food." I said I didn't see any harm in it, either.

The soldier was from East Point, a suburb of Atlanta, a stronghold of the kind of people who believe in Lester Maddox. His daddy was a policeman. "Makes it rough," he said. "I like to go to these bars, my favorite ones, and the cops come in and see me and first thing go tell my dad I was there." I asked him what he planned to do when he got out. He said he would be a computer operator, an ambition entirely out of my generation's experience, but sounding like a likely one.

"I still have to go back and finish high school; I got kicked out my senior year for dumping a whole big load of fireworks into a toilet in the boys' restroom. It blew out all the plumbing."

I laughed, but shouldn't have. He didn't, and I knew from my own son's recent experience with authority, with the close-knittedness nowadays of school and police authority (the educators are cops; the cops educate), that this wasn't a laughing matter anymore, that Huck Finn and Penrod are not tolerated in a society that is deadly serious, that he had felt the shiver of the threat of jail, of authoritarian power.

The army, he said, had matured him; he wouldn't ever do a fool stunt like that again. He had been to Vietnam. I fought off the juxtaposition of images, the guilty criminal putting fireworks in the boys' john and society's hero wreaking unspeakable havoc with the explosives and other chemicals they use in Vietnam: I'd had enough ironic juxtapositions for one trip. He said he had been wounded—showing me a scar on his wrist—by a grenade. "I know," he said (the plane was circling to land), "what we are fighting for over there."

"Oh yeah," I said, half-believing from the conviction in his voice that he did, that he would reveal a meaning in all this world of meaninglessness to me.

"They got my buddy," he said, "the same attack. A mortar. He didn't have a chance. And I said to myself right then, I'll kill every goddamn gook I can get my hands on. That's what this war is all about."

It was hot in Atlanta when we got down. The cab driver complained of the unrelenting quality of the god-damned heat in that ageless, always surprised, equinox after equinox, complaint of the Southerner. The Movement is dead, I said to myself. And there is no hope that lasts. They have known that for some time in other places: in France they have embodied it now into a philosophy; in India, they have nurtured their religion on it. Negroes in the South have known it, through slavery and since then—existing, making do. How did the SNCC kids, with all their reading of Camus miss that? Keeping on, those of them still at it, coining their rhetoric from the metal of hope, showing in all their hate-talk now only the other side of the love-talk, anything to avoid accepting hopelessness. Dr. King knew about that. Making do, as Southern Negroes always have done, with an irrelevant and irrational religion, he forged a world-view of staggering insight. Making do with the worst of his followers by drawing the best out of them, he built a movement that shook America, almost converted some of it, at the very least put an end to Southern institutionalization of racism. And then he had seen his philosophy and strategy of nonviolent change lose influence, had seen America steadily moving in the opposite direction from the one he sought. You get down to hopelessness, finally, his kind of hopelessness, and then you see that it is still possible to keep on, to find meaning in meaninglessness, like the Negroes with no food and no purpose, like the demonstrators in that driveway. "Keep on a-walking, children," Dr. King used to say in the hot, fervent, sacred little churches of the Movement's great days, "don't you get weary. We are headed toward the promised land."

New American Review, January 1969

Marks After the Campaign

by Steve Van Evera

MARKS, Miss.—One day last spring, the Poor People's Campaign began with a march from Memphis, Tenn., to Marks. Later, several Quitman County residents climbed aboard mule-drawn wagons here, to begin a grueling trip to Washington, D.C., and Resurrection City.

The last of these people returned from Washington in late July—tired but wiser. After their return, they talked about their experiences in the Poor People's Campaign.

"We did not get anything out of those people (Washington officials)," said Mrs. Mary Jones of Marks. But, she said, "I'm glad I went. I learned something from it. I found out they's just as bad there as these people down here.

"Nothing's changed at all," said Mrs. Jones, "and it made things worse back here, because now people pick at us. The so-called (police) patrol makes it so you can't hardly walk the street. Some people lost their jobs who went."

Kelson Taylor was one of those who lost their jobs. His 16-year-old son participated in a demonstration in Marks last April, and then left for Washington to join the Poor People's Campaign.

The day after the demonstration, Taylor said, he was "laid off" from his job with the Marks sanitation department, where he had worked for nine years.

"I didn't expect to get fired," he said. "It wasn't fair for them to do it. Yet, I'm still happy my son went. He was doin' something for our poor class of people."

Local leader William Franklin said he was bitter and disillusioned over the way the campaigners were received in Washington.

"We went all the way to Washington and didn't get a damn thing," Franklin said. "Ain't NOTHIN' changed! We feel like those people up there did us wrong. . . .

"They kept the only promise they made—with tear gas.

"We asked to get a factory here in Marks, schoolin' and milk and stuff for the children, and we got nothin'," Franklin continued. "A fellow from CBS News just came by askin' did we think we accomplished anything. I told him no, not a damn thing. . . .

"I thought we'd get something out of Washington. I honestly did. I thought if we would go and tell 'em face to face what it was like down here, if they had a heart in their body they'd help feed us, anyway. But we was just wastin' our time.

"In a way it was worth it, though," Franklin said. "You know the way up until now they always tell us, 'It's just them white folks in Mississippi that doin' it to you.' Well, now we know it ain't so. It's Washington—they's just as bad."

Franklin was particularly critical of Orville Freeman, U.S. Secretary Agriculture, and of U.S. Attorney General Ramsey Clark.

"We went into Orville Freeman's office, told them what we wanted, and they just sat an' looked at us," he recalled. "Finally, we said we'd give 'em ten days to give us an answer. They said they'd write us. We ain't heard from one of 'em yet.

"We went to Ramsey Clark," Franklin added, "and I swear he is as bad as ANYONE down here!"

Mrs. Lee Dora Collins went with Franklin to Washington. All she has to show for it, she said, is a $23 hospital bill and a bruised back.

"About the fourth day after we got into Washington, we were protesting around the Department of Agriculture," she explained. "Just standin' and prayin', not doin' anything, no profane language, not throwin' anything. Then the police come in, hittin' everybody with the clubs.

"We had the little children there with us, and we had to get them out of there, so they wouldn't get hurt. I got struck across the back, went to the hospital. It was a cop who hit me."

Was the campaign worth it?

"Well, I'm glad I went," said Mrs. Collins. "But I sure ain't pleased with the results. I was goin' for a purpose, to try to do all in my power to better conditions in my county. Hundreds and hundreds of people have no jobs here in Quitman County.

"We ought to give them one or two years, and if they still haven't done anything, we ought to go back to Washington and do the same thing," she said.

But Franklin disagreed. "We shouldn't go to Washington again," he said. "We got to do work right here in this town—get rid of these damn city commissioners, start politickin' against them the same way they politick against us.

"We got more than half colored folks in this town, so we can do it. We got to use politics on them. We got to get these Negroes together and decide what to do, and do it.

"Our conditions are just gettin' poorer and poorer," Franklin said. "We got to find some solution."

The Southern Courier, August 10–11, 1968

Fairfield Never Had a Negro Official— Until Last Month, When It Elected Six

by Bob Labaree

FAIRFIELD, Ala.—With few exceptions, the 1968 municipal elections were a disaster for Negro candidates. One of the biggest and most surprising exceptions was Fairfield.

In a record turn-out of voters of both races—about 60%—all six Negroes running at large for the City Council were elected outright on Aug. 13. They included Jimmie Lee Williams, Ernest McLin, Jerry D. Coleman, McKinley Kolb, Virgil Lee Pearson, and Joe L. Dubose.

(A seventh Negro candidate, Vernard F. Thomas, missed a quick victory over incumbent Lawrence G. Sides in a four-way race for president of the city council. In the Sept. 10 run-off, Sides edged Thomas by 200 votes.)

Fairfield's black community also claimed credit for electing a new mayor—a young white man named Joe H. King, who soundly defeated aging incumbent Claude Smithson (running for his fourth term) and two other white candidates on Aug. 13.

During the campaign, King openly courted voters from "the Hill," Fairfield's largest Negro section, and he was rewarded with an endorsement from community leaders. The endorsement no doubt helped bring him the majorities he needed in wards 3 and 4.

In return, according to several Negro leaders, King supported the seven black candidates. "He knew he couldn't win without us," said Demetrius Newton, a Fairfield native and an active leader in the campaign.

For some people, the change in administration is likely to be a shock. Literally overnight, Fairfield—a town which has never had a Negro officeholder—finds itself with six of its 12 city council seats filled by Negroes.

But if Negroes have never served in City Hall before, it's not because they haven't tried. In 1952—after a long period when, as one long-time Negro resident put it, "we never even raised our heads"—Edward Robinson broke the ice and became the first Negro to run for city council. He lost.

In 1956, Thomas and Newton tried again for city council positions, with the same results. There were no black candidates in the election four years later, but in 1964, Newton, Thomas, and another Negro ran again—and lost again.

Finally, said Newton, "we got our first taste of victory in 1966"—but not for a city office. That year, Newton won 62% of the vote in his race against two white men for Fairfield's one spot on the Jefferson County Democratic Executive Committee.

"Not long after that," Newton recalled, "they changed it so that Fairfield would be represented by three men instead of one."

Newton pointed out that his 1966 victory came at a time when "they (the whites) were out-voting us by quite a bit." But since then, said David Hood, Negro voting strength has equalled and even passed the whites'.

Hood estimated that, on paper at least, Negroes now make up about 52% of the electorate. The Negroes' losing streak "didn't change," he said, "until we managed to pack more Negroes in."

But—as many Black Belt counties with even larger Negro majorities have found—numbers aren't everything. Why, then, such a success in Fairfield, and why in this particular election?

"In the past, we've been waiting until the night before the election to ask for votes," was Hood's answer. "But not this time."

Much of the credit for the pre-election organization is given to Mrs. Louvenia Thomas, who first called the black candidates together shortly after they qualified in early July, and suggested something new—that they campaign together. They agreed.

Eventually, it was decided that the candidates would pool campaign funds, operate one campaign headquarters, appear on the same posters, and share a campaign staff—with Mrs. Thomas as campaign manager. The motto they adopted was "Moving Forward With Togetherness."

Long experience with NAACP voter-registration drives provided a model for the campaign organization, said Mrs. Thomas. Negro sections were divided up under ward captains, street captains, and block workers. People were assigned to carry others to register and to vote. Finally, said Mrs. Thomas, a voters list was prepared with telephone numbers, and "we made direct contact with each voter."

Every week, mass meetings were held to generate interest and to collect money. And as election time approached, cars with sound equipment passed through Negro areas, urging people to vote.

Newton said much of the interest shown in this election was the result of long-term efforts by the Rev. J. A. Salary, head of the Fairfield NAACP. "He's the one who started the ball rolling with school integration," said Newton, an attorney. Newton himself carried the schools issue into federal court in 1965.

About a month before the election, Newton filed another federal suit. This one charged city officials and others with using a privately-financed urban renewal project to squeeze Negroes out of Fairfield, and with discriminating against Negroes in municipal services. The hearings in court in early August were attended by many Fairfield people.

"I confess (that filing the suit so close to election time) was deliberate," said Newton, "and I don't care who knows it."

But other issues, too, brought people to the polls. Besides the slow pace of school integration—which has been the subject of much legal action and community bitterness—Negroes have complained about a lack of job opportunities downtown, discriminatory zoning, and an almost total lack of representation on city boards and agencies.

But whatever the specific grievances, said Mrs. Thomas, "the main thing in this election was we needed representation according to population."

Determined this time to leave nothing to chance, Hood made certain that the slim Negro majority would be "protected from corrupt practices," and from legal complications which have stolen victories elsewhere in the past.

"We've prepared for everything that might transpire," Hood said as the polls were about to close on Aug 13. Federal inspectors as well as the candidates' own poll-watchers had been engaged to observe the voting from beginning to end.

Hood also briefed the candidates on election procedures, especially the law requiring them to spend no more than a certain amount of money on their campaign and to report their expenditures by a certain date.

"If someone spent too much or didn't report it—either one would deny him an office if he won," Hood said.

Despite the precautions, though, there were complaints on Aug. 13 from people who said their polling place had been changed or their name was not on the rolls.

But City Clerk Grady Ellison discounted most of the complaints as misunderstandings. And with the returns so much in their favor, no one on the Hill seemed in the mood to press charges.

Perhaps because of King's support and perhaps because of wide-spread discontent with the old administration, several Negro candidates picked up substantial votes Aug. 13 in predominantly-white boxes.

At the Forest Hills box in ward 6, for example, Jimmy Lee Williams received 230 votes, and other Negro candidates got as many as 70.

On the other hand, some of the black candidates actually found themselves running their closest races in their own wards. This lack of solid backing in wards 3 and 4 was expected to—and did—hurt Thomas in his Sept. 10 run-off for council president.

The prospect of an integrated city government was apparently too much for some white people to take. The votes had scarcely been counted Aug. 13 before meetings were being called in one white section of town, to discuss the possibility of having Fairfield annexed by Birmingham.

Meanwhile, residents of another white section—not within city limits but receiving many of Fairfield's services—declared that they are seeking annexation to all-white Midfield.

In 1964, a proposed annexation by Birmingham was defeated by 400 votes. "We were for that (annexation) at one time," said Hood. "That was when we had no other recourse."

Only 50 to 100 signatures on a petition are needed to call a referendum vote on annexation. But, asked Thomas, "if they couldn't win the election (on Aug. 13), how do they think they can win a referendum?"

People from both City Hall and the Hill say an annexation vote can't succeed. Moreover, Hood and others have rejected the idea that Negroes are going to use their new power to "get even."

"We're not trying to control Fairfield," Hood said. "We're trying to make Fairfield a better place to live for all people."

The Southern Courier, September 21–22, 1968

S.N.C.C. in Decline After 8 Years in Lead

by C. Gerald Fraser

THE Student Nonviolent Coordinating Committee, which emerged from the rural South eight years ago to become a pace-setter in the national civil rights movement, is in serious decline.

It has lost much of its power and influence to the northern slum-born Black Panthers as the rights movement has grown into the "black liberation struggle." And it has also lost to the Panthers its leading apostle, Stokely Carmichael.

These losses, and this transition, have not come about without anxiety and pain.

Members of the Black Panthers walked into James Forman's office at the committee on Fifth Avenue in late July, according to Federal authorities. One of them produced a pistol and put it into Mr. Forman's mouth. He squeezed the trigger three times.

The gun went click, click, click. It was unloaded.

Mr. Forman, who is chairman of S.N.C.C.'s international affairs commission, suffers among other things from a nervous stomach—an occupational disease of many former civil rights workers. He was so upset after the incident that he checked into a hospital and later went on vacation in Puerto Rico.

It was shortly after this that Phil Hutchings, S.N.C.C.'s program director, announced that the alliance between his group and the Black Panthers was ended. It had lasted five months, but it never actually worked.

Another announcement "to S.N.C.C. staff and associates" read:

"By unanimous vote of the central committee meeting in Queens, New York . . . Stokely Carmichael's relationship to the organization was terminated."

Thus Carmichael was drummed out of the organization

whose early path he had followed down dusty road after dusty road in Mississippi and Alabama, whose work had taken him from one hot Southern jail to the next.

S.N.C.C. itself had changed, however, since the early nineteen-sixties, when Carmichael had come in as an organizer. Then S.N.C.C. had captured the conscience of black and white students, northern and southern, who wanted to help register Negro voters, set up co-operatives, establish health clinics and teach Negroes to read and write in rural areas of the South.

They came by the busloads during the summer vacations and contributions rolled into S.N.C.C. campaign chests.

Either alone or co-operating with groups like the Congress of Racial Equality or the Medical Committee for Human Rights, S.N.C.C. carried on a wide range of activities, including the founding of the Mississippi Freedom Democratic party and the Lowndes County Freedom Organization, the county-wide political party whose symbol was a black panther.

Now, before Carmichael's expulsion and even before its ill-starred alliance with the Black Panthers, S.N.C.C. seemed to most observers a shambles of an organization, only a shadow of what it had been in numbers, organization, resources and zeal.

Some observers have pronounced the emaciated S.N.C.C. a corpse.

"S.N.C.C.—as the old S.N.C.C.—I don't think has existed for some time," said Ella Baker, who, as executive secretary of the Southern Christian Leadership Conference, helped found S.N.C.C. in April, 1960.

Most S.N.C.C. members do not attribute the organization's decline to Carmichael, but some say he promoted a factionalism that they contend contributed to it.

The official reasons listed for his expulsion were:

¶"Failure to keep S.N.C.C. informed about his projects, activities, trips and Washington, D.C., operations."

¶"Failure to volunteer information concerning his personal life where it had obvious effect on the political direction of S.N.C.C."

¶"Engaging in a power struggle both within and outside of

S.N.C.C. with another organization member (Forman) which during the week of July 22 in New York City almost resulted in physical harm to S.N.C.C. personnel and threatened the existence of the organization."

While S.N.C.C.'s power and credentials in the black movement have diminished, Carmichael—a 28 year old Trinidadian-born naturalized American who was graduated from the Bronx High School of Science and Howard University—has remained in the movement's forefront.

A philosophy major in college, Carmichael was one of S.N.C.C.'s brain trust and took pride in being a theorist of the movement. Months ago he evidently became convinced that what militants refer to as the black liberation struggle was not being waged by S.N.C.C. and was not about to be.

He had become disenchanted with the American system after the Democratic National Convention in 1964 failed to seat the delegation of the Mississippi Freedom Democratic party. And he had announced in the summer of 1966 the turn that the civil-rights movement had already begun to take with his shouts, on Mississippi's Highway 51, for black power.

He came to believe, it seems, that the Panthers—wise to the ways of the slums, politically sophisticated and organized around the gun—had the nerve and the ability to carry on the struggle in America's urban communities.

Thus, by the time S.N.C.C. "terminated" his relationship, Carmichael had already left spiritually.

The main point in the opinion of most people in the movement is that the S.N.C.C. that Carmichael left is pre-Watts while the Panthers are post-Watts. They believe that the 1965 riots in the Watts area of Los Angeles marked the end of the middle-class-oriented civil rights movement.

Watts gave status to urban youth in northern black communities. Generations of Negro youth had bottled their resentment at America's racism. With the fires in Watts, the lid was off. The cathartic effect was a development of self-respect.

S.N.C.C. had brought middle-class black and white youths into the South at the height of the civil rights movement. They worked mainly among rural Negroes and developed among them an awareness that political self-determination was possible.

The Panthers were created out of an urban slum in Oakland, Calif. Its members are the youths in black communities who feel that with nothing to gain, they have nothing to lose.

Of the Panthers, one S.N.C.C. member said: "I can't work with anybody I don't feel right turning my back on." Eldridge Cleaver, the author and Panther minister of information, said S.N.C.C. members felt Panthers were a group of "bandits."

Of the members of S.N.C.C., Cleaver said: They are "black hippies . . . black college students who have dropped out of the middle class."

Since S.N.C.C. left the South, it has not developed a program around which it can organize. The Panthers have a program that they hope will lead to self-determination for black communities.

S.N.C.C. has eschewed white cooperation. The Panthers have cooperated with white radicals—notably the Peace and Freedom party.

The purpose of the alliance was to blend S.N.C.C.—the organization with the image—with the Panthers—the organization with the program. But it never really worked. H. Rap Brown and Mr. Forman of S.N.C.C. were named ministers of justice and foreign affairs, respectively. But they have since resigned.

S.N.C.C. finances, membership and programs are never discussed by the organization publicly, and some in the movement believe it does not now have a program. S.N.C.C. was never a large membership organization, and over the years its staff members have wandered off. Many former S.N.C.C. workers are now doing graduate study, are associated with poverty programs or with nonprofit groups, or are teaching or practicing law.

The current S.N.C.C. membership, believed to be far below 50, is formed of a nucleus of old-timers of the Southern movement. They are not significantly less "militant" or less "revolutionary" than the Panthers. And Carmichael is not necessarily more militant than S.N.C.C.

But what seems to have happened is that the bright, well-traveled Carmichael has continued to move, while S.N.C.C. has stumbled.

Miss Baker contends that S.N.C.C. was unable to make the transition from work in the South to work in the North.

"S.N.C.C. came North," she said, "when the North was in a ferment that led to various interpretations of what was needed to be done. With its own frustrations, it could not take the pace-setter role it took in the South.

"They were unable to sense that the milieu and factors of change were more than they had dealt with before. And the frustration that came to individuals that had gone through the Southern experience rendered them unable to make a historical decision that perhaps their days were over.

Carmichael was able, however, to make that switch.

While he was national chairman of S.N.C.C., in 1966 and 1967, he visited Scandinavia, France, Britain, Spain, Czechoslovakia, Cuba and North Vietnam. He has just returned from a trip to Africa.

He toured college after college and is said to have radicalized, single-handed, many classes of black students.

His speeches on foreign trips and college platforms, however, raised the hackles of some. A speech in Havana brought sharp criticism of both Carmichael and S.N.C.C. In it he said:

"We are preparing groups of urban guerrillas for our defense in the cities. . . . It is going to be a fight to the death."

One S.N.C.C. member exclaimed at the time, "My God, what is Stokely saying." But S.N.C.C., traditionally undisciplined, could not rein in Carmichael. And it alienated a portion of the Jewish community by publishing in a S.N.C.C. newsletter allegedly pro-Arab, anti-Jewish comments on the conflict in the Mideast.

Carmichael's personal life further alienated some S.N.C.C. staffers and members.

At the center of this was his marriage to Miriam Makeba, the South African–born singer. Miss Makeba has devoted time, talent and money to black liberation here and in Africa, but the marriage raised eyebrows because some of his associates thought he was going "bourgeois."

This notion gained momentum with a widely circulated but inaccurate report that the Carmichaels had purchased a $70,000 home in Washington. The couple do own a house in an expensive section of Washington, but Carmichael has said the price was far below $70,000.

In July S.N.C.C. purged itself of both the Panthers and Carmichael. "That cleared the air," said John Wilson, a deputy chairman of S.N.C.C.

"We had so many factions," Mr. Wilson continued, "the Carmichael faction, the Forman faction and so on. Now maybe we'll have just a S.N.C.C. faction, and we can get on with our program."

The New York Times, October 7, 1968

Jesse Jackson: Heir to Dr. King?

by Richard Levine

"POACHED eggs," muttered Jesse Jackson, sitting up in his Chicago hospital bed to get a better look at breakfast. "That's white folks' food." He winked at the group of Operation Breadbasket ministers and staff who vied for space in the tiny room with flowers from well-wishers, reached under the bed for a greasy paper bag, unwrapped it, and began taking in spoonfuls of sweet-potato pudding while leafing through the morning mail.

The ministers were there because Jackson had scheduled a ten o'clock press conference in the hospital lounge. Although Breadbasket had moved a long way from its original slogan— "Your ministers fight for jobs and rights"—they would provide a show of unity with occasional interjections of "Amen" and "Tell it, Jesse." The staff members were there to discuss the position of the organization on the Chicago Transit Authority's proposed bus-fare hike. (Jackson would talk about "taxation without representation"—there were no Negroes on the CTA board—and announce that if the CTA didn't shape up soon, Breadbasket would establish a BTA, a Black Transit Authority.)

Jesse Jackson was there because he had mononucleosis. He had been in the hospital for two weeks, darting past the disapproving glance of his doctor for important meetings and then back into bed again. Specialists at the hospital had determined that he suffered from sickle-cell trait, a blood disorder peculiar to Negroes of West African descent that protected against malaria but increased susceptibility to the more common viruses of Chicago, Illinois. Jackson was delighted with the diagnosis; mono was mono, but an African disease was a press release in itself.

Still, it was no time to be sick. At twenty-seven, Jesse Jackson was probably the most powerful Negro in Chicago. Breadbasket had become the only mass organization in the black community, a force to be reckoned with not just by white business interests in the ghetto but also by the politicians downtown, now that Jackson had begun endorsing candidates and speaking out on local political issues. Yet with all his success, he had serious problems, too. Breadbasket's quick growth in recent months had aggravated internal tensions between the ministers and the Negro businessmen, between the black and white staff members. And the thorniest problem of all was Jackson's attempt to build a consensus around his leadership in a black community plagued by factional rivalries and deep class hostility.

He lingered over one letter from the pile on his lap, finally reading it to the group. "Dear Reverend Jackson," wrote a fifteen-year-old girl, "when I first started attending the meetings my people thought you were a crook, but with the help of God I showed all but one that you weren't. I pray for Breadbasket every day and that I may some day commit my life to it." Jackson was puzzled. After three years of organizing Negroes in Chicago, bringing the largest chain stores in the city to heel with a series of boycotts, traveling around the country to set up other Breadbaskets, cradling Martin Luther King's head in his arms on the balcony of the Lorraine Motel in Memphis, gaining national prominence last June as manager of Resurrection City, finally landing in a hospital for "sins against my finitude," who could still think he was a crook?

Some people, even now. A great many more, three years ago. In the fall of 1965 Jesse Jackson was a student at the Chicago Theological Seminary, working part-time for the Coordinating Council of Community Organizations (CCCO), a shaky coalition of civil-rights groups which would provide Martin Luther King with his local support in the Chicago Freedom Movement the following spring and summer. A few months as a community organizer in the Kenwood-Oakland area of South Chicago taught Jackson that the most powerful forces in the ghetto were still the ministers rather than the professional organizers or the Negro politicians. The difficulty was that these ministers, mainly Baptist, were spending Sunday mornings, in the words of one now affiliated with Breadbasket, "shouting hallelujah and passing the plate." They were a generally conservative lot, ruling their churches like petty fiefs, intensely suspicious of rivals. Most had long since made their peace with the Daley machine. ("Negro ministers think they're servants of God, but they're servants of Daley," commented one independent black alderman. "Maybe that's the same thing.") Some of the more powerful—such as Dr. Joseph H. Jackson, president of the National Baptist Convention—were important cogs in the machine. Jesse Jackson, then twenty-four years old, seminary-trained, brash and ambitious by his own admission, seemed an unlikely candidate to win them over. Feelings ran so strong against him in those days that he was once turned out of a meeting of the Baptist Convention of Chicago at gunpoint. Yet by April of 1966, when Breadbasket launched its first campaign, many of these ministers were shouting hallelujah and announcing the boycott on Sunday morning.

"This may sound corny, but he's loved those ministers into support," says John McDermott, director of the Catholic Interracial Council. Jackson began to woo them by forming a friendship with the Reverend Clay Evans, then president of the Baptist Convention of Chicago, becoming associate pastor at Evans' church. Next he invited a group of ministers to meet regularly at the Chicago Theological Seminary with several professors. The talk at these meetings shuttled back and forth between traditional sin and—a favorite Jackson phrase—"institutional sin." (This remains the typical, often curious Breadbasket mix. One recent meeting of the organization's steering committee opened with a detailed documentation of the case against a small chain of food stores located exclusively in the ghetto—no Negroes in executive positions, unsanitary conditions, high prices for bad meat and bruised vegetables—and ended with the ministers, arms interlocked in a circle, offering up silent prayers for the salvation of the company president's soul.)

Gradually, Jackson was able to gain the ministers' confidence*, in part because he has a genuine respect for their role in the community. "The preacher is a psychotherapist," he says, "his congregation's soul doctor; if he drives a big Cadillac it's because his people want him to." He is also one of them in a way that was never the case, for example, with Mar-

*Though there are still some who have successfully resisted his appeal. Dr. J. H. Jackson speaks out frequently against Breadbasket. He was a long-time opponent of Martin Luther King, both because he doesn't believe in civil-

tin Luther King. "I'm just a country preacher doing some serious observing," he will say at a meeting, and the intention is half ironical, the effect humorous. In a real sense, though, it is true. Martin Luther King was middle-class Atlanta. He might speak of "the great washed and the great unwashed, the Ph.D.s and the no D.s," but you always knew *he* washed regularly and that it was *Dr.* King. Jesse Jackson was born in poverty in Greenville, South Carolina. He is well-educated, but speaks with a down-home accent—final "g's" in participles are dropped and "thing" becomes "thang." He is a sharp dresser—turtlenecks and suede sport jackets, occasionally a dashiki—but wears high-top country boots under his bell-bottom trousers. It is a nice touch. The ministers like it, and so do the kids.

By January 1966, when King brought the Southern Christian Leadership Conference into Chicago, sixty ministers were willing to form a steering committee and Operation Breadbasket was launched in the North—an Atlanta Breadbasket already existed—with Jackson as its director. Breadbasket's immediate model was a successful "selective buying" campaign conducted by the Reverend Leon Sullivan in Philadelphia in the early 1960s. At the start Jackson followed the familiar pattern. Breadbasket's goals were limited to jobs and its tactics were simple: ask a company with business in the ghetto for its employment figures, demand the hiring of Negroes at all levels equal to the percentage of the city's population that is black, throw up a picket line if the demands are not met, and wait by the phone.

It always rang. Between April and October of 1966 nine companies were contacted, milk companies in the spring ("That stuff can't stand around," Jackson explains), and soft-drink distributors when the weather turned hot. Four companies had to be picketed; the others heard the footsteps coming. Jackson held press conferences where the executives signed "covenants" which read more like confessions: they pledged adherence to "a program of creative employment and

---

rights protests and because King helped lead a splinter group out of the National Baptist Convention in 1962. His dislike of King and anyone connected with him is so intense that when the city of Chicago, in a belated tribute after King's death, renamed the street Dr. Martin Luther King, Jr. Drive, J. H. Jackson changed the address to a side entrance on 31st Street.

business development aimed at ending the economic indignities and injustices which have ravaged the Negro people physically and spiritually." He would then announce the organization's next target and leave—without a follow-up program or a specific hiring schedule.

Some businessmen called Jackson an extortionist, feeling that they were being forced to lower their standards, particularly in management positions. Jackson's stock answer was that if the Army can teach a Negro to build bridges in Vietnam after a six-month training program, a company doesn't need two years to teach him how to sell soda pop successfully. But the more typical reaction was simply bewilderment. Recalling his negotiations with the Breadbasket ministers two years ago, the vice president of a large milk company still shrugs his shoulders. "One minute they would be talking about how many Negro truck drivers we had to hire, and the next minute about man's relation to God."

Since those early days Breadbasket has grown enormously and changed its direction several times. If the organization has become more professional, it has also become more religious ("Breadbasket *is* my church" is a comment one hears frequently). But the religion would horrify most clergymen. Breadbasket "services" are held on Saturday morning at the Tabernacle Baptist Church. By 8:30 cars are triple-parked along Indiana Avenue and a small marketplace is in full session on the sidewalk outside the church. Boys hawk the Negro press, impeccably dressed young men offer the Muslim paper, *Muhammed Speaks.* There is a bookstall with works ranging from Eldridge Cleaver's *Soul on Ice* to a children's coloring book entitled *Color Me Brown.* African clothes, pastel drawings of Negro leaders, and a variety of buttons are also available. Inside the huge hangar-shaped church two or three thousand people are listening to the Breadbasket orchestra, actually a jazz band led by Ben Branch, the musician Martin Luther King was speaking to from the motel balcony just before he was shot.

The exact number of people at a given Saturday meeting depends on the guest celebrities expected (three main groups: white politicians, black athletes, and Jackson's Hollywood friends, black and white) and whether Breadbasket is involved in a boycott at the time, in which case picketing teams leave from the meeting. This particular Saturday the crowd is unusually large, for Coretta King is in Chicago and has promised to attend. Probably three-quarters of the people are women, mostly young, well-dressed, definitely middle-class. (Jackson, who is very conscious of his appeal to women, claims that he learned how to use his good looks to build a following from Adam Clayton Powell. In a recent "Pin-up Boy" poll conducted by a Chicago newspaper, he ranked, alphabetically, between Cary Grant and Jean-Claude Killy.) There are also pockets of whites in the audience and, perhaps more surprisingly, some tough-looking young blacks at the rear, their jackets indicating membership in one of the West Side gangs, the Conservative Vice Lords.

Now the Breadbasket choir, two hundred teenagers seated in tiers behind the pulpit, is warming up the audience with a hand-clapping rendition of "I Wish I Knew How It Would Feel to be Free." The song has become Breadbasket's "We Shall Overcome," and it will be sung often this morning, the audience joining in, each time more enthusiastically as the pace of the meeting picks up:

> I wish I knew how it would feel to be free,
> I wish I could break all these chains holding me;
> I wish I could say all the things I should say,
> Say 'em loud, say 'em clear, for the whole world to hear.

When the song is over, the guest speakers are introduced. Illinois Lieutenant Governor Paul Simon, who has been having a terrible time trying to look as though he always clapped and swayed to gospel music on Saturday morning, thanks Breadbasket for its endorsement of him before the November elections. The Reverend Willie Barrow, a fiery lady preacher who heads Breadbasket's women's division, gives the women a pep talk: "We've got a power in us, not because of how big our bust is, or how small our waist is, but because of how long our shopping list is." A high-school leader of a black student boycott explains his group's objectives: more Negro teachers and principals, courses in Afro-American history, holidays commemorating black heroes.

At 9:30 Jackson arrives from the hospital, the band moves into his theme song, "Hard Times," as he walks down the aisle, and the audience, standing now, breaks out in rhythmic clapping. Jackson lets the enthusiasm build for several minutes before taking the pulpit and motioning for quiet. He surveys the audience, unsmiling; the only indication of his illness is the sweat glistening on his forehead, though it is nearly freezing outside and not very much warmer inside.

"How many of you watch those cowboy movies on TV?" he asks, to a show of hands. "They're a lesson y'all got to learn. At first there ain't nothin' on the scene but pistols and money. Bang! Bang! A man holds up the stagecoach. Who has the most power? The man with the most money. He can be so ugly he looks like he's been made in a Headstart program and it don't matter.

"Now the rich man starts building up his economic base. Opens a saloon or a general store. Then he brings in the law. For justice? To make him give the money back? Course not. The law's there to make sure no one robs the rich man. He's the legislature, not only protects but decides who gets protected.

"Next the schoolmarm gets off the stagecoach. She interprets history and teaches culture. Since the rich man already has his money, he wants everybody else to be polite.

"Finally the preacher comes to town and forgives the rich man his original sin. Old folks who stole money start getting scared.

"That's how you go about forming a civilization. First the economic base, then the legislature to protect it—that's politics—then the culture to interpret it, finally religion to justify it. Y'all understand what I'm telling you? Say 'Amen.'"

Cries of "Amen" and "You're on the case, Jesse" amidst general laughter. Jackson, however, has more on his mind this morning than entertaining the audience with his own brand of social theory. "Saturday morning is hustling time," he had told a group of Negro businessmen the night before. "If you can't sell your product to three thousand people, hair growing long, lips thick, earrings dripping down, you can't sell your product period." He is about to prove his point.

"Black people are at the first stage of the cowboy movie,

building an economic base. Most of us don't think we produce but two or three things, the primary one being slums. But we produce all *these* things." Jackson points to a table beside the pulpit which holds the products of the black-owned businesses affiliated with Breadbasket, reaches for one of them and begins his pitch.

"You will show your blackness by buying Grove Fresh orange juice. Repeat after me: Say it loud, I'm black and I'm proud and I buy Grove Fresh orange juice." The audience responds on cue, as Jackson holds up one product after another.

"Say it loud, I use Mumbo barbecue sauce.

"Say it proud, I eat Staff of Life wheat bread.

"I use Swift Out. It opens up any drain. Why it's so strong if you pour it in your sink it'll open up the sewer down the block.

"Say it loud, I use King Solomon spray deodorant and I'm proud.

"Now Joe Louis milk does not come from a Negro cow. That milk has 400 U.S.P.s just like any other milk. It's written right here on the carton. Only difference is that your husband can make twelve thousand a year driving a truck for this company.

"Rather than looking through the yellow pages, you got to start looking through the black pages. Trouble is Negroes been programmed by white folks to believe their products are inferior. We've developed into a generation of Oreos—black on the outside, white on the inside.

"But I got news for you: a new hair-style does not constitute black power, a new life-style does. About the only thing can save us is waking up one morning with self-respect and willing to do some serious work. Cause the Lord don't make orange juice. He may make the ground fertile but Grove Fresh makes the orange juice and you got to buy it. That's what the Lord does to keep from being called a puppeteer."

After Jackson is finished, there is more singing and jazz while ushers move down the aisles taking up a collection. Then Coretta King is introduced, rather perfunctorily, as "the first lady of the civil-rights movement." Jackson was not too enthusiastic about her coming and there is obviously a certain amount of distrust between the two of them. "We'll take care of our business and then Mrs. King can do her women-power thing," he had told his staff during the week. (More women power is *not* what Negro organizations need, and it is certainly not what Breadbasket needs. Jackson was just then in the process of restructuring Breadbasket, primarily in order to eliminate the women's division, which was becoming too large and too independent, as a separate entity.)

For her part, Mrs. King has been sitting quietly behind the pulpit throughout the meeting, not looking entirely pleased with what is going on, and when she finally gets up to speak, she says: "The greatness of our movement is that it is basically a spiritual movement based on Christian precepts, and we must not forget this. If you believe in Dr. King's principles you have to believe that all people, no matter what color, are God's people." She gives a restrained tribute to "black women who have kept the faith over the centuries"—she is a lady of such enormous dignity that it is difficult to imagine her overdoing anything—and then there is a curious, awkward moment.

"After my last visit to Breadbasket," Mrs. King concludes, "I told my husband that Jesse Jackson will make a tremendous contribution to our society. I hoped then, and I still hope now, that he will remain with SCLC." Jackson is clearly caught off-guard and all he can think of doing in response is to raise Coretta King's right hand in a black power—she would call it soul power—salute. Modesty is not one of Jackson's virtues, and he is probably as much surprised by hearing his contribution to society put in the future tense as by the public suggestion that he might take Breadbasket out of SCLC.

And yet there have been rumors that he might, rumors which persist despite Jackson's denial of them. It is true that you can go to a number of Saturday meetings without ever hearing of SCLC, though you will invariably hear that Operation Breadbasket is the most viable civil-rights organization in this country, or words to that effect. It is also true that Jackson does not get along well with Ralph Abernathy and thinks him ineffective as head of SCLC, but their differences, except for one occasion, have been kept from public view.

The one occasion came last June when Jackson was replaced as manager of Resurrection City in Washington by Hosea Williams, and while he was given another assignment —organizing satellite Resurrection Cities around the country

—nothing much ever came of the plan, probably because nothing much was ever intended to come of it. Jackson's role in Resurrection City was partly to keep the young militants in the encampment (many of whom, including busloads of Blackstone Rangers, he had brought with him from Chicago) in line, but it soon became apparent that his desire for sharper confrontations with the Administration was closer to theirs than to Abernathy's and that he was turning morning prayer sessions into Operation Breadbasket meetings. By the time he led a group of marchers to the Agriculture Department cafeteria and let them run up a $292.66 lunch bill, then refused to pay it with the comment that the amount was a token of what the nation owed the poor, Abernathy had had enough and Jackson was reassigned.

More important than whether or not Jackson will separate from SCLC is that he could if he wanted to. The three thousand people on Saturday are committed to Breadbasket in Chicago not SCLC in Atlanta; or rather, they are committed to Jesse Jackson personally, which is why he must fly back to Chicago for the Saturday morning meetings no matter where in the country he may be on Friday night, and even get out of a hospital bed to attend, as he has been doing recently. Operation Breadbasket in Chicago is also the only financially independent program SCLC sponsors, with most of the money coming from collections at the meetings and regular contributions from the businessmen Jackson has helped so much over the past two years.

These Negro businessmen have become the core of Breadbasket. The huge meetings at Tabernacle Baptist Church are an outgrowth of Saturday breakfast meetings at the Chicago Theological Seminary beginning in the fall of 1966, where Jackson and a handful of businessmen, mainly small producers of food, cosmetics and houseware products, would discuss common problems and possible solutions. The problems were that they felt discriminated against by their natural outlets, the large food chains which do a high percentage of their business in the ghetto (forty of A&P's ninety stores in Chicago are located in the predominantly Negro South and West Sides of the city). When they weren't locked out completely, the businessmen complained, they were getting only token orders, unfavorable shelf space, and almost no advertising. The obvious solution was to force the chains to market their products with the threat of a Breadbasket boycott. The first store picketed turned out to be a Negro-owned franchise of Certified Grocers, a mistake which was never repeated. Within six months all of the major food chains that do business in the ghetto had negotiated covenants with Breadbasket.

The businessmen also held seminars with professors of the University of Chicago Business School, where they were instructed in accounting and marketing techniques. They hired a Negro advertising firm to give their products a new "black pride" image: "You don't have to be ~~Negro~~ black to drink Joe Louis milk. Just 'hip'"; "Afro-Sheen, a beautiful new hair product for a beautiful people."

Almost all of the companies increased their sales after affiliating with Breadbasket. One company, Argia B's Food Products, grew from virtually zero sales to a volume in six figures, and its single item, a barbecue sauce, now has 15 per cent of the entire Chicago market. But even an already substantial company like Joe Louis milk attributes a 20 to 30 per cent increase in sales over the past two years to Breadbasket negotiations. Occasionally, the organization's quick success proved disastrous, as when a bleach manufacturer failed because he could not meet the large orders from Jewel Tea.

New businessmen joining Breadbasket are questioned by an "attunement" committee to make sure they are black through and through—no Oreos, or, worse, an Oreo fronting for a "marshmallow," need apply—and treat their Negro employees accordingly. "If I thought we were just developing some more black capitalists with the same value system as white capitalists," Jackson told an early meeting of the businessmen, "I would leave this morning. The only thing dangerous about black power is that it might become like white power—compassionate toward machines, not people. What we need is white folks' technology and black folks' love." Breadbasket's directory of black businesses now includes over a hundred producers, financial institutions (two banks with predominantly Negro boards have quadrupled their resources in two years, although they are still both piggy banks by downtown standards), and a variety of services, all of which are negotiated into the covenants.

Last summer Breadbasket found that A&P was not living up to its original agreement. Although Negroes were being hired, others were being laid off and the net gain in jobs fell far short of the prescribed 770 new employees. After a fourteen-week boycott, a second covenant was signed, and Breadbasket considers it a model for future negotiations. In addition to the standard demands for jobs and the marketing of the businessmen's products, A&P has agreed to use black-owned scavenger, janitorial, and exterminating companies in its ghetto stores ("We have a monopoly on rats in the ghetto," Jackson likes to say, "and we're going to have a monopoly on killing them"), to contract with black construction companies for new stores, bank in the black banks, advertise in black media, employ a black public-relations firm, and meet monthly with Breadbasket just to make sure it does all this. As a further check, "sensitivity seminars" are held for A&P executives "to make management more aware of the effects of prejudice and assist them to develop action toward implementing this strengthened policy."

Since the businessmen have come to the fore, Jackson has been more vulnerable than ever to charges from black militants that he is only interested in helping a few dozen middle-class Negroes get rich quick, and doesn't concern himself with the masses of blacks for whom the "gut" issues are housing or welfare or whatever. One militant black leader of a West Side tenant union habitually referred to Jackson as "the Booker T. Washington of the late Sixties," and even when they conceded that he was effective in a limited area, it was with the faintest of praise. "If you're talking about pissing to fill up the Mississippi," another militant commented, "I guess every little bit helps."

The charges were the more damaging, of course, because they were substantially true. Breadbasket *was* a middle-class organization, and the decision to make it so had been taken very deliberately. Jackson felt that SCLC failed in Chicago in 1966 because Martin Luther King set himself up on the West Side, where the poorest blacks live, and then chose to organize them around the housing issue. The plain fact is that the poorest blacks are the most difficult to organize, and housing is the most complex of issues, with too many people making decisions—every slumlord or white homeowner who refuses to sell to a Negro, in fact—and too few people with the power to enforce an eventual rent or open-occupancy agreement. Jackson had been involved in organizing rent strikes and leading some of the marches into white neighborhoods, getting his head split open with a brick on one occasion, and he wasn't about to make the same mistake again. He would organize on the South Side among middle-class Negroes and choose black economic power as his issue, for although businessmen might be expected to take a what-have-you-done-for-me-lately attitude, if you managed to do something for them, they would stick by you.

And they did stick by him, showing up every Friday night for the workers' council meeting, where Jackson would give chalk-talks demonstrating his economic "theories." The island theory, for example—a little circle inside a big circle on the blackboard—which postulates that the black community is a colony inside the larger white community, so that money changes hands only twice, once when a Negro gets his salary and a second time when he spends it on the mainland. Or its complement, the kingdom theory—fence around the little circle—which explains that Negroes must make the ghetto their kingdom, buying only from one another within it, so that money changes hands continually, and whites who want to do business in the kingdom must pay a tax in the form of jobs and fair prices and marketing black products. "I don't know if you're ready for a kingdom," Jackson would sometimes conclude, "but I'm sure ready to be the king."

Jackson's political involvement began immediately after the death of Martin Luther King. At a City Council meeting the next day Mayor Daley read a eulogy: "The life of Dr. King and his ultimate total sacrifice provide us with the inspiration to deepen our dedication and commitment to the goals for which . . ." It was too much for Jackson. Wearing dark glasses to hide his fatigue and the same green turtleneck he had on the day before, now stained with King's blood, he told the packed chamber: "This blood is on the chest and hands of those who would not have welcomed him here yesterday. A fitting memorial to Dr. King would not be to sit here looking sad and pious and feeling bad, but to behave differently."

Four hundred people attended the Breadbasket meeting the Saturday before King's murder; four thousand attended a memorial service the following Saturday. Jackson now had the support he needed to become a political force in Chicago, and throughout the summer he issued a steady stream of press statements—against the passage of a "stop and frisk" law in Illinois, against Daley's "shoot to kill" order (the Mayor had also been watching cowboy movies, Jackson feared), against the police actions during the convention ("legalized klansmen and robots wound up by Mayor Daley"), in support of a group of black bus drivers striking the Chicago Transit Authority, in support of the black students' boycott.

"In the long run," a Breadbasket position paper explains, "one cannot hope to develop a strong black independent political movement without cultivating the economic resources of black people. . . . Where there are independent black entrepreneurs there is the possibility that they will support independent black candidates." Jackson endorsed two independent black Congressional candidates for the June primaries. Both lost. Then the national candidates began calling on Jackson— three thousand people every Saturday *is* a politician's church —and before the summer was over George McGovern and Eugene McCarthy had been received warmly at the meeting, and Nelson Rockefeller privately at Breadbasket headquarters.

In late October Jackson came out in support of Hubert Humphrey for President and Republican Richard B. Ogilvie for Governor of Illinois, though both endorsements were made with such little enthusiasm that a staff member of Breadbasket would describe Jackson's strategy as an attempt to sit down between two stools—the pun was intended— without falling. The Presidential endorsement was more an organizational obligation (Abernathy had spoken out for Humphrey) than a personal commitment, and came after some wavering on Jackson's part between McCarthy and Humphrey, as well as pressure from Nixon supporters, including, he charged, an attempted bribe to get him to back a planned "boycott" of the election by blacks. (Posters of Johnson as Clyde, Daley as Bonnie, and Humphrey as C. W. Moss, with a caption reading, "You white goats won't get our votes," were pasted up in the ghetto.) Jackson also endorsed Illinois Attorney General William G. Clark in the Senatorial contest, and this was done more enthusiastically, for the contrast between him and Everett Dirksen on civil rights was enough to make even the militants wax lyrical in his praise.

The Ogilvie endorsement was the most important of the three—Jackson announced his support "with some trepidation"—since the former president of the Cook County Board of Commissioners had never showed very much sensitivity to the black community, had indeed made better roads his principal issue in the campaign. But Ogilvie's opponent, Governor Samuel H. Shapiro, was a Daley man who had just signed the "stop and frisk" bill Jackson opposed so strongly, and here, the reasoning went, was an opportunity to hurt the machine. "Ogilvie is a Pharaoh and Shapiro is a Pharaoh," Jackson told the Saturday meeting before the election, "but Daley is a *Pharaoh's* Pharaoh."

It was understandable that Jackson's venture into politics had made him enemies in Chicago. Less understandable were the raised eyebrows among the politicians Jackson supported. He had a style which seemed tailor-made to offend the sensibilities of just those "good" liberal politicians who would normally be his closest allies in the white community if given half a chance. Saturday morning was his show, and every candidate came away knowing it. Introducing a Republican aspirant for a judgeship on the Cook County Circuit Court, Jackson raised the man's arm and shouted the old vaudeville gag line, "Here come de judge!" Adlai Stevenson III, Illinois State Treasurer and a Breadbasket hero since he put funds into the black banks, recalls the time he, William Clark, and Mayor Richard Hatcher were made to take up the collection at a Saturday meeting. "Now Adlai," Jackson directed the politicians, "you go up the center aisle, Bill, you take the left side, and Dick will flank out to the right."

When talking about Jesse Jackson, even some of his most enthusiastic admirers outside Breadbasket will admit they can't always figure him out. It is not just that he has a complex personality, but that he seems to have several personalities which fit together only very loosely, as if events have come too quickly and fame crowded too closely. He is still the campus hero, getting the adulation he needs from cheering crowds at Saturday morning meetings instead of at Saturday afternoon football games. He is a Baptist preacher, the Reverend Jesse Jackson, though certainly a new-style preacher, "the most secular one that walks," in the words of a close friend. He is most recently a powerful civil-rights leader, displaying great charisma and keen tactical sense, but it is often difficult—and perhaps it is unnecessary—to separate his intense commitment to his people from his equally intense commitment to himself.

Jesse Louis Jackson was born in Greenville, South Carolina, a large textile center, where his father is still a cotton sampler in a local mill. By the late 1940s Greenville had reached a certain level of sophistication in arranging a segregated society, and the public facilities, although definitely separate, were more or less equal. Jackson's earliest memory of the subtler effects of segregation comes from a picture in his second-grade geography book. It showed two boys standing back to back on the Equator. "There was John," he recalls, "dressed in knickers and a British-type jacket. He was facing North. Facing South was Bumble, his hair so hard it seemed like the sunlight was bouncing off it, and he didn't have nothin' on but a little string tied around his ass. None of us wanted to be like Bumble."

At Sterling High School Jackson's main interest was athletics, and he won letters in football and baseball. He also began to develop an attitude toward whites, a kind of bemused disdain for their foolishness, that is very characteristic of him today. Sterling High School played football on Thursdays, he remembers, and the white school, Greenville High, on Fridays. "For a while I would think, isn't it too bad I can't play with them. But we had the better team, so I soon began to think, isn't it too bad they can't play with us."

After high school Jackson received an athletic scholarship to the University of Illinois. He stayed one year and still talks about it with great bitterness. "Negroes were reduced to a subculture at Illinois. The annual interfraternity dance was *the* social event of the fall, only the three black fraternities weren't invited. My friends and I were down at the Veterans of Foreign Wars listening to 45s, while the white folks were jumping to Lionel Hampton in the gym. Live."

The second major phase of the civil-rights movement, after the Montgomery bus boycott of 1956, started during Jackson's freshman year at Illinois. On February 1, 1960, four Negro students from North Carolina Agricultural and Technical College in Greensboro sat down at a Woolworth lunch counter traditionally reserved for whites and ordered coffee. When the manager of the store closed down the counter, they took out their books and began to study. The Southern sit-ins were launched. Jackson saw the event on television, and a combination of homesickness, disgust with Illinois, and an as-yet-faint desire to join the movement, to be where the action was, led him to transfer to A&T when the year was over.

There he quickly became a kind of black version of the All-American Joe College—honor student, star quarterback, student body president, national officer (Second Vice Grand Basileus) of his fraternity. He began dating his future wife, Jacqueline. Then in the spring of 1963 he found himself, suddenly and almost accidentally, leading the protest marches in Greensboro. He had criticized the strategy and slow pace of the sit-in campaign during a conversation with two friends, members of CORE, and they challenged him to do better if he could. After a letterman's banquet the following day, he brought a group of athletes to a CORE meeting, where a decision was made to step up the organization's efforts. Almost daily for over a month Jackson led marches through downtown Greensboro. He would go into hotels, restaurants, and theaters alone, leaving, after service or tickets were refused, for the next "test," while white youths jeered the students and little kids ran along beside them chanting, "Two, four, six, eight, we ain't gonna integrate." These preliminary marches were followed by picketing, sit-ins, and mass arrests for criminal trespassing.

The demonstrations succeeded in desegregating downtown Greensboro, and Jackson gained statewide recognition for the achievement, becoming president of the newly formed North Carolina Intercollegiate Council on Human Rights.

More important for Jackson personally, the events of that spring left him with a strong commitment to civil rights and a determination to deliberately fashion himself into a Negro leader. He began to study the styles of such national figures as Malcolm X, Adam Clayton Powell, and Martin Luther King, looking for the best in each. "Malcolm had the capacity to respond quickly to whatever white folks threw at him," Jackson says. "The only question was how bad was he going to eat them up. Powell had the quality of defiance. At a time when Negroes could get arrested for restless eyeballing, he was walking around with white women. King had it all: he could deal with whites, he was courageous, plus he had intellectual respectability."

Although the two first became close during the Chicago Freedom Movement, Jackson feels that he owes much of his success to the example and encouragement of Martin Luther King ("my father figure, my brother figure, and my teacher"). He considers Operation Breadbasket King's legacy in Chicago and sees his own brief odyssey from civil-rights demonstrations to economic boycotts to political involvement as paralleling King's career and the development of his thinking. There is another, more explicit parallel. As a young man, Jackson has achieved a great deal in a short period of time, yet the problems he is faced with now are more difficult than the ones he has already solved, the expectations of his followers higher than ever. Lying in his hospital bed, he must have been thinking along the lines of a remark Martin Luther King made in a similar situation and at the same age. "I'm worried to death," King reportedly told a friend after the conclusion of the Montgomery bus boycott. "A man who hits the peak at twenty-seven has a tough job ahead. People will be expecting me to pull rabbits out of a hat for the rest of my life."

Jackson desperately needed to pull out his own rabbit now, one that could nibble away at several complex problems. Within the organization, the ministers and the businessmen were unhappy for different reasons. The ministers felt slighted because they had been pushed further and further to the sidelines as the influence of the businessmen grew. The businessmen were afraid that by moving from economic protest into politics, Jackson was spreading himself too thin.

"There is no such thing as being a little bit pregnant," one of them complained.

The conflict between the black and white staff members was probably inevitable, given Breadbasket's emphasis on self-help and black pride, as well as the general exodus of white liberals from civil-rights organizations across the country. Breadbasket was the last stand for many of these people in Chicago, the only aggressive organization where whites were still welcome, or at least tolerated, and they attended the Saturday meetings, picketed, even formed a North Shore for Breadbasket chapter. But the feeling was shared by several of the black staff members that the whites were assuming too much authority, in part, it was admitted, because they had more administrative experience. Organizational rivalry had reached the point where Jackson had threatened to quit if the whites were turned out.

Jackson's insistence that the whites stay was indicative of his role in the black community. He occupied the middle ground, serving as a link between the moderates and the militants, and this could be both a blessing and a curse. Jackson espoused nonviolence, yet occasionally the strain of this commitment showed, as when he admitted at a Saturday meeting soon after King's death that "every once in a while my jaws get pretty tight about white folks and I find myself in Whitey's chest beating his heart for him." Breadbasket remained an integrated organization, yet Jackson could tell a meeting of Chicago businessmen that white managers must leave ghetto stores immediately and white management ultimately. The success of his attempt to unite black organizations in Chicago around his leadership depended on his ability to stay inside the system while criticizing it, to sound like Whitney Young to the moderates and Stokely Carmichael to the militants. The difficulty was that he sometimes sounded like Whitney Young to the militants and Stokely Carmichael to the moderates.

This was, of course, the dilemma Martin Luther King faced in his last years; it would be the dilemma of any man in the middle, pressured from both sides. But Jackson had several advantages over King. He was younger, and so could speak the same language as the new generation of black militants. He was a better politician than King, sensitive to the problems of power and able to see issues in political as well as moral terms. Finally, he was simply more militant than King, for the middle ground had shifted in the civil-rights movement, and King had never quite succeeded in shifting with it.

There has been a power vacuum in Chicago's black community since Martin Luther King left, and Jackson was certainly the most likely candidate to fill it. A white lawyer who occasionally attends Breadbasket meetings recalls watching him after the memorial service for Martin Luther King as he stood by the church exit greeting the mourners. The whole spectrum of the black community filed by—politicians, NAACP officers, militant heads of small West Side community organizations, gang leaders, welfare mothers, businessmen—and the lawyer was amazed that Jackson had a personal word for each one, knew exactly when to give a black-power handshake and when a regular handshake. No other Negro in Chicago, perhaps in the nation, could have functioned as well in a similar situation, for Jackson was particularly adept at keeping lines of communication open to all groups. Reconciliation within the black community was the constant theme of Jackson's Saturday morning "sermons," and the results were beginning to show. Before the elections a reporter called Chester Robinson, a black militant who headed the West Side Organization, to get his reaction to the planned boycott. Robinson asked what Jackson had said, and when the reporter informed him that he had just come out for Humphrey, Robinson answered, "Well, I guess I'm a Humphrey man."

The rabbit that Jackson pulled from his hat was Black Christmas. It was a simple idea, not even completely original. Bob Lucas, former head of Chicago CORE, had called for a boycott by blacks of downtown stores during the Christmas season and Jackson at first supported the idea, then realized that "Negroes are going to buy—those Christmas lights are just too bright." Instead of merely boycotting downtown stores Jackson would ask them to shop exclusively in black-owned stores, buy gift packages of the businessmen's products in a special Black Christmas center that Breadbasket would run, or even open up accounts for their children in the black banks.

It was a simple idea, and it worked for Jackson on several levels. The ministers would be happy because he would emphasize the spiritual values of Christmas. The businessmen would be happy because they would be making money. The class antagonisms in the ghetto might be eased somewhat if Jackson could get enough middle-class Negroes to invite poor families into their homes for Christmas dinner. All groups in the black community would participate; who could be against Black Christmas?

Still in the hospital, Jackson began making telephone calls. Doug Andrews, militant head of the Garfield Organization, agreed to serve as co-chairman of Black Christmas and promised to get other West Side organizations involved. Lawrence Woods, an aide to Congressman Dawson, was willing to organize a parade through the ghetto to publicize the idea (Woods was a good choice; he wouldn't have any problem getting a permit). One by one, the businessmen agreed to rent floats in the parade ("Now, Mr. Johnson, you got a growing company. I think you need to rent *two* of those floats"). A call to Aretha Franklin took care of the entertainment after the parade. A friend consented to stuff his black dashiki and play Santa Claus ("We'll say you're a Soul Santa, a big fat black man from the *South* Pole"). Black Christmas might just work, but only if Jackson could get the word around the ghetto quickly. The first week in December was very late to start organizing; maybe not three hundred years too late, as he would tell the press, but a few weeks too late, anyway.

It is late Saturday night and the people in Lakemeadows Lounge are not thinking about Black Christmas. They are listening and dancing to music provided by Ben Branch's band. Jackson, out of the hospital a few days now, has dropped by because "my soul has a cavity that Ben's sound can fill." After the number Branch calls him up to the platform, where he receives a polite round of applause. But Jackson has a very portable pulpit, and where there is a large gathering of Negroes, he is not about to wave his hand in acknowledgment and take a seat.

"When I was a little boy growing up in the old country," he begins, "every winter Bing Crosby would come on the radio singing 'I'm Dreaming of a White Christmas.' It didn't snow in South Carolina but once in twenty years. When I grew up and visited Miami or Los Angeles or Hawaii, Bing Crosby would still be singing about a white Christmas, and you know he wasn't singing about *snow* in those places.

"White Christmas don't have nothin' to do with snow. It has to do with white merchants making up in the fourth economic quarter what they lost in the third. They can do it because Negroes don't live by quarters. We live day after day after day.

"Follow me now. There is a distinct difference between the Christmas rush and the Christmas celebration. Negroes participate in the Christmas rush. White people on State Street can't participate because they're too busy working. After we get through rushing, after we have signed our life away on new charge plates, all the vice presidents of the big companies fly off to the Caribbean Islands for the Christmas celebration. You know what they're celebrating? Our ignorance!

"Now, it does not have to snow to be a white Christmas, and it does not have to rain down coal for us to have Black Christmas. It just takes black folks getting together and deciding to determine our own destiny. Don't argue with a man who's got his game up tight. Worry about your own game. We got to put ourselves on the agenda. . . ."

Jackson is just warming up, and he will go on another fifteen minutes, interrupted occasionally by encouraging shouts from the audience, an approving toot from Ben Branch's saxophone, or a twang from Wayne Bennett's electric guitar. When it is over, he is sweating and visibly exhausted, for he is still weak from the mono and this is the fourth time he has preached about Black Christmas that day, with always the thought in the back of his mind that maybe it is too late, maybe even three hundred years too late. So that when a man comes over to his table and asks what he's been up to recently, Jackson sinks back in his chair and says, a little wearily, "Oh, just fightin' sin and organizin' Negroes."

Harper's Magazine, March 1969

from
Mau-Mauing the Flak Catchers

by Tom Wolfe

WHEN black people first started using the confrontation tactic, they made a secret discovery. There was an extra dividend
to this tactic. There was a creamy dessert. It wasn't just that
you registered your protest and showed the white man that
you meant business and weakened his resolve to keep up the
walls of oppression. It wasn't just that you got poverty money
and influence. There was something sweet that happened
right there on the spot. You made the white man quake. You
brought *fear* into his face.

Black people began to realize for the first time that the
white man, particularly the educated white man, the leadership, had a deep dark Tarzan mumbo jungle voodoo fear of
the black man's masculinity. This was a revelation. For two
hundred years, wherever black people lived, north or south,
mothers had been raising their sons to be meek, to be mild,
to check their manhood at the front door in all things that
had to do with white people, for fear of incurring the wrath
of the Man. The *Man* was the white man. He was the only
man. And now, when you got him up close and growled, this
all-powerful superior animal turned out to be terrified. You
could read it in his face. He had the same fear in his face as
some good-doing boy who has just moved onto the block
and is hiding behind his mama and the moving man and the
sofa while the bad dudes on the block size him up.

So for the black man mau-mauing was a beautiful trip. It
not only stood to bring you certain practical gains like money
and power. It also energized your batteries. It recharged your
masculinity. You no longer had to play it cool and go in for
pseudo-ignorant malingering and put your head into that
Ofay Pig Latin catacomb code style of protest. Mau-mauing
brought you respect in its cash forms: namely, fear and envy.

This was the difference between a confrontation and a demonstration. A demonstration, like the civil-rights march on Washington in 1963, could frighten the white leadership, but it was a general fear, an external fear, like being afraid of a hurricane. But in a confrontation, in mau-mauing, the idea was to frighten white men personally, face to face. The idea was to separate the man from all the power and props of his office. Either he had enough heart to deal with the situation or he didn't. It was like saying, "You—yes, you right there on the platform—we're not talking about the *gov*ernment, we're not talking about the *Off*ice of Economic Oppor*tun*ity— we're talking about *you*, you up there with your hands shaking in your pile of papers . . ." If this worked, it created a personal, internal fear. The internal fear was, "I'm afraid I'm not man enough to deal with these bad niggers!"

That may sound like a simple case of black people being good at terrifying whites and whites being quick to run scared. But it was more than that. The strange thing was that the confrontation ritual was built into the poverty program from the beginning. The poverty bureaucrats depended on confrontations in order to know what to do.

Whites were still in the dark about the ghettos. They had been studying the "urban Negro" in every way they could think of for fifteen years, but they found out they didn't know any more about the ghettos than when they started. Every time there was a riot, whites would call on "Negro leaders" to try to cool it, only to find out that the Negro leaders didn't have any followers. They sent Martin Luther King into Chicago and the people ignored him. They sent Dick Gregory into Watts and the people hooted at him and threw beer cans. During the riot in Hunters Point, the mayor of San Francisco, John Shelley, went into Hunters Point with the only black member of the Board of Supervisors, and the brothers threw rocks at both of them. They sent in the middle-class black members of the Human Rights Commission, and the brothers laughed at them and called them Toms. Then they figured the leadership of the riot was "the gangs," so they sent in the "ex-gang leaders" from groups like Youth for Service to make a "liaison with the key gang leaders." What they didn't know was that Hunters Point and a lot of ghettos were so disorganized, there weren't even any "key gangs," much less "key gang leaders," in there. That riot finally just burnt itself out after five days, that was all.

But the idea that the real leadership in the ghetto might be the *gangs* hung on with the poverty-youth-welfare establishment. It was considered a very sophisticated insight. The youth gangs weren't petty criminals . . . they were "social bandits," primitive revolutionaries . . . Of course, they were hidden from public view. That was why the true nature of ghetto leadership had eluded everyone for so long . . . So the poverty professionals were always on the lookout for the bad-acting dudes who were the "real leaders," the "natural leaders," the "charismatic figures" in the ghetto jungle. These were the kind of people the social-welfare professionals in the Kennedy Administration had in mind when they planned the poverty program in the first place. It was a truly adventurous and experimental approach they had. Instead of handing out alms, which never seemed to change anything, they would encourage the people in the ghettos to organize. They would help them become powerful enough to force the Establishment to give them what they needed. From the beginning the poverty program was aimed at helping ghetto people rise up against their oppressors. It was a scene in which the federal government came into the ghetto and said, "Here is some money and some field advisors. Now you organize your own pressure groups." It was no accident that Huey Newton and Bobby Seale drew up the ten-point program of the Black Panther Party one night in the offices of the North Oakland Poverty Center.

To sell the poverty program, its backers had to give it the protective coloration of "jobs" and "education," the Job Corps and Operation Head Start, things like that, things the country as a whole could accept. "Jobs" and "education" were things everybody could agree on. They were part of the free-enterprise ethic. They weren't uncomfortable subjects like racism and the class structure—and giving the poor the money and the tools to fight City Hall. But from the first that was what the lion's share of the poverty budget went into. It went into "community organizing," which was the bureaucratic term for "power to the people," the term for finding the real leaders of the ghetto and helping them organize the poor.

And how could they find out the identity of these leaders of the people? Simple. In their righteous wrath they would rise up and *confront* you. It was a beautiful piece of circular reasoning. The real leaders of the ghetto will rise up and confront you . . . Therefore, when somebody rises up in the ghetto and confronts you, then you know he's a leader of the people. So the poverty program not only encouraged mau-mauing it, it practically *demanded* it. Subconsciously, for administrators in the poverty establishment, public and private, confrontations became a ritual. That was the way the system worked. By 1968 it was standard operating procedure. To get a job in the post office, you filled out forms and took the civil-service exam. To get into the poverty scene, you did some mau-mauing. If you could make the flak catchers lose control of the muscles around their mouths, if you could bring fear into their faces, your application was approved.

Ninety-nine percent of the time whites were in no physical danger whatsoever during mau-mauing. The brothers understood through and through that it was a tactic, a procedure, a game. If you actually hurt or endangered somebody at one of these sessions, you were only cutting yourself off from whatever was being handed out, the jobs, the money, the influence. The idea was to terrify but don't touch. The term *mau-mauing* itself expressed this game-like quality. It expressed the put-on side of it. In public you used the same term the whites used, namely, "confrontation." The term *mau-mauing* was a source of amusement in private. The term *mau-mauing* said, "The white man has a voodoo fear of us, because deep down he still thinks we're savages. Right? So we're going to do that Savage number for him." It was like a practical joke at the expense of the white man's superstitiousness.

Almost every time that mau-mauing actually led to violence, you would find a revolutionary core to the organization that was doing it. If an organization was truly committed to revolution, then the poverty program, or the university, or whatever, was only something to hitch a ride on in the first place. Like at San Francisco State when the Black Students Union beat up the editor of the school newspaper, *The Gater*, and roughed up a lot of people during the strike. The BSU was allied with the Black Panthers. Stokely Carmichael, when he was with the Panthers, had come over to State and worked with the BSU, and given a speech that fired up the brothers for action. The willingness to be violent was a way of saying we are serious, we intend to go all the way, this *is* a revolution.

But this was a long way from the notion that all black militants in the ghetto were ready to be violent, to be revolutionaries. They weren't. A lot of whites seemed to think all the angry young men in the ghettos were ready to rise up and follow the Black Panthers at a moment's notice. Actually the Panthers had a complicated status in the ghettos in San Francisco. You talked to almost any young ace on the street, and he admired the Panthers. He looked up to them. The Panthers were stone courageous. They ripped off the white man and blew his mind and fucked him around like nobody has *ever* done it. And so on. And yet as an organization the Panthers hardly got a toehold in the ghettos in San Francisco, even though their national headquarters were just over the Bay Bridge in Oakland. Whites always seemed to think they had the ghetto's leaders identified and catalogued, and they were always wrong.

Like one time in an English class at San Francisco State there was a teacher who decided to read aloud to the class from *Soul on Ice* by Eldridge Cleaver. This teacher was a white woman. She was one of those Peter, Paul, and Mary–type intellectuals. She didn't wear nylons, she didn't wear make-up, she had bangs and long straight brown hair down to below her shoulders. You see a lot of middle-class white intellectual women like that in California. They have a look that is sort of Pioneer Hip or Salt of the Earth Hip, with flat-heeled shoes and big Honest Calves. Most of the students in her class were middle-class whites. They were the average English Literature students. Most of them hadn't even reached the Save the Earth stage, but they dressed Revolutionary Street Fighter. After the strike at State, middle-class students didn't show up on campus any more in letter sweaters or those back-to-school items like you see in the McGregor ads. They dressed righteous and "with the people." They would have on guerrilla gear that was so righteous that Che Guevara would have had to turn in his beret and get bucked down to company chaplain if he had come up against it. They would have on berets and hair down to the shoulders, 1958 Sierra Maestra style, and raggedy field jackets and combat boots and jeans, but not Levi's or Slim Jims or Farahs or Wranglers or any of those tailored hip-hugging jeans, but jeans of the people, the black Can't Bust 'Em brand, hod-carrier jeans that have an emblem on the back of a hairy gorilla, real *funky* jeans, and woolly green socks, the kind that you get at the Army surplus at two pair for twenty-nine cents. Or else they would go for those checked lumberjack shirts that are so heavy and woolly that you can wear them like a jacket. It's like the Revolution has nostalgia for the proletariat of about 1910, the Miners with Dirty Faces era, because today the oppressed, the hard-core youth in the ghetto—they aren't into the Can't Bust 'Ems with the gorilla and the Army surplus socks. They're into the James Brown look. They're into the ruffled shirts, the black belted leather pieces from Boyd's on Market Street, the bell-cuff herringbones, all that stuff, looking sharp. If you tried to put one of those lumpy lumberjack shirts on them, they'd vomit. Anyway, most of the students in this woman's English literature class were white middle class, but there were two or three students from the ghettos.

She starts reading aloud from *Soul on Ice*, and she's deep into it. She's got the whole class into Eldridge Cleaver's cell-block in San Quentin, and Cleaver is telling about his spiritual awakening and how he discovered the important revolution-ary thinkers. She goes on and on, a long passage, and she has a pure serene tone going. When she finishes, she looks up in the most soulful way, with her chin up and her eyes shining, and she closes the book very softly under her chin, the way a preacher closes the Bible.

Naturally all of the white kids are wiped out. They're sitting there looking at each other and saying, "Far out" . . . "Too much" . . . "Wow, that's heavy" . . . They're shaking their heads and looking very solemn. It's obvious that they just as-sume that Eldridge Cleaver speaks for all the black people and that what we need is a revolution . . . That's the only thing that will change this rotten system . . . In their minds they're now in the San Francisco State cellblock, and the only thing that is going to alter this shit is the Big Bust-out . . .

The teacher lets all this sink in, and then she says: "I'd like to hear some comments."

One of the ghetto brothers raises his hand, and she turns to him with the most radiant brotherly smile the human mind can imagine and says, "Yes?"

And this student, a funky character with electric hair, says: "You know what? Ghetto people would laugh if they heard what you just read. That book wasn't written for the ghettos. It was written for the white middle class. They published it and they read it. What is this 'having previously dabbled in the themes and writings of Rousseau, Thomas Paine, and Voltaire' that he's laying down in there? You try coming down in the Fillmore doing some *previously dabbling* and talking about Albert Camus and James Baldwin. They'd laugh you off the block. That book was written to give a thrill to white women in Palo Alto and Marin County. That book is the best su*burb*an jive I ever heard. I don't think he even wrote it. Eldridge Cleaver wouldn't write something like that. I think his wife wrote it . . . *Pre-vi-ously dab-bled . . .* I mean like don't dabble the people no previouslies and don't previous the people no dabblies and don't preevy-dabble the people with no split-level Palo Alto white bourgeois housewife Buick Estate Wagon backseat rape fantasies . . . you know? . . ."

As you can see, the man goes completely off his bean on this subject. He's saying every outrageous thing that bubbles up into his brain, because he wants to blow the minds of the whites in the room. They're all staring at him with congealed faces, like they just got sapped in the back of the neck. They hardly had a chance to get down into the creamy pudding of their romantic Black Hero trip, when this dude comes along and unloads on them. But they don't dare say a word against him, because he's hard-core, and he has that ghetto patter. He's the one who must know . . .

So mostly the fellow is trying to blow their minds because they are being so smug and knowing about The Black Man. He's saying, Don't try to tell *us* who our leaders are, because you don't know. And that's the truth. The Panthers were righteous brothers, but there were a lot of militants in the ghettos of San Francisco who had their own numbers going.

There were the Mission Rebels, the Cortland Progressives, the New Society, the United Council for Black Dignity, the Young Adults, the New Thang, the Young Men for Action . . . it was a list with no end . . . By the time you completed a list of all the organizations that existed at any given time, some new ones would have already started . . . Everybody had his own angle and his own way of looking at black power. The Panthers were on a very special trip. The Panthers were fighting The Pig. And the Pig was fighting the Panthers. If you joined the Panthers, you had to be ready to fight the police, because that was the trip you'd be on. One of the main things you stood to get out of it was a club up side your head, or a bullet. If you were a man who had really been worked over by the police, then you could relate to that and you were ready for that fight. The Panthers were like the Muslims in that respect. But as bad as things were in the ghettos, there weren't but so many aces who were ready to play it all-or-nothing that way.

The ghettos were full of "individualists" . . . in the sense the Russian revolutionaries used to use that word about the lumpenproletariat of Russia. The lumpenproletariat—the "underclass," as they say today—used to drive the Russian revolutionaries up the wall. Someone like Nikolai Bukharin would end up talking about them like he was some cracker judge from the year 1911: ". . . shiftlessness, lack of discipline, hatred of the old, but impotence to construct or organize anything new, an individualistic declassed 'personality,' whose actions are based only on foolish caprices . . ." He sounded like some Grand Kloogle on the bedsheet circuit.

In the ghettos the brothers grew up with their own outlook, their own status system. Near the top of the heap was the pimp style. In all the commission reports and studies and syllabuses you won't see anything about the pimp style. And yet there it was. In areas like Hunters Point boys didn't grow up looking up to the man who had a solid job working for some company or for the city, because there weren't enough people who had such jobs. It seemed like nobody was going to make it *by* working, so the king was the man who made out best by *not* working, by *not* sitting all day under the Man's bitch box. And on the street the king was the pimp. Sixty years ago Thorstein Veblen wrote that at the very bottom of the class system, down below the "working class" and the "honest poor," there was a "spurious aristocracy," a leisure class of bottom dogs devoted to luxury and aristocratic poses. And there you have him, the pimp. The pimp is the dude who wears the $150 Sly Stone–style vest and pants outfit from the haberdasheries on Polk and the $35 Lester Chambers–style four-inch-brim black beaver fedora and the thin nylon socks with the vertical stripes and drives the customized sun-roof Eldorado with the Jaguar radiator cap. The pimp was the aristocrat of the street hustle. But there were other lines of work that the "spurious aristocrats" might be into. They might be into gambling, dealing drugs, dealing in stolen goods or almost anything else. They would truck around in the pimp style, too. Everything was the street hustle. When a boy was growing up, it might take the form of getting into gangs or into a crowd that used drugs. There were plenty of good-doing boys who grew up under the shadows of their mothers and were aiming toward a straight life. But they were out of it in their own community. The status system on the block would be running against them, and they wouldn't "come out," meaning come out of the house and be on their own, until their late teens.

The pimp style was a supercool style that was much admired or envied. You would see some dude, just some brother from down the hall, walking down the street with his Rollo shirt on, and his black worsted bells with a three-button fly at the bell bottom of each pants leg, giving a spats effect, and he is walking with that rolling gait like he's got a set of ball-bearing discs in his shoulders and his hips, and you can say to the dude, "Hey, Pimp!" and he's not offended. He'll chuckle and say, "How you doing, baby." He's smiling and pleased with himself, because you're pulling his leg but at the same time you're saying that he's looking cool, looking sharp, looking good.

Sometimes a group of buddies who ran together, who were "stone pimp," as the phrase went, would move straight into the poverty program. They would do some fabulous, awesome, inspired mau-mauing, and the first thing you knew, they would be hanging out in the poverty scene. The middle-class bureaucrats, black and white, would never know what to make of an organization like this. They couldn't figure them out. There was one organization in a city just outside of San Francisco, in the kind of section that catches the bums, the winos, the prostitutes with the biscuits & gravy skin, the gay boys, the flaming lulus, the bike riders, the porno shops, peep shows, $8-a-week hotels with the ripped window shades flapping out. This area had everything you needed for a successful application for a poverty-program grant except for the one thing you need the most, namely, the militant youth. So that was when a remarkable ace known as Dudley showed up with a couple of dozen bonafide spurious aristocrats . . . his Ethnic Catering Service for skid row . . . There wasn't one of them that looked much under thirty, and nobody had ever heard of any black youth in that area before anyway, but they could mau-mau as if they had been trained by the great Chaser himself . . . They got a grant of nearly $100,000.

Every now and then the poverty bureaucrats from the Economic Opportunity Council or from City Hall would hold an area executive board meeting or some other kind of session at their clubhouse, and it was always a bear. A group of poverty workers and administrators would walk in there for the first time, and you could tell from the looks on their faces that something had hit them as different . . . and weird . . . They *felt* it . . . they *sensed* it . . . without knowing what it was. Actually it was a simple thing. The pimp-style aristocrats would be sitting around like a bunch of secretary birds.

There would be Dudley and the boys . . . Dudley, with his Fuzzy-Wuzzy natural and his welts. Dudley was a powerful man with big slabs of muscle like Sonny Liston and these long welts, like the welted seams on top of a pair of mocassins, on his cheeks, his neck, on the backs of his fists. These welts were like a historical map of fifteen years of Saturday night knife-fighting in the Bay Area. And Dudley's Afro . . . the brother had grown the rankest natural of all times. It wasn't shaped or anything close to it. It was growing like a clump of rumpus weed by the side of the road. It was growing every which way, and it wasn't even all one color. There was a lot of gray in it. It looked superfunky. It looked like he'd taken the stuffing

out of the seat of one of those old ripped-up chairs you see
out on the sidewalk with its insides spilling out after a fire on
Webster Street—it looked like he'd taken the stuffing out of
one of those chairs and packed it all over his head. Dudley
was the fiercest looking man in the Bay Area, but there would
be him and all his boys sitting around like a covey of secretary
birds.

That was the pimp look, the look of hip and supercool and
so fine. The white bureaucrats, and the black ones, too,
walked in trying to look as earthy and rugged as they could,
in order to be "with the people." They tried to walk in like
football players, like they had a keg of beer between their legs.
They rounded their shoulders over so it made their necks look
bigger. They thickened up their voices and threw a few
"mans" and "likes" and "digs" into their conversations.
When they sat down, they gave it that Honcho wide-open
spread when they crossed their legs, putting the right foot,
encased in a cordovan brogue with a sole sticking out like a
rock ledge, on the left knee, as if the muscles in their thighs
were so big and stud-like that they couldn't cross their legs all
the way if they tried. But the pimp-style aristocrats had taken
the manhood thing through so many numbers that it was beginning to come out through the other side. To them, by
now, being hip was striking poses that were so cool, so lan-
guid, they were almost feminine. It was like saying, "We've
got masculinity to spare." We've been through so much shit,
we're so confident of our manhood, we're so hip and so suave
and wise in the ways of the street, that we can afford to be refined and not sit around here trying to look like a bunch of
stud brawlers. So they would not only cross their legs, they'd
cross them further than a woman would. They would cross
them so far, it looked like one leg was wrapped around the
other one three or four times. One leg would seem to wrap
around the other one and disappear in the back of the knee
socket. And they'd be leaning forward in the chair with their
heads cocked to one side and their chins hooked over their
collarbones and their shades riding low on their noses, and
they'd be peering out over the upper rim of the shades. And
they'd have one hand cocked in front of their chins, hanging
limp at the wrist with the forefinger sticking out like some

kind of curved beak. They would look like one of those super-cool secretary birds that stand around on one long A-1 racer leg with everything else drawn up into a beautiful super-cool little bunch of fluffy feathers at the top.

They liked to run a meeting like everything else, namely, very cool. Dudley was conducting the meeting when in through the back door comes one of his boys, a tall dude with the cool rolling gait and his hands stuck in his pants pockets, which are the high Western-style pockets. The door he came in leads up a short flight of stairs and out onto an alley. This is a commercial district, and the alley is one of those dead-end slits they use for deliveries. It's always full of corrugated boxes and excelsior and baling wire and industrial wrapping paper and other debris. It's the kind of alley that has a little half side-walk on one side and there are always a couple of cars parked lopsided with two wheels up on the sidewalk and two on the alley. Anyway, the dude comes lolly-gagging in, as cool as you please, and walks over to where Dudley is sitting like a secretary bird and leans over and whispers something to him. Even the way he leans over is stone pimp-style. His legs don't bend and his back doesn't bend. It's like he's been cleaned, pressed, and Perma creased at hip level, right where his hand fits into his Western pocket, and he just jackknifes at the desired angle where the crease is. He keeps his hand in the pocket when he bends over. He just lets the hand bend backward at the wrist. It looks like his fingers are caught in his appendix.

"Say *what*, man?" says Dudley. "Don't you see I'm trying to hold a con-fer-ence in here?"

"But like man," says the Dude, "this is ve-ry im-por-tant."

"What the hell you into that's so im-por-tant, sucker?"

"Well, man, just wait a *min*-ute and let me tell you. You know that wino, Half and Half, that hangs out in the alley?"

"Yeah, I know him."

"Well, man, he's out there in the alley trying to burn down the buil-ding."

Dudley doesn't even move at first. He just peers out over his shades at his boys and at all the bureaucrats from down-town, and then he cocks his head and cocks his index finger in front of his chin and says, "We gonna have a tem-po-rary re-cess. The brother ask me to take care some business."

Then Dudley unwinds very casually and stands up, and he and the brother start walking toward the back door, but so cool and so slow, with the whole rolling gait, that it looks like Marcel Marceau doing one of those walks where he doesn't actually move off the spot he started on. They open the door like they're going out to check out the weather, but once they're on the other side—*whoosh!*—it's like somebody lit their after-burners. They're up those stairs like a rocket and out into the alley and on top of the wino, Half and Half, in just under one half a second.

This Half and Half is one of those stone winos who hang around there, one of those winos whose face is so weather-beaten it looks like a pebble-grain full-brogue oxblood shoe. He has white hair, but a full head of white hair, so thick it looks like every hair he ever had in his head was nailed in for good. All that boozing and drinking half-and-half, which is half sherry and half port, must do righteous things for the hair, because there are no old men in the world who have hair like the winos. This Half and Half is such a stone wino that the only clothes he has left are the green KP fatigues they hand out in the hospitals and the jails, because the rest have been ripped up, vomited on, or stolen. He has on the fatigues and a pair of black street shoes with thin white hospital socks. He has pushed the socks way down into the heels of the shoes because his ankles are swollen and covered with skin ulcers, which he swabs with paper towels he cops from out the public toilets. The old crock hates these black studs who have turned up down on his skid-row cul-de-sac, and he keeps trying to burn up the building. He has a big pile of paper and excelsior and other stuff shoved up against the wall and he has it smoldering in a kind of fogged-in wino way, trying to incin-e-rate the mother.

All of that is going on outside in the alley. From inside the clubhouse at first there's nothing: silence. Then you start to hear a sound that sounds like there is a paddlewheel from off a Mississippi steamboat out there in the alley, and to every paddle is attached a size 12E motorcycle boot, and as the wheel goes around every one of these boots hits the wino . . . *thunk . . . thunk . . . whop . . . whump . . . thunk . . . thunk . . . whop . . . whump . . .*

The white bureaucrats and the black bureaucrats look at Dudley's boys, and Dudley's boys just stare back over the top of their shades and sit there wound and cocked as coolly as the secretary bird . . .

thunk . . . thunk . . . whop . . . whump . . . thunk . . . thunk . . . whop . . . whump . . .

And then the white bureaucrats look at the black bureaucrats and the black bureaucrats look at the white bureaucrats, and one of the bureaucrats who is dressed in the Roos-Atkins Ivy League clothes and the cordovan shoes starts going "Unh, unh, unh." The thing is, the man thinks he doesn't have any more middle-class Uncle Tom mannerisms and attributes, but he just can't help going into that old preachery "Unh, unh, unh."

thunk . . . thunk . . . whop . . . whump . . .

"Unh, unh, unh."

thunk . . . thunk . . . whop . . . whump . . .

"Unh, unh, unh."

Then it stops and the door opens again, and Dudley and the Dude come walking back in even slower and more cool except for the fact that they're breathing hard, and they take their seats and cross their legs and get wound back up and cocked and perched, and Dudley peers out over his shades and says, "The meeting is resumed."

Brothers from down the hall like Dudley got down to the heart of the poverty program very rapidly. It took them no time at all to see that the poverty program's big projects, like manpower training, in which you would get some job counseling and some training so you would be able to apply for a job in the bank or on the assembly line—everybody with a brain in his head knew that this was the usual bureaucratic shuck. Eventually the government's own statistics bore out the truth of this conclusion. The ghetto youth who completed the manpower training didn't get any more jobs or earn any more money than the people who never took any such training at all. Everybody but the most hopeless lames knew that the only job you wanted out of the poverty program was a job *in* the program itself. Get on the payroll, that was the idea. Never mind *getting* some job counseling. *You* be the job counselor. You be the "neighborhood organizer." As a job counselor or a neighborhood organizer you stood to make six or seven hundred dollars a month, and you were still your own man. Like if you were a "neighborhood organizer," all you had to do was go out and get the names and addresses of people in the ghetto who wanted to relate to the services of the poverty center. That was a very flexible arrangement. You were still on the street, and you got paid for it. You could still run with the same buddies you always ran with. There was nobody looking over your shoulder. You didn't have to act like a convert, like the wino who has to sing hymns at the mission before he can get his dinner, to get something out of the poverty scene. In fact, the more outrageous you were, the better. That was the only way they knew you were a real leader. It was true that middle-class people who happened to live in the target areas got the top jobs, but there was still room for street types.

You'd run into some ace on the corner and you'd say, "Hey, man, what you doing?"

And he'd say, "Nothing, man, what you doing?"

And you'd say, "I'm a neighborhood organizer," or "I'm a job counselor, man" . . . and that gave you status, because it was well known that there were some righteous brothers in on the poverty program.

Some of the main heroes in the ghetto, on a par with the Panthers even, were the Blackstone Rangers in Chicago. The Rangers were so bad, the Rangers so terrified the whole youth welfare poverty establishment, that in one year, 1968, they got a $937,000 grant from the Office of Economic Opportunity in Washington. The Ranger leaders became job counselors in the manpower training project, even though most of them never had a job before and weren't about to be looking for one. This wasn't a case of the Blackstone Rangers putting some huge prank over on the poverty bureaucrats, however. It was in keeping with the poverty program's principle of trying to work through the "real leaders" of the black community. And if they had to give it the protective coloration of "manpower training," then that was the way it would have to be done. Certainly there was no one who could doubt that the Blackstone Rangers were the most powerful group in the Woodlawn area of Chicago. They had the whole place terrified. The Rangers were too much. They were champions. In San Francisco the champions were the Mission Rebels. The Rebels got every kind of grant you could think of, from the government, the foundations, the churches, individual sugar daddies, from everywhere, plus a headquarters building and poverty jobs all over the place.

The police would argue that in giving all that money to gangs like the Blackstone Rangers the poverty bureaucrats were financing criminal elements and helping to destroy the community. The poverty bureaucrats would argue that they were doing just the opposite. They were bringing the gangs into the system. Back in 1911 Robert Michels, a German sociologist, wrote that the bureaucracy provides the state with a great technique for self-preservation. The bureaucracy has the instinct to expand in any direction. The bureaucracy has the instinct to get all the discontented elements of the society involved and entangled in the bureaucracy itself. In the late 1960's it looked like he might be right. By the end of 1968 there were no more gangs in San Francisco in the old sense of the "fighting gangs." Everybody was into black power, brown power, yellow power, and the poverty program in one way or another. This didn't mean that crime decreased or that a man discontinued his particular hustles. But it did mean he had a different feeling about himself. He wasn't a hustler or a hood. He was a fighter for the people, a ghetto warrior. In the long run it may turn out that the greatest impact of the poverty program, like some of the WPA projects of the Depression, was not on poverty but on morale, on the status system on the streets. Some day the government may look back and wish it had given the Flak Catchers Distinguished Service medals, like the astronauts.

The poverty program, the confrontations, the mau-mauing, brought some of the talented aces something more. It brought them celebrity, overnight. You'd turn on the TV, and there would be some dude you had last seen just hanging out on the corner with the porkpie hat scrunched down over his eyes and the toothpick nodding on his lips—and there he was now on the screen, a leader, a "black spokesman," with whites in the round-shouldered suits and striped neckties holding microphones up to his mouth and waiting for The Word to fall from his lips.

from *Radical Chic &*
Mau-Mauing the Flak Catchers (1970)

from

Yazoo: Integration in a Deep-Southern Town

by Willie Morris

THE Fifth Circuit Court of Appeals, which of all the federal appellate courts has been the most active in implementing the racial decisions of the United States Supreme Court, gave the Yazoo schools, after a series of delays, until January 7, 1970, to comply with the law of the land. The law of the land now meant, as it pertained to Yazoo and the thirty Mississippi districts, complete school integration. The guidelines established by the Department of Health, Education, and Welfare would be followed in Yazoo City: the white high school would be the high school for the entire town, with the Negro students coming over en masse from their high school. The Negro high school would become the junior high school for the town; the white junior high students would move in a bloc to that building. Four other schools, including the previously all-black elementary school, would be integrated according to a racial pairing by grades. If every white student in town remained in the public schools, the high school under the HEW plan would be 42 per cent black, the junior high roughly 50 per cent black, and the various grade schools somewhere between 55 and 70 per cent black.

Since the October Supreme Court mandate, the white community in Yazoo had been undergoing an agony of survival. The Nixon Administration, with which that community sympathized, had tried to slow the pace of integration, but its deliberate conservatism had not prevented the Court from acting on its own. Many intelligent, well-meaning whites were baffled and perplexed. "We see on television that the Negro militants say integration doesn't matter any more," one of them said to me. "We hear the Administration doesn't believe in it, either. Does it or doesn't it matter? We're acting on the assumption down here that it does. We're trying to believe in it. Are we right or wrong?" Because there would be, under any circumstances, an exodus of white students to the private school which was already in operation in the white Methodist, Presbyterian, and Baptist churches, a predominantly black public school system was inevitable. The important question, as the January 7 deadline approached, was just how many white children would remain in the public schools, and with what consequences. Yazoo, and other places like it, was getting no inspiration from the President of the United States himself, and what they desperately needed at this juncture was some kind of effective inspiration. The town was alive with rumors and speculations. A number of whites predicted violence, and the great majority expected the public schools to collapse under the black presence. The private school was openly courting the disaffected whites. A prominent lawyer prophesied that not a single white child would turn up in any of the previously all-black schools on the appointed day. Criticism of the Supreme Court was as intense and pointed as ever; it was as if that leviathan had had a bad night, and woke up the next morning and said before breakfast, "We're going to do something today about Mississippi." Yet this time there was a difference. Even the most diehard white saw an inevitability now, and sensed that after sixteen years of legal delays, the blacks were indeed going to go into the white schools whether their children stayed with those schools or not. The full weight of our history, forged in bloodshed and laws and expressions of ideals, was about to fall on Yazoo, and the people knew it.

A leader of the local VFW wrote the Yazoo *Herald* late in December, in reference to Negro leadership, the boycott, and the integration of the schools: "To the many fine, colored people I can only say this: you are a part of our community, you have helped to raise our children, worked in our homes, but you have deserted us. You have left us to follow the outsiders who came here. They take your hard-earned money, tell you where to go, what to do, with whom to talk. And when you can give no more, they will leave you here. . . . May I suggest that you return to the churches you left, and kneel down and ask the good Lord's help. Then ask your troublemakers to go somewhere else, to let you live as you know you must." A white woman told me, "If I had a child, I'd go out and collect empty bottles if necessary to send him to private school." Another woman, describing the "sassy niggers" who used foul language and were unable to write a simple sentence, predicted that they would destroy the whole town and then celebrate its destruction. My mother, who teaches music in our house on Grand Avenue, had promised to drive every day at lunchtime to the junior high school, which is in the colored section and, as such things go in small Southern towns, a block from her house, to pick up two little white girls for their lessons so they wouldn't have to walk the few hundred yards through dangerous territory. Just before the opening day, the Negro teachers who would remain in the previously all-black junior high school organized a reception for the white parents who would be sending their children there. One white mother remarked to one of her acquaintances, who was sending her children to private school, "Why, everything was so clean, it smelt good, and they had electric typewriters and everything." And her friend replied, "Well, what do you expect? All the niggers were in the building the day before, sprayin' and scrubbin' with every sweet-smellin' thing they could get their hands on." Another white mother who went to the same reception came back and said a Negro teacher had introduced herself to her. "What do you teach?" the white mother asked, and she said the Negro teacher replied, *"I teaches English."*

Yet elsewhere, all over town, there were suggestions that something new was coming to the surface here, something never quite articulated with any degree of force or with the courage of numbers in many Deep-Southern towns, some painful summoning from deepest wellsprings. There were whites in town who fully intended to keep their children in the public schools, and who not only would say so openly, but who after a time would even go further and defend the very notion itself of integrated education as a positive encouragement to their children's learning. At first this spirit was imperceptible, but gradually, under the influence of some of Yazoo's white leaders and with the emergence of others of like mind, it became a movement with noticeable strength behind it. The economic health of the town, its attractiveness to outside industry, was the most consistent argument of the pro-public-school whites, but buttressing this, in the most unexpected places, were feelings infinitely more subtle and significant. There was the white Baptist preacher who said he could not live with himself if he did not keep his child in the public school; the white businessman who said he thought his son should be educated with as many different kinds of children as possible to prepare himself for "real life"; the white mother who said the two races must learn to live with each other or all of Mississippi would never amount to much of anything; the white Catholic nun who wrote to the newspaper that if white and black children—especially between the ages of kindergarten and junior high—"are not brought together in some way in this country, this state, this city, America will inevitably face deeper problems"; the white father who said he would not send his children to private school because the private school was based less on education than on "pure ole hate"; the white teacher who quoted Tocqueville and said the diversity of American experience demanded the need for integrated schooling; the white lawyer who said the South could show the North a thing or two about whites and blacks getting along together. For their part, the black leaders were encouraging the Negro students to make friends if possible, to make the best of a difficult situation if necessary. The confusion was not all on the white side. Some black parents were concerned too. There were to be uprootings of black children as well as white children, and this meant new transportation problems, disruption of school organizations, separation of classmates, and a new existence for many blacks.*

Setting the tone for the white moderates was the Yazoo *Herald*, the weekly newspaper. When I was growing up, I started writing sports for the *Herald* when I was twelve, using a strange argot that must have been incomprehensible to the occasional dirt farmer who might have followed my white-hot dispatches from the playing fields of Eden, Satartia, Flora, and Bentonia. The *Herald*'s editorial tone had changed considerably since those halcyon Dixiecrat days. Beginning with the

*W. F. Minor, *New South* (Winter 1970).

October Supreme Court decision, the *Herald* took a firm position behind the public schools, and became one of several forces of rationality in the community. "Yazoo City has been fortunate in many crises," one of its editorials said last fall, "because we seem to have a reservoir of enlightened readers (both black and white) willing to persevere through adversity and do what's right. We urge you all, our readers, to rise to the challenge of the transition being required of us. Certainly there will be perplexities and problems of human misunderstanding, but also opportunities and inspirations to all children of this community and their future."

The editors of the student newspaper in the white high school, the *Yazooan*, followed this example. In October, they editorialized: "Without a public school system a democratic society cannot exist. If a society limits the basic principle of equal opportunity by limiting the education which is available, it has become oligarchical and not democratic in nature. We of the *Yazooan* staff believe that Mississippi must give total support to the public school system as the best possible means of education for everyone." In December, three weeks before the deadline, the white students wrote:

> YHS faces massive integration for the first time next semester. We feel that all students who have begun school this year in the public schools should continue in them next semester because they will be receiving the best education available. The quality of education may even increase with the addition of students and teachers and the new influx of ideas. At the very least, whatever temporary inconveniences are created by overcrowdedness can be alleviated by the advantages of a better education in an accredited school for black students and the opportunity for white students to learn to handle racial problems more successfully than they have been handled in the past. Certainly we cannot even begin to attack the problems that surround us by running away from them, or ignoring them.

On the whole it was pragmatic economics, however, which was playing the leading role. Owen Cooper, the most powerful man in town as president of the Mississippi Chemical Corporation and one of the state's leading Baptists, was a quiet and effective influence. "Owen was almost alone among white establishment figures in Mississippi. He woke up one day a few years ago and all of a sudden realized blacks and whites have to live together," an editor from a delta town said to me. "He wants Yazoo to survive. With him it's a combination of good religion and good business." In the weeks leading to the school deadline, there was never any formal organization of the white moderates. Rather they were operating under what one leader called a "loose confederation" with several key members of the Chamber of Commerce, stressing the expense involved in sending a child to private school and the impossibility of establishing decent private facilities overnight.

On the night of November 24, "one of the largest crowds ever to gather in Yazoo City," as the *Herald* described it, and certainly the first integrated audience to meet "indoors," crowded into the high school auditorium—some one thousand whites and two hundred Negroes—to uphold the public schools. Twenty-five white leaders spoke, including the state senator, the state representative, all the school officials, businessmen, lawyers, coaches, and parents. A white Methodist preacher sought "divine help in removing hatreds, prejudices, and jealousies," and a white Baptist preacher prayed that people "won't abandon the legacy of the past, but instead provide for our children and our children's children." All this was considerably removed from the Citizens Council meeting I sat in on fifteen years before, when massive school integration had the support of fifty-three Negro names on a petition.

This mass meeting might have been the most dramatic espousal of integrated public schools in the history of Mississippi, and perhaps of the Deep South. Yet all through December, and into the first week of January, many advocates of the segregationist private schools scoffed at the notion that any substantial number of white children would tolerate wholesale mingling with blacks, and even among the white moderates there was a guarded pessimism. His Honor the Mayor of Yazoo expected violence. A white teacher told me the night before, "We're holding our breath and crossing our fingers, and those who know how to pray are praying pretty hard." That night I asked my grandmother Mamie, sitting hunched up on the edge of her bed, what she thought about the children going to school together. "Oh, son, I don't know," she said. "I just don't know. But I think they'll get along fine, if people'll just let 'em alone."

January 7, 1970, dawned clear and bitterly cold, a cold that rarely comes to Mississippi. It was 16 degrees on South Main Street, the trees along the older avenues were seared and deathly, and the water in the potholes of the roads in the Negro sections was frozen solid. All over Yazoo there was a cold eerie calm.

The "nationals" were out in force, for Yazoo is only forty-eight miles from the Jackson airport, and with its fifty-fifty population and its origins in both the hills and the delta, this was where the stories would go out from that day, telling the nation and many parts of the world how the first major test of massive school integration in America in a district with a black majority would work in a "typical Mississippi town." The *New York Times* was there, and the Washington *Post*, the TV networks, the wire services, the Boston *Globe*, *Time*, the Detroit *News*, and the Chicago *Sun-Times*.

At my high school, whites and blacks waited on the grounds or walked inside in separate groups; two police cars were parked nearby. I drove into the Negro section of town to the old black high school, which today was to become the town's junior high; across the street was a previously black grade school, about to become grades four and five for whites and blacks. (Three years or so ago, I gave a talk to the black high school, to a sea of black faces, and gave five autographed copies of *Invisible Man* to the school library. A white lady who was there came up to me later and said, "Who were you talkin' to? The little niggers didn't understand you," and I said I guessed I was talking to one person, and that was myself.) Cars were parked in all directions, some with Confederate flags on their windows or bumpers, and parents of both races were bringing their children into the school buildings. Roy Reed of the *Times*, a *Times* photographer, and I stood outside the front entrance to the junior high; we were soon to be joined by the Boston *Globe*. I went inside, to try to get a seat at the first meeting of the new student body of the amalgamated Yazoo Junior High.

"Winkie!" a booming voice shouted in my direction, using the nickname I have not been called since the sixth grade. "You're not allowed in there." I was escorted out by a man I did not recognize, rejoining the nationals at the front door. In a few moments, a Yazoo cop with the dimensions of any of

the L.A. Rams' front four, who would make Rod Steiger in
In the Heat of the Night seem benign and nunlike in comparison, came up to our group and shouted, "*You from the
press?*" Without waiting for anyone's answer, he said, "The
minute somebody tells you move, you *move!*"

"No one's asked us to move yet, Officer," Reed of the
Times, who traverses the South forever, as a man seeking lost
and holy visions, a wandering nomad of the Arab tribe of
Sulzberger, said, with some dignity.

"Move if anybody says move," the cop repeated, then
drifted away. I remembered him from the Greyhound station
fourteen years before, when I was putting a friend on the
midnight bus stopping briefly here between Memphis and
New Orleans. He got on the bus with a flashlight and went
up and down the aisle, and when he came out, I asked him if
there was any trouble. "No," he had said, "I was lookin' to
see if any niggers were sittin' up front."

By now the school assembly had begun, and everything
was oppressively quiet. It was much the same all over town.
At one of the grade schools later, black and white children
were playing together in the schoolyard. One group, dancing
in a circle for ring-around-a-rosy, were all white, but in the
circle next to them white and Negro children held hands and
kicked their feet. Over in the high school, where a meeting
of the student body was taking place, the situation was
slightly more dramatic. In a new twist, all the black students
sat together in the front seats of the auditorium, and all the
whites sat together in the back. When the student-body president of the black high school was introduced, the Negroes
applauded loudly and gave the black-power gesture, the
raised fist. When the white president was introduced, he received a sturdy round of support from the back seats. The
white principal spoke sternly about discipline. When the
black principal (now the *assistant* principal) stood to quote
from the Scriptures about the necessity of education, there
were the sudden makings of an incident; he has a physical deformity, and a number of the white students laughed out
loud.

By the middle of the day, however, it was quite apparent
that Yazoo City had indeed integrated its schools calmly and

deliberately, and that some 80 per cent of all the white children had chosen to stay.* Only two white teachers in the town had resigned. With the attrition to the private school, there was a black majority in every school, beginning with about 60 per cent in the high school and increasing toward the lower grades.

The nationals filed their stories, and within the next two days the town was praised on front pages, by the news weeklies, and by all the television networks. A Justice Department lawyer in Jackson said that Yazoo City had shown more strength in its schools than any other district in Mississippi, and pointed in contrast to the town of Canton just thirty miles away, where the white leaders and merchants had literally succeeded in destroying their public schools. The *Herald*'s editorials were captioned, "We Should Be Proud," and "Yazooans Show Character," and an outpouring of letters was published from all over the country. A typical one, from R. D. Cheatham, former star wingback on the Yazoo Indians of my era, now living in Las Vegas, said, "I have never been so proud of my home town than when I saw [the editor and the school superintendent] express a dynamic understanding of the changes taking place and Yazoo City's positive reaction to them. The coming months will not be easy, but I want you to know that I applaud your initial efforts. . . ." Another outside correspondent wrote, "We have been listening to the Yazoo City story on TV. We wish to commend you for your efforts. May Yazoo City lead the South out of its dreadful impasse." A white lady said to my mother, "When I read all the good things about integration here, it scares me. When I read anything critical, it makes me mad."

In the following days, an uneasy calm would settle on the town, an emotional labor survived but scarcely overcome. "ALL'S WELL IN YAZOO CITY, BUT WHAT ABOUT TOMORROW?" the Memphis *Commercial Appeal* wrote as its headline to a highly pessimistic analysis reporting that some white leaders "would rather judgment could be withheld. They do not appreciate the conclusions, however laudatory, reached in the

*The total enrollment in the city dropped by 480; 2,077 blacks and 1,362 whites began the new semester together.

fleeting moments of deadline by the correspondents from Detroit, Washington, St. Louis, New York, and even Copenhagen." The Memphis paper's pessimism was not entirely ill-founded. On the day after school integration, officials from the Justice Department in Jackson were in Yazoo to find out why its school officials had retained essentially the same classroom structure as before, which largely meant segregated classrooms in integrated buildings. There would be seeds of future trouble here, leading later to another NAACP suit.

But the predictions of the white conservatives had not materialized. Yazoo City came into a new era with remarkably strong and resilient leadership from both races, and while a number of other Mississippi schools, the first thirty districts in the national test, were being abandoned altogether to the blacks, the people of Yazoo would look ahead with considerable realism. "We've got to hold the whites," a young lawyer said. "This semester is critical. If we can hold them now, we can hold them from now on. And by God, I think we're going to do it." They saw few grand historical designs in what they had accomplished; they were more than willing to live with their experiment one day at a time. There had been, after all, a straightforward simplicity, a stark logic, in this act of compliance. Had the warnings of the white racists over the generations been so true?

The white high school had purchased an expensive machine, some time before, to spray the dressing rooms in the gymnasium and other places against athlete's-foot germs and the like. "I saw them put that big spray machine in the back of a pickup truck to take over to the colored school so they could spray it down before the white children started to school there," a white man told me. "When I saw them take that spray machine to the colored school, that was the day I knew integration was finally comin' after all the talk that it wouldn't—finally comin' after all."*

*Also, the black grade school had used a cowbell rather than an electrical bell system. This too was remedied before the advent of the whites.

from *Yazoo: Integration in a Deep-Southern Town* (1971)

The Two Nations at Wesleyan University

by Richard J. Margolis

"What atonement would the God of Justice demand for the robbery of black people's labor, their lives, their true identities, their culture, their history . . . ?"
—"THE AUTOBIOGRAPHY OF MALCOLM X" (1965)

"I came to America to convert the Indians; but oh! who shall convert me?"
—"THE JOURNAL OF JOHN WESLEY" (1738)

Middletown, Conn.

THE old John Wesley House, a splendid campus landmark with white Ionic columns, turned into the Malcolm X House one sunny day last April. Overnight it became a conspicuous presence on the startled New England landscape. The sky did not fall and the earth did not tremble; neither did the alumni withdraw their support. But Wesleyan, a small, estimable, historically white university in Middletown, would never be the same. "We have passed the point of no return," says a Wesleyan administrator. "The blacks are here in force and they are here to stay."

The first black who came to Wesleyan was Charles B. Ray, and he did not stay. He departed in 1832, soon after fellow students passed a resolution describing his presence there as "inexpedient." Ray's white friends deplored his banishment even while conceding it was "the wisest course." They wished him Godspeed.

After the Civil War, Wesleyan and the rest of the North discovered tokenism, and from time to time a few Negroes slipped through the academic mesh. Such lackluster integration as there was continued for a century. Then, in 1965, the present drama began to unfold when Wesleyan enrolled 14 black freshmen. More came the next year, and more the next. This year blacks and "other minorities" (mostly Puerto Ricans) make up 12 per cent of Wesleyan's 1,400 students and 20 per cent of the freshman class.

Compared with most other traditionally white universities, these figures are exceptionally high. Black enrollments at Yale and Harvard, for instance, are below 5 per cent, which suggests that in the intercollegiate-interracial sweepstakes Wesleyan is several lengths ahead. But the track has been treacherously mined and the finish line is nowhere in sight.

Nearly all of Wesleyan's glib and early assumptions about black-white integration—having to do both with its necessity and its ease of attainment—have by now gone the way of the John Wesley House, onto history's discard pile. "At first we thought all we had to do was recruit black students," notes Edwin D. Etherington, who in 1967 forsook the presidency of the American Stock Exchange for that of Wesleyan. "Now we know we have to do much more."

"Much more" has meant the appointment of 23 blacks to positions on the staff and faculty, and the establishment last spring of an Afro-American Institute in cooperation with the Martin Luther King Center in Atlanta. The institute, known to blacks as Ujamaa ("family" in Swahili), has its headquarters in the Malcolm X House and is the vital center of Wesleyan's black community. Designed in large measure by the black students, Ujamaa sponsors two courses in black history and culture and promotes such endeavors as an arts festival and a black repertory theater.

In times of racial crisis, which are frequent, Ujamaa's Central Committee is the blacks' chief spokesman and bargaining agent. Its pronouncements are a cheerless form of invective, full of phrases like "racist institution" and "white liberal swine." As a white English teacher has observed, the pronouncements "are the language of escalation. They have to be deciphered rather like statements from the Kremlin."

Membership in Ujamaa is open to all blacks in the vicinity, including Middletown blacks who would otherwise have no connection with the university. They thus constitute a "family" within the academic community that shelters them, but their loyalty to that community has been spotty to say the least.

All this has been allowed to occur, say administrators, in a sincere effort to satisfy black needs, and no one at North College—the school's administration building—is underestimating those needs. That particular mistake is already history.

"Back in 1965," explains Edgar W. Beckham, an associate provost and one of Wesleyan's few black alumni (class of '58), "we believed in what you might call automatic assimilation. We thought the black students would mysteriously merge into the white landscape. That might have worked in my day —there were so few of us, and Stokely hadn't shouted 'Black Power' yet—but it won't work today."

When Wesleyan's first sizable group of blacks was graduated last spring, their black brothers presented them with a plaque: "To the Vanguard Class of 1969." As Beckham explains, "Those guys had gone through their own special hell. The other blacks showed they understood." Their special hell, it would seem, was less a consequence of white prejudice than of white indifference; or, more precisely, of white determination to ignore blackness.

The blacks came to Wesleyan not knowing exactly what to expect; but they assumed, somewhat contradictorily, that they were entering a white paradise and also that they would be accepted—but not discriminated against—*as blacks*. They were wrong on both scores. "The whites were very condescending to us," a black student recalls. "They wanted us to pretend we were just like them." Most of the blacks played this game at first, on the historic premise that whites possessed all the secrets of superior life. Then, as the black student explains, "We began to see that the whites weren't supermen. They were just ordinary cats with ordinary hang-ups. That's when we stopped assimilating."

In pursuit of assimilation, school officials had carefully dispersed black students throughout all the dormitories and had provided each black with a white roommate. "The official policy was to keep us [blacks] apart," recalls Edwin C. Sanders Jr., a large black man from "the vanguard class" who is now co-director of Wesleyan's Afro-American Institute. "But it didn't take long for us to find each other."

The blacks soon learned to brandish their blackness. They cultivated Afro hairstyles, donned dashikis and sat at a "black table" in the dining hall. "I enjoyed shocking the whites," remembers Randy Miller, a senior this year. "Every morning I'd write out another quotation from Malcolm X or Stokely and nail it to my door. I had to show them who I was."

But most of the white students failed to get the message, and before long black gestures were yielding to black protest. A turning point came in December, 1967, at a Wilson Pickett "soul" concert which black students had arranged. Some of the more carefree whites in the audience shouted, hooted, made lavish use of the word "nigger" and, in a final act of gallantry, took off their pants. To everyone's surprise, the blacks protested. Thirty-seven of them signed a letter to The Argus, Wesleyan's student newspaper, deploring "the display of pale pink asses in the presence of our Black sisters." (Although Wesleyan went coeducational last year only a few of its girl students are black. Most of the "Black sisters" came from Middletown and cities nearby.) The letter concluded with what, in the fullness of time, turned out to be a typical threat: "The lid blew off, Baby. We're burning and we hope that the flame doesn't reach you."

It was the first time the blacks had ever spoken to Wesleyan with a single voice, and the voice stung. President Etherington issued a public apology. "The most disturbing thing about the evening," he declared, "was the undertone of racist slurs, punctuated by specific words and gestures." An Argus editorial dismissed the incident as the mere hi-jinks of "upper-class party boys of certain fraternities," but no one could entirely forget the show of black solidarity which the incident had inspired.

A year later, on the anniversary of Malcolm X's death, the blacks consolidated their gains by briefly taking over Fisk Hall, the school's main classroom building. "We seek to publicly memorialize . . . the death of a great American and a Black saint, Malcolm X," the demonstrators announced. Earlier the faculty had rejected (by a vote of 60 to 47) a black request to cancel classes on that day. But by midday of the take-over, Etherington was reminding teachers that although they had voted against suspension of all classes, individual teachers could do whatever they wished. As one professor remarked later, "It was tantamount to an order." By 2 P.M. Wesleyan was shut down.

In this way the blacks gradually compelled Wesleyan to put away childish thoughts of assimilation and to see through a glass darkly. The white missionaries were being converted. Yet aspects of the old dream have lingered. "We must learn to be comfortable with each other at Wesleyan," says Beckham, who, as a kind of ideological middleman between the blacks and the administration, knows the meaning of discomfort. And Etherington, a patient man, speaks wistfully of "many races, one community," a new dream for Wesleyan.

On the other hand, many white students remain infected with a tired old racism, and many black students respond with a fierce new separatism. The 1968 edition of Olla Podrida, Wesleyan's yearbook, contained hundreds of photographs depicting life at Wesleyan but only three that included black students. The blacks responded one night by burning four copies of Olla Podrida on the steps of North College. It was, they declared, "an outrageous, unforgivable insult to all Black people."

"Unforgivable" is the key word here, for it reflects a rising suspicion among blacks at Wesleyan that white people are beyond both pardon and salvation. As the suspicion grows, the goal of "many races, one community" fades. Matters have reached a point where Edwin Sanders, much of whose thinking was shaped as a student at Wesleyan, can look forward to a day when Wesleyan's enrollment is 90 per cent black. "I'll keep 10 per cent," he explains, "just to remember that the white folks still exist. I haven't found the button yet that will get rid of them."

These two contending visions, then, are what the struggle is all about at Wesleyan, as it is elsewhere in America, and the antagonisms they generate are never far below the surface. Ujamaa and the Malcolm X House—Wesleyan's crowning atonements to date—have come to symbolize both pride and prejudice. To blacks they are a safe haven and also a luminous proof of black power and dignity; to many whites they are a social irritant at best and a sinister sanctuary at worst. "Everybody knows they're hiding guns in there," comments an editor of The Argus, "but nobody's got the guts to go in and search." As an afterthought he adds, "Of course, we'd never print that. We have to live with each other, you know."

*

As soon as Worth Hayes set foot in the Hartford air terminal last August, he knew he was entering a new world, a world disturbingly unlike the black ghetto in St. Louis where he had grown up. "People were talking kind of proper," he recalls. "It was like a foreign language. I had a hard time understanding them." Hayes, one of 51 entering black freshmen in a class of 338, was groping toward Wesleyan; and Wesleyan, which had recruited Hayes with uncommon ardor and now awaited him with uncommon anxiety, was groping toward expiation, after more than 130 years of ethnic vanities. The whole unlikely experiment would depend largely on efforts by both parties to decipher each other's language.

Hayes, a tall, slim youth with a modest bush haircut, is typical of the kind of blacks Wesleyan is now attracting—bright, ambitious, shabbily educated and chock-full of "overall personal strength"—the quality Wesleyan admissions officers look for in black applicants. He was anxious to get to Wesleyan, but when he finally sat down in his dormitory room, he had trouble unpacking. "It was the dresser," he says. "I never had my own dresser before. I kept looking at it, wondering how do you space out the clothes."

Back home in St. Louis, he never had to wonder. He slept in a narrow corridor off the living room and shared a dresser with his brothers and sisters. Hayes's father is a hod carrier, hard-working and steady on the job; but the job does not pay enough and Hayes has had to work most of his life, starting as a newsboy when he was 10, then moving on to after-school jobs in supermarkets, restaurants and factory warehouses. "I worked at least 20 hours every week all through school," he says. "Maybe that's why I only got a B average."

Early in his senior year at Soldan public high school (3,100 blacks, two whites) Hayes began investigating colleges. "I've wanted to go to college ever since I was a little kid. My older brother, he graduated from high school but he never went to college. Now he's working 60 hours a week in a car wash." Hayes spent study-hall periods waiting to talk to his counselor about college, but his counselor had 499 other students to see and he never got around to Hayes. So Hayes wrote to colleges on his own, getting the names from brochures in the counselor's anteroom. "I'd never heard of most of them," he says. "They were just names to me."

Eventually he applied to 10 "names," including Harvard, Dartmouth, Wesleyan and the University of Missouri. He was not hopeful. "I knew I'd messed up my S.A.T.'s [Student Aptitude Tests]. I just can't put myself in a mood to take a test. I tense up and black out."

But Hayes was operating in an applicant's market; competition among colleges for promising black students was stiff, and there was a growing consensus that such traditional measuring sticks as S.A.T. scores and class rank were irrelevant to applicants from the ghetto. Wesleyan, pursuing these new tenets of enlightenment, accepts one-third of its black applicants and only one-fourth of its white applicants, although black S.A.T. scores are 130 points lower, on average, than white scores. (A perfect score is 800.)

In any case, Hayes was accepted by nine of the 10 colleges, and Harvard—the sole holdout—might have accepted him, too, had not Hayes picked Wesleyan before Harvard made up its mind. The way Hayes chose Wesleyan tells us much about both. He had decided on an Eastern college—"I'd heard they were better"—which narrowed the choice to Dartmouth and Wesleyan. Since he knew little about either school, he was delighted when Dartmouth invited him to an open house in a St. Louis suburb.

The catered affair took place at the home of a wealthy Dartmouth alumnus. "It was one of those big places," says Hayes, "with a circular driveway and Cadillacs, and servants all over the place. Most of the servants were black; they were the only black people in the place, except me and one or two other guys. I decided not to go to Dartmouth. I didn't want to be bought off."

A few weeks later Harold Murphy, a black senior at Wesleyan, came to St. Louis, his hometown, and telephoned Hayes. Murphy, who is majoring in social psychology, was in St. Louis on official university business—to sell Hayes and other black students in the area on the advantages of Wesleyan. "Our black students make the best recruiters of black prospects," notes William Roberts, an assistant dean of admissions. "We've learned to depend on them."

Hayes met Murphy, and asked him the question every black hopeful asks a brother who has experienced the white world: "What's it like out there?" Murphy's response was hardly a blanket endorsement, but he convinced Hayes that life was bearable at Wesleyan because a genuine black community existed there. "The black recruiter's pitch is very simple," observes Roberts: "'Look, man, if you're going to a honkie school, go to Wesleyan.'"

So Hayes went to Wesleyan, knowing he would not be alone, and not too afraid, in this world he'd never made. Along with most of the other black freshmen, Hayes arrived three weeks before classes were to start, because Wesleyan, in its eagerness to satisfy black needs, was preparing to "orient" them all. This proved to be a devious undertaking—or, in the opinion of a white professor, "an absolute disaster"—but it did serve to acquaint Hayes and his brothers with two incendiary forces on campus: black militancy and white obtuseness.

Most of the entering black freshmen were exposed to two kinds of orientation. One was the conventionally bland buffet of campus tours and welcoming speeches dished out to all freshmen regardless of race. (As we shall see, one of the speeches was not so bland.) The other was a week-long concoction designed as "a training experience in contract-building" between white faculty members and black freshmen and upperclassmen. It was given the innocuous rubric of "Me, My Goals and Wesleyan," but as at least one participating professor has observed, "It could as easily have been called 'Me, the Gallows and Wesleyan.' Somebody up there wanted to hang us."

"Me, My Goals and Wesleyan" was planned by Beckham with the help of a consulting firm, Systems for Change, Inc., a firm in Trenton, N.J., which specializes in mounting and producing confrontations. ("Don't say 'encounter,'" a company spokesman admonished. "That's not our bag.") This particular confrontation was aimed at giving black students a sense of where they were headed at Wesleyan, and at giving white faculty members a chance to probe their own dark misgivings. As the firm's president, Barry A. Passett, explains, the program was to be an adventure in diplomacy, with the two groups behaving rather like two opposing delegations at the

United Nations. During the first few days of orientation, each group would meet in private sessions and work out its strategies for later negotiations. The next three days would be spent at the bargaining table in head-to-head confrontation. Out of this adversary process were to come—for members of both sides—"self insight," "awareness of goals" and, inevitably, "more open channels of communication."

From the beginning the channels of communication were badly clogged. Ten faculty members volunteered for the program, though none had any precise notions of what they were getting into. "I'm afraid we were less than candid in our call for volunteers," Passett concedes. "No doubt most of them thought they were being asked to participate in a conventional orientation program."

Jeffrey E. Butler, a professor of history and one of the 10 volunteers, puts it another way. "We were intentionally misled," he says. "Passett admitted afterward that he didn't tell the whole story because he was afraid he wouldn't get any volunteers."

At the first session the professors were introduced to their "trainer," a young psychologist assigned by Systems for Change to lead discussions among the faculty. Faculty recollections of this session, admittedly blurred, go something like this:

"I thought this was an orientation session," one of the teachers said. "I don't see any students."

"You'll meet them later," the trainer said. "First we have to deal with the problems right in this room." The teachers were genuinely astonished; they wanted to know what problems he had in mind. "Well," said the trainer, using his best nondirective approach, "how do you feel about the black students?" Everyone said they felt just fine.

"I've heard it said that the faculty here is encapsulated," the trainer went on. "Does anyone want to comment on that?"

On the second day the faculty took a vote and agreed to dismiss the trainer.

On the third day, by prearrangement, the faculty members knocked on the door to the black caucus room, hoping to get in. There was no answer. The blacks had spent the night sitting-in at the headquarters of Teen-agers Organized for Productive Service (T.O.P.S.), a black antipoverty group in

Middletown. There'd been a rumor that T.O.P.S. was going to be closed down; hence the protest, and no meeting with the faculty that morning. The rumor about T.O.P.S. proved to be unfounded. (In its written evaluation, Systems for Change made much of this: "The trainers used the incident and the students' overreaction to lead into skills-training on rational problem-solving"—like checking out rumors.)

That afternoon Jeffrey Butler, representing his group, again knocked at the black door. This time two blacks came out and told Butler their group wasn't ready yet. "Look here," said Butler, "this is absurd." A discussion ensued. The faculty members, it developed, preferred to meet in small groups, "so that everyone has a chance to be heard." This looked to the blacks like white casuistry: divide and rule. To the teachers it looked like sound pedagogy: divide and reason. To an outsider it looked like both; Solomon would have been overwhelmed at Wesleyan.

Eventually the two groups did meet, and it is not clear what followed. According to Passett's evaluative report, the professors behaved badly—that is, like professors. They indulged in such dubious gambits as "'donnish' humor," "intellectual 'put-downs'" and "incessant verbiage." According to an administration official, "The faculty copped out."

And according to some of the faculty, the discussions were insulting. "The blacks began by demanding that we accept the proposition that Wesleyan is a racist institution," says Jeffrey Butler. "I told them that was rubbish. If it were a racist institution they wouldn't be here."

This line of reasoning, notes Jonathan Collett, an assistant professor of English who participated in the sessions, seemed to suggest to the blacks that they were expected to be *grateful* to Wesleyan for admitting them. Their reaction was described by still another faculty participant. "The blacks," he said colorfully, "turned livid with rage."

In fairness, many of the black freshmen said later that they had found the program helpful; it had given them more confidence in their ability to handle both Wesleyan and themselves. Such gains were not to be undervalued. Classes were scheduled to begin Sept. 17 and, precisely because of the questions which "Me, My Goals and Wesleyan" had tried to raise, the blacks would need all the confidence they could muster. The administration had not intended to hang the faculty, but it had hoped to rouse some of its members into examining these hard racial dilemmas of the classroom.

A distinguished professor in the social sciences pounds his palm with the bowl of his pipe and glares across the desk at his visitor. "Look," he says, "I'm not a racist. I'm simply saying we have a lot of very badly qualified students here, and we don't know how to cope with them. The danger is that our standards are diluted for the sake of getting black students through the curriculum." He relights his pipe. "No, it's not a danger, it's a problem that's already with us. Everybody on campus knows which are the 'gut' departments for blacks. Some of my colleagues give a ludicrously high proportion of A's to black students."

Some blacks would be surprised to hear they are getting A's. It is a commonplace among black students that "Wesleyan lets you in so they can flunk you out," and the claim contains a kernel of truth; according to Robert L. Kirkpatrick Jr., dean of admissions, black students do flunk out of Wesleyan at a somewhat higher rate than white students.

Wesleyan administrators are reluctant to examine the blacks' academic performance or to portray it as a special problem. But while denying the problem, they hunt for solutions. Thus far these solutions have been genuine but discouraging.

Back in 1965, the school sent entering black freshmen to various summer "compensatory-education programs," sponsored by preparatory schools or by other colleges, which alleged to impart such basic academic skills as English composition and algebra. But the programs did not teach and the students did not learn. Moreover, according to a recent report by Harold Davis, a black assistant dean of admissions, compensatory education was "offensive and degrading" to the black students. Davis, who was graduated from Wesleyan last year, was himself a beneficiary, or victim, of these programs. "The fact that special attention had been directed toward them (the black students)," he concludes, "gave them a sense of not being able to perform the work Wesleyan demanded."

In 1967 Wesleyan abandoned compulsory compensatory education. Only the premedical students now are offered a summer program, including short courses in the basic sciences. The rest must depend on voluntary tutorials offered by teachers or upperclassmen to anyone requesting extra help. The school also permits students in danger of sinking under too heavy a load to space out their course-work over a five-year period.

In this way Wesleyan has sought to give blacks sufficient academic support without smothering them in "special attention." It is a delicate balance, and maintaining it has probably improved the black student's chances of "making it" at Wesleyan.

But at the same time, efforts such as these have done nothing to improve relations between the faculty and the blacks, and relations have been deteriorating. "We can see signs of a liberal backlash among the faculty," notes John Maguire, an associate professor of religion who, along with Beckham, was one of a small cabal of reformers responsible for Wesleyan's social awakening five years ago. "Some of my colleagues deplore black incivility," Maguire continues. "They prefer the old Victorian virtues. Well, it's true the black do rage around a lot, but that's not the real point. The blacks aren't challenging Wesleyan's manners, they are challenging Wesleyan's morals, its whole system of social values."

Last October, shortly before Vietnam Moratorium Day, the faculty met to debate a resolution calling for U.S. withdrawal from Vietnam. A professor, speaking against the resolution, complained, "We wouldn't even be discussing Vietnam today if we hadn't started with this black thing." (The resolution was passed by a small majority.)

The logic may have been murky but the message was clear: blacks were luring Wesleyan away from traditional academic pursuits and into such questionable concerns as war and peace. A list of other concerns into which blacks have lured Wesleyan would include: the school's relationship to the Middletown ghetto, hiring practices by construction firms under contract to Wesleyan, and the school's investments in South Africa. "The blacks have been a fantastic leavening in the loaf," says Beckham. "They're creating a shift away from insular scholarship toward social action."

But the shift has been far from automatic; there are doubtless many teachers who would rather publish than picket. "My black students keep asking me what I've done to fight racism at Wesleyan," a teacher notes irritably. "I wasn't *hired* to fight racism. I was hired to *teach*." That, no doubt, was what the unhappy trainer meant by "encapsulated."

To many black students, the teacher is Wesleyan's *bête blanche*. "They never make a human effort," complains Harold Murphy, the junior who talked Hayes into coming to Wesleyan. "Once I asked a professor to define probability for me. He took me on a 45-minute trip and when he got done I still didn't know the meaning of probability. He wasn't *teaching*, man; he was just proving how much he knew."

Such complaints, of course, are voiced on all campuses by all races; but they run deeper with black students. Blacks complain that professors don't know their names—"They call us 'you'"—and don't treat them with respect. "If I try to say something in class," a black freshman observes, "the teacher, he'll get to smiling and walk over to my seat. It seems like he's surprised I can talk."

"Most of the white teachers here don't know how to teach blacks," says Dwight Green, a black senior who plans to go on to law school. "Maybe they can't teach *anybody*. Up until we got here they never had to try." But some professors are trying. They are scanning their course syllabi for signs of "ethnocentric bias," and they are adding black content to their lectures—"Baldwin and Wright mixed in with Dostoevski and Joyce," as Jonathan Collett says. In some music courses blacks are calling for African music to replace the "honkie music" of Bach, Mozart and Stravinsky. As a music teacher has quipped, "We're facing up to a Bach-lash."

There is, in fact, a desperate search for "black relevance" going on in Wesleyan classrooms—a response, in part, to black charges that Wesleyan teachers indulge in "colonization of the mind." But whatever pleases the black students seems to irritate the whites.

Last spring a visiting black drama professor, Dean Douglas Johnson, kicked his white students out of a course devoted to black drama. His explanation was interesting. "The whites could not participate in the lab sessions," he said, because they didn't understand the black world that was being dramatized. Instead, "they became observers. This served the archtype of the white man looking at the darkies." Whatever the merits of Johnson's case, white students reacted huffily. In a letter to The Argus, 16 whites accused him of "black racism." To be white at Wesleyan, they complained, "is to be a second-class citizen."

Increasingly nowadays, to be white at Wesleyan is to be angry and afraid. At the general orientation session for freshman last fall Dwight Green made a speech which he called "Faggots, Masturbators, and Whites." The blacks, most of whom sat in one corner of the room, applauded; the startled whites received the speech in silence. As one of them, a product of an all-white public school system on Long Island, recalls, "I walked out of there thinking there'd be a riot that night for sure."

It is a measure of Wesleyan's frustration that white students sensed peril where none existed, and that black students, wrapped up in their own grievances, failed to recognize white fears. "That white-fear stuff is just a cop-out," Green said later. "It takes racists off the hook. There was no reason for anybody to get hung up on the speech. I was using those terms as metaphors." At Wesleyan it is easier to mix metaphors than races.

All this heightens the black man's sense of alienation. From his first day on campus, he feels himself struggling among the scions of wealthy whites who cannot possibly understand his black world. The written personality test he is made to take asks, among other things, whether he prefers theater to travel. "Man, that test wasn't written for *me!*" he says to himself. On the same day an ingenuous white freshman, anxious to make a black friend, poses the inevitable question: "How does it really feel to be a Negro?" And that weekend he may learn that some of his white dormitory mates—the ones who had been especially friendly—have buzzed off to Smith College without asking him to come along. "They drink your wine and smoke your pot, but when it's time to meet some girls, they're gone."

"What we need around here," says Tom Morse, a white

junior from Rochester, N.Y., "is a black-white Emily Post, an etiquette for the races." Morse says he learned "good racial manners" the hard way. One day while talking with some black friends he lapsed into his W. C. Fields imitation. "That's right, my boy," he said in his best nasal drawl. The black faces froze. Later his black roommate told Morse what he had done. "You called us 'boy,'" he said. "You insulted your friends."

Last spring, in the wake of the black takeover of Fisk Hall, Morse organized the Student Action Movement (S.A.M.), an organization dedicated to stamping out white racism at Wesleyan. "I know a lot of guys around here," he says, "who say 'black' out loud and 'nigger' inside. The brothers aren't fooled; they've been around." White response to S.A.M., which claims about 50 members, has not been cheering. "Most of them look upon us as a bunch of guilty white liberals," Morse says. "White students generally don't worry about these things. They live from one football game to the next." If so, Wesleyan's Homecoming weekend last November, which featured both the last football game of the season and its first threat of organized racial violence, must have been annoying.

By half-time on Nov. 8 Wesleyan was in danger of suffering two defeats: in the stadium Williams was leading, 14–6; elsewhere the racists, both white and black, seemed to be carrying the day. Two dormitory incidents had heated up emotions to a point where Etherington had felt compelled to cancel the Homecoming dance and to get a court order enjoining members of Ujamaa from disrupting "athletic, social or academic events" that weekend.

As the fans munched hot dogs and awaited the second half, a voice boomed over the public-address system. "Wesleyan is a white racist institution," intoned Bernard Freamon, a black senior from Newark and a spokesman for Ujamaa. Etherington had given him permission to tell the blacks' side of the story. As Freamon finished, the fans gave forth with a wild cheer—their team had come back on the field. (It went on to win, 18–17.)

The story Freamon might have told began early this fall with a rash of burglaries in the dormitories. White students suspected three or four blacks who had been seen frequently wandering through the corridors of several dorms. One night a white student, hearing a knock at his door, and suspecting larcenous intentions, decided not to answer. The door opened and two blacks appeared. "Sorry," one of them said, "we thought this was the bathroom."

The white student made a sarcastic remark about the difficulties of finding clearly labeled bathroom doors. More words led to a fight with one of the black students, during which the other black, George Walker, pulled a knife—not to attack, he said later, but to prevent other whites who had rushed to the scene from interceding. It turned out that Walker was one of "the San Francisco five"—alleged Black Panthers from Wesleyan whom San Francisco police had arrested last spring and charged with illegal possession of weapons.

Thirteen days after the fight, Wesleyan's five-man Student Judiciary Board (S.J.B.—four whites, one black) put Walker and his friend on strict disciplinary probation, meaning that any further trouble would lead to automatic expulsion. At the same time S.J.B. issued an "official warning" to the white student, noting that his language may have been belligerent.

The decision triggered the next disaster. On Nov. 4, Jonathan Berg, a white senior from New Jersey, wrote a fiery letter to The Argus in which he called the S.J.B. ruling on the white student "just incredible" and called Walker "a common criminal" and "a punk." In black argot, and unknown to Berg, "punk" means homosexual. That night about a dozen blacks went to Berg's room and threatened him with physical harm if he did not retract his statement. The next night Walker paid another call on Berg, found him taking a shower, and beat him up. Walker was accompanied by Kerry Holman, a black junior from Washington, D.C., who also goes by the name of Kwasi Kibuyu.

At midnight Berg called both the police and David W. Adamany, a young associate professor of government who is also dean of students. Adamany, deciding to short-circuit S.J.B.'s creaky judicial machinery, promptly expelled Walker and suspended Holman.

The next night (two days before Homecoming) Ujamaa held a mass meeting attended by many blacks from Middletown. Ujamaa's newly elected Central Committee, which some white observers think represents "only the radical wing," had drawn up three demands to be made to Wesleyan: fire Adamany, restore Holman to full student status; and set up a separate, all-black student judiciary board to rule on cases involving black students. The meeting endorsed the proposals.

By 11 A.M. the next day spokesmen for Ujamaa were in Etherington's office listing their demands and giving him until 1 P.M. to decide, or else "suffer the very serious consequences." Etherington waited until 5 P.M. He then told the blacks he would neither dismiss Adamany nor approve an all-black judiciary; on the other hand, he had already reinstated Holman and turned his case over to S.J.B. (Holman is still at Wesleyan.)

Meanwhile, alumni bent on a jolly reunion were beginning to stream onto campus, and rumors of disruption were everywhere. Etherington, fearing the worst, then canceled the Saturday night Homecoming dance and got the injunction from Circuit Court Judge Aaron Palmer—the same judge who will preside over the coming Black Panther trial in New Haven—aimed at keeping the peace. In a way it worked —there was no violence that Homecoming weekend; but the action may have severed the gossamer tie of trust between Etherington and the blacks. By citing all members of Ujamaa, the injunction implied, as one black faculty member put it, that "all blacks were potential criminals." If it was true that some black moderates were trying to rein in the "radical" Central Committee, the injunction could hardly have strengthened their hand. "The injunction may have lowered the level of trust," Etherington concedes, "but it raised the level of reality."

In any case, the violence did not end there. On Nov. 19 a large fire at the door to Jonathan Berg's bedroom forced that unhappy letter-writer to jump to safety from his second-story window. Witnesses said it was a gasoline fire and that it had been started by two blacks. Middletown police promptly arrested Harold Williams, a black sophomore from New Haven and one of "the San Francisco five" apprehended last spring. Earlier that day Williams had been dropped as a student from Wesleyan for academic reasons. He faces charges of arson, but he is out on bail now, and the bail was supplied by a joint faculty-student fund, with both whites and blacks contributing. Many races, one community.

In early December shots were fired—aimed apparently at Rhahim Khabib, a black administrator. While entertaining three other blacks in his apartment one night, Khabib received a spurious phone call; the telephone was near a window, and soon after Khabib hung up bullets shattered the glass. No one was hit. Friends of Khabib speculated that the shooting was the work of white high-school students in Middletown. Weeks earlier Khabib had angered many whites by interceding in a controversial disciplinary case involving a black high-school student.

This incident was followed by a series of anonymous phone calls to the Wesleyan switchboard warning that bombs had been planted in various places on the campus, including the basement of the Malcolm X House. No bombs have been found, but by now many blacks are convinced there is a white conspiracy afoot to destroy Ujamaa.

Suspicion, in fact, has been increasing on both sides. When police, in response to the bomb scare at the Malcolm X House, limited their search to the basement, they were rebuked by both whites and blacks. The latter wanted the police to find a white bomb; the former, a black arsenal. Neither group doubted that its quarry existed somewhere in the Malcolm X House.

What worries some observers is that the search for guns and bombs precludes the search for understanding. It is clearly too late at Wesleyan for anything but understanding, yet with rare exceptions white students and black students do not even talk to each other. When Worth Hayes first got to Wesleyan he risked an occasional dinner with white friends and resented pressures from his brothers to keep him at "the black table." Nowadays there is no need for pressure; Hayes is content to associate with blacks only.

Similarly, a black artists' exhibition at the Malcolm X House, putatively open to everyone, has attracted few white students. Classroom announcements urging students to attend have been greeted with snickers from whites who view Malcolm X House less as a gallery than a fortress. "If the white man stays in his cocoon," says Hayes, "he'll never understand the black man."

But cocoons come in several colors at Wesleyan, as they do elsewhere in America. The blacks have their Ujamaa; the white have their centuries-old brotherhood of inherited wealth and power, the same brotherhood that expelled Charles B. Ray from Wesleyan in 1832; and the school's handful of Puerto Rican students have their newly formed Latin Leadership Conference, which specifically excludes Mexican-Americans.

If the analogy with cocoons means anything, it means that sooner or later they must give way to a freer, more mature form of living. That is what Wesleyan has been groping toward since 1965—"an experiment in hope," John Maguire calls it—and if moving ahead seems difficult, the alternative of turning back seems downright disastrous. "I am not discouraged," says Etherington. "We came out of this with a good deal of strength. Both our white students and our black students have a sharper awareness of each other's problems."

In the final analysis, only the students can insure the success of Wesleyan's experiment in hope, and they will not speed the day by giving aid and comfort to the armies of the night.

"It is no longer a choice now between violence and nonviolence," Martin Luther King told a Wesleyan audience at the 1964 commencement exercises. "It is either nonviolence or nonexistence."

The New York Times Magazine, January 18, 1970

The South Revisited
After a Momentous Decade

by Karl Fleming

ONCE more down the old familiar highways into that passionately alive and violent country. Days of smothering heat, pounding rain, exploding thunder, shards of lightning that split distant clouds. Nights of honeysuckle and pine needles, big buttery moons and the nocturnal gossip of bullfrogs and cicadas.

It all rolls past your car window and it all looks and sounds and smells the same. Kudzu vine and red ditchbanks and roadside stands laden with peaches, beans, tomatoes and dollar watermelons. The incessant, insistent shouting of the radio evangelists: "Glory be to *Jay*-sus, bless-ud be his nay-aim, hallelu*yah!*" Lazy creeks and rivers the color of dirty motor oil. Catfish and fried chicken and gourmet restaurants where the waitresses call you "honey" and the escargots come with black-eye peas and turnip greens. Mimosa and crepe myrtle and Negro shotgun shacks with backhouses and front gardens with a few pathetic collards struggling for life. Schools named Booker T. Washington and George Washington Carver. Honeymoon Fords and Chevies parked at motels with "Hot Springs Tonite" scrawled on the sides.

And the people. Open-faced friendliness and hard-eyed stares from the flush-faced whites riding around in pickups with whip antennas and gun racks in the back of the cab. The revival tents at the edge of town and the good ole boys around the country pool parlor, telling each other for maybe the thousandth time, "Boy, they got wimmin up 'ur in Atlanta, you give 'em $25 and they'll do *any*thang!" Toothpicks and crewcuts. Folks rocking on the front porch, waiting for the RFD mailman. Hopeless, listless Negro men getting drunk on busthead corn whisky down the muddy, weedy alleys where the pavement ends. Doubled-up names like Effie Dee and baby-talk names like Bubba. Church on Sunday morning and church on Sunday night.

The temptation, coming home, is to say that nothing has changed. Except for the encroachment of a few more factory buildings and a lot more plastic franchise eateries, the South looks just about the way it always has. Yet it has changed and changed profoundly in the decade since the sit-ins and the Freedom Rides. All the pain and all the blood have not been wasted. Black people are still poor and still imprisoned by their poverty. But they go places they have never been before—the "white" and "colored" signs have come down almost everywhere—and they think thoughts they have never dared think before. They vote now, and the politics of the South has begun to respond to their power. They have forced white people to recognize their common humanity, if not their claim to real equality. The Deep South used to say *never*; the extent to which it has changed since I left—and the extent to which it has acquiesced in the change—was stunning.

And yet there may be more pain and more blood still, precisely because the South is getting to be so much more like the North. Advanced agricultural technology is pushing Negroes off the land and into the cities faster than industrial growth can absorb them. So the cities breed unemployment, and unemployment breeds despair, and despair breeds militancy of a sort I know well from Watts but hadn't seen back home before. To many of the older Negroes I met, the changes seem important; the right to eat at the Holiday Inn is a triumph even if they can't afford it. But the younger blacks are different. The South as they see it is run by a cracker establishment that yields nothing except what government pressure or black power forces it to yield. They are less impressed by the Nixon Administration's promises to end school segregation this fall than by the fact that it has taken Washington sixteen years to get to that point. I heard about blacks and whites dancing together in Mississippi and was startled; dancing breached the next-to-the-last taboo. But a Negro kid in Jackson asked me bitterly, "What does it mean to me that I can dance with a white girl? How does that change my life?" And it was hard to tell him that he was wrong to ask.

Montgomery was where it all began. In Montgomery, fifteen years ago, the local blacks started a bus boycott willy-nilly and got the newest black preacher in town, Martin Luther King Jr., to run it for them. It worked; it made King a national hero and it transformed the face of Negro protest. The sit-in kids were King's children, and so were the Freedom Riders. The day their Greyhound came to town, bound for Jackson, a mob of whites beat them unmercifully and trapped them all one sweltering night in the First Baptist Church . . .

"Looks like trouble gonna start here," William Beasley remembers telling a friend that night. I found him one Sunday after services at the faded brick church; he is a stolid old man of 65, and he tells it like a war story he has told often before. "People began pouring into the church basement and then we were all hemmed in and couldn't get out. There was a lot of shouting and rock-throwing and the people inside were mighty scared. We were there all night and we might *never* have gotten out if it hadn't been for the U.S. marshals."

They did get out, and times changed in Montgomery, and now Beasley says, "It looks like everything worked out all right." At the Elite Café—people there pronounce it *E*-light —the Jaycees in rep ties and the fragile old ladies in blue-rinse hair-dos still spoon up bowls of gumbo; but now blacks eat gumbo there too. Jobs have opened to Negroes; so have the police force and the schools. And open season on black protesters no longer exists. "Bombings and beatings have gone out of style," C. J. Durr, 70, a retired lawyer and ex-FCC commissioner who lives up the road at Wetumpka, told me wryly. "The rule of law has finally arrived—you can go to jail for beating up a Negro now."

Montgomery has its town militant; his name is Richard Boone, and I found him standing in a fetid alley off Ripley Street talking with a black girl. She is 14, pregnant and unmarried. "She has to use everything she can to survive in this jungle," he says. "She'll have the baby and there'll be another mouth to feed. But we need all the black babies for the future. The revolution is coming." Boone, 30, thinks the old-time religion inhibits his people from "doing what's necessary —rioting, stealing, looting. When we can remove God from the minds of people," he says, "the explosion will come. A lot of preachers will be lynched."

But the preachers still hold sway in black Montgomery. "A lot of black folks ain't gonna see the face of God," the Rev. Larry Williams told his congregation at First Baptist the day I was there; he was pacing beside his little choir of eight, mopping his face with a handkerchief. "Some people got the idea all black folk are good," he said. "They are mighty, mighty wrong." And the whites cling to the distance that is left. "We got 45 per cent colored and we're the best damn folks in the world to 'em—hell, yeah!" George Wallace's cousin Cecil told me. Cecil runs a four-chair barbershop a half-mile from the capitol, where George will shortly resume his reign. "Us ole Alabama boys don't care about niggers eating in hotels and cafés and such. But they aren't setting down to dinner in our homes yet."

Philadelphia, Miss., was a place no one more than two counties away ever heard of until Mickey Schwerner, James Chaney and Andrew Goodman were jailed there one night in 1964— and never were seen again. The three, all CORE volunteers, went to Philadelphia to look into the burning of a Negro church; they were arrested and, so the government charged, released into the hands of a Klan lynch party. Their bodies were found three weeks later in an earthen farm dam. That summer, Claude Sitton, then of The New York Times, and I went to the courthouse to question Sheriff Lawrence Rainey and his deputy, Cecil Price, about the case. A crowd of whites met us in the lobby, led by a big-boned local insurance man, Clarence Mitchell. "We wouldn't be having all this nigger trouble if you Northern newsmen didn't come down here and stir them up," Mitchell told us. We mentioned weakly that Sitton was from Georgia and I was from North Carolina. Mitchell was unimpressed. He told us we would be killed if we didn't get out of town . . .

The rain was pouring hard off the corrugated steel awnings in the courthouse square the day I came back. Inside, there was nobody but a stooped old man in suspenders, hobbling with a cane toward a spittoon in the lobby. Price is in Federal prison for six years in the Schwerner-Chaney-Goodman case; Rainey was acquitted, but, once out of office, he couldn't find a job in Philadelphia and has moved to Kentucky. The schools are integrated. The star basketball player is a Negro who, at the end of the season, was hoisted to the shoulders of his white teammates and borne in triumph around the gym.

I looked up Mitchell, and this time he was friendly as could be. He told me that, if Schwerner, Chaney and Goodman had shown up in 1970 instead of 1964, "they might get the [obscenity] kicked out of them but they wouldn't be buried in a dam." Because times have changed even in Philadelphia, Miss. "If the niggers want to come to white schools, let 'em come," Mitchell said. "We don't care. We resent this forcing but there's no way to resist. It's like looking down the barrel of a cannon—you can't fight back with a pea shooter." Philadelphia used to have other ways of fighting. But this time, when I left town on my own volition, Clarence Mitchell grinned and told me, "Come on back anytime, boy. I won't let nobody hurt you."

Birmingham was a mean town in the old days—a place where bombings were so frequent that Negroes turned the city's official greeting around and told one another, "It's nice to bomb you in Havingham." In the spring and summer of 1963, they spilled by the hundreds out of the churches, with King in the lead, and marched through Kelly-Ingram Park—to be met by public-safety commissioner Bull Connor and his police dogs and fire hoses. Ultimately, they won the Civil Rights Act of 1964; but not without great cost. That spring, King's motel was bombed; late that summer, a dynamite charge killed four Negro girls at Sunday school at the Sixteenth Street Baptist Church. I remember finding a mimeographed church program in the ruins with a picture of Jesus on it, his face crayoned black by some black child . . .

The battle of Birmingham was about lunch counters, and the lunch counters are integrated now. So, to its own transcendent surprise, is Birmingham—at least in its public places. I met ancient A. G. Gaston, 78, said to be the richest black man in Alabama, outside his Gaston Motel—the same place the Kluxers bombed in 1963. A bloody riot followed; the law cracked a lot of heads. This time, sporty in a yellow porkpie hat, Gaston chortled, "Hell, I'm a depitty sheriff now."

"It isn't utopia," Gaston says, "and we're still fighting like hell, but everything is open now and there isn't any use standing in the hall knocking on the door when the door is already open. The whites don't want any more of that bombing stuff. They're scared as hell."

That was one side of it. A block away, near Kelly-Ingram Park, Perry Carlisle, 42, stands in front of his Afro-tinted variety store (a poster photo of Malcolm X hangs in the window) and holds angry court. Carlisle, massive, dark and bearded, marched in the 1963 demonstrations, but a cop spat in his face, and now he says, "You can't do it any more like Dr. King." The last time I was in Birmingham, it was all about lunch counters and nonviolence and love. Now, Carlisle purveys his line of shades, Afro combs and Malcolm posters, and he tells people, "Birmingham ain't no better than it was." And: "We're ready to kick some cracker asses if they don't stay out of the black community sucking blood."

Stone Mountain in Georgia used to be the Klan's favorite rallying place—the scene of an annual grand conclave and cross-burning. The decline and fall of the Invisible Empire was already well advanced the last time I went; I remember three wizened old Kluxers from Chattanooga standing in the dewy weeds and muttering disapprovingly about the amateurish way their younger brethren raised the cross and set it ablaze. "I don't think niggers ought to have better jobs," Imperial Wizard Bobby Shelton told us, "until they start improving their own status quo." They were a sorry lot; it wasn't easy to think of them as the knights of the torch, the bomb and the rope . . .

Stone Mountain is off limits to Kluxers now, but I found a KKK motorcade headed for a rally in a weed patch outside Lexington, Ga., and fell in. We were humming down the highway when a carload of blacks pulled alongside the Klan's lead car—an Olds 88 with an electric cross wired to the front bumper. Some words flew between the two cars. Out came pistols. Gunfire crackled. The blacks sped away. The motor-

cade pulled off the slab onto the shoulder. The only casualty
was Bill Ramsey, 48, who was pinked on the left eye. Bill's
wife, Marilyn, collapsed into his arms in shock.

There was some milling around and considerable complaining. "Hell wid 'em," one Kluxer said. "Let's shoot it out.
Don't think I won't kill a damn nigger." Another—an octo-
genarian with an ancient .38 on his hip—huffed indignantly,
"I've led about 300 motorcades and I've never had anything
like this happen before." But once everybody was satisfied
that Ramsey wasn't badly hurt, we ground on to Lexington
and the rally.

It was just what they came to hear. "I'm against the enemies of America," cried J. B. Stoner, an old-timey racist running for governor of Georgia, "and the enemies of America
are the Jews and the niggers."

"Don't forget the hippies," a voice said from near the
spluttering fiery cross. Only 150 people were there, and half of
them were children and reporters.

*Selma was the little Southwest Alabama town where King
and his followers finally shamed America into guaranteeing
Southern Negroes the right to vote. The blacks won it with their
blood that day at Edmund Pettus Bridge at the edge of town,
when Sheriff Jim Clark's mounted possemen and Col. Al Lingo's
state troopers clubbed and gassed a column of marchers . . .*

"Back then," says Dallas County's new sheriff, Wilson
Baker, "the community was being led by a small minority
shouting 'Never! Never!' when there was actually no way to
stop it." Baker, in the old days, ran the police force at constant cross-purposes with Clark. But now Clark is gone—he
scratched together the remnants of his glory and went to
work for a computer company in Birmingham—and Baker,
on the votes of combat-weary whites and newly franchised
blacks, was elected sheriff. One of his early official acts was
disbanding the old mounted posse. "We don't have a need for
it," he explains amiably. "People want peace."

The price of peace, as it turned out, was pathetically small:
the ballot, some jobs, desegregation in various public places.
I did find one bony, toothless white man, a "War One" vet
named Cleve Sims, 76, who thought even that was too much

—but still he accepted it. Sims was shelling field peas at a roadside stand. "I wish it would all stop but it ain't gonna," he told me. "I'm a pore man and I can't say much about it. But the Lord must have intended it this way."

By "this way," Sims meant the beginning new order between the races in the Alabama Black Belt. One can in fact see the changes in the day-to-day conditions of Negro life as trivial, in contrast to the poverty that plagues so many of them. But to do so would be to forget that even the simplest recognition of the human dignity of black people has been a painful concession for whites and a revolutionary triumph for the Negroes. Calvin Osborn, a one-armed black man, runs a sagging cotton gin on Jeff Davis Street. An urban-renewal project may grind him under and, even if it doesn't, economic reality may: the farmers around Selma are switching from cotton to soybeans and peanuts. But he told me how the local phone book has started listing Negro women as "Miss" or "Mrs." and that was something. The city directory quit putting a "(c)" for colored after the names of Negroes, and that was something. Whites used to call Osborn on business and start out, "Calvin." Now they say "Mr. Osborn," and that is something, too.

And so it all has changed. I can remember a thousand rallies in sweltering backwater churches, the bent old men in shapeless black suits and the gnarled old women with a few pennies for the Movement knotted up in handkerchiefs and the kids in freedom denims. They would sit with that endless patience, fanning themselves with paper fans from the local black funeral home. They would sing "Which Side Are You On?" and they always knew; they would sing "We Shall Overcome" and sometimes they did.

The millennium is not yet: the white South still has all its old genius for altering matters of etiquette and still preserving all the subtle arrangements of color and caste and distance. Some of the towns I visited were rushing into private schools they can't really afford; others have contrived to integrate their schools and segregate their classrooms as rigidly as ever. One evening in Jackson, two fiery young black women lectured me at passionate length to the effect that nothing is different, nothing is better and that the black revolution is coming. We happened to be sitting at Primo's Restaurant in a fancy white shopping center; we might have been mauled or even killed for making the attempt a decade ago, and now there we were, with a white waitress serving up stuffed flounder and asking my two black acquaintances, "Can I get you ladies anything else?"

The irony of it hit me hard. The white people I saw believe they have given up a lot; they kept telling me they don't like being forced or crowded, and a lot of them paste Wallace stickers on their cars, but not many of them say "never" any more. And yet now a new generation of black kids is coming up—kids who never heard of the Montgomery boycott or the Freedom Rides or Edmund Pettus Bridge—and they are full of the militant fever so familiar in the North.

Those kids don't remember John Lewis, an old and scarred SNCC warrior who not a decade ago was as young and full of fury as they. Lewis is only 30 now, but the dues in the old days were fearfully high—he was jailed 40 times and beaten often—and he seems older. He has come in out of the backwaters; he works at a desk in Atlanta now, organizing the registration of black voters. And now he says a little sadly: "When you look at the violence and suffering and dying that people went through in the last ten years, the changes seem very small. And the lives of poor black people *haven't* changed very much. What's happened is that the South is getting more like the North—more subtle and sophisticated in handling black people." He paused. "In the South," he said, "people still have a certain degree of hope and faith because they still have so far to go any change is a degree of progress. But if the frustration and bitterness continues and grows—it will be the North all over again."

Newsweek, August 10, 1970

The Revolutionary People's Constitutional Convention

by Nora Sayre

"We're chiefly interested in the survival of our people, but not at the expense of other people."
—Huey P. Newton

THE exhaust fumes from the Mister Softee truck mingled with the baby-powder smell of the creamy cones, while bongo drums thudded throughout the crowd of ten thousand waiting to hear Huey Newton speak at Philadelphia's Temple University—a crowd throbbing with suspense, elated by the anticipation of a leader. Political proximity has a new tang now: sniffing Softee, I remembered inhaling the mixture of tear gas and maple syrup that suffused a Washington waffle shop near the Department of Justice in November, 1969, where some of us raced for shelter. But one of the main lessons of the plenary session of the Revolutionary People's Constitutional Convention—which was sponsored by the Black Panthers and others in September—was the absence of CS gas or violence. And when an excited young group from North Philadelphia's ghetto started to march toward City Hall, the Panthers stopped them and made them go home. Just as they had been relentless peace-keepers on Yale's Mayday—when a few dustups began on the New Haven Green, while the Yale radio station repeated, "The Panthers ask you to go to your rooms"—so the Panthers wielded their authority in Philadelphia. When it came to the crunch, they saved skulls and probably lives, to the astonishment of some seasoned Philadelphians, who later said they'd been "sure of" a riot. The Panthers' military discipline (which often disturbs their liberal supporters) is acutely respected by many of the ghettos' young, and even by the white revolutionary trippers who appear half-stoned at Panther rallies. The Panthers distill a brand of control which some politicians and policemen might envy—although it's their privilege to deplore it.

In the week before the Philadelphia Convention, one policeman was killed and three were wounded. After five suspects from a group called The Revolutionaries were arrested, they were shown to be absolutely unconnected to the Panthers. Still, these events inspired a raid on the Panther offices. (A former Philadelphia policeman told me, "The best publicity any police department can have is a dead cop.") After a shootout, the police made fourteen Panthers strip naked against a wall and spread the cheeks of their buttocks so that "body cavities" could be thoroughly searched for weapons and explosives. (Bail was set at $100,000 apiece, as "preventive medicine," but was soon lowered to $2,500 and much less.) Police Commissioner Frank Rizzo, who at first referred to the Panthers as "yellow dogs" (because they submitted to the search), later tried to retract this image.

About snipers he said: "These creeps lurk in the dark and you never have a chance against them. They should be strung up—I mean within the law."

However, the savagery of Rizzo's troops had already generated lavish neighborhood support for the Philadelphia Panthers—which had been one of the Party's weakest chapters. The dean of Temple's School of Social Administration said that the raids were in response to dissent, rather than a reaction to any activities of the Panthers. One United States District judge issued a very unusual temporary order restraining the police—announcing at the same time that "a madman out of control shooting policemen is not much more dangerous to the community than a policeman who loses control and goes shooting up people's houses and raiding them"—while a black judge called the raids "outrageous," also "totally unnecessary, uncalled for and really improper." He added that white Philadelphians "were hopeful of violence [during the Convention, so] they could retaliate." The Panthers, who have labored for several years to be taken seriously as a political force, have succeeded to such an extent that some think Rizzo is trying to use them to make himself Mayor in 1971;

apprehensive Philadelphians say that both the Democrats and the Republicans would be glad to nominate him.

As a New Yorker, I found Philadelphia so jammed with hostilities and hatreds that Manhattan seems gentle and pastoral in comparison; although I'm often exasperated by Mayor Lindsay's many bunglings, I felt a wave of appreciation for his efforts to curb cops—as opposed to the police-camp vibes which shiver through Philadelphia or Chicago. (Rizzo: "The only thing we can do now is buy tanks and start mounting machine guns.") During the Convention, no white Philadelphian would give me street or bus directions to the ghetto; most just turned away, shrugging or scowling, though one cabdriver said, "You want to see stabbings and killings?" In fact, the only violence I saw was in the dining room of The Benjamin Franklin Hotel, where one middle-aged man began to slug another in the belly and the throat, finally pounding his head against the table. As they pummeled each other toward the doorway, a waiter said, "They're only brothers," and the audience of diners seemed relieved.

During the unviolent Convention, the Panther speeches—although pruned of much of last year's rhetoric—weren't lamblike. Michael Tabor (of the New York Panther 21, an ex-addict who is defending himself at his trial) and, later, Newton sounded as disgusted as William Lloyd Garrison must have been when he called the U.S. Constitution "a covenant with death, and an agreement with hell" which "should be immediately abolished"—because the document which gave whites their human rights excluded blacks. Both Tabor and Newton quoted the Declaration of Independence, concerning "the Right of the People to alter or abolish" a government which is destructive to their rights, "and to provide new Guards for their future security." Tabor, who spoke for over two hours, views the Nixon Administration as merely part of the native tradition: "What they're doing is the natural outgrowth" of our history and its Constitution. "The Founding Fathers started this show. . . . [Genocide has continued] since 1607 when those racist bandits first landed on that rock." Moreover, "Nixon ain't in control of this government . . . he's just a paranoid with a loser's complex." He unleashed contempt for the Pentagon, corporations and their directors—"They're the true dope fiends—hopelessly addicted to money"—white and black capitalists, all "murder on an international level," and said of Vietnam: "That war is over. It's over. The Vietnamese have won. So why is fighting still going on? Why? Because here in America, we have not done our job. . . ."

He said that "a lot of people are confused about the whole issue of self-defense." He cautioned that an unarmed man can't protect himself against a cop who menaces him at noon. "But, come sundown, when the streets are dark and deserted, and you go up on the roof, and you take your action out, fix up your sights, put your index on that trigger and you pull that trigger—that's self-defense, that's self-defense. Because if you don't get *him*, he's gonna get *you* the next day." (Roars of delight from the crowd.) He continued, "We have enemies who are dedicated to killing us, to offing us. If you're a masochist, then you'll just allow your life to be snuffed out. . . . History will look at you not as a martyr, but as a goddam fooool." He added that violence or nonviolence isn't the issue: "The issue is whether we want to live or we want to die. We're all here today because we want to *live.*

"America today has one foot in the graveyard and the other foot on a banana peel, and they're slipping fast, fast. . . ." (Cheers.) "Lots of people think they're going to get through this by playing cool. . . . But the name of the game in America is tag. And specifically, black people is *It.* . . . But I also think Kent State was It. . . . They have turned on their own sons and daughters." He repeated the Panthers' commitment to a class struggle as an alternative to racial war, and the need for a socialist government. (Actually, the Panthers' concept of socialism sounds quite similar to that of Clement Attlee after World War II: the skeleton of a Welfare State which has since had many bones snapped by British Socialists and Tories alike.) Tabor underlined the responsibilities of writing a new Constitution—and of preventing the U.S. from dispensing further death. "If we do not do our job effectively, mankind is through dancing . . . it'll be *all* over with."

After he finished, two tear-gas canisters were found near

the speakers' platform: which could have sent five thousand people stampeding up the wooden bleachers of Temple's gym —an ideal scenario for broken legs. Many had complained of the Panthers' stern security measures: all the frisking and "patting" which was required before anyone entered the gym. Yet the canisters had slid through; later, there were two telephone threats on Newton's life. Still, much of the crowd was unnerved by the searching; a jittering matron yelped at a boy behind her, "You blew on my neck!" When he apologized, she said severely, "I don't let even my *husband* do that." Otherwise, the waiting crowd was jubilant and cordial, although there were little clusters of racial shyness. About half of the mass was white. But the neighboring ghettos turned out more fully and eagerly than for any Panther gathering I've seen: it was a powerfully grass-roots audience.

The press was closed out of the hall for Newton's speech. Crammed up against a huge glass doorway, reporters rumbled with resentment, and one man began to mutter, "Press—op*press*ed, de*press*ed, sup*press*ed." In the past, all the Panthers I've seen have been helpful to reporters. But now, all journalists are associated with the oozing distortions of the media. And I can't be indignant—since I've seen how often the Panthers (and most dissidents) have been lushly misrepresented. (WBAI titles some of its reports, "Forgive us our Press-Passes.") Hence, in Philadelphia, many of us wanted to dissociate ourselves from the rest of the press; not wanting to be lumped with oink pig media pollution, we sometimes behaved as though the others had contagious cancer or inflammable V.D. (After two days of walking freely in and out of the Church of the Advocate, the Convention's information center, I was banished simply for standing next to two black reporters from The New York *Times* and The Washington *Star*. A Panther spokesman later apologized.) Still later, we were told that Newton was displeased at our exclusion supposedly due to "a mix-up with security." We also heard rumors that CBS—and perhaps ABC—had had a rumpus with the Convention's sponsors (which included the Muslims, African Unity, the Nationalist Separatist Front, the Black Vanguard, and others besides the Panthers) over the question of paying $25,000 for exclusive coverage. It was said that the sponsors had argued about the possible shakedown until Newton began to speak, and also that the networks had refused to deliver the sum.

For the next session, we were assured that we'd all get in; then, told that only one reporter would be allowed; then, that we ourselves must choose ten representatives—out of thirty. Soon, some of us loathed each other: it was a fine case of divide and conquer. Finally, everyone was admitted, after being made to march rapidly, two abreast, from one locked door to another, circling the building several times, yielding "anything sharp" such as a random nail file. In some ways, the hassle was a healthy reproof to those who control the established press: to the arrogance which has betrayed facts for too long. ("My editor rewrote it" gets no public forgiveness now. Reporters who can't be responsible for their published pieces will soon find all doors closed.) Still, if you consider yourself a reliable reporter—and yet refuse to be a flack for the movement—muck-ups of this kind will only become more frustrating. Who will be allowed to speak? Who will be allowed to hear—or read? Who's a pig in a poke? As Eldridge Cleaver said in a speech in '68, "People are so confused nowadays that they don't know who their enemies are and they don't know who their friends are."

So we heard Newton on tape and read his speech. His style was far cooler than Tabor's, but the vast audience was ecstatic. He said that U.S. history "leads us to the conclusion that our sufferance is basic to the functioning of the government," and that "a nation conceived in liberty and dedicated to life, liberty and the pursuit of happiness has in its maturity become an imperialist power dedicated to death, oppression, and the pursuit of profits." (Cataracts of applause.) ". . . we will not be blinded by small changes in form which lack any change in the substance of imperialistic expansion. Our suffering has been too long, our sacrifices have been too great, and our human dignity is too strong for us to be prudent any longer." ("RIGHT ON!") He stressed that the Constitutional Convention should produce "rational and positive alternatives." As for self-defense: "People are never violent . . . until they are aggressed."

Afterward, the crowd surged to the streets around the

Church of the Advocate. In this ghetto, the gashed sidewalks sparkle with broken glass—it's not yet paved with diamonds by the O.E.O. Standing on a ravaged curb, I learned from a former Urban Coalition staffer that this was a Model Cities area, where $25,000,000 had already been spent—too much of it on office space and salaries. He described job programs which allow participants to earn less than welfare recipients—"people working for their poverty"—and said that the techniques of "trying to create a golden ghetto" only intensify segregation; the housing plan ties residents to dwellings which they can't afford to leave, while the jobs which would pay them better are in the suburbs—remote from local transit systems. Around us, the packed streets seethed with hope that Newton would appear; he didn't, and it was then that the Panthers prevented a possible explosion.

Each of the next day's fifteen workshops produced a paper which served as a recommendation for the final draft of the Constitution (which was ratified in November, 1970). The two sessions I attended—on "The Distribution of Political Power" and "Control and Use of the Educational System"—kept breaking into smaller groups. Many delegates were haunted by the question of whether *any* eventual government can be trusted, and whether there's any alternative to voting. Later, I heard that some other workshops came close to punch-ups. But the proposals were finally thrashed out, and were then read aloud to all the delegates.

The recurrent themes were decentralization and self-government for numerous groups. Self-determination for women and homosexuals meant a radically new position for the Panthers, who, until recently, had derided both. But Newton wrote a supportive statement to Women's Liberation and Gay Liberation, admitting that "sometimes our first instinct is to want to hit a homosexual in the mouth and [to] want a woman to be quiet. We want to hit the homosexual . . . because we're afraid we might be homosexual; and we want to hit the woman or shut her up because we're afraid she might castrate us, or take the nuts we might not have to start with." (He added, "Friends are allowed to make mistakes"—a notion that's rare among revolutionaries.) From other workshops, there were repeated demands for community control

of the police; as a result of the Panther's conference in Oakland last year, they have already succeeded in qualifying this
proposal for a place on the ballot in Berkeley. Other workshops focused on the military ("No genocidal weapons shall
be manufactured or used"), the legal system, environment,
religious oppression, drugs and health (here, a demand for
socialized medicine), and "internationalism—relation with
liberation struggles around the world." The evening's biggest
ovation burst for "a redistribution of America's wealth to the
have-not nations of the world and acceptance of a more modest standard of living that such a move would require." Many
papers leaned on the phrase "*after* the revolution." The street
people's paper stated that acid, mescaline, and grass "are in-
strumental in developing the revolutionary consciousness."
The crowd whooped until the ceiling rang. However, "after
revolutionary consciousness has been achieved, these drugs
may become a burden." Small response. (Since the Panthers
work so fiercely against hard drugs, I doubt that the final
Constitution will recommend psychedelics.) But all in all the
new Constitution will insist on collectivism to a degree that's
guaranteed to fry the brains under most hard hats.

The next morning, while crowds swirled around the
Church of the Advocate, I listened to Charles X Kenyatta—
who was once Malcolm X's bodyguard, and was very active in
helping to calm Harlem streets after Martin Luther King was
killed—describing the International Congress of African People in Atlanta, which had taken place on the same September
weekend. The Congress, which included such diverse speakers
as Whitney Young, Le Roi Jones, and Roy Innis, largely
favored black separatism ("White cooperation is white
co-optation"), the use of the existing political system (by
running more black candidates), and nonviolence. Kenyatta
said that the Atlanta audience was middle-class and professional in contrast to the Philadelphia Convention, which had
drawn so many from the streets. He expressed his own doubts
about black-white alliances; he feels that the priorities are too
far apart. "The black radical is fighting for freedom, while the
white radical is fighting for power. The white's free already. . . ." At this point, a Philadelphia TV crew started to
interview Kenyatta. He said that he didn't believe in the gun,

although he would defend anyone's right to have it. Just as he began to say that the one thing he can't forgive whites is their ability to make blacks turn against each other, two teen-aged Panthers stopped the interview. The Party doesn't accept his criticism.

However, one Panther said that the leadership was trying to establish some "unofficial alliances" with separatists and cultural nationalists, despite the disagreements about working with whites. Newton told the Liberation News Service that "blacks have a moral right to separate," but that the Panthers feel that their "obligation is to transform this whole society," and hence separatism is a poor "political strategy." Later, a young Panther said of Ron Karenga (leader of the anti-white cultural nationalist U.S.), "Every time he opens his mouth, he's sick." He began to expand—"We're just as alien to African culture as the Atlantic is to the Pacific"—but someone down the block shouted, "Pigs are beating the sisters!" Warning the crowd to stay put, he and other Panthers dashed to the corner, and learned that the police had merely answered the house call of a brawling couple. The Panthers quickly killed the rumors that were rippling through the neighborhood.

Without question, the Panthers' strength has swelled in the last year. They may be the only group in the country which reaches both educated and uneducated people, and they try to show many different sorts of Americans what problems they have in common. (At a meeting of the poor during the 1969 Conference on Hunger, blacks, whites, and Mexicans withdrew and caucused. Finally, the blacks produced a list of demands, the whites had a list of goals, and the Mexicans presented grievances. The lists turned out to be very similar. That's the kind of point which the Panthers are trying to make.) Also, the Panthers' momentum has built from revealing lies and contradictions—from the brutal inadequacy of justice for black people to the many dysfunctions of democracy. And they've probably exposed more native failings than anyone since L.B.J. Although there's so much talk of death, the emphasis is on living; moreover, it's worth remembering that the threat of violence can be used as a substitute for violence itself. As Cleaver told Nat Hentoff in an interview for *Playboy*, "Perhaps if enough people recognize how possible [violence] is, they'll work all the harder for the basic changes that can prevent it." Admittedly, Washington still seems clueless: last May, when Nixon "talked to" students at the Lincoln Memorial, they later told CBS: "Someone asked [Nixon] about the Black Panthers, and whether he thought Bobby Seale had gotten his Constitutional rights in Chicago, and his answer was that when people stab other people with ice picks, they are still entitled to their Constitutional rights, and we . . . have no idea what that meant."

Still, the final point in Huey Newton's Philadelphia speech makes the choice quite clear:

"It is a fact that we will change the society. . . . It will be up to the oppressors if this is going to be a peaceful change."

Esquire, January 1971

Discovering One Another in a Georgia Town

by Marshall Frady

On a chill Friday evening last November, the football team of the Americus High Panthers met the squad from a neighboring Georgia town, the Cairo High Syrupmakers, in what has long been in the South a kind of seasonal demi-religious folk-festival. The two shallow banks of bleachers were filled with modest family galleries: the women wan of makeup, their neutral-colored hair fiercely scalloped and rippled from their afternoon beauty parlor appointments, the men beside them—with their cleanly clipped haircuts under little flannel fedoras and plaid shirts fastened tieless at their necks beneath snugly buttoned checkered sportscoats—tending to look like merely enlarged versions of the small boys sitting at their elbows. Along the waist-high wire fence immediately below the bleachers, there passed a ceaseless trudging processional of men who held anonymous white Styrofoam cups in their hands and who by halftime had already become a bit flushed and bawlingly convivial.

But there was, this particular evening, a discreet surreal alteration in the immemorial pageant. In the midst of whites in the stands who would release at every long gain by the Panthers those wild abject savage yodels that have lasted from Bull Run and Pickett's Charge, there was a significant population of blacks, students and parents, sitting somewhat more sober and subdued, but producing now and then patterings of circumspect applause. What's more, about half the players on the field below them were blacks—including a 16-year-old sophomore halfback named Calvin Prince who had already that season averaged 114 yards a game rushing. Now, as he was running back a punt for the first of his three touchdowns that evening, the cluster of primly groomed white matrons who had been dispensing hot chocolate and slabs of home-baked cake in the concession booth began bobbing up and down with ecstatic fluttering hand claps, squealing to one stranger's inquiry. "Calvin Prince! That's Calvin Prince! Who else?" Unlike the mammoth isolations of large city stadiums, here there was an immediate intimacy between the stands and field—nothing remote and detached about the half time performances of the integrated bands.

It has occasionally been fancied that football might one day help exorcise the old intractabilities in the South, and athletics, of course, have long served for black people as one of the few escape hatches out into an open if circumscribed respect and celebration. Considerably wider, however, were the implications of that Friday night in Americus. At last summer's end, that ultimate doomsday which has been looming before white Southerners ever since 1954—the total integration of their public schools—arrived at last in communities throughout the old Confederacy. Now, after the passage of many surprisingly placid months, a general suspicion is beginning to emerge that something both seismic and ironic may be transpiring in the South. For all the continuing scattered incidents of rear-guard viciousness, what is under way in communities like Americus, particularly among the youth, poses, even if flickeringly, the first authentic suggestion that it may be the South after all where the nation's general malaise of racial alienation first finds resolution. Not in the order of division prophesied by the old segregationist apologists, but in the formal advent of a single people, unique and richly dimensioned. The effusiveness at the football stadium, while only an incidental part of the progress taking place in Americus, offered a first fleeting sense of how ephemeral all human furies and irreconcilabilities might actually be.

Back during that brief eloquent decade in the South begun by the Montgomery bus boycott in 1956, during that saga of tabernacle mass meetings and courthouse confrontations which eventually became one of the most profound moral adventures through which the country has ever passed, certain sites such as Birmingham and Selma were apotheosized by their ordeals into legends. But innumerable other towns were vitally, if vagrantly, touched by the angers and agonies of those days. Among them, was Americus, whose 16,000 population includes some 8,000 blacks.

When Americus was visited by a series of demonstrations in 1963, local authorities captured five civil rights leaders and charged them under a century-old state law with "insurrection"—a rather total measure, since conviction could have carried a maximum penalty of death. Two years later, during a local election, city police arrested a Negro woman, who was a candidate for justice of the peace, as she was standing in a "white only" voting line. This artless lurch set off a long glowering summer of mass marches and wholesale jailings, and finally, one sullen evening in July, a white youth lounging with a collection of his fellows at a corner filling station was shot to death from a passing car of blacks. With that, the local county attorney—a hulking mild-spoken man named Warren Fortson —ventured a proposal for the formation of a biracial council to break through the blunderings of brute blind reflexes between the white and black communities. But as gentle as Fortson's recommendation might have seemed, within two months he found himself an exile in his own town, and finally fled.

That was five years ago. Today, a complete degree of school integration has been accomplished in Americus with startlingly serene dispatch. There are about 1,850 black students in a total enrollment of 3,105 in the city school system, ranging from about one white to four blacks in one lower elementary school to about one white to one black at Americus High. And though a program of instructional levels in each school has tended to pitch more blacks than whites into the slower classes, Americus has generally abstained from those nimble dissimulations devised by some other towns, such as the interior segregation of blacks from whites in separate classrooms.

Moreover, in the Americus school system's administrative offices, on the second floor of the turreted downtown edifice of mustard-colored brick with corridors that creak underfoot like a frigate's galley, there are displays of black studies programs, including pamphlets on Martin Luther King and Dred Scott and Frederick Douglass, as well as brochures entitled *Racism in America* and children's books about black cowboys. A number of school libraries contain books like *Patricia Crosses Town* ("A Negro girl in a newly integrated school learns about real friends"). In one English classroom at Americus High, among pictures of authors pinned along the walls, there is a poster of James Baldwin, with a quote from his work: "It is a terrible and inexorable law that one cannot deny the humanity of another without diminishing one's own: in the face of one's victim, one sees oneself." And in the county courthouse—whose tidy mown lawn bristled with state troopers and Negro demonstrators throughout the summer of 1965—there are now occasional evening discussions attended by blacks and whites. They ponder, with a fastidious precision, "the disadvantaged student" who "cannot be described by one factor." It is giddying in a town that only five years ago could be thrown into paroxysms by a proposal for a biracial council.

Some 135 miles below Atlanta, in south Georgia's outback of broom sage and scrub pine and peanut fields sprawling relentlessly level and limitless under a vast lonesome sky, the town appears abruptly—a meager and inauspicious collection of worn drab brick buildings infiltrated only by a few newly minted glassy geometric banks. Americus, a farming community partially sustained by incidental industry, has also recently acquired a Holiday Inn. Deposited in a gullied excavation of pale orange dirt on the outskirts of town, the motel has a cocktail lounge where on waning Saturday afternoons townsmen roost in their khakis and clay-spattered brogans amidst lush carpets and muted amber lights, sipping beer now not from the cans served up in nickel-plated chili cafes but from shell-thin glasses shaped like iris bulbs which they twirl between their fingers on wet napkins imprinted with mildly raffish cartoons.

When it became obvious that total school integration was at hand for these citizens, there was a minor but noticeable evacuation of some administrators and teachers out of the Americus school system, and they were accompanied by about 375 white students. Private schools multiplied over the area like an overnight backyard visitation of mushrooms. Generally dingy, dubious, makeshift affairs, one of them operates in the facilities of the Brooklyn Heights Baptist Church, another in a vacated squat mortar building near the center of town, where one finds oddly quiet children with pale blank gazes in its dim cramped corridors, empty RC Cola crates stacked in corners, and a vague sour rankness enclosed within its walls like the effluvium of a fox den. "Without a doubt, they the sorriest damn schools you ever saw," maintains one civic leader. "But as downright pathetic as they are, they maybe been a blessing. They've drawn off the reactionaries and allowed us to go on about our business, so when they fold up, we'll have the whole thing stabilized, and these folks will be coming back into the system on *our* terms."

Such meticulous calculations are only part of a general high diligent nervousness left, as one local citizen put it, "by all that disruption five years ago, which showed us the consequences of letting a situation develop without any positive and responsible leadership." Americus' new mayor is attorney Frank Myers, an amiable, deliberate, portly man with a flourish of sideburns on his moonlike face. Myers, who essayed his election by delicately maintaining a posture of moderate discretion, reports, "We decided we were going to have open house in all the schools right before the term began, just to let folks rub shoulders a little bit, let them go smell each other. At the elementary school my boy goes to, we had a meeting of the nominating committee for the PTA in the home of a black family—four blacks and two of us whites there. After the tea and cookies, we went on about our nominating business just like nothing had ever happened in this town."

During the open house at A. S. Staley School, the all-Negro high school that was converted this year into the integrated junior high, "some of the white parents would come into my office to meet me," recalls the principal, Kelsie Daniels. "They heard I was black, I guess, but somehow it still wasn't real to them until they actually saw me standing there. I just let them sit down and compose themselves after the shock, and I remember one lady finally said, in way of starting a pleasant little chat, 'Well, Mr. Daniels, how did you get to be an administrator, anyway?'"

For all that, admits the mayor, "the closest I ever came to a heart attack was just before school was to open, when somebody called me about 2 a.m. and, bless God, said somebody had set Staley on fire. Fortunately all that was burned was just a little old part of it right there in the front. About 75 black and white parents worked all the next day cleaning up the damage, and we opened that thing right on schedule—yessuh."

One hears the speculation among some white school officials that "people could be hanging in the public system, believing it's going to swing back sooner or later, that what we have now isn't normal." But according to Mary Myers, the mayor's daughter and a junior at the high school, "I haven't heard any students saying anything like that." A tall, effusive, coltish girl with long butterscotch-brown hair and a constant air of glad, dauntless, precipitous directness, she asserts, "It's so different now, it can't even be described. Frankly, I don't see why anyone would want it to swing back the way it was in Americus. Back during that summer five years ago, I remember everybody was so scared all the time. Who wants all that again?"

On the whole, as one Americus High student reports, "It seemed to the older folks this total integration thing was just something they had to do. There seemed to be a kind of reluctant resignation about it. But not with us. There might have been a few of us who thought it was bad being such a quick change, but it's probably good we didn't have to fret about it. Because as soon as it was certain, we really started looking forward to it. We were eager to see what it'd be like." The president of the Americus High student body, Johnny Sheffield, suggests that the school navigated the merger's first treacherous currents as gracefully as it did not so much because of the official precautionary policies and regulations of administrators, but as a result of "the little personal things among the students when they first got together. It's the personal moments that are carrying this thing.

"Instead of us coming together all at once in a totally new situation, for instance," says Sheffield, a hefty, freshly scrubbed youth who played fullback on the football team, "about a month before school started we had a football meeting in the gym. We started talking right away about how, if we could put their team and ours together, we might go all the way. Then, when we started our preseason practice, one of the drills was getting down on your hands and knees and locking heads with another player. I think I was the first one to come up on a colored boy, and I did feel a little funny there for a second—I mean, just to *touch* them was such a totally different situation. But I got down on all fours and locked heads with him, and after that everything went along real fine. I think if I had refused, you know, just a little thing like that right there could have turned the whole situation the other way."

Charles Warren, a sandy-haired youth who is the team's tight end, eventually began giving Calvin Prince lifts home after practice: "I could see folks staring at me when I passed through downtown, and later one of the boys on the team said to me, 'You gonna kiss him next time?' Well, that fella is one of Calvin's best friends now, and after a while it got to where, whenever I'd drive Calvin home, people downtown were waving to us." Some of the white players even began stopping by home now and then with black teammates, and one of them remembers, "My folks got kind of disturbed that first time, said I didn't have to actually bring him *in* the house, and I said, 'Well, what reason would *you* have given him for not inviting him in?'"

Certain awkward hesitations are still lingering in the transition. At Americus High these include retention of all-white cheerleaders and majorettes who were elected last spring, an abeyance of social occasions, the withdrawal off-campus of those school clubs sponsored by groups like the Kiwanis and Civitans. But these expediencies, almost exclusively, have been taken out of a solicitude for the paranoias of white parents.

"I know in the Key Club, which is sponsored by Kiwanis," Johnny Sheffield declares, "we'd already agreed that if some of the black fellas wanted to come in, we were going to bring them in. That's why they moved it off-campus. The rest of the year we'll just go our separate ways, I guess, but next year it's not going to be like this, with no black cheerleaders and no on-campus clubs and all that. . . ." A quiet youth possessed by an almost anguished shyness, Sheffield pauses a moment and then adds softly, "Really, the grown people are just not mature enough to accept it. I don't think they'll ever really change."

Lurking at the center of this queasiness on the part of white elders, of course, is the old hob-goblin of interracial liaisons. Mary Myers remembers that "Before school started, a lot of girls I talked to were scared to death because they'd heard all these horrible tales from their parents, you know." A number of teachers and administrators still cultivate a ferocious vigilance about the matter. "Sometimes, I'll just be standing around in the hall between classes," Calvin Prince allows, "and these white girls, they come up and start talking to you, and right away, man, those white teachers come blowing outta their rooms hollering, 'All right, everybody get on back in their classes, now, don't be congregating out here.' Shoot, man, it's the silliest thing, I don't understand why they want to be that way."

It was this brittleness on the part of white adults which produced the only serious moment of uncertainty during the early fall. "All the black kids had been having dances at the Astro Club after the games," explains Sheffield, "so the white kids decided we'd have a big dance for homecoming. I don't know what was wrong with us—we didn't really mean for it to be a restrictive kind of thing, but we just weren't thinking." Whatever, when the letters of invitation were prepared, some white parents intervened to add to them, "This dance will be private—no blacks admitted." A few of the letters even bore the further notation, "Make sure no blacks see this." But, inevitably, they did, precipitating chants by black students in the halls between classes and a threat of black defections from the football team. Charles Warren's signature had been printed on the letters—"Somebody's parents told Charles this was the right thing to do," says one student, "and he just took their word for it"—and now he watched aghast as the ramifications amplified about him. Finally, at a clamorous assembly meeting, he labored to explain and apologize, finishing with tears in his eyes. The dance was canceled, and gradually the school steadied again. "Afterward," Charles says, "a lot of black girls came up to me crying too, and said they were sorry for me and would help me the best way they could."

In more ways than one, black students have been indulgently and gently assisting white students in their efforts to recondition themselves. But one also comes across indications now of a smoldering cynicism and despair among some black students arising from a gap between their own expectations and the general exuberant optimism of white students. "There could have been just one black cheerleader," a black senior insisted recently, "that's all—just one. It would have made me feel much more like the school was mine too. I went over there with an open heart, but most of the black kids, when we got there, it wasn't really our school—because it seemed like everything was white. We had lost our own school, and all we had was the whites' school." Another black girl asserts, "There are a lot of them who feel right, sure, but they're afraid to show it for some reason. Whenever I'm with just nothing but girls, all the white girls seem to be nice and all. But just as soon as we get mixed and there's white boys around, they seem to turn and get nasty. Since all that with the homecoming dance, I just don't trust the whites anymore. It makes you wonder, if this is what it's come to, whether it's all been worth it—all those years of demonstrating and getting hit on the head and thrown in jail . . ."

Even Calvin Prince, a cheerful and ebullient youth, confesses to misgivings, "The whites are going to love you long as you playing football," he says, "but I don't trust them after that."

But whatever their disenchantments and resentments over the inadequacies and incompletions of the consolidation so far, the experience has brought to black students, as it has to whites, the single incalculable gift of liberation from the old illusions cultivated by the generations before them. "After all these years now," declares one black girl, "we realize that whites are just human beings, not supermen without any faults or weaknesses. I can sit there and look at them now and think, 'You're not like we been told—you're no different from me.' Maybe this is what the whites have been scared of all these years, us catching on to the fact that there are some of them just as dumb as anything ever walked on two feet. Why, a boy in one of my classes, he just sits there all the time eating pencils."

At the same time, the presence now of blacks in their schools should tend to tug white students out of that bland, blithe anesthesia which insulates white communities like that in Americus from the true throes at work in the affairs of the nation—a kind of innocent remoteness perhaps most eloquently indicated by the fact that the whimsical connotations of the Americus High nickname, the Panthers, not only do not seem to have disconcerted anyone, but even to have oc curred to anyone. White students in Americus are likely to feel themselves somewhat closer to the urgencies and desperations in which the destiny of the country is now involved, if only because the personae of those conflicts will become more immediate references for their understanding. But their release into a more expansive awareness, occasioned by the presence of blacks among them, is not likely to be limited to the realities of racial matters. One discovery begets further curiosity, which begets a legion of other curiosities.

"Two of my children are doing better than they ever did," Mayor Myers says. "The level of education ain't dropped a bit." What's more, says Myers, "Competition now between blacks and whites on the faculties is going to weed out the incompetents sooner or later. In the past, no one really cared enough to check whether a teacher was incompetent—just so they satisfied that basic social requirement of being white or black. There just ain't any way to count all the varieties of ways in which this business of keeping up two separate societies has stolen from all of us."

Probably the deepest misgiving haunting blacks now is that integration has stolen from black identity. But a black matron in Americus—Mrs. Thelma Barnum, wife of a prosperous funeral home director and a seasoned redoubtable partisan of the old civil rights battles in town—recently pronounced to a living room full of concerned black girls, "No, no, I don't think we'll be losing our identity." She shook her full sizzling fume of hair, her eyes glittering like bright agate. "We gonna give the whites a little soul. We gonna give 'em some *tone*."

Indeed, during football games white players would charge off the field after a score to exchange popping double-handed soul-slaps with black teammates. In the halls, according to one elementary school principal, "I been noticing just lately that our little white girls have begun trying to pick up that beat the little colored girls walk with." In general, reports one white Americus mother, "My oldest daughter, this year she's not anywhere near so—well, staid and serious and drudging about school as she always used to be. It's just not so grim anymore, there's some kind of zest and openness about it now."

A recent pep rally in the Americus High gymnasium began with a series of skits—primarily involving white girls and teachers costumed as beribboned dolls—which possessed a mirth and lustiness about equal to a Methodist Sunday school's Monday night social hour. Then, three woman teachers—two whites and a black—tripped out on the basketball court to perform a similarly airy dance to *Glow-Worm*, when suddenly a black drummer in the bleachers broke into the startling glad battering beat of a honky-tonk stripper show, bringing an explosion of cheers and howls and clapping. The three teachers, captured in the center of the court by that sleazy jubilant beat, began to twine and pump with fingers snapping high over their heads, as the entire band squalled and stomped after the drummer, with a shivering glee and exhilaration abruptly loosed in the air like a shout of mutual discovery.

There are occurring in Americus such casual and accidental moments of rapport that intimate a mutual accord, a potential for community beyond the bulk of the available evidence, beyond all the disappointed pessimisms and exasperations of the blacks, not to mention the agreeable concessions of whites. The custom evolved, for example, at a local radio station to invite the Americus team members, on the mornings after their games, to act as auxiliary disc jockeys on a program that plays phoned-in requests. On the Saturday after they won the regional AA Championship, the boys gathered at the station, and in the reception area one of the white players turned to the black player sitting beside him and mumbled, "Amerson, I noticed last night you had them four women waiting for you after the game again. Four women, and dawg, if you didn't go and pick out the *ugliest* one again . . ." Amerson chortled, "C'mon, man, you can't tell *me* about that woman. She so ugly, she smoke a pipe. She a tree . . ." Another white youth turned to Prince and said, "Calvin, you gonna wear that bracelet you got on your wrist to the next game maybe?"

Prince, grinning, said, "Watch out, man, you getting in my business now."

When they finally entered the broadcast booth, a black youth proclaimed, "I'm gonna put on some soul. I'm gonna put on *Heaven Help Me*." A white youth said, "I ain't ever heard of that one," and the black squawked, "Man, you mean you ain't ever heard that done by little Stevie Wonder?" The white youth smiled, "Yeah, actually, I guess I have, but I just can't understand it. It's sure got a good feeling to it, though."

"It's unbelievable," Mary Myers points out, "that in a small town like this, whites and colored were living right together all these years without ever actually knowing each other, doing anything together. But eventually, it's going to be like on TV, where a black boy will visit a little white boy at his home after school and all that and the cultures here will merge. I give it 10 years or so, really. Our own experience now in school, it's bound to change the community when we get up there— bound to open it up. Because we're going to know better."

Whenever white students in Americus are asked for a more specific explanation of their new dispositions toward blacks and integration, most of them fall mute. The most probable suggestion may be that, unlike their parents, they grew up witnessing personally or watching on television the challenges of the system they were born into. And there was spoken from those confrontations—the dogs of Birmingham, the Selma bridge—certain universal incontestable decencies and appeals that could not help but touch youths not yet clapped in the myths and defenses and simple habits of the society.

The homecoming dance crisis, in particular, proved to be a protean event in Americus High. For one thing, certain isolations were dispelled in the tension. "We know now we have to communicate between white and black students," says Mary Myers. "And we learned how to communicate through those two or three days there." Beyond that, says Mary, "We probably learned for all time not to assume anything from what we have heard from our parents. We know now that the black and white students have got to talk and trust only one another finally in this thing."

Even more, the crisis turned out to be a humanizing experience. Charles Warren, for one, admits, "People just weren't used to thinking very carefully about how something we might do or say would hurt a black man. We just had never put ourselves in their place. If we had, we would have realized it was going to make them mad, because it would have made me mad." The aftermath of the homecoming crisis suggests that this fresh generation of Southern white is finally and fully encountering in open daylight, even if under constraint and impressment, the black Southerner. And this experience alone might at last work a release from the elusive curse of those old myriad devious reflexes of mind, dullings of spirit and inward brutalizations which have endured from that primeval slave-system mentality in which white Southerners necessarily had to learn how to transform other humans into objects having no real connection to themselves.

But even while unrealized and unacknowledged, the white and black Southerners long ago became one people, or two halves of a single people artificially divided by arbitrarily consecrated laws and institutions. For almost 300 years up until the end of World War II, whites and blacks in the South were, save for the transitory intercession of the Civil War and Reconstruction, left more or less alone together, protagonists locked together in an unarticulated but profound common experience. The true communion between them—the unspoken interplay of frequencies, the underground merging of styles, visions, exuberances and relishes for life—is the unlit side of the moon of Southern history. An elderly white Georgia attorney pronounced some time ago, "There's no getting around it —the white Southerner has got a nigra personality: we both got the same sorta warm and easy feeling for life, the same sense of humor. It's actually been the nigra who's made the white Southerner different in nature from whites in the rest of the country. Hell, we even get the way we talk from them."

In a sense, this kinship could account for the guilts and brutalities that have largely characterized the white Southerner's open commerce with this secret shadow-brother of his. And while this intimacy between whites and blacks in the South has largely been compounded of exploitation and violence, it has also been, unlike the more polite detachments of the North, a humidly personal and existential communion, made up not only of violence but compassion, not only of guilt but shared savors, common hilarities and dreads and beguilements and love for their common earth. It is possible, then, that what has begun to be negotiated in the South is actually the immense transaction—after a kind of covert cruel 300-year-old common-law marriage—of formalizing and institutionalizing at last their common identity.

It has always seemed the lot of the South to serve as the crucible for the nation's ordeals of conscience over race. And if it is true that a racial dichotomy is the major crisis this country faces, then it may be that in goading and impelling the South toward an integration of its people, the rest of the nation has actually been prompting the South to deliver the entire country finally out of the danger of total racial schism. As is the case in Americus, the real peril now is that the impatience of blacks will constantly outstrip the pace of what whites regard as painful and substantial accommodations and accessions on their part. Through the next two or three years, Americus and numberless other communities like it will be embarked on a critical existential voyage, and the real toll will fall on the students, both black and white, whose lot it could be to purchase, with their own patience and compassion and endurance and belief, the future of the South itself.

On a soft and luminous November afternoon, Americus Mayor Frank Myers allowed, "I'll admit to you I'm still probably about 40% bigoted. There just ain't no way to grow up like I did without having prejudices. All I can do is just fight them the best I can. But I'll tell you one thing—my daughter now and my other two kids, they absolutely rid of *all* of them." And just as it took the passing of a generation during 40 years in the wilderness to purge the Israelites into a people prepared for the Promised Land, Myers declares, "It's gonna be our children finally who're going to deliver us out of this thing that's been going on down here ever since slavery. They the ones who'll do it."

Staying Home in Mississippi

by Alice Walker

JACKSON, Miss. Our bus left Boston before dawn on the day of the march. We were a jolly, boisterous crowd who managed to shout the words to "We Shall Overcome" without a trace of sadness or doubt. At least on the surface. Underneath our bravado there was anxiety: Would Washington be ready for us? Would there be violence? Would we *be* overcome? Could. *we* overcome? At any rate, we felt confident enough to try.

It was the summer of my sophomore year in college in Atlanta and I had come to Boston to find a job that would allow me to support myself through another year of school. No one else among my Boston relatives went to the march, but all of them watched it eagerly on TV. When I returned that night, they claimed to have seen someone exactly like me milling about just to the left of Martin Luther King Jr. But of course I was not anywhere near him. The crowds would not allow it. I was, instead, perched on the limb of a tree far from the Lincoln Memorial, and although I managed to see very little of the speakers, I could hear everything.

For a speech and drama term paper the previous year, my teacher had sent his class to Atlanta University to hear Martin Luther King lecture. "I am not interested in his politics," he warned, "only in his speech." And so I had written a paper that contained these lines: "Martin Luther King Jr. is a surprisingly effective orator, although *terribly* under the influence of the Baptist Church, so that his utterances sound overdramatic and too weighty to be taken seriously." I also commented on his lack of humor, his expressionless "Oriental" eyes, and the fascinating fact that his gray sharkskin suit was completely without wrinkles—causing me to wonder how he had gotten into it. It was a surprise, therefore, to find at the March on Washington that the same voice that had seemed ponderous and uninspired in a small lecture hall was now as electrifying in its tone as it was in its message.

Martin King was a man who truly had his tongue wrapped around the roots of Southern black religious consciousness, and when his resounding voice swelled and broke over the heads of the thousands of people assembled at the Lincoln Memorial, I felt what a Southern person brought up in the church *always* feels when those cadences—not the words themselves, necessarily, but the rhythmic spirals of passionate emotion, followed by even more passionate pauses—roll off the tongue of a really first-rate preacher. I felt my soul rising from the sheer force of Martin King's eloquent goodness:

> *There are those who are asking the devotees of civil rights, 'When will you be satisfied?' We can never be satisfied as long as the Negro is the victim of the unspeakable horrors of police brutality. We can never be satisfied as long as our bodies, heavy with the fatigue of travel, cannot gain lodging in the motels of the highways and the hotels of the cities. We cannot be satisfied as long as the Negro's basic mobility is from a smaller ghetto to a larger one. We can never be satisfied as long as our children are stripped of their selfhood and robbed of their dignity by signs stating 'For white only.' We cannot be satisfied as long as a Negro in Mississippi cannot vote and a Negro in New York believes he has nothing for which to vote. No, we are not satisfied and we will not be satisfied until justice rolls down like waters and righteousness like a mighty stream.*

And when he spoke of "letting freedom ring" across "the green hills of Alabama and the red hills of Georgia," I saw again what he was always uniquely able to make me see: that I, in fact, had claim to the land of my birth. Those red hills of Georgia were mine, and nobody was going to force me away from them, until I myself was good and ready to go.

> *. . . Some of you have come here out of great trials and tribulations. Some of you have come fresh from narrow jail cells. Some of you have come from areas where your quest for freedom left you battered by storms of persecution*

*and staggered by the winds of police brutality. . . . Go
back to Mississippi, go back to Alabama, go back . . . to
Georgia . . . knowing that somehow this situation can
and will be changed. . . . This is our hope. This is the
faith that I go back to the South with. With this faith we
will be able to hew out of the mountain of despair a stone
of hope.*

Later I was to read that the March on Washington was a
dupe on black people, that the leaders had sold out to the
Kennedy Administration and that all of us should have felt
silly for having participated. But whatever the Kennedy Administration may have done, or not done, had nothing to
do with the closeness I felt that day to my own people. To
King and John Lewis and thousands of others. And it is impossible to regret hearing that speech, because no black person I
knew had ever encouraged anybody to "Go back to Mississippi . . ." and I knew that if this challenge were taken up by
the millions of blacks who normally left the South for better
fortunes in the North, a change couldn't help but come.

This may not seem like much to other Americans, who
constantly move about the country with nothing but restlessness and greed to prod them, but to the Southern black person brought up expecting to be run away from home—
because of lack of jobs, money, power and respect—it was a
notion that took root in willing soil: We would fight to stay
where we were born and raised and destroy the forces that
sought to disinherit us. We would proceed with the revolution from our own homes.

I thought of my seven brothers and sisters who had already
left the South and I wanted to know: *Why did they have to
leave home to find a better life?*

I was born and raised in Eatonton, Ga., which is in the center of the state. It is a town with two streets and a large iron
rabbit on its courthouse lawn. It is also the birthplace of Joel
Chandler Harris. According to my parents Eatonton had
hardly changed at all since they were children. That being so,
on hot Saturday afternoons of my childhood I would gaze
longingly through the window of the corner drugstore where

white youngsters sat on stools in air-conditioned comfort and
drank Cokes and nibbled ice-cream cones. Black people could
come in and buy, but they couldn't eat what they bought inside. When the first motel was built in Eatonton in the late
fifties the general understanding of *place* was so clear the
owners didn't even bother to put up a Whites Only sign.

I was an exile in my town, and grew to despise its white
citizens almost as much as I loved the Georgia countryside
where I fished and swam and walked through fields of black-
eyed susans, or sat in contemplation beside the giant pine tree
my father "owned" because, when he was a boy and walking
five miles to school during the winter, he and his schoolmates
had built a fire each morning in the base of the tree, and the
tree still lived—although there was a blackened triangular
hole in it large enough for me to fit inside. This was my father's tree, and from it I had a view of fields his people had
worked (and briefly owned) for generations, and I could walk
—in an afternoon—to the house where my mother was born;
a leaning, weather-beaten ruin, it was true, but as essential to
her sense of existence as one assumes Nixon's birthplace in
California is to him. Probably more so, since my mother has
always been careful to stay on good terms with the earth she
occupies. But I would have to leave all this. Take my memories and run North. For I would not be a maid, and could not
be a "girl," or a frightened half-citizen, or any of the things
my brothers and sisters had already refused to be.

In those days, few blacks spent much time discussing hatred
of white people. It was understood that they were—generally
—vicious and unfair, like floods, earthquakes or other natural
catastrophes. Your job, if you were black, was to live with that
knowledge, as people in San Francisco live with the San An-
dreas Fault. You had as good a time (and life) as you could,
under the circumstances.

Not having been taught black history—except for the once-
a-year hanging up of the pictures of Booker Washington,
George Washington Carver and Mary McLeod Bethune that
marked Negro History Week—we did not know how much
of the riches of America we had missed. Somehow it was hard
to comprehend just how white folks—lazy as all agreed they
were—always managed to get ahead. When Hamilton

Holmes and Charlayne Hunter were first seen trying to enter the University of Georgia, people were stunned: Why did they want to go to that whitefolks' school? If they wanted to go somewhere, let them go to a school black money had built! It was a while before they could connect their centuries of unpaid labor with white "progress," but as soon as they did, they saw Hamp and Charlayne as the heroes they were.

I had watched Charlayne and Hamp every afternoon on the news when I came home from school. Their daring was infectious. When I left home for college in Atlanta in 1962, I ventured to sit near the front of the bus. A white woman (may her fingernails now be dust!) complained to the driver and he ordered me to move. But even as I moved, in confusion and anger and tears, I knew he had not seen the last of me.

My only regret when I left Atlanta for New York a year and a half later was that I would miss the Saturday morning demonstrations downtown that had become indispensable to education in the A. U. Center. But in 1965, I went back to Georgia to work part of the summer in Liberty County, helping to canvass voters and in general looking at the South to see if it was worth claiming. I suppose I decided it *was* worth something. After college, I received my first writing fellowship and made plans to leave the country for good and go to Senegal, West Africa, but I never went. Instead, I caught a plane to Mississippi, where I knew no one personally and only one woman by reputation. That summer marked the beginning of a realization that I could never live happily in Africa— or anywhere else—until I could live freely in Mississippi.

I was also intrigued by the thought of what continuity of place could mean to the consciousness of the emerging writer. The Russian writers I admired had one thing in common: a sense of the Russian soul that was directly rooted in the soil that nourished it. In the Russian novel, land itself is a personality. In the South, Faulkner, Welty and O'Connor could stay in their paternal homes and write because, although their neighbors might think them weird—and in Faulkner's case, trashy—they were spared the added burden of not being able to use a public toilet and did not have to go through intense emotional struggle over where to purchase a hamburger. What if Wright had been able to stay in Mississippi? I asked this not because I assumed an alternative direction to his life (since I rapidly admit that Jackson, Miss., with the stilling of gunfire, bombings and the surge and pound of black street resistance, is about the most boring spot on earth), but because it indicates Wright's lack of choice. And that a man of his talent should lack a choice is offensive. Horribly so.

Black writers have generally left the South as soon as possible. The strain of creation and constant exposure to petty insults and legally encouraged humiliations proved too great. But their departure impoverished those they left behind. I realized this more fully when I arrived in Jackson to live and discovered Margaret Walker, the author of "For My People," already here, like a natural force of nature, creating work under unimaginable pressures and by doing so keeping alive, in the thousands of students who studied under her, not only a sense of art but the necessity of claiming one's birthright at the very source. I do not know if, in her case, settling in the South was purely a matter of choice or preference, but in the future—for other black artists—it might and *must* be.

And so, 10 years after the March on Washington, the question is: How much has the mountain of despair dwindled? What shape and size is the stone of hope?

I know it is annoying this late in the day to hear of mere "symbols" of change, but since it is never as late in the day in Mississippi as it is in the rest of the country I will indulge in a few:

One afternoon each week, I drive to downtown Jackson to have lunch with my husband at one of Jackson's finest motels. It has a large, cool restaurant that overlooks a balalaika-shaped swimming pool, and very good food. My husband, Mel Leventhal, a human-rights lawyer who sues a large number of racist institutions a year (and wins—and who is now thinking of suing the Jackson Public Library because [1] they refused to issue me a library card in my own name, and [2] the librarian snorted like a mule when I asked for a recording of Dr. King's speeches, which the library didn't have) has his own reasons for coming here, and the least of them is that the cooks provide excellent charbroiled cheeseburgers. He remembers "testing" the motel's swimming pool in 1965: the angry insults of the whites as blacks waded in, and the tension that hung over everyone as the whites vacated the pool and stood about menacingly. I remember the cold rudeness of the waitresses in the restaurant a year later and recall wondering if "testing" would ever end (we were by no means alone in this; one of the new black school-board members still lunches at a different downtown restaurant each day—because she has been thrown out of all of them). It is sometimes hard to eat here because of those memories, but in Mississippi (as in the rest of America) racism is like that local creeping kudzu vine that swallows whole forests and abandoned houses; if you don't keep pulling up the roots it will grow back faster than you can destroy it.

One day, we sat relaxing in the restaurant and as we ate watched a young black boy of about 15 swimming in the pool. Unlike the whites of the past, the ones in the pool did not get out. And the boy, when he was good and tired, crawled up alongside the pool, turned on his back, drew up his knees— in his tight trunks—and just lay there, oblivious to the white faces staring down at him from the restaurant windows above.

"I could *swear* that boy doesn't know what a castration complex is," I said, thinking how the bravest black "testers" in the past had seemed to crouch over themselves when they came out of the water.

We started to laugh, thinking of what a small, insignificant thing this sight should have been. It reminded us of the day we saw a young black dude casually strolling down a street near the center of town arm-in-arm with his high-school sweetheart, a tiny brunette. We had been with a friend of ours who was in no mood to witness such "incorrect" behavior, and who moaned, without a trace of humor: "Oh, why is it that as soon as you do start seeing signs of freedom they're the wrong ones!"

But would one really prefer to turn back the clock? I thought of the time, when I was a child, that black people were not allowed to use the town pool, and the town leaders were too evil to permit the principal of my school to build a pool for blacks *on his own property*. Or when my good friend, a teen-ager from the North (visiting his grandmother, naturally), was beaten and thrown into prison because he stooped down on Main Street in broad daylight to fix a white girl's bicycle chain. And now, thinking about these two different boys, I was simply glad that they are still alive, just as I am glad we no longer have to "test" public places to eat, or worry that a hostile waitress will spit in our soup. They will inherit Emmett Till soon enough. For the moment, at least, their childhood is not being destroyed, nor do they feel hemmed in by the memories that plague us.

For it is memory, more than anything else, that sours the sweetness of what has been accomplished in the South. What we cannot forget and will never forgive. My husband has said that for her sixth birthday he intends to give our 4-year-old daughter a completely *safe* (racially) Mississippi, and perhaps that is possible. For her. For us, safety is not enough anymore.

I thought of this one day when we were debating whether to go for a swim and boat ride in the Ross Barnett Reservoir, this area's largest recreational body of water. But I remembered state troopers descending on us the first time we went swimming there, in 1966 (at night), and the horror they inspired in me; and I also recall too well the man whose name the reservoir bears. Not present fear but memory makes our visits there infrequent. For us, every day of our lives here has been a "test." Only for coming generations will enjoyment of life in Mississippi seem a natural right. But for just this possibility people have given their lives, freely. And continue to give them in the day-by-day, year-by-year hard work that is the expression of their will and of their love.

Blacks are coming home from the North. My brothers and sisters have bought the acres of pines that surround my mother's birthplace. Blacks who thought automatically of leaving the South 10 years ago are now staying. There are more and better jobs, caused by more, and more persistent, lawsuits: We have learned for all time that nothing of value is ever given up voluntarily. The racial climate is as good as it is in most areas of the North (one would certainly hesitate before migrating to parts of Michigan or Illinois), and there is still an abundance of fresh air and open spaces—although the frenetic rate of economic growth is likely to ugly up the landscape here as elsewhere. It is no longer a harrowing adventure to drive from Atlanta to Texas; as long as one has money, one is not likely to be refused service in "the motels of the highways and the hotels of the cities." The last holdouts are the truck-stops, whose owners are being dragged into court at a regular rate. Police brutality—the newest form of lynching— is no longer accepted as a matter of course; black people react violently against it and city administrations worry about attracting business and the city's "progressive" image. Black people can and do vote (poll watchers still occasionally being needed), and each election year brings its small harvest of black elected officials. The public schools are among the most integrated in the nation, and of course those signs, White Only and Colored, will not hurt my daughter's heart as they did mine—because they are gone.

Charles Evers, the famous Mayor of Fayette, is thinking— again—of running for the Mississippi governorship. James Meredith is—again—thinking of running for the same position. They make their intentions known widely on local TV. Charles Evers said in June at the 10th commemoration of his brother Medgar's assassination, "I don't think anymore that I will be shot." Considering the baldness of his political aspirations and his tenacity in achieving his goals, this is a telling statement. The fear that shrouded Mississippi in the sixties is largely gone. "If Medgar could see what has happened in Mississippi in the last few years," said his widow, Myrlie Evers, "I think he'd be surprised and pleased."

The mountain of despair *has* dwindled, and the stone of hope has size and shape, and can be fondled by the eyes and by the hand. But freedom has always been an elusive tease, and in the very act of grabbing for it one can become shackled. I think Medgar Evers and Martin Luther King Jr. would be dismayed at the lack of radicalism in the new black middle class, and discouraged to know that a majority of the black people helped most by the movement of the sixties have abandoned themselves to the pursuit of cars, expensive furniture, large houses and the finest Scotch. In fact, the very class that owes its new affluence to the movement now refuses to support the organizations that made its success possible, and has retreated from its concern for black people who are poor.

Ralph Abernathy recently threatened to resign as head of S.C.L.C. because of lack of funds and an $80,000 debt. This is more than a shame; it is a crime.

A friend of mine from New York who was in SNCC in the sixties came to Mississippi last week to find "spiritual nourishment." "But I found no nourishment," he wrote, "because Mississippi has changed. It is becoming truly American. What is worse, it is becoming the North."

Unfortunately, this is entirely possible, and causes one to search frantically for an alternative direction. One senses instinctively that the beauty of the Southern landscape will not be saved from the scars of greed, because Southerners are as greedy as anyone else. And news from black movements in the North is far from encouraging. In fact, a movement *backward* from the equalitarian goals of the sixties seems a facet of nationalist groups. In a recent article in The Black Scholar, Barbara Sizemore writes: "The nationalist woman cannot create or initiate. Her main life's goal is to inspire and encourage man and his children. Sisters in this movement must beg for permission to speak and function as servants to men, their masters and leaders, as teachers and nurses. Their position is similar to that of the sisters in the Nation of Islam. When Baraka is the guiding spirit at national conferences only widows and wives of black martyrs, such as Malcolm X and Martin Luther King Jr., and Queen Mother Moore can participate. Other women are excluded."

This is heartbreaking. Not just for black women who have struggled so *equally* against the forces of oppression, but for all those who believe subservience of any kind is death to the spirit. But we are lucky in our precedents, for I know that Sojourner Truth, Harriet Tubman—or a young Fannie Lou Hamer or Winson Hudson—would simply ignore the assumption that "permission to speak" *could be given them*, and would fight on for freedom of all people, tossing White Only signs and Men Only signs on the same trash heap. For in the end, freedom is a personal and lonely battle, and one faces down fears of today so that those of tomorrow might be attempted. And that is also my experience with the South.

And if I leave Mississippi—as I probably will one of these days—it will not be for the reasons of the other sons and daughters of my father. Fear will have no part in my decision, nor will lack of freedom to express my womanly thoughts. It will be because the pervasive football culture bores me, and the proliferating Kentucky Fried Chicken stands appall me, and the neon lights have begun to replace the trees. It will be because the sea is too far and mountains are few. But most of all, it will be because I have freed myself to leave; and it will be My Choice.

The New York Times Magazine, August 26, 1973

CHRONOLOGY 1941–1973

BIOGRAPHICAL NOTES

NOTE ON THE TEXTS

NOTES

INDEX

Chronology 1941–1973

abolish poll taxes in national elections are also passed by the House in 1943, 1945, 1947, and 1949, but are blocked in the Senate.) William Dawson is elected to the House of Representatives from Chicago on November 3, succeeding the retiring Arthur Mitchell as the sole black member of Congress.

1943   Members of the Committee of Racial Equality conduct sit-in protests in Chicago restaurants. (Organization is renamed Congress of Racial Equality in 1944.) FEPC continues to be hampered by its lack of legal enforcement powers. Fighting between African-Americans and whites in a city park in Detroit leads to rioting, June 20–23, in which 34 people are killed. Confrontation between a white police officer and a black soldier in Harlem section of New York City results in riot, August 1–2, in which six people are killed.

1944   On April 3 U.S. Supreme Court decides, 8–1, in *Smith* v. *Allwright* that the exclusion of African-Americans from voting in the Texas Democratic primary is a violation of the Fifteenth Amendment. (Case for the plaintiff was argued by Thurgood Marshall, executive director of the NAACP Legal Defense and Educational Fund from its founding in 1939 until 1961.) *An American Dilemma: The Negro Problem and Modern Democracy*, extensive study of race relations by Swedish economist Gunnar Myrdal, is published. Roosevelt is reelected on November 7, defeating Thomas Dewey 432–99 in the electoral voting and carrying all 11 Southern states (Virginia, North Carolina, South Carolina, Georgia, Florida, Tennessee, Alabama, Mississippi, Louisiana, Arkansas, and Texas). Adam Clayton Powell Jr. is elected to Congress from a district in Harlem and becomes the second African-American serving in the House of Representatives.

1945   Poll tax is abolished in Georgia on February 5. Roosevelt dies on April 12 and Vice-President Harry S. Truman becomes president. Congress votes to end funding for the FEPC after June 30, 1946. Japan surrenders on August 14, ending World War II.

1946   Attempts to create a permanent FEPC fail in both houses of Congress. In *Morgan* v. *Virginia* the Supreme Court rules 7–1 on June 3 that a Virginia law requiring segregated seating on interstate buses is an unconstitutional burden on interstate commerce. (Decision does not address intrastate travel or segregation on interstate lines that is the result of bus company policy.) Four African-Americans, Roger and Dorothy Malcolm and George and Mae Dorsey, are shot to death by a white mob at Moore's Ford, near Monroe, Georgia, on July 25 after Roger Malcolm wounded a white man in a scuffle. Murders attract widespread public attention along with other incidents of racial violence against African-Americans, including the beating of army veteran Isaac Woodard by two police officers in Batesburg, South Carolina, on February 13, which left Woodard blind, and the torture, mutilation, and murder of army veteran John Jones by a mob in Minden, Louisiana, on August 8. (Despite an extensive federal investigation, no one is ever charged in the Moore's Ford murders; one man is acquitted of federal charges in the assault on Woodard, and five men, including two deputy sheriffs, are acquitted of federal charges in the murder of Jones.) During a meeting held with Walter White on September 19 to discuss racial violence, Truman proposes creating a presidential committee on civil rights, and on December 5 appoints its 15 members, with Charles Wilson, president of General Electric, serving as its chairman.

1947   Fellowship of Reconciliation organizes "Journey of Reconciliation," April 9–23, in which integrated group of 16 activists rides interstate buses in Virginia, North Carolina, Tennessee, and Kentucky to test compliance with the *Morgan* decision. Four of the riders are arrested in Chapel Hill, North Carolina, and later sentenced to serve 30-day terms on a chain gang. Jackie Robinson plays his first game for the Brooklyn Dodgers on April 15, becoming the first African-American player in major league baseball since the 1880s. Presidential committee on civil rights submits its report on October 29; its recommendations include the creation of a civil rights division in the Department of Justice, a permanent national civil rights commission, and a permanent FEPC with enforcement powers; ending segregation in the armed forces; and federal legislation to punish lynching, secure voting rights, and abolish segregation in interstate transport.

1948   Truman sends message to Congress on February 2 en-
            dorsing many of the recommendations of the civil rights
            committee but, in the face of strong Southern opposition,
            does not submit civil rights legislation to Congress. Ran-
            dolph warns Truman at White House meeting on March
            22 that he will lead a civil disobedience campaign against
            the draft unless the armed forces are integrated, and op-
            position to continued military segregation is also ex-
            pressed by delegation of African-American leaders in
            meeting with Secretary of Defense James Forrestal on
            April 26. In case of *Shelley* v. *Kraemer*, Supreme Court
            rules 6–0 on May 3 that judicial enforcement of racially
            restrictive property convenants is a violation of the equal
            protection clause of the Fourteenth Amendment. After
            liberals force a floor fight, Democratic national conven-
            tion adopts platform plank on civil rights, July 14, that
            calls for a federal anti-lynching law, a new FEPC, the abo-
            lition of poll taxes, and desegregation of the armed
            forces. Adoption of plank causes split in Democratic
            party, and on July 17 Southern "Dixiecrats" hold a States'
            Rights convention and nominate Governor Strom Thur-
            mond of South Carolina for president. Truman issues two
            executive orders on July 26: 9980, establishing a Fair Em-
            ployment Board to promote nondiscriminatory employ-
            ment practices in the federal civil service, and 9981,
            declaring "equality of treatment and opportunity" in the
            armed services to be presidential policy. Randolph praises
            9981 and ends call for civil disobedience on August 18.
            Truman names seven-member committee to oversee inte-
            gration of the armed forces, September 18, and appoints
            Charles Fahy, a former solicitor general, as its chairman. In
            the presidential election, November 2, Truman wins 303
            electoral votes, Thomas Dewey 189, and Thurmond 39.
            Thurmond carries Louisiana, Mississippi, Alabama, and
            South Carolina, while Truman wins the other seven
            Southern states and also carries key states of Ohio, Illinois,
            and California with strong support from black voters.

1949   Senate votes 63–23 on March 17 to increase the majority
            needed for cloture from two-thirds of the Senators pres-
            ent and voting to two-thirds of the Senate; change in the
            rules strengthens ability of Southerners to block civil
            rights legislation with filibusters. Administration proposes
            legislation to make lynching a federal crime, create a new

FEPC, abolish poll taxes in national elections, and end segregation in interstate transportation, but none of the bills are brought to a vote in the Senate. Fahy Committee approves integration plans of the air force and navy, but encounters resistance to desegregation from the army. William Hastie, a former dean of the Howard Law School and a leading civil rights lawyer, is appointed by Truman to the Third Circuit Court of Appeals on October 15, becoming the first African-American federal appellate judge.

1950 Fahy Committee accepts army integration plan in January and submits its final report on May 22. Supreme Court decides three civil rights cases on June 5, all by 9–0 votes. In *Sweatt* v. *Painter*, the Court rules that separate law school established by the University of Texas does not provide equal educational opportunity and orders the university to admit African-Americans to its previously all-white law school; in *McLaurin* v. *Oklahoma State Regents*, it rules that the University of Oklahoma could not impose segregated seating arrangements on a black graduate student; and in *Henderson* v. *United States*, it rules that segregated seating on railroad dining cars denies the equal access to public accommodations guaranteed by the Interstate Commerce Act. (Although the NAACP attorneys arguing *Sweatt* and *McLaurin* had asked the Court to overturn the 1896 *Plessy* v. *Ferguson* decision establishing the "separate but equal" doctrine of constitutionally permissible segregation, the decisions do not rule on its continuing validity.) Korean War begins June 25. After meeting with NAACP attorneys and branch presidents, Thurgood Marshall decides to litigate against segregation in the public schools in a direct challenge to *Plessy*. (Public schools are segregated by law in all 11 Southern states as well as Delaware, Maryland, West Virginia, Kentucky, Missouri, Oklahoma, and the District of Columbia; laws in Kansas, New Mexico, and Arizona allow individual school districts to segregate.)

1951 Poll tax is abolished in South Carolina on February 13. NAACP attorneys argue school segregation cases in federal and state courts in South Carolina, Kansas, and Delaware, May–October. Harry Moore, a NAACP leader who campaigned against police brutality and led voter registration drives, is killed and his wife, Harriette Moore, a schoolteacher, is fatally wounded when their home in Mims, Florida, is bombed on December 25.

1952   Fourth school case is argued in federal court in Virginia in February. Republican Dwight D. Eisenhower wins presidential election, November 4, defeating Adlai Stevenson 442–89 in the electoral voting and carrying four Southern states (Texas, Tennessee, Florida, and Virginia). Supreme Court hears arguments on appeal in the four school cases, now consolidated as *Brown* v. *Board of Education of Topeka*, as well as *Bolling* v. *Sharpe*, case challenging school segregation in the District of Columbia, December 9–11.

1953   Divided Supreme Court orders reargument in *Brown* on June 8. Armistice is signed in Korea on July 27. Frederick Vinson, chief justice of Supreme Court since 1946, dies on September 8. Eisenhower appoints California governor Earl Warren as chief justice, October 2. Poll tax is abolished in Tennessee on November 3 (poll taxes remain in Texas, Arkansas, Mississippi, Alabama, and Virginia). *Brown* and *Bolling* are reargued, December 7–9. Warren begins working with other justices to bring about unanimous decision.

1954   On May 17 the Supreme Court rules 9–0 in *Brown* that public school segregation violates the equal protection clause of the Fourteenth Amendment. Writing for the court, Warren declares that the "separate but equal" doctrine has no place in public education and requests further argument concerning implementation. In companion case of *Bolling*, the Court rules 9–0 that school segregation in the District of Columbia violates the due process clause of the Fifth Amendment. *Brown* decision is denounced by many Southern elected officials. "Citizens' Council" is organized in Indianola, Mississippi, July 11, to oppose desegregation by political, legal, and economic means; by the end of the year chapters of the organization are founded in Texas, Louisiana, Alabama, Georgia, and Virginia, as well as throughout Mississippi. Desegregation begins in District of Columbia and Baltimore schools. Department of Defense announces on October 30 that the armed forces have been fully desegregated.

1955   Desegregation begins in St. Louis schools in February. Supreme Court hears arguments on implementation of *Brown*, April 11–14, and rules 9–0 on May 31 that school cases should be remanded to lower federal courts and instructs them to issue desegregation orders "with all deliberate speed" without setting a deadline for compliance. (Implementation of school desegregation decision will be obstructed by resistance, evasion, and delay by school authorities and state governments, as well as by reluctance of some federal judges to issue effective desegregation orders.) Emmett Till, a 14-year-old African-American boy visiting from Chicago, is beaten and shot to death in Tallahatchie County, Mississippi, on August 28 after he allegedly whistled at a white woman; his murder and the acquittal on September 23 of the two white men charged with the crime attract widespread public attention. Interstate Commerce Commission rules on November 7 that segregated seating on interstate buses and trains is a violation of the Interstate Commerce Act. Supreme Court rules in *Holmes* v. *Atlanta*, November 7, that municipal recreation facilities cannot be racially segregated. Rosa Parks, an active member of the NAACP, is arrested in Montgomery, Alabama, on December 1 for violating the municipal bus segregation ordinance. Montgomery Improvement Association is organized at mass meeting held on December 5 to conduct boycott of city buses, and Martin Luther King Jr., the pastor since 1954 of the Dexter Avenue Baptist Church, is elected as its president.

1956   King family escapes injury when their home is bombed on January 30. University of Alabama admits Autherine Lucy as its first African-American student, February 3, after prolonged litigation in federal court. White students and Tuscaloosa residents riot on February 6, and Lucy is suspended, allegedly for her own safety; she is later expelled for criticizing the university. "Southern Manifesto" is introduced in Congress on March 12; signed by 19 senators and 77 representatives, it denounces *Brown* as an "abuse of judicial power" and endorses resistance to integration by "any lawful means." Bus boycott begins in Tallahassee, Florida, on May 26. Alabama attorney general John Patterson obtains injunction against the NAACP in state court, June 1, on the grounds that it has failed to comply with state corporate registration laws, and July 9 obtains order directing the NAACP to turn over its membership lists. (Several other Southern states undertake legal campaigns to restrict the operations of the NAACP and the Legal Defense Fund.) Special session of the Virginia legislature in August adopts program of "massive resistance" to school desegregation that calls for the closing of schools under desegregation orders. Governor Frank Clement orders the National Guard to restore order in Clinton, Tennessee, on September 2 after white mobs attempt to block the desegregation of the high school. Eisenhower wins reelection on November 6, defeating Stevenson in the electoral voting 457–73 and carrying five Southern states (Texas, Louisiana, Tennessee, Virginia, and Florida). Supreme Court affirms ruling of lower federal court in *Browder* v. *Gayle* declaring segregation on Alabama intrastate buses to be unconstitutional, November 13. Montgomery boycott ends on December 21 as municipal buses begin operating on a desegregated basis. The Rev. Fred Shuttlesworth, a leading civil rights activist in Birmingham, Alabama, escapes injury when his parsonage is bombed on December 25.

1957   Southern Negro Leadership Conference on Transportation and Nonviolent Integration (later known as the Southern Christian Leadership Conference) is organized in Atlanta on January 11 with King as its chairman. Ghana becomes independent, March 6, beginning period of decolonization in sub-Saharan Africa. Malcolm X (born Malcolm Little), minister of Temple No. 7 of the Nation of Islam since 1954, leads demonstration outside a police station in Harlem, April 14, to protest the beating of a Black Muslim and demand his transfer to a hospital. First federal civil rights bill since 1875 is passed on August 29 after it is significantly weakened in the Senate to avoid a filibuster. The act creates a federal civil rights commission with investigatory powers; replaces the existing civil rights section of the Department of Justice with a division headed by an assistant attorney general; makes conspiring to deny citizens their right to vote in federal elections a federal crime; and gives federal prosecutors the power to obtain injunctions against discrimnatory practices used to deny citizens their voting rights. Federal district court orders nine African-American students admitted to Central High School in Little Rock, Arkansas, on September 3, but Governor Orval Faubus uses the National Guard to prevent them from entering the school. After the district court orders Faubus to end his interference on September 20, the governor withdraws the Guard, and on September 23 the students are attacked by a large mob. Eisenhower sends more than 1,000 paratroopers of the 101st Airborne Division to Little Rock on September 24 and places the Arkansas National Guard under federal control. Students are escorted to class by armed soldiers on September 25. Airborne troops are withdrawn from Little Rock, November 27, as federalized Guard continues to protect the students.

1958   Buses in Tallahassee begin desegregated service in May. Supreme Court rules 9–0 in *NAACP* v. *Alabama*, June 30, upholding on First Amendment grounds the refusal of the organization to turn its membership lists over to the Alabama authorities (injunction against the Alabama NAACP remains in effect). On September 12 the Court decides *Cooper* v. *Aaron*, unanimously overturning a district court decision allowing the Little Rock school board to postpone desegregation until 1960 because of the threat of continued violence. In opinion signed by all nine justices, Warren writes that governors and state legislators are bound by the Constitution to uphold Supreme Court decisions. (In response to decision, Little Rock high schools are closed for most of the 1958–59 school year, then reopen with token desegregation.) Schools under desegregation orders are closed in Norfolk, Charlottesville, and Warren County, Virginia. Bus boycott is organized in Birmingham in November but fails to end segregation on city buses.

1959   Virginia supreme court rules on January 19 that school closing law passed in 1956 violates the state constitution. Youth March for Integrated Schools held in Washington, D.C., on April 18 is attended by 25,000 people. Mack Charles Parker, an African-American man accused of raping a white woman, is taken from jail in Poplarville, Mississippi, and lynched by a mob on April 25. After Virginia legislature repeals its compulsory school attendance laws, Prince Edward County closes it schools on June 26 to avoid desegregation. *The Hate That Hate Produced,* television documentary on the Nation of

Islam, airs July 13–17 and brings Malcolm X to wider public attention.

1960   King moves to Atlanta, where the SCLC has its head-quarters, and becomes co-pastor with his father at the Ebenezer Baptist Church. Four African-American students stage sit-in at segregated lunch counter in Greensboro, North Carolina, on February 1. Sit-in movement spreads rapidly, and by the end of the month 31 lunch counter sit-ins are held in North Carolina, Maryland, Virginia, South Carolina, Georgia, Florida, Tennessee, Louisiana, and Texas, resulting in hundreds of arrests. Lunch counters are desegregated in San Antonio, Texas, on March 19, and in Nashville, Tennessee, and Winston-Salem, Charlotte, and Greensboro, North Carolina by July. Student Nonviolent Coordinating Committee (SNCC) is founded at conference organized by Ella Baker, executive director of the SCLC, and held in Raleigh, North Carolina, April 15–17. Civil rights act is passed by Congress, April 21; it provides criminal penalties for forcibly obstructing federal court orders; makes interstate flight after committing a bombing or arson a federal crime; and allows federal courts to appoint referees to register voters in cases where a pattern or practice of voting discrimination has been proven at trial. Survey of school desegregation records substantial desegregation efforts in the District of Columbia, West Virginia, Delaware, Kentucky, Maryland, Missouri, Oklahoma, and Texas; token desegregation in Arkansas, Florida, North Carolina, Tennessee, and Virginia; and no desegregation in Alabama, Georgia, Louisiana, Mississippi, and South Carolina. King is arrested during an Atlanta sit-in on October 19 and sentenced to four months in state prison for violating his probation on a traffic charge. Democratic presidential nominee Senator John F. Kennedy calls Coretta Scott King to express concern, and his brother, Robert F. Kennedy, calls the judge handling the case. King is released on bond, October 27, and his father publicly endorses Kennedy. On November 8 Kennedy narrowly defeats Richard M. Nixon with crucial support from African-American voters in key states of Illinois and Texas. Kennedy wins 303 electoral votes and Nixon 219, while 15 electors vote for Senator Harry Byrd, a leading segregationist. Nixon carries Virginia, Tennessee, and

Florida, while Kennedy wins the remainder of the Southern states with the exception of Mississippi and Alabama, whose unpledged electors vote mostly for Byrd. Limited school desegregation begins in New Orleans under federal court order, November 14, as federal marshals escort black elementary school pupils past hostile crowds. Supreme Court rules 9–0 in *Gomillion* v. *Lightfoot*, November 14, that the redrawing of the Tuskegee, Alabama, city boundaries in order to exclude black voters violates the Fifteenth Amendment. On December 5 the Court rules 7–2 in *Boynton* v. *Virginia* that segregation of facilities in interstate bus terminals violates the Interstate Commerce Act.

1961   Federal district court orders University of Georgia to admit Hamilton Holmes and Charlayne Hunter, January 6. They are suspended after a riot on campus by white students, January 11, but are reinstated by court order on January 13. James Farmer becomes national director of CORE on February 1 and begins planning "Freedom Rides" to test compliance with the *Boynton* decision. President Kennedy issues Executive Order 10925, March 6, establishing President's Committee on Equal Employment Opportunity to investigate racial discrimination by government contractors and recommend action by the Justice Department. First group of Freedom Riders leaves Washington May 4 and travels through Virginia, North Carolina, South Carolina, and Georgia to Atlanta. On May 14 they leave Atlanta for Birmingham on two buses, one of which is attacked by a mob and firebombed outside Anniston, Alabama; when the other bus arrives in Birmingham, the Freedom Riders are beaten by Klansmen. Group from CORE leaves Birmingham by air, and a new group of Freedom Riders is organized by SNCC activists in Nashville. Second group leaves Birmingham on May 20 and is attacked by a mob in the Montgomery bus station. Attorney General Robert F. Kennedy sends federal marshals to Montgomery to protect Freedom Riders while urging an end to the protest. Marshals use tear gas on May 21 against mob surrounding church of SCLC leader the Rev. Ralph Abernathy during civil rights meeting. In effort to avoid further involvement by federal marshals, Robert Kennedy arranges for Alabama and Mississippi National Guard to escort 27 Freedom Riders from

Montgomery to Jackson, Mississippi, where they are arrested at the bus station, May 24. Despite opposition from the Kennedy administration, Freedom Rides continue during the summer, with at least 1,000 people participating throughout the South and more than 300 people arrested in Jackson alone. (Many of the protestors arrested in Mississippi receive 60-day sentences on state prison farms.) Coalition of civil rights groups, including CORE, SNCC, NAACP, and SCLC, plans new effort to register African-Americans in the South; Voter Education Project receives funding from foundations and assistance from the Justice Department. In response to request from Robert Kennedy, the Interstate Commerce Commission issues new rules on September 22, effective November 1, forbidding interstate carriers to use segregated terminals. Herbert Lee, a farmer working with Robert Moses of SNCC to register black voters, is killed in Liberty, Mississippi, on September 25 by E. H. Hurst, a state representative. (Coroner's jury rules the killing to be self-defense, though Louis Allen, who witnessed the shooting, later tells the FBI Lee did not attack Hurst. Allen is murdered in 1964.) Coalition of civil rights groups and local African-American organizations in Albany, Georgia, forms Albany Movement, November 17, to conduct protest campaign against segregation. In series of demonstrations, December 10–16, more than 700 people are arrested, including King and Abernathy. Demonstrations are suspended December 18 to allow for negotiations with the city government.

1962   Boycott of city buses begins in Albany, January 12, as negotiations fail to reach an agreement on desegregation. Council of Federated Organizations (COFO) is organized in Mississippi in February by coalition of civil rights groups, including NAACP, CORE, and SNCC, to register black voters. In March Robert Kennedy approves FBI wiretapping of Stanley Levison, a close adviser to King who had been identified by FBI informers as a major clandestine fundraiser for the Communist party between 1952 and 1957. Justice Department officials begin warning King against associating with Levison, but he continues the relationship. Voter Education Project is launched in April. (In 1962 approximately 29 percent of eligible African-Americans in the South are registered to vote.)

Fifth Circuit Court of Appeals orders James Meredith admitted to the University of Mississippi, June 25. Mass demonstrations resume in Albany in late July but are suspended in August when local leadership decides to concentrate on voter registration. (Failure of the Albany Movement to achieve desegregation of public accommodations brings public attention to tensions among SCLC, SNCC, and NAACP activists over tactics and personalities.) Congress submits Twenty-fourth Amendment to the Constitution, abolishing poll taxes in federal elections, to the states for ratification on August 27. Mississippi Governor Ross Barnett gives televised address on September 13 in which he vows to resist any federal attempt to integrate the university. Barnett personally blocks attempts by Meredith to register on September 20 and 25 while secretly negotiating with Robert Kennedy to end the confrontation. Meredith, Deputy Attorney General Nicholas Katzenbach, and 400 federal marshals arrive on Oxford campus of the university on September 30 after President Kennedy federalizes the Mississippi National Guard. During the night a mob of more than 2,000 people repeatedly attack the marshals, who are reinforced by the Guard. Violence ends on morning of October 1 as U.S. army troops arrive from Memphis; two people are killed and more than 300 injured during the riot. Meredith registers on October 1 as army troops continue to arrive. (U.S. army deploys 12,000 men to Oxford area by October 2; the last troops are withdrawn on July 24, 1963.) Kennedy issues Executive Order 11063 on November 20, prohibiting racial discrimination in federally owned housing, in public housing built with federal funds, and in new housing built with loans from federal agencies.

1963   SCLC leaders meet in January to plan major campaign against segregation in Birmingham. Campaign begins with sit-in on April 3, and on April 12 King, Abernathy, and Birmingham civil rights leader Fred Shuttlesworth are arrested. King writes his "Letter from Birmingham Jail," justifying disobedience to unjust laws, before being released on bail on April 20. Mass marches by African-American high school students begin on May 2. Birmingham public safety commissioner Eugene (Bull) Connor orders police dogs and fire hoses used on the marchers, May 3, and the police make more than 2,400 arrests between May 2 and May 7. Demonstrations are suspended on May 8 for negotiations mediated by Justice Department officials. Agreement reached on May 10 establishes timetable for desegregation of downtown department stores, the establishment of a biracial civic committee, and the release on bond of jailed protestors. After Klansmen set off two bombs in Birmingham on night of May 11, rioting breaks out despite pleas of movement leaders for continued nonviolence. Supreme Court reverses convictions of sit-in protestors in series of cases decided on May 20, ruling that state enforcement of restaurant segregation is a violation of the Fourteenth Amendment. Campaign of sit-ins and demonstrations begins in Jackson, May 28, led by Medgar Evers, Mississippi field secretary of the NAACP since 1954. Two African-American students register at the University of Alabama at Tuscaloosa on June 11 after confrontation outside of administration building in which Katzenbach orders Governor George Wallace to cease his obstruction of the court order admitting the students. On the evening of June 11 President Kennedy gives televised address in which he calls racial discrimination "a moral crisis" and proposes passage of a new civil rights bill. Medgar Evers is assassinated outside his home early on June 12. National Guard is sent to Cambridge, Maryland, on June 14 after rioting breaks out during protest campaign against segregation. Administration submits civil rights bill prohibiting racial discrimination in public accommodations to Congress on June 19. Demonstrations are suspended in Jackson, June 20, after the city agrees to hire black police officers, promote black sanitation workers, and desegregate municipal facilities. Agreement is mediated by Justice Department in Cambridge, July 23, calling for limited school desegregation, the creation of a biracial committee, and holding a referendum on desegregating public accommodations. (During spring and summer of 1963, campaigns against segregation are also organized in Gadsen, Alabama; Savannah, Georgia; Plaquemine, Louisiana; Danville, Virginia; Raleigh, Greensboro, and Durham, North Carolina; and Charleston, South Carolina.) More than 200,000 people attend March for Jobs and Freedom in Washington, August 28, during which King delivers "I Have a Dream" speech. Klansmen bomb church in Birmingham on September 15, killing Denise McNair, age 11, Cynthia Wesley, 14, Carole Robertson, 14, and Addie Mae Collins, 14. After learning that King is continuing to communicate with Stanley Levison, Robert Kennedy authorizes FBI wiretapping of King on October 10. (Wiretapping continues until June 1966; the FBI will also repeatedly place microphones in King's hotel rooms.) President Kennedy is assassinated in Dallas on November 22 and Vice-President Lyndon B. Johnson becomes president. Johnson begins intensive effort to move civil rights bill through Congress.

1964   In January COFO leadership approves SNCC plan to bring hundreds of volunteers, mostly white Northern college students, to Mississippi during the summer. Ratification of the Twenty-fourth Amendment is completed on January 23. House of Representatives passes civil rights bill, 290–130, on February 10, and the Senate begins debate on the bill, March 9. Malcolm X resigns from the Nation of Islam on March 11. More than 280 people are arrested during sit-ins held in restaurants and hotels in St. Augustine, Florida, March 28–April 1. George Wallace enters three Democratic presidential primaries and receives 34 percent of the vote in Wisconsin (April 7), 30 percent in Indiana (May 5), and 43 percent in Maryland (May 19). Supreme Court rules 9–0 on May 25 that Prince Edward County, Virginia, must reopen its public school system, which has been closed since 1959. (In 1964, ten years after *Brown* decision, 55 percent of African-American students in the District of Columbia, Delaware, Kentucky, Maryland, Missouri, Oklahoma, and West Virginia attend integrated schools, while only 1.2 percent of black students in the 11 Southern states attend school with whites.) Series of mass demonstrations are held in St. Augustine, May 26–June 30. Supreme Court unanimously overturns Alabama ban on the NAACP, June 1, allowing the organization to operate in the state for the first time since 1956. Senate votes 71–29 on June 10 to limit further debate on the civil rights bill, ending the longest filibuster in Senate history, and passes revised civil rights bill, 73–27, on June 19. First of approximately 550 "Freedom Summer" volunteers begin arriving in Mississippi to register voters, work in community centers, and teach in "Freedom Schools" (another 400 volunteers go to Mississippi before the project ends in August). Civil rights workers Andrew Goodman, Michael Schwerner, and James Chaney are murdered near Philadelphia, Mississippi, June 21, by Klansmen who bury their bodies under an earthen dam. Malcolm X announces formation of the Organization of Afro-American Unity on June 28. House passes final version of civil rights bill on July 2 and Johnson signs it the same day. The act strengthens federal power to protect voting rights; prohibits discrimination in public accommodations; authorizes the attorney general to file suits for the desegregation of schools and public facilities; bars discrimination in federally assisted programs; prohibits discrimination by employers and unions; and establishes an Equal Employment Opportunity Commission with investigative and mediative powers. Senator Barry Goldwater, who voted against the civil rights bill, wins the Republican presidential nomination on July 15. Fatal shooting of an African-American youth by a police officer in New York City, July 16, leads to rioting in Harlem, July 18–21, in which one person is killed. The bodies of the three missing civil rights workers are discovered by the FBI on August 4. Newly founded Mississippi Freedom Democratic Party selects delegates on August 6 to attend the Democratic national convention and challenge the seating of the all-white regular Democrats, August 6. Convention credentials committee votes on August 25 to seat regular Democrats who pledge their loyalty to the national party while offering Freedom Democrats two at-large seats. Freedom Democrats reject offer, and all but three of the regular Mississippi Democrats walk out of the convention. King is awarded the Nobel Peace Prize on October 14. Johnson wins election on November 3, defeating Goldwater 486–52 in the electoral voting; Goldwater carries five Southern states (Louisiana, Mississippi, Alabama, Georgia, and South Carolina). FBI mails tape compiled from potentially compromising hotel room recordings to King on November 21, along with an anonymous letter in which he is urged to commit suicide in order to avoid public disgrace. On December 4 FBI agents arrest 19 people on federal civil rights charges in the murders of Goodman, Schwerner, and Chaney (seven defendants, including a deputy sheriff, are convicted by an all-white jury in 1967). In *Katzenbach* v. *McClung* and *Heart of Atlanta Motel* v. *United States*, both decided 9–0 on

December 14, the Supreme Court upholds the constitutionality of the public accommodations sections of the 1964 civil rights act.

1965   SCLC begins voter registration campaign in Selma, Alabama, intended to demonstrate need for a new federal voting rights law. Mass arrests begin at the Selma courthouse, January 19, and more than 700 people are arrested during a march on February 1. Jimmie Lee Jackson, a church deacon and woodcutter, is fatally wounded by a state trooper during a demonstration in nearby Marion, Alabama, on February 18. Malcolm X is assassinated in New York by members of the Nation of Islam on February 21. United States begins sustained bombing of North Vietnam on March 2. SCLC leaders organize 54-mile march from Selma to Montgomery, the state capital. Several hundred marchers are beaten and tear-gassed by state police and sheriff's deputies as they cross the Edmund Pettus bridge in Selma on March 7 (incident becomes known as "Bloody Sunday"). After a federal district judge issues a temporary restraining order against a second march, King leads 2,000 people across the bridge and then turns back into Selma on March 9. James Reeb, a Unitarian minister from Boston, is fatally beaten in Selma on the evening of March 9. Johnson addresses joint session of Congress on March 15 and calls for the passage of a new voting rights bill, which the administration submits on March 17. Federal judge lifts restraining order and enjoins state and local authorities from interfering with Selma to Montgomery march. Led by King, marchers leave Selma on March 21 under federal military protection. March ends with rally outside of state capitol in Montgomery on March 25 attended by 25,000 people. Viola Liuzzo, a civil rights volunteer from Detroit, is shot and killed by Klansmen in Lowndes County, Alabama, on the night of March 25. Senate votes 70–30 to end debate on voting rights bill, May 25, and passes the bill 77–19 on May 26. House of Representatives passes its version of the bill, 333–85, on July 9. Final version of bill is approved by the Senate on August 4 and signed by Johnson on August 6. The voting rights act prohibits the use of literacy tests in jurisdictions where less than 50 percent of the eligible population either was registered to vote on November 1, 1964, or voted in the 1964 presidential election (Alabama,

Georgia, Louisiana, Mississippi, South Carolina, Virginia, and parts of North Carolina); gives the federal government the power to register voters in these jurisdictions; and prohibits changes in voting procedures in the covered jurisdictions without approval from either the attorney general or a federal court panel. Justice Department begins registering voters in nine Southern counties on August 10. (Proportion of eligible African-Americans registered to vote in the South increases from 43 percent in 1964 to 62 percent in 1968.) Traffic stop by police leads to rioting in the Watts section of Los Angeles, August 11–16, in which 34 people are killed. Johnson issues Executive Order 11246 on September 24, requiring all federal contractors and subcontractors to take "affirmative action" to hire and promote persons without regard to race.

1966   Floyd McKissick is elected on January 3 to succeed James Farmer as national director of CORE. Civil rights activist Vernon Dahmer dies after his home is fire-bombed by Klansmen in Hattiesburg, Mississippi, on January 10. (At least 35 people are killed by white supremacist terrorism in the South between 1954 and 1967.) Robert C. Weaver becomes the first African-American cabinet member when he is sworn in on January 18 as Secretary of Housing and Urban Development. In *South Carolina* v. *Katzenbach*, March 17, the Supreme Court upholds 8–1 the constitutionality of the Voting Rights Act, and on March 24 it rules 6–3 in *Harper* v. *Virginia State Board of Elections* that the imposition of poll taxes in state and local elections violates the Fourteenth Amendment. Johnson submits new civil rights bill to Congress on April 28 that provides enforcement powers to the EEOC, expands federal protection for civil rights workers, prohibits discrimination in the sale, rental, or financing of housing, and seeks to prevent discrimination in jury selection. Lowndes County Freedom Organization, independent political party organized in Alabama by Stokely Carmichael and other SNCC activists, holds convention on May 3 and nominates all-black slate of candidates for county offices (LCFO slate is defeated in November election). John Lewis, national chairman of SNCC since 1966, is defeated for reelection by Carmichael on May 14. Carmichael announces that SNCC will no longer send white organizers into black communities. James Meredith begins one-man "walk against fear" through Mississippi on June 5 and is wounded in an ambush on June 6. King, McKissick, and Carmichael agree on June 7 to lead march along Meredith's intended route. Carmichael gives speech calling for "black power" at rally in Greenwood on June 16. "Meredith March" ends with rally in Jackson on June 26. SCLC and Chicago civil rights groups begin campaign against housing discrimination in Chicago with mass rally on July 10. (Leaders of the Chicago campaign include Jesse Jackson, who in 1967 becomes national director of Operation Breadbasket, SCLC program that uses boycotts to promote the hiring of African-Americans and create opportunities for black-owned businesses.) SCLC begins series of marches through white neighborhoods on July 30 that are often met with violence from mobs; during march on August 5 King is struck in the head by a rock. House of Representatives passes civil rights bill with weakened open housing provision 259–157 on August 9. King, Mayor Richard Daley, and Chicago realtors announce agreement on housing discrimination on August 26 that is denounced by SNCC and CORE as ineffectual. Attempt to close debate on civil rights bill fails in the Senate on September 19. (Open housing provision is opposed by Everett Dirksen, Republican leader whose support was crucial in the passage of 1964 and 1965 bills.) Black Panther Party is founded by Huey Newton and Bobby Seale in Oakland, California, on October 15. Edward Brooke, attorney general of Massachusetts, is elected to the Senate on November 8, becoming the first black senator since 1881 (all six African-American representatives are reelected in 1966).

1967   King gives speech strongly condemning American involvement in Vietnam, April 4, and addresses major anti-war rally in New York City on April 15. H. Rap Brown succeeds Stokely Carmichael as chairman of SNCC on May 12 and continues its commitment to "Black Power." Supreme Court rules 5–4 in *Reitman* v. *Mulkey*, May 29, that a California state constitutional amendment allowing racial discrimination by property owners violates the Fourteenth Amendment. In *Loving* v. *Virginia*, June 12, the Supreme Court rules 9–0 that laws prohibiting interracial marriage violate the Fourteenth Amendment. Johnson appoints Thurgood Marshall to be the first

African-American justice on the Supreme Court, June 13. Traffic arrest by police in Newark, New Jersey, leads to riot, July 12–17, in which 23 people are killed. Police raid on after-hours club in Detroit, July 23, leads to widespread rioting, and on July 25 Johnson sends 1,700 army paratroopers to reinforce the National Guard. Riot ends July 27 after 43 people are killed. Johnson appoints commission headed by Illinois Governor Otto Kerner to investigate recent civil disorders, July 27 (there are a total of 59 urban riots in 1967). House of Representatives passes bill extending protection for civil rights workers 326–93 on August 16. FBI director J. Edgar Hoover approves counterintelligence program (COINTELPRO) intended to disrupt black nationalist groups, August 25. Black Panther leader Huey Newton is arrested October 28 and charged in the shooting death of an Oakland police officer (incident is first in series of violent encounters between Black Panthers and the police). Carl Stokes wins election in Cleveland, Ohio, and Richard Hatcher is elected in Gary, Indiana, November 7, becoming the first black mayors of major cities. SCLC announces plans on December 4 for Poor People's Campaign.

1968   Three African-American students are shot to death by state highway patrolmen on campus of South Carolina State College in Orangeburg, February 8, after series of demonstrations prompted by continued segregation of a local bowling alley. Senate adds provision prohibiting racial discrimination in the sale, rental, or financing of housing to the civil rights bill passed by the House in 1967. Kerner Commission delivers report on March 1 warning that "the nation is moving toward two societies, one black, one white—separate and unequal." Senate votes to end debate on civil rights bill, March 4, after Dirksen reverses his earlier opposition to fair housing legislation, and passes the bill 71–20 on March 11. Johnson announces on March 31 that he will not seek reelection. King is assassinated in Memphis on April 4. Rioting in Washington, Chicago, Baltimore, Kansas City, and other cities, April 5–9, results in 46 deaths. House of Representatives passes Senate version of civil rights bill 250–172, April 10, and Johnson signs it on April 11. Abernathy succeeds King as president of the SCLC and leads Poor People's March to Washington, where protestors build "Resurrection City," plywood shantytown near the Washington Monument, on May 12. In *Green* v. *County School Board of New Kent County*, decided May 27, the Supreme Court rejects 9–0 "freedom of choice" desegregation plan adopted by a Virginia school district and orders it to take further action to end its dual school system. Senator Robert Kennedy is assassinated in Los Angeles on June 5 while campaigning for the Democratic presidential nomination. Supreme Court rules 7–2 in *Jones* v. *Alfred H. Mayer Co.*, June 17, that racial discrimination in housing sales violates the 1866 Civil Rights Act. Police evict remaining protestors from Resurrection City on June 24. Huey Newton is convicted of voluntary manslaughter on September 10. Richard M. Nixon wins presidential election on November 5, defeating Vice-President Hubert H. Humphrey and George Wallace, who ran as an independent. Nixon wins 301 electoral votes and carries Virginia, North Carolina, South Carolina, Florida, and Tennessee; Humphrey wins 191 electoral votes and carries Texas; and Wallace wins 46 electoral votes and carries Louisiana, Arkansas, Mississippi, Alabama, and Georgia. Black Panther leader Eldridge Cleaver flees the country on November 24 to avoid imprisonment for a parole violation and goes into exile in Algeria.

1969   Federal appellate judge Warren Burger succeeds Earl Warren as chief justice on June 23. Department of Labor announces "Philadelphia Plan," June 27, requiring federal building contractors in Philadelphia to meet specific "goals" for hiring minority workers. (Plan is criticized for establishing racial quotas, which are prohibited by the 1964 Civil Rights Act, but withstands challenge in the federal courts and is later extended to several other cities.) Nixon issues Executive Order 11478, August 8, requiring all federal agencies to adopt "affirmative programs for equal employment opportunity." Nomination of federal appellate judge Clement Haynsworth Jr. to the Supreme Court on August 18 is opposed by civil rights groups and labor unions. In *Alexander* v. *Holmes County Board of Education*, decided 8–0 on October 29, the Supreme Court declares the "all deliberate speed" standard is no longer constitutionally permissible and orders the immediate desegregation of 33 Mississippi school districts. (By close of the 1970–71 school year 33 percent of African-American

students in the South will attend white-majority schools.)
Haynsworth nomination is rejected by the Senate 55–45
on November 21, becoming the first Supreme Court appointment defeated in a confirmation vote since 1930.

1970   Nomination of federal appellate judge G. Harrold
Carswell to the Supreme Court on January 19 meets with
strong opposition from civil rights groups and is rejected
by the Senate, 51–45, on April 8. Huey Newton is released
from prison, August 5, after his manslaughter conviction
is overturned on appeal.

1971   Congressional Black Caucus is founded, February 2, with
13 members (12 Representatives and one nonvoting delegate from the District of Columbia). Black Panther party
splits into bitterly opposed factions headed by Newton
and Cleaver. In *Griggs* v. *Duke Power Company*, March 8,
the Supreme Court rules 8–0 in favor of black employees
who challenged the use of standardized tests by an employer with a past history of discrimination. (Decision
makes it easier to bring suit under the employment provisions of the 1964 Civil Rights Act in cases where there is
no evidence of discriminatory intent.) On April 20 the
Court rules 9–0 in *Swann* v. *Charlotte-Mecklenburg Board
of Education*, upholding a court-ordered busing plan designed to achieve racial balance in a de jure segregated
school system. Nomination of assistant attorney general
William Rehnquist to the Supreme Court is approved
68–26 on December 10 despite opposition from civil
rights groups. Jesse Jackson resigns from SCLC and
announces on December 18 the formation of his own organization, Operation PUSH (People United to Save
Humanity).

1972   Congress passes Equal Employment Opportunity Act,
March 24, giving the Equal Employment Opportunity
Commission the power to file class-action lawsuits and ex-
tending its jurisdiction to cover state and local govern-
ments and educational institutions. Nixon wins reelection
on November 7, defeating George McGovern 520–17 in
the electoral voting and carrying all 11 Southern states.
Andrew Young, a former aide to King, is elected to the
House of Representatives from Georgia, and Barbara
Jordan is elected to the House from Texas; they are the

first African-Americans elected to Congress from the South since 1898.

1973   Last American troops are withdrawn from South Vietnam on March 29. Tom Bradley wins election on May 29 and becomes the first African-American mayor of Los Angeles. In *Keyes* v. *Denver School District No. 1*, decided June 21, the Supreme Court upholds 7–1 descgregation order involving busing in Denver, Colorado, ruling that decisions by school officials had reinforced de facto segregation. Maynard Jackson wins election in Atlanta on October 16 and becomes the first African-American mayor of a major Southern city.

Biographical Notes

RENATA ADLER (October 19, 1938–) Born in Milan, Italy; raised mainly in Danbury, Connecticut. Educated at Bryn Mawr (B.A., 1959), the Sorbonne (D.d'E.S., 1961), and Harvard (M.A., 1962); later earned a law degree at Yale. Worked as *New Yorker* writer and reporter for twenty years beginning in 1962. Also served as *New York Times* film critic (1968–69) and taught theater and film at Hunter College of the City University of New York (1972–73). Author of *Toward a Radical Middle: Fourteen Pieces of Reporting and Criticism* (1969), *A Year in the Dark: Journal of a Film Critic, 1968–69* (1970), *Speedboat* (1976, novel), *Pitch Dark* (1983, novel), *Reckless Disregard: Westmoreland v. CBS et al.; Sharon v. Time* (1986), *Politics and Media: Essays* (1988), *Gone: The Last Days of the New Yorker* (1999), *Private Capacity* (2000), and *Canaries in the Mineshaft: Essays on Politics and Media* (2001).

ROBERT ANALAVAGE (January 8, 1939–June 5, 1976) Born in Pennsylvania. Worked as assistant editor (1966–70) of *Southern Patriot*, newspaper of the Southern Conference Educational Fund, reporting on civil rights and labor movement in Mississippi. Died in Los Angeles.

ROBERT E. ANDERSON Jr. (1929–) From the mid-1960s to the late 1970s, worked for the Southern Regional Council in Atlanta; published reports including *Atlanta Churches in Crisis* (1969), *Equal Housing Opportunities in the South* (1971, with Horace Barker), *Comprehensive Health Care: A Southern View* (1973, with Susan Morgan), *Poor, Rural, and Southern* (1978), and *A Report from the Southwide Meeting on Implementing Desegregation Plans in Public Higher Education* (1979).

RUSSELL BAKER (August 14, 1925–) Born in Loudoun County, Virginia. Graduated from Johns Hopkins University in 1947. After college worked for *Baltimore Sun*; joined *New York Times* Washington bureau in 1954, and wrote "Observer" column for *Times* from 1962 to 1998. Winner of 1979 Pulitzer Prize for commentary. Author of *City on the Potomac* (1958), *American in Washington* (1961), *No Cause for Panic* (1964), *All Things Considered* (1965), *Our Next President* (1968), *Poor Russell's Almanac* (1972), *The Upside Down Man* (1977), *So This Is Depravity* (1980), *Growing Up* (1982), *The Rescue of Miss Yaskell and Other Pipe Dreams* (1983), *The Good Times* (1989), *There's a Country in My Cellar* (1990), and *Looking Back* (2002).

GEORGE BARNER (July 2, 1928–) Born George Willard Barner in Emporia, Virginia; family moved to New York City when he was a child. Attended Columbia University (1953–55). Worked for *New York Amsterdam News* as reporter and later feature editor (1956–68); won New York State Press

Association awards for coverage of an execution at Sing Sing and for exclusive interview with Izola Ware Curry, who stabbed Martin Luther King Jr. in 1958. In 1969 named news service editor at the New School for Social Research in New York City; later worked as freelance writer and public relations consultant. Won 1974 Pulitzer Prize with *Newsday* team for series "The Heroin Trail." Lives in Albany, New York.

JOHN BEECHER (January 22, 1904–May 11, 1980) Born John Henry Newman Beecher in New York City; family moved to Birmingham, Alabama, when he was three years old. Expelled from Virginia Military Institute for refusing to testify in hazing case. Attended Cornell (1921–23), University of Alabama (B.A., 1926), Harvard (1926–27), the Sorbonne (1928), University of Wisconsin (M.A., 1930), and University of North Carolina (1933–34). Worked intermittently as steelworker and metallurgist, and as an English instructor; from 1934 to 1939 served in New Deal agencies including the Emergency Relief Administration and the Farm Security Administration. Took first job in journalism in 1940, working as associate editor of Birmingham *Age-Herald and News*. Beginning in late 1941 was senior field representative for President's Fair Employment Practice Committee (FEPC), responsible for Southern states; organized 1942 public hearings in Birmingham. Resigned in 1943; wrote *New York Post* and *New Republic* articles criticizing FEPC. From 1943 to 1945 served on the *Booker T. Washington*, first integrated ship in the U.S. Merchant Marine; published *All Brave Soldiers* (1945) about experience. Directed camps for displaced persons in Germany for United Nations Relief and Rehabilitation Administration; wrote popular history of Minnesota Farmer-Labor Party, *Tomorrow Is a Day* (first published 1979). Was assistant professor of sociology at San Francisco State College beginning in 1948; fired for refusal to sign loyalty oath. Received Ford Foundation grant to study California small farmers (1951–52); purchased ranch in Sonoma County, California. Founded Morning Star Press in 1956; taught English at Arizona State (1959–61). Reported on civil rights movement for *San Francisco Chronicle* and *Ramparts*. Taught literature and served as poet-in-residence at a number of colleges, including St. John's University (1970), Duke (1973–75), and San Francisco State (1977–80). Died in San Francisco. Author of *And I Will Be Heard: Two Talks to the American People* (1940), *Here I Stand* (1941), *Report to the Stockholders & Other Poems, 1932–62* (1962), *To Live and Die in Dixie and Other Poems* (1966), and *Collected Poems 1924–1974* (1974).

ART BERMAN (August 16, 1935–November 28, 1996) Born Arthur Malcolm Berman in New York City. Graduated from Antioch College in 1957. After college worked as reporter for Springfield, Ohio, *Daily News and Sun* (1957–59), Pasadena, California, *Star News* (1959–60), and Los Angeles *Mirror News* (1960–61). Joined staff of *Los Angeles Times* in 1962, working as reporter (1962–69), assistant metropolitan editor (1970–77), suburban editor (1978–82), "View" editor (1983–87), assistant national editor (1987–91), and assistant

"Calendar" editor (1992–96). Shared Pulitzer Prize in 1966 for reporting on Watts riots and 1969 Pulitzer Prize for series on municipal corruption.

HAMILTON BIMS (c. 1937–) Taught science and English in the Philippines as a Peace Corps volunteer, 1962–63. Late in 1963 began journalism career as reporter for *Ebony*, where he worked until 1976, eventually becoming associate editor; published articles on subjects including Haiti, baseball player Roberto Clemente, and teenage delinquency. Also studied cultural anthropology at Roosevelt University (B.A., 1970), University of Illinois (M.A., 1971), and University of Indiana (Ph.D., 1984); wrote master's thesis on urbanization in Guinea and doctoral dissertation on smallholder farming in Jamaica. Published academic articles during the later 1980s on Jamaican agriculture. Lives in Shrewsbury, Massachusetts.

EDWARD BRECHER (July 20, 1911–April 15, 1989) Born Edward Moritz Brecher in Minneapolis. Educated at University of Wisconsin (1928–30), Swarthmore College (B.A., 1932), University of Minnesota (M.A., 1934), and Brown University (1934–35). Worked for U.S. Senate Committee on Interstate Commerce as research supervisor (1938–41), as assistant to the chairman of the Federal Communications Commission (1941–46), as associate editor of *Consumer Reports* (1947–51), and as editor for the United Nations Technical Assistance Administration (1951–52). Beginning in 1952 earned living as freelance writer with wife, Ruth Brecher; they co-authored *Medical and Hospital Benefit Plans* (1961), *The Rays: A History of Radiology* (1969), and articles in *Harper's*, *Saturday Evening Post*, *Redbook*, and other national magazines; co-edited *An Analysis of Human Sexual Response* (1966). After wife's death in 1966 published *The Sex Researchers* (1969), *Licit and Illicit Drugs: The Consumers Union Report* (1972), *Methadone Treatment Manual* (1973), *Health Care in Correctional Institutions* (1975), *Treatment Programs for Sex Offenders* (1978), *Love, Sex, and Aging: A Consumers Union Report* (1982). Published *New York Times Magazine* article "Opting for Suicide" after colon cancer diagnosis; died by suicide in Cornwall, Connecticut.

RUTH BRECHER (February 21, 1911–October 21, 1966) Born Ruth Ernestine Cook in Ambler, Pennsylvania. Educated at Swarthmore (B.A., 1933) and Radcliffe (1933–38). Worked as research assistant in Harvard government department (1937–40), as reporter for *Executives War Digest* (1944–45), as assistant editor for *Consumer Reports* (1947–51), and beginning in 1951 as freelance writer with husband Edward Brecher (see biographical note above for their joint publications). Died in Torrington, Connecticut.

JIMMY BRESLIN (October 17, 1929–) Born in Jamaica, New York. Attended Long Island University (1948–50), working as copyboy for *Long Island Press* while in college. Reported on sports from 1950 to 1963 for *New York Journal-American* and other New York newspapers. Joined staff of New York *Herald-Tribune* in 1963 as sportswriter, eventually becoming columnist and reporter. Wrote columns for *New York Post* (1968–69), *New York Daily News* (1978–88), and *Newsday* (1988–   ). In 1969 ran for presidency of New York city council on Mailer-Breslin ticket. Contributed articles to *New York* magazine (1968–71) and wrote for *New Times* (1973); served as television commentator for New York ABC and NBC affiliates (1968–69; 1973). In 1977 was recipient of letters from "Son of Sam" serial killer David Berkowitz. Won 1986 Pulitzer Prize and 1986 George Polk award for commentary. Author of novels *The Gang That Couldn't Shoot Straight* (1969), *World Without End, Amen* (1973), *.44* (1978, with Dick Schapp), *Forsaking All Others* (1982), *Table Money* (1987), *He Got Hungry and Forgot His Manners* (1987), and *I Don't Want To Go to Jail* (2001), and nonfiction *Sunny Jim: The Life of America's Most Beloved Horseman, James Fitzsimmons* (1962), *Can't Anybody Here Play This Game?* (1963), *The World of Jimmy Breslin* (1967), *Running Against the Machine: The Mailer-Breslin Campaign* (contributor, 1970), *How the Good Guys Finally Won: Notes from an Impeachment Summer* (1975), *The World According to Breslin* (1984), *Damon Runyon* (1991), *A Slight Case of Amazing Grace: A Memoir* (1996), *I Want To Thank My Brain for Remembering Me: A Memoir* (1996), and *The Short Sweet Dream of Eduardo Gutierrez* (2002).

EARL CALDWELL (c. 1935–   ) Born in Clearfield, Pennsylvania. Educated at University of Buffalo. After college worked as apprentice sportswriter for *Clearfield Progress* and Lancaster, Pennsylvania, *Intelligencer Journal*. Hired as reporter for the *Democrat and Chronicle* in Rochester, New York. Joined staff of New York *Herald-Tribune* in 1966. Worked for *New York Times* as local and national reporter. Reported on assassination of Martin Luther King Jr. for *New York Times*, the only journalist present during the shooting. Refusal to provide information to FBI about Black Panthers led to landmark First Amendment case on reporters' right to protect confidential sources. Wrote column for *Washington Star* in the 1970s and for *New York Post* from 1979 until 1994. Was founding director of Institute of Journalism Education, training minority reporters. Author of *Black American Witness: Reports from the Front* (1994). Lives in New York City.

BOB CLARK New York City-based photographer assigned to cover the 1967 Detroit riots by the Black Star agency; had previously reported on a San Francisco race riot and interviewed Stokely Carmichael for a German magazine. In 1968 *Look* magazine published his photographs of a Harlem voodoo service; he interviewed actor Calvin Lockhart for *Essence* in 1970 and photographer-filmmaker Gordon Parks Jr. for *Encore* in 1973.

ROBERT COLES (October 12, 1929–   ) Born in Boston. Graduated from Harvard in 1950 and from Columbia University medical school in 1954. Served in U.S. Air Force as chief of neuropsychiatric service at Keesler Air Force Base, Biloxi, Mississippi (1958–60). From 1960 to 1962 was on psychiatric staff of Massachusetts General Hospital and a clinical assistant in psychiatry at Harvard Medical School; also worked as research psychiatrist for the Southern Regional Council, Atlanta. Was research psychiatrist at Harvard Medical School beginning in 1963; since 1978 has been professor of psychiatry and medical humanities. Received Pulitzer Prize for volumes 2 and 3 of *Children of Crisis* series in 1973, a MacArthur Foundation fellowship in 1981, and, in 1998, the Presidential Medal of Freedom. Author of series *Children of Crisis* (volume 1: *A Study in Courage and Fear*, 1967, volume 2: *Migrants, Sharecroppers, Mountaineers*, 1971; volume 3: *The South Goes North*, 1971; volume 4: *Eskimos, Chicanos, Indians*, 1977; volume 5: *Privileged Ones: The Well-Off and the Rich in America*, 1977), *Dead End School* (1968), *Still Hungry in America* (1969), *The Grass Pipe* (juvenile, 1969), *The Image Is You* (1969), *The Wages of Neglect* (1969, with Maria W. Piers), *Erik H. Erikson: The Growth of His Work* (1970), *The Middle Americans* (1971), *The Geography of Faith* (1971, with Daniel Berrigan), *Saving Face* (1972), *Farewell to the South* (1972, collected articles on civil rights movement), *A Spectacle Unto the World* (1973), *Riding Free* (1973), *The Old Ones of New Mexico* (1973), *The Buses Roll* (1974), *Irony in the Mind's Life: Essays on Novels by James Agee, Elizabeth Bowen, and George Eliot* (1974), *Headsparks* (1975), *William Carlos Williams: The Knack of Survival in America* (1975), *Mind's Fate: Ways of Seeing Psychiatry and Psychoanalysis* (1975), series *Women of Crisis* (with Jane Hallowell Coles, volume 1: *Lives of Struggle and Hope*, 1978; volume 2: *Lives of Work and Dreams*, 1980), *Walker Percy: An American Search* (1978), *Flannery O'Connor's South* (1980), *Sex and the American Teenager* (with Geoffrey Stokes, 1985), *The Moral Life of Children* (1986), *The Political Life of Children* (1986), *Simone Weil: A Modern Pilgrimage* (1987), *Dorothy Day: A Radical Devotion* (1987), *Harvard Diary: Reflection on the Sacred and the Secular* (1988), *The Red Wheelbarrow: Selected Literary Essays* (1988), *Times of Surrender: Selected Essays* (1988), *Learning by Example: Stories and the Moral Imagination* (1989), *Rumors of Separate Worlds* (poetry, 1989), *The Spiritual Life of Children* (1990), *Anna Freud: The Dream of Psychoanalysis* (1992), *The Call of Service: A Witness to Idealism* (1993), *The Mind's Fate: A Psychiatrist Looks at His Profession* (1995), *Doing Documentary Work* (1997), *The Moral Intelligence of Children* (1998), *The Secular Mind* (1999), and *Lives of Moral Leadership* (2000).

MARC CRAWFORD (December 14, 1929–March 20, 1996) Born Marwil Cooper Crawford in Detroit, Michigan; raised in small midwestern towns and in Detroit's Brewster Projects. Joined U.S. Army in 1946, serving in Germany and occupied Japan and during the Korean war as master sergeant. Beginning in 1953 worked as columnist for Texas edition of *Kansas City Call*. Attended Texas Southern University for a semester, then worked for Detroit edition of *Pittsburgh Courier*. Beginning in the mid-1950s reported for *Jet* and *Ebony*. Was kicked in the mouth and lost front teeth while covering integration of Central High School in Little Rock; later jailed and fined for allegedly biting his assailant in the foot. Also reported on crisis over Quemoy and Matsu and from Cuba. Did public relations work for musicians including B. B. King and Johnny Mathis, and for Chess Records; wrote album liner notes and freelance articles for *Look*, *Down Beat*, and other magazines. Traveled in Europe (1960–61); founded magazine *Tone*, a literary supplement syndicated in African-American newspapers, in 1961. Established Marc Crawford Agency, a Detroit public relations firm which organized June 21, 1963, Detroit civil rights rally. Worked as staff reporter for *Life* (1963–65); reported on demonstrations in St. Augustine, the Selma-to-Montgomery march, and Watts. Won 1966 National Headliners Club award for Watts reporting. Established Transmundo, a newsphoto agency. From 1968 to 1971 lived in Mexico, at work on novel; edited and wrote for *Mexico This Month* and *Gente*. Reported from Guyana and Ireland for *Encore* as foreign affairs editor; published short fiction in *Freedomways* and *Black World*. Taught creative writing at Livingston College of Rutgers University (1972–79). Founded *Time Capsule* magazine in 1976; worked as United Nations correspondent for Pacifica radio. From 1981 until 1995 taught creative writing and prose composition at New York University; established popular jazz appreciation course and produced NYU jazz concerts. Contributed feature articles to *Sepia*, *Amsterdam News*, and Brooklyn *Daily Challenge*; was U.S. correspondent for *Swing Journal* and *Jazz Podium*. Co-author of *The Lincoln Brigade: A Picture History* (1989, with William Loren Katz). Died in New York City.

PETER DE LISSOVOY (December 17, 1942–) Born in Evanston, Illinois. Graduated from Evanston Township High School. Attended Harvard University (1960–61, 1962–63); spent fifteen months in Africa, teaching with a Harvard project in Tanzania and working as reporter for Salisbury, Rhodesia, *Evening Standard*. Joined Youth Wing of Zimbabwe African National Union. In 1963 served as SNCC field worker in Albany, Georgia; organized marches and voter-registration work and was jailed in Atlanta, Albany, and Lee and Dougherty counties. In 1964 worked as speechwriter for congressional campaign of C. B. King and as assistant to Randy Battle, campaign's logistics manager; reported on Albany civil rights movement for *Harvard Crimson*, *Dissent*, and *The Nation*. Also in 1964, worked for a black-owned construction company in Albany. During 1970s and 1980s earned living as auto mechanic and cab driver while writing novels. Taught English and writing at Harvard University Extension School (1990–97) and Fitchburg State College (1998). Author of *Feelgood* (1970), a novel.

JERRY DeMUTH (September 11, 1937–) Born in Milwaukee, Wisconsin; grew up in Chicago area. Attended Northwestern University, where he edited campus magazine; received journalism degree from Southern Illinois University. After college was assistant editor at Regency Books. Spent 1962 and 1963 with American Friends Service Committee in Dayton, Ohio; wrote on civil rights and civil liberties for *Commonweal* and *York* (Pennsylvania) *Gazette and Daily*. Worked with SNCC in Atlanta (1964–65); reported on civil rights movement for *The Nation*, *New Republic*, and *Milwaukee Journal*. From 1966 to 1978 was a *Chicago Sun-Times* reporter and feature writer. In 1978 founded and edited a music business magazine. Has worked as freelance journalist since 1979, writing on film, music, small business, world trade, and other subjects.

JOAN DIDION (December 5, 1934–) Born in Sacramento; graduated from University of California–Berkeley in 1956. Worked as associate feature editor for *Vogue* (1956–63) and as columnist for *Saturday Evening Post*, *Life*, and *Esquire*. Author of novels *Run River* (1963), *Play It As It Lays* (1970), *A Book of Common Prayer* (1977), *Democracy* (1984), and *The Last Thing He Wanted* (1996); essay collections *Slouching Toward Bethlehem* (1968), *The White Album* (1979), *After Henry* (1992), and *Political Fictions* (2002); nonfiction *Salvador* (1983), and *Miami* (1987). Co-author, with John Gregory Dunne, of screenplays *The Panic in Needle Park* (1971), *Play It As It Lays* (1972), *A Star Is Born* (1976), *True Confessions* (1981), "Hills Like White Elephants" in *Women and Men: Stories of Seduction* (1990), *Broken Trust* (1995), and *Up Close and Personal* (1996).

MICHAEL DURHAM (June 26, 1935–) Born Michael Schelling Durham in New York City. Graduated from Harvard University in 1957. After two years in the U.S. Army took job as reporter for *Gloucester* (Massachusetts) *Daily Times*. Joined staff of *Life* magazine in 1961. In April 1963 was arrested and jailed with photographer Charles Moore while covering demonstrations in Birmingham. Also reported on murder of civil rights workers in Philadelphia, Mississippi, and Mississippi voter registration campaigns. Was correspondent in *Life*'s Paris bureau (1965–69) and a *Life* editor, based in New York City; later edited *Americana* magazine (1973–87) and worked as freelance writer. Currently lives in De Lancey, New York, and serves as an educator for the Alcohol and Drug Abuse Council of Delaware County. His books include *Powerful Days: The Civil Rights Photographs of Charles Moore* (1991); two volumes in the *Smithsonian Guide to Historic America* series; *The Miracles of Mary* (1995) and *Desert Between the Mountains* (1997).

LEZ EDMOND Currently Associate Professor of Social Sciences at St. John's University.

JERRY FARBER (March 21, 1935–) Born in El Paso, Texas. Was a radio actor in Los Angeles as a child. Wrote for *Daily Bruin*, as an undergraduate at UCLA, and later for *Los Angeles Free Press* (1965–68). Was active in the civil rights movement and the anti-war movement; arrested eight times and sentenced to jail several times between 1963 and 1968. Received Ph.D. in comparative literature from Occidental in 1970. Taught at California State University at Los Angeles (1962–68) and the University of Paris, VII (1974, 1977); since 1968 has been on the faculty at San Diego State University, where he is professor of comparative literature. Author of articles in academic journals and *The Student As Nigger* (1969), *The University of Tomorrowland* (1972), and *A Field Guide to the Aesthetic Experience* (1982).

JAMES FARMER (January 12, 1920–July 9, 1999) Born in Marshall, Texas. Educated at Wiley College in Marshall (B.A., 1938), and at Howard (B.D., 1941). Served as race relations secretary for the Fellowship of Reconciliation (1941–45); co-founded and served as national chairman of Congress of Racial Equality (1942–44, 1950, 1961–66). Worked as labor organizer for Upholsterer's International Union of North America (1945–47); lecturer on race and labor (1948–50); student field secretary of the League for Industrial Democracy (1950–54); international representative of the State, County, and Municipal Employees' Union (1954–59); NAACP program director (1959–61); leader of CORE Freedom Ride (1961); president, from 1965, of the Center for Community Action in Education; assistant secretary for administration, Department of Health, Education, and Welfare (1969–70); president of the Council on Minority Planning and Strategy (1973–76); and executive director of the Coalition of American Public Employees (1977–82). Ran unsuccessfully for Congress from New York (1968). Taught American studies, history, and social welfare at Mary Washington College, New York University, Lincoln University, and Antioch College. Awarded Presidential Medal of Freedom in 1998. Died in Fredericksburg, Virginia. Author of *Freedom—When?* (1965) and *Lay Bare the Heart: An Autobiography* (1985).

KARL FLEMING (August 30, 1927–) Born in Newport News, Virginia; grew up in church orphanage. Began career as police and court reporter for Wilson, North Carolina, *Daily Times* and reporter for *Atlanta Constitution*. Joined *Newsweek* in 1960 as civil rights correspondent. In 1965 became Los Angeles bureau chief; was seriously injured while reporting on Watts riots. Covered campaigns and political conventions for *Newsweek*. From 1978 to 1985 worked in television, as managing editor and on-air political editor for KNXT in Los Angeles; produced documentary *Watts Revisited* for CBS. From 1985 to 1987 was editor and publisher of *California Business*. Since 1988 has been president of Prime Time Communications, a media consulting firm. Author of *The First Time* (1975, with Anne Taylor Fleming).

BOB FLETCHER (December 12, 1938–) Born Robert E. Fletcher in Detroit, Michigan. Attended Fisk University for three years beginning in 1956; graduated from Wayne State in 1961. In 1963 was photographer and administrator in Detroit for tutorial program of National Student Association. Moved to New York, working at Harlem Education Project. From 1964 to 1968 was based in Mississippi as photojournalist for SNCC; taught in a Mississippi Freedom School. Showed photographs in exhibitions including "Us" (1965) and "Now" (1968). Returned to New York in 1969, working as freelance photojournalist and filmmaker and teaching photography. Worked on two documentary films about African independence movements, *A Luta Continua* ("The Struggle Continues," cinematographer and co-director, Angola, 1971), and *O Povo Organizado* ("The People Organized," cinematographer, Mozambique, 1975). Graduated from New York University School of Law in 1990. Currently practices law in New York City.

MARSHALL FRADY (January 11, 1940–) Born in Augusta, Georgia. Educated at Furman University (B.A., 1963) and University of Iowa. Worked for *Newsweek*'s Atlanta and Los Angeles bureaus as correspondent (1966–67); as staff writer on Atlanta bureau of *Saturday Evening Post* (1968–69); as contributing editor, based in Atlanta, for *Harper's* (1969–71) and *Life* (1971–73); as chief correspondent for *ABC News Close-up* (1979–86); and as correspondent for *Nightline* (1986–). Won 1982 Emmy award. Has contributed articles to *Esquire*, *New York Review of Books*, *Atlantic Monthly*, *New Yorker* and other periodicals. Author of *Wallace* (1968), *Across a Darkling Plain: An American's Passage Through the Middle East* (1971), *Billy Graham: A Parable of American Righteousness* (1979), *Southerners: A Journalist's Odyssey* (1980), *Jesse: The Life and Pilgrimage of Jesse Jackson* (1996), and *Martin Luther King Jr.* (2002), a volume in the Penguin Lives series.

C. GERALD FRASER (July 30, 1925–) Born Charles Gerald Fraser Jr. in Boston, Massachusetts. Graduated from University of Wisconsin in 1949 with B.A. in economics; worked on student newspaper *Daily Cardinal* and wrote newscasts for state-owned radio station WHA. Later earned M.A. in media studies at the New School for Social Research. Began professional career as reporter for *New York Amsterdam News* (1952–56); covered education and the criminal justice system. Received National Newspaper Publishers Association award for eyewitness report of a 1954 electrocution at Sing Sing. Edited military equipment manuals and a newspaper published by Building Service Employees Union, Local 144; wrote articles for Caribbean publications on United Nations activities. From 1963 to 1967 worked on New York *Daily News* national and foreign news desk; reported for *Daily News* on Alabama a year after the 1965 Selma-to-Montgomery march. Moved to *New York Times* in 1967 as metropolitan staff reporter; later worked on *Times*'s cultural news staff, writing columns in the daily paper, the weekly television guide, and the Sunday *Book Review*. Taught at Columbia University's Graduate School of Journalism and John Jay College of Criminal Justice. Beginning in 1991 joined *Earth Times*, a monthly focused on United Nations environmental and international development activities; has reported from every continent except Australia. Lives in New York City.

PAUL GOOD (March 11, 1929–) Born in Brooklyn, New York. Attended Brown University (1947) and Boston University (1948); served in U.S. Army (1951–53). Worked as rewriteman for New York *World Telegram & Sun* (1953–56), newswriter and editor for NBC (1958–60), correspondent and Atlanta bureau chief for ABC (1961–64), and as a freelance writer (1964–). Wrote column "The Old Sergeant" for *Army Times* for twelve years. Author of *The American Serfs: A Report on Poverty in the Rural South* (1968), *Once to Every Man* (novel, 1970), *The Trouble I've Seen: White Journalist/Black Movement* (1975), and two reports for the U.S. Commission on Civil Rights, *Cycle to Nowhere* (1968), and *Cairo, Illinois: Racism at Floodtide* (1973).

JEREMIAH S. GUTMAN (October 19, 1923–) Born Jeremiah Sheldon Gutman in Brooklyn, New York. Graduated from City College of New York in 1943. Served with U.S. Army, 1943–46. In 1949 received law degree from New York University, where he was editor-in-chief of law review. Made partner in firm Levy, Gutman, Goldberg & Kaplan, where he continues to practice. Traveled to Mississippi in summer of 1964 to defend civil rights workers; took depositions throughout state for Mississippi Freedom Democratic Party congressional vote challenge. Serves as president of the American/Israeli Civil Liberties Coalition, director of the New York Civil Liberties Union, and co-chair of the National Coalition Against Censorship. Lives in Hastings-on-Hudson, New York.

DAVID HALBERSTAM (April 10, 1934–) Born in New York City; educated at Harvard (B.A., 1955). After college took reporting job in Mississippi with *West Point Daily Times Leader* (1955–56); later worked for *Nashville Tennesseean* (1956–60), and as *New York Times* staff writer (1960–67). Shared Pulitzer Prize and George Polk award for foreign reporting, 1964. Left *Times* in 1967 to become contributing editor for *Harper's*. His books include *The Noblest Roman* (novel, 1961), *The Making of a Quagmire* (1965), *One Very Hot Day* (novel, 1968), *The Unfinished Odyssey of Robert Kennedy* (1969), *Ho* (1971), *The Best and the Brightest* (1972), *The Powers That Be* (1979), *The Breaks of the Game* (1981), *The Amateurs* (1985), *The Reckoning* (1987), *Summer of '49* (1989), *The Next Century* (1991), *The Fifties* (1993), *October 1964* (1994), *The Children* (1998), *War in a Time of Peace* (2001), and *Firehouse* (2002).

ELIZABETH HARDWICK (July 27, 1916–) Born in Lexington, Kentucky. Graduated from the University of Kentucky in 1938, and received master's degree in 1939; also did graduate work at Columbia (1939–41). Wrote for *Partisan Review*, *Harper's*, and other journals. In 1963 co-founded *New York Review of Books*, to which she continues to contribute. Author of novels *The Ghostly Lover* (1945), *The Simple Truth* (1955), and *Sleepless Nights* (1979), and nonfiction *A View of My Own: Essays in Literature and Society* (1962), *Seduction and Betrayal: Women and Literature* (1974), *Bartleby in Manhattan and Other Essays* (1984), *Sight Readings* (1998), *American Fictions* (1999), and *Herman Melville* (2000).

JOHN HERBERS (November 4, 1923–) Born in Memphis, Tennessee. Graduated from Emory University in 1949, after which he worked for Greenwood, Mississippi, *Morning Star* and Jackson, Mississippi, *Daily News*. From 1953 to 1963 reported from Mississippi for United Press International. Joined staff of *New York Times* in 1963; covered civil rights, Congress, presidential campaigns, and urban affairs. Appointed *Times* assistant national editor in 1975, deputy Washington bureau chief in 1977, and national Washington correspondent in 1979; retired in 1987. His books include *The Lost Priority: What*

Happened to the Civil Rights Movement in America? (1970), *The Black Dilemma* (1973), *No Thank You, Mr. President* (1976), and *The New Heartland: America's Flight Beyond the Suburbs and How It Is Changing Our Future* (1986).

CALVIN C. HERNTON (April 28, 1932–September 30, 2001) Born Calvin Coolidge Hernton in Chattanooga, Tennessee. Graduated from Talladega College in 1954 and received M.A. in sociology from Fisk University in 1956. Taught at Benedict College (1957–58), Alabama A&M (1958–59), Edward Waters College (1959–60), and Southern University and A&M (1960–61). Moved to New York in 1961, where he was employed as a social worker for New York State Department of Welfare. Co-founded *Umbra* magazine in 1963. From 1965 to 1969 was research fellow of the London Institute of Phenomenological Studies. Returned to U.S. in 1970, serving as writer-in-residence at Oberlin College. From 1973 until his death was professor of black studies and creative writing at Oberlin. Author of *The Coming of Chronos to the House of Nightsong: An Epical Narrative of the South* (1963, poetry), *Sex and Racism in America* (1965), *White Papers for White Americans* (1966), *Coming Together: Black Power, White Hatred, and Sexual Hangups* (1971), *Scarecrow* (1974, novel), *The Cannabis Experience: The Study of the Effects of Marijuana and Hashish* (1974, with Joseph Berke), *Medicine Man* (1976, poems), *Sexual Mountains and Black Women Writers: Adventure in Sex, Literature, and Real Life* (1987), and *The Red Crab Gang and Black River Poems* (1999).

JOHN HERSEY (June 17, 1914–March 24, 1993) Born John Richard Hersey in Tientsin, China; spent first ten years of life in China. Graduated Yale in 1936; attended Clare College, Cambridge (1936–37). During summer of 1937 worked as driver and private secretary for Sinclair Lewis. Joined staff of *Time* magazine in 1937 as editor and correspondent, reporting on war from China and Japan (1939), the South Pacific (1942), Sicily and the Mediterranean (1943), and Moscow (1944–45). Won 1945 Pulitzer Prize for novel *A Bell for Adano* (1944), about Allied occupation of Sicily. Traveled to Japan and China for *Life* and *New Yorker*, 1945–46; reported on atomic bombing of Hiroshima. Was master of Pierson College at Yale, 1965–70, and lecturer and professor at Yale from 1971 to 1984. Wrote *The Algiers Motel Incident* (1968) after Detroit riots, and *Letter to the Alumni* (1970) in wake of New Haven Black Panther trial. Also author of *Men on Bataan* (1942), *Into the Valley: A Skirmish of the Marines* (1943), *Hiroshima* (1946), *Here To Stay: Studies on Human Tenacity* (1962), *The President* (1975), *Aspects of the Presidency: Truman and Ford in Office* (1980), *Blues* (1987), *Life Sketches* (1989), *Fling and Other Stories* (1990), *Key West Tales* (stories, published posthumously in 1994), and novels *The Wall* (1950), *The Marmot Drive* (1953), *A Single Pebble* (1956), *The War Lover* (1959), *The Child Buyer* (1960), *White Lotus* (1965), *Too Far To Walk* (1966), *Under the Eye of the Storm* (1967), *The Conspiracy* (1972), *My Petition for More Space* (1974), *The Walnut Door* (1977), *The Call: An American Missionary in China* (1985), and *Antonietta* (1991).

WILLIAM BRADFORD HUIE (November 13, 1910–November 22, 1986) Born in Hartselle, Alabama. Graduated from University of Alabama in 1930. Worked as reporter for *Birmingham Post* (1932–36) and as associate editor of *American Mercury* (1941–43). Served in the U.S. Navy (1943–45), after which he returned to *Mercury* as editor and publisher, remaining until 1952. Later in the 1950s interviewed major political figures for CBS series *Chronoscope*. With Zora Neale Hurston, covered Florida murder case of Ruby McCollum; published *Ruby McCollum: Woman in the Suwannee Jail* (1956). In wake of 1967 novel *The Klansman*, a cross was burned on his lawn. Died in Guntersville, Alabama. His books of fiction include *Mud on the Stars* (1942), *The Revolt of Mamie Stover* (1951), *Wolf Whistle and Other Stories* (1959), *The Americanization of Emily* (1959), *The Hero of Iwo Jima and Other Stories* (1962), *Hotel Mamie Stover* (1963), *In the Hours of the Night* (1975); nonfiction, *The Fight for Air Power* (1942), *Seabee Roads to Victory* (1944), *Can Do!: The Story of the Seabees* (1944), *The Case Against the Admirals: Why We Must Have a Unified Command* (1946), *The Execution of Private Slovik* (1954), *The Hiroshima Pilot: The Case of Major Claude Eatherly* (1964), *Three Lives for Mississippi* (1965), *He Slew the Dreamer: My Search with James Earl Ray for the Truth about the Murder of Martin Luther King* (1970), *A New Life To Live: Jimmy Putnam's Story* (editor, 1977), *It's Me, O Lord!* (1979), *The Ray of Hope* (1984), and *To Live and Die in Dixie* (1985).

SNOW JAMES, pseud. See STETSON KENNEDY.

HAYNES JOHNSON (July 9, 1931–) Born Haynes Bonner Johnson in New York City. Graduated from University of Missouri in 1952 with degree in journalism. Served in U.S. Army in Korea from 1952 to 1955, becoming first lieutenant, after which he earned a master's in American history from University of Wisconsin–Madison. Began career as reporter at *Wilmington News-Journal* (1956–57). Moved to *Washington Star* in 1957, working as reporter, rewriteman, assistant city editor, and national assignments reporter (1957–69). Won 1966 Pulitzer Prize in national reporting for articles on Selma civil rights demonstrations. Served as *Washington Post* national correspondent (1969–73), assistant managing editor (1973–77), and columnist (1977–94). Taught journalism at Princeton (1975, 1978), Berkeley (1990), and George Washington University (1994–96); since 1998 has held Knight Chair at the Philip Merrill College of Journalism, University of Maryland. Has appeared as television commentator on *Washington Week in Review* (1967–94), *The Today Show* (1979–80), and *The News Hour with Jim Lehrer* (1994–). Author of *Dusk at the Mountain: The Negro, the Nation, and the Capital* (1963), *The Bay of Pigs: The Leaders' Story of Brigade 2506* (1964, with Manuel Artime, Jose Perez San Roman, Erneido Oliva, and Enrique Ruiz-Williams), *Fulbright: The Dissenter* (1968, with Bernard M. Gwertzman), *The Unions* (1972, with Nick Kotz), *Lyndon* (1973, with Richard Harwood), *The Working White House* (1975), *In the Absence of Power: Governing America* (1980), *The Landing* (novel, with

Howard Simons, 1986), *Sleepwalking Through History: America in the Reagan Years* (1991), *Divided We Fall: Gambling with History in the Nineties* (1994), *The System* (1996, with David S. Broder), and *The Best of Times: America in the Clinton Years* (2001).

MURRAY KEMPTON (December 16, 1917–May 5, 1997) Born James Murray Kempton in Baltimore. Worked as copyboy for H. L. Mencken at *Baltimore Evening Sun*. Educated at Johns Hopkins, where he was editor-in-chief of *Johns Hopkins News-Letter*. After graduation in 1939, worked for a short time as labor organizer, then joined staff of *New York Post*. Served in air force during World War II, returning to *Post* in 1949 as labor editor and later columnist. Also wrote for *Sun* and *World-Telegram* in New York. Edited *The New Republic*, 1963–64. In 1981 began writing regular column for *Newsday*, continuing until his death; also wrote for *New York Review of Books*. Won Pulitzer Prize for *Newsday* columns in 1985. His books include: *Part of Our Time: Some Ruins and Monuments of the Thirties* (1955), *America Comes of Middle Age: Columns 1950–1962* (1963), *The Briar Patch: The People of the State of New York v. Lumumba Shakur* (1973, winner of National Book Award), and *Rebellions, Perversities, and Main Events* (1994).

STETSON KENNEDY (October 5, 1916–) Born in Jacksonville, Florida. Studied at University of Florida (where he published column "News in the Nude" in *Florida Alligator*), the New School for Social Research, and the Sorbonne. From 1935 to 1942 worked as state director of folklore, oral history, and ethnic studies for Florida Federal Writers' Project; served on staff of *The Florida Guide* (1941). During World War II was based in Atlanta as editorial director of CIO political action committee; wrote column "Inside Out," syndicated in AFL–CIO newspapers (1945–48). Was research director, also in Atlanta, for Anti-Defamation League of B'nai B'rith (1946–49); conducted 1946 undercover investigation of Ku Klux Klan for Georgia Bureau of Investigation, later publishing exposés *Southern Exposure* (1946) and *I Rode with the Ku Klux Klan* (1954, reissued in 1990 as *The Klan Unmasked*). Traveled widely overseas from 1952 to 1960, spending three years in communist countries; published reports in *Pittsburgh Courier*. Edited Florida edition of *Pittsburgh Courier*, 1960–62; later wrote *Courier* column "Up Front Down South" under pseudonym "Daddy Mention." Was federal projects and development officer, Florida Memorial College, St. Augustine (1963–65); deputy director of Jacksonville Neighborhood Youth Corps (1965–67); and director of planning, training, and evaluation for Greater Jacksonville Economic Opportunity, Inc. Currently working on autobiography *Dissident-at-Large*. His other books include *Palmetto County* (1942), *Jim Crow Guide to the U.S.A.* (1959) and *After Appomattox: How the South Won the War* (1994).

E. W. KENWORTHY (September 23, 1909–January 25, 1993) Born Edwin Wentworth Kenworthy in Attleboro, Massachusetts. Earned undergraduate and graduate degrees from Oberlin College. Taught English at Indiana University. Worked for the Office of War Information during World War II; after the war wrote editorials for Baltimore *Evening Sun*, served as information officer for the U.S. Embassy in London, and was a correspondent for *Reporter* magazine. From 1949 to 1950 was executive secretary of the Committee on Equality of Treatment and Opportunity in the Armed Services (1949–50); published 1951 report "The Case Against Army Segregation." Contributed regular articles as freelance writer for "Week in Review" section of *New York Times* (1950–57). Became a full-time staffer at *Times* Washington bureau in 1957, remaining with paper until his retirement in 1977; reported mainly on Washington politics and the environment. Died in Washington, D.C.

PETER KIHSS (August 25, 1912–December 28, 1984) Born Peter Frederick Kihss in Brooklyn, New York; educated at Columbia. Began a long career in journalism soon after college, working for the Associated Press in Washington, as a part-time reporter for *New York Times* in Argentina and Uruguay (1933), for *Washington Post* (1934–36), *World-Telegram* (1936–43), *Herald-Tribune* (1943–51), and *New York Times* (1952–82). Reported for *Times* on enrollment of Autherine Lucy at University of Alabama and other school desegregation stories; nominated four times for Pulitzer Prize. Active in New York Newspaper Guild. Died at home of a heart attack in Jamaica Estates, New York.

ANDREW KOPKIND (August 24, 1935–October 23, 1994) Born Andrew David Kopkind in New Haven, Connecticut. Educated at Cornell (B.A., 1957), where he was editor of the *Cornell Daily Sun*; after college worked as a reporter for the *Washington Post* (1958–59) and studied at the London School of Economics (M.S., 1961). Joined staff of *Time* in 1961, reporting mainly from California. Served as *New Republic* associate editor (1965–67) and as correspondent for *New Statesman* (1965–69); reported on SNCC and SDS. Founded *Hard Times* in 1968; edited *Ramparts* (1970). Lived for part of 1970s in rural Vermont commune. From 1982 until his death wrote regularly for *The Nation*. Author of two collections of articles, *America: The Mixed Curse* (1969) and *The Thirty Years' Wars: Dispatches and Diversions of a Radical Journalist, 1965–1994* (published posthumously in 1995).

BOB LABAREE (1944–) Born in Philadelphia. Graduated from College of Wooster, where he majored in music, in 1966. Taught at Miles College in Birmingham, Alabama, for two years, reported for *Southern Courier* on aftermath of assassination of Martin Luther King Jr. and Poor People's Campaign. Was conscientious objector to military service during Vietnam War, working at St. Elizabeth's Hospital in Washington, D.C. Worked as high school teacher and musician. Earned Ph.D. in Ethnomusicology from Wesleyan University in 1988; since 1985 has been on the faculty of the Musicology Department at New England Conservatory in Boston, specializing in the music of Turkey. Founded conservatory's Intercultural Institute. Has performed and recorded Turkish music with the EurAsia Ensemble, which he co-founded in 1980. His solo CD, *Çengnağme*, was released in Istanbul in 2001.

ALICE LAKE (November 29, 1916–April 25, 1990) Born Alice Dannenberg in New York City. Educated at Vassar, after which she worked as a publicist for CBS (1937–40), and during the mid-1940s as a propaganda analyst, reporter for *St. Paul Dispatch*, and sewing machine operator. Afterward wrote freelance articles for *Ladies' Home Journal*, *McCall's*, *Good Housekeeping*, and *Redbook*. Died in New York City. Author of *Our Own Years: What Women over 35 Should Know About Themselves* (1979).

GEORGE B. LEONARD (August 9, 1923–) Born George Burr Leonard Jr. in Macon, Georgia. Educated at University of North Carolina. Served as combat pilot in U.S. Army Air Forces in South Pacific during World War II, and as intelligence officer during Korean War. Joined staff of *Look* magazine in 1953, reporting on education, foreign affairs, and civil rights movement. Left *Look* in 1970; worked as freelance writer and contributing editor for *Esquire*. Currently co-owner of Aikido of Tamalpais dojo in Mill Valley, California; serves as president of the Esalen Institute. His books include *The Decline of the American Male* (1958, with William Atwood and J. Robert Moskin), *Shoulder the Sky* (novel, 1959), *Education and Ecstasy* (1968), *The Man and Woman Thing, and Other Provocations* (1970), *The Transformation: A Guide to the Inevitable Changes in Humankind* (1972), *The Ultimate Athlete* (1975), *The Silent Pulse* (1978), *The End of Sex: Erotic Love After the Sexual Revolution* (1983), *Walking on the Edge of the World* (1988, memoir), *Mastery: The Keys to Long-Term Success and Fulfillment* (1992), *The Life We Are Given: A Long Term Program for Realizing the Potential of Body, Mind, Heart, and Soul* (1995, with Michael Murphy; program currently subject of studies at Stanford University Medical School), and *The Way of Aikido: Life Lessons from an American Sensei* (1999).

RICHARD LEVINE (June 19, 1942–) Born Richard Michael Levine in Brooklyn, New York. Graduated from Wesleyan University in 1963; later did graduate work in Slavic languages at Columbia and spent a year (1967–68) in Warsaw. Worked as associate editor of *New Leader* (1969–70), associate editor of *Newsweek*, senior editor of *Saturday Review* (1972–73), and as a freelance journalist, publishing in magazines including *Harper's*, *New York Times Magazine*, *Playboy*, *Rolling Stone*, and *Mother Jones*. Taught journalism at University of California–Berkeley; worked as media columnist for *New Times* and *Esquire*. Currently lives in Berkeley, California. Author of *Bad Blood: A Family Murder in Marin County* (1982).

LOUIS E. LOMAX (August 16, 1922–July 30, 1970) Born in Valdosta, Georgia. Educated at Paine College (B.A., 1942), American University (M.A., 1944), and Yale (Ph.D., 1947). Taught philosophy briefly at Georgia State College in Savannah. Worked as a newspaper reporter for Baltimore *Afro-*

American and *Chicago American*, until 1958; later a freelance magazine journalist and author of books including *The Reluctant African* (1960), *The Negro Revolt* (1962), *When the Word Is Given: A Report on Elijah Muhammad, Malcolm X, and the Black Muslim World* (1963), *Thailand: The War That Is, The War That Will Be* (1967), and *To Kill a Black Man* (1968). In 1959, with Mike Wallace, interviewed Malcolm X for documentary on Nation of Islam, *The Hate That Hate Produced*. From 1964 to 1968 hosted twice-weekly Los Angeles television show on KTTV; lectured widely on college campuses. Died in automobile accident near Santa Rosa, New Mexico.

JON LOWELL (July 15, 1938–   ) Born in Chicago. Graduated from Michigan State University in 1960. Worked as reporter for Michigan papers *Three Rivers Daily Commercial* (1960–62), *Muskegon Chronicle* (1962–65), and *Detroit News* (1965–68). Spent thirteen years as Detroit-based correspondent for *Newsweek* (1969–82) covering such stories as the Kent State shootings, the Attica prison riot, Jimmy Hoffa's disappearance, and Appalachian poverty. Coauthor, with Robert Kaiser, of *Great American Dreams: A Portrait of the Way We Are* (1979). From 1982 to 1985 was director of communications for Burroughs Corporation; since 1985 has specialized in coverage of the international auto industry and labor relations for a variety of print and broadcast organizations including *Ward's Auto World*, WXYZ-TV, WJR radio, and *Wired* magazine. Lives in Bloomfield Hills, Michigan.

RICHARD J. MARGOLIS (June 30, 1929–April 22, 1991) Born Richard Jules Margolis in St. Paul, Minnesota; educated at the University of Minnesota (B.A., 1952; M.A., 1953). Edited and published *Brooklyn Heights Press* (1956–60); worked as editorial director of Lerner Newspapers in Chicago (1960–62), and as a freelance writer. Author of a number of books of poetry and fiction for children including *Secrets of a Small Brother* (1984), articles in *Life, The Nation, New Leader*, and other magazines, and books *Something To Build On* (1966), *Homes of the Brave* (1981), and *Risking Old Age in America* (1990). Died in New Haven, Connecticut.

MARTIN MAYER (January 14, 1928–   ) Born in New York City; graduated from Harvard in 1947, after which he worked as a reporter for *New York Journal of Commerce*, associate editor of *Labor and Nation*, editor of *Real Detective* magazine, and at Hillman Books (1947–51). From 1951 to 1954 served as associate editor at *Esquire*. Since 1954 has published widely as freelance writer, and written many books including novels *The Experts* (1955) and *A Voice That Fills the House* (1959), and nonfiction *Wall Street: Men and Money* (1955), *Hi-Fi* (1956), *Madison Avenue, USA* (1958), *The Schools* (1961), *Where, When, and Why* (1963), *Emory Buckner* (1968), *All You Know Is Facts* (1969), *The Teacher's Strike: New York, 1968* (1969), *About Television* (1972), *The Bankers* (1974), *Today and Tomorrow in America* (1976), *The Builders: Houses, People, Neighborhoods, Governments, Money* (1978), *Trigger Points* (1979), *The Fate of the Dollar* (1980), *The Diplomats* (1983), *The Money*

Bazaars: Understanding the Banking Revolution Around Us (1984), *Grandissimo Pavarotti* (1986), *Markets: Who Plays, Who Risks, Who Gains, Who Loses* (1988), *The Greatest Bank Robbery Ever: The Collapse of the Savings and Loan Industry* (1990), *Whatever Happened to Madison Avenue?: Advertising in the '90s* (1991), *Stealing the Market* (1992), *Nightmare on Wall Street: Salomon Brothers and the Corruption of the Marketplace* (1993), *Making News* (1993), and *The Fed: The Inside Story of How the World's Most Powerful Financial Institution Drives the Markets* (2001).

AUGUST MEIER (April 30, 1923–   ) Born in New York City; raised in Newark, New Jersey. Graduated from Oberlin College in 1945; later, received Ph.D. from Columbia (1957). Taught history at Tougaloo (1945–49), Fisk (1953–56), Morgan State (1957–64), and Roosevelt University (1964–67). Served as secretary of Newark branch of NAACP (1951–52, 1956–57) and as adviser to SNCC in Baltimore from 1960 to 1964. Taught in history department, Kent State University, from 1967 until his retirement in 1993, as professor beginning in 1969. Editor of many books in the field of African-American studies, and author of *Negro Thought in America: Racial Ideologies in the Age of Booker T. Washington* (1963), *From Plantation to Ghetto: An Interpretive History of American Negroes* (1966, with Elliot Rudwick), *Time of Trial, Time of Hope: The Negro in America, 1919–1941* (1966, with Milton Meltzer), *CORE: A Study in the Civil Rights Movement, 1942–1968* (1973, with Elliot Rudwick), *Along the Color Line* (1976, with Elliot Rudwick), *Black Detroit and the Rise of the U.A.W.* (1979, with Elliot Rudwick), and a collection of essays, *A White Scholar and the Black Community, 1945–65* (1992).

JAMES H. MEREDITH (June 25, 1933–   ) Born James Howard Meredith in Kosciusko, Mississippi. Finished high school in St. Petersburg, Florida, where he lived with an aunt and uncle. Served in the U.S. Air Force from 1951 to 1960, becoming a sergeant; took extension courses while in the service. Attended Jackson State College from 1960 to 1962. Submitted application to University of Mississippi in January 1961; won legal battle over admission in June 1962 and graduated in August of the next year, first African-American to do so. Studied economics at University of Ibadan, Nigeria (1964–65); entered law school at Columbia University. In June 1966, on "March Against Fear" from Memphis, Tennessee, to Jackson, Mississippi, was victim of assassination attempt. In 1967 ran unsuccessfully for Congress in special election in New York City against Adam Clayton Powell Jr.; earned Columbia J.D. degree in 1968. Moved back to Jackson, Mississippi, in 1971; started several businesses and Reunification Under God Church, and lectured widely. Ran unsuccessfully in Republican primary in Mississippi, for congressional seat in 1972, and for a number of other public offices. Taught Afro-American Studies at University of Cincinnati (1984–85). In 1989 worked on staff of Senator Jesse Helms; in 1991 founded Meredith Publishing in Jackson. Author of *Three Years in Mississippi* (1966) and *Mississippi: A Volume of Eleven Books* (1994).

GILBERT MOORE (March 25, 1936–) Born Gilbert D. Moore in New York City; raised in Harlem and Jamaica, West Indies. Majored in English literature and journalism at City College (1954–60). Served in the U.S. Army (1960–62) at Fort Dix, New Jersey, and Kaiserslautern, Germany. Worked as a reporter for *Time* and as an assistant editor for *Life* and Time-Life Books. Taught English composition at Livingston College, Rutgers University, and writing in broadcast journalism at the Community Film Workshop Center in New York. Was editor of Community News Service in Harlem, local wire service funded by the Ford Foundation; contributed articles to *Time*, *Life*, *Newsweek*, *New York*, *Ms.*, *Essence*, and *Change*. Later worked as reporter, editor, and community organizer in field of historic preservation; founded Sugar Hill Historical Society. Currently completing a novel, *The Flight of the Black Swan*. Author of *A Special Rage* (1971).

WILLIE MORRIS (November 29, 1934–August 2, 1999) Born in Jackson, Mississippi. Educated at the University of Texas, graduating in 1956 with a Rhodes scholarship to New College, Oxford (M.A., 1960). Worked for the *Texas Observer* in Austin as associate editor and eventually editor-in-chief (1960–62), and then at *Harper's* magazine (1963–71), as editor-in-chief beginning in 1967. Author of novels *The Last of the Southern Girls* (1973) and *Taps* (published posthumously, 2002); a collection of stories, *After All, It's Only a Game* (1992); memoirs *North Toward Home* (1967), *James Jones: A Friendship* (1978), *New York Days* (1993), *My Dog Skip* (1995), and *My Cat Spit McGee* (1999); children's books *Good Old Boy* (1971) and *Good Old Boy and the Witch of Yazoo* (1989); essay collections *Terrains of the Heart* (1981) and *Always Stand in Against the Curve* (1983); and nonfiction *The South Today: 100 Years After Appomattox* (1965), *Yazoo: Integration in a Deep Southern Town* (1971), *The Courting of Marcus Dupree* (1983), and *The Ghosts of Medgar Evers* (1998).

MARLENE NADLE Born in Buffalo, New York. Graduated from the University of Buffalo in 1963 and did graduate work in English at Columbia University. Went to Africa to participate in an American Friends Service Committee student project. Began journalism career at *Village Voice* in 1963. Worked as a reporter for *Newark News* until the mid-1970s while continuing to write for *Voice*. Spent 1968 and 1969 in Latin America as reporter for *Voice* and *Ramparts*; was Senior Research Fellow for Council on Hemispheric Affairs. Since the 1980s has reported from Asia and Eastern Europe, publishing articles in *New York Times*, *Los Angeles Times*, *Boston Globe*, *Chicago Tribune*, and elsewhere; interviewed Vaclav Havel, Margaret Atwood, and others. Serves as associate of East and Central Europe Program at New School University. Lives in New York City.

JACK NELSON (October 11, 1929–) Born John Howard Jack Nelson in Talladega, Alabama. After high school worked as reporter for *Biloxi Daily Herald* (1947–51), then as reporter for *Atlanta Constitution* (1952–65); also served in the army (1951–52), and studied economics at Georgia State College (1953–57). Attended Harvard on Nieman fellowship, 1961–62. Joined staff of *Los Angeles Times* in 1965 as Southern bureau chief. Moved to Washington bureau in 1970, becoming bureau chief in 1975 and chief Washington correspondent in 1996. Won Pulitzer Prize for local deadline reporting, 1971. Author of *The Censors and the Schools* (1963, with Gene Roberts Jr.), *The Orangeburg Massacre* (1970, with Jack Bass), *The FBI and the Berrigans* (1972, with R. J. Ostrow), *Captive Voices* (1974), *Terror in the Night* (1993).

DAVID NEVIN (May 30, 1927–) Born in Washington, D.C. Served in U.S. Navy, Pacific theater (1944–46), and as a chief electrician in U.S. Merchant Marine. Attended Louisiana State (1946–47, 1949–50) and Texas Technological College (1948–49). Began career in journalism working as reporter on Texas dailies *Brownsville Herald* (1950–52), *Dallas Times Herald* (1952–54), and *San Antonio Light* (1954–60). Beginning in 1960 worked for *Life* magazine for ten years, afterward writing several books in Time-Life series. Author of *The Texans* (1968), *Muskie of Maine* (1972), *The Soldiers* (1973), *The Expressmen* (1973), *The Schools That Fear Built: Segregationist Academies in the South* (1976, with Robert E. Bills), *The American Touch in Micronesia* (1977), *The Mexican War* (1978), *The Pathfinders* (1980), *Architects of Air Power* (1981), *The Road to Shiloh* (1983), *Sherman's March* (1986), and four volumes in "American Story" series of historical novels, *Dream West* (1984), *1812* (1996), *Eagle's Cry* (2000), and *Treason* (2001).

GORDON PARKS (November 30, 1912–) Born in Fort Scott, Kansas. Attended high school in St. Paul, Minnesota. Earned living as busboy, bordello pianist, and waiter; worked as freelance fashion and society photographer in Minneapolis and Chicago (1937–42). Apprenticed as photographer at Farm Security Administration in Washington, D.C. (1942–43); photographed African-American 332nd Fighter Group for Office of War Information (1944). Worked as corporate photographer for Standard Oil Company in New Jersey (1945–48); also freelanced for *Vogue* and *Glamour*. Photo-essay on Harlem gang life led to position at *Life* magazine in 1948; remained on staff of magazine until 1972, working as reporter and photojournalist. Served as editorial director of *Essence* magazine (1970–73). Produced documentary films including *Diary of a Harlem Family* (1968); wrote, produced, and directed *The Learning Tree* (1969), and directed *Shaft* (1971), *Shaft's Big Score* (1972), *The Super Cops* (1974), *Leadbelly* (1976), *Solomon Northrup's Odysssey* (1984), and *Moments Without Proper Names* (1986). Author of technical books *Flash Photography* (1947) and *Camera Portraits: The Techniques and Principles of Documentary Portraiture* (1948); novels *The Learning Tree* (1963) and *Shannon* (1981); memoirs *A Choice of Weapons* (1968), *To Smile in Autumn* (1979), and *Voices in the Mirror* (1990); photo-illustrated books of poetry *A Poet and His Camera* (1968), *Whispers of Intimate Things* (1971), *In Love* (1971), *Moments Without Proper Names* (1975), and *Glimpses Toward In-*

finity (1996); and an essay collection, *Born Black* (1971). Lives in New York City.

ROY REED (February 14, 1930–) Born in Hot Springs, Arkansas. Educated at University of Missouri School of Journalism. Began journalism career at Joplin, Missouri, *Globe*. From 1956 to 1964 worked as reporter for *Arkansas Gazette*; attended Harvard as Nieman fellow (1963–64). Joined staff of *New York Times* in 1965, reporting on civil rights movement; subsequently reported for the *Times* from Washington, as New Orleans-based national correspondent, and from London (1976–78). Taught journalism at University of Arkansas in Fayetteville (1979–95) Currently lives in Hogeye, Arkansas. Author of *Looking for Hogeye* (1986) and *Faubus: The Life and Times of an American Prodigal* (1997).

ROBERT RICHARDSON (c. 1941–December 22, 2000) Born in Birmingham, Alabama. Family moved to Los Angeles when he was a child. Served in U.S. Army. Joined staff of *Los Angeles Times* in 1964, working as classified advertising salesman. In August 1965, hearing of violence in Watts, volunteered services as reporter (was the paper's only African-American employee covering the riots). Shared 1966 Pulitzer Prize for local reporting. Hired as reporter trainee, was dismissed a year later in wake of misdemeanor charge, subsequently dropped. Later worked for Los Angeles radio and television stations; suffered from alcoholism but gave up drinking eight years before his death. *Heat Wave*, a movie based on his experiences during the Watts riot, aired on Turner Network cable television in 1990. Died in West Los Angeles.

NAN ROBERTSON (July 11, 1926–) Born in Chicago. Graduated from Northwestern in 1948, after which she traveled to Europe, working as a reporter for *Stars & Stripes* in Germany (1948–49), as a fashion publicist in Paris (1950), and in Germany as a correspondent for *Milwaukee Journal* (1951–53) and feature writer and columnist for New York *Herald-Tribune* (1952–53); also reported for London *American Daily* (1953–54). Joined staff of *New York Times* on return to the U.S. in 1955, serving as reporter, feature writer, and correspondent in Washington and Paris; won 1983 Pulitzer Prize for article "Toxic Shock," based on her own nearly fatal attack of toxic shock syndrome. Retired from *Times* in 1988; taught journalism at University of Maryland. Author of *Getting Better: Inside Alcoholics Anonymous* (1988), and *The Girls in the Balcony: Women, Men, and The New York Times* (1992, a history of *Times* women and their 1974 gender-discrimination lawsuit).

NORA SAYRE (September 20, 1932–August 8, 2001) Born in Bermuda. Graduated from Radcliffe College in 1954. Worked as New York correspondent for the London *New Statesman* (1965–70), as *New York Times* film critic (1973–75), and as a freelance writer. Beginning in 1981 taught in the writing program at Columbia University; lectured in a number of writing workshops. Author of *Sixties Going on Seventies* (essays, 1973), *Running Time: Films of the*

Cold War (1982), *Previous Convictions: A Journey Through the 1950s* (history and memoir, 1995), and *On the Wing: A Young American Abroad* (2001). Died in New York City.

CAROL SCHMIDT (September 10, 1942–) Born Carolyne L. Schmidt in Dearborn, Michigan. Edited student newspaper at Marygrove College, Detroit, from which she graduated in 1964; was journalism research fellow at University of North Carolina–Chapel Hill (1964–65). Worked as reporter and editor at African-American newspaper *Michigan Chronicle* (1965–68), covering civil rights and other political events; later worked for *Macomb Daily* in suburban Detroit (1969–70). Moved to Los Angeles in 1970, where she was writer and editor for Brentwood Publishing (1970–78), and communications director of Harbor-UCLA Medical Center (1978–84). Contributed articles and columns to *Los Angeles Lesbian News, California NOW Times*, and other lesbian-feminist publications; named outstanding lesbian journalist of 1983 by National Gay and Lesbian Press Association. Co-founded Los Angeles organization White Women Against Racism (1981–84). Author of mystery novels *Silverlake Heat* (1993), *Sweet Cherry Wine* (1994), and *Cabin Fever* (1995). Lives in San Miguel de Allende, Guanajuato, Mexico.

CHARLES M. SHERROD (January 2, 1937–) Born in Petersburg, Virginia. Educated at Virginia Union University (B.A., 1958, B.D., 1961) and later at Union Theological Seminary in New York, receiving a master's in sacred theology in 1967. From 1961 to 1967 was SNCC field secretary in Albany, Georgia; also directed the Southwest Georgia Project for Community Education (1961–87) and New Communities, Inc., a cooperative farming project, from 1969 to 1985. Served on Albany City Commission from 1976 to 1990; in 1996 ran unsuccessfully for Georgia state senate. Currently works as chaplain at Georgia State Prison, Homerville, Georgia.

CLAUDE SITTON (December 4, 1925–) Born Claude Fox Sitton in Atlanta, Georgia. Served in U.S. Navy in the Pacific, 1943–46. Graduated from Emory University in 1949. After college worked as a wire service reporter, first for International News Service (1949–50), and then United Press (1950–55). After two years as U.S. Information Officer in Accra, Ghana (1955–57), joined *New York Times* staff as chief Southern correspondent; reported widely on civil rights movement (1958–64). From 1964 to 1968 was *New York Times* national news director. Became editorial director of Raleigh *News and Observer* and *Raleigh Times* in 1968; also served as editor of *News and Observer* and vice-president of News and Observer publishing company from 1970 until his retirement in 1990. Taught at Emory University from 1991 to 1994, and was a member of Board of Counselors of Emory's Oxford College (1993–2001). Won Pulitzer Prize for commentary (1983), George Polk career award (1991), and John Chancellor Award for excellence in journalism (2000). Lives in Oxford, Georgia.

SOL STERN (c. 1937–) Born in Tel Aviv; family moved to New York City when he was three years old. Educated at Stuyvesant High School, City College, University of Iowa, and University of California–Berkeley. Worked as editor and staff writer for *Ramparts* (1966–72) and as a freelance writer, publishing in *New York Times Magazine, New Republic, Village Voice,* and elsewhere. From 1985 to 1994 served in the office of the city council president in New York as director of issues, press secretary, and senior policy adviser; also served as executive director of New York State Commission on juvenile justice reform (1994). Currently lives New York City, where he writes about education reform for New York *Daily News, New York Post, Investor's Business Daily* and other publications; since 1997 has been a contributing editor of *City Journal.*

EKWUEME MICHAEL THELWELL (July 25, 1939–) Born in Ulster Spring, Jamaica; moved to U.S. in 1959. Attended Jamaica College and worked as public relations assistant for Jamaica Industrial Development Corp. (1958–59). Later educated at Howard University (B.A., 1964), where he edited the student newspaper, and University of Massachusetts at Amherst (M.F.A., 1969). Beginning in 1963 worked as director of the Washington, D.C., offices of SNCC, recruiting volunteers for Freedom Summer; also worked in Washington for the Mississippi Freedom Democratic Party (1964–65), running congressional challenge campaign. Since 1969 has been professor in the Afro-American Studies Department, University of Massachusetts at Amherst (served as founding chairman, 1970–75). Served as senior adviser on television series *Eyes on the Prize* (part 2). Currently editing the political autobiography of the late Kwame Ture (Stokely Carmichael). Author of two screenplays (*Washington Incident,* 1972; *Girl Beneath the Lion,* 1978, with Paul Carter Harrison); stories and articles in *Black Scholar, Negro Digest, Partisan Review, Village Voice,* and other publications; a novel (*The Harder They Come,* 1980); and a collection of essays (*Duties, Pleasures, and Conflicts,* 1987).

HUNTER S. THOMPSON (July 18, 1939–) Born Hunter Stockton Thompson in Louisville, Kentucky. Studied journalism at Columbia University. Served with the U.S. Air Force from 1956 to 1958; wrote for base magazine. Worked as Caribbean correspondent for *Time* and New York *Herald-Tribune* (1959–60), *National Observer* South American correspondent (1961–63), West Coast correspondent for *The Nation* (1964–66), columnist for *Ramparts* (1967–68) and *Scanlan's Monthly* (1969–70), national affairs editor for *Rolling Stone* (1970–84), *High Times* global correspondent (1977–82), and *San Francisco Examiner* media critic (1985–90). Author of books including *Hell's Angels: A Strange and Terrible Saga* (1966), *Fear and Loathing in Las Vegas: A Savage Journey to the Heart of the American Dream* (1972), *Fear and Loathing on the Campaign Trail '72* (1973), *The Great Shark Hunt: Strange Tales from a Strange Time* (1979), *The Curse of Lono* (1983), *Generation of Swine: Tales of Shame and Degradation in the '80s* (1988), *Songs of the*

Doomed: More Notes on the Death of the American Dream (1990), *Better Than Sex: Confessions of a Campaign Junkie* (1993), *The Proud Highway: Saga of a Desperate Southern Gentleman* (1997), *The Rum Diary* (1998), and *Screwjack and Other Stories* (2000).

CALVIN TRILLIN (December 5, 1935–   ) Born in Kansas City, Missouri. Graduated from Yale in 1957. Worked as reporter for *Time* from 1960 to 1963, after which he became a *New Yorker* staff writer (1963–   ). Also wrote columns for *The Nation* (1978–85), a syndicated column (1986–95), and columns for *Time* (1996–   ). His books include *An Education in Georgia* (1964), *Barnett Frummer Is an Unbloomed Flower* (1969), *U.S. Journal* (1971), *American Fried* (1974), *Runestruck* (1977), *Alice, Let's Eat* (1978), *Floater* (1980), *Uncivil Liberties* (1982), *Third Helpings* (1983), *Killings* (1984), *With All Disrespect* (1985), *If You Can't Say Something Nice* (1987), *Travels with Alice* (1989), *Enough's Enough* (1990), *American Stories* (1991), *Remembering Denny* (1993), *Deadline Poet* (1994), *Too Soon To Tell* (1995), *Messages from My Father* (1996), *Family Man* (1998), and *Tepper Isn't Going Out* (2001).

STEVE VAN EVERA (November 10, 1948–   ) Born in Duluth, Minnesota. During 1968 reported from Mississippi for *Southern Courier*, Alabama-based newspaper begun by civil rights workers. Graduated from Harvard in 1970 and received doctorate from University of California–Berkeley in 1984; taught at University of California–Davis, Tufts, and Princeton while in graduate school. Served as managing editor of *International Security* (1984–87). Author of articles in academic and policy journals, including studies on black politics in *New South* (1971) and *American Political Science Review* (1973), and two books: *Guide to Methods for Students of Political Science* (1997) and *Causes of War: Power and the Roots of Conflict* (1999). Currently associate professor of political science at Massachusetts Institute of Technology, specializing in international affairs and security studies.

ALICE WALKER (February 9, 1944–   ) Born Alice Malsenior Walker in Eatonton, Georgia. Graduated from Sarah Lawrence in 1966, working after college as a writer. Served as writer-in-residence at Jackson State College (1968–69) and Tougaloo (1970–71), and as lecturer in literature at Wellesley and University of Massachusetts–Boston (1972–73). Her books include *Once* (1968), *The Third Life of Grange Copeland* (1970), *Five Poems* (1972), *Revolutionary Petunias and Other Poems* (1973), *In Love and Trouble* (1973), *Langston Hughes: American Poet* (1973), *Meridian* (1976), *Goodnight, Willie Lee, I'll See You in the Morning* (1979), *You Can't Keep a Good Woman Down* (1981), *The Color Purple* (1982, winner of the Pulitzer Prize for fiction and the American Book Award), *In Search of Our Mothers' Gardens* (1983), *Horses Make a Landscape Look More Beautiful* (1984), *To Hell with Dying* (1988), *Living by the Word: Selected Writings, 1973–1987* (1988), *The Temple of My Familiar* (1989), *Her Finding the Green Stone* (1991), *Possessing the Secret of Joy* (1992), *Warrior Marks* (1993, with Pratibha Parmar), *Everyday Use* (1994),

Everything We Love Can Be Saved: A Writer's Activism (1997), *The Same River Twice* (1997), *By the Light of My Father's Smile* (1998), and *The Way Forward Is with a Broken Heart* (2001).

PAT WATTERS   (February 28, 1927–August 3, 1999)   Born Walter Patterson Watters in Spartanburg, South Carolina. Educated at Emory (B.A., 1951) and University of Iowa (M.A., 1953). After college worked on staff of *Atlanta Journal* as reporter (1952–59), city editor (1959–61), and columnist (1961–63); served as director of information for the Southern Regional Council (1963–75). Wrote articles for *Atlanta, Dissent, The Nation, New South,* and *New York Times Magazine,* among other publications. Taught journalism at the University of Louisiana–Lafayette (1991–93). His books include *Climbing Jacob's Ladder: The Arrival of Negroes in Southern Politics* (1967, with Reese Cleghorn), *The South and the Nation* (1970), *Down to Now: Reflections on the Southern Civil Rights Movement* (1971), *The Angry Middle-Aged Man* (1976), and *Coca-Cola: An Illustrated History* (1978). Died in Abbeville, Louisiana.

SANDRA A. WEST   Moved to Detroit in 1954; reported on Detroit riots for United Press International.

JAMES D. WILLIAMS   (November 5, 1926–October 24, 1997)   Born James DeBois Williams Jr. in Baltimore. Graduated from Temple University in 1948. Began career in journalism working as reporter for *Philadelphia Tribune* (1950–51) and city editor for *The Carolinian* (1951–53). Joined staff of *Afro-American* in 1953, serving as Baltimore city editor (1953–57), managing editor (1959–64), and Washington, D.C., editor and manager (1964–67). Was also visiting professor at Morgan State College (1961–63) and a writer and editor for *The Negro Almanac* (1967). Worked as director of public affairs for community action and deputy director in the Office of Economic Opportunity (1967–69) and as director of the office of information and publications with the U.S. Commission on Civil Rights (1970–72). From 1972 to 1986 served as director of communications for the National Urban League, and from 1986 to 1994 as national public relations director for the NAACP. Returned to *Afro-American* (1994–96) as editor-in-chief. Died in Baltimore.

GARRY WILLS   (May 22, 1934–   )   Born in Atlanta. Educated at St. Louis University (B.A., 1957), Xavier University, Cincinnati (M.A., 1958), and Yale (Ph.D., 1961). Was fellow at Harvard Center for Hellenic Studies (1961–62), associate professor of classics at Johns Hopkins (1962–67, adjunct 1968–80); Henry Luce professor of American culture and Public Policy at Northwestern (1980–88, adjunct 1988–   ). Since 1970 has written a syndicated column for Universal Press Syndicate. Author of articles in national magazines and books including *Chesterton* (1961), *Politics and Catholic Freedom* (1964), *Roman Culture* (1966), *Jack Ruby* (1967), *The Second Civil War* (1968), *Nixon Agonistes: The Crisis of the Self-Made Man* (1970), *Bare Ruined Choirs: Doubt,*

Prophecy, and Radical Religion (1972), *Inventing America* (1978), *At Button's* (thriller, 1979), *Confessions of a Conservative* (1979), *Explaining America* (1980), *The Kennedy Imprisonment: A Meditation on Power* (1982), *Lead Time* (1983), *Cincinnatus* (1984), *Reagan's America: Innocents at Home* (1987), *Under God: Religion and American Politics* (1990), *Lincoln at Gettysburg* (1992, winner of Pulitzer Prize for nonfiction), *Certain Trumpets: The Call of Leaders* (1994), *Witches and Jesuits: Shakespeare's Macbeth* (1994), *John Wayne's America: The Politics of Celebrity* (1997), *Saint Augustine* (1999), *A Necessary Evil: A History of American Distrust of Government* (1999), *Venice: Lion City* (2001), *Papal Sin: Structures of Deceit* (2001), and *Why I Am a Catholic* (2002).

DALE WITTNER (March 9, 1940–) Born in Evanston, Illinois; grew up in suburbs of Chicago and New York. Attended Duke University. Worked as copyboy in *New York Times* Sunday department. Moved to Arizona in 1961, covering police beat and courthouse for *Tucson Daily Citizen*; also wrote detective fiction under a pseudonyms and worked as a stringer for Time-Life. Hired by *Life* in 1967; reported on Newark riots, the Vietnam War, rural America, and the criminal justice system. Since 1972, when *Life* first ceased publication, has worked as a freelance magazine and corporate photographer; was contributing photographer to *People* magazine for twenty years. Lives in Seattle.

TOM WICKER (June 18, 1926–) Born Thomas Grey Wicker in Hamlet, North Carolina. Graduated from University of North Carolina in 1948 with a degree in journalism. After college edited two small North Carolina newspapers, Aberdeen *Sandhill Citizen* (1949) and Lumberton *Robesonian* (1949–50); also worked as director of the Southern Pines, North Carolina, Chamber of Commerce (1948–49) and as public information director for the North Carolina Board of Public Welfare (1950–51). Joined staff of *Winston-Salem Journal* in 1951, serving as copyeditor (1951–52) and, after two years with the U.S. Navy, as sports editor (1954–55), Sunday feature editor (1955–56), Washington correspondent (1957), and editorial writer and city hall correspondent (1958–59). Attended Harvard as Nieman fellow, 1957–58. Moved to the *Nashville Tennesseean* as associate editor (1959–60), and then to *New York Times*, working at the Washington bureau (1960–71, bureau chief 1964–68), as associate editor (1968–85), and columnist (1966–91). Author of three novels published under pseudonym Paul Connolly (*Get Out of Town*, 1951; *Tears Are for Angels*, 1952; *So Fair, So Evil*, 1955), and novels under his own name *The Kingpin* (1953), *The Devil Must* (1957), *The Judgment* (1961), *Facing the Lions* (1973), *Unto This Hour* (1984), *Donovan's Wife* (1992), and *Easter Lilly* (1998). His nonfiction works include *Kennedy Without Tears* (1964), *JFK and LBJ: The Influence of Personality upon Politics* (1968), *A Time To Die* (1975), *On Press* (1978), *One of Us: Richard Nixon and the American Dream* (1992), and *Tragic Failure: Racial Integration in America* (1996).

CHRISTOPHER S. WREN (February 22, 1936–) Born Christopher Sale Wren in Los Angeles; graduated from Dartmouth in 1957. After service in U.S. Army, obtained master's degree in journalism from Columbia University (1961). Began career as reporter for *Look*, covering civil rights movement and Vietnam War; was senior editor and Washington editor for *Look* until it ceased publication in 1971. Reported on national affairs for *Newsweek*. Joined *New York Times* staff in 1973 as metropolitan reporter; later worked as Moscow correspondent and bureau chief (1973–77), as bureau chief in Cairo (1977–81), Beijing (1981–84), Ottawa (1984–87), and Johannesburg (1988–92), as assistant financial desk editor (1994–95), and as United Nations correspondent (1995–) and foreign correspondent covering drug policy. Humorous memoir of overseas assignments published in 2000 as *The Cat Who Covered the World: The Adventures of Henrietta and Her Foreign Correspondent*. Other books include *Quotations from Chairman LBJ* (with Jack Shepherd, 1968), *The Almanack of Poor Richard Nixon* (with Jack Shepherd, 1968), *The Super Summer of Jamie McBride* (with Jack Shepherd, 1971), *Winners Got Scars Too: The Life and Legends of Johnny Cash* (1971), *The End of the Line: The Failure of Communism in the Soviet Union and China* (1990) and *Hacks* (1996). Lives in New York City.

TOM WOLFE (March 2, 1931–) Born Thomas Kennerly Wolfe Jr. in Richmond, Virginia; educated at Washington and Lee University and Yale, receiving a Ph.D. in American Studies in 1957. Began career in journalism as reporter for Springfield, Massachusetts, *Union* (1956–59); worked subsequently as *Washington Post* reporter and Latin American correspondent (1959–62), New York *Herald-Tribune* city reporter (1962–66), contributing editor for *New York* (1968–76) and *Esquire* magazines (1977–), and *Harper's* contributing artist (1978–81). His books include *The Kandy-Kolored Tangerine-Flake Streamline Baby* (1965), *The Electric Kool-Aid Acid Test* (1968), *The Pump House Gang* (1968), *Radical Chic & Mau-Mauing the Flak Catchers* (1970), *The Painted Word* (1975), *Mauve Gloves & Madmen, Clutter & Vine* (1976), *The Right Stuff* (1979), *In Our Time* (1980), *From Bauhaus to Our House* (1981), *The Purple Decades: A Reader* (1982), *The Bonfire of the Vanities* (1987), *A Man in Full* (1998), and *Hooking Up* (2000).

HOWARD ZINN (August 24, 1922–) Born in Brooklyn, New York. Served as bombardier during World War II. Received Ph.D. in history at Columbia in 1958 and was postdoctoral fellow in East Asian studies at Harvard. Appointed chairman of history department at Spelman College beginning in 1956; worked alongside SNCC activists in Alabama, Georgia, and Mississippi. Published articles about civil rights movement in *The Nation*, *Harper's*, *Freedomways*, and other magazines, and books *The Southern Mystique* (1964) and *SNCC: The New Abolitionists* (1964). From 1964 to 1988 was professor of history at Boston University. Flew to Hanoi with Father Daniel Berrigan during Vietnam War; wrote *Vietnam: The Logic of Withdrawal* (1967) and *Dis-*

obedience and Democracy: Nine Fallacies on Law and Order (1968), and later edited *The Pentagon Papers: Critical Essays* with Noam Chomsky. Also author of *La Guardia in Congress* (1959), *The Politics of History* (1970), *Post-War America* (1973), *A People's History of the United States* (1980), *Declarations of Independence: Cross-Examining American Ideology* (1990), *Failure to Quit: Reflections of an Optimistic Historian* (1993), and *The Zinn Reader: Writings on Disobedience and Democracy* (1997). An autobiography, *You Can't Be Neutral on a Moving Train: A Personal History of Our Times*, appeared in 1994.

Note on the Texts

This volume collects newspaper reports, magazine articles, and book excerpts first published between 1963 and 1973 and dealing with events connected with the African-American civil rights movement in the period between August 1963 and August 1973. Excerpts from books are taken from first editions; in some cases, the excerpts include material that had earlier appeared in periodicals in different form. The pieces included have been arranged in the approximate chronological order of the latest events they refer to or describe.

The following is a list of sources of the texts included in this volume, listed alphabetically by author.

Renata Adler. Letter from Selma: *The New Yorker*, April 10, 1965. Copyright © 1965 by Renata Adler. Reprinted by permission of Renata Adler.

Robert Analavage. Which Way in Grenada?: *The Southern Patriot*, August 1966.

Robert E. Anderson Jr. Welfare in Mississippi: Tradition vs. Title VI: *New South*, Spring 1967. Copyright © 1967 by the Southern Regional Council. Reprinted by permission.

Russell Baker. Capital Is Occupied by a Gentle Army: *The New York Times*, August 29, 1963. Copyright © 1963 by The New York Times Co. Reprinted by permission.

George Barner. We Ain't Taking No More: *New York Amsterdam News*, July 22, 1967. Reprinted by permission of the New York Amsterdam News.

John Beecher. McComb, Mississippi: *Ramparts*, May 1965. Reprinted by permission of Barbara M. Beecher.

Art Berman. Eight Men Slain; Guard Moves In: *Los Angeles Times*, August 14, 1965. Copyright © 1965 by Los Angeles Times Syndicate International. Reprinted by permission.

Hamilton Bims. Deacons for Defense: *Ebony*, September 1965. Copyright © Johnson Publishing Company, Inc. Reprinted by permission.

Ruth Brecher and Edward Brecher. The Military's Limited War Against Segregation: *Harper's*, September 1963. Copyright © 1963 by *Harper's Magazine*. All rights reserved. Reproduced by special permission.

Jimmy Breslin. Changing the South: New York *Herald-Tribune*, March 26, 1965. Copyright © 1965 by The New York Times Co. Reprinted by permission; Breslin on Riot: Death, Laughter, but No Sanity: *The Detroit News*, July 25, 1967. Reprinted by permission of *The Detroit News*.

Earl Caldwell. Martin Luther King Is Slain in Memphis: *The New York Times*, April 5, 1968. Copyright © 1968 by The New York Times Co. Reprinted by permission.

Bob Clark. Nightmare Journey: *Ebony*, October 1967. Copyright © Johnson Publishing Company, Inc. Reprinted by permission.

Robert Coles. Bussing in Boston: *The New Republic*, October 2, 1965. Reprinted by permission of *The New Republic*, © 1965, The New Republic, Inc.

Marc Crawford. The Ominous Malcolm X Exits from the Muslims: *Life*, March 20, 1964. Reprinted by permission of Abby London-Crawford.

Peter de Lissovoy. Gambler's Choice in Georgia: *The Nation*, June 22, 1964; "This Little Light . . .": *The Nation*, December 21, 1964. Reprinted by permission of *The Nation*.

Jerry DeMuth. Tired of Being Sick and Tired: *The Nation*, June 1, 1964. Reprinted by permission of Jerry DeMuth.

Joan Didion. Black Panther: *The Saturday Evening Post*, May 4, 1968. Reprinted with permission of *The Saturday Evening Post*, © 1968 BFL&MS, Inc.

Michael Durham. Ollie McClung's Big Decision: *Life*, October 9, 1964. Reprinted by permission of Michael S. Durham.

Lez Edmond. Harlem Diary: *Ramparts*, October 1964. Copyright © 1964 by Lez Edmond; reprinted by permission. See note 140.38–141.1 in this volume.

Jerry Farber. August, 1965: Jerry Farber, *The Student as Nigger* (North Hollywood: Contact Books, 1969), pp. 159–76. Reprinted by permission of Jerry Farber.

James Farmer. From "A Southern Tale": James Farmer, *Freedom—When?* (New York: Random House, 1965), pp. 3–19. Copyright © 1965 by The Congress of Racial Equality, Inc. Used by permission of Random House, Inc.

Karl Fleming. Birmingham: "My God, You're Not Even Safe in Church": *Newsweek*, September 30, 1963; The South Revisited After a Momentous Decade: *Newsweek*, August 10, 1970. Copyright © 1963, 1970, Newsweek, Inc. All rights reserved. Reprinted by permission.

Bob Fletcher. We're Gonna Rule!: *The Movement*, June 1967. Reprinted by permission of Bob Fletcher.

Marshall Frady. Discovering One Another in a Georgia Town: *Life*, February 12, 1971. Copyright © 1971, 1980 by Marshall Frady. Reprinted by permission of the author.

C. Gerald Fraser. S.N.C.C. in Decline after 8 Years in Lead: *The New York Times*, October 7, 1968. Copyright © 1968 by The New York Times Co. Reprinted by permission.

Paul Good. ". . . It Was Worth the Boy's Dying": *The Washington Post*, March 22, 1965; The Meredith March: *New South*, Summer 1966. Reprinted by permission of the Southern Regional Council. "No Man Can Fill Dr. King's Shoes"—But Abernathy Tries: *The New York Times Magazine*, May 26, 1968.

Jeremiah S. Gutman. Oktibbeha County, Mississippi: Leon Friedman, ed., *Southern Justice* (New York: Pantheon Books, 1965), pp. 80–87. Reprinted by permission of Jeremiah S. Gutman.

David Halberstam. The Second Coming of Martin Luther King: *Harper's*, August 1967. Copyright © 1967 by David Halberstam. Reprinted by permission of David Halberstam.

Elizabeth Hardwick. Selma, Alabama: The Charms of Goodness: *The New York Review of Books*, April 22, 1965. Reprinted with permission from *The New York Review of Books*. Copyright © 1965 NYREV, Inc.

John Herbers. Martin Luther King and 17 Others Jailed Trying To Integrate St. Augustine Restaurant: *The New York Times*, June 12, 1964. Copyright © 1964 by The New York Times Co. Reprinted by permission.

Calvin C. Hernton. And You, Too, Sidney Poitier!: Calvin C. Hernton, *White Papers for White Americans* (Garden City: Doubleday, 1966), pp. 53–70. Copyright © 1966 by Calvin C. Hernton. Used by permission of Doubleday, a division of Random House, Inc.

John Hersey. A Life for a Vote: *The Saturday Evening Post*, September 26, 1964. Reprinted with permission of *The Saturday Evening Post*, © 1964 BFL&MS, Inc.

William Bradford Huie. From *Three Lives for Mississippi*: William Bradford Huie, *Three Lives for Mississippi* (New York: WCC Books, 1965), pp. 193–219. Copyright © 1964, 1965, 1968 by William Bradford Huie. Reprinted by permission of Martha Hunt Huie. Photograph on p. 169 of this volume reprinted by permission of CBS Photo Archives.

Snow James (Stetson Kennedy, pseud.). "Seeing St. Aug." Proves Exciting: *The Pittsburgh Courier*, June 27, 1964. Reprinted by permission of GRM Associates, Inc., agents for *The Pittsburgh Courier*. Copyright © 1964 by *The Pittsburgh Courier*, copyright renewed 1992 by *The New Pittsburgh Courier*.

Haynes Johnson. Selma Revisited: 4 Months After Their "Finest Hour" Rights Forces Are in Disarray: *Washington Star*, July 26, 1965. Copyright © 1965, The Washington Post (Washington Star Collection). Reprinted with permission.

Murray Kempton. Gloria, Gloria: *The New Republic*, November 16, 1963. Reprinted by permission of *The New Republic*, © 1963, The New Republic, Inc.

E. W. Kenworthy. 200,000 March for Civil Rights in Orderly Washington Rally; President Sees Gain for Negro: *The New York Times*, August 29, 1963. Copyright © 1963 by The New York Times Co. Reprinted by permission.

Peter Kihss. Malcolm X Shot to Death at Rally Here: *The New York Times*, February 22, 1965. Copyright © 1965 by The New York Times Co. Reprinted by permission.

Andrew Kopkind. Selma: "Ain't Gonna Let Nobody Turn Me 'Round": *The New Republic*, March 20, 1965. Reprinted by permission of *The New Republic*, © 1965 The New Republic, Inc.

Bob Labaree. Fairfield Never Had a Negro Official—Until Last Month, When It Elected Six: *The Southern Courier*, September 21–22, 1968. Reprinted by permission of Robert Labaree.

Alice Lake. Last Summer in Mississippi: *Redbook*, November 1964.

George B. Leonard. Midnight Plane to Alabama: *The Nation*, May 10, 1965. Reprinted by permission of *The Nation*.

Richard Levine. Jesse Jackson: Heir to Dr. King?: *Harper's*, March 1969. Copyright © 1969 by *Harper's Magazine*. Reproduced by special permission. Lyrics from "I Wish I Knew How It Would Feel To Be Free" in this article copyright © 1964, Duane Music, Inc., and reprinted by permission.

Louis E. Lomax. Georgia Boy Goes Home: *Harper's*, April 1965. Reprinted by permission of Mrs. Louis Lomax.

Jon Lowell. Guerilla War Rips 12th: *The Detroit News*, July 26, 1967. Reprinted by permission of *The Detroit News*.

Richard J. Margolis. The Two Nations at Wesleyan University: *The New York Times Magazine*, January 18, 1970. Reprinted by permission of the Estate of Richard J. Margolis.

Martin Mayer. The Lone Wolf of Civil Rights: *The Saturday Evening Post*, July 11, 1964. Reprinted with permission of *The Saturday Evening Post*, © 1964 BFL&MS, Inc.

August Meier. On the Role of Martin Luther King: *New Politics*, Winter 1965. Copyright © 1992 by August Meier. Reprinted by permission of August Meier.

James H. Meredith. Big Changes Are Coming: *The Saturday Evening Post*, August 13, 1966. Reprinted with permission of *The Saturday Evening Post*, © 1966 BFL&MS, Inc.

Gilbert Moore. From *A Special Rage*: Gilbert Moore, *A Special Rage* (New York: Harper & Row, 1971), pp. 80–87. Copyright © 1971 by Gilbert Moore. Reprinted by permission of the author.

Willie Morris. From *Yazoo: Integration in a Deep-Southern Town:* Willie Morris, *Yazoo: Integration in a Deep-Southern Town* (New York: Harper's Magazine Press, 1971), pp. 28–50. Copyright © 1971 by Willie Morris. Reprinted by permission of Raines & Raines and the heirs of Willie Morris.

Marlene Nadle. The View from the Front of the Bus: *The Village Voice*, September 5, 1963; Malcolm X: The Complexity of a Man in the Jungle: *The Village Voice*, February 25, 1965. Copyright © 1963, 1965 by Marlene Nadle. Reprinted by permission of Marlene Nadle.

Jack Nelson. 2 Veteran Rights Leaders Ousted by SNCC: *The Los Angeles Times*, May 17, 1966. Copyright © 1966 by Los Angeles Times Syndicate International. Reprinted by permission.

David Nevin. A Strange, Tight Little Town, Loath to Admit Complicity: *Life*, December 18, 1964. Reprinted courtesy of David Nevin.

Gordon Parks. I Was a Zombie Then—Like All Muslims, I Was Hypnotized: *Life*, March 5, 1965; Whip of Black Power: *Life*, May 19, 1967. Copyright © 1965, 1967 by Gordon Parks. Reprinted by permission of Gordon Parks.

Roy Reed. Alabama Police Use Gas and Clubs to Rout Negroes: *The New York Times*, March 8, 1965. Copyright © 1965 by The New York Times Co. Reprinted by permission.

Robert Richardson. "Burn, Baby, Burn!": *Los Angeles Times* ("Get Whitey," Scream Blood-Hungry Mobs: August 14, 1965; "Burn, Baby, Burn" Slogan Used as Firebugs Put Area to Torch: August 15, 1965; Childhood Vanishes in Embers During Fearful Curfew Hours: August 16, 1965. Main title supplied for this volume from a phrase within Richardson's August 15 article.)

Nan Robertson. Mississippian Relates Struggle of Negro in Voter Registration: *The New York Times*, August 24, 1964. Copyright © 1964 by The New York Times Co. Reprinted by permission.

Nora Sayre. The Revolutionary People's Constitutional Convention: *Esquire*, January 1971. (Title, from a phrase within the article, supplied for this volume in place of "On Politics," the title of Sayre's regular *Esquire* column.) Copyright © 1996 by Nora Sayre. Reprinted by permission of Rutgers University Press.

Carol Schmidt. The White Community Asks Repeatedly, "Why?": *The Michigan Chronicle*, July 29, 1967. Reprinted by permission of Carol Schmidt.

Charles M. Sherrod. Mississippi at Atlantic City: *Grains of Salt* (Union Theological Seminary), October 12, 1964. Reprinted by permission of Charles M. Sherrod.

Claude Sitton. Birmingham Bomb Kills 4 Negro Girls in Church; Riots Flare; 2 Boys Slain: *The New York Times*, September 16, 1963; 3 in Rights Drive Reported Missing: *The New York Times*, June 22, 1964. Copyright © 1963, 1964 by The New York Times Co. Reprinted by permission.

Sol Stern. The Call of the Black Panthers: *The New York Times Magazine*, August 6, 1967. Reprinted by permission of Sol Stern.

Michael Thelwell. The August 28th March on Washington: Michael Thelwell, *Duties, Pleasures, and Conflicts: Essays in Struggle* (Amherst: University of Massachusetts Press, 1987), pp. 57–72. (Originally published as "Les Meandres de la 'Marche'," *Présence Africaine* [Paris], 1er trimestre 1964). Copyright © 1987 by the University of Massachusetts Press. Reprinted by permission; Fish Are Jumping an' the Cotton Is High: Notes from the Mississippi Delta: *Massachusetts Review*, Spring 1966. Copyright © 1966, The Massachusetts Review, Inc. Reprinted by permission.

Hunter S. Thompson. A Southern City with Northern Problems: *The Reporter*, December 19, 1963. Reprinted by permission of Hunter S. Thompson.

Calvin Trillin. U.S. Letter: Cleveland: *The New Yorker*, October 14, 1967. Copyright © 1967 by Calvin Trillin. Reprinted by permission of Lescher & Lescher, Ltd. All rights reserved.

Steve Van Evera. Marks After the Campaign: *The Southern Courier*, August 10–11, 1968. Reprinted with permission of Stephen W. Van Evera.

Pat Watters. "Keep on A-walking, Children": *New American Review*, January 1969. Reprinted by permission of Glenda Watters.

Alice Walker. Staying Home in Mississippi: *The New York Times Magazine*, August 26, 1973. Copyright © 1973 by Alice Walker. Reprinted by permission of Harcourt, Inc.; collected in Alice Walker, *In Search of Our Mothers' Gardens: Womanist Prose* (New York: Harcourt, Brace, Jovanovich, 1983).

Sandra A. West. Riot!—A Negro Resident's Story: *The Detroit News,* July 24, 1967. Reprinted by permission of *The Detroit News.*

Tom Wicker. Johnson Urges Congress at Joint Session to Pass Law Insuring Negro Vote: *The New York Times,* March 16, 1965. Copyright © 1965 by The New York Times Co. Reprinted by permission.

James D. Williams. First of 4 Birmingham Bomb Victims Is Buried: *The Afro-American* (Baltimore), September 28, 1963. Reprinted by permission of the Afro-American Newspapers Archives and Research Center.

Garry Wills. Martin Luther King Is Still on the Case!: *Esquire,* August 1968. © 1968 by Garry Wills. Reprinted with permission of The Wylie Agency.

Dale Wittner. The Killing of Billy Furr, Caught in the Act of Looting Beer: *Life,* July 28, 1967. Reprinted courtesy Time, Inc.

Tom Wolfe. From *Mau-Mauing the Flak Catchers:* Tom Wolfe, *Radical Chic & Mau-Mauing the Flak Catchers* (New York: Farrar, Straus and Giroux, 1970), pp. 119–42. Copyright © 1970 by Tom Wolfe. Reprinted by permission of Farrar, Straus and Giroux, LLC.

Christopher S. Wren. Personal Terror in Mississippi: *Look,* September 8, 1964. Reprinted by permission of Christopher S. Wren.

Howard Zinn. The Battle-Scarred Youngsters: *The Nation,* October 5, 1963. Reprinted by permission of *The Nation.*

Great care has been taken to trace all owners of copyrighted material included in this book; if any have been inadvertently omitted or overlooked, acknowledgment will gladly be made in future printings.

This volume presents the texts listed here without change except for the correction of typographical errors, but it does not attempt to reproduce features of their typographic design. The following is a list of typographical errors, cited by page and line number: 2.38, betweeen; 4.1, occured; 8.3, crudly; 9.11, truely; 9.23, enought; 11.24, now. Tens of dissolving fast now. ¶ These; 14.17, "We; 15.7, secrettary; 15.21, forums; 16.27, was right. 21.34, Carol; 23.20, The; 24.27, was; 25.1, S unday; 25.4, I; 25.6, to gether; 25.16, Slowly; 28.12, Carol; 30.34, Fred R.; 32.33, Carol; 52.15, which they; 53.25, of; 54.18, If; 60.9, then; 62.39, Dorcester; 108.16–17, Abernaty; 108.22, Davis The; 108.38, segregated. [no closing quote]; 114.18. demontrations; 119.29, now . . ."; 124.16, out"?; 124.32, coalition of patriotic; 125.22, Hoovers'; 139.19, Gravey; 140.39, warfare'; 174.19, violence?"; 180.28, white maids; 181.12, showly; 181.33, courtry; 181.39, committeed; 183.6, t that; 186.2, underprivilaged; 204.6, "they; 278.31, Butter.'; 279.10, bout; 279.29, overcome;; 299.34, Palm's; 302.37, sleep."; 304.12, now."; 304.15, self-respect."; 305.10, contrary, he; 307.22, Eiher; 312.35, assassins."; 315.1, Quiblah; 315.2, Llyasah; 319.28, Attallah; 325.31, witnessed; 340.37, Foreman's; 342.7, Foreman; 349.10, Erwin; 349.24–25, contended; 349.33, appeared in; 351.12, casts; 353.31, Jimme; 363.27, and old; 403.7, wods; 408.33, key,; 413.11, "I'd; 417.9, spontaneiously; 418.3, appraised; 418.11, exhausion; 440.3, Let; 456.39, give; 459.24, irresponsible"; 493.2, than than; 493.20, schocked; 504.28. it They; 511.29, Let's; 516.4,

Analavege; 517.35, Greneda's; 518.5, sub-marine; 536.6 Attempt; 537.9, out," 541.11, 'employable'; 545.20, national; 547.9, Alderman; 548.2, Government.";
549.26, spoted; 550.23, for; 565.15, Alban's; 591.12, estabilshed; 591.16, with an; 592.5, Charle; 597.15, rumaging; 598.12, on blind; 598.17, community,; 598.23, checking 10th; 600.17, exhileration; 607.17, 50–caliber; 608.26, wih; 618.20, 45; 629.20, .30–.30; 646.23, Negros; 648.3, 1965; 649.19, aagin; 659.39, Pharoah; 687.28, programing; 692.11, anethema; 703.3, precision; 756.15, here."; 757.1, gas."; 757.11, time."; 757.23, yet."; 758.3, County."; 758.13, it.";
764.21, commission suffers; 766.20, 50; 766.37, Souht; 768.6, peace-setter; 821.26, they were; 873.21, above; 875.29, or place.

Notes

In the notes below, the reference numbers denote page and line of this volume (the line count includes headings). No note is made for material included in standard desk-reference works. Biblical references are keyed to the King James Version. Footnotes and bracketed editorial notes within the texts were in the originals. For historical background see the Chronology in this volume; for further background and references to other studies, see *Encyclopedia of African-American Civil Rights*, edited by Charles D. Lowery and John F. Marszalek (Westport, Connecticut: Greenwood Press, 1992) and Ralph E. Luker, *Historical Dictionary of the Civil Rights Movement* (Lanham, Maryland: The Scarecrow Press, 1997).

1.30   CORE] Congress of Racial Equality, civil rights organization founded in 1942.

2.33   The Messenger] Elijah (Poole) Muhammad (1897–1975), leader of the Nation of Islam from 1934 to 1975.

3.4–5   Wagner . . . Spellman] Robert F. Wagner (1910–91), mayor of New York, 1954–65; Francis Spellman (1889–1967), Roman Catholic archbishop of New York, 1939–67.

3.27–28   Jim Peck . . . severe beating] Peck was beaten when the bus he was riding on stopped in Anniston, Alabama, on May 14, 1961, and again when it arrived in Birmingham later in the day. His head wounds required 53 stitches.

6.18–19   Freedom Walkers] William Moore, a white postal worker, was found shot to death near Attalla, Alabama, on April 23, 1963, while on a one-man "Freedom Walk" from Tennessee to Alabama. In May 1963 three groups of activists from SNCC (Student Nonviolent Coordinating Committee) and CORE attempted to complete his walk, but they were all arrested by Alabama authorities.

9.8   Lena Horne] African-American singer and actress, born 1917.

10.23   Ossie Davis] African-American actor and political activist, born 1917.

10.25   Josh White] White (1915–69) was an African-American blues and folk singer.

11.1   Dr. Ralph Bunche] Bunche (1904–71) held several high-ranking diplomatic posts at the United Nations from 1947 until 1971. He was the first

African-American to be awarded the Nobel Peace Prize, which he received in 1950 for his role in mediating the cease-fire agreements that ended the 1948–49 Arab-Israeli war.

11.16–17   Bob Dylan . . . song]   "Only a Pawn in Their Game," released in 1964 on the album *The Times They Are A-Changin'*.

11.17   Medgar Evers]   Evers (1925–63) was field secretary of the NAACP in Mississippi from 1954 to 1963. He was shot outside his home in Jackson on June 12, 1963.

16.16–19   "If we . . . to remove . . ."]   The passage is from Lincoln's Second Inaugural Address.

17.13   Odetta]   African-American folksinger, born Odetta Holmes in 1930.

20.26   arrest . . . the bombers]   In September 1963 the FBI launched an extensive investigation into the Birmingham church bombing. A memorandum submitted to FBI Director J. Edgar Hoover in 1965 identified four Klansmen—Robert Chambliss, Herman Cash, Thomas Blanton Jr., and Bobby Frank Cherry—as suspects in the case. Hoover did not inform prosecutors of the Bureau's findings, and the FBI closed its investigation in 1968. Alabama attorney general Bill Baxley reopened the investigation in 1971, and Chambliss was convicted of murder on November 18, 1977; he died in prison in 1985. Cash died in 1994 without ever having been charged. In 2000 Blanton and Cherry were charged with murder. Blanton was convicted on May 1, 2001, and Cherry was found guilty on May 22, 2002; both men were sentenced to life imprisonment.

23.28   Human Rights Movement]   The Alabama Christian Movement for Human Rights was founded in Birmingham on June 5, 1956, shortly after the state attorney general obtained a court injunction barring the NAACP from operating in Alabama. In 1957 the ACMHR became an affiliate of the Southern Christian Leadership Conference (SCLC).

24.6–7   "Suffer little . . . them not,"]   Mark 10:14, Luke 18:16.

29.14   Farley . . . Sims]   Farley was placed on probation for his role in the shooting, and Sims was sentenced to six months in juvenile detention.

32.20   Charles Longstreet Weltner]   Weltner (1927–92) served in Congress, 1963–67, and voted for the 1964 civil rights bill. Although he was nominated for a third term in 1966, he refused to take the party loyalty oath that would have required him to support Lester Maddox, the segregationist candidate for governor, and did not run for reelection.

42.21–22   Kennedy's . . . November 1962]   See Chronology.

54.36   Pete Seeger]   White folk singer and left-wing activist, born 1919.

55.15–16   Marian Wright]   Later Marian Wright Edelman, founder in 1973 of the Children's Defense Fund.

56.17–18 *federal government* . . . Albany] On April 12, 1963, an all-white jury in Columbus, Georgia, acquitted Sheriff L. Warren Johnson in a federal civil rights suit brought by Charles Ware, an African-American man Johnson had beaten and shot in 1961. One of the jurors, Carl Smith, owned a grocery store in a black neighborhood in Albany, Georgia. His business was subsequently picketed by civil rights activists as part of a campaign directed at stores that did not hire African-Americans. On August 9, 1963, a federal grand jury in Macon indicted three activists, including Dr. William G. Anderson, a leader of the Albany Movement, for jury interference, alleging that they had picketed Smith's store in retaliation for his vote in *Ware* v. *Johnson*. Another six activists in the Albany Movement were indicted for perjury for their testimony during the grand jury investigation of the picketing. The charges were eventually dismissed by a federal appeals court in 1966 on the grounds that African-Americans had been excluded from the grand jury.

57.8–9 Barnett . . . Lingo] Ross Barnett, governor of Mississippi, 1960–64; Laurie Pritchett, chief of police in Albany, Georgia, who arrested hundreds of civil rights protestors during the demonstrations in 1961 and 1962; Al Lingo, commander of the Alabama state police under Governor George Wallace.

57.12 the Debs case] In 1895 the Supreme Court unanimously refused to grant a writ of habeas corpus to Eugene Debs, president of the American Railway Union, who had been sentenced to six months' imprisonment for contempt of court after he defied a federal circuit court injunction forbidding the union from striking railroads using Pullman cars. Writing for the Court, Justice David Brewer upheld the injunction as a constitutionally valid means of removing obstructions to interstate commerce.

58.17 Bill Moore] See note 6.18–19.

64.30–31 Frazier . . . black bourgeois] Frazier (1894–1962) was professor of sociology at Howard, 1934–59, and author of *The Black Bourgeoisie* (1957).

77.1 1954] Rustin organized two youth marches. They were held on October 25, 1958, and April 18, 1959.

84.35–36 Telestar broadcast] Telstar was an early communications satellite. The first Telstar was launched on July 10, 1962, and relayed the first transatlantic television broadcast on July 11.

85.32–33 English version . . . *Conflicts* (1987)] This essay appeared in *Duties, Pleasures, and Conflicts: Essays in Struggle* (1987) with the following postscript:

> Like most Americans, I watched the event on television. A group of activist students—SNCC folk mostly—had been, by default and accident, left in possession of the headquarters tent when the March began spontaneously without the leadership. There being no possible

way to stop that sea of humanity, the assembled dignitaries had to scramble rather unceremoniously to overtake the masses they perceived themselves to be leading. A spectacle we found symbolically appropriate and funny.

Because we had just learned of the sanitizing of John's speech, as it turns out, for remarks critical of the Kennedy administration's civil rights agenda, our mood was not celebratory. Which is why we were quite ungracious when a messenger appeared with several large boxes of leis sent by sympathizers in Hawaii. The refrigerated garlands were accompanied by a message of heartfelt support and the hope that the leaders on the platform would wear them.

It was a touching gesture of solidarity, but in that moment it seemed entirely too festive. Besides which none of us, even were it possible, was in the mood to chase after those leaders to festoon them with the petals of orchids. So far as I know, the present was never acknowledged and the donors, watching from Hawaii, never saw their gifts on TV, nor learned what happened to them. (If they looked closely when the camera panned the crowd, they *may* have noticed that a number of attractive young women and some small children were indeed bedecked with bands of orchids.)

When the telecast began, the mood in the tent was mixed. We were respectful when the venerable A. Philip Randolph opened the program. "We are gathered here in the largest popular demonstration in the history of this nation . . . we are not an organization . . . not a pressure group . . . we are not a mob. We are the advance guard of a moral revolution. . . ."

But with each succeeding speaker, the mood in the headquarters tent grew grimmer and more sullen, all the more so because of the inescapable and confusing ambivalence we all felt—our deep-seated sense of co-optation and irrelevance in conflict with the sheer numbers and unprecedented size of the operation. So we hid our confused anger behind a screen of sarcasm. We mocked and jeered the "bullshit and rhetoric" so roundly that the few journalists who wandered in in search of "background" seemed visibly surprised and left hurriedly. Clearly they had expected jubilation.

Then something unforgettable happened. Martin Luther King, Jr., began to talk. We greeted him with crude witticisms about "De Lawd." Then that rich, resonant voice asserted itself and despite ourselves we became quiet. About half-way through as image built on stirring image, the voice took on a ringing authority and established its lyrical and rhythmic cadence that was strangely compelling and hypnotic. Somewhere in the artful repetitions of the "Let Freedom Ring" series, we began—despite our stubborn, intemperate hearts—to grunt punctuations to each pause. "Ahmen, Waal, Ahhuh."

By the time the oration triumphantly swept into its closing movement—an expression of faith and moral and political possibility, delivered in the exquisite phrasing and timing of the black preacher's art—we were transformed. We were on our feet, laughing, shouting, slapping palms, hugging, and not an eye was dry. What happened that afternoon in that tent was the most extraordinary, sudden, and total transformation of mood I have ever witnessed.

Then drowning the electronic sound from the set, like an eerie counterpoint, came the booming, indescribably deep and visceral roar of the real crowd—some 250,000 souls—half a mile away.

Seventeen days later, after I had mailed off the above, four young girls in Sunday school were murdered when their church was bombed. Two months later, in Dallas, Texas, John F. Kennedy was gunned down.—M. T. (1986)

88.2 "separate but equal"] Doctrine of constitutionally permissible segregation established by the Supreme Court in *Plessy* v. *Ferguson* (1896).

89.1–3 Murray Kempton . . . poor white."] See p. 60.23–24 in this volume.

90.34 ordinance . . . planning stage] An open housing ordinance was passed by the Louisville Board of Alderman on December 13, 1967, following a lengthy campaign by civil rights activists.

96.30–31 intemperate . . . Kennedy's assassination] While addressing a Nation of Islam rally in New York City on December 1, 1963, Malcolm X had described Kennedy as "twiddling his thumbs" at the recent killing of South Vietnamese president Ngo Dinh Diem and his brother, Ngo Dinh Nhu, and said that he "never foresaw that the chickens would come home to roost so soon." He then added: "Being an old farm boy myself, chickens coming home to roost never did make me sad; they've always made me glad."

106.3–4 Mrs. Hamer . . . elections] All of the African-American candidates were defeated in the June 2, 1964, primary, with Hamer receiving 621 votes and Whitten 35,218. The Freedom Democratic Party candidates then sought to run as independents in the November election, but their petitions were rejected by the Mississippi elections board and they were kept off the ballot. Supporters of the Freedom Democratic Party challenged the seating of the Mississippi House delegation in the new Congress on the grounds that black voters had been illegally prevented from participating in the 1964 elections, but the House voted 276–149 on January 4, 1965, to seat the Mississippi delegation while a committee investigated the allegations. The challenge was permanently dismissed in a 228–143 vote on September 17, 1965.

109.5 jail for a few days] King was released on bond on June 13, 1964.

111.15–17 scar . . . Campbell] King was attacked by Sheriff D. C. Campbell on July 29, 1962, after he went to the county jail in Albany to check on a SNCC worker who had been beaten by white inmates. The Justice Department declined to prosecute Campbell for the assault, which received national press attention at the time.

113.9   stump liquor]   Corn liquor.

114.18   first demonstrations in Albany]   In December 1961.

116.3   tonk]   A form of rummy.

116.23–24   Operation Crossroads Africa]   A private organization, founded in 1957, that sponsors exchange programs between the United States and Africa.

117.35–36   King will lose]   King (1923–88) was defeated in the 1964 primary. In 1970 he became the first African-American to run for governor of Georgia and received eight percent of the vote in the Democratic primary.

123.34   Dr. R. B. Hayling]   Robert B. Hayling, a dentist and former member of the NAACP, founded the St. Augustine chapter of SCLC in March 1964 and began organizing sit-ins in segregated restaurants and hotels.

124.17   John Birch Society]   An extreme right-wing political organization founded in Indiana in 1958 by Robert Welch (1899–1985) and named after John Birch (1918–45), an American intelligence officer killed by the Chinese Communists at the end of World War II.

124.36   Highlander Folk School]   The Highlander Folk School, founded in 1932 near Monteagle, Tennessee, conducted workshops and training sessions for labor organizers in the 1930s and 1940s, then shifted its focus during the 1950s to training civil rights activists. In 1961 the school had its charter revoked and its building seized by the state, but in 1964 it reopened in Knoxville as the Highlander Research and Education Center.

125.21   "Dan Smoot Report,"]   Weekly subscription newsletter first published in 1955 by Dan Smoot, a former FBI agent.

127.2–3   "Mrs. Peabody Slept Here."]   Mary Peabody, the wife of Malcolm Peabody, bishop of the Episcopal diocese of Massachusetts, and mother of Endicott Peabody, the governor of Massachusetts from 1963 to 1965, was arrested in St. Augustine on March 31, 1964, while sitting with an integrated group in a restaurant and was charged with trespassing and being an undesirable guest. She was released on bond on April 2.

127.10–11   Sarah Patton Boyle]   In *The Desegregated Heart: A Virginian's Stand in Time of Transition* (1962), Boyle, a white resident of Charlottesville, Virginia, described how she became a public supporter of school integration during the 1950s.

129.1   War Resisters League]   An American pacifist group, founded in 1923.

129.18   Freedom Ride . . . Reconciliation.)]   See Chronology, 1947.

129.23 Aldermaston Ban-the-Bomb protest] Several hundred anti-nuclear protestors marched from London to the Atomic Weapons Research Establishment at Aldermaston, Berkshire, on Easter Weekend, April 4–7, 1958. Subsequent marches were held annually on Easter Weekend through 1963.

129.25–26 the Sahara . . . explosion] A group of 19 protestors left Accra, Ghana, on December 6, 1959, hoping to drive to the test site at Reganne in southern Algeria. They were blocked by French troops in Upper Volta (Burkina Faso) and abandoned the attempt on January 17, 1960. The French nuclear device was successfully detonated on February 13, 1960.

132.39 morals charge] Rustin and two other men were arrested in Pasadena, California, on January 21, 1953, after they were discovered having sex in the back of a parked car. Rustin pleaded guilty and was sentenced to 60 days in jail.

133.3–4 Powell . . . innuendo] In June 1960 Democratic Representative Adam Clayton Powell publicly attacked plans by King and A. Philip Randolph to organize picketing at the Democratic national convention in Los Angeles and specifically criticized King's ties to Rustin. Shortly afterward, Powell privately warned King through an intermediary that he would accuse King and Rustin of having a homosexual relationship unless King withdrew from the Los Angeles protests. King attended the protests at the Democratic convention in July, but also accepted Rustin's offer to resign from his SCLC positions as special adviser and director of the New York office.

134.18–19 Trotsky trials . . . Hitler-Stalin pact] Three public show trials were held in Moscow in August 1936, January 1937, and March 1938, during which prominent Soviet Communists were falsely accused of conspiring with the exiled Leon Trotsky against Joseph Stalin and his regime. The German-Soviet nonaggression pact was signed in Moscow on August 23, 1939.

134.28–29 Second front.] Term used after the German invasion of the Soviet Union on June 22, 1941, for a major Anglo-American invasion of western Europe.

136.39 A. Philip Randolph Institute] The institute was founded in the spring of 1965 with a grant from the AFL-CIO. Rustin served as its executive director until his death in 1987.

138.4 *Saturday*] July 18, 1964.

138.8–9 Murphy . . . Commissioner] Michael J. Murphy was commissioner of the New York City Police Department from 1961 to 1965.

140.26 James Farmer] Farmer (1920–99) was the national director of CORE from 1961 to 1966.

140.35 Dr. Yosef Ben Jochannan] Ben-Jochannan (b. 1918) would later publish several books, including *African Origins of the Major "Western Religions"* (1970), *Africa: Mother of Western Civilization* (1971), and *Black Man of the Nile and His Family: African Foundations of European Civilization and Thought* (1972).

140.38–141.1   Gray, the Harlem . . . the police.]   Dr. Edmond communicated through his attorneys to the editors of this volume on May 7, 2002, that this statement was inaccurate and was included in the original published text of "Harlem Diary" by Warren Hinckle, the editor of *Ramparts* magazine, who copied the statement from *The New York Times*.

151.28   Progressive Labor Movement]   Maoist organization formed in 1962 by American Communists who favored China in the Sino-Soviet split. In 1965 it became the Progressive Labor Party.

153.30–31   Bedford-Stuyvesant]   A predominantly African-American neighborhood in Brooklyn.

158.11   Allen Dulles]   Dulles, a former director of the CIA (1953–61), visited Mississippi as a special emissary of President Johnson, June 24–25, 1964, and met separately with civil rights leaders and Governor Paul Johnson.

161.15–16   federal grand jury indictment]   On December 4, 1964, the FBI arrested 19 men, including Sheriff Lawrence Rainey and Deputy Sheriff Cecil Price, on charges of conspiring to deprive Chaney, Goodman, and Schwerner of their civil rights "under color of state law." A federal commissioner dismissed the charges on December 10, 1964, on the grounds that they were based on hearsay evidence, but on January 15, 1965, a grand jury indicted the 19 men. Federal district judge William Howard Cox dismissed the indictments against all of the accused except Rainey and Price on February 24, 1965, ruling that they had not been acting "under the color of state law," but in March 1966 the Supreme Court unanimously reversed his decision. The defendants went on trial in Meridian, Mississippi, on October 9, 1967, with assistant attorney general John Doar leading the prosecution. During the trial a former Klansman testified for the government that, after releasing the three civil rights workers from jail, Price had followed them, taken them into custody, and then turned them over to a party of Klansmen to be killed. On October 20, 1967, the all-white jury convicted Price and six other men, including Sam Bowers, the Imperial Wizard of the White Knights of the Ku Klux Klan, and Alton Wayne Roberts, the triggerman in the killings; acquitted eight men, including Rainey; and failed to reach verdicts on three defendants (one defendant received a directed acquittal before the case went to the jury). Judge Cox sentenced Bowers and Roberts to the maximum penalty of ten years in prison, Price to six years, and the other four men to terms of three to six years. Bowers and Roberts served six years before being paroled. In 1998 Bowers was convicted of murder in state court for the 1966 slaying of civil rights activist Vernon Dahmer in Hattiesburg, Mississippi, and was sentenced to life imprisonment.

170.30   Emmett Till murder]   See Chronology, 1955. "The Shocking Story of Approved Killing in Mississippi," the article Huie published in *Look* magazine about the Till case in 1956, is printed in *Reporting Civil Rights: American Journalism 1941–1963*, pp. 232–40.

170.32 Mack Parker] Mack Charles Parker, a black man awaiting trial on charges of raping a white woman, was taken from jail in Poplarville, Mississippi, on the night of April 24, 1959, and lynched. No one was ever charged in his murder.

170.33 Beckwith case] Byron de la Beckwith was arrested in Greenwood, Mississippi, on June 22, 1963, and charged with the murder of NAACP leader Medgar Evers in Jackson, Mississippi, ten days earlier. Two trials in state court ended in mistrials in 1964 when all-white juries voted 7–5 and 8–4 for his acquittal. The case was reopened in 1990, and a third trial before a racially mixed jury in 1994 ended in his conviction. Beckwith died in prison in 2001.

171.12 Joe Alsop wrote] Syndicated newspaper columnist Joseph Alsop (1910–89), in a column that appeared in *The Washington Post* on June 29, 1964.

173.23–24 FBI agents . . . a deal] The FBI reportedly paid an informer $30,000 to reveal where the bodies were buried.

180.18 recent constitutional amendment] See Chronology, 1962 and 1964.

180.31 The Saturday] August 22, 1964.

181.2 Senator Humphrey] Earlier in 1964 Senator Hubert H. Humphrey (1911–78) had served as the Senate manager of the civil rights bill. On August 26, 1964, President Johnson announced his choice of Humphrey to be the Democratic vice-presidential candidate.

181.13 Dawson of Chicago] William L. Dawson (1886–1970) served in the House of Representatives, 1942–70, and was the senior African-American member of Congress for the entire period of his service.

183.16 Jack Pratt] An attorney who did civil rights work in Mississippi on behalf of the Committee on Race and Religion of the National Council of Churches.

183.17 Forman, Ella Baker, Bob Moses.] James Forman (b. 1928) was executive secretary of SNCC, 1961–66. Ella Baker (1903–86) was the national director of branches for the NAACP, 1943–46, and associate director of SCLC, 1958–60. In 1960 she played a leading role in the founding of SNCC and served as an adviser to the group. Moses (b. 1935) was a leading SNCC organizer in Mississippi, 1961–65.

184.24 Klansmen freed in Georgia] On September 4, 1964, an all-white jury acquitted Howard Sims and Cecil Myers, two Klansmen charged with the July 11, 1964, murder near Colbert, Georgia, of Lemuel Penn, an African-American educator and lieutenant colonel in the army reserves who was driving back to his home in Washington, D.C. Sims and Myers were convicted in federal court on July 2, 1966, of conspiring to deprive Penn of his civil rights and sentenced to ten-year prison terms.

195.30   Cyprus] Intercommunal fighting broke out between Greek and Turkish Cypriots on December 21, 1963, and continued sporadically until August 9, 1964. More than 500 people were killed during the clashes.

197.9   Athens] A fictitious name. See p. 211.29 in this volume, where the scene of the episode described on pp. 197–202 is identified as Lexington, the seat of Holmes County, Mississippi; see also note 201.3–5 below.

198.7   Ittabala] A fictitious name.

201.3–5   whipping . . . whiskey] Leon McTatie was whipped to death by six white men on July 22, 1946, near Lexington in Holmes County, Mississippi, after he allegedly stole a saddle.

207.3–5   next year . . . Normandy] 1944.

211.29   Lexington] See note 197.9.

227.13–18   August 8 . . . explosion] On the night of August 8, 1964, an attempt was made to bomb the Freedom Center in Mileston, Mississippi, in the western part of Holmes County. On July 26, 1964, the car of a civil rights volunteer was firebombed in Mileston; cf. p. 222.5–9 in this volume.

233.23   four major civil rights groups] The NAACP, SCLC, SNCC, and CORE.

236.10–12   Travis . . . killed him.] Travis was wounded in Greenwood, Mississippi, on February 28, 1963, when the car in which he was riding with Moses was fired upon by men in another car.

248.9   American Gothic] Painting (1930) by Grant Wood (1891–1942).

251.24–25   Supreme Court upholds him] On December 14, 1964, the Supreme Court unanimously overturned the lower court decision in *Katzenbach* v. *McClung* (the name of the case changed after Nicholas Katzenbach succeeded Robert Kennedy as attorney general). The Court ruled that racial discrimination by restaurants with predominately local clienteles affected interstate travel, the interstate relocation of businesses, and the volume of interstate commerce in food, and that as a result Congress had the power under the commerce clause of the Constitution to forbid discrimination by such restaurants as part of the public accommodations section of the 1964 Civil Rights Act.

258.24   Max Schmeling defeated Joe Louis] Schmeling, a German prizefighter, knocked Louis out in the 12th round on June 19, 1936. In a rematch fought on June 22, 1938, after Louis had become the heavyweight champion, Louis knocked Schmeling out in the first round.

280.9   their arrest] See note 161.15–16.

283.7   indictment of Rainey and Price] Rainey, Price, and three other law
enforcement officers were indicted on October 2, 1964, for a series of beatings of black prisoners in Neshoba County. The indictments were dismissed
in October 1966 on the grounds that women and African-Americans had
been improperly excluded from the grand jury.

292.6   "All find . . . Yeats,] In "Crazy Jane and the Bishop" (1933).

305.23   Big Red] Malcolm X was known as "Big Red" and "Detroit
Red" in Harlem during the period, 1943–46, when he was a street hustler and
armed robber.

307.19–20   Freedom Now . . . Michigan] The party, formed in 1963, ran
39 candidates in the 1964 elections, then broke up.

308.9   *The Village Voice*, February 25, 1965] When this article appeared it
was accompanied by an editorial note explaining that it had been written before the assassination of Malcolm X on February 21, 1965.

309.7–8   Thomas Hagan . . . the killing] Thomas Hagan, also known as
Talmadge Hayer, a member of the Newark temple of the Nation of Islam, was
indicted for murder on March 11, 1965, along with two Black Muslims from
New York, Thomas 15X Johnson and Norman 3X Butler. All three men were
found guilty on March 10, 1966, and were sentenced to life terms. In an affidavit filed in 1977, Hayer admitted his involvement in the murder and stated
that his accomplices were four men from New Jersey, not Johnson and Butler.

310.25   Sullivan Law] New York State law, passed in 1911, that prohibits
possession of a handgun without a police permit.

312.4   WMCA] A New York radio station.

316.34   Mau Mau] A Kikuyu secret society that sought independence for
Kenya through attacks on European settlers and Africans considered loyal to
the colonial regime. The Mau Mau were suppressed by the British in a coun-
terinsurgency campaign, 1952–56, during which approximately 100 Europeans
and 13,000 Africans were killed. Kenya became independent in 1963.

318.1   Ben Bella] Ahmed Ben Bella (b. 1916), a leader in the Algerian independence movement, was prime minister of Algeria, 1962–63, and president, 1963–65. He was ousted in a coup led by defense minister Houari
Boumedienne on June 19, 1965.

319.34–35   bomb us . . . the house] Malcolm X's home in East Elmhurst,
Queens, was firebombed on February 14, 1965. His family escaped injury.

321.4–6   the mosque . . . no more."] The mosque was not attacked in
the aftermath of Malcolm X's assassination.

323.12   troops to the Congo] U.S. aircraft flew Belgian paratroopers to Stanleyville (Kisangani), where Belgian and American civilians were being held hostage by Congolese rebels, on November 24, 1964, and were then used to evacuate the freed hostages. A similar U.S.-Belgian operation was carried out at Paulis (Isiro) on November 26, 1964.

332.5   Mario Savio] Savio (1942–96) was a leader in the Free Speech Movement that successfully challenged restrictions on political organizing and advocacy at the University of California–Berkeley in the fall of 1964. During the summer of 1964 Savio had taught at a Freedom School in McComb County, Mississippi.

336.12   *John Brown's Body*] Narrative poem (1928) by Stephen Vincent Benét (1898–1943).

337.30–31   One . . . fatally beaten] The Rev. James Reeb (1927–65), a white Unitarian minister, was beaten on a Selma street on the evening of March 9 and died in a Birmingham hospital on March 11. Three men were indicted for his murder on April 13; they were acquitted on December 10, 1965.

339.5   LAST Tuesday] March 9, 1965.

340.11–12   Langston Hughes . . . crystal stair,"] From the poem "Mother to Son" (1922).

341.12   LeRoy Collins] Collins (1909–91) was the director, 1964–65, of the Community Relations Service, a federal agency established by the 1964 Civil Rights Act to conduct negotiations in situations of racial conflict. He had previously served as governor of Florida, 1955–61.

343.18   Bishop James Pike] Pike (1913–69) was the Episcopal bishop of the diocese of California, 1958–66.

346.14–15   hymn . . . to decide.'"] The words to "Once To Every Man and Nation" are taken from the poem "The Present Crisis" (1844) by James Russell Lowell (1819–91).

353.28   "Too Bad, Reeb"] See note 337.30–31.

357.10   Hollywood Ten] Ten screenwriters who refused on First Amendment grounds to answer questions about their membership in the Communist party when they were subpoenaed by the House Committee on Un-American Activities in 1947. They were subsequently convicted of contempt of Congress and served prison terms of up to one year.

358.29   *Herzog, Les Mots*] Novel (1964) by Saul Bellow; autobiography (1964) by Jean-Paul Sartre.

359.14   cloud of witnesses] Hebrews 12:1.

359.19   Billy Eckstine] Eckstine (1914–93) was an African-American jazz singer who made commercially successful recordings of popular ballads in the 1940s and 1950s.

383.30   Aldermaston] See note 129.23.

389.24   Gomillion . . . Reese] Gomillion (1900–95), a professor of sociology at Tuskegee Institute and a founder of the Tuskegee Civic Association, was the plaintiff in *Gomillion* v. *Lightfoot* (see Chronology, 1960). Reese, a Selma minister and schoolteacher, played a leading role in organizing the SCLC voting rights campaign that began in the city in 1965.

394.16   Liuzzo had been shot] Liuzzo (1925–65), a white civil rights volunteer from Detroit, Michigan, was killed in Lowndes County on March 25 while driving from Selma to Montgomery. The following day four Klansmen were arrested, including Gary Thomas Rowe, who had been a paid informant for the FBI since 1960. Despite Rowe's testimony, an all-white jury acquitted Leroy Wilkins, the alleged triggerman, of state murder charges on October 22, 1965. Wilkins, William Eaton, and Eugene Thomas were convicted on federal charges of conspiring to deprive Liuzzo of her civil rights by an all-white jury on December 3, 1965, and sentenced to ten-year prison terms. (The federal prosecution was led by assistant attorney general John Doar.) Eaton died from a heart attack on March 9, 1966, and Thomas was acquitted of state murder charges by a racially mixed jury on September 27, 1966. Rowe was indicted on state murder charges in 1978, but a federal judge blocked his extradition from Georgia and he was never tried.

399.15   Proposition 14, Cardinal McIntyre] Proposition 14 was a ballot initiative, approved by California voters in 1964, that amended the state constitution to prohibit the state from interfering with the right of property owners to sell, lease, or rent to persons of their own choosing. In 1967 the U.S. Supreme Court ruled 5–4 in *Reitman* v. *Mulkey* that the California amendment violated the equal protection clause of the Fourteenth Amendment of the U.S. Constitution. James Francis McIntyre (1886–1979), archbishop of the Roman Catholic diocese of Los Angeles from 1958 to 1970, was criticized for his attempts to prevent priests, nuns, and seminarians under his authority from speaking out on civil rights issues.

401.35   One morning . . . Allen] Allen was murdered on the night of January 31, 1964, one day before he planned to move to Milwaukee, Wisconsin.

408.33–34   Reese . . . charged] The charges against Reese were later dropped, and in 1972 he became one of the first African-Americans elected to the Selma City Council.

418.34–35   Fahrenkopf . . . recovers] Fahrenkopf survived and did not lose his eyesight.

428.12 N-VAC] Non-Violent Action Committee, a Los Angeles civil rights group.

437.2–4 Dean Acheson . . . John A. McCone's] Acheson (1893–1971) served as under secretary of state, 1945–47, and secretary of state, 1949–53. Stanley Mosk (1912–2001) was attorney general of California, 1959–64, and a justice of the California supreme court, 1964–2001. John A. McCone (1902–91) was chairman of the Atomic Energy Commission, 1958–60, and director of the Central Intelligence Agency from November 1961 to April 1965. Governor Brown appointed McCone as chairman of an eight-member investigating commission on August 19; the commission delivered its report on December 6, 1965.

456.5 *Stride Toward Freedom*] Published in 1958.

466.13–14 *Stormy Weather*] The film, directed by Andrew Stone, was released in 1943.

466.27 *Home of the Brave*] Released in 1949, the film was directed by Mark Robson and written by Carl Foreman, based on a play by Arthur Laurents. (In the play the soldier confronting prejudice was Jewish, not African-American.)

467.17–18 *A Man Is Ten Feet Tall*] Written by Robert Alan Arthur, the play was performed on the *Philco Television Playhouse* on October 2, 1955.

467.33 *Edge of the City*] Directed by Martin Ritt and written by Robert Alan Arthur, the film was released in 1957.

468.36 playing him . . . gladiator] Marshall played King Dick, a Haitian rebel, in *Lydia Bailey* (1952) and Glydon in *Demetrius and the Gladiators* (1954).

468.37–38 Marshall . . . in Europe] Marshall appeared in *Les Impures* (1955), directed by Pierre Chevalier, and *La Fille de Feu* (1958), directed by Alfred Rode.

469.4 "Something of Value"] In the film Poitier plays Kimani, a Kenyan who joins the Mau Mau rebels after being humiliated by white settlers. Released in 1957, the film was written and directed by Richard Brooks and was based on a novel by Robert Ruark.

469.8–9 *The Carpetbaggers . . . Huckleberry Finn*] Film released in 1964, directed by Edward Dmytryk and written by John Michael Hayes, based on the novel by Harold Robbins; film released in 1960, directed by Michael Curtiz and written by James Lee.

470.9 Elsewhere I have written] In *Sex and Racism in America* (1965).

470.25 *Paris Blues*] Released in 1961, the film was directed by Martin Ritt and written by Walter Bernstein, Lulla Adler, Irene Kamp, and Jack Sher, based on a novel by Harold Flender.

471.20   *The Long Ships*]   Directed by Jack Cardiff and written by Frans G. Bengtsson, Beverly Cross, and Berkely Mather, the film was released in 1963.

472.11   *Lilies of the Field*]   Released in 1963, the film was directed by Ralph Nelson and written by James Poe, based on a novel by William E. Barrett.

472.24–25   *The World, the Flesh, and the Devil*]   Directed and written by Ranald MacDougall, based on a novel by M.P. Shiel and a story by Ferdinand Reyher, the film was released in 1959.

473.17   *One Potato, Two Potato*]   Released in 1964, the film was directed by Larry Peerce and written by Orville H. Hampton and Raphael Hayes.

475.12–13   *A Raisin in the Sun*]   The film, released in 1961, was written by Hansberry and directed by Daniel Petrie.

475.16   *The Cool World . . . Nothing but a Man*]   *The Cool World* (1963), directed by Shirley Clarke and written by Clarke and Carl Lee, based on a play by Robert Rossen and Warren Miller and a novel by Miller, depicted life in Harlem. *Nothing but a Man* (1964), directed by Michael Roemer and written by Roemer and Robert M. Young, was set in the Deep South.

477.36–39   *Crossing . . . dissolve away.*"]   Cf. "Delta Autumn" in *Go Down, Moses* (1942).

478.11–14   *thick . . . even richer.*"]   Cf. "Delta Autumn" in *Go Down, Moses* (1942).

479.10–11   "In Your . . . Right."]   Slogan used in 1964 presidential campaign of Senator Barry Goldwater.

493.24   Last January]   The statement was issued on January 6, 1966.

493.33–34   Bond . . . a seat]   The Georgia House of Representatives voted 182–12 to deny Bond his seat on January 10, 1966. Bond sued, and on December 5, 1966, the U.S. Supreme Court unanimously ruled that the legislature's action had violated the First Amendment. Bond took his seat on January 9, 1967.

496.26–27   CORE and NAACP . . . meaning.]   At its 1966 national convention, held July 1–4, CORE endorsed the concept of "Black Power," repudiated the policy of nonviolence, and advocated self-defense in response to white violence. During the NAACP national convention, held July 5–9, its executive director Roy Wilkins criticized CORE and SNCC and described "Black Power" as "anti-white power" and "separatism."

497.12   Meredith was shot]   See Chronology, 1966.

498.13   "Ballad of the Green Beret"]   Song, written by Staff Sergeant Barry Sadler and Robin Moore and performed by Sadler, that was number one on the *Billboard* pop singles chart for five weeks in early 1966.

498.23–24 Charles Evers] Evers (b. 1922) became Mississippi field secretary of the NAACP in 1963 after the assassination of his brother Medgar.

498.24 Delta Ministry] A project of the National Council of Churches organized in September 1964 to undertake civil rights work and social welfare programs in Mississippi.

505.29 Sen. Fulbright] J. William Fulbright (1905–95) was a Democratic senator from Arkansas, 1945–75, and chairman of the Senate Foreign Relations Committee, 1959–74.

512.9–10 accused killer . . . jury.] Jonathan Daniels, a 26-year-old white seminary student and civil rights worker, was shot to death in Hayneville, Alabama, on August 20, 1965, by Tom Coleman, a special deputy sheriff. Coleman pled self-defense and was acquitted of manslaughter on September 30, 1965.

515.26 George Lee was murdered] The Rev. George Lee, an NAACP activist involved in voter registration efforts, was shot to death in Belzoni on May 7, 1955. No one was ever charged with the crime.

520.11 first town . . . in Mississippi] Meredith began his one-man march in Memphis, Tennessee.

522.19–20 A man stood . . . shotgun] Aubrey James Norvell, a resident of Memphis, pled guilty on November 21, 1966, to charges of assault and battery with intent to kill. He was sentenced to five years in prison, with three years of the sentence suspended.

535.11 James K. Vardaman] Vardaman (1861–1930) was governor of Mississippi, 1904–8, and a U.S. senator, 1913–19.

535.21–22 Title VI . . . Act of 1964] Title VI prohibited racial discrimination in programs receiving federal financial assistance.

535.24 HEW] Department of Health, Education, and Welfare. Established in 1953, it was divided in 1979 into the Department of Health and Human Services and the Department of Education.

538.5 Freedom Labor Union] The Mississippi Freedom Labor Union was organized in April 1965 by black farm laborers, tractor drivers, and domestic workers.

545.21 William Fitz Ryan] William Fitts Ryan (1922–72) was a Democratic congressman from New York City, 1961–72. In 1965 he led the challenge in the House of Representatives to the seating of the Mississippi delegation (see note 106.3–4).

552.28 equalizers] Guns.

553.17–18 Ron Karenga . . . US] Maulana Karenga (born Ronald Everett in 1941) founded US in Los Angeles in September 1965 and created the holiday of Kwanzaa in 1966. The US organization later fought with the Black

Panther party for control of the black studies program at UCLA, and on January 17, 1969, two Black Panthers were shot to death on the UCLA campus by members of US. (The conflict between the two organizations was intensified by covert actions carried out by the FBI as part of its campaign to disrupt black nationalist groups.) Karenga was imprisoned from 1971 to 1975 for assaulting two female members of US he suspected were trying to poison him, and in 1974 the organization dissolved.

566.4   succession laws] Gubernatorial elections were held every two years in Arkansas.

571.5   Stockholm] The Nobel Peace Prize is awarded in Oslo, Norway, where it was presented to King on December 10, 1964. King delivered his Nobel Lecture in Oslo on December 11, then visited Stockholm for two days.

575.33–34   leader . . . Ahmed] Fred (Ahmed) Evans (1931–78). Members of Evans' New Libya Movement opened fire on police in the Glenville section of Cleveland on July 23, 1968, beginning a gun battle in which three policemen, three New Libya supporters, and a bystander were killed. Evans was convicted of murder on May 12, 1969, and died in prison.

585.7–8   New Politics people] The National Conference for New Politics, formed in 1966 to support candidates opposed to the Vietnam War.

585.37   Spock] Dr. Benjamin Spock (1903–98), a pediatrician and author of *Baby and Child Care* (1946), was a prominent opponent of the Vietnam War.

586.29   your good Governor"] Ronald Reagan was elected governor of California in 1966.

590.1   Friday] July 14, 1967.

590.15   danshiki] A Yoruba word, later shortened in American usage to dashiki.

593.12–13   cab driver . . . other night] The Newark riot began on July 12, 1967, after police beat a cab driver they had arrested.

604.23   Harry Bennett's army] Harry Bennett was the head of the Service Department (security division) of the Ford Motor Company from the 1920s until his dismissal by Henry Ford II in 1945. In the 1930s his department employed several thousand men, many of them with criminal backgrounds, and became notorious for its use of intimidation and violence against members and supporters of the United Auto Workers.

611.4   Monday] July 24, 1967.

625.38–40   18 members . . . a felony] On July 20, 1967, Bobby Seale and five other Panthers pled guilty to misdemeanor charges and received sentences of up to six months. All of the remaining charges were dismissed.

632.38 Hunters Point riot] The riot began on September 27, 1966, after a white police officer fatally shot a 16-year-old African-American and ended the following day after 349 people were arrested and more than 3,000 National Guardsmen were deployed.

638.26 Law Director] City attorney.

643.21–22 Edward Brooke] Brooke (b. 1919), a Republican, was attorney general of Massachusetts, 1963–66, and a U.S. senator, 1967–79.

643.33–34 Stokes . . . Taft] Stokes defeated Taft, the grandson of President William Howard Taft, by a margin of about 1,600 votes.

645.6–7 distant gunman . . . escaped] On April 19, 1968, the FBI named James Earl Ray, an escaped convict, as a suspect in the assassination, and on June 8 he was arrested at Heathrow Airport outside of London. Ray pled guilty to murder charges on March 10, 1969, and was sentenced to 99 years. He died in prison in 1998.

653.39 J. P. Alley's "Hambone" cartoon] James Pinckney Alley (1885–1934) created the cartoon "Hambone's Meditations" in 1916. It was continued after his death by his son Calvin Alley (1915–70) until 1968.

655.39–40 Marc Connelly . . . The Green Pastures] Connelly (1890–1981) based his play The Green Pastures (1930) on Ol' Man Adam an' His Chillun (1928), a collection of stories by Roark Bradford (1896–1948) in which an African-American preacher retells stories from the Bible.

657.37 Birmingham] Montgomery; see Chronology, 1955.

669.19 city's great Civil War hero] Confederate cavalry commander General Nathan Bedford Forrest (1821–77).

670.21 Lester Maddox] Maddox, the governor of Georgia from 1967 to 1971, surrounded the state capitol with 160 state troopers on the day of King's funeral and refused to attend the ceremony.

672.37–38 April 4.] The meeting was held on April 3.

673.29–30 Professor Harold Hill] Character in the musical The Music Man (1957) by Meredith Willson (1902–84).

676.14 He is now awaiting trial] Newton was convicted of voluntary manslaughter on September 10, 1968, and sentenced to two to fifteen years in prison. His conviction was overturned by the state court of appeal on May 29, 1970, on the grounds that the judge had improperly instructed the jury, and Newton was released from prison on August 5, 1970. Two retrials in the fall of 1971 ended with juries deadlocked 11–1 for conviction and 6–6, and on December 15, 1971, the charges against Newton were dismissed. In his book The Shadow of the Panther: Huey Newton and the Price of Black Power in America (1994), author Hugh Pearson quoted two friends of Newton who recalled him boasting that he had killed Frey.

677.1   M-31]   A 12-gauge pump-action shotgun.

679.33   P-38]   A German nine-millimeter semiautomatic pistol.

679.37   Scottsboro boy]   In April 1931 nine black youths, aged 13 to 20, were tried in Scottsboro, Alabama, for allegedly raping two young white women onboard a freight train. After eight of the defendants were convicted and sentenced to death, the defense of the "Scottsboro Boys" became the focus of a nationwide campaign by civil rights groups and the Communist party. In 1932 the U.S. Supreme Court overturned the verdicts on the grounds that the inadequate counsel provided to the accused at their trial violated their right to due process under the Fourteenth Amendment. Four of the defendants were eventually retried and convicted, receiving sentences ranging from death (later commuted to life imprisonment) to 75 years. A fifth defendant received 20 years for assaulting a deputy while in custody, while charges against the remaining four defendants were dropped in July 1937. By 1950 all of the imprisoned men had either been paroled or had escaped from custody.

683.32–34   Bryant's . . . nothing"]   William Cullen Bryant (1794–1878), "The Battle-Field" (1837); cf. Thomas Carlyle (1795–1881), *Sartor Resartus* (1836), book II, chapter 7: "Is there no God, then; but at best an absentee God, sitting idle?"

690.7–8   black champion . . . Cassius Clay]   Muhammad Ali (Cassius Clay) was stripped of his heavyweight boxing title in 1967 after he refused to be inducted into the U.S. Army.

693.4–5   Senator Kennedy and Governor Rockefeller]   Robert F. Kennedy and Nelson Rockefeller.

699.23   *Black Rage*]   Book published in 1968 by William H. Grier and Price M. Cobbs, two African-American psychiatrists.

704.31–32   readers of *Life* magazine]   Moore had been assigned by *Life* to write a story about the Black Panthers.

707.15   Garrison]   Jim Garrison (1921–95), district attorney of New Orleans from 1962 to 1974, attracted widespread publicity in March 1967 when he indicted Clay Shaw, a prominent New Orleans businessman, on charges of conspiring to assassinate President Kennedy. Shaw was acquitted on March 1, 1969.

707.16   *MacBird!*]   Satirical play (1966) by Barbara Garson, inspired by Shakespeare's *Macbeth*, concerning the relationship between Lyndon Johnson and John and Robert Kennedy.

709.8   Solidarity Day]   June 19, 1968.

710.6   Wilbur Mills]   Mills (1909–92) was a Democratic representative from Arkansas, 1939–77, and chairman of the House Ways and Means Committee, 1958–74.

725.24   Senator McCarthy] Eugene McCarthy (b. 1916), Democratic senator from Minnesota, 1959–71, and an anti-war candidate for the Democratic presidential nomination in 1968.

725.26   New York primary] Of the 123 convention delegates chosen on June 18, 63 were pledged to McCarthy.

726.7–8   famous words . . . 1963 march] See pp. 15.32–16.3 and p. 84.11–28 in this volume.

728.12–13   Reies Lopes Tijerina] Tijerina (b. 1926) founded the Alianza Federal de las Mercedes (Federal Land Grant Alliance) in New Mexico in 1963 to press claims to Spanish and Mexican land grants. On June 5, 1967, he allegedly participated in an armed raid that freed several Alianza members who were being held on unlawful assembly charges in the county courthouse in Tierra Amarilla, New Mexico. While free on bail, Tijerina served as the southwestern coordinator of the Poor People's Campaign in 1968. He was acquitted of all charges relating to the courthouse raid on December 13, 1968.

729.38   Russell Long] Long (b. 1918) was a Democratic senator from Louisiana, 1948–87, and chairman of the Finance Committee, 1965–81.

730.24   C. Wright Mills] Mills (1916–62) was a professor of sociology at Columbia, 1946–62.

754.11   Penrod] Penrod Schofield, young protagonist of the novels *Penrod* (1914), *Penrod and Sam* (1916), and *Penrod Jashber* (1929) by Booth Tarkington.

764.14–19   Members of the . . . unloaded.] In his memoir *The Making of Black Revolutionaries* (1972) James Forman wrote that this incident never took place and described the newspaper story reprinted here as a "vicious lie."

773.39–40   renamed the street . . . 31st Street.] It is possible that some text was omitted in the original printing of this passage, which refers to the location on the corner of Martin Luther King Jr. Drive (formerly South Park Boulevard) and 31st Street of Olivet Baptist Church, where Joseph H. Jackson served as pastor from 1941 to 1990. Olivet Baptist Church presently lists its address as being on King Drive.

775.11   Jean-Claude Killy] French Alpine skier, born 1943, who won three gold medals at the 1968 Winter Olympics.

779.5   Blackstone Rangers] A Chicago street gang, later known as the Black P Stone Nation and then as El Rukns.

783.10   Daley's "shoot to kill" order] At a press conference held on April 15, 1968, Daley criticized police superintendent James Conlisk for not issuing clear instructions on the use of force during the rioting that followed the assassination of King and announced that he had told Conlisk to order police to "shoot to kill any arsonist or anyone with a Molotov cocktail in his hand" and to "shoot to maim or cripple" anyone looting.

783.25 George McGovern] Senator George McGovern announced his candidacy for the Democratic presidential nomination on August 10, 1968. In the balloting on August 28, he received 146.5 delegate votes out of 2,622, mostly from supporters of Robert Kennedy who refused to vote for either Hubert Humphrey or Eugene McCarthy.

784.2 C. W. Moss] A member of the Barrow-Parker gang in *Bonnie and Clyde* (1967); the character in the film is a fictitious composite.

786.4 Lionel Hampton] Hampton (1908–2002) was an African-American jazz vibraphonist and band leader.

795.38 beat up . . . *Gater*] James Vaszko was attacked on November 6, 1967, after he wrote to the Carnegie Corporation asking them not to fund programs sponsored by the Black Students Union.

795.39 during the strike] A student strike was called at San Francisco State University on November 6, 1968, by the Black Students Union and the Third World Liberation Front. It lasted until March 21, 1969.

804.4 Marcel Marceau] French mime, born 1923.

809.26 October Supreme Court mandate] See Chronology, 1969.

815.25 *Invisible Man*] Novel (1952) by Ralph Ellison (1913–94).

816.2 *In the Heat of the Night*] Film (1967), directed by Norman Jewison, in which Steiger plays the police chief of a small Mississippi town.

816.8–9 tribe of Sulzberger] Members of the Ochs-Sulzberger family have published *The New York Times* since 1896.

835.20–21 Black Panther trial in New Haven] On August 21, 1969, Bobby Seale and 11 other Black Panthers were indicted on charges relating to the kidnapping and murder of Alex Rackley, a young Panther from New York who was killed on May 21, 1969, after having been tortured for several days by members of the New Haven chapter who falsely suspected him of being a police informer. Two of the accused pled guilty and a third defendant was convicted of conspiracy to murder on September 1, 1970. After a lengthy trial, the jury hearing the case against Seale and Ericka Huggins deadlocked with large majorities (11–1 for Seale, 10–2 for Huggins) in favor of acquittal, and on May 25, 1971, the charges against them were dismissed. The charges against the remaining defendants were also dropped.

841.16 George . . . his reign] George Wallace (1919–98) was first elected governor of Alabama in 1962. Prevented by the state constitution from serving consecutive terms, Wallace ran his wife, Lurleen, as a surrogate candidate in 1966. Lurleen Wallace won the election but died in office on May 7, 1968, and was succeeded by Lieutenant Governor Albert Brewer. Wallace defeated Brewer in a bitter primary election in June 1970 and was elected to a second term in November 1970.

847.25–26   Yale's Mayday] A large rally was held in New Haven near the Yale campus on May 1, 1970, in support of the Black Panthers charged with the murder of Alex Rackley.

848.40   Rizzo . . . Mayor in 1971] Rizzo (1920–91) was elected mayor in 1971 and reelected in 1975. His campaigns for a third term in 1983 and 1987 were unsuccessful.

849.23   Tabor . . . Panther 21] On April 2, 1969, 21 people, many of them members of the Black Panther party, were indicted in New York City on charges of bombing four police stations and plotting to bomb several department stores. Opening arguments in the trial of 13 defendants, including Tabor, began on October 19, 1970. Tabor jumped bail in February 1971 and joined Eldridge Cleaver in Algeria; after his flight he was expelled from the Panthers by Huey Newton. All 13 defendants were acquitted on May 13, 1971.

850.29   Kent State] Four students protesting the American invasion of Cambodia were shot to death by Ohio National Guardsmen at Kent State University on May 4, 1970.

851.24   WBAI] A New York radio station, part of the left-wing Pacifica network.

854.29   Le Roi Jones, and Roy Innis] Amiri Baraka (b. 1934), also known as LeRoi Jones, writer and political activist; Roy Innis (b. 1934), national director of CORE since 1968. In 1970 both men were advocates of black nationalism.

856.5–6   Seale . . . Chicago] Seale was indicted on March 20, 1969, along with seven white radicals on federal charges of having conspired to incite riots in Chicago during the 1968 Democratic national convention. After the "Chicago Eight" trial began on September 24, 1969, Seale repeatedly disrupted the proceedings to protest the refusal of Judge Julius Hoffman to grant a delay while his attorney, Charles Garry, recovered from surgery. Hoffman had Seale bound and gagged in the courtroom from October 29 to November 3, then severed his case from the other defendants on November 5 and sentenced him to four years in prison on 16 counts of contempt of court. The government chose not to re-try Seale on the conspiracy charges, and his contempt conviction was overturned on appeal in 1972.

859.5–6   charged them . . . "insurrection"] The insurrection law was declared unconstitutional by a federal court on November 1, 1963.

867.13   Glow-Worm] Song (1952) with words by Johnny Mercer and music by Paul Lincke.

868.5–7 *Heaven Help Me . . .* Stevie Wonder] Possibly a reference to "Heaven Help Us All," from the album *Signed, Sealed and Delivered* (1970).

872.26–27 *justice rolls . . . mighty stream.*] Cf. Amos 5:24.

878.8 Emmett Till] See Chronology, 1955.

880.23 Baraka] See note 854.29.

880.25 Queen Mother Moore] Audley Moore (1898–1996) was born in New Iberia, Louisiana, and moved in 1922 to Harlem, where she became a leader in the Universal Negro Improvement Association founded by Marcus Garvey. After the collapse of the UNIA in 1927 Moore continued to be actively involved in civil rights, labor, black nationalist, and Pan-African causes and movements, including the granting of reparations to African-Americans. She received her honorific of "Queen Mother" of the Ashanti people during a visit to Ghana.

880.32 Winson Hudson] Hudson (b. 1916), a resident of the all-black rural community of Harmony and an NAACP leader in Leake County, Mississippi, was involved in voter registration and school desegregation campaigns in the late 1950s and the 1960s. In 1964 she participated in the Freedom Summer project and was a member of the Freedom Democratic Party delegation to Atlantic City.

Index

Mays, Benjamin, 575
McCarthy, Eugene J., 725, 783
McCarthy, Joseph R., 149, 752
McClendon, Emanuel, 8
McClung, Ollie, Jr., 251–54
McClung, Ollie, Sr., 251–54
McComb, H. S., 395–96
McComb, Mississippi, 395–405
McComb Enterprise-Journal, 395, 397
McCone, John A., 437
McDermott, John, 772
McGee, Silas, 503
McGovern, George, 783
McIntyre, Reverend, 125
McKissick, Floyd B., 18, 286, 509–11, 525, 527, 559, 582
McLaughlin, Alexander, 363
McLin, Ernest, 759
McNair, Denise, 21, 27–28, 32–33
McNair, Mrs., 28
McNamara, Robert, 42, 46, 552, 561
McShane, Jim, 362–63
Medical Committee for Human Rights, 498, 765
Medina, Leon, 135
Meier, August, *453–64*
Memphis, Tennessee, 238, 524–25, 651, 756; death of King, 645–50, 693; sanitation workers' strike, 646, 652–54, 657–63, 665–74, 719, 731
Memphis Commercial Appeal, 535, 654, 656–57, 669, 817–18
Memphis Press-Scimitar, 668
Mennonites, 237
Meredith, James H., 497, 499, 513–14, *520–32*, 648, 879
Meredith, John, 524
Meredith, June, 524
Meredith March, 495–532, 718
Meridian, Mississippi, 121, 157, 162, 236, 281
Meridian Star, 163–65
Merritt College, 631, 676
Methodists, 142, 284, 342, 749, 810, 814, 867
Mexican-Americans, 709, 712–13, 728, 837, 855
Meyer, Charles, 511
Michels, Robert, 807
Michigan, 307, 878; Detroit riots, 596–623

Michigan Chronicle, 601
Middlebrook, Harold, 410, 412
Middletown, Connecticut, 819–20, 822, 828, 830, 834–36
Midfield, Alabama, 29, 762
Miller, Bobby, 118–19
Miller, Mike, 55
Miller, Orloff, 389
Miller, Randy, 822
Miller, Steve, 442
Mills, C. Wright, 730
Mills, Wilbur, 710, 729
Minnesota, 351
Minnis, Jack, 493
Mission Rebels, 799, 807
Mississippi, 14, 43–44, 66, 74, 83, 89, 100–1, 104, 178, 194–96, 332–33, 380–81, 439, 444, 452, 457–58, 461, 562, 566, 576, 587, 659, 665–66, 709, 714, 730, 765–66, 839, 841–42, 845–46, 872–73, 875–81; congressional elections, 99–100, 102,105–6, 177; delegates to 1964 Democratic Convention, 105, 129, 176, 179–86, 224–25, 228, 245, 734; Delta race relations, 476–90; justice in, 187–93; McComb race relations, 395–405; Meredith March, 495–532; murder of civil rights workers, 120–22, 157–75, 236, 280–84; police brutality, 49, 52–54, 83, 102–3, 162, 283, 509–15, 518, 530, 696; Poor People's March, 685, 688–92, 696, 756–58; Sunflower race relations, 545–51; voter registration, 48–59, 99, 101–2, 104–6, 176–77, 179–80, 197–229, 231, 235, 240, 244–49, 281, 347, 351–52, 401, 501–3, 509, 515–17, 520, 527, 531, 543, 545–51, 734; welfare, 533–44; Yazoo City race relations, 809–18
Mississippi Freedom Democratic Party. *See* Freedom Democratic Party.
Mississippi Summer Project, 120–21, 168, 213–50, 281, 381, 463
Mitchell, Clarence, 841–42
Mitchell, Morris, 511
Mize, Sidney, 239
Mobile County, Alabama, 43
Model Cities program, 853
Mohammed, 143
Monroe, Joseph, 144–46

Monroeville, Alabama, 376–77
Montclair, New Jersey, 593
Montgomery, Alabama, 30, 76, 129, 322–23, 333, 339–40, 343, 348, 353, 358, 361–68, 370–72, 384, 386, 388–94, 406–7, 411–12, 453–54, 460–61, 463, 493, 496, 508, 525, 557, 569, 575, 663, 673, 682, 684, 687, 786–87, 840–41, 846, 858
Montgomery Advertiser, 384, 688
Montgomery County, Mississippi, 100, 102
Montgomery Improvement Association, 575, 687
Monroe, North Carolina, 626
Moore, Archie, 469
Moore, Bill, 58
Moore, Gilbert, 699–705; *A Special Rage*, 705
Moore, Jamie, 20
Moore, O'Neal, 443
Moore, Queen Mother, 880
Moore, Ronnie, 286, 288, 293, 295
Morehouse College, 574–75, 663, 670
Moreland, Mantan, 465
Morgan College, 65
Morris, Jesse, 236
Morris, Ruth, 334, 337
Morris, William, 334, 337
Morris, Willie, 809–18; *Yazoo*, 818
Morse, Tom, 832–33
Morse, Wayne, 183
Morsell, John, 583
Moses, 143, 461, 659, 661, 664
Moses, Bob, 53, 55–56, 183, 236, 238, 248
Moses, Donna, 236
Mosk, Stanley, 437
Mount Morris Presbyterian Church, 140
Mount Zion Methodist Church, 121
Movement, 551, 636
Movie industry, 465–75
Mudd, John, 544
Muhammad, Elijah, 2, 96–97, 300, 310–11, 316–17, 319–20, 430
Muhammad Speaks, 2, 320–21, 430, 774
Muilenberg, Pete, 380
Murphy, Harold, 825–26, 831
Murphy, Michael J., 138, 145
Murray, George, 703

Muslims, 2, 96–97, 143, 299, 303, 305, 317, 674–75. *See also* Nation of Islam.
Muste, A. J., 134
Myers, Frank, 861–62, 866, 87
Myers, Mary, 862, 864, 868
Myrtle Beach Air Force Base, 43

Nadle, Marlene, *1–6, 299–308*
Nashville, Tennessee, 116, 377, 491
Nasser, Gamal Abdel, 317
Natchez, Mississippi, 484
Nation, 59, 106, 119, 279, 338
Nation of Islam, 2, 4, 72, 94, 96–98, 299, 309–11, 314–21, 430, 441, 456, 570, 593, 615, 631, 637, 774, 799, 851, 880
National Association for the Advancement of Colored People, 10, 15, 17, 75, 77–78, 87, 94–95, 108, 126, 257, 266, 281, 336, 389, 392, 454, 457, 459–62, 471, 496, 498, 514, 526–27, 529–30, 541, 559, 583, 587, 626, 668, 671, 685, 761, 789, 818
National Baptist Convention, 574, 772
National Catholic Conference for Interracial Justice, 17
National Catholic Welfare Conference, 349
National Council of Churches, 17, 51, 235, 248, 690
National Guard, 19, 21, 61–62, 354, 369, 372–73, 414–16, 418, 426, 435–36, 514, 590, 597, 602, 604, 607–10, 612–21, 639, 645, 649
National Institute of Real Estate Brokers, 91
National States' Rights Party, 442
National Welfare Rights Organization, 709–10
Nationalism, black, 72, 96–98, 140–41, 299–300, 303, 309, 412, 491, 504, 519, 553, 559–60, 570, 575–77, 579, 587, 631, 634–35, 854–55, 880
Nationalist Separatist Front, 851
Native Americans, 157, 206, 254, 388, 478, 669, 684, 709, 712, 718, 728, 742, 745, 819
Navy, U.S., 34–35, 40–41, 45–47, 97, 158
Nazism, 82, 284, 328, 331, 359
NBC News, 688, 690
Negro Ministers' Association, 566

Panola County, Mississippi, 479

Parchman Prison, 51–55, 83, 216, 226, 482, 556

Paris Blues, 470–71

Parker, Mack Charles, 170

Parker, William, 310, 314

Parker, William H., 416, 418–19, 433, 436–37

Parks, Gordon, *316–21*, *552–62*

Parks, Rosa, 393, 575, 657, 674, 687

Pasadena, California, 414, 417

Passett, Barry A., 826–28

Passive resistance. *See* Nonviolence.

Paterson, New Jersey, 310

Peabody, Thomas, 693–94

Peace Corps, 3–4, 388

Peace and Freedom Party, 677, 700, 767

Peace movement. *See* Vietnam War.

Peacock, Willie, 55

Pearson, Virgil Lee, 759

Peck, James, 392; *The Freedom Riders*, 3

Pennsylvania, 185; Black Panthers in, 847–56

Perez, Leander, 285, 296

Perkins, Anthony, 387–88

Perkins, Mother, 55

Perry County, Alabama, 353, 371, 389, 393

Peter, Paul, and Mary, 10, 17, 391, 796

Petersburg, Virginia, 43

Philadelphia, Mississippi, 120–21, 157–63, 165, 170, 173–74, 215–16, 223–24, 236, 280–84, 508–9, 512, 514, 557, 841–42

Philadelphia, Pennsylvania, 74, 185, 347, 773; Black Panther convention, 847–56

Phillips, Rubel, 105

Phoenix, Arizona, 300, 320

Pickett, Wilson, 822

Pike, James, 343

Pilgrim Hill Baptist Church, 334

Pippen, M. W., 28

Pittsburgh Courier, 123, 127

Plaquemine, Louisiana, 285–98

Plaquemines Parish, Louisiana, 285

Plato: *Crito*, 664

Playboy, 855

Plymouth Rock Baptist Church, 287–88

Poafpybitty, Fran, 388

Poitier, Sidney, 465, 467–72, 475

Police brutality, 38, 57–58, 73, 81–82, 98, 125, 282, 297, 455, 556–57, 633, 711, 799, 872–73, 879; Alabama, 20, 29, 322–29, 343, 345, 353–54, 397, 604, 726, 842–44; Detroit, 616–21; Florida, 109; Los Angeles, 419, 429, 433–35, 437; Louisiana, 286–89, 295–96; Mississippi, 49, 52–54, 83, 102–3, 162, 283, 509–15, 518, 530, 696; New York City, 145–50, 152; Newark, 593–95; Virginia, 74; Washington, 750, 757

Polish-Americans, 566, 638–40

Poll taxes, 102, 180, 211, 213, 224, 352

Ponder, Annell, 49, 103, 236

Poole, Laura, 25

Poor People's Campaign, 681, 684–86, 688–93, 696–97, 706–40, 744–51, 753, 756–58, 771, 778–79. *See also* Resurrection City.

Poverty Program, 500, 714, 793–95, 800–1, 805–7. *See also* Welfare.

Powell, Adam Clayton, 133, 299, 675, 775, 787

Powell, Jimmy, 138

Pratt, Jack, 183

Prendergast, Thomas, 139–40

Presbyterians, 349, 810

Prescod, Martha, 55

Présence Africaine (Paris), 85

Preston, Robert, 630

Price, Cecil, 121, 157, 160–62, 166, 174–75, 280, 283, 508, 841–42

Prickett, Charles, 234, 238

Prickett, Juanita, 233–35

Prickett, Ralph, 233–35

Prickett, Ruth Kay, 230–50

Prince, Calvin, 857–58, 863–65, 867–68

Prince George County, Virginia, 43

Prinz, Joachim, 17

Pritchett, Laurie, 57, 115

Project Memphis, 656, 672

Pruitt, James Lee, 83–84

Public Health Service, 500

Puerto Ricans, 144, 153, 820, 837

Quakers, 129, 134, 511

Quin, Alyene, 404–5

Quitman County, Mississippi, 756, 758

Library of Congress Cataloging-in-Publication Data

Reporting civil rights
    p. cm.—(The Library of America; 137–138)
    Includes index.
    Contents: pt. 1. American journalism, 1941–1963—pt. 2 American
journalism, 1963–1973.
    ISBN 1–931082–28–6 (vol. 1: alk. paper)—ISBN 1–931082–29–4 (vol.
2: alk. paper)
    1. African Americans—Civil rights—History—20th century
Sources. 2. African Americans—Civil rights—Press coverage. 3. Civil
rights movements—United States—History—20th century—Sources.
4. Civil rights movements—Press coverage—United States. 5.
Journalism—United States—History—20th century. 6. United
States—Race relations—Sources. 7. United States—Race relations—
Press coverage. I. Title: Reporting civil rights. II. Series.
E185.61.R47   2003
323.1′196073′0904 dc—21   2002027459

THE LIBRARY OF AMERICA SERIES

The Library of America fosters appreciation and pride in America's literary heritage by publishing, and keeping permanently in print, authoritative editions of America's best and most significant writing. An independent nonprofit organization, it was founded in 1979 with seed money from the National Endowment for the Humanities and the Ford Foundation.

This book is set in 10 point Linotron Galliard,
a face designed for photocomposition by Matthew Carter
and based on the sixteenth-century face Granjon. The paper
is acid-free Domtar Literary Opaque and meets the requirements
for permanence of the American National Standards Institute. The
binding material is Brillianta, a woven rayon cloth made by
Van Heek-Scholco Textielfabrieken, Holland. The compo-
sition is by The Clarinda Company. Printing and
binding by R.R.Donnelley & Sons Company.
Designed by Bruce Campbell.